Principles

of Economics

Ninth edition

Richard G. Lipsey
K. Alec Chrystal

OXFORD
UNIVERSITY PRESS

OXFORD
UNIVERSITY PRESS

Great Clarendon Street, Oxford OX2 6DP

Oxford University Press is a department of the University of Oxford.
It furthers the University's objective of excellence in research, scholarship,
and education by publishing worldwide in

Oxford New York

Athens Auckland Bangkok Bogotá Buenos Aires Calcutta
Cape Town Chennai Dar es Salaam Delhi Florence Hong Kong Istanbul
Karachi Kuala Lumpur Madrid Melbourne Mexico City Mumbai
Nairobi Paris São Paulo Singapore Taipei Tokyo Toronto Warsaw

with associated companies in Berlin Ibadan

Oxford is a registered trade mark of Oxford University Press
in the UK and in certain other countries

Published in the United States
by Oxford University Press Inc., New York

British Library Cataloguing in Publication Data

Data available

Library of Congress Cataloging in Publication Data

Lipsey, Richard G., 1928–
Principles of economics / Richard G. Lipsey and K. Alec Chrystal.
— 9th ed.
p. cm.
Rev. ed. of: An introduction to positive economics. 8th ed. 1995.
Includes bibliographical references.
1. Economics. I. Chrystal, K. Alec, 1946– . II. Lipsey,
Richard G., 1928– Introduction to positive economics. III. Title.
HB171.L715 1999 330.1—dc21 98-48332

ISBN 0–19–877589–X.
ISBN 0–19–877588–1 (pbk.)

10 9 8 7 6 5 4 3 2

Typeset in Minion and Frutiger
by BookMan Services
Printed and bound in Italy by
Giunti Industrie Grafiche, Florence

Contents

Detailed contents

Part Two Consumers and producers

Why study economics?

Some of you will answer the question posed in the heading with 'It was part of my course of study, so I had no choice.' To that captive audience, and to those who chose economics from among several available alternatives, we offer hope. Economics covers topics that are highly relevant to many of the most pressing issues facing today's world—free markets versus government control, resource exhaustion, pollution, the population explosion, government taxes and spending, employment and unemployment, inflation, the EU, the euro, changing living standards in advanced nations, growth and stagnation among the world's poorer nations. These are some of the many issues that will be illuminated by what you study in this book.

One of the most important events in the first half of the twentieth century was the rise of communism. One of the most important events in the second half of that century was communism's fall. By 1999 the century-old battle between free markets and government planning as alternatives for organizing economic activity had been settled with a degree of decisiveness that is rare for great social issues. Understanding why market-oriented, capitalist economies perform so much better than fully planned or highly government-controlled economies is a core issue in economics. Economic theories are expressly designed to help us understand the successes (and, where they occur, the failures) of free-market societies.

The triumph of market-oriented economies suggests that income- and wealth-creating activities are usually best accomplished through the efforts of private citizens buying and selling in largely unregulated markets. But this is not the end of the story for at least three fundamental reasons.

First, although market economies certainly work better than planned economies, they do not work perfectly. One of today's great social issues is to reallocate the responsibilities of government, leaving it to do what it can best do and leaving free markets to do what they can best do. We ask: 'What are the important roles that governments can play in improving the functioning of a basically market-oriented economy?'

Second, market economies produce severe cycles as well as long-term growth. Long-term growth has raised the living standards of the ordinary working person from the horrors and degradations described by Charles Dickens to those of the property-owning workers of today, whose living standards are higher than those of 99 per cent of all the people of all classes who ever lived on the Earth. Yet capitalist growth is uneven growth. Severe business cycles operate around the rising trend of economic growth. In recessions, unemployment is high and living standards typically stand still or even fall. Although each cycle tends to leave living standards higher than all previous cycles, the ups and downs of uneven market-driven growth can be upsetting to those affected by it.

Third, although it is desirable to create income and wealth, we also care about how they are distributed among all citizens. Poverty for a minority in the midst of plenty for the majority has always been a problem in wealthy countries—just as poverty for the majority has always been a problem for poor countries. We ask: 'What is the place of government in pursuing social policies that alleviate the poverty and suffering of those who do not share in the income and employment that well-functioning market economies create for the majority?'

Economists have been in the forefront of analysing, explaining, and, where appropriate, offering solutions to all of the issues mentioned above—and many more. They have succeeded in these tasks mainly because economics has a core of useful theory that explains how markets work and that evaluates their performance. Although some economic analysis is extremely abstract, and sometimes even economists wonder about its value, the basic core of economic theory that is the secret of the subject's success can be understood by anyone who is willing to make the effort. This basic theory has an excellent record in illuminating issues in ways that lead both to deeper understanding and to useful policy recommendations.

When you take up this book, you are setting out on the study of a subject that, as the above discussion suggests, is highly relevant to understanding and improving the world in which we live.

Approached in the right way, your study will be an adventure. The basic theory must be mastered. Whether or not you find this effort fun in itself, you will find surprisingly early in your studies that theories can be used to understand many practical issues. The world is complex, and fully understanding its economic aspects requires much more economic theory than can be packed into one elementary textbook. But mastery of the subject to the level of this one book will contribute greatly to your understanding of many important issues and many of the policies directed at dealing with them.

Good luck and good studying!

RICHARD LIPSEY
ALEC CHRYSTAL

Vancouver, BC,
and London, England
July 1999

How to use this book

It may help you to know some of this book's devices that are designed to make learning easier.

Format

Figures, tags, and captions

Each figure caption begins with a tag line in bold type that states its main message. The full formal analysis related to each figure is given in a caption attached to that figure. This has the advantages of keeping the reasoning physically attached to its associated figure and allowing that reasoning to be studied at the point that seems best to you. The text is made self-sufficient by providing an intuitive explanation of the formal reasoning given in each figure caption. This means that the text can be read on its own, without the figure captions—say, on first reading or for revision. The basic analytical reasoning that is the core of economics is, however, given in the captions, *all of which you must study carefully at some time.*

Summaries

Every chapter ends with a set of summary points grouped under the chapter's main headings. These points provide a useful review as well as a warning that some of the chapter needs to be re-read when the reasoning behind one or more of the summary points cannot be reconstructed.

Topics for review

Every chapter also ends with a series of topics for review. These can be treated in the same way as the summaries: as checks on what has just been learned, and as signals during revision.

Discussion questions

The final item in each chapter is a set of questions for discussion. Sometimes these provide straight checks of your understanding of specific points and sometimes they ask you to roam a bit wider to apply what you have learned to a topic drawn from the press or some other source.

Boxes

Boxes are set off from the body of the chapter by a different type and a colour surround. Boxes cover many different types of material, such as empirical illustrations, more detailed elaboration of various points made in the text, points of historical interest, and occasional formal proofs, all of which may be of interest to some, but not all, readers. The main unifying point about all the boxes is that they contain material that can be omitted without loss of continuity. Thus all can be skipped, although we trust that you will find many of them interesting as well as useful.

Glossary

The first time a technical term is used extensively in the text it is printed in **bold** type so that it can be easily recognized as such. The definitions of all such terms are gathered together in a Glossary printed at the end of the book.

Supplements

The main text of *Principles of Economics* is accompanied by a good range of supplements. These have been carefully designed to complement the main text, explaining and developing key ideas and principles:

■ An Instructor's Manual discusses the main themes in each chapter and provides solutions to the end-of-chapter questions in the book, following each of these with a brief explanation.

■ A set of approximately one hundred Overhead Transparency Masters presents the most important figures from the book in an enlarged format suitable for projection in class or the lecture theatre. These will help lecturers to illustrate concepts in diagrammatic form during teaching.

Both of these products are available free of charge from Oxford University Press to tutors who adopt the main text.

More information on the text and ancillaries is available through the Internet on the web page http://www.oup.co.uk/best.textbooks/economics. Updates to this will cover some of the main policy topics in the book plus links to official sources such as the UK Treasury, the Bank of England, the International Monetary Fund, and the European Central Bank.

You can access further information about other Oxford University Press textbooks and products from this site: www.oup.com.

Approaches to studying economics

You need to study a book on economics in a different way from how you would study a book on, say, history or English literature. Economic theory has a logical structure that builds on itself from stage to stage. Thus if you only imperfectly understand some concept or theory, you will run into increasing difficulty when, in subsequent chapters, this concept or theory is taken for granted and built upon. Because of its logical structure, quite long chains of reasoning are encountered; if A then B, if B then C, if C then D, and if D then E. Each step in the argument may seem simple enough, but the cumulative effect of several steps, one on top of the other, may be bewildering on first encounter. Thus when, having followed the argument step by step, you encounter the statement 'it is now obvious that if A then E', it may not seem at all obvious to you. This is a problem that everyone encounters with chains of reasoning. The only way to deal with it is to follow the argument through several times. Eventually, as the reasoning becomes familiar, it will become obvious that *if A then E.*

Economics has its own technical language or jargon. At first you may feel that you are merely being asked to put complicated names to commonsense ideas. To some extent this is true. It is a necessary step, however, because loose thinking about vaguely formed ideas is a quick route to error in economics. Furthermore, when you begin to put several ideas together to see what follows from them, jargon—a clearly defined term to refer to each idea—becomes a necessary part of your equipment.

A book on economics is to be worked at, and understood step by step. It is usually a good procedure to read a chapter quickly in order to see the general run of the argument, and at this stage you might omit the captions to the figures. You then need to re-read the chapter carefully, making sure that the argument is understood step by step. On this reading, you *must* study the captions to all the figures carefully. If you do not understand the captions, you have not understood economics. You should not be discouraged if, occasionally at this stage, you find yourself spending quite a bit of time on only a few pages.

A pencil and paper are valuable adjuncts to your reading. Difficult arguments should be followed by building up your own diagram while the argument unfolds, rather than relying on the printed diagram, which is, perforce, complete from the beginning. Numerical examples can be invented to illustrate general propositions.

In short, the technical vocabulary aside, you must seek to understand economics, not to memorize it. Theories, principles, and concepts are always turning up in slightly unfamiliar guises. If you have understood your economics, this poses no problem; if you have merely memorized it, this spells disaster.

Write to us

Economics is a subject in which one never stops learning. We are grateful to many users—students and teachers—who have taken the trouble to write to us pointing out possible errors, making comments, and offering suggestions. We hope that readers will continue to teach us with as many further comments and criticisms as they have in the past. We try to acknowledge every such letter. If you write and do not hear from us, write again—the post (or our filing systems) have let us down!

Outlines for short or modular courses

This book provides a comprehensive coverage of basic economics suitable for a full one-year course. We have, however, designed the text to be flexible enough to cover shorter courses. To illustrate, we give our suggestions for the chapter content of several shorter courses.

A short Introduction to Economics course (twenty weeks)
Chapters 1, 3–4, 6 or 7, 8–10, 14–15, 18–19, 20–27, 30, 31, 35

A short course for Business students (twenty weeks)
Chapters 1, 3–4, 6 or 7, 8–12, 14–15, 18–19, 20–24, (25–27 optional), 35

An Introduction to Microeconomics course (one semester)
Chapters 1, 3–5, 6 or 7, 8–11, 14–15, 18–19

An Introduction to Macroeconomics course (one semester)
Chapters 20–27, 30, 31, 35 (alternatively, for a course with a growth emphasis include chapters **32** and **33**; for a course with an international emphasis the key chapters are **28** and **29** plus possibly **34**)

Acknowledgements

Finally we wish to say a word of thanks to those people who have made this book possible. In so far as the ideas and viewpoints expressed in the first edition—many of which have carried through to this edition—were novel, they were the common property of all of Lipsey's colleagues who in the late 1950s and early 1960s were members of the LSE *Staff Seminar on Methodology, Measurement and Testing in Economics.* In the first edition Lipsey gave his personal expression of this general viewpoint.

Joanna Lipsey and Robyn Wills have shown unlimited patience in providing the many and varied secretarial duties associated with the production of the book. Jason Pearce has been help-fully creative in his editing of the manuscript and setting of the text. At the OUP we are particularly grateful for the constant aid and encouragement provided by Ruth Marshall. The usual disclaimer of course holds here: for all remaining shortcomings and mistakes, the authors may blame each other, but the reader should blame us both.

R.G.L.
K.A.C.

Chapter 1
Economic Issues and Concepts

If you want a pint of milk, you go to the shop and buy it. It does not occur to you that farmers may have stopped producing milk or that dairies may have stopped delivering it to shops. When the shop owner needs more milk, he orders it from the distributor, who in turn gets it from the bottling plant, which in its turn gets it from the dairy farmer. The dairy farmer buys cattle feed and electric milking machines, and gets power to run all his equipment by putting a plug into a wall outlet where the electricity is supplied as he needs it. The milking machines are made from parts manufactured in several different places in the European Union and overseas, while these in their turn are made from materials mined and smelted in a dozen or more different countries.

As it is with the milk you drink, so it is with everything else that you buy. When you go to the appropriate shop, what you want is normally on the shelf. Those who make these products find that all the required components and materials are available when needed—even though these things typically come from many different parts of the world and are made by people who have no direct dealings with each other.

The complexity of the modern economy

The sales and purchases in which you are involved are only a small part of the fantastically complex set of transactions that take place every day in a modern society. Shipments arrive daily at our sea and airports. These include raw materials, such as iron ore and logs, parts, such as transistors and circuit boards, tools, such as screwdrivers and digging equipment, perishables, such as fresh flowers and fruits, and all kinds of manufactured goods, such as washing machines and TV sets. Rail and road shippers receive and dispatch these goods to thousands of different destinations. Some go directly to consumers. Others are used by local firms to manufacture their products—of which some will be sold domestically and some exported.

Most people who want to work can find work. They spend their working days engaging in the activities just described. In doing so they earn incomes, which they then spend on what they, and others like them, produce. Other people own firms that employ workers to assist in the many activities described above, such as importing things, making things, transporting things, and selling things. They earn their incomes as profits from their enterprises.

Self-organization

Economics began when thoughtful observers asked them-selves how such a complex set of dealings is organized. Who co-ordinates the whole set of efforts? Who makes sure that all the activities fit together, providing jobs to produce the things that people want and delivering those things to where they are wanted?

The answer is no one!

The great insight of the early economists was that an economy based on free-market transactions is self-organizing.

By following their own self-interest, doing what seems best and most profitable for themselves, and responding to the incentives of prices set on open markets, people produce a spontaneous social order. In that order, literally thousands of millions of transactions and activities fit together to produce the things that people want within the constraints set by the resources that are available to the nation.

The great Scottish economist and political philosopher Adam Smith, who was the first to develop this insight fully, put it this way:

It is not from the benevolence of the butcher, the brewer, or the baker, that we expect our dinner, but from their regard to their own interest. We address ourselves, not to their humanity but to their self-love, and never talk to them of our own necessities but of their advantages. Nobody but a beggar chuses to depend chiefly upon the benevolence of his fellow-citizens.

Smith is not saying that benevolence is unimportant. Indeed he praises it in many passages. He is saying, however, that the massive number of economic interactions that characterize a modern economy cannot all be motivated by benevolence. Although benevolence does motivate some of our actions, often the very dramatic ones, the majority of our everyday actions are motivated by self-interest. Self-interest, not benevolence, is therefore the foundation of economic order.

Efficient organization

Another great insight, which was hinted at by Smith and fully developed over the next century and a half, was that this spontaneously generated social order is relatively efficient. Loosely speaking (we will be more precise later), efficiency means that the resources available to a nation are organized to produce the maximum possible total output.

Smith said that market society produces ordered behaviour that makes it appear as if people are guided by a *hidden hand*. He did not literally mean that a supernatural presence guides economic affairs. Instead he referred to the amazing emergence of order out of so many independent decisions. The key to the explanation is that all individuals respond to the same set of prices, which are determined in markets that respond to overall conditions of national scarcities or plenty. Much of the first half of this book is devoted to a detailed elaboration of how this market order is generated.

A planned alternative

A century after Adam Smith, another great economist and political philosopher, Karl Marx, argued that although this market system would produce high total output, it would distribute that output in such a way that, over time, the rich would get richer and the poor poorer. He went on to argue that when societies became rich enough, they should dispense with the spontaneous social order. They should then replace it by a consciously created system, called a command economy, or communism, in which the government plans all of the transactions we have just described and, in so doing, creates a more equal and just distribution of the total output.

Beginning with the USSR in the 1920s, many nations listened to Marx and established systems in which conscious government **central planning** largely replaced the spontaneous order of the free market. For much of the twentieth century two systems, the centrally planned and the market, competed with each other for the favour of undecided governments. Then, within the last two decades of the century, governments of one communist country after another abandoned their central planning apparatus.

More and more economic transactions and activities were then left to be regulated by the self-organizing system of the market. Seldom has a great social issue been settled with such conclusiveness.

Adam Smith was right and Karl Marx was wrong.

Box 1.1 elaborates on some of the reasons for the failure of centrally planned economies. We hasten to add that Marx was right about many things, including the importance of technological change in raising living standards over the centuries. Where he was wrong, however, was in believing that the market could be replaced by central planning as a way of organizing all of a nation's economic activities.

In contrast to the failures of command economies the performance of the free-market price system is impressive. One theme of this book is *market success*—how the price system works to co-ordinate with relative efficiency the decentralized decisions made by private consumers and producers. However, this is not to conclude that doing things better means doing things perfectly. Another theme of this book is *market failure*—how and why the unaided price system sometimes fails to produce efficient results and fails to take account of social values that cannot be expressed through the marketplace.

In short, today, as in the time of Smith, economists seek to understand the self-organizing forces of a market economy, how well they function, and how governments may intervene to improve (but not to replace) its workings in specific situations.

Main characteristics of market economies

What then are the main characteristics of market economies that produce this spontaneous self-ordering?

■ Individuals pursue their own self-interest, buying and selling what seems best for themselves and their families

■ People respond to incentives. Other things being equal, sellers seek high prices while buyers seek low prices.

■ Prices are set in open markets in which would-be sellers compete to sell their wares to would-be buyers.

■ People earn their incomes by selling the services they own to those who wish to use them—their labour services, things they have produced, the services of the land and buildings that they own.

■ All of these activities are governed by a set of institutions largely created by the state. The most important are private property and freedom of contract. The nature of private property and contractual obligations are defined by the legislature and enforced by the police and the courts.

Box 1.1 The failure of central planning

The year 1989 signalled to the world what many economists had long argued: the superiority of a market-oriented price system over central planning as a method of organizing economic activity. The failure of central planning had many causes, but four were particularly significant.

The failure of co-ordination

In centrally planned economies a body of planners tries to co-ordinate all the economic decisions about production, investment, trade, and consumption made by the producers and consumers throughout the country. This proved impossible to do with any reasonable degree of efficiency. Bottlenecks in production, shortages of some goods, and gluts of others plagued the Soviet economy for decades. For example, in 1989 much of a bumper harvest rotted on the farm because of shortages of storage and transportation facilities, and for years there was an ample supply of black-and-white television sets and severe shortages of toilet paper and soap.

Failure of quality control

Central planners can monitor the number of units produced by any factory and reward those who overfulfil their production targets and punish those who fall short. It is much harder, however, for them to monitor quality. A constant Soviet problem was the production of poor-quality products. Factory managers were concerned with meeting their quotas by whatever means were available, and once the goods passed out of their factory, what happened to them was someone else's headache. The quality problem was so serious that in the 1990s very few Eastern European-manufactured products were able to stand up to the newly permitted competition with superior goods produced in the advanced market societies.

In market economies, poor quality is punished by low sales, and retailers soon give a signal to factory managers by shifting their purchases to other suppliers. The incentives that obviously flow from such private sector purchasing discretion are generally absent from command economies, where purchases and sales are planned centrally.

Misplaced incentives

In market economies relative wages and salaries provide incentives for labour to move from place to place, and the possibility of losing one's job provides an incentive to work diligently. This is a harsh mechanism that punishes losers with loss of income (although social programmes provide floors to the amount of economic punishment that can be suffered). In planned economies, workers usually have complete job security. Industrial unemployment is rare, and even when it does occur new jobs are usually found for those who lose theirs. Although the high level of security is attractive to many, it proved impossible to provide sufficient incentives to work reasonably hard and efficiently under such conditions. In the words of Oxford historian Timothy Garton Ash, who wrote eyewitness chronicles of the developments in Eastern Europe from 1980 to 1990, the social contract between the workers and the government in the Eastern countries was 'We pretend to work, and you pretend to pay us.'

Environmental degradation

Fulfilling production plans became the all-embracing incentive in planned economies, to the exclusion of most other considerations, including the environment. As a result, environmental degradation occurred in all the countries of Eastern Europe on a scale unknown in advanced Western nations. A particularly disturbing example occurred in central Asia, where high quotas for cotton output led to indiscriminate use of pesticides and irrigation. Birth defects are now found there in nearly one child in three. This is but one example of a general phenomenon which included toxic chemical dumps and atomic waste scattered throughout the land.

The failure to protect the environment stemmed from a combination of pressure to fulfil plans and lack of a political marketplace. The democratic process allows citizens to express views on the use of scarce resources for environmental protection. Imperfect though the system may be in democratic economies, their record of environmental protection has been vastly better than that of command economies.

Resources and scarcity

All of the issues discussed so far would not matter much if we lived in an economy of plenty where there was enough to satisfy everyone's wants. 'Ask and you shall receive' would be the motto of such an imaginary world. In contrast, the motto of our real economy is closer to 'Work for it and you may get at least some of it.'

Why is the economy of plenty impossible? The short answer is 'Because we live in a world of scarcity.' In relation to the known desires of individuals for such products as better food, clothing, housing, schooling, holidays, hospital care, and entertainment, the existing supplies of resources are woefully inadequate. They are sufficient to produce only a small fraction of the goods and services that people desire. This gives rise to the basic economic problem of choice under conditions of scarcity. If we cannot have everything we want, we must choose what we will and will not have.

To go further we need to clarify a few terms that you will need throughout your study of economics.

Kinds of resources

The nation's resources fall into four main categories:

■ All those gifts of nature, such as land, forests, minerals, etc., commonly called natural resources and known to economists as **land.**

■ All human resources, mental and physical, both inherited and acquired, which economists call **labour.**

■ All those man-made aids to further production, such as

Box 1.2 Judging definitions

The division of resources into land, labour, capital, and entrepreneurs, and the division of output into goods and services, are matters of definition. Definitions cannot be judged as we would matters of fact; they are to be judged instead on the grounds of usefulness and convenience. The question 'Is this fourfold division of factors likely to be a useful one?' can be discussed fruitfully. The question 'Is this fourfold division of factors the correct one?' is unlikely to give rise to fruitful discussion, and it certainly has no definite answer.

Useless arguments about the 'truth' of definitions are so common that they have been given a name. They are called *essentialist* arguments. Essentialist arguments concern purely semantic issues. They occur whenever we agree about the facts of the case but argue about what name to use to indicate the agreed facts. For example, we may agree about what happened in the Soviet Union between 1921 and 1989 but argue about whether that can be called true communism. We are then having an essentialist argument about definitions.

---

tools, machinery, and factories, which are used up in the process of making other goods and services rather than being consumed for their own sake, which economists call **capital.**

■ Those who take risks by introducing new products and new ways of making old products. They organize the other factors of production and direct them along new lines, and are called **entrepreneurs** or **innovators** by economists.

Collectively these resources are called **factors of production**—and sometimes just *factors* for short. In this section we have been concerned with definitions, and Box 1.2 discusses some issues concerning how definitions are to be assessed.

Ownership of resources

Private property is a key institution of a market economy. Individuals own the majority of the nation's factors of production. They also own the goods that they produce and the things that they buy. Some assets are owned by the state—roads, schools, public buildings, etc.—but most are, and must be, in private hands. People cannot make contracts to buy and sell what is not theirs. So without private ownership the market economy cannot function.

Kinds of production

Factors of production are used to make **goods** (also called products or commodities), which are tangible, such as cars and shoes, and **services,** which are intangible, such as haircuts and education. Economists often say 'goods' when they mean 'goods and services'.

The nation's total output of all goods and services over one year is called its **gross domestic product** or **GDP** for short. The act of making goods and services is called **production,** and the act of using these goods and services to satisfy wants is called **consumption.** Anyone who makes goods or provides services is called a **producer,** and anyone who consumes them to satisfy his or her wants is called a **consumer.**

Choice and opportunity cost

We value goods and services because they help us to satisfy our wants and desires. Goods and services are thus regarded as means to an end, the satisfaction of wants. We have said that a nation cannot produce enough goods and services to satisfy all of its citizens' wants. So choices must be made.

If you choose to have more of one thing, then, where there is an effective choice, you must have less of something else. Consider Cynthia, a young mother who is considering buying some additional bread for the week's meals. The cost of this extra bread could be measured as so many pence per loaf. A more revealing way of looking at the cost, however, is in terms of what other consumption Cynthia must forgo in order to obtain her bread. Say that she decides to give up some cinema attendances. If the price of a loaf is one-fifth of the price of a cinema seat, then the cost of five more loaves of bread is one cinema attendance; or, put the other way around, the cost of one more cinema attendance is five loaves of bread.

Now consider the same problem at the level of a whole society. If the government elects to build more roads, and finds the required money by building fewer schools, then the cost of the new roads can be expressed as so many schools per mile of road.

Opportunity cost is the economist's term for costs expressed in terms of forgone alternatives. If some course of action is adopted, there are typically many alternatives that might be forgone. For example, when the government decides to build the road, it might cut expenditure on schools, on research laboratories, or on a proposed modernization of the postal service. To get a precise measure of opportunity cost, economists count the sacrifice as that of the best available alternative. Thus, in the above example we ask, 'If the government had not built the roads, what was the best alternative use of its funds?' That alternative is what is given up to get the roads—it is the opportunity cost of the roads.

The concept of opportunity cost emphasizes the need for choice by measuring the cost of anything that is chosen in terms of the best alternative that could have been chosen instead. The amount of the sacrificed alternative measures the cost of obtaining what is chosen.

The production-possibility boundary

Now we are going to take a big step. We are going to show on a diagram some of the issues surrounding choice. Diagrams or figures pervade elementary economics books. They show the relation between things in which we are interested. The alternative is to express these relations in mathematical equations. Messy though some graphs may seem at times, most beginning students prefer to work through graphical reasoning rather than mathematical calculations. If you find graphs difficult to follow, you should study the section on graphs in Chapter 2 pages 21–5 in some detail.

Consider one choice that faces all economies today. How should the nation's productive resources be divided between the public and private sectors? All the things that governments provide, such as schools and defence and roads, are produced in what is called the public sector. Everything else, including all of the goods and services that you buy in shops and service establishments, is produced in the private sector. In this example we put all the goods and services that governments provide into one group called 'public sector goods'. The rest are provided by non-government organizations and we call these 'private sector goods'.

The choices that each country must make are illustrated in Figure 1.1. The horizontal axis measures the quantity of public sector goods while the vertical axis measures the quantity of private sector goods. The blue curve on the figure shows all those combinations of public and private goods that can be produced if all the nation's resources are fully employed. It is called a **production-possibility boundary**. Points outside the boundary show combinations that cannot be obtained because there are not enough resources to produce them. Points on the boundary are just obtainable: they are the combinations that can just be produced using all the available supplies of resources.

Choice, scarcity, and opportunity cost illustrated

A single production-possibility boundary illustrates three concepts that we have already discussed, scarcity, choice, and opportunity cost. *Scarcity* is shown by the unattainable combinations beyond the boundary. There are some things we just cannot have. *Choice* arises because of the need to select one of the attainable points on the boundary. No economy can be at more than one point at one time. One might have either the combination of public sector and private sector goods shown by point *a* or the combination shown by point *b*, but not both at the same time. *Opportunity cost* is shown by the negative slope of the

Figure 1.1 A production-possibility boundary
The negatively sloped boundary shows the combinations that are just attainable when all of the society's resources are efficiently employed. The quantity of public sector goods produced is measured along the horizontal axis, the quantity of private sector goods along the vertical axis. Any point on the diagram indicates some amount of each kind of good produced. The production-possibility boundary separates the blue-shaded attainable combinations, such as *a*, *b*, and *c*, from unattainable combinations, such as *d*. It is negatively sloped because in a fully employed economy more of one good can be produced only if resources are freed by producing less of other goods. Moving from point *a* (whose coordinates are c_0 and g_0) to point *b* (whose coordinates are c_1 and g_1) implies producing an additional amount of public sector goods, indicated by ΔG in the figure, at an opportunity cost of a reduction in private sector goods by the amount indicated by ΔC. Points *a* and *b* represent efficient uses of society's resources. Point *c* represents either an inefficient use of resources or a failure to use all the resources that are available.

boundary. As the economy moves along that boundary, more of one type of good is being obtained at the cost of less of the other type. For example, if the economy moves from point *a* to point *b*, it gains a quantity of public sector goods indicated in the figure by ΔG and gives up a quantity of private sector goods indicated by ΔC. Thus the opportunity cost of a unit of public sector goods is $\Delta C/\Delta G$. (The capital Greek letter delta, Δ, is commonly used to stand for a change. Thus ΔC means the change in C and ΔG means the change in G.)

Increasing opportunity cost The production-possibility curve of Figure 1.1 is drawn with a slope that gets steeper as one moves along it from left to right. The increasing slope indicates increasing opportunity cost as more and more of either product is produced. Consider, for example, starting at the vertical axis where all production is of private sector goods. A small increase in the production of public goods moves the economy slightly along the curve, indicating a reduction in the production of private sector goods. However, the flatness of the curve indicates that the loss of private sector goods is small. Now consider being at point *b*, where most production is of public sector goods. (Such a situation is not found in market economies except in the midst of a major war, when most of the public sector goods are war-related.) At *b* the curve is very steep. This indicates that, if even more public sector goods are to be produced, the sacrifice in civilian goods is very large.

The increasing steepness of the production-possibility curve as one moves along it from left to right indicates that the higher the production of either type of good, the greater is the opportunity cost of obtaining a further increase in its production.

The figure can also be used to illustrate another three important economic issues.

Three key issues

What should be produced How should the nation's scarce resources be allocated between the various possible kinds of production? The graphical expression of this key question is where to locate on the production-possibility boundary. Each point on the boundary indicates what is called a *production bundle*, a bundle of so many of each type of good. Alternative points indicate different allocations of the nation's resources to producing different bundles of goods and services. If point *a* is chosen, more resources are devoted to the private sector than if point *b* had been chosen. Conversely, if point *b* is chosen more of the nation's resources must be allocated to the public sector and less to the private sector than if point *a* had been chosen.

Efficient production If an economy is located inside its boundary more of everything could be produced. For example, if the economy is at point *c* it is possible to move towards the boundary and get more of both public and private sector goods. Such an economy faces no opportunity cost. It can have more of everything. If it goes from point *c* to any point of the boundary between *a* and *b*, it will get an increase in the production of all types of goods. There are two main reasons why an economy may produce inside its production boundary. First, some of its resources may be unemployed. Putting them back to work would raise production of some goods without having to lower the production of anything else. This is why economists speak of the deadweight loss of unemployment. Second, although its resources are fully employed, some of them may be inefficiently employed. If they could be used more efficiently, the production of some goods could be increased without having to produce less of anything else.

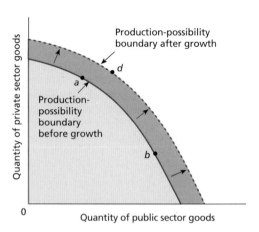

Figure 1.2 The effect of economic growth on the production-possibility boundary
Economic growth shifts the production-possibility boundary outward, allowing more of all commodities to be produced. Before growth in productive capacity points *a* and *b* were on the production-possibility boundary and point *d* was an unattainable combination. After growth point *d* becomes attainable, as do all points within the dark blue band.

We will have much more to say about inefficient uses of resources in later chapters.

These two possibilities help to reveal the source of opportunity cost.

If all of the nation's resources are fully employed, and none are employed inefficiently, then more of one good can be produced only by taking resources away from the production of a second good.

The lost production of the second good is the opportunity cost of the first.

Economic growth There is one other way an economy can get more of everything without having less of anything. If the economy's capacity to produce goods is increasing through time, the production-possibility boundary will be moving outwards over time, as illustrated in Figure 1.2. More of all goods can then be produced. This is what economic growth has accomplished from one decade to the next for the last several hundred years—and sporadically before then, back to the beginning of history. We will study this growth later in the book. In the meantime, we merely note that in the long term growth is driven by technological change. Over the years we learn to make existing products better and more cheaply and also to make many new products that satisfy old needs in new ways and create altogether new needs.

Box 1.3 deals with some of the sometimes confusing terminology that surrounds the concept of the production-possibility boundary.

Box 1.3 The terminology of production possibilities

We have used the term 'production-possibility boundary'. 'Boundary' emphasizes that the points on the line are maximum points. It is always possible to produce at points inside the line by not employing some factors of production, or by using them inefficiently. Two other terms, 'frontier' and 'curve', are often used instead of 'boundary'.

The words 'production possibility' emphasize the alternative possibilities available to a society. However, the term 'transformation' is often used instead. The idea behind the term 'transformation' is that society can, in effect, 'transform' one product into another by moving resources from the production of one product into the production of the other. Speaking of transforming one product into another stresses the idea of opportunity cost. Of course, one good is not literally transformed into another as ancient

alchemists sought to transform base metals into gold; but, by moving resources from producing one type of good to producing another, quantities of the first type of good are sacrificed to gain quantities of the second type.

You can make up six terms by combining the following words:

All six terms mean the same thing. All six are commonly used.

Who makes the choices and how

So choices have to be made, but who makes them and how are they made?

The flow of income and expenditure

Figure 1.3 shows the basic decision-takers and the flows of income and expenditure that they set up. Individuals own factors of production, including themselves. They sell the services of these factors to producers and receive payments in return. These are their incomes. Producers use the factors that they buy to make goods and services for consumption. They sell these to individuals, receiving payments in return. These are the incomes of producers. These basic flows of income and expenditure pass through markets. Individuals sell the services of the factor that they own in what are collectively called *factor markets*. Producers sell their outputs of goods and services in what are collectively called *goods markets*. The prices that are set in these markets determine the incomes that are earned and the purchasing power of those incomes. People who get high prices for their factor services earn high incomes; those who get low prices earn low incomes. The income each person earns expressed as a fraction of all incomes that are earned in the nation shows the share of total output that each person can command. The **distribution of income** refers to how the nation's total production is distributed among its citizens. This is largely determined by the price that each type of factor service can command in factor markets. Most of the first half of this book is an elaboration of how these markets work.

Maximizing decisions   In this story the basic decision-makers are individuals and producers. To these two groups we will shortly add a third, the government. The most important thing about how these two groups take their decisions is that everyone tries to do as well as possible for themselves. In the jargon of economics, they are *maximizers*. When individuals decide how many factor services to sell to producers and how many products to buy from

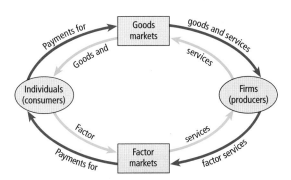

Figure 1.3 The circular flow of income and expenditure
The green line shows the flows of goods and services while the blue line shows the payments made to purchase these. Factor services flow from individuals who own the factors (including their own labour) through factor markets to firms which use them to make goods and services. These then flow through goods markets to those who consume them. Money payments flow from firms to individuals through factor markets. This becomes the income of individuals. When they spend this income buying goods and services, money flows through goods markets back to producers.

them, they make choices designed to maximize their well-being. When producers decide how many factor services to buy from individuals and how many goods to produce and sell to them, they seek to maximize their profits.

Marginal decisions The second key point about these choices is that they are all made at the margin. Let us see what this means. When you vote at a UK national election, you only have one vote and you must support one party over the others. You vote for everything that party stands for. You cannot say 'I vote for Labour on issue A and for the Conservatives on issue B.' You must make a total choice. In contrast, when you spend your income, you do not have to decide which product to spend your entire income on. You can, and do, decide to spread your expenditure among many products. Furthermore, having decided to buy some CDs, you do not have to buy a large number or none at all. You can buy any number you wish and, as your circumstances change, you can vary the number you buy each month, raising it or lowering it a bit. These are marginal decisions—decisions to buy a bit more or a bit less.

Maximizing individuals and producers are constantly making marginal decisions, whether to buy or sell a bit more or less of each of the things that they buy and sell.

Production choices

Producers decide what to produce and how to produce it. Production is a very complex process in any modern economy. A typical car manufacturer assembles a product out of thousands of individual parts. It makes some of these parts itself. Most are subcontracted to parts manufacturers and many of the major parts manufacturers subcontract some of their work out to smaller firms. This kind of production displays two characteristics noted two centuries ago by Adam Smith, and one that is more recent. These are specialization, the division of labour, and globalization.

Specialization

In ancient hunter–gather societies, and in modern subsistence economies, most people make most of the things they need for themselves. However, from the time that people first engaged in settled agriculture and some of them began to live in towns, people have specialized in doing particular jobs. Artisans, soldiers, priests, and government officials were some of the earliest specialized occupations. Economists call this allocation of different jobs to different people **specialization of labour.** There are two fundamental reasons why specialization is extraordinarily efficient compared with universal self-sufficiency.

First, individual abilities differ, and specialization allows each person to do what he or she can do relatively well while leaving everything else to be done by others. Even when people's abilities are unaffected by the act of special-izing, production is greater with specialization than with self-sufficiency. This is one of the most fundamental principles in economics. It is called the principle of **comparative advantage.** An example is given in Box 1.4 and a much fuller discussion is found in Chapter 34.

The second reason concerns changes in people's abilities that occur *because* they specialize. A person who concentrates on one activity becomes better at it than could a jack-of-all-trades. This is called **learning by doing.** It was a factor much stressed by early economists. Modern research into what are called *learning curves* shows that learning by doing is important in many modern industries.

The division of labour

Throughout most of history each artisan who was specialized in making some product made the whole of that product. Over the last several hundred years many technical advances in methods of production have made it efficient to organize agriculture and manufacturing into large-scale firms organized around what is called the **division of labour.** This term refers to specialization *within* the production process of a particular product.

Mass production In a mass-production factory work is divided into specialized tasks using specialized machinery. Each individual repeatedly does one small task that is a small fraction of those necessary to produce any one product. This is an extreme case of the division of labour.

Artisans and flexible manufacturing Two very recent changes have significantly altered the degree of specialization found in many modern production processes. First, individual artisans have recently reappeared in some lines of production. They are responding to a revival in the demand for individually crafted, rather than mass-produced, products. Second, many manufacturing operations are being reorganized along new lines called 'lean production' or 'flexible manufacturing', which was pioneered by Japanese car manufacturers. It has led back to a more craft-based form of organization within the factory. In this technique, which is discussed in more detail in Chapter 8, employees work as a team; each employee is able to do every team member's job rather than one very specialized task at one point on the assembly line.

Globalization

Market economies constantly change, largely as a result of the development of new technologies. Many of the recent changes are referred to as **globalization.** Globalized trade is an old phenomenon. But the usual pattern over most of the last two hundred years was manufactured goods being sent from Europe and North America to the rest of the world, with raw materials and primary products being sent in return. What is new in the last few decades is the globalization of manufacturing.

Box 1.4 Absolute and comparative advantage

A simple case will illustrate the important principles involved in the gains from specialization.

Absolute advantage

Suppose that, working full time on his own, Jacob can produce either 100 pounds of potatoes *or* 40 sweaters per year, whereas Maria can produce 400 pounds of potatoes *or* 10 sweaters. These productive abilities are shown in the first two columns of Table I. Maria has an absolute advantage in producing potatoes because she can grow more per year than Jacob can. However, Jacob has an absolute advantage over Maria in producing sweaters for the same reason. If they both spend *half* their time producing each commodity, the results will be as given in the columns (3) and (4) of Table I.

Now let Jacob specialize in sweaters, producing 40 of them, and Maria specialize in potatoes, producing 400 pounds. The final pair of columns in Table I, labelled 'Full specialization', shows that production of both commodities has risen because each person is better than the other person at his or her speciality. Potato production rises from 250 to 400, while sweater production goes from 25 to 40.

Table I

	Time spent fully producing one product or the other		Time divided equally between producing the two products		Full specialization	
	Potatoes	Sweaters	Potatoes	Sweaters	Potatoes	Sweaters
Jacob	either 100	or 40	50	20	—	40
Maria	either 400	or 10	200	5	400	—
Total			250	25	400	40

Comparative advantage

Now make things a little less obvious by giving Maria an absolute advantage over Jacob in both commodities. We do this by making Maria more productive in sweaters, so that she can produce 48 of them per year, with all other productivities remaining the same. This gives us the new data for productive abilities shown in the first two columns of Table II. Now, compared with Jacob, Maria is four times more efficient at producing potatoes and 20 per cent more efficient at producing sweaters. The second pair of columns in Table II gives the outputs when Jacob and Maria each divide their time equally between the two products.

It is possible to increase their combined production of both commodities by having Maria increase her production of potatoes and Jacob increase his production of sweaters. The final pair of columns in Table II gives an example in which Jacob specializes fully in sweater production and Maria spends 25

Table II

	Time spent fully producing one product or the other		Time divided equally between producing the two products		Jacob is fully specialized; Maria divides her time 25% and 75% between sweaters and potatoes	
	Potatoes	Sweaters	Potatoes	Sweaters	Potatoes	Sweaters
Jacob	either 100	or 40	50	20	—	40
Maria	either 400	or 48	200	24	300	12
Total			250	44	300	52

per cent of her time on sweaters and 75 per cent on potatoes. (Her outputs of sweaters and potatoes are thus 25 and 75 per cent of what she could produce of these commodities if she worked full time on one or the other.) Total production of potatoes rises from 250 to 300, while total production of sweaters goes from 44 to 52.

In this latter example Maria is absolutely more efficient than is Jacob in both lines of production, but her margin of advantage is greater in potatoes than in sweaters. Economists say that Maria has a **comparative advantage** over Jacob in the line of production in which her margin of advantage is greatest (potatoes, in this case). They also say that Jacob has a comparative advantage over Maria in the line of production in which his margin of disadvantage is least (sweaters, in this case).

This example is only an illustration; the principles can be generalized in the following way:

■ Absolute efficiencies are not necessary for there to be gains from specialization.
■ Gains from specialization occur whenever there are *differences* in the margin of advantage one producer enjoys over another in various lines of production.
■ Total production can always be increased when each producer becomes more specialized in the production of the commodity in which it has a comparative advantage.

A more detailed study of the important concept of comparative advantage and its many applications to international trade and specialization must await the chapter on international trade (which is sometimes studied in courses on microeconomics and sometimes in courses on macroeconomics). In the meantime, it is worth noting that the comparative advantage of individuals and of whole nations may change. Maria may learn new skills and develop a comparative advantage in sweaters that she does not currently have. Similarly, whole nations may develop new abilities and know-how that will change their pattern of comparative advantage.

Behind this phenomenon lie the rapid reduction in transportation costs and the revolution in information technology. The cost of moving products around the world has fallen greatly in recent decades owing to containerization and the increasing size of ships. Our ability to transmit and to analyse data has been increasing even more dramatically, while the costs of doing so have been decreasing, equally dramatically. For example, today £1,000 buys a computer that fits into a briefcase and has the same computing power as one that in 1970 cost £5 million and filled a large room. This revolution in information and communication technology (ICT) has made it possible to co-ordinate economic transactions around the world in ways that were difficult and costly fifty years ago and quite impossible a hundred years ago. This, combined with falling costs of transport, has decentralized manufacturing activities. Fifty years ago, if a car was to be assembled in Oxford, all the parts had to be made nearby. Today it is possible to make parts anywhere in the world and get them to Oxford exactly when they are required. As a result, manufacturing, which was formerly concentrated in the advanced industrial countries of Europe and North America, now takes place all over the world. A typical CD player, TV set, or car contains components made in literally dozens of different countries. We still know where a product is assembled, but it is becoming increasingly difficult to say where it is *made*.

Many *markets* are globalizing. For example, as some tastes become universal to young people, we can see the same designer jeans and leather jackets in virtually all big cities. Many *corporations* are globalizing, as more and more of them become what are called **transnationals.** These are massive firms with a physical presence in many countries and an increasingly decentralized management structure. MacDonald's restaurants are as visible in Moscow or Beijing as in London or New York. Many other brands are also virtually universal, such as Coca Cola, Kelloggs, Heinz, Nestlé, Guinness, Mercedes Benz, Rolls-Royce, Sony, and Hoover.

Today no country can take an isolationist economic stance and hope to take part in the global economy where an increasing share of jobs and incomes are created.

Markets and money

People who are specialized in doing only one thing, whether they are artisans, factory workers, or computer programmers, must satisfy most of their wants by consuming things made by other people. In early societies the exchange of goods and services took place by simple mutual agreement among neighbours. In the course of time, however, trading became centred on particular gathering places called *markets*. For example, the French markets or trade fairs of Champagne were well known throughout Europe as early as the eleventh century AD. Even now, many towns in Britain have regular market days. Today, however, the term 'market' has a much broader meaning. We use the term **market economy** to refer to a society in which people specialize in productive activities and meet most of their material wants through exchanges voluntarily agreed upon by the contracting parties.

Specialization must be accompanied by trade. People who produce only one thing must trade most of it to obtain all of the other things they require.

Early trading was by means of **barter,** the trading of goods directly for other goods. But barter is costly in terms of time spent searching out satisfactory exchanges. If a farmer has wheat but wants a hammer, he must find someone who has a hammer and wants wheat. A successful barter transaction thus requires what is called a *double coincidence of wants.*

Money eliminates the cumbersome system of barter by separating the transactions involved in the exchange of products. If a farmer has wheat and wants a hammer, he does not have to find someone who has a hammer and wants wheat. He merely has to find someone who wants wheat. The farmer takes money in exchange. Then he finds a person who wishes to trade a hammer and gives up the money for the hammer.

Money greatly facilitates specialization and trade.

Is there a practical alternative to the market economy?

The answer to the question in the above heading is no in one sense and yes in another. We answer no because the modern economy has no practical alternative to reliance on market determination. At the broad level we can distinguish only four main types of economic system.

Traditional systems

A **traditional economic system** is one in which behaviour is based primarily on tradition, custom, and habit. Young men follow their fathers' occupations—typically, hunting, fishing, and tool-making. Women do what their mothers did—typically, cooking and fieldwork. There are few changes in the pattern of goods produced from year to year, other than those imposed by the vagaries of nature. The techniques of production also follow traditional patterns, except when the effects of an occasional new invention are felt. The concept of private property is often not well defined, and property is frequently held in common. Finally, production is allocated among the members of society according to long-established traditions. In short, the answers to the economic questions of what to produce, how to produce, and how to distribute are determined by traditions.

Such a system works best in an unchanging environment. Under static conditions, a system that does not continually require people to make choices can prove effective in meeting economic and social needs.

Traditional systems were common in earlier times. The feudal system under which most people lived in medieval Europe was a largely traditional society. Today only a few small, isolated, self-sufficient communities still retain mainly traditional systems; examples can be found in the Canadian Arctic and the Himalayas. Also, in many of the world's poorer countries significant aspects of economic behaviour are still governed by traditional patterns.

Command systems

We have already seen that in command systems some central authority determines economic behaviour. It makes most of the necessary decisions on what to produce, how to produce it, and who gets it. Because centralized decision-makers usually lay down elaborate and complex plans for the behaviour that they wish to impose, the terms **command economy** and **centrally planned economy** are usually used synonymously.

The sheer quantity of data required for the central planning of an entire economy is enormous, and the task of analysing it to produce a fully integrated plan can hardly be exaggerated, even in the age of computers. Moreover, the plan must be a rolling process, continually changing to take account not only of current data but also of future trends in labour supplies, technological developments, and people's tastes for various goods and services. This involves the planners in the notoriously difficult business of forecasting the future.

A decade ago over one-third of the world's population lived in countries that relied heavily on central planning to deal with the basic economic questions. Today the number of such countries is small. Even in countries where planning is the proclaimed system, as in China, increasing amounts of market determination are being accepted, even encouraged.

Pure market systems

Earlier in this chapter we have seen the basics of a free-market economy. Millions of consumers decide what products to buy and in what quantities. A vast number of firms produce those products and buy the factor services that are needed to make them. Millions of owners of factors of production decide to whom and on what terms they will sell these services. These individual decisions collectively determine the economy's allocation of resources among competing uses and the distribution of its output among individual citizens.

In a **pure market economy,** all of these decisions, without exception, are made by buyers and sellers acting through unhindered markets. The state provides the background of defining property and protecting rights against foreign and domestic enemies but, beyond that, markets determine all resource allocation and income distribution.

Mixed systems

Fully traditional, fully centrally controlled, and fully free-market economies are useful concepts for studying the basic principles of resource allocation. When we look in detail at any real economy, however, we discover that its economic behaviour is the result of some mixture of central control and market determination, with a certain amount of traditional behaviour as well. The term **mixed economy** refers to an economy in which both free markets and governments have significant effects on the allocation of resources and the distribution of income.

In practice every economy is a mixed economy in the sense that it combines significant elements of all three systems—traditional, command, and market—in determining economic behaviour.

The degree of the mixture of free-market determination and government control varies from economy to economy and over time. There is more free-market determination in the UK and the USA than in France and South Korea. There is more free-market determination in the UK today than there was twenty-five years ago. The degree of the mix also varies from sector to sector within any one economy. For example, European agricultural markets have a substantial amount of government control. Under market determination, the average size of a farm would be much larger and agricultural prices much lower than they now are. In contrast, the markets for information and computer technologies are largely free from government intervention.

So the first answer to the question posed at the outset of this section is no. There is no real alternative to a mixed system with major reliance on markets but a substantial government presence in most aspects of the economy. The second answer is yes. Within the framework of a mixed economy there are substantial alternatives among many different and complex mixes of free-market and government determination of economic life.

Government in the modern mixed economy

Modern market economies in advanced industrial countries are based primarily on market transactions between people who voluntarily decide whether or not to engage in them. Private individuals have the right to buy and sell what they wish, to accept or refuse work that is offered to them, and to move to where they want when they want.

Key institutions are private property and freedom of contract, both of which must be maintained by active government policies. The government creates laws of ownership and contract and then provides the courts to enforce these laws.

In modern mixed economies governments go well beyond these important basic functions. They intervene in market transactions to correct what are called 'market failures'. These are well-defined situations in which free markets do not work well. Resources such as fishing grounds and common pastureland tend to be over-exploited to the point of destruction under free-market conditions. Some products, called public goods, are not provided at all by markets because, once produced, no one can be prevented from using them. So their use cannot be restricted to those who are willing to pay for them. Defence and police protection are public goods. In other cases private transactors impose costs called externalities on those who have no say in the transaction. This is the case when factories pollute the air and rivers. The public is harmed but has no part in the producers' decisions about what to make and how to make it. These are some of the reasons why free markets sometimes fail to function as we would like them to. They explain why citizens wish governments to intervene and alter the allocation of resources that would result from leaving everything to the market.

Also, there are important equity issues that arise from letting free markets determine people's incomes. Some people lose their jobs because firms are reorganizing to become more efficient in the face of new technologies. Others keep their jobs, but the market values their services so poorly that they face economic deprivation. The old and the chronically ill may suffer if their past circumstances did not allow them to save enough to support themselves. For many reasons of this sort we accept government intervention to redistribute income by taking from the 'haves' and giving to the 'have-nots'. Almost everyone supports some redistribution of incomes. Care must be taken, however, not to kill the goose that lays the golden egg. By taking too much from the haves, we risk eliminating their incentive to work hard and produce income, some of which is to be redistributed to the have-nots.

Governments also play a part in influencing the overall level of prices and in attempting to stabilize the economy against extreme fluctuations in income and employment. A stable price level and full employment are the two major goals of what is called the government's macroeconomic policy. These are dealt with in the second half of this book.

These are some of the reasons all modern economies are mixed economies. Throughout most of the twentieth century in advanced industrial societies the mix had been altering towards more and more government participation in decisions about the allocation of resources and the distribution of income. In the last two decades of the century, however, there has been a worldwide movement to lower the degree of government participation. The details of this shift in the market/government mix, and the reasons for it, are some of the major issues that you will study in this book.

Summary

The complexity of the modern economy
■ A market economy is self-organizing in the sense that when individuals act independently to pursue their own self-interest, responding to prices set on open markets, they produce co-ordinated and relatively efficient economic activity.

Resources and scarcity
■ Scarcity is a fundamental problem faced by all economies because not enough resources—land, labour, capital, and entrepreneurship—are available to produce all the goods and services that people would like to consume. Scarcity makes it necessary to choose among alternative possibilities: what products will be produced and in what quantities.

■ The concept of opportunity cost emphasizes scarcity and choice by measuring the cost of obtaining a unit of one product in terms of the number of units of other products that could have been obtained instead.

■ A production-possibility boundary shows all of the combinations of goods that can be produced by an economy whose resources are fully employed. Movement from one point to another on the boundary shows a shift in the amounts of goods being produced, which requires a reallocation of resources.

Who makes the choices and how
■ Modern economies are based on the specialization and

division of labour, which necessitate the exchange of goods and services. Exchange takes place in markets and is facilitated by the use of money. Much of economics is devoted to a study of how markets work to co-ordinate millions of individual, decentralized decisions.

■ Three pure types of economy can be distinguished: traditional, command, and free market. In practice, all economies are mixed economies in that their economic behaviour responds to mixes of tradition, government command, and price incentives.

■ Governments play an important part in modern mixed economies. They create and enforce important background institutions such as private property. They intervene to increase economic efficiency by correcting situations where markets do not effectively perform their co-ordinating functions. They also redistribute income and wealth in the interests of equity.

Topics for review

■ Factors of production

■ Self-organization

■ Goods and services

■ Scarcity, choice, and opportunity cost

■ Production-possibility boundary

■ Resource allocation

■ Growth in productive capacity

■ Specialization and the division of labour

■ Command, traditional, market, and mixed economic systems

Questions for discussion

1 Evidence accumulates that the use of chemical fertilizers, which increases agricultural production greatly, damages water quality. Use a production-possibility curve with agricultural output on the vertical axis and water quality on the horizontal axis to analyse the choice between more food and cleaner water. In what ways does this production-possibility curve reflect scarcity, choice, and opportunity cost? How would an improved fertilizer that increased agricultural output without further worsening water quality affect the curve?

2 Discuss the following statement by a leading economist: 'One of the mysteries of semantics is why the government-managed economies ever came to be called planned and the market economies unplanned. It is the former that are in chronic chaos, in which buyers stand in line hoping to buy some toilet paper or soap. It is the latter that are in reasonable equilibrium—where if you want a cake of soap or a steak or a shirt or a car, you can go to the store and find that the item is magically there for you to buy. It is the liberal economies that reflect a highly sophisticated planning system, and the government-managed economies that are primitive and unplanned.'

3 What is the difference between scarcity and poverty? If everyone in the world had enough to eat, could we say that food was no longer scarce?

4 List some of the things you actually do, or might easily do, that are characteristic of behaviour in (a) a market economy, (b) a command economy, and (c) a traditional economy.

5 How are specialization, division of labour, market economies, and money related to each other?

Chapter 2
How Economists Work

In Chapter 1 we discussed the basic question whose answer gave rise to economics. How do millions of producers and consumers, acting independently in their own self-interest, somehow become organized into a coherent system that delivers the goods and services where and when they are wanted and in about the quantities they are wanted? Economists study how this is done by the mixed market economies in which we live. Economists also identify situations in which markets fail to perform as well as they might. In such cases they ask, 'Could the economy be reorganized to deliver more goods to more people—or in some other way to perform more effectively?' Usually this involves government intervention of one form or another.

Economists then seek to evaluate the efficiency with which governments achieve their goals.

Having sought to understand what is happening in the mixed economy, the next step is often to give advice. 'After all,' one might ask, 'what is the point in understanding things if you cannot try to improve them?' Indeed economists give advice on a wide variety of topics. If you read a newspaper, watch television, or listen to the radio you will often notice some economist's opinions being reported. Perhaps it is on the prospects for unemployment, inflation, or interest rates, on some new tax, on the case for privatization or regulation of an industry, on reform of the National Health Service.

Positive and normative advice

Economists give two broad types of advice, called normative and positive. They sometimes advise that the government ought to try harder to reduce unemployment or to preserve the environment. When they say such things they are giving normative advice. They may be using their expert knowledge to come to conclusions about the costs of various unemployment-reducing or environment-saving schemes. But when they say that the government *ought* to do something, they are making judgements about the value of the various things that the government could do with its limited resources. Advice that depends on a value judgement is normative—it tells others what they ought to do.

Another type of advice is illustrated by the statement 'If the government wants to reduce unemployment, this is an effective way of doing so.' This is positive advice. It does not rely on a judgement about the value of reducing unemployment. Instead the expert is saying, 'If this is what you want to do, here are ways of doing it.'

The distinction between positive and normative is fundamental to any rational inquiry. Much of the success of modern science depends on the ability of scientists to separate their views on *what does*, or *might*, *happen* in the world, from their views on *what they would like to happen*. For example, until the eighteenth century almost everyone believed that the Earth was only a few thousand years old. Evidence then began to accumulate that the Earth was thousands of millions of years old. This evidence was hard for most people to accept since it ran counter to a literal reading of many religious texts. Many did not want to believe the evidence. Nevertheless, scientists, many of whom were religious, continued their research because they refused to allow their feelings about what they wanted to believe to affect their search, as scientists, for the truth. Eventually all scientists came to accept that the Earth is about 4,000 million years old.

Distinguishing what is true from what we would like to be, or what we feel ought to be, depends partly on being able to distinguish between positive and normative statements.

Normative statements depend on value judgements. They involve issues of personal opinion, which cannot be settled by recourse to facts. In contrast, **positive statements** do not involve value judgements. They are statements about what is, was, or will be, that is, statements that are about matters of fact.

Examples of both types of statement are given in Table 2.1. All five statements listed in the table as positive assert

Table 2.1   Positive and normative statements

Positive	Normative
A Raising interest rates encourages people to save.	F People should be encouraged to save.
B High rates of income tax encourage people to evade paying taxes.	G Governments should arrange taxes so that people cannot avoid paying them.
C Raising wage rates causes people to work harder.	H Firms should raise wage rates to provide a just reward for hard work.
D Lowering the price of tobacco causes people to smoke less.	I The government should raise the tax on tobacco to discourage people from smoking.
E The majority of the population would prefer a policy that lowered the level of unemployment to one that brought inflation down.	J The government ought to be more concerned with reducing unemployment than inflation.

things about the nature of the world in which we live. In contrast, the five statements listed as normative require value judgements.

Notice two things about the positive/normative distinction. First, positive statements need not be true. Statement D is almost certainly false. Yet it is positive, not normative. Second, the inclusion of a value judgement in a statement does not necessarily make the statement normative. Statement E is about the value judgements that people hold. We could, however, check to see if people really do prefer inflation to unemployment. We can ask them and we can observe how they vote. There is no need to introduce a value judgement in order to check the validity of the statement itself.

We leave you to analyse the remaining eight statements to decide precisely why each is either positive or normative. Remember to apply the two tests. (1) Is the statement only about actual or alleged facts? If so, it is a positive one. (2) Are value judgements necessary to assess the truth of the statement? If so, it is normative.

Economic theorizing

Economists seek to understand the world by developing theories and models that explain some of the things that have been seen and to predict some of the things that will be seen. What is a theory and what is a model?

Theories

Theories are constructed to explain things. For example, what determines the number of eggs sold in Newmarket in a particular week? As part of the answer to this question, and ones like it, economists have developed a theory of *demand*—a theory that we will study in detail in Chapter 3. Like any other theory, this one is distinguished by its definitions, assumptions, and predictions.

Definitions

The basic elements of any theory are its variables. A **variable** is a magnitude that can take on different possible values.

In our theory of egg purchases the variable *eggs* might be defined as a one-dozen box of grade-A eggs. The variable *price of eggs* is the amount of money that must be given up to purchase the one-dozen carton. The particular values taken on by those two variables might be *2,000 dozen* at a price of £1.80 on 1 July 1997, *1,800 dozen* at a

price of £2.00 on 8 July 1998, and *1,950 dozen* at a price of £1.90 on 15 July 1999.

For a theory of the demand for eggs we define the variable *demand* as the number of cartons of eggs consumers wish to purchase over a particular time-period.

Endogenous and exogenous variables   An **endogenous variable** is a variable that is explained within a theory. An **exogenous variable** influences endogenous variables but is itself determined by factors outside the theory. To illustrate, the quantity of eggs is an endogenous variable in our theory of the demand for eggs. It is determined from within our theory. The state of the weather is an exogenous variable. It affects the number of eggs people demand but we can safely assume that the state of the weather is not determined by economic conditions.[1]

Assumptions

A theory's assumptions concern motives, physical relations, lines of causation, and the conditions under which the theory is meant to apply.

Motives   The theories we study in this book make the

---

[1] Other words are sometimes used to make the same distinction. One frequently used pair is 'induced' for endogenous and 'autonomous' for exogenous. ('Autonomous' means self-governing or independent.)

Box 2.1 Prediction, prophecy, and forecasting

A scientific prediction is a conditional statement that takes the form '*If something is done, then* such and such will follow.' For example, if the government cuts taxes on firms, then investment will increase.

Prediction versus prophecy A prediction of this sort is different from the statement 'I prophesy that in two years' time there will be a large increase in investment because I believe the government will decide to cut tax rates.' The government's decision to cut tax rates in two years' time will be the outcome of many influences, both economic and political. If the prophecy about investment turns out to be wrong because in two years' time the government does not cut tax rates, then all that has been learned is that the person was not good at guessing the behaviour of the government. However, if the government does cut tax rates (in two years' time or at any other time) and investment does not then increase, a conditional scientific prediction in economic theory will have been contradicted.

Prediction versus forecasting Conditional prediction should not be confused with forecasting. Forecasting attempts to predict the future by discovering relations between economic variables such as that the value of Y at some future date depends primarily on the value of X today. If so future Y can be predicted by observing present X. Many conditional predictions are not of this form. Some theories relate the *current value* of Y to the current value of X. These theories provide significant and useful relations that allow us to predict 'if you now do this to X, Y will change now in some specified way', without allowing us to forecast the future. Second, other theories show that the value of X is one important determinant of the future value of Y without being the only determinant. These theories allow us to influence Y in the future without being able to forecast its precise value—because we cannot predict the changes in all the other forces that influence Y. The analogy often drawn between economics and weather forecasting relates to economic forecasting rather than to the wider and more interesting class of conditional—*if . . . then*—economic predictions.

fundamental assumption that everyone pursues their own self-interest when making economic decisions. People are assumed to know what they want, and to know how to go about getting it within the constraints set by the resources at their command.

Physical relations If egg producers buy more chicks and use more labour, land, and chicken feed, they will produce more eggs. This is an example of the most important physical relation in the theory of markets. It concerns assumptions about how the amount of output is related to the quantities of factors of production used to produce it. This relation is specified in what is called a production function.

Conditions of application Assumptions are often used to specify the conditions under which a theory is meant to hold. For example, a theory that assumes there is 'no government' does not mean literally the absence of government, but only that the theory is meant to hold when governments are not significantly affecting the situation being studied.

Direction of causation When economists assume that one variable is related to another, they are assuming some causal link between the two. For example, when the amount that consumers spend on holiday travel is assumed (and observed) to increase as their incomes increase, the causation is assumed to run from income to holiday travel. Consumers spend more on holiday travel *because* they have more income; they do not get more income *because* they spend more on holiday travel—it would be great if they did! Two useful terms are used to indicate this direction of causation. The variable that *does the causing* is called the **independent variable** and the variable that *is caused* is called the **dependent variable.** In

the above example income is the independent variable and expenditure on holiday travel is the dependent variable.

Predictions

A theory's predictions are the propositions that can be deduced from it. For example, a proposition in the theory of demand states, 'If the price of eggs rises, consumers will purchase fewer eggs.' This negative relation between a product's price and the amount people wish to buy applies to all commodities. These propositions are then taken as predictions about real-world events. For example, if the price of CDs is reduced, consumers will buy more of them. Box 2.1 discusses the distinction between predictions, forecasts, and prophecies

Models

Economists often proceed by constructing what they call **economic models.** This term has several different but related meanings.

Sometimes the term 'model' is used as a synonym for a theory, as when economists speak of the model of the determination of national income. Sometimes it may refer to a particular subset of theories, such as the Keynesian model or the neoclassical model of income determination.

More often, a model means a specific quantitative formulation of a theory. In this case, specific numbers are attached to the mathematical relationships defined by the theory, the numbers often being derived from observations of the economy. The specific form of the model can then be used to make precise predictions about, say, the behaviour of prices in the potato market, or the course of national income and total employment. Forecasting

Box 2.2 An illustrative model

It has been observed that the amount of research that goes into improving a new product often depends on the product's current sales—since the profits that finance much of a firm's research and development are generated by its sales. To gain insight into some possible consequences of this relation, we can build a very simple model in which the amount of current research to improve some product is positively related to the amount of that product's current sales. This creates what is called *positive feedback*, because the larger are current sales, the more research is done; the more research is done, the more rapidly the product improves; the more rapidly the product improves, the more current sales rise.

We may then elaborate the model by adding a second product, which competes with the first one. The model then shows that the product that gets the larger sales initially (for whatever reason) will attract more R&D, and hence will be improved more rapidly than the product with the smaller initial sales. This model will reveal one key tendency of positive feedback

systems: initial advantages tend to be reinforced, making it more and more difficult for competitors to keep up. No one believes that this simple model catches everything about the complex interactions when various new products compete with each other in the early stages of their development. But it does alert us to certain forces to watch for when we build more complex models or create more general theories of competition among new products and new technologies.

Interestingly, these self-reinforcing characteristics have been observed in many actual cases. These include the competition to be the power source of the first motor cars early in the twentieth century, the competition among alternative technologies to produce nuclear power in the middle of the century, and the recent competition to produce the operating system of personal computers (which was won by Microsoft). All of these are cases in which early success helped a particular technology to build up an unbeatable lead over competing technologies.

---

models used by the British government and the International Monetary Fund (IMF) are of this type.

The term 'model' is often used to refer to an application of a general theory in a specific context. So if we take our theory of consumer demand and apply it to the egg market in southern England we might speak of a model of the southern English egg market.

Finally, a model may be an illustrative abstraction, not meant to be elaborate enough to be tested. The circular flow in Figure 1.3 on page 7 is a model of this sort. By illustrating how income flows between consumers and producers, it helps us to understand how decisions of these two groups influence each other through factor markets and goods markets. However, the actual flows in any real economy are vastly more complex than the simple flows shown in the figure. The model helps us to understand what is going on without being detailed enough to yield specific testable predictions about real-world behaviour. In some ways, a model of this sort is like a political caricature. Its value is in the insights it provides that help us to understand key features of a complex world.

Box 2.2 gives another example of how an illustrative model may be used to understand some tendencies by studying them in isolation.

Evidence

Economists make much use of evidence, or, as they usually call it, empirical observation. Such observations can be used to test a specific prediction of some theory and to provide observations to be explained by theories.

Tests A theory is tested by confronting its predictions with evidence. Are events of the type contained in the theory followed by the consequences predicted by the theory? For

example, is an increase in the price of eggs met by a fall in the amount of eggs that consumers wish to buy. Generally, theories tend to be abandoned when they are no longer useful. A theory ceases to be useful when it cannot predict better than an alternative theory. When a theory consistently fails to predict better than an available alternative, it is either modified or replaced.

Theory and evidence, which came first? The old question of the chicken and the egg is often raised when discussing economic theories. In the first instance, it was observation that preceded economic theories. People were not born with economic theories embedded in their minds; instead economic theories first arose when people observed the co-ordination of market behaviour and asked themselves how such co-ordination occurred. But, once economics was established, theories and evidence interacted with each other. It has now become impossible to say that one now precedes the other. In some cases empirical evidence may suggest inadequacies that require the development of better theories. In other cases an inspired guess may lead to a theory that has little current empirical support but is subsequently found to explain many observations.

Box 2.3 discusses some more detailed aspects of testability.

Theories about human behaviour

So far we have talked about theories in general. But what about theories that purport to explain and predict human behaviour? A scientific study of human behaviour is only possible if humans respond in predictable ways to things that affect them. Is it reasonable to expect such stability?

Box 2.3 Testability

The way in which a positive statement can be tested against facts varies with the kind of positive statement that is under consideration.

A statement that something exists can be proven by finding a confirming example. But it cannot be conclusively disproved, because it is always possible that we have not looked hard enough and that someone will find a confirming example in the future. For example, the statement that extraterrestrials exist and frequently visit Earth in flying saucers could be proven if well-documented sightings were repeated in situations in which they could be confirmed by scientific measuring techniques—instead of occurring on isolated country roads to single individuals or small groups, as the alleged close-up sightings now do. But it can never be disproved. For no matter how long we look and wait, there always exists the possibility that in the future sightings will occur in a convincing form. In the meantime believers say the statement is true while sceptics say, 'not proven'.

In contrast, a statement that some relation always holds true can be refuted by one well-documented case in which it is does not hold. But it can never be proven, because there always exists the possibility that in the future we will observe a case in which it does not hold. For example, the theory of consumer demand predicts that the relation between a commodity's price and the amount consumers wish to purchase is negative—the lower the price, the higher are desired purchases. Occasional exceptions have been alleged (and we will study some of them in later chapters), but they have not been well documented or repeated enough to satisfy contemporary observers. So we can say that the evidence is consistent with the theory, but we cannot say that the theory is proven, because we cannot rule out the possibility that at some future date a case will be documented in which a price reduction reduces desired purchases.

The general point is:

A statement that something exists can be proven but not refuted. A statement that something always exists can be refuted but not proven.

The statement may refer to the existence of some phenomenon or a relation between two or more variables of the sort that we find in the theories of economics and other fact-based disciplines. In other words, we can show our theories to be consistent with observed facts but we cannot establish that they are true with certainty.

After all, we humans have free will and can behave in capricious ways if the spirit moves us.

Think, however, of what the world would be like if human behaviour were really unpredictable. Neither law, nor justice, nor airline timetables would be more reliable than the outcome of a single spin of a roulette wheel. A kind remark could as easily provoke fury as sympathy. Your landlady might evict you tomorrow or let you off the rent. One cannot really imagine a society of human beings that could work like this. In fact, we live in a world that is a mixture of the predictable, or average, or 'most of the people most of the time', and of the haphazard, contrary, or random.

How is it that human behaviour can show stable responses even though we can never be quite sure what one individual will do? Successful predictions about the behaviour of large groups are made possible by the statistical 'law' of large numbers. Very roughly, this 'law' asserts that (under a carefully specified set of conditions) random movements of a large number of items tend to offset one another.

For example, we might wonder if there is a relation between motorway speed limits and road accidents. When the speed limit is actually lowered, it will be almost impossible to predict in advance what changes will occur in any single individual's driving record. One individual whose record had been good may have a series of accidents after the speed limit is lowered because of deterioration in his physical or emotional health. Another person may have an improved accident record for reasons not associated with the alteration in the speed limit, for example because she purchases a more reliable car. Yet others may have altered driving records for no reasons that we can discern—we may have to put it down to an exercise of unpredictable free will.

If we study only a few individuals, we will learn nothing about the effects of the altered speed limit, since we will not know the importance of all the other causes that are at work. But if we observe 1,000 individuals, the effects of the change in the speed limit—if such effects do exist—will tend to show up in the average. If a lowered speed limit does discourage accidents, the group as a whole will have fewer accidents even though some individuals have more. Individuals may do peculiar things that, as far as we can see, are inexplicable, but the group's behaviour will none the less be predictable, precisely because the odd things that one individual does will tend to cancel out the odd things that some other individual does.

Why economists differ

When all their theories have been constructed and all their evidence has been collected, economists still disagree with each other on many issues. If you hear a discussion among economists on *Newsnight* or *The Money Programme*, or if you read about their debates in the daily press or weekly magazines, you will find that economists frequently disagree with each other. What should we make of this disagreement? Here are five of the many possible sources of disagreement.

First, different economists may be using different benchmarks. For example, inflation may be up compared with last year but down compared with the 1980s. When this sort of thing happens the disagreement is more apparent than real, although it can be confusing to observers.

Second, economists often fail to make it clear to their audience whether they are talking about short-term or long-term consequences. For example, one economist may be noting that a tax cut will stimulate consumption at the cost of lowering savings in the short run while another is pointing out that it will stimulate investment and saving in the long run. Here again the disagreement is more apparent than real, since both these short- and long-run effects command much agreement among economists.

Third, economists often fail to acknowledge the full extent of their ignorance. There are many things on which we know little, and even more on which our evidence is far from conclusive. Informed judgements are then required before an economist takes a position on even a purely positive question. If two economists' judgements differ, the disagreement is real. Evidence is not sufficient, and different people can come to different conclusions on the basis of such evidence as is available. What a responsible economist will do in such cases is to make clear the extent to which informed judgement is involved in any position he or she is taking.

Fourth, different economists have different values, and these normative views play a large part in most public discussions of policy. Many economists stress the importance of individual responsibility, while others stress the need for collective action to deal with certain issues. Different policy advice may stem from such differences in value judgements about what is socially important.

A fifth reason lies in the desire of the media to cover both sides of any contentious issue. As a result the public will usually hear one or two economists on each side of a debate, regardless of whether the profession is divided right down the middle or is nearly unanimous in its support of one side. Thus, the public will not know that in one case a reporter could have chosen from dozens of economists to present each side, whereas in another case the reporter had to spend three days finding someone willing to take a particular side because nearly all the economists supported the other side. In their desire to show both sides of all cases, however, the media present the public with the appearance of a profession equally split over all matters.

Anyone seeking to discredit some particular economist's advice by showing that there is disagreement among economists will have no trouble finding evidence of some disagreement. But those who wish to know if there is a majority view, or even a strong consensus, will find one on a surprisingly large number of issues.

Because the world is complex, and because no issue can be settled beyond any doubt, economists are never in *unanimous* agreement on any issue. None the less, the methods we have been discussing in this chapter have produced an impressive amount of agreement on many aspects of how the economy works and what happens when governments intervene to alter its workings. For example, a survey published in the *American Economic Review* showed strong agreement among economists on many propositions, including 'Rent control leads to a housing shortage' (85 per cent yes). Other examples of these areas of agreement will be found in countless places throughout this book.

Economic data

Economists seek to explain observations made of the real world. Why, for example, did the price of wheat rise last year even though the wheat crop increased? This case poses a problem in explanation only if we have numbers for the wheat crop and the price of wheat.

Economists also use real-world observations to test their theories. For example, did the amount that people saved last year rise—as the theory predicts it should have—when a large tax cut increased after-tax incomes? To test this prediction we need reliable data for people's incomes and their savings.

Political scientists, sociologists, anthropologists, and psychologists all tend to collect the data they use to formulate and test their theories. Economists are unusual among social scientists in mainly using data collected by others, often government statisticians. In economics there is a division of labour between collecting data and using it to generate and test theories. The advantage is that economists do not need to spend much of their scarce research time collecting the data they use. The disadvantage is that they are often not as well informed about the limitations of the data collected by others as they would be if they collected the data themselves.

Once data are collected they can be displayed in various ways, all of which we will see later in this chapter. They can be laid out in tables. They can be displayed in the various types of graph which we study later in this chapter. Where we are interested in relative movements rather than absolute ones, the data can be expressed in index numbers.

Index numbers

Table 2.2 shows how the prices of gold and silver varied over a six-year period from 1990 to 1995. How do these two sets of prices compare in volatility? It is difficult to tell

Table 2.2 Price of gold and silver, 1990–1995 (average July price; US$ per troy ounce)

	Gold	Silver
1990	$363.00	$4.90
1991	368.00	4.39
1992	353.00	4.06
1993	392.00	4.38
1994	385.00	5.39
1995	386.00	5.35

Source: *CRB Commodity Year Book* (Jersey City: Commodity Research Bureau, 1997).

Table 2.3 Calculation of an index of gold prices

1990	(363/363) × 100	=	100.0
1991	(368/363) × 100	=	101.4
1992	(353/363) × 100	=	97.2
1993	(392/363) × 100	=	108.0
1994	(385/363) × 100	=	106.1
1995	(386/363) × 100	=	106.3

Index numbers are calculated by dividing the given price by the base-year price and multiplying the result by 100. For example, the given year price in 1991 of $368 is divided by the base-year price of $363 for 1990 and multiplied by 100 to yield an index for 1991 of 101.4.
Source: Table 2.2.

Table 2.4 Index of gold and silver prices

	Gold	Silver
1990	100.0	100.0
1991	101.4	89.6
1992	97.2	82.9
1993	108.0	89.4
1994	106.1	110.0
1995	106.3	109.2

Sources: Tables 2.2 and 2.3.

from the table because the absolute values of the two prices fluctuate around different levels. It is easier to compare the series if we concentrate on relative rather than absolute price changes. (The absolute change is the actual change in the price; the relative change is the change in the price expressed in relation to some base price.)

Index numbers as relatives

Comparisons of relative changes can be made by expressing each price series as a set of **index numbers.** To do this we take the price at some point of time as the base to which prices in other periods will be compared. We call this the *base period*. In the present example we choose 1990 as the base period for both series. The price in that year is given a value of 100. We then take the price of gold in each subsequent year, called the *given year*, and express it as a ratio of its price in the base year and multiply the result by 100. This gives us an index number of gold prices. We then do the same for silver. The details of the calculations for gold are shown in Table 2.3.

The results, which are shown in Table 2.4, allow us to compare the relative fluctuations in the two series, even though their absolute values are quite different. It is apparent from the figures that silver prices have shown significantly more percentage variability than have gold prices.

The formula of any index number is:

$$\text{Value of index in given period} = \frac{\text{absolute value at given period}}{\text{absolute value in base period}} \times 100.$$

An index number merely expresses the value of some series in any given period as a percentage of its value in the base period. Thus the 1995 index of gold prices of 106.3 tells us that the 1995 price of gold was 106.3 per cent of the 1990 price. By subtracting 100 from any index we get the change from the base to the given year, expressed as a percentage of the base year. So in the above case the price of gold in 1995 was 6.3 per cent higher than in 1990. To take a second example, the silver index of 89.4 in 1993 tells us that the 1993 price of silver was only 89.4 per cent of the

1990 price. Or, what is the same thing, the price had fallen by 10.6 per cent between those two years.

Index numbers as averages

Index numbers are particularly useful if we wish to combine several different series into some average. Say, for example, that we want an index of precious metal prices and gold and silver are the only two commodities we need to worry about.

An unweighted index For any one year we could add the price indexes for gold and silver and average them. This would give us a precious metals index. But the index would give the two prices equal weight in determining the value of the overall index. Such an index is often called an unweighted index, but that is misleading. Actually it is an equal-weight index. It would be sheer luck if this were the appropriate thing to do.

In practice we need to weight each price by some measure of its relative importance, letting the more important prices have more weight than the less important prices in determining what happens to the overall index.

An output-weighted index In the present example we take the value of the outputs as weights. In the base year, gold and silver outputs were $25.4 billion and $2.6 billion respectively. In order to make the new index still have a

Table 2.5 Two indexes of precious metal prices

	Equal weights	Gold = 0.907 Silver = 0.093
1990	100.0	100.0
1991	95.5	100.3
1992	90.1	95.9
1993	98.7	106.3
1994	108.1	106.4
1995	107.8	106.6

Weight really matters. The equal-weight index is calculated for each year by adding the gold and silver indexes from Table 2.4 and dividing by two. The second index is calculated for each year by multiplying the gold index by 0.907 and the silver index by 0.093 and summing the result. The two series behave quite differently as a result of the different weights given to each of the two prices.

all of whom spend much more on accommodation than on sardines.

Graphing economic data

A single economic variable such as unemployment or GDP can come in two basic forms.

Cross-section The first is called **cross-sectional data,** which means a number of different observations on one variable all taken in different places at the same point in time. Figure 2.1 shows an example. The variable in the figure is unemployment as a percentage of the workforce. It is shown for ten selected EU countries for the year 1997.

Time-series The second type of data is called **time-series data.** It refers to observations taken on one variable at successive points in time. The data in Figure 2.2 show the

base period expressed as 100, the weights are all expressed as decimal fractions which sum to 1. To do this we express each value as a fraction of the total value of $28.0 billion. This gives us weights of 0.907 for gold and 0.093 for silver. In other words since the value of silver is only about one-tenth the value of gold, silver prices will be given only one-tenth the influence of gold prices in determining the overall index of precious metal prices. To get our weighted index of precious metal prices we multiply each index value in Table 2.4 by the metal's weight and sum the two to obtain the final index. The results are shown in Table 2.5. The quite different behaviour of the two indexes shows the importance of the choice of weights. When both prices are given equal weight, the index falls sharply in 1991. When gold is weighted by its importance in production, the precious metal index rises in that year.

An index that averages changes in several series is the weighted average of the indexes for the separate series, the weights reflecting the relative importance of each series.

Price indexes Economists make frequent use of indexes of the price level which cover a broad group of prices across the whole economy. One of the most important of these is the retail price index, RPI, which covers goods and services that individuals buy. This is described in detail in the appendix to Chapter 20.

All price indexes are calculated using the same procedure. First, the relevant prices are collected. Then a base year is chosen. Then each price series is converted into index numbers. Finally, the index numbers are combined to create a weighted average index series where the weights indicate the relative importance of each price series. For example, in any retail price series the price of sardines would be given a much smaller weight than the price of living accommodation, because what happens to the price of accommodation is much more important to consumers,

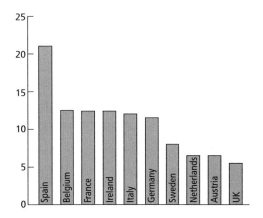

Figure 2.1 Unemployment for ten EU countries, 1997

Source: IMF, *World Economic Outlook*, May 1998.

Figure 2.2 UK unemployment claimant count as a percentage of the workforce, 1975–1998

Source: ONS, *Economic Trends*.

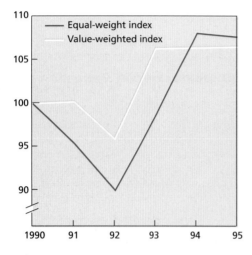

Figure 2.3 Two indexes of precious metals prices

Weights matter. The two series are constructed from the same prices for gold and silver. The difference is only in the weights. The equal-weighted series is a simple average of the indexes for each metal. The value-weighted series is constructed by multiplying the gold price index by 0.907 and the silver price index by 0.093. These weights conform to the relative proportion that each contributes to the total value of production.

Source: Table 2.5.

unemployment rate for the UK from 1975 to 1998. The large variations, with two peaks in the mid-1980s and mid-1990s, are readily apparent.[2] Figure 2.3 shows another time-series, this time for the two indexes of precious metal prices that we calculated in the section on index numbers.

Logarithmic scales Box 2.4 shows another type of series that is useful when relative or percentage changes are more important than absolute changes. When data are graphed on a logarithmic scale, equal distances indicate equal percentage changes rather then equal absolute changes.

Scatter diagrams Another way in which data can be presented is in a **scatter diagram.** This type of chart is more analytical than those above. It is designed to show the relation between two different variables, such as the price of eggs and the quantity of eggs sold. To plot a scatter diagram, values of one variable are measured on the horizontal axis and values of the second variable are measured on the vertical axis. Any point on the diagram relates a specific value of one variable to a corresponding specific value of the other.

The two series plotted on a scatter diagram may be either cross-sectional or time-series. An example of a cross-sectional scatter diagram is a scatter of the price of eggs and the quantity sold in July 1999 at two dozen different places in England. Each dot refers to a price–quantity combination observed in a different place at the same

Table 2.6 Income and savings for ten selected households

Household	Annual income	Annual savings
1	£70,000	£10,000
2	30,000	2,500
3	100,000	12,000
4	60,000	3,000
5	80,000	8,000
6	10,000	500
7	20,000	2,000
8	50,000	2,000
9	40,000	4,200
10	90,000	8,000

Savings tend to rise as income rises. The table shows the amount of income earned by ten selected households together with the amount they saved during the same year.

Figure 2.4 Savings and income

Savings tend to rise as income rises. The figure plots the incomes and savings for the ten households listed in Table 2.6. The number on each dot refers to the household in the corresponding row of the table. (Note that the scales are not the same on the two axes.)

time. An example of a scatter diagram using time-series data is the price and quantity of eggs sold in Newmarket for each month over the last ten years. Each of the 120 dots refers to a price–quantity combination observed at the same place in one particular month.

Table 2.6 shows data for the income and the savings of ten households in one particular year.[3] They are plotted on a scatter diagram in Figure 2.4. Each point in the figure stands for one household, showing its income and its saving. The positive relation between the two stands out. The higher income is, the higher saving tends to be.

[2] We are mainly concerned with the nature of charts. If we wished to make a careful study of variations in unemployment over the period, we would have to adjust for several changes in the definition of unemployment that have had the effect of lowering measured unemployment and that are discussed in Box 31.1 on page 530.

[3] Although our theory refers to individuals, data is often gathered for households, which are defined as a group of individuals who live under the same roof and make joint financial decisions.

Box 2.4 Ratio (logarithmic) scales and graphs

All the graphs in the text use axes that plot numbers on a natural or arithmetic scale. On a **natural scale** the distance between numbers is proportionate to the absolute difference between those numbers. Thus, 200 is placed halfway between 100 and 300. If proportionate rather than absolute changes in variables are important, it is more revealing to use a ratio or **logarithmic scale.** On a ratio scale the distance between two numbers is proportionate to the percentage difference between them (which can also be measured as the absolute difference between their logarithms). Equal distances anywhere on a ratio scale represent equal percentage changes rather than equal absolute changes. On a ratio scale, the distance between 100 and 200 is the same as the distance between 200 and 400, between 1,000 and 2,000, and between any two numbers that stand in the ratio 1:2 to each other. When a time-series is plotted with a natural scale on the horizontal axis (i.e. each year is the same distance apart) but with a ratio scale on the vertical axis, it is said to be plotted on a semi-log scale.

The table shows two series. Series A is growing by a constant absolute amount of 8 units per period while Series B is growing at a constant rate of 100 per cent per period. In the figure, the series are plotted first on a natural scale and then on a semi-log scale.

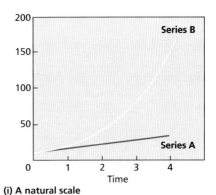

(i) A natural scale

Time-period	Series A	Series B
0	10	10
1	18	20
2	26	40
3	34	80
4	42	160

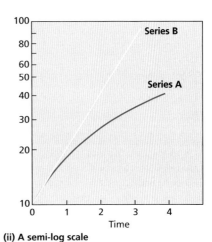

(ii) A semi-log scale

The natural scale makes it easy for the eye to judge absolute variations, and the logarithmic scale makes it easy for the eye to judge proportionate variations. Series A, which grows by a constant absolute amount, appears as a straight line on a natural scale but as a curve of diminishing slope on a semi-log scale, because the same absolute growth represents a decreasing percentage growth. Series B, which grows at a rising absolute rate but a constant percentage rate, appears as a curve of increasing slope on a natural scale but as a straight line on a semi-log scale. This is an important relation: when any economic variable is plotted on a semi-log scale, a constant slope (a straight line) indicates a constant rate of growth; an increasing or a decreasing slope indicates a rising or a falling rate of growth, respectively.

Graphing economic theories

Theories are built on assumptions about relations between variables. For example, the quantity of eggs purchased is assumed to fall as the price of eggs rises, and the total amount an individual saves is assumed to rise as his or her income rises. How can such relations be expressed? When one variable is related to another in such a way that to every value of one variable there is only one possible value of the second variable, we say that the second variable is a function of the first.[4] When we write this relation down,

[4] When two variables, X and Y, are related in some way, mathematicians say that there is a *correspondence* between them. When the relationship is such that to any value of the variable X there corresponds one and only one value of the variable Y, then Y is said to be a *function* of X. For example, in the relation, $Y = a + bX + cX^2$, Y is a function of X because each value of X gives rise to one and only one value of Y. In the text, we confine ourselves to functions. It is worth noting that Y being a function of X does not necessarily imply that X is a function of Y. For example, in the equation given in this footnote, X cannot be expressed as a function of Y because to many values of Y there correspond not one but two values of X.

we are expressing a functional relation between the two variables.

A functional relation can be expressed in words, in a numerical schedule, in mathematical equations, or in graphs.

To illustrate we take a specific example of a relation between a family's annual income, which we denote by the symbol Y, and the total amount it spends on goods and services during that period, which we denote by the symbol C.

1. **Verbal statement.** When income is zero, the family will spend £800 a year (either by borrowing the money or by consuming past savings), and for every £1 of income that it obtains it will increase its expenditure by £0.80.

2. **Schedule.** This shows selected values of the family's income and the amount it spends on consumption.

Annual income	Consumption	Reference letter
0	800	p
2,500	2,800	q
5,000	4,800	r
7,500	6,800	s
10,000	8,800	t

3. **Mathematical (algebraic) statement.** $C = £800 + 0.8Y$ is the equation of the relation just described in words. As a check, you can first see that when Y is zero C is £800. Then you can substitute any two values of Y that differ by £1, multiply each by 0.80, and add 800, and see that the corresponding two values of consumption differ by £0.80.

4. **Geometrical (graphical) statement.** Figure 2.5 shows both the points from the schedule above and the line representing the equation given in point 3.

Figure 2.5 Income and consumption
Consumption expenditure rises as income rises. The figure graphs the schedule and the equation for the consumption function discussed in the text.

Comparison of the values on the graph with the values in the schedule, and with the values derived from the equation just stated, shows that these are alternative expressions of the same relation between C and Y. All four of these modes of expression refer to the same relation between total consumption expenditure and total income.

Functions

Let us look in a little more detail at the algebraic expression of this relation between income and consumption expenditure. To state the expression in general form, detached from the specific numerical example above, we use a symbol to express the dependence of one variable on another. Using 'f' for this purpose, we write

$$C = f(Y). \qquad (1)$$

This is read 'C is a function of Y'. Spelling this out more fully, it reads 'The amount of consumption expenditure depends upon the household's income.'

The variable on the left-hand side is the dependent variable, since its value depends on the value of the variable on the right-hand side. The variable on the right-hand side is the independent variable, since it can take on any value. The letter 'f' tells us that a **functional relation** is involved. This means that a knowledge of the value of the variable (or variables) within the parentheses on the right-hand side allows us to determine the value of the variable on the left-hand side. Although in this case we have used 'f' (as a memory-aid for 'function'), any convenient symbol can be used to denote the existence of a functional relation. In practice Greek letters are often used to denote specific functions.

Functional notation can seem intimidating to those who are unfamiliar with it. But it is helpful. Since the functional concept is basic to all science, the notation is worth mastering.

Functional forms

The expression $C = f(Y)$ states that C is related to Y. It says nothing about the form that this relation takes. The term 'functional form' refers to the specific nature of the relation between the variables in the function. The example above gave one specific functional form for this relation:

$$C = £800 + 0.8Y. \qquad (2)$$

Equation (1) expresses the general assumption that consumption expenditure depends on the consumer's income. Equation (2) expresses the more specific assumption that C rises by 80p for every £1 that Y rises. A second form for the function in (1) would be $C = £600 + 0.9Y$. You should be able to say in words the behaviour implied in this relation.

There is no reason why either of these assumptions

must be true; indeed neither may be consistent with the facts. But that is a matter for testing. What we do have in each equation is a concise statement of a particular assumption.

Graphing functional relations

Different functional forms have different graphs, and we will meet many of these in subsequent chapters. Figure 2.5 is an example of a relation in which the two variables move together. When income goes up consumption goes up. In such a relation the two variables are said to be positively related to each other. (Figure 21.2 on page 362 shows the actual relation for the UK over the period 1955–97.)

Figure 2.6 gives an example of variables that move in opposite directions. As the amount spent on abating smoke pollution goes up the amount of pollution goes down. In such a relation the two variables are said to be negatively related to each other.[5]

Both of these graphs are straight lines. In such cases the variables are said to be *linearly related* to each other.

The slope of a straight line

Slopes are important in economics. They show you how fast one variable is changing as the other changes. The slope is defined as the amount of change in the variable measured on the vertical or *y*-axis per unit change in the variable measured on the horizontal or *x*-axis. In the case of Figure 2.6 it tells us how many tonnes of smoke pollution, symbolized by P, are removed per pound spent on pollution control, symbolized by E. As the figure shows, if we spend £2,000 more we get 1,000 tonnes less pollution. This is 0.5 tonnes per pound spent. On the graph the extra £2,000 is indicated by ΔE, the arrow indicating that E rises by 2,000. The 1,000 tonnes of pollution reduction is indicated by ΔP, the arrow showing that pollution falls by 1,000. (The Greek uppercase letter delta Δ stands for a change in something.) To get the amount of abatement per pound of expenditure we merely divide one by the other. In symbols this is $\Delta P/\Delta E$.

More generally, if we let X stand for whatever variable is measured on the horizontal axis and Y for whatever variable is measured on the vertical axis, the slope of a straight line is $\Delta Y/\Delta X$.

In Figure 2.5 the two variables change in the same direction, so both changes will always be either positive or negative. As a result their ratio, which is the slope of this line, is positive.

In Figure 2.6 the two variables change in opposite directions; when one increases the other decreases. So the two Δs will always be of opposite sign. As a result their ratio, which is the slope of the line, is always negative.

Notice also that straight lines have the same slope no matter where on the line you measure that slope. This tells us what inspection of the chart reveals, that the change in one variable in response to a unit change in the other is the same anywhere on the line. We get 0.5 tonnes of additional pollution abatement for every additional £1 that we spend on abatement no matter how much we are already spending.

Nonlinear functions

The world is seldom as simple as linear relations would make it seem. Although it is sometimes convenient to simplify a real relation between two variables by assuming them to be linearly related, this is seldom the case over their whole range. Nonlinear relations are much more common than linear ones. In the case of pollution abatement it is usually quite cheap to eliminate the first units of pollution. Then, as the smoke gets cleaner and cleaner, the cost of further abatement tends to increase because more

[5] Mathematicians refer to the slopes of curves as *positive* if both variables change in the same direction along the curve (i.e. if either they both increase or they both decrease) and as *negative* if the variables change in opposite directions along the curve (i.e. if one increases while the other decreases). Economists often read curves from left to right, calling negatively sloped curves 'downward-sloping' and positively sloped curves 'upward-sloping'. We stick mainly to the unambiguous terminology of positive and negative slopes.

Figure 2.6 Linear pollution abatement
Pollution falls linearly as expenditure on abatement rises. The slope of the line indicates the marginal reduction in pollution for every increase of £1 of abatement expenditure. It is constant at –0.5, indicating that every extra £1 spent on abatement reduces pollution by half a tonne.

Figure 2.7 Nonlinear pollution abatement

Pollution falls nonlinearly as abatement expenditure rises. When pollution is 8,000 tonnes per year, an additional expenditure of £3,000 reduces pollution by 2,000 tonnes. The marginal return for £1 additional expenditure is $\Delta P / \Delta E$ or 2,000/3,000, which is two-thirds of a tonne per £1 spent on abatement. However, when pollution has already been reduced to 3,000 tonnes, an extra £3,000 spent on abatement reduces pollution by only 500 tonnes. The marginal return for £1 of additional expenditure, $\Delta P / \Delta E$, is now only 500/3,000 or one-sixth of a tonne per £1 spent.

and more sophisticated and expensive methods need to be used. As a result, the graph relating expenditure on abatement and amount of pollution usually looks more like Figure 2.7 than Figure 2.6. Inspection of this figure shows that as more and more is spent, the benefit in terms of extra abatement for an additional £1 of abatement expenditure gets smaller and smaller. This is shown by the diminishing slope of the curve as we move rightward along it. As the figure shows, an extra £1 of expenditure yields two-thirds of a tonne of abatement (2,000/3,000) when pollution is 8,000 tonnes but only one-sixth of a tonne of abatement (500/3,000) when pollution is 3,000 tonnes.

Economists call the change in abatement when a bit more or a bit less is spent on abatement the *marginal* change. The figure shows that the slope of the curve at each point measures this marginal change. It also shows that, in the type of curve illustrated, the marginal return per pound spent is diminishing as abatement proceeds. There is always a payoff to more expenditure over the range shown in the figure, but the return diminishes as more is spent. This relation can be described as *diminishing marginal response*. We will meet such relations many times in what follows, so we emphasize now that diminishing marginal response does not mean that the total response is diminishing. In the figure the total amount of pollution continues to fall as more and more is spent on abatement. But diminishing marginal response does mean that the amount of abatement obtained for *each additional unit of expense* is diminishing as more and more pollution is abated.

Figure 2.8 shows a graph where the marginal return is increasing. It relates expenditure on navigational aids to the number of safe passages. At low levels of expenditure the curve is nearly flat. An additional unit of expenditure does not yield much additional protection. But as more and more is spent, it becomes possible to employ more efficient navigation aids that work together as a whole system. Each extra unit of expenditure yields more additional protection than each previous unit. In this case we have

what economists call *increasing marginal response*. The reason is that navigation aids encounter what are called network externalities. They are most effective not as single stand-alone bits, such as one lighthouse, but as an integrated whole. Each aid becomes more effective the more complex and interrelated is the whole system of which it is a part.

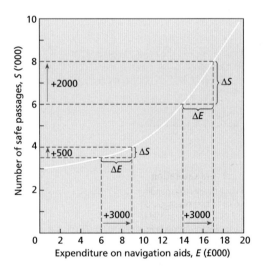

Figure 2.8 Navigation aids

Safe passages increase at an increasing rate as navigation aids are increased. The figure shows the number of safe passages varying positively with the amount spent on navigation aids. Because of network externalities, the number of safe passages increases at an increasing rate as more is spent on navigation aids. An increase in expenditure on navigation aids by £3,000 when expenditure is £6,000 raises safe passages by 500 from 3,500 to 4,000. The marginal return to £1 extra spent on navigation aids is then 500/3,000 or 0.167. In other words it takes £6 to get one more safe passage (3,000/500). When £14,000 is already being spent, a further increase of £3,000 increases safe passages by 2,000 from 6,000 to 8,000. The marginal return from £1 spent on aids is now 2,000/3,000 or 0.667. In other words it only takes £1.50 extra spending to get one more safe passage (3,000/2,000).

Functions with maxima and minima

So far all the graphs we have shown have had either a positive or negative slope over their entire range. But many relations change direction as the independent variable increases. Figures 2.9 and 2.10 extend our navigation and pollution examples over a larger range of the independent variables. We find that as more and more is spent on navigation aids, not only does the marginal contribution of each additional £1 spent begin to decline, but eventually the total safety begins to decline. The reason is that the signals begin to interfere with each other and confuse rather than aid navigators. So as expenditure on navigation aids increases, eventually the safety reaches a maximum and then begins to decline.

At the maximum point the curve is flat—it has a zero slope. Up to that point each £1 spent does increase safety —it has a positive marginal contribution. But after that point each additional unit lowers safety—it has a negative marginal contribution. At the maximum point the marginal contribution is zero.

Now look at Figure 2.10, which extends the pollution abatement example. Here we see that each £1 spent on pollution control adds to abatement up to the amount E_1, but after that abatement begins to decline. The reason in this case may be that the regulations become so costly that firms find ways of evading them and total enforcement gets less effective. Pollution reaches a minimum when E_1 is spent but rises thereafter. Notice that up to E_1 the curve has a negative slope, indicating that more expenditure is associated with less pollution, but that after E_1 the curve has a positive slope, indicating that more expenditure is associated with more pollution. At the point of minimum pollution the tangent to the curve shown by the line T has a slope of zero. (A tangent is a straight line that just touches a curve at some point and lies everywhere above or below the curve near that point.)

These two cases illustrate an important point, which we will see over and over in what follows:

At either a minimum or a maximum value of a function its marginal value is zero.

Figure 2.9 Aid saturation
Eventually increases in expenditure on navigation aids serve to reduce the number of safe passages. Up to E_1 expenditure on navigation aids encounters increasing marginal returns. Each additional £1 of expenditure allows a larger increase in safe passages than each previous £1 of expenditure. Between E_1 and E_2 expenditure encounters decreasing marginal returns. Each additional £1 spent increases the number of safe passages by less than the previous £1 of expenditure. At E_2 safe passages reach a maximum of S_2. Further expenditure encounters negative marginal returns. Each additional £1 spent lowers the number of safe passages. At the maximum point the slope of the tangent T (the straight line that just touches the curve at that point) is zero. At that point the number of safe passages shows no response to small changes in expenditure on navigation aids.

Figure 2.10 Abatement saturation
Beyond a certain point additional abatement expenditure increases pollution. Up to E_1 each additional £1 of expenditure reduces pollution, but at a diminishing amount for each £1. At expenditure E_1 pollution reaches a minimum of P_1. If further amounts are spent, pollution actually rises. At the minimum point the slope of the tangent line T is zero. At that point pollution shows no response to small changes in abatement expenditure.

Measuring marginal values

Economic theory makes much use of the marginal concepts that we have just introduced. Marginal cost, marginal revenue, marginal rate of substitution, and marginal propensity to consume are a few examples of concepts we will meet before too long. 'Marginal' means on the margin or border, and the concept refers to what will happen when there is a *small change* from the present position.

In the last section we gave some examples. Now we need to look at marginals a little more generally. A marginal value refers to functional relations, whether they are written as equations or drawn as graphs. The independent variable, which we call X and draw on the horizontal axis of any graph, determines the value of the dependent variable, which we call Y and draw on the vertical axis of any graph. We wish to know what will be the change in Y when X is changed by a small amount from its present value. The answer is referred to as 'the marginal value of Y' and is given various specific names depending on the economic variables that X and Y stand for.

Figure 2.11 summarizes what we have seen so far. The three lines in part (i) are all positively sloped, making Y positively related to X. The first is a straight line, which means it has a constant slope. The change in Y for a given change in X, the marginal value of Y, is the same no matter where on the line we measure it. The slope of the second line gets steeper as we move along it to the right. The response of Y to a change in X, the marginal value of Y, is increasing. The third line gets flatter as we move along it. The response of Y to a change in X, the marginal value of Y, is decreasing as we move along the line.

In part (ii) the three lines are all negatively sloped, so that Y is negatively related to X. Along the line labelled (4) the response of Y to a change in X is constant. On the line labelled (5) the response is increasing as the slope gets steeper and steeper. On the line labelled (6) the response of Y to a change in X, its marginal value, is decreasing as we move along it, as shown by the flattening of the curve.

So far we have measured marginal values by taking the ratio of the change in Y to the change in X ($\Delta Y/\Delta X$) between any two points on the curve in which we are interested. Actually, however, there is another, more exact measure, to which the ratios we have been using so far are only approximations. Because the exact measure uses differential calculus, introductory texts in economics usually use the ratio approximations, which depend only on simple algebra. This can be confusing, because the language of economic theory refers to the exact measure while introductory examples use the approximation. For this reason we need to explain both of them.

Figure 2.12 relates a firm's monthly output and the revenue that it earns from selling that output. (We assume that the firm only produces what it can sell.) The monthly output is designated by Q. It is plotted on the horizontal or x-axis because it is the independent variable—the one that does the determining. The firm's total revenue is denoted by R. It is plotted on the vertical or y-axis because it is the dependent variable—the one that is determined.

This relation can be expressed as a function, $R = \mathrm{f}(Q)$. It can also be expressed on a graph, as line TR in Figure 2.12 shows. We will see in Chapter 10 that Figure 2.12 corresponds to the shape of part of a monopolist's revenue function, but right now we may take its shape on trust.

The marginal concept that corresponds to this function is *marginal revenue*. It refers to the change in the firm's

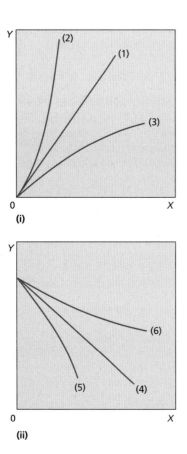

Figure 2.11 Positive and negative relations
Y is positively related to X in all three curves in part (i) and negatively related in all three curves in part (ii). The lines on the two graphs show the response of Y to a change in X. In (1) and (4) this response is constant. In curves (2) and (5) the response is increasing as we move along the curve to the right. In curves (3) and (6) the response is diminishing.

Figure 2.12 A total revenue curve

Total revenue *TR* rises at a diminishing rate, indicating decreasing marginal revenue. Incremental revenue when output goes from 10 to 30 is given by the ratio $\Delta R/\Delta Q$. True marginal revenue is given by the slope of the tangent *T* at 10 ($\Delta R_T/\Delta Q_T$). True marginal revenue at 30 is given by the slope of the tangent *T'* ($\Delta R_{T'}/\Delta Q_{T'}$).

revenue when output is altered slightly from its present level. But what do we mean by 'altered slightly'? The answer depends on which marginal concept we use.

The approximation to marginal revenue is called the incremental ratio, which is the measure we have used so far. In Figure 2.12 let the firm be selling 10 units, with corresponding total revenue of £250. Now the firm decides to increase its output and sales to 30 units. Revenue rises along the *TR* curve to £400. The increase in sales is 20 units and the increase in revenue is £150. Using the Δ notation for changes, we can write this as

$$\Delta R/\Delta Q = £150/20 = £7.50.$$

Thus incremental revenue is £7.50 per unit of additional sales when sales change from 10 to 30. This means that sales are increasing at an average rate of £7.50 per unit of commodity sold over the range from 10 to 30 units. We may call this the marginal revenue at 10 units of output but, as we will see, it is only an approximation to the true marginal revenue at that output.

Graphically, as Figure 2.12 shows, incremental revenue is the slope of the line joining the two points in question. (In geometry the line joining two points on a curve is called a chord.) In this case the two points are on the revenue function corresponding to outputs of 10 and 30. Look at the small triangle created by these points. Its base, shown by ΔQ, is 20 units in length and its vertical side,

shown by ΔR, is 150 units in height. The slope of the line joining the two points (the hypotenuse of the triangle we are considering) is 150/20 = 7.50, which is the incremental revenue. Visually it is clear that this slope tells us the average gradient or steepness of the revenue function over the range from $Q = 10$ to $Q = 30$. It thus tells us how fast revenue is changing *on average* as output changes over the range of Q from 10 to 30.

Incremental revenue will be different at different points on the function. For example, when output goes from 30 units to 50 units, revenue goes from 400 to 450. Using these changes we calculate the incremental revenue to be $\Delta R/\Delta Q = £50/20 = £2.50$.

This calculation confirms what visual inspection of the figure suggests: the larger is output over the ranges graphed in the figure, the less is the response of revenue to further increases in output. Marginal revenue is positive but declining.

The incremental ratio is an approximation to the true marginal concept, which in the present case measures the tendency for *R* to change as *Q* changes at each precise point on the curve. (Whereas the incremental ratio measures the average tendency over a range of the curve.) The value of this marginal revenue is given by the slope of the tangent to the point on the function in which we are interested. Thus the slope of the line *T*, which is the tangent to the curve at the point corresponding to 10 units of output, gives the 'true' marginal revenue at 10 units of output.[6] This slope is shown on the figure as $\Delta R_T/\Delta Q_T$, where the *T*s tell us that we are measuring this ratio along the line *T*. The slope of the line *T'* is indicated on the figure by the ratio $\Delta R_{T'}/\Delta Q_{T'}$. This tells us the precise marginal revenue at 30 units of output, the point at which *T'* is tangent to the *TR* curve.

Figure 2.12 shows that the incremental ratio declines as we measure it at larger and larger values of *Q*. It should be visually obvious that this is also true for true marginal revenue: the slope of the tangent to the function is smaller the larger is the value of *Q* at which the tangent is taken.

Now try measuring the incremental ratio starting at 10 units of output but for smaller and smaller changes in output. Instead of going from 10 to 30, go from 10 to 20. This brings the two points in question closer together and, in the present case, it steepens the slope of the line joining them. It is visually clear in the present example that as ΔQ is made smaller and smaller, the slope of the line corresponding to the incremental ratio starting from $Q = 10$ gets closer and closer to the slope of the tangent corresponding to the true marginal value evaluated at $Q = 10$. The degree

---

[6] Because of the thickness of the lines, the tangents in the figure sometimes seem to coincide with the curve over a range. It is of course impossible for a curve and a straight line to do this. The true tangents *T* and *T'* touch the curve *TR* at $Q = 10$ and $Q = 30$ respectively and lie above the curve for all other nearby values of *Q*.

of approximation of $\Delta R/\Delta Q$ to the slope of the tangent T is improving.

Now we can state our conclusions in general for the function $Y = f(X)$.

1. The marginal value of Y at some initial value of X is the rate of change of Y per unit change in X as X changes from its initial value.

2. The marginal value is given by the slope of the tangent to the curve graphing the function at the point corresponding to the initial value of X.

3. The incremental ratio $\Delta Y/\Delta X$ measures the average change in Y per unit change in X over a range of the function starting from the initial value of X.

4. As the range of measurement of the incremental ratio is reduced (i.e. as ΔX gets smaller and smaller), the value of the incremental ratio eventually approaches the true marginal value of Y. Thus, the incremental ratio may be regarded as an approximation to the true marginal value, the degree of approximation improving as ΔX gets very small.[7]

Moving between marginal and total values

We saw in a previous section that marginal revenue refers to the change in the total revenue as output changes. Figure 2.13(i) draws a new total revenue curve. Figure 2.13(ii) gives the corresponding marginal revenue curve.[8]

From totals to marginals

Assume that we have only the curve in part (i) of Figure 2.13, and that we wish to obtain the curve in part (ii). Graphically, the marginal curve is derived by measuring the slope of the tangent to the TR curve at each level of output and plotting the value of that slope against the same level of output in part (ii) of the figure. One example is shown in the figure. When output is 60 in part (i), the slope of the tangent to the curve is 40. This value of 40 is then plotted against output 60 in part (ii) of the figure. Looked at either as the slope of the tangent to the TR curve in part (i) or as the height of the MR curve in part (ii), this value tells us that revenue increases at a rate of 40 per unit increase in output when output is 60 units. Repeating this experiment we could discover the marginal revenue corresponding to each point on the TR curve and plot each value in part (ii). (Fortunately calculus provides a simpler way of finding the marginal revenue in one step.)

From marginals to totals

Now let us assume that we have only the curve in part (ii) of the figure, and that we wish to derive the curve in part

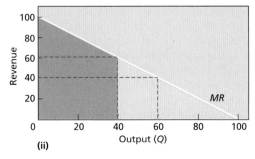

Figure 2.13 Total and marginal revenue curves

Total revenue rises at a diminishing rate, indicating positive but diminishing marginal revenue. In part (i) the slope of the tangent, T, to the TR curve at output 60 is 40. This is plotted in part (ii) as the marginal revenue at output 60. To reverse the procedure and go from marginal to total revenue, the area under the MR curve up to any point is summed, giving total revenue at that point. At output 40 the shaded area is 3,200, which is the total revenue.

(i). In other words, we know the marginal revenue associated with any specific output and we wish to deduce the corresponding total revenue. This is an operation that is frequently employed in economics and you need to understand it.[9]

---

[7] This footnote need only concern those who already know some calculus. We must be careful how we state conclusion 4 since, on a wavy function, the degree of approximation may alternately improve and worsen as ΔX gets smaller; but provided the conditions for a derivative to exist are met, there *must* be a small neighbourhood around the point in question within which the degree of approximation improves as ΔX gets smaller, with the 'error' going to zero as ΔX goes to zero

[8] We have drawn a new curve because in order to make the earlier points visually obvious we needed a TR curve with a sharply diminishing slope, which we drew freehand. Now we want a TR curve for which we actually know the marginal values at each point. To do this we take a curve with a specific algebraic formula. For the plotted curve we have chosen the formula $TR = 100Q - 0.5Q^2$.

[9] We can do this for the revenue that is determined by output but not for any amount that is not. In this case, we can be sure that sales revenue is zero when output is zero so all revenue will be associated with output. But if the firms had other sources of revenue that were independent of output we could not deduce these from knowledge of how revenue varied with output. (Mathematically this is a way of saying that integration is only determined up to an arbitrary constant.)

If we had a schedule of incremental ratios, all we would have to do is add up the necessary marginal values. This is illustrated in Table 2.7. For example, the total revenue when output is three units is calculated in the table as the sum of the contributions to total revenue of the first, the second, and the third units. This illustrates the fact that if we know what each unit adds to total revenue, we can calculate the total revenue associated with any amount of output, say 10 units, by summing the separate contributions to revenue of each of the 10 units.

Graphically, the same operation is done on a continuous curve by calculating the area under the marginal curve from 0 to any given level of output. For example, at output 40 in part (ii) of Figure 2.13, the shaded area under the *MC* curve gives total revenue, which is 3,200. The value of this area is the height of the *TR* curve in part (i) at output 40.[10]

The common sense of this relation is that the height of the *MR* curve at any given output tells us how much is being added to revenue by a change in output when output has the value in question. Adding all these heights, from zero to the output in question, means summing all the

Table 2.7 Total and marginal revenue associated with various levels of output

Output	Marginal revenue	Total revenue
1	£99.5	£99.5
2	98.5	198.0
3	97.5	295.5
4	96.5	392.0

Summing the marginal revenue yields the total revenue.

contributions to revenue from each unit of output from zero to the amount in question. On a continuous curve, this summation yields the area under the curve between zero and that output.

---

[10] You may notice that the scale on the vertical axis is different in the two figures. If we plotted *MR* on the same scale as *TR* you would hardly see it. Look where 100 would be plotted in part (i)! This is because the entire area in part (ii) is being related to the height of a line in part (i).

Summary

Positive and normative advice

■ A key to the success of scientific inquiry lies in separating positive questions about the way the world works from normative questions about how one would like the world to work.

Economic theorizing

■ Theories are designed to explain and predict what we see. A theory consists of a set of definitions of the variables to be employed, a set of assumptions about how things behave, and the conditions under which the theory is meant to apply.

■ A theory provides conditional predictions of the type '*if* one event occurs, *then* another event will also occur'. An important method of testing theories is to confront their predictions with evidence.

■ The term 'model' has a number of meanings, including (*a*) a synonym for theory, (*b*) a precise realization of a general theory, with a specific numerical relation in place of each general relation posited by the theory, (*c*) an application of a general theory to a specific case, and (*d*) a simplified set of relations designed to study one specific force in isolation.

Economic data

■ Index numbers express economic series in relative form. Values in each period are expressed in relation to the value in the base period, which is given a value of 100.

■ Economic data may be graphed in three different ways. Cross-section graphs show observations taken at the same time. Time-series show observations on one variable taken over time. Scatter diagrams show points each one of which refers to specific observations on two different variables.

Graphing economic theories

■ A functional relation can be expressed in words, in a schedule giving specific values, in a mathematical equation, or in a graph.

■ A graph of two variables has a positive slope when they both increase or decrease together and a negative slope when they move in opposite directions.

Measuring marginal values

■ The marginal value of a variable gives the amount it changes in response to a change in a second variable. When the variable is measured on the vertical axis of a diagram its marginal value is measured by the slope of the tangent line to the point in question and approximated by the slope of the line joining two nearby points.

Topics for review

■ Positive and normative statements

■ Endogenous and exogenous variables

■ Theories and models

■ Variables, assumptions, and predictions

- Time-series and cross-sectional graphs and scatter diagrams
- Functional relations
- Ways of expressing a relation between two variables
- Positive and negative relations between variables
- Positive and negatively sloped curves
- Marginal and incremental values
- Maximum and minimum values

Questions for discussion

1 Make five statements about unemployment. Classify each as either positive or normative. If your list contains all of one type or all of the other, add a sixth of the opposite type.

2 Write down the name of three variables which we might encounter in economics—one price, one quantity, and one that is neither. Sketch time-series charts, cross-sectional charts, and scatter diagrams in which each might be involved.

3 Name four pairs of things that depend on each other. In each relation, which is the dependent variable and which is the independent variable? Give symbols to each and express their dependencies in the form of a function and in a graph.

4 Draw three graphs in which the dependent variable increases at an increasing rate, at a constant rate, and at a diminishing rate. Then draw three where it decreases at an increasing, constant, and diminishing rate. Finally draw graphs where the variable reaches a maximum point and where it reaches a minimum point. For how many of these graphs can you think of real relations that might be described by them—other than the ones given in the text of this chapter?

5 A well-known economic theory predicts that if you raise people's wages they may work less. Draw a graph to illustrate this possibility. Does the possibility seem likely to you? Why or why not? How might you go about testing this prediction? (You can check your present answer when you read Chapter 15.)

Part One
Introduction to the Market Economy

Chapter 3
Demand, Supply, and Price

How do individual markets work? Now that the preliminaries are completed, we are ready to study this key question. The answer reveals what are called the laws of supply and demand. To derive them, we look first at the determinants of demand, then at those of supply, and then at how demand and supply interact to determine market price. Finally, we discuss the various types of market and the concept of a market economy together with its individual sectors.

Economics is about the behaviour of people. Much that we observe in the world, and that we assume in our theories, can be traced back to decisions taken by millions of individuals. Any person who makes decisions relevant to our theory is called an **agent.** To make the study of their behaviour more manageable, agents are consolidated into three groups: individuals, firms, and government. These are the *dramatis personae* of economic theory, and the stage on which their play is enacted is the market. In this chapter you will encounter both individuals as demanders and firms as suppliers.

Demand

Individuals and motives

The agents for demand theory are all assumed to be adult individuals who earn income by selling factor services (the services of their labour, land, or capital) and spend this income purchasing goods and services.

When one applies demand theory to real-world observations, however, the spending unit that must be studied is often not the individual but the household. A **household** is defined as all the people who live under one roof and who make joint financial decisions or are subject to others who make such decisions for them. Some economists such as the American Nobel Prize-winner Gary Becker have studied resource allocation within households. For purposes of developing the elementary theory of market behaviour, however, we view consumers as individuals.

Economists assume that each individual consumer seeks maximum *satisfaction*, or *well-being*, or *utility*, as the concept is variously called. The consumer 'maximizes utility' within the limits set by his or her available resources.

The nature of demand

The amount of a product that consumers wish to purchase is called the **quantity demanded.** Notice two important things about this concept. First, quantity demanded is a *desired* quantity. It is how much consumers *wish* to purchase, not necessarily how much they actually succeed in purchasing. We use phrases such as **quantity actually purchased** or **quantity actually bought and sold** to distinguish actual purchases from quantity demanded. Second, note that quantity demanded is a *flow*. We are concerned not with a single isolated purchase, but with a continuous flow of purchases. We must, therefore, express demand as so much per period of time—e.g. 1 million oranges *per day*, or 7 million oranges *per week*, or 365 million oranges *per year*. The important distinction between stocks and flows is discussed in Box 3.1.

The concept of demand as a flow appears to raise difficulties when we deal with the purchases of durable consumer goods (often called consumer durables). It makes obvious sense to talk about a person consuming oranges at the rate of 30 per month, but what can we say of a consumer who buys a new television set every five years? This apparent difficulty disappears if we measure the demand for the *services* provided by the consumer durable. Thus, at the rate of a new set every five years, the television purchaser is using the service (viewing TV programmes) at the rate of 1/60 of a set per month.

Box 3.1 Stocks and flows

Economics makes extensive use of both stock and flow variables and it is important not to confuse the two. A *flow variable* has a time dimension; it is so much per unit of time. The quantity of free-range eggs purchased in Glasgow is a flow variable. Being told that the number purchased was 2,000 dozen eggs conveys no useful information unless we are also told the period of time over which these purchases occurred. For example, 2,000 dozen per hour would indicate an active market in eggs, while 2,000 dozen per month would indicate a sluggish market.

A *stock variable* has no time dimension; it is just so much. Thus, the number of eggs in an egg producer's warehouse—for example, 20,000 dozen eggs—is a stock variable. All those eggs are there at one time, and they remain there until something happens to change the stock held by the producer. The stock variable is just a number, not a rate of flow of so much per day or per month.

Economic theories use both flow variables and stock variables, and it takes a little practice to keep them straight. The amount of income earned is a flow—so much per year or per month or per hour. The amount of a consumer's expenditure is also a flow—so much spent per week or per month. In contrast, the amount of money in your bank account is a stock—just so many pounds sterling. The key test for a variable being a flow is that a time dimension is required to give it meaning. Other variables are neither stocks nor flows; they are just numbers, for example the price of eggs.

The determinants of quantity demanded: the demand function

Six main variables influence the quantity of each product that is demanded by each individual consumer:

1. The price of the product
2. The prices of other products
3. The consumer's income and wealth
4. Various 'sociological' factors
5. The consumer's tastes
6. Forces outside human control, such as the weather

Making use of the functional notation that was introduced in Chapter 2, the above list is conveniently summarized in what is called a **demand function**:

$$q_n^{\text{d}} = \text{D}(p_n, p_1, \ldots, p_{n-1}, Y, S).$$

What do each of the terms in the above expression stand for? The term q_n^{d} stands for the quantity that the consumer demands of some product, which we call product n. The term p_n stands for the price of this product, while $p_1, \ldots, p_{n-1}$ is a shorthand notation for the prices of all other prod-

ucts. The term Y is the consumer's income. The term S stands for a host of sociological (and other) factors such as number of children, place of residence (e.g. big city, small town, country), and the state of the weather. Finally, the form of the function D is determined by the tastes of the consumer.

The demand function is just a shorthand way of saying that quantity demanded, which is recorded on the left-hand side, depends on the variables that are recorded on the right-hand side. The form of the function determines the nature of that dependence. (Recall that the 'form of the function' refers to the precise quantitative relation between the variables on the right-hand side of the equation and the variables on the left.)

We will not be able to understand the separate influences of each of the above variables if we ask what happens when everything changes at once. To avoid this difficulty, we consider the influence of the variables one at a time. To do this, we use a device that is frequently employed in economic theory. We assume that all except one of the variables in the right-hand side of the above expression are held constant. We then allow this one variable, say p_n, to change and see how the quantity demanded (q_n^{d}) changes. We are then studying the effect of changes in one influence on quantity demanded, *assuming that all other influences remain unchanged*, or, as economists are fond of putting it, **ceteris paribus** (which means 'other things being equal').

We can do the same for each of the other variables in turn, and in this way we can come to understand the effect of each variable. Once this is done, we can add up the separate influences of each variable to discover what will happen when several variables change at the same time—as they usually do in practice.

Demand and price

We are interested in developing a theory of how products get priced. To do this, we hold all other influences constant and ask, 'How will the quantity of a product demanded vary as its own price varies?'

A basic economic hypothesis is that the lower the price of a product, the larger the quantity that will be demanded, other things being equal.[1]

Why might this be so? A major reason is that there is usually more than one product that will satisfy any given desire or need. Hunger may be satisfied by meat or vegetables; a desire for green vegetables may be satisfied by broccoli or spinach. The need to keep warm at night may be satisfied by several woollen blankets, or one electric blanket, or a sheet and a lot of oil burned in the boiler. The

---

[1] In this chapter we introduce the hypothesis as an assumption. In Chapters 6 and 7 we derive it from more basic assumptions.

desire for a holiday may be satisfied by a trip to the Scottish Highlands or to the Swiss Alps, the need to get there by an aeroplane, a bus, a car, or a train; and so on. Name any general desire or need, and there will usually be several products that will contribute to its satisfaction.

Now consider what happens if we hold income, tastes, population, and the prices of all other products constant and vary the price of only one product.

First, let the price of the product rise. The product then becomes a more expensive way of satisfying a want. Some consumers will stop buying it altogether; others will buy smaller amounts; still others may continue to buy the same amount; but no rational consumer will buy more of it. Because many consumers will switch wholly, or partially, to other products to satisfy the same want, less will be bought of the product whose price has risen. For example, as meat becomes more expensive, consumers may switch some of their expenditure to meat substitutes; they may also forgo meat at some meals and eat less meat at others.

Second, let the price of a product fall. This makes the product a cheaper method of satisfying any given want. Consumers will buy more of it and less of other similar products whose prices have not fallen. These other products have become expensive *relative to* the product in question. For example, when a bumper tomato harvest drives prices down, shoppers buy more tomatoes and fewer other salad ingredients, which have now become relatively more expensive than tomatoes.

The demand schedule and the demand curve

An individual's demand A **demand schedule** is one way of showing the relationship between quantity demanded and price. It is a numerical tabulation that shows the quantity that will be demanded at some selected prices.

Table 3.1 shows one consumer's demand schedule for eggs. Alice often eats boiled eggs for breakfast, and living

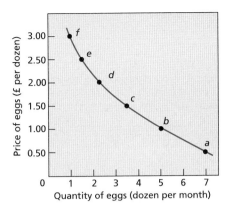

Figure 3.1 Alice's demand curve

This curve relates the price of a commodity to the amount that Alice wishes to purchase. Each point on the figure relates to a row in Table 3.1. For example, when the price is £3.00, 1 dozen are bought per month (point *f*), while when the price is £0.50, 7 dozen are bought (point *a*).

on her own, she often finds omelettes a convenient evening meal. But she does not have a lot of money, so she keeps an eye on the price of eggs when she does her weekly supermarket shopping. The table shows the quantity of eggs that she wishes to buy each month at six selected prices. For example, at a price of £1.50 per dozen Alice demands 3.5 dozen per month. For easy reference each of the price–quantity combinations in the table is given a letter.

Next we plot the data from Table 3.1 in Figure 3.1, with price on the vertical and quantity on the horizontal axis.[2] The smooth curve drawn through these points is called the demand curve. It shows the quantity that Alice would like to buy at every possible price; its *negative slope* indicates that the quantity demanded increases as the price falls.

A single point on the demand curve indicates a single price–quantity relation. *The whole demand curve shows the complete relation between quantity demanded and price.* Economists often speak of the conditions of demand in a

Table 3.1 Alice's demand schedule for eggs

Reference letter	Price (£ per dozen)	Quantity demanded (dozen per month)
a	0.50	7.0
b	1.00	5.0
c	1.50	3.5
d	2.00	2.5
e	2.50	1.5
f	3.00	1.0

The table shows the quantity of eggs that Alice demands at each selected price, other things being equal. For example, at a price of £1.00 per dozen she demands 5 dozen per month, while at a price of £2.50 per dozen she demands only 1.5 dozen.

[2] Readers trained in other disciplines often wonder why economists plot demand curves with price on the vertical axis. The normal convention, which puts the independent variable (the variable that does the explaining) on the horizontal axis and the dependent variable (the variable that is explained) on the vertical axis, calls for price to be plotted on the horizontal axis and quantity on the vertical axis.

The axis reversal—now enshrined by a century of usage—arose as follows. The analysis of the competitive market that we use today stems from the French economist Leon Walras (1834–1910), in whose theory *quantity* was the dependent variable. Graphical analysis in economics, however, was popularized by the English economist Alfred Marshall (1842–1924), in whose theory *price* was the dependent variable. Economists continue to use Walras's theory and Marshall's graphical representation, and thus draw the diagram with the independent and dependent variables reversed—to the everlasting confusion of readers trained in other disciplines. In virtually every other graph in economics the axes are labelled conventionally, with the dependent variable on the vertical axis.

Figure 3.2 The relation between individual and market demand curves

The market demand curve is the horizontal sum of the demand curves of all consumers in the market. The figure illustrates aggregation over two individuals, William and Sarah. For example, at a price of £2.00 per dozen William purchases 2.4 dozen and Sarah purchases 3.6 dozen and together they purchase 6 dozen.

particular market as 'given' or as 'known'. When they do so they are referring not just to the particular quantity that is being demanded at the moment (i.e. not just to a particular point on the demand curve). Instead they are referring to the whole demand curve, to the complete functional relation whereby desired purchases are related to all possible alternative prices of the product.

The market demand curve So far we have discussed how the quantity of a product demanded by one consumer depends on the product's price, other things being equal. To explain market behaviour, we need to know the total demand of all consumers. To obtain a market demand schedule, we sum the quantities demanded by each consumer at a particular price to obtain the total quantity demanded at that price. We repeat the process for each price to obtain a schedule of total, or market, demand at all possible prices. A graph of this schedule is called the *market demand curve*.

To avoid unnecessary complication, Figure 3.2 illustrates the summation graphically for only two consumers, Sarah and William. The figure illustrates the proposition that the market demand curve is the horizontal sum of the demand curves of *all* the individuals who buy in the market.

In practice, our knowledge of market curves is usually derived by observing total quantities directly. The derivation of market demand curves by summing individual curves is a theoretical operation. We do it to understand the relation between curves for individual consumers and market curves.

In Table 3.2 we assume we have data for the market demand for eggs. The schedule tells us the total quantity that will be demanded by all buyers in that market at selected market prices. The data are plotted in Figure 3.3, and the curve drawn through these points is the market demand curve.

Table 3.2 A market demand schedule for eggs

Reference letter	Price (£ per dozen)	Quantity demanded ('000 dozen per month)
U	0.50	110.0
V	1.00	90.0
W	1.50	77.5
X	2.00	67.5
Y	2.50	62.5
Z	3.00	60.0

The table shows the quantity of eggs that would be demanded by all consumers at selected prices, *ceteris paribus*. For example, row *W* indicates that if the price of eggs were £1.50 per dozen, consumers would want to purchase 77,500 dozen per month.

Determinants of demand once again

When we go from the individual consumer's demand curve to the market demand curve, we must reconsider item 3 in the above list of the determinants of demand. 'Consumer income' now refers to *the total income of all consumers*. If, for example, the population increases as a result of immigration and each new immigrant has an income, demands for most products will rise even though existing consumers have unchanged incomes and face unchanged prices.

A seventh determinant: income distribution among individuals When we take total income of all consumers as our income variable, we must add another factor to the major determinants of demand. Consider two societies with the same total income. In one society there are some rich people, many poor people, but only a few in the middle-income range. In the second society, most of the people have incomes that do not differ much from the average income for all consumers. Even if all other vari-

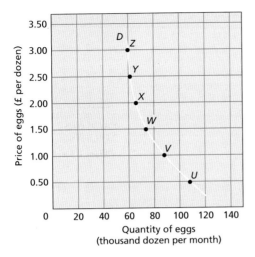

Figure 3.3 A market demand curve for eggs
The negative slope of the curve indicates that quantity demanded increases as price falls. The six points correspond to the six price–quantity combinations shown in Table 3.2. The curve drawn through all of the points and labelled *D* is the demand curve.

Table 3.3 Two alternative market demand schedules for eggs

(1)	(2) Price of eggs (£ per dozen)	(3) Quantity of eggs demanded at original level of personal income ('000 dozen per month)	(4) Quantity of eggs demanded when personal income rises to new level ('000 dozen per month)	(5)
U	0.50	110.0	140.0	U'
V	1.00	90.0	116.0	V'
W	1.50	77.5	100.8	W'
X	2.00	67.5	90.0	X'
Y	2.50	62.5	81.3	Y'
Z	3.00	60.0	78.0	Z'

An increase in total consumers' income increases the quantity demanded at each price. When income rises, quantity demanded at a price of £1.50 per dozen rises from 77,500 dozen per month to 100,800 dozen per month. A similar rise occurs at every other price. Thus the demand schedule relating columns (2) and (3) is replaced by the one relating columns (2) and (4). The graphical representations of these two schedules are labelled D_0 and D_1 in Figure 3.4.

ables that influence demand are the same, the two societies will have quite different patterns of demand. In the first there will be a large demand for Mercedes-Benz and Rolls-Royce cars and also for baked beans, bread, and chips. In the second, there will be a smaller demand for these products, but a large demand for skiing holidays, medium-sized cars, and other middle-income consumption goods. Clearly, the distribution of income is a major determinant of market demand.

Market demand: a recapitulation

We now summarize what we have learned about demand.

The total quantity demanded depends on the price of the product being sold, on the prices of all other products, on the income of the individuals buying in that market, on the distribution of that income among the individuals, and on their tastes. The market demand curve relates the total quantity demanded to the product's own price, on the assumption that all other prices, total income, its distribution among individuals, and tastes are held constant.

Shifts in the demand curve

The demand schedule and the demand curve are constructed on the assumption of *ceteris paribus*. But what if other things change, as surely they must? What, for example, if consumers find themselves with more income? If they spend their extra income, they will buy additional quantities of many products *even though market prices are unchanged*, as shown in Table 3.3. But if consumers in-

Figure 3.4 Two demand curves for eggs
The rightward shift in the demand curve from D_0 to D_1 indicates an increase in the quantity demanded at each price. The lettered points correspond to those in Table 3.3. When the curve shifts from D_0 to D_1, more is demanded at each price and a higher price is paid for each quantity. For example, at price £1.50 quantity demanded rises from 77,500 dozen (point *W*) to 100,800 dozen (point *W'*); while the quantity of 90,000 dozen, which was formerly bought at a price of £1.00 (point *V*), will be bought at a price of £2.00 after the shift (point *X'*).

crease their purchases of any product whose price has not changed, the new purchases cannot be represented by the original demand curve. The rise in consumer income *shifts* the demand curve to the right, as shown in Figure 3.4. This shift illustrates the operation of an important general rule.

A demand curve shifts to a new position in response to a change in any of the variables that were held constant when the original curve was drawn.

Any change that increases the amount consumers wish to buy at each price will shift the demand curve to the right, and any change that decreases the amount consumers wish to buy at each price will shift the demand curve to the left.

Changes in other prices We saw that demand curves have negative slopes because the lower a product's price, the cheaper it becomes relative to other products that can satisfy the same needs. Those other products are called **substitutes.** A product becomes cheaper relative to its substitutes if its own price falls. This also happens if the substitute's price rises. For example, eggs can become cheap relative to pizzas either because the price of eggs falls or because the price of pizzas rises. Either change will increase the amount of eggs consumers are prepared to buy. For example, Alice may eat more omelettes and fewer pizzas whenever she wants a quick meal.

A rise in the price of a product's substitute shifts the demand curve for the product to the right. More will be purchased at each price.

Thus, a rise in the price of pizzas may shift the demand curve for eggs from D_0 to D_1 in Figure 3.4, just as did a rise in income.

Products that tend to be used jointly with each other are called **complements.** Cars and petrol are complements; so are golf clubs and golf balls, bacon and eggs, electric cookers and electricity, an aeroplane trip to Austria and tickets on the ski lifts at St Anton. Since complements tend to be consumed together, a fall in the price of either will increase the demand for both. For example, a fall in the price of cars that causes more people to become car owners will, *ceteris paribus*, increase the demand for petrol.

A fall in the price of one product that is complementary to a second product will shift the second product's demand curve to the right. More will be purchased at each price.

Changes in total income If consumers receive more income, they can be expected to purchase more of most products even though product prices remain the same. Such a shift is illustrated in Table 3.3 and Figure 3.4. A product whose demand increases when income increases is called a **normal good.**

A rise in consumers' incomes shifts the demand curve for normal products to the right, indicating that more will be demanded at each possible price.

For a few products, called **inferior goods,** a rise in consumers' income leads them to reduce their purchases (because they can now afford to switch to a more expensive, but superior, substitute).

A rise in income will shift the demand for inferior goods to the left, indicating that less will be demanded at each price.

The distribution of income If total income and all other determinants of demand are held constant while the distribution of income changes, the demands for normal goods will rise for consumers gaining income and fall for consumers losing income. If both gainers and losers buy a good in similar proportions, these changes will tend to cancel out. This will not, however, always be the case.

When the distribution of income changes, demands will rise for those goods favoured by those gaining income and fall for those goods favoured by those losing income.

Sociological variables Changes in the many sociological variables that influence demand will cause demand curves to shift. For example, a reduction in the typical number of children per family, as has happened in this century, will reduce the demands for the things used by children. If the number of retired people increases, there will be a rise in the demands for goods consumed during leisure times.

Forces outside human control Changes in weather and other non-human forces can affect demand. From the point of view of our economic theory of demand these are exogenous forces, things that lie outside our theory affecting demand, sometimes greatly, but that are not themselves being explained by the theory. Box 3.2 illustrates the major influence that weather can exert on demand.

Changes in tastes If there is a change in tastes in favour of a product, more will be demanded at each price, causing the demand curve to shift to the right. In contrast, if there is a change in tastes away from a product, less will be demanded at each price, causing the entire demand curve to shift to the left.

Figure 3.5 summarizes our discussion of the causes of shifts in the demand curve. Notice that, since we are generalizing beyond our example of eggs, we have relabelled our axes 'price' and 'quantity', dropping the qualification 'of eggs'. The term *quantity* should be understood to mean quantity per period in whatever units the goods are measured. The term *price* should be understood to mean the price measured in pounds per unit of quantity for the same product.

Movements along demand curves versus shifts

Suppose you read in today's newspaper that carrot prices have soared because more carrots are being demanded. Then tomorrow you read that the rising price of carrots is greatly reducing the typical consumer's demand for carrots as shoppers switch to potatoes, courgettes, and peas. The two statements appear to contradict each other. The first

Figure 3.5 Shifts in the demand curve
A shift in the demand curve from D_0 to D_1 indicates an increase in demand; a shift from D_0 to D_2 indicates a decrease in demand. An increase in demand can be caused by a rise in the price of a substitute, a fall in the price of a complement, a rise in income, a redistribution of income towards groups who favour the commodity, or a change in tastes that favours the commodity.

A decrease in demand can be caused by a fall in the price of a substitute, a rise in the price of a complement, a fall in income, a redistribution of income away from groups who favour the commodity, or a change in tastes that disfavours the commodity.

associates a rising price with a rising demand; the second associates a rising price with a declining demand. Can both statements be true? The answer is that they can be, because they refer to different things. The first refers to a *shift* in the demand curve; the second refers to a movement *along a* demand curve in response to a change in price.

Consider first the statement that the increase in the price of carrots has been caused by an increased demand for carrots. This statement refers to a shift in the demand curve for carrots. In this case, the demand curve must have shifted to the right, indicating more carrots demanded at each price. This shift will, as we will see later in this chapter, increase the price of carrots.

Now consider the statement that fewer carrots are being bought because carrots have become more expensive. This refers to a movement along a given demand curve and reflects a change between two specific quantities being bought, one before the price rose and one afterwards.

So what lay behind the two stories might have been something like the following.

1. A rise in the population shifts the demand curve for carrots to the right as more and more are demanded at each price. This in turn is raising the price of carrots (for reasons we will soon study in detail). This was the first newspaper story.

2. The rising price of carrots is causing each individual consumer to cut back on his or her purchase of carrots. This causes a movement upward to the left along any particular demand curve for carrots. This was the second newspaper story.

To prevent the type of confusion caused by our two newspaper stories, economists have developed a specialized vocabulary to distinguish shifts of curves from movements along curves. **Demand** refers to one *whole* demand curve. **Change in demand** refers to a *shift* in the whole curve, that is, a change in the amount that will be bought at *every* price.

An increase in demand means that the whole demand curve has shifted to the right; a decrease in demand means that the whole demand curve has shifted to the left.

Any one point on a demand curve represents a specific

amount being bought at a specified price. It represents, therefore, a particular quantity demanded. A movement along a demand curve is referred to as a **change in the quantity demanded.**[3]

A movement down a demand curve is called an increase (or a rise) in the quantity demanded; a movement up the demand curve is called a decrease (or a fall) in the quantity demanded.

To illustrate this terminology, look again at Table 3.3.

First, at the original level of income, a decrease in price from £2.00 to £1.50 increases *the quantity demanded* from 67,500 to 77,500 dozen a month. Second, the increase in average consumer income *increases demand* from what is shown by column (3) to what is shown by column (4). The same contrast is shown in Figure 3.4, where a fall in price from £2.00 to £1.50 increases the quantity demanded from the quantity shown by point X to the quantity shown by point W. An increase in total consumers' income increases demand from curve D_0 to curve D_1.

Supply

First we introduce the agents that are responsible for the behaviour we are going to study.

Firms and motives

A **firm** is the agent on the supply side of the theory of market price. It is defined as the unit that employs factors of production to produce products that it sells. The firm's customers can be other firms, consumers, or government. For obvious reasons, a firm is often called a producer. Elementary economic theory gives firms several attributes.

First, each firm is assumed to make consistent decisions, as though it was composed of a single individual. This allows the firm to be treated, at least in elementary theory, as the individual unit of behaviour on the production or supply side of product markets, just as the consumer is treated as the individual unit of behaviour on the consumption or demand side.

Second, economists assume that, in their role as producers, firms are the principal users of the services of factors of production. In 'factor markets' where factor services are bought and sold, the roles of firms and individuals are thus reversed from what they are in product markets: in factor markets firms do the buying and individuals do the selling.

Economists assume that firms make their decisions with a single goal in mind: to make as much profit as possible. This goal of *profit maximization* is analogous to the consumer's goal of utility maximization. In Chapter 13 we ask what happens if firms have goals other than profit maximization.

The nature of supply

The amount of a product that firms are able and willing to offer for sale is called the **quantity supplied.** Supply is a

desired flow: how much firms are willing to sell per period of time, not how much they actually sell.

We make a brief study of supply in this chapter, establishing only what is necessary for a theory of price. In later chapters we study the behaviour of individual firms, and then aggregate individual behaviour to obtain the behaviour of market supply. For present purposes, however, it is sufficient to go directly to market supply, the aggregate behaviour of all the firms in a particular market.

The determinants of quantity supplied: the supply function

Three major determinants of the quantity supplied in a particular market are:

1. The price of the product

2. The prices of factors of production

3. The state of technology

This list can be summarized in a **supply function:**

$$q_n^s = S(p_n, F_1, \ldots, F_m),$$

where q_n^s is the quantity supplied of product n; p_n is the price of that product; $F_1, \ldots, F_m$ is shorthand for the prices of all factors of production; and the state of technology determines the form of the function S. (Recall, once again, that the form of the function refers to the precise quantitative relation between the variables on the right-hand side of the equation and the one on the left.)

---

[3] There is an alternative terminology in which a shift in the demand curve is referred to as an *expansion* or a *contraction* of demand, an expansion referring to what we have called an increase in demand and a contraction to a decrease in demand.

Supply and price

For a simple theory of price, we need to know how quantity supplied varies with a product's own price, all other things being held constant. We are only concerned, therefore, with the *ceteris paribus* relation, $q_n^s = S(p_n)$. We will have much to say in later chapters about this relation. For the moment, it is sufficient to state the hypothesis that, *ceteris paribus, the quantity of any product that firms will produce and offer for sale is positively related to the product's own price, rising when price rises and falling when price falls.*

In Chapter 9 we derive this hypothesis from basic assumptions about the firm's behaviour. In the meantime, all we need to note is that the basic reason behind this relation is the way in which costs behave as output changes. Typically, the cost of increasing output by another unit tends to be higher, the higher is the existing rate of output. So, for example, if the firm is already producing 100 units per week, the cost of increasing output to 101 units per week might be £1, while if 200 units were already being produced, the cost of increasing output to 201 units might be £2. Clearly, the firm will not find it profitable to increase output if it cannot at least cover the additional costs that are incurred. As the price of the product rises, the firm can cover the rising costs of more and more additional units of output. As a result, higher and higher prices are needed to induce firms to make successive increases in output. The result is a positive association between market price and the firm's output. Do not worry if this does not seem obvious; it will become so after you have studied Chapter 9.

The **supply schedule** given in Table 3.4 is analogous to the demand schedule in Table 3.2. It records the quantity all producers wish to produce and sell at a number of alternative prices, rather than the quantity consumers wish to buy.

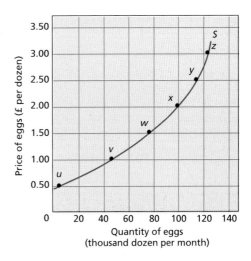

Figure 3.6 A supply curve for eggs
This supply curve relates quantity of eggs supplied to the price of eggs; its positive slope indicates that quantity supplied increases as price increases. The six points correspond to the price–quantity combinations shown in Table 3.4. The curve drawn through these points, labelled *S*, is the supply curve.

The six points corresponding to the six price–quantity combinations shown in the table are plotted in Figure 3.6. The curve drawn through the six points is a **supply curve** for eggs. It shows the quantity produced and offered for sale at each price.[4]

The supply curve in Figure 3.6 has a positive slope. This is a graphical expression of the following assumption:

The market price and the quantity supplied are positively related to each other.

Shifts in the supply curve

A shift in the supply curve means that, at each price, a different quantity is supplied. An increase in the quantity supplied at each price is illustrated in Table 3.5 and plotted in Figure 3.7. This change appears as a rightward shift in the supply curve. A decrease in the quantity supplied at each price causes a leftward shift.

For supply-curve shifts there is an important general rule similar to the one stated earlier for demand curves:

When there is a change in any of the variables (other than the product's own price) that affect the amount of a product that firms are willing to produce and sell, the whole supply curve for that product will shift.

Table 3.4 A market supply schedule for eggs

Reference letter	Price (£ per dozen)	Quantity supplied ('000 dozen per month)
u	0.50	5.0
v	1.00	46.0
w	1.50	77.5
x	2.00	100.0
y	2.50	115.0
z	3.00	122.5

The table shows the quantities that producers wish to sell at various prices, *ceteris paribus*. For example, row *y* indicates that if the price were £2.50 per dozen, producers would wish to sell 115,000 dozen eggs per month.

---

[4] Since we are not considering individual firms in this chapter, all supply curves are market curves showing the aggregate behaviour of the firms in the market. Where that is obvious from the context, the adjective 'market' is usually omitted.

Table 3.5 Two alternative market supply schedules for eggs

(1)	Price of eggs (£ per dozen) (2)	Original quantity supplied ('000 dozen per month) (3)	New quantity supplied ('000 dozen per month) (4)	(5)
u	0.50	5.0	28.0	u′
v	1.00	46.0	76.0	v′
w	1.50	77.5	102.0	w′
x	2.00	100.0	120.0	x′
y	2.50	115.0	132.0	y′
z	3.00	122.5	140.0	z′

An increase in supply means a larger quantity is supplied at each price. For example, the quantity that is supplied at £2.50 per dozen rises from 115,000 dozen to 132,000 dozen per month. A similar rise occurs at every price. Thus the supply schedule relating columns (2) and (3) is replaced by the one relating columns (2) and (4).

Figure 3.7 Two supply curves for eggs

The rightward shift in the supply curve from S_0 to S_1 indicates an increase in the quantity supplied at each price. For example, at the price of £1.00 the quantity supplied rises from 46,000 dozen to 76,000 dozen per month.

The major possible causes of such shifts are summarized in the caption of Figure 3.8 and are considered briefly below.

Prices of inputs All things that a firm uses to produce its outputs—such as, in the case of an egg producer, chicken feed, labour, and egg-sorting machines—are called the firm's *inputs*. Other things being equal, the higher the price of any input used to make a product, the less will be the profit from making that product. Thus, the higher the price of any input used by a firm, the lower will be the

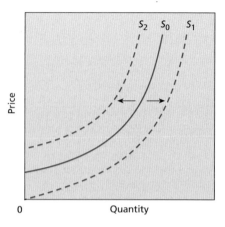

Figure 3.8 Shifts in the supply curve

A shift in the supply curve from S_0 to S_1 indicates an increase in supply; a shift from S_0 to S_2 indicates a decrease in supply. An increase in supply can be caused by improvements in technology or decreases in the costs of inputs that are important in producing the commodity.

A decrease in supply can be caused by increases in the costs of inputs that are important in producing the commodity or by changes in technology that increase the costs of production (although such changes are rare).

amount that the firm will produce and offer for sale at any given price of the product.

A rise in the price of any input shifts the supply curve to the left, indicating that less will be supplied at any given price; a fall in the price of inputs shifts the supply curve to the right.

Technology At any time, what is produced and how it is produced depend on the technologies in use. Over time, knowledge and production technologies change; so do the quantities of individual products supplied.

A technological change that decreases costs will increase the profits earned at any given price of the product. Since increased profitability leads to increased production, this change shifts the supply curve to the right, indicating an increased willingness to produce the product and offer it for sale at each possible price.

Movements along supply curves versus shifts

As with demand, it is essential to distinguish between a movement along the supply curve (caused by a change in the product's own price) and a shift of the whole curve (caused by a change in something other than the product's own price). We adopt the same terminology as with demand: **quantity supplied** refers to a particular quantity actually supplied at a particular price of the product, and **supply** refers to the whole relation between price and quantity supplied. Thus, when we speak of an *increase* or a *decrease in supply*, we are referring to shifts in the supply curve such as the ones illustrated in Figures 3.7 and 3.8.

When we speak of a *change in the quantity supplied*, we mean a movement from one point on the supply curve to another point on the same curve.[5]

The determination of price

So far we have considered demand and supply separately. We now come to a key question: how do the two forces of demand and supply interact to determine price?

The concept of a market

Markets are basic economic concepts. Originally the term designated a physical place where products were bought and sold. Once developed, however, theories of market behaviour were easily extended to cover products such as wheat, which can be purchased anywhere in the world at a price that tends to be uniform the world over. The concept of 'the wheat market' extends our viewpoint well beyond the idea of a single place to which the consumer goes to buy something.

For present purposes a **market** may be defined as an area over which buyers and sellers negotiate the exchange of some product or related group of products. It must be possible, therefore, for buyers and sellers to communicate with each other and to make meaningful deals over the whole market.

Individual markets differ in the degree of competition among the various buyers and sellers. In the next few chapters we will confine ourselves to markets in which the number of buyers and sellers is sufficiently large that no one of them has any appreciable influence on price. This is a very rough definition of what economists call *perfectly competitive markets*. Starting in Chapter 10, we will consider the behaviour of markets that do not meet this competitive requirement.

The graphical analysis of a market

Table 3.6 brings together the demand and supply schedules from Tables 3.2 and 3.4. Figure 3.9 shows both the demand and the supply curves on a single graph; the six points on the demand curve are labelled with uppercase letters, while the six points on the supply curve are labelled with lowercase letters, each letter referring to a common price on both curves.

Quantity supplied and quantity demanded at various prices

Consider first the point at which the two curves in Figure 3.9 intersect. Both the figure and Table 3.6 show that the market price is £1.50, the quantity demanded is 77,500 dozen, and the quantity supplied is the same. At that price consumers wish to buy exactly the same amount as producers wish to sell. Provided that the demand curve is negatively sloped and the supply curve positively sloped throughout their entire ranges, there will be no other price at which the quantity demanded equals the quantity supplied.

Now consider prices below £1.50. At these prices consumers' desired purchases exceed producers' desired sales. It is easily seen, and you should check one or two examples, that at all prices below £1.50 the quantity demanded exceeds the quantity supplied. Furthermore, the lower the price, the larger the excess of the one over the other. The amount by which the quantity demanded exceeds the

Table 3.6 Demand and supply schedules for eggs and equilibrium price

Price per dozen (£)	Quantity demanded ('000 dozen per month)	Quantity supplied ('000 dozen per month)	Excess demand (quantity demanded minus quantity supplied) ('000 dozen per month)
0.50	110.0	5.0	105.0
1.00	90.0	46.0	44.0
1.50	**77.5**	**77.5**	**0.0**
2.00	67.5	100.0	−32.5
2.50	62.5	115.0	−52.5
3.00	60.0	122.5	−62.5

Equilibrium occurs where quantity demanded equals quantity supplied so that there is neither excess demand nor excess supply. These schedules are repeated from Tables 3.2 and 3.4. The equilibrium price is £1.50. For lower prices there is excess demand; for higher prices there is excess supply, which is shown as negative excess demand.

[5] As with demand, an alternative terminology refers to an increase in supply as an *expansion of supply* and a reduction in supply as a *contraction of supply*.

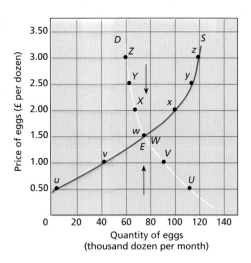

Figure 3.9 Determination of the equilibrium price of eggs
The equilibrium price corresponds to the intersection of the demand and supply curves. Point *E* indicates the equilibrium. At a price of £1.50 per dozen quantity demanded (point *W*) equals quantity supplied (point *w*). At prices above equilibrium there is excess supply and downward pressure on price. At prices below equilibrium there is excess demand and upward pressure on price. The pressures on price are represented by the vertical arrows.

quantity supplied is called the **excess demand,** which is defined as quantity demanded *minus* quantity supplied $(q^d - q^s)$. This is shown in the last column of Table 3.6.

Finally, consider prices higher than £1.50. At these prices consumers wish to buy less than producers wish to sell. Thus, quantity supplied exceeds quantity demanded. It is easily seen, and again you should check a few examples, that for any price above £1.50 quantity supplied exceeds quantity demanded. Furthermore, the higher the price, the larger the excess of the one over the other. In this case there is negative excess demand $(q^d - q^s < 0)$. This is also shown in the last column of Table 3.6.

Negative excess demand is usually referred to as **excess supply,** which measures the amount by which supply exceeds demand $(q^s - q^d)$.

Changes in price when quantity demanded does not equal quantity supplied

Whenever there is excess demand, consumers are unable to buy all they wish to buy; whenever there is excess supply, firms are unable to sell all they wish to sell. In both cases some agents will not be able to do what they would like to do. How will they react?

To develop a theory of how the market behaves in the face of excess demand or excess supply, we need to make two further assumptions. First, we assume that *when there*

is excess supply, the market price will fall. Producers, unable to sell some of their goods, may begin to offer to sell them at lower prices; purchasers, observing the glut of unsold output, may begin to offer lower prices. For either or both of these reasons, the price will fall.

Second, we assume that *when there is excess demand, market price will rise.* Individual consumers, unable to buy as much as they would like to buy, may offer higher prices in an effort to get more of the available goods for themselves. Suppliers, who could sell more than their total production, may begin to ask higher prices for the quantities that they have produced. For either or both of these reasons, prices will rise.

The equilibrium price

Our theory now tells us that for any price of eggs above £1.50 the price will fall; while for any price below £1.50 the price will rise. At a price of £1.50 there is neither excess demand creating a shortage, nor excess supply creating a glut; quantity supplied is equal to quantity demanded, and there is no tendency for the price to change. The price of £1.50, where the supply and demand curves intersect, is the price towards which the actual market price will tend. It is called the **equilibrium price:** the price at which quantity demanded equals quantity supplied. The amount that is bought and sold at the equilibrium price is called the **equilibrium quantity.** The term 'equilibrium' means a state of balance; it occurs when desired purchases equal desired sales.

When quantity demanded equals quantity supplied, we say that the market is in **equilibrium.** When quantity demanded does not equal quantity supplied we say that the market is in **disequilibrium.**

Summary

We have now developed one of the most famous and powerful theories in all of economics and it is worth summarizing what we have done.

Assumptions concerning a competitive market:

1. All demand curves have negative slopes throughout their entire range.

2. All supply curves have positive slopes throughout their entire range.

3. Prices change if, and only if, there is excess demand; rising if excess demand is positive and falling if excess demand is negative.

Implications:

1. There is no more than one price at which quantity demanded equals quantity supplied: equilibrium is unique.

2. Only at the equilibrium price will the market price remain constant.

3. When the demand or the supply curve shifts, the equilibrium price and quantity will change.

The laws of demand and supply

Earlier in this chapter, we studied shifts in demand and supply curves. Recall that a rightward shift in the relevant curve means that more is demanded or supplied *at each market price*, while a leftward shift means that less is demanded or supplied *at each market price*. How does a shift in either curve affect price and quantity?

The answers to this question are called the 'laws' of supply and demand. Each of the laws summarizes what happens when an initial position of equilibrium is upset by some shift in either the demand or the supply curve, and a new equilibrium position is then established. The sense in which it is correct to call these propositions 'laws' is discussed in Box 3.3.

To discover the effects of each of the curve shifts that we wish to study, we use the method known as **comparative statics.** We start from a position of equilibrium and then introduce the change to be studied. The new equilibrium position is determined and compared with the original one. The differences between the two positions of equilibrium must result from the change that was introduced, for everything else has been held constant.

The four laws of demand and supply are derived in Figure 3.10, the caption of which must be carefully studied. The analysis of that figure generalizes our specific discussion about eggs. Because it is intended to apply to any product, the horizontal axis is simply labelled 'quantity' and the vertical axis 'price'.

The laws of supply and demand are:

1. A rise in the demand for a product (a rightward shift of the demand curve) causes an increase in both the equilibrium price and the equilibrium quantity bought and sold.

2. A fall in the demand for a product (a leftward shift of the demand curve) causes a decrease in both the equilibrium price and the equilibrium quantity bought and sold.

3. A rise in the supply of a product (a rightward shift of the supply curve) causes a decrease in the equilibrium price and an increase in the equilibrium quantity bought and sold.

4. A fall in the supply of a product (a leftward shift of the supply curve) causes an increase in the equilibrium price and a decrease in the equilibrium quantity bought and sold.

In Figures 3.5 and 3.8 we summarized the many events that cause demand and supply curves to shift. Using the four 'laws' derived in Figure 3.10, we can understand the link between these events and changes in market prices

---

Box 3.3   The 'laws' of demand and supply

As with all theories, the implications of the theory of demand and supply may be looked at in two quite distinct ways. First, they are logical deductions from a set of assumptions about behaviour. When we consider the truth of the implications, we are concerned with whether or not they are logically correct deductions. If we discovered that we made mistakes in our reasoning process, then we would conclude that the alleged implications are false in the sense that they do not follow from the assumptions of the theory. Second, the implications are predictions about real-world events. When we consider the truth of the implications, we are concerned with whether or not they are empirically correct. If one or more of the assumptions are empirically incorrect, the predictions of the theory are likely to be factually incorrect. In this case we would conclude that the predictions are false in the sense that they are contradicted by real-world observations.

Consider an example. The sentence 'If the demand curve for cars is negatively sloped, and if the supply curve is positively sloped, then an increase in demand for cars will raise their equilibrium price' is logically correct in the sense that the 'then' statement follows logically from the two 'if' statements. The single statement 'A rise in the demand for motor cars will increase the price of motor cars' is one that may or may not be empirically true. If any one of the assumptions of the theory is not empirically correct for motor cars, the statement may be found to be empirically false, even though it is a correct logical deduction from the theory's assumptions. If, for example, the market

for cars does not respond to excess demand with a rise in price, the statement may be empirically false: even though a rise in demand for motor cars does create excess demand, market price will not rise.

Economists are concerned with developing implications that are correct in both senses: that they follow logically from the assumptions of a theory, and that they are factually correct.

Use of the term 'laws' in the popular phrase 'the laws of supply and demand' suggests that the four implications have been shown to be true in the empirical sense. We must remember, however, that these 'laws' are nothing more than predictions that are always open to testing. There is considerable evidence that the predictions are consistent with the facts in many markets. In other markets, especially those for durable consumer goods such as cars and TV sets, it is not so clear that they are fully consistent with all relevant empirical observations.

Strictly, the theory of demand and supply applies only to cases in which no single buyer or seller has any influence over the market price. In Chapter 5, however, we will learn to extend demand and supply analysis to situations in which those price-taking assumptions are not true for suppliers. The theory may still generate useful predictions, but the proof of the value of these extensions is an empirical one: does the theory generate predictions that agree with the facts?

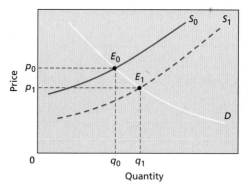

(i) The effect of shifts in the demand curve

(ii) The effect of shifts in the supply curve

Figure 3.10 The 'laws' of demand and supply

The effects on equilibrium price and quantity of shifts in either demand or supply are called the laws of demand and supply.

An increase in demand. In part (i) assume that the original demand and supply curves are D_0 and S, which intersect to produce equilibrium at E_0, with a price of p_0 and a quantity of q_0. An increase in demand shifts the demand curve to D_1, taking the new equilibrium to E_1. Price rises to p_1 and quantity rises to q_1.

A decrease in demand. In part (i) assume that the original demand and supply curves are D_1 and S, which intersect to produce equilibrium at E_1, with a price of p_1 and a quantity of q_1. A decrease in demand shifts the demand curve to D_0, taking the new equilibrium to E_0. Price falls to p_0 and quantity falls to q_0.

An increase in supply. In part (ii) assume that the original demand and supply curves are D and S_0, which intersect to produce an equilibrium at E_0, with a price of p_0 and a quantity of q_0. An increase in supply shifts the supply curve to S_1, taking the new equilibrium to E_1. Price falls to p_1 and quantity rises to q_1.

A decrease in supply. In part (ii) assume that the original demand and supply curves are D and S_1, which intersect to produce an equilibrium at E_1, with a price of p_1 and a quantity of q_1. A decrease in supply shifts the supply curve to S_0, taking the new equilibrium to E_0. Price rises to p_0 and quantity falls to q_0.

Box 3.4 Demand and supply: what really happens

'The theory of supply and demand is neat enough,' said the sceptic, 'but tell me what really happens.'

'What really happens,' said the economist, 'is that demand curves have negative slopes; supply curves have positive slopes; prices rise in response to excess demand and fall in response to excess supply.'

'But that's theory,' insisted the sceptic. 'What about reality?'

'That is reality as well,' said the economist.

'Show me,' said the sceptic.

The economist produced the following passages from the press:

■ *OPEC countries once again fail to agree on output quotas. Output soars and prices plummet.* (June 1995)

■ *Oil prices surge on move by producers to cut output.* (July 1998)

■ *The price of cashew kernels has fallen nearly 6 per cent in 10 months as Viet Nam has begun to challenge India and Brazil, the world's two largest exporters.*

■ *How deep is the art market's recession? In today's unforgiving economic climate, the sales of contemporary, impressionist, and modern works of art took hits at this week's auctions. Sales totalled just under £60 million compared with £500 million just one year ago. Many paintings on offer went unsold, and those that did sell went for well under their predicted price.*

■ *Coffee prices at the London Commodity Exchange staged another spectacular rise, putting them above their level at the start of the year. The president of the Association of Coffee Producing Countries said that the supply shortages that are underpinning prices would last quite some time.*

■ *Increased demand for macadamia nuts causes price to rise above competing nuts. A major producer now plans to double the size of its orchards during the next five years.*

■ *The effects of deregulation of US airlines were spectacular: cuts in air fares of up to 70 per cent in some cases, record passenger jam-ups at the airports, and a spectacular increase in the average load factor* [the proportion of occupied seats on the average commercial flight].

The sceptic's response is not recorded, but you should be able to tell which clippings illustrate which of the economist's four statements about 'what really happens'.

Box 3.5 The market for computer chips

According to an article in the *Financial Times* (28 June 1996),

It is only nine months since the world semiconductor industry was forging ahead. Demand for chips was so great that there was a shortage, analysts were forecasting record growth and manufacturers were unveiling plans for dozens of $1bn chip factories. . . .

The euphoria has been short lived. The shortage rapidly turned into surplus, and the price of dynamic random access memory (D-Ram) chips—the basic memory chips for PCs—has dropped by about 65 per cent over the past six or seven months. . . .

Commodity chip prices normally fall by 20 per cent to 30 per cent each year as manufacturing costs fall. But with manufacturers scrambling to protect market share, international spot market prices have fallen below the break-even point of some Asian manufacturers.

The story points to two key elements to the developments in this market. First, the technology of producing computer chips is evolving rapidly. This causes the market supply curve to shift rightwards continually. The second element is the negatively sloped demand curve, which shifts in some periods.

The trend decline of '20 per cent to 30 per cent each year' is clearly shown in the chart. So is the abnormal period between 1992 and 1995 when chip prices actually rose slightly before falling back sharply in 1996, as discussed above. What is the explanation?

In normal times the primary influence is that the shifting supply curve moves to the right along a nearly static demand curve. Chip prices fall and quantity demanded increases. In the 1992–5 period, however, the demand curve shifted sharply to the right. This increase in demand was due to the increased availability and reduced price of such complementary software products as multimedia games and educational programs. By 1996 the demand curve had stopped shifting to the right but the supply curve had not. Hence prices returned to their downward trend.

Notice that the price rises associated with the temporary boom in demand between 1992 and 1995 would have increased the quantity supplied on each rightward-shifting supply curve because the high profitability of chip production encouraged higher production at each level of capacity. The fall in price in 1996 no doubt reduced the quantity supplied along the supply curve that existed at that time. However, despite the fall in price, the supply curve continued to shift to the right in successive periods as technical progress continued to reduce costs of production.

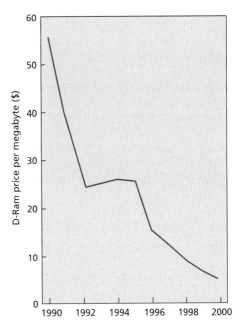

A subsequent article (*Financial Times*, 29 May 1998) showed that the steady decline in prices had continued as expected:

The performance of Japan's leading electronics conglomerates has been hit by the triple blow of a collapse in semi-conductor prices, dire domestic consumer demand and the Asian economic crisis. . . . Both NEC and Mitsubishi Electric were hit by last year's contraction of the Japanese personal computer market. . . . Poor demand in Asia caused Hitachi's consumer products business to slide into loss and sales of Mitsubishi's consumer products to slide.

Ceteris paribus, the fall in prices associated with cost reductions should cause state-of-the-art firms no great difficulty. If their costs fall as fast as prices, they can maintain their profitability. But when demand declined in what had been an expanding industry even the most efficient producers ran into difficulties.

and quantities. To take one example, a rise in the price of butter will lead to an increase in both the price of margarine and the quantity bought. This is because a rise in the price of one product causes a rightward shift in the demand curves for its substitutes, and 'law' 1 tells us that such a shift causes price and quantity to increase.

We will see in subsequent chapters that the theory of the determination of price by demand and supply is beautiful in its simplicity and yet powerful in its range of applications. In the meantime, Box 3.4 suggests some simple applications and Box 3.5 details one specific case.

Prices in inflation

Up to now we have developed the theory of the prices of individual products under the assumption that all other prices remain constant. Does this mean that the theory is inapplicable during an inflationary period when almost all prices are rising? Fortunately, the answer is no.

We have mentioned several times that what matters for demand and supply is the price of the product in question relative to the prices of other products. The price of the product expressed in money terms is called its **money price** or its **absolute price;** the price of a product expressed in relation to other prices is called its **relative price.**

In an inflationary world changes in a product's relative price can be measured by changes in the product's own price relative to changes in the average of all other prices, which is called the *general price level.* If, during a period when the general price level rose by 40 per cent, the price of oranges rose by 60 per cent, then the price of oranges rose relative to the price level as a whole. Oranges became *relatively* expensive. However, if the price of oranges had risen by only 30 per cent when the general price level had risen by 40 per cent, then their relative price would have fallen. Although the money price of oranges rose, oranges became *relatively* cheap.

In Lewis Carroll's famous story *Through the Looking-Glass,* Alice finds a country where everyone has to run in order to stay still. So it is with inflation. A product's price must rise as fast as the general level of prices just to keep its relative price constant.

It has been convenient in this chapter to analyse a change in a particular price in the context of a constant price level. The analysis is easily extended, however, to an inflationary period. Any force that raises the price of one product when other prices remain constant will, given general inflation, raise the price of that product relative to the average of all other prices. Consider the example of a change in tastes in favour of eggs that would raise their price by 20 per cent when other prices were constant. If, however, the general price level goes up by 10 per cent, then the price of eggs will rise by 32 per cent.[6] In each case the price of eggs rises 20 per cent *relative to the average of all prices.*

In price theory whenever we talk of a change in the price of one product, we mean a change relative to the general price level.

Individual markets, sectors, and the economy

In this final section we start with the concept of an economy as a whole and then consider various subdivisions of the economy, which are called *sectors.*

The concept of an economy

An **economy** is any broad collection of interrelated productive activities. It may refer to productive activity in a region of one country, such as *the economy of eastern Canada*; it may refer to one country, such as *the UK economy*, or it may refer to a group of countries, such as *the economy of Western Europe.*

A typical economy consists of thousands and thousands of individual markets. There are markets for wheat, strawberries, steel, cement, coal, oil, new cars, used cars, TVs, shirts, skis, CDs, haircuts, video rentals, air travel, financial consulting, accounting services, consumer loans, mortgages, foreign currencies, and the many other goods and services.

Goods and factor markets

For many purposes it is useful to group these markets into two types. **Goods markets** are those where goods and services are bought and sold.[7] The sellers in such markets are usually firms; the buyers may be consumers, other firms, or the government. **Factor markets** are those where factor services are bought and sold. The sellers in

such markets are the owners of factors of production (usually individuals, but sometimes firms); the buyers are usually firms and governments. As we will see many times throughout this book, demand and supply analysis helps us to understand the operation of both factor markets and goods markets. Factor markets determine how much we earn; goods markets determine how much our income will buy.

Relations among markets

Although each of the individual markets referred to above is distinct, all are interrelated and we need to see why.

The separation of individual markets Markets are separated from each other by the product sold, by natural economic barriers, and by barriers created by governments. To illustrate, consider one example of each type of separation. First, the market for men's shirts is different from the market for refrigerators because different products are sold in each. Second, the market for cement in the United

---

[6] Let the price level be 100 in the first case and 110 in the second. Let the price of eggs be 120 in the first case and x in the second. To preserve the same relative price, we need x such that $120/100 = x/110$, which makes $x = 132$.

[7] Since these markets include both goods and services, it might seem better to refer to them as *commodity markets.* Unfortunately, this term is in common use in the business world to refer to markets where basic commodities such as rubber, tin, and jute are sold. To avoid confusion, economists often speak of 'goods markets' where, in their own terminology, 'commodity markets' would be better.

Kingdom is distinct from the market for cement in the western United States. The costs of transporting cement are so high that UK purchasers would not buy American cement even if its market price in the western United States were very much lower than its market price in Britain. Third, the market for textiles is separated among many countries since government-imposed quotas severely limit the amount that firms in one country can sell to consumers in another.

Because markets are distinct we can use demand and supply analysis to study the behaviour of markets one at a time, as we have done in this chapter and will do in much more detail in Chapter 5.

The interlinking of individual markets   Although all markets are to some extent separated, most are also interrelated. Consider again the three causes of market separation: different products, spatial separation, and government intervention. First, the markets for different kinds of products are interrelated because all products compete for consumers' income. Thus, if consumers spend more in one market, they will have less to spend in other markets. Second, the geographical separation of markets for similar products depends on transport costs. Products whose transport costs are high relative to their production costs tend to be produced and sold in geographically distinct markets. Products whose transport costs are low relative to their production costs tend to be sold in what amounts to one world market. But whatever the transport costs, there will be some price differential at which it will pay someone to buy in the low-priced market and ship to the high-priced one. Thus, there is always some potential link between geographically distinct markets, even when shipping costs are high. Third, markets are often separated by policy-induced barriers, such as tariffs (which are taxes paid when goods come into a country from abroad). Although high tariffs tend to separate markets, they do not do so completely. If price differences become large enough, it will pay buyers in the high-price market to import from the low-price market and producers in the low-price market to export to the high-price one, even though they have to pay the tariff as a result.

Because markets are interrelated we must treat them as a single interrelated system for many purposes. *General equilibrium analysis* studies markets as a single inter-related system in which individual demands and supplies depend on all prices, and what happens in any one market will affect many other markets—and in principle could affect all other markets.

Sectors of an economy

Markets are often aggregated into groups called *sectors*. Three of the most common types of aggregation are used to distinguish various physical types of production, the public and private sectors, and the marketed and non-marketed sectors.

Types of production   It is often useful to aggregate the production that passes through the nation's markets into three broad classes called primary, secondary, and tertiary. The *primary* sector includes the harvesting of natural re-sources, especially agricultural crops, fish, forests, minerals, and sources of energy such as coal, oil, and natural gas. These provide foodstuffs, basic raw materials, and power on which other production depends. The *secondary* sector comprises all of manufacturing and construction. The *tertiary* sector covers the production of all services, such as transport, entertainment, personal services, commerce, retailing, government, finance, and professions. The overall sizes of these three broad sectors in the UK as well as the details for the manufacturing sector are given in Box 3.6.

The public and private sectors   The productive activity of a country is often aggregated in a different way to obtain the private and the public sectors. The **private sector** refers to all production that is in private hands; the **public sector** refers to all production that is in public hands. The distinction between the two sectors depends on the legal distinction of ownership. In the private sector individuals or other firms own the organization that does the produc-ing; in the public sector it is owned by the state. The public sector includes all production of goods and services by government agencies, plus all production by nationalized industries that is sold to consumers through ordinary markets. Privatization, the sale of nationalized industries to private owners, has greatly reduced the size of the UK public sector over the last two decades.

In both the public and the private sectors, demand and supply analysis is useful. For example, whether the producer is privately or publicly owned, the consequences of setting a disequilibrium price will be the same—excess demand or excess supply. Furthermore, both publicly and privately owned firms in secondary industries must usually buy their primary products in competitive markets. Both will suffer similar consequences if alterations in the market conditions cause large changes in primary product prices.

Market and non-market sectors   The third type of aggregate which we consider distinguishes the two basic ways in which products may pass from those who make them to those who use them. First, products may be sold by producers and bought by consumers. When this happens, the producers must cover their costs by the revenues they obtain from the sale of the product. Such production is called *marketed production*, and this part of the country's activity belongs to the **market sector**. Second, the product may be given away. In this case the costs of production

Box 3.6 Size of production sectors

The charts show the relative sizes of some UK sectors classified by types of production. In these charts size is gauged by employment, not value of output. The left-hand pie shows that primary production—agriculture, mining, fishing, energy, and water production—is a small sector. The secondary sector—manufacturing and construction—although much larger, is still small (at least in terms of employment) relative to the tertiary sector.

The middle bar shows the relative employment of the major UK industries across all three of these sectors. While manufacturing is one of the largest single sectors, it accounts for less than 20 per cent of all employment—down from figures in the mid-30s which were typical of the first eight decades of the twentieth century.

The right-hand pie shows the relative sizes of the various manufacturing industries. Engineering is the largest manufacturing industry, employing one in every five factory workers. Paper, printing, and publishing; mineral products; and food, drink, and tobacco are the three next largest groups. Together with engineering, these industries account for the employment of about 65 per cent of the manufacturing workforce. Among other industries, transportation equipment, textiles and clothing products, petroleum and chemical products, rubber and plastics, and wood products are sufficiently important to be separately distinguished.

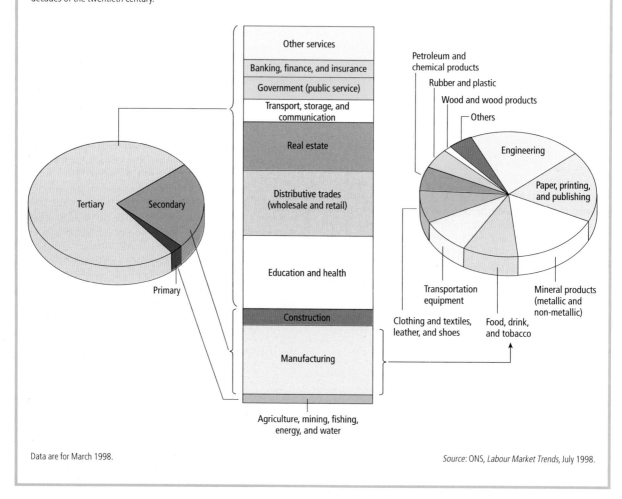

Data are for March 1998.

Source: ONS, *Labour Market Trends*, July 1998.

must be covered by some means other than sales revenues. This production is called *non-marketed production* and belongs to the **non-market sector.** In the case of private charities, the money required to pay for factor services may be raised from the public by voluntary subscriptions. In the case of production by the government—which accounts for the great bulk of non-marketed production—the money is provided from government revenue, which in turn comes mainly from taxes levied on firms and consumers. Government production is discussed in Chapters 18 and 19.

Supply and demand analysis is directly applicable to marketed goods, whose prices tend to fluctuate with changing market conditions. It is also useful, although in less obvious ways, in studying non-marketed production. For instance, if a good is supplied free of charge, the quantity demanded will be determined at the point where the demand curve cuts the quantity axis. If the government is unwilling to supply everything that is demanded at that price, as is often the case, then the government must find some way of rationing the supply that it does make available—since price is prevented from doing this job.

Conclusion

Whatever the market in which we are interested, whatever the level of aggregation that we wish to study, and whatever the method by which production is financed, the theory of market price is an invaluable tool. Eventually we will need to expand our theory to consider new situations —particularly those where there are only a few buyers or sellers. We can, however, understand much economic behaviour, and make sense of much seemingly peculiar behaviour, using nothing more than the simple theoretical tools now at our command—plus just one more: the concept of elasticity, which we study in the next chapter.

Summary

■ The decision-taking units in economic theory are called agents. They are (a) individuals, for demand in goods markets and for supply in factor markets; (b) firms, for supply in goods markets and demand in factor markets; and (c) governments, for supply of some goods and for regulation and control of the private sector (see Chapter 5). Given the resources at their command, each individual is assumed to maximize his or her satisfaction, and each firm is assumed to maximize its profit.

Demand

■ An individual consumer's demand curve shows the relation between the price of a product and the quantity of that product the consumer wishes to purchase per period of time. It is drawn on the assumption that all other prices, income, and tastes remain constant. Its negative slope indicates that the lower the price of the product, the more the consumer wishes to purchase.

■ The market demand curve is the horizontal sum of the demand curves of all the individual consumers. The demand curve for a normal good shifts to the right when the price of a substitute rises, when the price of a complement falls, when total income rises, when the distribution of income changes in favour of those with large demands for the product, and when tastes change in favour of the product. It shifts to the left with the opposite changes.

■ A movement along a demand curve indicates a change in quantity demanded in response to a change in the product's own price; a shift in a demand curve indicates a change in the quantity demanded at each price in response to a change in one of the conditions held constant along a demand curve.

Supply

■ The supply curve for a product shows the relationship between its price and the quantity that producers wish to produce and offer for sale per period of time. It is drawn on the assumption that all other forces that influence quantity supplied remain constant, and its positive slope indicates that the higher the price, the more producers wish to sell.

■ A supply curve shifts in response to changes in the prices of the inputs used by producers, and to changes in technology. The shift represents a change in the amount supplied at each price. A movement along a supply curve indicates that a different quantity is being supplied in response to a change in the product's own price.

The determination of price

■ At the equilibrium price the quantity demanded equals the quantity supplied. Graphically, equilibrium occurs where the demand and supply curves intersect. At any price below equilibrium there will be excess demand and price will tend to rise; at any price above equilibrium there will be excess supply and price will tend to fall.

■ A rise in demand raises both equilibrium price and quantity; a fall in demand lowers both. A rise in supply raises equilibrium quantity but lowers equilibrium price; a fall in supply lowers equilibrium quantity but raises equilibrium price. These are the so-called 'laws' of supply and demand.

■ Price theory is most simply developed in the context of a constant price level. Price changes discussed in the theory are changes relative to the average level of all prices. In an inflationary period, a rise in the relative price of one product means that its price rises by more than the rise in the general price level; a fall in its relative price means that its price rises by less than the rise in the general price level.

Individual markets, sectors, and the economy

■ Markets are partially separated from each other because different products are sold in each, and because of barriers to the movement of products among markets such as transport costs (a natural barrier) and tariffs (a policy-induced barrier).

■ For various types of study, data for individual markets are aggregated into sectors. Examples are primary, secondary, and tertiary, a distinction depending on the types of goods produced; private and public, a distinction depending on ownership; and market and non-market, a distinction depending on whether or not the costs of production are recovered by selling products to their users.

Topics for review

- Quantity demanded and the demand function
- The demand schedule and the demand curve for an individual and for the market
- Shifts in the demand curve and movements along the curve
- Substitutes and complements
- Quantity supplied and the supply function
- The supply schedule and the supply curve
- Shifts in the supply curve and movements along the curve
- Excess demand and excess supply
- Equilibrium and disequilibrium prices
- The 'laws' of demand and supply
- Money prices and relative prices
- Goods and factor markets
- Sectors of the economy

Questions for discussion

1 Describe in words the meaning of a positively sloped demand curve and a negatively sloped supply curve. Why does such behaviour seem implausible?

2 Consider the statements quoted by the economist in Box 3.4 on page 48. Explain each in terms of demand and supply curves.

3 Classify the effect of each of the following as (i) a decrease in the demand for fish, (ii) a decrease in the quantity of fish demanded, or (iii) other. Illustrate each diagrammatically. (a) The government of Canada closes the Atlantic Cod fishery. (b) People buy less fish because of a rise in fish prices. (c) The Catholic Church relaxes its ban on eating meat on Fridays. (d) The price of beef falls, and as a result consumers buy more beef and less fish. (e) Fears of mercury pollution lead locals to shun fish caught in nearby lakes. (f) Strong evidence shows that eating fish is better for one's health than eating meat.

4 Use demand and supply curves to explain the following two events and to show why they are not inconsistent. (a) Rising demand for housing causes prices of new houses to soar. (b) Many families refuse to buy houses, as prices become prohibitive for them.

5 State clearly what is meant by a sector of the economy. Distinguish the public and the private sector. Name three organizations that are in each. Answer the same question for the market and the non-market sector.

Chapter 4
Elasticity of Demand and Supply

In this chapter we develop and apply measures of the responses of the quantity demanded and the quantity supplied to changes in the variables that determine them, particularly prices and incomes. These measures are called *elasticities*, and we need to learn how to calculate and interpret them.

To illustrate why we want to have these measures, consider the effects of a new government subsidy on each kilogram of carrots grown. This will shift the supply curve of carrots to the right because more will be produced at each price. If the demand for carrots is as shown in part (i) of Figure 4.1, the effect of the government's policy will be to reduce carrot prices slightly, while greatly increasing the quantity grown and consumed. If, however, the demand is as shown in part (ii) of Figure 4.1, the effect of the policy will be to reduce carrot prices greatly but to increase carrot

production and consumption by only a small amount. If the purpose of the subsidy is to increase the quantity that is produced and consumed, then the policy will be a great success when the demand curve is similar to the one shown in part (i), but a failure when the demand curve is similar to that shown in part (ii). If, however, the main purpose of the subsidy is to achieve a large reduction in the price of carrots, the policy will be a failure when demand is as shown in part (i) but a great success when demand is as shown in part (ii).

This example illustrates that it is often not enough to know whether quantity rises or falls in response to some change; it may be important to know by how much. To measure this in a useful way, we use the concept of *elasticity*.

(i)

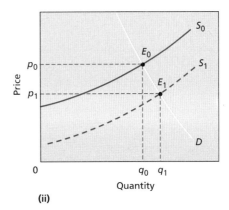
(ii)

Figure 4.1 The effect of the shape of the demand curve
The flatter the demand curve, *ceteris paribus*, the less the change in price and the greater the change in quantity. Both parts of the figure are drawn on the same scale. Both show the same initial equilibrium price p_0 and quantity q_0, the same shift of the supply curve from S_0 to S_1, and a new equilibrium at p_1 and q_1. In part (i) the effect of the shift in supply is a slight fall in the price and a large increase in quantity. In part (ii) the effect of the identical shift in the supply curve is a large fall in the price and a relatively small increase in quantity.

Demand elasticity

In the first part of this chapter we deal with quantity demanded and start by considering its response to changes in the product's own price.

Price elasticity of demand

The degree to which quantity demanded responds to changes in the product's own price is called the *responsiveness of demand*. Sometimes we wish to know how the responsiveness of one product changes over time, or we may wish to compare the responsiveness of several products or several alternative demand curves for one product. In Figure 4.1, we were able to compare the responsiveness of quantity demanded along the two demand curves because they were drawn on the same scale. But you should not try to compare two curves without making sure that the scales are the same. Also, you must not leap to conclusions about responsiveness of quantity demanded on the basis of the apparent steepness of a single curve. The hazards of so doing are illustrated in Figure 4.2. Both parts of the figure plot the same demand curve, but the choice of scale on the 'quantity' and 'price' axes serves to make one curve look steep and the other flat.

Measuring the responsiveness of demand to price

In order to get a measure of responsiveness that is independent of the scale we use, and that can be compared across products, we need to deal in percentage changes. A given percentage change in the quantity of carrots will be the same whether we measure it in tonnes, kilograms, or pounds. Similarly, although we cannot easily compare the absolute changes in tonnes of carrots and barrels of oil, we can compare their two percentage changes.

These considerations lead us to the concept of the **price elasticity of demand,** which is defined as the percentage change in quantity demanded *divided by* the percentage change in price that brought it about.[1] This elasticity is usually symbolized by the lowercase Greek letter eta, η:

$$\eta = \frac{\text{percentage change in quantity demanded}}{\text{percentage change in price}}. \quad (1)$$

Many different elasticities are used in economics. To distinguish η from the others, the full term 'price elasticity of demand' can be used. Since η is by far the most commonly used elasticity, economists often drop the adjective 'price' and refer to it merely as *elasticity of demand*, or sometimes just *elasticity*. When more than one kind of elasticity could be involved, however, η should be given its full title.

[1] Elasticity is an example of what mathematicians call a *pure number*, which is a number whose value is independent of the units in which it is calculated. Slope, $\Delta p/\Delta q$, is not a pure number. For example, if price is measured in pence, $\Delta p/\Delta q$ will be 100 times as large as $\Delta p/\Delta q$ along the same demand curve where price is measured in pounds sterling.

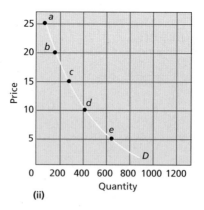

Figure 4.2 One demand curve drawn on two different scales
Suitable choice of scale can make any demand curve appear steep or flat. Parts (i) and (ii) plot the same demand curve. Because the same distance on the quantity axes stands for twice as much in part (ii) as in part (i), and the same distance on the price axes stands for half as much, the curve is steeper when plotted in graph (ii) than when plotted in graph (i).

The sign of the measure Because of the negative slope of the demand curve, the price and the quantity will always change in opposite directions. One change will be positive and the other negative, making the measured elasticity of demand negative. This would pose no problem except for two unfortunate habits of economists. First, either by carelessness or by design, the minus sign is often dropped and elasticity is reported as a positive number. Second, it is almost universal practice when comparing two elasticities to compare their absolute, not their algebraic, values. For example, if product X has an elasticity of −2 while product Y has an elasticity of −10, economists will say that Y has a greater elasticity than X (in spite of the fact that −10 is *less than* −2). As long as it is understood that absolute and not algebraic values are being compared, this usage is acceptable.[2] After all, the demand curve with the larger absolute elasticity *is* the one where quantity demanded is more responsive to price changes. For example, an elasticity of −10 indicates greater response of quantity to price than does an elasticity of −2.

This need not cause us trouble as long as we remember the basics:

Demand elasticity is measured by a ratio: the percentage change in quantity demanded divided by the percentage change in price that brought it about; for normal, negatively sloped demand curves, elasticity is negative, but two elasticities are compared by comparing their absolute values.

Table 4.1 shows the calculation of two demand elasticities, one that is quite large and one that is quite small. The larger elasticity indicates that quantity demanded is highly responsive to a change in price. The smaller elasticity indicates that the quantity demanded is relatively unresponsive to a change in price.

Table 4.1 Calculation of two demand elasticities

	Original	New	% change	Elasticity
Good A				
Quantity	100	95	−5%	$\frac{-5}{10}=$ **−0.5**
Price	£1	£1.10	10%	
Good B				
Quantity	200	140	−30%	$\frac{-30}{20}=$ **−1.5**
Price	£5	£6	20%	

Elasticity is calculated by dividing the percentage change in quantity by the percentage change in price. With good A, a rise in price of 10p on £1, or 10 per cent, causes a fall in quantity of 5 units from 100, or 5 per cent. Dividing the 5 per cent reduction in quantity by the 10 per cent increase in price gives an elasticity of −0.5. With good B, a 30 per cent fall in quantity is caused by a 20 per cent rise in price, making elasticity −1.5.

Figure 4.3 Three constant-elasticity demand curves
Each curve has a constant elasticity. D_1 has *zero elasticity*: the quantity demanded does not change at all when price changes. D_2 has *infinite elasticity at the price p_0*: a small price increase from p_0 decreases quantity demanded from an indefinitely large amount to zero. D_3 has *unit elasticity*: a given percentage increase in price brings an equal percentage decrease in quantity demanded at all points on the curve; it is a rectangular hyperbola for which price *times* quantity is a constant.

Interpreting price elasticity

The value of price elasticity of demand ranges from zero to minus infinity. In this section, however, we concentrate on absolute values, and so ask by how much the absolute value *exceeds zero*.

Elasticity is zero if quantity demanded is unchanged when price changes, namely when quantity demanded does not respond to a price change. A demand curve of zero elasticity is shown as curve D_1 in Figure 4.3. It is said to be *perfectly* or *completely* inelastic.

As long as there is some positive response of quantity demanded to a change in price, the absolute value of elasticity will exceed zero. The greater the response, the larger the elasticity. Whenever this value is less than one, however, the percentage change in quantity is less than the percentage change in price and demand is said to be **inelastic.**

When elasticity is equal to one, the two percentage changes are then equal to each other. This case, which is called **unit elasticity,** is the boundary between elastic and inelastic demands. A demand curve having unit elasticity over its whole range is shown as D_3 in Figure 4.3.

When the percentage change in quantity demanded exceeds the percentage change in price, the elasticity of demand is greater than one and demand is said to be **elastic.** When elasticity is infinitely large, there exists some small price reduction that will raise demand from zero to infinity. Above the critical price, consumers will buy nothing. At the critical price, they will buy all that they can obtain (an infinite amount, if it were available). The graph of a demand curve with infinite price elasticity is shown as

[2] The absolute value is the magnitude without the sign. Thus, for example, −3 is smaller in algebraic value than 2 but larger in absolute value.

Box 4.1 The terminology of elasticity

TERM	SYMBOL	NUMERICAL MEASURE OF ELASTICITY	VERBAL DESCRIPTION
Price elasticity of demand (supply)	η (ε_s)		
Perfectly or completely inelastic		Zero	Quantity demanded (supplied) does not change as price changes
Inelastic		Greater than zero, less than one	Quantity demanded (supplied) changes by a smaller percentage than does price
Unit elasticity		One	Quantity demanded (supplied) changes by exactly the same percentage as does price
Elastic		Greater than one, but less than infinity	Quantity demanded (supplied) changes by a larger percentage than does price
Perfectly, completely, or infinitely elastic		Infinity	Purchasers (sellers) are prepared to buy (sell) all they can at some price and none at all at a higher (lower) price
Income elasticity of demand	η_y		
Inferior good		Negative	Quantity demanded decreases as income increases
Normal good		Positive	Quantity demanded increases as income increases:
Income-inelastic		Less than one	less than in proportion to income increase
Income-elastic		Greater than one	more than in proportion to income increase
Cross-elasticity of demand	η_{xy}		
Substitute		Positive	The quantity demanded of some good and the price of a substitute are positively related
Complement		Negative	The quantity demanded of some good and the price of a complement are negatively related

D_2 in Figure 4.3. Such a demand curve is said to be *perfectly* or *completely elastic*. (This unlikely looking case will turn out to be important later when we study the demand for the output of a single firm with many competitors.)

Box 4.1 summarizes the discussion of this and subsequent sections. The terminology in the table is important, and you should become familiar with it.

Elasticity and total revenue

How does consumers' total expenditure react when the price of a product is changed? Notice that the total expenditure of the product's buyers is equal to the revenues of the product's sellers plus any taxes that the government levies on the product. (In what follows we ignore any taxes on the commodity so that sellers' revenue is equal to buyers' expenditure.)

The simplest example will show that buyers' expenditure and sellers' revenue may rise or fall in response to a decrease in price. Suppose 100 units of a product are being sold at a unit price of £1. The price is then cut to £0.90. If the quantity sold rises to 110, the total expenditure falls from £100 to £99. But if quantity sold rises to 120, total expenditure rises from £100 to £108.

The change in total expenditure brought about by a change in price is related to the elasticity of demand. If elasticity is less than unity, the percentage change in price will exceed the percentage change in quantity. The price change will then be the more important of the two changes, so that total expenditure will change in the same direction as the price changes. If, however, elasticity exceeds unity, the percentage change in quantity will exceed the percentage change in price. The quantity change will then be the more important change, so that total expenditure will change in the same direction as quantity changes (that is, in the opposite direction to the change in price).

1. When elasticity of demand exceeds unity (demand is elastic), a fall in price increases total expenditure on the good and a rise in price reduces it.

2. When elasticity is less than unity (demand is inelastic), a fall in price reduces total expenditure on the good and a rise in price increases it.

3. When elasticity of demand is unity, a rise or a fall in price leaves total expenditure on the good unaffected.[3]

You should now return to the example in Table 4.1 and calculate what happens to total revenue when price changes in each case. In the case of product A, whose demand is inelastic, you will see that a rise in price raises the revenue of sellers. In contrast, the rise in the price of good B, whose demand is elastic, lowers sellers' revenue.

Some complications

We now need to look a little more closely at the elasticity measure. Let us first write out in symbols the definition that we have been using, which is percentage change in quantity divided by percentage change in price:

$$\eta = \frac{\dfrac{\Delta q}{q} \cdot 100}{\dfrac{\Delta p}{p} \cdot 100}.$$

We can cancel out the 100s and multiply the numerator and denominator by $p/\Delta p$ to get

$$\eta = \frac{\Delta q}{q} \cdot \frac{p}{\Delta p}.$$

Since it does not matter in which order we do our multiplication (i.e. $q \cdot \Delta p \equiv \Delta p \cdot q$), we may reverse the order of the two terms in the denominator and write

$$\eta = \frac{\Delta q}{\Delta p} \cdot \frac{p}{q}. \qquad (2)$$

We have now split elasticity into two parts: $\Delta q/\Delta p$, the ratio of the change in quantity to the change in price, which is related to the slope of the demand curve; and p/q, which is related to the place on the curve at which we made our measurement.

Figure 4.4 shows a straight-line demand curve. If we wish to measure the elasticity at a point, we take our p and q at that point and consider a price change, taking us to another point, and measure our Δp and Δq between those two points. The slope of the straight line joining the two points is $\Delta p/\Delta q$. (If you have forgotten this, refer to page 25.) The term in equation (2), however, is $\Delta q/\Delta p$, which is the reciprocal of $\Delta p/\Delta q$. Thus, the first term in the elasticity formula (2) is the reciprocal of the slope of the straight line joining the two price–quantity positions under consideration.[4] The second term is the ratio of price to quantity at the point where elasticity is measured.

Now we can use the expression in (2) to discover a number of things about our elasticity measure.

First, the elasticity of a negatively sloped straight-line demand curve varies from infinity at the price axis to zero

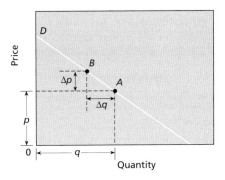

Figure 4.4 Elasticity on a linear demand curve

Elasticity depends on the slope of the demand curve and the point at which the measurement is made. Starting at point A and moving to point B, the ratio $\Delta p/\Delta q$ is the slope of the line, while its reciprocal $\Delta q/\Delta p$ is the first term in the percentage definition of elasticity. The second term is p/q, which is the ratio of the coordinates of point A. Since the slope $\Delta p/\Delta q$ is constant, it is clear that the elasticity along the curve varies with the ratio p/q, which is zero where the curve intersects the quantity axis and 'infinity' where it intersects the price axis.

at the quantity axis. We first notice that a straight line has a constant slope, so that the ratio $\Delta p/\Delta q$ is the same anywhere on the line. Therefore, its reciprocal, $\Delta q/\Delta p$, must also be constant. We can now infer the changes in η by inspecting changes in the ratio p/q as we move along the demand curve. At the price axis $q = 0$ and p/q is undefined. However, if we let q approach zero, without ever quite reaching it, we see that the ratio p/q increases without limit. Thus elasticity increases without limit as q approaches zero. Loosely, we say elasticity is infinity when q is zero. Now move the point at which elasticity is being measured down the demand curve. As this happens, p falls and q rises steadily; thus the ratio p/q is falling steadily, so that η is also falling. At the q-axis the price is zero, so the ratio p/q is zero. Thus elasticity is zero.

Second, with a straight-line demand curve the elasticity measured from any point (p, q), according to equation (2) above, is independent of the direction and magnitude of the change in price and quantity. This follows immediately from the fact that the slope of a straight line is a constant. If we start from some point (p, q) and then change price,

---

[3] Algebraically, total revenue is price *times* quantity. If, for example, the equilibrium price and quantity are p_1 and q_1, then total revenue is $p_1 q_1$. On a demand-curve diagram price is given by a vertical distance and quantity by a horizontal distance. It follows that on such a diagram total revenue is given by the *area* of a rectangle the length of whose sides represent price and quantity. Total revenue to the supplier and total expenditure by consumers are identical in these examples.

[4] If economists followed normal mathematical practice of plotting the demand curve with the dependent variable (quantity in this case) on the vertical axis, the ratio in (2) would be the slope of the demand curve rather than its reciprocal.

the ratio $\Delta q/\Delta p$ will be the same whatever the direction or the size of the change in p.

Our third point takes us back to the beginning of this chapter, where we warned against judging elasticity from the apparent shape of a demand curve. Since we frequently need to compare elasticities on two curves, it is fortunate that this can be done by inspection for the elasticities of two intersecting straight-line demand curves. These can be compared *at the point of intersection* merely by comparing the slopes of the two curves. The steeper curve is the less elastic. Figure 4.5 shows two intersecting curves and proves that the steeper curve is less elastic than the flatter curve when elasticity is measured at the point where the two curves intersect. The intuitive reason is that at the point of intersection p and q are common to both curves, so all that differs in the elasticity formula is their relative slopes. This is a valuable result, which we will use many times in later chapters.

Measured at the point of intersection of two demand curves, the steeper curve has the lower elasticity.

Our final point is that when equation (2) is applied to a nonlinear demand curve, the elasticity measured at any one point varies with the direction and magnitude of the change in price and quantity. Figure 4.6 shows a nonlinear demand curve with elasticity being measured at one point. The figure makes it apparent that the ratio $\Delta q/\Delta p$, and hence the elasticity, will vary according to the size and the

Figure 4.6 Elasticity on a nonlinear demand curve

Elasticity measured from one point on a nonlinear demand curve and using the percentage formula varies with the direction and magnitude of the change being considered. Elasticity is to be measured from point A, so the ratio p/q is given. The ratio $\Delta p/\Delta q$ is the slope of the line joining point A to the point reached on the curve after the price has changed. The smallest ratio occurs when the change is to point C and the highest ratio when it is to point E. Since the term in the elasticity formula, $\Delta q/\Delta p$, is the reciprocal of this slope, measured elasticity is largest when the change is to point C and smallest when it is to point E.

direction of the price change. This result is very inconvenient. It happens because the ratio $\Delta q/\Delta p$ gives the average reaction of q to a change in p over a section of the demand curve, and, depending on the range that we take, the average reaction will be different.

A more precise measure

The measure defined in (2) gives the elasticity over some range, or *arc*, of the demand curve. This measure is sometimes used in empirical work where elasticity is measured between two observed price–quantity situations. In theoretical work, however, it is normal to use a concept that gives a unique measure of the elasticity at each specific point on the demand curve. Instead of using the changes in price (Δp) and quantity (Δq) over some range of the curve, this elasticity measure uses the concept of how quantity is *tending* to change as price changes at each specific point on the curve.

If we wish to measure the elasticity in this way, we need to know the reaction of quantity to a change in price at each point on the curve, not over some range on the curve. We use the symbol dq/dp to refer to this concept and define it as *the reciprocal of the slope of the straight line (i.e. $\Delta q/\Delta p$) that is tangent to the demand curve at the point in question.* Figure 4.7 illustrates the use of this measure to calculate the elasticity of demand at the point a. It is the ratio p/q (as

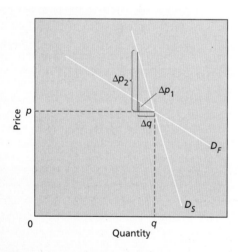

Figure 4.5 Two intersecting demand curves

At the point of intersection of two demand curves, the steeper curve has the lower elasticity. At the point of intersection p and q are common to both curves, and hence the ratio p/q is the same. Therefore, elasticity varies only with $\Delta q/\Delta p$. The absolute value of the slope of the steeper curve, $\Delta p_2/\Delta q$, is larger than the absolute value of the slope, $\Delta p_1/\Delta q$, of the flatter curve. Thus, the absolute value of the ratio $\Delta q/\Delta p_2$ on the steeper curve is smaller than the ratio $\Delta q/\Delta p_1$ on the flatter curve, so that elasticity is lower.

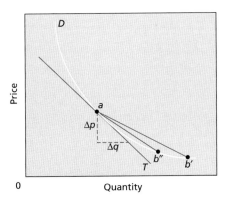

Figure 4.7 Elasticity by the exact method
When elasticity is related to the slope of the tangent to the demand curve at some point, there is a unique measured value of elasticity at that point. In this method the ratio $\Delta q/\Delta p$ is taken as the reciprocal of the slope of the line that is tangent to point a. Thus there is only one measured elasticity at point a. It is p/q multiplied by $\Delta q/\Delta p$ measured along the tangent T. There is no averaging of changes in p and q in this measure because only one point on the curve is used.

it has been in all previous measures) now multiplied by the ratio $\Delta q/\Delta p$ measured along the straight line that is tangent to the curve at a.[5] This definition may now be written as

$$\eta = \frac{dq}{dp} \cdot \frac{p}{q}. \qquad (3)$$

This elasticity measure is the one normally used in economic theory. Elasticity measured by the percentage formula $(\Delta q/\Delta p)(p/q)$ may be regarded as an approximation to this expression. It is obvious from inspecting Figure 4.7 that the elasticity measured from $(\Delta q/\Delta p)(p/q)$ will come closer and closer to that measured by $(dq/dp)(p/q)$, the smaller the price change used to calculate the value of $\Delta q/\Delta p$. Thus, if we consider the percentage definition of elasticity as an approximation to the precise definition, the approximation improves as the size of Δp diminishes. Box 4.2 further investigates some of the properties of the percentage definition and shows a practical way of avoiding some of its undesirable aspects.

[5] Although the expression dq/dp, as we have defined it, is the differential-calculus concept of the derivative of quantity with respect to price at the point (p, q), you can understand the concept without knowing the calculus.

Box 4.2 Measuring elasticity over a range

We have seen that the percentage formula gives different answers for the elasticity at any point on a nonlinear demand curve depending on the size and the direction of the change being considered. Many textbooks just give the percentage elasticity formula, without warning the reader of this property. Inquisitive students usually discover this property with a shock the first time they try to calculate some elasticities from numerical data.

One common way in which students discover the problem is when they try to calculate the elasticity on a unit-elasticity curve. Using the percentage formula the answer never comes out to be 1. For example, the demand curve

$$p = \pounds 100/q \qquad (i)$$

is a unit-elastic curve because expenditure, pq, remains constant at £100 whatever the price. But if you substitute any two prices into the above equation and calculate the elasticity according to the percentage formula, you will *never* get an answer of 1, whatever two prices you take. For example, the equation tells us that if price rises from £2 to £3, quantity falls from 50 to 33.3. If we take the original price as £2, we have a price change of 50 per cent and a quantity change of −33.3 per cent, making an elasticity of −0.667. If we take the original price as £3, the elasticity comes out to be −1.5.

This is unsatisfactory. The problem can be avoided when measuring elasticity between two separate points on the curve by taking p and q as the average values between the two points on the curve. This measure has two convenient properties. First, it is independent of the direction of the change and, second, it gives a value of unity for any point on a demand curve whose true value is unity.

In the above example the average p is £2.5 and the average q is 41.667.

This makes the percentage change in price 40 per cent ($(1/2.5) \times 100$) and the percentage change in quantity also 40 per cent ($(16.667/41.667) \times 100$). So elasticity is correctly measured as 1. Whatever two prices you put into equation (1), you will always get a value of unity for the elasticity, provided you use the average of the two prices and of the two quantities when calculating the elasticity. Readers who enjoy playing with algebra can have fun proving this proposition.[*]

The best approximation to the correct measure when elasticity is measured between two separate points on a demand curve is obtained by defining p and q as the average of the prices and quantities at the two points on the curve.

The above is the best way to measure elasticities given readings from any two points on a curve when that is all that is known. As we have seen in the text, for theoretical purposes the way out of the problem is to measure the ratio $\Delta q/\Delta p$ as the slope of the tangent to one point on the curve rather than between two points on the curve. To do this we need to know a portion of the demand curve around the point in question.

In practice economists do not usually estimate elasticity on the basis of only one observation. It is more common to report an elasticity measure that is valued at the mean of two p and q data points. This is analogous to the averaging we suggest here.

[*] What you need to prove is that

$$\frac{q_2 - q_1}{p_2 - p_1} \cdot \frac{(p_1 + p_2)/2}{(q_1 + q_2)/2} = 1.$$

What determines elasticity of demand?

The main determinant of elasticity is the availability of substitutes. Some products, such as margarine, cabbage, lamb, and Ford Mondeos, have quite close substitutes—butter, other green vegetables, beef, and Vauxhall Cavaliers. When the price of any one of these products changes, *the prices of the substitutes remaining constant*, consumers will substitute one product for another. When the price falls, consumers buy more of the product and less of its substitutes. When the price rises, consumers buy less of the product and more of its substitutes. More broadly defined products, such as all foods, all clothing, cigarettes, and petrol, have few if any satisfactory substitutes. A rise in their price can be expected to cause a smaller fall in quantity demanded than would be the case if close substitutes were available.

A product with close substitutes tends to have an elastic demand; one with no close substitutes tends to have an inelastic demand.

Closeness of substitutes—and thus measured elasticity—depends both on how the product is defined and on the time-period under consideration. This is explored in the following sections. One common misconception about demand elasticity is discussed in Box 4.3.

Definition of the product There is no substitute for food; it is a necessity of life. Thus for food taken as a whole demand is inelastic over a large price range. It does not follow, however, that any one food, such as Weetabix or Heinz tomato soup, is a necessity in the same sense; each of these has close substitutes, such as Kellogg's Cornflakes and Campbell's tomato soup. Individual food products can have quite elastic demands, and they frequently do.

Durable goods provide a similar example. Durables as a whole have less elastic demands than do individual durable goods. For example, after a rise in the price of TV sets, many consumers replace their lawnmower or their vacuum cleaner instead of buying a TV. Thus, although their purchases of television sets will fall, their total purchases of durables will fall by much less.

Because most specific manufactured goods have close substitutes, they tend to have price-elastic demands. Hats, for example, have been estimated to have an elasticity of −3.0. In contrast, all clothing taken together tends to be inelastic.

Any one of a group of related products will tend to have an elastic demand, even though the demand for the group as a whole may be inelastic.

Long-run and short-run elasticity of demand Because it takes time to adjust fully to some price change, a demand that is inelastic in the short run may prove elastic when enough time has passed. For example, before the first OPEC oil price shocks of the mid-1970s, the demand for

---

Box 4.3 Elasticity and income

It is often argued that the demand for a product will be more inelastic the smaller the proportion of income spent on it. The argument runs as follows. When only a small proportion of income is spent on some product, consumers will hardly notice a price rise. Hence they will not react strongly to price changes one way or the other. The most commonly quoted example of this alleged phenomenon is salt.

Salt is, however, a poor example for the argument being advanced. Although it does take up a very small part of consumers' total expenditure, it also has few close substitutes. Consider another product, say one type of mint. These mints no doubt account for only a small portion of the total expenditure of mint-suckers, but there are many close substitutes—other types of mints and other sucking sweets. The makers of Polo mints, for example, know that if they raise Polo prices greatly, mint-suckers will switch to other brands of mint and to other types of sucking sweets. They thus face an elastic demand for their product.

Similar considerations apply to any one brand of matches. If the makers of Swan Vesta matches raise their prices significantly, people will switch to other brands of matches rather than pay the higher price.

What this discussion shows is that *goods with close substitutes will tend to have elastic demands whether they account for a large or a small part of consumers' incomes.*

There is, however, another aspect of the influence of income. To see this, consider any good that has an inelastic demand. A rise in its price causes more to be spent on it. If consumers spend more on that product, they must spend less on all others taken as a group. But the higher is the proportion of income spent on the product, the less likely are they to spend more on it when its price rises. After all, if a consumer spends all of his or her income on potatoes, demand must have unit elasticity. As price rises, purchases must then fall in proportion since the consumer has only a given income to spend. Thus, *for a good to have a highly inelastic demand it must have few good substitutes, and it must not take up too large a proportion of consumers' total expenditure.*

---

petrol was thought to be highly inelastic because of the absence of satisfactory substitutes. But the large price increases over the 1970s led to the development of smaller, more fuel-efficient cars and to less driving. The elasticity of demand for petrol was measured as −0.6 soon after the price rose. However, when the first five years of quantity adjustment had been allowed for the elasticity had become −1.2.

For many products the response of quantity demanded to a given price change, and thus the measured price elasticity of demand, will tend to be greater the longer the time-span considered.

The different quantity responses can be shown by different demand curves. Every demand curve shows the response of consumer demand to a change in price. For such products as cornflakes and ties, the full response occurs quickly and there is little reason to worry about longer-term effects. For these products a single demand curve will suffice. Other products are typically used in connection with highly durable appliances or machines. A change in price of, say, electricity or petrol may not have its major effect until the stock of appliances and machines using these products has been adjusted. This adjustment may take a long time, making it useful to identify two kinds of demand curve for such products. A *short-run demand curve* shows the response of quantity demanded to a change in price, *given* the existing quantities of the durable goods that use the product, and *given* existing supplies of substitute products. A different short-run demand curve will exist for each such structure of durable goods and substitute products. The *long-run demand curve* shows the response of quantity demanded to a change in price after enough time has passed to allow all adjustments to be made.

The relation between long-run and short-run demand curves is shown in Figure 4.8. Assume, for example, that there is a large rise in the price of electricity. The initial response will be along the short-run demand curve. There will be some fall in quantity demanded, but the percentage drop is likely to be less than the percentage rise in price, making short-run demand inelastic. Over time, however, many people will replace their existing electric cookers with gas cookers as they wear out. New homes will be equipped with gas rather than electric appliances more often than they would have been before the price rise. Over time, factories will switch to relatively cheaper sources of power. When all these types of long-run adaptations have been made, the demand for electricity will have fallen a great deal. Indeed, over this longer period of time, the percentage reduction in quantity demanded may exceed the percentage increase in price. If so, the long-run demand for electricity will be elastic.

The principal conclusion in the discussion of elasticity is:

The long-run demand curve for a product that is used in conjunction with durable products will tend to be substantially more elastic than any of the short-run demand curves.

This distinction will prove valuable in several of the chapters that follow.

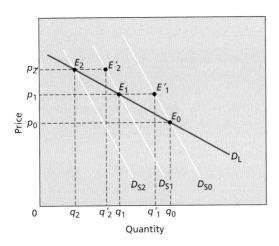

Figure 4.8 Short-run and long-run demand curves
The long-run demand curve is more elastic than the short-run curves. D_L is the long-run demand curve showing the quantity that will be bought after consumers become fully adjusted to each given price. Through each point on D_L there is a short-run demand curve. It shows the quantities that will be bought at each price when consumers are fully adjusted to the price at which that particular short-run curve intersects the long-run curve. So at every other point on the short run curve consumers are not fully adjusted to the price they face, possibly because they have an inappropriate stock of durable goods.
When consumers are fully adjusted to price p_0, they are at point E_0 consuming q_0. Short-run variations in price then move them along the short-run demand curve D_{S0}. Similarly, when they are fully adjusted to price p_1, they are at E_1 and short-run price variations move them along D_{S1}. The line D_{S2} shows short-run variations in demand when consumers are fully adjusted to price p_2.

Other demand elasticities

So far we have discussed *price elasticity of demand*, the response of the quantity demanded to a change in the product's own price. The concept of demand elasticity can, however, be broadened to measure the response to changes in *any* of the factors that influence demand. How much, for example, do changes in income and the prices of other products affect quantity demanded?

Income elasticity

Economic growth has raised the real income of the average citizen of Europe and North America quite dramatically over the past two centuries. At low levels of income most money is spent on such basics as food, clothing, and shelter. As income rises an increasing proportion of expenditure tends to fall on manufactured goods, particularly such durables as cars, TV sets, and refrigerators. At yet higher levels of income more and more of any additional income goes to services such as foreign travel, entertainment, and education.

The responsiveness of demand for a product to changes in income is termed **income elasticity of demand,** and is defined as

$$\eta_y = \frac{\text{percentage change in quantity demanded}}{\text{percentage change in income}}.$$

For most products increases in income lead to increases in quantity demanded, and income elasticity is therefore positive. If the resulting percentage change in quantity demanded is larger than the percentage increase in income, η_y will exceed unity. The product's demand is then said to be **income-elastic.** If the percentage change in quantity demanded is smaller than the percentage change in income, η_y will be less than unity. The product's demand is then said to be **income-inelastic.** In the boundary case, the percentage changes in income and quantity demanded are equal, making η_y unity. The product is said to have a *unit income elasticity of demand.*

While virtually all observed price elasticities are negative, income elasticities are observed to be both positive and negative.

We have already encountered these relations on pages 39–40, where we argued that a change in income would shift the demand curve for a product. If the product is a normal good, a rise in income causes more of it to be demanded, other things being equal, which means a rightward shift in the product's demand curve. If the product is an inferior good, a rise in income causes less of it to be demanded, which means a leftward shift in the product's demand curve. So normal goods have positive income elasticities while inferior goods have negative income elasticities. Finally, the boundary case between normal and inferior goods occurs when a rise in income leaves quantity demanded unchanged, so that income elasticity is zero.

The important terminology of income elasticity is summarized in Figure 4.9 and in Box 4.1 on page 58. You should spend time studying this terminology and committing it to memory. Figure 4.9 illustrates all possible reactions by showing a product whose income elasticity goes from zero to positive to negative. Specific goods do not need to show all of these. For example, a good may have a positive income elasticity at all levels of income. (You should be able to explain why no good can, however, have a negative income elasticity at *all* levels of income.) A graph that directly relates quantity demanded to income, such as Figure 4.9, is called an *Engel curve* after Ernst Engel (1821–96), the German economist who used this device to establish a systematic relationship between household income and expenditure on necessities.

Cross-elasticity

The responsiveness of quantity demanded of one product to changes in the prices of other products is often of considerable interest. Producers of, say, beans and other meat substitutes find the demands for their products rising when cattle shortages force the price of beef up. Producers of large cars found their sales falling when the price of

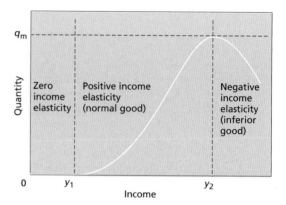

Figure 4.9 The relation between quantity demanded and income

Normal goods have positive income elasticities; inferior goods have negative elasticities. Nothing is demanded at income less than y_1, so for incomes below y_1 income elasticity is zero. Between incomes of y_1 and y_2, quantity demanded rises as income rises, making income elasticity positive. As income rises above y_2, quantity demanded falls from its peak at q_m, making income elasticity negative.

petrol rose dramatically after the 1973 and 1979 oil price rises.

The responsiveness of demand for one product to changes in the price of another product is called **cross-elasticity of demand.** It is defined as

$$\eta_{xy} = \frac{\text{percentage change in quantity demanded of one commodity}}{\text{percentage change in price of another commodity}}.$$

Cross-elasticity can vary from minus infinity to plus infinity. Complementary goods have negative cross-elasticities and substitute goods have positive cross-elasticities.

Bread and butter, for example, are complements. A fall in the price of butter causes an increase in the consumption of both products. Thus, changes in the price of butter and in the quantity of bread demanded will have opposite signs. In contrast, butter and margarine are substitutes: a fall in the price of butter increases the quantity of butter demanded but reduces the quantity of margarine demanded. Changes in the price of butter and in the quantity of margarine demanded will, therefore, have the same sign. The terminology of cross-elasticity is also summarized in Box 4.1.

Box 4.4 provides some examples of the importance of taking elasticity into account when making many practical decisions.

Box 4.4 Elasticity matters

Elasticities are rather boring concepts to learn about and to calculate. But they are powerful tools. Practical people who scorn theory ignore elasticity considerations at their peril. Here are a few cautionary tales.

■ Many years ago the government of the former USSR was trying to earn enough US dollars to buy some strategic materials that it lacked at home. It had few exports at the time but it did have large stocks of gold, which it dumped on the world market to earn US dollars. Since it was desperate for the money it adopted desperate measures, selling a large amount quickly. This drove the price down substantially. Indeed the price fell more than in proportion to the increased quantity brought to the market. If you had been advising the Communist government just after reading this chapter, you would have known enough to point out the error of its ways. Since the world demand was inelastic it needed to be careful not to try to sell too much. It could have earned more by selling less!

■ Not long ago the executive of a professional association introduced a

motion at the annual meeting 'to increase dues by 10 per cent so as to increase our revenues by 10 per cent'. You could have told them that they were optimistically assuming the elasticity of demand for membership was zero. If the elasticity differed at all from zero, revenues would rise by less than 10 per cent. If the elasticity proved to be greater than unity, they would actually suffer a loss of revenue as a result of the rise in dues.

■ A local bus company fearfully raised its prices two years ago by 10 per cent in an attempt to cover increased costs. It was pleased to see its revenues rise by 5 per cent. This year it confidently raised its prices again and was surprised and dismayed to find that its revenues fell by 2 per cent. The manager was reported in the local press as saying, 'It is hard to do business when our customers are so erratic.' You could have told him that there was nothing erratic about the customers' behaviour. The manager was unreasonably assuming that the elasticity of demand for bus rides was constant over the whole relevant range. All that happened is that the second increase took fares into the range where the market demand curve was inelastic.

Supply elasticity

We have seen that elasticity of demand measures the response of quantity demanded to changes in any of the factors that influence it. Similarly, elasticity of supply measures the response of quantity supplied to changes in any of the factors that influence it. Because we wish to focus on the product's own price as a factor influencing its supply, we will be mainly concerned with *price elasticity of supply*. The usual practice is to drop the adjective 'price', referring to 'elasticity of supply' or 'supply elasticity' whenever there is no ambiguity in this usage.

Supply elasticities are important in economics. Our treatment is brief for two reasons: first, much of what has been said about demand elasticity carries over to the case of supply elasticity and does not need repeating; second, we will have more to say about the determinants of supply elasticity later in this book.

A definition

The **price elasticity of supply** is defined as the percentage change in quantity supplied divided by the percentage change in price that brought it about. Letting the lowercase Greek letter epsilon, ε, stand for this measure, its formula is

$$\varepsilon_S = \frac{\text{percentage change in quantity supplied}}{\text{percentage change in price}}.$$

Supply elasticity is a measure of the degree of responsiveness of quantity supplied to changes in the product's own price.

Since supply curves normally have positive slopes, supply elasticity is normally positive.[6]

Interpreting supply elasticity

Figure 4.10 illustrates three cases of supply elasticity. The case of zero elasticity is one in which the quantity supplied does not change as price changes. This would be the case, for example, if suppliers persisted in producing a given quantity and dumping it on the market for whatever it would bring. Infinite elasticity occurs at some price if nothing is supplied at lower prices but an indefinitely large amount will be supplied at that price. Any straight-line supply curve drawn through the origin, such as the one shown in part (iii) of the figure, has an elasticity of unity. The reason is that, for any positively sloped straight line, the ratio of p/q at any point on the line is equal to the ratio $\Delta p/\Delta q$ that defines the slope of the line. Thus in the

[6] As with demand elasticity, the unique measure of supply elasticity at any point on a supply curve as given by the formula $(\mathrm{d}q/\mathrm{d}p)(p/q)$ where $\mathrm{d}q/\mathrm{d}p$ is the reciprocal of the slope of the tangent to the supply curve at the point (p, q)—which is the same thing as the calculus concept of the *derivative* of quantity supplied with respect to price.

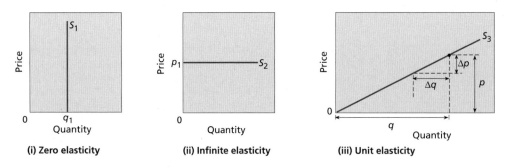

Figure 4.10 Three constant-elasticity supply curves

All three curves have constant elasticity. Curve S_1 has a *zero elasticity*, since the same quantity, q_1, is supplied whatever the price. Curve S_2 has an *infinite elasticity at price* p_1; nothing at all will be supplied at any price below p_1, while an indefinitely large quantity will be supplied at the price of p_1. Curve S_3, as well as all other straight lines through the origin, has a *unit elasticity*, indicating that the percentage change in quantity equals the percentage change in price between any two points on the curve.

formula $(\Delta q/\Delta p)(p/q)$ the two ratios cancel each other out.[7]

The case of unit supply elasticity illustrates that the warning given earlier for demand applies equally to supply. Do not confuse geometric steepness of supply curves with elasticity. Since *any* straight-line supply curve that passes through the origin has an elasticity of unity, it follows that there is no simple correspondence between geometrical steepness and supply elasticity. The reason is that varying steepness (when the scales on both axes are unchanged) reflects varying *absolute* changes, while elasticity depends on *percentage* changes. The terminology of supply elasticity is summarized in Box 4.1 on page 58.

What determines elasticity of supply?

What determines the response of producers to a change in the price of the product that they supply? First, the size of the response depends in part on how easily producers can shift from the production of other products to the one whose price has risen. If agricultural land and labour can be readily shifted from one crop to another, the supply of any one crop will be more elastic than if labour cannot easily be shifted. Here also, as with demand, length of time for response is critical. It may be difficult to change quantities supplied in response to a price increase in a matter of weeks or months, but easy to do so over a period of years. An obvious example concerns the planting cycle of crops. Also, new oilfields can be discovered, wells drilled, and pipelines built over a period of years, but not in a few months. Thus, the elasticity of supply of oil is much greater over five years than over one year. Second, elasticity is strongly influenced by how costs respond to output changes. This issue will be treated at length in later chapters.

Measurement of demand and supply

Much of what economists do to earn a living uses measurements of demand and supply elasticities. Will a fare increase help to ease the deficit of London Underground or the Panama Canal? The answer requires knowledge of price elasticity of demand. The United Nations Food and Agriculture Organization (FAO), and producers' co-ops, use income elasticities of demand to predict future changes in demand for food. Over the past decade, many industries have estimated their products' cross-elasticities of demand with petroleum in order to predict the effects of sharply changing petroleum prices. Members of the Organization of Petroleum Exporting Countries (OPEC)

wish to know supply elasticities in non-member countries in order to predict the reaction to price increases manipulated by OPEC. The methods for obtaining this information are dealt with in econometrics courses. Solutions to two of the most troubling problems concerning demand measurement are discussed below.

---

[7] The proof can be seen by referring to the two triangles in part (iii) of Figure 4.10. One has sides p, q, and the S curve, while the other has sides Δp, Δq, and the S curve. Clearly, they are similar triangles. It follows that the ratios of their sides are equal, i.e. $p/q = \Delta p/\Delta q$. Elasticity of supply is $\varepsilon = (\Delta q/\Delta p)\cdot(p/q)$. Substituting $p/q = \Delta p/\Delta q$ (since, as we have just seen, these two are equal) into the definition of elasticity gives $(\Delta q/\Delta p)\cdot(\Delta p/\Delta q)$, which is unity.

Problems of demand measurement

The explosion of knowledge of elasticities in recent decades came about when econometricians overcame major problems in measuring demand (and supply) relationships.

Everything is changing at once

When quantity demanded changes over time, it is usually because *all* of the influences that affect demand have been changing at the same time. How, then, can the separate influence of each variable be determined?

What, for example, is to be made of the observation that the quantity of butter consumed per capita rose by 10 per cent over a period in which average consumer income rose by 5 per cent, the price of butter fell by 3 per cent, and the price of margarine rose by 4 per cent? How much of the change is due to income elasticity of demand, how much to price elasticity, and how much to the cross-elasticity between butter and margarine? If this is all we know, the question cannot be answered. If, however, there are many observations showing, say, quantity demanded, income, price of butter, and price of margarine every month for four or five years, it is possible to discover the separate influence of each of the variables. The standard technique for doing so is called *multiple regression analysis*.

Separating the influences of demand and supply

A second set of problems concerns the separate estimation of demand and supply curves. We do not observe directly what people wish to buy and what producers wish to sell. Rather, we see what they do buy and what they do sell. The problem of how to estimate both demand and supply curves from observed market data on prices and quantities actually traded is called the **identification problem.**

To illustrate the problem, we assume in Figure 4.11 that all situations observed in the real world are equilibrium ones, in the sense that they are produced by the intersection of demand and supply curves. The first two parts of the figure show cases where only one curve shifts. Observations made on prices and quantities then trace out the curve that has not shifted. The third part of the figure, however, shows that when both curves are shifting, observations of prices and quantities are not sufficient to identify the slope of either curve.

The identification problem is surmountable. The key to identifying the demand and supply curves separately is to bring in variables other than price, and then to relate demand to one set and supply to *some other* set. For example, supply of the product might be related not only to the price of the product but also to its cost of production, and

demand might be related not only to the price of the product but also to consumers' incomes. Provided that these other variables change sufficiently, it is possible to determine the relation between quantity supplied and price as well as the relation between quantity demanded and price. The details of how this is done will be found in a course on econometrics.

Econometricians allow for the identification problem when estimating demand curves. In more popular discussions, however, the problem is sometimes ignored. Whenever you see an argument such as 'We know that the foreign elasticity of demand must be very low because the price of whisky rose by 10 per cent last year while whisky exports hardly changed at all', you should ask if the author has really identified the demand curve. If the rise in price was due to a rise in foreign demand for whisky, we may actually have discovered that the short-run *supply curve* of whisky is very inelastic (since whisky takes several years to manufacture). The general proposition to keep in mind is:

Unless we know that one curve has shifted while the other has not, price and quantity data alone are insufficient to reveal anything about the shape of either the demand or the supply curve.

Measurements of specific elasticities

The solution of the statistical problems associated with demand measurement has led to a large accumulation of data on demand elasticities. The value of these data to the applied economist shows the usefulness of demand theory.

Price elasticities

Much of the early work on demand measurement concentrated on the agricultural sector. Large fluctuations in agricultural prices provided both the incentives to study this sector and the data on which to base estimates of price elasticities of demand. Nobel Laureate Professor Richard Stone in the United Kingdom (1913–91) and Professor Henry Schultz (1893–1938) in the United States did much of the pioneering work. Many agricultural research centres extended their work and even today are making new estimates of the price elasticities of foodstuffs. The resulting data mostly confirm the existence of low price elasticities for food products as a whole, as well as for many individual products. The policy payoff of this knowledge in terms of understanding agricultural problems has been enormous; it represents an early triumph of empirical work in economics. (See the discussion in Chapter 5.)

Although the importance of the agricultural problem led early investigators to concentrate on the demand for

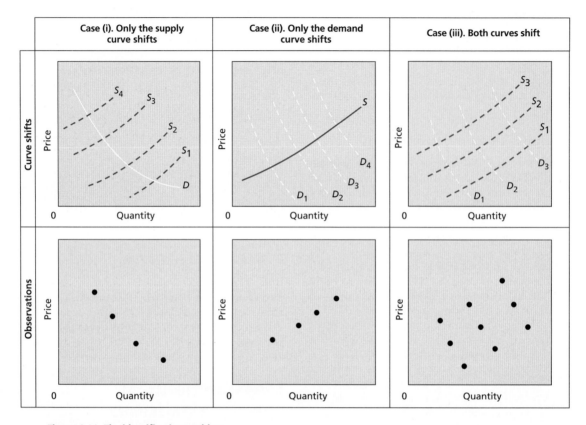

Figure 4.11 The identification problem

Observations on prices and quantities are sufficient to identify the slope of one of the curves only when it is stationary while the other shifts. In each case the curves in the top row shift randomly from one numbered position to another, generating the observations shown by the points in the corresponding bottom row. In case (i) the observations trace out the shape of the demand curve. In case (ii) they trace out the supply curve. In case (iii) neither curve can be identified from the observed prices and quantities.

foodstuffs, modern studies have expanded to include virtually the whole range of products on which consumers spend their incomes. The demands for consumer durables such as cars, radios, refrigerators, television sets, and houses are of particular interest because they constitute a large fraction of total demand, and because they can vary markedly from one year to the next. A durable product can usually be made to last for another year; thus, purchases can be postponed with greater ease than can purchases of nondurables such as food and services. If enough consumers decide simultaneously to postpone purchases of durables for even six months, the effect on the economy can be substantial.

Durables as a whole have an inelastic demand, while many individual brands of durable have elastic demands. This is another example of the general proposition that the broader the category, the fewer the close substitutes and hence the lower the elasticity. Indeed, whether durable or nondurable, most specific manufactured goods have close

substitutes, and studies show that they tend to have price-elastic demands.

Table 4.2 shows some recent measures of price elasticity for food products.

Income elasticities

Table 4.2 also shows some measured income elasticities for the United Kingdom. Note the low income elasticities for all of the food products consumed by consumers that are listed in the table.

Note also the interesting contrast between the data for price and income elasticities. Many meat products that are price-elastic have zero income elasticities. This tells us that changes in relative prices will cause substantial substitution among different types of meat—hence the greater-than-unity price elasticities—but that increases in incomes cause almost no increases in overall meat consumption—hence the low income elasticity. Of the products shown,

Table 4.2 Estimated price and income elasticities of demand for selected foods in the UK, 1989

Product	Price elasticity	Income elasticity
Carcass meats	−1.37	−0.01*
Cheese	−1.20	0.19
Frozen peas	−1.12	0.15*
Cereals	−0.94	0.03*
Fruit juices	−0.80	0.94
Bacon and ham	−0.70	−0.28
Fresh green vegetables	−0.58	0.13
Other fresh vegetables	−0.27*	0.35
Fresh potatoes	−0.21	−0.48
Bread	−0.09*	−0.25

Most foodstuffs have very low income elasticities, while price elasticities cover a wider range. Notice that although carcass meats have a zero income elasticity, they have a high price elasticity of 1.37. All demands are measured as being negatively related to price, as theory predicts. Three of the products—bread, potatoes, and bacon—show statistically significant negative income elasticities which classify them as inferior goods.

* Indicates not significantly different from zero on a standard statistical test.

Source: Ministry of Agriculture, Food, and Fisheries, *Household Food Consumption and Expenditure, 1992* (London: HMSO).

bacon and ham, potatoes, and bread have negative income elasticities, indicating that they are inferior goods at current levels of consumer incomes. Thus, although reductions in relative prices lead to increased purchases—normal price elasticities—the goods are inferior with respect to increases in income.

Cross-elasticities

In many countries monopoly is illegal. Measurement of cross-elasticities has helped courts to decide on the allegation that a monopoly exists. To illustrate, assume that the government of a particular country brings a suit against a company for buying up all the firms making aluminium cable, claiming the company has created a monopoly of the product. The company replies that it needs to own all the firms in order to compete efficiently against the several firms producing copper cable. It argues that these two products are such close substitutes that the firms producing each are in intense competition, so that the sole producer of aluminium cable cannot be said to have an effective monopoly over the market for cable. Measurement of cross-elasticity can be decisive in such a case. A cross-elasticity of 10, for example, would support the company by showing that the two products were such close substitutes that a monopoly of either would not be an effective monopoly of the cable market. A cross-elasticity

of 0.5, on the other hand, would support the government's contention that the monopoly of aluminium cable *was* a monopoly over a complete market.

Elasticities and economic growth

One of the most interesting constants in the behaviour of elasticities is the strong tendency for both income and price elasticities of demand for food to fall as nations get richer. Over the decades, economic growth has been increasing the real incomes of many countries throughout the world. As this happens the demand for foodstuffs increases, but at a slower and slower rate. At the same time the demand becomes less and less sensitive to price fluctuations. For example, the price elasticity of demand for food is only about 0.1 in the USA, the country with the highest per capita income. As we go down the income scale, price elasticities rise, being about 0.3 in the UK, 0.45 in Israel, 0.55 in Peru, and around 0.7 in India. Over the same income range, income elasticities also fall. They go from about 0.15 in the USA, 0.35 in the UK, 0.5 in Israel, and 0.65 in Peru to almost 0.8 in India.

This phenomenon of price and income elasticities that fall as economic growth raises per capita income has many important consequences, as we will see in the next chapter.

Other variables

Modern studies show that demand is often influenced by a wide variety of socioeconomic factors—family size, age, geographical location, type of employment, wealth, and income expectations—not included in the traditional theory of demand. Although significant, the total contribution of all these factors to changes in demand tends to be small. Typically, less than 30 per cent of the variations in demand are accounted for by these 'novel' factors and a much higher proportion is explained by the traditional variables of current prices and incomes.

Why the measurement of demand is important

The empirical measurements of demand elasticity help to provide the theory of price with empirical content. If we knew *nothing* about demand elasticities, then all of the exercises we have gone through in previous chapters would have very little application to the real world. As time goes by, further evidence accumulates, and economists are far beyond merely wondering if demand curves have negative slopes. Not only do we now know the approximate shape of many demand curves; we also have information about how demand curves shift. Our knowledge of demand relations increases significantly every year.

Summary

Demand elasticity

■ Elasticity of demand (also called price elasticity of demand) is defined as the percentage change in quantity divided by the percentage change in price that brought it about.

■ When the percentage change in quantity is less than the percentage change in price, demand is inelastic and a fall in price lowers the total amount spent on the product. When the percentage change in quantity is greater than the percentage change in price, demand is elastic and a fall in price raises total spending on the product.

■ A more precise measure that gives a unique value for elasticity at any point on any demand curve replaces $\Delta q/\Delta p$ measured between two points on the curve with $\Delta q/\Delta p$ measured along the tangent to the curve at the point in question (symbolized by dq/dp).

■ The main determinant of the price elasticity of demand is the availability of substitutes for the product. Any one of a group of close substitutes will have a more elastic demand than the group as a whole.

■ Elasticity of demand tends to be greater the longer the time over which adjustment occurs. Items that have a few substitutes in the short run may develop ample substitutes when consumers and producers have time to adapt.

■ Income elasticity is the percentage change in quantity demanded divided by the percentage change in income that brought it about. The income elasticity of demand for a product will usually change as income varies.

■ Cross-elasticity is the percentage change in quantity demanded divided by the percentage change in the price of some other product that brought it about. Products that are substitutes for one another have positive cross-elasticities; products that complement one another have negative cross-elasticities.

Supply elasticity

■ Elasticity of supply measures the ratio of the percentage change in the quantity supplied of a product to the percentage change in its price.

■ A commodity's elasticity of supply depends on how easy it is to shift resources into the production of that commodity and how the costs of producing the commodity vary as its production varies.

Measurement of demand and supply

■ Over the years, economists have measured many price, income, and cross-elasticities of demand. Being able to do so requires the use of statistical techniques to measure the separate influences of each of several variables when all are changing at once. It also requires a solution of the identification problem, which refers to measuring the separate shapes of the demand and supply curves. This cannot be done from price and quantity data alone.

Topics for review

■ Price, income, and cross-elasticity of demand
■ Zero, inelastic, unitary, elastic, and infinitely elastic demand
■ The relation between price elasticity and changes in total expenditure
■ Determinants of demand elasticity
■ Income elasticities for normal and inferior goods
■ Cross-elasticities between substitutes and complements
■ Long- and short-run elasticity of demand
■ Elasticity of supply and its determinants

Questions for discussion

1 Draw a demand curve that fits the following specifications. Nothing is demanded above a price of £2. For every reduction in price of 10p quantity demanded rises by 20 tonnes. Calculate the elasticity of demand at a price of £1.50, £1, and £0.50. What happens to elasticity as one moves downward to the right along the demand curve? Can you suggest why?

2 From the following quotations, what, if anything, can you conclude about elasticity of demand? (a) 'Good weather has resulted in record wheat harvests and sent wheat prices tumbling. The result has been disastrous for many wheat farmers.' (b) 'Bus use always went up when bus fares came down, but the increased patronage was never enough to prevent a decrease in overall revenue.' (c) 'As the price of compact disc players fell, producers found their revenues soaring.' (d) 'Coffee to me is an essential good—I must have it no matter what the price.' (e) 'The soaring price of flats does little to curb the strong demand in London.'

3 What elasticity measures would be useful in answering the following questions? (a) Will cheaper transport into the city centre help to keep in-town shopping centres profitable? (b) Will raising the bulk postage rate increase the revenues for the Post Office? (c) Are producers of toothpaste and mouthwash in competition with each other? (d) What effect will rising petrol prices have on the sale of cars that use propane gas?

4 Suggest products that you think might have the following patterns of elasticity of demand: (a) high income elasticity, high price elasticity; (b) high income elasticity, low price elasticity; (c) low income elasticity, low price elasticity; (d) low income elasticity, high price elasticity.

5 A stamp collector buys the only two existing copies of a stamp at an auction. After the purchase, the collector goes to the front of the room and burns one of the stamps in front of the shocked audience. What must the collector believe for this to be a rational, wealth-maximizing action?

Chapter 5
Price Theory in Action

Demand and supply analysis provides a powerful tool for understanding the world around us. Although there is more to be learned, especially about how firms affect supply, this chapter provides some real payoff to what you have learned in the previous chapters. It shows how to use demand and supply to understand real events.

In the first part of this chapter we apply demand and supply to two real-world situations, a newspaper price war and the impact of the Channel Tunnel. In the rest of the chapter, we study the effects of various government interventions into specific markets.

Throughout the chapter we use the method of comparative statics. Here is how it works. We start with a market in equilibrium. We then introduce the change in which we are interested. We then determine the new equilibrium. The differences between the first and the second equilibria must be the result of the change we introduced, since that is the only disturbance that is operating. (Appropriate corrections can be made if we wish to apply the results to cases in which the industry is initially in disequilibrium.)

Keeping up with *The Times*: demand analysis in action

In September 1993 the owners of *The Times* newspaper unilaterally lowered the price of *The Times* by one-third. Initially all the major competing newspapers kept their prices constant and carried on as if nothing had happened. Only later did a price war break out.

Table 5.1 provides price and sales figures for the five major national broadsheet newspapers—*The Times*, the *Guardian*, the *Daily Telegraph*, the *Financial Times*, and the *Independent*. Since consumers' average incomes changed only slightly over the period and newspapers have a low income elasticity, we would expect total sales to have remained constant, unless there had been a major change in tastes over the period in question. The data suggest that tastes did not change significantly, since the combined sales of all the newspapers held constant at around 2.5 million copies daily. Hence, the existing suppliers were fighting for a share of a stable market. If one gained more customers, it had to be at the expense of rival suppliers.

Observed price elasticities

Table 5.1 shows us that a 33.3 per cent price reduction of the price of *The Times* led to a 19.14 per cent increase in its sales. This indicates a price elasticity of demand for *The Times* of –0.57 (calculated as percentage change in quantity divided by percentage change in price or 19.14/–33.3). As a result, *The Times*'s daily sales revenue fell from £169,576 (376,836 × £0.45) to £134,689 (448,962 × £0.30). Only if the price elasticity had been greater than 1 would total revenue have increased.

The competing papers suffered, and the *Independent* suffered most, with a 14.1 per cent loss of sales. This would suggest that the *Independent* was the closest substitute for *The Times*. The cross-elasticity of demand implied by these figures was –14.1/–33.3 = 0.42. (This is positive as both the sales and the price changes were negative.) The cross-elasticity for the *Guardian* was –4.39/–33.3 = 0.13, and the cross-elasticity for the *Daily Telegraph* was –1.93/–33.3 = 0.06.

The *Financial Times* had a small increase in sales over this period. Its cross-elasticity was 0.58/–33.3 = –0.017. Taken at face value, this means that the *Financial Times* is (very weakly) complementary to *The Times*. However, the change is very small, and it is more likely that the two papers serve different markets (and hence have a cross-elasticity of zero) and that the slight rise in sales of the *Financial Times* was for reasons unrelated to the

Table 5.1   Changes in demand for newspapers

	Price		Average daily sales		Percentage change	
	Pre-Sept. '93	Post-Sept. '93	Pre-Sept. '93	Post-Sept. '93	Price	Sales
The Times	45p	30p	376,836	448,962	−33.3	+19.14
Guardian	45p	45p	420,154	401,705	0.0	−4.39
Daily Telegraph	45p	45p	1,037,375	1,017,326	0.0	−1.93
Independent	50p	50p	362,099	311,046	0.0	−14.10
Financial Times	65p	65p	289,666	291,119	0.0	+0.58
			2,486,130	2,470,158		

The Times led but no one followed. The table shows the fall in the price of *The Times* and the less-than-proportionate increase in sales. It also shows the constant prices of the other papers, with declining sales (except for the *Financial Times*) as they lost readers to *The Times*.

Source: Audit Bureau of Circulation. The sales figures are daily average circulation for September 1992 to February 1993 and for September 1993 to February 1994.

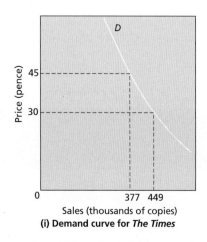

(i) Demand curve for *The Times*

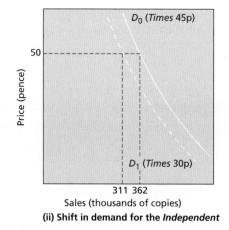

(ii) Shift in demand for the *Independent*

Figure 5.1   Demand for *The Times* and the *Independent*

A cut in the price of *The Times* shifted the *Independent*'s demand curve to the left. Part (i) shows the price cut for *The Times*. When its price was lowered from 45p to 30p, sales rose from 377,000 to 449,000 copies per day. Part (ii) shows the shift in demand for the *Independent* as a result of the fall in the price of *The Times*. At a constant price of 50p sales fell from 362,000 to 311,000.

fall in the price of *The Times*. Further study of the demand for the *Financial Times* would be required to settle this issue.

Applying demand and supply

The theory of demand and supply developed in Chapters 3 and 4 assumes that there are many buyers and many sellers, each one of whom must accept the price that is determined by overall demand and supply. Newspapers fit this theory on the demand side, since there are tens of thousands of buyers each of whom can do nothing to affect the price. On the supply side, however, there are

only a few newspapers and each sets the price of its own product. We can handle the supply side if we note that each newspaper then sells all the copies that are demanded at the price that it sets. Graphically, this is shown by a horizontal supply curve at each newspaper's fixed price. The elasticity of supply is infinite at the set price.

Figure 5.1 illustrates the effect of the price cut both on *The Times* and on the *Independent*. Notice that, since each newspaper is a distinct product, there is no industry supply curve for newspapers. Each supplier simply sets a price and lets demand determine its sales.

Rival newspapers may not have followed *The Times* in cutting prices because they believed that their demands would prove as inelastic as *The Times*'s. If so, they would have lost more revenue by cutting their prices than they did by leaving prices unchanged. As it was, the *Independent* suffered a daily loss of revenue of a little over £25,000 (just over 50,000 sales at 50p each).

The puzzle is why *The Times* persisted with its price drop even though it lost sales revenue. One possibility is that the increased circulation led to an increase in advertising revenue. Newspapers' advertising rates are related to their circulation. If *The Times* increased its advertising revenue by more than about £35,000, the price reduction would have increased its profit.

The *Independent* was known to be in financial difficulty, and it is possible that the managers of *The Times* thought that their price cut might force the *Independent* out of business—a strategy sometimes referred to as *predatory pricing* (see Chapter 11). Had it succeeded, a high proportion of *Independent* readers would have moved over to *The Times*, since the cross-elasticities show that the *Independent* was the closest substitute for *The Times*. Soon after, however, the *Independent* was taken over by the Mirror Group, which had more financial resources. Hence, if *The*

Times had been following a predatory strategy it failed. Later the Mirror Group sold the *Independent* to an Irish newspaper group.

A third possibility is that its managers expected that *The Times*'s demand elasticity would increase over time. If so, sales could eventually have risen sufficiently to compensate for the price cut. Indeed, *The Times* did continue to increase its market share beyond the period studied in Table 5.1. In June 1994 the *Telegraph* reacted to *The Times*'s growing market share by cutting its price, and the *Independent* followed. *The Times* responded to this by cutting its own price still further, although prices settled down at slightly higher levels soon after. To some extent this third explanation has proven correct. At the time of writing (July 1998) *The Times*'s price was 35p (20p on Monday) while the *Guardian, Telegraph,* and *Independent* were at 45p. *The Times*'s sales were well over 800,000, almost double what they had been just after the first gains following the outbreak of the price war. In contrast the *Independent*'s sales were 210,000, less than 60 per cent of what they were just before the price war began.

The Channel Tunnel

The opening of the Channel Tunnel to full passenger and freight services between Folkestone and Calais in 1995 had a big impact on the cross-Channel travel market as it involved a massive increase in capacity, that is, an increase in supply.

The impact of the tunnel

We deal with the market in cross-Channel journeys.[1] Although things other than price, such as speed and convenience, will affect the division of demand among the various types of travel, we hold these factors constant and focus on the average price of cross-Channel journeys. The supply comes from the tunnel, several shipping firms, hovercraft, and airlines. Although firms operating each of these types of travel have power over price, it is safe to assume that the total amount they will all wish to supply will vary positively with the price, that is to say that the supply curve of cross-Channel transport is positively sloped.

Figure 5.2 analyses the market. Part (i) shows the total demand and supply for cross-Channel journeys. Part (ii) shows the demand for journeys on air and sea services, which were the only suppliers before the tunnel opened. Initially the demand curve facing sea and air operators was the same as the total market demand curve. The opening of the tunnel shifted the market supply curve to the right

in part (i) while shifting the demand curve for air and sea journeys to the left in part (ii). (One way to think of the effect on demand for air and sea journeys is that the price of a substitute, tunnel journeys, has fallen from infinity to some positive number.) Notice that it does not matter for the general analysis whether tunnel journeys are cheaper or more expensive than other methods of travel, although the quantitative effects will depend on this. All that matters is that tunnel travel is cheap enough so that some passengers who would have gone by air or sea now go by rail.

The first prediction derived from Figure 5.2 is that the opening of the tunnel will cause a fall in the average price of cross-Channel journeys and an increase in the quantity purchased. The size of the increase depends on the size of the price reduction and the demand elasticity.

The second prediction is that the air and sea operators will experience a fall in demand because a new substitute comes into being. Initially, this would be seen entirely in empty seats and car decks, because prices are set in advance (though some lower prices may have been set in anticipation of a demand fall). Very soon, however, there would be special cut-price deals, and, eventually, sustained price-cutting even for regular fares.

---

[1] Readers who think that we are being wise after the event in this section should consult our previous edition, pp. 108–10, in which we set out essentially the same analysis, written a year before the Channel Tunnel opened.

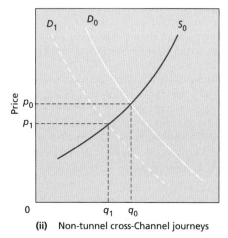

Figure 5.2 The market for cross-Channel journeys
The opening of the tunnel added to total supply but reduced demand for non-tunnel travel. Before the tunnel opened, the demand and supply curves were D_0 and S_0 in both parts of the figure. Price and quantity are thus the same in both parts, shown as P_0, Q_0 in part (i) and p_0, q_0 in part (ii). The opening of the tunnel shifted the supply curve to the right from S_0 to S_1 in part (i). With a given demand curve D_0 this lowered price and increased quantity from P_0 and Q_0 to P_1 and Q_1. Part (ii) shows the demand and supply curves for non-tunnel journeys (air and sea). The availability of a new substitute, tunnel travel, shifted the demand curve for other forms of travel to the left from D_0 to D_1. The price and quantity accordingly fell to p_1 and q_1. In part (i) the total of cross-Channel journeys Q_1 is split between Q_2 going by air and sea and $Q_1 - Q_2$ going via rail.

It was estimated (prior to the tunnel being built) that after the tunnel opened there would be an approximate market size of 70 million journeys per year. Of these, it was thought that the tunnel might take a market share of about 40 per cent, or about 28 million passenger journeys. Up to about half of these 28 million journeys were expected to be diverted from air and sea services, and the rest were expected to be new journeys stimulated by the new lower prices.

What happened?

The above predictions, based on the application of simple demand and supply analysis, turned out to be remarkably accurate. We illustrate this by direct quotes from a series of newspaper reports.

In September 1995, shortly after the tunnel came into full operation, the *Financial Times* wrote:

Eurotunnel has grabbed a big slice of the ferry operators' business on the cross-Channel market over the crucial summer months. Stena Sealink, the second largest ferry company on the Dover–Calais route, admitted its passenger volume fell 10 per cent and freight volumes 13 per cent in July compared with the same month last year. These trends have continued during August . . . Eurotunnel's own July traffic figures showed an 11.5 per cent increase over the previous month in the number of cars carried. . . . The price war in the cross-Channel market is growing in intensity, with the ferry companies maintaining discounts of up to 25 per cent on published prices throughout the summer. Eurotunnel has also offered a number of incentives to customers.

A month later *The Economist* had this to say:

In June . . . the number of passengers flying from London's Heathrow to Paris's Charles de Gaulle—traditionally the world's busiest airline route—was down 35% from the same time last year. . . . On the London–Brussels route, the numbers fell by 6% from Heathrow and 22% from Gatwick. Worse still . . . Eurostar has forced down average airline economy fares by 25–30%.

In May 1996 the *Financial Times* wrote:

The cut-throat cross-Channel price war intensified yesterday when Eurotunnel, the Anglo-French operator of the Channel tunnel, announced that it is to halve the standard return fare over the summer to £129. The main ferry companies responded immediately, saying they would match any bargain fares offered by Eurotunnel for comparable trips. . . . Eurotunnel has a market share of Dover–Calais traffic of about 45 per cent . . .

The price war took place in the context of an overall growth in the cross-Channel journey market (as predicted by the negative slope of the overall market demand curve). The *Investors Chronicle* (12 April 1996, p. 10) estimated this market to have grown by 25 per cent in 1995 and by a further 20 per cent in 1996. Also the *Economist* article referred to above quotes the total seat capacity on the London–Paris/Brussels routes as being 690,000 per week in July 1994 but having risen to 1,297,000 in July 1995.

The latter information tells us about the amount that the supply curve shifted and the magnitude of the elasticity of demand.

Assessment

The events referred to in the newspaper stories show that the predictions of our demand and supply analysis were amply borne out in practice. First, the prices of cross-Channel journeys fell and the quantity demanded increased. Second, the airlines, ferry, and hovercraft companies suffered a fall in demand. They have all responded with aggressive price-cutting. The airlines have also shifted some of their capacity onto other routes. The ferries have not been so quick to cut capacity. In 1998 the two major companies, P&O and Stena, merged their cross-Channel operations, presumably so that they could co-ordinate their competition with the other forms of transport and manage the needed capacity reduction.

Government intervention in markets

Before we continue with this chapter, we need to introduce a third set of players on the economic stage. We have called decision-takers *agents*, and in Chapter 3 we introduced two sets of agents: consumers and firms. The third set is most accurately called the *central authorities* but is more commonly, if loosely, referred to as the **government** or the state. This broad class of agents includes all public agencies, government bodies, and other organizations belonging to, or owing their existence to, either central or local governments. They exist at the centre of legal and political power and exert some control over the rest of us.[2]

We saw in Chapter 1 that governments play important parts in modern mixed economies. Among other things, governments sometimes seek to alter market outcomes. They can influence the prices at which goods are sold by taxing or subsidizing either their production or their consumption. They can influence the terms on which goods and services are offered for sale by imposing quality standards or regulating the terms of hire-purchase agreements. These, and many other methods that we will encounter throughout this book, are collectively referred to as *government intervention*.

Price controls

If the government wishes to influence the price at which some product is bought and sold, it has two main alternatives. First, it may change the equilibrium price by altering the product's demand or supply. Second, it may enact legislation that regulates the price. **Price controls** refer to the latter alternative: influencing price by laws, rather than by market forces.

Disequilibrium trading

If controls are used to hold price at a disequilibrium level, what determines the quantity actually traded on the market?

Any voluntary market transaction requires both a willing buyer and a willing seller. Thus, if quantity demanded is less than quantity supplied, demand will determine the amount actually traded, and the excess supply will remain in the hands of the unsuccessful sellers. If quantity supplied is less than quantity demanded, however, supply will determine the amount actually traded and the excess demand will take the form of desired purchases by unsuccessful buyers. This is shown graphically in Figure 5.3.

At any disequilibrium price, quantity exchanged is determined by the lesser of quantity demanded and quantity supplied.

This result is often expressed by the maxim that in disequilibrium the short side of the market dominates (i.e. determines what is bought and sold).

Box 5.1 discusses the problems that arise when governments provide road services at a zero price.

Maximum-price legislation

In this section we concentrate on laws setting *maximum* permissible prices, which are often called 'price ceilings'. Over the years, such laws have had many purposes. Governments of medieval cities sometimes sought to protect their citizens from the consequences of crop failures by fixing a maximum price at which bread could be sold. In modern times, many governments have employed rent controls in an attempt to make housing available at a price that could be afforded by lower-income groups. Governments

---

[2] It is *not* a basic assumption of economics that the central authorities always act in a consistent fashion as if they were a single individual. Indeed, conflict among different central-authority agencies is often an important component in theories that analyse government intervention in the economy.

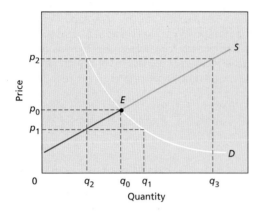

Figure 5.3 Disequilibrium quantity
In disequilibrium, quantity exchanged is determined by the lesser of quantity demanded and quantity supplied. Market equilibrium is at point E. For prices below p_0 the quantity exchanged will be determined by the supply curve. For example, q_2 will be exchanged at price p_1 in spite of the excess demand of $q_1 - q_2$. For prices above p_0 the quantity exchanged will be determined by the demand curve. For example, q_2 will be exchanged at price p_2 in spite of the excess supply of $q_3 - q_2$. Thus the dark blue and dark yellow portions of the S and D curves show the actual quantities exchanged at each price.

Box 5.1 Road pricing

Some goods and services are provided free, but this does not mean that everyone can have as much as they like all the time. Unless the amount supplied equals the amount demanded at zero price, excess demand will develop. It will have to be handled by some non-price allocation mechanism. Examples include waiting lists for health services and congestion on the roads.

In the seventeenth and eighteenth centuries many main roads in Britain were 'turnpikes' and travellers had to pay a fee to travel on them. This fee was used to maintain the road. Throughout the twentieth century, road provision in the United Kingdom has been paid for by the state out of the revenue from general taxation. (Specific taxes on cars such as the road fund licence have not been linked directly to expenditure on roads.) Some other countries have charges on some major roads, such as the autostrade of Italy, the autoroutes of France, some turnpikes in the United States, and new motorways in Mexico.

The recent growth of car ownership has been such that demand for road use continually outstrips supply when the price of using the roads is zero. For example, the M25 orbital motorway around London has had frequent jams from the day it opened. Also, many town centres suffer severe traffic congestion during rush hours, and in some cases for most of the day.

This congestion is, in effect, rationing by queuing. It imposes the highest cost on those whose time is most valuable.

Road pricing can be used to reduce the quantity demanded to the available supply. Users are then able to use road services without congestion. Travellers with essential business and other urgent needs will pay. Others will take less crowded routes, use public transport, or postpone their journeys.

Many roads are congested at peak periods but have excess capacity during off-peak periods. If the price for using such roads were higher in periods of peak demand and lower in off-peak periods, demand would equal the given supply during both periods. A form of this type of pricing has been operating for some time in Singapore—a country with many people but little space. Licences to drive only at weekends are considerably cheaper than licences to drive at any time, and there is a surcharge for driving in the central area during peak traffic times. Also, the number of licences issued is limited. As a result of this and other supporting measures, such as a first-class public transport system, Singapore has one of the few urban road systems in the whole of Southeast Asia that is not heavily congested and polluted. In contrast, Bangkok and Manila are suffering near traffic paralysis from road congestion.

Pricing of specific bits of road with limited access presents no technical problem. Hence, for example, the UK already has tolls on the Severn Bridge, the Dartford Crossing, the Forth Bridge, and the Mersey Tunnel. Although the pricing of road use in, say, central London presents greater problems, these will soon be solved by the electronic tagging of cars, now in the experimental stage. An electronic meter will soon be able to record the identity of each car passing over city streets and motorways. Drivers can then be billed for miles travelled just as householders are now billed for gas or electricity used. This may seem futuristic, but the UK government announced in 1993 that it intended to introduce electronic road pricing by 1998. Although that timetable was not met, road pricing seems inevitable at some time in the not-too-distant future.

Free goods can be consumed without restriction only if the supply continues to equal (or exceed) demand at zero price. Where the free good is a gift of nature, pricing soon appears when the resource becomes scarce. Where the free good is provided by the state, pricing is often preferable to other rationing mechanisms. It leads people to economize on the use of the scarce resource and ensures that those who value it most highly will be its most frequent users.

in many poor countries set the prices of some basic foodstuffs well below their market equilibrium values.

The effects on price and quantity Most price ceilings actually specify the highest permissible price that producers may legally charge. If the ceiling is set above the equilibrium price, it has no effect, since the equilibrium remains attainable. If, however, the ceiling is set below the equilibrium price, it determines the price—in which case the ceiling is said to be *binding*. The key consequences of price ceilings are shown in Figure 5.4.

The setting of a maximum price has no effect if the price is set at or above the equilibrium price. If the maximum

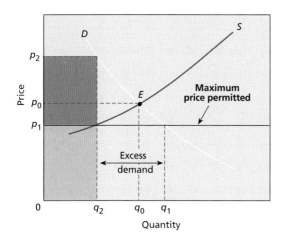

Figure 5.4 Black-market pricing

A price ceiling set below the equilibrium price causes excess demand and invites a black market. Equilibrium price is at p_0. If a price ceiling is set at p_1, the quantity demanded will rise to q_1 and the quantity supplied will fall to q_2. Quantity actually exchanged will be q_2. Excess demand is $q_1 - q_2$. Black marketeers would buy q_2 at the controlled price of p_1, paying the amount shown by the light blue area p_1q_2. They would sell at the price p_2, earning profits shown by the dark blue area between p_1 and p_2.

price is set below the equilibrium price, a shortage will develop and quantity actually bought and sold will fall below its equilibrium value.

Allocation of available supply In the case of a binding price ceiling, production is insufficient to satisfy everyone who wishes to buy the product. Since price is not allowed to rise so as to allocate the available supply among the would-be purchasers, some other method of allocation must be found. Theory does not predict what this other method will be, but experience has shown several possibilities.

If shops sell to the first customers who arrive, people are likely to rush to those stores that are rumoured to have any stocks of the scarce product. Long queues will develop, and allocation will be on the basis of luck, or to those knowing enough to gain from the principle of 'first come, first served'. This system was commonly found in the command economies of Eastern Europe during the Communist era, where queuing was a way of life.

Sometimes shopkeepers themselves decide who will get the scarce products and who will not. They may keep products under the counter and sell only to regular customers or only to people of a certain colour or religion. Such a system is called allocation by **sellers' preferences.**

If the government dislikes the allocation that results from price ceilings, it can ration the goods, giving out coupons sufficient to purchase the available supply. The

coupons might be distributed equally, or on such criteria as age, sex, marital status, or number of dependants. Rationing by coupons was used in Britain and most of the other belligerent countries during the Second World War (1939–45). Rationing persisted in Britain for another nine years after the war, until 1954.

Any official rationing scheme substitutes the government's preferences for the sellers' preferences in allocating a product that is in excess demand because of a binding price ceiling.

Black markets A binding price ceiling, with or without rationing, is likely to give rise to a **black market.** This is a market in which goods are sold illegally at prices that violate the legal restrictions. Many products have only a few manufacturers but many retailers. Although it is easy to police the producers, it is difficult even to locate, much less to control, all those who are, or could be, retailing the product.

Figure 5.4 shows the result of a price ceiling that determines the price that producers get but does not control the price at which retailers sell to the public. Output is restricted by the low price received by producers, while consumers must pay the high price that equates demand to the available supply. The difference between what consumers pay and what producers get goes as profits to the black marketeers.

It is unlikely that all of the output will be sold on the black market—both because there are many honest people in every society and because the government usually has some power to enforce its price ceilings on retailers. Thus, the normal case is not the extreme result shown in the figure. Instead, some of the limited supplies will be sold at the controlled price and some at the black-market price.

Economists can evaluate a black-market situation only when the government's objectives are known. Where the purpose is to keep prices down, the policy is a failure to the extent that black marketeers succeed in raising prices; it is a success to the extent that sales actually occur at the controlled prices. If, however, the government wishes to restrict production in order to release resources for other, more urgent needs, such as war production, the policy works effectively, if somewhat unfairly.

Evidence There is much evidence confirming these predictions. During the First and Second World Wars governments set binding ceilings on many prices. The legislation of maximum prices was always followed by shortages, then by either the introduction of rationing or the growth of some private method of allocation (such as sellers' preferences), and then by the rise of some sort of black market. The ceilings were more effective in limiting consumption than in controlling prices, although they did restrain price increases to some extent. Until recently, many of the former socialist countries of Eastern Europe followed a policy of controlling food prices at levels that were below the equilibrium prices. Chronic shortages, queues, allocation by sellers' preferences, and black markets were the result.

Rent controls

Our study of the consequences of maximum-price legislation has an important application in rent-control legislation, which is just a special case of price ceilings. Controls are usually imposed to freeze rents at their current levels at times when equilibrium rents are rising. Demand may be shifting rightward, owing to forces such as rising population and income, or supply may be shifting leftward, owing to forces such as rising costs. The result is that the controlled rents are soon well below the free-market equilibrium level, and excess demand appears. The further the controlled price falls below the free-market price, the stronger are the consequences. The discrepancy often grows in periods of inflation. Typically the controlled rents are not increased as fast as the general price level is rising, causing the *relative price* of rented accommodation to fall.

Predictions The following predictions about rent controls are simply applications to the housing market of the results concerning binding price controls in any competitive market.

1. There will be a shortage of rental accommodation; quantity demanded will exceed quantity supplied.

2. The quantity of accommodation occupied will be less than if free-market rents had been charged.

3. The short-term effects of controls are to lower rents for an unchanged supply of accommodation. The reason is that the short-run supply curve of rental accommodation tends to be quite *inelastic* at the level of the quantity currently supplied. The long-term effects are a growing housing shortage. The reason is that the long-run curve is quite *elastic* since rental accommodation will not be replaced as it is converted to other uses or wears out unless it offers a market rate of return to its owners.

4. Black markets will appear. Landlords may require large lump-sum entrance fees from new tenants, and may evict existing tenants so as to collect this fee. Sitting tenants are reluctant to move from their present accommodations, even when they are no longer suitable. If they do move, they may sublet their accommodation, charging the market price while themselves paying only the controlled price.

5. As a political response to the forces just outlined, governments typically pass security-of-tenure laws, which protect the tenant from eviction and thus give existing tenants priority over potential new tenants. By making it harder to evict undesirable tenants, these laws reduce the expected return from any given rental price. Landlords may resort to illegal harassment to evict tenants and become even less willing to replace accommodation as it wears out over the years.

Evidence These and other consequences have been observed throughout the world wherever binding rent controls have been imposed. Here are a few examples.

UK Rent controls were first introduced in 1914 and were gradually extended to cover the entire rental market. Over a period of sixty years, the market for privately owned unfurnished rental accommodation was largely eliminated! From 45 per cent of households in privately owned rental accommodation in 1945, the figure fell steadily, until by the 1980s it was only 8 per cent. Finally in 1989 the British government announced measures to phase out rent controls. They also used subsidies to encourage housing associations, which are non-profit-making providers of rental accommodation. None the less, the long-term consequences of rent controls will persist in the UK housing market well into the twenty-first century because of the small stock of housing available to rent and the high levels of owner-occupation. Both of these influences are the consequences of over half a century of controls that made being a landlord unprofitable and becoming a new tenant nearly impossible.

In other countries rent control has also caused severe housing shortages. In the United States, rent control is in the hands of individual cities. For example, rent control in the Queens borough of New York City was accompanied by severe housing shortages; whole blocks of buildings were abandoned because the controlled rent did not even cover operating costs, although the buildings could have lasted for decades. Uncontrolled markets in the southwestern United States have seen supplies increase rapidly to meet the growing demands for housing as more people moved there. Rent control on lower-rent properties was introduced in the Canadian province of Ontario in 1975, and extended to all rental accommodation in 1985. Since that time the construction of rental accommodation has halted, except where it is subsidized. Conversions to owner-occupancy soared and were then made illegal, entrance fees and subletting have become common, and would-be renters have often resorted to increasingly desperate measures, ranging from bribes to searching out the families of newly deceased tenants.

The problems of agriculture

To the casual observer the agricultural sector of almost any advanced Western economy presents a series of apparent paradoxes. Food is a basic necessity of life. Yet over the last century agricultural sectors have been declining in relative importance. The number of farmers and farm workers in the original six EC member states fell from nearly 10.5 million in 1960 to under 5 million in the 1990s, and many of those persons who have remained on the land have been receiving incomes well below national averages. Were it not for the EU's Common Agricultural Policy (the CAP), the number of farmers would be much less than it now is and farm incomes would be even lower.

Governments of many countries have felt it expedient to intervene in agricultural markets, and have resorted to a bewildering array of controls and subsidies. These have often led to the accumulation of vast surpluses, which have sometimes rotted in storage and sometimes been sold abroad at subsidized prices. The theory of demand and supply can help us gain some insight into these, and other, agricultural problems.

Short-term fluctuations in prices and incomes

Agricultural production is subject to large variations resulting from factors that are beyond human control; for example, bad weather reduces output below that planned by farmers, while exceptionally good weather pushes output above planned levels. Figure 5.5 shows how variations in farm output cause prices to fluctuate in the opposite direction to crop sizes. A bumper crop sends prices down;

a poor crop sends them up. The price changes will be larger the less elastic is the demand curve.

Because farm products often have inelastic demands, large price fluctuations accompany unplanned changes in production.

The effects on farmer's incomes follow from the results established on page 58 concerning elasticity and total revenue.[3]

When demand is inelastic unplanned variations in output will cause producers' revenues to vary in the opposite direction as output varies and to fluctuate more the further the elasticity of demand diverges from unity in either direction.

Since most agricultural products have inelastic demands, farmers typically see their incomes dwindling when nature is unexpectedly kind in producing a bumper crop, while their incomes rise when crops are poor. Notice that every individual farmer's income need not rise (after all, some farmers may have nothing to harvest); it follows only that the aggregate revenue earned by *all* farmers must rise.

Agricultural stabilization programmes

In free-market economies agricultural incomes often tend to fluctuate around a low *average* level. As a result

---

[3] While we can make predictions in this section only about sales revenues, such receipts are closely related to farmers' incomes. We can, therefore, without risk of serious error, extend these predictions to incomes.

Figure 5.5 Unplanned fluctuations in output

Unplanned fluctuations in output lead to much sharper fluctuations in price if the demand curve is inelastic than if it is elastic. Suppose that the expected price is p_0 and the planned output is q_0. The two curves D_i and D_e are alternative demand curves. If actual production always equalled planned production, the equilibrium price and quantity would be p_0 and q_0 with either demand curve. Unplanned fluctuations in output, however, cause quantity to vary year by year between q_1 (a bad harvest) and q_2 (a good harvest). When demand is inelastic (shown by the yellow curve), prices will show large fluctuations. When demand is elastic (shown by the blue curve), prices will show much smaller fluctuations. (In both cases elasticity is measured around point E.)

agricultural stabilization programmes often have two goals: to reduce the fluctuations, and to raise the average level of farm incomes. We will see that these two goals of stable incomes and high incomes often conflict with each other.

What will happen if the government attempts to stabilize the incomes of farmers in the face of unplanned market fluctuations by buying and selling in the open market? In a typical scheme of this sort, the government holds a stockpile, adds to it when there is a surplus, and sells from it when there is a shortage. How can the government stabilize farmers' incomes through its own purchases and sales in the open market?

Figure 5.6 shows the required policy.[4] Farmers sell their whole crop each year. When production unexpectedly exceeds normal output, the government buys in the market. It allows price to fall, but only by the same proportion that production has increased. When production unexpectedly falls short of normal output, the government enters the market and sells some of its stocks. It allows price to rise, but only by the same proportion that production has fallen below normal. Thus, as farmers encounter unplanned fluctuations in their output, they encounter exactly offsetting fluctuations in prices, so that their revenues are stabilized. In effect, the government has converted the elasticity of demand from being inelastic to being unitary. With a unit elasticity the total revenue of sellers does not change as quantity changes, because given percentage changes in quantity are offset by equal percentage changes of price but in the opposite direction.

Appropriate government intervention into agricultural markets can reduce price fluctuations and stabilize producers' revenues.

Government schemes of this sort can be self-financing. If we ignore costs of storage, the schemes can show a profit, for the government buys at low prices—the lower the price, the more it buys—and sells at high prices—the higher the price, the more it sells.

Problems with stabilization policies

If the type of stabilization scheme we have just studied has the advantages we outlined, why is there so much trouble with such schemes in practice?

Choosing the proper price Farmers can often use political pressure to exploit the uncertainty of agricultural markets. Since demand and supply curves are never known exactly, the government does not know how much will be produced at each possible price. It does not know, therefore, exactly what level of income it can try to achieve while also keeping average sales from its own stocks equal to its average purchases for these stocks. Since farmers have votes, there is strong pressure on any government to be overgenerous. If the price, and hence the level of income,

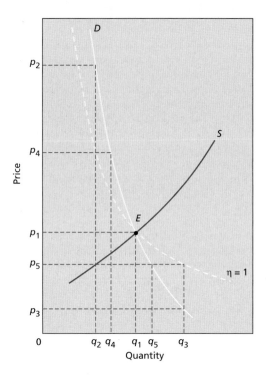

Figure 5.6 Income stabilization

Income stabilization is achieved by allowing prices to fluctuate in inverse proportion to output. D is demand, S is planned supply, and equilibrium is at E. However, actual production fluctuates between q_2 and q_3, and these fluctuations cause the free-market price to fluctuate between p_2 and p_3.

A curve of unit elasticity over its whole range is drawn through E and labelled $\eta = 1$. To stabilize income, any given output must be sold at a price determined by this curve. The government buys or sells an amount equal to the horizontal distance between the $\eta = 1$ curve and the demand curve.

When production is q_3, market price must be held at p_5 if income is to be unchanged. But at market price p_5 the public wishes to purchase only q_5 and the government must buy up the remaining production, $q_3 - q_5$, and add it to its stocks. Farmers' total sales are q_3 at price p_5, and since the broken yellow curve is a rectangular hyperbola, income $p_5 \times q_3$ is equal to income $p_1 \times q_1$.

When production is equal to q_2, price must be allowed to rise to p_4 (by construction the area p_4q_2 is equal to the area p_1q_1). But at price p_4 the public will wish to buy q_4, so that the government must sell $q_4 - q_2$ out of its stocks.

[4] Stabilization policies are intended to reduce cyclical fluctuations as well as the short-term fluctuation studied in the text. Agricultural markets often show substantial cyclical instability. In periods of prosperity employment and wages are high, which implies a strong demand for most products. In periods of depressed business activity employment and wages are diminished, which implies a weaker demand for most products. Thus the demand curves for most products rise and fall as business activity ebbs and flows. Given a highly inelastic short-run supply curve, cyclical fluctuations in agricultural prices are often large.

is fixed too high, then the government will have to buy unsold crops in most years. Thus, stocks will build up more or less continuously (forming 'butter mountains' and 'wine lakes', in well-known EU terminology). Sooner or later the accumulating surpluses will have to be destroyed, given away, or dumped on the market for what they will bring, thus forcing the market price down, defeating the purpose for which the crops were originally purchased. If they are dumped on foreign markets, this will disrupt markets in foreign countries, many of which are already much poorer than the countries of the EU.

The government's plan will now show a deficit, which will have to be covered by taxation. This means that people in cities will be paying farmers for producing goods that cannot be sold at prices covering their costs of production. The next step is often to try to limit the production of each farmer. Quotas are assigned to individual farmers, penalties are imposed for exceeding them, and bonuses are paid for leaving land idle. Such measures attempt to avoid the consequence of there being too many resources allocated to the agricultural sector by preventing these resources from producing all that they could.

Government policies that stabilize prices at too high a level will cause excess supply, a rising level of unsold stocks, and pressure for further government intervention to restrict output.

The long-term problem of resource allocation Even if the temptation to set too high a price is avoided, there is still a formidable problem facing the managers of agricultural stabilization programmes. Output and real incomes have been rising at an average rate of about 2 per cent per year over the last 100 years in the countries that now form the European Union. Assume for simplicity that productivity expands more or less uniformly in all industries. The demand for products with low income elasticities will be expanding more slowly than output; excess supplies will develop, prices and profits will be depressed, and it will be necessary for resources to move out of these industries. Exactly the reverse will happen for products with high income elasticities: demand will expand faster than supply, prices and profits will tend to rise, and resources will move into those industries.

With continuous productivity increases there will be a continuous tendency towards excess supply of products with low income elasticities and excess demand for products with high income elasticities. Adjustment to these changes requires a continuous movement of resources out of industries producing the former type of products into industries producing the latter.

In a free-market economy, this reallocation will take place under the incentives of low prices, wages, and incomes in the declining sector and high prices, wages, and incomes in the expanding sector. Because of the tendency

towards excess supply in the agricultural sector, prices will fall, taking producers' incomes down with them. There will be a decline in the demand for farm labour and the other factors of production used in agriculture, and the earnings of these factors will also decline. At the same time the opposite tendencies will be observed in sectors with high income elasticities. Here demand will be expanding faster than supply; prices will be rising, taking producers' incomes up with them. The demand for the factors of production used in these industries will be rising, causing factor prices and factor incomes to increase.

The need to reallocate resources has been strongly felt in agriculture, where not only is the income elasticity of demand low, but productivity growth has been high. For example, between 1970 and 1990 cereal yields per acre nearly doubled in the EU. Milk yields in France and the Netherlands, sugar yields in Italy, and rape yields in Germany increased by almost 50 per cent over the same period. In France and Italy, the potato yield more than doubled between 1960 and the 1990s.

Stabilization schemes that guarantee a 'reasonable' income to farmers remove the incentive for resources to transfer out of the agricultural sector. Unless other means are found to persuade resources to transfer, a larger and larger proportion of the resources currently devoted to agriculture become redundant.

Economics cannot prove that governments ought, or ought not, to interfere with the price mechanism. However, by providing some insight into the workings of that mechanism, economics can predict some of the gains and losses resulting from intervention. It can also point out problems that must be solved if intervention is to be successful.

The EU's agricultural policy

The Common Agricultural Policy of the European Union, nicknamed the CAP, amply illustrates the applicability of the theories just outlined. The policy has held agricultural prices well above their market equilibrium values within the EU. To prevent the flood of imports that would have been attracted by these high prices, the imports of all agricultural goods that receive EU price support have been subject to a high tariff. (The EU imports more than it exports by value, but its imports are mainly tropical fruits, such as bananas, and those that are out of season in Europe.) The high European prices cause EU production to exceed EU consumption. Surpluses pile up, only to be destroyed or sold abroad at a fraction of their production costs. EU farmers gain, while taxpayers, consumers, and efficient foreign producers are the losers. The payments to farmers have risen so much over the years that they put serious strain on the EU budget. Expenditure on agriculture reached a peak of nearly 65 per cent of the entire EU budget in 1986, but has fallen over the last decade, reaching around 50 per cent at the end of the century. In contrast, at the end of the century agriculture accounted for a little less than 2 per cent of total EU production of all goods and services (down from 4.8 per cent in 1973).

Efficient agricultural producers in the developing countries have found their livelihoods threatened by subsidized exports of surplus EU products. The attempt to restrain these exports has caused great strains on the relations between the EU and other agricultural producing countries. These were focused in the long-running Uruguay Round of trade negotiations, as a result of which the EU has agreed to relatively minor alterations to the CAP. (These negotiations took place under the auspices of an international organization called the GATT.) A phased reduction in intervention prices started in 1993 and has helped

to reduce the proportion of total EU budget devoted to agricultural support, as noted above. It seems likely that price supports will soon be replaced by direct subsidies. In many cases these subsidies will be payments for non-production. For example, the 'set-aside' policy pays farmers to keep some of their land idle. Thus, while the nature of intervention in the EU is changing, it is not disappearing. Consumers may gain from the price reductions planned (over time), but taxpayers will continue to carry the burden of the costs of intervention.

Box 5.2 presents a brief report on EU farm policy taken from *The Economist*. Readers should determine what pieces of analysis given earlier in this chapter explain the economic forces lying behind the various issues raised in the article.

Box 5.2   The EU's Common Agricultural Policy

The following excerpt appeared in *The Economist* (3 October 1987). Such is the power of farmers that the only change needed to make the discussion fully applicable today would be to increase the quoted US dollar values (which we have not done).

Farming in most rich countries is in a classic mess. As food prices have tumbled on world markets, subsidies to farmers (paid through taxes or propped-up food prices) have spiralled to more than $100 billion a year. Such protectionism only sharpens the appetite for more; it never achieves its proclaimed goals. Farmers' incomes and land prices are falling; bankruptcies are rising. Now the Americans have urged the EC to agree to abolish all subsidies and barriers to agricultural trade within ten years. The Americans have good reasons for wanting a change: their own spending on farm support has trebled in the past three years. The main way in which the EU's common agricultural policy supports farmers is by Eurocrats setting guaranteed prices for dairy products, beef, cereals, sugar. If market prices fall below the floor, intervention agencies buy the surpluses. This rigged system is buttressed by import levies and export subsidies, and its benefits go mainly to the wrong people. Three-quarters of EU farm support reaches the biggest and richest 25% of farmers, concentrated in the wealthier northern countries. They get nearly $10,000 a year each from Europe's taxpayers. The other quarter goes to the poorer, southern 75% of farmers. They get about $1,000 a year each. Because German and French politicians want their farmers to have average German and French incomes, the EU pays Karl and Jacques to produce butter at five times the price at which New Zealanders can do it; some of this butter is dumped on world

markets at under one-fifth of its true cost, making economic New Zealand butter unsaleable.

Europe's farm ministers recognise some of these absurdities, but prefer to tackle the symptoms (eg, through curbing surpluses of milk and sugar by imposing production quotas) rather than the cause (which is the gap between Community prices and world prices). Quotas have sometimes made the gap worse, because farmers have received higher prices to compensate them for not being allowed to produce so much of what is not wanted. Quotas also freeze market shares. Trading in quotas mitigates this, but creates nonsense of its own. In parts of Britain a farmer's milk quotas are now worth more than his land. Curbs on milk output can just mean more beef or cereals. When everything is in surplus, quotas are a nightmare of red tape, with each farmer having to account for his production down to the last bunch of radishes.

Every statesman knows that a better solution would be sharp cuts in support prices, but these are called politically impossible.

Since this passage was written, the problems facing the European Union's agricultural policy have not lessened. Overproduction is unabated, and payments to farmers continue to take up the majority of the EU's entire budget. One of the latest measures is the 'set-aside' policy, under which farmers are paid for not producing. The more they do not produce, the more they earn! The day has not yet come when a new entrant can earn a large income by setting up a farm designed to non-produce a range of agricultural commodities, but that nightmare vision is only an exaggeration of trends visible in the European Union's current policies.

Some general lessons about the price system

The cases studied in this chapter suggest four widely applicable lessons.

Costs may be shifted, but they cannot be avoided

The average standard of living depends on the amount of resources available to the economy and on the efficiency with which these resources are used. Production, whether in response to free-market signals or to government controls, uses resources; thus, it involves costs to members of society. If it takes 5 per cent of the nation's resources to provide housing at some stated average standard, those resources will not be available to produce other products. If resources are used to produce unwanted wheat, those resources will not be available to produce other products. For society, there is no such thing as free housing or free wheat. Rent controls or subsidies to agriculture can change the share of the costs paid by particular individuals or groups, lowering the share for some and raising the share for others, but they cannot make the costs go away.

Different ways of allocating the costs may also affect the total amount of resources used and thus the amount of costs incurred. For example, controls that keep prices and profits of some product below free-market levels will lead to increased quantities demanded and decreased quantities supplied. Unless government steps in to provide additional supplies, fewer resources will be allocated to producing the product. If government chooses to supply all the demand at the controlled prices, more resources will be allocated to it, which means that fewer resources will be devoted to other kinds of goods and services.

Free-market prices and profits encourage efficient use of resources

Prices and profits in a market economy provide signals to both demanders and suppliers. Prices that are high and rising (relative to other prices) provide an incentive to purchasers to economize on the product. They may choose to satisfy the want in question with substitutes whose prices have not risen so much (because they are less costly to provide) or to satisfy less of that want by shifting expenditure to the satisfaction of other wants.

On the supply side rising prices tend to create rising profits. Short-term profits that bear no relation to current costs repeatedly occur in market economies. High profits, however, attract further resources into production. They cause resources to move into profitable industries until profits fall to levels that can be earned elsewhere in the economy.

Falling prices and falling profits provide the opposite

motivations. Purchasers are inclined to buy more; sellers are inclined to produce less and to move resources into more profitable undertakings.

The price system responds to a need for change in the allocation of resources, say, in response to an external event such as the loss of a source of a raw material or the outbreak of a war. Changing relative prices and profits signal the need for change, to which consumers and producers respond.

Government intervention affects resource allocation

Governments intervene in the price system sometimes to satisfy generally agreed-upon social goals and sometimes to help politically influential interest groups. Government intervention changes the allocation of resources that the price system would achieve.

Interventions have allocative consequences because they inhibit the free-market mechanism. Some controls, such as rent controls, prevent prices from rising (in response, say, to an increase in demand with no change in supply). If the price is held down, the signal is not given to consumers to economize on a product that is in short supply. On the supply side, when prices and profits are prevented from rising, the profit signals that would attract new resources into the industry are never given. The shortage continues, and the movements of demand and supply that would resolve it are not set in motion.

Other controls, such as agricultural price supports, prevent prices from falling (in response, say, to an increase in supply with no increase in demand). This leads to excess supply, and the signal is not given to producers to produce less or to buyers to increase their purchases. Surpluses continue, and the movements of demand and supply that would eliminate them are not set in motion.

Intervention requires alternative allocative mechanisms

Intervention typically requires alternative allocative mechanisms. During times of shortages, allocation will be by sellers' preferences, on a first-come, first-served basis, or by some system of government rationing. During periods of surplus there will be unsold supplies unless the government buys and stores the surpluses. Because long-run changes in demand and costs do not induce resource reallocations through private decisions, the government will have to step in. It will have to force resources out of industries in which prices are held too high, as it has tried to do in agriculture, and into industries in which prices are held too low, as it can, for example, by providing public housing.

Intervention almost always has both benefits and costs.

Economics cannot answer the question of whether a particular intervention into free markets is desirable, but it can clarify the issues by identifying benefits and costs and who will enjoy or bear them. In doing so, it can identify the competing values involved. These matters will be discussed in detail in Chapters 18 and 19.

Summary

The Times and the tunnel

■ Demand and supply theory is a potent tool for analysing many real-world situations such as the effects of the Channel Tunnel and price-cutting among British newspapers.

Government intervention in markets

■ Effective price ceilings lead to excess demand, black markets, and non-price methods of allocating the scarce supplies among would-be purchasers.

■ Rent controls are a form of price ceiling. Their major consequence is a shortage of rental accommodation that gets worse because of a slow but inexorable decline in the quantity of rental accommodation.

The problems of agriculture

■ On the free market many agricultural prices are subject to wide fluctuations as a result of weather-induced, year-to-year fluctuations in supply operating on inelastic demand curves, and cyclical fluctuations in demand operating on inelastic supply curves.

■ Governments can stabilize agricultural incomes by reducing price fluctuations. They achieve this by holding stocks, which they add to through purchases in times of surplus and sell from in times of shortage.

■ The long-term problems of agriculture arise from productivity growth on the supply side combined with low income elasticity on the demand side. This means that, unless many resources are being transferred out of agriculture fairly rapidly, quantity supplied tends to increase faster than quantity demanded year after year.

■ Stabilization schemes that hold prices above their free-market levels on average, over short-term and cyclical swings, frustrate the long-term adjustment process and lead to ever-growing surpluses—as has the EU's Common Agricultural Policy (the CAP).

Some general lessons about the price system

■ Some major lessons about the price system are: costs may be shifted, but they cannot be avoided; free-market prices and profits encourage economical use of resources; government intervention affects resource allocation; and intervention requires alternative allocative mechanisms.

Topics for review

■ Maximum, or ceiling, prices
■ Alternative allocation systems under excess demand
■ Short- and long-run effects of rent controls
■ Minimum, or floor, prices
■ Causes of fluctuations in agricultural prices and incomes
■ Schemes for income stabilization
■ The CAP

Questions for discussion

1 Governments sometimes try to assist producers of some product by forcing their price above what it would be in a completely free market. What specific actions would accomplish this result by (a) shifting the supply curve, (b) shifting the demand curve, and (c) forcing the price up without shifting either curve. Compare the consequences of these three types of policies.

2 Who will gain and who will lose in the short and long runs from rent controls that force the prices of rental accommodation well below their equilibrium?

3 Who gains and who loses from the EU's Common Agricultural Policy (the CAP)?

4 Some time ago the Kenya Meat Commission (KMC) decided that it was undemocratic to allow meat prices to be out of reach of the ordinary citizen. It decided to fix meat prices at low levels. Six months later, in a press interview, the managing commissioner of the KMC made the following statements. (a) 'Cattle are scarce in the country, but I do not know why.' (b) 'People are eating too much beef, and unless they diversify their eating habits and eat other foodstuff, the shortage of beef will continue.' Can you explain to the commissioner why these things have happened?

5 A co-operative covering all producers of some agricultural crop whose demand fluctuates widely decides to stabilize its members' income by storing some of the crop in times of high harvest and selling some of its stocks in times of low harvest. What should its price policy be? Show the required behaviour using demand and supply curves. The government now takes over the co-operative, buying the farmers' crops in times of high harvest and selling them in times of poor harvest. What should the policy be? Explain why the co-operative and the government must adopt different pricing policies to achieve the same objectives of stabilizing farmers' incomes.

Part Two
Consumers and Producers

Chapter 6
What Determines Demand? I: Marginal Utility Theory

In Chapter 3 we used market demand and supply curves to enable us to develop the theory of market prices. In order to deepen our understanding of market behaviour we now need to study both the consumer behaviour that lies behind demand curves and the firm behaviour that lies behind supply curves. The theory of demand is covered in Chapters 6 and 7 and the theory of supply is covered in Chapters 8–11.

We deal with demand first. Why do consumers and producers respond to price and income changes in the way they do? Is it irrational for consumers to spend more on some commodities when their prices fall but to spend less on other commodities when they undergo a similar price reduction? Why are consumers willing to pay high prices for many luxury goods such as emeralds and rare postage stamps, while being unwilling to do the same for goods that are necessary to life, such as food and water?

The history of demand theory has seen two major breakthroughs. The first was the marginal utility theory, which assumed that the utility or satisfaction that people got from consuming products could be measured quantitatively. By distinguishing total and marginal utilities, this theory was able to show that some consumer behaviour that seemed strange or even paradoxical could be seen as a rational pursuit of the consumer's own self-interest.

The second breakthrough came with indifference theory, which dispensed with the dubious assumption of quantitatively measurable utility on which marginal utility theory was based. In this new theory, all that was needed was the assumption that consumers could say which of two consumption bundles they preferred without having to say by how much. In this and the next chapter, we deal with these two theories in their historical order.

The utility theory of demand

In this chapter we distinguish marginal from total utility, see that the shape of the demand curve depends on the former, and then go on to see how the individual consumer maximizes utility by equating marginal utility to price. From this insight, it is an easy step to derive the negative slope of the demand curve from utility theory and to explain some of what seems like paradoxical behaviour.

Marginal and total utility

We begin with a single product. The satisfaction a consumer receives from consuming that product is called utility. **Total utility** refers to the *total satisfaction* from the amount of that product consumed. **Marginal utility** refers to the change in satisfaction resulting from consuming a little more or a little less of that product. For example, the total utility of consuming 14 eggs a week is the total satisfaction provided by 14 eggs. The marginal utility of the fourteenth egg consumed is the additional satisfaction provided by the consumption of that unit. Thus, marginal utility of the fourteenth egg is the difference in total utilities gained from consuming 13 eggs per week and from consuming 14 per week.

Diminishing marginal utility

Here is the basic assumption of utility theory, which is sometimes called the *law of diminishing marginal utility*:

The marginal utility that any consumer derives from successive units of a particular product diminishes as his or her total consumption of that product increases, while holding constant the consumption of all other products.

Water provides an excellent example. We consume it in many forms: tap water, soft drinks, bottled water, or water flavoured with such things as tea leaves and coffee grounds. However we consume it, water is necessary to our very existence. Anyone denied water is soon dead. So we value the minimum of water needed to sustain life as much as we value life itself. For most of us this is quite a lot! We would be willing, therefore, to pay quite a lot if this were the only way to obtain the amount of water needed to sustain life. Thus, the utility of that much water is extremely high. More than this bare minimum will be drunk, but the marginal utility of successive amounts of water drunk over any period of time will decline steadily. Furthermore, water has many uses other than for drinking. A fairly high marginal utility will be attached to some minimum quantity for bathing, but much more than this minimum will be used only for more frequent baths, or for having a water level in the tub higher than is absolutely necessary. The last weekly gallon used for bathing is likely to have a low marginal utility. Again, some small quantity of water is necessary for tooth brushing, but many people leave the water running while they brush. The water going down the drain between wetting and rinsing the brush surely has a low utility. When all the extravagant uses of water by the modern consumer are considered, it is certain that the marginal utility of the last, say, 30 per cent of all units consumed is very low, even though the total utility of *all* the units consumed is extremely high.

Utility schedules and graphs

For the moment we assume that we can measure a person's

Table 6.1 Total and marginal utility schedules

Number of films attended per month	Total utility	Marginal utility
0	0.00	
1	15.00	15.00
2	25.00	10.00
3	31.00	6.00
4	35.00	4.00
5	37.50	2.50
6	39.00	1.50
7	40.25	1.25
8	41.30	1.05
9	42.20	0.90
10	43.00	0.80

Total utility rises, but marginal utility declines as consumption increases. The marginal utility of 10, shown as the second entry in the last column, arises because with attendance at the second film total utility increases from 15 to 25, a difference of 10. Although total utility rises with more attendance, each additional visit adds less to the total.

utility in some units which we will call 'utils'. We will soon be able to drop this assumption and work in money units, but for the moment we use utils.

The schedule in Table 6.1 illustrates the assumptions that have been made about utility, using the number of times one consumer, Carol, attends the cinema. The table shows her total utility rising the more films she attends each month. Everything else being equal, more films means more satisfaction—at least over the range shown in the table. But Carol's marginal utility of each *additional* film per month is less than that of the previous one, even though each film adds something to her total satisfaction. The schedule shows that marginal utility declines as quantity consumed rises.

Maximizing utility

We saw in Chapter 3 that a basic assumption of the theory of consumer behaviour is that consumers try to obtain as much satisfaction as they possibly can in the circumstances in which they find themselves. In other words, consumers seek to maximize their total utility.

Equilibrium for one product

If we hold the consumption of all but one product constant, we can study Carol's maximizing behaviour and derive her demand curve from a marginal utility schedule such as the one shown in Figure 6.1.

To do this, we need to convert utils into a money measure. How much is a util worth? To answer this question, we ask how much utility Carol could get if she spent £1 of income on some commodity other than cinema attendances where it would yield her most utility. Say this is CDs, where £1 worth of expenditure yields one util. Then a util is worth £1 and we can change all the util figures in Table 6.1 into pounds. Notice that if £1 worth of CDs had yielded 2 utils, then 1 util would be worth £0.50. We would then have to divide the util figures in Table 6.1 by 2 to turn them into money equivalents.

From now on we work with money equivalents and plot these in Figure 6.1.

Now let Carol be faced with a given market price of some product. The price shows what she must sacrifice to obtain each unit of the product. The marginal utility schedule, or graph, shows the value she places on each unit of the product. Clearly, Carol can increase her utility by adding to her purchases as long as the value that she places on each additional unit exceeds the amount she must pay for that unit. It follows that our utility-maximizing consumer will adjust her purchases of a product until the marginal utility of the last unit purchased (measured in money units) is equal to the price of a unit of that product.

For example, at a price of £6 Carol will see three films

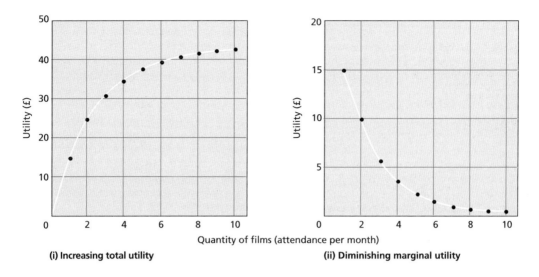

(i) Increasing total utility   **(ii) Diminishing marginal utility**

Figure 6.1 Total and marginal utility curves

As consumption increases, total utility rises but marginal utility falls. The dots correspond to the points listed in Table 6.1; smooth curves have been drawn through them. They show total utility rising, while marginal utility is positive but declining, as the amount consumed per period of time rises. The utility-maximizing consumer equates marginal utility to price by attending 2 films when the price is £10, 4 when the price is £4, 8 when the price is £1.05, and so on.

per month, since she values the first and second attendance more highly than the price she pays for them and the third just at its price. This is shown in part (ii) of the figure.

When the consumption of all but one product is held constant, the marginal utility schedule for the variable product is that product's demand curve.

Equilibrium for many products

Now let us drop the artificial assumption that the consumption of all other products is held constant. How can Carol adjust her expenditure among more than one product so as to maximize her total utility? Should she go to the point at which the marginal utility of each product is the same, that is, the point at which she would value equally the last unit of each product consumed? This would make sense only if each product had the same price per unit. But if Carol must spend £3 to buy an additional unit of one product and only £1 for a unit of another, the first product would represent a poor use of her money if the marginal utility of each were equal. Carol would be spending £3 to get satisfaction she could have acquired for only £1.

To maximize utility consumers allocate expenditure among products so that equal utility is derived from the last unit of money spent on each.[1]

Imagine that Carol is in a position in which the utility of

the last £1 spent on the cinema yields three times the utility of the last £1 spent on CDs. In this case total utility can be increased by switching £1 of expenditure from CDs to cinema attendances and gaining the difference between the utilities of £1 spent on each.

Carol will continue to switch expenditure from CDs to the cinema as long as £1 spent on cinema attendance yields more utility than £1 spent on CDs. But this switching reduces the quantity of CDs consumed, which raises their marginal utility. At the same time, the switching increases the quantity of cinema attendances consumed, thereby lowering their marginal utility.

Eventually the marginal utilities will have changed enough so that Carol's utility from £1 spent on cinema attendance is just equal to her utility from £1 spent on CDs. At this point there is nothing to be gained by a further switch of expenditure from CDs to cinema attendance. If Carol persists in reallocating her expenditure, this will further reduce the marginal utility of cinema attendance (by consuming more of them) and raise the marginal utility of CDs (by consuming fewer of them). Total utility

---

[1] By the 'last unit' we do not refer to money spent over successive time-periods. Instead we refer to buying more or fewer units at one point in time. We refer, that is, to alternative allocations of expenditures at a moment of time, not to successive allocations over time.

will no longer be at its maximum because the utility of £1 spent on CDs will exceed the utility of £1 spent on cinema attendance.

The conditions for maximizing utility can be stated more generally. Denote the marginal utility of the last unit of product X by MU_X and its price by p_X. Let MU_Y and p_Y refer respectively to the marginal utility of a second product Y and its price. The marginal utility per pound spent on X will be MU_X/p_X. For example, if the last unit adds 30 units to utility and costs £2, its marginal utility per pound is $30/2 = 15$.

The condition required for any consumer to maximize utility is that the following relation should hold, for all pairs of products:

$$\frac{MU_X}{p_X} = \frac{MU_Y}{p_Y}. \tag{1}$$

This merely says in symbols what we earlier said in words. Consumers will allocate expenditure so that the utilities gained from the last £1 spent on both products are equal.

This is the fundamental equation of utility theory. Each consumer demands each good up to the point at which the marginal utility per pound spent on it is the same as the marginal utility of a pound spent on each other good. When this condition is met, the consumer cannot shift a pound of expenditure from one product to another and increase total utility.

Now we see why when we first put a money value on a unit of utility it did not matter which line of alternative expenditure we selected. We asked what the utility would be of another £1 spent on CDs. But when the consumer is in equilibrium the utility of £1 is the same in all lines of expenditure.

Another view

If we rearrange the terms in equation (1), we can gain additional insight into consumer behaviour:[2]

$$\frac{MU_X}{MU_Y} = \frac{p_X}{p_Y}. \tag{2}$$

The right-hand side of this equation states the *relative* price of the two goods. It is determined by the market and is beyond Carol's control. She reacts to these market prices but is powerless to change them. The left-hand side of the equation states the *relative ability* of the two goods to add to her satisfaction, and is within her control. In determining the quantities of different goods she buys, Carol determines also what her marginal utilities of the goods will be. Looking at Table 6.1, we see, for example, that if Carol attends three cinema performances a month the marginal utility of the last performance to her will be 6, while if she attends six performances her marginal utility for the last performance attended will be 1.5.

If the two sides of equation (2) are not equal, Carol can increase her total satisfaction by rearranging purchases. Assume, for example, that the price of a unit of X is twice the price of a unit of Y ($p_X/p_Y = 2$), while the marginal utility of a unit of X is three times that of a unit of Y ($MU_X/MU_Y = 3$). Under these conditions, it pays Carol to buy more X and less Y. For example, reducing purchases of Y by two units frees enough purchasing power to buy a unit of X. Since one extra unit of X bought yields 1.5 times the satisfaction of two units of Y forgone, the switch is worth making. What about a further switch of X for Y? As Carol buys more X and less Y, the marginal utility of X falls and the marginal utility of Y rises. In this example Carol will go on rearranging purchases—reducing Y consumption and increasing X consumption—until the marginal utility of X is only twice that of Y. At this point, total satisfaction cannot be further increased by rearranging purchases between the two products.

Consider what Carol is doing. She is faced with a set of prices that she cannot change. She responds to these prices and maximizes her satisfaction by adjusting the things that can be changed—the quantities of the various goods purchased—until equation (2) is satisfied for all pairs of products.

We see this sort of equation frequently in economics—one side representing the choices the outside world presents to decision-takers and the other side representing the effect of those choices on their welfare. It shows the equilibrium position reached when decision-takers have made the best adjustment they can to the external forces that limit their choices.

When they enter the market, all consumers face the same set of market prices. When they are fully adjusted to these prices, each one of them will have identical ratios of their marginal utilities for each pair of goods. Of course, a rich consumer may consume more of each product than a poor consumer. However, the rich and the poor consumer (and every other consumer) will adjust their *relative* purchases of each product so that the relative marginal utilities are the same for all. Thus, if the price of X is twice the price of Y, each consumer will purchase X and Y to the point at which his or her marginal utility of X is twice the marginal utility of Y. Consumers with different tastes will, however, have different marginal utility schedules. So they will consume differing relative quantities of products. None the less, when they have maximized their utility, the ratios of their marginal utilities will be the same for all of them.

Box 6.1 illustrates the general applicability of the insight that maximizing behaviour implies balancing things at the margin. Marginal not average values are what matter for maximization.

---

[2] This is done by multiplying both sides of the equation by p_X/MU_Y.

The consumer's demand curve

To derive the consumer's demand curve for some product, say sugar, take equation (2) and let X stand for sugar and Y for all other products. What will happen if, with all other prices constant, the price of sugar rises?

We start by observing that for most consumers sugar absorbs only a small proportion of total expenditure. If, in response to a change in its price, expenditure on sugar changes by £2 per month, this might represent a large change in sugar consumption but would require only a negligible change in the consumption of each of many other products. Hence we proceed in the text by assuming that the marginal utilities of other products do not change when the amount spent on sugar changes. The appendix to this chapter gives the major alternative treatments.

Let some consumer, Gerald, start from a position of equilibrium in which

$$\frac{MU \text{ of sugar}}{MU \text{ of } Y} = \frac{price \text{ of sugar}}{price \text{ of } Y}. \qquad (3)$$

When the price of sugar rises, Gerald will now be in a position in which

$$\frac{MU \text{ of sugar}}{MU \text{ of } Y} < \frac{price \text{ of sugar}}{price \text{ of } Y}. \qquad (4)$$

To restore equilibrium, he must buy less sugar, thereby raising his marginal utility until once again equation (2) is satisfied (where X is sugar). The common sense of this is that the marginal utility of sugar *per £1* spent on it falls when its price rises. Gerald begins with the utility of the last £1 spent on sugar equal to the utility of the last £1 spent on all other goods, but the rise in sugar prices changes this. Gerald buys less sugar (and more of other goods) until the marginal utility of sugar rises enough to make the utility of a pound spent on sugar the same as it was originally.

This analysis leads to the basic prediction of demand theory.

A rise in the price of a product (with income and the prices of all other products held constant) will lead to a decrease in the quantity of the product demanded by each consumer.

If this is what each consumer does, it is also what all consumers taken together do. Thus the theory predicts a negatively sloped market demand curve.

Box 6.1 Marginals matter

A consumer interested in maximizing utility must allocate expenditure between the things she can buy until the utility of the last penny spent on each is the same. This principle applies to *all* situations in which something is being maximized. It is one of economists' greatest insights. Yet it is a principle that is often forgotten in practice. Consider the following:

A firm is allocating workers between two production teams nicknamed GO and DO. A manager notices that GO's output per person is higher than DO's. As far as he can see the workers in each team are more or less the same so the differences must be caused by how each team is organizing its work. He then reasons that since those working in the GO team are more productive than those working in the DO group, he could increase production by moving some workers from DO to GO. As he does this, he notices that the output per person starts to fall in the GO group and rise in the DO group. But it is still higher in GO than in DO so he continues to transfer workers. Finally he reaches a situation in which the output per worker is the same in both groups. So he reasons that he has found the optimal size of each group since workers are now equally productive in each group.

Can you see what is wrong with the manager's reasoning?

What he has done is to equate average output per worker. What he should have done is to equate marginal outputs of a worker in each group. He does this by transferring workers as long as the reduction in output

caused by a worker leaving the DO group (which is his marginal contribution to DO's output) is less than the increase in output when the worker enters the GO group (which is his marginal contribution to GO's output). This is another way of saying that the marginal contribution of a worker is higher in the GO group than in the DO group. He should stop moving workers when the last worker causes the output in the DO group to fall by as much as he causes production in the GO group to rise. At this point the manager has equated the marginal contribution of a worker in each group so there is no gain in any further transfer of workers from one group to the other.

As this example shows, equating averages across groups, whatever the groups are, has a seductive appeal. Yet it does not maximize the total value of whatever the groups are doing.

To help persuade yourself that the rule of equating averages is not the right maximizing rule, work out the following simple illustration. The GO group's output is 20 with one worker, 31 with two workers, and remains at 31 no matter how many further workers are added. The DO group's output is 10 with one worker, 20 with two workers, and rises by ten for every additional worker. Assume that the manager has nine workers to allocate between the two groups. How many would he allocate to each if he came as close as possible to equating the average output per worker in each group? How many would he allocate if he equated the marginal contribution of a worker in each group? Which rule maximizes the total output?

Consumers' surplus

The concept

The negative slope of demand curves has an interesting consequence:

All consumers pay less than they would be *willing* to pay for the total amount of any product that they consume.

The difference between what they would be willing to pay—which is the value of the total utility that they derive from consuming the product—and what they do pay—which is their total expenditure on that product—is called **consumers' surplus.**

For example, in Table 6.1 Carol attends the cinema five times a month when the price is £2.50 per visit and hence spends £12.50 per month on the cinema. However, the total value placed on these attendances—that is, the maximum Carol would pay rather than forgo *all* attendances—is £37.50. So Carol's surplus is £25.

This concept is important enough to deserve further elaboration. Table 6.2 gives hypothetical data for the weekly consumption of milk by one consumer, Ms Green. The second column, labelled 'Total utility', gives the total value she places on consumption of so many glasses per week (when the alternative is zero). The third column, labelled 'Marginal utility', gives the amount she would pay

Table 6.2 Consumer's surplus

Glasses of milk consumed per week (1)	Total utility (2)	Marginal utility (3)	Consumer's surplus on each glass if milk costs £0.30 per glass (4)
1	£3.00	£3.00	£2.70
2	4.50	1.50	1.20
3	5.50	1.00	0.70
4	6.30	0.80	0.50
5	6.90	0.60	0.30
6	7.40	0.50	0.20
7	7.80	0.40	0.10
8	8.10	0.30	0.00
9	8.35	0.25	—
10	8.55	0.20	—

Consumer's surplus on each unit consumed is the difference between the market price and the maximum price the consumer would pay to obtain that unit. The table shows the value that Ms Green puts on successive glasses of milk consumed each week. As long as she is willing to pay more than the market price for any glass, she obtains a consumer's surplus when she buys it. The marginal glass of milk is the eighth. This is the one she values at just the market price and on which she earns no consumer's surplus.

to add the last glass indicated to weekly consumption. Thus, for example, the marginal utility of £0.80 listed against four glasses gives the value Ms Green places on increasing consumption from three to four glasses. It is the difference between the total utilities she attaches to consumption levels of three and four glasses per week.

If Ms Green is faced with a market price of £0.30, she will maximize utility by consuming eight glasses per week because she values the eighth glass just at the market price, while valuing all earlier glasses at higher amounts. Because she values the first glass at £3.00 but gets it for £0.30, she makes a 'profit' of £2.70 on that glass. Between her £1.50 valuation of the second glass and what she has to pay for it, she clears a 'profit' of £1.20. She clears £0.70 on the third glass. And so on. These 'profits', which are called her consumer's surpluses on each unit, are shown in the final column of the table. The total surplus is £5.70 per week. In the table, we arrive at Ms Green's surplus by summing the surpluses on each glass. We arrive at the same total, however, by first summing what Ms Green would pay for all the glasses bought (which is £8.10 in this case) and then subtracting the £2.40 that she does pay.

The value placed by each consumer on his or her total consumption of some product can be estimated in at least two ways. The valuation that the consumer places on each successive unit may be summed, or the consumer may be asked how much he or she would pay to consume the amount in question if the alternative were to have none.[3]

While other consumers would put different numerical values into Table 6.2, diminishing utility implies that the figures in the final column would be declining for each person. Since a consumer will go on buying further units until the value placed on the last unit equals the market price, it follows that there will be a consumers' surplus on every unit consumed except the last one.

The data in columns (1) and (3) of Table 6.2 give Ms Green's demand curve for milk. It is her demand curve because she will go on buying glasses of milk as long as she values each glass at least as much as the market price she must pay for it. When the market price is £3.00 per glass she will buy only one glass; when it is £1.50 she will buy two glasses; and so on. The total consumption value is the

---

[3] This is only an approximation, but it is good enough for our purposes. More advanced theory shows that the calculations presented here slightly overestimate consumers' surplus because they ignore the income effect. Although it is sometimes necessary to correct for this bias, none of the corrections that are called for would upset our basic conclusion: *when consumers can buy all the units they require at a single market price, they pay much less than they would be willing to pay if faced with the choice between having the quantity they consume and having none.*

area below her demand curve, and consumers' surplus is that part of the area that lies above the price line. This is shown in Figure 6.2.

Figure 6.3 shows that the same relation holds for the smooth market demand curve that indicates the total amount all consumers would buy at each price.[4]

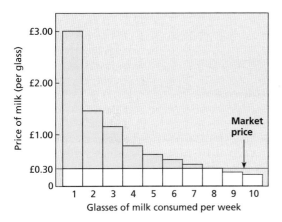

Figure 6.2 Consumer's surplus for an individual

Consumer's surplus is the sum of the extra valuations placed on each unit above the market price paid for each. This figure is based on the data in Table 6.2. Ms Green pays the yellow area for the 8 glasses of milk she consumes per week when the market price is £0.30 a glass. The total value she places on these 8 glasses of milk is the entire shaded area (yellow and green). Hence her consumer's surplus is the light green area.

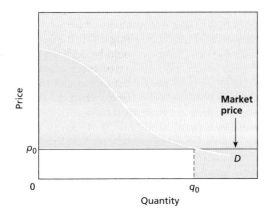

Figure 6.3 Consumers' surplus for the market

Total consumers' surplus is the area under the demand curve and above the price line. The area under the demand curve shows the total valuation that consumers place on all units consumed. For example, the total value that consumers place on q_0 units is the entire area shaded yellow and green under the demand curve up to q_0. At a market price of p_0 the amount paid for q_0 units is the yellow area. Hence consumers' surplus is the green area.

Applications

In subsequent chapters we will find many uses for the concept of consumers' surplus. In this chapter we show how it can be used to resolve some very old problems.

The paradox of value

Early economists, struggling with the problem of what determines the relative prices of products, encountered what they called the *paradox of value*: many necessary products, such as water, have prices that are low compared with the prices of luxury products, such as diamonds. Does it not seem odd, these economists asked, that water, which is so important to us, has such a low market value while diamonds, which are much less important, have a much higher market value? It took a long time to resolve this apparent paradox, so it is not surprising that, even today, similar confusions persist and cloud many policy discussions.

The key to resolving the 'paradox' lies in the distinction between total and marginal utility. We have already seen in the previous section that the area under the demand curve measures the *total utility* that consumers place on *all* of the units consumed. In Figure 6.3 the total consumption value of q_0 units is the entire shaded area (yellow and green) under the demand curve.

What about the value that the consumer places on having *one more* or *one less* than the q_0 units she is currently consuming? Faced with a market price of p_0, the consumer buys all units on which she puts a value of p_0 or greater, but she does not purchase any units that she values at less than p_0. It follows that the value consumers place on the last unit consumed of any product, its marginal utility, is equal in equilibrium to the product's price.

Now look at the total amount spent to purchase the product—the price paid for it multiplied by the quantity bought and sold—which we can call its *total market value* or *sale value*. In Figure 6.3 this is shown by the yellow rectangle with sides p_0 and q_0.

We have seen that the total utility consumers derive from a given amount of a product exceeds its total market value. The two values do not, however, have to bear any constant relation to each other. Figure 6.4 shows two goods, one for which total market value is a very small fraction of its total utility and another for which total market value is a much higher fraction of total utility.

The resolution of the paradox of value is that a good that is very plentiful, such as water, will have a low price. It will be consumed, therefore, to the point where all

---

[4] Figure 6.2 is a bar chart because we allowed the consumer to vary her consumption only in discrete units, one at a time. Had we allowed her to vary her consumption continuously, we could have traced out a continuous curve for Ms Green similar to the one shown in Figure 6.3.

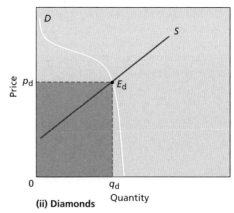

Figure 6.4 Total utility versus market value

The market value of the amount of some commodity bears no necessary relation to the total utility that consumers derive from that amount. The total utility that consumers derive from water, as shown by the area under the demand curve in part (i), is great—indeed, we cannot possibly show the curve for very small quantities, because people would pay all they had rather than be deprived completely of water. The total utility that consumers derive from diamonds is shown by the area under the demand curve in part (ii). This is less than the total utility derived from water. The supply curve of diamonds makes diamonds scarce and keeps diamonds high in price. Thus when equilibrium is at E_d, the total market value of diamonds sold, indicated by the dark blue area of $p_d q_d$, is high. The supply curve of water makes water plentiful and makes water low in price. Thus when equilibrium is at E_w, the total market value of water consumed, indicated by the dark blue area of $p_w q_w$, is low.

purchasers place a low value on the last unit consumed, whether or not they place a high value on their total consumption of the product; that is, marginal utility will be low whatever the value of total utility. On the other hand, a product that is relatively scarce will have a high market price. Consumption will, therefore, stop at a point at which consumers place a high value on the last unit consumed whatever value they place on their total consumption of the good; that is, marginal utility will be high whatever the value of total utility.

We have now reached an important conclusion:

The market price of a product depends on demand and supply. Hence no paradox is involved when a product on which consumers place a high total utility sells for a low price, and hence has only a low total market value (i.e. a low amount spent on it).

Total utility, marginal utility, and elasticity

In ordinary discussion people often distinguish between products that are difficult to do without, such as food and water, and products that can be fairly easily dispensed with, such as camembert cheese, electric curtain openers, and diamond rings. In the previous section we learned to measure these total utilities by the areas under demand curves. Using this terminology, we could say that an indispensable product has a very large total utility as measured by the area under its demand curve; a dispensable one has a smaller total utility.

A frequent error occurs when people try to use knowledge of total utilities to predict demand elasticities. It is sometimes argued that since dispensables can be given up, they have highly elastic demands; when their prices rise, consumers can stop purchasing them. Conversely, it is argued that indispensable products have highly inelastic demands because, when prices rise, consumers have no choice but to continue to buy them.

But elasticity of demand depends on marginal utilities, not on total utilities. The relevant question for predicting the response to a price change is 'How much do consumers value a bit more of the product?', not 'How much do they value *all* that they are consuming?' When the price of a product rises, each consumer will reduce his or her purchases of that product until he or she values the last unit consumed at the price that must be paid for that unit.

Elasticity of demand depends on the value consumers place on having a bit more or a bit less of the product (marginal utility); it bears no necessary relation to the value they place on total consumption of the product (total utility).

Attitude surveys

Attitude surveys often ask people which of several alternatives they prefer. Such questions measure *total rather than marginal utilities*. Where the behaviour being predicted involves an either–or decision, such as to vote for the Labour or the Conservative candidate, the total utility that is attached to each party or candidate will indeed be what matters, because the voter must choose one and reject the other. Where the decision is a marginal one regarding a little more or a little less, however, total utility is not what will determine behaviour. If one attempts to predict behaviour in these cases from knowledge of total utilities, even if the information is correct, one will be hopelessly in error.

Here are two examples of how surveys can be misleading. A market research survey asked people to name the household device they thought was most important. Suppliers of a new version of this device used the survey to predict demand but subsequently found that it had failed to do so. A post-mortem revealed that most people did not respond to the sales promotion because they already had

the product and were unwilling to pay the advertised price for a second one. In other words, although the total utility they got from the device was high, the marginal utility they attached to another unit of it was low.

For a second example, a political party conducted a survey to determine what types of public expenditure people thought most valuable. Unemployment benefits rated very high. The party was subsequently surprised when it aroused great voter hostility by advocating an increase in unemployment benefits. Although the party was surprised, there was nothing inconsistent or irrational in the voters' feeling that protection of the unemployed was a very good thing, providing a high total utility, but that additional payments were unnecessary, and therefore had a low marginal utility.

Summary

The utility theory of demand

■ Marginal utility theory distinguishes between the total utility that each consumer gets from the consumption of all units of some product and the marginal utility each consumer obtains from the consumption of one more unit of the product.

■ The basic assumption in utility theory is that the utility the consumer derives from the consumption of successive units of a product diminishes as the consumption of that product increases.

■ Each consumer reaches a utility-maximizing equilibrium when the utility he or she derives from the last £1 spent on each product is equal. Another way of putting this is that the marginal utilities derived from the last unit of each product consumed will be proportional to their prices.

■ Demand curves have negative slopes because when the price of product X falls, each consumer restores equilibrium by increasing his or her purchases of X. The increase must be enough to lower the marginal utility of X until its ratio to the new lower price of X is the same as it was before the price fell. This restores the equality of the ratio to what it is for all other products.

Consumers' surplus

■ Consumers' surplus is the difference between (1) the value consumers place on their total consumption of some product and (2) the actual amount paid for it. The first value is measured by the maximum they would pay for the amount consumed rather than go without it completely. The second is measured by market price times quantity consumed.

■ It is important to distinguish between total and marginal values because choices concerning a bit more and a bit less

cannot be predicted from knowledge of total values. The paradox of value involves confusion between total and marginal values.

■ Elasticity of demand is related to the marginal value that consumers place on having a bit more or a bit less of some product; it bears no necessary relationship to the total value that consumers place on all of the units consumed of that product.

Topics for review

■ Marginal and total utility
■ Diminishing marginal utility
■ Derivation of a demand curve
■ Consumers' surplus
■ Paradox of value

Questions for discussion

1 Which of these choices involves marginal utility and which total utility? (a) You fill your shopping basket at the local supermarket. (b) You decide to live with one partner rather than another. (c) You decide to vote for one party rather than another. (d) You consider upgrading your computer.

2 Estimate your consumer's surplus on some product that you buy regularly by comparing what you do spend on it with what you would be willing to spend on it if the alternative were to consume none of it.

3 What is wrong with the following statement? 'I don't maximize utility because I get much more satisfaction from

the last glass of beer that I buy each month than for the last loaf of bread.' What comparison would you need to make to know if the speaker was optimally allocating expenditure between beer and bread?

4 How are diminishing marginal utilities and negatively sloped demand curves related? How much would a consumer buy of a product whose marginal utility increased the more of it she consumed?

5 Mary is willing to pay £10 for the first widget she purchases each year, £9 for the second, £8 for the third, and so on down to £1 for the tenth and nothing for the eleventh. How many widgets will she buy, and what will be her consumer's surplus, if widgets cost £3 each? What will happen if the price of widgets rises to £5? Can you state a generalization about the relation between consumers' surplus obtained and the price of a commodity?

Appendix Derivation of a demand curve from marginal utility theory

Marginal utility theory can derive the negatively sloped demand curve for one product only by making some key simplifying assumptions. In this appendix we investigate some of the alternative assumptions that can be used. We consider deriving the demand curve for some product, say sugar (S).

Case 1 In the simplest case we hold the consumption of all other products constant and the equilibrium is given by

$$p_S = MU_S. \tag{A1}$$

Diminishing marginal utility then yields a negatively sloped demand curve. The problem here is that, if demand has any elasticity other than unity, adjusting sugar purchases to a change in the price of sugar implies altering purchases of other products as well.

Case 2 To deal with the problem just mentioned, we allow for n products. First we divide (A1) by MU_S to get

$$\frac{p_S}{MU_S} = 1. \tag{A2}$$

Then we observe that there will be a similar equation for each product. Since the right-hand sides of each are all unity, we can equate the left-hand sides to get the following:

$$\frac{p_1}{MU_1} = \frac{p_2}{MU_2} = \frac{p_3}{MU_3} = \cdots = \frac{p_n}{MU_n}. \tag{A3}$$

Sugar is now product one and n is a very large number. The dots indicate the equivalent ratios for all goods other than the four listed.

Since the consumption of each of the goods from 2 to n will change only a little when sugar purchases are altered in response to a change in its price, we can *assume* their marginal utilities are constant. In this case, when p_1 changes, MU_1 must change in the opposite direction to keep the ratio of the two values equal to the *unchanged* ratios of all other MUs to their respective prices.

Case 3 Next we let money stand for all other goods, since money is general purchasing power. This reduces (A3) to

$$\frac{MU_1}{p_1} = \frac{MU_M}{p_M}. \tag{A4}$$

MU_M is the marginal utility of money, which is the additional utility derived from spending £1 of additional purchasing power distributed optimally among all products. Since the price of £1 of money is by definition £1, cross-multiplication reduces (A4) to

$$MU_1 = p_1 MU_M. \tag{A5}$$

This is the same as (A1) except for the multiple MU_M, the marginal utility of money. Each increment of income permits an increment of consumption of all products, and the utility of this increment must be declining since the utility of successive units of each product that make it up is declining.

A problem now arises because a fall in the price of sugar makes it possible to buy more of *all* products and hence will reduce the marginal utility of money. This is why, when equations (A1) or (A3) are used, it is necessary to assume that the product in question only takes up a small part of total expenditure so that the change in MU_M caused by a change in p_1 is negligible and so can be assumed to be zero.

In marginal utility theory the negative slope of the demand curve is derived using *ceteris paribus* assumptions about the marginal utilities of all other goods or, equivalently, about the marginal utility of money.

These have the effect of eliminating (by assumption) what we will learn in Chapter 7 to call the income effect. There we will see that it is the income effect which prevents us from being able to show in general that the demand curves for each and every product must *invariably* be negatively sloped.

Chapter 7
What Determines Demand? II: Indifference Theory

This chapter deals with the second major approach to explaining consumer behaviour.[1] It dispenses with the questionable assumption that the utility people obtain from consuming a good can be directly measured, and that various changes in utility can be compared.

In this chapter we will first use indifference curves to describe consumers' tastes and then introduce a budget line to describe the consumption possibilities open to them. After that, we show how consumers reach equilibrium by consuming the bundle that allows them to reach the highest possible levels of satisfaction. We can then see how any consumer alters behaviour when income or prices change, and go on to derive the negative slope of the demand curve in a more satisfactory fashion than is done with marginal utility theory.

There are two great advantages of this approach to consumer behaviour. First, it allows us to distinguish between two effects of a change in price which are called the income and the substitution effects, which have important practical applications. Second, it allows us to understand the rare but interesting exception to the prediction that all demand curves are negatively sloped, which arises with a so-called Giffen good. Box 7.1 compares the assumptions of the two theories for those readers who have studied Chapter 6.

---

[1] It was originated by the Italian economist Vilfredo Pareto (1848–1923) and introduced to the English-speaking world (and greatly elaborated) by two British economists, John Hicks (1904–89) and R. G. D. Allen (1906–83).

Box 7.1 Utility and indifference theory contrasted

To explain the difference between the marginal utility and indifference curve approaches, think of a consumer comparing alternative amounts of several goods. A collection that contains a given amount of each good is called a *bundle* of goods. For example, bundle one (signified by b_1) might have 6 apples, 3 oranges, and 5 lemons, while bundle two (signified by b_2) has 8 apples, 2 oranges, and 4 lemons, and bundle three (signified by b_3) has 7 apples, 4 oranges, and 2 lemons.

In utility theory all consumers are assumed not only to be able to say that they are better or worse off when their consumption bundle changes, say, from bundle b_1 to b_2 to b_3, but also to be able to compare the magnitudes of these changes. One consumer might say, for example, that the increase in her utility when going from b_1 to b_2 exceeded the increase in her utility when going from b_2 to b_3. When this can be done, utility is said to be *cardinally measurable*.

Indifference theory uses a much weaker assumption. Consumers are only assumed to be able to *order* various consumption bundles, saying for example that b_3 is preferred to b_2, which is preferred to b_1; they are not as-

sumed to be able to say *by how much* each bundle is preferred to the other. Under this assumption utility is said to be only *ordinally measurable*.*

Consider, for example, Table 6.1 on page 88. In marginal utility theory the consumer is assumed to be able to say not only that she prefers three cinema attendances to two and two to one, but that the increase in utility in going from one to two (10 units in the table) exceeds the increase in going from two to three (6 units in the table). This is the meaning of diminishing marginal utility. In indifference theory, the consumer is assumed to be able to say *only* that she prefers two to one and three to two cinema attendances per month. This is a much weaker assumption, but it is all that is needed to develop demand theory.

---

* Under ordinal measurability the consumer can order bundles, saying for example that $b_3 > b_2 > b_1$, where the $>$ sign indicates the bundle on the left has a larger utility and hence is preferred to the bundle on the right. Under cardinal measurability the consumer can order *first differences*, saying for example $b_3 - b_2 > b_2 - b_1$; that is, in this example the change in utility in going from b_2 to b_3 *exceeds* the change in going from b_1 to b_2.

How the consumer reaches equilibrium

Our first task is to discover consumers' equilibrium in this new framework. Once that is done, we will be able to study consumers' responses to changes in such things as prices and incomes.

The consumer's preferences

In indifference theory the consumer's tastes or preferences, as they are variously called, are shown by indifference curves.

A single indifference curve

We start by developing a single indifference curve. To do this we give our imaginary consumer, Kevin, some quantities of each of two products, say 18 units of clothing (C) and 10 units of food (F). This bundle is plotted as point b in Figure 7.1. We first consider points in the two shaded areas defined by a vertical and a horizontal line drawn through b. To do so, we introduce our first assumption about tastes:

Assumption 1. Other things being equal, the consumer always prefers more of any one product to less of that same product.

As Figure 7.1 shows, assumption 1 implies that the consumer will prefer bundles that have more of all products to those that have less. But what about bundles that have more of some products and less of others? Further assumptions about the consumer's tastes are needed if such bundles are to be ranked.

To show preferences in these situations we start at bundle b in Figure 7.1, which has 18C and 10F. We then imagine offering Kevin an alternative bundle—say, 13 units of clothing and 15 units of food. This alternative has 5 units fewer of clothing and 5 units more of food than bundle b. Whether he prefers this bundle depends on the relative value that he places on 5 units more of food and 5 units fewer of clothing. If he values the extra food more than the forgone clothing, he will prefer the new bundle to the original one. If he values the food less than the clothing, he will prefer the original bundle. There is a third alternative: if Kevin values the extra food the same as he values the forgone clothing, he would gain equal satisfaction from the two alternative bundles. In this case the consumer is said to be *indifferent* between the two bundles.

Assume that we have identified a number of bundles, shown in Table 7.1, each of which gives Kevin equal satisfaction. There will, of course, be other bundles that yield him the same level of satisfaction. All of these that lie within the confines of Figure 7.2 are shown by the smooth curve passing through the points plotted from the table. This curve is an indifference curve.

An indifference curve shows combinations of products that yield the same satisfaction to the consumer. A consumer is indifferent between the combinations indicated by any two points on one indifference curve.

Now we can rate bundles in the two unshaded portions of Figure 7.1. Points above and to the right of the curve in Figure 7.2 show combinations of food and clothing that

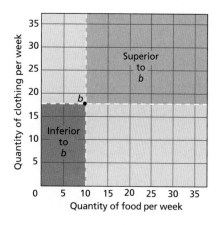

Figure 7.1 Some consumption bundles compared

According to assumption 1, bundle *b* is superior to bundles that have less of both goods and inferior to all bundles that have more of both. All points in the dark blue area are regarded as inferior to bundle *b* because they contain less of both commodities (except on the boundaries, where they have less of one and the same amount of the other).

Table 7.1 Bundles conferring equal satisfaction

Bundle	Clothing	Food
a	30	5
b	18	10
c	13	15
d	10	20
e	8	25
f	7	30

Since each of these bundles gives Kevin equal satisfaction, he is indifferent among them. None of the bundles contains more food and more clothing than any of the other bundles. Kevin's assumed indifference among these bundles is not, therefore, in conflict with the assumption that more is preferred to less of each product.

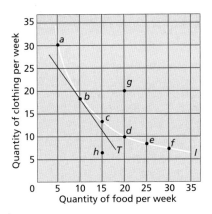

Figure 7.2 An indifference curve

The indifference curve shows combinations of food and clothing that yield equal satisfaction and among which the consumer is indifferent. Points a to f are plotted from Table 7.2 and an indifference curve is drawn through them. Compared with any point on the curve, point g is superior while point h is inferior. The slope of the tangent T gives the marginal rate of substitution at point b. Moving down the curve from b to f, the slope of the tangent flattens, showing that the more food and the less clothing Kevin has, the less willing he will be to sacrifice further clothing to get more food.

Kevin would prefer to combinations indicated by points on the curve. Consider, for example, the combination of 20F and 20C, which is represented by point g in the figure. Although it might not be obvious that this bundle is preferred to bundle a (which has more clothing but less food), assumption 1 tells us that g is preferred to bundle c, because g has more clothing *and* more food than c. Inspection of

the graph shows that *any* point above the curve will be obviously superior to *some* points on the curve in the sense that it will contain both more food and more clothing than those points on the curve. But since all points on the curve are equally valuable in Kevin's eyes, any point above the curve must, therefore, be superior to *all* points on the curve. By a similar argument, points such as *h*, which are below and to the left of the curve, represent bundles of goods that Kevin regards as inferior to all bundles on the curve. These comparisons are summarized in Figure 7.3.

Diminishing marginal rate of substitution

We now make a second assumption:

Assumption 2. The less of one product that is presently being used by a consumer, the smaller the amount of it that the consumer will be willing to forgo in order to increase consumption of a second product.

This assumption is usually referred to as **diminishing marginal rate of substitution**. It is illustrated in Table 7.2, which is based on the example of food and clothing shown in Table 7.1. As we move down the table through points *a* to *f*, Kevin has bundles with less and less clothing and more and more food. In accordance with the hypothesis of diminishing marginal rate of substitution, he is willing to give up smaller and smaller amounts of clothing to further increase his consumption of food by one unit. When Kevin moves from *c* to *d*, for example, the table tells us that he is prepared to give up 0.6 units of clothing to get a further unit of food. When he moves from *e* to *f*, he will give up only 0.2 units.

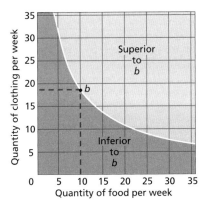

Figure 7.3 Consumption bundles compared

The indifference curve allows any bundle such as *b* to be compared with all others. Kevin regards all bundles in the dark blue area as inferior and all bundles in the light blue area as superior to *b*. The indifference curve is the boundary between these two areas. All points on the curve yield equal satisfaction and Kevin is, therefore, indifferent among them.

Table 7.2 Diminishing marginal rate of substitution

Movement	Change in clothing (1)	Change in food (2)	Marginal rate of substitution (3)
From *a* to *b*	−12	5	2.4
From *b* to *c*	−5	5	1.0
From *c* to *d*	−3	5	0.6
From *d* to *e*	−2	5	0.4
From *e* to *f*	−1	5	0.2

The marginal rate of substitution measures the amount of one product a consumer must be given to compensate for giving up one unit of the other. This table is based on the data in Table 7.1. When Kevin moves from *a* to *b*, he gives up 12 units of clothing and gains 5 units of food, a rate of substitution of 12/5 or 2.4 units of clothing sacrificed per unit of food gained. When he moves from *b* to *c*, he sacrifices 5 units of clothing and gains 5 of food (a rate of substitution of 1 unit of clothing for each unit of food). Note that the marginal rate of substitution (MRS) is the absolute value of the ratio of ΔC to ΔF. Since these two changes always have opposite signs, the MRS is obtained by multiplying this ratio by −1.

The geometrical expression of this hypothesis is found in the shape of the indifference curve. Look closely, for example, at the slope of the curve in Figure 7.2. Its negative slope indicates that if Kevin is to have less of one product, he must have more of the other to compensate. Diminishing marginal rate of substitution is shown by the fact that the curve is convex viewed from the origin: moving down the curve to the right, its slope gets flatter and flatter. The absolute value of the slope of the curve is the marginal rate of substitution, the rate at which the consumer is willing to reduce his consumption of the product plotted on the vertical axis in order to increase his consumption of the product plotted on the horizontal axis.

The slope of the indifference curve at any point is measured by the slope of the tangent to the curve at that point. The slope of tangent T drawn to the curve at point b shows the marginal rate of substitution at that point. It can be seen that, moving down the curve to the right, the slope of the tangent, and hence the marginal rate of substitution at each point, gets flatter and flatter.[2]

The indifference map

So far we have constructed only a single indifference curve. There must, however, be a similar curve through other points in Figures 7.2 and 7.3. Starting at any point, such as g, there will be other combinations that will yield Kevin equal satisfaction. If the points indicating all of *these* combinations are connected, they will form another indifference curve. This exercise can be repeated many times, generating a new indifference curve each time.

It follows from the comparisons given in Figure 7.3 that the further away any indifference curve is from the origin, the higher is the level of satisfaction given by the consumption bundles that it indicates. We refer to a curve that confers a higher level of satisfaction as a *higher curve*.

A set of indifference curves is called an **indifference map**. An example is shown in Figure 7.4. It specifies any consumer's tastes by showing, for every level of consumption of the two products, his or her rate of substitution between them. When economists say that a consumer's tastes are *given*, they do not mean merely that the consumer's current consumption pattern is given: rather, they mean that the consumer's entire indifference map is given.

Of course, there must be an indifference curve through *every* point in Figure 7.4. To graph them, we only show a few, but all are there. Thus, as Kevin moves upwards to the right starting from the origin, his utility is rising continuously. As he follows a route such as the one shown by the arrow, consuming ever more of both products, he can be thought of as climbing a continuous utility mountain. We show this 'mountain' by selecting a few equal-utility contours, labelled I_1 to I_5. But every point between each of the contours shown must also have a curve of equal utility passing through it.

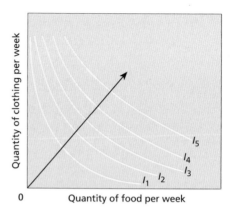

Figure 7.4   An indifference map

A set of indifference curves is called an indifference map. The further the curve from the origin, the higher the level of satisfaction it represents. If Kevin moves along the arrow, he is climbing a 'utility mountain', moving to ever-higher utility levels and crossing ever-higher equal-utility contours, which we call indifference curves.

If we assumed cardinal (i.e. measurable) utility, we could attach a specific utility number to each curve. Perhaps every point on I_1 would confer 50 utils, every bundle on I_2 100 utils, on I_3 140 utils, on I_4 170 utils, etc. In this case, we could say by how much utility was increasing as we moved from I_1 through to I_5. As we have chosen the numbers, utility would be rising at a diminishing rate as utility rose by 50, 40, and 30 between the curves I_1, I_2, I_3, and I_4.

In indifference theory we do not make such a strong assumption. Instead, all we say is that the utility attached to I_5 exceeds that attached to I_4, which in turn exceeds the utility attached to I_3, and so on. We can say that the consumer is climbing a utility mountain as he moves along the arrow starting from the origin, but we cannot say if the mountain is gentle or steep.

Box 7.2 shows some specific shapes of indifference curves that correspond to some specific taste patterns.

The choices available to the consumer

An indifference map tells us what any consumer *would like* to do: reach the highest possible indifference curve, that is,

---

[2] Table 7.2 calculates the rate of substitution between distinct points on the indifference curve. Strictly speaking, these are the incremental rates of substitution between the two points. Geometrically, the slope of the chord joining the two points gives this incremental rate. The marginal rate refers to the slope of the curve at a single point and is given by the slope of the tangent to the curve at the point. The discussion of the relation between marginal and incremental rates given on pages 28–31 of Chapter 2 should be read, or reread, at this point.

Box 7.2 Shapes of indifference curves

Any taste pattern can be illustrated with indifference curves. This box shows a few examples that will help you to understand how indifference curves work. In each case the curve labelled I_2 indicates a higher utility than the curve labelled I_1.

Perfect substitutes: part (i) Drawing pins that came in red packages of 100 would be perfect substitutes for identical pins that came in green packages of 100 for a colour-blind consumer. He would be willing to substitute one type of package for the other at a rate of one for one. The indifference

curves would thus be a set of parallel lines with a slope of −1, as shown in part (i) of the figure. *Indifference curves for perfect substitutes are straight lines whose slopes indicate the rate at which one good can be substituted for the other.*

Perfect complements: part (ii) Left- and right-hand gloves are perfect complements, since one of them is of no use without the other. This gives rise to the indifference curves shown in part (ii) of the figure. There is no rate at which any consumer will substitute one kind of glove for the other when she starts with equal numbers of each. *Indifference curves for perfect complements are 'L-shaped'.*

A good that gives zero utility: part (iii) When a good gives no satisfaction at all, a person would be unwilling to sacrifice even the smallest amount of other goods to obtain any quantity of the good in question. Such would be the case for meat for a vegetarian consumer, whose indifference curves are horizontal straight lines. *Indifference curves for a product yielding zero satisfaction are parallel to that product's axis.*

An absolute necessity: part (iv) There is some minimum quantity of water, w_0, that is necessary to sustain life. As consumption of water falls towards w_0, increasingly large amounts of other goods are necessary to persuade the consumer to cut down on his water consumption. Thus each indifference curve becomes steeper and steeper as it approaches w_0, and the marginal rate of substitution increases. *The marginal rate of substitution for an absolute necessity approaches infinity as consumption falls towards the amount that is absolutely necessary.*

A good that confers a negative utility after some level of consumption: part (v) Beyond some point, further consumption of many foods and beverages, films, plays, or cricket matches would reduce satisfaction. Figure (v) shows a consumer who is *forced* to eat more and more food. At the amount f_0 she has all the food she could possibly want. Beyond f_0 her indifference curves have positive slopes, indicating that she gets *negative* value from consuming the extra food, and so would be willing to sacrifice some amount of other products to avoid consuming it. *When, beyond some level of consumption, the consumer's utility is reduced by further consumption, the indifference curves have positive slopes.*

This case does not arise if the consumer can dispose of the extra unwanted units at no cost. The indifference curves then become horizontal.

A good that is not consumed: part (vi) Typically, a consumer will consume only one or two of all of the available types of cars, TV sets, dishwashers, or tennis rackets. If a consumer is in equilibrium consuming a zero amount of say, green peas, she is in what is called a *corner solution* (as shown in part (vi) of the figure by the budget line *ab* and the curve I_1). *When a good is not consumed, the indifference curve cuts the axis of the non-consumed good with a slope flatter than the budget line.*

climb as high up the utility mountain as possible. To see what that consumer *can* do, we need another construction, called the budget line.

We start by considering a single consumer, Jessie, who is allocating the whole of her money income between two goods, called food and clothing.[3]

The budget line

The **budget line** shows all those combinations of the goods that are just obtainable given Jessie's income and the prices of the products that she buys.[4]

Assume, for example, that Jessie's income is £120 per week, the price of clothing is £4 per unit, and the price of food is £2 per unit. As in the earlier discussion, we denote food by *F* and clothing by *C*. Thus, for example, a bundle containing 20 units of food and 10 units of clothing is written as 20*F* and 10*C*. Table 7.3 lists a few of the bundles of food and clothing available to Jessie, while the blue line running from *z* to *w* in Figure 7.5 shows all the possible bundles. Point *w*, for example, indicates that Jessie is spending all her income to buy 60*F* and no clothing, while point *z* indicates that she is spending all her income to buy 30*C* and no food. Points on the line between *z* and *w* indicate how much Jessie could buy of both products.

The slope of the budget line

Figure 7.5 highlights two points from Table 7.3. They are labelled *y* and *x*. It is clear from the figure that the absolute value of the slope of the budget line measures the ratio of the change in *C* to the change in *F* as we move along the line. This ratio, Δ*C*/Δ*F*, is 0.5 in our present example (10/20).

How does the slope of the budget line relate to the prices of the two goods? This question is easily answered if we remember that all points on the budget line represent bundles of goods that just exhaust Jessie's whole income.

Table 7.3 Data for Jessie's budget line

Quantity of food	Value of food	Quantity of clothing	Value of clothing	Total expenditure
60	£120	0	£0	£120
50	100	5	20	120
40	80	10	40	120
30	60	15	60	120
20	40	20	80	120
10	20	25	100	120
0	0	30	120	120

The table shows combinations of food and clothing available to Jessie when her income is £120 and she faces prices of £4 for clothing and £2 for food. Any row indicates a bundle of food and clothing that exactly exhausts Jessie's income.

Figure 7.5 Jessie's budget line

The budget line shows the quantities of goods available to Jessie, given her money income and the price of the goods she buys. With an income of £120 a week and prices of £2 per unit for food and £4 per unit of clothing, the coloured line is Jessie's budget line showing all combinations of *F* and *C* that are obtainable. Bundle *u* (10*C* and 20*F*) does not use all of her income. Bundle *v* (35*C* and 40*F*) requires more than her present income.

If Jessie moves from point *y* (20*F* and 20*C*) to point *x* (40*F* and 10*C*), she consumes 20 more *F* and 10 fewer *C*. These amounts are indicated by Δ*F* and Δ*C* in the figure. Thus the opportunity cost of each unit of *F* added to consumption is 10/20 = 0.5 units of clothing forgone. This is the absolute value of Δ*C*/Δ*F*, which is the slope of the budget line *zw* in the figure.

It follows that when she moves from one point on the budget line to another, the change in expenditure on *C* must be of equal value, but opposite in sign, to the change in expenditure on *F*. Letting Δ*C* and Δ*F* stand for the changes in the quantities of clothing and food respectively, and p_c and p_f stand for the money prices of clothing and food respectively, we can write this relation as follows:

$$\Delta C p_c = -\Delta F p_f.$$

There is nothing difficult in this. All it says is that if any amount more is spent on one product, the same amount less must be spent on the other. A given income imposes this discipline on any consumer.

If we divide the above equation through, first by Δ*F*, and then by p_c, we get the following:

[3] These assumptions are not as restrictive as they at first seem. Two goods are used so that the analysis can be handled graphically; the argument can easily be generalized to any number of goods with the use of mathematics. Savings are ignored because we are interested in the allocation of expenditure among commodities for current consumption. Saving and borrowing can be allowed for, but doing so affects none of the results in which we are interested here.

[4] A budget line is analogous to the production-possibility boundary shown in Figure 1.1 on page 5. The budget line shows the combinations of commodities available to one consumer given her income and prices, while the production-possibility curve shows the combination of commodities available to the whole society given its supplies of resources and techniques of production.

$$\frac{\Delta C}{\Delta F} = \frac{p_f}{p_c}.$$

So the slope of the budget line is the negative of the ratio of the two prices (with the price of the good that is plotted on the horizontal axis appearing in the numerator).

Notice that the slope of the budget line depends only on the relation between the two prices, not on their absolute values. To check this, consider an example. If clothing costs £4 and food costs £2, then Jessie must forgo 0.5 units of clothing in order to be able to purchase one more unit of food. If clothing costs £8 and food costs £4, Jessie must still forgo 0.5 units of clothing to be able to purchase one more unit of food. As long as the price of clothing is twice the price of food, Jessie must forgo half a unit of clothing in order to be able to purchase one more unit of food.

More generally, the amount of clothing that must be given up to obtain another unit of food depends only on *the relation between* their two prices. If we take the money price of food and divide it by the money price of clothing, we have the opportunity cost of food in terms of clothing (the quantity of clothing that must be forgone in order to be able to purchase one more unit of food). This may be written:

$$\frac{p_f}{p_c} = \text{opportunity cost of food in terms of clothing.}$$

It is apparent that changing income and/or changing both prices in the same proportion leaves the ratio p_f/p_c unchanged.[5]

This discussion helps to clarify the distinction between money prices and relative prices that was introduced in Chapter 3. Both p_f and p_c are money prices, while the ratio p_f/p_c is a relative price.

The consumer's equilibrium

The budget line tells us what consumers *can* do: they can select any consumption bundle on, or below, the line, but not above it. To see what consumers *want* to do, we introduce our third assumption:

Assumption 3. Consumers seek to maximize total satisfaction, which means reaching the highest possible indifference curve.

We have now developed representations of a consumer's tastes and available choices. Figure 7.6 brings together the budget line and the indifference curves for another consumer, Paul. Any point on the budget line can be attained. Which one will Paul actually choose?

Inspection of the figure shows that if Paul is at a point where an indifference curve cuts his budget line, a higher indifference curve can be reached by moving along the line. When Paul is at a point of tangency between the indiffer-

ence curve and the budget line, he cannot reach a higher indifference curve by varying the bundle consumed.

Satisfaction is maximized at the point where an indifference curve is tangent to a budget line. At that point, the slope of the indifference curve—which measures the consumer's marginal rate of substitution—is equal to the slope of the budget line—which measures the opportunity cost of one good in terms of the other as determined by market prices.

Notice that Paul is presented with market prices that he cannot change. He adjusts to these prices by choosing a bundle of goods such that, at the margin, his own relative valuation of the two goods conforms to the relative valuations given by the market. Paul's relative valuation is given by the slope of his indifference curve, while the market's relative valuation is given by the slope of his budget line.

When Paul has chosen the consumption bundle that maximizes his satisfaction, he will go on consuming that bundle unless something changes. The consumer is thus in equilibrium.

Figure 7.6 The equilibrium of a consumer

Equilibrium occurs at *E*, where an indifference curve is tangent to the budget line. Paul has an income of £150 a week and faces prices of £5 a unit for clothing and £6 a unit for food. A bundle of clothing and food indicated by point *a* is attainable, but by moving along the budget line to points such as *b* and *c*, higher indifference curves can be reached. At *E*, where the indifference curve I_4 is tangent to the budget line, Paul cannot reach a higher curve by moving along the budget line. If he did alter his consumption bundle by moving from *E* to *d*, for example, he would move to the lower indifference curve I_3 and thus to a lower level of satisfaction.

---

[5] Those who prefer an algebraic derivation may refer now to the proof of this proposition on pages 112–13, in the appendix to this chapter.

How the consumer responds to changes

We are now ready to consider how consumers respond to various changes in their incomes and the prices that they face. To do this, we take Karen's tastes as given and present her with some alternative budget lines.

Parallel shifts in the budget line

A change in money income A change in Karen's money income will, other things being equal, shift her budget line. For example, if income rises, Karen will be able to buy more of both goods. Her budget line will, therefore, shift out parallel to itself to indicate this expansion in her consumption possibilities. (The fact that it will be a parallel shift is established by our demonstration on page 102 that the slope of the budget line depends only on the relative price of the two products.)

A change in the consumer's income shifts the budget line parallel to itself, outwards when income rises and inwards when income falls.

The effect of income changes is shown in Figure 7.7. For each level of income, there is an equilibrium position at which an indifference curve is tangent to the relevant budget line. Each such equilibrium position means that Karen is doing as well as she possibly can for that level of income. If we join up all the points of equilibrium, we trace out what is called her **income–consumption line**. This line shows how the consumption bundle changes as income changes, with prices held constant.[6]

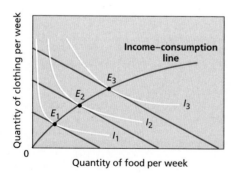

Figure 7.7 An income–consumption line
This line shows how Karen's purchases react to changes in income with relative prices held constant. Increases in income shift the budget line out parallel to itself, moving the equilibrium from E_1 to E_2 to E_3. The blue income–consumption line joins all these points of equilibrium.

A proportionate change in all prices If all prices are cut in half Karen can buy twice as much of both products. This causes the same shift in the budget line as when Karen's income doubles with prices held constant. On the other hand, a doubling of all prices will cause her budget line to shift inwards in exactly the same way as if her money income had halved with prices held constant.

This illustrates a general result (which is also proven in the appendix to this chapter):

An equal proportionate change in all money prices, with money income held constant, shifts the budget line parallel to itself, towards the origin when prices rise and away from the origin when prices fall.

From this point on the analysis is the same as in the previous section, since changing money prices proportionately has the identical effect to changing money income.

Offsetting changes in money prices and money incomes The results in the last two sections suggest that we can have offsetting changes in money prices and money incomes. Consider a doubling of money income that shifts Karen's budget line outwards. Let this be accompanied by a doubling of all money prices that shifts her budget line inwards. The net effect is to leave her budget line where it was before the changes in her income and the market prices. This illustrates a general result (which is also proven in the appendix to this chapter):

Multiplying money income by some constant, λ, and simultaneously multiplying all money prices by λ leaves the budget line unaffected and hence leaves consumer purchases unaffected.

The symbol λ is the lowercase Greek letter lambda, which is often used for some constant multiple.

Changes in the slope of the budget line

A change in relative prices We already know that a change in the relative prices of the two goods changes the slope of the budget line. At a given price of clothing, Karen has an equilibrium consumption position for each possible price of food. Connecting these positions traces out a **price–**

---

[6] This income–consumption line can be used to derive the curve relating quantity demanded to income that was introduced on page 64. This is done by plotting the quantity of one of the goods consumed at the equilibrium position against the level of money income that determined the position of the budget line. Repeating this for each level of income produces the required curve.

Figure 7.8 The price–consumption line

This line shows how a consumer's purchases react to a change in one price with money income and other prices held constant. Decreases in the price of food (with her money income and the price of clothing constant) pivot Karen's budget line from *ab* to *ac* to *ad*. Her equilibrium position moves from E_1 to E_2 to E_3. The blue price–consumption line joins all such equilibrium points.

consumption line, as is shown in Figure 7.8. Notice that, as the relative prices of food and clothing change, the relative quantities of food and clothing purchased also change. In particular, as the price of food falls, Karen buys more food.

Real and money income

The preceding analysis allows us to look deeper into the important distinction between two concepts of income that were first introduced at the end of Chapter 3. **Money income** measures a consumer's income in terms of some monetary unit; for example, so many pounds sterling or so many dollars. **Real income** measures the *purchasing power* of the consumer's money income. A rise in money income of *x* per cent combined with an *x* per cent rise in all money prices leaves a consumer's purchasing power, and hence his or her real income, unchanged. When we speak of the real value of a certain amount of money, we are referring to the goods and services that can be bought with the money, that is, to the purchasing power of the money.

Allocation of resources: the importance of relative prices

Price theory shows why the allocation of resources depends on the structure of relative prices. If the money value of all prices, incomes, debts, and credits were doubled, there would, according to our theory, be no noticeable effects. We have already seen that doubling money income and all money prices leaves each consumer's budget line un-

changed. So, according to the theory of consumer behaviour, the combination of these changes gives the consumer no incentive to vary any purchases. As far as producers are concerned, if the prices of all outputs and inputs double, the relative profitabilities of alternative lines of production will be unchanged. Thus, producers will have no incentive to alter production rates so as to produce more of some things and fewer of others. The same set of relative prices and real incomes would exist, and there would be no incentive for any reallocation of resources. The economy would function as before.

In contrast, a change in *relative* prices will cause resources to be reallocated. Consumers will buy more of the relatively cheaper products and less of the relatively more expensive ones, and producers will increase production of those products whose prices have risen relatively, and reduce production of those whose prices have fallen relatively (since the latter will be relatively less profitable lines of production).

The theory of price and resource allocation is a theory of relative, not absolute, prices.

Inflation and deflation: the importance of absolute prices

The average level of all money prices is called the general price level, or more usually just the **price level.** If all money prices double, we say that the price level has doubled. An increase in the price level is called an **inflation,** a decrease is called a **deflation.** If a rise in all money prices and incomes has little or no effect on the allocation of resources, it may seem surprising that so much concern is expressed over inflation. Clearly, people who spend all their incomes, and whose money incomes go up at the same rate as money prices, lose nothing from inflation. Their real income is unaffected.

Inflation, while having no effect on consumers whose incomes rise at the same rate as prices, does none the less have many serious consequences. These arise mainly because all prices do not rise at the same rate. These consequences are studied in detail later in this book. In the meantime, *we assume that the price level is constant.*

Under these circumstances a change in one money price necessarily changes that price *relative* to the average of all other prices. As we saw in Chapter 3, the theory extends to situations in which the price level is changing. Under inflationary conditions, whenever shifts in demand or supply require a change in a product's relative price, its price rises *faster* (its relative price rising) or *slower* (its relative price falling) than the general price level is rising. Explaining this each time can be cumbersome. It is, therefore, simpler to deal with relative prices in a theoretical setting in which the price level is constant. It is important to realize, however, that, even though we develop the theory in this way, it is not limited to such situations. The propositions we develop can be applied to changing price levels merely by making explicit what is always implicit: in the theory of relative prices, 'rise' or 'fall' *always* means rise or fall *relative to the average of all other prices.*[7]

The consumer's demand curve

To derive the consumer's demand curve for any product, we need to depart from the world of two products. We are now interested in what happens to the consumer's demand for some product, say petrol, as the price of that product changes, *all other prices being held constant.*

Derivation of the demand curve

In part (i) of Figure 7.9 a new type of indifference map is plotted in which the horizontal axis measures litres of petrol and the vertical axis measures the value of all other goods consumed. We have in effect used *everything but petrol* as the second product. The indifference curves now give the rate at which Mr Phillips is prepared to substitute petrol for money (which allows him to buy all other goods).

The derivation of a demand curve is illustrated in Figure 7.9. For a given income each price of petrol gives rise to a particular budget line and a particular equilibrium position. Plotting the quantity of petrol that Mr Phillips consumes against the price that determined the position of the budget line yields one point on his demand curve. Each such price yields a different point. Taken together these give Mr Phillips's whole demand curve.

The slope of the demand curve

The price–consumption line in part (i) of Figure 7.9 indicates that as price decreases, the quantity of petrol demanded increases. But one can draw Mr Phillips's indifference curves in such a way that his response to a decrease in price is for less to be consumed rather than more. This possibility gives rise to the positively sloped demand curve for a good, referred to as a **Giffen good** after the Victorian economist Sir Robert Giffen (1837–1910), who is reputed to have documented a case of such a curve. Let us see how the conditions leading to this case can be analysed using indifference curves.

Income and substitution effects The key is to distinguish

Figure 7.9 Derivation of an individual's demand curve
The points on a price–consumption line provide the information needed to draw a demand curve. In part (i) Mr Phillips has an income of £200 per month and alternatively faces prices of £0.75, £0.50, and £0.25 per litre of petrol, choosing positions E_0, E_1, and E_2. The information for the number of litres he demands at each price is then plotted in part (ii) to yield his demand curve. The three points x, y, and z in (ii) correspond to the three equilibrium positions E_0, E_1, and E_2 in (i).

between what are called the income effect and the substitution effect of a change in price. The separation of the two effects according to indifference theory is shown in Figure 7.10. We can think of it as occurring in the following way. After the price of the good has fallen, we reduce money income *until the original indifference curve can just be obtained.* Mr Phillips is now on his original indifference

---

[7] The rest of this chapter can be skipped without loss of continuity as long as one is willing to accept the negative slope of demand curves on the basis of the intuitive arguments given in Chapter 3.

Figure 7.10 The income and substitution effects

The substitution effect is defined by sliding the budget line around a fixed indifference curve; the income effect is defined by a parallel shift of the budget line. The original budget line is ab and a fall in the price of petrol takes it to aj. The original equilibrium is at E_0 with q_0 of petrol consumed, and the final equilibrium is at E_2 with q_2 of petrol consumed. To remove the income effect, imagine reducing Mr Phillips's income until he is just able to attain his original indifference curve at the new price. We do this by shifting the line aj to a parallel line nearer the origin until it just touches the indifference curve that passes through E_0. The intermediate point E_1 divides the quantity change into a substitution effect, $q_1 - q_0$, and an income effect, $q_2 - q_1$. The point E_1 can also be obtained by sliding the original budget line ab around the indifference curve until its slope reflects the new relative prices.

curve but facing the new set of relative prices. His response is defined as the **substitution effect**: the response of quantity demanded to a change in relative price, real income being held constant (meaning staying on the original indifference curve). Then, to measure the income effect, we restore money income. Mr Phillips's response to this is defined as the **income effect**: the response of quantity demanded to a change in real income, relative prices held constant. The distinction between income and substitution effects is one of the trickiest bits of basic economic theory. Readers are advised, therefore, to study Figure 7.10 with great care.

In Figure 7.10 the income and substitution effects work in the same direction, both tending to increase quantity demanded when price falls. Is this necessarily the case? The answer is no. It follows from the convex shape of indifference curves that the substitution effect is always in the same direction: more is consumed of a product whose relative price has fallen. The income effect, however, can be in either direction: it can lead to more or less being consumed of a product whose price has fallen. The direction of the income effect depends on the distinction we drew earlier between normal and inferior goods.

The slope of the demand curve for a normal good For a normal good an increase in any consumer's real income, arising from a decrease in the price of the product, leads to increased consumption, reinforcing the substitution

effect. Because quantity demanded increases, the demand curve has a negative slope. This is the case illustrated in Figure 7.10.

The slope of the demand curve for an inferior good Figure 7.11 shows indifference curves for inferior goods. The income effect is negative in each part of the diagram. This follows from the nature of an inferior good: as income rises, less of the good is consumed. In each case the substitution effect serves to increase the quantity demanded as price decreases and is offset to some degree by the negative income effect. The final result depends on the relative strengths of the two effects. In part (i) the negative income effect only partially offsets the substitution effect, and thus quantity demanded increases as a result of the price decrease, though not as much as for a normal good. This is the typical pattern for inferior goods, and it too leads to negatively sloped demand curves, often relatively inelastic ones.

In part (ii) the negative income effect actually outweighs the substitution effect and thus leads to a positively sloped demand curve. This is the Giffen case. For this to happen the good must be inferior. But that is not enough; the change in price must have a negative income effect *strong enough* to more than offset the substitution effect. Most economists believe that these circumstances are unusual ones; they believe that a positively sloped market demand curve is a rare exception to the general rule that demand curves have negative slopes.

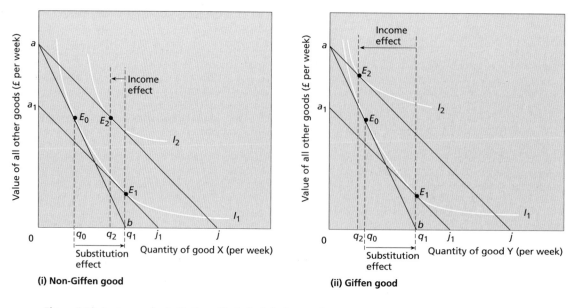

Figure 7.11 Income and substitution effects for inferior goods
A large enough negative income effect can outweigh the substitution effect and lead to a decrease in consumption in response to a fall in price. In each part of the diagram Mr Phillips is in equilibrium at E_0, consuming a quantity q_0 of the good in question. The price then decreases and the budget line shifts to aj, with a new equilibrium at E_2 and quantity consumed q_2. In each case the substitution effect increases consumption from q_0 to q_1. In (i) there is a negative income effect of $q_1 - q_2$. Because this is less than the substitution effect, the latter dominates, so good X has a normal, negatively sloped demand curve. In (ii) the negative income effect $q_1 - q_2$ is larger than the substitution effect, and quantity consumed actually decreases. Good Y is a Giffen good.

Criticisms of demand theory

Readers new to economics often find demand theory excessively abstract and feel that it is unrealistic. In this section we first consider the charge that demand theory is unrealistic and then consider some alleged exceptions to the law of demand that have been suggested by economists themselves. Box 7.3 discusses one of the many practical applications of the distinction between the income and substitution effects of a price change.

Is demand theory in conflict with everyday experience?

It is easy to show that people do not *always* behave in the manner assumed by demand theory. Fortunately, the existence of a relatively stable, negatively sloped market demand curve does not require that all consumers in-

variably behave in the manner assumed by the theory. Such fully consistent behaviour on the part of everyone at all times is sufficient but not necessary for a stable market demand curve. Consider two other possibilities. First, some consumers may always behave in a manner contrary to the theory. Consumers who are emotionally disturbed are one obvious possibility. The erratic behaviour of such consumers will not cause market demand curves for normal goods to depart from their downward slope. Provided that the consumers account for a small proportion of purchases of any product, their behaviour will be swamped by the normal behaviour of the majority of consumers. Second, an occasional irrationality on the part of every consumer will not upset the downward slope of the market demand curve for a normal good. As long as these are unrelated across consumers, occurring randomly, their effect will be swamped by the normal behaviour of most consumers most of the time.

Box 7.3 Income and substitution effects in practice

Although they sound highly abstract and 'theoretical' when first encountered, the income and substitution effects turn out to be useful tools. They help us to deal with many problems such as: Do high rates of income tax act as disincentives to work? Would cutting the rate of income tax increase the amount of work people do? Would raising the wage rate of workers in some industry lead to a reduction in absenteeism?

Such questions frequently face decision-takers and they are often surprised at the results that the market produces. For example, many years ago the National Coal Board, which used to run the UK coal industry, raised miners' wages in an attempt to boost coal production and was surprised to find miners working fewer rather than more hours. In several countries increases in rates of income tax (within a moderate, not a confiscatory, range) have been found to be associated with people working more hours rather than fewer; at other times reductions in tax rates seem to have caused people to work less.

The surprise in all these cases was the same. Intuition suggests that if you pay people more they will work more; experience shows that the result is often the opposite: more pay, less work; less pay, more work.

The explanation of this surprising behaviour lies in distinguishing the income effect from the substitution effect of a change in the reward for work.

Think of Luke starting with an endowment of 24 hours per day and deciding to consume some of it as 'leisure' (including sleeping time) and to trade the rest for income by working. If Luke works 9 hours a day at an after-tax rate of £10 per hour, he is consuming 15 hours a day of leisure and trading the other 9 for £90 worth of income which can be used to buy goods and services.

Now let the after-tax wage rate rise to £12 an hour, either because the wage rate rises or because the rate of personal income tax falls to produce that increase in after-tax earnings. Luke's response to this change will have an income and a substitution component.

The substitution effect works the way intuition suggested: more wages, more work. Gaining income is now cheaper in terms of the leisure Luke must sacrifice per £1 worth of income gained. At the new wage rate 1/12 of an hour (i.e. 5 minutes) of work earns Luke £1 worth of income, whereas before

it took 1/10 of an hour (6 minutes). Looked at the other way around, consuming leisure is now more expensive per amount of income that Luke must give up. An extra hour of leisure consumed requires sacrificing £12 of income instead of £10. The substitution effect leads to an increased consumption of the thing whose relative price has fallen—income in this case—and a reduced consumption of the thing whose relative price has risen—leisure.

So far so good. The surprise lies in the income effect. The rise in the after-tax wage rate has an income effect in the sense that Luke can have more goods *and* more leisure. He could, for example, consume an extra hour of leisure by cutting his hours worked from 9 to 8 while at the same time raising his income from £90 a day (9 hours @ £10) to £96 a day (8 hours @ £12). The income effect leads him to consume more goods and more leisure, that is, to work fewer hours.

Only if the substitution effect is strong enough to overcome the income effect will the rise in the wage rate induce Luke to work more. If the substitution effect is strong enough, Luke might for example work 9½ hours instead of 9 and increase his income from £90 to £114 a day. This means, however, choosing this combination of income and leisure in preference to all combinations that give more income and more leisure, such as 8¾ hours of work (down from 9) and £105 of income (up from £90).

So we should not be surprised if increases in the after-tax hourly wage lead to less work; this merely means that the income effect is stronger than the substitution effect.

The above analysis helps to explain why employers separate higher overtime rates from normal rates of pay. If the normal rate of pay is increased, the income effect is quite large, whereas if only the overtime rate is raised, the income effect is much smaller but the substitution effect is unchanged. In the above example, raising the normal wage rate from £10 to £12 increases Luke's income by £18 if he continues to work an unchanged 9 hours a day. But introducing an overtime rate has an income effect only in so far as overtime hours are already being worked. If, in the previous example, the employer introduced a £15 hourly rate for work of over 9 hours a day, the income effect would be zero; Luke must work more in order to gain any benefit from the higher overtime rate.

The negative slope of the demand curve requires only that at any moment in time most consumers are behaving as is predicted by the theory. This is quite compatible with behaviour contrary to the theory by some consumers all of the time and by all consumers some of the time. Thus, we cannot test the theory of market demand by observing the behaviour of a few isolated consumers.

Demand and taste changes

Some critics have argued that including changes in tastes as one cause of shifts in demand makes a demand theory untestable. Propositions about tastes are not really testable unless we have some way of measuring them. Since we do not have such a measure, what we usually do is infer tastes from the data for demand. We make such statements as 'In spite of the rise in price, quantity purchased increased, so

there must have been a change in tastes in favour of this product.' More generally, we are likely to use prices and incomes to account for as many changes in demand as possible, and then assert that the rest must be due to changes in tastes (and to errors of measurement). Anything that does not seem to agree with our theory can then be explained away by saying that tastes must have changed.

Say, for example, *incomes and other prices were known to be constant*, while the price of some product X rose and, at the same time, more X was observed to be bought. This gives us observations such as the two illustrated in Figure 7.12(i). The demand curve for X might be positively sloped in this case, but another explanation is that the rise in price coincided with a change in tastes, so that the demand curve shifted just as price changed. With only two observations, we are unable to distinguish between these possibilities, since we have no independent way of telling

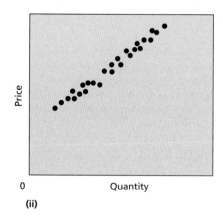

(i)   (ii)

Figure 7.12 Which way does the demand curve slope?

Taste changes may explain isolated contradictions but not repeated ones. These observations may have been generated by changes in tastes that shifted a normal demand curve from D_1 to D_2 along an upward-sloping supply curve or by a supply curve that shifted along a positively sloped demand curve D_3. Part (ii) shows twenty-six weekly observations over a period when the product's price rose and fell (with incomes and other prices constant). The explanation that supply-curve shifts are operating on a positively sloped demand curve is more likely than the explanation that tastes changed each week to shift a normally sloped demand curve leftwards and rightwards along a upward-sloping supply curve.

whether or not tastes changed. If, however, we have many observations, we can get some idea of where the balance of probabilities lies between the two explanations. Consider, for example, a product whose price has changed each week over a period of six months, sometimes increasing and sometimes decreasing. *After using appropriate statistical procedures to remove the effects due to changes in income and other prices*, we have the twenty-six observations illustrated in Figure 7.12(ii). We will be hard-pressed to avoid the conclusion that the evidence conflicts with the hypothesis of a negatively sloping demand curve.

Of course, we can always explain away these observations by saying that tastes must have changed in favour of this product each time its price rose and against the product each time its price fell. This 'alibi' can certainly be used with effect to explain away a single conflicting observation, but we would be uncomfortable using the same alibi twenty-six times in six months. Indeed, we should begin to suspect a fault in the hypothesis that demand and price vary inversely with each other.

We now have a problem in statistical testing. We are not prepared to throw away a theory after only one or two conflicting observations, but we are prepared to abandon it once we accumulate a mass of conflicting observations that were very unlikely to have occurred if the theory was correct.[8] Thus, statistically, the theory is testable. Fortunately, there is, as we have seen, a great deal of evidence that most demand curves do have negative slopes. With a few possible exceptions, the predictions of the theory have been found to be in agreement with the facts.

Alleged exceptions to the law of demand

The prediction that demand curves have negative slopes has long been known as *the law of demand*. Over the years, a number of exceptions to this law have been alleged.

Giffen goods and the law of demand

Great interest attached to a refutation of the law of demand based on observations supposedly made by Sir Robert Giffen. He was reputed to have observed that an increase in the price of wheat led to an increase in the consumption of bread by nineteenth-century English peasants. If this observation is correct, it does refute the hypothesis that demand curves always have negative slopes. Does it refute the modern theory of demand? The answer is no, because that is just the type of rare exception to the normal case that is envisaged by the modern indifference theory and was studied earlier in this chapter.

The modern theory of demand makes an unequivocal prediction only when we have extraneous information

---

[8] If changes in tastes are not related to changes in price, we can easily calculate the odds that the observations in Figure 7.12 are consistent with a negatively sloped, but continually shifting, demand curve. If tastes changed randomly each week, there is a 50–50 chance that tastes changed in the direction needed to offset the first week's price change. In the second week there is also a 50–50 chance. The chance that they changed the 'right' way in both weeks is $\frac{1}{2} \times \frac{1}{2} = \frac{1}{4}$, and the chance that they changed the right way for twenty-five successive weeks is $(\frac{1}{2})^{25} = 1/33,544,432$!

about income elasticities of demand. Since incomes change continuously as a result of economic growth, we do have such information about many products. When we know that the income effect is positive (income elasticity of demand exceeds zero), as it is for most products, we can predict in advance that the quantity demanded will be negatively related to its price. When we know the income effect is negative (i.e. the good is inferior), we cannot be sure of the result. The only thing we can then say is that the smaller is the proportion of total expenditure accounted for by this product, the less important the income effect will be, and, hence, the more likely we are to get the normal result of price and quantity varying negatively with each other. Finally, if we have no knowledge about the income effect, we can still hazard a probabilistic statement:

The great weight of existing evidence suggests that, if we had to guess with no prior knowledge whether the demand for some product X was negatively or positively related to price, the former choice would be the odds-on favourite.

Alternative theories of the sources of consumer satisfaction

The only exception to the law of demand admitted within indifference theory is the Giffen good. Further exceptions all arise from making assumptions that contradict those of indifference theory.

Assume, for example, that Rose's satisfaction depends not only on the quantities of the various products that she consumes but also on the prices she has to pay for them. She may, for example, buy diamonds not because she particularly likes diamonds *per se*, but because she wishes to show off her wealth in an ostentatious but socially acceptable way. Rose values diamonds precisely because they are expensive; thus, a fall in price might lead her to stop buying diamonds and switch to a more satisfactory object of ostentatious display. Consumers such as Rose have positively sloping demand curves for diamonds: the lower

the price, the fewer they will buy. If enough consumers act similarly, the *market* demand curve for diamonds could be positively sloped as well.

Does this mean that if a salesperson offers a discount to a rich purchaser of diamonds, she would be less likely to buy? Not necessarily. The ostentatious value depends on the price others *think* she paid for the diamonds. Thus, although the demand may be positively associated with published price, it may also be negatively associated with the price as known only to the buyer and seller.

But a positively sloping *market* demand curve for diamonds and other similar products has never been observed. Why? A moment's thought about the industrial uses of diamonds, and the masses of lower-income consumers who would buy diamonds only if they were sufficiently inexpensive, suggests that positively sloping individual demand curves for a few rich consumers are much more likely than a positively sloping *market* demand curve for the same product. Recall the discussion earlier in the chapter about the ability of the theory of the negatively sloping demand curve to accommodate odd behaviour on the part of a small group of consumers. (This time the 'odd' group is the rich, rather than the emotionally disturbed.)

Conclusion

Today we not only believe that most demand curves have negative slopes, we also have a good idea of many of their elasticities. This is fortunate, because we need reasonably precise knowledge about demand curves if we are to apply price theory to real-world cases. We need this knowledge to predict in advance the effects of changes in many things such as taxes, costs, and the amount of competition in particular markets. The more accurate is our knowledge of the shape of demand curves, the smaller will be the margin of error in such predictions. Fortunately, as we have seen earlier, economists have accumulated a large stock of the requisite empirical knowledge.

Summary

How the consumer reaches equilibrium

■ Indifference theory assumes only that individuals can order alternative consumption bundles, saying which bundles are preferred to which but not by how much.

■ A single indifference curve shows combinations of products that give the consumer equal satisfaction, and among which he or she is therefore indifferent. An indifference map is a set of indifference curves.

■ The basic assumption about tastes in indifference curve

theory is that of a diminishing marginal rate of substitution: the less of one good and the more of another good the consumer has, the less willing he or she will be to give up some of the first good to get more of the second. This implies that indifference curves are negatively sloped and convex to the origin.

■ While indifference curves describe the consumer's tastes and, therefore, refer to what he or she *would like* to purchase, the budget line describes what the consumer *can* purchase.

■ Each consumer achieves an equilibrium that maximizes his or her satisfaction at the point at which an indifference curve is tangent to the budget line.

How the consumer responds to changes

■ The income–consumption line shows how quantity consumed changes as income changes with relative prices constant.

■ The price–consumption line shows how quantity consumed changes as relative prices change. The consumer will normally consume more of the product whose relative price falls.

■ The price–consumption line relating the purchases of one particular product to all other products contains the same information as an ordinary demand curve. The horizontal axis measures quantity, and the slope of the budget line measures price. Transferring this information to a diagram whose axes represent price and quantity leads to a conventional demand curve.

The consumer's demand curve

■ A change in price of one product, all other prices and money income constant, changes both relative price and the real incomes of those who consume it. The effect of changes on consumption is measured by the substitution effect and the income effect.

■ Demand curves for normal goods have negative slopes because both income and substitution effects work in the same direction, a decrease in price leading to increased consumption.

■ A decrease in price of an inferior good leads to more consumption via the substitution effect and less consumption via the income effect. In the exceptional case of a Giffen good, the income effect more than offsets the substitution effect, causing the product's demand curve to have a positive slope.

Criticisms of demand theory

■ Observed demand curves are negatively sloped in spite of odd behaviour on the part of some people some of the time. Such behaviour tends to cancel out as long as individuals behave independently of each other.

■ The Giffen good, although a genuine exception to the law of demand, is consistent with indifference theory. Other exceptions, based on such things as snob appeal, are not consistent with indifference theory because they assume that people value goods for reasons other than the utility they get from consuming them. All these possible exceptions are rarely if ever observed in practice.

Topics for review

■ An indifference curve and an indifference map

■ Slope of an indifference curve and diminishing marginal rate of substitution

■ Budget line

■ Absolute and relative prices, and the slope of the budget line

■ Response of a consumer to changes in income and prices

■ Derivation of the demand curve from indifference curves

■ Income and substitution effects

■ Normal goods, inferior goods, and Giffen goods

Questions for discussion

1 The prices of food and clothing are £2 and £6 per unit respectively. What are the values of: (a) the relative price of food, (b) the relative price of clothing, (c) the opportunity cost of food measured in units of clothing, (d) the opportunity cost of clothing measured in food, (e) the slope of the budget line drawn with food on the horizontal and clothing on the vertical axis, and (f) the slope of the budget line drawn with the two commodities on the opposite axes?

2 What would it imply about a consumer's tastes if his indifference curve between two products was a negatively sloped *straight line*. What would his equilibrium be with respect to these two commodities?

3 Distinguish carefully between the income and the substitution effects. What commodity in your consumption bundles is likely to have the largest income effect? How would a 50 per cent fall in the price of this product affect your general consumption behaviour?

4 Could a person's indifference curves ever cross? What would it mean if they did?

5 Draw an income–consumption line for an inferior good. Explain why a good that is inferior over some ranges of income must be a normal good over other income ranges.

Appendix The algebra of the budget line

In this appendix we use simple algebra to prove the propositions asserted in the chapter.

Let the consumer's money income be M. Let p_x and p_y be the prices of food and clothing, and let X and Y be the quantities of food and clothing. Total expenditure is thus $p_x X + p_y Y$. For a consumer who spends all his income on these two goods

$$p_x X + p_y Y = M. \tag{A1}$$

Rearrangement of terms yields the equation of the budget line as it is plotted in Figure 7.5. To do this, we subtract $p_x X$ from both sides, and then divide through by p_y to obtain

$$Y = \frac{M}{p_y} - \frac{p_x}{p_y} X. \tag{A2}$$

This is a linear equation of the form

$$Y = a - bX, \tag{A3}$$

where $a = M/p_y$ and $b = p_x/p_y$. The intercept a is the number of units of Y that can be purchased by spending all of M on Y, i.e. money income divided by the price of Y. The slope b is the relative price p_x/p_y.

We first prove that the opportunity cost, the slope of the budget line, and the relative price are identical. First-differencing (A1) yields

$$p_x \Delta X + p_y \Delta Y = \Delta M.$$

This says that the change in the value of purchases of X and Y must be equal to the change in income.

Along a budget line expenditure is constant, so we can write

$$p_x \Delta X + p_y \Delta Y = 0,$$

which says that if income does not change the change in the total value of purchases must be zero. Manipulation yields

$$p_x/p_y = -\Delta Y/\Delta X. \tag{A4}$$

$\Delta Y/\Delta X$ is the opportunity cost of X measured in units of Y, i.e. the amount of Y sacrificed (gained) per unit of X gained (sacrificed). From (A4) this is equal to the relative price of X, which, from (A2), is the slope of the budget line.

We may now prove the five propositions used in the text.

Proposition 1 A change in money income, with money prices constant, shifts the budget line parallel to itself (p. 104).

Proof. If we change the value of M in (A2), we change the value of a in (A3) in the same direction: $\Delta a = \Delta M/p_y$. But b is unaffected since M does not appear in that term. Thus changing M shifts the budget line inwards ($\Delta M < 0$) or outwards ($\Delta M > 0$) but leaves the slope unaffected.

Proposition 2 An equal percentage change in all absolute prices with money income unchanged shifts the budget line parallel to itself (p. 104), inwards towards the origin when prices rise, and outwards away from the origin when prices fall.

Proof. Multiplying both prices in (A2) by the same constant λ gives

$$Y = \frac{M}{\lambda p_y} - \frac{\lambda p_x}{\lambda p_y} X.$$

Since the λs cancel out of the slope term, b is unaffected; the a term, however, is changed. If $\lambda > 1$, then a is diminished, while if $\lambda < 1$ then a is increased.

Proposition 3 Multiplying all money prices by the same constant, λ, while holding money income constant has exactly the same effect on the budget line as multiplying money income by $1/\lambda$ while holding money prices constant.

Proof. Multiply both money prices in (A2) by λ:

$$Y = \frac{M}{\lambda p_y} - \frac{\lambda p_x}{\lambda p_y} X.$$

Cancelling the λ from the slope term gives

$$Y = \frac{M}{\lambda p_y} - \frac{p_x}{p_y} X.$$

Finally, bringing the λ from the denominator to the numerator of the constant term gives

$$Y = \frac{(1/\lambda)M}{p_y} - \frac{p_x}{p_y} X.$$

Proposition 4 A change in relative prices causes the budget line to change its slope (p. 102).

Proof. The relative price p_x/p_y in (A2) is the slope term, b, in (A3). Thus changing the relative price is necessary and sufficient for changing the slope of the budget line.

Proposition 5 Equal percentage changes in all absolute prices and in money income leave the budget line unaffected (p. 105).

Proof. Multiply M and both prices in (A2) by λ:

$$Y = \frac{\lambda M}{\lambda p_y} - \frac{\lambda p_x}{\lambda p_y} X.$$

Cancel out the λ from the intercept and the slope terms to obtain equation (A2) once again.

Chapter 8
Firms, Cost, and Profits

In Chapters 6 and 7 we went behind the demand curve to understand how it is determined by the behaviour of consumers. In this and the next two chapters we go behind the supply curve to understand how it is determined by the behaviour of firms. These chapters also provide a first step towards dealing with a host of policy questions, such as: Is it always in the public interest to encourage competition? Do consumers always suffer when industries are monopolized? Why did the Organization of Petroleum Exporting Countries (OPEC) succeed so spectacularly in holding up the price of oil in the 1970s and early 1980s and fail so dramatically in trying to do the same thing in the late 1980s and the 1990s?

We begin by comparing the firms that we see in the real world with those that appear in economic theory. Next we introduce the concepts of costs, revenues, and profits and

outline the key place that profits play in determining the allocation of the nation's resources. To determine the most profitable amount for a firm to produce and supply to the market, we need to see how its costs vary with its output, which we do in the last three parts of this chapter. The first of these deals with the short run, when a firm can vary only some of its inputs and output is governed by the famous 'law of diminishing returns'. The next part deals with the long run, when the firm can alter all of its inputs. Here we pay special attention to scale economies, where increases in total output lead to reductions in the cost of producing each unit of output. In the final section we study how firms alter their production capabilities by research and development, in response to such economic signals as rising costs of particular inputs.

Firms as agents of production

We start by taking a brief look at the basic unit of production, the firm. After briefly studying firms as we see them in the real world, we go on to see how firms are treated in economic theory.

Firms in practice

In our brief look at actual firms we ask: How are they organized? How are they financed? What are their goals?

Organization

A firm can be organized in any one of five different ways. A **single proprietorship,** or sole trader, has one owner–manager who is personally responsible for everything that is done. An **ordinary partnership** has two or more joint owners, each of whom is personally responsible for all of the partnership's debts. The **limited partnership,** which is less common than ordinary partnerships, provides for two types of partner. *General partners* take part in the running

of the business and are liable for all the firm's debts. *Limited partners* take no part in the running of the business, and their liability is limited to the amount they actually invest in the enterprise.[1] A **joint-stock company** (called a *corporation* in the United States) is a firm regarded in law as having an identity of its own; its owners are not personally responsible for anything that is done in the name of the firm, though its directors may be. In the United Kingdom joint-stock companies are indicated either by the initials PLC after the firm's name, standing for *public limited company,* or Ltd (limited), which indicates a *private* limited-liability company. 'Private' in this context means that its shares are not traded on any stock exchange, while 'public' means that shares are traded on some public exchange. In the UK many limited companies are wholly owned subsidiaries of PLCs, while most PLCs own many sub-

---

[1] Limited partnerships are mainly used for high-tech start-ups, where inventors have full liability and backers only risk what they have invested. However, it is in the interest of the general partner (inventor) to convert to 'Ltd' fairly quickly.

sidiary companies. A **public corporation** is set up to run a nationalized industry. It is owned by the state but is usually under the direction of a more or less independent, state-appointed board. Although its ownership differs, the organization and legal status of such a public corporation are similar to those of a joint-stock company.

A sixth method of organizing production differs from all the others in that the output is not sold. Instead, it is provided to consumers free (or at a nominal price), while costs of production are paid from tax revenue (in the case of government production) or charitable donations (in the case of private production). Important examples found in all countries are government agencies providing defence, roads, and education, as well as private charities. In the United Kingdom we must also add the National Health Service to this list. (In countries without nationalized medical services, hospitals and doctors behave just as other firms do, gaining revenue by selling their services to people who wish to purchase them.)

The first five types of organization comprise what in Chapter 3 we called the market sector of the economy. The sixth type comprises the non-market sector.

Joint-stock companies that have locations in more than one country are often called **multinational enterprises (MNEs)**, although the United Nations officially designates them as **transnational corporations (TNCs)**. Their num-

bers and importance have increased greatly over the last few decades. They are discussed in more detail in Box 8.1.

Financing

The money a firm raises for carrying on its business is sometimes called its financial capital (or its *money capital*), as distinct from its real capital (or *physical capital*), which are the firm's physical assets such as factories, machinery, offices, and stocks of materials and finished goods. Although the use of the term 'capital' to refer to both an amount of money and a quantity of goods can be confusing, it will usually be clear from the context which sense is being used. The two uses are not independent, for much of the financial capital raised by a firm will be used to purchase the capital goods that the firm requires for production. The basic types of financial capital used by firms are equity (funds provided by the owners) and debt (funds borrowed from outside the firm).

Owners' capital In individual proprietorships and partnerships, one or more owners provide much of the required funds. A joint-stock company acquires funds from its owners in return for stocks, shares, or equities (as they are variously called). These are basically ownership certificates. The money goes to the company and the shareholders become owners of the firm, risking the loss of their money,

Box 8.1 Transnational corporations

Over the past half century the concept of a *national* economy has become less precise as firms have produced what they require in more than one country. Such firms used to be called *multinational corporations*, but the United Nations now officially calls them *transnational corporations* (TNCs).* TNCs encourage global competition as well as the transfer of technological know-how among countries. Their number has been increasing steadily over the years. Although large firms still dominate the TNC scene, the role of medium-sized and small TNCs is significant and growing.

At the beginning of the 1990s there were about 37,000 TNCs in the world and they controlled about 170,000 foreign affiliates. Ninety per cent of these TNCs are headquartered in developed countries; the five major home countries being France, Germany, Japan, the United Kingdom, and the United States. About 60 per cent of all parent TNCs are in manufacturing, 37 per cent are in services, and 3 per cent are in primary production such as forestry and mining.

The main way in which firms used to develop foreign operations was foreign direct investment (FDI), which means acquiring the controlling interest in foreign production facilities either by purchasing existing facilities or by building new ones. More recently, however, FDI has fallen dramatically, and other methods have become more common. The most important of these are joint ventures with domestic firms located in countries where the TNCs wish to develop an interest, and licensing arrangements whereby a domestic firm produces a TNC's product locally.

There are many reasons for a company to transfer some of its production

beyond its home base (thus becoming a TNC) rather than producing everything at home and then exporting the output. First, products become more sophisticated and differentiated; locating production in large local markets allows more flexible responses to local needs than can be achieved through centralized production 'back home'. Second, trade barriers make location in large foreign markets, such as the United States and the European Union, less risky than sending exports from the home base. Third, many TNCs are in the rapidly developing service industries such as advertising, marketing, public management, accounting, law, and financial services, where a physical presence is needed to produce a service in any country. Fourth, the computer and communications revolutions have allowed production to be 'disintegrated' on a global basis. Components of any one product are often manufactured in many countries, each component being made where its production is cheapest.

This globalization of production has brought benefits to many less developed countries, which have gained increasing employment at wages that are low by world standards but high by their own. TNCs now account for a large proportion of the foreign trade of many developed countries. As the United Nations puts it, 'This dynamic aspect of the growth of TNCs is one of the major channels by which economic change is spread throughout the world.'

* The material in this box is drawn from *Transnational Corporations in World Development: Trends and Prospects* (New York: United Nations, 1988).

Box 8.2 Kinds of debt instruments

Most debt instruments can be grouped into three broad classes. First, some debt is in the form of *loans* from financial institutions. These are private agreements between the firm and the institution usually calling for the periodic payment of interest and repayment of the principal, either at a stipulated future date or 'on demand', meaning whenever the lending institution requests repayment.

Second, *bills* and *notes* are commonly used for short-term loans of up to a year. They carry no fixed interest payments, only a principal value and a redemption date. Interest arises because the borrowing firm sells the new bills that it issues at a price below their redemption value. If, for example, a bill promising to pay £1,000 in one year's time is sold to a lender for £950, this gives the lender an interest payment of £50 in one year's time when the bill that he bought for £950 is redeemed for £1,000. This makes an interest rate of 5.26 per cent per year ((50/950) × 100). Bills are *negotiable*, which

means they can be bought and sold. So if I buy a 90-day bill from some firm and want my money back 30 days later, I can sell the bill on the open market. The purchaser must be prepared to assume the loan to the firm for the 60 days that it still has to run.

The third type of instrument carries a fixed redemption date, as does a bill, and the obligation to make periodic interest payments, as do most loans. These instruments have many different details and correspondingly many different names, such as *bonds*, *stocks*, and *debentures*. They are commonly used for long-term loans—up to 20 or 30 years. A firm that issues a 7 per cent 30-year instrument of this sort with redemption value of £1,000 is borrowing money now and promising to pay £70 a year for 30 years and then to pay £1,000. All such instruments are negotiable. This is important, because few people would be willing to lend money for such long periods of time if there were no way to get it back before the redemption date.

---

and gaining the right to share in the firm's profits. Profits that are paid out to shareholders are called dividends.

One easy way for an established firm to raise money is to retain current profits rather than paying them out to shareholders. Financing investment from *undistributed profits* has become an important source of funding in modern times. Reinvested profits add to the value of the firm, and hence raise the market value of existing shares; they are capital provided by owners.

Debt The firm's creditors are not owners; they have loaned money in return for some form of loan agreement, or IOU. There is a bewildering array of such agreements, which are collectively called **debt instruments** in the business world and **bonds** in economic theory. Each has its own set of characteristics and its own name, and some types are discussed in Box 8.2. Two characteristics are, however, common to all debt instruments issued by firms. First, they carry an obligation to repay the amount borrowed, called the **principal** of the loan. Second, they carry (explicitly or implicitly) an obligation to make some form of payment to the lender called **interest.** The time at which the principal is to be repaid is called the **redemption date** of the debt. The amount of time between the issue of the debt and its redemption date is called its **term.**

Goals

Firms are in business to make profits, which they do by making and selling goods and services. They must pay all their costs of production. The cost of labour includes wages, pensions, and other payments that must be made whenever labour is employed. The cost of borrowed capital is the interest they pay to those who have lent them money. The cost of intermediate goods and services covers the inputs they buy from other firms. The cost of rented inputs covers whatever they rent rather than own, often land and

buildings. Firms must also impute costs for using their own capital equipment such as buildings, machinery, and office equipment. This cost, which is called depreciation, is correctly measured by the reduction in the value of the assets that will occur if the firm uses them over the period in question. After deducting all these costs, the remainder is what firms call their profits. It is the return to their owners' capital. Some of this may be distributed to the shareholders in the form of dividends while the rest is retained for reinvestment. If the investments are sound, the value of the firm increases and this adds to the owners' capital.

Firms in theory

In Chapter 3 we defined the firm as the unit that takes decisions with respect to the production and sale of goods and services. This concept of the firm includes all types of business organization, from the single proprietorship to the joint-stock company. It also covers the whole variety of business sizes and methods of financing, from the single inventor operating in his garage and financed by whatever he can extract from a reluctant bank manager, to vast undertakings with many thousands of shareholders and customers.

The boundaries of the firm

If firms require something, either a specific input such as a specialized part, or a service such as cleaning their shop floor, they have two options. Either they can do it themselves—-making the part and providing their own service—or they can buy what they need from some other firms. The boundary between what firms do for themselves and what they buy from outside differs among firms and changes over time. Why is this so?

The answer was provided by British-born economist Ronald Coase, who received the 1991 Nobel Prize in economics for this, and other, path-breaking work. His analysis is based on the concept of **transaction costs,** which are the costs associated with all market transactions. For example, when a firm purchases some good or service, it must identify the market and then find what different quantities and qualities are available at what prices. This takes time and money, and it usually involves some uncertainty. When the firm decides to do the job itself 'in house', it uses the *command principle*: it orders the product to be made, or the service to be performed, to its desired specifications. The market transaction costs are avoided but the advantages of buying in a competitive market are lost. Furthermore, as the firm gets larger, the inefficiencies of the command system tend to rise relative to efficiencies involved in decentralizing decision-taking through the market system.

All firms must choose when to transact internally and when to transact through the market. For example, a car manufacturer must decide whether to purchase a certain component from an independent parts manufacturer or to produce the component itself. Most firms do both, buying many of their components from other firms and producing others for themselves.

Coase's insight was to see the firm as an institution that economizes on transaction costs. The market works best when transaction costs are low. When transaction costs are high, there is an incentive for the firm to reduce these by using the internal mechanisms of the command system in place of market transactions.

Firms exist as an alternative to a pure market structure of transactions. Inside a firm there is a command economy. Managers of firms have always to be asking what activities should be done inside the firm and what should be obtained in the market from other suppliers.

Changes in technology alter the relative advantages of these two types of activity. For example, the modern information and communications revolution, centred on the computer, has greatly reduced the transactions costs associated with many market activities. So the costs of obtaining things through the market have fallen relative to the costs of doing them in house. As a result firms do many fewer things in house than they used to do. Instead, they 'contract out' both the production of many parts and the performance of many services. Large firms are then able to concentrate on what they call their 'core competencies', the main things they do. Smaller firms that specialize in producing single services, such as lift maintenance, office cleaning, accounting, and product design, are often able to perform these services more efficiently than a large multi-purpose business unit can.

Goals

The theory of the firm that we study in this book is called neoclassical. It is based on two key assumptions. First, all firms are profit-maximizers, seeking to make as much profit for their owners as is possible. Second, each firm can be regarded as a single, consistent decision-taking unit.

The desire to maximize profits is assumed to motivate all decisions taken within a firm, and such decisions are assumed to be unaffected by the peculiarities of the persons taking the decisions and by the organizational structure in which they work.

These assumptions allow the theory to ignore the firm's internal organization and its financial structure, although the firm must still decide on the boundary between what it provides internally and what it obtains through the market. Using their assumptions, economists can predict the behaviour of firms. To do this, they first study the choices open to the firm, establishing the effect that each choice would have on the firm's profits. They then predict that the firm will select the alternative that will produce the largest profits.

Chapter 13 considers some limitations of theories that are based on these simple but powerful assumptions, as well as some alternative theories that use such factors as internal organization and financing to assist in explaining and predicting firm behaviour.

Production, costs, and profits

We must now specify a little more precisely the concepts of production, costs, and profits that are used by economists.

Production

In order to produce the goods or services that it sells, each firm needs inputs. Hundreds of inputs enter into the production of any specific output. Among the many inputs entering into car production, for example, are sheet steel, rubber, spark plugs, electricity, the site of the factory, machinists, cost accountants, spray-painting machines, forklift trucks, painters, and managers. These can be grouped into four broad classes: (1) those that are inputs to the car firm but outputs to some other firm, such as spark plugs, electricity, and sheet steel; (2) those that are provided directly by nature, such as land; (3) those that are provided directly by people, such as the services of workers and managers; and (4) those that are provided by the factories and machines used for manufacturing cars.

The items that make up the first class of inputs, goods and services produced by other firms, are called *intermediate products*. For example, one firm mines iron ore and sells it to a steel manufacturer. Iron ore is an intermediate product: an output of the mining firm and an input for the steel plant. These appear as inputs only because the stages of production are divided among different firms. If these intermediate products are traced back to their sources, all production can be accounted for by the services of the three kinds of input which we first discussed in Chapter 1, and which are called *factors of production*. These are the gifts of nature, such as soil and raw materials, called *land*; physical and mental efforts provided by people, called *labour*; and factories, machines, and other man-made aids to production, called *capital*.

The **production function** relates inputs to outputs. It describes the technological relation between the inputs that a firm uses and the output that it produces. When using this function, remember that production is a flow: it is so many units *per period of time*. For example, when we say that production rises from 100 to 101 units, we do not mean 100 units are produced this month and 1 unit next month. Instead we mean that the rate of production has risen from 100 units *each month* to 101 units *each month*.

Using functional notation, the production function is written as

$$q = \psi(f_1, \ldots, f_m), \qquad (1)$$

where q is the quantity of output of some good or service and $f_1, \ldots, f_m$ are the quantities of m different inputs used in its production, everything being expressed as rates per period of time.[2] The Greek letter ψ tells us that q is a function of the fs; that is, the fs determine q.

---

[2] If you have any trouble with this form of expression, you should review Chapter 2 pages 24–7 at this time.

Box 8.3 Measuring depreciation: why bygones are bygones

Accountants commonly use the historical cost method when calculating depreciation. This starts with the price that was originally paid for the asset and an estimate of its life. Annual depreciation is then calculated by multiplying the asset's original cost by the fraction of the total life made up by one year. For example, if an asset costs £60,000 and is estimated to last for six years, then depreciation will be calculated at £10,000 each year. While such methods are often useful approximations, they may, in some cases, seriously differ from the depreciation required by correct principles. Here are two examples of possible errors.

Example 1 Clara, who owns a small firm, buys a £12,000 car that she intends to use for six years for business purposes and then discard. She may think this will cost her £2,000 per year. But if after one year the value of her car on the used-car market is £9,000, it has cost her £3,000 to use the car during the first year. Why should she charge herself £3,000 depreciation during the first year? After all, she does not intend to sell the car for six years. The answer is that one of her alternatives is to buy a one-year-old car and operate it for five years. Indeed, that is the very position she is in after the first year. Whether she likes it or not, she has paid £3,000 for the use of the car during the first year of its life. If the market had valued her car at £11,000 after one year (instead of £9,000), the correct depreciation charge would have been only £1,000.

Example 2 A firm has just purchased a set of machines for £100,000. The machines have an expected lifetime of ten years and the firm's accountant calculates the 'depreciation cost' of these machines at £10,000 per year.

The machines have no alternative uses and no scrap value. Assume that, when the machines are used to produce the firm's product, the cost of all other inputs is £25,000 per year. Immediately after purchasing the machines, the firm finds that the price of the product in question has unexpectedly fallen, so that the output can now be sold for only £29,000 per year instead of the £35,000 that had originally been expected. What should the firm do?

If in calculating its costs the firm adds in the historically determined 'depreciation costs' of £10,000 a year, the total cost of operation comes to £35,000; with the revenue at £29,000 the firm 'loses' £6,000 per year. It appears that the product should not be made. But this is not correct. Since the machines have no alternative use the opportunity cost of using them is zero. The total cost of producing the output is thus only £25,000 per year, and the whole current operation shows a return over cost of £4,000 per year rather than a loss of £6,000. (If, hoping to avoid losses, the firm did not produce the goods, it would earn £4,000 per year less than if it carried on with production.)

Of course, the firm would not have bought the machines had it known that the price of the product was going to fall. Once it has bought them, however, the cost of using them is zero. It is thus profitable to use them as long as they yield any net revenue whatsoever over all other costs.

Both of these examples illustrate an important maxim:

Bygones, often called sunk costs, should have no influence in deciding what is currently the most profitable thing to do.

Costs and profits

The production function specifies the amount of output that can be obtained from any given amounts of inputs. We have seen that firms arrive at what they call profits by taking the revenues they obtain from selling their output and deducting all the costs associated with their inputs, including depreciation of their own capital. Charging for depreciation can be tricky. Box 8.3 deals with some errors that commonly arise when inappropriate methods are used. When all costs have been correctly deducted the resulting 'profits' are the return to owners' capital.

Economists use somewhat different concepts of costs and profits. They add the opportunity cost of the owner's capital, both the pure return and the risk premium, to the firm's other costs. This is not just the depreciation of the capital, but an estimate of what the capital, and any other special advantages owned by the firm, could have earned in their best alternative uses. When this larger set of costs is deducted from revenues, the remainder is called **pure** or **economic profits,** or, where there is no room for ambiguity, just profit.

What is the owners' opportunity cost of the financial capital they have tied up in a firm? The answer is best broken into two parts. First, ask what could be earned by lending this amount to someone else in a riskless loan. The owners could have purchased a government bond, which has no significant risk of default. Say the return on this is 8 per cent per annum. This amount is called the pure return, or risk-free rate of return on capital. It is clearly an opportunity cost, since the firm could close down operations, lend out its money, and earn an 8 per cent return. Next, ask what the firm could earn in addition to this amount by lending its money to another firm where risk of default was equal to the firm's own risk of loss. Say this is an additional 6 per cent. This is called the risk premium and it is clearly also a cost. If the firm does not expect to earn this much in its own operations, it could close down and lend its money out to some other equal-risk use earning 14 per cent (8 per cent pure return plus 6 per cent risk premium).

Next suppose a firm owns a valuable patent or a highly desirable location, or produces a product with a popular brand name such as Guinness, Tizer, Triumph, or Player's. Each of these involves an opportunity cost to the firm in production (even if it was acquired free), because if the firm did not choose to use the special advantage itself, *it could sell or lease it to others.* The firm must, therefore, charge itself for using the special advantage if it chooses to do so.

Tables 8.1 and 8.2 compare the concepts of costs and profits as used by firms in practice and by economists in their theories. (Notice that Table 8.1 divides the firm's costs between those that vary with output, called *variable costs,* and those that do not, called *fixed costs,* a distinction that is considered in detail later in this chapter.)

What firms call profit is the return to the owners' capital. Economists deduct from this profit figure the imputed opportunity cost of the owners' capital (and any marketable special advantages owned by the firm) to obtain their concept of pure or economic profits.

Since there are two different concepts it would be better if two different terms were used to denote them. What

Table 8.1 Profit and loss account for XYZ Company for the year ending 31 December 1999

Expenditure		Income
Variable costs		
Wages	£200,000	Revenue from sales £1,000,000
Materials	300,000	
Other	100,000	
Total VC	600,000	
Fixed costs		
Rent	50,000	
Managerial salaries	60,000	
Interest on loans	90,000	
Depreciation allowance	50,000	
Total FC	250,000	
Total costs	850,000	
Profit		150,000

The profit and loss account shows profits as defined by the firm. The table gives a simplified version of a real profit and loss statement. The total revenue earned by the firm, minus what it regards as costs, yields profits. (Note that costs are divided into those that vary with output, called variable costs, and those that do not, called fixed costs. This distinction is discussed later in this chapter.)

Table 8.2 Calculation of pure profits

Profit as reported by the firm	£150,000
Opportunity cost of capital	
Pure return on the firm's capital	−100,000
Risk premium	−40,000
Pure or economic profit	10,000

The economist's definition of profit excludes the opportunity cost of capital. To arrive at the economist's definition of profit, the opportunity cost of capital—the return on a riskless investment plus any risk premium—must be deducted from the firm's definition of profit. What is left is pure profit.

firms call their profits might be referred to as the return to owners' capital. But business does call these 'profits'. So when there is any possibility of confusion, economists speak of economic or pure profits. But since this is always what economists mean when they are dealing with their own theories they usually just use the word 'profits' to mean the return to the firm over and above the opportunity costs of capital (the pure risk-free return *and* the risk premium).[3]

Is one of these concepts better than the other? No. Businesses are interested in the return to their owners and seek to maximize this, which is what they call profits. They must also conform with tax laws which define profits the way they do. In contrast, economists are interested in how profits affect resource allocation and their definition is best for that purpose.[4]

Profits and resource allocation   When resources are valued by the opportunity-cost principle, their costs show how much these resources would earn if used in their best alternative uses. If the revenues of all the firms in some industry exceed opportunity cost, the firms in that industry will be earning pure profits. Thus, the owners of factors of production will want to move resources into the industry, because the earnings potentially available to them are greater there than in alternative uses of their resources. If, in some other industry, firms are incurring economic losses, some or all of this industry's resources are more highly valued in other uses, and owners of the resources will want to move them to those other uses.

Profits and losses play a crucial signalling role in the workings of a free-market system.

Pure profits in an industry are the signal that resources can profitably be moved into the industry. Losses are the signal that the resources can profitably be moved elsewhere. Only if there are zero economic profits is there no incentive for resources to move into or out of an industry.

Profit-maximizing output

To develop a theory of supply, we need to determine the level of output that will maximize a firm's profit, to which we give the symbol π (the lowercase Greek letter pi). This is the difference between the revenue each firm derives from the sale of its output, R, and the cost of producing that output, C:

$$\pi = R - C.$$

Thus what happens to profits as output varies depends on what happens to revenue and costs. In the rest of this chapter we develop a theory of how input costs vary with output. This theory is common to all firms. In the chapters that follow we consider how revenue varies with output. Costs and revenues are then combined to determine the profit-maximizing equilibrium for firms in various market situations. The resulting theory can then be used to predict the outcome of changes in such things as demand, costs, taxes, and subsidies, which we do in Chapter 13. This may seem like quite a long route to get to a theory of supply, *and it is*, but the payoff when we get there is in being able to understand and evaluate a great deal of economic behaviour.

We start with inputs. Suppose that a firm wishes to increase its rate of output. To do so, it must increase the inputs of one or more factors of production. For the rest of this chapter, we consider a very simple example relating to the production of some industrial product. We can best focus on essentials by dealing with only two inputs. The first is labour, to which we give the symbol L. The second is capital, to which we give the symbol K. This means that we are ignoring land and all intermediate inputs and dealing with the simplified version of the production function introduced earlier in this chapter:

$$q = \psi(L, K), \qquad (2)$$

where q is quantity of output per period of time, L is labour employed in production, and K is units of capital services used measured in such flows as machine and factory hours. The Greek letter ψ again stands for the relation that links the inputs to the outputs; this time it links K and L to q.

The firm cannot vary all of its factors with the same degree of ease. It can vary labour on short notice, but time is needed to install more capital. To capture the fact that different inputs can be varied with different speeds, we abstract from the more complicated nature of real decisions and think of each firm as making three distinct types of decisions. These are (1) how best to employ its existing plant and equipment; (2) what new plant, equipment, and production processes to select, within the framework of existing technology; and (3) what to do about encouraging the development of new technology. The first set of decisions is said to be made over the *short run*; the second over the *long run*; and the third over the *very long run*.

---

[3] An alternative terminology avoids the potential confusion arising from using the same term to refer to two different things. We mention it here because you may encounter it elsewhere, since it is still used in some elementary textbooks—but seldom in more advanced theory. This terminology calls the opportunity cost of capital *normal profit*. Any excess of revenue over normal profits is then called *supernormal profits*.

[4] Note that any activity that maximizes one concept of profit also maximizes the other. The only difference is that by subtracting the opportunity cost of capital from the firm's concept of profits, economists make positive or negative pure profits the signal for resources to enter or leave an industry.

Costs in the short run

The **short run** is defined as the period of time over which the inputs of some factors, called **fixed factors,** cannot be varied. The factor that is fixed in the short run is usually an element of capital (such as plant and equipment), but it might be land, or the services of management, or even the supply of skilled, salaried labour. What matters is that at least one significant factor is fixed. The inputs that can be varied in the short run are called **variable factors.**

The short run is not of the same duration in all industries. In the electric power industry, for example, where it takes three or more years to build new power stations, an unforeseen increase in demand must be served as well as possible with the existing capital equipment for several years. At the other end of the scale, a machine shop can acquire new equipment in a few weeks, and thus the short run is correspondingly short. The length of the short run is influenced by technological considerations such as how quickly equipment can be manufactured and installed. These things may also be influenced to some extent by the price the firm is willing to pay to increase its capacity *quickly.*

Short-run variations in input

In the short run we are concerned with what happens to output and costs as more, or less, of the variable factor is applied to a given quantity of the fixed factor. In the simplified production function given above, we assume that capital is fixed and labour is variable. Our firm starts with a fixed amount of capital—it might be machine months. It then contemplates applying various amounts of labour to it. Table 8.3 shows three different ways of looking at how output varies with the quantity of the variable factor. As a preliminary step, some terms must be defined.

Total product (*TP*) means just what it says: the total amount produced during some period of time by all the factors of production that the firm uses. If the inputs of all but one factor are held constant, the total product will change as more or less of the variable factor is used. This variation is illustrated in column (2) of Table 8.3, which gives a total product schedule. Figure 8.1(i) shows such a schedule graphically. (The shape of the curve will be discussed shortly.)

Average product (*AP*) is merely the total product per unit of the variable factor, which is labour in the present illustration:

$$AP = \frac{TP}{L}.$$

Table 8.3 Total, average, and marginal products in the short run

Quantity of labour (*L*) (1)	Total product (*TP*) (2)	Average product (*AP*) (3)	Marginal product (*MP*) (4)
			43
1	43	43	
			117
2	160	80	
			191
3	351	117	
			249
4	600	150	
			275
5	875	175	
			277
6	1,152	192	
			220
7	1,372	196	
			164
8	1,536	192	
			120
9	1,656	184	
			94
10	1,750	175	
			65
11	1,815	165	
			45
12	1,860	155	

The relation of output to changes in the quantity of the variable factor can be looked at in three different ways. Capital is assumed to be fixed at 10 units. As the quantity of labour increases, the rate of total output increases, as shown in column (2). The average product in column (3) is found by dividing the total product in column (2) by the labour requirement shown in the corresponding row of column (1). The marginal product is shown between the rows because it refers to the change in output from one level of labour input to another.

Average product is shown in column (3) of Table 8.3. Notice that as more of the variable factor is used, average product first rises and then falls. The point where average product reaches a maximum is called the *point of diminishing average returns.* In the table, average product reaches a maximum when 7 units of labour are employed.

Marginal product (*MP*) is the change in total product resulting from the use of one more (or one less) unit of the variable factor:[5]

$$MP = \frac{\Delta TP}{\Delta L},$$

where ΔTP stands for the change in the total product and

---

[5] Strictly speaking, the text defines what is called 'incremental product', that is, the rate of change of output associated with a discrete change in an input. Marginal product refers to the rate at which output is tending to vary as input varies at a particular output. Students familiar with elementary calculus will recognize the marginal product as the partial derivative of the total product with respect to the variable factor. In symbols $MP = \partial q/\partial L$. In the text we refer only to finite changes, ΔL and ΔTP, but the phrase 'a change of one unit' should read 'a very small change'. At this time it would be helpful to read, or reread, the discussion of the marginal concept on pages 28–31 of Chapter 2.

(i) Total product

(ii) Average and marginal product

Figure 8.1 Total, average, and marginal product curves

Total product (*TP*), average product (*AP*), and marginal product (*MP*) curves often have these shapes. The curves are plotted from the data in Table 8.3. In part (i) the *TP* curve shows the total product steadily rising, first at an increasing rate, then at a decreasing rate. This causes both the average and the marginal product curves in part (ii) to rise at first and then decline. Where *AP* reaches its maximum, *MP* = *AP*.

ΔL stands for the change in labour input that caused *TP* to change.

Computed values of the marginal product appear in column (4) of Table 8.3. Marginal Product in the example reaches a maximum between $L = 5$ and $L = 6$ and thereafter declines. The level of output where marginal product reaches a maximum is called the *point of diminishing marginal returns*.

Figure 8.1(ii) shows the average and marginal product curves plotted from the data in Table 8.3. Notice, first, that *MP* reaches its maximum at a lower level of *L* than does *AP*, and, second, that *MP* = *AP* when *AP* is a maximum. These relations are discussed in more detail below.

Finally, bear in mind that the schedules of Table 8.3, and the curves of Figure 8.1, all assume a specified quantity of the fixed factor. If the quantity of capital had been, say, 14 instead of the 10 units that were assumed there would be a different set of total, average, and marginal product curves. The reason is that if any specified amount of labour has more capital to work with, it can produce more output. Its total, average, and marginal products will be greater.

The law of diminishing returns

We now consider the variations in output that result from applying different amounts of a variable factor to a given quantity of a fixed factor. These variations are the subject of a famous hypothesis called the **law of diminishing returns.**

The law of diminishing returns states that if increasing quantities of a variable factor are applied to a given quantity of a fixed factor, the marginal product, and the average product, of the variable factor will eventually decrease.

As illustrated in Figure 8.2, the law of diminishing returns is consistent with marginal and average product curves that decline over the whole range of output (part (i) of the figure), or that increase for a while and only later diminish (part (ii) of the figure). The latter case arises when it is impossible to use the fixed factor efficiently with only a small quantity of the variable factor (if, say, one man were trying to farm 1,000 acres). In this case increasing the quantity of the variable factor makes possible more efficient division of labour, so that the addition of another unit of the variable factor would make all units more productive than they were previously. According to the hypothesis of diminishing returns, the scope for such economies must eventually disappear, and sooner or later the marginal and average product of additional workers must decline.

Notice that when various amounts of labour are applied to a fixed quantity of capital, the proportion in which the two factors are used is being varied.

The law of diminishing returns is also called the 'law of variable proportions', because it predicts the consequences of varying the proportions in which factors of production are used.

The common sense of diminishing marginal product is that the fixed factor limits the amount of additional output that can be obtained by adding more of the variable

(i) *MP* and *AP* decline
over all ranges of output

(ii) *MP* and *AP* first rise,
then decline

Figure 8.2 Alternative average and marginal product curves

According to the law of diminishing returns, average and marginal product must eventually decline as output increases. The law of diminishing returns permits the average and marginal product curves to decline at all positive levels of output, as shown in part (i). The law also allows the average and marginal products to rise over an initial range of output and only then decline, as shown in part (ii).

factor. Were it not for the law of diminishing returns, there would be no need to fear that rapid population growth will cause food shortages in poorer countries. If the marginal product of additional workers who were employed on a fixed quantity of land was constant, then a country's food production could be expanded in proportion to the increase in population merely by keeping the same proportion of the population on farms. As it is, diminishing returns means an inexorable decline in the marginal product of each additional labourer as an expanding population is applied, with static techniques, to a fixed supply of agricultural land. Thus, unless there is a continual improvement in the techniques of production, a population increase among subsistence farmers in a poor country must bring with it declining living standards.[6]

The relation between marginal and average product curves Notice that in Figure 8.2(ii) the *MP* curve cuts the *AP* curve at the latter's maximum point. It is important to understand why. The key is that the average product curve slopes upward as long as the marginal product curve is above it; it makes no difference whether the marginal curve is itself sloping upwards or downwards. The common sense of this relation is that if an additional worker is to raise the average product of all workers, the worker's output must be greater than the average output of all existing workers. It is immaterial whether his contribution to output is greater or less than the contribution of the worker hired immediately before him; all that matters is that his contribution to output exceeds the average output of *all* the workers hired before him. Since *AP* slopes upwards or downwards depending on whether *MP* is above or below *AP*, it follows that *MP* must equal *AP* at the highest point on the *AP* curve.[7]

Short-run variations in cost

We have now seen how output varies with factor inputs in the short run. By correctly valuing these inputs, we can discover how a firm's output is related to its cost of production. For the time being we consider firms that are not in a position to influence the prices of the factors of production that they employ.

We now define cost concepts that are closely related to the product concepts introduced earlier.

Total cost (*TC*) means just what it says. It is the total cost of producing any given rate of output. Total cost is divided into two parts, total fixed costs (*TFC*) and total variable costs (*TVC*). **Fixed costs** are those costs that do not vary with output; they will be the same if output is 1 unit or 1 million units. These costs are also often referred to as *overhead costs* or *unavoidable costs*. All of those costs that vary positively with output, rising as more is produced and falling as less is produced, are called **variable costs.** In our present example, since labour is the variable factor of

---

[6] This has not happened everywhere in the world because rapid technological advances have increased productivity in agriculture faster than the increase in population. However, in many poorer countries farmers subsist mainly on what they themselves grow and use relatively static techniques. For them, rising population in combination with the law of diminishing returns means declining output per person and hence declining living standards.

[7] This is easily proved for those who know elementary calculus. Our definitions are $TP = q(n)$, $AP = q(n)/n$, and $MP = q'(n)$, where the single prime mark indicates the first derivative and n is the quantity of the variable factor employed. A necessary condition for the maximum of the *AP* curve is that its first derivative, $[nq'(n) - q(n)]/n^2$, be equal to zero. Setting the above expression equal to zero, adding $q(n)/n^2$ to both sides, and multiplying through by n yields $q'(n) = q(n)/n$, which is to say $MP = AP$.

production, the cost of labour would be a variable cost. Variable costs are often referred to as *direct costs* or *avoidable costs*. The latter term is used because the costs can be avoided by not hiring the variable factor.[8]

Average total cost (*ATC*) is the total cost of producing any given output divided by the number of units produced, or the cost per unit. *ATC* may be divided into **average fixed costs** (*AFC*) and **average variable costs** (*AVC*) in just the same way as total costs were divided.

Marginal cost (*MC*) is the increase in total cost resulting from raising the rate of production by one unit. The marginal cost of the tenth unit, for example, is the change in total cost when the rate of production is increased from nine to ten units per period.

These three measures of cost are merely different ways of looking at a single phenomenon, and they are mathematically interrelated.[9] Sometimes it is convenient to use one, and sometimes another.

Short-run cost curves

The relations just outlined are most easily understood if we show them as cost curves. To illustrate how this is done, we take the production relationships in Table 8.3 and assume that the price of labour is £20 per unit and the price of capital is £10 per unit. In Table 8.4 we present the cost schedules computed for these values. (It is important that you see where the numbers come from.[10] If you do not, review Tables 8.3 and 8.4 and the definitions of cost just

---

[8] This twofold division of costs is sufficient for an introductory treatment. More detailed study of the firm requires the use of further categories of costs. For example, what we have called fixed costs can be divided into two classes. The first covers those costs that cannot be avoided as long as the firm stays in existence, such as the costs of the firm's debt. The second covers those that do not vary over all positive ranges of output but can be avoided by shutting down a plant's operations, such as the salaries of management and supervisory staff.

[9] Mathematically, average total cost is total cost divided by output while marginal cost is the first derivative of total cost with respect to output.

[10] There is one problem associated with our numerical example that has not so far been discussed. We have derived the data in Tables 8.3 and 8.4 by letting inputs of labour vary by one unit at a time. This gives rise to variation in output of more than one unit. Marginal cost is defined as the change in cost when output varies one unit at a time. To calculate marginal cost, we divide the *increase in costs when labour inputs rise by one unit* by the *increase in output*. This gives us the increase in costs *per unit of output* over the range of output being considered. This problem does not arise when marginal variables are defined as derivatives.

Table 8.4 Variation of costs with capital fixed and labour variable

Inputs		Output (q)	Total cost			Average cost			Marginal cost (MC)[d]
Capital (1)	Labour (L) (2)	(3)	Fixed (TFC) (4)	Variable (TVC) (5)	Total (TC) (6)	Fixed (AFC)[a] (7)	Variable (AVC)[b] (8)	Total (ATC)[c] (9)	(10)
10	1	43	£100	£20	£120	£2.326	£0.465	£2.791	£0.465
10	2	160	100	40	140	0.625	0.250	0.875	0.171
10	3	351	100	60	160	0.285	0.171	0.456	0.105
10	4	600	100	80	180	0.167	0.133	0.300	0.080
10	5	875	100	100	200	0.114	0.114	0.228	0.073
10	6	1,152	100	120	220	0.087	0.104	0.191	0.072
10	7	1,372	100	140	240	0.073	0.102	0.175	0.091
10	8	1,536	100	160	260	0.065	0.104	0.169	0.122
10	9	1,656	100	180	280	0.060	0.109	0.169	0.167
10	10	1,750	100	200	300	0.057	0.114	0.171	0.213
10	11	1,815	100	220	320	0.055	0.121	0.176	0.308
10	12	1,860	100	240	340	0.054	0.129	0.183	0.444

The relation of cost to the rate of output can be looked at in several different ways. These cost schedules are computed from the product curves of Table 8.3, given the price of capital of £10 per unit and the price of labour of £20 per unit. Marginal cost (in column (10)) is shown between the lines of total cost because it refers to the *change* in cost divided by the *change* in output that brought it about. Marginal cost is calculated by dividing the increase in costs by the increase in output when one additional unit of labour is used. This gives the increase in cost per unit of output over that range of output. For example, the *MC* of £0.08 is the increase in total cost of £20 (from £160 to £180) divided by the 249 unit increase in output (from 351 to 600). This tells us that when output goes from 351 to 600 (because labour inputs go from 3 to 4), the increase in costs is £0.08 per unit of output. In constructing a graph, marginal costs should be plotted midway in the interval over which they are computed. The *MC* of £0.08 would thus be plotted at output 475.5.

[a] Col. (4) ÷ col. (3).   [c] Col. (6) ÷ col. (3) = col. (7) + col. (8).
[b] Col. (5) ÷ col. (3).   [d] Change in col. (5) from one row to the next ÷ corresponding change in col. (3).

(i) Total cost curves   **(ii) Marginal and average cost curves**

Figure 8.3 Total cost, average cost, and marginal cost curves

Total cost (*TC*), average cost (*AC*), and marginal cost (*MC*) curves often have the shapes shown here. These curves are plotted from Table 8.4. Total fixed cost does not vary with output. Total variable cost and the total of all costs (*TC* = *TVC* + *TFC*) rise with output, first at a decreasing rate, then at an increasing rate. The total cost curves in (i) give rise to the average and marginal curves in (ii). Average fixed cost (*AFC*) declines as output increases. Average variable cost (*AVC*) and average total cost (*ATC*) fall and then rise as output increases. Marginal cost (*MC*) does the same, intersecting the *ATC* and *AVC* curves at their minimum points. Capacity output is at the minimum point of the *ATC* curve, which is an output of 1,500 in this example.

given.) Figure 8.3(i) shows the total cost curves; Figure 8.3(ii) plots the marginal and average cost curves that are derived in Table 8.4.

How cost varies with output

Since total fixed cost (*TFC*) does not vary with output, average fixed cost (*TFC/q*) is negatively related to output while marginal fixed cost is zero. In contrast, variable cost is positively related to output, since to produce more requires more of the variable factor. Average variable cost may, however, be negatively or positively related to output. If output rises faster than total variable costs, average variable costs will be falling as output rises; if total output rises less fast than costs rise, average variable cost will be rising. Marginal variable cost is always positive, indicating that it always costs something to increase output, but, as we will soon see, marginal cost may rise or fall as output rises.

Notice that the marginal cost curve cuts the *ATC* and *AVC* curves at their lowest points. This is another example of the relation (discussed above) between a marginal and an average curve. The *ATC* curve, for example, slopes downwards as long as the marginal cost curve is below it; it makes no difference whether the marginal cost curve is itself sloping upwards or downwards.

In Figure 8.3 the average variable cost curve reaches a minimum and then rises. With fixed factor prices, when

average product per worker is at a maximum, average variable cost is at a minimum. The common sense is that each new worker adds the same amount to cost but a different amount to output, and when output per worker is rising the cost per unit of output must be falling, and vice versa.

The law of diminishing returns implies eventually increasing marginal and average variable cost.

Short-run *AVC* curves are often drawn U-shaped. This reflects the assumptions (1) that average productivity is increasing when output is low, but (2) that average productivity eventually begins to fall fast enough to cause average total cost to increase.[11]

The definition of capacity The output that corresponds to the minimum short-run average total cost is very often called **capacity**. Capacity in this sense is not an upper limit

---

[11] This point is easily seen if a little algebra is used. (The only new symbols used here are *w*, which stands for the price of a unit of labour and a dot to indicate multiplication.) By definition, *AVC = TVC/q*. But *TVC = L·w*, and *q = AP·L* (since *AP = q/L*). Therefore

$$AVC = (L \cdot w)/(AP \cdot L)$$
$$= w/AP.$$

In other words average variable cost equals the price of the variable factor divided by the average product of the variable factor. Since *w* is constant, it follows that *AVC* and *AP* vary inversely with each other, and when *AP* is at its maximum value *AVC* must be at its minimum value.

on what can be produced, as you can see by looking again at Table 8.4. In the example, capacity output is between 1,536 and 1,656 units, but higher outputs can be achieved. A firm producing *below capacity* is producing at a rate of output less than the one for which average total cost is a minimum. A firm producing *above capacity* is producing more than this amount. It is thus incurring costs per unit of output that are higher than the minimum achievable.

A family of short-run cost curves   A short-run cost curve shows how costs vary with output for a given quantity of the fixed factor—say a given size of plant.

There is a different short-run cost curve for each quantity of the fixed factor.

A small plant for manufacturing nuts and bolts will have its own short-run cost curve. A medium-sized and a very large plant will each have their own short-run cost curves. If a firm expands by replacing its small plant with a medium-sized plant, it will move from one short-run cost curve to another. This change from one size of plant to another is a long-run change. We now study how the short-run cost curves of different-sized plants are related to each other.

Costs in the long run

In the short run, with only one factor variable, there is only one way to produce a given output: by adjusting the input of that factor until the desired rate of output is achieved. Thus, once the firm has decided on a rate of output, there is only one technically possible way of achieving it.

By contrast, in the long run all factors are variable. The firm must decide both on a level of output *and* on how to produce that output. Specifically, this means that firms in the long run must choose the nature and amount of plant and equipment, as well as the size of their labour force.

In making this choice, the firm will wish to avoid being technically inefficient, which means using more of *all* inputs than is necessary. Being technically efficient is not enough, however. To be economically efficient, the firm must choose, from among the many technically efficient options, the one that produces a given level of output at the lowest possible cost.

Long-run decisions are risky because the firm must anticipate what methods of production will be efficient, not only today, but also for many years in the future, when the costs of labour and raw materials will no doubt have changed. The decisions are also risky because the firm must estimate how much output it will want to produce. Is the industry to which it belongs growing or declining? Will new products emerge to render its existing products less useful than an extrapolation of past sales suggests?

Profit maximization and cost minimization

Any firm seeking to maximize its profits in the long run must select the economically efficient method, which is the method that produces its output at the lowest possible cost. This implication of the hypothesis of profit maxim-

ization is called **cost minimization**: from the alternatives open to it, the profit-maximizing firm will choose the least costly way of producing whatever specific output it chooses.

Choice of factor mix

If it is possible to substitute one factor for another in such a way that output remains constant while total cost falls, the firm is not using the least costly combination of factors. The firm should then substitute one factor for another factor. Such profit-increasing substitutions are always possible whenever the marginal product of the one factor per £1 expended on it is greater than the marginal product of the other factor per £1 expended on it. The firm has not minimized its costs as long as these two magnitudes are unequal. For example, if an extra £1 spent on labour produces more output than an extra £1 spent on capital, the firm can reduce costs by spending less on capital and more on labour.

If we use K to represent capital, L to represent labour, and p to represent the price of a unit of the factor, the necessary condition for cost minimization is as follows:

$$\frac{MP_K}{p_K} = \frac{MP_L}{p_L}. \qquad (3)$$

Whenever the two sides of equation (3) are not equal, there are possibilities for factor substitutions that will reduce costs.

To see why this equation must be satisfied if costs of production are to be minimized, consider a situation where the equation is not satisfied. Suppose, for example, that the marginal product of capital is 20 and its price is £2, making the left side of equation (3) equal to 10. Suppose that the marginal product of labour is 32 and its price is £8, making the right side of equation (3) equal to 4. Thus the last £1 spent on capital adds 10 units to output, whereas the last £1 spent on labour adds only 4 units to output. In such a case the firm could maintain its output level and reduce costs by using £2.50 less of labour and spending £1.00 more on capital. Making such a substitution of capital for labour would leave output unchanged and reduce costs by £1.50. Thus the original position was not cost-minimizing.[12]

We can take a different look at cost minimization by multiplying equation (3) by p_K/MP_L to obtain

$$\frac{MP_K}{MP_L} = \frac{p_K}{p_L}. \qquad (4)$$

The ratio of the marginal products on the left-hand side of the equation compares the contribution to output of the last unit of capital and the last unit of labour. If the ratio is 4, this means that 1 unit more of capital will add 4 times as much to output as 1 unit more of labour. The right-hand side of the equation shows how the cost of 1 unit more of capital compares with the cost of 1 unit more of labour. If the ratio is also 4, the firm cannot reduce costs by substituting capital for labour or vice versa. Now suppose that the ratio on the right-hand side of the equation is 2. Capital, which is four times as productive as labour, is now only twice as expensive. It will pay the firm to switch to a method of production that uses more capital and less labour. If, however, the ratio on the right-hand side is 6 (or *any* number more than 4), it will pay to switch to a method of production that uses more labour and less capital.

We have seen that when the ratio MP_K/MP_L exceeds the ratio p_K/p_L, the firm will substitute capital for labour. This substitution is measured by changes in the **capital–labour ratio,** which is merely the amount of capital per worker. So if the firm uses £1m worth of capital and employs 100 workers, its capital–labour ratio is 10,000 (1,000,000/100), indicating that there is £10,000 worth of capital for each worker.

How far does the firm go in making this substitution? There is a limit, because the law of diminishing returns tells us that as the firm uses more capital, the marginal product of capital falls, and as it uses less labour, the marginal product of labour rises. Thus, the ratio MP_K/MP_L falls. When it reaches 2, the firm does not need to substitute further. The ratio of the marginal products is equal to the ratio of the prices.

Equation (4) shows how the firm can adjust the elements over which it has control (the quantities of factors used, and thus the marginal products of those factors) according to the prices of the factors given by the market.

Long-run equilibrium of the firm

The firm will have achieved its equilibrium capital–labour ratio when there is no opportunity for cost-reducing substitutions. This occurs when the marginal product per pound spent on each factor is the same (equation (3)) or, equivalently, when the ratio of the marginal products of factors is equal to the ratio of their prices (equation (4)).

The principle of substitution

Suppose that a firm is meeting the cost-minimizing conditions shown in equations (3) and (4) and that the cost of labour increases while the cost of capital remains unchanged. The least-cost method of producing any output will now use less labour and more capital than was required to produce the same output before the factor prices changed.

Methods of production will change if the relative prices of factors change. Relatively more of the cheaper factor and relatively less of the more expensive factor will be used.

This is called the **principle of substitution,** and it follows from the assumption that firms minimize their costs.

The principle of substitution plays a central role in resource allocation, because it relates to the way in which individual firms respond to changes in relative factor prices that are caused by the changing relative scarcities of factors in the economy as a whole. When a factor becomes scarcer to the economy as a whole, its price will tend to rise. This motivates individual firms to use less of that factor. When some other factor becomes more plentiful to the economy as a whole, its price will tend to fall. This motivates individual firms to use more of it. Firms need never know the relative scarcities of the various factors. As long as relative factor prices reflect relative scarcities, firms will tend to substitute plentiful factors for scarce factors. They do this through their own cost-minimizing responses to the changes in the prices of their inputs.

The appendix to this chapter gives a formal analysis of the firm's choice of factor proportions and of its factor substitution in response to changes in relative factor prices. The analysis uses the concept of isoquants, which are the firm's equivalent of consumers' indifference curves: an indifference curve shows all those combinations of products that give the consumer the same satisfaction, while an isoquant shows all those combinations of factor inputs that give the firm the same output. Those who wish to study this formal analysis of the subject matter of this section should read the appendix now. Those who are content with the intuitive discussion in the text can read on in the text. Box 8.4 discusses the broader significance of the principle of substitution.

---

[12] The argument in this paragraph assumes that the marginal products do not change when expenditure changes by a small amount.

Box 8.4   The economy-wide significance of the principle of substitution

In free markets, relative factor prices reflect the relative scarcities (in relation to demand) of different factors of production. Abundant factors have prices that are low relative to the prices of factors that are scarce. Firms seeking their own private profit and responding to relative factor prices will be led to make lavish use of the factors with which the whole country is plentifully endowed, and to be frugal in their use of the factors that are in scarce supply.

For example, a country with a great deal of land and a small population will experience a low price of its plentiful land and a high price of its scarce labour. Firms producing agricultural goods will tend to make lavish use of the cheap land and to economize on the expensive labour. In contrast a small country with a large population will have expensive land and cheap labour. Firms producing agricultural goods will tend to economize on land by using a great deal of labour per unit of land.

In recent decades construction workers' wages have risen sharply relative to the wages of factory labour and the cost of machinery. In response builders have shifted from on-site construction to panelization, a method of

building that uses standardized modules. The wiring, plumbing, insulation, and painting of these standardized modules are all done at the factory. The bulk of the factory work is performed by machinery and by assembly-line workers whose wages are only half those of on-site construction workers.

These are examples of the price system operating as an automatic control mechanism. No single firm need be aware of national factor surpluses and scarcities. Since these are reflected in relative market prices, individual firms that never look beyond their own private profits are led to economize on factors that are scarce in the nation as a whole. We should not be surprised, therefore, to discover that methods of producing the same product differ in different countries. In Europe, where labour is highly skilled and very expensive, a manufacturer may use very elaborate equipment to economize on labour. In China, where labour is abundant and capital scarce, a much less mechanized method of production may be appropriate. The Western engineer who feels that the Chinese are behind because they are using methods abandoned in the West as inefficient long ago may be missing the significance of economic efficiency.

Cost curves in the long run

When all factors can be varied, there is a least-cost method of producing each possible level of output. Thus, with given factor prices, there is a minimum achievable cost for each level of output; if this cost is expressed as a quantity per unit of output, we obtain the long-run average cost of producing each level of output. When this least-cost method of producing each output is plotted on a graph, the result is called a **long-run average cost curve** ($LRAC$). Figure 8.4 shows one such curve.

This cost curve is determined by the industry's current technology and by the prices of the factors of production. It is a 'boundary' in the sense that points below it are unattainable; points on the curve, however, are attainable if sufficient time elapses for all inputs to be adjusted. To move from one point on the $LRAC$ curve to another requires an adjustment in all inputs, which may, for example, require building a larger, more elaborate factory.

The $LRAC$ curve is the boundary between cost levels that are attainable, with known technology and given factor prices, and those that are unattainable.

Just as the short-run cost curves discussed earlier in this chapter are derived from the *production function* describing the physical relationship between factor inputs and output, so is the $LRAC$ curve. The difference is that in deriving the $LRAC$ curve there are no fixed factors, so all factors are treated as variable. Because all input costs are variable in the long run, we do not need to distinguish between average variable cost (AVC), average fixed cost (AFC), and average total cost (ATC), as we did in the short

run. In the long run, there is only one long-run average cost ($LRAC$) for any given set of input prices.

The shape of the long-run average cost curve

As the firm varies its output, average cost may vary for two distinct reasons. First, the prices of its inputs may change. Second, the physical relation between its inputs and outputs may change. To separate these two effects we assume for the moment that all input prices remain constant.

Now look at the $LRAC$ curve shown in Figure 8.4. This curve is often described as U-shaped, although empirical studies suggest it is often 'saucer-shaped'.

Decreasing costs   Over the range of output from zero to q_m, the firm has falling long-run average costs: an expansion of output permits a reduction of costs per unit of output. Technologies with this property are said to exhibit **economies of scale.** (Of course, when output is increased, such economies of scale will be realized only after enough time has elapsed to allow changes to be made in all factor inputs.) Recall that the prices of factors are assumed to be constant for the moment. Thus the decline in long-run average cost must occur because output is increasing *more than* in proportion to inputs as the scale of the firm's production expands. Over this range of output, the decreasing-cost firm is often said to enjoy long-run **increasing returns.** This is an extremely important phenomenon, and its sources are discussed in the next section. Ouput q_m is called the **minimum efficient scale,** defined as the lowest level of output at which all scale economies are exploited.

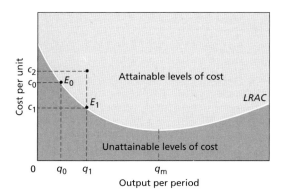

Figure 8.4 A long-run average cost curve
The long-run average cost (*LRAC*) curve is the boundary between attainable and unattainable levels of cost. Since the lowest attainable cost of producing q_0 is c_0 per unit, the point E_0 is on the *LRAC* curve. Suppose a firm producing at E_0 desires to increase output to q_1. In the short run it will not be able to vary all factors, and thus unit costs above c_1, say c_2, must be accepted. In the long run a plant that is the optimal size for producing output q_1 can be built and costs of c_1 can be attained. At output q_m the firm attains its lowest possible per-unit cost of production for the given technology and factor prices.

Increasing costs Over the range of outputs greater than q_m, the firm encounters rising long-run unit costs. An expansion in production, even after sufficient time has elapsed for all adjustments to be made, will then be accompanied by a rise in average costs per unit of output. Since input prices are still assumed to be constant, the firm's output must be increasing *less than* in proportion to the increase in inputs. When this happens, the increasing-cost firm is said to encounter long-run **decreasing returns.** Decreasing returns imply that the firm suffers some diseconomy of scale. As its scale of operations increases, diseconomies are encountered that increase its per-unit cost of production.

These diseconomies may be associated with the difficulties of managing and controlling an enterprise as its size increases. For example, planning problems do not necessarily vary in direct proportion to size. At first there may be scale economies as the firm grows, but sooner or later planning and co-ordination problems may multiply more than in proportion to the growth in size. If so, management costs per unit of output will rise. Another source of scale diseconomies concerns the possible alienation of the labour force as firm size increases. Also, providing appropriate supervision becomes difficult as more and more tiers of supervisors and middle managers come between the person at the top and the workers on the shop floor. Control of middle-range managers may also become more difficult. As the firm becomes larger, managers may begin to pursue their own goals rather than devote all of

their efforts to making profits for the firm. (This is the principal–agent problem, which is discussed in detail in Chapter 13.)

Constant costs In Figure 8.4 the firm's long-run average cost falls until output reaches q_m and rises thereafter. Another possibility should be noted. The firm's *LRAC* curve might have a flat portion over a range of output around q_m. With such a flat portion, the firm would be encountering constant costs over the relevant range of output. This means that the firm's long-run average costs per unit of output do not change as its output changes. Because factor prices are assumed to be fixed, the firm's output must be increasing *exactly in proportion to* the increase in inputs. A firm in this situation is said to be encountering **constant returns.**

Sources of increasing returns

Whenever a firm finds that it can increase its output per unit of input, that firm is enjoying economies of large-scale production. These economies are important, and wherever they exist they encourage large plants and/or large firms. Three important sources of scale economies are geometrical relations, one-time costs, and the technology of large-scale production.

Geometrical relations One important source of scale economies lies in the geometry of our three-dimensional world. To illustrate how geometry matters, consider a firm that wishes to store liquid. The firm is interested in the *volume* of storage space. However, the amount of material required to build the container is related to the *area* of its surface. When the size of a container is increased, the storage capacity, which is determined by its volume, increases faster than its surface area.[13] This is a genuine case of increasing returns—the output, in terms of storage capacity, increases proportionally more than the increase in the costs of the required construction materials. Another of the many other similar effects concerns smelters. The heat loss is proportional to the smelter surface area, while the amount of ore smelted depends on its volume. Thus, there is a scale economy in heat needed per tonne of ore smelted as smelters get larger. In practice, however, the size of the smelter is limited by the need to deliver a smooth flow of air to all of the molten ore. When improved forced-air pumps were invented in the nineteenth century, smelters could be built larger and unit costs fell.

---

[13] For example, consider a cubic container with metal sides, bottom, and lid, all of which measure 1 metre by 1 metre. To build this container, $6m^2$ of metal is required (six sides, each $1m^2$), and it will hold 1 cubic metre of gas or liquid. Now increase all of the lengths of each of the container's sides to 2m. Now $24m^2$ of metal is required (six sides, each $4m^2$), and the container will hold $8m^3$ of gas or liquid ($2m \times 2m \times 2m$). So increasing the amount of metal in the container's walls fourfold has the effect of increasing its capacity eightfold.

One-time costs A second source of increasing returns consists of inputs that do not have to be increased as the output of a product is increased, even in the long run. For example, the research and development (R&D) costs to design a new generation of aeroplanes, or a more powerful computer, have to be incurred only once for each product. Hence they are independent of the scale at which the product is subsequently produced. Even if the product's *production costs* increase in proportion to output in the long run, average total costs, including *product development costs*, will fall as the scale of output rises. The influence of such once-and-for-all costs is that, other things being equal, they cause average total costs to be falling over the entire range of output.[14] (The significance of such once-and-for-all costs is further discussed in Chapter 11.)

The technology of large-scale production A third and very important source lies in technology. Large-scale production can use more specialized and highly efficient machinery than smaller-scale production. It can also lead to more specialization of human tasks, with a resulting increase in human efficiency.

Even the most casual observation of the differences in production techniques used in large and small plants will show that larger plants use greater specialization. An example, drawn from the electricity industry, is discussed in Box 8.5.

These differences arise because large, specialized equipment is useful only when the volume of output that the firm can sell justifies employment of that equipment. For example, assembly-line techniques, body-stamping machinery, and multiple-boring engine block machines in car production are economically efficient only when individual operations are repeated thousands of times. Use of elaborate harvesting equipment (which combines many individual tasks that would otherwise be done by hand and by tractor) provides the least-cost method of production on a big farm but not on a few acres.

Typically, as the level of planned output increases, capital is substituted for labour and complex machines are substituted for simpler ones. Robotics is a contemporary

---

[14] This phenomenon is popularly referred to as 'spreading one's overhead'. It is similar to what happens in the short run when average fixed costs fall with output. The difference is that fixed short-run production costs are variable long-run production costs. If the firm increases its scale of output for some product, it will incur more capital costs in the long run as a larger plant is built. However, its costs of developing that product are not affected.

Box 8.5 Economies of scale in the electricity industry

In the 1940s, 1950s, and 1960s major economies of scale in electricity generation in the UK came from the use of larger and larger generators: from 30 MW (= 30,000 kilowatt) generating sets in 1948 to 100 MW sets in 1956, 200 MW sets in 1959, and 500 MW sets in 1966.

Since the 1970s there has been little increase in the size of generators, with the largest now being installed at 660 MW. Furthermore, total generating capacity has been declining since 1980. The cause is a decline in the demand for energy, because of the decline of British manufacturing and the superior energy efficiency of newer technologies such as chips and fibre optics.

In spite of the absence of further economies in the size of generators after 1970, and in spite of the decline in overall capacity after 1980, methods of gaining scale economies were still being found. The new method was to reduce the *number* of power stations, each station having several generators. As a result, the average capacity of each power station has continued to rise significantly, bringing a different type of economy of scale. The number of power stations fell from 233 in 1965 to 174 in 1978 to 78 in 1987. The average capacity of these stations rose from 147 MW in 1965 to 324 MW in 1974 to 671 MW in 1987.

Costs were also reduced by exploring economies of scale in bulk transmission of electricity. The 'Supergrid' of 400 kV (= 400,000 volt) transmission lines which was built in the 1960s replaced three lines operating at 275 kV and eighteen lines operating at 132 kV, without a corresponding increase in costs.

Economies of scale have allowed the industry to cope with rising *real* prices of its main inputs—coal and labour—without raising the real price of electricity. During the 1960s the real price of oil, the major alternative fuel, was falling owing to the increasing exploitation of economies of scale in oil tankers delivering crude oil from the Middle East. In response the UK electricity industry was able to reduce the real price of electricity, which is one of the reasons why electricity was adopted more and more widely in preference to other fuels.

Privatization did not change the cost structure of the industry immediately, partly because producers were locked into three-year contracts to buy coal. After this period shifts were made to cheaper, imported coal and, where new capacity was required, to the adoption of the cheaper technology of combined cycle gas turbines (CCGT). There are mild economies of scale with current technology as size increases from 240 MW to 480 MW, but bigger generators do not deliver significant further scale economies.

Strictly speaking, scale economies refer to the effects of increasing output *along* a negatively sloped *LRAS* curve as a result of rising output within the confines of known technology, while changes in technological knowledge *shift* the *LRAS* curve. As this example shows, the two forces usually become mixed in most real-world applications. The rise in demand for electricity in the three decades of the 1950s, 1960s, and 1970s required an increase in output. The rise in output made the use of higher-capacity equipment possible and thus provided an incentive for the development of such equipment. No fundamental new knowledge was required, but the details of the technology of larger generators had to be developed through research rather than being taken from already existing blueprints.

Competitive forces continue to put pressure on producers to reduce costs. The main pressures now are on cutting costs through productivity gains rather than exploiting further economies of even-larger-scale production of individual plants and distribution systems.

Box 8.6 The revolution in flexible manufacturing

Production techniques have recently been revolutionized by the introduction, in many industries and in many countries, of *flexible manufacturing*, or, as it is sometimes called, *lean production techniques*.* This is the most fundamental change to occur since Henry Ford brought mass production to full development early in the twentieth century.

Mass-production methods are based on specialization and division of labour. They use skilled personnel to design products and production methods, and then the employment of relatively unskilled labour to produce standardized parts and to assemble them using highly specialized, single-purpose machines. The result is a standardized product, made in a fairly small number of variants and produced at low cost with moderate quality. The work is repetitive, and workers are regarded as variable costs to be laid off or taken on as the desired rate of production varies.

Flexible manufacturing techniques, which were pioneered by the Japanese car industry, combined the flexibility and high quality standards of craft production with the low cost of mass-production techniques. They are lean because they use fewer of all inputs, including time, labour, capital, and inventories, compared with either of the other techniques. They are flexible because the costs of switching from one product line to another are minimized. Workers are organized as teams. Each worker is able to do all the tasks assigned to the team, using equipment that is less highly specialized than that used in mass-production techniques. This emphasizes individuality and initiative rather than a mind-numbing repetition of one unskilled operation. It also helps workers to identify places where improvements can be made and encourages them to follow up on these.

In mass-production plants stopping an assembly line to correct a problem at one point stops work at all points. So stopping the line is regarded as a serious matter, and keeping the assembly line running is the sole responsibility of a senior line manager. To reduce stoppages, large stocks of each part are held, and defective parts are discarded. Faults in assembly are left to be corrected until after the product has been assembled—often an expensive procedure. Stoppages are none the less frequent to correct materials-supply and co-ordination problems.

In flexible manufacturing every worker has the ability to stop production whenever a fault is discovered. Parts are delivered by the suppliers to the work stations 'just in time'. Defective parts are put aside for their source to be identified. When lean methods are first introduced, stoppages are frequent as problems are identified and investigated. As the sources are found and removed, work stoppages diminish, and the typical mature lean production line—where any worker can stop the line—stops much less frequently than the typical mass-production assembly line, where only the line foreman can press the stop button.

Mass-production firms try to reduce the costs of product design using specialist designers. This creates problems both in co-ordinating the work of various designers and in getting good feedback from parts producers and assembly-line workers. The product design must be worked out in detail before the machine makers begin to design the specialized equipment needed to do the work.

Lean producers use design teams that work closely with production engineers and parts producers. As the new product begins to take shape, the tool designers can begin to work on their outline plans; as the product design becomes better specified, the design of the tools can likewise be more fully developed.

Although flexible manufacturing still has scale economies—unit costs fall as the volume of output increases—its main effect is to shift the whole long-run cost curve dramatically downward. These methods are also effective in the very long run in developing successful new products. Japanese motor car manufacturers using these methods have been able to achieve unit costs of production below those of mass-production-based North American and European car factories that have twice their volume of output. They have also been able to lead in international competition to design new products efficiently and rapidly.

* The material in this box is adapted from J. P. Womack, D. T. Jones, and D. Roos, *The Machine That Changed the World* (New York: Maxwell Macmillan, 1990).

example. Electronic devices can handle huge numbers of operations quickly, but unless the level of production requires such a large volume of operations, robotics or other forms of automation will not provide the least-cost method of production.

Until very recently large-scale production meant mass production, sometimes referred to as 'Fordism', a system that was introduced early in the twentieth century. It was based on a very detailed division of jobs, often on a production line, in which each person did one repetitive task in co-operation with such very specialized machinery (called dedicated machinery). In this technology size was very important. Very high rates of output were required in order to reap all the scale economies available to this type of production.

In recent decades production technology has been revolutionized by what is called *flexible manufacturing*. This is a much less specialized type of production in which workers do many tasks in co-operation with machinery

that is also less specialized. One of its most important characteristics is its ability to achieve maximum efficiency with low average costs at much smaller rates of output than are required for mass-production techniques. This is further discussed in Box 8.6.

The relationship between long-run and short-run costs

The short-run cost curves and the long-run cost curves are all derived from the same production function. Each curve assumes given prices for all factor inputs. In the long run all factors can be varied; in the short run some must remain fixed. The long-run average cost (*LRAC*) curve shows the lowest cost of producing any output when all factors are variable. Each short-run average total cost (*SRATC*) curve shows the lowest cost of producing any output when one or more factors are held constant at some specific level.

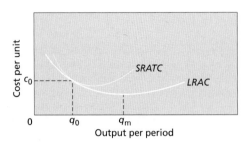

Figure 8.5 Long-run average cost and short-run average total cost curves

The short-run average total cost (*SRATC*) curve is tangent to the long-run average cost (*LRAC*) curve at the output for which the quantity of the fixed factors is optimal. The curves *SRATC* and *LRAC* coincide at output q_0, where the fixed plant is optimal for that level of output. For all other outputs there is too little or too much plant and equipment, and *SRATC* lies above *LRAC*. If some output other than q_0 is to be sustained, costs can be reduced to the level of the long-run curve when sufficient time has elapsed to adjust the size of the firm's fixed capital.

The output q_m is the lowest point on the firm's long-run average cost curve. It is called the firm's *minimum efficient scale* (MES), and it is the output at which long-run costs are minimized.

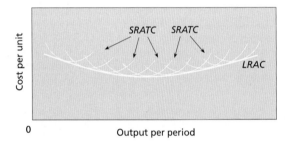

Figure 8.6 The envelope long-run average cost curve

For every point on the long-run average cost (*LRAC*) curve there is an associated short-run average total cost (*SRATC*) curve tangent to that point. Each short-run curve shows how costs vary if output varies, with the fixed factor held constant at the level that is optimal for the output at the point of tangency. As a result, each *SRATC* curve touches the *LRAC* curve at one point and lies above it at all other points. This makes the *LRAC* curve the envelope of the *SRATC* curves.

No short-run cost curve can fall below the long-run curve, because the *LRAC* curve represents the lowest attainable cost for each possible output. As the level of output is changed, a different-sized plant is normally required to achieve the lowest attainable cost. This is shown in Figure 8.5, where the *SRATC* curve lies above the *LRAC* curve at all outputs except q_0.

As we observed earlier in this chapter, a short-run cost curve such as the *SRATC* curve shown in Figure 8.5 is one of many such curves. Each curve shows how costs vary as output is varied from a base output, holding the fixed factor at the quantity most appropriate to that output. Figure 8.6 shows a family of short-run average total cost curves along with a single long-run average cost curve. The long-run average cost curve is sometimes called an **envelope** because it encloses a series of short-run average total cost curves by being tangent to them. Each *SRATC* curve *is tangent to* the long-run average cost curve at the level of output for which the quantity of the fixed factor is optimal, and lies above it for all other levels of output.

Shifts in cost curves

The cost curves derived so far show how cost varies with output, given constant factor prices and fixed technology. Changes in factor prices will cause the entire family of short-run and long-run average cost curves to shift. If a firm has to pay more for any factor that it uses, the cost of producing each level of output will rise; if the firm has to pay less for any factor that it uses, the cost of producing each level of output will fall.

A rise in factor prices shifts the family of short-run and long-run average cost curves upward. A fall in factor prices, or a technological advance, shifts the entire family of average cost curves downward.

Although factor prices usually change gradually, sometimes they change suddenly and drastically. For example, in the mid-1980s oil prices fell dramatically. As a result there was a fall in the cost curves of all firms that used oil and oil-related products as inputs.

The very long run: endogenous technical change

In the long run profit-maximizing firms do the best they can to produce known products with the techniques and the resources currently available. This means being *on*, rather than above, their long-run cost curves. In the very long run, production techniques change. This means that the production function itself alters so that the same inputs produce more output. This in turn causes long-run cost curves to shift.

The decrease in costs that can be achieved by choosing from among the available factors of production, known techniques, and alternative levels of output is necessarily limited. In contrast, improvements by invention and innovation are potentially limitless. Hence sustained growth in living standards is critically linked to *technological change*. This was once thought to be mainly a random process, brought about by inventions made by crackpots and eccentric scientists working in garages and scientific laboratories. Recent research has shown that this is an incorrect view.

Changes in technology are often *endogenous responses* to changing economic signals; that is, they result from responses by firms to the same things that induce the substitution of one factor for another within the confines of a given technology.[15]

In our discussion of long-run demand curves in Chapter 3 we looked at just such technological changes in response to rising relative prices when we spoke of the development of smaller, more fuel-efficient cars in the wake of rising petrol prices. Similarly, much of the move to substitute capital for labour in manufacturing, transportation, communications, mining, and agriculture in response to rising wage rates has taken the form of inventing new labour-saving methods of production.

Most microeconomic theory analyses only the short- and long-run responses of the firm to various changes. In the short run, firms can change price and output within the confines of fixed plant and equipment. In the long run,

they can change all inputs but within the confines of fixed technology. Such an analysis is incomplete whenever technological change is an endogenous response to economic signals. Consider, for example, a rise in the price of an important input in one country. In the short run, firms that use the input will cut back production in response to the rise in costs. In the long run, they will substitute other inputs for the one whose price has risen. When all adjustments have been made, however, firms still find themselves at a cost disadvantage compared with competitors in other countries who have not suffered the rise in the price of their inputs. In the very long run, the domestic firms may engage in research and development designed to further reduce the use of the newly expensive inputs. If the firms succeed, they may develop processes that allow them to lower costs below those of their competitors in other countries who did not suffer the increased input prices and so did not have the same incentive to innovate.

Modern research into induced technological development has documented several such instances. As a result,

---

[15] Many scholars on both sides of the Atlantic have been influential in establishing this key result. One of the most important books on this issue is N. Rosenberg, *Inside the Black Box: Technology and Economics* (Cambridge University Press, 1982).

Box 8.7 Endogenous materials design: a new industrial revolution?

A new industrial revolution has been in progress since the mid-1980s. It is the 'Materials Revolution'. Throughout history, an important source of technological advancement has been the development of new materials. Indeed, we label stages of history by the materials that were used—the stone age, the bronze age, and the iron age. Many key twentieth-century advances in manufacturing would not have been possible without materials such as steel and hydrocarbons. Today, important technical progress is built upon polymers, composites, and ceramics.

Previous materials advances were usually the outcome of a process of trial and error—Edison allegedly tried many thousands of different materials and designs before he 'invented' the light bulb. Today, however, scientists are able to use knowledge of the microstructure of matter, combined with advanced computing power, to design the materials to be used in production simultaneously with the engineering of production itself. This is having profound effects on the design of most new products and processes.

An example is found in a long-term co-operative venture between Audi and Alcoa to develop an aluminium-intensive car:

The result has been a quantum leap in weight reduction technology and automotive structural manufacturing. This revolution is embodied in the development of the aluminium space frame (ASF) and in the ability to integrate the design of the material, the product, and the manufacturing process. The ASF concept breaks away from design and manufacturing mindsets and requirements associated with steel monocoque car body structures. Moreover, the aluminium-

intensive vehicle introduced by Audi in 1994 represents a significant first step towards the development of a 'green' car which is cost effective, high-performance, low emission and recyclable. Lower weight facilitates greater fuel efficiency and the reduction of carbon dioxide emissions while at the same time increasing stiffness and passenger safety. . . . Despite a minimum 40% reduction in weight in the spaceframe, it is an extremely strong structure and provides exceptional safety for the car occupants. Aluminium absorbs more energy, on a weight to weight basis, than steel. The aluminium body structure absorbs more energy in a collision than today's steel monocoque body structures. Audi claims that the standard of safety and crashworthiness offered by the ASF has not been seen before in conventional cars. *

Another example of new materials technology can be found in sports equipment. When Björn Borg won the Wimbledon tennis tournament five times in the late 1970s he played with a wooden racket. Jimmy Connors won it in 1982 playing with an aluminium alloy racket. Pete Sampras has been the men's champion five times since 1993 playing with a graphite composite racket, a product of the materials revolution.

---

* Lakis C. Kaounides, 'New materials and simultaneous engineering in the car industry: the Alcoa–Audi alliance in lightweight aluminium car body structures', ch. 1 of *Manufacturing Technology* (London: Institute of Mechanical Engineers, July 1996).

the response of firms to changes in such economic signals as output prices and input costs must be studied in three steps:

1. the short-run response that consists of altering the variable factor;

2. the long-run response that consists of adjusting *all* factors; and

3. the research and development response in which firms seek to innovate their way out of difficulties caused by reductions in their product prices and/or increases in their input prices.

Studies that ignore the third set of responses ignore what are often the most important effects, once several years have elapsed.

In this context it is interesting to note that flexible manufacturing (see Box 8.6 on page 131), which is revolutionizing production in most industrialized countries, was first developed by the Japanese car producers in response to a scale disadvantage. They were unable to reach the efficient scale of production when they were selling only in their small, protected, home market. In response, they innovated their way out of these difficulties. They developed techniques that allowed them to produce a superior product at lower prices than did their American and European competitors and so turned a long-run disadvantage into a very-long-run advantage.

Box 8.7 deals with another revolutionary change, the ability of modern science to design new materials that are appropriate for newly designed products. This ability to create new materials on demand links technological change even more closely to economic incentives than it has been in the past.

Summary

Firms as agents of production

■ Production is organized either by private sector firms, which take four main forms—sole traders, ordinary partnerships, limited partnerships, and joint-stock companies—or by state-owned enterprises called public corporations.

■ Modern firms finance themselves by selling shares, reinvesting their profits, or borrowing from lenders such as banks.

■ Firms are in business to make profits, which they define as the difference between what they earn by selling their output and what it costs them to produce that output. This is the return to owners' capital.

■ The boundaries of firms are determined by the relation between the costs of making transactions in the market and the costs of producing what is required within the firm.

■ Neoclassical economic theory assumes that all firms make consistent decisions designed to maximize their profits.

Production, costs, and profits

■ The production function relates inputs of factor services to outputs.

■ In addition to what firms count as their costs, economists include the imputed opportunity costs of owners' capital. This includes the pure return, what could be earned on a riskless investment, and a risk premium, what could be earned over the pure return on an equally risky investment. Pure or economic profits are the difference between revenues and all these costs.

■ Pure profits play a key role in resource allocation. Positive pure profits attract resources into an industry; negative pure profits induce resources to move elsewhere.

Costs in the short run

■ Short-run variations in output are subject to the law of diminishing returns: equal increments of the variable input sooner or later produce smaller and smaller additions to total output and, eventually, a reduction in average output per unit of variable input.

■ Short-run average and marginal cost curves are U-shaped, the rising portion reflecting diminishing average and marginal returns. The marginal cost curve intersects the average cost curve at the latter's minimum point, which is called the firm's capacity output.

■ There is a family of short-run average and marginal cost curves, one for each amount of the fixed factor.

Costs in the long run

■ In the long run, the firm will adjust all factor inputs to minimize the cost of producing any given level of output. This requires that the ratio of a factor's marginal product to its price be the same for all factors.

■ The principle of substitution states that when relative factor prices change, firms will substitute relatively cheaper factors for relatively more expensive ones.

■ Long-run cost curves are often assumed to be U-shaped, indicating decreasing average costs (increasing returns to scale) followed by increasing average costs (decreasing returns to scale). The long-run cost curve may be thought of as the envelope of the family of short-run cost curves, all of which shift when factor prices shift.

The very long run

■ In the very long run, innovations introduce new methods

of production that alter the production function. These innovations often occur as response to changes in economic incentives such as variations in the prices of inputs and outputs. They cause cost curves to shift downwards.

Topics for review

- Forms of business organization
- Methods of financing modern firms
- Profit maximization
- Imputed costs
- Alternative definitions of profits
- The production function
- The short, long, and very long runs
- The law of diminishing returns
- Short-run average, marginal, fixed, and total costs
- Conditions for long-run cost minimization
- The principle of substitution
- The long-run envelope cost curve
- Constant, increasing, and decreasing long-run costs
- Invention and innovation in the very long run

Questions for discussion

1 Explain why the existence of economic profit is necessary to attract entrants into an industry but the existence of what firms call profits is not sufficient to do so.

2 The shapes of which cost curves are explained by the law of diminishing returns. To what 'runs' (short, long, and very long) does it not apply? Why?

3 Here are data for total production costs of a manufacturing firm at various levels of output:

Output (units)	Total cost (£)
0	1,000
20	1,200
40	1,300
60	1,380
100	1,600
200	2,300
300	3,200
400	4,300
500	5,650
1,000	13,650

(a) Calculate average variable cost (AVC), average total cost (ATC), and average fixed cost (AFC). (Hint: fixed costs have to be incurred even when output is zero and do not vary with the production level in the short run.) (b) Calculate marginal or incremental cost over each production range for which data are given. (c) If this firm can sell as much as it wants at a price of £11, what is its profit-maximizing output? (d) How much profit is made? (e) At output levels shown in the table immediately on either side of the profit-maximizing output, what is the level of profit.

4 The long-run average cost curve can be thought of as consisting of a series of points, one taken from each of a number of short-run average total cost curves. Explain in what sense any point on the long-run average cost curve is also on some short-run average total cost curve. What is the interpretation of a move from one point on a long-run average cost curve to another point on the same curve? Contrast this with a movement along a short-run average total cost curve.

5 In *The Competitive Advantage of Nations*, Professor Michael Porter of Harvard University reported, 'Faced with high relative labour cost . . . American consumer electronics firms moved to locate labour-intensive activities in . . . Asian countries, leaving the product and production process essentially the same . . . Japanese rivals . . . set out instead to eliminate labour through automation. Doing so involved reducing the number of components which further lowered cost and improved quantity. Japanese firms were soon building assembly plants in the United States, the place American firms had sought to avoid.' Discuss these reactions in terms of changes over the long run and the very long run.

Appendix Isoquants: an alternative analysis of the firm's long-run input decisions

The long-run choices of factor proportions that we have just studied can be shown graphically by using a new concept. This concept, which is called an *isoquant*, is defined below.

A single isoquant

Table 8A.1 gives a hypothetical illustration of those combina-tions of two inputs (labour and capital) that will produce a given quantity of output. The data from Table 8A.1 are plotted in Fig-ure 8A.1. A smooth curve is drawn through the points to indicate that there are additional ways, not listed in the table, of produc-ing 6 units. The curve is called an **isoquant.** It shows the set of technologically efficient possibilities for producing a given level of output—here it is 6 units. The isoquant in this example is

Table 8A.1   Alternative methods of producing six units of output: points on an isoquant

Method	K	L	ΔK	ΔL	Rate of substitution $\Delta K/\Delta L$
a	18	2			
b	12	3	−6	1	−6.0
c	9	4	−3	1	−3.0
d	6	6	−3	2	−1.5
e	4	9	−2	3	−0.67
f	3	12	−1	3	−0.33
g	2	18	−1	6	−0.17

An isoquant describes the firm's alternative methods for producing a given output. The table lists some of the methods indicated by a production function as being available to produce six units of output. The first combination uses a great deal of capital (K) and very little labour (L). As we move down the table, labour is substituted for capital in such a way as to keep output constant. Finally, at the bottom, most of the capital has been replaced by labour. The rate of substitution between the two factors is calculated in the last three columns of the table. Note that as we move down the table, the absolute value of the rate of substitution declines.

Figure 8A.1   An isoquant for output of six units

Isoquants are negatively sloped and convex. The lettered points are plotted from the data in Table 8A.1. The convex shape of the isoquant reflects a diminishing marginal rate of substitution; moving along the isoquant to the right, its slope becomes flatter. Starting from point *a*, which uses relatively little labour and much capital, and moving to point *b*, 1 additional unit of labour can substitute for 6 units of capital (while holding production constant); but from *b* to *c*, 1 unit of labour substitutes for only 3 units of capital; and so on.

analogous to an indifference curve that shows all combinations of commodities that yield a given utility. It is derived from the production function in equation (2) of the text, by altering L and K in such a way as to keep q constant.

As we move from one point on an isoquant to another, we are *substituting one factor for another* while holding output constant. The **marginal rate of substitution** (*MRS*) measures the rate at which one factor is substituted for another with output held constant. Graphically, this is measured by the absolute value of the slope of the isoquant at a particular point. The table shows the calculation of some rates of substitution between various points of the isoquant.[16]

Let us now see how the marginal rate of substitution is related to the marginal products of the factors of production. An example will illustrate this relation. Assume that, at the present level of inputs of labour and capital, the marginal product of a unit of labour is 2 units of output while the marginal product of capital is 1 unit of output. If the firm reduces its use of capital and increases its use of labour so as to keep output constant, it needs to add only 0.5 units of labour for 1 unit of capital given up. If, at another point on the isoquant with more labour and less capital, the marginal products are 2 for capital and 1 for labour, then the firm will have to add 2 units of labour for every unit of capital it gives up. The general proposition this example illustrates is:

The magnitude of the marginal rate of substitution between two factors of production is equal to the ratios of their marginal products.

Isoquants satisfy two important conditions: they are negatively sloped, and they are convex viewed from the origin. What is the meaning of each of these conditions?

The negative slope indicates that each factor of production has a positive marginal product. If the input of one factor is reduced and that of the other is held constant, output must fall. Thus, if one input is reduced, production can be held constant only if the other input is increased. This gives the marginal rate of substitution a negative value: decreases in one factor must be balanced by increases in the other factor if output is to be held constant.

Now consider what happens as the firm moves along the isoquant in Figure 8A.1 downwards and to the right. This movement means that labour is being added and capital reduced so as to keep output constant. If capital is cut by successive increments of exactly one unit, how much labour must be added each time? The key to the answer is that both factors are assumed to be subject to the law of diminishing returns. Thus, the gain in output associated with each additional unit of labour added is *diminishing*, while the loss of output associated with each additional unit of capital forgone is *increasing*. It therefore takes ever larger increases in labour to offset equal reductions in capital in order to hold production constant. This implies that the isoquant is convex viewed from the origin.

An isoquant map

The isoquant drawn in Figure 8A.1 referred to 6 units of output. There is another isoquant for 7 units, and for every other output. Each isoquant refers to a specific output; it connects alternative combinations of factors that are technologically efficient methods of achieving that output. If we plot a representative set of these isoquants on a single graph, we obtain an **isoquant map**. Such a map is shown in Figure 8A.2. The higher the level of output along a particular isoquant, the further away from the origin it will be.

---

[16] The table shows the incremental rate. The true marginal rate is the partial derivative of K with respect to L, holding output constant.

Figure 8A.2 An isoquant map

An isoquant map shows a set of isoquants, one for each level of output. The figure shows four isoquants drawn from the production function and corresponding to 4, 6, 8, and 10 units of production. The higher the level of output, the further is the isoquant from the origin.

Isoquants and the conditions for cost minimization

Finding the efficient way of producing any output requires finding the least-cost factor combination. To do this when both factors are variable, factor prices need to be known. Suppose, to continue the example, that capital is priced at £4 per unit and labour at £1. We can now draw what are called **isocost lines,** each one of which shows all of the combinations of the two factors that can be purchased for a given outlay. Four such lines are shown in

Figure 8A.3 Isocost lines

An isocost line shows alternative factor combinations that can be purchased for a given outlay. The graph shows the four isocost lines that result when labour costs £1 a unit and capital £4 a unit and expenditure is held constant at £12, £24, £36, and £48 respectively. The line labelled $TC = £12$ represents all combinations of the two factors that the firm could buy for £12. Point a represents 2 units of K and 4 units of L.

Figure 8A.3. For given factor prices, the parallel isocost lines reflect alternative levels of expenditure on factors. The higher the expenditure, the further from the origin is the isocost line. Note that the isocost line is similar to the budget line introduced in Chapter 7, which shows all the combinations of two goods that can be bought with a given income.

In Figure 8A.4 the isoquant and isocost maps are brought together. A careful study of that figure reveals the following important results. If the isoquant cuts the isocost line, it is possible to move along the isoquant and reach a lower level of cost. Where the isoquant is tangent to the isocost line, however, a movement in either direction along the isoquant is a movement to a higher level of cost. Thus:

The least-cost method of producing any given output is shown graphically by the point of tangency between the relevant isoquant and an isocost line.

Notice that point A in Figure 8A.4 indicates not only the lowest level of cost for 6 units of output but also the highest output for £24 of cost. Thus we find the same solution if we set out either to minimize the cost of producing a given output or to maximize the output that can be produced for a given cost. One problem is said to be a *dual* of the other.

The absolute value of the slope of the isocost line is given by the ratio of the prices of the two factors of production. The slope of

Figure 8A.4 The determination of the least-cost method of output

Least-cost methods are represented by points of tangency, such as A, between isoquant and isocost lines. The isoquant map of Figure 8A.2 and the isocost map of Figure 8A.3 are brought together here. Consider point A. It is on the 6-unit isoquant and the £24 isocost line. Thus it is possible to achieve an output of 6 units for a total cost of £24. There are, however, other ways to achieve this output. For example, at point B 6 units are produced, but at a total cost of £48.

Now consider moving along the isocost line, say from point A to point C. Although costs are held constant, output falls from 6 to 4 units.

Point A thus shows both the least-cost method of producing 6 units of output and the maximum output that can be produced for an outlay of £24. Moving along the isoquant from point A in either direction clearly increases cost.

the isoquant is given by the ratio of their marginal products. (Both statements refer to absolute values.) When the firm reaches its least-cost position, it has equated the price ratio (which is given to it by the market prices) with the ratio of marginal products (which it can adjust by varying the proportions in which it hires the factors). In symbols

$$\frac{MP_K}{MP_L} = \frac{p_K}{p_L}.$$

This is equation (4) on page 127. We have now derived this result by use of the isoquant analysis of the firm's decisions.

Isoquants and the principle of substitution

Suppose that with technology unchanged—that is, with the isoquant map fixed—the price of one factor changes. Figure 8A.5 shows why the change in price changes the least-cost method of producing a given output. An increase in the price of one factor pivots the isocost line inwards and thus increases the cost of producing any output. It also changes the slope of the isocost line and thus changes the least-cost method of production. Costs at the new least-cost point C are higher than they were before the

price increase, but not as high as if the factor substitution had not occurred. The slope of the isocost line has changed, making it efficient to substitute the now relatively cheaper capital for the relatively more expensive labour.

This result illustrates the principle of substitution.

Changes in relative factor prices will cause a partial replacement of factors that have become relatively more expensive by factors that have become relatively cheaper.

Of course, substitution of capital for labour cannot fully offset the effects of a rise in the cost of labour, as Figure 8A.5(i) shows. This means that if production is to be held constant, higher costs must be accepted—but because of substitution it is not necessary to accept costs as high as would be needed to accompany an unchanged factor proportion.

This leads to the following prediction:

A rise in the price of one factor with all other factor prices constant will (1) shift upwards the cost curves of commodities that use that factor, and (2) lead to a substitution of factors that are now relatively cheaper for the factor whose price has risen.

Both of these predictions were stated in this chapter; they have now been derived formally using the isoquant technique.

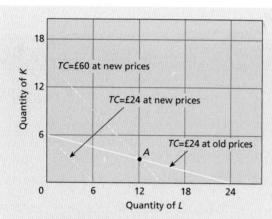

(i) The effect on the isocost line of an increase in the price of labour

(ii) Substitution of capital for labour resulting from an increase in the price of labour

Figure 8A.5 The effects of a change in factor prices on costs and factor proportions

An increase in the price of labour pivots the isocost line inwards and thus increases the cost of producing any given output. It also changes the slope of the isocost line and thus changes the least-cost method of producing any given output. In part (i) the rise in price of L from £1 to £4 a unit (with price of K constant at £4) pivots the $TC = £24$ line inwards. Any output previously produced for £24 will cost more at the new prices if it used any amount of labour. The new cost of producing at A rises from £24 to £60. In part (ii) the steeper isocost line is tangent to the 6-unit isoquant at C, not A. Total cost at C is £48, which is higher than before the price increase but not as high as it would be if the factor substitution had not occurred.

Chapter 9
Perfect Competition

In this chapter we derive the supply curves that we assumed to exist in earlier chapters. We do this for industries that economists call perfectly competitive. In these industries there are so many firms that no one of them can affect the market price simply by varying its own output. After deriving supply curves, we go on to study how an industry reacts to various forces that affect it, including changes in demand and costs.

Since each firm in a perfectly competitive industry takes its price as given, its sales revenue varies in proportion to its output. For example, doubling the amount produced and sold at any constant price doubles sales revenue. In contrast, relating revenue to output proves to be more complicated when firms can influence the prices of their products. This is done in Chapters 10 and 11.

The degree to which firms can influence the price of their product through their own actions is an important determinant of what is called market structure, a concept which we must understand at the outset.

Market structure and firm behaviour

Does Shell compete with BP in the sale of petrol? Does Lloyds Bank compete with Barclays? Does a wheat farmer from Yorkshire compete with a wheat farmer from Somerset? If we use the ordinary meaning of the word 'compete', the answer to the first two questions is plainly yes, and the answer to the third is no.

Shell Oil Company and BP both advertise extensively to persuade car drivers to buy *their* products. Gimmicks such as new mileage-stretching additives and free airmiles are used to tempt drivers to buy one brand of petrol rather than another. Most town centres in England and Wales have not only Barclays and Lloyds Banks but also Midland and National Westminster. They all provide similar services but work hard to attract customers from each other. For example, they all offer incentives for students to open bank accounts in the hope that they will stay with that bank for life.

When we shift our attention to firms producing wheat, however, we see that there is nothing that the Yorkshire farm family can do to affect either the sales or the profits of the Somerset farm family. There would be no point in doing so even if they could, since the sales and profits of the Somerset farm have no effect on those of the Yorkshire farm.

To sort out the questions of who is competing with whom and in what sense, it is useful to distinguish between the behaviour of individual firms and the *type of market* in which they operate.

Market structure and behaviour

The term **market structure** refers to the type of market in which firms operate. Markets are distinguished by such features as the number of firms in the market and the type of product that they produce and sell.

Competitive market structure The competitiveness of the market refers to the extent to which individual firms have power to influence market prices or the terms on which their product is sold. *The less power an individual firm has to influence the market in which it sells its product, the more competitive that market is.*

The extreme form of competitive structure occurs when each firm has zero market power. In such a case many firms sell an identical product and each must accept the price set by the forces of market demand and market supply. The firms can sell as much as they choose at the prevailing market price and have no power to influence that price.

This extreme is called a *perfectly competitive market structure*. (Usually the term 'structure' is dropped and economists speak of a *perfectly competitive market.*) In it, there is no need for individual firms to compete actively with one another, since one firm's ability to sell its product does not depend on the behaviour of any other firm. For example, the Yorkshire and Somerset wheat farmers operate in a perfectly competitive market over which they have no power.

Competitive behaviour In everyday language the term 'competitive behaviour' refers to the degree to which individual firms actively compete with one another. For example, Shell and BP certainly engage in competitive behaviour. Both companies also have some real power over their market. Either firm could raise its prices and still continue to attract customers. Each has the power to decide, within limits set by buyers' tastes and the prices of competing products, the price that people will pay for their petrol and oil. So although they actively compete with each other, they do so in a market that does not have a perfectly competitive structure.

In contrast, the Yorkshire and Somerset wheat farmers do not engage in competitive behaviour, because the only way they can affect their revenues is by changing their outputs of (or their costs of producing) wheat.

Behaviour versus structure The distinction that we have just made explains why firms in perfectly competitive markets (e.g. the Yorkshire and the Somerset wheat producers) do not compete actively with each other, whereas firms that do compete actively with each other (e.g. Shell and BP) do not operate in perfectly competitive markets.

The significance of market structure

The firms that produce a product, or a closely related set of products, constitute an **industry.** The market demand curve for any particular product is the demand curve facing the *industry* that produces that product.

When firms make their production and sales decisions, they need to know what quantity they can sell at various prices. Their concern is, therefore, not with the *market* demand curve for their industry's product, but rather with the demand curve for their own output of that product. If a firm's managers know the demand curve that their own firm faces, they know the sales that their firm can make and the revenue it will earn at each price it could charge. If they also know their costs of producing the product, they can calculate the profits that would be associated with each rate of output. With this information, they can choose the output that maximizes their profits.

The structure of the market in which a firm operates determines the relationship between the market demand curve for the industry's product and the demand curve facing each individual firm in that industry—the firm's own demand curve. To reduce the analysis of market structure to manageable proportions, economists focus on four theoretical market structures that cover most actual cases. These are called perfect competition, monopoly, monopolistic competition, and oligopoly. Perfect competition will be dealt with in the rest of this chapter; the others will be dealt with in the chapters that follow.

Elements of the theory of perfect competition

The perfectly competitive market structure—usually referred to simply as *perfect competition*—applies directly to a number of real-world markets. It also provides an important benchmark for comparison with other market structures.

Assumptions of perfect competition

The theory of **perfect competition** is built on a number of key assumptions relating to the firm and to the industry.

■ **Assumption 1.** All the firms in the industry sell an identical product. Economists describe this by saying that the firms sell a **homogeneous product.**

■ **Assumption 2.** Customers know the nature of the product being sold and the prices charged by each firm.

■ **Assumption 3.** The level of output at which each firm's long-run average total cost reaches a minimum is small relative to the industry's total output.

■ **Assumption 4.** Each firm is a **price-taker.** This means that each firm can alter its rate of production and sales without significantly affecting the market price of its product. This is why a firm operating in a perfectly competitive market has no power to influence that market through its own individual actions. It must passively accept whatever happens to be the ruling price, but it can sell as much as it wants at that price.[1]

---

[1] To emphasize its importance, we identify price-taking as a separate assumption, although strictly speaking it is implied by the first three assumptions.

Box 9.1 Demand under perfect competition: firm and industry

Because all products have negatively sloped market demand curves, *any* increase in the industry's output will cause *some* fall in the market price. The calculations given below show, however, that any conceivable increase that one wheat farm could make in its output has such a negligible effect on the industry's price that the farmer correctly ignores it. (For our purposes the farm is a firm producing wheat.*)

The calculations given below arrive at the elasticity of demand facing one wheat farmer in two steps. Step 1 shows that a 200 per cent variation in the farm's output leads to only a very small percentage variation in the world price. Thus, as step 2 shows, the elasticity of demand for the farm's product is very high: 71,429!

Although the arithmetic used in reaching these measures is unimportant, understanding why the wheat farmer is a price-taker in these circumstances is vital.

Here is the argument that the calculations summarize. The market elasticity of demand for wheat is approximately 0.25. This means that if the quantity of wheat supplied in the world increased by 1 per cent, the price would have to fall by 4 per cent to induce the world's wheat buyers to purchase the extra wheat.

Even huge farms produce a very small fraction of the total world crop. In a recent year, one large farm produced 1,750 metric tonnes of wheat; this was only 0.0035 per cent of the world production of 500 million metric tonnes. Suppose that the farmer decided in one year to produce nothing and in another year managed to produce twice the normal output of 1,750 metric tonnes; this is an extremely large variation in one farm's output. The increase in output from zero to 3,500 metric tonnes represents a 200 per cent variation measured around the farm's average output of 1,750 metric tonnes. Yet the percentage increase in world output is only (3,500/500,000,000) × 100 = 0.0007 per cent. The calculations show that this increase would lead to a decrease in the world price of 0.0028 per cent (2.8p in £1,000) and give the farm's own demand curve an elasticity of over 71,000. This is an enormous elasticity of demand. The farm would have to increase its output by over 71,000 per cent to bring about a 1 per cent

decrease in the price of wheat. It is not surprising, therefore, that the farmer regards the price of wheat as unaffected by any change in output that his one farm could conceivably make. For all intents and purposes, the wheat-producing firm faces a perfectly elastic demand curve for its product; *it is a price-taker.*

We will now proceed with the calculation of the firm's elasticity of demand (η_f) from market elasticity of demand (η_m), given the following figures:

World elasticity of demand (η_m) = 0.25,
World output = 500,000,000 metric tonnes.

A large farm with an average output of 1,750 metric tonnes varies its output between 0 and 3,500 tonnes. The variation of 3,500 tonnes represents 200 per cent of the farm's average output of 1,750 metric tonnes. This causes world output to vary by only (3,500/500,000,000) × 100 = 0.0007 per cent.

Step 1: Find the percentage change in world price. We know that the market elasticity is 0.25. This means that the percentage change in quantity must be one-quarter as big as the percentage change in price. Put the other way around, the percentage change in price must be four times as large as the percentage change in quantity. We have just seen that world quantity changes by 0.0007 per cent, so world price must change by 0.0007 × 4 = 0.0028 per cent.

Step 2: Find the firm's elasticity of demand. This is the percentage change in its *own output* divided by the resulting percentage change in the world price. This is 200 per cent divided by 0.0028 per cent. Clearly, the percentage change in quantity vastly exceeds the percentage change in price, making elasticity very high. Its precise value is 200/0.0028 or 2,000,000/28, which is 71,429.

* Strictly speaking this box applies to wheat farmers outside of the EU. It will apply directly when the EU lowers its support price to the world price or removes it altogether. In the meantime, EU wheat farmers do face a perfectly elastic demand curve because the Commission stands ready to buy all the wheat that is legally produced at its support price.

■ **Assumption 5.** The industry is assumed to be characterized by *freedom of entry and exit*; that is, any new firm is free to enter the industry and start producing if it so wishes, and any existing firm is free to cease production and leave the industry.

The difference between the wheat farmers that we considered earlier and Shell is in *degree of market power*. Each firm that is producing wheat is an insignificant part of the whole market and thus has no power to influence the price of wheat. The oil company does have power to influence the price of petrol because its own sales represent a significant part of the total sales of petrol. Box 9.1 explores further the reasons why each firm producing wheat finds the price of wheat to be beyond its influence.

A perfectly competitive market is one in which individual firms have zero market power.

Demand and revenue for a firm in perfect competition

A major distinction between firms operating in perfectly competitive markets and firms operating in any other type of market is in the shape of the firm's own demand curve.

In perfect competition each firm faces a demand curve that is horizontal, because variations in the firm's output have no noticeable effect on price.

The horizontal (perfectly elastic) demand curve does not mean that the firm could actually sell an infinite amount at the going price. What it does mean is that the variations in output *that it will normally be possible for the firm to make* will leave price virtually unchanged because they have only a negligible effect on the industry's total

(i) Competitive industry's demand curve

(ii) Competitive firm's demand curve

Figure 9.1 The demand curve for a competitive industry and for one firm

The industry's demand curve is negatively sloped; the firm's demand curve is virtually horizontal. Notice the difference in the quantities shown on the horizontal scale in each part of the figure. The competitive industry has output of 200 million tonnes when the price is £3. The individual firm takes that market price as given and considers producing up to, say, 60,000 tonnes. The firm's demand curve in part (ii) is horizontal because any change in output that this one firm could manage would leave price virtually unchanged at £3.

output. Figure 9.1 contrasts the demand curve for the product of a competitive industry with the demand curve facing a single firm in that industry.

To study the revenues that each firm receives from the sales of its products, economists use three related concepts called total, average, and marginal revenue. These are the revenue counterparts of the concepts of total, average, and marginal cost that we considered in Chapter 8.

Total revenue (TR) is the total amount received by the seller from the sale of a product. If q units are sold at a price of p pounds each,[2] $TR = p \cdot q$.

Average revenue (AR) is the amount of revenue per unit sold. This is equal to the price at which the product is sold.

Marginal revenue (MR), sometimes called *incremental revenue*, is the change in a firm's total revenue resulting from a change in its rate of sales by one unit. Whenever output changes by more than one unit, the change in revenue must be divided by the change in output to calculate marginal revenue. For example, if an increase in output of three units per month is accompanied by an increase in revenue of £1,500, the marginal revenue resulting from the sale of *one extra unit* per month is £1,500/3, or £500. At any existing rate of sales, marginal revenue shows the extra revenue the firm would gain by selling one unit more and the revenue it would lose by selling one unit fewer.[3]

To illustrate each of these revenue concepts, consider a firm that is selling an agricultural product in a perfectly competitive market at a price of £3 per tonne. Because every tonne brings in £3, the average revenue per tonne sold is clearly £3. Furthermore, because each *additional* tonne sold brings in £3, the marginal revenue of an extra tonne sold is also £3. Table 9.1 shows calculations of these revenue concepts for a range of outputs between 10 and 13 tonnes.

The important point illustrated in the table is that as long as the market price is unaffected by the amount the firm sells, its marginal revenue is equal to its average revenue (which is *always* equal to the price at which the

Table 9.1 Revenue concepts for a price-taking firm

Quantity sold (units) (q)	Price (p)	TR = p·q	AR = TR/q	MR = ΔTR/Δq
10	£3.00	£30.00	£3.00	
11	3.00	33.00	3.00	£3.00
12	3.00	36.00	3.00	3.00
13	3.00	39.00	3.00	3.00

When price is fixed, average revenue, marginal revenue, and price are all equal to each other. The table shows the calculation of total (*TR*), average (*AR*), and marginal revenue (*MR*) when market price is £3.00 and the firm varies its quantity over the range from 10 to 13 units. Marginal revenue is shown between the lines because it represents the change in total revenue in response to a change in quantity. For example, when sales rise from 11 to 12 units, revenue rises from £33 to £36, making marginal revenue $(36 - 33)/(12 - 11) = £3$ per unit.

output is sold). Graphically, as shown in part (i) of Figure 9.2, average revenue and marginal revenue are the same horizontal line drawn at the level of market price. Because the firm can sell any quantity it chooses at this price, the horizontal line is also the *firm's demand curve*; it shows that any quantity the firm chooses to sell will be associated with this same market price.

If the market price is unaffected by variations in the firm's output, the firm's demand curve, its average revenue

---

[2] Four common ways of indicating that two variables such as p and q are to be multiplied together are $p \cdot q$, $p \times q$, $(p)(q)$ and pq.

[3] Total revenue is a function of output. Because we use numerical examples in the text, we are, strictly speaking, using the concept of *incremental revenues*, $\Delta TR/\Delta q$. Marginal revenue is defined geometrically as the slope of the tangent to the total revenue curve at the point in question. It is defined mathematically as the first derivative of total revenue with respect to output, dTR/dq. For small changes, incremental revenue may be regarded as an approximation of marginal revenue, which we do in the text. The material in Chapter 2 pages 28–31 is once again relevant at this point.

Figure 9.2 Revenue curve for a firm

The demand curve for a perfectly competitive firm is a horizontal straight line. The graph shows the data in Table 9.1. Because price does not change, neither marginal nor average revenue varies with output—both are equal to price. When price is constant, total revenue is a straight line through the origin whose positive slope is the price per unit.

curve, and its marginal revenue curve all coincide in the same horizontal line.

This result can be stated in a slightly different way, which turns out to be important for our later work:

For a firm in perfect competition, price equals marginal revenue.

This means, of course, that total revenue rises in direct proportion to output, as shown in part (ii) of Figure 9.2.

Short-run equilibrium

The next step is to combine information about the firm's costs and revenues to determine the level of output that will maximize its profits. We have just learned how the revenue of each price-taking firm varies with its output. In the short run, the firm has one or more fixed factors such as its plant and machinery, and the only way in which it can change its output is by altering the inputs of the variable factors such as labour. Thus, the firm's short-run cost curves are relevant to its output decision.

Rules for all profit-maximizing firms

We start by stating three rules that apply to *all* profit-maximizing firms, whether or not they operate in perfectly competitive markets.[4]

Should the firm produce at all?

The firm always has the option of producing nothing. If it exercises this option, it will have an operating loss that is equal to its fixed costs. If it decides to produce, it will add the variable cost of production to its costs and the receipts from the sale of its product to its revenue. Therefore, it will be worthwhile for the firm to produce as long as it can find some level of output for which revenue exceeds variable cost. However, if its revenue is less than its variable cost at *every* level of output, the firm will actually lose more by producing than by not producing.

Rule 1. A firm should not produce at all if, for *all* levels of output, the total variable cost of producing that output exceeds the total revenue derived from selling it or, equivalently, if the average variable cost of producing the output exceeds the price at which it can be sold.

The shutdown price The price at which the firm can just cover its average variable cost, and at which it is indifferent between producing and not producing, is often called the **shutdown or break-even price**. At any price below it, the firm will shut down. Such a price is shown in part (i) of Figure 9.6 on page 146. At the price of £2 the firm can just cover its average variable cost by producing q_0 units. Any other output would not produce enough revenue to cover variable costs. For any price below £2 there is no output at which variable costs can be covered. The price of £2 in part (i) is thus the shutdown price.

How much should the firm produce?

If a firm decides that (according to rule 1) production is worth undertaking, it must decide how much to produce.

---

[4] Students who know elementary calculus may like to study the mathematical derivation of these rules given in the appendix to this chapter.

Common sense dictates that, on a unit-by-unit basis, if any unit of production adds more to revenue than it does to cost, producing and selling that unit will increase profits. However, if any unit adds more to cost than it does to revenue, producing and selling that unit will decrease profits. Using the terminology introduced earlier, a unit of production raises profits if the marginal revenue obtained from selling it exceeds the marginal cost of producing it; it lowers profits if the marginal revenue obtained from selling it is less than the marginal cost of producing it.

Now let a firm with some existing rate of output consider increasing or decreasing that output. If a further unit of production will increase the firm's profits, the firm should expand its output. However, if the last unit produced reduced profits, the firm should contract its output. From this it follows that the only time the firm should leave its output unaltered is when the last unit produced adds the same amount to costs as it does to revenue. These results yield the following rule:

Rule 2. Whenever it is worthwhile for the firm to produce some output, it should produce the output at which marginal revenue equals marginal cost.

Maximization not minimization

Figure 9.3 shows that it is possible to fulfil rule 2 and yet have profits at a minimum. Rule 3 is needed to distinguish minimum-profit from maximum-profit positions:

Rule 3. An output where marginal cost equals marginal revenue may be either profit-maximizing or profit-minimizing. Profit maximization requires that marginal cost be less than marginal revenue at slightly lower outputs and that marginal cost exceed marginal revenue at slightly higher outputs.

The geometric statement of this condition is that at the profit-maximizing output, the marginal cost curve should intersect the marginal revenue curve from below. This ensures that *MC* is less than *MR* to the left of the profit-maximizing output and greater than *MR* to the right of the profit-maximizing output.

The optimum output

The above three rules determine the output that will be chosen by any firm that maximizes its profits in the short run. This output is called the firm's **profit-maximizing output,** and sometimes its **optimum output:**

■ The firm's optimum output is zero if total revenue is less than total variable cost at all levels of output; the optimum output is positive if there is any output for which total revenue exceeds total variable cost.

■ When the firm's optimum output is positive, it is where marginal cost equals marginal revenue.

■ If output is reduced slightly from the optimum level,

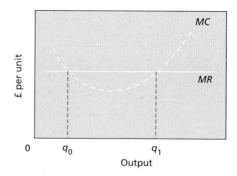

Figure 9.3 Two outputs where marginal cost equals marginal revenue

The equality of marginal cost and marginal revenue is necessary, but not sufficient, for profit maximization. $MC = MR$ at outputs q_0 and q_1. Output q_0 is a minimum-profit position because a change of output in either direction would increase profit: for outputs below q_0 marginal cost exceeds marginal revenue and profits can be increased by *reducing* output, while for outputs above q_0 marginal revenue exceeds marginal cost and profits can be increased by *increasing* output. Output q_1 is a maximum-profit position, since at outputs just below it marginal revenue exceeds marginal cost and profit can be increased by *increasing* output towards q_1; while at outputs just above it marginal cost exceeds marginal revenue and profit can be increased by *reducing* output towards q_1.

marginal cost must be less than marginal revenue; if output is increased slightly from the optimum level, marginal cost must exceed marginal revenue.

Rule 2 applied to price-taking firms

Rule 2 tells us that any profit-maximizing firm that produces at all will produce at the point where marginal cost equals marginal revenue. However, we have already seen that for price-taking firms marginal revenue is the market price. Combining these two results gives an important conclusion:

A firm that is operating in a perfectly competitive market will produce the output that equates its marginal cost of production with the market price of its product (as long as price exceeds average variable cost).

In a perfectly competitive industry the market determines the price at which the firm sells its product. The firm then produces the output that maximizes its profits. We have seen that this is the output for which price equals marginal cost.

When the firm has reached a position where its profits are maximized, it has no incentive to change its output, because it is doing as well as it can do given the market situation. Therefore, unless prices or costs change, the firm will continue to produce that output. The firm is in *short-run equilibrium*, as illustrated in Figure 9.4. (The long run is considered later in this chapter.)

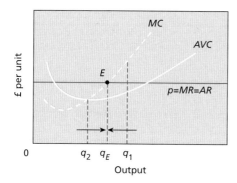

Figure 9.4 The short-run equilibrium of a firm in perfect competition
The firm chooses the output for which $p = MC$ above the level of AVC. When price equals marginal cost, as at output q_E, the firm loses profits if it either increases or decreases its output. At any point left of q_E, say q_2, price is greater than the marginal cost, and it pays to increase output (as indicated by the left-hand arrow). At any point to the right of q_E, say q_1, price is less than the marginal cost, and it pays to reduce output (as indicated by the right-hand arrow).

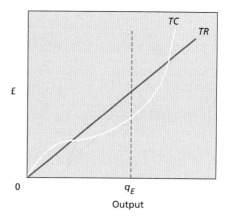

Figure 9.5 Total cost and revenue curves
The firm chooses the output for which the gap between the total revenue and the total cost curves is the largest. At each output the vertical distance between the TR and TC curves shows by how much total revenue exceeds or falls short of total cost. In the figure the gap is largest at output q_E, which is thus the profit-maximizing output.

In a perfectly competitive market each firm is a price-taker and a quantity-adjuster. It pursues its goal of profit maximization by producing the output that equates its short-run marginal cost with the price of its product that is given to it by the market.

Figure 9.4 shows the equilibrium of the firm using average cost and revenue curves. We can, if we wish, show the same equilibrium using total cost and revenue curves. Figure 9.5 combines the total cost curve first drawn in Figure 8.3 with the total revenue curve first shown in Figure 9.2. It shows the profit-maximizing output as the output with the largest positive difference between total revenue and total cost. This must of course be the same output as we located in Figure 9.4 by equating marginal cost and marginal revenue.

Short-run supply curves

We have seen that in a perfectly competitive market the firm responds to a price that is set by the forces of demand and supply. By adjusting the quantity it produces in response to the current market price, the firm helps to determine the market supply. The link between the behaviour of the firm and the behaviour of the competitive market is provided by the *industry supply curve*, which is also called the *market supply curve*.

The supply curve for one firm The firm's supply curve is derived in part (i) of Figure 9.6, which shows a firm's marginal cost curve and four alternative prices. The horizontal line at each price is the firm's demand curve when the market price is at that level. The firm's marginal cost curve gives the marginal cost corresponding to each level of output. We require a supply curve that shows the quantity that the firm will supply at each price. For prices below average variable cost, the firm will supply zero units (rule 1). For prices above average variable cost, the firm will equate price and marginal cost (rule 2, modified by the proposition that $MR = p$ in perfect competition). This leads to the following conclusion:

In perfect competition the firm's supply curve is its marginal cost curve for those levels of output for which marginal cost is above average variable cost.

The supply curve of an industry To illustrate what is involved, Figure 9.7 shows the derivation of an industry supply curve for an industry containing only two firms. The general result is as follows:

In perfect competition the industry supply curve is the horizontal sum of the marginal cost curves of all firms in the industry (above the level of average variable cost).

The reason for summing the marginal cost curves is that each firm's marginal cost curve shows how much it will supply at each given market price, and the industry supply curve is the sum of what each firm will supply. The reason for the qualification 'above the level of average variable cost' is that, as rule 1 shows, the firm will not produce at all if price is less than its average variable cost.

This supply curve, based on the short-run marginal cost curves of all the firms in the industry, is the industry's supply curve that was first encountered in Chapter 3. We have now established the profit-maximizing behaviour of

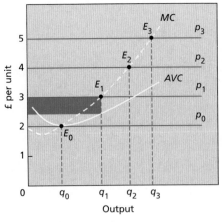

(i) Marginal cost and average
variable cost curves

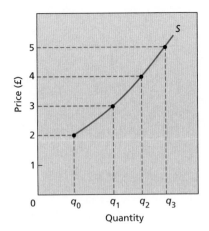

(ii) The supply curve

Figure 9.6 The supply curve for a price-taking firm

For a price-taking firm the supply curve has the same shape as its *MC* curve above the level of *AVC*. The point E_0, where price p_0 equals *AVC*, is the shutdown point. As price rises from £2 to £3 to £4 to £5, the firm increases its production from q_0 to q_1 to q_2 to q_3. If, for example, price were £3, the firm would produce output q_1 and be earning the contribution to fixed costs shown by the shaded rectangle.

The firm's supply curve is shown in part (ii). It relates market price to the quantity the firm will produce and offer for sale. It has the same shape as the firm's *MC* curve for all prices above *AVC*.

(i) Firm A

(ii) Firm B

(iii) Firms A and B

Figure 9.7 The supply curve for a group of firms

The industry supply curve is the horizontal sum of the supply curves of each of the firms in the industry. At a price of £3 firm A would supply 4 units and firm B would supply 3 units. Together, as shown in part (iii), they would supply 7 units. In this example, because firm B does not enter the market at prices below £2, the supply curve S_{A+B} is identical to S_A up to price £2 and is the sum of S_A and S_B above £2.

individual firms that lies behind that curve. It is sometimes called a **short-run supply curve** because it is based on the short-run, profit-maximizing behaviour of all the firms in the industry. This distinguishes it from a *long-run supply curve*, which relates quantity supplied to the price that rules in long-run equilibrium when there are no fixed factors (which we study later in this chapter).

Short-run equilibrium price

The price of a product sold in a perfectly competitive market is determined by the interaction of the industry's short-run supply curve and the market demand curve. Although no one firm can influence the market price significantly, the collective actions of all firms in the industry (as shown by the industry supply curve) and the collective actions of consumers (as shown by the market demand curve) together determine the equilibrium price. This occurs at the point where the market demand curve and the industry supply curve intersect.

At the equilibrium price each firm is producing and selling a quantity for which its marginal cost equals price. Given their fixed factors, all firms are maximizing their

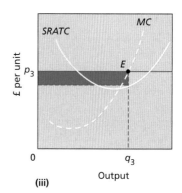

Figure 9.8 Alternative short-run equilibrium positions for a firm in perfect competition
When it is in short-run equilibrium, a competitive firm may be suffering losses, breaking even, or making profits. The diagram shows a firm with given costs faced with three alternative prices, p_1, p_2, and p_3. In each part E is the point at which $MC = MR$ = price. Since in all three cases price exceeds AVC, the firm is in short-run equilibrium.

In part (i) price is p_1. Because price is below average total cost, the firm is suffering losses shown by the light blue area. Because price exceeds average variable cost, the firm continues to produce in the short run. Because price is less than ATC, the firm will not replace its capital as it wears out.

In part (ii) price is p_2 and the firm is just covering its total costs. It will replace its capital as it wears out since its revenue is covering the full opportunity cost of its capital.

In part (iii) price is p_3 and the firm is earning pure profits in excess of all its costs, as shown by the dark blue area. As in part (ii) the firm will replace its capital as it wears out.

profits and so have no incentive to alter output in the short run. Because total quantity demanded equals total quantity supplied, there is no reason for market price to change. Thus the market and all the firms in the industry are in short-run equilibrium.

Short-run profitability of the firm

We know that when an industry is in short-run equilibrium, each firm is maximizing its profits. However, we do not know *how large* these profits are. It is one thing to know that a firm is doing as well as it can, given its particular circumstances; it is another thing to know how well it is doing.

Figure 9.8 shows three possible positions for a firm in short-run equilibrium. In all cases the firm is maximizing its profits by producing where price equals marginal cost, but the size of the profits is different in each case. In part (i) the firm is suffering losses. In part (ii) it is just covering all of its costs—it is just breaking even. In part (iii) it is making pure profits because average revenue exceeds average total cost. In part (i) we could say that the firm is minimizing its losses rather than maximizing its profits, but both statements mean the same thing. In all three cases the firm is doing as well as it can, given its costs and the market price.

The allocative efficiency of perfect competition

We saw in Chapter 1 that economics began when observers wondered about the systematic way in which resources were allocated by markets in which people made independent decisions motivated by self-interest. Not only do resources get allocated in a self-organizing manner, under certain conditions they are *optimally* or *efficiently* allocated. (These two words mean the same thing in this context.) The nation's resources are efficiently allocated if there is no other allocation that would allow someone to be made better off while no one was made worse off. To put this the other way around, resources are inefficiently allocated if the allocation could be changed in such a way as to make at least one person better off while making no one worse off. For example, if resources could be reallocated so as to make fewer hats and more shoes and someone made better off by the change while no one was made worse off, then the current allocation cannot be efficient.

It can be shown that a perfectly competitive economy would allocate its resources efficiently. However, a number of other conditions also need to be fulfilled, as we will see in Chapter 18. In the meantime we will show one way in which the tendency for perfect competition to produce an optimal allocation of resources can be established. We do this using the concepts of consumers' and producers' surplus.

We saw in Chapter 6 that consumers' surplus is the difference between the total value that consumers place on all the units consumed of some product and the payment that they actually make for the purchase of that product. The total value that they place on the amount they consume is the area under the demand curve, which represents the summation of all the marginal valuations they place on each separate unit consumed. What they pay is the area representing the price multiplied by the quantity consumed. The difference between these two is shown in Figure 9.9 as consumers' surplus.

Producers' surplus is a new concept. It is analogous to consumers' surplus. It occurs because all units of each firm's output are sold at the same market price, while, given a rising supply curve, the marginal costs of all but the

last unit are less than the market price. **Producers' surplus** is defined as the amount that producers are paid for a product less the total variable cost of producing the product. The total variable cost of producing any output is shown by the area under the supply curve up to that output, which represents the summation of the marginal costs of producing each unit of output.[5] Thus producers' surplus, which is shown in Figure 9.9, is the area above the supply curve and below the line giving the market price. (Do not forget that all firms are either directly or indirectly owned by people, so producers' surplus is really owners' surplus.)

If the total of consumers' and producers' surplus is not maximized, the industry's output could be altered to increase that total. The additional surplus could then be used to make some people better off without making any others worse off.

Allocative efficiency occurs where the sum of consumers' and producers' surplus is maximized.

The allocatively efficient output occurs under perfect competition where the demand curve intersects the supply curve, that is, at the point of equilibrium in a competitive market. This is shown graphically in Figure 9.10. For any output that is less than the competitive output, the demand curve lies above the supply curve, which means that the value consumers put on the last unit of production exceeds its marginal cost of production. Suppose, for example, that the current output of shoes is such that an additional pair of shoes that costs £60 to make is valued by consumers at £70. If the shoes are sold at any price between £60 and £70, both producers and consumers gain; there is £10 of potential surplus to be divided between the two. In contrast, the last unit produced and sold at competitive equilibrium adds nothing to either consumers' or producers' surplus. This is because consumers value it at exactly its market price, and it adds the full amount of the market price to producers' cost.

If production were pushed beyond the competitive equilibrium, the sum of the two surpluses would fall. Assume, for example, that firms were forced to produce and sell further units of output at the competitive market price and that consumers were forced to buy these extra units at that price. (Note that neither group would do so voluntarily.) Firms would lose producers' surplus on those extra units because their marginal costs of producing them would be above the price that they received for them. Purchasers would lose consumers' surplus because the

Figure 9.9 Consumers' and producers' surplus

Consumers' surplus is the area under the demand curve and above the market price line. Producers' surplus is the area above the supply curve and below the market price line. The equilibrium price and quantity are p_0 and q_0. The total value that consumers place on q_0 units of the product is given by the sum of the dark yellow, light yellow, and dark blue areas. The amount that they pay is p_0q_0, the rectangle that consists of the light yellow and dark blue areas. The difference, shown as the dark yellow area, is *consumers' surplus.*

The receipts to producers from the sale of q_0 units are also p_0q_0. The area under the supply curve, the blue-shaded area, is total variable cost, the minimum amount that producers require to supply the output. The difference, shown as the light yellow area, is *producers' surplus.*

[5] Recall from Chapter 2 pages 30–1 that the area under a marginal cost curve up to any output is the variable cost of producing that output. Graphically, taking the area under a marginal cost curve is equivalent to summing all the marginal costs to get total variable cost. Similarly, summing the area under the demand curve yields the total amount that consumers would be willing to pay if offered each unit one at a time, i.e. the total valuation they place on all the units.

Figure 9.10 The allocative efficiency of perfect competition

Competitive equilibrium is allocatively efficient because it maximizes the sum of consumers' and producers' surplus. At the competitive equilibrium E consumers' surplus is the dark yellow area above the price line, while producers' surplus is the light yellow area below the price line.

Reducing the output to q_1 but keeping price at p_0 lowers consumers' surplus by area 1 and lowers producers' surplus by area 2. If producers are forced to produce output q_2 and to sell it to consumers, who are in turn forced to buy it at price p_0, producers' surplus is reduced by area 3 (the amount by which variable costs exceed revenue on those units), while consumers' surplus is reduced by area 4 (the amount by which expenditure exceeds consumers' satisfactions on those units). Only at the competitive output, q_0, is the sum of the two surpluses maximized.

valuation that they placed on these extra units, as shown by the demand curve, would be less than the price that they would have to pay.

The sum of producers' and consumers' surplus is maximized when a perfectly competitive industry is in equilibrium. The resulting level of output is allocatively efficient.

Long-run equilibrium

The key to long-run equilibrium under perfect competition is entry and exit.

The effect of entry and exit

We have seen that when firms are in *short-run equilibrium* they may be making profits, suffering losses, or just breaking even. Because costs include the opportunity cost of capital, firms that are just breaking even are doing as well as they could do by investing their capital elsewhere. Thus, there will be no incentive for such firms to leave the industry. Similarly, if new entrants expect just to break even, there will be no incentive for firms to enter the industry, because capital can earn the same return elsewhere in the economy. If, however, existing firms are earning revenues in excess of all costs, including the opportunity cost of capital, new capital will enter the industry to share in these profits. If existing firms are suffering losses, capital will leave the industry because a better return can be obtained elsewhere in the economy. Let us now consider this process in a little more detail.

An entry-attracting price First, let all firms in the competitive industry be in the position of the firm shown in part (iii) of Figure 9.8 on page 147. Attracted by the profitability of existing firms, new firms will enter the industry. Suppose that, in response to the high profits that the

100 existing firms are making, 20 new firms enter. The market supply curve that formerly added up the outputs of 100 firms must now add up the outputs of 120 firms. At any price, more will be supplied because there are more producers.

With an unchanged market demand curve, this shift in the short-run industry supply curve means that the previous equilibrium price will no longer prevail. The shift in supply will lower the equilibrium price, and both new and old firms will have to adjust their output to this new price. This is illustrated in Figure 9.11. New firms will continue to enter, and the equilibrium price will continue to fall, until all firms in the industry are just covering their total costs. Firms will then be in the position of the firm shown in part (ii) of Figure 9.8, which is called a *zero-profit equilibrium*.

Profits in a competitive industry are a signal for the entry of new firms; the industry will expand, pushing price down until the profits fall to zero.

An exit-inducing price Now let the firms in the industry be in the position of the firm shown in part (i) of Figure 9.8. Although the firms are covering their variable costs, the return on their capital is less than the opportunity cost of capital. They are not covering their total costs. This is a signal for the exit of firms. Old plants and equipment will not be replaced as they wear out. As a result the industry's

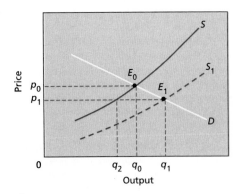

Figure 9.11 New entrants shift the supply curve
The supply curve shifts to the right and the equilibrium price falls. The entry of new firms shifts the supply curve to S_1, the equilibrium price falls from p_0 to p_1, while output rises from q_0 to q_1. Before entry only q_2 would have been produced at this price. The extra output is supplied by the new firms.

short-run supply curve shifts leftward, and the market price rises. Firms will continue to exit, and the market price will continue to rise, until the remaining firms can cover their total costs, that is, until they are all in the zero-profit equilibrium illustrated in part (ii) of Figure 9.8. The exit of firms then ceases.

Losses in a competitive industry are a signal for the exit of firms; the industry will contract, driving the market price up until the remaining firms are covering their total costs.

The break-even price Because firms exit when they are motivated to do so by losses and enter when they are motivated by profits, this conclusion follows:

The long-run equilibrium of a competitive industry occurs when firms are earning zero profits.

The firm in part (ii) of Figure 9.8 is in a zero-profit, long-run equilibrium. For that firm, the price p_0 is its shutdown or break-even price. It is the price at which all costs, including the opportunity cost of capital, are being covered. The firm is just willing to stay in the industry. It has no incentive to leave, nor do other firms have an incentive to enter.

In the preceding analysis we see profits serving the function of providing signals that guide the allocation of scarce resources among the economy's industries. It is also worth noting that freedom of entry will tend to push profits towards zero in any industry, whether or not it is perfectly competitive.

Marginal and intramarginal firms When considering possible exit from an industry, it is sometimes useful to distinguish marginal from intramarginal firms. The mar-

ginal firm is just covering its full costs and would exit if price fell by even a small amount. The intramarginal firm is earning profits and would require a larger fall in price to persuade it to exit. In the pure abstract model of perfect competition, however, all firms are marginal firms in long-run equilibrium. All firms have access to the same technology, and all, therefore, will have identical cost curves when enough time has passed for full adjustment of all capital to be made. In long-run industry equilibrium, all firms are thus in position (ii) in Figure 9.8. If price falls below p_2 in that figure, all firms wish to withdraw. Exit must then be by some contrived process, such as random lot, since there is nothing in the theory to explain who will exit first.

In real-world situations firms are not identical, since technology changes continually and different firms have different histories. A firm that has recently replaced its capital is likely to have more efficient, lower-cost plant and hence lower cost curves than a firm whose capital is ageing. The details of each practical case will then determine the identity of the marginal firm that will exit first when price falls. For one example, assume that all firms have identical costs and differ only in the date at which they entered the industry. In this case, the firm whose capital comes up for replacement first will be the marginal firm. It will exit first because it will be the first to confront the long-run decision about replacing its capital in a situation where no firms are covering long-run opportunity costs.

A more detailed analysis of the long run

Consider the position of the firms and the industry when both are in long-run equilibrium. There is no change that any firm could make, over the short or the long run, that would increase its profits. This requirement can be stated as three distinct conditions:

1. *No firm will want to vary the output of its existing plants.* Short-run marginal cost (*SRMC*) must equal price.

2. *Profits earned by existing plants must be zero.* This implies that short-run *ATC* must equal price—that is, firms must be in the position of the firm in Figure 9.8(ii).

3. *No firm can earn profits by building a plant of a different size.* This implies that each existing firm must be producing at the lowest point on its long-run average cost curve.

We have already seen why the first two conditions must hold. The reasoning behind the third condition is shown in Figure 9.12. Although the firm with the average cost curve *SRATC*$_0$ is in short-run equilibrium, it is not in long-run equilibrium because its *LRAC* curve lies below the

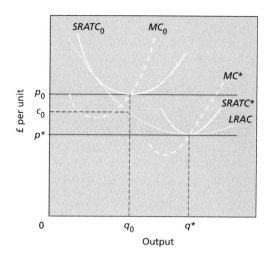

Figure 9.12 Short-run and long-run equilibrium of a firm in perfect competition

A perfectly competitive firm that is not at the minimum point on its *LRAC* curve cannot be in long-run equilibrium. The firm's existing plant has short-run cost curves $SRATC_0$ and MC_0 while market price is p_0. The firm produces q_0, where MC_0 equals price and total costs are just being covered. Although the firm is in short-run equilibrium, it can earn profits by building a larger plant and so moving downwards along its *LRAC* curve. Thus the firm cannot be in long-run equilibrium at any output below q^*, because average total costs can be reduced by building a larger plant.

If all firms do this, industry output will increase and price will fall until long-run equilibrium is reached at price p^*. Each firm is then in short-run equilibrium with a plant whose average cost curve is $SRATC^*$ and whose short-run marginal cost curve, MC^*, intersects the price line p^* at an output of q^*. Because the *LRAC* curve lies above p^* everywhere except at q^*, the firm has no incentive to move to another point on its *LRAC* curve by altering the size of its plant. The output q^* is the firm's minimum efficient scale.

market price at some higher levels of output.[6] The firm can, therefore, increase its profits by building a plant of larger size, thereby lowering its average total costs. Since the firm is a price-taker, this change will increase its profits.

A price-taking firm is in long-run equilibrium only when it is producing at the minimum point on its *LRAC* curve.

All three of the conditions listed above are fulfilled when each firm in the industry is in the position shown in Figure 9.12 by the short-run cost curve $SRATC^*$.[7]

Long-run response to a change in demand

Now suppose that the demand for the product increases. Price will rise to equate demand with the industry's short-run supply. Each firm will expand output until its short-run marginal cost once again equals price. Each firm will

earn profits as a result of the rise in price, and the profits will induce new firms to enter the industry. This will shift the short-run supply curve to the right and force down the price. Entry will continue until all firms are once again just covering average total costs.

Now consider a fall in demand. The industry starts with firms in long-run equilibrium as shown in Figure 9.12, and the market demand curve shifts left and price falls. There are two possible consequences.

First, the decline in demand may force price below *ATC* but leave it above *AVC*. Firms are then in the position shown in Figure 9.8(i). They can cover their variable costs and earn some return on their capital, so they remain in production for as long as their existing plant and equipment lasts. Exit will occur, however, as old capital wears out and is not replaced. As firms exit, the short-run supply curve shifts left and market price rises. This continues until the remaining firms in the industry can cover their total costs. At this point, it will pay to replace capital as it wears out, and the industry will stop declining. This adjustment may take a long time, for the industry shrinks in size only as existing plant and equipment wears out.

The second possibility is that the decline in demand is large enough to push price below the level of *AVC*. Now firms cannot even cover their variable costs, and some will shut down immediately. Reduction in capital devoted to production in the industry occurs rapidly because some existing capacity is scrapped or shifted to other uses. The decline in the number of firms reduces supply and raises the equilibrium price. Once the price rises enough to allow the remaining firms to cover their variable costs, the rapid withdrawal of capital ceases. Further exit occurs more slowly, as described in the previous paragraph.

Entry of new capital into a profitable industry can take place only as fast as new plants can be built and new equipment installed. Exit of existing capital from an unprofitable industry with losses will occur very quickly when price is less than average variable cost, but only at the rate at which old plant and equipment wears out when price exceeds average variable cost.

This adjustment process is examined in greater detail in the following section.

---

[6] Because all inputs are variable in the long run, no distinction is needed between variable and fixed costs. We have only one long-run average cost curve.

[7] The text discussion implies that all existing firms and all new entrants face identical *LRAC* curves. This means that all firms face the same set of factor prices and have the same technology available to them. Do not forget that we are in the long run, *where technological knowledge is given and constant*, and where all firms have had a chance to adjust their capital to the best that is available. This is a theoretical construction designed to analyse tendencies. In any industry in which technological change is ongoing, long-run equilibrium will never be established and a wide variety of different technologies will be used by different firms at each point in time.

The long-run industry supply curve

Possible adjustments of the industry to the kinds of changes in demand just discussed are shown by the **long-run industry supply (LRS) curve.** This curve shows the relation between equilibrium price and the output that firms will be willing to supply after all desired entry or exit has occurred.

The long-run supply curve connects positions of long-run equilibrium after all demand-induced changes have occurred.

When induced changes in factor prices are considered, it is possible for the LRS curve to be horizontal or to be positively or negatively sloped. The various cases are illustrated in Figure 9.13.

In Figure 9.13(i) the long-run supply curve is horizontal. This indicates that, given time, the industry will adjust its size to provide whatever quantity is demanded at a constant price. That price is set by the minimum point of the firm's long-run average cost curve. An industry with a horizontal long-run supply curve is said to be a *constant-cost industry*.

This case occurs when an alteration in the size of the industry leaves the long-run cost curves of existing firms unchanged, which requires that the industry's input prices do not change as the whole industry's output expands or contracts. Since all firms have access to the same technology and face the same factor prices, all firms have identical cost curves. Under these circumstances the long-run equi-

librium with price equal to minimum long-run average total cost of each and every firm can be re-established only when price returns to its original level.

Changing factor prices and rising long-run supply curves When an industry expands its output it needs more inputs. The increase in demand for these inputs may bid up their prices.[8]

If costs rise with increasing levels of industry output, so too must the price at which the producers are able to cover their costs. As the industry expands, the short-run supply curve shifts outwards but the firms' *SRATC* curves shift upward because of rising factor prices. The expansion of the industry comes to a halt when price is equal to minimum *LRAC* for existing firms. This must occur at a higher price than ruled before the expansion began, as illustrated in Figure 9.13(ii). A competitive industry with rising long-run supply prices is often called a *rising-cost industry*.

Can the long-run supply curve decline? So far we have suggested that the long-run supply curve may be horizontal or positively sloped. Could it ever decline, thereby

---

[8] In a fully employed economy the expansion of one industry implies the contraction of some other industry. What happens to factor prices depends on the proportions in which the expanding and the contracting industries use the factors. The relative price of the factor used intensively by the expanding industry will rise, causing the costs of the expanding industry to rise relative to those of the contracting industry. In a two-sector, two-factor model a rising long-run industry supply curve is normal because of the effect that changes in industry outputs have on relative factor prices.

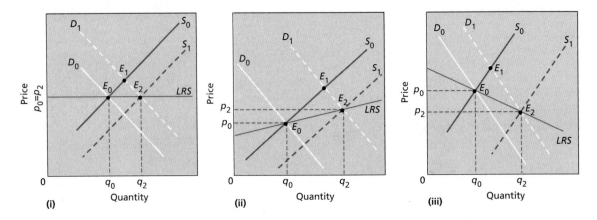

Figure 9.13 Long-run industry supply curves
The long-run industry supply curve may be horizontal, or positively or negatively sloped. In all three parts the initial curves are at D_0 and S_0, yielding equilibrium at E_0 with price p_0 and quantity q_0. A rise in demand shifts the demand curve to D_1, taking the short-run equilibrium to E_1. New firms now enter the industry, shifting the short-run supply curve outwards and pushing price down until pure profits are no longer being earned. At this point the supply curve is S_1 and the new equilibrium is E_2 with price at p_2 and quantity q_2. In part (i) price returns to its original level, making the long-run supply curve horizontal. In part (ii) profits are eliminated before price falls to its original level, giving the *LRS* curve a positive slope. In part (iii) the price falls below its original level before profits return to normal, giving the *LRS* curve a negative slope.

indicating that higher outputs are associated with lower prices in long-run equilibrium?

It is tempting to answer yes, because of the opportunities of more efficient scales of operation using greater mechanization and more effective specialization of labour. But this answer would not be correct for perfectly competitive industries, because each firm in long-run equilibrium must already be at the lowest point on its *LRAC* curve. If a firm could lower its costs by building a larger, more mechanized plant, it would be profitable to do so without waiting for an increase in demand. Since any single firm can sell all it wishes at the going market price, it will be profitable to expand the scale of its operations as long as its *LRAC* is falling.

The scale economies that we have just considered are within the control of the firm; they are said to be **internal economies.** A perfectly competitive industry might, however, have falling long-run costs if industries that supply its inputs have increasing returns to scale. Such effects are outside the control of the perfectly competitive firm and are called **external economies.** Whenever expansion of an industry leads to a fall in the prices of some of its inputs, the firms will find their cost curves shifting downwards as they expand their outputs.

As an illustration of how the expansion of one industry could cause the prices of some of its inputs to fall, consider the early stages of the growth of the car industry. As the output of cars increased, the industry's demand for tyres grew greatly. This, as suggested earlier, increased the demand for rubber and tended to raise its price, but it also provided the opportunity for tyre manufacturers to build larger plants, which exploited some of the economies available in tyre production. These economies were large enough to offset any factor-price increases, and tyre prices charged to car manufacturers fell. Thus, car costs fell, because of lower prices of an important input. This case is illustrated in part (iii) of Figure 9.13. An industry that has a negatively sloped long-run supply curve is often called a *falling-cost industry.*

Notice that although the economies were external to the car industry, they were internal to the tyre industry. However, if the tyre industry had been perfectly competitive, all its scale economies would already have been exploited. So this case refers to a perfectly competitive industry that uses an input produced by a non-competitive industry, whose own scale economies have not yet been fully exploited because demand is insufficient. Another example is provided by perfectly competitive agricultural industries, which buy their farm machinery from the farm implement industry, which is dominated by a few large firms.

Can perfectly competitive industries have scale economies?

The key to answering the question posed in this heading lies in the size of the firm relative to the size of the market.

A competitive firm will never be in equilibrium on the falling part of its *LRAC*—if price is given and costs can be reduced by increasing the scale of output, profits can also be increased by doing so. Thus, firms will grow in size until all scale economies are exhausted. Provided that the output that yields the minimum *LRAC* for each firm is small relative to the industry's total output, the industry will contain a large number of firms and will remain competitive. If, however, reaching the minimum *LRAC* makes firms so large that each one has significant market power, they will cease to be price-takers and perfect competition will also cease to exist. Indeed, scale economies may exist over such a large range that one firm's *LRAC* is still falling when it serves the entire market. That firm will then grow until it monopolizes the entire market. This case, which economists call a *natural* monopoly, is considered further in later chapters.

A necessary condition for a long-run perfectly competitive equilibrium is that any scale economies that are within the firm's control should be exhausted at a level of output that is small relative to the whole industry's output.

Summary

Market structure and firm behaviour

■ Competitive *behaviour* refers to the extent to which individual firms compete with each other to sell their products. Competitive *market structure* refers to the power that individual firms have over the market—perfect competition occurring where firms have no market power and hence no need to react to each other.

Elements of the theory of perfect competition

■ The theory of perfect competition is based on the following assumptions: firms sell a homogeneous product; customers are well informed; each firm is a price-taker; the industry can support many firms, which are free to enter or leave the industry.

Short-run equilibrium

■ Any firm maximizes profits by producing the output where its marginal cost curve intersects the marginal revenue curve from below—or by producing nothing if average variable cost exceeds price at all outputs.

■ A perfectly competitive firm is a quantity-adjuster, facing a perfectly elastic demand curve at the given market price and maximizing profits by choosing the output that equates its marginal cost to price.

■ The supply curve of a firm in perfect competition is its marginal cost curve, and the supply curve of a perfectly competitive industry is the sum of the marginal cost curves of all its firms. The intersection of this curve with the market demand curve for the industry's product determines market price.

The allocative efficiency of perfect competition

■ Perfect competition produces an optimal allocation of resources because it maximizes the sum of consumers' and producers' surplus by producing equilibrium where marginal cost equals price.

Long-run equilibrium

■ Long-run industry equilibrium requires that each individual firm be producing at the minimum point of its *LRAC* curve and be making zero profits.

■ The long-run industry supply curve for a perfectly competitive industry may be (i) positively sloped, if input prices are driven up by the industry's expansion, (ii) horizontal, if plants can be replicated and factor prices remain constant, or (iii) negatively sloped, if some other industry that is not perfectly competitive produces an input under conditions of falling long-run costs.

Topics for review

■ Competitive behaviour and competitive market structure

■ Behavioural rules for the profit-maximizing firm

■ Price-taking and a horizontal demand curve

■ Average revenue, marginal revenue, and price under perfect competition

■ Relation of the industry supply curve to its firms' marginal cost curves

■ The role of entry and exit in achieving long-run equilibrium

■ Exhaustion of scale economies in perfectly competitive long-run equilibrium

Questions for discussion

1 Which of the following observed facts about an industry are inconsistent with its being perfectly competitive? (*a*) Different firms use different methods of production. (*b*) The industry's product is extensively advertised by a trade association. (*c*) Individual firms devote a large fraction of their sales receipts to advertising their own product brands. (*d*) There are twenty-four firms in the industry. (*e*) All firms made economic profits in 1995. (*f*) All firms are charging the same price.

2 Which of the assumptions of the theory of perfect competition does the following newspaper story relate to? 'Recently, Ken Chapman booked a US$932 round-trip ticket at noon. While he slept that night, a new computer program searched for a better deal. Sixteen hours later, a new fare became available, and Chapman is now ticketed to travel for US$578.' Will this new procedure make the airline industry more or less competitive? Will it make it perfectly competitive? Why or why not?

3 Suppose all of the potentially arable land in some country is currently being used for growing either wheat or barley. Both crop markets are in equilibrium. Discuss exactly how decentralized competitive markets would respond to shift resources following a report that barley helps to reduce cancer risk.

4 Why would the existence of entry barriers make it unlikely that an industry would be perfectly competitive? What types of entry barriers do you think are important in practice? How can the existence of economies of scale affect the degree of competitiveness in a market?

5 How does technical progress affect the equilibrium of a firm and of the perfectly competitive industry in which it operates? Why do some industries decline while others grow? At what point should firms quit a declining industry?

Appendix A mathematical derivation of the rules of profit maximization

In this brief appendix we provide formal derivations of the three rules for profit maximization. The first derivation uses only algebra and can be read by anyone. The second and third use elementary calculus and should not be attempted by those who are unfamiliar with simple derivatives.

Condition 1 Profits, π, are defined as follows:

$$\pi = R - (F + V),$$

where R is total revenue, F is total fixed cost, and V is total variable cost. Now let subscript n stand for a state where there is no production and p for one where there is production. It pays the firm to produce if there is at least one level of production for which

$$\pi_p \geq \pi_n.$$

When the firm does not produce, R and V are zero, so the above condition becomes

$$R - F - V \geq -F$$

or

$$R \geq V.$$

Dividing both sides by output, q, we get:

$$\text{price} \geq AVC.$$

Condition 2

$$\pi = R - C,$$

where C is total cost $(F + V)$. Both revenues and costs vary with output, i.e. $R = R(q)$ and $C = C(q)$. Thus we may write

$$\pi = R(q) - C(q).$$

A necessary condition for the maximization of profits is[9]

$$\frac{\mathrm{d}\pi}{\mathrm{d}q} = R'(q) - C'(q) = 0$$

or

$$R'(q) = C'(q).$$

But these derivatives define marginal revenue and marginal cost, so we have

$$MR = MC.$$

Condition 3 To ensure that we have a maximum and not a minimum for profits, we require

$$\frac{\mathrm{d}^2\pi}{\mathrm{d}q^2} = R''(q) - C''(q) = \frac{\mathrm{d}MR}{\mathrm{d}q} - \frac{\mathrm{d}MC}{\mathrm{d}q} < 0$$

or

$$\frac{\mathrm{d}MR}{\mathrm{d}q} < \frac{\mathrm{d}MC}{\mathrm{d}q},$$

which means that the algebraic value of the slope of the marginal cost curve must exceed, at the point of intersection, the algebraic value of the slope of the marginal revenue curve. This translates into the geometric statement that the marginal cost curve should cut the marginal revenue curve from below.

---

[9] Note the convenient use of a prime for a derivative. Thus for the function $F(X)$, the two notations $\mathrm{d}/\mathrm{d}X$ and $F'(X)$ mean the same thing, as do $\mathrm{d}^2/\mathrm{d}X^2$ and $F''(X)$.

Chapter 10
Monopoly

In this chapter we study the market structure called monopoly which is at the opposite extreme from perfect competition. A **monopoly** occurs when one firm, called a monopolist or a monopoly firm, produces an industry's entire output. In contrast to perfectly competitive firms, which are price-takers, a monopolist sets its own market price.

We see that when a monopoly firm must charge a single price for its output, it will produce less, charge a higher price, and earn greater profits than do firms operating under perfect competition. Next we see why all monopoly firms have an incentive to charge different prices to different classes of users or on different units sold to the same user. We also see that monopoly profits provide a strong incentive for new firms to enter the industry and that this will happen unless there are effective barriers to entry, either of a natural or of a man-made variety. Finally we study how groups of firms can band together to form a cartel that raises profits by acting as if it were a monopoly.

A single-price monopolist

The first part of this chapter deals with a monopoly firm that charges a single price for its product. The firm's profits, like those of all firms, will depend on the relationship between its production costs and its sales revenues.

Cost and revenue in the short run

We saw in Chapter 8 that U-shaped short-run cost curves are a consequence of the law of diminishing returns. Because this law applies to the conditions under which goods are produced rather than to the market structure in which they are sold, monopoly firms have U-shaped short-run cost curves just as perfectly competitive firms do.

Because a monopoly firm is the sole producer of the product that it sells, its demand curve is identical to the market demand curve for that product. The market demand curve, which shows the total quantity that buyers will purchase at each price, also shows the quantity that the monopoly firm will be able to sell at each price. Thus, the monopoly firm, unlike the perfectly competitive firm, faces a negatively sloped demand curve. This means that it faces a trade-off between the price it charges and the quantity it sells. Sales can be increased only if price is reduced, and price can be increased only if sales are reduced.

Average and marginal revenue

Starting with the market demand curve, the monopoly firm's average and marginal revenue curves can be readily derived. When the monopoly firm charges the same price for all units sold, average revenue per unit is identical to price. Thus, the market demand curve is also the firm's *average revenue curve.*

Now consider the monopoly firm's *marginal revenue* resulting from the sale of an additional (or marginal) unit of production. Because its demand curve is negatively sloped, the monopoly firm must lower the price that it charges on *all* units in order to sell an *extra* unit.

It follows that the addition to its revenue resulting from the sale of an extra unit is less than the price that it receives for that unit (less by the amount that it loses as a result of cutting the price on all the units that it was selling already).

The monopoly firm's marginal revenue is less than the price at which it sells its output.

This proposition is illustrated in Figure 10.1.

To clarify these relations, we consider a numerical example of a specific, straight-line demand curve. Some points on this curve are shown in tabular form in Table 10.1 while the whole curve is shown in Figure 10.2. Notice in the table that the change in total revenue associated with a change of £0.10 in price is recorded between the rows

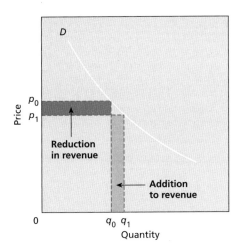

Figure 10.1 The effect on revenue of an increase in quantity sold

Because the demand curve has a negative slope, marginal revenue is less than price. A reduction of price from p_0 to p_1 increases sales by one unit from q_0 to q_1 units. The revenue from the extra unit sold is shown as the medium blue area. But to sell this unit, it is necessary to reduce the price on each of the q_0 units previously sold. The loss in revenue is shown as the dark blue area. Marginal revenue of the extra unit is equal to the *difference* between the two areas.

Table 10.1 Total, average, and marginal revenue

Price $p = AR$	Quantity q	Total revenue $TR = p \cdot q$	Marginal revenue $MR = \Delta TR/\Delta q$
£9.10	9	£81.90	
			£8.10
9.00	10	90.00	
			7.90
8.90	11	97.90	

Marginal revenue is less than price because price must be lowered to sell an extra unit. The marginal revenue of the eleventh unit is total revenue when 11 units are sold minus total revenue when 10 units are sold. This is £7.90, which is less than the price of £8.90 at which all 11 units are sold. Marginal revenue is the £8.90 gained from selling the extra unit at £8.90 minus £0.10 lost on each of the 10 units already being sold when their price falls from £9.00 to £8.90.

that refer to specific prices. We do this, as we have done in previous tables, because the data refer to what happens when the price is changed from the value shown in one row to the value shown in the adjacent row.

Notice also from Figure 10.2 that when price is reduced starting from £10, total revenue rises at first and then falls. The maximum total revenue is reached in this example at a price of £5. Because marginal revenue gives the change in total revenue resulting from the sale of one more unit of output, marginal revenue is positive whenever total

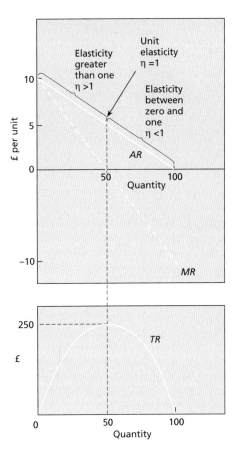

Figure 10.2 Revenue curves and demand elasticity

Rising *TR*, positive *MR*, and elastic demand all go together, as do falling *TR*, negative *MR*, and inelastic demand. In this example, for outputs from 0 to 50 marginal revenue is positive, elasticity is greater than unity, and total revenue is rising. For outputs from 50 to 100 marginal revenue is negative, elasticity is less than unity, and total revenue is falling. (All elasticities refer to absolute not algebraic values.)

revenue is increased by selling more, but it is negative whenever total revenue is reduced by selling more.[1]

The proposition that marginal revenue is always *less than* average revenue, which has been illustrated numerically in Table 10.1 and graphically in Figure 10.2, provides an important contrast with perfect competition. You will recall that in perfect competition the firm's marginal revenue from selling an extra unit of output is *equal to* the price at which that unit is sold. The reason for the difference is not difficult to understand. The perfectly competitive firm is a price-taker; it can sell all it wants at the given

---

[1] Notice that the marginal revenue shown in the table is obtained by subtracting the total revenue associated with one price from the total revenue associated with another, lower, price and then apportioning the change in revenue among the extra units sold. In symbols, it is $\Delta TR/\Delta q$.

market price. The monopoly firm faces a negatively sloped demand curve; it must reduce the market price in order to increase its sales.

Marginal revenue and elasticity

In Chapter 4 we discussed the relationship between the elasticity of the market demand curve and the total revenue derived from selling the product. Figure 10.2 summarizes this earlier discussion for a linear demand curve and extends it to cover marginal revenue.[2]

Over the range in which the demand curve is elastic, total revenue rises as more units are sold; marginal revenue must therefore be positive. Over the range in which the demand curve is inelastic, total revenue falls as more units are sold; marginal revenue must therefore be negative.

Short-run monopoly equilibrium

To show the profit-maximizing equilibrium of a monopoly firm, we bring together information about its revenues and its costs and then apply the two rules developed in Chapter 9. First, the firm should not produce at all unless there is some level of output for which price is at least equal to average variable cost. Second, if the firm does produce, its output should be set at the point where marginal cost equals marginal revenue.

When the monopoly firm equates marginal cost with marginal revenue, it reaches the equilibrium shown in Figure 10.3. The output is where marginal cost equals marginal revenue. The demand curve shows the price that corresponds to that output.

Notice that because marginal revenue is always less than price for the monopoly firm, when it equates marginal revenue to marginal cost, both are less than price.

When a monopoly firm is in profit-maximizing equilibrium, its marginal cost is always less than the price it charges for its output.

Competition and monopoly compared The comparison between monopoly and perfect competition is important. In perfect competition, firms face perfectly elastic curves, so that price and marginal revenue are the same. Thus, when they equate marginal cost to marginal revenue, they ensure that marginal cost also equals price. In contrast, a monopoly firm faces a negatively sloped demand curve for which marginal revenue is less than price. Thus, when it equates marginal cost to marginal revenue, it ensures that marginal cost will be less than price.

The relationship between elasticity and revenue discussed above has an interesting implication for the monopoly firm's equilibrium. Because marginal cost is always

Figure 10.3 The equilibrium of a monopoly
The monopoly maximizes its profits by producing where marginal cost equals marginal revenue. The monopoly produces the output q_0 for which marginal revenue equals marginal cost (rule 2). At this output the price of p_0—which is determined by the demand curve—exceeds the average variable cost (rule 1). Total profits are the profits per unit of $p_0 - c_0$ multiplied by the output of q_0, which is the dark blue area.

greater than zero, a profit-maximizing monopoly (which produces where $MR = MC$) will always produce where marginal revenue is positive, that is, where demand is elastic. If the firm were producing where demand was inelastic, it could reduce its output, thereby increasing its total revenue and reducing its total costs. No such restriction applies to firms in perfect competition. Each reacts to its own perfectly elastic demand curve, not to the market demand curve. Thus, the equilibrium can occur where the market demand curve is either elastic or inelastic.

A profit-maximizing monopoly will never sell in the range where the demand curve is inelastic.

Monopoly profits The fact that a monopoly firm produces the output that maximizes its profits tells us nothing about how large these profits will be or even whether there will be any profits at all. Figure 10.4 illustrates this by

---

[2] It is helpful when you are drawing these curves to remember that if the demand curve is a negatively sloped straight line, the MR curve is also negatively sloped and exactly twice as steep. Its price intercept (where $q = 0$) is the same as that of the demand curve, and its quantity intercept (where $p = 0$) is one-half of that of the demand curve. This is easily established for those who know calculus. A linear demand curve is $p = a - bq$. Total revenue (TR) is $pq = aq - bq^2$. Marginal revenue is $\mathrm{d}TR/\mathrm{d}q = a - 2bq$, which is a straight line of twice the slope of the demand curve. Average revenue is TR/q, and dividing the expression for TR by q gives $AR = a - bq$, which is, of course, the demand curve, since price is average revenue.

Figure 10.4 Alternative profit possibilities for a monopolist

Profit maximization means only that the monopoly is doing as well as it can do. The figure shows one demand curve and three alternative cost curves. With the curve ATC''' there is no positive output at which the monopolist can avoid making losses. With the curve ATC'' the monopolist covers all costs at output q_1, where the ATC curve is tangent to the D curve. With the curve ATC' profits can be made by producing at any output between q_2 and q_3. (The profit-maximizing output will be some point between q_2 and q_3, where $MR = MC$, which is not shown on the diagram.)

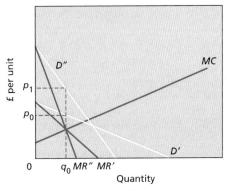

The same output at different prices

Figure 10.5 No supply curve under monopoly

There is no unique relation between price and the quantity sold. The demand curves D' and D'' both have marginal revenue curves that intersect the marginal cost curve at output q_0. But because the demand curves are different, q_0 is sold at p_0 when the demand curve is D', and at p_1 when the demand curve is D''.

For a monopoly firm there is no unique relationship between market price and quantity supplied.

showing three alternative average total cost curves: one where the monopoly firm can earn pure profits, one where it can just cover its costs, and one where it makes losses at any level of output.

No supply curve for a monopoly In describing the monopolist's profit-maximizing behaviour, we did not introduce the concept of a supply curve, as we did in the discussion of perfect competition. In perfect competition the industry short-run supply curve depends only on the marginal cost curves of the individual firms. This is true because, under perfect competition, profit-maximizing firms equate marginal cost with price. Given marginal costs, it is possible to know how much will be produced at each price. In contrast, a monopoly firm's output is not solely determined by its marginal cost. Let us see why.

As with all profit-maximizing firms, the monopolist equates marginal cost to marginal revenue; but marginal revenue does not equal price. Hence the monopoly does *not* equate marginal cost to price. In order to know the amount produced at any given price, we need to know the market demand curve as well as the marginal cost curve. Under these circumstances, it is possible for different demand conditions to cause the same output to be sold at different prices. This is illustrated in Figure 10.5 by an example in which two monopolists facing the same marginal cost curves but different demand curves sell identical outputs at different prices.

Firm and industry Because the monopolist is the only producer in an industry, there is no need for separate theories about the firm and the industry, as is necessary with perfect competition. The monopoly firm *is* the industry. Thus, the short-run, profit-maximizing position of the firm, as shown in Figure 10.3, is also the short-run equilibrium of the industry.

Box 10.1 deals with an interesting variation of monopoly theory, the pricing of limited editions.

A multi-plant monopoly

So far we have implicitly assumed that the monopoly firm produces all of its output in a single plant. Fortunately, the analysis easily extends to multi-plant monopolists. Assume, for example, that the firm has two plants. How will it allocate production between them? The answer is that any given output will be allocated between the two plants so as to equate their marginal costs. Assume, for example, that plant A was producing 30 units per week at a marginal cost of £20, while plant B was producing 25 units at a marginal cost of £17. Plant A's production could be reduced by one unit, saving £20 in cost, while plant B's production was increased by one unit, adding £17 to cost. Overall output is held constant while costs are reduced by £3. The generalization is that, whenever two plants are producing at

Box 10.1 Demand for once-off production

An interesting case of monopoly pricing occurs with 'limited editions'. These are works of art—sometimes lithographs, etchings, or woodcuts by famous artists and sometimes products with less artistic merit, as in the following examples.

Not long ago one had only to pick up a London telephone directory to see the words 'Limited Edition Print Offer: See inside back cover' in the bottom right-hand corner of a coloured sketch which decorated the front cover of each of the four volumes of the directory. Information on the inside cover revealed that the four watercolours were 'specially commissioned' and would be reproduced 'in a limited edition of 500 prints' to be sold at £25 each or £85 for the set of four. 'Only 500 prints will be made of each image following which the plates will be destroyed.' This suggested that British Telecom felt that limiting the quantity supplied to 500 was necessary to make £25 a viable price, in the sense that the quantity demanded at £25 would be around 500.

Similar examples can be seen in the booklets sent to credit card users with their monthly statements. A Wedgwood 'collector's plate produced on fine bone china' and depicting 'Meadows of Wheatfields' was offered to holders of Midland Bank's Access card, with the promise that production

would be 'limited to 150 firing days' and that a numbered certificate would accompany the plate. In fact, the sellers must have overestimated the quantity that would be demanded at their price of £16.65 (including postage and packing), as the offer was repeated a few months later.

Analysing this case helps to illustrate the flexibility of theory when used imaginatively. The normal demand curve is for a repeated flow of purchases, period after period. In this case, the demand is for a stock to be produced and purchased once only—because the smaller the total number of items produced, the more people value each item and the higher the price that can be charged. This gives rise to a negatively sloped demand curve.

If producers know the curve exactly and know their marginal cost of production, choosing the profit-maximizing price–quantity combination is simple. They equate marginal cost with marginal revenue. But since limited-edition production and sales are not repeated period after period, producers have no chance to learn the shape of the demand curve. They must guess on the basis of the sales of earlier, more or less similar, limited editions. If they set the price too low, they will sell all their output but not at its profit-maximizing price. If they set the price too high, they will be left with unsold output, which they must destroy or re-advertise at considerable expense.

different marginal costs, the total cost of producing their combined output can be reduced by reallocating production from the plant with the higher marginal cost to the plant with the lower marginal cost.

A multi-plant, profit-maximizing monopoly firm will always operate its plants so that their marginal costs are equal.

How does the multi-plant monopoly firm determine its overall marginal cost? Assume, for example, that both plants are operating at a marginal cost of £10 per unit and one is producing 14 units per week while the other is producing 16. The firm's overall output is 30 units at a

marginal cost of £10. This illustrates the following general proposition:

The monopoly firm's marginal cost curve is the horizontal sum of the marginal cost curves of its individual plants.

This sum tells us the total output of all the firm's plants when each is producing at any given marginal cost.

It follows that the analysis in this chapter applies to any monopolist, no matter how many plants it operates. The marginal cost curve we have used is merely the sum of the marginal cost curves of all the plants. In the special case in which there is only one plant, the *firm's MC* curve is that *plant's MC* curve.

The allocative inefficiency of monopoly

We saw in Chapter 9 that the perfectly competitive equilibrium maximizes the sum of consumers' and producers' surpluses. It follows immediately that the lower monopoly output must result in a smaller total of consumers' and producers' surpluses.

The monopoly equilibrium is not the outcome of a voluntary agreement between the one producer and the many consumers. Instead, it is imposed by the monopoly firm by virtue of the power it has over the market. When the monopoly chooses an output below the competitive level, market price is higher than it would be under perfect

competition. As a result, consumers' surplus is diminished, and producers' surplus is increased. In this way, the monopoly firm gains at the expense of consumers. This is not, however, the whole story.

When output is below the competitive level, there is always a *net* loss of surplus. Consumers give up more surplus than the monopolist gains. Some surplus is lost by society, because output between the monopolistic and the competitive levels is not produced. This loss of surplus is called the *deadweight loss of monopoly*. It is illustrated in Figure 10.6

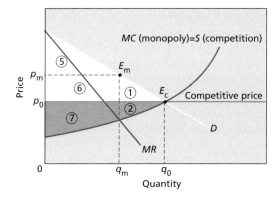

Figure 10.6 The deadweight loss of monopoly
Monopoly is allocatively inefficient because it does not maximize the sum of consumers' and producers' surpluses. At the perfectly competitive equilibrium E_c consumers' surplus is the sum of the yellow shaded areas 1, 5, and 6. When the industry is monopolized, price rises to p_m and consumers' surplus falls to area 5. Consumers lose area 1 because that output is not produced; they lose area 6 because the price rise has transferred it to the monopolist. Producers' surplus in a competitive equilibrium is the sum of the dark blue areas 7 and 2. When the market is monopolized and price rises to p_m, the surplus area 2 is lost because the output is not produced. However, the monopolist gains area 6 from consumers. Area 6 is known to be greater than 2 because p_m maximizes profits. Thus areas 1 and 2 are lost to society. They represent the deadweight loss resulting from monopoly and account for its allocative inefficiency.

It follows that there is a conflict between the private interest of the monopoly producer and the public interest of all the nation's consumers.

This creates a rational case for government intervention to prevent the formation of monopolies if possible, and, if that is not possible, then to control their behaviour.

A multi-price monopolist: price discrimination

So far in this chapter we have assumed that the monopoly firm charges the same price for every unit of its product, no matter where or to whom it sells that product. A monopoly firm will also find it profitable, as we will soon see, to sell different units of the same product at different prices whenever it gets the opportunity. Because this practice is also prevalent in markets that contain a few large firms, called *oligopolistic* markets, the range of examples quoted covers both types of market structure. We deal with price discrimination here because it naturally arises whenever monopoly is discussed.

Raw milk is often sold at one price when it is to be used as fluid milk but at a lower price when it is to be used to make ice cream or cheese. Doctors in private practice often charge for their services according to the incomes of their patients. Cinemas often have lower admission prices for children than for adults. Railroads charge different rates per tonne per kilometre for different products. Electricity producers sell electricity at one rate to homes and at a lower rate to firms. Airlines often charge less to people who stay over a Saturday night than to those who come and go within the week.

Price discrimination occurs when a seller charges different prices for different units of the same product for reasons not associated with differences in cost. Not all price *differences* represent price *discrimination*. Quantity discounts, differences between wholesale and retail prices, and prices that vary with the time of day or the season of the year may not represent price discrimination, because the same product sold at a different time, in a different

place, or in different quantities may have different costs. If an electric power company has unused capacity at certain times of the day, it may be cheaper for the company to provide service at those hours than at peak demand hours. If price differences reflect cost differences, they are not discriminatory. In contrast, when a price difference is based on different buyers' valuations of the same product, price discrimination does occur.

Why price discrimination is profitable

Why should it be profitable for a firm to sell some units of its output at a price that is well below the price that it receives for other units of its output? Persistent price discrimination is profitable either because different buyers are willing to pay different amounts for the same product or because one buyer is willing to pay different amounts for different units of the same product. The basic point about price discrimination is that, in either of these circumstances, sellers may be able to capture some of the consumers' surplus that would otherwise go to buyers.

Discrimination among units of output Look back to Table 6.2 on page 92, which shows the consumers' surplus when a person buys eight glasses of milk at a single price. If the supplier could sell each glass separately, it could capture this surplus. It would sell the first unit for £3.00, the second unit for £1.50, the third unit for £1.00, and so on until the eighth unit was sold for £0.30. The firm would get total revenues of £8.10 rather than the £2.40 obtained from selling eight units at the single price of £0.30 each.

In this example the firm is able to discriminate perfectly and to extract the entire consumers' surplus.

Perfect price discrimination occurs when the firm obtains the entire consumers' surplus. This usually requires that each unit be sold at a separate price. In practice, perfect discrimination is seldom possible. Suppose, however, that the firm could charge two different prices, one for the first four units sold and one for the next four units sold. If it sold the first four units for £0.80 and the next four units for £0.30, it would receive £4.40—less than it would receive if it could discriminate perfectly but more than it would receive if it sold all units at £0.30.

Discrimination among buyers in one market Think of the demand curve in a market that is made up of individual buyers, each of whom has indicated the maximum price that he or she is prepared to pay for the single unit each wishes to purchase. Suppose, for the sake of simplicity, that there are only four buyers, the first of whom is prepared to pay any price up to £4, the second of whom is prepared to pay £3, the third £2, and the fourth £1. Suppose that the product has a marginal cost of production of £1 per unit for all units. If the selling firm is limited to a single price, it will maximize its profits by charging £3, thereby selling two units and earning profits of £4. If the seller can discriminate among each of the buyers, it could charge the first buyer £4 and the second £3, thus increasing its profits from the first two units to £5. Moreover, it could also sell the third unit for £2, thus increasing its profits to £6. It would be indifferent about selling a fourth unit because the price would just cover marginal cost.

Discrimination among markets Many monopoly firms sell in two different markets. Some firms are the only sellers in a tariff-protected home market while being price-takers in foreign markets where there is much competition. The firm will equate its marginal cost to the price in the foreign market, as does any perfect competitor. But in the domestic market it equates marginal costs to marginal revenue, as does any monopolist. As a result, it charges a higher price on sales in the home market than on sales abroad. This case is elaborated in the appendix to this chapter.

Price discrimination more generally Demand curves have a negative slope because different units are valued differently, either by one individual or by different individuals. This fact, combined with a single price for a product, gives rise to consumers' surplus.

The ability to charge multiple prices gives a seller the opportunity to capture some (or, in the extreme case, all) of the consumers' surplus.

The larger the number of different prices that can be charged, the greater is the firm's ability to increase its revenue at the expense of consumers.

It follows that if a selling firm is able to discriminate through price, it can increase revenues received (and thus also profits) from the sale of any given quantity. However, price discrimination is not always possible, even if there are no legal barriers to its use.

When is price discrimination possible?

Discrimination among units of output sold to the same buyer requires that the seller be able to keep track of the units that a buyer consumes in each period. Thus, the tenth unit purchased by a given buyer in a given month can be sold at a price that is different from the fifth unit *only* if the seller can keep track of who buys what. This can be done by an electric company through its meter readings or by a magazine publisher by distinguishing between renewals and new subscriptions. It can also be done by distributing certificates or coupons that allow, for example, a car wash at a reduced price on a return visit.

Discrimination among buyers is possible only if the buyers who face the low price cannot resell the goods to the buyers who face the high price. Even though the local butcher might like to charge the banker twice as much for buying steak as he charges the taxi driver, he cannot succeed in doing so. The banker can always shop for meat in the supermarket, where her occupation is not known. Even if the butcher and the supermarket agreed to charge her twice as much, she could hire the taxi driver to shop for her. The surgeon, however, may succeed in discriminating (especially if other reputable surgeons do the same) because it will not do the banker much good to hire the taxi driver to have her operation for her.

Price discrimination is possible if the seller can either distinguish individual units bought by a single buyer or separate buyers into classes such that resale among classes is impossible.

The ability to prevent resale tends to be associated with the character of the product or the ability to classify buyers into readily identifiable groups. Services are less easily resold than goods; goods that require installation by the manufacturer (e.g. heavy equipment) are less easily resold than movable goods such as household appliances.

An interesting example where resale is impossible occurs in the case of plate glass. Small pieces of plate glass are much cheaper to buy per square metre than bigger pieces, but the person who needs glass for a picture window that is 2 metres by 3 metres cannot use four pieces of glass that are 1 metre by 1.5 metres

Of course, it is not enough to be able to separate different buyers or different units into separate classes. The seller must also be able to control the supply going to each group. There is no point, for example, in asking more than the competitive price from some buyers if they can simply go to other firms who sell the good at the competitive price.

Transportation costs, tariff barriers, and import quotas separate classes of buyers geographically and may make discrimination possible.

Consequences of price discrimination

In the appendix to this chapter we show that a monopoly firm that is able to discriminate between two markets will allocate its output between those two markets so as to equate the marginal revenues in the two. If this is not done, total revenue can always be increased by reducing sales by one unit in the market with the lower marginal revenue and raising sales by one unit in the market with the higher marginal revenue. This reallocation of sales raises total revenue by the difference between the two marginal revenues. If the demand curves are different in the two markets, having the same marginal revenues means charging different prices.

Two important consequences of price discrimination follow from this result.

Proposition 1. For any given level of output the most profitable system of discriminatory prices will provide higher total revenue to the firm than the profit-maximizing single price.

Remember that a monopolist with the power to discriminate could produce exactly the same quantity as a single-price monopolist and charge everyone the same price. Therefore, it need never receive *less* revenue, and it can do better if it can raise the price on even one unit sold, as long as the price need not be lowered on any other.

Proposition 2. Output under price discrimination will generally be larger than under a single-price monopoly.

Remember that a monopoly firm that must charge a single price for a product will produce less than would all the firms in a perfectly competitive industry because it knows that selling more depresses its price. Price discrimination allows the firm to avoid this disincentive. To the extent that the firm can sell its output in separate blocks, it can sell another block without spoiling the market for the block that is already being sold. In the case of perfect price discrimination, in which every unit of output is sold at a different price, the profit-maximizing monopolist will produce every unit for which the price charged is greater than or equal to its marginal cost. It will therefore produce the same quantity of output as does the perfectly competitive industry.

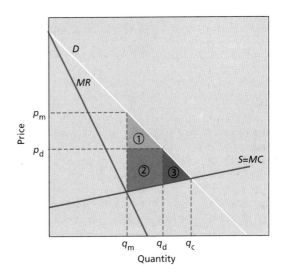

Figure 10.7 A price-discriminating monopolist
Price discrimination reduces the deadweight loss of monopoly. Initially the monopolist produces output q_m where $MC = MR$ instead of the competitive output q_c where MC equals demand (which is consumers' marginal utility). The deadweight loss is the sum of the three blue shaded areas labelled 1, 2, and 3. A second group of consumers is then isolated from the first. This group, who would buy nothing at the original price of p_m, will buy an amount that would increase total output to q_d at a price of p_d. The monopoly firm's profits now rise by the shaded area 2, which is the difference between its cost curve and the price p_d that is charged to the new group who buy the amount between q_m and q_d. Consumers' surplus rises by the shaded area labelled 1 and total deadweight loss falls to the shaded area labelled 3.

Figure 10.7 illustrates the output-expanding effects of price discrimination. It shows a case in which a monopoly firm has maximized profits selling at a single price. The firm then finds that it can isolate a group of potential buyers who were unwilling to purchase at the monopoly price. Perhaps it forms a buying club from which members of the first group are excluded. A lower price can be used to attract the new group of buyers without having to lower the price charged to its original customers. As long as the new price exceeds the marginal cost of producing the extra output, the monopoly firm adds to its profits. But consumers' surplus is also increased, since a new group of buyers is now in the market. So both the monopolist and consumers earn additional surplus.

Normative aspects of price discrimination

There are two quite separate issues involved in evaluating any particular example of price discrimination. The first concerns the effect of discrimination on the level of

Box 10.2 Examples of price discrimination

The principle of charging different customers different prices has been around for a very long time. The earliest example we have come across is from the Egyptian kingdom of Rameses the Great in the period 1304–1237 BC.* In what is now southern Lebanon the Egyptians maintained a toll road on an important route across a range of hills. There were other routes, but they were considerably more tortuous than this one. The servant of the Egyptian ruler sent to administer this toll road found that he had some discretion over pricing. He wrote to his employers asking for guidelines on charges. The reply came back: 'Charge what the traffic will bear.' So famous is this instruction that the phrase has become something of a cliché. It is based upon the insight, set out in the text, that setting different prices increases revenue. In practice the discriminating monopolist charges each traveller the maximum that he or she would be prepared to pay to use the road.

Here are two more recent examples from transport. The first shows price discrimination in action. The second shows that problems can arise when price discrimination does not occur.

Air fares In June 1994 a standard fare on British Airways from London Heathrow to Rome was £445. This fare covered return the same day or within the week. However, if you stayed over Saturday night, the fare was only £176! This difference for the same class of fare on the same planes discriminates between the business traveller and the tourist. Such discrimination is profitable because the elasticities of demand for these two types of travel are different, being lower for business than for pleasure travel.

A similar price discrimination applies to transatlantic airfares. In early 1996 a standard economy return fare between London and New York on a reputable airline cost around £900. However, the Apex fare for anyone prepared to book fourteen days in advance and stay at least seven days was around £400, and in the off-peak season even better deals were available. Again, these substantial differences reflect a segmentation of the market between business travellers, who presumably get their fares paid by their company, and tourists who are paying out of their own pocket.

British Rail This case illustrates the problems that arise when segmentation is not allowed even though both producers and consumers could be better off if it were. Some years ago British Rail (the nationalized industry that operated all British railways) was not allowed to charge different prices to passengers travelling on different lines. In the interest of equity, a fixed fare per passenger mile was laid down by government and had to be charged on all lines whatever the density of their passenger traffic and whatever the elasticity of demand for their services. In the interests of economy, branch lines were closed down when they could not cover their costs. This meant that some lines closed even though the users preferred rail transport to any of the available alternatives and the strength of their preferences was such that they would voluntarily have paid a price sufficient for the line to cover its costs. The lines were none the less closed because it was thought inequitable to charge the passengers on one line more than the passengers on other lines.

---

*   We are grateful to Professor Arie Melnik of Haifa University for this example.

---

output. Discrimination usually results in a higher output than would occur if a single price were charged. As we saw in Figure 10.7, price discrimination tends to reduce the deadweight loss of monopoly and therefore leads to a more efficient allocation of resources than does a single-price monopoly.

Often, however, it is the effect on income distribution that accounts for people's strong emotional reactions to price discrimination. Compared with perfect competition, price discrimination transfers income from buyers to sellers. When buyers are poor and sellers are rich, this may seem undesirable. However, the case is often more complex. For example, doctors in countries with market-based medical systems often vary their charges with their patients' incomes. This enables them to serve their poorer patients in ways that they could not if they had to charge everyone a single price for their services. Another example is the prevalent practice of giving discounts to old-age pensioners or airline passengers who stay on over a weekend. These practices often allow lower-income persons to buy a product that they would be unable to afford if it were sold at the single price that maximized the producers' profits.

Box 10.2 outlines some interesting cases of price discrimination.

Long-run monopoly equilibrium

In both monopolized and perfectly competitive industries losses and profits provide incentives for exit and entry.

If the monopoly firm is suffering losses in the short run, it will continue to operate as long as it can cover its variable costs. In the long run, however, it will leave the industry unless it can find a scale of operations at which its full opportunity costs can be covered.

If the monopoly firm is making profits, other firms will wish to enter the industry in order to earn more than the opportunity cost of their capital. If such entry occurs, the equilibrium position shown in Figure 10.3 will change, and the firm will cease to be a monopolist.

Entry barriers

Impediments that prevent entry are called **entry barriers;** they may be either natural or created.

If a monopoly firm's profits are to persist in the long run, effective entry barriers must prevent the entry of new firms into the industry.

Barriers determined by technology

Natural barriers most commonly arise as a result of economies of scale. When the long-run average cost curve is negatively sloped over a large range of output, big firms have significantly lower average total costs than small firms.

You will recall from Chapter 9 that perfectly competitive firms cannot be in long-run equilibrium on the negatively sloped segment of their long-run average cost curve (see Figure 9.12 on page 151).

Now suppose that an industry's technology is such that any firm's minimum achievable average cost is £10, which is reached at an output of 10,000 units per week. Further, assume that at a price of £10 the total quantity demanded is 11,000 units per week. Under these circumstances only one firm can operate at or near its minimum costs.

A **natural monopoly** occurs when, given the industry's current technology, the demand conditions allow no more than one firm to cover its costs while producing at the minimum point of its long-run cost curve. In a natural monopoly, there is no price at which two firms can both sell enough to cover their total costs.

Another type of technologically determined barrier is *set-up cost*. If a firm could be catapulted fully grown into the market, it might be able to compete effectively with the existing monopolist. However, the cost to the new firm of entering the market, developing its products, and establishing such things as its brand image and its dealer network may be so large that entry would be unprofitable.

Policy-created barriers

Many entry barriers are created by conscious government action and are, therefore, officially condoned. Patent laws, for instance, may prevent entry by conferring on the patent-holder the sole legal right to produce a particular product for a specific period of time.

A firm may also be granted a charter or a franchise that prohibits competition by law. Regulation and licensing of firms, often in service industries, can restrict entry severely. For example, the 1979 Banking Act required all banks in the UK to be authorized by the Bank of England. The 1986 Financial Services Act required all sellers of investment products to be authorized by the Securities and Investment Board (SIB) or some other recognized regulatory body. Regulation and authorization of all financial firms, including banks, was effectively transferred to the Finan-

cial Services Authority in 1998, although the legal change awaited the passage of the necessary legislation.

Other barriers can be created by the firm or firms already in the market. In extreme cases the threat of force or sabotage can deter entry. The most obvious entry barriers of this type are encountered in the production and sale of illegal goods and services, where operation outside the law makes available an array of illegal but potent barriers to new entrants. The drug trade is a current example. In contrast, legitimate firms must use legal tactics intended to increase a new entrant's set-up costs. Examples are the threat of price-cutting, designed to impose unsustainable losses on a new entrant, and heavy brand-name advertising. (These and other created entry barriers will be discussed in much more detail in Chapter 11.)

The significance of entry barriers

Because there are no entry barriers in perfect competition, profits cannot persist in the long run.

Profits attract entry, and entry erodes profits.

In monopoly, however, profits can persist in the long run whenever there are effective barriers to entry.

Entry barriers frustrate the adjustment mechanism that would otherwise push profits towards zero in the long run.

'Creative destruction'

In the very long run technology changes. New ways of producing old products are invented, and new products are created to satisfy both familiar and new wants. What has this to do with entry barriers? The answer is that a monopoly that succeeds in preventing the entry of new firms capable of producing its product will sooner or later find its barriers circumvented by innovations. One firm may be able to use new processes that avoid some patent or other barrier that the monopolist relies on to bar entry of competing firms. Another firm may compete by producing a new product that, although somewhat different, still satisfies the same need as the monopoly firm's product. Yet another firm might get around a natural monopoly by inventing a technology that produces the good at a much lower cost than the existing monopoly firm's technology. The new technology may subsequently allow several firms to enter the market and still cover costs.

Joseph Schumpeter (1883–1950) argued that entry barriers were not a serious problem in the very long run. According to Schumpeter, the possibility of obtaining monopoly profits provides a major incentive for people to risk their money by financing inventions and innovations. The large short-run profits of a monopoly encourage others to try to capture some of these profits for themselves. If a frontal attack on the monopolist's barriers to entry is not possible, the barriers will be circumvented by such means as the development of similar products against which the monopolist will not have entry protection.

Schumpeter called the replacing of an existing monopoly by one or more new entrants through the invention of new products or new production techniques the *process of creative destruction*. He argued that this process precludes the very-long-run persistence of barriers to entry into industries that earn large profits.

Cartels as monopolies

Until this point in our discussion a monopoly has meant that there is only one firm in an industry. A second way in which a monopoly can arise is for many firms in an industry to agree to co-operate with one another, to behave as if they were a single seller, in order to maximize joint profits by eliminating competition among themselves. Such a group of firms is called a **cartel,** or sometimes just a producers' association. A cartel that includes *all* firms in the industry can behave in the same way as a single-firm monopoly that owned all of these firms. The firms can agree among themselves to restrict their total output to the level that maximizes their joint profits.[3]

The effects of cartelization

Perfectly competitive firms accept the market price as given and increase their output until their marginal cost equals price. In contrast, a monopoly firm knows that increasing its output will depress the market price. Taking account of this, the monopolist increases its output only until marginal revenue is equal to marginal cost. If all the firms in a perfectly competitive industry form a cartel, they too will be able to take account of the effect of their *joint output* on price. They can agree to restrict industry output to the level that maximizes their joint profits (where the industry's marginal cost is equal to the industry's marginal revenue). One way to do this is to establish a quota for each firm's output. Say that the profit-maximizing output is two-thirds of the perfectly competitive output. When the cartel is formed, each firm could be given a quota equal to two-thirds of its competitive output.

The effect of cartelizing a perfectly competitive industry and of reducing its output through production quotas is shown in part (i) of Figure 10.8.

Problems facing cartels

Cartels encounter two characteristic problems. The first is ensuring that members follow the behaviour that will maximize the industry's *joint* profits, and the second is preventing these profits from being eroded by the entry of new firms.

Enforcement of output restrictions The managers of any cartel want the industry to produce its profit-maximizing output. Their job is made more difficult if individual firms either stay out of the cartel or enter and then cheat on their output quotas. Any one firm has an incentive to do just this: to be either the one that stays out of the organization or the one that enters and then cheats on its output quota. For the sake of simplicity, assume that all firms enter the cartel, so enforcement problems are concerned strictly with cheating by its members.

If Firm X is the only firm to cheat, it is in the best of all possible situations. All other firms restrict output and hold the industry price near its monopoly level. They earn profits, but only by restricting output. Firm X can then reap the full benefit of the other firms' output restraint and sell some additional output at the high price that has been set by the cartel's actions. However, if all of the firms cheat, the price will be pushed back to the competitive level, and all of the firms will return to their zero-profit position.

This conflict between the interests of the group and the interests of the individual firm creates the cartel's dilemma. Provided that enough firms co-operate in restricting output, all firms are better off than they would be if the industry remained perfectly competitive. However, any one firm is even better off if it remains outside the cartel, or joins it and then cheats by exceeding its output quota. If all firms act on this incentive, all will be worse off than if they had joined the cartel and restricted output.

Cartels tend to be unstable because of the strong incentives for individual firms to violate the output quotas needed to enforce the monopoly price.

The conflict between the motives for co-operation and for independent action is analysed in more detail in part (ii) of Figure 10.8.

Cartels and similar output-restricting arrangements have a long history. For example, schemes to raise farm

---

[3] In this chapter we deal with the simple case in which *all* of the firms in a perfectly competitive industry form a cartel in order to act as if they were a monopoly. Cartels are sometimes formed by a group of firms that account for a significant part, but not all, of the total supply of some commodity. The effect is to turn the industry into what is called an *oligopoly*. The most famous example of this type is the Organization of Petroleum Exporting Countries, best known as OPEC. We will return to this type of cartel in Chapter 11.

(i) Market equilibrium   **(ii) Firm equilibrium**

Figure 10.8 Conflicting forces affecting cartels

Co-operation leads to the monopoly price, but individual self-interest leads to production in excess of the monopoly output. Market conditions are shown in part (i), and the situation of a typical firm is shown in part (ii). (Note the change of scale between the two graphs.) Initially the market is in competitive equilibrium, with price p_0 and quantity Q_0. The individual firm is producing output q_0 and is just covering its total costs.

The cartel is formed and then enforces quotas on individual firms that are sufficient to reduce the industry's output to Q_1, the output that maximizes the joint profits of the cartel members. Price rises to p_1. The typical firm's quota is q_1. The firm's profits rise from zero to the amount shown by the dark blue area in part (ii). Once price is raised to p_1, however, the individual firm would like to increase output to q_2, where marginal cost is equal to the price set by the cartel. This would allow the firm to earn profits shown by the blue hatched area. If all firms violate their quotas, industry output will exceed Q_1, and the profits earned by all firms will fall.

incomes by limiting crops bear ample testimony to the accuracy of the predicted instability of cartels. In the past, industry agreements to restrict output often broke down as individual farmers exceeded their quotas. This is why most crop-restriction plans are now operated by governments rather than by private cartels. Production quotas backed by the full coercive power of the state can force monopoly behaviour on existing producers and can effectively bar the entry of new ones.

Restricting entry A cartel must not only police the be-haviour of its members, but must also be able to prevent the entry of new producers. In an industry with no strong natural entry barriers, to maintain its profits in the long run it must create its own barriers. Otherwise new firms will enter and force down price until the profits disappear. Successful cartels are often able to license the firms in the industry and to control entry by restricting the number of licences. At other times the government has operated a quota system and has given it the force of law. If no one can produce without a quota and the quotas are allocated among existing producers, entry is precluded.

Summary

A single-price monopolist

■ A monopoly is an industry containing a single firm. The monopoly firm maximizes its profits by equating marginal cost to marginal revenue, which is less than price. Production under monopoly is less than it would be under perfect competition, where marginal cost is equated to price.

The allocative inefficiency of monopoly

■ Monopoly is allocatively inefficient. By producing less than the perfectly competitive output it transfers some consumers' surplus to its own profits and also causes deadweight loss of surplus that would have resulted from the output that is not produced.

A multi-price monopolist

■ If a monopolist can discriminate among either different units or different customers, it will always sell more and earn greater profits than if it must charge a single price.

■ For price discrimination to be possible, the seller must be able to distinguish individual units bought by a single buyer or to separate buyers into classes among whom resale is impossible.

Long-run monopoly equilibrium

■ A monopoly can earn positive profits in the long run if there are barriers to entry. These may be man-made, such as patents or exclusive franchises, or natural, such as economies of large-scale production.

Cartels as monopolies

■ The joint profits of all firms in a perfectly competitive industry can always be increased if they agree to restrict output. After agreement is in place, each firm can increase its profits by violating the agreement. If they all do this, profits are reduced to the perfectly competitive level.

Topics for review

■ Relationship between price and marginal revenue for a monopolist

■ Relationships among marginal revenue, total revenue, and elasticity for a monopolist

■ Short- and long-run monopoly equilibrium

■ Natural and created entry barriers

■ Price discrimination among different units and different buyers

■ Individual versus group profits in a cartel

Questions for discussion

1 A firm owns a mineral spring in an area where no other source of water is available. It can produce indefinitely once certain pipes are installed. What is the firm's profit-maximizing price? What is the elasticity of demand at that price? Is this the appropriate pricing policy if the water monopoly is owned by the municipal government and operated in the public interest?

2 Using the same cost information as for the firm described in question 3 of Chapter 8 (page 135), you are now given information about demand. The table shows the price at which the corresponding quantity can be sold:

Sales (units)	Price (£)
20	19.20
40	18.40
60	17.60
100	16.00
200	12.00
300	8.00
400	4.00
500	0.00
1,000	—

(You might like to know that this is a straight-line demand curve that can be expressed as $p = 20 - 0.04q$, where p is price and q is quantity sold.) (a) What is the marginal revenue for each level of sales? (b) What are the approximate profit-maximizing levels of sales and price? (c) Draw a graph showing total costs, total revenue, and profit at each level of sales.

3 What does it mean to say that a perfectly competitive firm (a) faces a horizontal demand curve, (b) is a price-taker, and (c) does not compete with anyone?

4 Transatlantic airline fares are higher in summer than in winter. Some railroads charge lower passenger fares during the week than on weekends. Electric companies charge consumers lower rates the more electricity they use. On many airline trips you get a reduced fare if you stay over Saturday night. Are these all examples of price discrimination? What additional information would you need before answering this question?

5 Suppose now that the firm in question 2 above has constant marginal costs of £4.00 per unit (i.e. ignore previous information about costs) and that it faces two segmented markets. One has the demand curve above in question 2, and the other has the following demand curve:

Sales (units)	Price (£)
20	9.60
40	9.20
60	8.80
100	8.00
200	6.00
300	4.00
400	2.00
500	0.00
1,000	—

(If it helps, this demand curve can be written $p = 10 - 0.02q$.) (a) What quantity will the firm sell in each market? (b) What price will be charged in each market?

Appendix A formal analysis of price discrimination among markets

Consider a monopoly firm that sells a single product in two distinct markets, A and B, with demand, marginal revenue, and cost curves as shown in Figure 10A.1. Resale among customers is impossible and a single price must be charged in each market.

What is the best price for the firm to charge in each market? The simplest way to discover this is to imagine the firm deciding how best to allocate any given total output Q^* between two markets. Since output is fixed arbitrarily at Q^*, there is nothing the monopolist can do about costs. The best thing it can do, therefore, is to maximize the revenue that it gets by selling Q^* in the two markets. *To do this it will allocate its sales between the markets until the marginal revenues are the same in each market.* Consider what would happen if the marginal revenue in market A exceeded the marginal revenue in market B. The firm could keep its overall output constant at Q^* but reallocate a unit of sales from B to A, gaining a net addition in revenue equal to the difference between the marginal revenues in the two markets. Thus, it will always pay a monopoly firm to reallocate a given total quantity between its markets as long as marginal revenues are not equal in the two markets.

If we assume that marginal cost is constant, we can determine the profit-maximizing course of action from Figure 10A.1. The MC curve in both parts shows the constant marginal cost. The firm's total profits are maximized by equating MR in each market to its constant MC, thus selling q_A at p_A in market A and q_B at p_B in market B. Marginal revenue is the same in each market ($c_A = c_B$) so that the firm has its total output correctly allocated between the two markets, and marginal cost equals marginal rev-

enue, showing that the firm would lose profits if it produced more or less total output.

Next, assume that marginal cost varies with output, being given by MC' in Figure 10A.2(iii). Now we cannot just put the MC curve on to the diagram for each market, since the marginal cost of producing another unit for sale in market A will depend on how much is being produced for sale in market B and vice versa. To determine what overall production should be, we need to know overall marginal revenue. To find this, we merely sum the separate quantities in each market that correspond to each particular marginal revenue. If, for example, the tenth unit sold in market A and the fifteenth unit sold in market B each have a marginal revenue of £1 in their separate markets, then the marginal revenue of £1 corresponds to overall sales of 25 units (10 units in A and 15 in B). This example illustrates the general principle: the overall marginal revenue curve for a discriminating monopolist is the horizontal sum of the marginal revenue curves in each of its markets. This overall curve shows the marginal revenue associated with an increment to production on the assumption that sales are divided between the two markets so as to keep the two marginal revenues equal.

This overall MR curve is shown in Figure 10A.2(iii) and is labelled MR'. The firm's total profit-maximizing output is at Q_1, where MR' and MC' intersect (at a value of c_1). By construction, marginal revenue is c_1 in each market although price is different. To find the equilibrium price and quantity in each market, find the quantities, q_A and q_B, that correspond to this marginal revenue; then find the prices in each market that correspond to q_A and q_B. All of this is illustrated in parts (i) and (ii) of the figure.

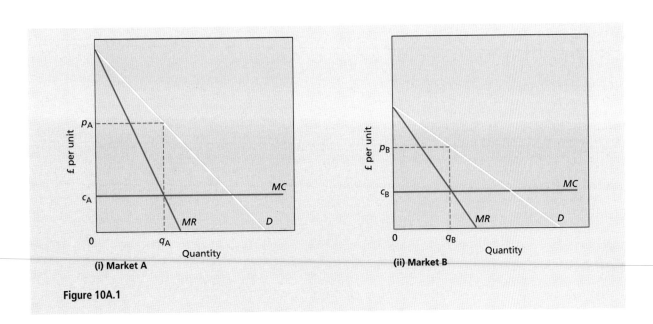

(i) Market A   (ii) Market B

Figure 10A.1

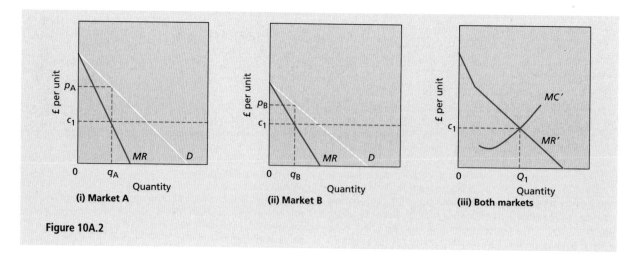

Figure 10A.2

An application

In some industries firms sell competitively on international markets while enjoying a home market that is protected from foreign competition by tariffs or import quotas. To illustrate the issues involved, consider the following extreme case. A firm is the only producer of product X in country A. There are thousands of producers of X in other countries, so that X is sold abroad under conditions of perfect competition. The government of country A grants the firm a monopoly in the home market by prohibiting imports of X. The firm is now faced with a negatively sloped demand curve at home and a perfectly elastic demand curve abroad at the prevailing world price of X.

What will it do? To maximize profits, the firm will divide its sales between the foreign and the home markets so as to equate marginal revenues in the two. On the world market its average and marginal revenues are equal to the world price. Thus, the firm will equate marginal revenue in the home market with the world price, and since price exceeds marginal revenue at home (because the demand curve slopes downwards), price at home must exceed price abroad.

The argument is illustrated in Figure 10A.3. The home market is shown in (i), the foreign market in (ii), and the sum of the marginal revenue curves in (iii). Provided that the marginal cost curve cuts the marginal revenue curve to the right of the kink (i.e. *MC* does not exceed the world price when only the home market is served), the two markets will be served at prices of p_H at home and p_F abroad. The total quantity sold will be Q, of which q_H is allocated to the home market and the rest ($q_F = Q - q_H$) is sold abroad.

Figure 10A.3

Chapter 11
Imperfect Competition

Most firms involved in the production, distribution, and retailing of consumer goods and services, as well as capital goods, operate under intermediate market structures rather than the two extremes of perfect competition and monopoly. On the one hand, they are not monopolies because their industries contain several firms, which often compete actively against each other. Firms manufacturing cars, refrigerators, TV sets, breakfast cereals, and many other consumer goods are in industries containing several close rivals, usually both foreign and domestic. Even in small towns, residents find more than one chemist, garage, hairdresser, and supermarket competing for their patronage. On the other hand, they do not operate in perfectly competitive markets because the number of competing firms is often small, and, even when the number is large, *the firms are not price-takers*.

In this chapter we study firm behaviour in two intermediate market structures. One, which is called monopolistic competition, is close to perfect competition with one important difference. Firms do not sell a homogeneous product. The second, called oligopoly, deals with industries that typically contain a few large firms, which compete actively with each other.

Patterns of concentration in manufacturing

One measure of the extent to which firms in some industry have potential market power is called a **concentration ratio**. This measures the fraction of total sales in the nation that are controlled by some specified number of the industry's largest sellers. Common types of concentration ratios cite the share of an industry's total market sales made by the largest three or five firms. For example, the UK five-firm concentration ratio for soaps and toilet preparations is 53.5 per cent. This means that the largest five firms in that industry account for 53.5 per cent of the industry's total sales.

Table 11.1 gives the five-firm concentration ratios for thirteen UK manufacturing industries.[1] The data show that in most of these industries the largest five firms are

Table 11.1 UK selected concentration ratios, 1990 (% of total industry value added produced by largest five enterprises)

Industry	Concentration ratio
Tobacco	99.3
Motor vehicles	87.7
Cycles and motorcycles	76.7
Domestic electric appliances	61.2
Ice-cream and sweets	58.8
Spirit distilling	56.1
Pharmaceuticals	55.8
Soap and toilet preparations	53.5
Rubber products	49.5
Brewing	43.0
Paints, varnishes, and ink	31.9
Toys and sports goods	24.7
Leather goods	12.4

UK concentration ratios vary greatly across manufacturing industries. The largest five firms account for virtually all of the output of tobacco products but only 12 per cent of the output of leather products.

Source: CSO Census of Production, published in *Business Monitor* (PA1002).

too large a part of the total market to be price-takers. Yet none of these industries is a single-firm monopoly.

Although national concentration ratios provide useful information, care must be taken in interpreting them. For example, markets often extend across national borders. A single firm operating in the United Kingdom does not have a monopoly if it is competing in the UK market against products imported from several foreign producers. The globalization of competition, brought about by the falling costs of transportation and communication, has been one of the most significant developments in the world economy in recent decades. Global competition has greatly reduced the number of secure monopolies that exist in national markets. This important development is discussed further in Box 11.1.

[1] The census on which these figures are based occurs only once every decade. The results of the most recent census should be available by the end of the century but were not available at the time of writing.

Box 11.1 Globalization of production and competition

A mere 150 years ago people and news travelled by sailing ship, so that it took months to communicate across various parts of the world. Advances in the first 60 years of the twentieth century sped up both communications and travel. In the past three decades the pace of change in communications technology has accelerated. The world has witnessed a communications revolution that has dramatically changed the way business decisions are made and implemented.

Four decades ago telephone links were laboriously and unreliably connected by operators; satellites were newfangled toys for rocket scientists; photocopying and telecopying were completely unknown; mail was the only way to send hard copy, and getting it to overseas destinations often took weeks; computers were in their infancy; and jets were just beginning to replace the much slower and less reliable propeller aircraft. Today direct dialling is available to most parts of the world, at a fraction of what long-distance calls cost forty years ago. Faxes, satellite links, fast jet travel, computer networks, cheap courier services, and a host of other developments have made communication that is reliable, and often instantaneous, available throughout the world.

The communications revolution has been a major contributor to the development of what has become known as the 'global village', three important characteristics of which are a *disintegration* of production, an increase in competition, and a decline in the power of the nation-state.

Production The communications revolution has allowed many large international companies, known as transnational corporations (TNCs), to decentralize their production process (see Box 8.1). They are now able to locate their research and development (R&D) where the best scientists are available. They can produce various components in dozens of places, locating each activity in the country where costs are cheapest for that type of production. They can then ship all the parts, as they are needed, to an assembly factory where the product is 'made'.

The globalization of production has brought employment, and rising real wages, to people in many less developed countries. At the same time, it has put less skilled labour in the developed countries under strong competitive pressures.

Competition The communications revolution has also caused an internationalization of competition in almost all industries. National markets are no longer protected for local producers by high costs of transportation and communication or by consumers' ignorance of similar foreign products. Walk into a local supermarket or department store today and you will have no trouble in finding products representing most of the UN member states.

Consumers gain by being able to choose from an enormous range of goods and services. Firms that are successful gain worldwide sales. Firms that fall behind even momentarily may, however, be wiped out by competition coming from many quarters. Global competition is fierce competition, and firms that want to survive must be fast on the uptake of their own and other people's new ideas.

Economic policy The globalization of production, and consequently of competition, has greatly reduced the scope for individual countries to implement distinctive economic policies. Today, firms of all sorts, from large transnationals to individuals operating out of homes through computer links, can relocate production easily. So tough national policies that reduce local profitability are often self-defeating, as firms move production elsewhere. Generous policies that seek to attract production may succeed only in attracting small and specialized parts of it.

To measure potential market power appropriately, concentration ratios need to measure the fraction of sales made in the relevant market by the largest firms operating in that market, whether they are located at home or abroad.

Imperfectly competitive market structures

The market structures that we are now going to study are called *imperfectly competitive*. The word 'competitive' emphasizes that we are not dealing with monopoly, and the word 'imperfect' emphasizes that we are not dealing with perfect competition.

We first note patterns of firm behaviour that are typical of all imperfectly competitive market structures.

Firms create their own products

If a new farmer enters the wheat industry, the full range of products that can be produced is already in existence. If he decides to produce No. 1 Durham wheat, it will be the same as the No. 1 Durham wheat produced by all other farmers. In contrast, if a new firm enters the computer software industry, that firm must decide on the characteristics of the new computer programs that it is to produce. It will not produce programs that are identical to those already in production. Rather, it will develop, at substantial cost, one or more new programs, each of which will have its own distinctive characteristics. This is true of firms in virtually all consumer and capital goods industries. As a result, firms in these industries sell a range of differentiated products. The term **differentiated product** refers to a group of products that are similar enough to be considered variations on one generic product but dissimilar enough that they can be sold at different prices.

Most firms in imperfectly competitive market structures sell differentiated products. In such industries, the firm itself must decide on the characteristics of the products it will sell.

Firms choose their prices

In imperfectly competitive markets firms typically have several product lines that differ more or less from each other and from the competing product lines of other firms. No market sets a single price for razor blades, television sets, face soap, or word-processing packages by equating overall demand with overall supply. Instead, *each* variety of the differentiated product has a price that must be set by its maker. Of course, a certain amount of haggling is possible, particularly at the retail level; but this is usually within well-defined limits set by the price charged by the producers.

In such circumstances economists say that firms *administer* their prices and are **price-makers** rather than price-takers. An **administered price** is a price set by the conscious decision of an individual firm rather than by impersonal market forces.

Each firm has expectations about the quantity that it will sell at the price that it sets for each of its product lines. *Unexpected* market fluctuations then cause unexpected variations in the quantities that are sold at the administered prices.

In market structures other than perfect competition, firms set their prices and then let demand determine sales. Changes in market conditions are signalled to the firm by changes in the quantity that the firm sells at its current administered price.

The changed conditions may or may not then lead firms to change their prices.

Short-run price stability   In perfect competition prices change continually in response to changes in demand and supply. In markets for differentiated products, prices often change less frequently. Manufacturers' prices for motor cars, computers, television sets, and men's suits do not change with anything like the frequency that prices change in markets for basic materials or shares and bonds. (Retail mark-ups are, however, varied more often in response to short-term fluctuations in market conditions.)

Modern firms that sell differentiated products typically have hundreds, or even thousands, of distinct products on their price lists. Changing such a long list of administered prices involves costs. These include the costs of printing new list prices and notifying all customers, the difficulty of keeping track of frequently changing prices for purposes of accounting and billing, and the loss of customer and retailer goodwill owing to the uncertainty caused by frequent changes in prices.

Because firms producing differentiated products must administer their own prices, they must decide on the *frequency* with which they change these prices.

In making this decision, each firm will balance the cost of making price changes against the revenue lost by not making price changes. Clearly, the likelihood that the firm will make costly price changes rises with the size of the disturbance to which it is adjusting and the probability that the disturbance will not be reversed. Thus, transitory fluctuations in demand may be met by changing output with prices constant, while changes in costs that are thought to be permanent are passed on through price increases.[2]

Other aspects of the behaviour of firms

Several other important aspects of the observed behaviour of firms in imperfect competition could not occur under either perfect competition or monopoly.

Non-price competition   Many firms spend large sums of money on advertising. They do so in an attempt both to shift the demand curve for the industry's product and also to attract customers from competing firms. Firms often offer competing standards of quality and product guarantees. Any kind of sales promotion activity undertaken by a single firm would not happen under perfect competition since each firm can sell any amount at the going market price. Any such scheme directed at competing firms in the same industry is, by definition, inconsistent with monopoly. According to some recent theories, firms also use advertising to signal their commitment to quality and service. Again this is something a perfect competitor would never do, and something a pure monopolist is unlikely to need to do.

Unexploited scale economies   Many firms in industries that contain more than one firm appear to be operating on the downward-sloping portions of the long-run average cost curves for many of the individual product lines that they produce. Although this is possible under monopoly, firms in perfect competition must, in the long run, be at the minimum point of their long-run average cost curves (see Figure 9.12 on page 151).

---

[2] Over fifty years ago the British economist Paul Sweezy offered an explanation of oligopolistic price stickiness called the 'kinked demand curve'. This explanation has long since been discredited on both empirical grounds (no evidence for it) and theoretical grounds (the behaviour it assumes can be shown to be inconsistent with profit maximization). It will not be found in any modern textbook on industrial organization, although it still survives in a few elementary textbooks and the occasional examination paper.

One set of reasons for this is found in the high development costs and short product lives of many modern products. For example, the manager of a large telecommunications firm recently stated that 80 per cent of the products his firm sells today did not exist five years ago! In such cases, firms face steeply falling long-run average total cost curves. The more units that are sold, the lower are the fixed development costs per unit. Given perfect competition, these firms would go on increasing outputs and sales until rising marginal costs of production just balanced their falling fixed average costs, bringing their average total cost to a minimum. As it is, they often face falling average total cost curves all through each product's life-cycle.

Entry prevention Firms in many industries engage in activities that appear to be designed to hinder the entry of new firms, thereby preventing existing pure profits from being eroded by entry. We will consider these activities in much more detail later in the chapter.

The two main market structures designed to capture the key elements of imperfect competition are monopolistic competition and oligopoly. We consider these in turn.

Monopolistic competition

The American economist Edward Chamberlin (1899–1967) was the originator of the theory of **monopolistic competition,** which refers to imperfect competition among many firms.[3]

The theory

Assumptions

The theory is based on four key assumptions.

1. *Each firm produces one specific variety, or brand, of the industry's differentiated product.* Each firm thus faces a demand curve that, although it is negatively sloped, is highly elastic, because other varieties of the same product that are sold by other firms provide many close substitutes.

2. *The industry contains so many firms that each one ignores the possible reactions of its many competitors when it makes its own price and output decisions.* Each firm makes decisions based on its own demand and cost conditions and does not consider any response that may be made by the other firms in the industry.

3. *There is freedom of entry and exit in the industry.* If existing firms are earning profits, new firms have an incentive to enter. When they do, the demand for the industry's product must be shared among more brands.

4. *There is symmetry.* When a new firm enters the industry selling a new version of the differentiated product, it takes customers equally from all existing firms. For example, a new entrant that captured 5 per cent of the existing market would do so by capturing 5 per cent of the sales of each existing firm.

Equilibrium

Short-run equilibrium Because each firm has a mono-poly over its own product, each firm faces a negatively sloped demand curve. But the curve is rather elastic because similar products sold by other firms provide many close substitutes. The negative slope of the demand curve provides the potential for monopoly profits in the short run, as illustrated in part (i) of Figure 11.1.

Long-run equilibrium Freedom of entry and exit forces profits to zero in the long run. If existing firms in the industry are earning profits, new firms will enter. Their entry will mean that the demand for the product must be shared among more and more brands. Thus, the demand curve for each existing firm's brand shifts to the left.[4] Entry continues until profits fall to zero as shown in part (ii) of Figure 11.1.

Excess capacity

The absence of positive profits requires that each firm's demand curve be nowhere above its long-run average cost curve. The absence of losses, which would cause exit, requires that each firm be able to cover its costs. Thus, average revenue must equal average cost at some output. Together these requirements imply that, when a monopolistically competitive industry is in long-run equilibrium, each firm will be producing where its demand curve is tangent to (i.e. just touching at one point) its average total cost curve.

Two curves that are tangent at a point have the same

---

[3] Another attempt to reconcile theory with the same evidence was made by the British economist Joan Robinson (1903–83). She assumed that each industry was monopolized. Although her work led to important clarifications of the theory of monopoly, it proved a dead-end in explaining the behaviour of manufacturing industries. Instead, it was Chamberlin's work that set the direction that more modern explanations have successfully followed.

[4] The shift in the demand curve is determined by Chamberlin's critical *symmetry assumption*: a new entrant takes sales in equal proportion from all existing firms.

(i) Short-run equilibrium

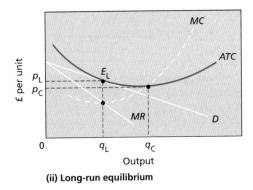

(ii) Long-run equilibrium

Figure 11.1 Equilibrium of a typical firm in monopolistic competition

In the short run a typical firm may make pure profits, but in the long run it will only cover its costs. In part (i) a typical monopolistically competitive firm is shown in short-run equilibrium at point E_S. Output is q_S, where $MC = MR$, price is p_S, and profits are the dark blue area.

In part (ii) the firm is in long-run equilibrium at point E_L. Entry of new firms has pushed the existing firm's demand curve to the left until the curve is tangent to the ATC curve at output q_L. Price is p_L, and total costs are just being covered. Excess capacity is $q_C - q_L$. If the firm did produce at capacity, its costs would fall from p_L per unit of output to p_C.

Note that to make the points q_L and q_C visually distinct, the demand curve in part (ii) has been drawn more steeply sloped than in part (i). The flatter demand curve of part (i) is what is expected in monopolistic competition. If it were drawn on part (ii), q_L would more realistically be closer to q_C, but the differences being illustrated by the figure would be harder to see.

slope at that point. If a negatively sloped demand curve is to be tangent to the *LRAC* curve, the latter must also be negatively sloped at the point of tangency. This situation is shown in Figure 11.1(ii): the typical firm is producing an output less than the one for which its *LRAC* reaches its minimum point.

This is the famous **excess capacity theorem** of monopolistic competition. Each firm is producing its output at an average cost that is higher than it could achieve by producing its capacity output. In other words, each firm has *unused* or *excess* capacity. So:

The theory of monopolistic competition shows that an industry can be competitive, in the sense of containing numerous competing firms, and yet contain unexploited scale economies, in the sense that each firm is producing on the negatively sloped portion of its average cost curve.

This implies that firms typically invest in capacity that is not fully utilized.

Is excess capacity wasteful? The long-run equilibrium of a monopolistically competitive industry might seem inefficient. Production costs are not as low as they could be if firms produced at the lowest point on their average cost curves, and firms typically invest in some capacity that goes unused.

But this is not necessarily inefficient, because people value diversity and are prepared to pay a price for it. For example, each brand of breakfast food, stereo, car, word-processing package, and watch has its sincere devotees. Increasing the number of differentiated products has two effects. First, it increases the amount of excess capacity in the production of each product, because the total demand must be divided among more products. Second, the increased diversity of available products will better satisfy diverse tastes.

Now consider how to maximize consumers' satisfactions in these circumstances.

Consumers' satisfactions are maximized when the number of differentiated products is increased until the marginal gain in consumers' satisfaction from an increase in diversity equals the loss from having to produce each existing product at a higher cost.

For this reason, among others, the worry that large-group monopolistic competition would lead to inefficiency in the use of resources is not well founded.[5]

Empirical relevance

A long controversy raged over several decades as to the empirical relevance of monopolistic competition. Although, product differentiation is an almost universal phenomenon in industries producing consumer goods and capital goods, many economists maintain that the monopolistically competitive market structure is found

---

[5] Important demonstrations of this result were given in the 1970s by several economists, including Kelvin Lancaster, formerly of the London School of Economics and now at Columbia University in New York.

only infrequently in practice. To understand this position we need to distinguish between products and firms. Although many industries produce a vast array of differentiated products these are often produced by only a few firms. For example, a mere three firms produce most of the many breakfast foods. Similar circumstances exist in soap, chemicals, cigarettes, and numerous other industries where many competing products are produced by a few very large firms. These industries are clearly not perfectly competitive and neither are they monopolies. Are they monopolistically competitive? The answer is no, because they contain few enough firms for each to take account of the others' reactions when determining its own behaviour (thus violating the second assumption above). Furthermore, these firms often earn large profits without attracting new entry (thus violating the prediction of zero profits in the long run). In fact, the few firms in each of these industries operate under a market structure called oligopoly, which we consider in the next section.[6]

While accepting that many differentiated products are produced by industries that are not monopolistically competitive, some economists feel that the theory is useful in analysing industries that contain many relatively small firms producing differentiated products.[7]

Oligopoly

Oligopoly is the theory of imperfect competition among the few; it refers to an industry that contains only a few competing firms. Each firm has enough market power to prevent its being a price-taker, but each firm is subject to enough interfirm rivalry to prevent it considering the market demand curve as its own. In most modern economies this is the dominant market structure for the production of consumer and capital goods as well as many basic industrial materials such as steel and aluminium. Services, however, are often produced in industries containing a larger number of firms—although universal product differentiation prevents them from being perfectly competitive.

In contrast to a monopoly, which has *no* competitors, and to a monopolistically competitive firm, which has *many* competitors, an oligopolistic firm faces *a few* competitors. Because there are only a few firms in an oligopolistic industry, each firm realizes that its competitors may respond to any move it makes. The prudent firm will take such possible responses into account. In other words oligopolists are aware that all the decisions made by the various firms in the industry affect the other firms.

This is the key difference between oligopolists on the one hand and perfect competitors, monopolistic competitors, and monopolies on the other hand. The behaviour of oligopolists is **strategic,** which means that they take explicit account of the impact of their decisions on competing firms and of the reactions they expect from competing firms. In contrast, firms in perfect and monopolistic competition engage in **non-strategic** behaviour, which means they make decisions based on their own costs and their own demand curves without considering any possible reactions from their large number of competitors. The behaviour of a monopolist is also non-strategic. It has no competitors with whom to interact.

Oligopolistic industries are of many types. In some industries there are only a few firms (three in the case of cigarettes). Oligopoly is also consistent with a large number of small sellers, called a 'competitive fringe', as long as a 'big few' dominate the industry's production. For example, about 500 banks operate in the United Kingdom, but the big four—Barclays, Lloyds, NatWest, and Midland—dominate the UK's commercial banking industry.

In oligopolistic industries prices are typically administered. Products are usually differentiated. Firms engage in the type of rivalrous behaviour described on pages 139–40, although its intensity varies greatly across industries and over time. This variety has invited extensive theorizing and empirical study.

Why bigness?

Several factors contribute to explaining why a few large firms dominate so many industries. Some of these factors are 'natural', and some are created by the firms themselves.

---

[6] At first sight retailing may appear to be closer to the conditions of large-group monopolistic competition than is manufacturing. Every city has many retailers selling any one commodity, each of them differentiated from the others mainly by geographical location. Each firm, however, tends to have only a few close neighbours and many more distant ones. Thus a model of interlocking oligopolies, with every firm in strong competition with only a few close neighbours, seems to be a better model for retailing than the model of large-group monopolistic competition, in which every firm competes directly, and equally, with all other firms in the industry.

[7] Micro-based mathematical theories that cover the whole economy and depart from the assumption of perfect competition almost always use monopolistic competition in preference to oligopoly. This is because monopolistic competition can be expressed mathematically and its results aggregated to predict unique behaviour across the whole economy. One famous example is found in G. Grossman and E. Helpman, *Innovation and Growth in the Global Economy* (Cambridge, Mass.: MIT Press, 1991).

Natural causes of bigness

Economies of scale Much factory production uses the principle of the division of labour that we first studied in Chapter 1. The production of a product is broken up into hundreds of simple, repetitive tasks. This type of division of labour is the basis of the assembly line, which revolutionized the production of many goods in the early twentieth century, and it still underlies economies of large-scale production in many industries. The division of labour is, as Adam Smith observed long ago, dependent on the size of the market. If only a few units of a product can be sold each day, there is no point in dividing its production into a number of specialized tasks. So big firms have an advantage over small firms whenever there is great potential for economies based on division of labour. The larger the scale of production the lower their average variable costs of production.

Fixed costs It is costly to design, prove, and market a new product. In technologically dynamic industries it may be a matter of only a few years before each new version is replaced by some superior version of the same basic product. Yet the fixed costs of product development must be recovered in the revenues from sales of the product. The larger the firm's sales, the lower the cost that has to be recovered from each unit sold. Consider a product that costs £1 million to develop and market. If 1 million units can be sold before the product is replaced by a superior version, £1 of the selling price of each unit must go towards recovering the development costs. If, however, the firm expects to sell 10 million units, each unit need contribute only 10 pence to these costs, and the market price can be lowered accordingly. With the enormous development costs of some of today's high-tech products, firms that can sell a large volume have a distinct pricing advantage over firms that sell a smaller volume. Firms with large product development costs face downward-sloping average total cost curves even if their average variable costs are constant.

Economies of scope A third type of economy is related to financing and marketing. It is costly to enter a market, to establish a sales force, and to make consumers aware of a product. These and other similar costs are often nearly as high when sales are small as when they are large. Thus, the smaller the volume of the firm's sales, the higher the price must be if the firm is to cover all of these costs. Notice that these economies are related to the overall size of the firm. They are not related either to the amount the firm produces of any one of its differentiated products, or to the size of any one of its plants as are scale economies. Economies that depend on the overall size of the *firm* rather than on the size of its *plants* or the volume of production of any one product are called the **economies of scope**. By lowering the firm's non-production costs, they shift the total cost curves of all its products downward.

Where size confers a cost advantage, through economies either of scale or of scope, there may be room for only a few firms, even when the total market is quite large. This cost advantage of size will dictate that the industry be an oligopoly, unless government regulation prevents the firms from growing to their efficient size.

Firm-created causes of bigness

The number of firms in an industry may be decreased while the average size of the survivors rises owing to the *strategic* behaviour of the firms themselves. Firms may grow by buying out rivals (acquisitions), or merging with them (mergers), or by driving rivals into bankruptcy through predatory practices. This process increases the size and market shares of the survivors and may, by reducing competitive behaviour, allow them to earn larger profit margins. But these high profits will attract new entrants unless the surviving firms can create and sustain barriers to entry. Although most firms would like to behave in this manner, it is no easy task to create effective entry barriers when natural ones do not exist. We will have more to say about such barriers later in the chapter.

Is bigness natural or firm-created?

Most observers would agree that the general answer to the question posed in the heading to this section is 'It is some of both'. Some industries have high concentration ratios because the efficient size of the firm is large relative to the overall size of the industry's market. Other industries may have higher concentration ratios than efficiency considerations would dictate because the firms are seeking enhanced market power through large size plus entry restriction. The issue that is debated is the relative importance of these two forces, the one coming from the efficiencies of large scale and scope, and the other coming from the desire of firms to create market power by growing large.

Harvard economist Alfred D. Chandler, Jr is a champion of the view that the major reason for the persistence of oligopolies in the manufacturing sector is the efficiency of large-scale production. His monumental work *Scale and Scope*[8] argues this case in great detail for the United States, the United Kingdom, and Germany.

The basic dilemma of oligopoly

Oligopolistic behaviour is necessarily *strategic* behaviour. In deciding on strategies, oligopolists face a basic dilemma between competing and co-operating.

---

[8] A. D. Chandler, Jr, *Scale and Scope: The Dynamics of Industrial Capitalism* (Cambridge, Mass.: Harvard University Press, 1990).

The firms in an oligopolistic industry will make more profits as a group if they co-operate; any one firm, however, may make more profits for itself if it defects while the others co-operate.

This behaviour is similar to that established in Chapter 10 for the cartelization of a perfectly competitive industry.[9] In a perfectly competitive industry, however, there are so many firms that they cannot reach the co-operative solution unless some central governing body is able to force the necessary behaviour on all firms. In contrast, the few firms in an oligopolistic industry will themselves recognize the possibility of co-operating to avoid the loss of profits that will result from competitive behaviour.

The co-operative solution

If the firms in an oligopolistic industry co-operate, either overtly or tacitly, to produce among themselves the monopoly output, they can maximize their joint profits. If they do this, they will reach what is called a **co-operative solution,** which is the position that a single monopoly firm would reach if it owned all the firms in the industry.

The non-cooperative equilibrium

Our analysis of a cartel in Chapter 10 shows that if all the firms in an oligopolistic industry are at the co-operative solution, it will be profitable for any one of them to cut its price or to raise its output, as long as the others do not do so. However, if all do the same thing, they will be worse off as a group and may all be worse off individually. An equilibrium that is reached by firms when they proceed by calculating only their own gains, without co-operating with others, is called a **non-cooperative equilibrium** or a **Nash equilibrium.** This type of equilibrium is named after the US mathematician John Nash, who developed the concept in the 1950s and received the 1994 Nobel prize in economics for this work. It is an equilibrium in which each firm's best strategy is to maintain its present behaviour, *given the present behaviour of the other firms.*

An example from game theory

The **theory of games** is a study of rational decision-making when each player knows that the other players will react to its moves, and takes account of their expected reactions when making moves. For example, firm A asks, 'Shall I raise or lower my price or leave it unchanged?' Before arriving at an answer, it asks, 'What will the other firms do in each of these cases, and how will their actions affect the profitability of whatever decision I make?'

When game theory is applied to oligopoly, the players are firms, their game is played in the market, their strategies are their price/output decisions, and the payoffs are their profits.

Figure 11.2 The oligopolist's dilemma: to co-operate or to compete

Co-operation to determine the overall level of output can maximize joint profits, but it leaves each firm with an incentive to alter its production. The figure gives what is called a payoff matrix for a two-firm duopoly game. Only two levels of production are considered in order to illustrate the basic problem. A's production is indicated across the top, and its profits (measured in millions of pounds) are shown in the blue circles within each square. B's production is indicated down the left side, and its profits (in millions of pounds) are shown in the green circles within each square. For example, the top right square tells us that if B produces one-half, while A produces two-thirds, of the output that a monopolist would produce, A's profits will be £22 million, while B's will be £15 million.

If A and B co-operate, each produces one-half the monopoly output and earns profits of £20 million, as shown in the upper left box. In this 'co-operative solution' either firm can raise its profits by producing two-thirds of the monopoly output, provided that the other firm does not do the same.

Now let A and B behave non-cooperatively. A reasons that whether B produces either one-half or two-thirds of the monopoly output, A's best output is two-thirds. B reasons similarly. They then reach the non-cooperative equilibrium, where each produces two-thirds of the monopoly output, and each makes less than it would if the two firms co-operated.

A game-theory illustration of the basic dilemma of oligopolists, to co-operate or to compete, is shown in Figure 11.2 for the case of a two-firm oligopoly, called a **duopoly.** The simplified game, adopted for the purposes of illustration, allows only two strategies for *each firm.* Each firm must produce an output equal to either one-half of the monopoly output or two-thirds of the monopoly output. Even this simple game, however, is sufficient to illustrate several key propositions in the modern theory of oligopoly.

---

[9] The basic reason is that when only one firm increases its output by 1 per cent, the price falls by less than when all firms do the same. Thus, when the point is reached at which profits will be *reduced* if all firms expand output together, it will still pay one firm to expand output *if* the others do not do the same.

Figure 11.2 presents what is called a *payoff matrix*. The data in the matrix show the profits that result from the four possible combinations of strategies.

The co-operative solution If both sides co-operate, *each producing* one-half of the monopoly output, they achieve the co-operative solution and jointly earn the monopoly profits by *jointly producing* the output that a monopolist would produce. As a group, they cannot do better.

Non-cooperative equilibrium It is easy to see that there is one Nash equilibrium in Figure 11.2. In the bottom-right cell, the best decision for each firm, given that the other firm is producing two-thirds of the monopoly output, is to produce two-thirds of the monopoly output itself. Between them they produce a joint output of one-and-a-third times the monopoly output. Neither firm has an incentive to depart from this position, except through co-operation with the other. In any other cell, each firm has an incentive to alter its output, *given the output of the other firm.*

The basis of a Nash equilibrium is rational decision-making in the absence of co-operation. Its particular importance in oligopoly theory is that it is the only type of equilibrium that is *self-policing.* It is self-policing in the sense that there is no need for group behaviour to enforce it. Each firm has a self-interest to maintain it because no move that it can make on its own will improve its profits, given what other firms are currently doing.

If a Nash equilibrium is established—by any means whatsoever—no firm has an incentive to depart from it by altering its own behaviour. It is self-policing.

Strategic behaviour The Nash equilibrium will be attained if each firm behaves strategically, by choosing its optimal strategy taking into account what the other firm may do. Let us see how this works.

Suppose that firm A reasons as follows: 'B can do one of two things; what is the best thing for me to do in each case? First, what if B produces one-half of the monopoly output? If I do the same, I receive a profit of 20, but if I produce two-thirds of the monopoly output, I receive 22. Second, what if B produces two-thirds of the monopoly output? If I produce one-half of the monopoly output, I receive a profit of 15, whereas if I produce two-thirds, I receive 17. Clearly, my best strategy is to produce two-thirds of the monopoly output in either case.'

B will reason in the same way. As a result, they end up by jointly producing one-and-a-third times the monopoly output, where each earns a profit of 17.

This type of game, where the non-cooperative equilibrium makes both players worse off than if they were able to co-operate, is called the **prisoner's dilemma.** The reason for this curious name, and some further applications, are discussed in Box 11.2. The important insight following from prisoner's dilemma games is that individual maximization does not always lead to an optimum allocation of resources. In the Nash equilibria of the prisoner's dilemma games shown in Figure 11.2 and Box 11.2, both players can be made better off if they co-operate and so move to the top left-hand box. But if both make individual maximizing decisions, they end up in the bottom right-hand box.

Breakdown of co-operation The Nash equilibrium is attained by the strategic reasoning just outlined. It can, however, be used to give an intuitive argument for why oligopolistic co-operation tends to break down.

Assume that the co-operative position has been attained. Each firm is producing one-half of the monopoly output and each is earning a profit of 20. The data in

Box 11.2 The prisoner's dilemma

The game shown in Figure 11.2 is often known as a 'prisoner's dilemma' game. This is the story that lies behind the name:

Two men, John and William, are arrested for jointly committing a crime and are interrogated separately. They know that if they both plead innocent they will get only a light sentence. Each is told, however, that if either protests innocence while the other admits guilt, the one who claims innocence will get a severe sentence while the other will be let off. If they both plead guilty, they will both get a medium sentence.

The table shows the payoff matrix for that game.

John reasons as follows: 'If William pleads innocent, I get a light sentence if I also plead innocent, but no sentence at all if I plead guilty, so guilty is my better plea. Second, if William pleads guilty, I get a severe sentence if I plead innocent and a medium sentence if I plead guilty. So once again guilty is my

		John's plea	
		Innocent	Guilty
William's plea	Innocent	J light sentence W light sentence	J no sentence W severe sentence
	Guilty	J severe sentence W no sentence	J medium sentence W medium sentence

preferred plea.' William reasons in the same way, and, as a result, they both plead guilty and get a medium sentence, whereas if they had been able to communicate, they could both have agreed to plead innocent and get off with a light sentence.

Figure 11.2 show that if A cheats by increasing its output, its profits will increase. However, B's profits will be reduced. A's behaviour drives the industry's prices down, so B earns less from its unchanged output. Because A's cheating takes the firms away from the joint profit-maximizing monopoly output, their joint profits must fall. This means that B's profits fall by more than A's rise.

Figure 11.2 shows that similar considerations also apply to B. It is worthwhile for B to depart from the joint maximizing output, as long as A does not do so. So both A and B have an incentive to depart from the joint profit-maximizing level of output.

Finally, Figure 11.2 shows that, when either firm does depart from the joint-maximizing output, the other has an incentive to do so as well. When each follows this 'selfish' strategy, they reach a non-cooperative equilibrium at which they jointly produce one-and-a-third times as much as the monopolist would. Each then has profits that are lower than at the co-operative solution.[10]

Game theory is an extremely flexible tool that has been applied to many branches of economics. Box 11.3 elaborates on some of the theory's basic concepts.

Types of co-operative behaviour

We have seen that although oligopolists have an incentive to co-operate, they may be driven, through their own individual decisions, to produce more and earn less than they would if they co-operated. Our next step is to look in more detail at the types of co-operative and competitive behaviour that oligopolists may adopt. We can then go on to study the forces that influence the balance between co-operation and competition in actual situations.

When firms agree to co-operate in order to restrict output and to raise prices, their behaviour is called **explicit collusion.** Collusive behaviour may occur with or without an actual agreement to collude. Where explicit agreement occurs, economists speak of *overt* or *covert collusion*, depending on whether the agreement is open or secret. Where no explicit agreement actually occurs, economists speak of **tacit collusion.**

Explicit collusion The easiest way for firms to ensure that they will all maintain their joint profit-maximizing output is to make an explicit agreement to do so. Such collusive agreements have occurred in the past, although they have been illegal for a long time in the United Kingdom. When they are discovered today, they are prosecuted. However, such agreements are not illegal everywhere in the world, and are often supported by national governments.

When firms get together to act in this way in international markets, it is called a cartel. Cartels, which we first met in Chapter 10, illustrate the basic conflict between co-operation and competition that we just discussed. Full co-operation always allows the industry to achieve the result of monopoly. It also always presents individual firms with the incentive to cheat. The larger the number of firms, the greater the temptation for any one of them to cheat. After all, the cheating of one small firm may not be noticed, because it will have a negligible effect on price.

When cartels are formed by a group of firms that would otherwise be in an oligopolistic market, the firms may let their joint interest in co-operating guide their behaviour. Although cheating may still occur, the few firms in the industry can easily foresee that the outcome of an outbreak of rivalry among themselves will be lower profits for all.

Tacit co-operation While collusive behaviour that affects prices is illegal, a small group of firms that recognizes the influence that each has on the others may act without any explicit agreement to achieve the co-operative equilibrium. In terms of Figure 11.2 Firm A decides to produce one-half of the monopoly output, hoping that Firm B will do the same. Firm B does what A expects, and they achieve the co-operative equilibrium without ever explicitly co-operating.

In such *tacit* agreements the two forces that push towards co-operation and competition are still evident. First, firms have a common interest in co-operating to maximize their joint profits at the co-operative solution. Second, each firm is interested in its own profits, and any one of them can usually increase its profits by behaving competitively.

Types of competitive behaviour

Although the most obvious way for a firm to violate the co-operative solution is to produce more than its share of the joint profit-maximizing output, there are other ways in which rivalrous behaviour can break out.

Competition for market shares Even if *joint* profits are maximized, there is the problem of market shares. How is the profit-maximizing level of sales to be divided among the competing firms? Competition for market shares may upset the tacit agreement to hold to joint maximizing behaviour. Firms often compete for market shares through various forms of non-price competition, such as advertising and variations in the quality of their product. Such costly competition may reduce industry profits.

Covert cheating In an industry that has many differentiated products and in which sales are often by contract between buyers and sellers, covert rather than overt cheating may seem attractive. Secret discounts and rebates can allow a firm to increase its sales at the expense of its competitors while appearing to hold to the tacitly agreed monopoly price.

---

[10] This is why we do not speak of the co-operative *equilibrium*. It is a solution to the problem of finding the best co-operative behaviour; but it is not an equilibrium, since, once achieved, each firm has an incentive to depart from it.

Box 11.3 Strategies and equilibrium concepts in game theory

A *dominant strategy* occurs when there is one best choice for A to make whatever B does, and one best choice for B to make whatever A does. The equilibrium in Figure 11.2 is a dominant strategy since it is always best for each to produce two-thirds of the monopoly output whatever the other produces. The prisoner's dilemma game in Box 11.2 also has a dominant strategy, which is for each to confess no matter what the other does.

All dominant strategies are Nash equilibria, but not all Nash equilibria are dominant strategies. Consider, for example, a hypothetical payoff matrix which arises when two firms, A and B, are trying to decide which independent R&D laboratory to hire in order to develop some new technology that they both want to use. (In each cell in Table I, A's payoff is written before the comma and B's payoff after it.) When both firms employ the same laboratory, there is a much bigger payoff than when the research funds are divided between the two laboratories, neither of which may have enough funding to develop the best new technique.

Table I		Firm A employs	
		Lab. Q	Lab. R
Firm B employs	Lab. Q	20, 20	5, 8
	Lab. R	8, 5	15, 15

If A chooses to employ laboratory Q, the best thing B can do is also to employ Q. But if A chooses to employ laboratory R, B should also employ R. The difference between this game and the one in the text is that the biggest payoffs come when both make the same choice and the smallest payoffs when they make different choices. In such cases, each person's best choice depends on the choice made by the other. There are two Nash equilibria in which both firms make the same choice. Although the choice of laboratory Q is better for both than the choice of R, if either firm chooses R, the best the other can do is also to choose R.

Some games, including the one just considered, have more than one Nash equilibrium (equilibrium is not unique). In others no Nash equilibrium exists, as in the payoff matrix in Table II. In this game, if A chooses *U*, B wants to choose *T*. But if B chooses *T*, A wants to choose *V*. But if A does choose *V*, B wants to choose *S*, and if B does choose *S*, A wants to choose *U*. There is thus no combination of choices where each will be satisfied with his or her own choice given the other player's choice.

So far we have implicitly assumed that the game is played only once. In *repeated games* the players play the same game many times, and we need to distinguish between *pure strategies*, which are strategies that do not change, and *mixed strategies*, whereby each player alternates randomly be-

Table II		Player A chooses	
		U	*V*
Player B chooses	*S*	10, 10	2, 10
	T	10, 20	30, 2

tween each of the available choices with pre-assigned probabilities. In the game whose payoffs are shown in Figure 11.2, one firm might choose half the monopoly output with probability 5/6 and two-thirds the monopoly output with probability 1/6. (The managers could roll a die and choose half the monopoly output if any number from 1 to 5 turned up and two-thirds the monopoly output if a 6 turned up.) The other firm might choose either output with a probability of 1/2. It is an interesting theorem in game theory that, whatever the payoff matrix, there always exists a Nash equilibrium in mixed strategies for a wide class of games. In other words, there is some set of probabilities for making choices among the alternatives by each player that leaves *each player* satisfied with his or her choice of strategy, given the other player's current choice of strategy.

Repeated games give a possibility of avoiding the non-optimal prisoner's dilemma solution. In a game that is repeated for ever, called an *infinite game*, one can establish a reputation by punishing a person who does the 'wrong thing' and rewarding him if he does the 'right thing'. In Figure 11.2, call half the monopoly output the 'right choice'. A can adopt the following strategy. If B makes the right choice A will make the right choice the next time the game is played; but if B makes the wrong choice A will punish B by also making the wrong choice on the next round of play. This strategy is called *tit for tat*. In computer experiments this simple strategy outperforms many other, more complex, strategies. The moral is that both players can learn that co-operation pays if the game is played long enough for them to discover that non-cooperation is followed by a competitive reaction that hurts both players.

Perhaps surprisingly, a repeated game that is played for only a finite number of moves provides no such simple resolution to the prisoner's dilemma. The last move of any finite repeated game is exactly the same as a one-time game, since there are no reputation effects to worry about in a game that will not be played again. Thus, the best strategy for either player on the last play of the game is to sell two-thirds of the monopoly output. But if that is so, then the second-to-last move also carries no penalty for non-cooperation. And so, by what is called backward induction, we conclude that, as long as co-operation cannot be ensured by some binding agreement, there is no incentive to co-operate at any point in a finite repeated game.

Very-long-run competition As we first discussed in Chapter 10, very-long-run considerations may also be important. When technology and product characteristics change constantly, there may be advantages to behaving competitively. A firm that behaves competitively may be able to maintain a larger market share and earn larger profits than it would if it co-operated with the other firms in the industry, even though all the firms' joint profits are lower. In our world of constant change, a firm that thinks it can *keep* ahead of its rivals through innovation has an incentive to compete even if that competition lowers the joint profits of the whole industry. Such competitive behaviour contributes to the long-run growth of living standards and may provide social benefits over time that outweigh any losses arising from the restriction of output at any point in time.

For these and for other reasons, there are often strong incentives for oligopolistic firms to compete rather than to maintain the co-operative solution, even when they understand the inherent risks to their joint profits.

Long-run behaviour: the importance of entry barriers

Suppose that firms in an oligopolistic industry succeed in raising prices above long-run average total costs and earn substantial profits that are not completely eliminated by non-price competition. In the absence of significant barriers to entry, new firms will enter the industry and erode the profits of existing firms, as they do in monopolistic competition. Natural barriers to entry are an important part of the explanation of the persistence of profits in many oligopolistic industries. Where such natural barriers do not exist, oligopolistic firms can earn profits in the long run only if they can create entry barriers.

Brand proliferation

By altering the characteristics of a differentiated product, it is possible to produce a vast array of variations on the general theme of that product. Think, for example, of cars with a little more or a little less acceleration, braking power, top speed, cornering ability, petrol mileage, and so on, compared with existing models.

Although the multiplicity of existing brands is no doubt partly a response to consumers' tastes, it also discourages the entry of new firms. Say, for example, that an industry contains three large firms, each selling one brand of cigarettes, and say that 30 per cent of all smokers change brands in a random fashion each year. If a new firm enters the industry, it can expect to pick up one-third of the smokers who change brands.[11] This would give the new firm 10 per cent (one third of 30 per cent) of the total market the first year merely as a result of picking up its share of the random switchers, and it would keep increasing its share for some time thereafter. If, however, the existing three firms have five brands each, there would be fifteen brands already available. A new firm selling one new brand could then expect to pick up only one-fifteenth of the brand switchers, giving it 2 per cent of the total market the first year, with smaller gains also in subsequent years. This is an extreme case, but it illustrates a general result:

The larger the number of differentiated products sold by existing oligopolists, the smaller the market share available to a new firm entering with a single new product.

An example of brand proliferation drawn from the alcoholic drinks industry is given in Box 11.4.

---

[11] Since there are now four brands to choose from, you might think that the new brand would pick up one-quarter of the switchers. But this is not correct because, by definition, the switcher rejects his old brand and chooses one of the others. Each switcher's choice-set therefore consists of three brands—two of the pre-existing brands and the one new brand.

Box 11.4 Brand proliferation in alcoholic drinks

What used to be Allied Lyons PLC and is now Allied Domecq PLC is one of Britain's largest companies. This is partly because of the diversity of its activities—manufacturing and selling beers and other alcoholic drinks, producing a wide variety of food products, and operating restaurants including Baskin-Robins and Dunkin' Donuts, which are big sellers in North America.

Even within a limited field like alcoholic drinks, the range of apparently competing brands for which the company is responsible is staggering. In addition to the beers produced by the original Ind Coope group and Benskins in the South of England, Allied is responsible for Tetley Bitter, Ansells Bitter, John Bull Bitter, and Draught Burton Ale, all of which originated in the North of England or the Midlands but are increasingly being found in the South. It also produces Double Diamond beer. Even if the Scottish brewers in the group—Drybrough Brewery and Alloa Brewery Company—do not compete much with those further south, there is a wealth of lager brands from which to choose: Lowenbrau, Castlemaine XXXX, Skol, and Oranjeboom. If you want to encourage competition in the cider field, it's no good switching from Gaymer's Olde English to Whiteways: they're both made by Allied. Of course, you could ponder the situation while sipping a whisky: Allied won't mind whether you choose Ballantine's or Teacher's as they own both, while having a 50 per cent share in Grant's Steadfast and Glenfiddich. Switch to Hiram Walker, Irish Mist, or Laphroaig, and you are still drinking Allied. Try a

Lamb's Navy Rum for a change, or Courvoisier brandy or Kahlúa and Tia Maria liqueurs, and you're still buying from Allied. You may prefer fortified wines like Harvey's sherries or Cockburn's ports; your sophisticated friends go for Tico mixer sherry; your less sophisticated acquaintances for British wines like VP or Rougemont Castle—you're all drinking Allied products.

Of course, Allied is not the only multi-brand producer; most of Allied's few competitors are also very large firms. For example, Diageo, which was formed by a merger of Guinness and Grand Metropolitan, now sells many alcoholic products, including Dimple, Black and White, Vat 69, Gordons, I.W. Harper, Rebel Yell, Tanqueray, Johnnie Walker, Old Parr, White Horse, Harp, Kaliber, Guinness, Hennessy, Moet and Chandon, Hine, Cossack Vodka, Pimm's, Booths, Haig, Dewar's, Bell's, Cardhu, Oban, Talisker, Glen Ord, Glen Elgin, Ushers, Canadian LTD, Mercier, Glenkinchie, and Lagavulin, and many food products, including Haagen Dazs, Old El Paso, Green Giant, and Pillsbury.

The production of such a wide range of differentiated products helps to satisfy consumers' clear demand for diversity. It also has the effect of making it more difficult for a new firm to enter the industry. If the new firm wishes to compete over the whole range of differentiated products, it must enter on a massive scale. If it wishes to enter on only a small scale it faces a formidable task of establishing brand images and customer recognition with only a few products over which to spread the expenses of entry.

Set-up costs

Existing firms can create entry barriers by imposing significant fixed costs on new firms that enter their market. This is particularly important if the industry has only weak natural barriers to entry because the minimum efficient scale occurs at an output that is low relative to the total output of the industry.

Advertising serves the useful function of informing buyers about their alternatives, thereby making markets work more smoothly. Indeed, advertising is essential to make consumers aware of new products whether produced by existing firms or new entrants.

None the less, advertising can also operate as a potent entry barrier by increasing the set-up costs of new entrants. Where heavy advertising has established strong brand images for existing products, a new firm may have to spend heavily on advertising to create its own brand images in consumers' minds. If the firm's initial sales are small, advertising costs *per unit sold* will be large, and price will have to be correspondingly high to cover those costs.

An application

The combined use of brand proliferation and advertising as an entry barrier helps to explain one apparent paradox of everyday life—that one firm often sells multiple brands of the same product, which compete actively against one another as well as against the products of other firms.

The soap and cigarette industries provide classic examples of this behaviour. Because quite small plants can realize all available scale economies, both industries have few natural barriers to entry. Both contain a few large firms, each of which produces an array of heavily advertised products. The numerous existing products make it harder for a new entrant to obtain a large market niche with a single new product. The heavy advertising, although it is directed against existing products, creates an entry barrier by increasing the set-up costs of a new product that seeks to gain the attention of consumers and to establish its own brand image.

Predatory pricing

A firm will not enter a market if it expects continued losses after entry. One way in which an existing firm can create such an expectation is to cut prices below costs whenever entry occurs and to keep them there until the entrant goes bankrupt. The existing firm sacrifices profits while doing this, but it sends a discouraging message to potential future rivals, as well as to present ones. Even if this strategy is costly in terms of lost profits in the short run, it may pay for itself in the long run by creating *reputation effects* that deter the entry of new firms at other times or in other markets that the firm controls.

Predatory pricing is controversial. Some economists argue that pricing policies that appear to be predatory can be explained by other motives and that existing firms only hurt themselves when they engage in such practices instead of accommodating new entrants. Others argue that predatory pricing has been observed and that it is in the long-run interests of existing firms to punish the occasional new entrant even when it is costly to do so in the short run.

Contestable markets and potential entry

The theory of contestable markets shows that pure profits may be eliminated even though the industry contains only a few firms and experiences no actual entry. *Potential* entry can do the job just as well as actual entry, as long as two conditions are fulfilled. First, entry must be easy to accomplish, and, second, existing firms must take potential entry into account when making price and output decisions.

Entry is usually costly to the entering firm. It may have to build a plant, it may have to develop new versions of the industry's differentiated product, or it may have to advertise heavily in order to call attention to its product. These and many other initial expenses are often called **sunk costs of entry,** which are defined as costs that a firm must incur to enter the market and that cannot be recovered if the firm subsequently exits.

A market which new firms can enter and leave without incurring any sunk costs of entry is called a perfectly **contestable market.** A market can be perfectly contestable even if the firm must pay some costs of entry, as long as these can be recovered when the firm exits. Because all markets require at least some sunk costs of entry, contestability must be understood as a variable. The lower the sunk costs of entry, the more contestable the market.

In a contestable market the existence of profits, even if they are due to transitory causes, will attract entry. Firms will enter to gain a share of these profits and will exit when the transitory situation has changed.

Consider, for example, the market for air travel on the lucrative London–Paris route. This market would become quite contestable, once EU regulations are phased out, *if* counter and loading space were easily available to new entrants at the two cities' airline terminals. An airline that was not currently serving the cities in question could shift some of its existing planes to the market with small sunk costs of entry. Some training of personnel would be needed for them to become familiar with the route and the airport. This is a sunk cost of entry that cannot be recovered if the cities in question are no longer to be served. However, most of the airline's costs of entering the London–Paris market are not sunk costs. If it subsequently decides to leave a city, the rental of terminal space will stop, and the aeroplanes and the ground equipment can be shifted to another location. The former head of the American Civil Aeronautics Board, and architect of airline deregulation, captured this point by referring to commercial aircraft as 'marginal cost with wings'.

Sunk costs of entry constitute an entry barrier. The larger they are, the larger the profits of existing firms can be without attracting new entrants. The flip side of this coin is that firms operating in markets without large sunk costs of entry will not earn large profits. Strategic considerations will lead them to keep prices near the level that would just cover their total costs. They know that if they charge higher prices, firms will enter to capture the profits while they last and then exit.

Contestability, where it is possible, is a force that can limit the profits of existing oligopolists. Even if entry does not occur, the ease with which it could be accomplished may keep existing oligopolists from charging prices that would maximize their joint profits.

Contestability is just another example, in somewhat more refined form, of the key point that the possibility of entry is the major force preventing the exploitation of market power. Notice that the entrants do not have to be new firms. They can be domestic firms entering new domestic markets or foreign firms entering the domestic market.

Oligopoly and the functioning of the economy

Oligopoly is found in many industries and in all advanced economies. It typically occurs in industries where both perfect and monopolistic competition are made impossible by the existence of major economies of scale or of scope (or both). In such industries, there is simply not enough room for a large number of firms, all operating at or near their minimum efficient scales.

Three questions are important for the evaluation of the performance of the oligopolistic market structure. First, do oligopolistic markets allocate resources very differently from perfectly competitive markets? Second, in their short-run and long-run price–output behaviour, where do oligopolistic firms typically settle between the extreme outcomes of earning zero profits and earning the profits that would be available to a single monopolist? Third, how much do oligopolists contribute to economic growth by encouraging innovative activity in the very long run? We consider each of these questions in turn.

The market mechanism under oligopoly

We have seen that under perfect competition prices are set by the impersonal forces of demand and supply, and

changes in the market conditions for both inputs and outputs are signalled by changes in the prices of a firm's inputs and outputs. The market signalling system works slightly differently when prices are administered by oligopolists. Changes in prices still signal changes in market conditions for inputs. However, changes in the market conditions for outputs are typically signalled by changes in the volume of their sales at the administered prices.

Increases in costs of inputs will shift cost curves upward, and oligopolistic firms will be led to raise prices and lower outputs. Increases in demand will cause the sales of oligopolistic firms to rise. Firms will then respond by increasing output, thereby increasing the quantities of society's resources that are allocated to producing that output. They will then decide whether or not to alter their administered prices.

The market system reallocates resources in response to changes in demands and costs in roughly the same way under oligopoly as it does under perfect competition.

Profits under oligopoly

Some firms in some oligopolistic industries succeed in coming close to joint profit maximization in the short run. In other oligopolistic industries firms compete so intensely among themselves that they come close to achieving competitive prices and outputs.

In the long run those profits that do survive competitive behaviour among existing firms will tend to attract entry. These profits will persist only in so far as entry is restricted either by natural barriers, such as large minimum efficient scales for potential entrants, or by barriers created, and successfully defended, by the existing firms.

Very-long-run competition

Once we allow for the effects of technological change, we need to ask which market structure is most conducive to the sorts of very-long-run changes that we discussed in Chapter 8. These changes are the driving force of the economic growth that has so greatly raised living standards over the last two centuries. They are intimately related to Schumpeter's concept of creative destruction, which we first encountered in our discussion of entry barriers in Chapter 10 (pages 164–6).

Examples of creative destruction abound. In the nineteenth century, railways began to compete with horse-drawn wagons and barges for the carriage of freight. In the twentieth century, lorries operating on newly constructed highways began competing with rail. During the 1950s and 1960s, aeroplanes began to compete seriously with lorries and rail.

In recent years the development of facsimile transmission and electronic mail has eliminated the monopoly of the Post Office in delivering hard-copy (as opposed to oral) communications. In their myriad uses, computers for the home and the office have swept away the markets of many once-thriving products and services. For instance, in-store computers answer customer questions, decreasing the need for salespeople. Aided by computers, 'just in time' inventory systems greatly reduce the investment in inventories required of existing firms and new entrants alike. Computer-based flexible-manufacturing systems allow firms to switch production easily and inexpensively from one product line to another, thereby reducing the minimum scale at which each can be produced profitably. Computers are involved in book production, having replaced the author's hand- and type-written copy and the publisher's laborious page-makeup procedures. One day soon the multimedia CD-rom, or its successor, may replace the textbook altogether.

An important defence of oligopoly relates to this process of creative destruction. Some economists argue that intermediate market structures, such as oligopoly, lead to more innovation than would occur in either perfect competition or monopoly. Oligopolists face strong competition from existing rivals and cannot afford the more relaxed life of the monopolist. At the same time, however, oligopolistic firms expect to keep a good share of the profits that they earn from their innovative activity.

Everyday observation provides some confirmation of this view. Leading North American firms that operate in highly concentrated industries, such as Kodak, IBM, Microsoft, Du Pont, Xerox, General Electric, and 3M, have been highly innovative over many years. UK examples include Rolls-Royce, Glaxo, Wellcome, and GEC. Also, most of the innovations that have vastly raised agricultural productivity over the last century have come from oligopolistic producers of farm machinery and from government-supported research laboratories, not from perfectly competitive farmers.

A final word

Oligopoly is an important market structure in modern economies because there are many industries in which the minimum efficient scale is simply too large to support many competing firms. The challenge to public policy is to keep oligopolists competing, rather than colluding, and using their competitive energies to improve products and lower costs, rather than merely to erect entry barriers.

Summary

Imperfectly competitive market structures
■ Firms in market structures other than perfect competition face negatively sloped demand curves and must administer their prices.

Monopolistic competition
■ In the theory of large-group monopolistic competition, many firms compete to sell differentiated products. Each may make pure profits in the short run. In the long run, freedom of entry shifts its demand curve until it is tangent to the *ATC* curve, leading to excess capacity and production at average costs above the minimum possible level.

Oligopoly
■ Competitive behaviour among oligopolists may lead to a non-cooperative equilibrium. It is self-policing in the sense that no one has an incentive to depart from it unilaterally. The prisoner's dilemma game is a case in point.

■ Oligopolistic profits can persist only if there are entry barriers. Natural barriers include economies of large-scale production and large fixed costs of entering the market. Artificial barriers include brand proliferation and high levels of advertising.

■ In qualitative terms the workings of the allocative system under oligopoly are similar (but not identical) to what they are under perfect competition. Oligopolistic industries appear to have contributed much more to the technological changes that underlie the long-run growth of productivity than have perfectly competitive industries.

Topics for review

■ The assumptions of monopolistic competition
■ Excess capacity under monopolistic competition
■ The co-operative solution and the non-cooperative equilibrium
■ Entry barriers
■ Resource allocation under oligopoly

Questions for discussion

1 It is sometimes said that there are many more chemists and petrol stations than are really needed. In what sense might this be correct? Does the consumer gain anything from this duplication of retail outlets?

2 Compare the effects on the car and the wheat industries of each of the following: (a) a large rise in demand, (b) a

large rise in the costs of production, (c) a temporary cut in supplies of components and other inputs owing to a three-month rail strike, and (d) a rush of cheap foreign imports. In the light of your answers discuss ways in which oligopolistic industries fulfil the same general functions as perfectly competitive industries.

3 Evidence suggests that the profits earned by all the firms in many oligopolistic industries are less than the profits that would be earned if the industry were monopolized. Why might this be so?

4 'Creative destruction can work without the entry of new firms. New products developed by existing firms will do just as well.' Explain the reasoning behind this quotation and say why you agree or disagree.

5 Two firms are making sealed bids on a contract. Only two bids are permitted, one at a high price and one at a low price. The high price yields a profit of £10 million whereas the low price yields a profit of £7 million. If the firms bid the same price, they share the job and each earns half the profits. If they give different bids, the whole job and its profits go to the lower bidder. Draw up a payoff matrix and determine the outcomes under co-operative and non-co-operative behaviour. (*Hint*: this is a prisoner's dilemma game.)

Chapter 12
Risk and Uncertainty

Nothing in life is certain. So economic transactions, just like everything else we do, involve some element of risk. In some cases the risk does not significantly affect what is done and can be ignored. In other cases the riskiness of the transactions seriously affects the behaviour of those involved in them. In this chapter we consider some important examples of this latter set of cases.

We first ask how we can characterize and measure risk. We then consider insurance and gambling, both of which relate to risk. We ask why there are markets in which people willingly supply and demand both insurance and gambling. We also look at some of the problems that arise in two common situations. First, the existence of insurance may influence how people behave. Second, the buyers and sellers of insurance may have different amounts of information about the risks that are being insured against. Later in the chapter we consider the problems of investing in financial assets which carry different amounts and types of risk. This leads to the important issue of portfolio diversification.

The behaviour of the consumer under risk

So far we have studied the behaviour of consumers when they are presented with choices that involve outcomes that are certain. We asked, for example, if a consumer would prefer bundle A, containing 10 units of food and 5 units of clothing, to bundle B, containing 6 units of food and 12 units of clothing. In so doing, we assumed implicitly that the bundle chosen could be obtained with certainty. What happens, however, if the consumer is faced with only a *probability* of obtaining each bundle?

This is not the type of choice that normally faces a shopper. Usually, he knows that if he pays his money, he will get what he has paid for with certainty. Sometimes, however, the shopper is uncertain about the quality of the various products offered for sale. The shopper may think that the more expensive brand X will last longer and require less maintenance expenditure than the cheaper brand Y. He may not, however, be sure of how *much* longer it will last, and how *much* less maintenance will be involved.

Other types of choice involve more serious kinds of risk. Buying a flat in area A rather than area B may reduce the chances of being burgled, as may installing a burglar alarm or bars on the ground-floor windows. But by how much?

Many of the principles discussed in this chapter were first developed by analysing games of chance such as roulette or coin-tossing. The same principles arise in consumption and production decisions involving risk, but they can often be more easily appreciated in the kind of games that the early theorists studied. Many of the ideas are quite subtle. To handle them rigorously requires careful definitions and some complex analysis. This chapter gives only an intuitive overview.

The characterization of risk

How are choices made when the outcome of any choice is not certain? To study this question we need two important concepts. The first is called **expected value.** It is defined as the most likely outcome if some situation is repeated over, and over, and over. The second is called the **degree of risk.** This is measured by the dispersion of possible outcomes if some situation is repeated over and over. Under certainty there is only one possible outcome to any given choice. This outcome is thus the expected value and the dispersion of the outcomes is zero, indicating no risk. Under uncertainty more than one outcome is possible and the most likely outcome is the expected value and the spread of possible outcomes is the degree of risk.

Expected value Say you choose to play a game in which the proprietor tosses a coin *once every minute*. The coin is fair in that there is an equal chance of throwing a head or a tail. The probability of throwing a head is said to be 0.5 or ½, and the probability of throwing a tail is also 0.5 or ½.[1] The proprietor pays you £1 if the result is a head and you pay her £1 if the result is a tail.[2] If you play the game for 10 minutes, you may have a lucky run and win £10 in 10 minutes. There is an equal chance that you will have an unlucky run and lose £10. It is much more likely, however, that you will get some heads and some tails and end up winning or losing a sum much smaller than £10. The single most likely outcome is that you will exactly break even. This is because there are more sequences of 10 tosses that will end up with 5 heads and 5 tails than any other single combination of heads and tails. For the same reason, the two next most likely results are that you will win £1 (6 heads and 4 tails) or that you will lose £1 (6 tails and 4 heads). Outcomes with larger gains and larger losses are less likely. The two least likely results are winning £10 or losing £10.

Now consider playing the game repeatedly day after day. It is still quite possible that you will end up winning £10 or losing £10. For example, if you have broken even after many days of play, the chance that you will now encounter 10 heads in a row is the same as it was on your first 10 tosses of the coin. But as you go on playing, the average return *per minute spent playing the game* gets smaller and smaller. This return can be expressed as $(H - T)/n$, where H is the number of heads, T is the number of tails, and n is the number of minutes you have spent playing the game, which is the same as the number of tosses. Every time the game is played, n increases by one; the only way the numerator can increase by the same amount is if *every* toss is an H, or every toss is a T. So if your sequence of losses contains a mixture of heads and tails, the average gain or loss per play will tend to decline. Indeed, it can be shown that, as you go on playing for longer and longer periods of time, so that n increases without limit, the value of $(H - T)/n$ tends to zero. This is the expected value of the game.

The expected value tells you the most likely outcome for a small number of tosses and what you can expect to earn as an average per toss if you play the game for a long time—in this case zero.

Another way of calculating the expected value of the outcome of any game is to add up the various outcomes, each multiplied by its probability of occurrence. The coin-tossing game we are considering has two outcomes on each toss: either you win £1 with probability 0.5 or you lose £1 with probability 0.5. The expected value of the outcome is £1(0.5) – £1(0.5) = £0.50 – £0.50 = 0.

Degree of risk In the above game you stood to win £1 per toss or lose £1 per toss. If you contract to play for 10 minutes, your maximum possible loss is £10. Now suppose you play the same game, one toss per minute, but this time you win £100 for each head and lose £100 for each tail. The

expected value of the outcome is still zero. But you risk more if you play it for any given amount of time. There is the same chance that you will encounter an unlucky run of 10 tails, but now you stand to lose £1,000 in this event. Clearly there is more risk attached to the second game than to the first. Risk refers to the dispersion of the possible results. In the first game the possible results from 10 minutes play are dispersed over a range running from +£10 to –£10; in the second game the possible results are dispersed over a range running from +£1,000 to –£1,000.

The risk attached to any choice refers to the variation in the possible outcomes resulting from making that choice.[3]

Fair and unfair games

The penny-toss game that we have considered so far is a mathematically fair game in the sense that you have just as much chance of winning as of losing. A lottery in which all of the ticket money is paid out is also a fair game. Say, for example, that 100 lottery tickets are sold for £1 each, and a draw then determines which one of the ticket-holders wins £100. This is a fair game because each ticket-holder has 1 chance in 100 of winning £99 (the person's own £1 back and £99 of winnings) and 99 chances out of 100 of losing £1. To find the expected value of this gamble, we multiply the winnings of £99 by the chance of winning it (1 chance in 100) and subtract the loss multiplied by the chance of losing it (99 chances in 100). This gives:

$$£99(1/100) - £1(99/100) = £0.99 - £0.99 = 0.$$

A mathematically fair game is one for which the expected value of the outcome is zero.

If you play a fair game repeatedly, you may end up winning or losing, depending on the 'luck of the toss', but the *average gain or loss per play* calculated over all plays will tend towards zero as time passes.

Now consider playing the coin-tossing game under the rules that heads the proprietor pays you £2, tails you pay the proprietor £1. The expected value of the outcome of this game is £2(0.5) – £1(0.5) = £1 – £0.50 = £0.50. If you play the game only once, you will either win £2 or lose £1. If you play it repeatedly, however, your average gain will

---

[1] These are equivalent expressions. The first 0.5 is the ratio of the expected number of heads to the overall number of tosses. The second ½ says there is one chance in two of throwing a head (since there are two equally likely outcomes on any one toss).

[2] This game is called a *zero-sum game*, which is defined as any game in which the sum of the winnings and losses of all the players is always zero. In other words what someone in the game wins, someone else in the game must have lost.

[3] For many purposes the variation can be satisfactorily measured by what is called the *variance* of the possible results, which is the average of the sum of the squares of the deviations of each result from the average, or most likely, result. It is also often measured by the *standard deviation*, which is the square root of the variance.

tend towards £0.50 per toss. This is not a fair game. Instead it is biased in your favour (and hence biased *against* the proprietor). (However, it is still a zero-sum game, since your gain is exactly equal to the proprietor's loss.)

What about the kind of lottery that typically exists? The organizers take a proportion of the ticket revenue as their profit and distribute the rest as prize money. All such lotteries are not fair games. They are biased against the participants in the sense that the expected value of participating in the game is negative. (Also, they are not zero-sum games, since the losses of those whose tickets are not selected exceed the gains for those whose tickets are winners.)

To illustrate, take our previous lottery where 100 tickets are sold at £1 each. Now, however, assume that the organizers take £50 as their profit and pay out the other £50 to the winning ticket. The expected value of a lottery ticket is now £49(1/100) − £1(99/100) = £0.49 − £0.99 = −£0.50. The negative value shows that this is not a fair game; instead, it is biased against anyone who plays it.

Another way of seeing this is to ask yourself what would happen if you bought all the tickets. You would spend £100 and win back £50, thus making a loss of £50. This is a loss of £0.50 per ticket, which, we have already seen, is the expected value of each ticket. (What do you now think about someone who buys two tickets instead of one and tells you he does this in order 'to increase my chances of coming out a winner'?)

Consumers' tastes for risk

Economists distinguish three kinds of decision-takers when risk is involved. Those who are **risk-neutral** will be indifferent about playing a fair game, will willingly play one that is biased in their favour, but will not play one that is biased against them. Those who are **risk-averse** will only play games that are sufficiently biased in their favour to overcome their aversion to risk, and will be unwilling to play fair games, let alone ones that are biased against them. Finally, people who are **risk-loving** are willing to play games even when they are biased against them, the extent of the love of risk being measured by the degree of bias that a person is willing to accept. (No one would knowingly buy a ticket in a lottery in which the prize was zero, but some extreme risk-lovers might enter a lottery in which only 10 per cent of the ticket money was paid out as prize money.)

What will be the typical person's attitude towards risk? Is it just as likely that John or Amanda will be risk-lovers as that they will be risk-averse? To answer this question, we use a basic assumption first introduced in Chapter 6.

According to the *assumption of diminishing marginal utility of income*, individuals get less and less satisfaction from successive, equal increases in their income and wealth.

The argument is that if you earn only £1,000 per year, you will spend it satisfying your most urgent wants. If your income is increased by £1,000, you will also spend it on quite important needs, but the additional needs will be a little less urgent than those satisfied by the first £1,000. If your income is increased progressively by £1,000 increments, needs that are less and less urgent will be satisfied by the expenditure of each additional £1,000 of income. The general idea, therefore, is that people can arrange their wants in order and will satisfy the ones that give them most utility first, and then, as their incomes increase, those wants that give them progressively less and less utility. It follows from this assumption that the utility each consumer will attach to successive equal increments of income will decrease steadily as income increases; or, put the other way around, the utility attached to successive equal reductions of income will increase steadily as income is decreased.

Figure 12.1 shows an illustrative utility curve for income for one individual, Amanda. The curve relates any income received with certainty to the utility Amanda derives from it. The curve is based on the assumption that we can measure her utility in some units (although all that matters is that utility be increasing at a diminishing rate as income rises, the precise numbers being for illustrative purposes only).

Amanda must now choose between two different occupations. The first is an office job that pays her a definite income of £15,000. The second is as a salesperson working on commission. If she is good at the job she will earn £20,000,

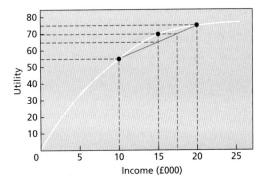

Figure 12.1 The utility of income

Diminishing utility of income implies risk-aversion. The curve shows the total utility attached to various incomes to be received with certainty. Amanda's utility from an income of £15,000 for certain is 70. An occupation that gives a 50 per cent chance of either £10,000 or £20,000 has an expected value of £15,000 but an expected utility of only 65. To make her accept a risky income source, its expected value would have to be £17,500 (which yields a utility of 70 as does the certain income of £15,000).

but if she is poor at it she will earn only £10,000. She is uncertain about her sales ability and reckons that she is equally likely to be good or bad at the job. So she assigns a probability of 0.5 to each of the two possible outcomes. Thus the expected value of the income from the sales job is £15,000—that is, (0.5)(£10,000) + (0.5)(£20,000). If she were risk-neutral, she would be indifferent between these two occupations, since they both yield the same expected income. But the risky alternative yields her either £5,000 more or £5,000 less than the certain one. Because of diminishing utility of income she assigns a smaller utility to £5,000 more than the office job salary than she assigns to £5,000 less than it. The graph tells us that the utility of the certain income of £15,000 is 70 while the utilities attached to £20,000 and £10,000 are 75 and 55 respectively. Although the expected incomes from the two occupations are the same, the expected utilities are not. The sales job yields either £10,000 with a probability of 0.5 or £20,000 also with a probability of 0.5. So the expected utility associated with this job is only 65—(55)(0.5) + (75)(0.5). So she prefers the job with the certain income of £15,000 to the job with the uncertain income that has the same expected value of £15,000. Amanda is risk-averse.[4]

A moment's reflection will show that this conclusion is independent of the particular utility values that we selected. All that it requires is diminishing marginal utility of income. This means that the addition of utility resulting from an income that is above average by some amount is less than the subtraction from utility resulting from an income that is below average by the same amount.

What would the expected value of the risky alternative have to be to leave her indifferent between the two occupations? The answer is read off the curve in Figure 12.1. The expected value of the risky income needs to be £17,500 to obtain the same utility from the sales job as the office job offers. The difference between the actual expected value of the sales job and the expected value she would need to leave her indifferent between the risky and the riskless job measures her cost of risk. This is what we would have to give her to leave her indifferent between a certain income and an uncertain one with the same expected value.

Diminishing marginal utility of income makes utility-maximizing people risk-averse.

The demand for insurance

The Smiths, who own a house valued at £200,000, estimate that there is 1 chance in 1,000 that it will be destroyed by fire during their period of ownership and 999 chances in 1,000 that there will be no fire. The most likely outcome is that nothing will happen at all, but there is a small chance of a really big loss. Someone offers them a mathematically fair insurance policy that avoids this big loss. The policy

costs £200 paid now. If they buy the policy, they give up £200. However, if the disaster occurs, they will be fully compensated.

So the Smiths have a choice between two alternatives:

- **Alternative A, the status quo.** If they choose not to buy the policy, they have 1 chance in 1,000 of losing £200,000 and 999 chances out of 1,000 of losing nothing. Multiplying these possible losses of £200,000 and zero by their probabilities gives the expected value of this alternative as −£200 (i.e. −£200,000(1/1,000) + £0(999/1,000) = −£200).
- **Alternative B, purchase the policy.** In this case £200 is spent for certain but there is no chance of losing £200,000.

The insurance policy represents a fair bargain because the expected value of the status quo is equal to the certain cost of the policy. Not buying the insurance is, however, a much riskier course of action for the homeowners than buying it. If they are lucky, they save the £200 insurance premium; if they are unlucky, they lose £200,000. What should they do?

Normal risk-averse individuals will buy the policy. The expected value of the outcome is the same as if they did not buy the policy, but they have eliminated the risk of a large monetary loss.

One further complication needs to be mentioned. Since insurance companies must themselves make money, they do not offer their policyholders mathematically fair policies such as the one just described. In the above case, where the risk to the insurance company is 1 chance in 1,000 of losing £200,000, it would charge a premium of more than £200, possibly £220. The insurance company expects to pay out an average of £200 per policy, so the £20 per policy goes to cover its costs and to earn an income.

For the purchaser the certain cost of buying the policy is now −£220. But the expected value of not buying remains at −£200. A risk-neutral person would not buy the policy, which requires spending £220 to avoid a situation (no insurance) whose expected value is −£200.

People with diminishing marginal utility of wealth are willing to buy insurance policies that are not mathematically 'fair' because they value the reduction of risk more than they value the reduction in their expected wealth when they buy the policy.

[4] This footnote explains how expected income and utility vary as Amanda's probability of being good at her sales job varies. Let the probability of Amanda being good at the job be p and of being bad at it be $1 - p$. The expected value of the income associated with the sales job is then $(£20,000)(p) + (£10,000)(1 - p) = £10,000 + £10,000p$. The expected utility is the utility attached to the high income multiplied by the probability of achieving the high income plus the utility attached to the low income multiplied by the probability of achieving the low income. In the case shown in Figure 12.1, this is $(75)(p) + 55(1 - p) = 55 + 20p$. So, as p varies between 0 and 1, the point showing the expected value of the income and the utility arising from the sales job varies along a straight line joining the two points (£10,000, 55) and (£20,000, 75). This is the straight line shown in Figure 12.1.

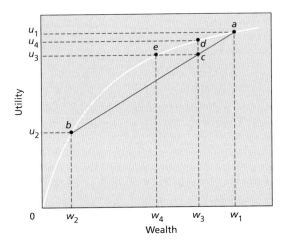

Figure 12.2 Purchasing insurance

Diminishing marginal utility of wealth makes a mathematically unfair insurance policy attractive to utility-maximizing consumers. Without insurance the homeowners will have *either* wealth of w_1 with utility of u_1 if there is no fire (point *a*) *or* wealth of w_2 and utility u_2 if there is a fire (point *b*). The expected value of their wealth is w_3 with an associated utility of u_3 (point *c*). Point *c* is closer to *a* than to *b* because the fire is an unlikely event. A mathematically fair insurance policy would charge a premium that reduced the owners' wealth to w_3 for certain. The utility associated with w_3 achieved with certainty is u_4, which is higher than u_3. The maximum the owners would be prepared to pay for a mathematically unfair policy is the amount that would reduce their wealth to w_4. Paying that amount would make their wealth w_4 for certain (point *e*), yielding them the same utility as is associated with not buying insurance (point *c*).

Figure 12.2 shows the decision facing our homeowners.[5]

The demand to gamble

We now know that diminishing marginal utility of income and wealth lead people to be risk-averse and thus to insure against losses. Why do people gamble? Why do they buy lottery tickets, enter the football pools, and bet on horse races? These are different from insurance, where one pays money to avoid the risk of a large loss. In gambling one pays money to purchase the chance of a gain.

Earlier in this chapter we considered a lottery consisting of 100 tickets sold for £1 each, with a single prize of £100 going to the winning ticket. If you buy a ticket you have 99 chances out of 100 of losing £1 and 1 chance in 100 of winning £99. (If you win, you get your £1 back and £99 more.) This is a mathematically fair game, since the expected value of a ticket is zero (£99(1/100) − £1(99/100)). But, given diminishing marginal utility of income, the utility you get from winning £100 will be less than 100 times the utility you sacrificed by giving up £1. Thus, because the expected value of the ticket measured in money is zero, the

expected value of the ticket measured in utility is negative. If you are a utility maximizer and have diminishing marginal utility of income, you would not buy the ticket.

The lottery is a mathematically fair gamble. However, most betting games are biased against the player. The proprietor of the game takes out some of the money wagered to cover costs and provide a profit (the government may also take some as a betting tax). Only the remainder is distributed as prize money. This is true of all private and government-run commercial gambling, including lotteries, pools, dog and horse races, and casino gambling. (The gambling games individuals play at home with each other are usually fair in the sense that the value of what is won is equal to the value of what is lost, so that the expected value of playing the game is zero.)

Gambling on any event in which the organizers take a profit, and/or on which the government levies a tax, has a negative expected value and is thus inconsistent with utility-maximizing risk-averse participants who are subject to diminishing marginal utility of income.

Yet we observe such behaviour every day. How can we explain it? At least four possibilities suggest themselves.

One possibility is that people have increasing marginal utilities of income. This could explain why they gamble on games that have negative expected values. It would, however, be inconsistent with their buying insurance policies with negative expected values. So this explanation would work only if there were one class of people who gambled (those with increasing marginal utility of income) and another class who bought insurance (those with decreasing marginal utility of income). The common observation that there are many people who do both rules out this possibility as a general explanation.

A second possibility is that people derive utility from gambling for its own sake. Although they would not engage in gambling as a way of maximizing the money values of their income and wealth, they get pleasure out of the very act of gambling. In this sense, they are giving up some income to purchase the pleasure of gambling just as if they purchased a ticket to obtain the pleasure of attending the theatre. In the case of gambling games with massive wins, such as the football pools, the appeal may be somewhat different. Diminishing marginal utility of increases in income may not hold for massive wins that could change one's whole life-style in ways that would otherwise be quite beyond the gambler's reach. It may not matter that the average player will lose money over his or her lifetime. The gamblers are sustained by the mere thought that, against all the odds, they might win a sum large enough to

---

[5] Here we deal with wealth rather than the income that we considered when Amanda was selecting a job. Wealth is merely the present value of all current assets including any expected future income. Thus diminishing marginal utility of either implies diminishing marginal utility of the other.

Box 12.1 The ethics of gambling

Throughout the world both private firms and governments run gambling activities. In many lotteries and pools the payout ratio is quite low. For example, in the UK National Lottery less than 50 per cent of the money wagered is returned in prizes. Also, the average income of those who buy tickets is well below the national average income.

Critics argue that this and other similar lotteries are a tax on poverty and ignorance. They point out that those with higher incomes and more knowledge tend to avoid such poor bets. Supporters argue that the poor are the main purchasers of lottery tickets just because, for most of them, escape into a better life-style is beyond anything they could achieve by their own efforts. So they are buying a remote possibility of an otherwise unachievable gain, a dream that may give them utility in itself. The supporters' argument has more weight when fully informed persons buy tickets for the value of the dream. It has less weight when badly informed persons buy tickets in the mistaken belief that they are playing either a fair game or one that they can influence by their own supernatural powers.

What do you think?

own odds after they know the amounts bet, they are on the right side of a mathematically unfair game from which they must win. Assume, for example, that you run a lottery and are free to take for yourself what you wish from the funds raised and then distribute the rest as prizes. You cannot lose.

Firms providing this type of gambling service sometimes have a government monopoly and sometimes are subject to competition from other firms. If there is competition, then there will be pressure to keep the payout ratio high, provided that ticket purchasers are aware of the prizes given out by competing lotteries. If the lottery has a monopoly, there will be an optimum payout ratio that will maximize the profits of the firm running the game. As the payout ratio goes to one, profits go to zero, since all money taken in is paid out. As the payout ratio goes to zero, profits will also go to zero, since fewer and fewer people will be willing to wager money as the size of the winnings and/or the number of winners get smaller.

Somewhere in between a ratio of zero and one will be the optimum payout ratio that maximizes the profits of a monopoly firm running a lottery or other betting game.

transform an otherwise hard life, in the same way that Cinderella's fairy godmother transformed her life.

A third possibility is that people are badly informed. They may not know the expected values of the gambles that they take. It is probably true that many people do not realize the magnitude of the negative expected value of many gambles. (The smaller the *payout ratio*—the ratio of money paid out to money taken in—the larger the magnitude of the negative expected value of the game.)

A fourth possibility is that people are superstitious, as many people are observed to be. They do not believe that the law of averages applies to them. They think that by choosing lucky numbers, or engaging in various rituals, they will beat the odds. These people do not care that they are playing mathematically unfair games. They believe that their personal powers will influence the results in some way or another—as those who choose what they regard as lucky numbers are observed to believe.

Box 12.1 considers the ethics of gambling.

The supply of gambling

So much for consumers. Why are firms willing to supply such services as insurance and gambling games to consumers who demand them? We first consider the easy case of gambling and then go on to the more difficult, but also more interesting, case of insurance.

There is no difficulty in understanding why firms are willing to provide such gambling opportunities as the pools or betting on horse or dog races. If firms make their

The supply of insurance

In the gambling case the firm could decide how much to pay out after it knew how much it had taken in. Insurance is a different matter. The insurance firm takes your money and agrees to pay out a certain sum if the unlucky event strikes you. Conceivably the insurance firm could have a run of bad luck in which, in the limit, all of the people it insures suffer loss at the same time. The basis for profitable insurance firms is not, therefore, being on the right side of an unfair game. Instead, it lies in the mathematics of what are called *pooled risks*.

Risk-pooling

To see what is involved in the pooling of risks, consider two individuals, John and June, who receive incomes which vary according to the toss of a coin. (Once again, the coin toss stands for any source of risk.) Each individual tosses a coin each month. If a head comes up, John gets £500; if a tail, he gets nothing. The same applies to June: she gets £500 if she tosses a head and nothing if a tail comes up. The expected value of their income is £500(0.50) = £250 per month. Over a long period of time, their monthly incomes will indeed average close to £250 each. But neither of them may like the possibility of going from £500 to nothing on the toss of a coin each month. Suppose they decide to pool their incomes each month and each take half of the resulting amount. The expected value of the pooled income is £500 while the expected value of each individual income is unchanged at £250 per month.

Importantly, however, the variation from month to month in each income will be diminished. The result is shown in Table 12.1. When they were operating on their own, each income deviated from its expected value by £250 each month; in good months it was £250 over, and in bad months it was £250 below. When the two incomes are pooled, the expected value is reached whenever one is lucky and the other unlucky, which will tend to be about half the time. Only in one-quarter of the outcomes will income be £250 above, and in one-quarter will it be £250 below. These two results require that both John and June are lucky at the same time or that both are unlucky.

If three people pool their incomes, the extreme cases of £500 each and zero each occur only when all three are lucky or unlucky at the same time. These cases each occur with a probability of 1 chance in 8. (There is 1 chance in 2 that any one person will get a head, and $(1/2)(1/2)(1/2) = 1/8$ that all three will get heads at once. Similarly, there is 1 chance in 8 that all three will toss tails at the same time.) So the extreme cases in which everyone gets *either* £500 *or* zero occur only one-quarter of the time. If four people pool their incomes, the extreme cases of *either* £500 *or* zero income per person will occur only with probability 2/16. By the time ten people are involved, the two extreme cases will occur only twice in two raised to the tenth power (2^{10}) times, which is a very small fraction indeed.

The larger the number of independent events that are pooled, the less likely is it that extreme results will occur.

The key to this proposition is that the events must be independent; the result of John's coin toss must not be in any way related to the result of June's. In the unpooled case, the extreme result occurs to one of them when he or she is unlucky or lucky. The probability of the extreme result is less likely when they pool their incomes because it requires that both be unlucky or lucky at the same time.

The same reasoning applies to all kinds of events that may be regarded as chance occurrences, as long as they are independent of each other. There is some probability that any given house in the country will burn down in any given year; let us say it is 1 in 1,000. An insurance company takes a premium from house-owners and offers them full compensation if their house burns down. If the company is so small that it insures only ten houses, it may be unlucky in having ten owners who just happen to be careless at the same time and burn their houses down accidentally. This is unlikely, but not impossible. A bad bit of luck over all ten houses insured would ruin the company, which could not meet all of its insured risks at the same time. But let the company be large enough to insure 100,000 houses. Now it is pooling risk over a large number, and the chances are that very close to 1 house in every 1,000 insured houses will burn down. With 100,000 houses insured, the most likely outcome is that 100 houses will burn down. The company might be unlucky and have 110 burn down or lucky and have only 90 burn down. But to have 200 burn down is very unlikely indeed, as long as a fire in one house is independent of a fire in another.

This requirement of independence explains why insurance policies normally exclude wars and other situations where some common cause acts on all the insured units. A war may lead to a vast number of houses being destroyed. Since the cause of the loss of one house is not independent of the cause of the loss of another, the insurance company has a high probability, should a war break out, of suffering ruinous losses.

The basic feature of insurance is the pooling of independent events, which is what makes extreme outcomes unlikely. A common cause that seriously affects all insured items in the same way defeats the principle on which insurance is based.

The typical insurance company, therefore, deals with repeated events such as fires or death in which the probability of each insured person becoming a claimant is independent of the probability of any other person becoming a claimant.

Risk-sharing

A further practice of insurance companies allows them to extend their coverage to events that are not repeated and where the loss might be large enough to ruin any one company.

Say that a famous pianist wants to insure her hands against any event that would stop her from playing the piano. The amount insured would be colossal, amounting to all the income she would earn over her lifetime if her

Table 12.1 Risk-pooling

Coin toss	Risks are not pooled		Risks are pooled:
	John gets	June gets	both get
T–T	0	0	0
T–H	0	500	250
H–T	500	0	250
H–H	500	500	500

Pooling of independent risks reduces risk. Both John and June toss a coin, and each gets an income of £500 if he or she tosses a head (H) and nothing for a tail (T). There are four possible results, in two of which one head and one tail occur. In the other two there are either two tails or two heads. When each accepts his or her own risks, each expects an income of £500 half the time and zero the other half. When the incomes are pooled then split, only one combination in four gives them zero income, while half of the time they will get £250. Pooling leaves the expected value of their incomes unchanged but lowers the average amount of variation around that value.

hands stayed unharmed. The company can calculate the chances that any randomly chosen female in the population will suffer such a loss to her hands. But it is not insuring the whole population. Only one person is involved. If there is no catastrophe, the company will gain its premium. If there is a catastrophe, the company will suffer a large loss.

The trick in being able to insure the pianist, or any single person or thing where the loss would be large, lies in *risk-sharing* (or re-insurance, as it is sometimes called). One company writes a policy for the pianist and then breaks the policy up into a large number of subpolicies. Each subpolicy carries a fraction of the payout and earns a fraction of the premium. The company then sells the subpolicies to many different firms.

Assume, for illustration, that 100 firms each write one such primary policy—one on a pianist's hands, one on a footballer's legs, one on a rare treasure being flown to Japan for exhibit, etc. Each then breaks its primary policy up into 100 subparts and sells a part to each of the other 99 firms. Each firm ends up holding risks that are independent of each other, no one of which is large enough to threaten the firm should it give rise to a claim. This is what Lloyd's of London does. It is a syndication of a large number of insurance underwriters. Each is prepared to insure almost anything as long as a claim would not break all of the firms when the risk is spread over a large number of them.[6]

We return to risk in the context of financial investments later in this chapter.

Problems with insurance

Economists have been prominent in helping us to understand two major problems with insurance, called moral hazard and adverse selection.

Moral hazard

If the contents of your flat are valuable but are not insured for theft, you are likely to be careful in locking your door every time you leave and will take other sensible, anti-break-in precautions. If you take out an insurance policy, you may be less careful. Say, for example, that you get ten minutes down the road and realize that you forgot to lock up. You may decide to press on, reasoning that you cannot afford the time you would lose in returning to lock up, that being visited by burglars on any particular day is unlikely, and that anyway you are insured against burglary.

The existence of the insurance policy has altered your behaviour. You take more risks, making a loss from burglary more likely than if you were uninsured.

This behaviour, called **moral hazard,** is defined as an insurance-induced alteration of behaviour that makes the event insured against more likely to occur.

Moral hazard occurs in many lines of insurance. For example, people are observed to be more careless about fire prevention when they are insured than when they are not. Fire insurance is clearly socially beneficial in allowing people to pool risks, thus avoiding the chances of a large loss in return for a relatively small payment. However, there is an offsetting social loss if the very existence of fire insurance leads to more destruction by fire than would occur without it.

Adverse selection

When the person on one side of a bargain knows more about what is being bought and sold than the person on the other side, we have a situation of *asymmetrical information*. This can lead to undesirable consequences.

For example, a person who is considering taking out life insurance may know more about her health than the insurance company can find out in one medical examination and a few life-style questions. The insurance company will quote a rate that covers the average risk for all persons in some category, such as middle-aged female non-smokers in apparent good health. Those who believe their health is better than average know they are being asked for a premium that is high relative to their individual risk. In contrast, those who know they are less healthy than the average in their group know they are being offered a bargain: insurance at a rate that is low relative to their own individual risk. As a result, a higher proportion of people who are above the average risk will insure themselves than those who are below the average risk.

Adverse selection refers to the tendency for people who are more at risk than the average to purchase insurance and for those who are less at risk than the average to reject insurance. It occurs whenever individuals within a group that is offered a common insurance rate know which way their own risk deviates significantly from the average risk within the group. Those at high risk relative to the average are offered a bargain; those at low risk are offered expensive insurance.

This problem would be serious if all people were charged the same rate as the customer with the average risk. Young healthy non-smokers would be heavily penalized and much less inclined to take out insurance. In contrast, older smokers with chronic ailments would be subsidized and have a strong inducement to insure themselves.

The result would be that the average risk of the group who took out insurance would rise above the average risk in the whole population. Rates would then have to be raised

---

[6] This is also what bookmakers do when they cannot control the odds themselves. When they take bets at odds set by others, one large bet could ruin them by requiring a payout greater than their current assets. To avoid such risks, they lay off part of the bet with other bookmakers. In this way no one ends up holding bets that are big enough to threaten their solvency if they suffer an unlucky run of payouts.

Box 12.2 Used-car prices: the problem of 'lemons'

It is common for people to regard the large loss of value of a new car in the first year of its life as a sign that consumers are overly style-conscious and will always pay a big premium for the latest in anything. The US economist George Akerlof suggests a different explanation, based on the proposition that the flow of services expected from a one-year-old car that is *purchased on the used-car market* will be lower than that expected from an *average* one-year-old car on the road.

Any particular model year of motor cars will include a certain proportion of 'lemons'—cars that have one or more serious defects. There were faults in their assembly, or in the parts assembled, that went undetected. Purchasers of new cars of a certain year and model take a chance on their car turning out to be a lemon. Those who are unlucky and get a lemon are more likely to resell their car than those who are lucky and get a well-functioning

car. Hence, the used-car market will contain a disproportionately large number of lemons for sale. Because it is difficult to identify a lemon or a badly treated used car before buying it, the purchaser is prepared to buy a used car only at a price that is low enough to offset the increased probability that it is of poor quality.

This is a rational consumer response to asymmetric knowledge between the seller of a car and its eventual buyer. It helps to explain why one-year-old cars typically sell for a discount that is somewhat larger than can be explained by the physical depreciation that occurs in one year in the *average* car of that model. The larger discount reflects the lower services that the purchaser can expect from a used car because of the higher probability that it will be a lemon.

---

to cover the average risk of the insured groups, and this would provide an even stronger incentive for those who have below-average risks to go uninsured.

Insurance companies try to cope with this problem by defining a number of groups distinguished from each other by characteristics that affect their risk. They then charge each group a different rate based on the average risk of that group. For example, rates for theft insurance in London vary with the postal code. This certainly helps, but it is always true that there will be variations within any one group. Those who know they are more at risk than the average in their group are offered a bargain, while those who know they are less at risk than the average are offered what is, for them, expensive insurance.

Insurance companies sometimes make surprising offers such as life insurance for people over 55 with no medical examination. When it does this a company is consciously choosing to avoid obtaining relevant medical knowledge. This increases the degree of knowledge asymmetry between the company and the policy purchaser and thus strengthens the tendency towards adverse selection. If the company is to earn a profit, its rates for this kind of policy

will have to be set higher than the rates on otherwise equivalent policies that require a medical examination. For very-high-risk people the policy may still be a bargain—possibly the only way they can get life insurance. For average- and low-risk people the rates must be higher than they could obtain by purchasing a policy that required a medical examination.

Adverse selection also applies in banking. Banks tend to expand by merger or acquisition, not by organic growth. The reason is that the marginal customers obtained by attracting new custom are not the ones banks want to lend to. They are riskier than average. However, when one bank buys another bank it gets the whole set of that bank's existing customers. It knows their average characteristics and it picks up good customers as well as bad.

All the large UK banks have grown up from mergers of existing banks. None of their major components is less than 150 years old. (NatWest, Lloyds, Barclays, and Midland all fit this story.)

Box 12.2 outlines a different case of moral hazard; in this case it is the sellers who know more about the product than do the buyers.

Financial choices and risk

An important function of any financial system is to channel funds from one set of agents, who have money to lend, to another set of agents, who wish to borrow. Savers are investing their own money in the hope of receiving an interest return on that investment. They also have to consider risk, because borrowers may default. Even if default is not likely, many forms of investment involve risks of capital gains and losses, which occur when the

market value of the investment changes. Accordingly, all investors have to take into consideration not just the expected return on their investment, but also the risks involved.

The analysis of risk and return as applied to finance has created a vast literature. Here we can develop only a few of the key ideas that help in understanding a wide range of financial behaviour.

Portfolio diversification

'Don't put all your eggs in one basket' is a well-known proverb which summarizes the message that there may be benefits to diversification. If you carry your breakable items in several baskets, there is a chance that one will be dropped, but you are unlikely to drop all your baskets on the same trip. Similarly, if you invest all your wealth in the shares of one company, there is a chance that the company will go bust and you will lose all your money. Since it is unlikely that all companies will go bust at the same time, a portfolio of shares in several companies will be less risky.

This may sound like the idea of risk-pooling, which we discussed earlier in this chapter, and risk-pooling is certainly an important reason for many elements of diversification. We will use the notion of risk-pooling to explain some forms of financial behaviour, but a full understanding of portfolio diversification involves a slightly wider knowledge of the nature of risk than what is involved in coin-tossing.

The key difference about risk in the real world of finance, as opposed to coin-tossing, is that many of the potential outcomes are not independent of other outcomes. If you and I toss a coin, the probability of yours turning up heads is independent of the probability of my throwing a head. However, the return on an investment in, say, BP is not independent of the return on an investment in Shell. This is because these two companies both compete in the same industry. If BP does especially well in attracting new business, it may be at the expense of Shell. So high profits at BP may be associated with low profits at Shell, or vice versa.

The fact that the risks of individual investments may not be independent has important implications for investment allocations, or what is now called *portfolio theory*. Investments can be combined in different proportions to produce risk and return characteristics which cannot be achieved through single investments, although institutions have grown up to take advantage of the benefits of diversification, as we will see below.

Diversified portfolios may produce combinations of risk and return which dominate non-diversified portfolios.

This is a very important statement, which requires a little closer investigation. It will help to identify the circumstances under which diversification is beneficial. It will also clarify what we mean by the word 'dominate'.

Table 12.2 sets out two simple examples. In both there are two assets that an investor can hold, and there are two possible situations which are equally likely to arise. Thus, there is a probability of 0.5 attached to each situation and the investor has no advance knowledge of which is going to happen. The two situations might be a high exchange rate and a low exchange rate, a booming and a depressed economy, or any other alternatives that have different effects on the earnings of different assets.

Table 12.2 Combinations of risk and return

	Situation 1	Situation 2
(i) Returns are negatively correlated		
Asset A	10%	30%
Asset B	30%	10%
(ii) Returns are positively correlated		
Asset A	10%	30%
Asset B	0%	40%

Assets differ in expected return and variability in returns. Part (i) illustrates the return on two assets in two different situations. Asset A has a high return in situation 2 and a low return in situation 1. The reverse is true for asset B. A portfolio of both assets has the same expected return but lower risk than a holding of either asset on its own. In (ii) both assets have a high return in situation 2 and a low return in situation 1. For the risk-averse investor asset A dominates asset B.

Consider part (i) of the table. In this case both assets have the same expected return (20 per cent) and the same degree of risk. (The possible range of outcomes is between 10 and 30 per cent on each asset.) If all that mattered in investment decisions were the risk and return of individual shares, the investor would be indifferent between assets A and B. Indeed, if the choice were between holding only A or only B, all investors should be indifferent (whether they were risk-averse, risk-neutral, or risk-loving) because the risk and expected return are identical for both assets. However, this is not the end of the story, because the returns on these assets are not independent. Indeed, there is a perfect negative correlation between them: when one is high the other is low, and vice versa.

What would a sensible investor do if permitted to hold some combination of the two assets? Clearly, there is no possible combination that will change the overall expected return, because it is the same on both assets. However, holding some of each asset can reduce the risk. Let the investor decide to hold half his wealth in asset A and half in asset B. His risk will then be reduced to zero, since his return will be 20 per cent whichever situation arises. This diversified portfolio will clearly be preferred to either asset alone by risk-averse investors. The risk-neutral investor is indifferent to all combinations of A and B because they all have the same expected return, but the risk-lover may prefer not to diversify. This is because, by picking one asset alone, the risk-lover still has a chance of getting a 30 per cent return and the extra risk gives positive pleasure.

Risk-averse investors will choose the diversified portfolio, which gives them the lowest risk for a given expected rate of return, or the highest expected return for a given level of risk.

Diversification does not always reduce the riskiness of a portfolio, so we need to be clear what conditions matter.

Consider the example in part (ii) of Table 12.2. As in part (i), both assets have an expected return of 20 per cent. However, now asset B is riskier than asset A and it has returns that are positively correlated with A's. Portfolio diversification does not reduce risk in this case. Risk-averse investors would be likely to invest only in asset A, while risk-lovers might invest only in asset B. Combinations of A and B are always riskier than holding A alone. Thus we could say that for the risk-averse investor asset A *dominates* asset B, as asset B will never be held so long as asset A is available. The key difference between the example in part (ii) of Table 12.2 and that in part (i) is that in the second example returns on the two assets are positively correlated while in the former they are negatively correlated.[7]

The risk attached to a combination of two assets will be smaller than the sum of the individual risks if the two assets have returns that are negatively correlated.

Diversifiable and non-diversifiable risk

Not all risk can be eliminated by diversification. The specific risk associated with any one company can be diversified away by holding shares of many companies. But even if you held shares in every available traded company, you would still have some risk, because the stock market as a whole tends to move up and down over time. Hence we talk about market risk and specific risk. *Market risk* is non-diversifiable, whereas *specific risk* is diversifiable through risk-pooling.

Beta It is now common to use a coefficient called Beta to measure the relationship between the movements in a specific company's share price and movements in the market. A share that is perfectly correlated with an index of stock market prices will have a Beta of 1. A Beta higher than 1 means that the share moves in the same direction as the market but with amplified fluctuations. A Beta between 1 and 0 means that the share moves in the same direction as the stock market but is less volatile. A negative Beta indicates that the share moves in the opposite direction to the market in general. Clearly, a share with a negative Beta would be in high demand by investment managers, as it would reduce a portfolio's risk.

The *capital asset pricing model*, or CAPM, predicts that the price of shares with higher Betas must offer higher average returns in order to compensate investors for their higher risk.

For any given market conditions there is a trade-off between risk and return. Investments with higher risk will be priced to offer higher expected returns than those with low risk.

Mutual funds

Many small investors do not have enough wealth to invest in company shares to gain the benefits of a diversified portfolio. Yet the average returns on investing in shares are higher than those on safe assets, such as National Savings Certificates or bank and building society deposits. Hence there is a role for institutions that sell to small investors a share in a much bigger and more diversified portfolio.

Such institutions are generally known as mutual funds. They are like clubs in which savers pool their funds and then jointly own a diversified set of investments. In the UK they are known as unit trusts and investment trusts.

Mutual funds play an especially important role in helping small investors to achieve international diversification. Just as diversification across UK companies is beneficial in improving the risk–return trade-off, so international diversification improves it still further. Small investors find it very difficult and costly to buy and sell foreign shares, but mutual funds are able to access foreign markets and spread the costs over large numbers of investors. Investment opportunities for small investors are thereby greatly enhanced.

Financial intermediaries

Mutual funds are a form of financial intermediary. They take in money from savers and invest the money in company shares or bonds. Banks and building societies are also important financial intermediaries. Some other financial arrangements which help companies or individuals to manage risk are discussed in Box 12.3.

The traditional building society takes in deposits from savers and makes loans (mortgages) to house purchasers. Why do savers not lend directly to house-buyers rather than through this intermediary? The building societies' costs could then be avoided and lenders and borrowers could, perhaps, get better terms. (The spread between building society deposit rates and loan rates could be split between the lender and the borrower.)

There are several reasons why both lenders and borrowers prefer not to deal with each other directly.

First, there are transaction or search costs for lenders and borrowers before they can meet. The intermediary provides a 'trading post' where depositors know they can find a willing borrower at all times and homebuyers know they can find a willing lender.

Second, the characteristics of the loan that a saver wants to make may differ from those the ultimate borrower would be happy with. A typical saver may want to get her money back at short notice; a typical house buyer wants to borrow money for twenty or twenty-five years. The

---

[7] Readers who have studied statistics will recall that if two statistical series A and B are added together, the variance of the combined series is equal to the variance of A plus the variance of B plus twice the covariance of A and B. The covariance of A and B will be negative if A and B are negatively correlated, hence the combined variance will be less than the sum of its parts.

Box 12.3 Derivatives: dealing with risk in financial markets

Many modern financial instruments create markets in various aspects of risk. Agents who wish to avoid or reduce risk can deal on these markets with others who are willing to accept the risk (for a price). The financial products that are most commonly traded are not primary loans or securities, but can be used to change the risk characteristics of some underlying asset or liability position. They are often referred to as 'derivatives'.

Futures and forward contracts These enable agents to buy, at a price agreed today, some product or asset which will be delivered and paid for at some time in the future. Thus, a farmer might sell his wheat crop six months before it is harvested in order to hedge against the risk of the price falling at harvest time. A tyre manufacturer might buy rubber ahead of production needs to lock in a particularly favourable supply price. An importer of American jeans who will have to pay the producer in dollars in nine months' time may buy the dollars with pounds sterling in the forward foreign exchange market in order to avoid the risk that the dollar might appreciate against the pound in the meantime. *Futures contracts* are contracts traded in standard sizes on organized exchanges (such as the London International Financial Futures Exchange, LIFFE). *Forward contracts* are contracts that are typically made between a customer and a bank and are custom made in terms of characteristics (hence they are said to be traded in the over-the-counter market, or OTC).

Swaps Swaps are used to manage interest rate risk. Agents who hold fixed interest rate assets and floating interest rate liabilities will be exposed to losses if interest rates rise, because the cost of borrowing will rise while the return on assets will not. Swapping either the fixed asset rate into floating, or the floating liability rate into fixed will reduce risk. The principle involved here is referred to as 'matching' because it creates assets and liabilities that will move up or down together.

Options Options come in two varieties. A *call option* is the right (but not the obligation) to buy some commodity or security at a specific price called the *exercise price*. A *put option* is the right (but not the obligation) to sell some commodity or security at a specific price. With a forward or futures contract you are committed to a future transaction; with an option you have the right to go ahead but you can walk away from the deal if you prefer. A wheat farmer who has sold his crop on the futures market must fulfil the contract. (If his crop falls short of what he has sold, he must buy at the market price to make up the shortfall.) With a put option, however, he could choose not to deliver if the market price turned out to be much higher than the exercise price of his contract. Options thus have favourable characteristics. They limit the downside of risk without limiting the upside. Naturally, there is a price which has to be paid for this one-way bet, which is known as the *option premium*. Those who sell options must charge a premium high enough to cover their losses when options are exercised at prices that are much better than the existing market price.

borrower may default. A building society can spread the risk over a wide range of different borrowers and a wide range of different types of dwellings. Building societies with nationwide coverage grew up to take advantage of the fact that wide diversification of loans across different industries and regions is safer than, say, lending only to coalminers in South Yorkshire. Hence, minimizing overall risk is a central part of any financial intermediary's *raison d'être*.

A fourth reason for the existence of financial intermediaries is the provision of loans that are not secured by any asset. In such cases the lending institutions must make judgements about who is likely to pay them back and who is not. Banks and building societies are well placed to do this because they will normally lend only to people with whom they have an ongoing banking relationship. They can see how much money a customer is earning because it passes through her account. They therefore have better information about the creditworthiness of a potential borrower than any other potential lender could have.

Banks have superior information about the risks involved, and they are in a good position to monitor the financial progress of their customers over time.

Thus, again, the existence of risk is central to the need for banks to play this role, and the nature of their relationship with customers puts them in an ideal position to monitor (and possibly control) those risks.

Financial intermediaries allow savers to find relatively safe outlets for their savings which pay a competitive rate of interest. (Financial intermediaries compete for business just like the other firms that we have discussed.) Those who wish to borrow are also able to do so in a well-developed market for loans. Such savings-and-loans markets are important for the functioning of a market economy. In particular, they enable consumers to move consumption either forward or backward in time, thereby greatly enhancing the range of choices available. Saving postpones consumption for the future. Borrowing permits consumption today that will be paid for in future, or the purchase of large durable product like a house or a car, the services of which will be consumed over future periods.

Conclusion

All economic activity is inherently risky. Goods are produced or bought today for sale in the future. Contracts commit producers, customers, and borrowers to exchanging goods and services in the future, and lenders to various actions in the future. Because the future can never be known with certainty, these essential economic activities all carry risks.

One of the triumphs of the market economy is its ability to facilitate a specialization of tasks. For a fee specialists in

building society can make long-term loans by taking in a whole series of different short-term deposits.

Third, a typical saver could lend to no more than one or two house-buyers. Any single house may collapse, or the risk assume the risks that others must take. In the process, they reduce the total amount of risk because of risk-sharing and their own specialized knowledge of risky situations. Insurance grew up when overseas trade became important in the post-medieval world. It allowed merchants who were specialists in markets to pass the risks of the voyage on to insurers who were specialists in marine risks. The joint-stock company grew up in the postindustrial period as a way of allowing vast amounts of capital to be accumulated with acceptable risks to the individual investors.

Today's specialists in risks are many and varied. They often act as financial intermediaries, standing between savers and borrowers. They facilitate complex transactions which, among other things, allow many economic agents to specialize in what they can best do while allowing others to assume the risks that are inherent in these activities.

Summary

The behaviour of the consumer under risk

■ Many economic decisions taken by firms and consumers involve risky choices which can often be characterized by the expected value of the outcome and the degree of risk as measured by the dispersion of the possible outcomes.

■ Because those providing the insurance, or gambling games, must make profits, those gambling or buying insurance do not take mathematically fair gambles. Diminishing marginal utility explains why people are risk-averse and therefore buy insurance policies, but it also predicts that such people would not gamble. Gambling where there is a small chance of a very large gain may be explained by the value placed on the hope (however small) of transforming one's life. Gambling where small gains and losses are involved may be explained by enjoyment of gambling in itself.

■ From the firm's point of view, providing gambling games where the odds can be set endogenously is a no-lose situation. Providing insurance is risky, but the pooling of independent risks minimizes the risk.

■ Two problems with insurance are moral hazard, when the existence of insurance alters people's behaviour in a socially costly way, and adverse selection, which arises under conditions of asymmetric information.

Financial choices and risk

■ Portfolio diversification is a method of reducing an investor's risk by holding a broad spectrum of financial assets. This is partly the pooling of the return on assets whose risks are independent of each other and partly the pooling of assets whose risks are correlated with each other but of different magnitude. Optimum portfolio diversification allows investors to choose a bundle of assets that minimizes the risk on any given expected rate of return.

■ Mutual funds allow even small investors to hold highly diversified portfolios.

■ Financial intermediaries are institutions that stand between savers and borrowers. Their specialized knowledge and large volume of transactions reduce the transaction costs of matching savers and lenders and reduce risk.

Topics for review

■ Expected value and risk
■ Fair and unfair games
■ Attitudes to risk
■ Risk-sharing and risk-pooling
■ The demand for insurance
■ Portfolio diversification
■ The Beta coefficient
■ Mutual funds
■ Financial intermediaries

Questions for discussion

1 Toss a coin and keep track of the number of heads after (a) 5 tosses, (b) 10 tosses, (c) 15 tosses, and (d) 20 tosses. How far does your number of heads differ from the mathematically expected value after each run of a larger and larger number of tosses? What do you think would happen if you had the persistence to toss the coin 100 times and 1,000 times? Now get a group of friends each to toss a coin 5 times and count each head as a £1 win. Observe the dispersion of winnings among your friends. What would happen if you all agreed to pool your winnings and share the result equally? What does this tell you about risk-pooling and risk-sharing?

2 John drives to the betting shop in an uninsured car. What does this tell you about his preferences for risk?

3 What are moral hazard and adverse selection? How would each arise if it were possible to insure against failing an examination?

4 What is a zero-sum game? By how much do betting on (a) the price of a stock, (b) a horse race, (c) the football pools, and (d) the National Lottery diverge from zero-sum games?

5 The riskier a company is, the higher is the rate of interest it pays on its bonds. Why do profit-maximizing investors not rush to buy all of these assets in order to obtain the high returns? Why do they not all shun them completely in order to avoid the high risk?

Chapter 13
Consumer and Producer Theory in Action

In this chapter we apply the theory of market behaviour to a number of real-world problems. As well as helping you to understand some important issues, this chapter provides essential practice in using the theory you have been learning. Mastering economics lies not in just repeating what you have learned, but in being able to use the theory to study new situations as they arise.

The first half of the chapter deals with changes in supply or demand. We see how the economy responds to changes in costs brought about by changes in input prices, production technology, and taxes. We study reactions to shifts in demand, paying close attention to the economics of declining industries. Finally, we use the Organization of Petroleum Exporting Countries (OPEC) as a case study to illustrate how the market reacts in the short, long, and very long runs to disturbances that impinge on it.

The second half of the chapter looks into the internal working of the firm, which we have so far taken for granted. We look at how the organization and size of firms adapt to economic changes, particularly those caused by changes in technology. We see how mergers, takeovers, and buyouts help to accomplish some of the required adjustments. Finally, we raise questions about the basic assumption that firms are profit-maximizers. We see that there is serious debate about this issue. We conclude, however, that the competitive price system allocates resources and deals with change in the ways predicted by maximizing theory —at least in broad outline, even if not in every detail.

In this chapter we use the method called *comparative statics* that we first introduced in Chapter 3. We start with a market in equilibrium and then introduce one change that takes the market to a new equilibrium. The differences between the two equilibria must be the result of the one change we introduced, since everything else has been held constant.

Cases on demand and supply

Changes in costs

In this section we use the theory of perfect competition to understand how a competitive industry responds to changes in its costs. Such changes can result from changes in government policy, in input prices, or in technology. We start with the general effects of a change in costs whatever its origin.

The effects of changes in cost of production are familiar from our study of perfectly competitive firms and industries in Chapter 9. A fall in the cost of production causes a downward shift in each firm's marginal cost curve. As a result the short-run supply curve, which is the sum of the individual firms' marginal cost curves, shifts downwards. This leads to a higher output and a lower price. The price will fall, however, by less than the fall in costs, while profits will now be earned because of the lower costs of production. These changes are shown in Figure 13.1.

In the short run under perfect competition a fall in variable cost causes price to fall, but by less than the reduction in marginal cost. The benefit of the reduction in cost is thus shared between consumers, in terms of lower prices, and producers, in terms of profits.

In the long run, however, profits cannot persist in an industry with freedom of entry. New firms will enter the industry, increasing output and reducing price until all profits are eliminated. Entry shifts the short-run supply curve until price falls to p_2 in the figure. Now each firm, old and new, just covers its total costs by producing at the minimum point on $SRATC_1$.

In the long run under perfect competition all of the bene-

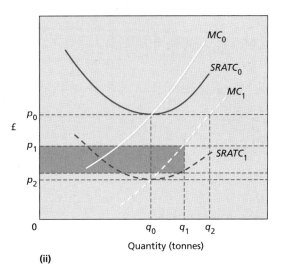

Figure 13.1 A fall in costs in a competitive industry

A fall in costs in a competitive industry leads to a fall in price, an increase in output, and the emergence of profits. In part (i) the original demand and supply curves of D and S_0 intersect at E_0 to yield a price and quantity of p_0 and q_0. When each firm's production costs fall, the supply curve—which is the sum of the marginal cost curves of all firms in the industry—shifts downward by the amount of the fall in costs, to S_1. If price fell by the full amount that costs had fallen, price would become p_2. Instead, price falls to p_1 while quantity rises to q_1, at the new equilibrium E_1.

In part (ii) the typical firm is shown in equilibrium at price p_0 with cost curves $SRATC_0$ and MC_0. The cost curves then shift to $SRATC_1$ and MC_1. The firm would be willing to produce output q_0 at price p_2. Instead, price falls only to p_1, and the firm increases its output to q_1. At this price–quantity combination it earns profits shown by the dark blue area.

fits of lower costs are passed on to consumers in terms of higher output and lower prices.

The case of a rise in costs is just the reverse. In the short run the effects will be shared between consumers, in terms of higher prices, and producers, in terms of losses. In the long run, however, firms will leave the industry until those remaining can cover all their costs. Therefore, the long-run effects of higher costs are fully borne by consumers in terms of lower output and higher prices.

Changes in input prices

If cost curves shift because of a change in input prices, the above analysis applies directly with no amendment. So if, for example, the cost of imported raw materials used in a particular industry increases, the price charged by the industry will rise and its output will fall in the short run. In the long run the losses suffered by individual firms will cause the industry to contract, shifting the short-run supply curve to the left until prices rise enough to allow the surviving firms to cover their full costs.

Changes in technology

Technological change alters costs. We look at two cases, a once-and-for-all change and a continuous series of changes.

A once-and-for-all change To study the effects of a single advance in an industry's production technology, assume that the industry starts in long-run equilibrium where each firm is earning zero profits. Some technological development in the industry's production process now lowers the production costs of newly built plants. Old plants cannot use the technology because it must be embodied in new plant and equipment. Since initially the price was just equal to the average total cost for the existing plants, new plants will be able to earn profits and they will be built immediately. But this expansion in capacity shifts the industry's short-run supply curve to the right and drives price down.

The expansion in capacity and the fall in price will continue until price is equal to the average total cost of the new plants. At this price old plants will not be covering their long-run costs. As long as price exceeds their average variable cost, however, they will continue in production. As the outmoded plants wear out, they will gradually disappear. Eventually a new long-run equilibrium will be established in which all plants use the new technology. Output will be larger, price will be lower, and the new plants will be just covering their total costs.

Ongoing changes Now ask what happens in a competitive industry in which this type of technological change occurs more or less continuously. Plants built in any one year will

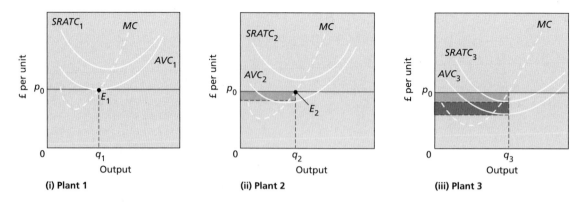

Figure 13.2 Plants of different ages when technical progress is continuous

Entry of progressively lower-cost firms forces price down. Plant 1 is the oldest plant in operation. It is just covering its average variable costs, and it will close down when price falls below p_0. Plant 2 is of intermediate age. It is covering its variable costs and earning some contribution towards its fixed costs as shown by the shaded area in part (ii). Plant 3 is the newest plant with the lowest costs. It is fully covering its fixed costs as shown by the dark shaded area in (iii). It is also making additional profits (shown by the light shaded area) which will offset the losses it expects to suffer later, when firms with newer technology enter the industry.

tend to have lower costs than plants built in any previous year. Figure 13.2 illustrates such an industry. It will have a number of interesting characteristics.

First, plants in operation will be of many different ages and at different levels of efficiency. This is dramatically illustrated by the variety of types and vintages of generator found in any long-established electricity industry. Critics who observe the continued use of older, less efficient plants and urge that the industry be modernized miss the point of economic efficiency. If the plant is already there, it can be operated profitably as long as it can cover its variable costs. As long as a plant can produce goods that are valued by consumers at an amount above the value of the resources currently used up by its operation (variable costs), the value of society's total output is increased by producing these goods.

A second characteristic of such an industry is that price will be governed by the minimum average total cost of the most efficient plants. Entry will continue until plants of the latest vintage are just expected to cover the opportunity cost of their capital over their lifetimes. This means that new plants must earn pure profits when they enter to balance the losses they expect later in life when newer firms with superior technologies enter the industry. The benefits of the new technology are passed on to consumers, because all units of the product, whether produced by new or old plants, are sold at a price that is related solely to the average total costs of the new plants. Owners of older plants find their returns over variable costs falling steadily as increasingly efficient plants drive the price down.

A third characteristic is that old plants will be discarded when the price falls below their average total costs. This may occur well before the plants are physically worn out.

In industries with continuous technical progress, capital is usually discarded because it is economically obsolete, not because it has physically worn out. This illustrates the economic meaning of 'obsolete':

Old capital is obsolete when its average variable cost exceeds the average total cost of new capital.

Taxes on price and output

There are many kinds of taxes that affect the costs of firms. We will consider three of them here: a tax that is levied on each unit produced, a tax that is a fixed amount independent of how much is produced, and a tax that is a fixed percentage of profits. The first is called a per-unit tax, the second a lump-sum tax, and the third a profits tax.

Per-unit tax Box 13.1 shows two methods of analysing the effects of a per-unit tax. The method that we use in what follows adds the tax to the firm's costs. From the firm's point of view a tax on each unit produced is just another cost of production. It shifts each firm's marginal cost curve vertically upwards by the amount of the tax, where marginal cost now refers to the firm's total outlay—costs and taxes—associated with each additional unit of production.

The upward shift in marginal cost curves makes the industry's supply curve shift upward by the amount of the tax. Now all we need to do is to recall the results established in the previous section on cost changes.

The effects of a per-unit tax on the output of a competitive industry are as follows:

1. in the short run the price will rise, but by less than the amount of the tax, so that the burden will be shared by

Box 13.1 Alternative methods of analysing a per-unit tax

(i)

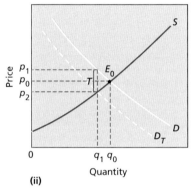

(ii)

The two parts of the figure show a competitive market in equilibrium with the demand and supply curves D and S intersecting at E_0 to produce equilibrium price and output of p_0 and q_0. A tax of T per unit is then placed on the product.

Part (i) analyses the effect of the tax by adding it to the supply curve. The 'costs' of producers now comprise production costs plus the tax that must be paid to the government. Every point on the supply curve shifts vertically upwards by the amount of the tax. The intersection of the new supply curve S_T and the demand curve D yields the new quantity and market price of q_1 and p_1. Producers' after-tax receipts are read from the original supply curve S and are p_2 ($= p_1 - T$) per unit.

Part (ii) analyses the same tax by subtracting it from the demand curve. The new curve D_T tells us the after-tax receipts of producers. Its intersection with the supply curve S yields the after-tax equilibrium. The new equilibrium quantity is q_1, producers get after-tax receipts of p_2 per unit, while the market price is p_1.

These are two alternative ways of studying the same tax and they give identical results, as can be seen by comparing the two figures.

3. if the cost curves of firms remaining in the industry are unaffected by the contraction in the size of the industry, price will rise in the long run by the full amount of the tax.

The second of the above consequences is an example of a most important general proposition. This is that in an industry with freedom of entry or exit and where there is room for a large number of firms, profits will always be pushed to zero in the long run. Thus any temporary advantage or disadvantage given to the industry by any public policy or private action must be dissipated in the long run—free entry and exit always ensures that surviving firms earn zero pure profits.

Government intervention in a competitive industry can influence the size of the industry, the total volume of its sales, and the price at which its goods are sold; but intervention cannot influence the long-run profitability of the firms that remain in the industry.

Many a government policy has started out to raise the profitability of a particular industry and ended up only increasing the number of firms, each operating at an unchanged level of profits. It illustrates that any policy by any group will fail to secure economic profits in the long run.

Box 13.2 gives a further illustration of this important point, this time related to market intervention by producers rather than by governments.

Lump-sum tax Lump-sum taxes increase the fixed costs of the firm but do not increase marginal costs. As long as a firm is able to cover its variable costs, it will remain in production. Since both marginal costs and marginal revenues are unaffected by the taxes, the profit-maximizing level of output must be unchanged.

A lump-sum tax leaves the short-run equilibrium price and output unchanged in all market structures, unless the tax is so high that it causes firms to abandon production at once.

In the long run there will be effects. If the industry was in equilibrium with zero profits before the tax was instituted, the tax will cause losses to occur. Although nothing will happen in the short run to price and output, equipment will not be replaced as it wears out. Thus in the long run the industry will contract, and price will rise until the whole tax has been passed on to consumers and the firms remaining in the industry are again covering their total costs.

A lump-sum tax will have no effect on a competitive industry in the short run, but in the long run it will cause the exit of firms; output will fall and price will rise until the whole of the tax is borne by consumers.

Taxes on profits A famous prediction is that a tax levied as

consumers, who pay a higher price, and by producers, who do not cover their average total costs;

2. in the long run the industry will contract, losses will disappear, and the whole burden will fall on consumers;

Box 13.2 The price of haircuts and the profits of hairdressers

Suppose that there are many hairdressers and freedom of entry into the industry: anyone can set up as a hairdresser. Assume that the going price for haircuts is £7.50 and that at this price all hairdressers believe their incomes are too low.

The hairdressers hold a meeting and decide to form a trade association. The purpose of the association is to impose a price of £10 for haircuts. What is the result?

We need to distinguish between the short-run and the long-run effects of an increase in the price of haircuts. In the short run the number of hairdressers is fixed. Thus, in the short run the answer depends only on the elasticity of the demand for their services. If demand elasticity is less than 1, total expenditure will rise and so will the incomes of hairdressers; if demand elasticity exceeds 1, the hairdressers' revenues will fall. Thus, to answer the question we need some knowledge about the size of the elasticity of demand for haircuts. Assuming it to be inelastic, hairdressers will be successful in raising incomes in the short run.

What about the long run? If hairdressers were just covering costs before the price change, they will now be earning economic profits. Hairdressing will become an attractive trade relative to others requiring equal skill and training, and there will be a flow of new entrants into the industry. As the number of hairdressers rises, the same amount of business must be shared among more and more of them, so the typical hairdresser will find business —and thus earnings—decreasing.

Profits may also be squeezed from another direction. With fewer customers coming their way, hairdressers may compete against one another for the limited number of customers. Their agreement does not allow them to compete through price cuts, but they can compete in service. They may spruce up their shops, offer their customers expensive magazines to read, and so forth. This kind of non-price competition will raise operating costs.

These changes will continue until hairdressers are just covering their opportunity costs, at which time the attraction for new entrants will vanish. The industry will settle down in a new long-run equilibrium in which individual hairdressers make incomes only as large as they did before the price rise. There will be more hairdressers than there were in the original situation, but each one will be working for a smaller fraction of the day and will be idle for a larger fraction. (The industry will have excess capacity.) Customers will have shorter waits even at peak periods, and they will get to read a wide choice of magazines, but they will be paying £10 for haircuts.

If the association adopted the plan in order to raise the average income of hairdressers, it will have failed. It has created more jobs for hairdressers, but not a higher income for each.

The general lesson is clear: one cannot raise income by raising price above the competitive level unless one can prevent new entry or otherwise reduce the quantity of the product or service provided.

---

a percentage on what economists call profits will have no effect on price and output under any market structure. Let us first see how the prediction is derived, and then consider its application to real-world situations.

Given free entry there will be no profits in long-run equilibrium. Thus, the firms in a perfectly competitive industry will pay no profit tax in the long run. (X per cent of zero is zero.) It follows that the tax does not affect any firm's long-run behaviour and hence has no effect on industry price and output.

A tax on profit as defined in economics affects neither price nor output of a competitive industry in equilibrium. Hence it does not affect the allocation of resources.

Does this prediction apply to those taxes on firms' profits that are actually levied in many countries? The answer is no, because profits are defined in tax law according to accountants' rather than economists' usage. In particular the tax-law definition includes the opportunity cost of capital and the reward for risk-taking. To economists this is a cost; for tax purposes it is profit. (The discussion on pages 119–20 is relevant to this point.)

Consider some of the consequences of a tax on the return to capital. First, perfectly competitive firms will pay such taxes even in long-run equilibrium, since they use capital and must earn enough money to pay a return on it. Second, the tax will affect costs differently in different industries. To see this, compare two industries. One is very

labour-intensive, so that 90 per cent of its costs of production go to wages and only 10 per cent to capital and other factors. The other is very capital-intensive, so that fully 50 per cent of its costs (in the economist's sense) are a return to capital. The tax on the return to capital will take a small part of the total earnings of the first industry and a large part of those of the second industry. If the industries were equally profitable (in the economist's sense) before the tax, they would not be afterwards, and producers would be attracted into the first industry and out of the second one. This would cause prices to change until both industries became equally profitable, after which no further movement would occur.

A tax on profits as they are defined in tax law does affect price and output and hence alters the allocation of resources.

Changes in demand

So much for changes in costs. Now ask how a competitive industry will respond to a change in demand. These effects have already been analysed on pages 150–3 of Chapter 9. For completeness we summarize them.

In the short run a rise in demand in a competitive industry will cause:

1. price to rise;

2. an increase in the quantity supplied by each firm and hence by the industry;

3. each firm to earn profits.

The long-run effects follow from the third prediction. Profits will attract new investment. New entry will cause an increase in supply that will force the price below the previously established, short-run equilibrium. This will continue until profits have returned to zero.

In the long run a rise in demand in a competitive industry will cause:

1. the scale of industry to expand;

2. profits to return to zero;

3. the new equilibrium price to be above, below, or equal to the original price; but (i) constant factor prices and (ii) identical, and unchanged, cost curves for new and old firms ensure that price returns to its original level.

The effects of a fall in demand are the opposite. In the above colour passage, read contract instead of expand in 1 and losses instead of profits in 2, while 3 is unchanged.

Now that we know what happens in general, we can apply these results to any case of changes in demand. Here is one important illustration.

Declining industries

What happens when a competitive industry begins to suffer losses because the demand for its output begins to decline? The market price will begin to fall, and firms that were previously covering average total costs will no longer be able to do so. They find themselves in the position shown in part (i) of Figure 9.8 on page 147. Firms suffer losses instead of breaking even; the signal for the exit of capital is given, but exit takes time.

The response of firms The economically efficient response to a steadily declining demand is to continue to operate with existing equipment as long as its variable costs of production can be covered. As equipment becomes obsolete because it cannot cover even its variable cost, it will not be replaced unless the new equipment can cover its total cost. As a result the capacity of the industry will shrink. If demand keeps declining, capacity must keep shrinking.

Declining industries typically present a sorry sight to the observer. Revenues are below long-run total costs, and as a result new equipment is not brought in to replace old equipment as it wears out. The average age of equipment in use thus rises steadily. The untrained observer, seeing the industry's plight, is likely to blame it on the old equipment.

Box 13.3 The economics of declining industries

The view that public control was needed to save an industry from the dead hand of third-rate, unenterprising private owners was very commonly held about the British coal industry between the First and Second World Wars. It was undoubtedly a factor leading to the nationalization of coal in 1946.

The late Sir Roy Harrod argued, however, that the run-down state of the industry in South Wales and Yorkshire, and the advanced state of the pits in Nottinghamshire and Derbyshire, represented the correct response of the owners to the signals of the market. He wrote:

The mines of Derbyshire and Nottinghamshire were rich, and it was worth sinking capital in them. If similar amounts of capital were not sunk in other parts of the country, this may not have been because the managements were inefficient, but simply because it was known that they were not worth these expenditures. Economic efficiency does not consist in always introducing the most up-to-date equipment that an engineer can think of but rather in the correct adaptation of the amount of new capital sunk to the earning capacity of the old asset. In not introducing new equipment, the managements may have been wise, not only from the point of view of their own interest, but from that of national interest, which requires the most profitable application of available capital . . . it is right that as much should be extracted from the inferior mines as can be done by old-fashioned methods (i.e. with equipment already installed), and that they should gradually go out of action. *

Declining industries always present a sorry sight to the observer. Because revenues have fallen below long-run costs, new equipment is not installed to replace old equipment as it wears out. The average age of equipment in use thus rises steadily. A declining industry will always display an old age-structure of capital, and thus 'antiquated' methods. The superficial observer, seeing the industry's very real plight, is likely to blame the antiquated equipment, which is actually the effect, not the cause, of the industry's decline.

To modernize at high capital costs merely makes the plight worse, since output and costs will rise in the face of declining demand and prices. To nationalize a declining industry, as was done with coal, in order to install new plant and equipment which privately owned firms were unwilling to install (at least in some areas) was to use the nation's scarce resources inefficiently. Capital resources are scarce: if investment occurs in mines, there is less for engineering, schools, roads, computer research, and a host of other things. To re-equip a declining industry that cannot cover its capital costs is to use scarce resources where, by the criterion of the market, their product is much less valuable than it would be in other industries. The efficient response to a steadily declining demand is not to replace old equipment, but to continue to operate existing equipment as long as it can cover its variable costs of production.

* Roy Harrod, *The British Economy* (New York: McGraw Hill, 1963), p. 54.

The antiquated equipment in a declining industry is often the effect rather than the cause of the industry's decline.

Box 13.3 covers an interesting illustration of the above point that had profound effects on British economic policy some fifty years ago.

The response of governments Governments are often tempted to support declining industries because they are worried about the resulting job losses. Experience suggests, however, that propping up genuinely declining industries only delays their demise—at significant national cost. When the government finally withdraws its support, the decline is usually more abrupt and hence more difficult to adjust to than it would have been had the industry been allowed to decline gradually under the market force of steadily declining demand.

Once governments recognize the decay of certain industries and the collapse of certain firms as an inevitable aspect of economic growth, a more effective response is to provide temporary income support and retraining schemes that cushion the impacts of change. These can moderate the effects on the incomes of workers who lose their jobs and make it easier for them to transfer to expanding industries. Intervention that is intended to increase mobility while reducing the social and personal costs of mobility is a viable long-run policy. In contrast, trying to freeze the existing industrial structure by shoring up a declining industry is not viable in the long run.

OPEC: a case study of a cartel

Cocoa producers in West Africa, farmers in the European Union, coffee growers in Brazil, oil producers, taxi drivers in many cities, and labour unions throughout the world have all sought to obtain, through collective action, some of the benefits of departing from the price-taking aspects of perfect competition. In all of these cases the sellers were so numerous that each one had no individual market power. Acting individually, each had to accept the market price that was determined by forces beyond its control. Acting collectively, they were able to influence prices by restricting supply. Cases of this sort are worth studying because they occur frequently and in various guises.

In Chapter 10 we studied the behaviour of perfectly competitive firms that organized themselves into a cartel. We reached two important conclusions:

1. It always pays the producers in a perfectly competitive industry to enter into an output-restricting agreement.

2. Each individual cartel member can increase its profits by violating the output restrictions, provided that the other members do not violate theirs.

These two conclusions highlight the dilemma of any cartel that is composed of firms which, acting individually, would be price-takers—whether it be the Organization of Petroleum Exporting Countries (OPEC) or a local producers' association. Each firm is better off if the cartel is effective in restricting output and so raising price. But each is even better off if everyone else co-operates while it cheats. Yet if all cheat, all will be worse off.

The behaviour of OPEC provides an example of the cartelization of an industry that contained a large number of price-taking firms. Because it did not cover all of the firms in the industry, it created an oligopoly rather than a monopoly. Its behaviour illustrates both the problems of oligopolistic industries and the general functioning of the competitive price system in all the runs—short, long, and very long.

Early success

OPEC did not attract world attention until 1973, when its members voluntarily agreed to restrict their outputs by negotiating quotas. At the time OPEC countries accounted for about 70 per cent of the world's supply of crude oil and 87 per cent of world oil exports. So, although it was not quite a complete monopoly, the cartel had substantial market power. As a result of the output restrictions, the world price of oil nearly quadrupled within a year, from about $3 to nearly $12 a barrel. (Oil prices are customarily stated in US dollars.) What happened is analysed in more detail in Figure 13.3.

OPEC's policy succeeded for several reasons. First, the member countries provided a large part of the total world supply of oil. Second, other producing countries could not quickly increase their outputs in response to price increases. Third, as Figure 13.3 shows, the world demand for oil proved to be highly inelastic in the short run.

The higher prices were maintained for the remainder of the decade. As a result, OPEC countries found themselves suddenly enjoying vast wealth. The increase in their wealth was so great that the temptation to cheat, in order to gain even more, was small during the rest of the 1970s. By the end of the decade, however, the OPEC countries had become used to their vast wealth and were spending more and more on arms, as well as on economic development. Eager for yet more income, they engineered a second output restriction that pushed prices from the $10–$12 range to over $30 a barrel. New income poured in, and OPEC's power to hold the oil-consuming world to ransom seemed limitless.

Longer-term market forces, however, were inexorably working against OPEC.

Pressure on the cartel

Monopolistic producers always face a long-run dilemma. The closer are their prices to the profit-maximizing level, the greater their short-term profits, but also the greater the

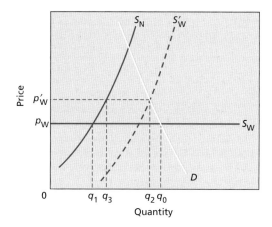

Figure 13.3 OPEC as a successful cartel

Given a rising non-OPEC supply curve of oil, OPEC could determine equilibrium price by choosing its contribution to total supply. The curve S_N represents the non-OPEC supply curve of oil. When the OPEC countries were prepared to supply all that was demanded at the world price p_W, the world supply curve was S_W. At that price production was q_1 in non-OPEC countries and $q_0 - q_1$ in OPEC countries.

By fixing its production, OPEC shifted the world supply curve to S'_W, where the horizontal distance between S_N and S'_W is OPEC's production. The world price rose to p'_W. Production became q_3 in non-OPEC countries and $q_2 - q_3$ in OPEC countries.

OPEC increased its oil revenues because, although sales fell, the price rose more than in proportion. Non-OPEC countries gained doubly because they were free to produce more and to sell it at the new, higher world price.

incentive for market reactions that will reduce their profits in the longer term. In OPEC's case the market reactions came from both the demand and the supply sides of the market.

Increasing world supply The high prices and high profits achieved by the OPEC cartel spurred major additions to the world's oil supply by non-OPEC producers. This was, in effect, new entry and a rightward shift in the non-OPEC supply curve. In 1973 OPEC produced more than 70 per cent of the world's oil; by 1979 its share was less than 60 per cent, and by 1985 it was only 30 per cent! The increased supply of non-OPEC oil tended to drive the world price down. To maintain the price, OPEC had to reduce its own output more and more so as to hold world output constant.

Declining world demand The market demand curve for oil in Figure 13.3 shows how variations in the price of oil affect purchases, other things being equal. Other things being equal, there was little that users could do to reduce their consumption of petroleum products in response to the price rise. Over a longer period of time, however, other things did not remain equal. A host of long-term adapta-

tions—including smaller cars, more efficient insulation on oil-heated buildings, and more economical diesel engines—economized on petroleum products within known technology. The long-run demand curve proved to be much more elastic than the short-run demand curve. (See Figure 4.8 on page 63, for an elaboration of the distinction between short- and long-run demand curves.)

Very-long-run forces were also unleashed. The high price of petroleum led to a burst of scientific research to develop more petroleum-efficient technologies and alternatives to petroleum. Solar-heating technology was advanced, as was technology concerning many longer-term alternatives such as tidal power and heat from the interior of the Earth. Had the price of petroleum remained at its 1980 peak, this research would have continued at an intense pace and would have borne increasing fruits in the decades that followed.

The shrinking market for OPEC oil at the high world price necessitated ever stiffer production limitations if the cartel was to maintain that price. By 1981, OPEC exports were only 18 million barrels per day, two-thirds of the 1973 level, and by 1985 maintaining prices required production to be cut to only 15 million barrels.

The pressure to cheat As world output of oil grew, OPEC output had to be reduced substantially to maintain the high prices. As a result incomes in OPEC countries declined sharply and the instabilities inherent in any cartel began to be felt. In 1981 the cartel price was about five times as high as the 1972 price (measured in constant dollars), but production quotas were less than half of OPEC's capacity. Upset by declining incomes, OPEC producers began to violate their quotas. They met every few months to debate quotas, deplore cheating, and argue about strategy. But the agreements that were reached proved impossible to enforce, and at the end of 1985 OPEC eliminated production quotas. The price fluctuated considerably and then settled down near $18 a barrel, which is a little higher than the price before OPEC's restrictions began (allowing for inflation)—the slightly higher price being accounted for by the modest output restrictions that OPEC was still able to enforce.

Since that time attempts to re-establish new quota restrictions have failed. The price of crude oil moved in the range of $12–$14.50 per barrel in 1998, which is below the real price that held before OPEC first began its market interventions.[1] This price is consistent with competitive market determination in an industry in which technological advances have significantly lowered production costs.

---

[1] The real price of oil is the money price corrected for inflation. Doing this expresses the price relative to the general level of all prices. Since the general level of all dollar prices has risen about fourfold since 1970, a nominal price of $3.40 in 1970 and $15 in 1998 indicates an approximately unchanged real price.

The relevance of the OPEC experience

OPEC's experience illustrates some basic problems of output restriction schemes.

1. Where demand is inelastic, restriction of output to below the competitive level can lead to immense profits in the short term.

However, supply is likely to increase when, as Schumpeter long ago predicted, new producers find ways of overcoming entry barriers in order to share in the large profits. Furthermore, demand is likely to decrease as new substitutes are invented and produced. These long-term adjustments limit the market power of monopolies and cartels, but only with a significant time-lag.

2. Maintaining market power becomes increasingly difficult as time passes.

The closer the cartel pushes price to the monopoly level, the higher are the short-run profits, but the greater is the incentive for longer-term, profit-reducing reactions from both the supply side and the demand side of the market.

3. Producers with market power face a basic trade-off between profits in the short term and profits in the longer term.

When there are many producers it is difficult to force them all to maintain the output restrictions, because each one has an incentive to cheat. This is particularly so if declining demand and increasing competition from new sources, or new products, lead to a steadily shrinking share of the market and falling profits.

4. Output restriction by voluntary agreement among several producers is difficult to maintain over any long period of time.

For a while OPEC massively exploited the non-OPEC world. But in the end the forces of the free market came to the rescue.

The firm in more detail

We began Chapter 8 by observing that there were many forms of business organization, running from the sole trader to the joint-stock company. From then on, however, we have treated the firm as a black box. We have not been concerned with what goes on inside it. Instead we have assumed firms to be profit-maximizing agents whose internal structure does not affect their performance. It is now time to go beyond that very useful simplification and look at the firm in more detail.

Organization as a variable

Different forms and sizes of business organization have varying efficiencies in different circumstances. When the circumstances change, so must the organization change.

The most common cause of changing circumstances to which the firm must react is changes in the technologies of the products it makes (called *product technology*) and in the processes it uses to make them (called *process technology*). At the beginning of the twentieth century technological changes made large scale efficient in many—but not all—manufacturing activities. The result was a wave of mergers as many smaller firms were united to make fewer large firms. Towards the end of the twentieth century developments in information and communications technology have again altered the relative efficiencies of different sizes and forms of business organization. In many activities, small size has become efficient. Large firms have shed many peripheral activities that are now undertaken by smaller, more specialized firms. This allows the larger firms to concentrate on what they call their 'core competencies'. Within many large firms, the old hierarchical organization, with hoards of middle managers passing information and commands upwards and downwards, is now obsolete. A newer, more loosely controlled, lateral form of organization is proving more efficient in many situations. In the process of adjustment, many middle-range managers have lost their jobs. In the global economy that has been created by the information and communications revolution, some activities are most efficiently undertaken on a very large scale. For example, banks and other financial institutions have been increasing in size and scope. Also, many specific activities, such as marketing, distribution, and financing, have large scale economies in the globalized marketplace. These are most efficiently undertaken by large units. In contrast, many production activities are more efficiently undertaken in units that are much smaller than were the typical manufacturing firms in the days of mass production. As a result many sectors are seeing simultaneous growth in the size of firms, while firms' internal organization is becoming less hierarchical.

If the market economy is to function efficiently, these changes in size and structure of firms must be made whenever they are needed. One way in which the size of firms is varied is by combining several existing firms into a larger single unit. Such combinations are negotiated in what is called the **market for corporate control.** Instead of the more familiar markets for products and factors, this is a market in which firms themselves are bought and sold.

The market for corporate control

A **takeover** occurs when Company A buys Company B (which then becomes a part of A). In a friendly takeover, both sides wish to make the transaction. A hostile takeover occurs when it is opposed by the current management of the target firm. A **merger** occurs when Companies A and B join together, often combining even their names. A **buyout** occurs when a group of investors, rather than an existing firm, buys up a firm or one of its subsidiaries. In a management buyout the existing management buys its firm from the present owners. In one form of management buyout the managers of a wholly owned subsidiary buy their firm from the group that owns it. From then on it becomes an independent firm.

Buyouts, mergers, and takeovers are transactions in the market for corporate control.

The buyers in this market are those who wish to acquire the rights to control a firm. The sellers are the current owners of the firm's equity. As in other markets, the expected outcome is that the assets being bought and sold will wind up in the hands of those who value them most.

The effects of takeovers

Takeovers, mergers, and buyouts tend to come in waves. Some are driven by technological changes that increase the minimum efficient scale of firms in many industries. They tend to have long-lasting effects. Such was the merger wave at the beginning of this century in the United States. Some are based on experiments that prove to be either outright failures or far less valuable than originally thought. Such was the wave of conglomerate mergers in the 1970s that often united firms selling widely different products in widely different markets (hence the name 'conglomerate'). Although some of the conglomerates formed in that period have survived, many have been dismantled. Some went in the wave of buyouts that occurred in the 1980s. Others were dismantled from within, as when Hanson PLC was split into five separate companies in 1996/7.

Do takeovers improve economic efficiency? The main argument for answering yes is that after a takeover the new management can make more efficient use of the target firm's assets. The acquiring firm should be able to exploit profit opportunities that the target management was not exploiting. This can be done in many ways after the take-over. The target firm may be operated more efficiently. It may be provided with funds that it could not obtain on its own. It may be able to enter markets that would be too expensive for it to access on its own. Or it might just be moved towards the most efficient size, which may have been changed by technological advances in the industry. If any of these situations hold, the value of the target firm will rise in response to an imminent takeover, reflecting the expectation of increased future profits. Further, it is often argued that if the acquiring firm's managers are acting in the best interest of their stockholders, the value of the acquiring firm should also rise when it looks like it is about to succeed in its takeover bid.

Returns to shareholders

Evidence strongly supports the proposition that takeover bids benefit the shareholders of target firms. Estimates of the magnitude of the gains for UK and US shareholders of target firms typically show that on average they sell their shares for about 20 per cent over the pre-takeover share price. Some specific cases have produced gains to shareholders well in excess of this amount.

In contrast, the benefits to shareholders in the acquiring firms vary greatly from takeover to takeover. Sometimes the benefit is large; at other times it is negative (the takeover lowers the value of the acquiring firm's shares). However, the accumulated evidence seems to show that the average benefit to acquiring firms in both the United States and the United Kingdom has been very close to zero, or possibly slightly negative.

It may seem strange that firms taking over other firms do not actually benefit from such actions on average. However, this is what we would expect if the market for corporate control were competitive. A typical takeover starts when an existing firm is perceived to be undervalued. This may be for any of the reasons mentioned above. Other firms will want to take the firm over and will bid up the value of its shares to reflect the perceived undervaluation.

The result of such bidding wars is a rise in the price of the target firm's shares to the benefit of the owners, whereas the firm that finally makes the successful takeover pays about the price that makes its investment yield a normal return (including a risk premium).

However, expectations about the potential profitability of the target firm are subject to a wide margin of error. So some takeovers turn out to be more valuable than expected and the acquiring firm gains, while others turn out to be less valuable than expected and the acquirer loses. If, however, the market judges correctly on average, takeovers will only prove normally profitable on average (no excess returns) for the firm making the takeover. The inevitability that some takeover bids will be a mistake is known as the winner's curse. This is discussed in Box 13.4.

Box 13.4 The winner's curse

In any auction market the sale price is determined by what the highest bidder is prepared to pay. In a standard auction, the price keeps rising until all but one bidder drops out. The highest bidder, who ends up acquiring the object for sale, is often described as 'the winner'. However, the winner of an auction, especially in the context of the 'winner' of a takeover bid, may not be a winner at all.

The winner of a takeover fight has to pay a price so high that not only are the existing owners prepared to sell, but also all other bidders have dropped out. This means that the so-called winner has paid a price for the target firm that is higher than the valuation placed on it by any other party in the auction.

The winner may know something about the value of the target firm that nobody else knows. More often, however, all bidders have roughly the same information. But there is always some uncertainty about how to assess the importance of this information. The uncertainty gives rise to differences in the potential purchasers' assessments of the true value of the target firm. The auction guarantees that the winner will be the bidder with the most optimistic estimate. If the average of all the bidders' estimates is close to the true value, the firm that wins will always pay more than the true value. Fortunately for the winner, uncertainty is such that sometimes even the most optimistic estimate is less than the true value. Also the target firm is sometimes worth more to the winner than to any other bidder. In such cases the winner really wins.

In other cases, however, the firm that wins a takeover battle does not increase the value of its own company. Indeed, in a hotly contested bidding war in which there are rival bidders and the winning bid is well above the initial bid, the successful bidder may end up paying more than the target firm is really worth. This is why this phenomenon is known as **the winner's curse.**

The true winners in a takeover war may be not only the shareholders of the target company but also the rival bidders who failed to 'win'. The shareholders win because they sell their shares for more than they are really worth, at least in the opinion of most potential buyers. The losing bidders win because their rival who 'won' the auction may be saddled with a capital loss that could weaken its ability to compete in other ways.

A good example of this phenomenon is the takeover of the Crocker Bank of California by the UK's Midland Bank. This so weakened Midland that it ended up being taken over itself by HSBC. Another example is the takeover in 1987 of US employment agency Manpower by the much smaller UK employment agency Blue Arrow. This effectively turned Blue Arrow from a fast-growing stock market star into a basket case overnight. The best example of all is the takeover of RJR Nabisco by Kolberg Kravis and Roberts (KKR) in one of the most famous (and biggest—$25 billion) takeover auctions of all time. KKR survived, but the firm's ability to raise capital for other activities was severely dented for most of the following decade. The firm would probably have been a much bigger force on Wall Street in the last decade if it had lost that bid.

The winner's curse applies not just to takeover bids but also to any transaction in which there is competitive bidding, such as for supply contracts which go to the lowest bidder. That bidder may have underestimated the true costs and hence may lose on the deal.

Benefits to the economy?

There is considerable controversy about whether the threat of takeover is always a good thing. Critics of hostile takeovers argue that they encourage 'short-termism'. Managers cannot take appropriate long-term investment decisions because short-term weakness in the share price may lead to the firm being taken over and the management replaced. In Germany and Japan institutional arrangements make hostile takeovers difficult, if not impossible, so managers do not have to worry about being deposed in this way.

Supporters emphasize several positive values. First, the possibility of such hostile takeovers may be a useful discipline on entrenched but inefficient managers. Second, the possibility may restrain managers from acting in non-maximizing ways. For example, managers may be more interested in securing their own high salaries than in taking the kind of risk on which long-term business success depends. Third, each new bout of takeovers (whether hostile or friendly) and mergers helps to chart new waters. Changes in technology change the advantages of scale and scope resulting from changes in production techniques, market demand, and market boundaries.

The new forms of organization that are often made necessary by technological changes are sometimes effected through mergers, takeovers, and buyouts (and sometimes through the downsizing of firms). When firms react to rapidly changing circumstances, they must learn by experience. It is not surprising that even though people generally move in the right direction, some make mistakes. In particular, a merger movement may go too far, so that among the profit-increasing mergers, takeovers, or buyouts, there are also some profit-reducing ones. Over time the successful ones will be solidified and unsuccessful ones abandoned.

We would expect to find such experimentation in a world of rapidly changing circumstances where people must learn appropriate responses through experience. It makes assessment of any current wave of mergers, buyouts, or takeovers difficult until the whole process is completed.

Until all the dust has settled, it is hard to distinguish between some spectacular, attention-getting failures that are an inevitable part of the learning process and a more general failure of the concept behind the wave.

One reason why a firm may be taken over by another is that it is not maximizing its profits. The new management may believe that after the takeover it can exploit profitable opportunities that are being ignored by the present management. In this section and the one that follows, we discuss a number of alternative theories, all of which suggest that firms do not routinely succeed in maximizing their profits.

Alternative maximizing theories

The view that many firms may systematically maximize something other than profits is made plausible by the nature of the modern corporation. One hundred years ago the small firm, whose manager was its owner, was common in many branches of industry. In such firms the single-minded pursuit of profits would be expected. Today, however, ownership of many firms is diversified among thousands of shareholders, and these firms' managers are rarely its owners. Arranging matters so that managers always act in the best interests of shareholders is, as we will see, anything but straightforward. Thus, there is potential for managers to maximize something other than profits.

The separation of ownership from control

In corporations the shareholders elect directors, who appoint managers. Directors are supposed to represent shareholders' interests and to determine the broad policies that the managers will carry out. In order to conduct the complicated business of running a large firm, a full-time professional management group must be given broad powers of decision. Although managerial decisions can be reviewed from time to time, they cannot be supervised in detail.

The links between shareholders, directors, and managers are typically weak enough that it is often top management that really controls the corporation over long periods of time.

Although the managers are legally employed by the shareholders, they remain largely independent from them. This separation of ownership from management does not matter unless the managers pursue interests that are different from the shareholders' interests. Do the interests of the two groups diverge? To study this question we need to look at what is called principal–agent theory.

Principal–agent theory

If you (the principal) hire a gardener (your agent) to mow your lawn while you are away, all you can observe is how the lawn looks when you come back. He could have mowed it every ten days, as you agreed, or he could have waited until two days before you were due home and mowed it only once. By prevailing on a neighbour to monitor your

employee's behaviour, you could find out what he actually did, but only at some cost.

When you hire a solicitor it is almost impossible for you to monitor his effort and diligence on your behalf. You have not studied law, and much of what the solicitor does will be a mystery to you.

This latter situation is close to the relationship that exists between shareholders and managers. The managers have information and expertise that the shareholders do not have—indeed, that is why they are the managers. The shareholders can observe profits, but they cannot directly observe the managers' efforts. To complicate matters further, even when the managers' behaviour can be observed, the shareholders do not generally have the expertise to evaluate it. Everyone can see the firm's revenues, but it takes very detailed knowledge to estimate how large those revenues could have been if the managers had acted differently. Boards of directors, who represent the firm's shareholders, can acquire some of the relevant expertise and monitor managerial behaviour, but again this is costly.

These examples illustrate the **principal–agent problem**. This is the problem of designing mechanisms that will induce agents to act in their principals' interests. In general, unless there is costly monitoring of agents' behaviour, the problem cannot be completely solved. Hired managers (like hired gardeners) will generally wish to pursue their own goals. They cannot ignore profits, because if they perform badly enough they will lose their jobs. Just how much latitude they have to pursue their own goals at the expense of profits depends on many things, including the degree of competition in the industry and the possibility of takeover by more profit-oriented management.

Principal–agent analysis shows that when ownership and control are separated, the self-interest of agents will tend to make profits lower than in a 'perfect', frictionless world in which principals act as their own agents.

We know that in the case of firms the shareholders, who are the principals, are interested in maximizing profits. Will the managers who are their agents have different motives?

Sales maximization

If agents do not maximize profits on behalf of the principals, what do they do? One possibility is that they seek to maximize sales. Suppose that the managers need to make some minimum level of profits to keep the shareholders satisfied; beyond this they are free to maximize their firm's sales revenue. This is a self-interested policy on the part of management, because salary, power, and prestige all rise with the size of a firm as well as with its profits. Generally, the manager of a large, normally profitable corporation will earn a salary that is considerably higher than the salary

Figure 13.4 Profit maximizing, sales maximizing, and satisficing

The 'best' level of output depends on the motivation of the firm. The curve shows the profits associated with each output. A profit-maximizing firm produces output q_m and earns profit π_m. A sales-maximizing firm with a minimum-profit constraint of π_t produces the output q_1. A satisficing firm with a target level of profits of π_t is willing to produce any output between q_0 and q_1.

earned by the manager of a small but highly profitable corporation.

The sales maximization hypothesis says that managers of firms seek to maximize their sales revenue, subject to a profit constraint.

As shown in Figure 13.4, sales maximization subject to a profit constraint causes a firm's managers to sacrifice some profits by setting price below and output above their profit-maximizing levels.

Non-maximizing theories

Some experts on corporate behaviour, particularly economists based in business schools, criticize the profit maximization assumption from a perspective different from that given by principal–agent theory. They believe that corporations are profit-oriented in the sense that, other things being equal, more profits are preferred to less profits. They do not believe, however, that corporations are profit-maximizers.

Failure to minimize costs

The sales maximization hypothesis implies that the firm's managers will choose to produce more than the profit-maximizing level of output. Would the firm's managers ever decide to produce their chosen output at greater than minimum achievable cost?

There are many possible answers, but the most straightforward one is that minimizing costs requires much detailed managerial attention, and if management can avoid doing so, it would prefer not to make the effort. Moreover, it is usually costly for a firm to change its routine be-

haviour. If this is so, even if one firm operates at a higher cost than another, it may still not be worthwhile for the first firm to copy the behaviour of the second firm. The transaction costs of making the change could outweigh the benefits. As with sales maximization, pressure from shareholders, competition from other firms, and threat of takeover will limit the extent to which economic or technological inefficiency can survive, but they may not eliminate inefficiency.

Full-cost pricing

Most manufacturing firms are price-setters: they must quote a price for their products rather than accept a price set on some impersonal competitive market. Simple profit-maximizing theory predicts that these firms will change their prices in response to every change in demand and cost that they experience. In the short run, prices of manufactured goods do not vary in response to every shift in the firm's demand. Instead, they appear to change rather sluggishly.

This short-run behaviour is consistent with the hypothesis of full-cost pricing, which was first advanced following a series of detailed case studies of actual pricing decisions made in Oxford in the 1930s. Case studies in the intervening decades have continued to reveal the widespread use of full-cost pricing procedures.

The full-cost pricer, instead of equating marginal revenue with marginal cost, sets price equal to average cost at normal-capacity output plus a conventional mark-up.

The firm changes its prices when its average costs change substantially (as a result of such events as a new union contract or a sharp change in the prices of key raw materials), and it may occasionally change its mark-up. But it changes output rather than price when its demand fluctuates over the short run. This makes its short-run pricing behaviour appear somewhat conventional rather than fully profit-maximizing.

Modern critics of profit-maximizing theory accept the evidence that full-cost prices are sometimes changed in the profit-maximizing direction. They hold, however, that the prevalence of conventional full-cost practices shows that prices are typically not at their profit-maximizing level. They also hold that the prevalence of full-cost pricing shows that firms are creatures of custom that make profit-oriented changes at infrequent intervals.

We saw in Chapter 11 that the short-term stickiness of oligopolistic prices can be accounted for under profit-maximizing theory by the fact that it is quite costly for a multi-product firm to change its list prices. If so, the possible conflict between full-cost and profit-maximizing theory concerns only the setting of the mark-up that relates prices to costs. If mark-ups are conventional and are only rarely revised, then there is a conflict. If, however, the mark-up is the profit-maximizing one for normal-capacity output, full-cost pricing is consistent with profit maximization when it is costly to change prices.

Satisficing theory

A major group of critics of profit maximization develop their argument as follows. Firms operate in highly uncertain environments. Their long-term success or failure is determined largely by their ability to administer innovation and change. But the risks of innovation are large, and the outcomes are highly uncertain. Rational firms tend, therefore, to be quite risk-averse. They develop routines of behaviour that they follow as long as they are successful. Only when profits fall low enough to threaten their survival do they adopt risky courses of action.

Supporters of this view include economists such as the American business school professor Michael Porter, who argues on the basis of considerable evidence that firms react to the stick of threatened losses of existing profits more than to the carrot of possible increases in profits. Other supporters of this view argue that firms simply cannot handle the task of scrutinizing all possibilities, calculating the probable outcomes, and then choosing among these so as to maximize their expected profits. Instead, in their view, firms carry on with existing routines as long as these produce satisfactory profits, and only when profits fall to unacceptably low levels do the firms search for new ways of doing old things or for new lines of activity.

The theory of satisficing provides one way of formalizing these views. It was first put forward by American Professor Herbert Simon, who was awarded the 1978 Nobel Prize in economics for his work on the behaviour of firms. He wrote, 'We must expect the firm's goals to be not maximizing profits but attaining a certain level or rate of profit, holding a certain share of the market or a certain level of sales.' In general a firm is said to be satisficing if it does not change its behaviour, provided that a satisfactory (rather than optimal) level of performance is currently being achieved.

According to the satisficing hypothesis, firms could produce any one of a range of outputs that produce profits at least equal to the target level. This contrasts with the unique output that is predicted by profit-maximizing theory. Figure 13.4 on page 212 compares satisficing behaviour with sales- and profit-maximizing behaviour.

The theory of satisficing predicts not a unique equilibrium output but a range of possible outputs that includes the profit-maximizing output.

Evolutionary theories

The modern evolutionary theories of the firm owe their first systematic development to the American economists Richard Nelson and Sidney Winter. They built on the earlier theories of full-cost pricing and satisficing. Nelson and Winter and the evolutionary theorists who followed them have gathered much evidence to show that tradition often dominates firms' planning. The basic effort at the early stages of planning is directed, they argue, towards the problem of performing reasonably well in established markets and maintaining established market shares. They quote evidence to show that suggestions made in preliminary planning documents to do radically new things are usually weeded out in the reviewing process. They believe that most firms spend very little effort on planning to enter entirely new markets, and still less on direct efforts to leave, or even reduce their share in, long-established markets. Their theories make some key analogies with the theory of biological evolution. Here are two illustrations.

Genes In biological theory behavioural patterns are transmitted over time by genes. Rules of behaviour fulfil the same function in the evolutionary theory of the firm. In Nelson and Winter's words, 'A great deal of firm decision behaviour is routinized [covering such] decision situations from pricing practices in retail stores to such "strategic" decisions as advertising or R and D effort, or the question of whether or not to invest abroad.' Nelson and Winter talk of firms 'remembering by doing' according to repetitive routines. They add that government policymakers tend to have unrealistic expectations about firms' flexibility and responsiveness to changes in market incentives. These expectations arise from the maximizing model, whose fatal flaw, Nelson and Winter allege, is to underestimate the importance, and the difficulty, 'of the task of merely continuing the routine performance, i.e. of preventing undesired deviations'.

Mutations In the theory of biological evolution mutations are one vehicle of change. In the evolutionary theory of the firm this role is played by innovations. The most common innovations concern product and production techniques. However, a further important class of innovations in evolutionary theory is the introduction of new rules of behaviour. Sometimes innovations are thrust on the firm; at other times the firm consciously plans for, and creates, this type of innovation. According to maximizing theory, innovations are the result of incentives—the 'carrot' of new profit opportunities. In evolutionary theory the firm is much more of a satisficer. It usually innovates only under the incentive of the 'stick', either of unacceptably low profits or of some form of external prodding. Firms change routines when they get into trouble, not when they see a chance to improve an already satisfactory performance. For example, in the growing markets of the 1960s and 1970s many firms adopted wasteful practices, which they shed fairly easily when their profits were threatened in the more difficult economic climate of the 1980s and 1990s.

The importance of non-maximizing theories

An impressive array of empirical and theoretical evidence can be gathered in support of non-maximizing theories. What would be the implications if they were accepted as being better theories of the behaviour of the economy than the 'standard model', which is based on the assumption of profit maximization?

To the extent that existing non-profit-maximizing theories are correct, the economic system does not perform with the delicate precision that follows from profit maximization. Firms will not always respond quickly and precisely to small changes in market signals from either the private sector or government policy. Nor are they certain to make radical changes in their behaviour even when the profit incentives to do so are large.

The non-maximizing theories imply that in many cases firms' responses to small changes in market signals will be of uncertain speed and direction.

According to all existing theories, both maximizing and non-maximizing, firms will tend to sell more when demand increases and less when it decreases. They will also tend to alter their prices and their input mixes when they face sufficiently large changes in input prices. Moreover, there are limits to the extent to which non-maximizing behaviour can survive in the marketplace. Failure to respond to profit opportunities can lead to takeover by a more profit-oriented management. Although this does not mean that profits are being precisely maximized at all times, it does put real limits on the extent to which firms can ignore profits.

Profits are a potent force in the life and death of firms. The resilience of profit-maximizing theory and its ability to predict the economy's reactions to many major changes (such as the dramatic variations in energy prices that have occurred since 1973) suggest that firms are at least strongly motivated by the pursuit of profits.

Three key points are at issue here:

1. To what extent do firms respond predictably to changes in such economic signals as output and input prices, taxes, and subsidies, particularly when the changes are small?

2. To what extent does non-maximizing behaviour provide scope for profit-oriented takeovers, mergers, and buyouts?

3. How do firms manage very-long-run changes?

One of the most important lessons learned by economists in the last decade is that much oligopolistic competition takes place in product or process innovation. How firms perform relative to their domestic and foreign competitors with respect to innovation is a major determinant of their competitive performance, and indeed of their very survival, over the period of a decade or so. These matters require making decisions on highly uncertain issues relating to the very long run. Many investigators argue that the innovative performance of firms is best understood by theories that take account of firms' organizational structures and the routines that they use to guide their decision-making.

In the 1980s and 1990s the question of how firms behave in detail has received renewed attention from both economists and organization theorists. Almost everyone in the field agrees that firms do not exactly maximize profits at all times and in all places. At the same time, almost everyone agrees that firms cannot stray too far from the goal of profit maximization. Just how far is too far depends on the circumstances in which firms operate and on the mechanisms that firms' owners can use to influence managers.

Profit maximization as an evolutionary equilibrium

The US economist Armen Alchian has suggested that in long-run equilibrium firms will evolve to become profit-maximizers. His argument is based on the principle of 'survival of the fittest'. In a competitive environment firms that pursue goals or adopt rules that are inconsistent with profit maximization will be unable to stay in business; firms that either choose or happen upon rules that are closer to profit maximization will undersell and displace those that do not. Eventually only the profit-maximizing firms will survive in the marketplace. He concludes that even if no firm starts out with the intention of maximizing profits, in the long run the firms that survive in the marketplace will tend to be those that come closest to profit maximization.

In contrast, many evolutionary theorists point out that evolutionary equilibrium is unlikely ever to be achieved. As technology and tastes change over time, so too does the behaviour that will maximize profits. Without a fixed target, a firm's behaviour will continually evolve, but it will never reach an equilibrium. The target refuses to stay put.

Evolutionary theorists argue that although firms never end up being profit-maximizers, the competitive market does reward the successful line of behaviour and successful types of experiments while punishing the unsuccessful ones. For example, when a wave of merger mania sweeps over investors, both good and bad mergers occur. But the market then sorts out the wheat from the chaff. Those that improved things will persist and those that made things worse will be undone, possibly because the firms involved fail. Thus when circumstances change, the market produces results that are not too different from what would occur if all firms were profit-maximizers. This will happen as long as there are enough firms to experiment with many different responses and as long as the market rewards success and punishes failure. This pushing of profitable and suppressing of unprofitable behaviour, in spite of each firm not being a profit-maximizer, is what Nelson and Winter call the 'evolutionary hand' of the competitive market.

Whether it is because firms make maximizing decisions internally or because the market sorts out good decisions from bad ones by rewarding the former with profits and punishing the latter with losses, the competitive economy tends to produce behaviour that continually adapts to changing circumstances.

On this much both sides agree. Those who accept profit-maximizing say that the adaptations that we observe are optimal. Those who accept evolutionary theory say that the adaptations end up being more or less as good as could be expected but not in any sense perfect. Some subtle issues in advanced economics turn on which view is accepted. However, the overall view on how the market economy works to adapt and innovate as circumstances change is pretty well agreed.

Summary

Cases on demand and supply

■ Changes in costs can be induced by change in the prices of inputs, by technological improvements, and by government taxes. In competitive industries the benefits of technological changes are passed fully on to the consumer in the long run.

■ Under competitive conditions taxes and subsidies will affect profits in the short run. In the long run they will affect price and output but will not affect profits.

■ A declining industry will show an old capital structure, which is the consequence not the cause of decline.

■ An industry's profits can always be increased if firms co-operate to depart from a perfectly competitive equilibrium and reduce output until marginal cost equals the industry's marginal revenue. At this co-operative solution, each firm can increase its profits by increasing its output. If all try to do this simultaneously, price will be driven back to its perfectly competitive level.

■ OPEC's experience shows the profits that can be earned by restricting output to below the perfectly competitive level, as well as the difficulties of maintaining the co-operative solution over time. It also shows the economy's powerful response to price signals: high relative prices and profits induce increased supplies and long-term reductions in demand.

The firm in more detail

■ Principal–agent theory gives support to the idea that corporate managers may pursue their own interests rather than simply maximizing profits. Sales maximization is an example of such a pursuit.

■ Another class of theories claims that firms do not maximize anything. This may be because they lack sufficient knowledge, or because they choose not to do so.

■ Full-cost pricing with conventional mark-ups makes firms creatures of convention. The same theory, with mark-ups determined at the profit-maximizing level for normal-capacity output (plus the assumption that changing prices is costly), is consistent with profit maximization.

■ Organization theory assumes that the firm satisfices— which means that it is satisfied with any level of output and prices which meets its minimum-profit constraint.

■ Evolutionary theories see firms as profit-oriented but not profit-maximizing. Firms follow rules of behaviour that have been shown to work and change these only when forced to by major changes in market conditions.

■ Even if individual firms do not always maximize profits, it is possible that the industry will be characterized by behaviour that is approximately profit-maximizing. The reason is that those firms that come closest to maximizing profits will prosper and grow while those further away from profit maximization will shrink or fail altogether.

Topics for review

■ The effects of changes in demand and in costs
■ The effect of taxes on output and profits
■ The gains from monopolizing a perfectly competitive industry
■ OPEC
■ The incentives to cheat on a cartel
■ Mergers, takeovers, and buyouts
■ Sales maximization
■ Satisficing
■ Evolutionary theories
■ Takeovers as a constraint on non-maximizing behaviour

Questions for discussion

1 Explain what is meant by the principal–agent problem. How would it arise if teachers wanted to maximize what their students learned while students merely wanted to pass their exams? What incentive structures might induce the agents (students) to come closer to fulfilling the principals' (teachers') goals?

2 Why might a principal–agent problem arise between a firm's shareholders and its senior management? What incentives might be used to alleviate the problem?

3 Compare the conditions you would expect to find in two industries, one, such as computers, where technology is changing rapidly and one, such as steel manufacture, where technology is *relatively* stable.

4 A perfectly competitive industry is in equilibrium with its product selling for £10 a unit. Compare the effects of a tax of £2 a unit with those of a tax of 20 per cent of the market price. (*Hint*: at first sight these may seem to be identical in effect but they are not.)

5 What bearing did each of the following have on the current oil price at the time and on the eventual ability of OPEC to maintain a price for oil well above the competitive equilibrium price? (*a*) Between 1979 and 1985 OPEC's share of the world oil supply decreased by half. (*b*) During the 1970s government policies in many oil-importing countries protected consumers from oil price shocks by subsidizing domestic prices to hold them well below OPEC's price. (*c*) The former USSR increased its oil exports massively in the 1980s, but exports then dwindled in the 1990s as the industry fell into disrepair. (*d*) In the late 1980s Iran became increasingly concerned with maximizing its own oil revenues in order to pay for its war with Iraq. (*e*) Iraq occupied Kuwait, and many of its large stock of wells were set on fire when Iraq was driven out in 1991. (*f*) Other OPEC countries were able to make up for the lost Kuwaiti production by raising their outputs at marginal costs far below the current world price.

Part Three
How Income is Earned

Chapter 14
How Income is Generated

In this chapter we study how incomes are determined in competitive markets, those in which individual buyers and sellers have no market power over prices. We first study the forces that determine the demand for factors, then the forces that determine supply, and finally how these interact to determine both the prices of factors of production and the share of the nation's total income going to each factor. In subsequent chapters we allow for market power exercised in factor markets by a few larger sellers and/or buyers.

Why does the market system reward some people with high incomes, while others earn very little? It is tempting to give superficial answers such as 'People are paid what they are worth.' But we may wonder: worth what, and to whom? What gives them value? Sometimes it is said that people earn according to their ability. But note that incomes are distributed more unequally than any measured index of ability such as IQ or physical strength. If answers couched in terms of worth and ability seem superficial, so are answers such as 'It's all a matter of luck' or 'It's just the system'.

The theory in outline

In this section we explain the meaning of some overlapping terms that often cause confusion. We then outline the basic insights of the theory and conclude with two of its key assumptions. After that we are ready to study the theory in more detail, which we do in the major sections that follow.

Some definitions

The theory that deals with the questions outlined above is variously called the theory of distribution, the theory of factor pricing, the neoclassical theory, and the marginal productivity theory. This can be confusing. So we take a moment to explain these terms. The term **distribution theory** refers to any theory that explains how the total national income is divided up among the nation's citizens. The division of total income can be viewed at the level of individuals or of groups of any type or size. We may be interested in why average incomes differ between geographical areas, or occupations, or skill classes, or different factors of production such as land and capital. The theory that we study in the next few chapters seeks to explain distribution on the basis of market forces that determine the prices of factors of production and the quantities employed. Any theory that explains distribution on the basis

of market forces is a **factor price theory** of distribution. Theories of this type use factors' marginal products (first studied in Chapter 8) to explain their demands. They are thus often called **marginal productivity theories** after their demand part. Marginal productivity theories were first developed by a group of economists writing about a century ago. We call them neoclassical economists, hence the term **neoclassical theory of distribution.**

All of this matters only because all of these terms are in common use. For our purposes we need to remember only two things. First, any theory that explains how income is divided up among any set of groups in which we are interested is called distribution theory. Second, the theory that we study explains distribution as a result of the market forces of demand and supply.

Early economists were interested in explaining the distribution of income among the major factors of production: labour, land, and capital. This is called the **functional distribution of income** because it divides income by functional classes, the three groups that provide the services of labour, land, and capital.

Modern economists are more concerned with another way of looking at the distribution of incomes, called the **size distribution of income.** This term refers to the distribution of income among different households without reference to the source of their incomes or each individual's social class.

Figure 14.1 A Lorenz curve of individual pre-tax income in the UK, 1996

The size of the shaded area between the Lorenz curve and the diagonal is a measure of the inequality of income distribution. If there were complete income equality, the Lorenz curve would coincide with the diagonal line. The extent of income inequality (e.g. the lower 20 per cent receive only 7 per cent of the income) determines how far the Lorenz curve lies below the diagonal.

Source: ONS, *Annual Abstract of Statistics*, 1998.

The functional and size distributions of income refer, respectively, to the shares of total national income going to each of the major factors of production, and to various groups of individuals. One focuses on the source of income, the other on its size.

The current size distribution of income in the UK is shown graphically in Figure 14.1. This curve is called a **Lorenz curve** and it shows how much of total income is accounted for by given proportions of the nation's income earners. (The further the curve bends away from the diagonal, the more unequal is the distribution of income.) The curve shows, for example, that the bottom 20 per cent of all UK individuals receive only 7 per cent of all taxable income earned, while the bottom 80 per cent receive only 57 per cent of total taxable income. The remaining 43 per cent goes to the top 20 per cent of income-earners. The income measured is taxable income, which is income before taxes.[1]

Figure 14.2 shows how UK income inequalities have changed over time. Average income has been rising over time, so it does not tell us anything about the level of income. But it does tell us that inequalities have increased

---

[1] The data refer only to income with some tax liability and therefore exclude all income that escapes the notice of the tax authorities or is otherwise exempt from income tax.

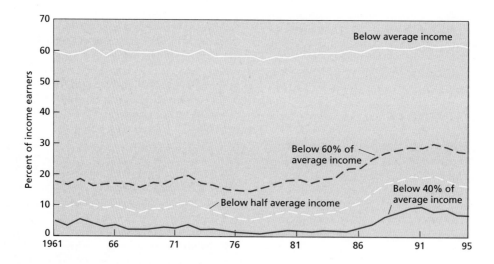

Figure 14.2 Income inequalities in the UK, 1961–1995

The figure shows the percentage of people whose income is below various fractions of average income. The proportion of people with incomes below the average has been almost constant at 60 per cent over the period from 1960. The proportion who were below 40 per cent of the average income began to rise in the 1980s, reached a peak in the early 1990s, and has declined somewhat since then. Similar comments apply to those with incomes less than 60 per cent of the average income.

Source: ONS, *Social Trends*, 1998.

over time. For example, while about 18 per cent of the population had incomes that were less than 60 per cent of the national average in 1961 the figure was close to 30 per cent in 1995.

Today economists devote most of their attention to the size distribution of income rather than the functional distribution. If someone is poor, it matters little whether that person is a landowner or a worker. Moreover, some capitalists, such as the owners of small retail stores, are in the lower part of the income scale, and some wage-earners, such as professional athletes, are at the upper end. Furthermore, the vast majority of company shares are owned by wage-earners through pension funds and life insurance policies. This fact alone makes irrelevant to the modern world the old Marxist class division between workers who supply labour and the capitalists who own the means of production. In most cases, workers are owners and owners are workers. Class distinctions may still exist, but they do not divide those who are and are not the owners of firms.

We follow modern economists in dealing with the size distribution of income, concentrating on various groups of interest. At the end of the chapter we pay some brief attention to the functional distribution.

The link between output and input decisions

In Chapter 8 we saw how firms' costs varied with their outputs and how they could achieve cost minimization by finding the least costly combination of factors to produce any given output. In Chapter 9 we saw that firms in perfect competition decided how much to produce by equating their marginal costs to given market prices. We also saw how the market supply curve interacted with the market demand curve in each goods market. This interaction determines the market price as well as the quantity that is produced and consumed.

These events in goods markets have implications for factor markets. The decisions of firms on how much to produce and how to produce it imply specific demands for various quantities of the factors of production. These demands, together with the supplies of the factors of production (which are determined by the owners of the factors), come together in factor markets. Together they determine the quantities of the various factors of production that are employed, their prices, and the incomes earned by their owners.

The above discussion shows that there is a close relationship between the production and pricing of the goods and services produced by firms on the one hand and the pricing, employment, and incomes earned by the factors of production they hire on the other hand. These are two aspects of a single set of economic activities relating to the production of goods and services and the allocation of the nation's resources among their various possible uses. This discussion provides a brief introduction to one of the great insights of economics:

When demand and supply interact to determine the allocation of resources among various lines of production, they also determine the incomes of the factors of production that are used in making the outputs.

This insight is the basis of what is called the neoclassical theory of distribution. According to this theory, the distribution of income is nothing more than a special case of price theory. The way this works can be summarized in the following three points.

1. The income of any factor of production (and hence the amount of the national product that it is able to command) depends on the price that is paid for the factor and the amount that is used.

2. Demands and supplies in factor markets determine factor prices and quantities in exactly the same way that the prices and quantities of commodities are determined in product markets.

3. All that is needed to explain distribution is to identify the main determinants of the demand for, and supply of, factors of production and allow for any intervention into free markets by governments, unions, or other similar institutions.

Figure 14.3 illustrates the neoclassical theory by showing how competitive market forces determine one factor's income. The rest of this chapter is an elaboration of this

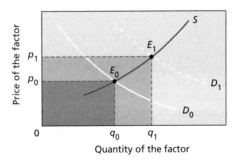

Figure 14.3 Factor income determined in competitive markets

The interaction of demand and supply in competitive factor markets determines a factor's equilibrium price and quantity, and hence its income. The original demand and supply curves are D_0 and S. Equilibrium is at E_0, with price p_0 and quantity employed q_0. The factor's income is shown by the dark blue area in the figure. When the demand curve shifts to D_1, equilibrium shifts to E_1, with price p_1 and quantity q_1. The factor's income rises by the amount of the medium blue area.

important theme. We first study the demand for factors, then their supply, and finally how they come together to determine factor prices and quantities.

Two assumptions

Before we begin, we need to make two assumptions designed to facilitate the analysis.

Other prices constant In order to ensure that we are speaking of relative and not just absolute prices and quantities, we make the following assumption. When the changes studied in Figure 14.3 occur, *the prices of all other factors of production, the prices of all goods, and the level of national income are given and constant.*[2] Under these circumstances fluctuations in a factor's equilibrium price and quantity cause fluctuations (1) in the money earnings of that factor, (2) in its earnings relative to other factors, and (3) in the share of national income going to the factor. Assume, for example, that the money price of one factor changes from some value p_0 to a higher value p_1, while the

quantity employed changes from q_0 to q_1. This means that (*a*) the factor's *relative price* rises from p_0/F to p_1/F, where F is the constant, average price of *all* other factors; and (*b*) because the factor's total earnings change from p_0q_0 to p_1q_1, the share of income going to this factor changes from p_0q_0/Y to p_1q_1/Y, where Y is the constant total national income.

Competitive markets In this chapter we confine ourselves to perfectly competitive markets. This means that individual firms are price-takers in both goods and factor markets. On the one hand they face a given price for the product they produce, and that price is both their average and marginal revenue. On the other hand they face a given price of each factor that they buy, and that price is both the average and marginal cost of the factor.

Dealing first with firms that are price-takers in product and factor markets allows us to study the principles of factor price determination in the simplest context. Once these are understood, it is relatively easy to allow for monopolistic elements in either or both types of markets. This is done in Chapter 15.

The demand for factors

Firms use the services of land, labour, capital, and natural resources[3] as inputs. They also use products, such as steel, plastics, and electricity that are produced by other firms. These products are in turn made by using land, labour, capital, natural resources, and other produced inputs. If we continue following through the chain of outputs of some firms that are used as inputs by other firms, we can account for all of the economy's output in terms of inputs of the basic factors of production—land, labour, capital, and natural resources. The theory of factor pricing applies to *all* inputs used by a firm. The theory of distribution explains the division of total national income among the owners of the basic factors: land, labour, capital, and natural resources.

Firms require inputs not for their own sake but as a means to produce goods and services. For example, the demand for computer programmers and technicians is growing as more and more computers are used. The demand for carpenters and building materials rises and falls as the amount of housing construction rises and falls. Thus, demand for any input is derived from the demand for the goods and services that it helps to produce; for this reason, the demand for a factor of production is called a **derived demand.**

Derived demand provides a link between the markets for output and the markets for inputs.

The most important relation concerning factor demand is that the amount demanded varies negatively with its price. As its price falls more is demanded and as its price rises less is demanded. In other words:

The demand curve for a factor is negatively sloped, price and quantity demanded always varying in the opposite direction.

The reasons for the negative slope to factor demand curves differ in the long and the short runs.

Factor demand in the long run

In the long run all factors are variable. In this case both the substitution and the income effects contribute to the negative slope of the demand curve. We consider the case

---

[2] We make these assumptions because we are concerned with a factor's relative share of total national income. As we observed in Chapter 3, these assumptions are only a simplifying device for our analysis; they do not prevent it from being applied to inflationary situations.

[3] Although natural resources are often included with land as a single factor of production, they have so many important special characteristics that it is sometimes worthwhile treating them as a separate factor. Some of the issues involved with pricing natural resources are discussed in Chapter 16.

of a price reduction and leave a price rise as a simple variation which you can work through for yourself.

The substitution effect A fall in a factor's price makes it less expensive relative to other factors and more of it will be used relative to others whose price has not fallen. This is true at all levels of aggregation. It is true if the price of all labour falls relative to capital or if the price of one type of labour falls relative to other types of labour. We saw in Chapter 8 that a fall in the price of all types of labour will lead profit-maximizing firms to substitute labour for capital. According to the principle of substitution (see page 127), they will use more of the now cheaper factor and less of the relatively more expensive ones. A fall in the price of one type of labour will lead to more of that type being used as a replacement for other types of labour whose price has not fallen. For example, some time ago the wages of building labour rose dramatically. This led builders to substitute prefabricated parts made in factories for parts made to order on the building site. Window frames, door jambs, walls, and a host of other parts of buildings that used to be custom made on the site were prefabricated to standard designs in factories where wages were much less than those on construction sites. In effect, factory labour whose price had not risen was substituted for building labour whose price had risen.

The income effect A fall in the price of a factor of production reduces the cost of making all products that use that factor. The cost curves of these products thus shift downwards, shifting the sum of the marginal cost curves —which is the industry supply curve. As a result more will be sold. To make more output, an increase in all the inputs is required. This leads to a rise in the amount demanded of the factor whose price has fallen, as well as a rise in the demand for all other factors that co-operate with it in production.

Factor demand in the short run

In the short run some factors are fixed and only some can be varied. If we think of an extreme situation in which only one factor can be varied, we can derive a famous proposition that is true for each and every factor as long as the firms that hire them are maximizing their profits.

The maximizing firm

In Chapter 9 we established the rules for the maximization of a firm's profits in the short run. When one factor is fixed and another is variable, the profit-maximizing firm increases its output until the last unit produced adds just as much to cost as to revenue, that is, until marginal cost equals marginal revenue. Another way of stating that the

firm maximizes profits is to say that *the firm will increase production up to the point at which the last unit of the variable factor employed adds just as much to revenue as it does to cost.*

The addition to total cost resulting from employing one more unit of a factor is its price. (Recall that the firm is assumed to buy its factors in competitive markets.) So if one more worker is hired at a wage of £15 per hour, the addition to the firm's costs is £15.

The amount that a unit of a variable factor adds to revenue is the amount that the unit adds to total output multiplied by the change in revenue caused by selling an extra unit of output.

In Chapter 8 we called the variable factor's addition to total output its *marginal product*. When dealing with factor markets, economists use the term **marginal *physical* product** (*MPP*) to avoid confusion with the revenue concepts that they also need to use.

The change in revenue caused by selling one extra unit of output is just the price of the output, p (since the firm is a price-taker in the market for its output). The resulting amount, which is $MPP \times p$, is called the factor's **marginal revenue product** and given the symbol *MRP*.

For example, if the variable factor's marginal physical product is two units per hour and the price of a unit of output is £7.50, then the factor's marginal revenue product is £15 (£7.50 × 2).

We can now state the condition for a firm to be maximizing its profits in two ways. First,

$$\text{Addition to total costs caused by hiring another unit of the variable factor} = \text{The factor's marginal revenue product } (MRP). \quad (1)$$

First note that if the firm is a price-taker in input markets the left-hand side is just the price of a unit of the variable factor, which we now call w. Also note that as long as the firm is a price-taker in the market for its output, the right-hand side is the factor's marginal physical product, *MPP*, multiplied by the price at which the output is sold, which we call p. We can now restate (1) as follows:

$$\text{Price of a unit of the variable factor} = \text{The factor's marginal physical product multiplied by the product's market price} \quad (2)$$

and in symbols,

$$w = MPP \times p. \quad (2')$$

To check your understanding of equation (2), consider an example. Suppose that the variable factor is available to the firm at a cost of £10 a unit ($w = £10$). Suppose also that employing another unit of the factor adds three units to output ($MPP = 3$). Suppose further that output is sold for £5 a unit ($p = £5$). Thus, the additional unit of the variable factor adds £15 to the firm's revenue and £10 to its costs. Hiring one more unit of the factor brings in £5 more than it costs. *The firm will take on more of the variable factor whenever its marginal revenue product exceeds its price.*

Now alter the example so that the last unit of the variable factor taken on by the firm has a marginal physical product of one unit of output—it adds only one extra unit to output—and so adds only £5 to revenue. Clearly, the firm can increase profits by cutting back on its use of the factor, since laying off one unit reduces revenues by £5 while reducing costs by £10. *The firm will lay off units of the variable factor whenever its marginal revenue product is less than its price.*

Finally, assume that another unit of the factor taken on, or laid off, has an *MPP* of two units, so that it increases revenue by £10. Now the firm cannot increase its profits by altering its employment of the variable factor in either direction. *The firm cannot increase its profits by altering employment of the variable factor whenever the factor's marginal revenue product equals its price.*

This example illustrates what was said earlier. We are doing nothing that is essentially new; instead, we are merely looking at the firm's profit-maximizing behaviour from the point of view of its inputs rather than its output. In Chapter 9 we saw the firm varying its output until the marginal cost of producing another unit was equal to the marginal revenue derived from selling that unit. Now we see the same profit-maximizing behaviour in terms of the firm varying its inputs until the marginal cost of another unit of input is just equal to the revenue derived from selling the unit's marginal product.

The firm's demand curve

It is now easy to see why in the short run with only one variable factor the firm's demand curve for that factor is negatively sloped. Let the firm begin in equilibrium. The relation shown in (2) above must hold, which means that that factor's marginal revenue product is equated to its price. Now the price of the factor falls. The unchanged marginal revenue product is now higher than the lowered price. So it pays the firm to hire more of the factor. As it takes on more units the marginal physical product falls, and since the firm is a price-taker so does the marginal revenue product. The firm goes on hiring more units of the variable factor until the marginal revenue product falls to the level of the new lower price. What this tells us is that

In the short run with only one variable factor, the firm's demand for its variable factor is negatively sloped as a result of the operation of the law of diminishing returns.

This is all we need to know about the short-run demand for a factor. The appendix to this chapter, however, gives a more elaborate graphical derivation of the short-run demand curve for those who would like to study it.

The industry's demand curve for a factor

So far we have seen how a single firm that takes its market price as given will vary its quantity demanded for a factor as that factor's price changes. But when a factor's price changes and *all firms* in a competitive industry vary the amount of the factor that they demand in order to vary their output, the price of the industry's product changes. That change will have repercussions on desired output and the quantity of the factor demanded.

For example, a fall in carpenters' wages will reduce the cost of producing houses, thus shifting the supply curve of houses to the right. Price-taking construction firms would plan to increase construction, and hence increase the quantity of carpenters demanded, by some specific amount if the price of houses does not change. Because the demand curve for houses is negatively sloped, however, the increase in output leads to a fall in the market price of houses. As a result each individual firm will increase its desired output *by less* than it had planned to do before the market price changed.

An increase in carpenters' wages has the opposite effect. The cost of producing houses rises, the supply curve shifts to the left, and the price of houses rises. As a result the individual firm will cut its planned output and employment of factors of production by less than it would have done if market price had not changed.

The industry's demand curve for a factor is steeper when the reaction of market price is allowed for than it would be if firms faced an unchanged product price.

It may be useful to summarize the reasoning used so far.

1. In the short run the derived demand curve for a factor of production on the part of a *price-taking* firm will have a negative slope because of the law of diminishing returns. As more of the factor is employed in response to a fall in its price, its marginal product falls. No further units will be added once its marginal revenue product falls to the factor's new price.

2. An industry's short-run demand curve for a factor is less elastic than suggested by point 1. As the industry expands output in response to a fall in a factor's price, the price of the firm's output will fall, causing the final increase in each firm's output, and hence its demand for factor services, to be less than it would be if the output price remained unchanged.

Elasticity of factor demand

The elasticity of demand for a factor measures the *degree* of the response of the quantity demanded to a change in its price. The influences that were discussed in the preceding sections explain the *direction* of the response; that is, the quantity demanded is negatively related to price. You should not be surprised, therefore, to hear that the amount of the response depends on the strength with which these influences operate. This section gives the four principles of derived demand that come from the work of the British economist Alfred Marshall (1842–1924).

Diminishing returns

The first influence on the slope of the demand curve is the diminishing marginal productivity of a factor. If marginal productivity declines rapidly as more of a variable factor is employed, a fall in the factor's price will not induce many more units to be employed. Conversely, if marginal productivity falls only slowly as more of a variable factor is employed, there will be a large increase in quantity demanded as price falls.

The faster the marginal productivity of a factor declines as its use rises, the lower is the elasticity of each firm's demand curve for the factor.

For example, both labour and fertilizers are used by market gardeners who produce vegetables for sale in nearby cities. For many crops additional doses of fertilizers add significant amounts to yields over quite a wide range of fertilizer use. Although the marginal product of fertilizer does decline, it does so rather slowly as more and more fertilizer is used. In contrast, although certain amounts of labour are needed for planting, weeding, and harvesting, there is only a small range over which additional labour can be used productively. The marginal product of labour, although high for the first units, declines rapidly as more

and more labour is used. Under these circumstances, market gardeners will have an elastic demand for fertilizer and an inelastic demand for labour.

Substitution

In the long run all factors are variable. If one factor's price rises, firms will try to substitute relatively cheaper factors for it. For this reason, the slope of the demand curve for a factor is influenced by the ease with which other factors can be substituted for the factor whose price has changed.

The greater the ease of substitution, the greater is the elasticity of demand for the factor.

The ease of substitution depends on the substitutes that are available and on the technical conditions of production. It is often possible to vary factor proportions in surprising ways. For example, in car manufacturing and in building construction glass and steel can be substituted for each other simply by varying the dimensions of the windows. Another example is that construction materials can be substituted for maintenance labour in the case of most durable consumer goods. This is done by making the product more or less durable and more or less subject to breakdowns and by using more or less expensive materials in its construction.

Such substitutions are not the end of the story. Plant and equipment are being replaced continually, which allows more or less capital-intensive methods to be built into new plants in response to changes in factor prices. Similarly, engines that use less petrol per mile tend to be developed when the price of petrol rises severely.

Box 14.1 provides an example of substitution in the electricity industry.

Box 14.1 Electricity generation: substitution in practice

The principle of substitution has been important in the choice of fuels used to generate electricity, but it has not always worked in the same direction.

During the 1950s and 1960s increasing economies of scale in shipping crude oil from the Middle East to Western Europe made oil-based fuels more and more competitive. The relative price of fuels for industrial use fell by even more than the production cost of petrol, as it was the demand for petrol that was mainly responsible for the derived demand for crude oil. Other outputs of the oil-refining process were byproducts. The Central Electricity Generating Board, as it was then called (it has since been privatized as National Power and Powergen), responded to the falling relative price of 'bunker' oil by building more and more oil-fired power stations and gradually closing down (or converting) the older coal-fired stations. From 85–7 per cent of electricity generated from coal and 11–14 per cent from oil in 1962–5, the CEGB steadily changed the 'mix', so that by 1971–4 it was generating 63–6 per cent from coal and 24–6 per cent from oil.

Then came the 'oil shocks' of 1973–4 and 1979–80, when the OPEC

countries dramatically raised the price of crude oil, leading to correspondingly dramatic increases in the prices of all oil products. Even though people in coalmining saw an opportunity to raise coal prices substantially, the *relative* price of oil was significantly higher in the 1980s than it had been in the 1960s and early 1970s. The CEGB accordingly switched back to increasing reliance on coal-firing, generating 77–81 per cent of its electricity from coal and only 5–7 per cent from oil in 1982–4.

Nevertheless, the CEGB clearly retained the ability to switch back to oil rapidly if required. In 1984/5 a coalminers' strike which lasted almost the whole year led to an amazing 41 per cent of electricity being generated from oil (with total output slightly higher than the previous year) and only 42 per cent from coal. After the strike, the figures quickly returned to their 1982–4 levels. However, the proportion of coal used declined again in the late 1980s and early 1990s owing to the growing use of natural gas and nuclear power. By 1996 the percentages of fuels used in electricity generation were coal 42, nuclear 28, gas 21, oil 5, and other 4.

Importance of the factor

Other things being equal, the larger the fraction of the total costs of producing some product that are made up of payments to a particular factor, the greater is the elasticity of demand for that factor.

To see this, suppose that wages account for 50 per cent of the costs of producing a good and raw materials for 15 per cent. A 10 per cent rise in the price of labour raises the cost of production by 5 per cent (10 per cent of 50 per cent), but a 10 per cent rise in the price of raw materials raises the cost of the product by only 1.5 per cent (10 per cent of 15 per cent). The larger the increase in the cost of production, the larger is the shift in the product's supply curve, and hence the larger the decreases in quantities demanded of both the product and the factors used to produce it.

Elasticity of demand for the output

The fourth, and last, principle of derived demand is:

Other things being equal, the more elastic the demand for the product that the factor helps to make, the more elastic is the demand for the factor.

If an increase in the price of the product causes a large decrease in the quantity demanded—that is, if the demand for the product is elastic—there will be a large decrease in the quantity of a factor needed to produce it in response to a rise in the factor's price. However, if an increase in the price of a product causes only a small decrease in the quantity demanded—that is, if the demand for the product is inelastic—there will be only a small decrease in the quantity of the factor required in response to a rise in its price.

In Box 14.2 the forces affecting the elasticity of the derived demand curves that have just been discussed are related more specifically to the market for the industry's output.

Box 14.2 The principles of derived demand

This box demonstrates two of the four principles of derived demand using demand and supply curves.

1. The larger the proportion of total costs accounted for by a factor, the more elastic is the demand for it.

Consider part (i) of the figure. The demand curve for the *industry's product* is D and, given the factor's original price, the *industry supply curve* is S_0. Equilibrium is at E_0 with output at q_0.

Suppose that the factor's price then falls. If the factor accounts for a small part of the industry's total cost, each firm's marginal cost curve shifts downward by only a small amount. So also does the industry supply curve, as illustrated by the supply curve S_1. Output expands only a small amount to q_1, which implies only a small increase in the quantity of the variable factor demanded.

If the factor accounts for a large part of the industry's total costs, each firm's marginal cost curve shifts downward a great deal. So also does the industry supply curve, as illustrated by the curve S_2. Output expands greatly to q_2, which implies a large increase in the quantity of variable factor demanded.

2. The more elastic the demand curve for the product made by a factor, the more elastic is the demand for the factor.

Consider part (ii) of the figure. The original demand and supply curves for the industry's product intersect at E_0 to produce an industry output of q_0. A fall in the price of a factor causes the industry's supply curve to shift downward to S_1.

When the demand curve is relatively inelastic, as shown by the curve D_i, the industry's output increases by only a small amount to q_1. The quantity of the variable factor demanded will increase by a correspondingly small amount.

When the demand curve is relatively elastic, as shown by the curve D_e, the industry's output increases by a large amount to q_2. The quantity of the variable factor demanded will then increase by a correspondingly large amount.

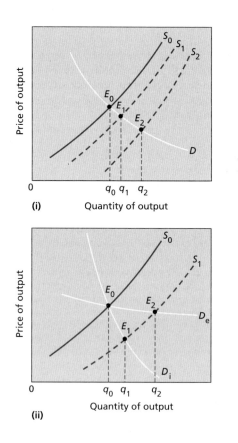

The supply of factors

When we consider the supply of any factor of production, we must consider the amount supplied to the economy as a whole, to each industry and occupation, and to each firm. The elasticity of supply of a factor will normally be different at each of these levels of aggregation. We start with the highest level of aggregation, the total supply of each factor to the economy as a whole.

The total supply of factors

At any one time the total quantity of each factor of production is given. For example, in each country the labour force is of a certain size, there is so much arable land available, and there is a given supply of discovered petroleum. However, these supplies can and do change in response to both economic and non-economic forces. Sometimes the change is very gradual, as when climatic changes slowly turn arable land into desert or when a medical discovery lowers the rate of infant mortality and hence increases the rate of population growth. Sometimes the changes can be quite rapid, as when the UK discovered oil in the North Sea, or when a boom in business activity brings retired persons back into the labour force, or when a rise in the price of agricultural produce encourages the draining of marshes to add to the supply of arable land.

Total supply of capital

The supply of capital in a country consists of the stock of existing machines, factories, equipment, and so on. Capital is a manufactured factor of production, and its total quantity is in no sense fixed, although it changes only slowly. Each year the stock of capital goods is diminished by the amount that becomes physically or economically obsolete and is increased by the amount that is newly produced. The difference between these is the net addition to, or net subtraction from, the capital stock. On balance, the trend has been for the capital stock to grow from decade to decade over the past few centuries. In Chapter 16 we will consider in some detail the determinants of investment in capital.

Total supply of land

The total area of dry land in a country is almost completely fixed, but the supply of *fertile* land is not fixed. Considerable care and effort are required to sustain the productive power of land. If farmers earn low incomes, they may not provide the necessary care and the land's fertility may be destroyed within a short time. In contrast, high earnings

from farming may provide the incentive to increase the supply of arable land by irrigation and other forms of reclamation.

Total supply of labour

The number of people willing to work is called the *labour force*; the total number of hours they are willing to work is called the **supply of effort** or, more simply, the **supply of labour.** The supply of effort depends on three influences: the size of the population, the proportion of the population willing to work, and the number of hours worked by each individual. Each of these is partly influenced by economic forces.

Population Populations vary in size, and these variations are influenced to some extent by economic forces. There is some evidence, for example, that the birth rate and the net immigration rate (immigration minus emigration) are higher in good times than in bad. Much of the variation in population is, however, explained by factors outside economics.

The labour force The proportion of the total population, or of some subgroup such as men, women, or teenagers, that is willing to work is called that group's **labour force participation rate.** This rate varies in response to many influences. One non-economic influence is change in attitudes and tastes. The enormous rise in female participation rates in the last half of the twentieth century is a case in point. One economic influence is change in the demand for labour. A rise in demand is usually accompanied by a rise in earnings. This then leads to an increase in the proportion of the population willing to work. More married women and elderly people enter the labour force when the demand for labour is high. For the same reasons the labour force tends to decline when earnings and employment opportunities decline.

Hours worked Not only does the wage rate influence the number of people in the labour force (as we observed above), it is also a major determinant of hours worked. By giving up leisure in order to work, workers obtain the incomes they need to buy goods. They can, therefore, be thought of as trading leisure for goods.

A rise in the wage rate implies a change in the relative prices of goods and leisure. Goods become cheaper relative to leisure, since each hour worked buys more goods than before. The other side of the same change is that leisure becomes more expensive, since each hour of leisure consumed is at the cost of more goods forgone.

This change in relative prices has both the income and

Box 14.3 The supply of labour

The discussion in the text can be formalized using indifference curves. The key proposition is the following:

Because a change in the wage rate has an income effect and a substitution effect that pull in opposite directions, the supply curve of labour may have a positive or a negative slope.

Part (i) of the figure plots leisure (in hours) on the horizontal axis and the consumption of goods (measured in pounds) on the vertical axis. The budget line always starts at 24, indicating that everyone is endowed with 24 hours a day that may be either consumed as leisure or traded for goods by working.

At the original wage rate the individual could obtain q_a of goods by working 24 hours (i.e. the hourly wage rate is $q_a/24$). Equilibrium is at E_0, where the individual consumes l_0 of leisure and works $24 - l_0$ hours in return for q_0 of goods.

The wage rate now rises, so that q_b becomes available if 24 hours are worked (i.e. the hourly wage rate is $q_b/24$). Equilibrium shifts to E_1.

Consumption of leisure falls to l_1, and the individual works $24 - l_1$ hours in return for a consumption of q_1 goods. The rise in wages increases hours worked.

The hourly wage rate now rises further to $q_c/24$, and equilibrium shifts to E_2. Consumption of leisure rises to l_2, whereas $24 - l_2$ hours are worked in return for an increased consumption of q_2 goods. This time, therefore, the rise in the wage rate lowers hours worked.

Part (ii) of the figure shows the same behaviour as in part (i), using a supply curve. It plots the number of hours worked against the wage rate. At wage rates of up to w_1 the individual is not in the labour force, since no work is offered. As the wage rate rises from w_1 to w_2, more and more hours are worked so the supply curve of effort has the normal, positive slope. The wage rates that result in E_0 and E_1 in part (i) of the figure lie in this range. Above w_2 the quantity of effort falls as wages rise, so that the supply curve has a negative slope. This latter case is often referred to as a *backward-bending supply curve of labour*. The wage that gives rise to equilibrium E_2 in part (i) lies in this range.

(i) Indifference curves

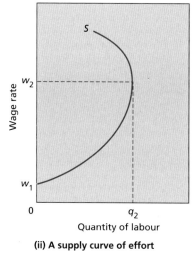

(ii) A supply curve of effort

the substitution effects that we studied on pages 107–9. The substitution effect leads the individual to consume more of the relatively cheaper goods and *less* of the relatively more expensive leisure—that is, to trade more leisure for goods. The income effect, however, leads the individual to consume more goods and *more* leisure, since the rise in the wage rate makes it possible for the individual to have more of both. For example, if the wage rate rises by 10 per cent and the individual works 5 per cent fewer hours, more leisure and more goods will be consumed.

Because the income and the substitution effects work in the same direction for the consumption of goods, we can be sure that a rise in the wage rate will lead to a rise in

income earned and goods consumed. Because, however, the two effects work in opposite directions for leisure,

A rise in the wage rate leads to less leisure being consumed (more hours worked) when the substitution effect is the dominant force and to more leisure being consumed (fewer hours worked) when the income effect is the dominant force.

Box 14.3 provides an optional analysis of these two cases using indifference curves.

Much of the long-run evidence tends to show that as real hourly wage rates rise for the economy as a whole, people wish to reduce the number of hours they work.

The supply of factors for a particular use

Most factors have many uses. A piece of land can be used to grow any one of several crops, or it can be subdivided for a housing development. A computer programmer in Oxford can work for one of several firms, for the government, or for the University. A lathe can be used to make many different products, and it requires no adaptation when it is turned for one use or another. Plainly, it is easier for any one user to acquire more of a scarce factor of production than it is for all users to do so simultaneously.

One user of a factor can bid resources away from another user, even though the total supply of that factor may be fixed.

When we are considering the supply of a factor for a particular use, the most important concept is *factor mobility*. A factor that shifts easily between uses in response to small changes in incentives is said to be *mobile*. Its supply to any one of its uses will be elastic, because a small increase in the price offered will attract many units of the factor from other uses. A factor that does not shift easily from one use to another, even in response to large changes in remuneration, is said to be *immobile*. It will be in inelastic supply in any one of its uses, because even a large increase in the price offered will attract only a small inflow from other uses. Often a factor may be immobile in the short run but mobile in the long run.

An important key to factor mobility is time. The longer the time interval, the easier it is for a factor to convert from one use to another.

Consider the mobility of factors among particular uses of each of the three key factors of production.

Capital Some kinds of capital equipment—lathes, lorries, and computers, for example—can be shifted easily among uses; many others are difficult to shift. A great deal of machinery is quite specific: once built, it must be used for the purpose for which it was designed, or it cannot be used at all. (It is the immobility of much fixed capital equipment that makes the exit of firms from declining industries the slow and difficult process described in Chapter 13.)

In the long run, however, capital is highly mobile. When capital goods wear out, a firm may simply replace them with identical goods, or it may exercise other options. It may buy a newly designed machine to produce the same goods, or it may buy machines to produce totally different goods. Such decisions lead to changes in the long-run allocation of a country's stock of capital among various uses.

Land Land, which is physically the least mobile of factors, is one of the most mobile in an economic sense. On agricultural land one crop can be harvested and a totally different crop can be planted. A farm on the outskirts of a growing city can be sold for a housing development at short notice—as long as planning permission is forthcoming. Once land is built on, its mobility is much reduced. A site on which a hotel has been built can be converted into a warehouse site, but it takes a large differential in the value of land use to make that transfer worthwhile, because the hotel must be torn down.

Although land is highly mobile among alternative uses, it is completely immobile as far as location is concerned. There is only so much land within a given distance of the centre of any city, and no increase in the price paid can induce further land to be located within that distance. This locational immobility has important consequences, including high prices for desirable locations and the tendency to build tall buildings to economize on the use of scarce land, as in the centre of large cities.

Labour Labour is unique as a factor of production in that the supply of the service often requires the physical presence of the person who owns it. Labour must be physically present if it is helping in the direct production of most goods, such as cars, and of some services, such as haircuts. In other cases, however, labour services, such as consulting, designing a product, or writing advertising copy, can be supplied at a distance and their product communicated to the purchaser by such means as phone, fax, email, or the postal service.

Absentee landlords, while continuing to live in the place of their choice, can obtain income from land that is located in remote parts of the world. While physical capital needs to be present at the production site, its owner need not be. However, when a worker who is employed by a firm that produces men's ties in York decides to supply labour service to a firm that produces women's shoes in Northampton, the worker must physically travel to Northampton. This has an important consequence.

Because of the need for labour's physical presence when its services are provided for the production of many commodities, non-monetary considerations are much more important for the supply of labour than for other factors of production.

People may be satisfied with, or frustrated by, the kind of work that they do, where they do it, the people with whom they do it, and the social status of their occupation. Since these considerations influence their decisions about what they will do with their labour services, they will not always move just because they could earn a higher wage.

Nevertheless, labour does move among industries, occupations, and areas in response to changes in the signals provided by wages and opportunities for employment. The ease with which movement occurs depends on many forces. For example, it is not difficult for a secretary to shift from one company to another in order to take a job in

Cheltenham instead of in Hull, but it can be difficult for a coalminer to become an editor, a model, a machinist, or a doctor within a short period of time. Workers who lack ability, training, or inclination find certain kinds of mobility to be difficult or impossible.

Some barriers to movement may be virtually insurmountable once a person's training has been completed. It may be impossible for a farmer to become a surgeon or for a lorry-driver to become a professional athlete, even if the relative wage rates change greatly. However, the *children* of farmers, doctors, lorry-drivers, and athletes, when they are deciding how much education or training to obtain, are not nearly as limited in their choices as their parents, who have already completed their education and are settled in their occupations.

In any year some people enter the labour force directly from school or further education, and others leave it through retirement or death. The turnover in the labour force owing to these causes is 3 or 4 per cent per year. Over a period of ten years the allocation of labour can change dramatically merely by directing new entrants to jobs other than the ones that were left vacant by workers who left the labour force.

The role of education in helping new entrants adapt to available jobs is important. In a society in which education is provided to all, it is possible to achieve large increases in the supply of any needed labour skill within a decade or so. These issues are discussed at greater length in the first part of Chapter 15.

The labour force as a whole is mobile, even though many individual members of it are not.

The supply of factors to individual firms

Most firms usually employ a small proportion of the total supply of each factor that they use. As a result they can usually obtain their factors at the going market price. For example, a firm of management consultants can usually augment its clerical staff by placing an advert in the local paper and paying the going rate for clerks. In doing so, the firm will not affect the rate of pay earned by clerks in its area. Thus, most individual firms are price-takers in factor markets.

The operation of factor markets

The determination of the price, quantity, and income of a factor in a single market poses no new problem. Figure 14.3 on page 221 has already shown a competitive market for a factor in which the intersection of the demand and supply curves determines the factor's price and the quantity of it that is employed. As we saw at that time, the factor's price times its quantity employed is its total income, and that amount, divided by the total income earned by all factors in the economy (so-called national income), represents that factor's share of the nation's total income. (We will study total national income and total national output in some detail in Chapter 20.)

Factor-price differentials

If every labourer were the same, if all benefits were monetary, and if workers moved freely among markets, then the price of labour would tend to be the same in all uses. Workers would move from low-priced jobs to high-priced ones. The quantity of labour supplied would diminish in occupations in which wages were low, and the resulting labour shortage would tend to force those wages up; the quantity of labour supplied would increase in occupations in which wages were high, and the resulting surplus would

force wages down. The movement would continue until there were no further incentives to change occupations, that is, until wages were equalized in all uses.

As it is with labour, so it is with other factors of production. If all units of any factor of production were identical and moved freely among markets, all units would receive the same remuneration in equilibrium.

In fact, however, different units of any one factor receive different remunerations. These differentials may be divided into two distinct types: those that exist only in disequilibrium situations and those that persist in equilibrium.

Disequilibrium differentials lead to, and are eroded by, factor movements; equilibrium differentials are not eliminated by factor mobility.

Disequilibrium differentials

Some factor-price differentials reflect a temporary state of disequilibrium. They are brought about by circumstances such as the growth of one industry and the decline of another. The differentials themselves lead to reallocation of factors, and such reallocations in turn act to eliminate the differentials.

Over the past century there has been a steady rise in the demand for air transport and a decline in the demand for rail transport. In factor markets the airline industry's demand has increased while the railroad industry's demand has decreased. Relative factor prices have gone up in airlines and down in railroads. The differential in factor prices caused a net movement of factors from the railroad industry to the airline industry, and this movement itself caused the differentials to lessen. How long such a process takes depends on how easily factors can be reallocated from one industry to the other, that is, on the degree of factor mobility.

The behaviour that causes the erosion of disequilibrium differentials is summarized in the assumption of the *maximization of net advantage*: the owners of factors of production will allocate them to uses that maximize the net advantages to themselves, taking both monetary and non-monetary rewards into consideration. If net advantages were higher in occupation A than in occupation B, factors would move from B to A. The increased supply in A, and the lower supply in B, would drive factor earnings down in A and up in B until net advantages were equalized, after which no further movement would occur. This analysis gives rise to the prediction of *equal net advantage*:

In equilibrium units of each kind of factor of production will be allocated among alternative possible uses in such a way that the net advantages in all uses are equalized.

Although non-monetary advantages are important in explaining differences in levels of pay for labour in different occupations, they tend to be quite stable over time. As a result monetary advantages, which vary with market conditions, lead to changes in *net advantage*.

A change in the relative price of a factor between two uses will change the net advantages of the uses. It will lead to a shift of some units of that factor to the use whose relative price has increased.

This implies a positively sloped supply curve for a factor in any particular use. When the price of a factor rises in that use, more will be supplied to that use. This factor supply curve (like all supply curves) can also *shift* in response to changes in other variables. For example, an improvement in the safety record in a particular occupation will shift the labour supply curve to that occupation.

Equilibrium differentials

Some factor-price differentials persist in equilibrium without generating any forces that will eliminate them. These **equilibrium differentials** can be explained by intrinsic differences in the factors themselves and, for labour, by differences in the cost of acquiring skills and by different non-monetary advantages of different occupations. They are also called *compensating differentials* and were introduced over two hundred years ago by Adam Smith.

Intrinsic differences If various units of a factor have different characteristics, the market price will differ among these units. For example, if intelligence and dexterity are required to accomplish a task, intelligent and manually dextrous workers will earn more than less intelligent and less dextrous workers. If land is to be used for agricultural purposes, highly fertile land will earn more than poor land. These differences will persist even in long-run equilibrium.

Acquired differences If the fertility of land can be increased by costly methods, then more fertile land will command a higher price than less fertile land. If it did not, owners would not incur the costs of improving fertility. The same holds true for labour. It is costly to acquire most skills. For example, a mechanic must train for some time, and unless the earnings of mechanics remain sufficiently above what can be earned in less skilled occupations, people will not incur the cost of training.

Non-monetary advantages Whenever working conditions differ among various uses for a single factor, that factor will earn different equilibrium amounts in its various uses. The difference between a test pilot's wage and a chauffeur's wage is only partly a matter of skill; the rest is compensation to the worker for facing the higher risk of testing new planes as compared with driving a car. If both were paid the same, there would be an excess supply of chauffeurs and a shortage of test pilots.

Academic researchers commonly earn less than they could earn in the world of commerce and industry because of the substantial non-monetary advantages of academic employment, such as long holidays from teaching, which can be devoted partly to research and partly to leisure. If chemists were paid the same in both sectors, many chemists would prefer academic to industrial jobs. Excess demand for industrial chemists and excess supply of academic chemists would then force chemists' wages up in industry until the two types of jobs seemed equally attractive on balance.

The same forces account for equilibrium differences in regional earnings of otherwise identical factors. People who work in remote logging or mining areas are paid more than people who do jobs requiring similar skills in large cities. Without higher pay, not enough people would be willing to work at sometimes dangerous jobs in unattractive or remote locations.

Pay equity

The distinction between equilibrium and disequilibrium factor-price differentials raises an important consideration for policy. Trade unions, governments, and other bodies often have explicit policies about earnings differentials, sometimes seeking to eliminate them in the name of equity. The success of such policies depends to a great extent on the kind of differential that is being attacked.

Policies that attempt to eliminate equilibrium differentials will encounter severe difficulties.

Some government legislation seeks to establish *equal pay for work of equal value*, or *pay equity*. These laws can work as intended whenever they remove pay differentials that are due to prejudice. They run into trouble, however, whenever they require equal pay for jobs that have different non-monetary advantages.

To illustrate the problem, say that two jobs demand equal skills, training, and everything else that is taken into account when deciding what is work of equal value but that, in a city with an extreme climate, one is an outside job and the other is an inside job. If some pay commission requires equal pay for both jobs, there will be a shortage of people who are willing to work outside and an excess of people who want to work inside. Employers will seek ways to attract outside workers. Higher pensions, shorter hours, longer holidays, overtime paid for but not worked, and better working conditions may be offered. If these are allowed, they will achieve the desired result but will defeat the original purpose of equalizing the monetary benefits of the inside and outside jobs. They will also cut down on the number of outside workers that employers will hire, since the total cost of an outside worker to an employer will have risen. If the authorities prevent such 'cheating', the shortage of workers for outside jobs will remain.

In Chapter 15 we discuss the effects of discrimination on wage differentials. Although discrimination is often important, it remains true that many factor-price differentials are a natural market consequence of supply and demand conditions that have nothing to do with inequitable treatment of different groups in society.

Policies that seek to eliminate factor-price differentials without considering what caused them or how they affect the supply of the factor are likely to have perverse results.

Economic rent

One of the most important concepts in economics is that of *economic rent*. A factor must earn a certain amount in its present use to prevent it from moving to another use. This is called its **reservation price** (Alfred Marshall called it the factor's *transfer earnings*). If there were no non-monetary advantages in alternative uses, the factor's reservation price would equal what it could earn elsewhere (its opportunity cost). This relation usually holds for capital and land. Labour, however, gets non-monetary advantages that differ among different jobs. It must earn enough in one use to equate the two jobs' total advantages—monetary and non-monetary.

Any excess that a factor earns over its reservation price is called its **economic rent**. Economic rent is analogous to economic profit as a surplus over the opportunity cost of

capital. The concept of economic rent is crucial in predicting the effects that changes in earnings have on the movement of factors among alternative uses. However, the terminology of rent is confusing because economic rent is often called simply *rent*, which can of course also mean the full price paid to hire something, such as a house or a piece of land. How the same term came to be used for these two different concepts is explained in Box 14.4.

Box 14.4 Origin of the term 'economic rent'

In the early nineteenth century there was a public debate about the high price of wheat in England. The price was causing great hardship because bread was a major source of food for the working class. Some people argued that wheat had a high price because landlords were charging high rents to tenant farmers. In short, it was argued that the price of wheat was high because the rents of agricultural land were high. Some of those who held this view advocated restricting the rents that landlords could charge.

David Ricardo, a great British economist who was one of the originators of classical economics, argued that the situation was exactly the reverse. The price of wheat was high, he said, because there was a shortage, which was caused by the Napoleonic Wars. Because wheat was profitable to produce, there was keen competition among farmers to obtain land on which to grow wheat. This competition in turn forced up the rent of wheat land. Ricardo advocated removing the tariff so that imported wheat could come into the country, thereby increasing its supply and lowering both the price of wheat and the rent that could be charged for the land on which it was grown.

The essentials of Ricardo's argument were these. The supply of land was fixed. Land was regarded as having only one use, the growing of wheat. Nothing had to be paid to prevent land from transferring to a use other than growing wheat because it had no other use. No landowner would leave land idle as long as some return could be obtained by renting it out. Therefore, all the payment to land—that is, rent in the ordinary sense of the word—was a surplus over and above what was necessary to keep it in its present use.

Given a fixed supply of land, the price of land depended on the demand for land, which depended on the demand for wheat. *Rent*, the term for the payment for the use of land, thus became the term for a surplus payment to a factor over and above what was necessary to keep it in its present use.

Later two facts were realized. First, land often had alternative uses, and, from the point of view of any one use, part of the payment made to land would necessarily have to be paid to keep it in that use. Second, factors of production other than land also often earned a surplus over and above what was necessary to keep them in their present use. Television stars and great athletes, for example, are in short and fairly fixed supply, and their potential earnings in other occupations are often quite moderate. However, because there is a huge demand for their services as television stars or athletes, they may receive payments greatly in excess of what is needed to keep them from transferring to other occupations. This surplus is now called *economic rent*, whether the factor is land, labour, or a piece of capital equipment.

The division of factor earnings

In most cases economic rent makes up part of the actual earnings of a factor of production. The distinction is most easily seen, however, by examining two extreme cases. In one case everything a factor earns is rent; in the other none is rent.

The possibilities are illustrated in Figure 14.4. When the supply curve is perfectly inelastic (vertical), the same quantity is supplied whatever the price. Evidently, there is no minimum that the factor needs to be paid to keep it in its present use, since the quantity supplied does not decrease no matter how low the price goes. In this case the whole of the payment is economic rent. The price actually paid allocates the fixed supply to those who are most willing to pay for it.

When the supply curve is perfectly elastic (horizontal), none of the price paid is economic rent. If any lower price is offered, nothing whatsoever will be supplied. All units of the factor will transfer to some other use.

The more usual situation is that of a gradually rising supply curve. A rise in the factor's price serves the

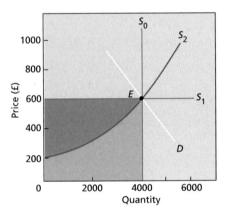

Figure 14.4 The determination of rent in factor payments
The amount of rent in factor payments depends on the shape of the supply curve. A single demand curve is shown with three different supply curves. In each case the competitive equilibrium price is £600, and 4,000 units of the factor are hired. The total payment (£2.4 million) is represented by the entire dark and medium blue areas.

When the supply curve is vertical (S_0), the whole payment is economic rent, because a decrease in price would not lead any units of the factor to move elsewhere.

When the supply curve is horizontal (S_1), none of the payment is rent, because even a small decrease in price offered would lead all units of the factor to move elsewhere.

When the supply curve is positively sloped (S_2), part of the payment is rent. Although the 4,000th unit is receiving just enough to persuade it to offer its services in this market, the 2,000th unit is earning well above what it requires to stay in this market. The aggregate of economic rents is shown by the dark blue area, and the aggregate of what must be paid to keep 4,000 units in this market is shown by the light blue area.

allocative function of attracting more units of the factor into the market in question, but the same rise provides additional economic rent to all units of the factor that are already employed. We know that the extra pay that is going to the units already employed is economic rent because the owners of these units were willing to supply them at the lower price. The general result for a positively sloped supply curve is stated as follows:

If there is an upward shift in the demand for a factor in any sector, its price will rise. This will serve the allocative function of attracting additional units into that sector. It will also increase the economic rent going to all units of the factor already employed in that sector.[4]

Determinants of the division

The proportion of a given payment to a factor that is economic rent varies from situation to situation. We cannot point to a factor of production and assert that some fixed fraction of its income is always its economic rent. The proportion of its earnings that is rent depends on the alternatives that are open to it.

Focus first on a narrowly defined use of a given factor, say its use by a particular firm. From that firm's point of view the factor will be highly mobile, since it could readily move to another firm in the same industry. The firm must pay the going wage or risk losing that factor. Thus, from the perspective of the *single firm* a large proportion of the payment made to a factor is needed to prevent it from transferring to another use.

Focus now on a more broadly defined use, for example the factor's use in an entire industry. From the industry's point of view the factor is less mobile, because it would be more difficult for it to gain employment quickly outside the industry. From the perspective of the particular *industry* (rather than the specific *firm* within the industry), a larger proportion of the payment to a factor is economic rent.

From the even more general perspective of a particular *occupation*, mobility is likely to be less, and the proportion of the factor payment that is economic rent is likely to be more. It may be easier, for example, for a carpenter to move from the construction industry to the furniture industry than to retrain as a computer operator.

The often controversial large salaries that are received by some highly specialized types of labour, such as superstar singers and professional athletes, illustrate these distinctions. These performers have a style or a talent that cannot be duplicated, whatever the training. The earnings that they receive are mostly economic rent from the viewpoint of the occupation: these performers enjoy their occupations and would pursue them for much less than the

[4] In this context the term 'sector' can stand for occupation, industry, or geographical area.

high remuneration that they actually receive. For example, Ryan Giggs would choose football over other alternatives even at a much lower salary than he was earning in 1998. However, because of Giggs's skills as a football player, most teams would pay handsomely to have him, and he is able to command a high salary from the team he does play for. From the perspective of the firm, Manchester United, most

of Giggs's salary is required to keep him from switching to another team and hence is not economic rent. From the point of view of the 'football industry', however, much of his salary is economic rent.

Similar arguments apply to famous entertainers such as the Spice Girls, who earned several million pounds each in 1997/8 from record sales and concerts.

The functional distribution of income

The founders of classical economics, Adam Smith and David Ricardo, were concerned with the distribution of income among what were then the three great social classes of workers, capitalists, and landowners. To match these classes, they defined three factors of production: labour, capital, and land. The return to each factor determined the share of total national income going to each social class. This is why the theory of factor pricing is also called the theory of distribution.

There was a long and heated debate about how the distribution of income would be affected by what they called the progress of society. By this term they meant rising population, accumulation of capital, and advancing technological knowledge. Would all three social groups benefit from the progress of society? In contrast, would capitalists and/or landowners receive a larger and larger share of the national income while the workers received an ever-shrinking share?

These nineteenth-century debates focused on the functional distribution of income, defined as the distribution of total income among the major factors of production.

Figure 14.5 shows the functional distribution by income class. The amount shown as 'Employment income' includes cash benefits received from the government and pension income as well as incomes received in return for the current sale of factor services in such forms as wages and salaries, income from self-employment, and investment and rental income. As the figure shows, the share of total income going to those earning income from employment has remained relatively stable over the years.[5]

In contrast to the classical theory of income distribution, the neoclassical theory that we have studied in this chapter concentrates on the pricing of factors in each of the economy's many markets and hence on the size distribution of income. The theory has little to say about the

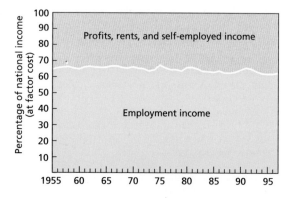

Figure 14.5 The UK functional distribution of income, 1955–1997

The share of national income going to employed persons has been remarkably stable over the years. The figure shows the proportion of national income going to income from employment (shaded green) and to other incomes, mainly profits of private and public enterprises, rent, and income from self-employment (shaded blue). Employment income fluctuated between 62 and 69 per cent from 1955 to 1997. The income figure used here is national income at factor cost, which excludes that part of the value of output that goes to pay indirect government taxes, mainly the VAT.

Source: ONS, *Economic Trends*.

question of what determines the functional distribution of income among land, labour, and capital. Indeed many modern economists would argue that the classical question is not an interesting one and is probably unanswerable in any case. This issue is briefly discussed in Box 14.5.

[5] The official definitions of the breakdown of income changed in 1996. The new categories are set out in Table 20.3 on page 346.

Box 14.5 The functional distribution of income

Questions of the functional distribution of income among the main social classes of society—labourers, landlords, and capitalists—were central issues to classical economics. With the development of marginal analysis in the second half of the nineteenth century, emphasis shifted to the determination of factor prices and quantities in millions of individual markets.

The theory that grew out of this development (often called 'marginal productivity theory' after its demand half) offers few general predictions about the broad functional distribution of income. It holds that to discover the effect of some change—say, a tax or a new trade union—on the functional distribution between wages, profits, and rent, we would need to be able to discover what would happen in each individual market of the economy and then aggregate to find the overall result. To do this, we would need to know the degree of monopoly and monopsony power exercised in each market; we would need to be able to predict the effect on oligopolists' prices and outputs of changes in their costs; and we would need to have a theory of the outcome of collective bargaining in situations of monopoly and monopsony. We would also need to know how much factor substitution would occur in response to any resulting change in relative factor prices. Finally, we would need a general equilibrium theory linking all these markets together.

In recent years the development of computable general equilibrium models has gone a long way towards providing such knowledge! None the less, with our present state of knowledge, marginal productivity theory provides few if any predictions about the effects on the broad functional

distribution of such changes as shifts in total factor supplies, taxes on one factor, and the rise of trade unions.

This conclusion is not necessarily a criticism of the theory. It may well be that relative shares are determined by all the detailed interactions of all the markets in the economy. It may also be that predictions about the effects of various events on labour or capital in general can be obtained only after we have enough knowledge to solve the general equilibrium problem outlined above. Nor does this conclusion mean that we can never identify forces that will affect the functional distribution in a predictable way. For example, the decline of unions has reduced the relative wage differential between union and non-union workers. But this tells us nothing about effects on the relative share of national income going to labour as a whole.

Some economists argue that we should not expect to get further than this. They hold that the great questions about the functional distribution on the scale of labour versus capital are largely unanswerable. They argue that it makes sense to talk about laws governing functional distribution between the three classes of factors only if labour, capital, and land are each relatively homogeneous and are each subject to a set of influences not operating on the other two factors. In fact, so goes the argument, there is as much difference in demand and supply conditions between two kinds of labour as between one kind of labour and one kind of machine. Thus, there is no more reason to expect that there should be simple laws governing the distribution of income among land, labour, and capital than to expect that there should be simple laws governing the distribution between all blondes on the one hand and all brunettes on the other hand.

Summary

The theory in outline

■ The functional and size distributions of income refer to the shares of total national income going, respectively, to each of the major factors of production and to various groups of individuals. One focuses on the source of income, the other on its size.

■ The income of a factor of production depends on the price paid per unit of the factor and the quantity of the factor used.

The demand for factors

■ The firm's decisions on how much to produce and how to produce it imply demands for factors of production, which are said to be *derived* from the demand for goods that they help to produce.

■ A profit-maximizing firm equates a factor's marginal cost to its marginal revenue product, which is its marginal physical product multiplied by the marginal revenue associated with the sale of another unit of output. When the firm is a price-taker in input markets, the marginal cost

of the factor is its price per unit. When the firm sells its output in a competitive market, the marginal revenue product is the factor's marginal physical product multiplied by the market price of the output.

■ A firm's demand for a factor is negatively sloped in the long run because cheaper factors will be substituted for dearer ones and a fall in a factor's price leads to an increase in the output of the commodities it is used to make. It is negatively sloped in the short run because of the law of diminishing returns.

■ The industry's demand for a factor will be more elastic: (a) the faster the marginal physical product of the factor declines as more of the factor is used, (b) the easier it is to substitute one factor for another, (c) the larger is the proportion of total variable costs accounted for by the cost of the factor in question, and (d) the more elastic is the demand for the good that the factor helps to make.

The supply of factors

■ The total supply of land and capital is fixed at any moment but can vary over time. The total supply of labour varies with the size of the population, the participation rate, and hours worked. The latter two vary with the wage rate. A rise in the wage rate has a substitution effect, which tends to induce more work, and an income effect, which tends to induce less.

■ The supply of a factor to a particular use is more elastic than its supply to the whole economy because one user can bid units away from other users. The elasticity of supply to a particular use depends on factor mobility, which tends to be greater the longer the time allowed for a reaction to take place.

The operation of factor markets

■ Disequilibrium factor-price differentials induce factor movements that eventually remove the differentials. Equilibrium differentials persist indefinitely.

■ Whenever the supply curve is positively sloped, part of the total pay going to a factor is needed to prevent it from transferring to another use, and the rest is rent. The proportion of each depends on the mobility of the factor.

The functional distribution of income

■ The largest share in the functional distribution of income goes to labour, and the share fluctuates somewhat from year to year.

Topics for review

■ Functional distribution and size distribution of income
■ Derived demand
■ Marginal physical product
■ Marginal revenue product
■ Factor mobility
■ Disequilibrium and equilibrium differentials
■ Equal net advantage
■ Economic rent

Questions for discussion

1 Consider the effects on the overall level of income inequality of each of the following situations: (a) increasing participation of women in the labour force as many women shift from work in the home to full-time jobs in the workplace, (b) increasing use by fruit growers of guest workers from low-income countries, (c) increasing numbers of minority group members studying law and medicine, (d) cuts in the standard rate of income tax, together with the elimination of some personal income tax deduction.

2 How much of the following payments for factors services is likely to be economic rent? (a) the £600 per month that a landlord receives for a flat leased to students, (b) the salary of the Prime Minister, (c) the large annual income of recording stars such as Céline Dion, Brian Adams, All Saints, and Gary Barlow, (d) the salary of a window cleaner who says, 'It's dangerous and dirty work, but it beats driving a lorry.'

3 The demands listed below have been increasing rapidly in recent years. What derived demands would you predict have also risen sharply? Where will the extra factors of production that are demanded be drawn from? (a) demand for natural gas, (b) demand for medical services, (c) demand for international and interregional travel.

4 A recent *Wall Street Journal* article asks, 'Why do football players earn millions of pounds for their negligible contribution to society while major contributors—such as schoolteachers, policemen, firemen, and ambulance drivers—earn barely enough to survive?' Can you offer an answer based on what was discussed in the chapter?

5 Draw an indifference curve diagram to illustrate an individual's choice in the following situations. (a) The individual faces a fixed wage rate of £6 per hour and chooses to work 8 hours. (b) The wage rate is raised to £9 per hour. (c) The wage rate remains at £6 but overtime is paid at £9 per hour for all work over 8 hours per day. (d) The wage rate stays at £6 but a lump-sum bonus of £6 is paid for anyone who works 10 hours or more in one day.

Appendix Marginal productivity and factor demand

In this appendix we derive the firm's demand curve for a factor in the short run. This was done intuitively in the text but is done more formally in the appendix.

One variable factor

Equation (2′) on page 223 in the text is repeated below as equation (A1):

$$w = MPP \times p. \qquad (A1)$$

It tells us what determines the quantity of a variable factor a firm

will demand when faced with some specific price of the factor and some specific price of its output. The firm's demand curve shows how much the firm will buy at *each* price of the variable factor. To derive this curve, we start by considering the right-hand side of equation (A1), which tells us that the factor's marginal revenue product is composed of a physical component and a value component.

The physical component of *MRP* As the quantity of the variable factor varies, output will vary. The hypothesis of diminishing returns, first discussed in Chapter 8, predicts what will happen. As the firm adds further units of the variable factor to a given

(i) The *MPP* curve

(ii) The *MRP* and demand curve

Figure 14A.1 From marginal physical product to demand curve
Each additional unit of the factor employed adds a certain amount to total product (part (i)) and hence a certain amount to total revenue (part (ii)), and this determines the amount of the factor that firms will demand at each price. Part (i) assumes data that are consistent with marginal productivity theory; it shows the addition to the firm's *output* produced by additional units of labour hired. The curve is negatively sloped because of the law of diminishing returns.

Part (ii) shows the addition to the firm's *revenue* caused by the employment of each additional unit of labour. It is the marginal physical product from part (i) multiplied by the price at which that product is sold. In this case the price is assumed to be £5. (The multiplication is by market price because the firm is assumed to be a price-taker in the market for its output.)

Since the firm equates the price of the variable factor, which in this case is labour, to the factor's marginal revenue product, it follows that the *MRP* curve, in part (ii), is also the demand curve for labour, showing how much will be employed at each price.

quantity of the fixed factor, the additions to output will eventually get smaller and smaller. In other words the factor's marginal physical product will decline. This is illustrated in part (i) of Figure 14A.1, which uses hypothetical data that have the same general characteristics as the data in Table 8.3 on page 121. The negative slope of the *MPP* curve reflects the operation of the law of diminishing returns: each unit of labour adds less to total output than the previous unit.

The value component of *MRP* To convert the marginal physical product curve of Figure 14A.1(i) into a curve showing the marginal revenue product of the variable factor, we need to know the value of the extra physical product. As long as the firm sells its output on a competitive market, this value is simply the marginal physical product multiplied by the market price at which the firm sells its product.

This operation is illustrated in part (ii) of Figure 14A.1, which shows a marginal revenue product curve for labour on the assumption that the firm sells its product in a competitive market at a price of £5 a unit. This curve shows how much would be added to revenue by employing one more unit of the factor *at each level of total employment of the factor*.

Profit-maximizing firms should equate the addition to cost of buying another unit of a variable factor with the addition to revenue caused by selling the output of that unit, which we call the factor's marginal revenue product, *MRP*. The *MRP* is always composed of a physical component, which is the factor's *MPP*, and a value component, which is the marginal revenue of selling those extra physical units of output. Because our firms are price-takers in their output markets, the marginal revenue is just the price that they face in that market. If the firms faced a negatively sloped demand curve for their output, we know from Chapter 10

that the addition to revenue from selling further units is not the market price because marginal revenue is less than price.

From *MRP* to the demand curve Equation (A1) states that the profit-maximizing firm will employ additional units of the factor up to the point at which the *MRP* equals the price of the factor. If, for example, the price of the variable factor were £2,000 per month, then it would be most profitable to employ 60 workers. There is no point in employing a sixty-first, since that would add just less than £2,000 to revenue but a full £2,000 to costs. So the profit-maximizing firm hires the quantity of the variable factor that equates the marginal revenue product with the price of the variable factor. Thus, the curve that relates the quantity of the variable factor employed to its *MRP* is also the curve that relates the quantity of the variable factor the firm wishes to employ to its price.

The *MRP* curve of the variable factor is the same as the demand curve for that variable factor.

More than one variable factor

When a firm can vary the amounts of several factors that it uses, profit maximization requires that the last £1 it spends on each factor brings in the same amount of revenue.

To see how this works out for two factors, call their prices p_A and p_B and their marginal revenue products MRP_A and MRP_B. The amount of extra revenue per £1 spent on hiring more factor A is MRP_A/p_A, while the amount of extra revenue per pound spent on hiring more factor B is MRP_B/p_B. For example, if one more unit of A costs £3 and adds £6 to revenue, it yields £2 of revenue per £1 spent on it. If one more unit of B costs £5 and adds £10 to revenue, it too yields £2 of revenue per £1 spent on it. If the firm wants to equate these *MRP*s per pound spent on the factor, it must set

$$\frac{MRP_A}{p_A} = \frac{MRP_B}{p_B}.$$ (A2)

The marginal revenue product is the marginal physical product multiplied by the product's selling price. We now have three prices, two for the variable inputs and one for output. To prevent confusion, we call the output price p_S, which stands for selling price. So $MRP = MPP \times p_S$. So we can rewrite equation (A2) as:

$$\frac{MPP_A \times p_S}{p_A} = \frac{MPP_B \times p_S}{p_B}.$$ (A3)

If we eliminate the common p_S term, we have

$$\frac{MPP_A}{p_A} = \frac{MPP_B}{p_B}.$$ (A4)

This is equation (3) in Chapter 8 page 126, except that we are now

calling the factor's marginal product *MPP* (to distinguish it from *MRP*), whereas we called it *MP* in the text treatment, because there was no possibility of confusion there.

Equation (A4) can be rewritten as follows:

$$\frac{MPP_A}{MPP_B} = \frac{p_A}{p_B}.$$ (A5)

Those who have studied the appendix to Chapter 8 have seen the analysis given here carried out with isoquants, where the slope of the isoquant is given by the ratio of the two factor's marginal physical products.

Equation (A5) should be compared with equation (2) on page 90 of Chapter 6. In equation (A5) the firm is given prices of the two factors, and it adjusts to these by altering the quantities of the two inputs until it has the profit-maximizing amount of each. This behaviour is similar to that of the consumer described on page 90. The consumer is given the prices of two commodities and she adjusts her consumption until her utility is maximized (which she does by making the ratios of the marginal utilities equal the ratio of their prices).

Chapter 15
The Income of Labour

In this chapter we look specifically at labour markets. The first part of the chapter is devoted to explaining wage differentials between different types of labour. We learn that these are due partly to different skills and educational attainments, partly to age and sex, and partly to the type of market in which labour services are supplied. Labour does best when it is organized as a single seller dealing with a large number of buyers, and worst when it is unorganized but sells to a single buyer. Cases in which both sides are competitive fall in between these two extremes. We then go on to consider minimum-wage laws and unions. Although much less powerful than they were twenty or thirty years ago, unions are still an important part of the economic landscape. The theory helps us to understand quite a bit about union behaviour.

This part of the chapter uses market-clearing theories of wage determination which assume that wages are set in competitive markets that clear in the sense that neither excess demand nor excess supply persists. This is so unless strong buyers or sellers are able to exercise power over the market to prevent it from clearing. We see that these theories can explain quite a bit about the forces that create wage differentials in the real world. But they are not the whole story.

Today more and more employees are hired for their brain rather than their brawn. This adds many complications to the labour market. People are heterogeneous, their contributions to the firm's success are difficult to assess. Their motives may not always conform to the firm's objective of maximizing its profits. In the final part of the chapter we study the many institutions and practices that have evolved to deal with these modern labour market problems.

In reading this chapter, do not forget that by 'labour' we mean all human resources of both workers and management, and by 'labour income', or 'wages', we mean all income earned from work, whether in the form of wages or salaries.

Wage differentials

We noted in the previous chapter that if labour were a homogeneous factor of production, and were sold in perfectly competitive markets, every person would earn the same income in equilibrium. Disequilibrium differentials in wages would arise whenever demand or supply curves shifted. However, workers would then move from the lower-income to the higher-income jobs until the differentials had disappeared. In reality some workers scrape out a bare living, others earn modest but adequate incomes, while yet others earn enough to afford many of life's luxuries. These are equilibrium differentials that persist even after all markets have reached equilibrium.

■ *Incomes vary with the type of job.* Dustmen and charwomen earn less than electricians and computer operators.

■ *Incomes vary with education.* Average earnings of people with university degrees exceed the average earnings of those with only A-levels, which in turn exceed the average earnings of those with only GCSEs.

■ *Incomes vary with age.* Average earnings rise until a person's mid-40s and fall thereafter.

■ *Incomes vary with years on the job.* Generally, the longer one stays with one firm, the higher the income one earns.

■ *Incomes vary with sex and race.* On average, men earn more than women, and members of some minority ethnic groups earn less than members of majority groups—even when differences in education and experience are allowed for.

■ *Incomes vary with the type of market in which labour sells its services.* Workers who sell their labour in markets dominated by unions often earn more than similar persons who sell their labour in more competitive markets.

In what follows we study some of the major causes of these equilibrium differentials in the earnings of various types of labour.

Differentials due to basic differences: non-competing groups

More highly skilled jobs pay better wages than less highly skilled jobs. Why does a movement from the latter to the former not erode these differentials?

One obvious answer lies in human differences that are either innate or acquired so early in life as to be beyond each individual's personal control. Some people are brighter than others; some people are more athletic; others are better endowed with manual skills. In an extreme case people might be separated by their natural endowments of intelligence, skills, and abilities into separate groups between which no movement was possible. We would then have a series of *non-competing groups* which did not interact with each other. They would be selling their services in a series of *segmented labour markets.*

Figure 15.1 shows that wage differentials among non-competing groups arise from the positions of both the demand and the supply curves. One group will earn higher incomes than another only if its supply is low *relative to the demand for it.* It is not good enough to have a rare skill; that skill must be rare in relation to the demand for it.

Over time wage differentials change. On the demand side economic growth constantly alters the derived demand for many specific groups of labour, creating new differentials and eroding old ones. On the supply side there may be exogenous shifts. For example, a new group of immigrants may alter the mix of skills available in the local market. Furthermore, human differences notwithstanding, substantial mobility between groups does occur—particularly in the long run, when older people with specific skills leave the labour force and young people with different skills enter.

None the less, the lesson of the simple theory of non-competing groups is important:

Some income differentials arise because basic human characteristics cause the supplies of some types of labour to remain low relative to the demand for them, even in the long run.

Differentials due to human capital

The key to mobility among occupations is education. Many skills are learned rather than inherited. These may be thought of as a stock of human capital acquired by each worker.

A machine is physical capital. It requires an investment of time and money to create it, and, once built, it yields valuable services over a long time. In the same way, the

(i) Occupation 1

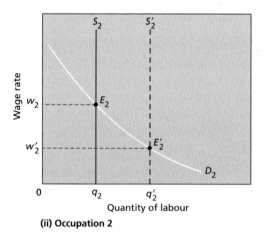

(ii) Occupation 2

Figure 15.1 Wage differentials in segmented labour markets

When labour cannot move from one market to another, wage differentials of any size can persist. Because of basic differences in abilities the supply of labour is fixed at q_1 in occupation 1 and at q_2 in occupation 2. Demand and supply curves intersect at E_1 and E_2 to produce the high wage of w_1 in occupation 1 and the low wage of w_2 in occupation 2.

A fall in demand from D_1 to D_1' in occupation 1 takes equilibrium to E_1', lowering its wage to w_1'. A rise in supply in occupation 2, to q_2', takes equilibrium to E_2', lowering its wage to w_2'.

acquisition of labour skills requires an investment of time and money, and, once acquired, these skills yield an increased income to their owner over a long time. Since investment in labour skills is similar to investment in physical capital, acquired skills are called **human capital.**

Because acquiring human capital is costly, the more highly skilled the job, the more it must pay if enough people are to be attracted to train for it.

The stock of skills acquired by individual workers is called human capital; investment in this capital is usually costly, and the return is higher labour productivity and hence higher earning power.

The two main ways in which human capital is acquired are through formal education and on-the-job training.

Formal education

Compulsory education provides some minimum human capital for all citizens. Some people, either through luck in the school they attend or through their own efforts, profit more from their early education than do others. They acquire more human capital than their less fortunate contemporaries. Those who decide to stay in school beyond the years of compulsory education are deciding to invest voluntarily in acquiring further human capital.

Costs and benefits The cost of further education is the income that could have been earned if the person had entered the labour force immediately after compulsory education, plus any out-of-pocket costs for such things as fees and equipment, minus any student grant or scholarship. The return is the difference between the income that would have been earned if one had left school and the income that is earned as a result of going on to higher education. (There is also a consumption return whenever higher education is something that students enjoy more than work.) These costs and benefits are analysed in Figure 15.2.

Changes in costs and benefits If the demand for labour with low amounts of human capital falls, as it has in recent times, the earnings of such persons will fall. This will lower the costs of staying on in school, since the earnings forgone by not going to work are reduced. A rise in unemployment will also lower the costs, because the probability of earning a steady income will be reduced, and this will reduce the expected loss from not entering the labour force early. If the demand for labour having more human capital rises, the earnings of such labour will rise. This will raise the expected return to those currently deciding whether or not to make the investment themselves.

Individual decisions For any *given* state of these incentives, why do some people decide to acquire human capital while others do not?

First, there are differences among individuals. For reas-

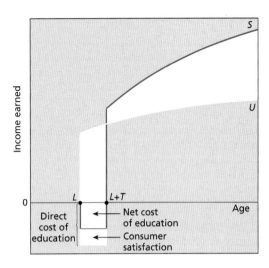

Figure 15.2 The costs and benefits of formal education

Acquiring human capital through formal education beyond minimum school-leaving age implies costs now and benefits later. Age is plotted on the horizontal axis and income earned on the vertical axis. Income is zero until age *L*, which is the minimum school-leaving age. After that the yellow line *U* shows the income of a typical person who leaves school at age *L* and takes the relatively unskilled job for which his or her human capital is suitable.

The blue line *S* shows the more complicated stream of payments and income receipts of someone who stays on for *T* years of formal training after age *L*. At first receipts are negative, reflecting the net out-of-pocket expenses related to attending school and university. Deducting the consumption value placed on being at school rather than at work (light yellow area) yields the net cost associated with being in school. Adding this to the income that could have been earned by going directly into the labour force at age *L* yields the total cost of the education, which is the medium yellow area.

The benefit is shown by the dark yellow area, representing the difference between the income earned in the skilled job that is acquired at year *L* + *T* (line *S*) and the income that would have been earned if the labour force had been entered at age *L* (line *U*). The investment in human capital could not possibly be worthwhile unless the dark yellow benefit area exceeded the medium yellow cost area. The net benefit to a particular individual depends on how much he or she discounts the more distant gain in order to compare it with the more immediate costs.

ons related to genetics or to early educational experience, some people at the age of 16 correctly decide that they have a low chance of profiting from further formal education. For them the return from such education is lower than for others who have the necessary aptitudes.

Second, some people have special talents for types of work that do not require further human capital. For them the cost of acquiring more human capital is higher than it is for others; the earnings they would forgo by not entering the labour force are higher than the earnings that would be forgone by the average school-leaver.

Third, different people have different time-preferences.

The cost of acquiring human capital is forgone income *now*, and the return is a *probability* of higher income *later*. Tastes differ. Some people put a high value on income now and are not willing to pay the cost of postponing it. Others place a higher value on income to be earned later in life and are willing to have less now in return for the chance of much more later on.

Fourth, different people put different values on the consumption aspects of education. Those who enjoy the experience find the costs of acquiring human capital lower than those who do not. Those who would prefer to be at work rather than at school find the cost increased by the negative value they place on the educational experience.

Market forces adjust the overall costs and benefits of acquiring human capital, while individuals respond according to their varying personal evaluation of the costs and the benefits.

In the long run decisions to acquire human capital help to erode disequilibrium differentials in incomes. Market signals change the costs and benefits of acquiring human capital in such specific forms as skill in electronics, accountancy, law, or medicine. By reacting to these signals, young people increase the supplies of high-income workers and reduce the supplies of low-income workers, thus eroding existing disequilibrium differentials.

On-the-job education

Wage differentials according to age are readily observable in most firms and occupations. To a significant extent these differentials are a response to human capital acquired on the job. This type of human capital falls into two types.

Firm-specific human capital   Learning how one firm does such things as recording and retrieving its information, how it makes decisions, and how the personal relations among its employees are to be used to advantage are all firm-specific. As employees acquire this knowledge, they become more valuable to the firm. But the knowledge is not valuable to other firms; workers who move to similar jobs with other firms will have to learn the new firm-specific characteristics of their jobs.

Firms do not want to lose long-term employees with large amounts of firm-specific human capital since other employees will then have to be trained. But, being firm-specific, the capital is of no value to other firms. So if the firm pays the employee a wage that reflects the productivity conferred by this capital, employees have an incentive to stay in the job rather than to move to another firm where their value would be much less.

General human capital   If a firm trains a junior secretary through various ranks up to a senior secretary, able to run the life of its general manager, the secretary's skills will be useful to other firms. Some of the secretary's human capital can be acquired only through on-the-job training; hence it must be acquired within the firm. However, unlike the firm-specific capital, a secretary who is paid the value of his or her marginal product at all times has no monetary incentive to stay with the firm that taught these general skills. The same is true of any non-specific human capital acquired through on-the-job experience by any of the firm's employees.

Firms have no incentive to provide freely what can immediately be transferred to another firm. The solution is to pay each worker less than his or her marginal product in the early years and more later on. The low pay can be seen as the employee's payment to the firm for helping them to acquire marketable human capital. The high pay later in life is a return on that capital.

Human capital acquired through on-the-job experience provides a reason why earnings rise with the length of time spent with a firm. Firms tend to pay employees the value of their current marginal products for firm-specific capital, but for general human capital they pay less than the marginal products early in life and more later in life.

Another reason for the same pattern of lifetime wages is that competition tends to be strongest at the initial point of entry into the firm and to weaken thereafter, when promotion posts typically go to internal candidates. This will tend to hold wages down to competitive levels at entry points but allow them to drift above those levels for personnel with years of seniority and experience.

Market solutions   The above analysis shows the subtlety of market solutions to the issues posed by the human capital acquired through on-the-job experience. What looks arbitrary, or unfair, to the casual observer is often a rational response that has evolved to handle some aspect of the market—such as the fact that on-the-job training creates capital that is sometimes firm-specific and sometimes general.

To illustrate the significance of this lesson, consider two jobs that employ persons with equal initial requirements. One provides on-the-job training that is mainly firm-specific, and the wage follows the time-path of the employee's evolving marginal product fairly closely. The second job provides general training, and the wage paid is less than marginal product for younger employees and greater for older ones. Now assume that government policymakers get worried about the discrimination between workers in different jobs and introduce legislation requiring equal pay for 'work of equal value'. Both types of employees must now be paid the value of their marginal products. Firms then become reluctant to invest in helping their employees acquire general human capital, because it is now illegal to use a time-pattern of wages that allows the firm to cover the cost of providing this capital. However fair it may appear to some, this government policy, designed to enhance equity, may not be in the interests of the workers affected by it.

Differentials due to sex and race

Crude statistics show that incomes vary by race and sex. More detailed studies suggest that much of these differences can be explained by such influences as amount of human capital acquired through both formal education and on-the-job experience. When these influences are taken into account, however, a core of difference remains

that is consistent with discrimination based on race and sex. This is further discussed with respect to male–female earnings differentials in Box 15.1.

Some forms of discrimination make it difficult, or impossible, for certain groups to take certain jobs, even if skill and education equip them for these jobs. Until very recently, non-whites and women found many occupations closed to them. Even today, when overt discrimination in hiring is illegal, many feel that more subtle forms of discrimination are applied.

To the extent that such discrimination occurs, it reduces the supply of labour in the exclusive jobs—by keeping out the groups who are discriminated against. It also increases the supply in non-exclusive jobs, which are the only ones

Box 15.1 Why are women paid less than men?

Wage discrimination can affect women (or any other group that is discriminated against) in at least two ways. They may earn less than men when doing the same job, or they may be forced into jobs that typically pay lower wages than the jobs from which they are excluded. Non-discriminatory wage differentials arise when men and women differ on average in relevant labour market characteristics. For example, men and women differ significantly in their average educational qualification and in their labour market experience, with women typically spending somewhere between five and ten years out of the labour market raising children.

Across the whole economy, the average pay of women is less than that of men. This has been known since at least the 1880s, when reliable records started. Indeed, at the Trade Union Congress of 1888 a motion was passed stating that where men and women do the same jobs they should get the same pay. However, it was 1970 before the Equal Pay Act finally legislated that pay must be the same 'for the same or broadly similar work'.

Up to 1970, the data show that on average women were paid just over 60 per cent of the average male wage. However, by the late 1970s this had narrowed to a little over 70 per cent and by the late 1990s to about 80 per cent. Researchers have been unable to explain this narrowing in any other way than as a result of the legislation. This suggests that some previously existing discrimination has been eliminated. The figure shows current differentials in major sectors in·the UK.

Further research has looked at the remaining differentials. Correcting for differing lengths of labour market experience would increase female pay to over 85 per cent of male. Other differences between the sexes, such as years of schooling, account for another 5 or 6 percentage points, leaving fewer than 10 percentage points unexplained. This could be due to discrimination.

On a narrow interpretation the pay differentials according to different labour market experiences are a reflection of the resulting lower marginal products. On a wider view of discrimination, however, these different experiences are merely convenient excuses for paying women less. This wider view is given some plausibility by the fact that in Sweden, the most egalitarian country in Europe, female earnings average fully 90 per cent of male earnings.

It is harder to estimate the effects of discrimination that excludes women from certain jobs and crowds them into others. Studies suggest, however, that if the discrimination in type of employment were eliminated, wages in occupations that are currently dominated by females would rise by as much

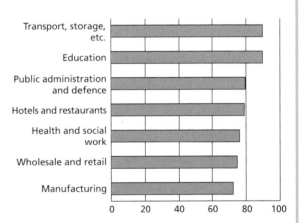

UK women's earnings as a percentage of men's earnings by industry, April 1997

Source: New Earnings Survey, Office for National Statistics and Department of Economic Development, Northern Ireland.

as 50 per cent! In contrast, wages in male-dominated jobs would fall by only a few percentage points.

These estimates put *upper bounds* on the effects of discrimination. To some extent the crowding of women into certain types of jobs may reflect their own preferences for these types of jobs, and the amount of human capital that they are willing to acquire. To the extent that this is true the crowding into certain occupations and the resulting lower female earnings represent the outcome of female preferences. However, to the extent that crowding is due to discriminatory practices on the part of employers, the wage differentials are not an efficient market outcome.

All of the research results reported here are tentative, since this type of estimation is no easy matter. However, the evidence does suggest two things. First, there is almost certainly some discrimination against women remaining in labour markets today. Second, we have to be very careful in interpreting the raw data. The measured average differentials have to be adjusted for labour force characteristics in order to identify any residual that is due to discrimination.

open to the groups subject to discrimination. This raises the wages in the exclusive jobs and lowers them in the non-exclusive jobs. Since discrimination prevents movement from the lower- to the higher-wage jobs, the resulting wage differences are equilibrium, not disequilibrium, differentials.

A model of labour market discrimination

To isolate the effects of discrimination, we begin by considering a non-discriminating labour market. We then introduce discrimination between two groups of equally qualified workers called group X and group Y. The analysis applies to workers who are distinguished on any grounds other than their ability, such as female and male, black and white, alien and citizen, Catholic and Protestant.

Suppose that, except for the fact that half of the people are marked with X and the other half are marked with Y, the groups are the same. Each has the same number of members, the same proportion who are educated to various levels, identical distributions of talent, and so on. Suppose also that there are two occupations. Occupation E (for elite) requires people of above-average education and skills, and occupation O (ordinary) can use anyone. If wages in the two occupations are the same, employers in occupation O will prefer to hire the above-average worker. Finally, suppose that the non-monetary advantages of the two occupations are equal.

In the absence of discrimination the wages in E occupations will be bid up above those in O occupations in order that the E jobs attract the workers of above-average skills. Both Xs and Ys of above-average skill will take the E jobs, while the others, both Xs and Ys, will have no choice but to seek O jobs. Because skills are equally distributed, each occupation will employ one-half Xs and one-half Ys.

Now discrimination enters in an extreme form. All E occupations are hereafter open only to Xs; all O occupations are hereafter open to either Xs or Ys. The immediate effect is to reduce by 50 per cent the supply of job candidates for E occupations; candidates must now be *both* Xs and above average. The discrimination also increases the supply of applicants for O jobs by 50 per cent; this group now includes all Ys and the below-average Xs.

Wage-level effects As shown in Figure 15.3 wages now rise in E occupations and fall in O occupations.

Discrimination, by changing supply, can decrease the wages and incomes of a group that is discriminated against.

In the longer run further changes may occur. Notice that total employment in the E industries falls. Employers may find ways to utilize slightly below-average labour and thus lure the next-best-qualified Xs out of O occupations. Although this will raise O wages slightly, it will also make these occupations increasingly 'Y occupations'. If discrim-

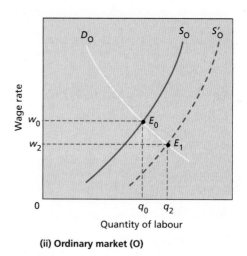

(i) Elite market (E)   (ii) Ordinary market (O)

Figure 15.3 Economic discrimination

If market E discriminates against one group and market O does not, the supply curve will shift to the left in E and to the right in O. Market E requires above-average skills, while market O requires only ordinary skills. When there is no discrimination, demands and supplies are D_E and S_E in market E, and D_O and S_O in market O. Initially the wage rate is w_0 and employment is q_0 in each market. (The actual wage in market E will be slightly higher than the wage in market O.) When all Ys are barred from E occupations, the supply curve shifts to S'_E and the wage earned by the remaining workers, all of whom are Xs, rises to w_1. Ys put out of work in the E occupations now seek work in the O occupations. The resulting shift in the supply curve to S'_O brings down the wage to w_2 in the O occupations. Because all Ys are in O occupations, they have a lower wage than many Xs. The average X wage is higher than the average Y wage.

ination has been in effect for a sufficient length of time, Ys will learn that it does not pay to acquire above-average skills. Regardless of ability, Ys are forced by discrimination to work in unskilled jobs.

Now suppose that a long-standing discriminatory policy is reversed. Because they will have responded to discrimination by acquiring fewer skills than Xs, many Ys will be locked into the O occupations, at least for a time. Moreover, if both Xs and Ys come to expect that Ys will have less education than Xs, employers will tend to look for Xs to fill the E jobs. This will reinforce the belief of Ys that education does not pay. This, and other kinds of subtle discrimination, can persist for a very long time, making the supply of Ys to O jobs higher than it would be in the absence of the initial discrimination, thus depressing the wages of Ys and poor Xs.

The kind of discrimination that we have considered in our model is extreme. It is similar to South Africa's former apartheid system (which was eliminated by 1994), in which blacks were excluded by law from prestigious and high-paying occupations. In most Western countries labour market discrimination against a specific group usually occurs in somewhat less obvious ways. First, it may be difficult (but not impossible, as in our model) for members of the group to get employment in certain jobs. Second, members of groups subject to discrimination may receive lower pay for a given kind of work than members of groups not subject to discrimination.

It is interesting to note that falling transport and communication costs over the past century have expanded firms' choice of location for the production of goods, from local markets, to national markets, to wider regional markets, and now often to global markets. This has greatly reduced the power of local prejudices to impose discrimination on maximizing firms. If firms give in to local pressure, the production can be transferred to other sites and the customers will quickly lose any concern about, or even awareness of, the nature of the far-distant workforce that makes the products they consume.

Differentials due to labour market structures

In this section we see how differences in the degree of competition can contribute to income differentials across markets. We then go on to study unions in a little more detail.

The determination of wages without unions

When labour is supplied competitively in an individual labour market, each individual worker must take the existing wage rate as given and decide how much labour

services to supply at that wage. We have seen that each worker has a supply curve showing how much effort he or she will supply at each wage (see page 228). The sum of these curves yields a market supply curve showing the total supply of effort to this market as a function of the real wage rate. The determination of wages under competitive supply now falls into three cases, distinguished by whether labour is bought by competitive purchasers, a single-wage monopsonist, or a discriminating monopsonist.

Case 1: a competitive market We first assume that there are so many purchasers of labour services that no one of them can influence the market wage rate. Instead, each merely decides how much labour to hire at the current rate. Since both demanders and suppliers are price-takers and quantity-adjusters, this labour market is perfectly competitive. Demand and supply as shown in Figure 14.3 on page 221 then determine the wage rate and volume of employment.

Case 2: a single-wage monopsonist—a single purchaser Now consider a labour market containing only a few firms. For simplicity we deal with a case in which the few purchasers form an employers' association and act as a single decision-taking unit in the labour market. In this section the single buyer is restrained to paying a single wage to all workers of one type that it employs.

When there is a single purchaser in any market, that purchaser is called a **monopsonist**. A monopsonist can offer any wage rate it chooses, and workers must either work for that wage or move to other markets (i.e. change occupation or location).

Suppose that the monopsonist decides to hire some specific quantity of labour. The labour supply curve shows the wage that it must offer. To the monopsonist this wage is the *average cost curve* of labour. In deciding how much labour to hire, however, the monopsonist is interested in the marginal cost of hiring additional workers. It wants to know how much its costs will rise if it takes on more labour.

Whenever the supply curve of labour has a positive slope, the marginal cost of employing extra units will exceed the average cost (the wage) because the increased wage rate necessary to attract an extra worker must also be paid to *everyone already employed*.

Consider an example. If 100 workers are employed at £2 per hour, then total cost is £200 and average cost per worker is £2. If an extra worker is employed and this drives the wage rate up to £2.05, then total cost becomes £207.05 (101 × £2.05); the average cost per labourer is £2.05, but the total cost has increased by £7.05 as a result of hiring one more labourer.

Monopsony results in a lower level of employment and a lower wage rate than when labour is purchased competitively.

The reason is that the monopsonistic purchaser is aware

that, by purchasing more, it is driving up the price against itself. It will, therefore, stop short of the point that is reached when the factor is purchased by many different firms, none of which can exert an influence on its price.

Case 3: a discriminating monopsonist What happens if the monopsonist can discriminate among different units of a single type of labour that it hires? As with the discriminatory monopolists that we studied in Chapter 10, the ability to discriminate has two effects:

A discriminating monopsonist will hire more labour and earn more profits than will a monopsonist who must pay the same wage to everyone.

In Figure 15.4 the monopsonist who must pay the same wage to all did not hire more labour, because doing so drove up the wage of its existing workers. For this reason the monopsonist's marginal cost of hiring labour exceeds the average costs. If the monopsonist can split its labour into groups, it can hire a second group without driving up the price of the first group. Consider the extreme case in which the monopsonist can make a separate bargain with each worker, paying just what is needed to persuade that person to accept a job. The supply curve is then the marginal cost curve of labour and the monopsonist employs the same amount of labour as would a perfectly competitive industry.

In Figure 15.4 the perfectly competitive employment is q_c with a wage of w_c, so that labour earns $w_c q_c$. A perfectly discriminating monopsonist will also employ q_c of labour, but, by paying each worker his or her supply price, the total wage bill is reduced to the area under the supply curve. Thus, the area between the supply curve and the perfectly competitive wage is added to the monopsonist's profits.

This is the extreme case. As long, however, as the monopsonist can discriminate between two or more groups, employment and profits will be higher than when a single wage must be paid.

The determination of wages with unions

Unions affect wages and employment in two ways, depending on whether labour is hired competitively or monopsonistically.[1]

Case 4: monopoly—a single seller Suppose a union enters a competitive labour market and raises the wage above its equilibrium level. By so doing, it is establishing a minimum wage below which no one will work. The industry can hire as many units of labour as are prepared to work at the union wage, but none at a lower wage. Thus, the industry (and each firm) faces a supply curve that is horizontal at the level of the union wage up to the quantity of labour willing to work at that wage.

This is shown in Figure 15.5. The intersection of this horizontal supply curve and the demand curve establishes

Figure 15.4 A monopsonist facing many sellers

Under monopsony employment and wages are less than under competition. The competitive wage and employment are w_c and q_c, where the demand and supply curves intersect. The monopsonist that must pay the same wage to all equates the marginal cost of hiring labour with labour's marginal revenue product, which occurs at point E_m. The firm hires q_m workers at a wage of w_m. (According to the supply curve, w_m is the wage at which q_m workers will be supplied.) Labour's income is shown by the dark yellow and dark blue areas enclosed by q_m and w_m.

A perfectly discriminating monopsonist can pay each worker his or her supply price, so the S curve is also its marginal cost curve. It will hire q_c labour and pay labour a total income equal to the dark and medium blue areas *under* the S curve. The light yellow area between w_m and w_c is now part of the monopsonist's profits, as is the dark yellow area between w_m and the S curve (whereas under perfect competition both yellow areas are part of labour's income).

a higher wage rate, and a lower level of employment, than would occur at the competitive equilibrium.

There will be a group of workers who would like to obtain work in the industry or occupation but cannot. Pressure to cut the wage rate may develop among the unemployed, but the union must resist this pressure if the higher wage is to be maintained.

A union can raise wages above the competitive-market level, but only at the costs of lowering employment and creating an excess supply of labour with its consequent pressure for wage-cutting.

Case 5: a monopsony versus a monopoly We now consider the effects of introducing a union into the monopsonistic labour market first illustrated in Figure 15.4.

The (single-wage) monopsonistic employers' organization now faces a monopoly union, and the two sides will settle the wage through collective bargaining. The outcome of this bargaining process will depend on the objective

---

[1] For simplicity we deal here with only the single-wage monopsonist. Combining a union with a discriminating monopsonist complicates the analysis substantially without adding any new insights. Theoretically inclined readers may, none the less, like to do this for themselves as an exercise.

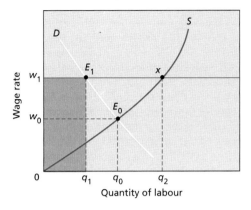

Figure 15.5 A single union facing many employers
A union that faces many employers can raise wages above the competitive level. Competitive equilibrium is at E_0. When the union sets the wage at w_1, it creates a perfectly elastic supply curve of labour up to the quantity q_2, which is the amount of labour willing to work at the wage w_1. Equilibrium is at E_1, with q_1 workers employed and $q_2 - q_1$ willing to work at the going wage rate but unable to find employment. Labour income is shown by the dark blue area.

Figure 15.6 A single union facing a single employer
A union can raise both the wage and employment above their monopsonistic levels. The monopsonist facing competitively supplied labour is in the equilibrium analysed in Figure 15.4, with q_m workers employed at a wage of w_m. If a newly entering union sets its wage at w_0, the supply curve runs from w_0 to E_0 and then rises along the line S. Equilibrium is at E_0 with employment at q_0.

If the union seeks a wage higher than w_0, it must accept a lower level of employment than q_0. The union can, for example, set a wage of w_u, creating a supply curve that runs from w_u to x then up the S curve. This yields the same level of employment, q_m, as when the monopsonist dominated the market, but at the much higher wage of w_u. At that wage rate there are $q_2 - q_m$ people who would like to work but who are unable to find employment.

that each side sets and on the skill that each has in bargaining for its objective. We have seen that, left to itself, the employers' organization will set the monopsonistic wage shown as w_m in Figure 15.4.

To understand the range over which the wage may be set after the union enters the market, let us ask what the union would do if it had the power to set a wage below which its members would not work. There is now no point in the employers' holding off hiring for fear of driving the wage up or of reducing the quantity demanded in the hope of driving the wage rate down. Here, just as in the case of a wage-setting union in a competitive market, the union presents the employer with a horizontal supply curve (up to the maximum number of workers who will accept work at the union wage). As demonstrated in Figure 15.6, the union can raise wages *and employment* above the monopsonistic level.

Because the union turns the firm into a price-taker in the labour market, it can stop a firm from exercising its monopsony power and thus raise both wages and employment to the competitive level.

The union may not be content merely to neutralize the monopsonist's power. It may choose to raise wages further. If it does, the outcome will be similar to that shown in Figure 15.5. If the wage is raised above the competitive level, the employer will no longer wish to hire all the labour that is offered at that wage. The amount of employment will fall, and unemployment will develop. This is also shown in Figure 15.6. Notice, however, that the

union can raise wages substantially above the competitive level before employment falls to a level as low as it was in the pre-union monopsonistic situation.

So now we know that the employer would like to set the monopsonistic wage and that the union would not want a wage below the competitive wage. The union may target a still higher wage depending on what trade-off it is willing to make between employment for its members and the wage that they earn. If the union is willing to accept the resulting low amount of employment, it could target a wage rate substantially higher than the competitive wage.

Simple demand and supply analysis can take us no further. As we have already observed, the actual outcome will depend on such other things as the target wage that the two sides seek to achieve, their relative bargaining skills, how each side assesses the cost of concessions, and how serious a strike would be for each.

Differentials due to product market structures

The ability of a union to raise wages above the competitive level depends partly on the profitability of the industry in which it is operating. Some industries are highly competitive because they contain a large number of small firms and entry and exit are easy. Typically firms in such industries will be earning enough to cover the opportunity cost of their capital, but no pure profits. A strong union might still raise wages in such an industry. This would increase costs and lead to exit until prices rose sufficiently for the remaining firms fully to cover their now higher costs. Thus, the rise in wages would be accompanied by a fall in output and employment. However, even this limited gain may not be possible. If the union does not have a closed shop, new firms may enter, with lower costs achieved by hiring non-union labour. Also, if there is competition from foreign firms that do not face strong unions, the domestic industry may suffer a drastic contraction.

In other industries scale economies allow only a few firms, each one of which may earn significant pure profits. Government regulation that restricts competitive behaviour can also create economic profits over and above the opportunity cost of capital. Evidence suggests that unions can appropriate a share of these profits through aggressive collective bargaining. This was illustrated when several US industries were deregulated, subjecting their firms to greatly increased competitive pressures. Wages fell significantly in most of these industries, showing that their employees had succeeded in obtaining significant rents in excess of what they could have earned elsewhere.

Minimum-wage laws

When unions set wages for their members, they are in effect setting a minimum wage. Governments can cause similar effects by legislating specific *minimum wages*, which define the lowest wage rates that may legally be paid. Such minimum wages are common in the United States and Canada and are a part of the European Union. The UK introduced the minimum wage in April 1999 with a minimum wage of £3.60 an hour for adult workers and £3.00 for 18–21 year olds (rising to £3.20 in June 2000), while 16- and 17-year-olds are exempt.

To the extent that minimum wages are effective, they raise the wages of employed workers. However, as our analysis in Chapter 5 indicated, an effective floor price (which is what a minimum wage is) may well lead to a market surplus—in this case, unemployment. Thus, minimum wages benefit some groups of workers while hurting others.

The problem is more complicated than the analysis of Chapter 5 would suggest, both because not all labour markets are competitive and because only a small proportion of the labour force is affected by minimum-wage laws. Moreover, some groups in the labour force, especially youth and minorities, are affected more than is the average worker.

A comprehensive minimum wage

Consider a minimum-wage law that, like the UK one, applies uniformly to all occupations. The occupations and the industries in which minimum wages are effective will be those paying the lowest wages. They will usually involve unskilled or, at best, semi-skilled labour. In most of them the workers will not be members of unions. Thus the market structures in which minimum wages are likely to be most effective include both those in which competitive conditions obtain and those in which employers exercise monopsony power. The effects on employment are different in the two cases.

Competitive labour markets The consequences for employment of an effective minimum wage are unambiguous when the labour market is competitive. By raising the wage that employers must pay, minimum-wage legislation leads to a reduction in the quantity of labour that is demanded and an increase in the quantity of labour that is supplied. As a result, the actual level of employment falls, and unemployment is generated. This situation is exactly analogous to the one that arises when a union succeeds in setting a wage above the competitive equilibrium wage, as was illustrated in Figure 15.5. The excess supply of labour at the minimum wage also creates incentives for people to evade the law by working below the legal minimum wage.

In competitive labour markets effective minimum-wage laws raise the wages of those who remain employed but also create some unemployment.

Monopsonistic labour markets By effectively flattening out the labour supply curve, a minimum-wage law can simultaneously increase both wages and employment in monopsonistic labour markets. The circumstances in which this can happen are the same as those in which a union that is facing a monopsonistic employer succeeds in setting a wage above the wage that the employer would otherwise pay, as was shown in Figure 15.6. Of course, if the minimum wage is raised above the competitive wage, employment will start to fall, as in the union case. When it is set at the competitive level, however, the minimum wage can protect workers against monopsony power *and* lead to increases in employment.

Evidence from North America

Empirical work on the effects of minimum-wage laws in North America, where they are commonly used, reflects these mixed theoretical predictions. There is some evidence that those who keep their jobs gain when the minimum wage is raised. There is also evidence that some groups suffer a decline in employment consistent with the effect of a minimum wage in a competitive market. At other times and places, there is evidence that both wages earned and employment rise when the minimum wage rises, as is consistent with monopolistic labour markets.

The gains and losses are not neatly segregated by group. Within any affected group, such as the young and inexperienced, those who keep their jobs gain while the losers are those who are unable to find work owing to a high minimum wage. Supporters tend to stress the benefits to those who gain, while detractors stress the losses of those who suffer. One worrying problem arises because critical job experience is gained from one's first job, particularly for those with minimum school training. Only part of a young inexperienced person's wage is in the form of money, the rest comes in the form of training. Those who have their first employment postponed because of the unemployment created by a minimum wage lose time before they get the critical first-job training. The long-term effects on these people can be serious. So, as with any group, the policy helps some and can seriously hurt other young and inexperienced persons.

Forecasts for the UK

Many years will have to pass before the effects of the new minimum-wage law are apparent in the UK. In the meantime all that is known is who will be affected and how various groups have reacted. The Low Pay Commission, whose recommendations for a minimum wage were adopted by the government, estimated that 2 million persons will have their wages raised by it.

The pay of 1.5 million women workers will rise by 25 per cent, while the pay for 250,000 18–20-year-olds will rise by 33 per cent. On the occupation side, cleaning, catering, and cloth cutting and shaping will be most heavily affected. These are large enough increases to cause concern about the employment effects, particularly on those under 21 years of age. The potential for adverse employment effects was great enough to worry Treasury officials. The Chancellor of the Exchequer was quoted in the press as being concerned that the minimum wage would undermine his Welfare to Work programme. He also expressed concern that many young workers whose pay had been rising at a rate of about 4 per cent per year owing to market forces would find themselves unemployed instead of working at a rate that, although below the new minimum, was rising steadily.

Unions

Having concluded our discussion of the causes of equilibrium wage differentials with a study of the influence of unions, it is appropriate to raise some further issues related to unions. We begin by discussing the rise of unions.

The rise of unions

One reason for the rise of unions was to turn cases 1, 2, and 3 that we studied on pages 245–6 above into cases 4 and 5. Another was to provide the many workers with a collective, and hence an effective, voice in dealing with the few employers on such other conditions of work as safety, hours, holidays, and non-wage benefits.

Since early unions did not have large resources, employers had to be attacked where they were weakest. The unions that succeeded first were those that covered skilled artisans rather than semi-skilled or unskilled workers. Economic theory provides reasons that help to explain their success—reasons coming from both the demand and the supply side of the market.

Demand forces Highly skilled specialists usually faced quite inelastic demands for their services, and thus could raise wages without facing major losses of employment. Inelastic demands are explained by two of the principles outlined in Chapter 14. First, these specialists were difficult to dispense with since their services had no real substitutes (see the substitution rule on page 225). Second, labour in any one skilled occupation usually accounted for a very small proportion of total production costs, since large quantities of unskilled labour were employed in most production processes (see the importance rule on page 226).

Supply forces We have seen that one of the problems of raising wages above their competitive levels is the emergence of a supply of workers who would like to work at the going wage rate but cannot find employment. These would-be employees are tempted to work for less than the union wage, and thus can undercut the union's ability to maintain a high wage rate.

The skilled workers normally had guilds, and other associations that controlled entry into their profession. Thus, they did not have to rely on the strategy of fixing the wage and letting the employer decide quantity. Instead, they could restrict supply by restricting entry into their trade, and then accept the free-market wage rate. This method of raising wages, which is studied in Figure 15.7, had the advantage of avoiding a pool of unemployed workers ready to undercut the prevailing wage. Such a method was not, however, available to the semi-skilled and unskilled workers.

This is a method that has been used at many times and in many places. The key requirement is that the supply

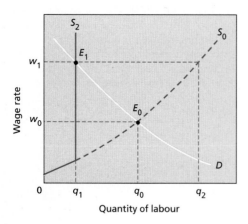

Figure 15.7 Raising wages by restricting supply

If wages are raised by restricting supply, any target wage can be maintained without creating a pool of unemployed workers. With free entry into the occupation the supply curve S_0 and the demand curve D intersect at E_0 to produce an equilibrium wage of w_0 with employment of q_0. If entry is restricted to the quantity q_1, the supply curve becomes vertical at that quantity (the blue supply curve in the figure labelled S_2). The competitive market now reaches equilibrium at E_1, determining the wage rate at w_1. There is no excess supply.

If instead the wage had been fixed at w_1 without controlling entry, the supply of persons willing to work at that wage but unable to find employment would have been $q_2 - q_1$.

of persons offering themselves for employment can be controlled. This can be done by unions that can restrict membership and have closed-shop agreements preventing non-members from being employed. Professional

associations that license those allowed to practise the profession can also do it; entry can then be reduced by raising standards for entry. This makes it difficult to decide whether the public is being protected by ensuring that practitioners are of a reasonable standard, or is being exploited by restricting entry through the imposition of unnecessarily high standards.

Unions today

Box 15.2 discusses some of the major institutions that characterize modern unions. Table 15.1 shows the wide variations in union membership among advanced industrial countries. Although union membership has been falling in the United Kingdom it is currently close to the average for all of these countries. Modern unions do many things, including bargaining about pay and working conditions.

Collective bargaining

In collective bargaining between firms and unions there is usually a substantial range over which wages may be set. An example is shown in Figure 15.8.

Economic theory can put limits on the outcome, but where it settles within those limits may depend on a host of considerations. Just as in oligopolistic competition between firms, the outcome may be significantly influenced by such political and psychological factors as skill in bargaining, ability to bluff, and one side's assessment of the other side's reactions to its own moves. For example, the employers will ask, 'How much can we resist without

---

Box 15.2 Union institutions

Modern unions are organized throughout the world along two main lines. In **trade** (or **craft**) **unions** workers with a common set of skills are joined in a common association, no matter where, or for whom, they work. In **industrial unions** all workers in a given plant, or a given industry, are collected into a single union, whatever their skills.

Industrial unions are common in the United States. Because of them many firms, including the great American automobile companies, deal with one union. So also do American steel companies. A single agreement over wages, working conditions, or union practices is sufficient to change the situation throughout the entire industry.

A single union covering an entire industry is less common in the United Kingdom (and in many other countries) because the main basis of organization is the trade union. As a result, a typical employer has to deal with many unions—twenty or more within a single firm is not uncommon in the United Kingdom. Under these circumstances, agreement between labour and management can be hard to reach.

Unions do many things designed to influence the wages and conditions

of work of their members. What they are able to accomplish depends partly on the institutional setting within which they operate.

Modern unions bargain under two basic types of arrangement: the open shop and the closed shop. In an **open shop** a union represents its members but does not have exclusive negotiating rights for all the workers of one kind; membership of the union is not a condition of getting or keeping a job. Unions usually oppose such an arrangement, and it is easy to see why. Consider an open-shop negotiating situation. If, on the one hand, employers accede to union demands, the non-members achieve the benefits of the union without paying dues or sharing the risks. If, on the other hand, employers choose to fight the union, they can run their plants with the non-union members, thus weakening the power of the union.

In a **closed shop** only union members can be employed. (Closed shops may be either 'pre-entry', where the worker must be a member of the union before being employed, or 'post-entry', where the worker must join the union on becoming employed.) These were once common in the United Kingdom, but under the 1980 Employment Act they were virtually abolished.

provoking the unions into calling a costly strike?' The union will ask, 'Will the employers force us to strike only for a token period so they can tell their shareholders they *tried* to resist, or do they intend to hold out to the bitter

Table 15.1 Percentage of the non-agricultural labour force in unions, 1994–1995

Country	%
Sweden	77
Denmark	68
Norway	52
Belgium	38
Austria	37
Ireland	36
Italy	31
Canada	31
Germany	30
UK	26
Netherlands	22
Switzerland	20
Japan	19
USA	13
France	6

The importance of trade unions varies greatly across the advanced industrial countries.

Source: World Labour Report 1997–8.

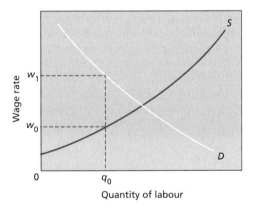

Figure 15.8 Collective bargaining between one union and one employer

There is often more than one mutually acceptable outcome to the bargaining process. The supply curve of persons who would like to work in the job in question is given by *S*, but the union is assumed to have restricted entry to q_0. The single employer (one firm or an employers' association) has a demand curve for this labour of *D*. The supply curve indicates that q_0 workers would be willing to work for w_0. The *D* curve indicates that the employer would be willing to employ q_0 workers at any wage up to w_1. Both sides would prefer any wage between w_0 and w_1 rather than have no agreement at all.

end against any strike that we might call?' It is because monopoly versus monopsony allows more than one acceptable economic solution that these non-economic factors become so important.

Wages versus employment

We have already seen that in many situations the union faces a trade-off between wages and employment: an increase in wages can be obtained only at the cost of lowered employment. In some cases, however, it is possible to avoid the conflict between wages and unemployment by bargaining with the employer about both wages and employment. This can sometimes be accomplished in one small sector of the economy by manning agreements that force employers to use more labour than they need for a given level of output. Such agreements, which push employers off their demand curves, were common in the United Kingdom from 1945 to 1980, but most had disappeared by 1990.

When faced with such behaviour, employers are given a strong incentive to develop new technology that will eliminate the unneeded workers by replacing their jobs with machines. Workers may fight the introduction of the new technology, but they cannot resist it indefinitely. When it is introduced, the demand curve shifts left and employment may be less than it would have been if employers had not been pushed off their demand curves in the first place. This is a reasonable description of the long battle between printers' unions and newspaper owners in the UK, in which unions forced the owners off their demand curves for years while they successfully held off the introduction of new technology. Finally, when the new technology was introduced, many of the union members lost their jobs.

Where it is not possible to push employers off demand curves, unions will be more aware of the wage–employment trade-off the closer the bargaining process is to being nationwide. In firm-by-firm bargaining unions know that if they push wages up high enough to reduce employment, the displaced workers can get jobs elsewhere. However, when a single union bargains with an employers' federation over the whole economy, there is no 'elsewhere'. The union thus tends to be much more restrained by the wage–employment trade-off than are small unions. In their book *The Unemployment Crisis* (Oxford University Press, 1994), three British economists—Richard Layard, Stephen Nickell, and Richard Jackman—present data for several countries that seem to support this view that wage bargaining is more likely to create unemployment the more decentralized it is.

Unions and the structure of relative wages

So far we have considered the influence of one particular union, operating in a small section of the total labour market, on the wages of its members. Our theory predicts that a powerful union can in such circumstances raise the wages earned by its members, possibly at the expense of increased unemployment. This prediction seems to be supported by substantial empirical evidence that in the past British unions were able to raise wages on average around 10 per cent above what wages would have been under competitive wage determination. If one group got a larger share of total national income, some other groups must have got less. A substantial amount of the extra earnings of unionized labour appears to have been at the expense of lower wages for some groups of unorganized workers and unemployment for some workers who would have had jobs at the competitive wage rate.

Evidence also suggests that by the early 1990s union-induced wage differentials had all but disappeared in the UK. This decline in union power over wages had several causes. First, union power had been broken in many of the industries where unions had been powerful. For example, computer-based composition finally destroyed the power of the old printers' union, which had been able to hold wages substantially above competitive levels (and in the process made it more difficult for UK publishing firms to compete with foreign rivals). Second, many of the industries in which unions were strong, such as coal, steel, and the docks, are all in decline, employing small and shrinking numbers of workers. Third, in the one place where unions may still be maintaining a major wage differential which would not exist in their absence—the public sector—contracting out is becoming common (usually to non-union firms). Over time, therefore, unions in that sector can be expected to become less and less effective in imposing wage differentials between their workers and those in the private sector.

Unions were effective in many ways, but any large wage differentials over and above what market forces would have determined could not persist indefinitely. Instead the high wages encouraged a form of Schumpeterian creative destruction. It took time, but eventually the market forces of substitution among factors, international competition from lower-wage producers, and induced technological innovation that was labour-saving eroded both the wage differentials and the union power that created them.[2]

Heterogeneity, incentives, and monitoring costs

In the first part of this chapter we studied the broad forces that create wage differentials between different market structures and between very different groups such as senior management, junior management, shop supervisors, and assembly-line workers. In these contexts it is a useful simplification to regard each group as being composed of identical individuals. But to understand other labour market issues we need to recognize heterogeneity and several other phenomena left out of our analysis so far. Labour market institutions evolve in subtle ways to cope with the following problems.

Heterogeneity Individuals are different. They all respond to the same incentives, but they respond differently; given the same wage, some will work harder than others. Some have more ability than others; with the same amount of effort some produce more and better results than others. This applies to all employees whether working in production, design, planning, or supervision.

Asymmetric information Firms might like to reward good workers more than indifferent workers, but it is difficult to know one from the other in most complex work situations. Generally workers know more about their effectiveness than does their employer.

Adverse selection We first met this problem in Chapter 12, where, faced with the same rates, high-risk persons were more inclined to take insurance than low-risk persons. In labour markets a firm seeking to hire people usually advertises a particular job with an associated pay, or pay range. From the pool of those who meet the paper specifications, applicants are more likely to be lower-quality workers who find that wage a good bargain than higher-quality workers who know they can get a good wage elsewhere. This would be no problem if the employer knew as much about his prospective employees as did the employees themselves. But this is an obvious case of asymmetric information. You know more about yourself, your work habits, and your strengths and weaknesses than any outsider (except possibly your psychoanalyst).

Costly monitoring It is difficult and costly for management to monitor its employees to find out how well each is contributing to its goal of maximizing profits.

The principal–agent problem The management wishes to motivate employees to work in the firm's best interest,

---

[2] Notice that these last two paragraphs give positive statements about what happened and why it happened. These do not imply any normative judgement about whether the reported changes were desirable or undesirable (which will, to a great extent, depend on the point of view of the person making the judgement).

while employees often have different and conflicting motivations. Management would like to design incentive systems that motivate workers to provide the type of effort that it requires. This is the principal–agent problem that we first encountered in Chapter 13, where we used it to study the relation between shareholders and senior management. Here we use the same theory to help us understand the relationship between senior management and all other employees.

Contracts and performance monitoring

When you purchase a haircut, you have a clear idea of what you expect to get and you can accurately judge the quality of the service you receive. When a firm hires a divisional manager, it knows that it wants good work but cannot say specifically what the manager should be doing at each moment in her work day. Furthermore, it is not easy to judge how much of the division's subsequent performance is due to the manager's efforts and how much to forces beyond the manager's control. Many modern employment situations are better thought of as an ongoing relationship rather than as the equivalent of a purchase of a specific, exactly definable labour service. Hence employment contracts are often referred to as *relational contracts*.

These contracts do not attempt to cover all of the many contingencies that could arise in a job. Instead, they set out general functions to be fulfilled in the post and leave the details to be decided by an evolving interaction between employer and employee. In many modern jobs it is not even desirable in principle to establish an exact job description because the nature of the work is continually evolving. For example, as recently as the 1980s a secretary's job involved taking handwritten manuscripts and creating hard copy using a typewriter. Today the same job typically involves taking draft documents on a floppy disc and reformatting them using a word-processor package. Instead of typing memos, the secretary will now be sending email messages. A precise 1980 job description would have been a hindrance to progress.

Under relational contracts neither employer nor employee has an exact or agreed expectation of each other's detailed behaviour.

The firm does not know the marginal product of each employee. The employees do not know precisely what they need to do to get promoted and avoid being sacked. Neither workers nor firms can make accurate decisions based upon full information.

An obvious principal–agent problem that arises with relational contracts, from the perspective of the firm, is that employees have some range of discretion about how hard they work, and they may have objectives of their own that are different from those of the employer.

The firm (the principal) cannot monitor accurately the performance of many of its employees (the agents). It is often too costly even to try, and in many jobs it is impossible even if money is no object. In such circumstances the firm needs to design mechanisms that will induce its employees to act in the firm's interests. In general, unless there is costly monitoring of the agents' behaviour, the problem cannot be completely solved.

Principal–agent analysis shows that when employees have some range of discretion, their self-interested behaviour will make profits lower than in a 'perfect', frictionless world in which principals act as their own agents, or agents always do exactly what the principals want.

Much labour market behaviour that seems odd at first sight has evolved to deal—more or less effectively—with the principal–agent problem. For example, people put in positions of trust are often paid much more than is needed to induce them to take these jobs. Why should principals pay their agents more than they need to pay to fill the jobs? The explanation is that agents who are paid much more than they could earn in other jobs have an incentive not to violate the trust placed in them. If they do violate the trust and are caught, they lose the premium attached to the job.

Efficiency wages

The theory of competitive markets predicts that excess supply causes price to fall until the excess supply is eliminated—that is, until demand equals supply. Often this does not happen in labour markets. In the face of excess supply, firms do not typically cut wages, even though such a move would seem to enhance profits. Why?

Employers are worried about the quality and performance of the heterogeneous workers that they hire as well as just their price. The wage that yields the best combination of price and quality of worker is known as the **efficiency wage.**

The theory of the *efficiency wage* helps to explain why it may be optimal for firms to set wages that are permanently above the level that would clear the labour market. Efficiency wage theory applies to hiring, to productivity on the job, and to worker turnover.

Efficiency in hiring Firms do not know the characteristics of specific workers until after they have sunk costs into hiring and training them. Good workers know who they are and are likely to have a higher reservation wage than bad workers. The reservation wage is the lowest wage at which a person is prepared to work for a particular firm. By lowering the wage that it offers, a firm will significantly lower the average ability of the workers who apply for its jobs. This tendency for a firm that pays lower wages to attract poor-quality workers is a case of adverse selection. As a result paying lower wages can make the firm worse off.

In labour markets with informational asymmetries, where unobserved characteristics of workers are correlated with the reservation wage, it will generally be optimal for firms to pay wages that exceed their employees' reservation wages.

Efficiency on the job If wages are so low that workers are just indifferent between staying and losing their job, they are unlikely to do more than the minimum required. Workers are likely to give greater effort if they feel they are being well rewarded. Workers will then expect to be much worse off if they lose their current job, and they will be aware of a queue of good-quality workers prepared to work for the high wage. The high wage improves on-the-job efficiency.

Minimizing turnover Many firms find high quit rates are costly because they must invest in training their workers. Firms are thus reluctant to lower wages for existing workers, even in the face of an excess supply of labour. Workers who are already inside the company and know its work practices are worth retaining, even at premium wages. New workers, though possibly cheaper, may not be as good, and will be costly to train.

Efficiency wage theory says that firms will find it advantageous to pay high enough wages that working is a clearly superior alternative to being laid off. This will minimize labour turnover and improve the quality of workers' effort.

When considering the supply curve of labour, we saw that high wages may induce less work from workers who can choose their hours—because of an income effect that is stronger than the substitution effect (see page 228). High efficiency wages give the workers a different choice, which is to work hard for a high reward or not to work at all (or, perhaps, to work in another job at the much lower average wage). By posing an all-or-nothing choice, employers alleviate the disincentive effects of high wages. Workers who do not work hard enough risk losing their high-paying job. This *potential-loss-of-income effect* reinforces the substitution effect, and for many workers encourages them to adopt the hard-work/high-pay solution—at least among those who are fortunate enough to have this choice.

Signalling

Participants in markets with asymmetric information will develop informal criteria for signalling information about some of these unseen characteristics. Employers who pay a high efficiency wage signal that they are interested in

high-quality staff and are prepared to pay them well. Educational qualifications provide a signal from potential employees. Hopefully your university degrees, or higher education certificate, will indicate that you have acquired some useful knowledge and skills. However, another important function of the degree you will acquire is to convince potential employers that you are ambitious, hard working, intelligent, and committed to self-improvement —just the kind of person that every employer is looking for! The degree creates a signal about your personal characteristics independent of the subject of the degree. In selection situations the signal about who you are may play as important a role as what you have learned.

Internal labour markets

Most manual and other unskilled workers have little or no expectation of advancement or even of long-term employment. They are often paid an hourly rate and have little job security. In contrast, many skilled manual workers, most white-collar workers, and virtually all technical, managerial, and professional staff have a long-term employment relationship, which provides a career path within the firm. Typically, there are limited entry points into the firm and most senior posts are filled by promotions from within the firm. These workers operate in what is known as an **internal labour market,** composed of a firm and its long-term employees—that is, the market is internal to the firm. Such a market has only limited connections with external labour markets and its structure reflects the needs and traditions of each specific firm. The market offers a *job ladder* for the firm's long-term employees, with most employees starting somewhere near the bottom of the ladder and working their way up throughout their career.

Pay and promotion

Firms with internal labour markets do not generally try to assess their employees' marginal productivity and then pay them accordingly. Instead, firms have a number of defined job grades with pay rates being attached to the job rather than to any individual's productivity. Individuals generally improve their pay by moving up the ladder of promotion. Good work in the current job has a potential payoff more in terms of promotion prospects than in terms of dramatically increased current pay.

There are at least three reasons why internal labour markets may be more efficient than tying individuals' pay to their individual performance. First, most of the covered jobs involve a great deal of learning. A long-term employment relationship, with a potential for promotion, creates an incentive for employees to invest in acquiring skills that will benefit the firm. These firm-specific skills will take time to acquire and will take even longer to generate a payoff to the firm. Hence, to achieve the benefits of this learning effect, firms have to offer the prospect of both long-term employment and of future promotion.

The second reason why internal labour markets may be efficient derives from efficiency wage theory. The incentives for good performance built into the efficiency wage require a long-term employment relationship. The 'good' workers are attracted to the firm by high rewards and also by a commitment on the part of firms to a high degree of employment stability and 'good prospects'. Hence, both employees and employers are likely to generate a more productive relationship via mutual longer-term commitment, rather than via temporary employment contracts and minimal mutual commitment.

The third factor supporting internal labour markets is that successful firms require long-term strategic thinking from their senior staff. The ability to take and implement long-term strategies is not something that shows up or can be tested over a short horizon. Hence, successful firms have significant numbers of senior managers who have been selected as a result of observing their performance within the company, and who have sufficient expectation of continuing employment that they are prepared to take a long-term view. A manager who does not expect to stay with a firm very long may postpone important investments, while one who sees his own future as tied to the success of the firm will want to ensure its continued survival.

The internal labour market increases the convergence of interests between the employee and the firm, thereby reducing principal–agent problems.

Tournaments

One way to think of an internal labour market is as a *tournament*. Workers enter the tournament when they join a firm on the lower rungs of the ladder. Workers at each level compete with each other to show the senior management that they are most worthy of promotion. Periodically, when a more senior job becomes vacant, someone from the grade immediately below the vacant post is chosen to progress up the ladder. As there are fewer senior jobs than junior jobs, not everybody can progress up the ladder at the same pace. The winner of the tournament is the one who reaches the post of chief executive.

In an internal labour market tournament the pay of senior executives is as much about motivating everybody in the organization as it is about paying a 'fair' compensation for the incumbent of any specific post. The £1 million salary paid to a chief executive officer (CEO) may be more important in terms of motivating junior staff to strive to rise to that exalted post than in terms of rewarding the current CEO for his efforts. Even though those who enter a golf or tennis tournament know that they cannot all win, tournaments with the greatest prize for winning still attract the best players and tend to bring out the best in them.

The tournament structure of rewards has three advantages for firms. First, when a candidate is selected for promotion, only enough information is needed to make relative judgements among potential candidates. No absolute or detailed performance measures are needed. This economizes on the need to acquire costly information, which may in any case be unreliable.

The second advantage is that pay ranges are set in advance for each job, so time is not wasted on individual pay negotiations with each and every employee. An employee who wants more pay must work for a promotion. So bargaining time is saved. Equally, there is no incentive for employers to argue about performance in order to avoid having to pay bonuses.

The third advantage is that tournaments reduce the problems of asymmetric information. Employees who are chosen for promotion from within the firm will have become well known to their superiors, and so there is little uncertainty about their characteristics. Equally, employees who are promoted already know a great deal about the functioning of the company, so they can become effective in their new position more quickly than would be likely with an outsider.

The promotion path in an internal labour market can be thought of as a tournament in which higher pay rates in more senior jobs create an incentive for employees to progress up the career ladder.

Seniority and *MRP*

The incentive issues discussed above suggest that where there is a long-term relationship between firm and workers, firms will find it efficient to reward loyalty and long service. Hence, it will generally be true that longer-serving workers will get higher rewards than younger workers. The rewards for long service will come via higher wages and company pension schemes, which will naturally reward long service with a higher pension. A pension can be thought of as deferred wages.

The need to reward long service means that on average there is a cross-subsidy passing from young workers, who get less than their current marginal revenue products, to older workers, who get more. However, the young workers have the encouragement of knowing that they themselves will eventually benefit from this cross-subsidy when they themselves become older workers. Thus, *ceteris paribus*, expectations of lifetime earnings will be the same for both groups.

Conclusion

Labour is the most important input into any modern firm. A hundred years ago it was just the manual effort of workers that was being hired. Today, however, the vast majority of workers are not hired for their physical strength. Rather they are hired for their mental skills. Today brainpower rather than muscle power drives business success.

Brainpower is a much more complicated input to manage than was muscle power. The mental ability of potential new employees is difficult to assess and the effort of brain

workers is hard to monitor accurately. Yet the success of a firm in the long term depends crucially upon selecting, keeping, and motivating a stock of corporate brainpower. The institutions and practices discussed in this section have evolved to provide the structure within which a company's most talented employees are nurtured, motivated, and developed.

Summary

Wage differentials

■ Equilibrium wage differentials can arise among jobs because (a) each requires different degrees of physical or mental abilities, (b) each requires different amounts of human capital acquired through costly formal education or on-the-job training, (c) some jobs are closed to people who could fill them as a result of discrimination, and (d) the factor markets related to different jobs have different competitive structures.

■ In perfectly competitive factor markets wages are set by demand and supply and there is no unemployment in equilibrium. In monopsonistic markets wages and employment are less than their competitive levels, but there is no unemployment in equilibrium.

■ If a union enters a perfectly competitive market, it can raise wages above the competitive level at the cost of lowering employment and creating a pool of persons who would like to work at the union wage but cannot. If a union enters a monopsonistic labour market, it can raise wages *and* employment to the competitive level. If it raises wages beyond that point, employment will fall.

■ Unions and professional associations can sometimes restrict the supply of labour and thereby achieve wages above the competitive equilibrium without creating a pool of unemployed.

■ Minimum-wage laws have a similar effect to the setting of wages by unions. If the market was monopsonistic before the minimum wage is imposed, wages *and* employment can be raised. If it was competitive, wages can be raised only at the expense of increased unemployment.

Unions

■ Modern unions are organized either on trade or on industrial lines, and they bargain either in open or closed shops. Collective bargaining between a union with monopoly power and firms with monopsony power can lead to a wide range of possible outcomes depending on factors other than demand and supply.

Heterogeneity, incentives, and monitoring costs

■ Real-world employment is complicated by the fact that

labour is heterogeneous but the full characteristics of individual workers are hard to discern.

■ Many employment contracts are relational contracts, which do not specify in detail what workers have to do. This creates the potential for principal–agent problems, where the hired employees act, in part, in their own interest rather than that of the employer.

■ Solutions to the principal–agent problem involve some combination of incentives and monitoring.

■ Most skilled, managerial, and professional workers now find themselves in an internal labour market that has some of the characteristics of a tournament. Here the main incentive for lower- and middle-ranking staff is to achieve promotion. Higher pay generally attaches to more senior jobs, and the competition to gain promotion can be thought of as a tournament.

Topics for review

■ Causes of equilibrium wage differentials
■ Human capital
■ Formal education and on-the-job training
■ Wage differentials due to departure from perfect competition on the demand and the supply sides of labour markets
■ The significance of unions
■ Relational contracts
■ Principal–agent problems in labour markets
■ Efficiency wages
■ Signalling in the labour market
■ Internal and tournament labour markets

Questions for discussion

1 During the late 1980s and early 1990s British industry underwent a restructuring that eliminated many middle-management jobs. As a result, a relatively large group of workers in their forties and fifties were thrown back into

the job market. Many of these people had difficulty finding new work and attributed this problem to age discrimination. What are some factors *other than prejudice* that could place such workers at a competitive disadvantage relative to their younger counterparts?

2 This chapter discusses several supply-side origins of discrimination in the labour market. Recall from Chapter 14 that the demand for a factor of production is equal to that factor's marginal revenue product. In the light of this can you identify any source of discrimination that might originate on the demand side of the labour market?

3 Use this chapter's analysis of minimum-wage laws, and of heterogeneity and asymmetric knowledge, to predict as many effects as you can, favourable and unfavourable, of raising the typical wage paid to 18–20-year-olds by 33 per cent through government intervention.

4 What are the characteristics and the advantages of internal and tournament-style labour markets?

5 How do moral hazard, adverse selection, and the principal–agent problem affect labour markets where labour is heterogeneous?

Chapter 16
Capital, Land, and Natural Resources

In this chapter we discuss the two important cases of physical capital and non-renewable resources. Resources that can be replaced, either by being manufactured, as is the case with machines, or by reproducing themselves, as do people or fish, are called **renewable resources**. Resources that cannot be replaced, such as fossil fuels, are called **non-renewable** or **exhaustible resources**. Physical capital and non-renewable resources are similar factors of production in that each is a stock of valuable things that gets used up in the process of producing goods and services. They are different in that physical capital can be replaced while non-renewable resources cannot. A new machine can always be created to replace one that wears out, but when a barrel of oil is used there is a permanent reduction in the world's total stock of oil.

Capital

The nation's capital stock consists of all those produced goods that are used in the production of other goods and services. Factories, machines, tools, computers, roads, bridges, houses, and railroads are but a few of the many examples. Because capital is a produced factor of production, it is a renewable resource.

The pure return on capital

To calculate the income going to capital, which we call the *return on capital*, we take the receipts from the sale of the output that the capital helps to make and subtract all variable costs of production. This gives us the **gross return on capital**.[1] It is convenient to divide this gross return into four components using concepts defined in Chapter 8 (see pages 117–20).

1. *Depreciation* is an allowance for the decrease in the value of a capital good over time resulting from its use in production and its obsolescence. Most theories take depreciation to occur at a constant rate, independent of use.

2. The *pure return on capital* is the amount that capital could earn in a riskless investment in equilibrium. When expressed as a return per £1 worth of capital invested, the result is called the **pure rate of interest**.

3. The *risk premium* compensates the owners for the actual risks of the enterprise.

4. *Pure* or *economic profit* is the residual after all other deductions have been made from the gross return. It may be positive, negative, or zero.

The *gross return* on capital is the sum of these four items. The *net return* is the sum of the last three—that is, the gross return minus depreciation.

In a competitive economy positive and negative pure profits are a signal that resources should be reallocated, because earnings exceed opportunity costs in some lines of production and fall short of costs elsewhere. Economic profits are thus a product of disequilibrium.

To study the return to capital in its simplest form, we consider an economy that is in equilibrium with respect to the allocation of existing factors of production among their possible uses. Thus, economic profits are zero in every productive activity. This does not mean that the owners of capital get nothing; it means only that the gross return to capital does not include an element signalling the need to reallocate resources. The *equilibrium* net return on capital is composed of components 2 and 3 minus 1.

---

[1] This simplified example assumes that capital is the only fixed factor of production.

To simplify things further at the outset, we deal with a world of perfect certainty: everyone knows what the return to an existing new unit of capital will be in any of its possible uses. Since there is no risk, the gross return to capital does not include a risk premium.

We have now simplified to the point where the net return to capital is all pure return (item 2 on the above list), while the gross return is pure return plus depreciation (items 1 and 2). Our study is directed at understanding what determines this pure return on capital.

Do we now have a case that is too unrealistic to be interesting? The answer is no. All we have done is to focus on the pure return to capital. This is the return that varies from time to time and from place to place under the influences of economic forces. Risk and disequilibrium differentials are merely additions to that pure return.[2]

Implications of durability

Next we must consider an important complication that arises because factors of production are durable—a machine lasts for years, a labourer for a lifetime, and land more or less for ever. *It is convenient to think of a factor's lifetime as being divided into the shorter periods that we refer to as production periods, or rental periods.* The present time is the current period. Future time is one, two, three, and so on, periods hence.

The durability of factors makes it necessary to distinguish between the factor itself and the flow of services that it provides in a given production period. We can, for example, rent the use of a piece of land for some period of time, or we can buy the land outright. This distinction is just a particular instance of the general distinction between flows and stocks that we first encountered in Box 3.1 on page 36.

Although what follows applies to any durable factor, applications to capital are of most importance, so we limit the discussion to capital. Box 16.1 discusses some of these issues as they apply to labour.

If a firm hires a piece of capital equipment for some period of time—for example, one lorry for one month—it pays a price for the privilege. If the firm buys the lorry outright, it pays a different (and higher) price for the purchase. Consider in turn each of these prices.

Rental price

The *rental price of capital* is the amount that a firm pays to obtain the services of a capital good for a given period of time. The rental price of one week's use of a piece of capital is analogous to the weekly wage rate that is the price of hiring the services of labour.

Just as a profit-maximizing firm operating in competitive markets continues to hire labour until its marginal revenue product (*MRP*) equals its wage, so will the firm go on hiring capital until its *MRP* equals its rental price, which we call *R*. Since in a competitive market all firms will face the same rental price, all firms that are in equilibrium will have the same *MRP* of capital.

A capital good may also be used by the firm that owns it. In this case the firm does not pay out any rental fee. However, the rental price is the amount that the firm could charge if it leased its capital to another firm. It is thus the *opportunity cost* to the firm of using the capital good itself. This rental price is the *implicit* price that reflects the value to the firm of the services of its own capital that it uses during the current production period.

Whether the firm pays the rental price explicitly or calculates it as an implicit cost of using its own capital, the

---

[2] We are implicitly assuming a constant price level. Under inflationary conditions we need to distinguish the nominal return on capital, where everything is measured in nominal monetary units, from the real return, where nominal values are deflated by a price index. This distinction is considered in detail in Chapter 3.

Box 16.1 The rental and purchase price of labour

If you wish to farm a piece of land, you can buy it yourself, or you can rent it for a specific period of time. If you want to set up a small business, you can buy your office and equipment, or you can rent them. The same is true for all capital and all land; a firm often has the option of either buying or renting.

Exactly the same would be true for labour if we lived in a slave society. You could buy a slave to be your assistant, or you could rent the services either of someone else's slave or of a free person. Fortunately, slavery is illegal throughout most of today's world. As a result, the labour markets that we know deal only in the services of labour; we do not go to a labour market to buy a worker, only to hire his or her services.

You can, however, buy the services of a labourer for a long period of time. In professional sports, multi-year contracts are common, and ten-year con-

tracts are not unknown. The late Herbert von Karajan was made conductor for life of the Berlin Philharmonic Orchestra. Publishers sometimes tie up their authors in multi-book contracts, and film and television production firms often sign up their actors on long-term contracts. In all cases of such *personal service contracts*, the person is not a slave, because his or her personal rights and liberties are protected by law. The purchaser of the long-term contract is none the less buying ownership of the person's services for an extended period of time. The price of the contract will reflect the person's expected earnings over the contract's lifetime. If the contract is transferable, the owner can sell these services for a lump sum or rent them out for some period. As with land and capital goods, the price paid for this *stock* of labour services depends on the expected rental prices over the contract period.

profit-maximizing firm equates the rental price of a capital good over the current production period to its marginal revenue product.

Purchase price

The price that a firm pays to buy a capital good is called the *purchase price of capital*. When a firm buys such a good outright, it obtains the good's expected marginal revenue product over its lifetime. The price that the firm is willing to pay is, naturally enough, related to the total value that it places now on this stream of *expected* receipts over future time-periods.

The term 'expected' emphasizes that the firm is usually uncertain about the prices at which it will be able to sell its outputs in the future. For the sake of simplicity we assume that the firm knows the future *MRP*s.

Present value of future returns

Consider the stream of future income that is provided by a capital good. How much is that stream worth *now*? How much would someone be willing to pay now to buy the right to receive that flow of future payments? The answer is called the good's *present value*. In general, **present value** (*PV*) refers to the value *now* of one or more payments to be received *in the future*.

Present value of a single future payment

One period hence To study present value, we start with the simplest possible case. How much would a firm be prepared to pay *now* to purchase a capital good that will produce a single marginal physical product valued at £100 in one year's time, after which time the good will be useless? One way to answer this question is to discover how much the firm would have to lend out in order to have £100 a year from now. Suppose for the moment that the interest rate is 5 per cent, which means that £1.00 invested today will be worth £1.05 in one year's time.[3]

If we use *PV* to stand for this unknown amount, we can write *PV*(1.05) = £100. (The left-hand side of this equation means *PV* multiplied by 1.05.) Thus, *PV* = £100/1.05 = £95.24. This tells us that the present value of £100, receivable in one year's time, is £95.24 when the interest rate is 5 per cent. Anyone who lends out £95.24 for one year at 5 per cent interest will get back £95.24 plus £4.76 in interest, which makes £100 in total. When we calculate this present value, the interest rate is used to *discount* (i.e. reduce to its present value) the £100 to be received one year hence. The maximum price that a firm would be willing to pay for this capital good is £95.24 (assuming that the interest rate relevant to the firm is 5 per cent).

To see why, let us start by assuming that firms are offered the capital good at some other price. Say that the good is offered at £98. If, instead of paying this amount for the capital good, a firm lends its £98 out at 5 per cent interest, it would have at the end of one year more than the £100 that the capital good will produce. (At 5 per cent interest, £98 yields £4.90 in interest, which, together with the principal, makes £102.90.) Clearly, no profit-maximizing firm would pay £98—or, by the same reasoning, any sum in excess of £95.24—for the capital good. It could do better by using its funds in other ways.

Now say that the good is offered for sale at £90. A firm could borrow £90 to buy the capital good and would pay £4.50 in interest on its loan. At the end of the year, the good yields £100. When this is used to repay the £90 loan and the £4.50 in interest, £5.50 is left as profit to the firm. Clearly it would be worthwhile for a profit-maximizing firm to buy the good at a price of £90 or, by the same argument, at any price less than £95.24.

The actual present value that we have calculated depended on our assuming that the interest rate was 5 per cent. What if the interest rate is 7 per cent? At that interest rate the present value of the £100 receivable in one year's time would be £100/1.07 = £93.46.

These examples are easy to generalize. In both cases we have found the present value by dividing the sum that is receivable in the future by 1 plus the rate of interest.[4] In general, the present value of £*R* one year hence at an interest rate of *i* per year is

$$PV = \frac{R}{(1+i)}. \tag{1}$$

Several periods hence Now we know how to calculate the present value of a single sum that is receivable one year hence. The next step is to ask what would happen if the sum were receivable at a later date. What, for example, is the present value of £100 to be received *two* years hence when the interest rate is 5 per cent? This is £100/(1.05 × 1.05) = £90.70. We can check this by seeing what would happen if £90.70 were lent out for two years. In the first year the loan would earn an interest of (0.05)(£90.70) = £4.54, and hence after one year the firm would receive £95.24. In the second year the interest would be earned on this entire amount; interest earned in the second year would equal (0.05)(£95.24) = £4.76. Hence in two years the firm would have £100. (The payment of interest in the second year on the interest income earned in the first year is known as *compound interest*.)

---

[3] The analysis in the rest of this chapter assumes *annual* compounding of interest.

[4] Notice that in this type of formula the interest rate, *i*, is expressed as a decimal fraction; for example, 7 per cent is expressed as 0.07, so (1 + *i*) equals 1.07.

In general, the present value of £R after t years at i per cent is

$$PV = \frac{R}{(1 + i)^t}. \qquad (2)$$

All that this formula does is discount the sum, R, by the interest rate, i, repeatedly, once for each of the t periods that must pass until the sum becomes available. If we look at the formula, we see that the higher i or t is, the higher is the whole term $(1 + i)^t$. This term, however, appears in the denominator, so PV is *negatively* related to both i and t.

The formula $PV = R/(1 + i)^t$ shows that the present value of a given sum payable in the future will be smaller the more distant the payment date and the higher the rate of interest.

Present value of a stream of future payments

Now consider the present value of a stream of receipts that continues indefinitely, as might the *MRP* of a very long-lived piece of capital. At first glance that PV might seem very high, because the total amount received grows without reaching any limit as time passes. The previous section suggests, however, that people will not value the far-distant money payments very highly.

To find the PV of £100 a year, payable for ever, we ask how much you would have to invest now, at an interest rate of i per cent per year, to obtain £100 each year. This is simply $iPV = £100$, where i is the interest rate and PV the investment required. Dividing through by i shows the present value of the stream of £100 a year for ever to be

$$PV = \frac{£100}{i}. \qquad (3)$$

For example, if the interest rate were 10 per cent, the present value would be £1,000. This merely says that £1,000 invested at 10 per cent yields £100 per year, for ever. Notice that, as in the previous sections, PV is negatively related to the rate of interest: the higher the interest rate, the less is the present value of the stream of future payments.

In the text we have concentrated on finding the present value of amounts available in the future. Box 16.2 reverses the process and discusses the future value of sums available in the present.

Conclusions

From the foregoing discussion we can put together the following important propositions about the rental and purchase prices of capital.

1. The rental price of capital paid in each period is the flow of net receipts that the capital good is expected to produce during that period, that is, the marginal revenue product of the capital good.

Box 16.2 The future value of a present sum

In the text we have concentrated on the present value of amounts to be received in the future. We can, however, turn the question around and ask, 'What is the future value of an amount of money that is available in the present?'

Assume that you have £100 available to you today. What will that sum be worth next year? If you lend it out at 5 per cent, you will have £105 in one year. Letting PV stand for the sum you have now and FV for the value of the sum in the future, we have $FV = PV(1.05)$ in this case. Writing the interest rate as we have in the text, we get

$$FV = PV(1 + i).$$

If we divide through by $(1 + i)$, we get equation (1) in the text. (In the text we denote the future value by R.)

Next, if we let the sum build up by reinvesting the interest each year, we get

$$FV = PV(1 + i)^t.$$

If we divide both sides by $(1 + i)^t$, we get equation (2) in the text.

This tells us that what we did in the text is reversible. If we have an amount of money today, we can figure out what it will be worth if it is invested at compounded interest for some number of future periods. Similarly, if we are going to have some amount of money at some future date, we can figure out how much we would need to invest today to get that amount at the specified date in the future.

Our argument tells us that the two sums, PV and FV, are linked by the compound interest expression $(1 + i)^t$. To go from the present to the future, we *multiply* PV by the interest expression, and to go from the future to the present we *divide* FV by the interest expression.

The so-called rule of 72 is a convenient way of going from PV to FV by finding out how long it takes for FV to become twice the size of PV at any given interest rate. According to the rule, the time it takes for any amount to double in size is given approximately by $72/100i$. So, for example, if i is 0.1 (an interest rate of 10 per cent), any present sum doubles in value in $72/10 = 7.2$ years.

---

2. The maximum price that a firm would pay to purchase a capital good is the discounted present value of the flow of net receipts (i.e. the rental values) that the good is expected to produce over its lifetime.

3. The maximum purchase price that a firm would pay for a capital good is positively associated with its rental price and negatively associated with both the interest rate and the amount of time that the owner must wait for payments to accrue.

Equilibrium of the firm

When putting a present value on future income flows, each firm will discount them at a rate that reflects its own opportunity cost of capital, often called its *internal rate of discount.* With perfect capital markets in which the firm can borrow all that it needs, the internal rate of discount will equal the market rate of interest (suitably adjusted for risk in each case). The evidence suggests, however, that most firms do not face perfect capital markets and have internal rates of return that exceed market rates. They thus have internal rates of discount that exceed the relevant market rate of interest. The general points made in the text are not affected by this complication, as long as i is interpreted in each case to mean the 'appropriate rate of discount'. In what follows we assume, for simplicity, that firms face perfect capital markets so that the internal rate of discount is equal to the market rate of interest.

In adjusting to market forces, an individual firm faces a given interest rate and given purchase prices of capital goods. The firm can vary the quantity of capital that it employs, and, as a result, the marginal revenue product of its capital varies. The law of diminishing returns tells us that the more capital the firm uses, the lower its capital's *MRP*.

The decision to purchase capital

A firm is deciding whether or not to add to its capital stock. It can borrow (and lend) money at an interest rate of 10 per cent per year. The first thing the firm needs to do is to estimate the expected marginal revenue product of the new piece of capital over its lifetime. Then it discounts this at the appropriate rate, 10 per cent in this example, to find the present value of that stream of receipts the machine will create.[5] Let us say it is £5,000.

The present value, by its construction, tells us how much any flow of future receipts is worth now. If the firm can buy the machine for less than its *PV*, this is a good buy. If it must pay more, the machine is not worth its price.

It is always worthwhile for a firm to buy another unit of capital whenever the present value of the stream of future *MRP*s that the capital provides exceeds its purchase price.

The size of the firm's capital stock

The *MRP* of each addition to the firm's capital stock declines as the amount of capital is increased. The firm will go on adding to its capital stock until the *present value* of the flow of *MRP*s conferred by the last unit added is equal to the purchase price of that unit. The firm then has its equilibrium amount of capital.

The equilibrium capital stock of the firm is such that the present value of the stream of net income that is provided by the marginal unit of capital is equal to its purchase price.

Now let the firm be in equilibrium with respect to its capital stock and ask what would cause it to buy more capital. Given the price of the machines, anything that in-

Figure 16.1 The firm's demand curve for capital
The firm's desired capital stock is negatively related to the rate of interest. The lower is the interest rate, the higher is the present value of any given stream of marginal revenue products, and hence the more capital the firm will wish to use.

creases the present value of the flow of income that the machines produce will have that effect. Two things will do this job. First, the *MRP*s of the capital may rise. That will happen, for example, if technological changes make capital more productive so that each unit produces more than before. (This possibility is dealt with later in the chapter.) Second, the interest rate may fall, causing an increase in the present value of any given stream of future *MRP*s. For example, suppose that next year's *MRP* is £1,000. This has a *PV* of £909.09 when the interest rate is 10 per cent and £952.38 when the interest rate falls to 5 per cent.

So when the interest rate falls, the firm will wish to add to its capital stock. It will go on doing so until the decline in the *MRP*s of successive additions to its capital stock, according to the law of diminishing returns, reduces the present value of the *MRP*, at the new lower rate of interest, to the purchase price of the capital.

The size of a firm's desired capital stock increases when the rate of interest falls, and it decreases when the rate of interest rises.

This relationship is shown in Figure 16.1. It can be considered as the firm's demand curve for capital plotted against the interest rate. It shows how the desired stock of capital varies with the interest rate. (It is sometimes called the *marginal efficiency of capital curve.*)

---

[5] Suppose that the machine has an *MRP* of £1,000 each period. First, suppose the machine only lasts this period. The present value is then £1,000. Next, suppose it lasts two periods. The *PV* is then £1,000 + £1,000/1.10 = £1,909.09. If it lasts three periods, the *PV* is £1,000 + £1,000/1.10 + £1,000/(1.10)^2 = £2,735.53, and so on. Each additional period that it lasts produces an *MRP* of £1,000, but at a more and more distant date, so that the *present value* of that period's revenue gets smaller owing to heavier discounting. The details of the calculation do not need to concern us. We only need to know that such a present value can be calculated.

Equilibrium for the whole economy

The term **capital stock** refers to some aggregate amount of capital. The *firm's capital stock* has an *MRP*, showing the net increase in the firm's revenue when another unit of capital is added to its existing capital stock. The *economy's capital stock* also has a marginal revenue product; this is the addition to total national output (GDP) that is caused by adding another unit of capital to the economy's total stock. This capital stock also has an average product, which is total output divided by the total capital stock (i.e. the amount of output per unit of capital).

The same analysis that we used for one firm in the previous section applies to the whole economy. The lower the rate of interest, the higher is the desired stock of capital that all firms will wish to hold. Such a curve is shown as the economy's demand curve in Figure 16.2.

Short-run equilibrium

In the short run the economy's capital stock is given, but for the economy as a whole the interest rate is variable. Whereas the firm reaches equilibrium by altering its capital stock, the whole economy reaches equilibrium through variations in the interest rate.

For the economy as a whole the condition that the present value of the *MRP*s should equal the price of capital goods determines the equilibrium interest rate.

Let us see how this comes about. If the price of capital were less than the present value of its stream of future *MRP*s, it would be worthwhile for all firms to borrow money to invest in capital. For the economy as a whole, however, the stock of capital cannot be changed quickly. As a result, the main effect of this demand to borrow would be to push up the interest rate until the present value of the *MRP* equals the price of a unit of capital goods. Conversely, if the price of capital is above its present value, no one would wish to borrow money to invest in capital, and the rate of interest would fall. This is also illustrated in Figure 16.2.

Accumulation of capital in the long run

In an economy with positive saving, more capital is accumulated over time and the stock of capital grows slowly. As this happens, the *MRP* falls. This will cause the equilibrium interest rate to fall over time, as is also shown in Figure 16.2.

Changing technology in the very long run

In the very long run technology changes. As a result the capital stock becomes more productive as the old, obsolete capital is replaced by newer, more efficient capital. This shifts the *MRP* curve outward, which in turn tends to increase the equilibrium interest rate associated with any particular size of the capital stock. This, of course, is also the equilibrium return on capital. However, the accumulation

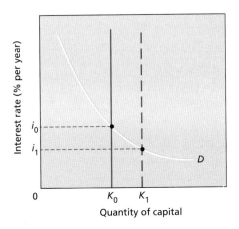

Figure 16.2 The equilibrium interest rate

In the short run the interest rate equates the demand for capital with its fixed supply. The economy's desired capital stock is negatively related to the interest rate, as shown by the curve D. In the short run, when the stock is K_0, the equilibrium interest rate is i_0. When the capital stock grows to K_1 in the long run, the equilibrium interest rate falls to i_1.

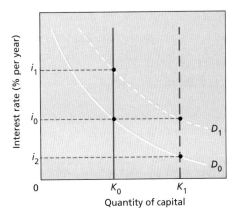

Figure 16.3 Changes in technology and the capital stock

Increases in technological knowledge and in the capital stock have opposite effects on the interest rate. The original demand curve D_0 and capital stock K_0 produce an interest rate of i_0. Technological improvements shift the desired capital stock curve to D_1 and, with a constant stock of capital, would raise the interest rate to i_1. However, the capital stock increases to K_1, which *ceteris paribus* would lower the interest rate to i_2. In the figure the two effects exactly offset each other, and the interest rate remains unchanged at i_0, where K_1 and D_1 intersect.

of capital moves the economy downward to the right along any given *MRP* curve, and that tends to lower the return on capital associated with any one *MRP* curve. The net effect on the return on capital of both of these changes may be to raise it, to lower it, or to leave it unchanged, as shown in Figure 16.3. The very-long-run effects of changing technology, combined with a growing capital stock, are studied further in Chapter 32.

So we see that the income going to capital is the pure rate of return (multiplied by the amount of capital in use), plus a risk premium, plus any pure profits or minus any pure losses. The pure return serves to allocate capital to its most productive uses. All uses that yield more than the pure rate of return (plus any necessary risk premium) will be exploited; all uses that earn less than the pure rate will not be taken up.

Non-renewable resources

The world's minerals and fossil fuels are examples of non-renewable resources; the total amount in existence is fixed. However, since some of the world's total stock is as yet undiscovered, the *known* stock of each resource is not fixed over time. New discoveries increase the known stock, and current use reduces it.

Are we exhausting our supply of non-renewable resources too quickly? Some people advocate conserving more of our resources to pass on to our children and grandchildren. Others are willing to let future generations take care of themselves. 'After all,' they argue, 'they will be richer than we are in any case.'

How does the price system regulate the use of a non-renewable resource? Does it lead to overly rapid exploitation? Does it lead to too much conservation of a resource, which may in any case be rendered less useful by future technological change?

Determining the rate of extraction

To focus on the basic issues, it helps to begin with a few simplifying assumptions. First, assume that all the petroleum in existence has already been discovered, so that every unit that is used permanently diminishes the stock by one unit. Second, assume that many different firms own the land that contains the oil supply, so that each must accept the world price as given. Third, assume that their current extraction costs are virtually zero. They have invested money in discovering the oil, drilling wells, and laying pipelines. All they have to do is turn their taps on, and the oil flows at any desired rate to the petroleum markets.

The last two of these assumptions are close to reality for the oil industry. Although large groups of producers, such as OPEC, can influence the price of oil by agreeing to alter the rate of current production, no one producer has that kind of market power—and even OPEC's power is quite

limited over any longish period of time. Also, most of the costs of producing oil are incurred discovering fields, proving them, drilling wells, and building such transport facilities as pipelines and oil ports. Once all this has been done, the variable cost of producing another barrel from established fields is quite small. The only one of our three assumptions that is far from the mark for oil is that the total existing supply has already been discovered and developed. As we will see, much new oil is continually being discovered. This has important consequences, but to understand them we need first to see what happens with any non-renewable resource whose total supply is already known and available for current production.

Optimal firm behaviour

What should each firm do if it wishes to maximize its profits? It could extract all of its oil in a great binge of production this year, or it could husband the resource for some future rainy day and produce nothing this year. In practice, it is likely to adopt some intermediate policy, producing and selling some oil this year and holding stocks of it in the ground for extraction in future years. But *how much* should it extract this year and *how much* should it carry over for future years?

Its profit-maximizing course of action depends on three things: the current market price, the price the firm expects to rule next year, and the interest rate. Let us see why.

Each firm can do two things with its oil. First, it can leave it in the ground to be available for extraction next year. If the price rises next year, the firm will have gained the difference between the current price and next year's price. Second, it can extract and sell the oil at the current price, yielding revenue this year. How does the firm compare these two amounts, one earned now and one available next year?

There are two ways of arriving at the answer.[6] One way

---

[6] Box 16.2 shows that these two methods are equivalent. In the text we use the second method.

is to take the expected gain in value of a barrel of oil over the coming year and discount that amount to get its present value today. The other is to turn the value of the revenue from the sale of the oil now into an amount available next year that can be compared with the estimated value of the oil in the ground next year. If the money earned by selling the oil now is invested at the current rate of interest it will be increased in value next year by the interest that it earns. The firm will decide to extract the oil now or leave it in the ground depending on which of two values is the greater. The first is the amount it could earn by selling the oil now and investing the revenue for a year. The second is the increase in the value of the oil if it is left in the ground. To illustrate this important result, assume that next year's price is expected to be £1.05 per barrel and that the rate of interest is 5 per cent. Now suppose the current price is £1.04 per barrel. Clearly, it pays to produce more now, since the £1.04 that is earned by selling a barrel now can be invested to yield approximately £1.09 (£1.04 × 1.05), which is more than the £1.05 that the oil would be worth in a year's time if it is left in the ground. Next, suppose that the current price is £0.90 per barrel. Now it pays to reduce production, since oil left in the ground will be worth 16.66 per cent more next year ((1.05/0.90) × 100). Extracting it this year and investing the money will produce a gain of only 5 per cent. Finally, let the current price be £1.00. Now oil producers make the same amount of money whether they leave £1.00 worth of oil in the ground to be worth £1.05 next year or sell the oil for £1.00 this year and invest the proceeds at a 5 per cent interest rate.

The price response

How will the world market price for oil respond if all firms decide their current production by making the comparison just outlined?

First, suppose the price of oil is expected to rise by less than the interest rate. Oil extracted and sold now will have a higher value than oil left in the ground. All firms will, therefore, extract more oil this year. But although no one firm is large enough to affect the world price, the price will react when they *all* decide to produce more. Because the demand curve for oil has a negative slope, raising the world extraction rate will lower the current price. Production will rise, and the current price will fall until the expected price rise between this year and next year is equal to the interest rate.[7] The firms will then be indifferent at the margin between producing another barrel this year and leaving that barrel in the ground for next year. (Of course, next year each firm can make the same calculation and decide to leave some of its oil in the ground for a further year.)

Second, suppose that the price is expected to rise by more than the interest rate. Firms will prefer to leave their oil in the ground, where they earn a higher return than

could be earned by selling the oil this year and investing the proceeds at the current interest rate. Thus, firms will cut their current rate of production, which will raise this year's price. When the current price has risen so that the gap between the current price and next year's expected price is equal to the interest rate, firms will put equal value on a barrel of oil extracted and one left in the ground.

In a perfectly competitive industry the profit-maximizing equilibrium for a completely non-renewable resource occurs when the last unit currently produced earns just as much for each firm as it would if it had been left in the ground for future use.

The actual price

What we have established so far determines the pattern of prices over time: if stocks are given and unchanging, prices should rise over time at a rate equal to the rate of interest. But what about the level of prices? Will they start low and rise to only moderate levels over the next few years, or will they start high and then soar to even higher levels? The answer depends on the total stock of the resource that is available (and, where some new discoveries are possible, on the expected additions to that stock in the future). The scarcer is the resource relative to the demand for it, the higher its market price will be at the outset.

Profit-maximizing behaviour on the part of many producers will cause the resource's price to rise over time at a rate equal to the rate of interest, while the height of that whole price profile will depend on the resource's scarcity relative to current demand.

Optimal social behaviour

Petroleum is a valuable social resource. The value to consumers of one more barrel produced now is the price that they would be willing to pay for it, which is the current market price of the oil (in this example assumed to be £1.00). If the oil is extracted this year and the proceeds are invested at the rate of interest (the proceeds might be used to buy a new capital good), they will produce £1.05 worth of valuable goods next year. If that barrel of oil is not produced this year and is left in the ground for extraction next year, its value to consumers at that time will be next year's price of oil. It is not socially optimal, therefore, to leave the oil in the ground unless it will be worth £1.05 to consumers next year. More generally, society obtains

---

[7] The discussion is simplified by assuming next year's expected price to be given. The decision to produce more this year may also affect next year's price. If the total supplies are small, next year's expected price might rise. The argument proceeds exactly as in the text, except that the equilibrium gap between two prices is achieved by the present price falling and the expected future price rising, rather than by having next year's expected price remaining constant and all the adjustment coming through this year's price.

increases in the value of what is available for consumption by conserving units of a non-renewable resource only if the price of the units is expected to rise at a rate that is at least as high as the interest rate.

How much of a non-renewable resource is it socially optimal to consume now? The US economist Harold Hotelling (1895–1973) provided the answer to this question many years ago. His answer is very simple, yet it specifically determines the optimal profile of prices over the years. It is interesting that the answer applies to all non-renewable resources. It does not matter whether there is a large or a small demand, whether that demand is elastic or inelastic, or whether the remaining stock is large or small. In all cases the answer is the same:

The socially optimal rate of extraction of any non-renewable resource should be such that its price increases at a rate equal to the interest rate.

For example, if the rate of interest is 4 per cent, then the price of the resource should be rising at 4 per cent per year. If it is rising by more, there is too much current extraction; if it is rising by less, then there is not enough current extraction. We have already seen that this is the rate of extraction that will be produced by a competitive industry.

The actual rate of extraction

What about the actual rate at which the resource will be extracted *if the competitive market fulfils Hotelling's rule for optimal extraction rates*? The answer to this question *does* depend on market conditions. Specifically, it depends on the position and the slope of the demand curve. If the quantity demanded at all prices is small, the rate of extraction will be small. The larger the quantity demanded at each price, the higher the rate of extraction will tend to be.

Now consider the influence of the slope of the demand curve. A highly inelastic demand curve suggests that there are few substitutes and that purchasers are prepared to pay large sums rather than do without the resource. This will produce a relatively even rate of extraction, with small reductions in each period being sufficient to drive up the price at the required rate. A relatively elastic demand curve suggests that people can easily find substitutes once the price rises. This will encourage a great deal of consumption now and a rapidly diminishing amount over future years, since large reductions in consumption are needed to drive the price up at the required rate.

Figure 16.4 illustrates this working of the price mechanism with a simple example in which the whole stock of oil of 200,000 barrels must be consumed in only two periods, this year and next year. At a 10 per cent interest rate the price in the second year must be 10 per cent higher than the price in the first year. With a relatively elastic curve this requires that the quantities differ substantially over the two years, while on the relatively inelastic curve the quantity in the second year is only slightly smaller than in the first year. (Because the two curves are drawn on the same scale, the steeper curve is also the more inelastic at each price.) The general point is as follows:

The more inelastic the demand curve, the more even the rate of extraction (and hence the rate of use) will be over the years; the more elastic the demand curve, the more uneven the rate of extraction will be over the years.

(i) Relatively flat demand curve

(ii) Relatively steep demand curve

Figure 16.4 The extraction rate for non-renewable resources

The shape of the demand curve determines the extraction profile over time. The two conditions—that the whole supply be used over two periods and that the price rise by 10 per cent between the two periods—determine price and quantities. In part (i), with a relatively flat demand curve, quantity and price are 120,000 barrels at £1.00 in the first period and 80,000 barrels at £1.10 in the second period. In part (ii), with a relatively steep demand curve, the values are 104,000 barrels at £1.50 in the first period and 96,000 barrels at £1.65 in the second.

An elastic demand curve will lead to a large consumption now and a rapid fall in consumption over the years. An inelastic demand curve will lead to a smaller consumption now and a less rapid fall in consumption over the years. In each case, quantities consumed are varying over time in such a way as to equate the rate of price increase with the rate of interest. The difference between the two lies in the different patterns of quantity variation that are required along demand curves of different slopes if prices are to rise at the same rate.

Rents to natural resources

The incomes earned by the owners of the oil resources are *rents* in the sense defined in Chapter 14. This is because the owners would be willing to produce the oil at a price that covers the direct costs of extraction, which in this example is zero. (In real cases the direct cost of extracting the resource is positive, and the rent is the income earned above that amount.) Thus the incomes they do earn over their costs of extraction are not needed to get the product produced, since any non-zero price would do that. They do, however, fulfil the important function of determining the extraction rate, and hence the use of the resource, *over time*. As we have seen, the price profile determines the use of the resource and hence the amount of resources allocated to its production *over time*.

The price system as a conservation mechanism

In the above discussion we see the price system playing its now familiar role of co-ordinator. By following private profit incentives, firms are led to conserve the resource in a manner that is consistent with society's needs.

The role of rising prices

We have seen that from society's viewpoint the optimal extraction pattern of a totally non-renewable resource occurs when its price rises each year at a rate equal to the interest rate. The rising price fulfils a number of useful functions.

First, the rising price encourages conservation. As the resource becomes scarcer and its price rises, purchasers will be motivated to be more and more economical in its use. Uses of oil that yield low returns may be abandoned altogether, and uses that yield high returns will be pursued only as long as their value at the margin is enough to compensate for the high price.

Second, the rising price encourages the discovery of new sources of supply—at least in cases in which the world supply is not totally fixed and already known. Unlike our simple example given above, the world's supply of petro-

leum is not completely known. High prices, when they do occur, encourage exploration, which adds to known reserves; low prices discourage it.

Third, the rising price encourages innovation. New products that will do the same job may be developed, as well as new processes that use alternative resources.

How might the price system fail?

Three basic ways in which the price system might fail to produce the optimal rate of resource extraction are discussed below. We look at examples of each of these and ask if each justifies government intervention.[8]

Ignorance   Private owners might not have sufficient knowledge to arrive at the best estimate of the rate at which prices will rise. If they do not know the world stocks of their commodity and the current extraction rate, they may be unable to estimate the rate of the price rise and thus will not know when to raise or lower their current rates of extraction. For example, if all firms mistakenly think that prices will not rise greatly in the future, they will all produce too much now and conserve too little for future periods.

The government could not do better, unless it had access to some special knowledge that private firms do not possess. If it did have such knowledge, the government could make it public, leaving the firms to do the rest. In practice whatever knowledge does exist about both the proven reserves of non-renewable resources and their current extraction rates is usually freely and openly available.

Inadequate property rights   Some non-renewable resources have the characteristics of what is called a *common property resource*. Such property cannot be exclusively owned and controlled by one person or firm. For example, one person's oil-bearing land may be adjacent to another person's, and the underground supplies may be interconnected. If one firm holds off producing now, the oil may end up being extracted by the neighbour. In such cases, which are sometimes encountered with petroleum, there is a tendency for a firm to extract the resource too fast, because a firm's oil that has been left in the ground may not be available to that firm at a future date. (Similar issues arise with any common property resource such as fishing grounds, and they are discussed in more detail in Chapter 18.)

This problem arises because of inadequate property rights. Since the resource will be worth more in total value when it is exploited at the optimal extraction rate than when small firms exploit it too quickly, there will be an incentive for individual owners to combine until each self-contained source of supply is owned by only one firm. After that the problem of overexploitation will no longer

---

[8] This discussion partly anticipates Chapter 18, which studies market successes and market failures in more general terms.

arise. Government ownership is not necessary to achieve this result. What is needed, at most, is intervention to ensure that markets can work to provide the optimal size of individual units so that the private owners can apply proper extraction management.

Political uncertainty can provide another source of inadequate property rights. For example, the owners of the resource may fear that a future election or a revolution will establish a government that will confiscate their property. They will then be motivated to exploit the resource too quickly, on the grounds that certain revenue now is more valuable than highly uncertain revenue in the future. The current rate of extraction will tend to increase until the expected rate of price rise exceeds the interest rate by a sufficient margin to compensate for the risks that supplies left in the ground may be confiscated at some future date. The problem arises here because property rights are not secure over time.

Unequal market and social values   Normally in a competitive world the real interest rate indicates the rate at which it is optimal to discount the future over the present. Society's investments are valuable if they earn the market rate of return, and are not valuable if they earn less (because the resources could be used in other ways to produce more value to consumers). In certain circumstances, however, the government may have reasons to adopt a different rate of discount. It is then said that the *social rate of discount*—the discount rate that is appropriate to the society as a whole—differs from the private rate, as indicated by the market rate of interest. In such circumstances there is reason for the government to intervene to alter the rate at which the private firms would exploit the resource. If the government owns the resources, it must be careful to use the social rate of discount in all of its decisions about exploiting the resource.

Critics are often ready to assume that profit-mad producers will despoil most non-renewable resources by using them up too quickly. They argue for government intervention to conserve the resource by slowing its rate of extraction. Yet unless the social rate of discount is *below* the private rate, there is no clear social gain in holding the resources in the ground.

Since governments must worry about their short-term popularity and their chances of re-election, there is no presumption that government intervention will slow down the rate of extraction, even if the social discount rate is below the private rate. Instead, governments often extract resources faster than would free markets. This is because governments, being concerned primarily with the next election, may have a rate of discount much higher than either the social or the market rate.

A good example is provided by the Hybernia oil field that lies off the Newfoundland coast of Canada. When development began, the costs of developing the field and extracting the oil exceeded its current market value. It would thus not have been developed under free-market conditions. Instead, Canadian taxpayers' money was used to produce oil whose market value was less than its full costs of production. If left in the ground, the field would one day have developed a positive value, if either the price of oil rose or the costs of production fell.

Actual price profiles

Many non-renewable resources do not seem to have the steadily rising profile of prices that the theory predicts. The price of petroleum, having been raised artificially by the OPEC cartel, returned in the late 1980s to an inflation-adjusted level that was at or a little below where it was in 1970, and has remained there ever since. The price of coal has not soared; nor has the price of iron ore.

In many cases the reason lies in the discovery of new supplies, which have prevented the total known stocks of many resources from being depleted. In the case of petroleum, for example, the ratio of known reserves to one year's consumption is no lower now than it was two or even four decades ago. Furthermore, most industry experts believe that large quantities of undiscovered oil still exist under both the land and the sea.

In these cases the amount firms spend on exploration depends on their expectations of future prices. Even a small rise in the expected price can lead to a large increase in exploration activity. As a result the proven supply rises. In such an industry the price behaves more like it would in a competitive industry with a very elastic long-run supply curve. Eventually, if an oil substitute is not developed, undiscovered supplies will diminish. Then the price will begin to behave as predicted by the theory of the pricing of non-renewable resources with completely fixed supplies.

In other cases the invention of new substitute products has unexpectedly reduced the demand for some of these resources. For example, plastics have replaced metals in many uses, fibre optics have replaced copper wire in many types of message transmission, and newer fuels have replaced coal in many of its uses. The interesting case of the coal industry's decline in the face of massive unused resources is discussed in Box 16.3.

In yet other cases the reason is to be found in government pricing policy. An important example of this type is the use of *non-renewable* water for irrigation in much of the United States. Vast underground reserves of water lie in aquifers beneath many areas of North America. Although these reserves were accumulated over millennia, they are being used up at a rate that will exhaust them in a matter of decades. The water is often supplied by government water authorities at prices that cover only a small part of total costs and that do not rise steadily to reflect the dwindling stocks.

Such a constant-price policy for *any* non-renewable

Box 16.3 The abdication of king coal

The British coal industry has witnessed a dramatic decline in output and employment stretching over most of this century. Many have argued that this decline must be the outcome of a political decision designed to reduce the power of the National Union of Mineworkers. However, the underlying economics of the industry has had more influence on events than have political vendettas.

Peak output for the coal industry was achieved immediately before the First World War, when 290 million tonnes were produced and over 1 million workers were employed. About a third of this output was exported. A significant decline in production during the inter-war period (1919–39) resulted from the loss of export markets. However, in 1955 output was still 225 million tonnes; there were 850 working collieries and nearly 750,000 miners.

Substitution in favour of oil and natural gas, combined with a sharp decline in demand for coal for domestic heating (following the Clean Air Act of 1956), caused coal output to decline to 125 million tonnes, produced in 133

pits by just over 150,000 workers, in 1975. Substitution towards cheaper imported coal, combined with greater use of other energy sources, including electricity imported from France and hydroelectric power, caused output to fall by 1991/2 to just over 30 million tonnes, produced by only 50 pits, employing fewer than 50,000 workers.

The main driving force behind this decline in demand for British coal was the availability of imported coal at a cheaper price. A second reason for the industry's decline is that coal is a greater producer of harmful gases than most alternative fuels. Furthermore, British coal has nearly twice the acid-rain-producing sulphur content of imported coal. Gas turbine generation produces about half the greenhouse gas emissions of coal. The high costs of building clean coal technology (such as flue gas desulphurization) will induce a continued decline in the already low demand for British coal.

Thus the decline in the British coal industry was the result of fundamental economic and environmental pressures.

---

resource creates three characteristic problems. First, the resource will be exhausted much faster than if price were to rise over time. A constant price will lead to a constant rate of extraction to meet the quantity demanded at that price until the resource is completely exhausted. Second, no signals go out to induce conservation, innovation, and exploration. Third, when the supply of the resource is finally exhausted, the adjustment will have to come all at once. If the price had risen steadily each year under free-market conditions, adjustment would have taken place little by little each year. The controlled price, however, gives no signal of the ever-diminishing stock of the resource until all at once the supplies run out. The required adjustment will then be much more painful than it would have been if it had been spread over time in response to steadily rising prices.

Summary

Capital

■ Because capital goods are durable, it is necessary to distinguish between the stock of capital goods and the flow of services provided by them, and thus between their purchase price and their rental price. The linkage between them relies on the ability to assign a present value to future returns. The present value of a future payment will be lower when the payment is more distant and the interest rate is higher.

■ The rental price of capital in each period equals its marginal revenue product in that period. It is the amount that is paid to obtain the flow of services that a capital good provides for a given period. The purchase price is the amount that is paid to acquire ownership of the capital, and in equilibrium it is equal to the present value of the future net income stream generated by the capital. This is the present value of capital's future stream of marginal revenue products.

■ An individual firm will invest in capital goods as long as the present value of the stream of future net incomes that

are provided by another unit of capital exceeds its purchase price. For a single firm and for the economy as a whole, the size of the total capital stock demanded varies negatively with the rate of interest.

Non-renewable resources

■ The socially optimal rate of exploitation for a completely non-renewable resource occurs when its price rises at a rate that is equal to the rate of interest. This is also the rate that will be established by a profit-maximizing, competitive industry.

■ Resources for which the demand is highly elastic will have a high rate of exploitation in the near future and a fairly rapid fall-off over time. Resources for which the demand is highly inelastic will have a lower rate of exploitation in the near future and a smaller fall-off over time.

■ Rising prices act as a conservation device by rationing the consumption over time according to people's preferences. As prices rise, conservation, discovery of new sources of supply, and innovation to reduce demand are all encouraged.

■ The price system can fail to produce optimal results if (a) people lack the necessary knowledge, (b) property rights are inadequate to protect supplies left for future use by their owners, or (c) the social rate of discount differs significantly from the market rate.

■ Controlling the price of a non-renewable resource at a constant level speeds up the rate of exploitation and removes the price incentives to react to the growing scarcity.

Topics for review

■ Rental price and purchase price of capital
■ Present value
■ The interest rate and the capital stock
■ Hotelling's rule
■ The role of rising prices of non-renewable resources

Questions for discussion

1 Suppose you are offered, free of charge, one from each of the following pairs of assets: (a) a perpetuity that pays £20,000 per year for ever, or an annuity that pays £100,000 per year for five years; (b) an oil-drilling company that earned £100,000 after corporate taxes last year, or British government bonds that paid £100,000 in interest last year;

(c) a 1 per cent share in a new company that has invested £10 million in a new cosmetic that is thought to appeal to middle-income women or a £100,000 bond that has been issued by the same company. What considerations would determine your choice in each case?

2 How would you go about evaluating the present value of each of the following? (a) the existing reserves of a relatively small oil company, (b) the total world reserves of an exhaustible natural resource with a known, completely fixed supply, (c) a long-term bond, issued by a very unstable Third World government, that promises to pay the bearer £1,000 per year for ever, (d) a lottery ticket that your neighbour bought for £10 which was one of one million tickets sold for a draw to be held in one year's time that will pay £2 million to the single winner.

3 A ten-year bond issued by a central African investment corporation pays £100 a year interest and sells for £400. What do you infer about the corporation's prospects? Divide the interest into its components such as the pure rate, the risk premium, etc.

4 List some resources that are renewable if they are exploited at one rate and non-renewable if they are exploited at other, higher rates.

5 Species that are on the verge of extinction—beluga whales, African elephants, mountain gorillas, and California condor—might be classified as non-renewable resources; once they disappear, there will be no regeneration. Does the market create appropriate incentives to ensure that extinction will not occur? How might market signals be devised to do so?

Chapter 17
Factor Market Theory in Action

In this chapter we illustrate the explanatory power of the theory of factor markets. We start by restating the basic outlines of the theory, which is variously called the theory of factor pricing or the theory of distribution. We then look at some of the impressive evidence, first, that market conditions do strongly influence factor prices and, second, that factors of production do respond to the price incentives created by factor markets. In doing this, we give a number of case studies in which factor market theory explains commonly observed events, some of which seem strange at first sight.

The theory restated

The previous chapters have developed the neoclassical theory of factor markets in several contexts, repeating what is basically the same analysis in applications to land, labour, and capital. This repetition helps to develop a 'feel' for the workings of the price system that is very important to the economist. It has the disadvantage, however, of making the theory appear to be more complex than it actually is. In fact, the whole theory depends on a very few basic hypotheses about the behaviour of factor owners and firms. Before going on, it will be useful to repeat its underlying structure.

The neoclassical theory of factor markets and income distribution maintains that factor prices can be explained by supply and demand. The theory of factor supply is based on the assumption that factors will move among occupations, industries, and places in search of the highest net advantage, taking both monetary and non-monetary rewards into account, until the net advantages in all possible uses are equalized. Because there are impediments to the mobility of factors, there may be lags in their response to changes in prices. The elasticity of supply will depend on what factor is being discussed and what time-horizon is being considered.

The demand side of the neoclassical theory is based on profit maximization and is called the marginal productivity theory (of factor demand). The demand for a factor is a derived demand. It depends for its existence on the demand for the product made by the factor. The elasticity of an industry's demand curve for a factor is higher in the long run than in the short run, since more substitution is possible the longer the time considered. Also, as we saw in

Chapter 3, the demand for any product made by the factor will itself be more elastic in the long run than in the short run—thus making the derived demand for the factors that it uses correspondingly more elastic.

In equilibrium *all* profit-maximizing firms will employ their variable factors up to the point at which the marginal unit of each type of factor adds as much to cost as to revenue. When these firms are *price-takers in the markets for their inputs*, they employ factors up to the point at which the price paid for the last unit of each factor equals the increase in revenue resulting from the sale of that factor's addition to output. When firms are *price-takers in the markets for their outputs*, the increase in revenue is the marginal physical product times the price; when firms face *negatively sloped demand curves* for their products, the increase in revenue is marginal physical product times marginal revenue.

The relations just described all hold in equilibrium. They apply to all firms that succeed in maximizing their profits and can be stated in two equivalent ways. First, a firm that is not equating the marginal revenue product of each of its factors with that factor's price is not maximizing its profits. Second, a firm that is maximizing its profits is necessarily equating each factor's price to its marginal revenue product, whether or not it knows it is doing so. The theory of factor demand thus stands or falls with the theory of profit maximization. It is merely an implication of profit maximization, and the only reason for spelling it out in detail is that this helps us to develop interesting and useful insights into the effects of various changes in the economy on the markets for factors of production.

When one thinks of all the heated arguments over the neoclassical theory of distribution, and of all the passionate denunciations and defences that it has occasioned over more than a century, it is surprising to observe how uncontroversial most of its predictions seem today. These propositions, which are supported by much evidence, do not seem the sort that would create heated debate. They are important since they frequently apply to practical issues of policy. Some of the strong feelings about the theory may have been aroused by the argument advanced by some past supporters that distributing income according to marginal product created a just distribution of income. There may also have been a feeling, no longer a real worry today, that there was something highly suspect, possibly demeaning, about reducing human behaviour to theories that can be expressed in impersonal mathematics.

One of the present authors recalls hearing, when he was a graduate student, a paper denouncing marginal productivity theory for reducing glorious and diverse human behaviour to two mere curves: the labour supply curve and the marginal revenue curve.

Such emotive criticisms are no longer taken seriously. Either the theory works or it does not. How well it works depends on how well it explains and predicts what we see happening in factor markets. If factor markets are to allocate the nation's productive resources effectively, as the theory says they do, two things are necessary. First, factor prices must be determined by the demand and supply condition in factor markets, changing in response to changes in these conditions. Second, factors must move in response to changes in their relative prices and earnings. We consider these in turn.

Market conditions determine factor prices

To see market conditions determining factor prices we need to look separately at markets for raw materials, land, capital, labour, and special factors.

Raw materials

The prices of copper, tin, rubber, petroleum, and hundreds of other basic commodities fluctuate daily in response to changes in their demands and supplies. Prices fluctuate in response to several different types of forces. First, short-term fluctuations in demand and supply create shortages and gluts that are almost always signalled by price changes. Second, there is often a distinct seasonal pattern in these prices. For example, the price of fuel oil is higher in winter, when demand is high, and lower in summer. Furthermore, a really cold and prolonged winter results in significantly higher prices than a mild winter. These prices also show a strong cyclical component. They rise on the upswing of the business cycle, when their (derived) demand rises, and fall on the downswing, when their (derived) demand falls. They also show long-term secular shifts. For example, traditional materials, such as copper and nickel, are displaying weak prices as their demands fall in response to the development of many new materials that are part of the materials revolution (see Box 8.7 on page 133).

Of course, if monopoly elements arise, the theories of factor pricing under monopoly or monopsony need to be applied. For example, OPEC's drastic restriction of oil supplies in the 1970s and early 1980s led to a large rise in the prices of petroleum and its derivatives, which are inputs into many production processes. This in turn led to rapid rises in the prices of such diverse products as fertilizers and plastics.

Land values

Values of land in the centres of growing cities rise in response to increasing demand. The London and New York skylines are monuments to the high value of urban land. The increase in the price of land on the periphery of every growing city is another visible example of the workings of the market.

Case study 1: the economics of land prices and skyscrapers

The larger is a city's population, the larger is the demand for all the inputs that are required to run its industries and to service its residents. One of these inputs is land. So, according to the principles of derived demand, the larger the city, the higher the demand for land on which to site all of its activities. A high demand for labour in the city will attract more people to come to the city. But land cannot move from one place to another. So the higher the demand for land the higher its rental and purchase prices.

Since land in the centre of cities is more desirable as sites for most of any city's activities than land on the periphery, the demand for central land is higher than that for land on the periphery. As a result virtually all cities show a 'rent gradient' with rents and property prices looking like a tent, highest in the centre and declining towards the edges. Figure 17.1 shows typical gradients for two cities, one larger than the other. If land were physically mobile, it would be

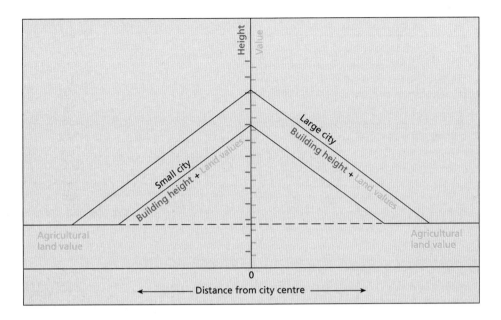

Figure 17.1 Rent and height profiles

Both land rents and building heights tend to be highest at the city centre. The figure shows two typical rent gradients for cities of two different sizes. Rents are highest at the city centre and fall towards the periphery. At the boundary between the city and the countryside, the rent that urban uses can pay just equals the rent that can be paid for the same land in agricultural uses. Building heights will show a similar profile, being highest at the centre and tending to fall as one moves towards the periphery.

reallocated until these gradients disappeared. Since it is immobile, the gradients persist indefinitely.

Case study 2: New York and London skylines

What determines the height of buildings? Construction costs per square metre of usable space rise as the height of buildings rises. There are many reasons for this, including the requirements that higher buildings be stronger with more and faster lifts than smaller buildings. Profit-maximizing developers will go on adding to a building's designed height until the extra cost per square metre can just be covered by rentals. So for any piece of land, the larger the city and the closer to the centre is its location, the higher the demand for the space it provides—thus the higher the building that can be profitably erected on it. For this reason most large cities display a profile of average height of building that is similar to their rent profile, highest in the centre and lowest at the peripheries.

Why is this predicted profile much clearer in New York than in London? The reason is that until the last half of the twentieth century, construction technology did not permit the erection of very high buildings on the clay that underlies London. In contrast, New York is largely built on rock, and for more than a hundred years technology has been adequate for the construction of very high buildings on rock. When the technology of construction improved

in the last half of the twentieth century, the average height of new London buildings began to increase.

Why, when the technology changed, did London's profile not immediately change to mimic New York's? One reason is related to sunk costs. We saw in Chapter 13 that it takes a long time for physical capital to exit a declining industry. Similarly, it takes a long time for old buildings to wear out and be replaced. The buildings are already there, and all the associated construction costs are sunk. They cannot be recovered by exiting. A new building must earn, over and above what the old building can earn, enough to repay the full costs of construction. So, as the theory predicts, we see large variations in the sizes of buildings, even on the most expensive land in the centre of the city. But old buildings are eventually demolished, either because they reach the limit of their age, or because their productivity falls sufficiently below what a new building would earn on the same site. So old and new coexist, but gradually the old go and new higher buildings take their place.

A second reason is related to government regulations. Many of the older London boroughs and hamlets had long-standing restrictions on building heights. These tended to push the new higher buildings away from the very centre of the city to the nearest convenient location where these restrictions did not apply. Canary Wharf and Docklands are literally and figuratively monuments to the new construction technologies and the response of the market to economic and political forces.

What these case studies tell us is that a city is an evolving entity whose past history determines much of its present character. None the less, how it evolves over time is determined to a great extent by the size and type of buildings that the market shows to be most profitable.

Case study 3: the evolution of agricultural land prices

Writing in the early nineteenth century, the classical economists predicted that as population and the demand for agricultural products grew, the price of the fixed supply of land would rise enormously. To the contrary, however, the free-market price of agricultural land has not skyrocketed worldwide. The demand for agricultural produce did expand in the predicted fashion because of the rise in population. However, the productivity of agricultural land increased in quite unexpected ways with the invention of the vast range of new machines, crops, and farming techniques that characterize modern agriculture. A century ago over half of the workforce of Western nations was producing food to feed the rest. Today, a mere 3–5 per cent of the workforce produces enough to feed everyone in the Western nations, with substantial margins left over for export. The prediction of rising land prices and increasing food shortages in advanced countries was falsified, not because the price of agricultural land is insensitive to market forces, but because some of the market forces were incorrectly foreseen. Technological advances in food production caused supply to expand much faster than rising populations and incomes caused demand to grow.

Case study 4: policy-created high prices

The European Union's Common Agricultural Policy (CAP) has insulated the European market from cheap foreign imports and has held up food prices. As a result, the prices of agricultural land in Europe, and the gross earnings of landowners, have been much higher than prices and incomes for comparable land in such other food-producing countries as Australia and Canada. For example, when Ireland entered the European Union and became eligible for CAP subsidies and market restraints, prices of agricultural land increased by between 100 and 500 per cent, a strong testimony both to the power of the CAP and to the applicability of the theory of derived demand.

Capital

We saw in the previous chapter that the return to capital is made up of a pure return, which responds to demand and supply, plus a risk premium. The effect of risk is easily observable. Interest rates are high in countries where economic and political conditions are unstable. Interest rates are higher on loans to consumers than on loans to large firms, because the risk of default is larger.

Over past centuries loans to the major European governments commanded very high rates. In more recent times, however, such loans have commanded the lowest rates in the market. The reason is that the risk of default on loans to governments was enormous in most previous centuries while the risk of lending to modern governments has fallen dramatically. Governments have developed high capacity to tax their citizens and have obtained control of their domestic money supply, allowing them to print new money to pay their bills if necessary.

It is interesting to note that both of these conditions are changing. First, the common European currency, the euro, removes the capacity of individual governments to create money to pay their debts. Second, by making capital and enterprise extremely mobile, the information/communication revolution is making it increasingly difficult for one government to charge taxes that are out of line with those ruling in other jurisdictions. As a result governments will either have to curtail their borrowing or face rising interest rates on their large debts.

Supply and demand conditions determine the pure rate of interest. For example, over the past few decades Japan has had remarkably low interest rates. The Japanese were exceptionally high savers. Although their economy was booming, the domestic supply of funds was more than adequate to meet high demand for capital to invest. The result was interest rates that were much lower than those typically found in Europe and North America.

Labour

We saw in Chapter 15 that the theory of factor markets can explain most of the pay differentials between major classes of labour.

Non-competitive elements can also be handled. For example, strong unions succeed in raising wages and incomes when they operate in small sections of the whole economy. The high earnings attract others to enter the occupation or industry. Thus the privileged position can be maintained only if entry can be effectively restricted. Closed-shop laws are one obvious way of doing this. With the end of much of the power of unions to restrict entry, union-induced wage differentials have narrowed substantially in the UK, as shown in Table 17.1.

Not only can monopoly elements raise incomes above their competitive levels, they can also prevent incomes from falling and reflecting decreases in demand. Of course, if demand disappears more or less overnight (as it did for silent-film stars and carriage-makers) unions cannot maintain incomes. But the story may be different if, as is more usual, demand shrinks slowly over a few decades. In this

Table 17.1 Union wage differentials, UK, 1984–1990

% extra for union in	1984	1990
Unskilled	10.5	7.5
Semi-skilled	10.5	6.5
Skilled	3.5	1.5

Unions' power has diminished over recent decades. The fall in union power is manifested in the reduced differentials between union and non-union wages in each of the three skill categories.

Source: M. Stewart, 'Union wage differentials in an era of declining unionisation', *Oxford Bulletin of Economics and Statistics*, 1995.

case unions that are powerful enough to stop new labour from entering the industry can often hold wages up in the face of declining demand. The industry's labour force thus declines, through death and retirement, despite the relatively high wage being paid to the employees who remain.

Wages also respond to long-term changes in demand and supply that are driven by new technologies. Consider some examples from the past. With the advent of the motor car many skilled carriage-makers found the demand for their services declining rapidly. Earnings fell, and many craftsmen who were forced to leave the industry found that they had been earning substantial rents for their scarce, but highly specific, skills. When the demand for silent films grew, music-hall stars whose talents did not project on to the flat, flickering screen of the early silent films suffered disastrous cuts in income and sank into oblivion. A similar fate later hit many silent-screen actors whose voices were unsuitable for the 'talkies'. Later still, falling incomes beset many radio personalities who were unable to make the transition to television and had to compete in a greatly reduced market for radio talent.

This type of variation in factor earnings is caused by changes in market conditions, not by changes in our notions of the intrinsic merit of various activities. To illustrate, ask yourself why, if you have the ability, you can make a lot of money writing copy for a London advertising agency, whereas even if you have great talent you are unlikely to make a lot of money writing books of poetry. This is not because any economic dictator or group of philosophers has decided that advertising is more valuable than poetry. Instead the explanation lies in the large demand for advertising and the tiny demand for poetry.

The following two case studies show how the theory can be used, with suitable elaboration, to explain what at first sight may seem to be strange outcomes.

Case study 5: the earnings of superstars

Small groups of people in many professions are often paid extraordinarily large salaries. Newcastle United is reported to have paid Blackburn Rovers £15 million for the services of Alan Shearer, and Middlesbrough were reported to be

paying Fabrizio Ravanelli nearly £50,000 a week in 1996/7. Phil Collins the rock star is reputed to have earned £8 million in 1995, and Damon Hill was on a contract worth £7 million even before he became the 1996 Formula 1 world motor racing champion. Similar examples also arise in business and the professions. In October 1996 NatWest Bank bought corporate finance specialist company Hambro Magan. Several of its key employees were tied into contracts worth in excess of £1 million per year. Luciano Pavarotti, Placido Domingo, and a few other top tenors earn vastly more than did Enrico Caruso and Beniamino Gigli who sang just as well nearly a century previously.

Why are superstars so highly paid? Should not market incentives encourage others to compete for these large rewards, with the end result that the massive rewards for a few would fall and be replaced by more modest rewards for the many. On the contrary, forces in the modern economy appear to be increasing the gap between superstars and the rest. There are three components to the explanation.

First, the general increase in real wealth over time has created an increase in demand for output in the sectors in which superstars perform.

Second, in some of these activities there is a premium to being the very best over what the merely competent can command. For example, if you are wealthy and need a lawyer or a heart surgeon, you are going to pay for the best. Someone who is good but not the best will not do. Equally, if you want your team to win the Premier League, you need the best striker in the country. Coming second is commendable but not good enough. Hence, those who are 'the best' may be only, say, 10 per cent better than a bunch behind them, but they may command a substantial wage premium just because there is no one better. (The *MRP* of being the best greatly exceeds the *MRP* of being second.)

Third, modern communications have increased the size of the market over which stars compete. What used to be a series of local markets where the person who was the best in each market earned a moderately high income has become a single global market in which people compete to be the best in the world. The winners earn huge sums because they serve huge markets. TV, movie, and pop stars are the obvious examples. Why listen to a local opera company when you can listen to Pavarotti and Domingo on a CD? Why listen to a local band when you can access the latest global music hits, played by those who wrote them? The marginal revenue products of top stars have been vastly increased by modern communications media that allow them to reach audiences thousands of times larger than could be reached a century ago.

Case study 6: CEO pay— fat cats or optimal incentives?

Can chief executives of large companies possibly be 'worth' their very large salaries? Multi-million dollar salaries are not uncommon in the United States, as are salaries of £1 million or more for UK chief executives and chairmen. To put this in context, the typical Japanese chief executive officer (CEO) is paid less than twenty times as much as the average Japanese worker, while the typical US CEO earns over one hundred times as much as the average US worker. Furthermore, CEO pay among the largest US companies grew four times faster in the 1980s than the pay of the average worker.

Some people believe that these high salaries for British and American CEOs are an inefficiency caused by the principal–agent problem. In this view, CEOs have escaped shareholders' control. Their high pay is evidence that shareholders are being ripped off. If this were true, the solution would be to give genuinely independent non-CEOs more power in setting compensation, or to give shareholders a vote on CEO pay.

There are good economic reasons, however, why high payments to CEOs are needed for the incentives they create within the company. There are three elements to the incentive issue.

One is the tournament model of internal incentives that we studied in Chapter 15. High pay for CEOs provides an incentive for all the workers in the firm to aspire to the top job. Hence, the pay is not justified solely by the perform-ance of the specific incumbent CEO. Rather, it is desirable for the extra effort it motivates from those who have any serious prospects of eventually becoming CEO. For them, high CEO pay may increase loyalty and the ambition to achieve promotion.

The second element is that the CEO does have to be motivated by his rewards, because there is no further pro-motion available. Hence, while middle-managers may be motivated partly by the prospect of moving up the promo-tion ladder, the CEO needs other motivation.

The third element relates to the incentives in place to take risks. If employees are risk-averse, they will take the safe option rather than take a chance of being fired for making a risky decision. However, in a modern dynamic economy, firms need to be at least risk-neutral, if not risk-takers. This means that CEOs need an incentive to take risks in the interest of the long-term health of the com-pany. One way to encourage them is to offer a reward if risk-taking pays off, while imposing no penalty when failures occur. Just such a reward profile is offered by share options. These options become valuable if the company's shares rise in value, but carry no cost to the CEO if the options expire worthless. Share options may encourage senior executives to take risks. A significant proportion of CEO compensation does involve just such incentives.

One further important use of employment-contingent options to buy shares in the future is to bind managers to the firm. A young firm in a dynamic industry may not be able to pay its executives a large current salary. It thus risks having them leave, taking their firm-specific experience with them. As well as providing an incentive to take risks,

options to buy the firm's shares in the future reduce the incentive to leave for a higher-paying job. After all, the stock options become worthless when the manager leaves.

Special factors, the legal right to produce

In many instances the right to produce is restricted by regulations enforced by governments. The instrument that gives the right to produce, whether it is a licence, quota, or patent, becomes a factor of production. Without it production is impossible. When the right to produce is saleable, its market value becomes the present value of the monopoly profits that arise from the output restriction. Suppose, for example, that each tonne of a crop that is produced under quota restriction earns £1,000 of pure profit per year, that is, £1,000 of revenue in excess of the return necessary to persuade farmers to go on producing it. People who obtain the quota to produce a tonne of the product can make £1,000 per year more than they could by producing in some other industry where freedom of entry and exit forces pure profits to zero. The quota will thus sell in the open market for the present value of a flow of £1,000 per year, which is $1,000/i$. At a 10 per cent rate of interest this is £10,000.[1] As the demand for the product fluctuates and the supply restriction is held constant, the profits, and hence the present value of the quota, fluctuates.

New entrants do not earn pure profits because they must buy the quota, whose price is the present value of those profits. So entry becomes even more costly since, as well as the normal expenses of setting up in business, the price of the quota must be found. Farmers do gain in the long run, however, as long as the market in which they operate is expanding. If demand is growing while the supply of quotas is held constant, prices and profits will rise. These extra profits are reflected in an enhanced value of the quotas, which increases the wealth of their present owners. In contrast, if there were no restrictions, a rise in demand would induce new entry until profits were pushed back to zero. So the existing farmers would get no long-term gain from a rise in demand. The big losers are con-sumers, who must pay higher prices compared to what they would pay if entry were free.

Case study 7: taxis in Toronto and London

The system of regulating taxicabs in London is very differ-ent from the one in use in Toronto. The theory successfully predicts the consequences of these different regulatory rules.

---

[1] Where, as we saw in Chapter 16, i is the rate of interest expressed as a decimal fraction; for example, $i = 0.1$ means a 10 per cent rate of interest. In practice there will be a further discounting because of the risk that govern-ment policy will change.

The supply of Toronto taxicabs, and the fares they charge, are rigidly controlled by a licensing system. The number of cabs is kept well below what it would be in a free-market situation. The medallion, which confers the right to operate a cab, acquires a scarcity value. In 1998 it sold for about CAN$90,000 (which was about £40,000). As the population increases and people earn higher incomes, the demand for the services of taxicabs rises. In a free market fares would rise, increasing the earnings of taxi owners. The higher earnings would attract new entrants until earnings had been reduced to what could be earned in other comparable lines of activity. But neither of these things can happen, so existing cabs spend less time empty and hence earn more for their owners. Since investment in a taxi would now earn more than comparable other investments, investors would like to enter the industry. The only way to do so, however, is to buy one of the fixed supply of medallions. So the market price of medallions is bid up. The price rises to equal the present value of the extra earnings that can be obtained by investing in a taxicab rather than other comparable lines of activity. As a result new entrants earn only normal returns on their investment, which includes the price of the medallion. Eventually the regulating authority raises fares in response to the excess demand. If the demand proves inelastic, the gross income from operating a cab rises. But the price of the medallion is bid up correspondingly. The fare increase thus amounts to a free gift to the current holders of medallions; it does nothing to raise the net incomes of cab operators newly entering the industry.

In London the fares of black cabs are rigidly regulated, but entry is free to anyone who can pass a set of tests. The fares of minicabs are completely unregulated and entry is free (but they are prohibited from cruising the streets in search of fares). Periodically black cab fares are raised in an effort to raise incomes. If demand is inelastic, incomes do rise in the short run. But this attracts new entrants, who continue to enter until each existing cab is carrying just enough fares to cover its full opportunity cost, at which price economic profits have been reduced to zero. This case is analytically identical to the case of hairdressers discussed in Box 13.2 on page 204.

Factors move in response to changes in factor prices

Changes in earnings are signals that induce resources to move from where they are not needed to where they are needed. Once again the details of how this works differ among the various factors of production.

Land

Does physical land move among uses according to economic signals? One might at first think the answer would be no because land is totally physically immobile. Yet land is observed to be highly mobile in its economic uses. Land is transferred from one crop to another in response to changes in the relative profitability of the crops. Land on the edge of town is transferred from rural to urban uses as soon as it can earn substantially more as a building site than as a corn field (and provided planning permission can be obtained).

Case study 8: support policies and land allocation

When free markets determine agricultural prices, farmers often plant more than one crop as insurance against expected price fluctuations. This is the kind of risk-sharing that we studied in Chapter 12. Instead of having all their eggs in one product basket, farmers diversify among several products. This reduces the risk of extreme income fluctuations, which, under diversification, require unexpectedly high or low prices for several crops at the same time, rather than for just one.

The agricultural support policies adopted by many governments, including the European Union's CAP, remove much of this uncertainty. Farmers can then calculate the most profitable crop to plant with something close to certainty. The incentive is to produce the single crop, or small set of crops, that promises the highest yields. The results can be unfortunate. Gluts of crops whose support prices are out of line can often occur. More importantly the land can suffer from exhaustion of specific minerals and other valuable properties as a result of repeated planting of one crop rather than a diversified set of crops.

Although these responses to price and profit signals are undesirable, they provide strong evidence that agricultural resources do move according to price and profit incentives. This type of response is what makes government intervention into otherwise competitive markets so fraught with danger. Economists cannot prove that governments ought not to try, but they can reveal the difficulties inherent in such attempts. Difficulties typically arise when some excellent-sounding scheme sets up unsuspected incentives to behave in ways that are then seen to be undesirable. This is also the reason for the maxim that 'controls breed controls'. The government is likely to react to these unexpected events by introducing new measures to prevent them. These new measures may in turn create unsuspected incentives with further undesirable consequences. Further schemes are then introduced to remove these consequences. Such a progression is not inevitable but it often does occur. Where it does, it is a monument to the fact that owners of resources do respond to incentives and that such incentives are often subtle in nature.

Natural resources

Markets for the use of natural resources often do not work efficiently. In many cases this is not because resource owners are unresponsive to incentives but because the incentives themselves are perverse. An important source of perverse incentive is imperfect or non-existent property rights. We will discuss these in more detail in Chapter 18. In the meantime we can note that the incentive to use resources efficiently over the long run is absent if the users do not themselves have a property right to the resource over the long run.

Case study 9: imperfect property rights

We noted in Chapter 16 that when individual properties within one oil field are too small, owner A can extract the oil under owner B's land by pumping too much oil out of his well. Neither owner then has an incentive to extract at the socially optimal rate, preserving most of the oil for future extraction. After all, the oil may not be there when owner B plans to extract it; his neighbour may already have done so. This is a case of imperfect property rights.

Case study 10: property rights that reside with the wrong agents

It has been seriously argued that some of the incentives for non-sustainable logging in the vast forests of Western Canada are created by the system of property rights in place there.[2] The government owns the forests and leases them out to the lumber companies for specific periods of time. As a result the company logging a particular area has little incentive to act in a way that is compatible with efficient reforestation. So laws are needed to force the companies to behave in the way that they would behave if they owned the land themselves. Once the laws are in place they must be enforced, which is not always easy, particularly in remote areas. If the logging companies owned the land they would have a self-interest in preserving the forests for their own future logging. More efficient logging practices and more effective reforestation would be the result.

Capital

The location of, and the products produced by, a country's factories have changed greatly over the last two centuries. Over a period of fifty years or so the change can be dramatic. From one year to the next it is small. Most plant and machinery is relatively specific. Once installed, it will be used for the purpose for which it was designed, as long as the variable costs of production can be covered. But if full long-run opportunity costs are not covered, the capital will not be replaced as it wears out. Investment will take place in other industries instead.

Long-run movements in the allocation of physical capital clearly occur in response to market signals.

The mechanism works as long as there is freedom of entry and exit. Exit is difficult to prevent (other than by government legislation and subsidy), but monopolies and oligopolies, government regulations, and nationalized industries do erect barriers to entry. Where entry is blocked, profits of monopolists or oligopolists do not induce flows of new investment. Thus, such barriers serve no apparent long-run allocative function.

Case study 11: underinvestment by nationalized industries

After the end of the Second World War in 1945 many industries were nationalized in the UK and other European countries. Many nationalized public utilities typically did not invest enough to meet the demand at the prices they were charging. The telephone industry was a good case in point. For most of the post-war period service was poor, phones were hard to get, with long waiting-lists, and in many areas private lines were almost impossible to obtain. Customers had to put up with shared lines through which two or more private residences had to use the same line. When the industry was privatized in the 1980s, whatever else good or bad happened, the waiting-lists vanished very quickly. Motivated by the profits that could be earned by satisfying customer demands, investment in telephone capacity rose to meet consumer requirements.

Although the profits that arise from the market power of private firms do not cause capital to move when entry is blocked in the long run, we cannot be so sure about this in the very long run. Profits may cause other firms to develop competing products and to innovate in other ways so as to attack the firms with market power. This is a process that Joseph Schumpeter called creative destruction. Because this incentive is important, monopoly profits do influence

---

[2] Much of the concern of environmentalists is with another issue: whether or not the remaining first-growth lands should be logged at all. Our concern here is with the efficient management of those areas which it is agreed will be logged.

the allocation of capital in the very long run. Furthermore, creative destruction takes place not only when there is monopoly, but also when oligopolistic firms compete through the development of new product and process technologies. In such cases the market allocates capital investment into research and development when firms anticipate that they can better satisfy consumers' wants by creating new products or new ways of producing old products.

Case study 12: creative destruction— an endless process

The steel-nibbed pen eliminated the quill pen with its sharpened bird's feather nib. The fountain pen eliminated the steel pen and its accompanying inkwell. The ball-point pen or 'biro' virtually eliminated the fountain pen. Rolling-ball and fibre-tipped pens have partly replaced the biro. Who knows what will come next in writing implements.

The hand-cranked adding machine replaced the Dickensian clerk adding up long columns of figures in his head. (This *was* an all-male occupation.) The electrically driven mechanical desk calculator eliminated the hand-cranked version. The electronic desk calculator eliminated the mechanical calculator, while the pocket calculator eliminated the slide rule (which was a device for doing calculations based on logarithms). The mainframe computer largely replaced the electronic calculator during the 1960s and 1970s (except for pocket use). In the late 1980s and early 1990s the increasingly powerful personal computer largely replaced the mainframe. IBM, then the world's largest producer of computer equipment, suffered seriously from its misjudgement of this shift in demand. Each step vastly increased the speed and accuracy with which calculations could be completed. A modern PC will do in a fraction of a second what the Dickensian clerk did in a week, and what a desk calculator could do in half a day.

The silent film eliminated vaudeville. The 'talkies' eliminated the silent film, and colour largely eliminated black-and-white films. The TV seriously reduced the demand for films (and radio) while not eliminating either of them. Satellites reduced the demand for direct TV reception by offering better pictures and a more varied selection, and cable may do the same to satellite transmission.

In the 1920s and 1930s the American supermarket threatened the small grocery store as the main shopping place for the typical family. The small store fought back with assistance from the courts and the regulators, and was able to slow the advance of the supermarkets. But in the end the big stores were seen to offer a superior product and they pushed the small operations into the niche of the convenience store or corner shop. In the 1960s supermarkets spread throughout Britain. In the 1980s and 1990s out-of-town shopping malls and hypermarkets threatened town-centre supermarkets.

For long-distance passenger travel by sea the steamship eliminated the sailing vessel around the late nineteenth century. The aeroplane eliminated the ocean liner in the 1950s and 1960s. For passenger travel on land the train eliminated the stagecoach, while the bus competed with the train without eliminating it. The aeroplane wiped out the passenger train in most of North America while leaving the bus still in a low-cost niche used mainly for short and medium distances. In Europe distances are such that bus, train, and plane all compete over many routes while air transport dominates the longer trips.

The above are all product innovations. Production processes also undergo the same type of creative destruction. The laborious hand-setting of metal type for printing was replaced by the linotype, which allowed the type to be set by a keyboard operator but which still involved a costly procedure for making corrections. The linotype was swept away by computer typesetting, and many of the established printing shop operations have recently been replaced by desktop publishing.

Masses of assembly-line workers, operating highly specialized and inflexible machines, replaced the craftsman when Henry Ford perfected the techniques of mass production at the beginning of the twentieth century. A smaller number of less specialized flexible-manufacturing workers, operating sophisticated and less specialized machinery, have now replaced the assembly-line workers who operated the traditional factory in many industries.

The list of such cases can be extended almost indefinitely, and they all illustrate the same general lesson. Creative destruction transforms the products we consume, how we make those products, and how we work. It continually sweeps away positions of high income and economic power established by firms that were in the previous wave of technological change and by those who work for them. It is an agent of dynamism in our economy, an agent of change and economic growth. But it is not without its dark side, as attested by the periodic loss of privileged positions on the part of the replaced firms and their many workers.

Labour

Labour clearly moves in response to monetary incentives. High relative wages attract and hold labour in such unattractive parts of the world as the North Sea oil fields, the Canadian North, Siberia, and the Amazon jungles, while occupations with much leisure and pleasant working conditions pay lower wages, *ceteris paribus*. There is a supply as well as a demand element at work here. Unpleasant but unskilled jobs are often poorly paid because anyone can do them, but even so electricians working in the frozen Canadian North are paid more than electricians working in Vancouver because, otherwise, they would not stay in the unattractive climate.

At the risk of grossly oversimplifying a complex situation, the following generalizations seem consistent with the evidence:

1. There exists a fairly mobile component of labour in any group. It tends to consist of the younger and more adaptable members of the group.

2. This mobile group can be attracted from one area, occupation, or industry to another by relatively small changes in economic incentives. It can also be induced to invest in skills that are newly in high demand and are hence being highly remunerated.

3. Provided that the pattern of demand for resources does not shift too quickly, this mobile group can accomplish most of the necessary reallocation. Of course, the same individual need not move over and over again. New entrants into the labour force are constantly replenishing this group.

4. As we go beyond these very mobile persons, we get into ranges of lower and lower mobility until, at the very bottom, we find those who are completely immobile. The most immobile are the old, those with capital sunk in non-marketable assets, the timid, the weak, and those who receive high rents in their present occupation or location. In extreme cases even the threat of starvation may not be enough to induce movement, since some people believe they will starve even if they do move.

Thus shifts in earnings may create substantial inflows of workers into an expanding occupation, industry, or area and an outflow of workers from a depressed occupation, industry, or area. Over long periods of time, outflows have been observed from depressed areas such as the Highlands of Scotland, the former Welsh mining areas, the Appalachian region in the United States, the Maritime Provinces of Canada, southern Italy, and the rural parts of central France. Although some outmigration occurs readily, it is difficult for large transfers to take place in short periods of time. When demand falls rapidly, pockets of poverty tend to develop. Workers have been leaving each of the geographical areas mentioned above, but poverty has increased too. The reason is that the rate of exit has been slower than the rate of decline of the economic opportunities in each area. Indeed, the exit itself causes further decline, because when a family migrates all the locally provided goods and services that it once consumed suffer a reduction in demand, leading to a further decline in the demand for labour.

Unemployment   Factor market theory does well in ex-plaining earnings and factor allocations, but it has one implication that seems to conflict with observations. A competitive market should clear in the sense that there is neither excess demand nor excess supply. So in labour markets there should be no one who is willing to work at the prevailing wage but who cannot find a job. Yet we observe what appear to be substantial amounts of this type of unemployment. Theories that seek to explain why are studied in Chapter 31. Some theories deny that such involuntary unemployment exists. Other theories accept its existence and seek to explain why modern methods of wage determination do not yield the type of wage flexibility that would quickly remove involuntary unemployment. Broadly speaking, the answer seems to be that wages in labour markets do not fluctuate with sufficient rapidity to prevent large pockets of unemployment from persisting. Over the long term relative wages do respond to the conditions of demand and supply. Over the long term labour does move in response to market signals. But over shorter periods of time, which may be several years, wages respond to many influences other than demand and supply. As a result pockets of excess demand and excess supply can persist.

So markets do work in providing incentives and in allocating labour among its various uses, but they do not seem to work in such a way as to prevent long-term persistent unemployment among some groups of workers.

It is one thing to say that factors move in response to price signals, for which there is much evidence; it is quite another thing to say that they always move fast enough that equilibrium theory is all we need to understand what we see in the world. There is also much evidence that factor movements are quite sluggish at various times and in various markets. Sluggish movement can give rise to many effects, some of which come under the heading 'hysteresis'. The amount of human capital that workers acquire depends, among other things, on the time that they are employed. Long bouts of unemployment may not only reduce their accumulated experience but can also create attitudes that lower their future abilities to get work and to command high wages even if they do find employment. It is quite possible for factor markets to work qualitatively in the directions that we have discussed above while in many cases working slowly enough that their behaviour can be regarded as less than satisfactory. Quantitative studies of how well and how fast labour markets work are important in modern labour economics. This problem is briefly discussed in Chapter 31, and it is discussed in detail in books and courses devoted to labour economics.

Summary

The theory restated

■ The neoclassical theory of distribution is an implication of profit maximization. Each factor is paid the value of its marginal revenue product, and units of the factor move among uses to equalize net advantages, taking monetary and non-monetary rewards into account.

■ The satisfactory working of factor markets depends on two conditions. Factor prices must reflect market conditions, and factors must move in response to changes in relative factor prices.

Market conditions determine factor prices

■ Urban land values respond to demand by showing a typical tent shape, highest in the city centre and lowest in the suburbs. Rural land values have not risen to the extent predicted by the classical economists because rising agricultural productivity has increased food supplies faster than rising population and rising incomes have increased food demand.

■ The earnings of superstars and top business executives reflect the high demand for the *very best* talent and for trust and initiative.

■ Saleable production quotas have market values that eliminate monopoly profits once the cost of the quota is included as a cost of production.

Factors move in response to changes in factor prices

■ Land and natural resources are constantly being reallocated among their various possible uses in response to changes in market prices.

■ Inefficiencies can arise when property rights do not confer long-term ownership of resources on those currently making use of them. These are particularly serious in the use of natural resources.

■ In the long and very long runs capital moves into industries making pure profits, using creative destruction to break down entry barriers when necessary.

■ Problems arise when resources do not move with sufficient speed even though they do move in the directions indicated by market signals. Early experience of prolonged unemployment can affect a person's ability to gain employment and earn a satisfactory wage for the rest of his or her life.

Topics for review

■ The size and functional distributions of income
■ The effect of licences and quotas
■ The effect of market conditions on factor prices
■ The effect of factor prices on the allocation of factors among uses

Questions for discussion

1 Governments around the world frequently seek to raise the incomes of groups of producers by imposing a minimum price that is well above the free-market price for their products. Who benefits and who loses? Why are such schemes difficult to maintain in the long run?

2 Concern is sometimes expressed that serious food shortages will arise because urban growth is taking so much land out of food production. Explain how the market mechanism determines how much land is allocated to urban and to agricultural uses. Explain why serious food shortages are unlikely to arise for the reason alleged above.

3 Suppose that the huge earnings of superstars were judged to be immoral and their earnings were capped legally at £200,000. What would be the consequences in the various industries in which stars now earn much more?

4 How do effective property rights provide incentives to conserve resources? How do ineffective ones provide incentives to squander them?

5 What would be the consequences of a policy of controls that fixed the rents of unfurnished accommodation on the basis of construction and operating costs but did not allow them to reflect local conditions of demand and supply (a policy followed for decades in the UK)?

Part Four
The Government in the Economy

Chapter 18
Market Success and Market Failure

An unkind critic of economics once said that economists have two great insights: *markets work* and *markets fail*. An unkind critic of politics once added that economics was thus a step ahead of both the political left and the political right, each of which accepts only one of these insights. Whatever may be true of other disciplines, we will see in this Part how economists attempt the critical step of showing when each of these insights applies, and why.

In this chapter we first look at the basic functions that all governments have undertaken since the dawn of history. These are providing security of life, limb, and property. We see that if those functions are reasonably well performed, the free-market economy will allocate resources with relative efficiency. Indeed, an idealization of the free market, in which there is perfect competition in all markets, allocates resources optimally. We go on to see that in the real world markets fail to do an efficient job under a number of well-defined circumstances, including common property resources, public goods, harmful externalities, and excessive market power. These market failures provide the potential for government intervention to improve market efficiency. We see what government policies could do this job under ideal circumstances. In Chapter 19 we study how well or poorly actual governments do this job.

Basic functions of government

Governments are as old as organized economic activity. They arose shortly after the neolithic agricultural revolution turned people from hunter–gatherers into settled farmers. An institution that has survived that long must be doing something right! Over the intervening 100 centuries the functions undertaken by government have varied enormously. But through all that time the function that has not changed is to provide what is called a *monopoly of violence*. Violent acts can be conducted by the military and the civilian police arms of government, and through its judicial system the government can deprive people of their liberty by incarcerating them or, in extreme cases, by executing them. This is a dangerous monopoly that is easily abused, as is any monopoly, but with more serious consequences than when monopolies over production are abused. For these reasons satisfactory societies have systems of checks and balances designed to keep the government's monopoly directed to the general good rather than to the good of a narrow government circle.

The importance of having a monopoly of violence can be seen in those countries whose governments do not have it. Somalia in recent decades and China in the 1920s provide examples of countries in which individual warlords commanded armies that could not vanquish each other. Colombia, and to some extent Russia, provide examples of organized crime having substantial power to commit violence that the government cannot control. In extreme cases where many groups have almost equal ability to exert military violence, power struggles can create havoc with normal economic and social life. Life then becomes 'nasty, brutish, and short'—to use the words of the seventeenth-century English political philosopher Thomas Hobbes.

The importance of having checks on the arbitrary use of its monopoly by a selfish government is seen in the disasters that ensue in the many dictatorships that misuse their power. The USSR under Stalin, Uganda under Idi Amin, Nigeria under Sanni Abacha, and Cambodia under Pol Pot are a few of the many modern-day examples.

When the government's monopoly of violence is secure and functions with reasonable restraints against its arbitrary use, citizens can safely carry on their ordinary economic and social activities.

So governments are, as they always have been, institutions to which people give over a monopoly of violence in return for the enforcement of 'law and order'. A related government activity is to provide security of property. Governments define and enforce property rights that give people a secure claim to the fruits of their own labour. These property rights include clear definition and enforcement of the rights and obligations of institutions such as joint-stock companies, banks, insurance companies, and stock exchanges.

As the founder of British classical economics, Adam Smith, put it a long time ago:

The first duty of the sovereign [is] that of protecting the society from the violence and invasion of other independent societies. . . . The second duty of the sovereign [is] that of protecting, as far as possible, every member of the society from the injustice or oppression of every other member of it.[1]

In a modern complex economy, providing these 'minimal' government services is no simple task. Countries whose governments are not good at doing these things have seldom prospered economically.

[1] Adam Smith, *The Wealth of Nations* (1776; New York: Random House, 1937 edn., pp. 653, 669).

Market efficiency

Within a secure framework of law and order, and well-defined and enforced property rights, a modern economy can function at least moderately well without further government assistance. In this section we see how and why this is so. In subsequent sections we study government functions that arise when free markets fail to produce acceptable results.

Free markets are impressive institutions. Consumers' tastes and producers' costs help to generate price signals. These signals co-ordinate separate decisions taken by millions of independent agents, all pursuing their own self-interest and oblivious to national priorities. In doing so, they allocate the nation's resources without conscious central direction. Markets also determine the distribution of income by establishing prices of factors of production, which provide incomes for their owners. Furthermore, modern market economies, where firms compete to get ahead of each other by producing better goods more cheaply, generate the technological changes that have raised average living standards fairly steadily at least over the past two centuries.

How markets work

The most general case in support of market economies is that they fulfil their functions better than any known alternative. We observed that this *was* so in Chapter 1, but now we have developed a deeper insight into *why* this is so.

Better information   Market-generated prices convey an enormous amount of information about constantly changing market conditions. The central planners of the former Soviet Union found that generating this information by conscious planning was a massive job. For example, the Soviet authorities had to set prices for over 5 million items. Yet their economy was much simpler than any Western economy because the planners suppressed most of the vast range of product differentiation that is available to consumers in modern industrial economies.

Greater flexibility Compared with any known alternative, the decentralized market system is more flexible and leaves more scope for personal adaptation at any moment in time. If, for example, a scarcity of oil raises its price, one individual can elect to leave her heating on full and economize on her car's petrol consumption, while another may wish to do the opposite. In order to obtain the same overall reduction in consumption by non-price rationing, the government typically forces the same reduction in heating and driving on both individuals, independent of their tastes, doctor's advice, and other perceived needs.

Better adaptability In market economies prices change as conditions change. Decentralized decision-takers can react continuously to these changing signals, whereas government quotas, allocations, and rationing schemes are slower to adjust. Millions of adaptations to millions of changes in tens of thousands of markets are required every year. The Eastern European planners discovered that it is a Herculean task to anticipate these and plan the necessary adjustments.

Decentralization of power   The market economy decentralizes power and thus requires less coercion of individuals than do other types of economy. Governments must coerce if markets are not allowed to allocate people to jobs, and products to consumers. The power to allocate creates major opportunities for bribery, corruption, and allocation according to the tastes of the central administrators. If, at the going prices and wages, there are not enough flats or coveted jobs to go around, the bureaucrats must allocate them. Some will go to those who pay the largest bribe, some to those with religious beliefs, hairstyles, or political views that they like, and only the rest to those whose names come up on the waiting-list.

Of course, large firms and large unions exercise substantial economic power in market economies. However, that power tends to be constrained both by the competition of other large entities and by the emergence of new products and firms.

The efficiency of perfect competition

While they accept the general case for the superiority of the market economy just outlined, professional economists want to be more precise about just what the market economy does so well. This is done by proving that an idealization of the market economy (perfect competition) leads, in equilibrium, to an optimum, or efficient, allocation of resources. This is often referred to as **Pareto optimality** after the great Italian economist Vilfredo Pareto (1848–1923), who studied it in great detail.

In Chapter 9 we showed that perfect competition was efficient because it maximized the sum of producers' and consumers' surplus. In Chapter 10 we showed that monopoly was not efficient because it restricts output below what is required to maximize these surpluses. In this section we develop an alternative proof of the proposition that perfect competition leads to efficient allocation of resources. As a first step we first enquire in a little more depth into the meaning of this efficiency.

Productive efficiency

Production is efficient when it is impossible to reallocate resources so as to produce more of some product without producing less of some other product. Watch the double negative! An allocation of resources is productively inefficient when it is possible to produce more of some product without producing less of any other product. It is efficient when this cannot be done—in other words when the only way to produce more of one product is to produce less of some other product.

Productive efficiency has two aspects, one concerning the allocation of resources within each firm, and one concerning the allocation of resources among the firms in an industry. The first condition for productive efficiency is that each firm should produce any given output at the lowest possible cost. Any firm that is not being productively efficient is producing at a higher cost than is necessary. This must reduce its profits. Thus any perfectly competitive profit-maximizing firm will be productively efficient.[2]

The second condition for productive efficiency is that all firms producing the same product should have the same marginal cost. This ensures that the total output of each industry is allocated among its individual firms in such a way that the total cost of producing the industry's output is minimized. If all firms' marginal costs were not the same, resources could be transferred from the firm with the highest marginal cost to the firm with lowest. The same output would be produced but at a lower cost.

Perfect competition produces productive efficiency. First, all firms are motivated to produce at the lowest possible cost. Second, since firms in any one industry face the same price to which they equate their marginal cost, all firms have the same marginal cost.

Look again at the production-possibility curve in Figure 1.1 on page 5. An economy that is productively inefficient will be at some point inside the curve such as point *c*. It will be possible to produce more of some goods without producing less of others.

Productive efficiency implies being on, rather than inside, the economy's production-possibility curve.

Allocative efficiency

Allocative efficiency relates to the allocation of resources to the production of all the goods and services that are produced. In other words,

Allocative efficiency relates to the choice among alternative points on the production-possibility curve.

It concerns, for example, the choice between points such as *a* and *b* in Figure 1.1 on page 5. Changing the allocation of resources implies producing more of some goods and less of others, which in turn means moving from one point on the production-possibility curve to another.

Allocative inefficiency means that resources can be reallocated from their present uses so as to make at least one person better off while making no other person worse off. Conversely, **allocative efficiency** means that it is impossible, by producing a different bundle of goods, to make any one person better off without making at least one other person worse off.

How is it achieved? How do we find the allocatively efficient point on the production-possibility curve? For example, how many shoes, dresses, and hats should be produced to achieve allocative efficiency? The answer is as follows:

The economy's allocation of resources is efficient when

---

[2] We must restrict this result to price-taking firms because inefficient production, using more fixed capital than is necessary, can be an entry-barring strategy for oligopolistic firms. It may pay firms in such markets to produce above the minimum attainable cost in order to maximize profits in the long run by restricting entry.

the marginal cost of producing each good is equal to its market price.

To understand the reasoning behind this answer, we need to look at the significance of price and marginal cost.

First, look at price. Recall a point that was established in our discussion of consumers' surplus in Chapter 6. The price of any product indicates the value that each consumer places on the last unit purchased of that product. Faced with the market price of some product, the consumer goes on buying units until the last one is valued exactly at its price. Consumers' surplus arises because each consumer would be willing to pay more than the market price for all but the last unit bought. On the last unit bought (i.e. the marginal unit), however, the consumer only 'breaks even', because the valuation placed on it is just equal to its price.

Now consider marginal cost. It is the value of the resources used to produce the last unit of output. Thus, when marginal cost is equated to price, the value that consumers place on the last unit they consume is exactly equal to the value of the resources required to produce that unit of output.

For the next step in the argument suppose that the entire economy is perfectly competitive. Marginal cost will then equal price in all lines of production. The value that consumers place on the last unit of each and every commodity that they consume will be equal to the cost of producing that unit.

In a perfectly competitive economy £1 worth of resources reallocated from the production of any one product would produce £1 worth of value for consumers whatever product it was then used to produce.

To illustrate, assume that marginal cost equals price in all lines of production except blue jeans. Jeans sell for £25 but initially cost £30 to produce at the margin. If one pair of jeans fewer is produced, consumers lose the £25 of value that they place on it. But resources worth £30 are freed. If those resources move to any industry in which marginal cost equals price, they will produce £30 worth of value. Society will have gained £5 in total value and it will be possible to make someone better off by £5 worth of consumption without making anyone else worse off.

Now let the output of jeans fall until they only cost £20 to produce at the margin but still sell for £25. If one more pair of jeans is now produced, resources worth £20 will have to be withdrawn from some other line of production. But since marginal cost equals price in all other lines, only £20 worth of consumer satisfaction will be lost when these resources move. When they produce one more pair of jeans, consumers get a product they value at £25. So there is a net gain of £5 on the transfer.

Finally let the output of jeans increase until the marginal cost of the last pair produced is equal to its £25 price.

If *one pair of jeans fewer* is produced, £25 worth of value is sacrificed and the £25 worth of resources that are freed could produce £25 worth of value anywhere else in the economy. If *one more pair of jeans* is produced, the producers of jeans create £25 of value but £25 worth of value is lost when the resources are taken from some other industry. So there is no gain in reallocating resources either into or out of the production of blue jeans. The current allocation is efficient.

When marginal cost equals price in all industries it is impossible to reallocate resources between alternative lines of production and increase consumer satisfaction. The economy is allocatively efficient.

A perfectly competitive economy is allocatively efficient because it equates marginal cost to price in all lines of production and (as we saw in earlier chapters) because it maximizes the sum of producers' and consumers' surplus.

How markets fail

The term **market failure** describes the failure of the market economy to achieve an efficient allocation of resources. We observed in Chapter 11 that firms in most lines of production have some market power over their prices because they face negatively sloped rather than perfectly elastic demand curves for their products. Since when firms face negatively sloped demand curves, price will exceed marginal cost in equilibrium, no real market economy has ever achieved perfect allocative efficiency. The conditions for efficiency are meant only as a benchmark to help in identifying sources of allocative inefficiency, called market failures. These sources are candidates for government intervention designed to improve market efficiency—even if not to achieve complete efficiency.

There are several important circumstances under which markets fail to allocate resources with reasonable efficiency, let alone to achieve the optimal allocation of resources:

1. where producers with excess capacity set positive prices

2. where there are resources that can be used by everyone but belong to no one—called common property resources

3. where there are goods whose consumption cannot be restricted to those who are willing to pay for them—called public goods

4. where people not party to some market bargain are none the less significantly affected by it—called externalities

5. where one party to a market transaction has fuller knowledge of its consequences than is available to the other party—a situation referred to as asymmetric information

6. where needed markets do not exist

7. where substantial monopoly power causes prices to diverge from marginal costs

Coping with these market failures provides governments with major functions in addition to the law and order functions discussed earlier. In the rest of this chapter we study these sources of market failure and how government policies could conceivably alleviate them. In Chapter 19 we study how well government policies actually work in coping with market failures and in achieving all the other goals that governments set for themselves.

Non-rivalrous and non-excludable goods

Economies must allocate resources between the production and consumption of the four major classes of goods and services that are shown in Table 18.1. A good is **rivalrous** if no two persons can consume the same unit. For example, if you buy and eat an apple, no one else can buy and eat that same apple. A good is **excludable** if people can be prevented from obtaining it. Excludability requires that an owner be able to exercise effective property rights over the good or service in order to determine who uses it—typically only those who pay for the privilege.

Most of the goods and services that you and I buy are rivalrous and excludable. If I buy a chocolate bar and eat it, no one else can buy and eat that bar, and the owner can prevent me from having it if I am unwilling to pay for it

(unless I steal it). If an airline sells you a seat on a particular flight, it cannot let more than one person occupy that seat.

Obvious though these characteristics may seem, there are important classes of goods and services that lack one or both of them. Goods and services are **non-rivalrous** when the amount that one person consumes does not affect the amount that other people can consume. They are **non-excludable** when, once produced, there is no way to stop anyone from consuming them.

Rivalrousness is usually fixed once and for all by the nature of the good or service. An apple is rivalrous; a work of art is not. In contrast, excludability depends on the specific circumstances and the state of technology.

Circumstances The Fastnet lighthouse guides all shipping making a landfall on southwest Ireland and there is no way to force passing ships to pay for its services. The New Brighton lighthouse illuminates the entrance to the River Mersey and the Port of Liverpool, and if its operators had turned it off (prior to the invention of radar), many ships would have passed on to another, better-lit harbour entrance. In this case private owners could sell the lighthouse's services, not to passing ships, but to the port authorities, who knew they needed it in order to compete with rival ports.

Technology Early TV programmes were all broadcast openly to anyone who had a set. But the development of satellites, encoded signals, and cable transmission allowed some forms of TV signals to be provided only to those who pay for the service. The programmes are still non-rivalrous in the sense that there is no limit to the number of people who can watch a given programme. But the new technologies made them excludable so that private companies would provide them. For another example, until recently it has been impracticable to charge tolls for the use of urban roads and exclude non-payers because of the excessive costs involved in the many tollbooths needed to service a road in a densely populated urban area. Today it is possible to implant in each car a device that tracks its location at very small cost. Fees for the use of urban roads can now be assessed and non-payers denied use of the roads.

Table 18.1 Four types of goods

	Excludable	Non-excludable
Rivalrous	*Normal goods*	*Common property*
	Apples	Fisheries
	Dresses	Common land
	TV sets	Wildlife
	Computers	Air
	A seat on an aeroplane	Streams
Non-rivalrous (up to capacity)		*Public goods*
	Art galleries	Defence
	Museums	Police
	Fenced parks	Public information
	Roads	Broadcast signals
	Bridges	Some navigation aids

Markets cope best with rivalrous excludable goods. The table gives examples of items in each of the four categories. The market can produce goods that are excludable but non-rivalrous, but their efficient use requires a zero price. Goods that are non-excludable but rivalrous are common property resources, which get overused by free markets. Goods that are non-rivalrous and non-excludable are public goods, which will usually not be produced at all by the free market.

Cost In some cases it is technically possible to make a good excludable but too costly to do so. One could put a fence around the Lake District National Park and charge hikers a fee for walking in the area, but the cost of erecting and policing the fence makes it uneconomic to exclude non-payers.

In what follows we look at the characteristics of goods and services that fall into the four possible combinations of excludable and non-excludable and rivalrous and non-rivalrous as shown in Table 18.1.

Excludable goods

Private agents who produce goods and services for sale on the free market must be able to prohibit consumption of their output by those who will not pay for the privilege. Otherwise the producers cannot gain the revenue they need to cover their production costs.

So excludability is necessary for a good to be produced by a firm for sale on the market.

Ordinary goods: excludable and rivalrous

The market works best when goods and services are rivalrous and excludable. Private firms can produce and sell them. Furthermore, these firms will fulfil the condition for allocative efficiency by operating where marginal cost equals price as long as they are price-takers.

Art galleries, museums, and parks: excludable but non-rivalrous

Some excludable goods and services are non-rivalrous, at least up to a large capacity constraint. This is the first reason on our list of market failures. A park with a fence around it provides an excludable service, but one person's use does not interfere with another person's use—at least until there are so many users that overcrowding becomes a serious problem. Such goods can be provided by private firms, but since the marginal cost of adding another user is zero (until capacity is reached), any admission fee that the owner charges will result in a non-optimal use of the facility. It costs nothing to add another user, but to cover their costs the providers must charge each user a fee. Thus, under private provision price will exceed marginal cost and some people who are willing to pay more than this marginal cost but less than the price do not use it. This market failure is called inefficient exclusion.

To avoid inefficient exclusions, the government often provides non-rivalrous but excludable goods and services.

The costs are then met out of taxation, and the service is provided free. Parks, art galleries, roads, and bridges often come under this category. Box 18.1 reviews the debate that arose in the early 1990s when the Conservative government in the UK reduced the grants to galleries and museums and the trustees of some felt they had little option but to levy charges for admission.

Box 18.1 Pricing of galleries and museums

Art galleries, museums, fenced parks, bridges, and similar public institutions are examples of goods that are excludable—admission is easily controlled at entrances—but non-rivalrous at least up to substantial capacity. Except on crowded days, one person's use does not reduce another person's ability to use the facility. The efficient solution is to allow everyone to use the facility free of charge on non-crowded days but to charge a price on days on which the crowds do make the facility's use a rivalrous activity.

The argument *against* the policy of free admission runs along the following lines. Many taxpayers who never use the facility, and do not even care that it exists, are forced to help to pay for it. Many of these people may have lower-than-average incomes and be less well educated. So the free-admission policy is to a great extent a subsidy for middle-class persons with particular tastes. In times of financial stringency, those who want the facility should pay for it.

Whatever the reasons, in the early 1990s the Conservative government in the UK decided to curtail its support for the arts drastically. In response many museum and gallery trustees decided that the only course open to them was to institute admission charges, although others did not. Controversy was sustained and often bitter. However, the decision is now past and the current policy of charging for admission to some such facilities raises little current protest. Nor was there great protest when two of the major

holdouts, the National Gallery and the British Museum, instituted entrance fees in 1998.

Those who opposed the imposition of charges argued several points. The admission fees would lead to inefficient exclusion. Institutions that were underused and could add more visitors would be excluding potential users by their not insignificant charges. Those excluded would be from lower-income classes that had contributed little to the costs of operation in the past because they paid little in income tax.

There is no easy resolution of such debates. They tend to pit those who worry about equity against those who worry about efficiency. But even that is not always a clear division. It is an equity argument that those who benefit from the facilities should pay for them. But it is also an equity argument that positive admission fees should not be used to preclude the poor from taking part in an activity that has a zero marginal cost.

In the latest development in this saga the UK Labour government announced in mid-1998 that it was moving the pendulum well back in the direction of free admission. Money will be made available to all national collections sponsored by the Department of Culture, Media, and Sport to introduce free access for children in 1999–2000, for pensioners in 2000–1, and for everyone in 2001–2. One wonders if the government was swayed more by concerns about equity or efficiency in reaching this decision.

Non-excludable goods

This class provides the next two sources on our list of major market failures, those associated with common property resources and public goods.

Common property: non-excludable but rivalrous

If you catch a fish in the open ocean, I cannot catch it, so it is rivalrous. But in a free market there is no way for you to exclude me from catching it, so it is non-excludable. This is the second reason on our list of causes of market failures. A **common property resource** is one that is rivalrous but non-excludable. No one has an exclusive property right to it, and it can be used by anyone. No one owns the ocean's fish until they are caught. No one owns common grazing land. The world's international fishing grounds are common property for all fishermen, as is common grazing land for all livestock owners. If, by taking more fish, one fisherman reduces the catch of other fishermen, he does not count this as a cost, although it is a cost to society. If, by grazing her own sheep, a peasant reduces the feed available for other people's goats, she does not count this as a cost. The result has been called *the tragedy of the commons*—the tendency for commonly held property to be overexploited, often to the extent of destruction.

It is socially optimal to add to a fleet that is fishing any given fishing area until the last boat increases the *value of the fleet's total catch* by as much as it costs to operate the boat. Similarly, it is optimal to add another sheep to the flock that grazes on the commons as long as the total supply of meat (and milk) is increased by as much as the cost of maintaining the extra animal. These are the sizes of fishing fleet and flock of sheep that a social planner or a private monopolist would choose.

The socially optimal exploitation of a common property resource occurs when the marginal cost of the last user equals the value of the marginal addition to total output.

The free market will not, however, produce that result. Consider the fishery. Potential new entrants will judge entry to be profitable if the *value of their own catch* is equal to the costs of operating their boats. But a new entrant's catch is *partly* an addition to total catch and *partly* a reduction of the catch of other fishermen—because of congestion each new boat reduces the catch of all other boats. Thus, under competitive free entry there will be too many boats in the fleet and too many sheep on the common.

How does a potential new fisherman judge the value of entering the industry? He will expect to do about as well as the average boat. So it pays to enter, adding a new boat to the fleet, until the *average* value of the catch of a typical boat in the fleet is equal to the cost of running the newly entering boat.[3]

Figure 18.1 Overfishing of a common property fishery
A common property resource is exploited beyond the socially optimal level. Adding boats to the fleet adds to the total catch but at a diminishing rate up to 140 boats, after which additional boats lower the total catch. With the old technology, the cost (capital and current) of running each boat is £10,000, giving the steeper of the two total cost curves. The socially optimal level is 35 boats, where the addition to total catch, as shown by the slope of the tangent to the total catch curve, just equals the addition to the total cost of running one more boat, as shown by the slope of the total cost curve. At that point there is a surplus of revenue over total cost of £150,000. At that fleet size, a new boat expects to catch about £14,300 (i.e. £500,000/35) worth of fish, so entry is profitable from the private point of view. When the fleet reaches 100 boats, a new boat expects to catch £10,000 worth of fish, which just matches its cost. With new technology, each boat costs only £4,000 to run. The fleet expands to 200 boats catching £800,000 worth of fish. This yields revenue of £4,000 per boat, which just matches cost. Production has been pushed beyond the point of negative marginal returns.

The free market will add users to a common property resource until the marginal cost of the last entrant equals the *average* output of all existing producers.

At this point, however, the *net* addition to the *total* catch brought about by the last boat will be substantially less than the cost of operating the boat, and it may even be negative.

With common property resources the level of output will be too high because each new entrant will not take account of the cost that he or she imposes on existing producers.

This tendency to overexploitation of a common property resource is illustrated by the example in Figure 18.1. Free-market entry proceeds until the cost of the last boat,

---

[3] This subtle point is the same as the difference between the perfectly competitive producer and the monopolist. The monopolist knows that if it sells more, it will reduce the market value of what it is already selling. The perfect competitor must take the market price as given and so values a marginal unit of production at the market price, i.e. at the *average value* of all units already being sold.

which is average total cost per boat, equals the revenue it expects, which is the average revenue per boat. This is the same as saying total cost equals total revenue—so there are no economic profits to attract further entrants. The surplus over cost that could be earned with a smaller fleet is dissipated by entry. In this example, the fishing fleet is 100 vessels. Each boat costs £10,000 to run and catches £10,000 worth of fish. If the fleet was restricted to 35 boats, each £10,000 boat would catch fish worth just over £14,000. The new technology reduces the cost of running each. Entry then proceeds well beyond the 140-boat level where each additional boat actually begins to reduce the total catch.

Fishing grounds, common pastures, and other common property resources often show a pattern of overexploitation.

This is true of almost all of today's fishing grounds, except where the catch is effectively regulated by government intervention. Box 18.2 discusses this case in more detail.

One solution to the common property problem is to agree on the optimal level of use and then police the resource to reduce its use to that level. This is done with such items as fishing quotas and hunting licences. The problem here is to enforce the restrictions. It is possible to control the number of fish caught in the high seas, but doing so is difficult and costly, as attested by the frequent international disputes over alleged quota violations.

Another method is for the state to create property rights that make the resource excludable. Its private owners then have an incentive to exploit it efficiently. The English enclosure movement that peaked between 1793 and 1815 did just that. Although those who had previously used the common grazing land were hurt by the measure, the land was much more efficiently used under private ownership. Issuing licences for the use of each particular wavelength can control the airwaves. State forests which are being destroyed by excessive wood gathering can be sold to private owners. Property rights to wildlife can be given to local villages. And so on. This last case is controversial and is further discussed in Box 18.3.

All of these cases show the common problem of a trade-off between efficiency and equity. When a common property resource is 'privatized', the efficiency of its use typically rises but the former users typically suffer. The difficult issue of trading off efficiency of the resource's use against

---

Box 18.2 Endangered fish

The fish in the ocean are a common property resource, and theory predicts that such a resource will be overexploited if there is a high enough demand for the product and suppliers are able to meet that demand. In past centuries there were neither enough people eating fish nor efficient enough fishing technologies to endanger stocks. Over the last fifty years, however, the population explosion has added to the demand for fish and advances in technology have vastly increased the ability to catch fish. Large boats, radar detection, and more murderous nets have tipped the balance in favour of the predator and against the prey. As a result the overfishing prediction of common property theory has been amply borne out. Today fish are a common property resource; tomorrow they could become no one's resource.

Overfishing

Since 1950 the world's catch has increased fivefold. The increase was only sustained by substituting smaller, less desirable fish for the diminishing stocks of the more desirable fish and by penetrating ever further into remote oceans. Today, all available stocks are being exploited, and now even the total tonnage is beginning to fall. The UN estimates that the total value of the world's catch could be increased by nearly $30 billion if fish stocks were properly managed by governments interested in the total catch, rather than exploited by individuals interested in their own catch.

The developed countries have so overfished their own stocks that Iceland and the European Union could cut their fleets by 40 per cent and catch as much fish as they do today. This is because more fish would survive to spawn, allowing each boat in a smaller fleet to catch about 40 per cent more than does each boat in today's large fishing fleet.

The problem has become so acute that Canada shut down its entire Atlantic cod fishing industry in 1985 and its Pacific salmon industry in 1988.

Tens of thousands of Newfoundland residents lost their livelihoods in the demise of what had been the province's largest industry—the catching, freezing, and canning of fish—an industry that had flourished for five centuries. Canada and the European Union have since been in conflict over what Canada claims is predatory overfishing by EU boats just outside Canadian territorial waters.

The Mediterranean has been so overfished that seafood that was once the staple for the poor is now an expensive luxury eaten mainly by rich tourists.

Policy response

The European Union has a common fishing policy covering the Atlantic territorial waters of its member countries. Since 1983, total allowable catches for all main species have been set annually and divided up into catch quotas for each member country. Minimum mesh size on nets and other ways of protecting young fish are also imposed. Inspection and monitoring measures are rigorously applied to give force to the regulations. So far, however, the regulations apply only to the Atlantic. There is no equivalent set of policies to protect the seriously overfished Mediterranean.

Some developing countries are following similar lines, but the majority are encouraging rapid expansion of their own fishing fleets with the all-too-predictable results that their domestic waters will soon be seriously overfished.

Worldwide action saved most species of whales. It remains to be seen how many types of fish will be caught to extinction and how many will recover as individual nations slowly learn the lesson of economic theory. Common property resources need central management if they are not to be overexploited to an extent that risks extinction.

Box 18.3 Buffaloes, cows, and elephants

For centuries North American bison—commonly called buffaloes—were a common property resource for the Plains Indians, whose populations were small enough that they could kill all they needed without endangering the ability of the herds to reproduce themselves. In a little over a decade following the end of the American Civil War in 1865, white hunters decimated the herds. Buffalo Bill Cody may have been a folk hero, but he, and those like him, were the buffalo's executioners.

The buffalo was replaced by cattle, which did not follow the buffalo into extinction. The difference was that cattle were the private property of the ranchers. Rustlers and other predators attacked the herds, but the self-interest of ranchers made it worthwhile for them to protect their cattle.

Many people, watching the decimation of wildlife in Africa and Asia, have argued that property rights should be used to turn these animals from the modern equivalent of the buffalo into the modern equivalent of cattle. Wildlife is a common property resource. When it becomes endangered, laws are passed to prevent predatory hunting. But no one has any profit motive in enforcing these laws. Government officials are employed to do this job,

but they are often few in number and poorly paid. Some become corrupted by the large sums poachers are willing to pay to avoid enforcement. Others find the policing job impossible, given the inadequate resources that their governments devote to enforcement.

Some African governments have dealt with the problem by giving ownership of the wild animals to local villages and allowing them to use the animals as a commercial asset. The animals are the subjects of camera safaris whose organizers pay the locals for the privilege. They are also prey for hunters who pay large sums for licences to kill a selected number of animals. Local tribesmen control poachers and keep the licensed kill rate below the reproduction rate because they have a profit motive in protecting what has become their very valuable property.

These schemes have many opponents as well as many supporters. Some opponents object to any permissible 'sports hunting' and other commercial use of wild animals. They argue for more effective public enforcement of anti-poaching laws. Supporters counter that leaving the animals as common property is bound to result in their extinction. Farming them is, they argue, better than presiding over their extinction.

justice for the present users has no easy resolution. What is sure, however, is that if the resource is being exploited to the point of destruction, little is achieved for either equity or efficiency by preserving its common property status.

Public goods: non-excludable and non-rivalrous

Goods that are neither excludable nor rivalrous are called **public goods,** or sometimes **collective consumption goods.** They are the third reason on our list of causes for market failure. The classic case is national defence. An army of a given size protects all the nation's citizens equally no matter how many citizens there are and whether or not a particular individual pays taxes to support it. Similarly, a police force that keeps the streets safe protects all of the street's users, no matter how many there are. If some do not pay their share of the costs, they cannot be denied protection as long as they continue to use the safe street. Information is often a public good. It is clearly non-rivalrous and often non-excludable. Suppose a certain food additive causes cancer. The cost of discovering this needs to be borne only once. The information is then of value to everyone who might have used the additive. Once it is in the public domain, no one can be stopped from learning about the information. Other public goods include lighthouses (in most but not all circumstances) and weather forecasts.

Because public goods are non-excludable, private firms will not provide them.

The obvious remedy in these cases is for the government to provide the good and pay for its provision out of general tax revenue.

When should a public good be provided? To illustrate the basic principle, consider a community composed of just two consumers. The government is considering whether or not to provide a park. Arthur is prepared to pay up to £200 for use of the park, while Julia is willing to pay up to £100. The total value to the two individuals of having the park is £300. If it can be produced for £225, there is a £75 gain on its production since it provides services that the community values at £300 at a cost of only £225.

The optimal quantity of a public good The above example reveals a key point about public goods. If one person consumes a unit of an ordinary good, another person cannot also consume that unit. Thus to satisfy all the demand at any given price, the sum of all the quantities demanded must be produced. With a public good, however, a given unit can be consumed by everyone. Thus the demand for any unit of the good is represented by the sum of the prices that each individual consumer would be willing to pay for that unit. Therefore, the community's demand curve for a public good is the vertical sum of the demand curves of the individual consumers.

If the amount of a public good can be varied continuously, the optimal quantity to produce is that quantity for which the marginal cost of the last unit is just equal to the sum of the prices all consumers would be willing to pay for that unit.

This equilibrium, which is analysed in Figure 18.2, guarantees that the last unit of the public good costs as much to produce as the value that it gives to all of its consumers.

Who pays? One way to pay for a public good is to charge

Figure 18.2 A public good

The society's demand curve for a public good is the vertical sum of all the individuals' demand curves. The demand curves D_a and D_b refer to two individuals. Their collective demand is shown by D_m, which is the vertical summation of D_a and D_b. For example, individual a would pay p_0 for quantity q_0, while individual b would pay p_1 for the same quantity. Together they are willing to pay the sum of p_0 and p_1, which is p_2.

The optimal quantity of the good to produce is q_0, where the marginal cost curve MC cuts the collective demand curve. At this point the marginal cost of another unit is just equal to the sum of the values that each person places on that unit.

each person the same proportion of the maximum amount he or she would be prepared to pay rather than go without the good, while fixing that proportion so as to cover the total costs of production. In the two-person community discussed above, Arthur is prepared to pay £200 and Julia £100 for the park rather than go without. If it costs £150 to produce, then each person can be charged one-half of their own maximum, making £100 for Arthur and £50 for Julia.

Each of them gets the use of the park for half of what he or she is prepared to pay. Their payments just cover total costs of production, leaving £150 of total consumers' surplus.

The practical problem in using any formula based on what people are willing to pay for the public good lies in getting people to reveal their preferences. Suppose, for example, that the government is considering building a public park to serve a community of 1,000 people. It asks each of them how much he or she is prepared to pay. If I am one of those 1,000, it is in my interests to understate my true valuation, as long as everyone else does not do the same. Indeed, I might say I valued the park at zero, while others reported enough value to cover the costs. The public good would then be produced, and I would get the use of it for no payment at all.

The **free rider problem** refers to each person's motivation to understate the value of a non-rivalrous good in the hope that others will end up paying for it. This motivation makes it difficult to cover the costs of such goods by any formula based on people's individual valuations.

The free rider problem can be avoided by covering the costs of public goods out of tax revenue.

Goods such as national defence, weather forecasts, navigation aids, police, and fire protection are typically paid for from tax revenue and provided free to all users. This allows the goods to be produced above the levels at which the free market would produce them (often the free market would produce nothing). It also avoids the problem of inefficient exclusion. Those who value a particular good higher than the average valuation gain more than those who value it below the average valuation. The hope is that, over a large number of public goods, these individual differences will cancel out. Everyone will then gain on balance as a result of the government's provision of public goods out of tax revenue.

Externalities

We have seen that a perfectly competitive economy allocates resources optimally because price equals marginal cost in all lines of production. For this to be true, it is necessary that all costs are incurred by the producers and all benefits are reaped by their customers. This localization of costs does not occur when there are **externalities,** which are costs or benefits of a transaction that are incurred or received by other members of the society but not taken into account by the parties to the transaction. They are also called *third-party effects* and sometimes *neighbourhood effects*, because parties other than the primary participants in the transaction (the consumers and the producers) are

affected. Externalities are the fourth item on our list of causes of market failure.

Externalities arise in many different ways, and they may be beneficial or harmful. A harmful externality occurs, for example, when a factory generates pollution. Individuals who live and work in the neighbourhood bear costs arising from the factory's production, including adverse health effects and clean-up costs. Profit-maximizing factory owners do not take these effects into account when they decide how much to produce. The element of social cost that they ignore is external to their decision-making process.

A beneficial externality occurs, for example, when I paint my house and enhance my neighbours' views and the values of their properties. Other cases arise when some genius—an Einstein, a Mozart, a Van Gogh—gives the world discoveries and works of art whose worth is far in excess of what he or she is paid to create them.

Externalities create a divergence between the private benefits and costs of economic activity and the social benefits and costs. **Private costs** are those costs that are incurred by the parties directly involved in some economic activity. When a good is produced, the private costs are those borne by the producing firm. **Social costs** are the costs incurred by the whole society. These are the private costs *plus* any costs borne by third parties. **Private benefits** are the benefits received by those involved in the activity. In the case of a marketed good these are the utilities obtained by buyers. **Social benefits** are the benefits to the whole society. They are the private benefits *plus* any benefit to third parties.

Society's resources are optimally allocated when social marginal cost equals social marginal benefit.

When this is so, there can be no social benefit in reallocating resources among different lines of production. Free markets will not produce social optimality when there are discrepancies between private and social costs and private and social benefits. The reason is that under perfect competition *private* marginal cost is equated to *private* marginal benefit (the price of the product).

Two important results follow immediately:

1. The outputs of firms that create harmful externalities will exceed the socially optimal levels.

This is the reason. When marginal private cost is equated to price and hence to marginal private benefit, marginal social cost, which is higher because of harmful externalities, will exceed marginal social benefit.

2. The outputs of firms that create beneficial externalities will be less than the socially optimal levels.

This is the reason. When marginal private cost is equated to price and hence to marginal private benefit, the marginal social benefit, which is higher because of beneficial externalities, will exceed marginal social cost.

Consider a simple example in which a standard kitchen gadget sells for £10 and 1,000 units are produced at a marginal cost of £10. If there are no externalities, this is the socially optimal output, because the £10 valuation that each consumer puts on the last unit consumed is equal to the £10 opportunity cost of producing that unit. Now let there be £5 of negative externalities created when each unit is produced. Marginal social cost of £15 exceeds the marginal social benefit of £10 on the last unit produced. To move towards the social optimum, output should be reduced. Alternatively assume the externality is beneficial

Figure 18.3 Private and social cost

Negative externalities cause marginal social cost to exceed price in competitive equilibrium. Marginal social cost, MC_s, exceeds marginal private cost, MC_p, by the amount of the external cost imposed on others. At the competitive output, q_0, marginal private cost equals price, but marginal social cost exceeds it. The socially optimal output is q^*, where MC_s = price. For every unit between q^* and q_0 marginal social cost exceeds price and hence its production involves a social loss.

instead of harmful, conferring external benefits valued at £6 a unit on third parties. Now marginal social benefit of £16 exceeds marginal social cost of £10. To approach a social optimum, output should be increased.

To achieve the optimal allocation of resources in the face of externalities, governments need to encourage production of goods with positive externalities and discourage production of those with negative externalities, compared with what would be produced under free-market conditions.

Figure 18.3 illustrates the market failures caused by externalities as well as their optimal correction.

Unregulated markets tend to produce excessive amounts of environmental damage. Zero environmental damage, however, is neither technologically possible nor economically efficient.

Externalities and the Coase theorem

Externalities arise because of a lack of property rights. A factory throws its liquid waste into the river and its smoke into the atmosphere because no one owns them. Both the river and the air are common property resources. If they were in private hands, the owners would have a self-interest in preserving them. Let us see how this might come about.

An example

Say, for example, that a manufacturing plant needs pure water for one of its processes. It gets this from a short mountain stream which then tumbles into the ocean. A chemical plant is established upstream and dumps its waste into the river. The river is a common property resource so the plant cannot be stopped from imposing negative externalities on the downstream user, who must now set up an expensive water-purification system.

A downstream owner Assume that the downstream plant owns the stream. Its owner might say to the chemical plant's managers, 'Do not dump *your* waste into *my* stream.' The managers might counter that they were willing to pay for the privilege. The downstream owner asks, 'How much?' After considering the cost of alternative waste-disposal mechanisms, the chemical plant's managers answer, '£6 per tonne of waste'. The owner of the downstream plant determines that the cost of purifying the water in the stream is £8 per tonne of waste. 'No deal,' she says. The upstream chemical plant opens an alternative waste-disposal system at a cost of £6 and the least costly method of dealing with the waste is thus used.

Later, technological improvements in water purification allow the downstream plant to purify its water for only £3 per tonne. The owner calls the upstream managers and says, 'I hear your disposal plant is coming up for renewal next year. I am prepared to let you dump the waste in my stream for a fee of £4 per tonne.' 'Done,' say the upstream managers, and next year the waste is disposed of in the river. The water is then cleaned up by the downstream user at a cost of £3 per tonne, instead of at a cost of £6 when the chemical plant treated the waste. Once again, the cheapest method of disposal and use is adopted.

An upstream owner What would have happened if the river had been owned by the chemical plant instead of the downstream user? The managers of the chemical plant decide to use their stream for disposing of their waste. But the downstream users of water complain and offer to pay for the use of the fresh water. Their costs of making the water usable are £8 per tonne of waste. So they can offer up to that much to dissuade the chemical plant from dumping its waste. That plant can use an alternative waste-disposal method at a cost of £6 per tonne. So the managers say, 'Yes, how about giving us £7 for every tonne of our waste that we do not dump into our river?' A deal is struck and the cheapest method is undertaken.

Later, when the new water-purification technology is developed, the downstream users can purify the water at a cost of only £3 per tonne. So they will offer no more than that to prevent the chemical plant from dumping its waste. When the upstream plant's alternative waste-disposal system wears out, it will not be replaced. The waste will be dumped and the downstream plant will purify its water at

a cost of £3 per tonne. Once again the cheapest method of dealing with the waste will have been adopted.

The theorem

This example illustrates a remarkable result developed some years ago by the British-born economist Ronald Coase, who received the 1991 Nobel Prize in economics. The result is now called the **Coase theorem**:

If the two sides to an externality—the one causing it and the one suffering from it—can bargain together, they will produce the efficient use of resources.

What is needed is that one of the two has a property right that forces the other side to bargain. Surprisingly, however, it does not matter which side has the property right. We saw this in the above example, where the same result was arrived at independently of who owned the river. Property rights will determine who gets most of the consumers' surplus on the bargain, because they determine who has to pay whom. But, given that both sides bargain for their own self-interest, the allocation of resources to deal with the externality will be independent of where the property right resides.

High transaction costs

What makes the Coase theorem work is that someone has a property right over what is affected by the externality *and* that both sides can bargain effectively together. This latter condition is a matter of transaction costs. It was easy enough for the owners of the two plants to talk on the phone and reach an efficient bargain. It is another matter for all the citizens of the cities of London or São Paulo to bargain with the hundreds of factory owners, car drivers, and other producers of pollution in order to reach an efficient solution to dealing with air and water pollution in and around their cities.

In cases in which property rights cannot be assigned and/or where transaction costs are excessive, there are only two possibilities. We may accept the externality and learn to live with it, or governments may intervene on our behalf to deal with it.

We will see, however, that although governments often do improve matters somewhat, arriving at the most efficient solution is no easy task.

The control of pollution

In this section we illustrate government policies with respect to negative externalities in the context of one of their most important applications, environmental damage caused by pollution. Steel plants produce heat and smoke in addition to steel. Farms produce chemical runoff as well as food. Household consumption produces human waste and refuse. Indeed, there are few human activities that do not produce some negative pollution externalities.

For this reason it is impossible to reduce pollution to zero. Instead, the optimal amount of pollution abatement occurs when the marginal benefit of a unit of abatement is just equal to the marginal cost of abatement.

Pollution control through direct regulation

Direct controls are a common method of environmental regulation. For example, UK car emissions standards must be met by all new cars, and by cars over three years of age when they take their annual MOT test. Many cities and towns prohibit the private burning of leaves and other rubbish because of the air-pollution problem that the burning would cause. The 1956 UK Clean Air Act obliged people to switch from coal to smokeless fuels. Similarly, the government gradually reduced the amount of lead allowed in petrol and provided tax incentives for drivers to switch to unleaded petrol. Since the mid-1970s, petrol consumption has increased by about 50 per cent while lead emissions have fallen by about 75 per cent.

Problems with direct controls Direct controls are often economically inefficient. This is because controls typically mandate the same response from different polluters independently of their costs of pollution abatement. Although these requirements may seem reasonable, they will be inefficient unless the polluters face identical pollution abatement costs. Alternative, more flexible, methods can often provide the same amount of abatement at a lower cost.

Direct pollution controls are usually inefficient because, by mandating the same response from all agents, they do not minimize the cost of any given amount of pollution abatement.

Efficient allocation of pollution abatement between firms with different prevention costs is analysed in Figure 18.4. As long as one firm has a lower abatement cost than another firm, it pays to reallocate a given amount of abatement. The lower-cost firm should abate more and the higher-cost firm less. The general conclusion is that

Efficient abatement requires that each firm have the same marginal cost of the last unit of abatement undertaken.

None the less, direct controls are effective when it is important not to exceed certain dangerous thresholds. They are also useful in situations where production is undertaken by a very small number of publicly owned natural monopolies. In other cases policies that create economic incentives not to pollute are more effective than those that operate on the command principle.

Control through emissions taxes

The great British economist A. C. Pigou (1877–1959), who did path-breaking work on externalities of all sorts, was a pioneer in developing public policy tools for their control. His name is associated particularly with pollution taxes, which provide an alternative method to direct controls. The advantage of such taxes is that they **internalize the externality**, which means increasing the firm's private cost by the amount of the external cost. This makes private and social costs the same, with the result that efficient outcomes can result from decentralized decisions made by individual producers.

Look again at the example in Figure 18.4. If all firms are required to pay a tax of £80 on each unit of pollution, profit maximization will lead them to reduce emissions to the point at which the marginal cost of further reduction is equal to the tax. This means that firm B will reduce emissions much more than firm A, and that in equilibrium both will have the same marginal cost of further abatement, which is required for efficiency.

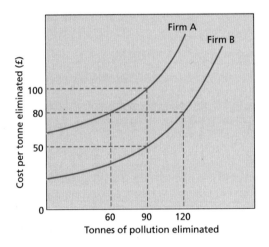

Figure 18.4 Pollution abatement

Efficient methods of abating pollution take account of differences in costs of abatement among firms. The figure shows the different marginal costs of pollution abatement for two firms. For any given amount of abatement, firm A has a higher cost of a further unit of abatement than has B. When they are both mandated to reduce pollution by 90 units, A's marginal cost of £100 exceeds B's marginal cost of £50. This is inefficient. A could cut its abatement by one unit, saving £100, while B increased its abatement by one unit, adding £50 to its costs. Total abatement would then be unchanged but costs would fall by £50.

An emissions tax of £80 per tonne of pollution is now imposed. Low-cost firm B now abates pollution by 120 tonnes, while high-cost firm A abates by 60 tonnes. This is the efficient way of producing 180 tonnes of abatement since the two firms have the same abatement costs at the margin, thus minimizing the total cost of reducing pollution by 180 tonnes.

A second great advantage of using emissions taxes is that they do not require the regulators to specify how polluters should abate pollution. Firms can be left to find the most efficient abatement techniques. The profit motive will lead them to do so, because they will want to minimize their tax bill.

In principle emissions taxes can perfectly internalize pollution externalities, so that profit-maximizing behaviour on the part of firms will lead them to produce the efficient amount of pollution abatement at minimum cost.

Emissions taxes in practice Emissions taxes can work only if it is possible to measure emissions accurately. In some cases this does not pose much of a problem, but in many other cases there are no effective measuring devices that can be installed at reasonable cost. One important example is automotive pollution. It would be very expensive to attach a reliable monitor to every car and lorry and then to assess taxes based on readings from the monitor. In this case, as in many others, direct controls are the only cost-effective method.

Another problem involves setting the tax rate. The regulatory agency needs to estimate the marginal social damage caused per unit of each pollutant and set the tax equal to this amount. This would perfectly internalize the pollution externality. However, the required information is often difficult to obtain. If the regulatory agency sets the tax rate too high, too many resources will be devoted to pollution control. If the tax is set too low, there will be too much pollution.

Control through tradable emissions permits

Tradable emissions permits can solve many of the problems associated with direct controls and emissions taxes. To use them, the regulator must decide how much pollution to permit. In Figure 18.4 the original regulations required each firm to reduce its total pollution by 90 tonnes. This is exactly the same as permitting the firms to pollute by their original amount of pollution *minus* 90 tonnes. To pose the problem this way, the regulators issue to each firm a right to pollute by that amount. To illustrate, if each firm had been generating 150 tonnes of pollution, exactly the same reduction occurs if firms are ordered to reduce pollution by 90 tonnes or if they are permitted to pollute to a maximum of 60 tonnes.

Tradable permits in theory Now, however, comes the new twist. A large efficiency gain can be achieved by making these rights to pollute tradable. This allows the firm with the low cost of pollution abatement to sell its right to pollute to the high-abatement-cost firm. Total pollution and total pollution abatement will be unchanged, but more abatement will be done by the firm with the low abatement cost (which sold its rights to pollute to the other firm),

Figure 18.5 Tradable pollution permits

Tradable permits achieve the same results as the most efficient tax. Each firm produces 150 tonnes of pollution when no abatement procedures are followed. Abatement reduces the amount of pollution but at a rising marginal cost. Each firm is originally given an endowment of permits to emit 60 tonnes of pollution. If no trading is allowed, the marginal costs of abatement are then £120 for A and £50 for B. With trading, B sells 30 tonnes' worth of permits to A. Firm A then pollutes by 90 tonnes and firm B by 30 tonnes. The price of a permit is £80, which is the same as both firms' marginal cost of abatement at their new levels of pollution.

thus reducing the total cost of meeting the target for any given amount of pollution reduction.

Figure 18.5 illustrates this case. Where Figure 18.4 showed the amount of abatement, Figure 18.5 shows the amount of emissions. The cost curves now rise to the left instead of to the right as they did in Figure 18.4. Starting from the 150 tonnes of pollutants that each firm is emitting with zero abatement, the abatement cost rises as less and less pollution is allowed. Production with zero pollution is impossible, so the costs rise rapidly as very low pollution levels are achieved. The government wishes to cut pollution from its existing level of 300 tonnes to 120 tonnes. So it gives each firm 60 tonnes' worth of pollution permits. When they each cut their pollution to 60 tonnes, firm A has a much higher marginal cost than firm B. So B sells A some permits. B abates more and A pollutes more. Total pollution is unchanged but total abatement costs fall. Trade will be profitable as long as A's marginal abatement costs exceed B's. In the final equilibrium, both firms have the same marginal cost of abatement, which equals the price of a permit to abate by 1 tonne. Now each firm is indifferent between abating by 1 tonne and buying a permit to avoid abating by 1 tonne. The cost of abatement is minimized and both firms have gained. A has saved more clean-up costs than the cost of the permits it has bought. The prices of the permits that B sells exceed the cost of the extra abatement it must incur because of having fewer permits.

Everyone is better off. Society gets its abatement at the least cost in terms of valuable resources. Both firms have more money in their pockets than if each had been ordered to cut pollution by an identical amount.

Notice that the £90 price of a permit to produce 1 tonne of pollution is the same as the pollution tax required to induce 150 tonnes of abatement at the least cost. The difference is that permits require less information than taxes. The authorities just issue the number of permits they decide upon and let the market fix the price. If taxes are to be used, the government must determine the best tax rate and then impose it.

Tradable emissions permits can be used to achieve the same allocation of resources as would occur with emissions taxes, while reducing the amount of information required by the regulatory authorities.

Tradable emissions permits in practice Tradable permits and emissions taxes pose difficult problems of implementation. Some of these involve technical difficulties in measuring pollution and in designing mechanisms to ensure that firms and individuals comply with regulations. None the less their use is growing in the USA as firms and governments become more used to them. One interesting phenomenon has been the steady fall in the price of pollution permits particularly for SO_2 emissions. This reflects the development of newer, less polluting technologies under the incentive of having to pay for polluting by purchasing a pollution permit. As less and less pollution is produced, the price of the rights to produce a fixed amount of pollution is declining. Canada is also beginning to experiment with these imaginative methods which harness market incentives, and the EU would be well advised to consider following these leads.

Conclusion

Much environmental pollution is caused by the failure of markets to account for externalities. At the same time market-like mechanisms can be used to internalize the externalities. Pollution is an example of a problem in which markets themselves can be used to correct market failure.

The problem of externalities arises because of the absence of property rights. For example, the polluting firm uses the free air to dump its waste. If it owned the air, it would worry about the loss of the value of its property caused by the pollution. If those affected by the pollution owned the air, they would not allow it to be used unless they were paid sufficient compensation.

Since many externalities arise from an absence of property rights, the externality can be internalized if appropriate property rights can be created.

Box 18.4 outlines some of the main policies that governments have used to give effect to desired environmental control.

Asymmetric information

Markets work best when everyone is well informed. People cannot make maximizing decisions if they are poorly informed about the things they are buying or selling. Lack of relevant information is the fifth item on our list of reasons for market failure.

Rules requiring that products and prices be described correctly are meant to improve the efficiency of choices by providing people with correct and relevant information. In many cases where the consequences of errors are not dramatic, consumers can be left to discover, through trial and error, what is in their own best interests. In other cases, however, the results of error can be too drastic to allow consumers to learn from their own experiences which products are reliable and which unreliable. For example, botulism, caused by poorly preserved foods, can cause death. In such cases the state intervenes to impose standards and testing requirements in the consumers' own best interests.

Standards are also set in the workplace. Some people argue that firms should be left to set their own safety standards. High-risk firms would then have to pay wage premiums to induce workers to accept these risks voluntarily. Those who favour government regulation of work standards argue it on two grounds. First, firms are often better informed than workers on changing safety conditions in work, particularly in small factories. Government regulation then compensates for the inefficiencies caused by this unequal access to information. Second, people who are desperate for work will take risks that are socially unacceptable, or that their own desperation causes them to assess imperfectly. In this case the purpose of government intervention is either to impose social values not held by specific individuals or to act paternalistically in the belief that the state can assess the self-interests of the workers better than the workers can do for themselves.

In some situations governments cannot easily remove the differences in information available to buyers and sellers. The party with the superior knowledge can then use it to change the nature of the transaction itself. For example, doctors, lawyers, and other specialists typically know much more than their clients about what they are doing. They can, therefore, influence the demand for their services by what they do and do not tell their clients. In countries where doctors are paid for on a fee-for-service basis—whether by the government, private insurers, or individual patients—elective surgery is often observed to vary with doctors' other workloads. It is low in regions

Box 18.4 Policies for environmental regulation

Governments throughout the world are experimenting with many of the methods of environmental control discussed in the text. Here is a sampling of some of these policies:

■ In the United Kingdom the Environmental Protection Act of 1989 lays down minimum standards for all emissions from thousands of chemical, waste incineration, and oil-refining factories. Performance is monitored by HM Inspectorate of Pollution, the costs of which are paid for by the factory owners themselves. The release of genetically engineered bacteria and viruses is also regulated. Strict regulations are imposed on waste-disposal operations and on most forms of straw and stubble burning. Litterers are subject to on-the-spot fines of up to £1,000.

■ The 'Environmental Action Programmes' of the European Union set specific standards for minimum acceptable levels of water quality for drinking and for bathing. Bathing beaches are regularly monitored.

■ In the 1992 Copenhagen Agreements nearly 100 countries agreed to phase out chlorofluorocarbons (CFCs) by the year 1996, four years earlier than had previously been agreed. The Copenhagen Agreements also regulated other ozone-damaging substances, such as methyl bromide, used in preserving fruit and grain, the output of which was to be held at 1991 levels by the year 1995.

■ The Kyoto Protocol signed in 1998 called for major reductions in greenhouse gas emissions over the next fifteen years. Once again the developed countries had more success in agreeing on reductions among themselves than in persuading developing nations to follow suit. Many observers wondered if the reductions agreed to by some of the developed nations could be realized at an acceptable cost. Following the conference the UK environment minister was quoted (on the government's web site) as saying

that measures such as voluntary agreements, adoption of best practice, regulations, and market instruments such as trading or taxation would all have a part to play. Until such measures could be devised, he called on business for voluntary co-operation in meeting objectives for reductions in emissions.

■ Under the United States Clean Air Act utilities must cut emissions of sulphur dioxide from a national total of 19 million tonnes to 9 million tonnes by the year 2000. This is being accomplished by issuing 9 million tonnes worth of tradable permits to pollute.

■ According to the 'polluter-pays' principle used by the OECD, the polluter is to bear the cost of government-imposed measures designed to reduce pollution. This principle has been adopted in all member states so as to avoid the distortions in trade flows that could arise if countries tackled environmental problems in widely different ways with widely different effects on prices. In other cases it is the sufferer who is paying. For example, Sweden assists Poland to reduce the acid rain that is damaging Swedish lakes and forests. Similarly, the Montreal Protocol includes provisions by which developing countries are to be compensated by richer countries for agreeing to limit their use of CFCs.

■ The UK strategy for water pricing gives water companies the freedom to pass on any extra costs of environmental improvements and ensures that those companies have an economic incentive to undertake such improvements. The policy violates the 'polluter-pays' principle by putting the costs on the consumer. Non-market incentives are also widely applied to water. Under the UK Control of Pollution Act, a licence is required for the discharge of pollutants into rivers and coastal waters. These licences, called Discharge Consents, are issued by the National Rivers Authority. They specify the type and quantity of substances that may be discharged.

where doctors are busy and high in regions where doctors are underemployed. The explanation lies not in the different needs of patients in these various areas, but in the varying demands for these services created by the different advice that doctors give to their patients.

Two important sources of market failure that arise when privately held information is bought and sold have already been discussed in Chapter 12. (The discussion on pages 194–5 should be reviewed at this point.) These are *moral hazard* and *adverse selection*. Since they were discussed earlier, we need say little more here beyond two observations. First, when insurance leads people to take risks that they would avoid in the absence of insurance (*moral hazard*), social costs are unnecessarily high. For example, more houses are destroyed by fire because insured people take risks that they would avoid if they had to bear the full cost of any fire losses themselves. Second, when buyers and sellers have unequal knowledge about their transactions, *adverse selection* may cause the outcome to be less efficient than if they were equally well informed. This happens, for example, when some types of insurance are bought heavily by those who know better than the insurers that they are bad risks and is avoided by

those who know better than the insurers that they are good risks.

Missing markets

In the 1950s two American economists, Kenneth Arrow and Gerard Debreu, who were subsequently awarded Nobel Prizes in economics studied necessary conditions for optimality in resource allocation. One of the conditions is that there must exist a separate market in which each good and service can be traded to the point where the marginal benefit equals the marginal cost. Missing markets are the sixth item on our list of causes of market failure.

Not only do markets not exist for such prominent things as public goods and common property resources; they are also absent in a number of less obvious but equally important cases.

One important set of missing markets involves risk. You can insure your house against its burning down. This is because your knowledge of the probability of this occurrence is not much better than your insurance company's, and because the probability of your house burning down is normally independent of the probability of other houses burning down.

If you are a farmer, you cannot usually insure your crop against bad weather. This is because the probabilities of yours and your neighbour's crop suffering from bad weather are interrelated. If the insurance company has to pay you, the probabilities are it will also have to pay your neighbour and everyone else in the county—perhaps even throughout the country. An insurance company survives by pooling independent risks. It cannot survive if the same event affects all its clients in the same way. (This is why, although you can insure your house against a fire from ordinary causes, you cannot insure it against fires caused by war.)

If you are in business, you cannot insure against bank-ruptcy. Here the problem is adverse selection. You know much better than does your would-be insurance company the chances that your business will fail. If insurance were offered against such failure, it would mainly be taken out by people whose businesses had recently developed a high chance of failure.

Another set of missing markets concerns future events. You can buy certain well-established and unchanging products, such as corn or oil, on futures markets. But you cannot do so for most manufactured products, such as cars and TV sets, because no one knows the precise speci-fications of future models. Futures markets for these products are missing, so there is no way that the costs and benefits of planned future expenditure on these products can be equated by economic transactions made today.

Public policy towards monopoly and competition

The seventh and last item on our list of reasons for market failure concerns market power. Cartels and price-fixing agreements among oligopolists, whether explicit or tacit, have long met with public suspicion and official hostility. These, and other non-competitive practices, are collectively referred to as monopoly practices. Note that these are not just what monopolists do. They include non-competitive behaviour of firms that are operating in other market structures such as oligopoly. The laws and other instruments that are used to encourage competition and discourage monopoly practices make up competition pol-icy and are used to influence both the market structure and the behaviour of individual firms.

The goal of controlling market power provides ration-ales both for competition policy and for economic regu-lation. Competition can be encouraged and monopoly practices discouraged by influencing either the *market structure* or the *market behaviour* of individual firms. By and large UK competition policy has sought to create more competitive market structures where possible. Where such structures could not be established, policy has sought to discourage monopolistic practices and to encourage com-petitive behaviour. In addition the government employs economic regulations, which prescribe the rules under which firms can do business, and in some cases determine the prices that businesses can charge for their output.

We study three aspects of these policies: the direct control of natural monopolies, the direct control of oligo-polies, and the creation of competitive conditions. The first is a necessary part of any competition policy, the second has been important in the past but is less so now, and the third constitutes the main current thrust of UK competition policy.

Direct control of natural monopolies

The clearest case for public intervention arises with a na-tural monopoly, an industry in which economies of scale are so dominant that there is room for only one firm to operate at the minimum efficient scale. UK policymakers have not wanted to insist on the establishment of several smaller, less efficient producers whenever a single firm would be much more efficient; neither have they wanted to give a natural monopolist the opportunity to restrict out-put, raise prices, and reap monopoly profits.

One response to natural monopoly is for government to assume ownership of the single firm, setting it up as a na-tionalized industry. The government appoints managers who are supposed to set prices guided by their under-standing of the national interest. Another response has been to allow private ownership but to regulate the monopoly firm's behaviour. Until the 1980s, and particularly after the Second World War, UK policy favoured public ownership. Recently such industries have been privatized—that is, sold to members of the public—and then to some extent regulated. Examples are telecommunications, gas, water, and electricity. Whichever choice the government makes, it will exert an influence on the behaviour of these indus-tries.

Short-run price and output

What is the correct price–output policy that the govern-ment should encourage these industries to adopt?

Marginal cost pricing   Sometimes the government

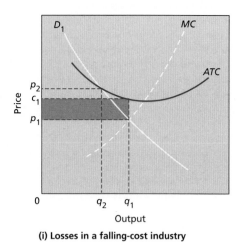

(i) Losses in a falling-cost industry

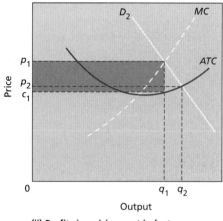

(ii) Profits in a rising-cost industry

Figure 18.6 Pricing policies for natural monopolies

Marginal cost pricing leads to profits or losses; average cost pricing is inefficient. In each part the output at which marginal cost equals price is q_1 and price is p_1.

In part (i) average costs are falling at output q_1, so marginal costs are less than the average cost of c_1. There is a loss of $c_1 - p_1$ on each unit, making a total loss equal to the dark blue area.

In part (ii) average cost of c_1 is less than price at output q_1. There is a profit of $p_1 - c_1$ on each unit sold, making a total profit equal to the dark blue area.

In each part of the diagram the output at which average cost equals price is q_2 and the associated price is p_2. In part (i) marginal cost is less than price at q_2, so output is below its optimal level. In part (ii) marginal cost exceeds price at q_2, so output is greater than its optimal level.

dictates that price should be set equal to short-run marginal cost so as to maximize consumers' plus producers' surpluses. According to economic theory, this policy, which is called marginal cost pricing, provides the efficient solution.

Marginal cost pricing does, however, create some problems. The natural monopoly may still have unexploited economies of scale and may hence be operating on the falling portion of its average total cost curve. In this case marginal cost will be less than average total cost and pricing at marginal cost will lead to losses. This is shown in Figure 18.6.

A falling-cost natural monopoly that sets price equal to marginal cost will suffer losses.

Average cost pricing Sometimes natural monopolies are directed to produce the output that will just cover total costs, thus earning neither profits nor losses. This means that the firm produces to the point where average revenue equals average total cost, which is where the demand curve cuts the average total cost curve. Figure 18.6 shows that for a falling-cost firm this pricing policy requires producing at less than the optimal output in order to avoid the losses that would occur under marginal cost pricing.

Average cost pricing is usually allocatively inefficient.

The very long run

Natural monopoly is a long-run concept, meaning that, given existing technology, there is room for only one firm to operate profitably. In the very long run, however, technology changes. Not only does today's competitive industry sometimes become tomorrow's natural monopoly, but also today's natural monopoly sometimes becomes tomorrow's competitive industry.

A striking example is the telecommunications industry. Not long ago the transmissions of voice and hard-copy messages were thought to be natural monopolies. Now technological developments such as satellite transmission, electronic mail, the Internet, and fax machines have made these activities highly competitive. Also, new firms can be given access to existing infrastructure such as cables, thus greatly lowering set-up costs and encouraging competition from new entrants. As a consequence in many countries an odd circumstance arose: nationalized industries, such as the UK Post Office and the telephone system, sought to maintain their profitability by prohibiting entry into what would otherwise have become a fluid and competitive industry. Since it has the full force of the legal system behind it, the public firm may be more successful than the privately owned firm in preserving its monopoly long after technological changes have destroyed its 'naturalness'.

Government policies need to be adjusted frequently to keep them abreast with more or less continuous technological change.

When the UK telephone system was privatized to become British Telecom, it was given a near monopoly for five years, with Cable and Wireless, another privatized company, as its only competitor. This legal restriction of competition was presumably designed to raise the value of the shares that the government sold to the public.

Regulation of natural monopolies

Now that most UK nationalized industries have been privatized, those that are natural monopolies are being regulated by newly formed public regulatory authorities, such as OFTEL (telephones), OFGAS (gas), and OFWAT (water). In the United States, such regulatory bodies were often captured by the firms they were supposed to regulate and ended up working against the interests of consumers (see Box 18.5). An opposite pitfall that some worry about in the United Kingdom is that prices may be pushed so far down in the short-term interests of consumers that the regulated industries will have little incentive to invest in technological innovations. In response to this worry firms were given the right to appeal if they feel prices are being pushed too low. In today's world of rapid technological

change this could work to the long-term disadvantage of consumers.

This worry is often raised in connection with the so-called RPI − X formula, which has been used to regulate the prices charged by privatized firms. The permitted price increase is the increase in the retail price index (RPI) minus some amount designed to pass on some of the firm's cost reductions to its customers. For example, if X is 2 per cent and the price index rises by 5 per cent, the firm can raise its prices by 3 per cent. This is all very well, provided X is not set too high or adjusted too rapidly whenever the firm succeeds in cutting its costs. Large profits provide the incentive to spend money and take risks in developing new cost-cutting innovations. If prices are forced down as soon as the cost reductions are effective, the incentive to innovate will quickly be dissipated.

The UK water industry is being regulated under an RPI + K formula, rather than RPI − X. This is to allow for the fact that the water companies have an obligation to undertake significant expenditures on capital projects, both to improve the reliability and quality of tap water and to reduce pollution of rivers and beaches. The K factor, announced by Ian Byatt, head of OFWAT, in July 1994 for the rest of the decade, was an average of 1.5 per cent. (It was different for each company.) This means that water companies will be permitted to raise the price charged to consumers each year by an average of 1.5 per cent above the rate of increase of retail prices.

UK regulation of privatized industries is still in its early

Box 18.5 Regulation as protection against competition

North American regulatory bodies have all too frequently protected firms rather than consumers. For example, Canadian and American railroad rates were originally regulated in order to keep profits down by establishing schedules of maximum rates. By the 1930s, however, concern had grown over the railroads' depressed economic conditions and the emerging vigorous competition from road transportation. The regulators then became the protectors of the railroads, permitting them to establish minimum rates for freight of different classes, allowing price discrimination, and encouraging other restrictive practices. Moreover, the regulators became leading advocates of including road haulage under the regulatory umbrella, restricting entry and setting *minimum* rates for the large road transport firms. As a result, the big firms lost out to small, unregulated road haulage firms, who could cut rates and draw away customers without fear of retaliation. To eliminate the rate competition, regulation was extended to the small firms. The only reason for regulating the highly competitive road carriers was to control their competition with the railroads.

Airline regulation provides another example. When US airline routes and fares were first regulated, there was arguably so little demand that competition could not have been effective. By the mid-1960s, however, the regulations were plainly designed to shield the major North American carriers from competition. (Unlike Europe, where most carriers have been

government-owned, North America is served by many competing privately owned airlines.) In the 1970s most US regulation, except for safety and other related matters, was swept away. Fares tumbled. Fierce competition broke out. Many small airlines arose and were then absorbed into the big airlines. Some big airlines went under or were absorbed by competitors. The end result, however, was fares on competitive routes that are often less than half those paid by the average air traveller in Europe, where regulations are only slowly being relaxed, decades after they were swept away in the USA.

Why did American regulatory bodies shift from protecting consumers to protecting firms? One thesis, championed by the American Nobel Prize-winner George Stigler (1911–91), is that the firms they were supposed to regulate gradually captured the regulatory commissions. In part this capture was natural enough. When regulatory bodies were hiring staff, they needed people who were knowledgeable in the industries they were regulating. Where better to go than to people who had worked in these industries? Naturally, these people tended to be sympathetic to firms in their own industries. Also, since many of them aspired to go back to those industries once they had gained experience within the regulatory bodies, they were not inclined to arouse the wrath of industry officials by imposing policies that were against the firms' interests.

days. One can only hope that the regulators will remain flexible as experience accumulates and will avoid, as far as possible, excessively favouring either firms or consumers at the expense of the other.

Direct control of oligopolies

Governments have from time to time intervened in industries that were oligopolies, rather than natural monopolies, seeking to enforce the type of price and entry behaviour that was thought to be in the public interest. Such intervention has typically taken two distinct forms. In the United Kingdom from 1945 to 1980 it was primarily nationalization of whole oligopolistic industries such as airlines, railways, steel, and coalmining, which were then run by government-appointed boards. In the United States firms in such oligopolistic industries as airlines, railways, and electric power were left in private hands, but their decisions were regulated by government-appointed bodies that set prices and regulated entry.

Deregulation and privatization

The last two decades of the twentieth century witnessed a movement in virtually all advanced industrial nations, and the vast majority of less developed nations as well, to reduce the level of government control over industry. As a result nationalized industries are being sold to private sector buyers throughout the world. Also, privately owned oligopolies are being subjected to much less detailed control than they were only a couple of decades ago.

Causes

A number of forces had been pushing in this direction:

■ Regulatory bodies often sought to reduce, rather than increase, competition (as discussed in Box 18.5).

■ Expectations that nationalized industries would be superior to private firms in the areas of efficiency, productivity growth, and industrial relations were falsified by experience.

■ Falling transportation costs, and the information and communications revolutions, are exposing local industries to much more international competition than they have previously experienced domestically. This has lowered concern over high national concentration ratios.

■ In spite of being allocatively inefficient because price exceeds marginal cost (by virtue of each firm's negatively sloped demand curve), oligopolistic market structures provided much of the economic growth of the twentieth century. New products, and new ways of producing old products, have followed each other in rapid succession, all leading to higher living standards and higher productivity. Many of these innovations have been provided by firms in oligopolistic industries such as motor cars, agricultural implements, steel, petroleum refining, chemicals, and telecommunications. As long as governments can keep oligopolists competing with each other rather than co-operating to produce monopoly profits, most economists see no need to regulate such things as the prices at which they sell their products and the conditions of entry into their industries.

The worldwide movement towards privatization and deregulation is part of a growing belief among policymakers that private firms operating in free markets are more efficient producers and innovators than governments.

The call is for a diminished role of government in resource allocation—but not for a zero role. Although the belief that government intervention has been excessive is almost worldwide, there are many reasons why the public interest may still require significant intervention. Externalities and other market failures are some of the reasons why it is not necessarily efficient to leave the free market to decide all issues of resource allocation.

The natural outcome of these revised views has been the privatization of nationalized industries and the deregulation of privately owned ones. This latter policy was intended, among other things, to return price-setting and entry decisions to market determination.

Privatization has gone a long way in the United Kingdom. The majority of the nationalized industries, both those containing a few large firms and those containing many smaller firms, have been returned to private ownership. Some details are given in Box 18.6.

The evidence on the effects of privatization is largely encouraging. Prices have fallen markedly in the gas, electricity, and telecommunications industries. At the same time all have had rising stock market values. Some former state-owned companies have become world leaders in a manner that would have been unlikely under state control. The most obvious examples are BT, Cable and Wireless, and British Airways. Many have been attractive targets for takeover bids by foreign utilities. All of this is strong evidence that their performance has been improved by being transferred to private ownership.

Privatization has also spread to other EU countries. For example, Deutsche Telekom was privatized in 1996. Part of the pressure to privatize has come from stiff competition from efficient foreign firms and part from the Maastricht Treaty, which limits public spending and government borrowing. There has also been a trend towards deregulation of many markets. Major pressure in this direction has been exerted by the Single Market Act, which is discussed in Chapter 34. A notable example is air travel, where state-imposed restrictions, often designed to protect state-

Box 18.6 Privatization in the United Kingdom

Privatization has been a complex development in the United Kingdom. Some nationalized industries were sold outright; in others, the government maintained substantial holdings while selling off the rest of its shares. In yet other cases, profitable parts of unprofitable enterprises were separated off and sold. In still other cases, the government sold shares that it held in private companies that had never been nationalized.

The first step towards UK privatization was the sale of council houses, which began in 1979. Over the succeeding decade there was a major reduction in the stock of publicly owned housing, with almost 700,000 dwellings being sold to their occupiers.

The next phase covered a number of relatively small operations in markets where competition was strong. These included the British Sugar Corporation, British Rail Hotels, Sealink Ferries, British Ports, Jaguar, and British Aerospace. These companies have operated successfully, under relatively competitive conditions, since their privatization.

The third phase covered the great industrial giants. It began with British Telecom in 1984 and continued with British Gas in 1986, British Airways in 1987, and British Steel in 1988. Sale of shares in the publicly owned electricity industry began in 1990, with water following soon thereafter. Sale of the remaining coal pits was completed in 1994. The privatization of British Rail was completed by 1997, with the track going to Railtrack and the train services going to several private operators.

A more widely accepted criticism concerns the ways in which privatization has been conducted. When selling off its industrial giants, the UK government faced a dilemma:

Selling an industry as a single unit maximizes the government's sale price, but this also maximizes the industry's subsequent allocative inefficiency.

The government could sell off a giant, such as British Airways or British Gas, as a single unit. This maximizes the monopoly power of its private owners, and hence maximizes the price that they will pay for it. Alternatively, the giant could be broken up and sold in separate units as far as is feasible. This could have been possible, for example, in the sale of British Gas and British Telecom. While this minimizes the monopoly power of the private purchasers (which would still be substantial), it also minimizes the price that will be paid for the industry by private investors.

Up until 1990 the government appeared to have succumbed to the temptation to maximize the selling price by marketing each giant as a single unit. This policy is likely to create more regulatory problems a decade or two from now than if the government had sacrificed some short-term financial gain for the long-term advantages of enhanced competition. One indication of second thoughts on this policy was the splitting in two of British Gas and the introduction of competition in the gas market in 1998.

In later cases of privatization the government seems to have responded to its critics by breaking up the monopoly before selling it to the public. This was the case, for example, of the electricity industry, which was broken up into many constituent parts before being privatized in 1990 (distribution) and 1991 (generation). When the railways were privatized, one firm, Railtrack, owned the lines but many different operating companies were set up to run the trains. Examples are Virgin Trains and Stagecoach.

owned national airlines, are being phased out. Many new private carriers are entering the industry, such as Easyjet based in the UK. The ensuing competition is pushing many fares down, although they still have a long way to go to reach the low fares per mile achieved by the highly competitive US airline industry.

Criticisms

Only a minority of economists today support public over private ownership in industries that can support several competing firms. There is more disagreement, however, over natural monopolies such as gas and electricity. Supporters of privatization argue that there are no natural monopolies in the very long run and that private ownership will encourage the technological dynamism that will erode any natural monopoly. They argue that in the meantime the private firms can be prevented from charging monopoly prices by effective regulation. Opponents argue that a privately owned monopoly will not be more technologically progressive and will behave more like a monopolistic profit-maximizer than would a publicly owned firm. There is no simple resolution to this part of the debate. The behaviour probably depends on the relative abilities of the managements of the publicly owned and privately owned firms, and on the nature of the regulations to which they are subjected.

Intervention to keep firms competing

The least stringent form of government intervention is designed to create conditions of competition by preventing firms from merging unnecessarily or from engaging in certain anti-competitive practices such as colluding to set monopoly prices. Such policies seek to create the most competitive market structure possible and then to prevent firms from reducing competition by engaging in certain forms of co-operative behaviour.

Why worry?

For some time up until the early 1990s industrial concentration increased in Britain, with the percentage of industrial production accounted for by the five largest firms growing steadily. Two major causes were the growth of large firms at the expense of smaller ones and mergers of existing firms. Although more recent data are difficult to come by—the last Census of Production was in 1990—those that exist suggest that recent developments have been mixed. Concentration increased, for example, in pharmaceuticals when Glaxo merged with Wellcome. In other industries, however, large firms have been broken up by their owners, reducing concentration ratios.

Globalization—the growing internationalization of competition—is one reason why this increasing domestic concentration in production has not necessarily implied less market competition. The size of most markets now extends well beyond the boundaries of a single nation as a result of such developments as the removal of almost all trade barriers within the European Union, the decline in world transportation costs, and the steady reduction of worldwide tariffs under the auspices of the GATT and its successor, the World Trade Organization (WTO). A firm with an apparent monopoly in the United Kingdom may well be operating in a highly competitive international market that includes German, French, and Japanese firms. None the less, some intervention to keep firms competing rather then colluding is still thought necessary in most countries.

UK competition policies

Ultimate responsibility for competition policy in the United Kingdom lies with the Secretary of State for Trade and Industry. For many years key elements of monitoring and enforcement have been delegated to three important institutions: the Restrictive Practices Court (RPC), the Office of Fair Trading (OFT), and the Monopolies and Mergers Commission (MMC). At the end of 1998 proposals for reform were under active consideration including abolishing the MMC and merging its functions with the OFT.

There is an important difference between the legislation affecting restrictive practices and that affecting the potential creation of a monopoly by a merger. Restrictive practices must be registered and demonstrated to be in the public interest. The OFT can investigate cases that are not already approved and refer them to the RPC for judgement. By contrast, the onus is entirely on the authorities to prove that a merger is not in the public interest; otherwise it must be permitted to proceed. Here decisions are made by the Secretary of State on the basis of recommendations made by the MMC.

Unsettled questions: market structure in the very long run

The case against monopoly and monopolistic practices concerns the allocation of resources within the context of a fixed technology. In the very long run, however, tech-

nology is constantly changing as a result of both the discoveries of lower-cost methods of producing old products and the introduction of new and improved products. Does market structure affect the rate of innovation in the very long run?

The incentive to innovate

Who gets the profits? Both the monopolist and the perfect competitor have a profit incentive to introduce cost-reducing innovations. A monopoly can always increase its profits if it can reduce costs. Furthermore, since it is able to prevent the entry of new firms into the industry, these additional profits will persist into the long run. Thus, a firm that is either a monopoly or an oligopolist with entry barriers has both a short- and a long-run incentive to reduce its costs.

Firms in perfect competition have the same incentive in the short run, but not in the long run. In the short run a reduction in costs will allow a firm that was just covering costs to earn profits. In the long run other firms will be attracted into the industry by these profits. Existing firms will copy the cost-saving innovation, and new firms will enter the industry using the new techniques. This will go on until the profits of the innovator have been eliminated.

Monopolies and oligopolists with entry barriers have both a short- and a long-run incentive to innovate; perfectly competitive firms have only a short-run incentive.

How effective are profits as an incentive for perfectly competitive firms to develop cost-reducing innovations? The answer depends on the magnitude of the extra profits, and on how long they persist. For example, if an innovation can be copied in a few months, the profits earned over that period may not be sufficient to compensate the innovating firm for the risks involved in making the innovation.

Funds for research and development The large profits available to oligopolistic firms provide a ready fund out of which research and development can be financed. The typical perfectly competitive firm, however, is earning only enough to cover all its production costs, and it will have few funds to spare for research and development. As an empirical illustration, farmers producing under perfect competition did not develop the innovations that have vastly raised agricultural productivity over the last century. Rather, they were developed by a few oligopolistic manufacturers of farm equipment and by researchers in universities and in government-financed research institutions.

Schumpeter's defence of oligopoly and monopoly

Joseph Schumpeter, whom we have met earlier in the book, was a strong critic of the classical preference for perfect competition. In his theory monopolistic and oligo-polistic market structures are more conducive to growth than perfect competition.[4] He claimed that since it is the incentive of profits that leads individuals and firms to take the great risks of innovation, market power is much more important than perfect competition in providing the climate under which innovation occurs. The large short-run profits earned by firms with market power provide the incentive for others to try to usurp some of these for themselves. Oligopolistic firms compete for each other's profits, as well as for the new profits that will be generated by major innovations. If they do not compete, or if they have a genuine monopoly, outsiders will seek to enter in order to share in the profits of the sitting firm or firms. If a frontal attack on the major barriers to entry is not possible, then the barriers will be circumvented by such dodges as the development of similar products against which the established firms will not have entry protection. Schumpeter called the replacing of one entrenched posi-tion of market power by another through the invention of new products or new production techniques the *process of creative destruction.*

In Schumpeter's theory monopoly and oligopoly are more conducive to growth-creating innovations than is perfect competition. It follows that the 'inefficient' alloca-tion of resources that results from oligopoly is more con-ducive to a rapid rate of innovation and growth than an 'efficient' allocation that results from perfect competition.

What we have got to accept is that it [the profit that stems from market power] has come to be the most powerful engine of progress and in particular of the long-run expansion of total output not only in spite of, but to a considerable extent through, this strategy [i.e. creating market power], which looks so restrictive when viewed in the individual case and from the individual point of time.

In this respect, perfect competition is not only impossible but inferior, and has no title to being set up as a model. It is hence a mistake to base the theory of government regulation of industry on the principle that big business should be made to work as the respective industry would work in perfect competition.[5]

This important hypothesis cannot be handled with normal long-run theory, because long-run theory *assumes* constant technology.

Schumpeter's theory is not easy to test. None the less, business school studies of firm behaviour show that much, probably most, interfirm competition is in product and process innovation. Firms rarely fail because they set the wrong prices—for one reason, it is easy to alter prices that turn out to be uncompetitive. Firms do fail, however, when they fall behind their competitors in the constant battle to produce new and better products by ever more cost-efficient methods.

The future of competition policy

Even though governments on the whole are no longer in the business of owning industries or tightly controlling their pricing and output decisions, they are certainly not indifferent to industry performance. Government has an important role as both rule-maker and referee of the market economy. So long as monopoly and restrictive practices continue to be seen as a threat to the efficient working of the economy, governments will regard the behaviour of firms as something that requires appropriate monitoring and occasional control. Even the strongest advocates of Schumpeter's theory of creative destruction accept that the public interest is better served when oligo-polists are induced to compete with each other rather than colluding to avoid such rivalrous activity.

Conclusion

Anarchists see everything that the government does as evil and would do away with government altogether. The all-important function of providing the background against which the free market can effectively function—by maintaining a monopoly of violence and defining and protecting property rights—discredits the anarchist case.

Minimalists would take government activity no further. Just provide an effective background, they say, and the miracle of Adam Smith's hidden hand will do the rest. Most people, although not quite all, reject this view. The case against the minimalists lies in what we observed at the outset of this chapter: although markets work—and work very effectively much of the time—markets also fail—and sometimes fail quite disastrously.

[4] At the time that Schumpeter first wrote, economists only recognized two market structures, perfect competition and monopoly. He thus applied his arguments about creative destruction to monopolies. Now that oligopoly is seen to be the dominant market form in manufacturing, it is clear that his arguments apply with more force in oligopoly, where the threat of com-petition is more immediate, than in monopoly.
[5] Joseph Schumpeter, *Capitalism, Socialism and Democracy*, 3rd edn. (New York: Harper & Row, 1950), p. 106.

Now that you have studied the whole of this chapter, you know a great deal about the *why*, *how*, and *where* of these market failures. You also know quite a bit about what might be done to alleviate the most serious of these failures.

Facilities with excess capacity such as roads, bridges, and art galleries at off-peak times are most efficiently offered at zero prices, which a profit-maximizing firm would never do. Public goods such as police, courts, and urban traffic control must be provided by the government or not provided at all. Common property resources, such as fishing grounds and forests, must be controlled by the government or they will succumb to the tragedy of the commons—as all too many fishing grounds and forests have already done. Externalities in production and consumption are inevitable and ubiquitous. They run from minor nuisances, such as the neighbour's loud radio, through serious health hazards, such as second-hand smoke, to threats to our very existence, such as depletion of the ozone layer. Either we accept them or we use the government to control them. Government regulation and information provision can sometimes correct for asymmetric information and missing markets. Substantial monopolistic and monopsonistic market power, although not always undesirable, can only be restrained by government activity where it is thought to be undesirable.

In the next chapter we will raise concerns about how well governments actually deal with these market failures. Whatever the conclusion about those concerns, there is no doubt about three points. First, markets do fail in many important ways. Second, governments provide the only institutions available to deal with many of these failures. Third, economists have designed many instruments, some of them highly subtle, by which governments can deal with these failures.

As Adam Smith long ago observed (see Chapter 1), altruism, no matter how valuable a motive in many situations, cannot be the basis for the day-to-day functioning of a market economy, which must be based on the pursuit of self-interest. Similarly, altruism, although often a highly effective motive behind locating and publicizing market failures, cannot be the basis for a systematic and sustained handling of these failures. Instead they are best coped with by creating incentives that direct self-interested behaviour in the direction of alleviating them.

Summary

Basic functions of government

■ Effective governments have a monopoly of violence. They also define and protect the rights and obligations of property owned by individuals and institutions.

■ Key characteristics of market economies are (*a*) their ability to co-ordinate decentralized decisions without conscious control, (*b*) their determination of the distribution of income, and (*c*), compared with the alternatives, their minimization of arbitrary economic power.

Market efficiency

■ A perfectly competitive economy is allocatively efficient because it produces where price, which measures the value consumers place on the last unit produced, equals marginal cost, which measures the value to consumers that the resources used to produce the marginal unit could produce in other uses. This maximizes the sum of producers' and consumers' surpluses.

■ Free markets can fail to achieve efficiency because of inefficient exclusion of users from facilities with excess capacity, common property resources, public goods, externalities, asymmetric information, missing markets, and market power.

Non-rivalrous and non-excludable goods

■ The optimal price for the service of a facility with excess capacity is zero. Since private owners will charge a positive price, their facility will be inefficiently underused.

■ The private market will exploit a common property resource to the point where the average revenue per producer equals the production cost of a new entrant instead of to the socially optimal level, where the marginal addition to total product caused by a new entrant equals its production cost.

■ The optimal quantity of a public good is provided when the marginal cost of production is equal to the sum of the prices that all its consumers would be willing to pay for the marginal unit produced. This is difficult to attain because of the free rider problem—the incentive for individuals to understate the true value that they place on a public good.

Externalities

■ The Coase theorem shows that if those parties that create an externality and those that are affected by it can bargain together with minimal transaction costs, all inefficiencies can be removed.

■ Where private bargaining is impossible, the government can alleviate externalities by imposing rules and regulations or, more efficiently, by internalizing externalities through such measures as taxes and tradable permits to pollute.

Public policy towards monopoly and competition

■ Government policy with respect to market power is designed to encourage competitive practices and discourage monopolistic ones. It seeks to regulate natural monopolies either by running them as nationalized industries (the UK solution in the past) or by putting them in private hands and regulating them (the typical UK solution today).

■ Direct control of pricing and entry conditions of some key oligopolistic industries has been common in the past, but deregulation is reducing such control. The move to deregulation was largely the result of the experiences that oligopolistic industries are a major engine of growth, as long as their firms are kept competing; that direct control of such industries has produced disappointing results in the past; and that forced cross-subsidization can have serious consequences for some users.

■ An important issue concerns the effect of market structure on economic growth. Schumpeter's theory and substantial evidence suggest that the productively inefficient resource allocation that results whenever firms have market power may be more conducive to the technological change that underlies long-term economic growth than is the productively efficient allocation that results from perfect competition.

Topics for review

■ Government as a monopolist of violence and a protector of property rights
■ The efficiency of a perfectly competitive economy
■ Rivalrous and non-rivalrous goods
■ Excludable and non-excludable goods
■ Inefficient exclusion
■ Common property resources and the tragedy of the commons
■ Rules for providing and pricing public goods
■ Harmful and beneficial externalities
■ Emissions taxes
■ Tradable emissions permits
■ Government control of market power
■ Marginal and average cost pricing

■ Competition policy
■ Privatization
■ Deregulation

Questions for discussion

1 Your local authority undoubtedly provides a police station, a fire brigade, and a public library. What are the market imperfections, if any, that each of these seeks to correct? Which of these are closest to being public goods? Which are furthest? What would happen if governments were prevented from offering these services?

2 Not counting the ones mentioned in the text, how many goods and services can you think of that are (a) non-rivalrous but excludable, (b) non-excludable but rivalrous, and (c) non-rivalrous and non-excludable?

3 'There would be no externalities, harmful or beneficial, if everyone were well informed and could bargain with each other with no transactions cost.' Explain why you agree or disagree.

4 An industry consists of two firms producing the same product but using different technologies. Each emits 50 tonnes of pollution each year. One can clean up the first tonne at a cost of £1,000, while the cost of each additional tonne cleaned up rises by £1,000 per tonne until the last tonne costs £50,000. The second firm's cost for the first tonne cleaned up is £20,000, and the cost rises by £1,000 per tonne until the fiftieth tonne is cleaned up at a cost of £70,000. The government wishes to cut the industry's total emissions from 100 to 50 tonnes a year. It gives each firm 25 tradable permits, each one allowing 1 tonne of pollution. What will be the equilibrium price of a permit to pollute by 1 tonne. How many permits will be traded? By how much will each firm clean up its own pollution? What would you infer if, in a subsequent year, the price of a pollution permit fell by 50 per cent?

5 Why do we worry about the behaviour of natural monopolies and about collusion among oligopolists? What can be done to prevent the undesirable effects of their behaviour without stifling technological advance?

Chapter 19
Government Success and Government Failure

In Chapter 18 we established some important results. First, free markets are effective ways of co-ordinating decentralized decision-taking. Second, although markets work quite well most of the time, they fail in the presence of certain well-defined circumstances. Third, government policy can alleviate some of these market failures, either by imposing more efficient behaviour by rules, regulations, and public ownership or by internalizing externalities.

In this chapter we introduce the government more explicitly. We outline the objectives that it has in addition to dealing with the market failures that we studied in Chapter 18. We then deal with the many tools that are available to the government to achieve its policies, showing how these tools can be applied to areas other than market failure. After that we allow for the *costs* of government activity. These must be offset against the benefits in order to assess the net value of any proposed government intervention. Finally, we deal with government failure, which occurs when governments consciously act in ways that encourage either inefficiency rather than efficiency in resource allocation or undesirable inequities in income distribution.

Government objectives

Governments have multiple objectives, only some of which we studied in the previous chapter. Aside from looking after the welfare of elected officials and civil servants—which we will look at later in the chapter—governments seek many more socially acceptable objectives. The main ones are as follows:

1. to protect life and property by exercising a monopoly of violence and establishing property rights

2. to improve economic efficiency by addressing the various causes of market failure

3. to achieve some accepted standard of equity

4. to protect individuals from others and from themselves

5. to influence the rate of economic growth

6. to stabilize the economy against income and price level fluctuations

The first two of these objectives were considered in the previous chapter. The next three are considered in this chapter. The last is a major subject of the second half of this book, which deals with macroeconomic theory and policy.

Policies for equity

Markets generate reasonably efficient allocations of the nation's resources because, most of the time, the information that they need to perform well is derived from agents' desires to improve their private circumstances. No one should be surprised, therefore, that markets do not efficiently allocate resources towards achieving such broad social goals as establishing an 'equitable' distribution of income and promoting shared community values. Markets do not directly foster these goals, precisely because individuals do not seek to achieve them by purchasing goods and services in markets. Instead we look to the political system to achieve desired results in these directions.

The distribution of income

An important characteristic of any market economy is the *distribution* of income that it determines. People whose skills are scarce relative to supply earn large incomes, whereas people whose skills are plentiful relative to supply earn much less.

As we have seen in earlier chapters, differentials in

earnings serve the important function of motivating people to adapt. The advantage of such a system is that individuals can make their own decisions about how to alter their behaviour when market conditions change. The disadvantage is that temporary rewards and penalties are dealt out as a result of changes in market conditions that are beyond the control of the affected individuals. The resulting differences in incomes will seem inequitable to many—even though they are the incentives that make markets work.

Concerns about equity have two dimensions, horizontal and vertical equity. **Horizontal equity** means that persons in similar circumstance should be treated similarly. Although this type of equity appeals to many people as desirable, it is not always a goal of government policies. For example, people who are exposed to similar natural risks are given more government assistance when they are planting crops than when they are mining ore, cutting trees, or extracting oil. This may be because farmers have more political power than others, or it may stem from a gut feeling on the part of the electorate that food production is more basic than any other economic activity. **Vertical equity** means the different treatment of people in different economic situations in order to reduce inequalities between them.

Redistributive policies are of two general types. Some, such as the progressive income tax, are concerned with vertical equity. They seek to alter the size distribution of income in quite general ways. High marginal rates of income tax, combined with a neutral expenditure system that benefits all income groups more or less equally, will narrow income inequalities.

Other policies seek to mitigate the effects of markets on particular individuals. They do not seek to narrow income gaps in general but to deal with specific unfortunate events. Should heads of households be forced to bear the full burden of their misfortune if they lose their jobs through no fault of their own? Even if they lose their jobs through their own fault, should they and their families have to bear the whole burden, which may include starvation? Should the ill and the aged be thrown on the mercy of their families? What if they have no families? Policies designed to deal with such situations usually seek horizontal equity in treating similarly all those who fall into some group.

Both private charities and a great many government policies are concerned with modifying the distribution of income that results from such things as one's parents' abilities, luck, and how one fares in the labour market.

The distribution of wealth

It is sometimes argued that egalitarian economic policy should devote more concern than it does to the distribution of wealth and less to the distribution of income.

Wealth confers economic power, and wealth is more unequally distributed than is income. Heavy estate duties in the United Kingdom, however, caused a gradual reduction in the inequality of wealth distribution during the twentieth century. The trend has slowed, if not reversed, over the last two decades, but largely because of the buildup of pension wealth in the hands of 50–70-year-olds. None the less, in the mid-1990s just less than 20 per cent of all marketable wealth was held by the top 1 per cent of people in the UK wealth distribution, and an impressive 93 per cent of all marketable wealth by those in the top half of the distribution.

There are two main ways in which inequalities in the distribution of wealth can be reduced. The first is to levy taxes on wealth at the time that wealth is transferred from one owner to another, either by gifts during the lifetime of the owner or by bequest after death. In Britain such transfers used to be subject to a capital transfer tax. The rate of tax was progressive and rose to 60 per cent on taxable transfers in excess of £2 million. Currently, however, gifts among individuals during their lifetime are potentially exempt from tax. They become taxable if made within seven years of the donor's death. In 1998 inheritance tax was set at the rate of 40 per cent on all estates over £233,000.

The second method is an annual tax on the value of each person's wealth. A wealth tax of this sort has been considered in the past but it has not been actively debated since 1979.

Equity versus efficiency

Problems arise when government measures designed to improve equity seriously inhibit the efficient operation of the price system.

Often the goal of a more equitable distribution conflicts with the goal of a more efficient economy.

Say that we were so extreme as to believe that equity demanded that everyone receive the same income. All incentives to work hard and to move from job to job would be eliminated. Some command economies came close to this extreme position, and the results were predictably disastrous. Suppose that, to be less extreme, we believed that factor earnings should not reflect short-term fluctuations in demand and supply. The UK controls on rented accommodation did just that in the 1960s and 1970s, as do controls in several other countries today. If such intervention is effective, the incentive system for resource allocation is eliminated. A rise in demand creates extra earnings, which attract resources to meet the demand. Remove the price reaction and there is no reason for the resource reallocation to occur. Some of the problems that this conflict between efficiency and equity can create in policy debates are further discussed in Box 19.1

Box 19.1 Distribution versus efficiency—the 'leaky bucket'

Economists recognize that government actions can affect both the allocation of resources and the distribution of income. Resource allocation is easier to talk about, simply because economists have developed precise definitions of *efficient* and *inefficient* allocations. Distribution is more difficult, because we cannot talk about *better* or *worse* distributions of income without introducing normative considerations. Partly because of this, much of economics focuses on efficiency and neglects effects on the distribution of income. Many disagreements about economic and social policy can be understood in terms of differences in emphasis on efficiency and distribution. Distribution, of course, is often more important as a political matter, because it is distribution (especially one's own share) that people care about most, not the overall efficiency with which the economy is operating.

Moreover, economic efficiency is necessarily reduced to some extent whenever society chooses to redistribute income. The image of the 'leaky bucket' illustrates the problem. Suppose we have a well-supplied reservoir of water and we wish to get some water to a person who is not able to come to the reservoir. The only vessel available for transporting the water is a leaky bucket; it works, in that water can be delivered to the intended location, but it works at a cost, in that some of the water is lost on the trip. Thus, in order to get a gallon of water to its intended destination, more than a gallon of water has to be removed from the reservoir. It may be possible to design better or worse buckets, but all of them will leak to some extent.

The analogy to an economy is that the act of redistributing income (carrying the water) reduces the total value of goods and services available to the economy (by the amount of 'water' that 'leaks' on the trip). Transferring a pound or a euro to the poor reduces the resources available to everyone else by more than a pound or a euro.

Why is the bucket always leaky?

First, consider income redistribution. There is no way to redistribute income without changing the incentives faced by consumers and producers. Generally, a programme that takes income from the rich and gives it to the poor will reduce the incentives of both the rich and the poor to earn income.

Second, consider a policy of subsidizing goods that are deemed to be important, such as food, shelter, or oil. This will cause the market prices of those goods to be lower than marginal costs. Thus the resources used to produce those goods could be used to produce goods of higher value elsewhere in the economy—another leak in the bucket.

Measuring the efficiency costs of redistribution is an important area of economic research. Most economists would agree that programmes that directly redistribute income are more efficient (per pound of resources made available to a given income group) than programmes that subsidize the prices of specific products. One reason for the greater efficiency of direct redistribution is that price subsidies apply even when high-income people purchase the products in question.

Although redistribution almost always entails some efficiency loss, this *does not imply* that redistribution should not be undertaken. (That buckets leak surely does not imply that they should not be used to transport water, given that we want to transport water and that buckets are the best available tools.) Whatever the social policy regarding the redistribution of income, economics has an important role to play in measuring the efficiency costs and distributional consequences of different programmes of redistribution. Put another way, it has useful things to say about the design and deployment of buckets in ways that minimize leakages.

Policies to protect individuals

Protection from others People can use and even abuse other people for economic gain in ways that the members of society find offensive. Child labour laws and minimum standards of working conditions are responses to such actions. Yet direct abuse is not the only example of this kind of market failure. In an unhindered free market, the adults in a household would usually decide how much education to buy for their children. Selfish parents might buy no education, while egalitarian parents might buy the same education for all of their children, regardless of their abilities. The members of society may want to interfere in these choices, both to protect the child of the selfish parent and to ensure that some of the scarce educational resources are distributed according to ability rather than the family's wealth. All households are forced to provide a minimum of education for their children, and a number of inducements are offered—through public universities, scholarships, and other means—for talented children to consume more education than they or their parents might choose if they had to pay the entire cost themselves.

Protection from oneself Members of society, acting through the government, often seek to protect adult (and presumably responsible) individuals not from others, but from themselves. Laws prohibiting the use of heroin, crack cocaine, and other drugs, and laws prescribing the installation and use of car seat belts, are intended primarily to protect individuals from their own ignorance or shortsightedness. This kind of interference in the free choices of individuals is called **paternalism.** Whether such actions reflect the wishes of the majority in society or whether they reflect the interference of overbearing governments, there is no doubt that the market will not provide this kind of protection. Buyers do not buy what they do not want, and sellers have no motive to provide it.

Paternalism is often closely related to **merit goods.** Merit goods are goods that society, operating through the government, deems to be especially important or that those in power feel individuals should be encouraged to consume. Housing, education, health care, and certain cultural activities are often cited as merit goods. Critics argue that the concept is merely a way of imposing the tastes of an elite group on others.

Policies to promote social obligations

In a free-market system if you can persuade someone else to clean your house in return for £20, both parties to the transaction are presumed to be better off. You prefer to part with £20 rather than to clean the house yourself, and the person you hire prefers to have £20 than to avoid cleaning your house. Normally society does not interfere with people's ability to negotiate mutually advantageous contracts.

Most people do not feel this way, however, about activities that are regarded as social obligations. For example, during major wars when military service is compulsory, contracts similar to the one between you and your house-keeper could also be negotiated. Some persons, faced with the obligation to do military service, could no doubt pay enough to persuade others to do their tour of service for them. By exactly the same argument as we just used, we can presume that both parties will be better off if they are allowed to negotiate such a trade. Yet such contracts are usually prohibited as a result of widely held values that cannot be expressed in the marketplace. In times of major wars, of the sort that were experienced twice in the twentieth century, military service by all healthy males is held to be a duty that is independent of an individual's tastes, income, wealth, or social position.

Military service is not the only example of a social obligation. Citizens are not allowed to buy their way out of jury duty or to sell their votes, even though in many cases they could find willing trading partners. Even if the price system allocated goods and services with complete efficiency, members of a society do not wish to rely solely on the market for all purposes, since they have other goals that they wish to achieve.

Policies for economic growth

Over the long haul economic growth is the most powerful determinant of living standards. Whatever their policies concerning efficiency and equity, people who live in economies with rapid rates of growth find their living standards rising on average faster than those of people who live in countries with low rates of growth. Over a few decades these growth-induced changes tend to have much larger effects on living standards than any policy-induced changes in the efficiency of resource allocation or the distribution of income.

For the last half of the twentieth century most economists viewed growth mainly as a macroeconomic phenomenon related to total savings and total investment. Reflecting this view, most textbooks do not even mention growth in the chapters on microeconomic policy.

More recently there has been a shift back to the perspective of earlier economists, who saw technological change as the engine of growth, with individual entrepreneurs and firms as the agents of innovation. This is a microeconomic perspective, which is meant to add to, not replace, the macroeconomic stress on total savings and total investment.

Although most basic textbooks have not yet caught up with the change to a microeconomic perspective on growth, governments have. Today few microeconomic policies escape being exposed to the question 'Even if this policy achieves its main goal, will it have unfavourable effects on growth?' Answering yes is not a sufficient reason to abandon a specific policy. But it is a sufficient reason to think again. Is it possible to redesign the policy so that it can still achieve its main objective, while removing its undesirable side-effects on growth?

Tools and performance

The main sets of tools available to governments to achieve their goals are taxes, expenditure, rules, and public ownership. In this section we discuss these tools and show how they are used to achieve the specific objectives outlined earlier.

Taxation

Taxes and expenditures are by far the most important items on this list. Governments spend money to achieve many purposes, and that money must be either borrowed or raised through taxes. We leave borrowing aside as it is only a temporary measure. Interest must be paid on borrowed money and, if that too is borrowed, the total government debt eventually explodes to unmanageable proportions.

So sooner or later all government expenditure must be paid for out of taxes. Borrowing only postpones the need to tax.

Table 19.1 shows the major sources of tax revenues, along with the major classes of government expenditures, for the UK in 1997.

Table 19.1 Expenditure and revenue of UK central and local government, 1997

Expenditure	£ billion	Revenue	£ billion
Health	43.9	Income taxes	70.0
Education	36.2	Corporation taxes	29.9
Defence	23.4	Expenditure taxes	87.2
Other current spending	43.9	Social security	
Capital	10.6	contributions	47.7
		Other tax revenue	35.2
All goods and services	158.0	Total taxes	270.0
Social security	115.8	Operating surplus,	
Other (including interest		interest, and	
on debt)	42.2	other receipts	32.0
		Borrowing	14.0
Total expenditure	316.0	Total revenue	316.0

Source: ONS, UK national accounts.

As well as providing the revenues needed to finance all of the government's activities, taxes are also used as tools in their own right for a wide range of purposes. They can be used to alter the incentives to which private maximizing agents react, and to alter the distribution of income.

Indirect taxes

Taxes are divided into two broad groups, depending on whether persons or transactions are taxed. An **indirect tax** is levied on a transaction and is paid by an individual by virtue of being involved in that transaction. Taxes and stamp duties on the transfer of assets from one owner to another are indirect taxes, since they depend on the assets being transferred. Inheritance taxes, which depend on the size of the estate being inherited and not on the circumstances of the beneficiaries, are also an indirect tax.

The most important indirect taxes in today's world are those on the sale of currently produced products. These taxes are called excise taxes when they are levied on manufacturers, and sales taxes when they are levied on the sale of goods from retailer to consumer. The EU countries levy a comprehensive tax of this sort on all transactions, whether at the retail, wholesale, or manufacturer's level, called the **value added tax** (VAT). Value added is the difference between the value of factor services and materials that the firm purchases as inputs and the value of its output. It therefore represents the value that a firm adds by virtue of its own activities. VAT is an indirect tax because it depends on the value of what is made and sold, not on the wealth or income of the maker or seller. Thus, two self-employed fabric designers, each with a value added of £50,000 in terms of designs produced and sold, would pay the same VAT even if one had no other source of income while the other was independently wealthy.

Indirect taxes may be levied in two basic ways. An **ad valorem tax** is a percentage of the value of the transaction on which it is levied. The UK's 17.5 per cent VAT on most transactions is an ad valorem tax. A **specific** or **per-unit tax** is a tax expressed as so many pence per unit, independent of the commodity's price. Taxes on cinema and theatre tickets, and on each litre of petrol or alcohol, and on each packet of cigarettes are all specific, indirect taxes.

Direct taxes

Taxes in the second broad group are called **direct taxes.** These are levied on persons and vary with the status of the taxpayer. The most important direct tax is the income tax. The personal income tax falls sometimes on the income of households and sometimes separately on each member of the household. It varies with the size and source of the taxpayer's income and various other characteristics, such as marital status and number of dependants.

Firms also pay taxes on their incomes. This is a direct tax, both in the legal sense that the company is an individual in the eyes of the law, and in the economic sense that the company is owned by its shareholders so that a tax on the company is a tax on them. An expenditure tax—as advocated some years ago for the United Kingdom by the Royal Commission headed by Nobel Prize-winning economist James Meade (1909–96)—is also a direct tax. It is based on what a person spends, rather than on what he or she earns, and has exemptions that are specific to the individual taxpayer. A poll tax, which is simply a lump-sum tax levied on each person, is also a direct tax.

It is important for many purposes to distinguish average from marginal rates of any tax. The *average rate* of income tax paid by a person is that person's total tax divided by his or her income. The *marginal rate* of tax is the rate he or she would pay on another unit of income.

Progressivity The general term for the relation between the level of income and the percentage of income paid as a tax is **progressivity.** A **regressive tax** takes a *smaller percentage* of people's incomes the larger is their income. A **progressive tax** takes a *larger percentage* of people's incomes the larger is their income. A **proportional tax** is the boundary case between the two since it takes the *same percentage* of income from everyone. Taxes on food, for example, tend to be regressive, because the proportion of income spent on food tends to fall as income rises. Taxes on alcoholic spirits tend to be progressive, since the proportion of income spent on spirits tends to rise with income. Taxes on beer, on the other hand, are regressive. Different types of progressivities are shown in Figure 19.1.

Progressivity can be defined for any one tax or for the tax system as a whole. Different taxes have different characteristics. Inevitably, some will be progressive and some regressive. The impact of a tax system as a whole on high-, middle-, and low-income groups is best judged by

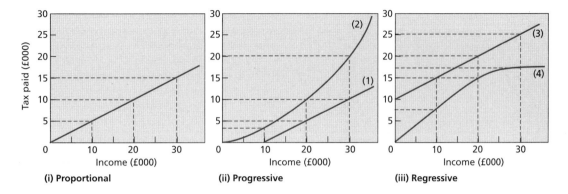

Figure 19.1 Income taxes with different progressivities

Income taxes may be proportional, progressive, or regressive. In part (i) the proportional tax's average and marginal rates remain unchanged at 50 per cent as income changes. In part (ii) tax (1) has a constant marginal rate of 50 per cent. But the average rate rises with income, being zero at income £10,000, 25 per cent at income £20,000, and 33.3 per cent at income £30,000. With tax (2) both the marginal and the average tax rates rise as income rises. In part (iii) tax (3) has a constant marginal rate of 50 per cent. But the average rate falls as income rises, being 150 per cent at £10,000, 100 per cent at £20,000, and 83.3 per cent at £30,000. With tax (4) both the marginal and the average rates fall as income rises.

looking at the progressivity of the whole set of taxes taken together. For example, income taxes are progressive in the United Kingdom, rising to a maximum marginal rate of 40 per cent. The overall tax system is also progressive, but much less so than one would guess from studying only the income tax rates. This is because much revenue is raised by indirect taxes, which are much less progressive than income taxes.

Expenditure

Some government expenditures are in return for goods and services that count as part of current output. When the government buys the services of factors of production and uses them to produce goods and services in the public sector of the economy, the factors are unavailable to produce private sector output. This type of expenditure is sometimes called **exhaustive expenditure.** Among their many uses exhaustive expenditures are the tool for filling in gaps in what the free market provides. For example, public goods, such as national defence, the legal system, and coastal navigation aids, must be produced by the government or not at all. In those cases the failure of the free market, and the potential for a remedy by government action, are obvious.

The remainder of government expenditure consists of **transfer payments,** which are payments *not* made in return for any contribution to current output. Old-age pensions, unemployment insurance and supplementary benefits, welfare payments, disability payments, and a host of other expenditures made by the modern welfare state are all

transfer payments. They do not add to current marketable output; they merely transfer the power to purchase output from those who provide the money (usually taxpayers) to those who receive it. Their main purpose, therefore, is to alter the *distribution* of income. Tax-induced redistributions are not just from rich to poor. They also make transfers from those working to those retired and unemployed, from the healthy to the sick, and from city-dwellers to farmers (through CAP subsidies in the EU). None of these transfer payments represents a claim by the government on real productive resources. Revenue must none the less be raised to finance them. Table 19.2 shows UK government spending expressed as a proportion of the nation's national income.

Figure 19.2 shows the overall redistributive effect of the UK tax–expenditure system. In spite of all the concerns associated with the welfare changes instituted by the Thatcher governments in the 1980s, the system still redistributes incomes from rich to poor. The main benefits

Table 19.2 UK government spending as a percentage of GDP

Spending on	1956	1976	1997
Goods and services	20.7	25.9	20.8
Transfer payments	13.2	21.0	18.6
Total spending	33.9	46.9	39.2

Source: ONS, UK national accounts.

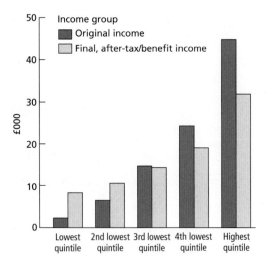

Figure 19.2 UK households' original and final income, 1996/7

The distribution of original income is much more unequal than the distribution of final income. Original income obtained from private sector activities is altered by the subtraction of direct and indirect taxes and the addition of cash benefits and benefits in kind to obtain final, or after-tax/benefit, income.

to lower-income groups come from cash payments, such as welfare and unemployment benefits, and in-kind benefits, mainly education and the NHS. High-income groups contribute to the income redistribution because although they receive many benefits, they pay even higher amounts of both direct and indirect taxes.

Rules and regulations

Rules and regulations are potent tools for redressing market failures. Governments use rules both to set the framework within which market forces operate and to alter the workings of unhindered markets. Rules pervade economic activities. Shop hours and working conditions are regulated. Rules govern the circumstances under which various types of unions can be formed and operated. Discrimination between labour services provided by males and females is illegal in the UK and in many other countries. Children cannot be served alcoholic drinks. They must attend school in most countries, and be inoculated against communicable diseases in many. Laws prohibit people from selling or using certain drugs. Prostitution is prohibited in many societies even though it usually involves a willing buyer and a willing seller. In many countries you are forced to purchase insurance for the damage you might do to others with your private motor car. In some countries people who offer goods for sale

cannot refuse to sell them to someone just because they do not like the customer's colour or religion. There are rules against fraudulent advertising and the sale of substandard, adulterated, or poisonous food. In some countries, such as the United States, anyone can purchase a variety of firearms ranging from pistols to machine-guns; in other countries, such as the United Kingdom, it is difficult for a private citizen to obtain a handgun.

As we saw in Chapter 18, most business practices have some control exerted on them by rules and regulations. In many countries agreements among oligopolistic firms to fix prices, or divide up markets, are illegal. The mere existence of monopoly is outlawed in some countries. When large economies of scale create a natural monopoly, the prices that firm can charge, and the return it can earn on its capital investment, are often regulated.

Public ownership

In the past many governments have used public ownership of nationalized industries as a tool for achieving policy goals. In the UK today most of these industries have been privatized—although other EU countries, particularly France, still retain a substantial number of nationalized industries. The remaining publicly owned industries in the UK are the Post Office, state education, and the National Health Service (NHS). The Post Office is in the market sector in the sense that it finances its activities by selling its services on the open market. We say nothing more about it here. We deal briefly with education and then in more detail with the NHS. The provision of both of these services, education and health, has been largely removed from the UK private sector and provided free to consumers.

The inefficiency of free goods

Of course, there is no such thing as a costless good or service. The production of anything requires resources, which have opportunity costs. So a 'free good' is not a costless good, only one whose costs are not borne by its users. Instead, the costs of state-provided free goods are borne by taxpayers.

Providing any good or service freely to its users poses efficiency problems. To illustrate, consider a product that has neither positive nor negative externalities so that private and social costs and benefits coincide. If such a product is provided free and all demand is met, then people will go on consuming it until the last unit has a zero value to them. But that unit will have a positive marginal cost of production which represents the value to consumers that the resources used in its production could create in other lines of activity.

In short, the provision of free goods is allocatively inefficient because its price (of zero) is less than its marginal cost.

Figure 19.3 shows the resource waste. It is obvious that the size of the waste will depend on the elasticity of the demand curve for the subsidized product. With a highly inelastic demand curve the policy induces only a small increase in output, so only a small quantity of resources is inefficiently allocated. With a highly elastic demand the quantity of misallocated resources is large.

From the point of view of improving equity in income distribution, free goods also have major shortcomings. Much of the money spent goes to subsidize their consumption by higher-income groups. Since there are few goods that are not bought by all income groups, the policy is much like shooting at a target with a shotgun—the bull's-eye will be hit, but so will almost everything else.

Transfer payments can be targeted at specific income groups; free goods cannot.

This lack of targeting makes the free-good policy an unnecessarily expensive way of helping low-income groups.

A further problem with free goods is that the government often does not provide a sufficient quantity to meet the demand at zero price. Some alternative rationing scheme must therefore arise. Sometimes queues do the rationing. At other times sellers' preferences do the job, as first discussed in Chapter 5. This happens, for example,

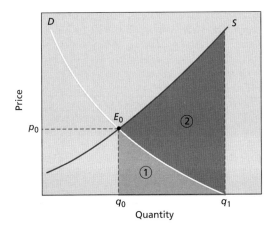

Figure 19.3 The inefficiency of free goods
Consumption of a free good exceeds what it would be at the efficient competitive equilibrium. Competitive equilibrium is at E_0 with price p_0 and quantity q_0. At a zero price q_1 is consumed. Since each extra unit that is produced adds its marginal cost to the total cost of production, total costs rise by the area under the industry's marginal cost curve (its supply curve). The two shaded areas 1 and 2 show this extra cost. The additional consumers' surplus is given by the medium blue shaded area 1. So the efficiency loss is the dark shaded area 2.

when those considered most worthy by administrators or doctors are given expensive health care while others get cheaper alternatives.

Education

Education could be left completely to the private sector. Those who were willing to pay would choose from the many schools at all levels that the private sector would no doubt provide. Most countries leave a substantial amount of education to be provided in this way. In the UK in 1996/7 about 6 per cent of primary and secondary students were being educated in the private sector. Thus state schools still account for the majority of students. This raises three questions that are distinct although often confused. First, why is education made compulsory? Second, who should pay for education? Third, who should provide it?

Why compulsion?   There are three main reasons for making education compulsory up to some allowable school-leaving age, which is typically around 15 or 16—it is 16 in the UK. The first is protection of children. If selfish parents decided to spend money on themselves and nothing on their children, they would hamper their children's ability to function in the economy when they grew up. The second is income redistribution. It is held that no one should be prevented from gaining some minimum level of education because of lack of parental income. The third reason is externalities. Everyone gains from living in a society where everyone else has some minimum level of education. A well-trained person is seldom of value on his or her own. It is only by working in groups that people are productive. One machinist in a society with no others would not be able to take most jobs that machinists do because they are done with other similarly trained workers. Because of externalities we insist that everyone attends school up to some legal leaving age.

Why free?   If an expensive service is made compulsory because it is of benefit to everyone, the obvious way to pay for it is through taxes. This is more acceptable because the proposition that free goods are consumed in inefficient amounts does not apply to any good or service whose consumption is compulsory. Because everyone of school age must attend school, the elasticity of demand for such education is zero. Thus the amount of resources allocated to compulsory education is independent of who pays for it. The method of payment will affect the distribution of income but will not cause any allocative inefficiency.

Who should provide it?   There is no universal agreement on the question of provision. In the UK many parents opt out of the system and provide private education for their children. For this they must pay (in addition to the taxes that they already pay to support the state system). Those who go through the state system have little choice. They must go to the local school (possibly choosing between two nearby ones if space is available). They must accept the current curriculum and whatever educational experiments are currently being mandated. They cannot purchase educational experiments that do not currently have ministry approval. In short, as with any other nationalized industries, there is little market choice available and experimentation is centralized.

Here are some of the arguments commonly advanced for state provision of education. It creates a desirable uniformity of standards. Pay and working conditions will be the same throughout the system. The state with all its educational experts knows better than the child and its parents what educational experience is in the child's best interest. Ministries can research new methods and techniques and institute them efficiently when they seem to be improvements on current practices.

Opponents of the state monopoly in the provision of state-funded education argue for more market determination. Many systems could provide this. The state could give every child education vouchers to the value of what the state is providing. These vouchers could be used to purchase education in any establishment that accepts them. The school then redeems the vouchers for government cash. Proponents of this type of system argue several alleged advantages. It would give parents more choice among various schools. Parents and their children usually have a better idea of what kind of education is needed and of whether or not they are getting it at the school currently being attended. This would penalize schools with poor academic and discipline records. Salaries would not be uniform across all schools; instead the earnings of schools and the salaries of teachers would vary with the success of individual schools in attracting students. Poorer schools would get few vouchers and hence little revenue out of which to pay their staff. The system would also encourage experimentation. Anyone with a new idea could try it out providing only that she could fill one classroom with students. The small amount of current centralized experimentation would be replaced with a large amount of decentralized experimentation. If some new educational ideal or fad gained majority acceptance it would not be forced on all students. Anyone that disagreed with it would need only find a school that was not following the herd.

These are some of the arguments advanced for exposing education to market forces while ensuring that it remains available to everyone. Many others worry about exposing education to market forces and prefer the system of state monopoly.

Although state financing of education is not in dispute in modern countries, the value of a state monopoly in providing free education is debated. Some think it the best system; others wish to inject market competition into the provision of free education.

Health and medical care

The case for providing hospital and medical services at a price below cost (zero in the limit) rests on three considerations. First, private provision is prone to market failure. Second, it is alleged that the inefficiencies of free medical care are not large. Third, serious equity issues arise when health care is left to private markets.

Market failure In the previous chapter we studied the types of market failure that emerge when all sides to a transaction are not equally informed. So we merely need note how these failures apply to the market for medical and health care. First, doctors are better informed about their patients' needs than are the patients themselves. In other words doctors are in a position to influence the demand for their services rather than respond to the demands of their patients. As a result elective surgery and other treatments of non-life-threatening medical conditions are observed to vary with the supply of doctors. (See Chapter 18 pages 299–300 for a fuller discussion.) Second, patients are better informed than their medical insurers on the state of their own health. This creates the problem of adverse selection first studied in Chapter 12, page 194. Third, people who are fully insured are likely to be more careless with their health than those who must pay themselves. This is the problem of moral hazard also studied in Chapter 12. It is worth noting that the first problem exists with any fee-for-service system no matter who pays the bill. The second exists only when insurance companies pay the bill, while the third exists in all systems where anyone but the patient pays.

With medical care social and private costs and benefits are thought to diverge substantially. If I do not cure my infectious disease, the effects are not felt by me alone. More generally everyone gains by living in a healthy rather than a disease-ridden society. Thus there are arguments for reducing the private costs of these services below the market rate by means of a subsidy.

Insurers can do little to avoid some adverse selection, but they will not insure those whom they know to be already ill or serious risks for other reasons. This means that a considerable number of people just cannot get medical insurance under free-market provision. This group includes those who were born with serious health problems or acquired them while still living at home. It also includes those with serious health problems whose medical coverage runs out when they leave their present employer to change firms or retire. When they try to reinsure themselves in a private plan they often find themselves uninsurable.

Small inefficiencies Recall that the magnitude of the resource cost of a free-good policy depends on the slope of the demand curve between the free-market price and the subsidized price. Studies suggest low incidence of unnecessary hospitalization in free-hospital systems. If the demand for services is not much larger than it would be in the free market (where most people would be privately insured) then the magnitude of the waste caused by divergence between the zero price and the positive marginal cost will be small.

Other potential inefficiencies also exist. Governments typically do not provide facilities to meet all the demand for free services. So scarce funds must be allocated within the system. However, bureaucratic decisions are seldom efficient in allocating scarce funds so that their marginal benefits are the same in all uses. In the mid-1990s a controversial internal-market mechanism was introduced into the NHS. Patients got treatment free, but doctors had a notional budget that they used to buy services from hospitals. Hospitals priced operations, and these prices varied substantially over the country. Services were also rationed among patients. This was done partly by having long queues for many kinds of non-life-threatening care, partly by inadequate provision of emergency services, and partly by unofficial allocation by doctors and hospitals of scarce treatment facilities to particular types of patients. This latter is the 'allocation by sellers' preferences' that we first encountered in Chapter 5. This internal-market system was criticized by the Labour Party before the 1997 election made them the governing party. At the end of 1998 it was still not clear if the system would survive.

Equity considerations There are also more subtle arguments about social values. It has been argued that in richer societies decisions about basic medical care should be taken out of the economic arena. It is degrading for a person to have to balance medical care for a child against the other family needs. Therefore, it is argued, the inefficiency cost of freely provided basic medical care is worth accepting in order to produce a society where choices about basic medical services are eliminated.

Notice the use of the word 'basic' in the previous paragraph. The above position is arguable if it is confined to basic services for all. Modern medical technology is so expensive that the state could not afford to make all conceivable services freely available to all. The more expensive services must be rationed. This can be done either by prices or by decisions about need taken by medical and hospital authorities.

For all its problems the NHS remains one of the most popular of the government's many activities. It seems likely, therefore, to stay in place for a long time to come. As a result understanding its shortcomings and using economic analysis to alleviate the worst of its inefficiencies is an important social activity.

Economic growth

We saw earlier that modern concern about the interface between microeconomic policies and economic growth is relatively new. Concern is largely about unintentional side-effects on growth of policies with other primary objectives. Concern is directed to a lesser extent at micro policies that are directly focused on growth. But, as we will see below, both types of concerns are relevant when policy tools are chosen.

Taxation policies for growth

Almost all taxes can affect growth by altering incentives either to save, to work, or to take risks.

Taxation of consumption or income Income taxes apply to income when it is earned; spending taxes (such as VAT) apply only to that part of income that is spent on consumption.

Consider a woman in the 40 per cent marginal tax bracket who earns an extra £1,000 and pays £400 income tax. If she spends her after-tax income, she will be able to buy £600 worth of goods. If she saves the money, she will be able to buy a £600 bond. If the bond pays, say, a 4 per cent real return, she will earn £24 interest per year. But a 40 per cent tax must then be paid on the interest earnings, leaving only a £14.40 annual income. This is a 2.4 per cent after-tax return on the bond and a 1.44 per cent after-tax return on the original £1,000 income!

This 'double taxing' of savings is a disincentive. Economists who wish to encourage saving, which helps to finance growth-creating investment, argue for taxes on consumption, not on income. Under an expenditure tax any income that is saved is untaxed. Our saver in the previous paragraph would be taxed only when the interest earned on the savings was actually spent on consumption. In the 1980s the Conservative government took a major step in this direction by significantly reducing income tax rates and making up for the lost revenue by raising the VAT rate.

Steeply progressive rates of tax Steeply progressive tax rates are an incentive to emigrate or at least move one's business abroad. They also penalize people with fluctuating incomes, such as authors, self-employed builders, and small-scale innovators. Consider an innovator who tries to introduce one new product each year. She only covers costs on her first four attempts and then has a success that yields £250,000 over costs in the fifth year. Her income over the five years is the same as a salaried employee who earns £50,000 for each of these five years. Yet under a steeply progressive tax regime she will pay much more tax than he will. This was a really serious problem when the maximum rate of tax in the United Kingdom was 70 per cent. (Right after the Second World War in 1945 it was well over 90 per cent!) As we have already noted, in the 1980s the maximum rate was cut to 40 per cent, which greatly reduces the tax penalty paid by someone with a highly fluctuating income. But it is still there. In 1998/9, the lady innovator would have paid £96,295 in taxes, while over the same five-year period the salaried man would have paid £74,585 (assuming each had no dependants).

Here we see one of the many possible conflicts between growth and equity. One may favour steeply progressive tax rates on grounds of equity but be persuaded to moderate the degree of progressivity in the interest of encouraging the risk-taking that is necessary for promoting growth.

Adjustment policies for growth

The innovations in products and production processes that underlie growth require continual changes and adaptations throughout the economy. If government policies discourage change, growth will be slowed. The realization that many policies designed to improve equity can discourage change has led to some policy re-evaluations.

Labour market policies   When people lose jobs because of economic change, the various measures that constitute the welfare safety net provide them with income support. Although such passive support provides immediate relief, it provides no incentive for recipients to change their situation and can sometimes even discourage such efforts.

An alternative is to make some or the entire support conditional on adjusting to change, for example by re-training or relocating. The UK government, for example, has funded Training and Enterprise Councils (TECs), through which all young people out of work and not in higher education are encouraged to undergo a period of training or work experience.

Support of firms and industries   Governments are always tempted to support declining industries. Over the past century both Labour and Conservative governments have done a lot of this. Such policies reduce unemployment in the short run, but if economic forces are leading to a continual decline, the policies are only costly ways of postponing the inevitable. Furthermore, when it finally does come, the adjustment often comes suddenly. This is because the government support is withdrawn all at once when the growing cost of the support finally becomes unacceptable.

Industrial policies for growth

Earlier we considered government policies towards industry that were directed primarily at efficiency. Other policies have long-term growth as their primary objective. Many of the disagreements over such policies depend on differing views on the micro-conditions needed to encourage growth-creating innovations. Some economists feel that maximizing the amount of competition at any point in time is the most important condition for growth. Others follow Schumpeter in holding that the existence of monopoly and oligopoly profits at any point in time is a powerful incentive to growth-creating innovations.

Patents   Some economists, who believe that competitive market structures best serve consumers by assuring them low prices, worry about a possible lack of incentives to innovate under competition. If an innovation can be easily copied, new firms may enter an industry so quickly that the innovating firm is not compensated for the costs and risks of innovation. The innovation is, in effect, a public good, and private firms are not motivated to produce it.

Patent laws are designed to provide the needed incentives. They create a temporary property right over the invention, extending the short-run period during which the invention's owner can earn profits as a reward for inventing. Once the patent expires, other firms can legally copy the innovation. If there are no other barriers to entry, production will then expand until profits fall to normal.

Reduction of entry barriers   Those who accept Schumpeter's theory hold that anti-monopoly policy and public utility regulations are unnecessary as policies to influence behaviour in the very long run. They worry that state intervention will inadvertently create entry barriers that will protect existing firms from the growth-creating process of creative destruction. They believe that government policies directed at minimizing entry barriers are the only industrial and competition policies that are needed.

Nationalization   Those who reject Schumpeter's theory often support anti-monopoly and public utility regulation policies. They feel that such policies are required to prevent monopolies from earning large profits at the expense of consumers.

Supporters of Schumpeter's theory argue that nationalization and public regulation will defeat their own purposes in the long term by inhibiting the process of creative destruction. A government monopoly provides the most enforceable entry barrier. It may inhibit the introduction of new products, and of new ways to produce old products, that would have occurred when new firms attacked the entrenched positions of existing firms. Supporters of this view point to the former Soviet Union's need to buy technology from Western countries, and argue that the rapid development of new products and processes in the oligopolistic and monopolistic industries operating in market-oriented economies gives some support to Schumpeter's view. Box 19.2 deals with an important court case in which different groups took different positions on the issue of the importance of monopoly power and creative destruction.

A short-term/long-term trade-off?   Economists who accept both the force of the argument that monopolistic firms can earn large exploitative profits in the short term *and* Schumpeter's argument about the very long run face a policy dilemma. In the short term firms that gain monopoly power may earn very large profits at the expense

Box 19.2 The great Microsoft anti-trust case

Some of the greatest innovations in information and communications technology have been due to Bill Gates and his firm Microsoft. Now in his early thirties, Gates is one of the world's wealthiest persons. He is a classic entrepreneur who entered the PC software industry when it was new, fiercely competitive, and rapidly developing. His Windows operating system achieved instant customer approval and now dominates the industry.

In 1998 the United States Department of Justice brought an anti-trust suit against Microsoft for alleged monopoly practices. The firm was accused of tactics designed to make entry difficult for smaller firms selling specialized products that competed with some parts of Microsoft's array. In particular, when customers buy any new version of the Windows operating system, they are automatically provided with Microsoft's Internet browser. This bundling of Microsoft products undoubtedly makes competition more difficult for smaller firms producing one type of product.

The suit reveals all the conflicting views that can be taken about competition and technical change.

■ Technological innovations have transformed the lives of ordinary people several times since the first industrial revolution in the mid-eighteenth century.

■ A new industry producing a wholly new range of products typically starts off as highly competitive as did cars, aircraft, and computers. Soon, however, the winners in the race to expand and improve the range of products eliminate most of the weaker competitors. They emerge as oligopolists in a mature industry.

■ The dominant firm in the technological race often establishes something close to a monopoly position. This dominance is partly a result of continued successful innovation—established oligopolies have been the source of much growth-inducing technological change over the past 150 years. It is also partly a result of the firm's ability to suppress competition from smaller upstart firms.

■ Over the long haul, even if the oligopolist becomes something close to a monopolist, it cannot perpetuate its position indefinitely—new firms with new products eventually arise to challenge and unseat the established firms.

So how should the US government react? Should it constrain Microsoft in order to create more growth-enhancing competition? Or should it accept Microsoft's dominant position in the industry as the reward for its amazing record as an innovator? Should it accept Schumpeter's argument that, in the very long run, neither Microsoft nor any other dominant firm will be able to maintain its position unless it outperforms actual and potential competitors in the race to provide consumers with more, better, and cheaper products?

Faced with that decision, the US Department of Justice took the line that Microsoft's behaviour was designed to stifle competition. Later a US appeals court took the opposite line on a 2–1 split decision. Whatever the final outcome, these early differences in legal opinions illustrate the difficulty in distinguishing successful competitive behaviour from behaviour designed to suppress competition.

of consumers. In the very long term, however, attempts to control these monopolies may inhibit the creative destruction that helps to raise living standards through productivity growth.

The policy world is not a simple place, and policies that help to achieve desired goals over one time-span must be constantly scrutinized for undesired effects over other time-spans.

The costs of government intervention

We have seen that governments have many reasons to take action. We also know that governments have many tools that may help them to achieve their goals. This, however, is not the end of the story. To evaluate government intervention, we need to consider costs as well as benefits.

Large potential benefits do not necessarily justify government intervention, nor do large potential costs necessarily make it unwise. What matters are net benefits—the balance between benefits and costs.

Three types of cost of government intervention need to be considered. These are costs that are internal to the government, costs that are external to the government but directly paid by others in the sector where the intervention occurs, and costs that are external to the government and felt more generally throughout the entire economy.

Internal costs

Everything the government does uses resources. It costs money when government inspectors visit plants to check on compliance with government-imposed health standards, industrial safety, or environmental protection. The inspectors and their support staff must be paid and their offices maintained. The salaries of the judges, the clerks, and the court reporters that are needed when an anti-monopoly case is heard are costs imposed by the regulation.

Armies of clerks, backed up by computers and other modern equipment, keep track of income tax and VAT receipts. Inspectors take the field to enforce compliance, and the courts deal with serious offenders. Unemployment and supplementary benefits must be administered. The size of the body of public employees at the national and local levels attests to the significant resource costs of government activity, costs that need to be set against the benefits produced. In 1996 the income payments made in the three major parts of the UK public sector expressed in billions of pounds and as percentages of GDP were as follows: public corporations £26bn (3.5 per cent), central government £27bn (3.5 per cent), and local authorities £38bn (5.1 per cent), which sums to £91bn or 12.1 per cent of GDP. These are not inconsiderable figures.

Direct external costs

External costs are costs that the government's action imposes on others; they may be either direct or indirect. Direct external costs fall on agents with whom the government is directly interacting.

Increases in production costs Regulation and control often add directly to the costs of producing goods. For example, firms must inspect machinery to ensure that it meets government safety standards.

Costs of compliance Much business activity is devoted to understanding, reporting, and contesting regulatory provisions. Occupational safety and environmental control have increased the number of employees not working on the shop floor. The legal costs of a large company can run to large sums each year. The same can be said of the costs of complying with tax laws. Firms, and wealthy individuals, spend substantial sums on lawyers and accountants. These advisers help them to comply with tax laws. They also assist in choosing tax-minimizing courses of action. These resources have alternative uses. So do firms' time and planning energies, whose social product might be higher if devoted to maximizing growth potential rather than minimizing their tax payments.

Losses in productivity Quite apart from the actual expenditures, government intervention may reduce the incentive for experimentation, innovation, and the introduction of new products. Requiring advance government clearance before introducing a new method or product (on grounds of potential safety hazards or environmental impact) can reduce the incentive to develop it. New lines of investment may be chosen more for their tax implications than for their potential for reducing production costs and so contributing to productivity growth.

Indirect external costs

Indirect external costs are costs of the government's action that spread beyond those immediately affected by it—sometimes to the entire economy. Here is a sampling of the many costs of this type.

Externalities

Ironically, government intervention to offset adverse externalities can create new adverse externalities. For example, government regulations designed to ensure the safety of new drugs delay the introduction of all drugs, including those that are safe. The benefits of these regulations are related to the unsafe drugs kept off the market. The cost includes the delayed availability of new safe drugs.

Tax shifting The shifting of taxes often causes major externalities. **Shifting** refers to the passing of the incidence of a tax from the person who initially pays it to someone else. The **incidence** refers to who actually bears the tax. One major problem with the use of taxes to achieve a social goal such as redistributing income is that market forces may shift the burden of the tax from the person who initially pays it to others. In Chapter 13, pages 202–3, we studied the effects of a tax levied in a single market and concluded:

If the supply curve is positively sloped, and the demand curve negatively sloped, the burden of a tax is shared between producers and consumers.

This outcome does not depend on who actually makes the tax payment to the government. If producers initially pay the tax, the upward shift in the market supply curve will raise the price and pass some of the tax burden on to consumers. If consumers initially pay the tax, the downward shift in their after-tax demand curve will lower the price received by producers. This passes some of the burden on to producers.

There will also be repercussions in other markets. As the price of one product rises, the demand curves for substitutes will shift to the right, while the demand curves for complements will shift to the left. The resulting changes in their market prices will induce changes in other related markets. The effects of a tax on one market will thus spread throughout the economy, making the final distribution of the burden difficult to ascertain.

Inefficiencies

Almost all government interventions have some adverse efficiency effects. These have played an important part in the so-called supply-side criticisms of government policy, and we need to look at them in some detail.

Taxation First, consider a sales tax on one specific good. The tax raises the relative price that consumers face for that good, so they will buy less of it and more of other products. Production falls below the competitive equilibrium level, which is the one that maximizes the sum of consumers' and producers' surplus. The result, as shown in Figure 19.4, is a loss of consumers' surplus exactly analogous to the deadweight loss of monopoly.

This result applies to any taxes that affect the prices of products in different proportions and hence change

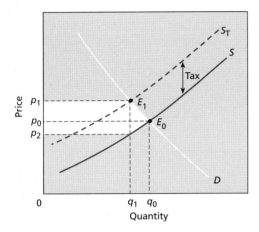

Figure 19.4 The efficiency loss from an indirect tax

The tax causes a loss of consumers' surplus, which is a deadweight loss. The tax shifts the supply curve from S to S_T. This moves equilibrium from E_0 with price p_0 and quantity q_0 to E_1 with price p_1 and quantity q_1. Consumers pay p_1, while the after-tax receipts of producers are p_2. The government gains tax revenue equal to the light yellow area, which is p_1 minus p_2 (the tax) multiplied by q_1. Part of this comes from producers and part from consumers. Consumers also lose surplus of the dark yellow area. Producers also lose surplus of the medium shaded area. Since no one gets the surpluses that consumers and producers lose, they are the deadweight loss of the tax.

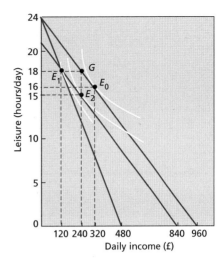

Figure 19.5 An income tax and the work–leisure choice

An income tax results in an inefficient choice between work and leisure. This person earns £40 an hour. His budget line runs from 24 hours (no work) to £960 (no sleep!). He maximizes utility at E_0 with 16 hours of leisure (8 hours of work) and income of £320 per day. An income tax of 50 per cent shifts his after-tax budget line to run from 24 hours to £480 (no sleep). He maximizes utility by moving to E_1 with 18 hours of leisure (6 hours of work) and a gross pay of £240. This yields him an after-tax income of £120.

The government could raise its £120 through a tax that did not alter the income–leisure trade-off (say a poll tax). The after-tax budget line in this case shifts in to 21 hours (the tax is the equivalent of 3 hours' work) and £840. The individual now moves from E_0 to E_2, consuming 15 hours of leisure (working 9 hours) and consuming £240 worth of goods. E_2 is superior to E_1 because it lies on a higher indifference curve.

relative prices. It thus applies to VAT whenever different products are taxed at different rates. The key is that

Consumers equate their marginal utilities to prices including tax, while producers equate their marginal costs to the price net of the tax. Hence the tax causes inefficiency, since the value that consumers place on the last unit consumed exceeds the marginal cost of making it.

Next consider the income tax. It creates inefficiency by distorting the work–leisure choice. Employers pay one wage (pre-tax) and employees receive another wage (post-tax). Employees, reacting to after-tax wage rates, see a rate of substitution between work and leisure that differs from the rate implied by the pre-tax wage the employer is prepared to pay.

To understand the source of the inefficiency, compare the income tax with a **poll tax,** which takes the same lump sum from everyone. Because it is not related to income, a poll tax leaves the marginal rate of substitution between goods and leisure unaffected. The tax exerts no disincentive to work at the margin, and thus is more efficient than the income tax.

Figure 19.5 demonstrates the inefficiency of the income tax. It shows that each individual achieves a higher indifference curve when he or she is forced to pay a given amount of tax revenue through a poll tax, rather than through an income tax. The poll tax is more efficient

because it leaves each person facing a choice at the margin that reflects the wage rate actually paid by employers in the labour market.

The importance of the figure lies in its demonstration that any practical tax does have negative efficiency effects, because it distorts relative price signals. The only tax that does not do so, under normal conditions, is the poll tax. It has no negative efficiency effects because the amount paid does not vary with the taxpayer's economic income or wealth or any of his or her economic decisions. It is precisely for this reason that most people find it *unacceptable* on equity grounds as anything other than a minor source of revenue.[1]

---

[1] The argument in the text assumes a closed economy in which everyone actually pays the tax. In practice, however, even the poll tax will have some efficiency effects. A large enough poll tax will cause people to emigrate. It will also cause some people to choose jobs, and life-styles, that facilitate evasion. People with no fixed addresses, and no regular jobs, find evasion easier than people who are stuck with one job and own their own houses or flats. Thus, at the margin, the poll tax will influence some people's job and residence decisions, which means it does have some adverse efficiency effects.

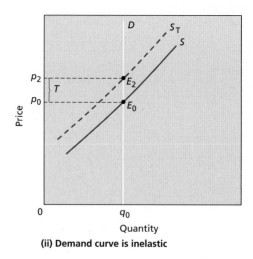

(i) Supply curve is inelastic

(ii) Demand curve is inelastic

Figure 19.6 Taxes that do not cause inefficiencies

A tax that does not change the allocation of resources causes no allocative inefficiency. In both parts of the figure the original curves are D and S with equilibrium at E_0. A tax of T is then imposed. In part (i) the supply curve is completely inelastic so the quantity provided remains constant. The net-of-tax demand curve shifts to D_T and producers' revenue falls to p_1 per unit. In part (ii) the demand curve is completely inelastic. The tax-inclusive supply curve shifts up to S_T and market price rises by the full amount of the tax to p_2. There is no change in quantity and consumers bear the whole burden of the tax.

Exceptional circumstances Two extreme circumstances provide exceptions to the rule that all taxes upset efficiency conditions. These occur, as shown in Figure 19.6, where either the demand or the supply curve is perfectly inelastic. In either case the same amount will be bought and sold both before and after the tax. Because the quantity is insensitive to the price changes caused by the tax, the tax does not have adverse efficiency effects. If decisions do not respond to changes in the price signals, then these changes have no effects, unfavourable or favourable.

There are few, if any, markets where these extreme conditions are met. It is sometimes alleged that taxes on cigarettes and alcohol come close because demand is highly inelastic. But there is plenty of room for substitution among types of alcohol, with people shifting to cheaper sources as prices rise. Furthermore, there is international substitution whenever tax rates differ between countries. In the European Union, for example, consumers take day trips to buy from adjacent countries with lower taxes on specific products such as alcohol and tobacco. This has become a major phenomenon since the Single Market rules permitted unlimited purchases 'for personal use' and created a new blue channel for passengers returning from other EU countries.

For these and other similar reasons, although elasticities of demand for alcohol and tobacco may be less than unity, they are not zero. Thus, taxes on these products have efficiency effects. The very high rates charged on them may be justified on grounds of negative externalities, since a

significant proportion of medical and hospital care goes to treat alcohol- and tobacco-related ailments. They may also be explained, however, by a government seeking to maximize its tax revenue from products which, although inelastic in demand, are not regarded socially as necessities.

Disincentive effects

The disincentive effects of high marginal rates of income tax are still subject to debate. If we consider a 'closed economy' where there is no possibility of emigration, then marginal rates of up to 40 or 50 per cent do not seem to have strong disincentive effects. Some people work less hard, but others work harder in order to restore their after-tax incomes to what they would have been if tax rates had been lower. At some point, however, high marginal tax rates begin to have more serious disincentive effects. As marginal rates approach 100 per cent, the disincentive effect becomes absolute.

Steeply progressive rates also have inefficient allocative effects among types of employment. People whose incomes are high for a few years and low thereafter pay high taxes relative to others that have the same lifetime incomes but have them spread more evenly over the years.

In an open society where emigration is possible, very high marginal rates of tax have major effects. Authors, artists, pop groups, and others who 'strike it rich' are strongly tempted to emigrate to countries that will allow them to keep a higher proportion of their incomes. The

Table 19.3 UK marginal rates of income tax (tax rate on an extra £1 of income)

Taxable income* (1990 £)	Marginal tax rate (%)	
	1978–79	1997–98
2,500	34	20
6,000	34	24
18,000	45	24
24,000	50	24
30,000	65	40
36,000	70	40
54,000	83	40

UK income taxes are much less progressive than they used to be. The figures have been converted to 1990 pounds to make them comparable. Currently, the maximum marginal rate of 40 per cent sets in at about £30,000 taxable income. Twenty years earlier the marginal rate at that level of income was a full 65 per cent.

* Income after deducting allowances.

Source: ONS Financial Statement and Budget Report.

temptation is particularly strong when there are countries with common linguistic and cultural environments and substantially lower tax rates. Emigration of successful people of this type from the United Kingdom to the United States was significant between 1945 and 1980, when UK marginal rates of income tax were often double those in the United States.

From the point of view of maximizing tax revenues and reducing tax burdens on middle- and lower-income groups it would be better to have high-income people still in the country paying tax rates of 40–50 per cent than out of the country avoiding higher tax rates.

Governments throughout the world have come to accept that very high marginal rates of tax do exert various important disincentive effects. Table 19.3 shows marginal rates of income tax in the UK for 1978–79 and 1997–98. It is worth noting that the higher rate in 1978 was much lower than the highest marginal rate of 97.5 per cent levied in the UK in the period shortly after the Second World War. (This enormous rate included a surtax on investment income.)

Income taxes and the supply of effort Do high rates of income tax cause people to work less? Would a reduction of income tax rates cause people to work more?

Economic theory makes no general prediction about how altering income tax rates will affect the supply of effort. On page 228 and in Box 7.3 we showed that a rise in the wage rate might increase, or decrease, the supply of effort, and, similarly, a fall in the wage rate might have either effect. Now observe that the after-tax wage rate is lowered by a rise in the rate of income tax, and raised by a

fall in the rate. It follows immediately that any given change in the rate of income tax may either raise or lower the supply of effort.

The Laffer curve A cut in the rate of tax might increase the supply of effort so much that tax revenues actually increase. This possibility is illustrated in a famous figure called the **Laffer curve,** named after an American exponent of supply-side economics, Professor Arthur Laffer.

The general shape of the curve, which is shown in Figure 19.7, is argued as a matter of simple logic. At a zero tax rate, no revenue will be collected. Similarly, at an average tax rate of 100 per cent, revenues will again be zero because no one would bother to earn taxable income just to support the government. At intermediate rates, people will earn taxable income and pay taxes. Government tax revenues will reach a maximum value at some rate of taxation between zero and 100 per cent. For rates higher than the rate that produces this maximum, every increase in tax rates will lead to a decrease in tax revenues. The curve cannot be a guide to practical policy, however, until we know where this maximum occurs. An interesting early precursor of Laffer's curve is discussed in Box 19.3.

Welfare measures and the supply of effort Payments designed to help certain low-income groups are often means-tested. Sometimes the welfare payments are reduced by £1 for every £1 of income received by welfare recipients. The person in effect faces a marginal tax rate of 100 per cent on every unit of income earned up to the level of the benefit payments. The effect, called the poverty trap, is a severe disincentive to work, and we should not be surprised when people respond rationally to these market signals.

Say, for example, benefit payments are £25 a day and are cut by £1 for every £1 of income earned. If the person

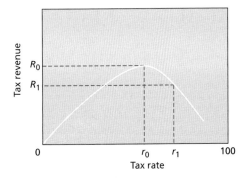

Figure 19.7 The Laffer curve
Increases in tax rates beyond some level will decrease tax revenue. The curve relates the government's tax revenue to the tax rate. Revenue reaches a maximum level of R_0 at average tax rate r_0. If the tax rate was r_1, reducing it to r_0 would increase revenue to the government.

Box 19.3 The Laffer curve 600 years before Laffer

Complaints about the disincentive effects of heavy taxation are as old as governments. Here is one perceptive example from the fourteenth-century Arabic philosopher Ibn Khaldun. Although the language sounds archaic to our ears, his observations have a remarkably modern ring. Note that by 'assessments' he means tax rates and by 'cultural activity' he means everything beyond the production of such basic necessities as food and clothing.

At the beginning of the dynasty, taxation yields a large revenue from small assessments. At the end of the dynasty, taxation yields a small revenue from large assessments. . . .

[At first] the dynasty [displays] kindness, reverence, humility, respect for the property of other people, and disinclination to appropriate it, except in rare instances. Therefore, the individual imposts and assessments, which together constitute the tax revenue, are low. When tax assessments and imposts upon the subjects are low, the latter have the energy and desire to do things. Cultural enterprises grow and increase, because the low taxes bring satisfaction. When cultural enterprises grow, the number of individual imposts and assessments mounts. In consequence, the tax revenue . . . increases.

When the dynasty continues in power and their rulers follow each other in succession . . . qualities of moderation and restraint disappear.

As a result, the individual imposts and assessments upon the subjects, agricultural labourers, farmers and all the other tax-payers, increase. Gradual increases in the amount of assessments succeed each other regularly . . . Eventually, the taxes will weigh heavily upon the subjects and overburden them. Heavy taxes become an obligation and tradition, because the increases took place gradually, and no one knows specifically who increased them or levied them. They lie upon the subjects like an obligation and tradition.

[Eventually] the assessments increase beyond the limits of equity. The result is that the interest of the subjects in cultural enterprise disappears, since when they compare expenditures and taxes with their income and gain and see the little profit they make, they lose all hope. Therefore, many of them refrain from all the activity. The result is that the total tax revenue goes down.

Finally, civilization is destroyed, because the incentive for cultural activity is gone.*

* *From the Muqaddimah: An Introduction to History*, translated from the Arabic by Franz Rosenthal (Bollingen Series XLIII. Copyright 1958 and 1967 by Princeton University Press. Reprinted by permission of Princeton University Press.)

employment that they would have accepted if the schemes had not existed.

Benefit payments are required to help those in real need. If they are income-related, however, they tend to discourage recipients from working.

This does not argue against welfare payments. It does suggest, however, that welfare schemes should be designed to minimize their effects on efficiency.

Starting in 1997 the new Labour government in the UK instituted a package of measures called Welfare to Work designed to reduce the disincentives associated with welfare schemes. The scheme was to assist young persons and single parents and the long-term unemployed to find work. It also sought to upgrade schools, since poor performance in school is one of the root causes of long-term youth unemployment. To assist these groups to move from welfare to work measures were introduced to reduce the high implicit tax rate of 70–90 per cent suffered by

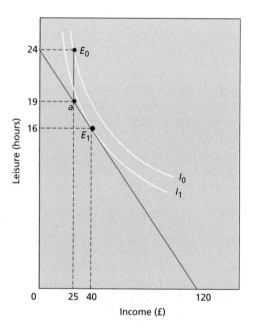

Figure 19.8 Disincentives of welfare schemes

Income-tested benefits provide disincentives to work. The individual is not employed but is receiving benefits of £25 per day from some income-related scheme. This puts him at point E_0, consuming 24 hours of leisure and receiving £25 pounds of income. He is now offered work at £5 per hour, presenting him with a budget line that ends at £120 (for 24 hours' work). In the absence of the benefit he would locate at E_1, consuming 16 hours of leisure (working 8 hours) and earning £40 of income. But for every £1 he earns he loses £1 of benefit, so the budget line starts at E_0 and is vertical to point a, where he is working 5 hours and still getting £25 but now all from work. Further work nets him £5 an hour, so the budget line has its normal slope below a. Since the indifference curve through E_1 is lower than the curve through E_0, his rational choice is not to work.

makes £5 a day, benefits fall to £20; if £10 is earned, benefits fall to £15, and so on. Only when more than £25 per day is earned will the person's disposable income begin to rise. Even if the benefits are reduced at a less sharp rate, say 50p per £1 earned, the disincentive of the high implicit tax rate is strong. Figure 19.8 illustrates this disincentive effect by showing how such schemes induce many people to reject

---

Box 19.4 Welfare to Work

The Welfare to Work programme was introduced in the UK in the Budget of 1997 and extended in the Budget of 1998. It was financed by a one-off tax on the 'excess profits' of privatized utility companies and topped up with funds from the National Lottery. It had four 'New Deal' components, to which were added a major reform of the tax–benefit system.

A New Deal for the young unemployed This provides the opportunity of a job, a work placement, or a place on a training course to young persons under 25 who have been unemployed for long periods.

A New Deal for the long-term unemployed A subsidy is provided to firms who take on persons who have been unemployed for over two years.

A New Deal for lone parents The 60 per cent of lone parents who do not work will be encouraged to work by various incentives. Lone parents whose youngest child is aged 5 or older will be offered individualized case-managed assistance, job search help and advice, training and re-skilling, and help with child care.

A New Deal for schools £1.3 billion is being invested in modernizing the school infrastructure. Schools will be equipped with information technology to assist students to acquire skills required by modern knowledge-intensive production.

Making work pay When the lower earning limit for National Insurance payments is reached, a contribution of £3.20 a week must be paid, making an implicit income tax rate of well *over* 100 per cent! This anomaly is to be removed. The Working Family Tax Credit (WFTC) removes the high implicit tax rates by guaranteeing that every family which earns £100 a week will have an after-benefit income of £180 and that families earning less than £220 a week (half the national average) will pay no tax.

This is a brave experiment. Only time will tell if these structural reforms will significantly alleviate the problems of unemployment and welfare dependency.

---

many groups when the source of their incomes changed from transfer payments to earned income. Some details are given in Box 19.4.

Costs versus benefits

It is difficult to estimate the overall direct and indirect costs of general government activity. About the most that can be said is that they are not insignificant. The level of uncertainty is great enough that those who wish to reduce the scope of government activity can argue that these costs are high, while those who wish to maintain or enlarge the present scope of government can argue that the benefits greatly outweigh the costs.

The costs are often clearer when specific government activities are considered, rather than taking everything in one lump. For example, when it became generally accepted that high marginal rates of income tax had serious consequences, governments (eventually) moved to lower these rates. When it became accepted that government-run business enterprises were no more efficient than privately run ones, and often much less efficient, many governments moved to privatize the industries that they owned. A great debate has raged over the costs of environmental regulation. Although full indirect costs are hard to measure, most estimates do not show these costs to be prohibitive. But the costs and inefficiencies of direct mandates to specific firms have seemed large enough that governments have searched for more efficient, less costly methods. In many cases the best solution seems to be tradable pollution permits.

So the lesson is that there is no general lesson about too much or too little government but that government activity *is* costly and, in some circumstances, can be very costly. So every activity, existing or projected, needs to be assessed on its individual merits. Only if the benefits appear to outweigh the measurable costs and the best guess about the unmeasurable costs should the activity be initiated or continued.

Government failure

So far we have dealt with a government that is trying its best to achieve the goals that we laid out at the beginning of this chapter. It may impose costs, some expected and some unexpected, but it is seeking, as best it can, to achieve socially acceptable goals.

Is this too naïve a view of government and the political process? Today, many observers of the political scene, including not a few economists, would answer with an emphatic yes.

Without doubt governments are far from perfect. This is not because bureaucrats and politicians are worse than other people, more stupid, more rigid, or more venal. Instead it is because they are like others, with flaws as well as virtues and with motives of their own. So having found potential net benefits from perfect but costly government intervention, the final issue is whether the imperfect governments that we encounter in the real world would achieve some of these benefits. Where they do not succeed in achieving potential benefits that exceed the full direct and indirect costs, we speak of **government failure.**

Governments may sometimes make isolated mistakes just as private decision-makers do. What is interesting, however, are the reasons why governments tend, under certain circumstances, to be more systematically in error than would unhindered markets. Here are a few of the many possible causes of systematic government failure.

Rigidities

Rules and regulations, tax rates, and expenditure policies are hard to change. Market conditions, however, change continually and often rapidly. A rule requiring the use of a certain method to reduce pollution may have made sense when the cost of that method was low. It may, however, become a wasteful rule when some alternative becomes a less costly method.

Today's natural monopolies are often made into tomorrow's competitive industries by technological innovations. For example, the near monopoly of the early railways was eliminated by the development of cheap road transport, and the falling cost of air transport is currently providing potent competition for surface transport in the movement of many products. One danger of government intervention is that it will be too slow in adapting to a constantly changing environment.

A centralized decision-taking body has difficulty in reacting to changing conditions as fast as decentralized decision-takers react to market signals.

As well as rigidities in reacting to changing market conditions, governments are often slow to admit mistakes even when they become aware of them. It is often politically easier to go on spending money on a project that has turned sour than to admit fault. A classic example was the development of Concorde. Successive governments realized it was an enormous money-loser, but went on supporting it long after any chance of commercial success was gone.

Markets are much harsher in judging success. When people are investing their own money, the principle that bygones are bygones is usually followed. No firm could raise fresh financial capital for what was currently a poor prospect just because the prospects had seemed good in the past. Nor could it do so because much money had already been spent on it, or because those who supported it in the past would lose face if it were now dropped.

Decision-makers' objectives

By far the most important cause of government failure

arises from the nature of the government's own objectives. Until recently, economists did not concern themselves greatly with the motivation of government. The theory of economic policy implicitly assumed that governments had no objectives of their own. As a result economists only needed to identify places where the market functioned well on its own, and places where government intervention could improve the market's functioning. Governments would then stay out of the former markets and intervene as necessary in the latter.

This model of government behaviour never fitted reality, and economists were gradually forced to think more deeply about the motivation of governments. Why was economists' advice followed closely in some cases, while it was systematically ignored in others? Today economists no longer assume that governments are faceless robots doing whatever economic analysis shows to be in the social interest. Instead they are modelled just as are producers and consumers—as units with their own objectives, which they seek to maximize.

Governments undoubtedly do care about the social good to some extent, but public officials have their careers, their families, and their prejudices as well. Public officials' own needs are seldom wholly absent from their consideration of the actions they will take. Similarly, their definition of the public interest is likely to be influenced heavily by their personal views of what policies are best. The resulting problems are similar to the principal–agent issues mentioned earlier as a source of market failure. In the present case the *principals* are the public; they want governments to do certain things. However, their *agents*—elected and appointed—are motivated by considerations that sometimes pull against what the public wishes.

Modelling governments as maximizers of their own welfare, and then incorporating them into theoretical models of the working of the economy, was a major breakthrough. One of the pioneers of this development was the American economist James Buchanan, who was awarded the 1986 Nobel Prize in economics for his work in this field. The theory that he helped to develop is called *public choice theory*.

The key breakthrough was to view the government as just another economic agent engaging in its own maximizing behaviour. When this view is adopted, there is still room for many competing theories, depending on what variables are in the government's preference function (i.e. what things the government cares about). Consider the other two main decision-taking bodies in orthodox economics. Firms have only profits in their utility functions, and they seek to maximize these. Consumers have only goods and services in their utility functions, and they seek to maximize their satisfactions from consuming them. An analogous theory of the government allows only one variable in its utility function, the variable being votes!

Such a government takes all its decisions with a view to maximizing its votes at the next election.

Public choice theory

Full-blown public choice theory deals with three maximizing groups. Elected officials seek to maximize their votes. Civil servants seek to maximize their salaries (and hence their positions in the hierarchy). Voters seek to maximize their own utility. To this end, voters look to the government to provide them with goods and services and income transfers that raise their personal utility. No one cares about the general interest!

On the one hand this surely is not a completely accurate characterization of motives. Elected statesmen have acted in what they perceive to be the public interest, hoping to be vindicated by history even if they know they risk losing the next election. Some civil servants have exposed inside corruption even though it cost them their jobs. And some high-income individuals vote for the political party that advocates the most, not the least, income redistribution.

On the other hand the characterization is close to the mark in many cases. Those who have seen the UK TV series *Yes Minister* have seen civil servants that fit the public choice model very well. Most of us have read of politicians whose only principle is 'What will get me most votes?' And many voters ask only 'What is in it for me?' This is why the theory can take us a long way in understanding what we see, even though real behaviour is more complex.

Here is one example. Why, in spite of strong advice from economists, have governments persisted in subsidizing agriculture for decades, until many governments now have major farm crises on their hands? Public choice theory looks at the gainers and the losers among the voters.

The gainers from agricultural supports are farmers. They are a politically powerful group, and are aware of what they will lose if farm supports are reduced. They would show their disapproval of such action by voting against any government that even suggests it. The losers are the entire group of consumers. Although they are more numerous than farmers, and although their total loss is large, each individual consumer suffers only a small loss. For example, a policy that gives £50 million a year to British farmers need only cost each citizen £1 per year.[2] Citizens have more important things to worry about, and so do not vote against the government just because it supports farmers. As long as the average voters are unconcerned about, and often unaware of, the losses they suffer, the vote-maximizing government will ignore the interests of the many and support the interests of the few. The vote-maximizing government will consider changing the agricultural policy only when the cost of agricultural support becomes so large that ordinary taxpayers begin to count the cost. What is required for a policy change,

according to this theory, is that those who lose become sufficiently aware of their losses for this awareness to affect their voting behaviour.

The ability of elected officials and civil servants to ignore the public interest is strengthened by a phenomenon called **rational ignorance.** Many policy issues are extremely complex. For example, even the experts are divided when assessing the pros and cons of the UK's decision to stay out of the first wave of membership in the euro, the common European currency. Much time and effort is required for a layperson even to attempt to understand the issue. Similar comments apply to the evidence for and against capital punishment or lowering the age of criminal liability. Yet one person's vote has little influence on which party gets elected or on what they really will do about the issue in question once elected. So the costs are large, the benefits small. Thus a majority of rational, self-interested voters will remain innocent of the complexities involved in most policy issues.

Who will be the informed minority? The answer is those who stand to gain or lose a lot from the policy, those with a strong sense of moral obligation, and those policy junkies who just like this sort of thing.

Inefficient public choices

A major principle of most people's idea of democracy is that each citizen's vote should have the same weight. One of the insights of public choice theory is that resource allocation based on the principle of one-person–one-vote will often be inefficient because it fails to take into account the *intensity of preferences*.

To illustrate this problem, consider three farmers, Abraham, Bob, and Charles. Farmers Abraham and Bob want the government to build an access road to each of their farms, each road to cost £6,000. Suppose that the road to Abraham's farm is worth £7,000 to Abraham and that the road to Bob's farm is worth £7,000 to Bob. (Charles's farm is on the main road and so requires no new access road.) Suppose that, under the current taxing rules, the cost of building each road would be shared equally among the three farmers—£2,000 each. It is efficient to build both roads, since each generates net benefits of £1,000 (£7,000 gross benefits to the farmer helped, less £6,000 total cost). But each would be defeated 2–1 in a simple majority vote. (Bob and Charles would vote against Abraham's road; Abraham and Charles would vote against Bob's road.)

Now suppose that we allow Abraham and Bob to make a deal: 'I will vote for your road if you will vote for mine.'

---

[2] 'Why worry?' you may ask. 'Isn't the small loss to each consumer a reasonable price to pay?' It may be in this one case. The problem, however, lies not in one such policy, but in the cumulative effects of many. If each of many special-interest groups secures a policy that costs each member of the public a small amount, the total bill over all such policies can be, and in many countries is, very large indeed.

Although political commentators often decry such deals, the deal enhances efficiency. Both roads now get 2–1 majorities, and both roads get built. However, such deals can just as well reduce efficiency. If we make the gross value of each road £5,000 instead of £7,000 and let Abraham and Bob make their deal, each road will still command a 2–1 majority because the total cost is £4,000 to each farmer while Abraham and Bob each gain £5,000 worth of road. It is, however, socially inefficient to build the roads, since the gross value of each road is now only £5,000, while the cost is still £6,000. Abraham and Bob will be using democracy to appropriate resources from Charles while reducing economic efficiency.

This case can be interpreted in a different way. Instead of being the third farmer, Charles might be all of the other voters in the county. Instead of bearing one-third of the costs, Abraham and Bob might each bear only a small portion of the costs. To the extent that Abraham and Bob are able to go to the local government and forcefully articulate the benefits that they would derive from the roads, they may be able to use democracy to appropriate resources from taxpayers in general. Much of the concern with the power of 'special interests' stems from the fact that the institutions of representative democracy tend to be responsive to benefits that focus on particular, identifiable, and articulate groups. Often the costs are diffused among all taxpayers, who hardly notice them and in any case are rationally ignorant about them.

This potential bias applies to regulations as well as to direct government provisions. Chapter 18 discussed a number of cases in which economic regulations are used to benefit the affected industry. Similarly, as we saw in Chapter 5, rent control can be interpreted, at least in part, as benefiting existing tenants at the expense of future potential tenants. The latter group tends to have no political power at all.

The effects of government failure

Suppose that, for any of the reasons discussed above, the government makes a mistake in regulation. Say it mistakenly specifies a method of pollution control that is less effective than the best method. If it insists on the level of control appropriate to the best method, but chooses the poorer method, it can convert a social gain from con-

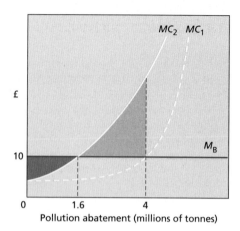

Figure 19.9 Government failure

Choice of an unnecessarily costly method of control reduces the optimal amount of abatement. Each tonne of pollution imposes a social cost of £10, so the marginal social benefit of abatement is £10 per tonne as shown by the M_B line. The most efficient method of control has a marginal cost curve of MC_1, making it socially optimal to prevent 4 million tonnes of pollution. The government misguidedly chooses an abatement procedure that has a marginal cost curve of MC_2. Optimal abatement is now only 1.6 million tonnes. If the government insists on having 4 million tonnes abated, there is a loss of the light shaded area above marginal benefit curve and below the MC_2 curve. That loss may exceed the benefit, which is given by the dark shaded area between the M_B curve and the MC_2 curve. If so, the programme causes a net social loss. Having no programme would then be better than having the inefficient one imposed at too high a level of abatement.

trol into a social loss. This possibility is illustrated in Figure 19.9.

If governments pursue their own objectives such as vote-maximizing, they may sometimes fail to act in the voters' interest by design rather than by mistake. If government economists foresee that a politically popular policy will increase the degree of market failure in the long term, while seeming beneficial in the short term, the government may adopt the harmful policy, in spite of the unfavourable long-run consequences. The government could plead in such cases that it was only being democratic in following the public will. But if governments are to follow exactly where public opinion leads, they do not require experts who are able to foresee consequences that are not obvious to casual observers who are rationally ignorant about complex issues.

Government intervention today

Do governments intervene too little, or too much, in response to market failure? This question reflects one aspect of the continuing debate over the role of government in the economy.

The role of analysis

Economics can help to eliminate certain misconceptions that cloud and confuse the debate. We have earlier noted one such misconception: the optimal level of a negative externality such as pollution is not, as some urge, zero.

Another mistake is to equate market failure with the greed of corporations. Externalities do not require callous, thoughtless, or deliberately deceptive practices on the part of private firms. Externalities occur whenever the signals to which rational decision-takers respond exclude significant benefits and costs. Local authorities and nationalized industries pollute just as much as privately owned industries when they neglect externalities in their operations, as they often do. Most dramatically, pollution in the centrally planned former Soviet Union vastly exceeded the pollution in any industrialized Western market economy.

A third mistake is to think that industrial profits are related to externalities. Both profitable industries such as chemicals, and unprofitable ones such as coal, are capable of spending too little on pollution control or on safety. They may also spend too much. The existence of profits provides no clue one way or the other.

The role of ideology

While positive analysis has a part to play, there are reasons why ideology plays a large role in evaluating government intervention. First, measuring the costs of government intervention is difficult, particularly with respect to indirect costs, because some of the trade-offs are inherently uncertain. How important and how unsafe is nuclear power? Does the ban on some pesticides cause so much malnutrition as to offset the ecological gains that it brings? What cannot be readily measured can be alleged to be extremely high, or low, by opponents, or supporters, of intervention.

Second, classifying the actual pattern of government intervention as successful or not is partly subjective. Has government safety regulation been (choose one) useful if imperfect, virtually ineffective, or positively adverse? All three views have been advocated.

Third, specifying what constitutes market failure is sometimes difficult. For example, does product differentiation represent market success, by giving consumers the variety they want, or failure, by foisting unwanted variations on them?

Over the last two decades in most of the advanced industrial countries the mix of free-market determination and government ownership and regulation has been shifting towards more market determination. No one believes that government intervention can, or should, be reduced to zero. Do we still have a long way to go in reversing the tide of big intrusive government that flowed through most of the twentieth century? Or perhaps we have gone too far and have given some things to the market that governments could do better? These will be some of the great social debates of the early decades of the twenty-first century.

Summary

Government objectives

- Governments seek to protect life and property, improve economic efficiency, protect individuals from others and (sometimes) from themselves, influence the rate of economic growth, and stabilize the economy against fluctuations in national income and the price level.

- Policies for equity include making the distribution of income and wealth somewhat less unequal.

- Equity, efficiency, and growth often come into conflict. Policies to increase equity can reduce efficiency and/or growth, while policies to increase efficiency or growth can make some situations less equitable.

Tools and performance

- Governments may seek to achieve their policies using the tools of taxes, expenditure, rules and regulations, and public ownership.

The costs of government intervention

- Government activity incurs many types of cost. Internal costs refer to the government's own costs of administering its policies. Direct external costs refer to the costs imposed on those directly affected by these policies in such terms as extra production costs, costs of compliance, and losses in productivity. Indirect external costs refer to the efficiency losses that spread throughout the whole economy as a result of the alteration in price signals caused by government tax and expenditure policies.

Government failure

■ As well as showing the potential for benefits to exceed costs in a world where the government functioned perfectly, it is necessary to consider the likely outcome in the imperfect world of reality. Government failure—not achieving some possible gains—can arise because of rigidities causing a lack of adequate response of rules and regulations to changing conditions, poorer foresight on the part of government regulators compared with private participants in the market, and government objectives—such as winning the next election—that conflict with such objectives as improving economic efficiency.

Topics for review

■ Direct and indirect taxes
■ Progressive, regressive, and proportional taxes
■ The benefits and costs of government intervention
■ Sources of government failure
■ Public choice theory
■ Rational ignorance

Questions for discussion

1 What inefficiencies will be caused by (*a*) VAT, (*b*) the personal income tax, (*c*) farm subsidies, (*d*) free health care, (*e*) free elementary school education, (*f*) welfare payments to non-working persons.

Explain why such inefficiencies do not provide *sufficient* reasons to end the activity.

2 It is often asserted, on the basis of nearly a century of US experience with the regulation of many industries, that regulatory agencies ultimately come to be controlled by those they are supposed to regulate. Has this happened so far with the UK bodies set up to regulate the newly privatized (formerly nationalized) industries? Why did this happen in the USA? How can the independence of the UK regulatory bodies be protected?

3 How many rules, regulations, prohibitions, and other 'command-type' tools of government policy can you think of that could be replaced by market-based incentive schemes?

4 Mention a few government programmes that would have effects on all three goals of *equity*, *efficiency*, and *growth*. Select those programmes that have desirable effects on some and undesirable effects on others of these three goals. (Assume that your equity criterion is to have a less unequal distribution of income.) Discuss the trade-offs involved in these policy conflicts.

5 Discuss the relative efficiency and equity effects of two programmes designed to assist certain needy groups. One programme provides coupons that reduce the purchase price of groceries by 50 per cent. (The shop returns the coupons to the government and gets back the discount that it gave to the coupon-holder.) The other programme gives a money income supplement that has the same value as the food coupons.

6 List some things that *only* governments can do and some things that the government can do better than the private sector. Can you think of anything that the British government did thirty years ago, or that it does now, that the private sector could probably do better? Can you think of anything that the private sector did thirty years ago, or is doing now, that the government could probably do better?

Part Five
Modelling the Economy as a Whole

Chapter 20
Macroeconomic Issues and Measurement

Macroeconomics addresses issues affecting the economy as a whole, such as inflation, unemployment, recession, and competitiveness. Microeconomics, in contrast, is concerned with analysing specific product markets or the behaviour of agents such as firms and consumers. Of course, all agents in the economy need to be concerned about the state of the economy as a whole, as well as the markets in which they buy or sell their goods and services. Firms are concerned about how inflations, recessions, and foreign competition affect their profits, and perhaps even their survival. Governments worry about how to prevent recessions, reduce inflation, increase competitiveness, and increase employment. Adults of working age are anxious to avoid the unemployment that comes with recessions,

and to obtain rising real incomes. Pensioners are keen to protect themselves against the hazards of inflation, which can lower the value of their savings.

Each of the concerns just mentioned plays a major role in macroeconomics. In this chapter we explain how macroeconomics differs in approach from the microeconomics of the first half of this book and outline the main issues addressed. We then look in detail at how the activity of the economy as a whole is measured before discussing the interpretation of these measures. In subsequent chapters we are concerned with explaining how the national product or national income is determined, and what government policy can do to influence it.

What is macroeconomics?

Macroeconomics is the study of how the economy behaves in broad outline without dwelling on much of its interesting, but sometimes confusing, detail. Macroeconomics is largely concerned with the behaviour of economic *aggregates*, such as total national product, total investment, and exports for the entire economy. It is also concerned with the average price of all goods and services, rather than the prices of specific products. These aggregates result from activities in many different markets and from the behaviour of different decision-makers such as consumers, governments, and firms. In contrast, *microeconomics* deals with the behaviour of individual markets, such as those for wheat, computer chips, or strawberries, and with the detailed behaviour of individual agents, such as firms and consumers.

In macroeconomics we add together the value of cornflakes, beer, cars, strawberries, haircuts, and restaurant meals along with the value of all other goods and services produced, and we study the aggregate *national product*. We also average the prices of all goods and services consumed and discuss the *general price level* for the entire economy—

usually just called the price level. In practice the averages of several different sets of prices are used. For example, one important index measures the average price of the goods and services bought by the typical consumer. In Britain it is known as the **Retail Price Index** (RPI), while the equivalent in some other countries is called the *consumer price index* (CPI). An appendix to this chapter discusses how the RPI is calculated.

We know full well that an economy that produces much wheat and few cars differs from one that produces many cars but little wheat. We also know that an economy with cheap wheat and expensive cars differs from one with cheap cars and expensive wheat. Studying aggregates and averages often means missing such important differences, but in return for losing valuable detail we are able to view the big picture.

In macroeconomics we look at the broad range of opportunities and difficulties facing the economy as a whole. When national product rises, the output of most firms, and the incomes of most people, usually rise with it. When interest rates rise, most borrowers, including firms and homeowners, have to make bigger payments on their debts, though many savers will get a higher return on their savings. When the price level rises, virtually everyone in the economy is forced to make adjustments, because of the lower value of money. When the unemployment rate rises, workers are put at an increased risk of losing their jobs and suffering losses in their incomes. These movements

in economic aggregates are strongly associated with the economic well-being of most individuals: the health of the sectors in which they work and the prices of the goods that they purchase. These associations between the health of the macroeconomy and the economic fortunes of many people are why macroeconomic aggregates (particularly inflation, unemployment, interest rates, and the balance of payments) are often in the news.

Why do we need macroeconomics?

We need a separate subject called macroeconomics because there are forces that affect the economy as a whole that cannot be fully or simply understood by analysing individual markets and individual products. A problem that is affecting all firms, or many workers, in different industries may need to be tackled at the level of the whole economy. Certainly, if circumstances are common across many sectors of the economy, then analysis at the level of the whole economy may help us to understand what is happening. Let us look at some of the issues that are best thought about in a macroeconomic context.

Major macroeconomic issues

Business cycles

The economy tends to move in a series of ups and downs, called *business cycles*, rather than in a steady pattern. The 1930s saw the greatest worldwide economic depression in the twentieth century, with nearly one-fifth of the UK labour force unemployed for an extended period. In contrast, the twenty-five years following the Second World War were a period of sustained economic growth, with only minor interruptions caused by modest recessions. Then the business cycle returned in more serious form. There have been three major recessions in the United Kingdom during the last three decades (1973–5, 1979–81, and 1990–2), and most other major countries have experienced a similar pattern. Figure 24.7 on page 417 shows the path of real GDP and GDP growth in the UK for the last century, and Figure 27.1 on page 460 shows the cycle in activity in the USA and Germany over the last three decades.

An understanding of business cycles is important for the owners and managers of firms. During recessions many businesses go bust, while profits fall for the survivors. In contrast, during booms demands for most products rise,

profits rise, and most businesses find it easy to expand. Understanding the business cycle is, thus, important for successful businesses. Expanding capacity during the onset of a recession could be a recipe for disaster, while having too little capacity during a boom may be a lost opportunity. Most importantly, although business cycles are beyond the control of individual firms, firms do need to understand that the economy moves in cycles. Governments sometimes claim that their policies will bring stable growth and the end to cycles, but business cycles have been around for a long time, and they are likely to be with us for much longer yet. Box 20.1 outlines some of the terminology associated with a stylized business cycle.

Macroeconomics as a subject was invented to help produce policies that could ameliorate economic fluctuations. Much of what follows is devoted to explanations of why the economy goes through these ups and downs, and what, if anything, the government can do about them.

Overall living standards

Both total and per capita output have risen for many decades in most industrial countries. These long-term trends have produced rising average living standards. In the United Kingdom the real value of the average wage doubled in the twenty years between 1953 and 1973. It stagnated for a while in the 1970s but then grew steadily again in the 1980s and 1990s.

Although long-term growth gets less media attention than does the current inflation or unemployment rate, it is the predominant determinant of living standards and the material constraints facing a society from decade to decade and generation to generation. Among the most important issues in macroeconomics is identifying policies that increase the chances that worldwide growth will continue without the type of slowdown that happened in the 1970s or the serious recessions of the early 1980s and early 1990s.

Box 20.1 The terminology of business cycles

The yellow line shows the hypothetical path of national output relative to trend, or potential, over time. Although the phases of business fluctuations are described by a series of commonly used terms, no two cycles are the same.

Trough A trough is characterized by high unemployment and a level of demand that is low in relation to the economy's capacity to produce. There is thus a substantial amount of unused productive capacity. Business profits are low; for some individual companies they are negative. Confidence about economic prospects in the immediate future is lacking, and as a result many firms are unwilling to risk making new investments.

Recovery The characteristics of a recovery, or expansion, are many—rundown equipment is replaced; employment, income, and consumer spending all begin to rise; and expectations become more favourable as a result of increases in production, sales, and profits. Investments that once seemed risky may be undertaken as the climate of business opinion starts to change from one of pessimism to one of optimism. As demand rises, production can be increased with relative ease merely by re-employing the existing unused capacity and unemployed labour.

Peak A peak is the top of a cycle. At the peak existing capacity is utilized to a high degree; labour shortages may develop, particularly in categories of key skills; and shortages of essential raw materials are likely. As shortages develop in more and more markets, a situation of general excess demand develops. Costs rise, but since prices rise also business remains profitable.

Recession A recession, or contraction, is a downturn in economic activity.

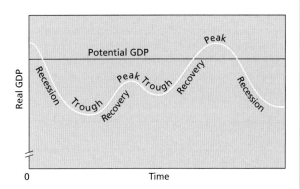

Common usage defines a recession as a fall in real GDP for two quarters in succession. Demand falls off, and as a result production and employment also fall. As employment falls so do personal incomes. Profits drop, and some firms encounter financial difficulties. Investments that looked profitable with the expectation of continually rising demand now appear unprofitable. It may not even be worth replacing capital goods as they wear out, because unused capacity is increasing steadily. In historical discussions, a recession that is deep and long-lasting is often called a **depression**.

Booms and slumps Two nontechnical but descriptive terms are often used. The bottom of an abnormally deep recession is called a *slump*, and the top of an abnormally strong recovery is called a *boom*.

Inflation

The annual UK inflation rate was over 25 per cent in 1975. This was the highest level reached in peacetime for at least three centuries, and at that rate inflation halves the purchasing power of money in three years. The government of Margaret Thatcher was elected in 1979 on the promise of eliminating inflation from the British economy. Inflation did fall below 5 per cent by 1984, but it rose again to around 10 per cent before the end of the decade. By the late 1990s the annual rate of inflation had fallen to around 2–3 per cent, which was the lowest level since the early 1960s. In May 1997 the incoming Labour government set a target level of inflation of 2.5 per cent and gave the Bank of England the power to set interest rates in order to achieve this target. (We will discuss the implementation of this move and other important monetary policy changes involved in the setting up of the European Central Bank in Chapter 25 below.)

Swings in economic activity have accompanied swings in inflation. Generally, attempts by governments to control high inflation have helped to bring about recessions. However, the pattern of booms and recessions has been very similar across many different countries, so it cannot all be attributed to domestic government policy alone. Also the relationship between inflation and recession seems to change over time. The 1979–81 UK recession was accompanied by inflation in the mid-teens, while the 1990–2 recession was accompanied by only single-figure inflation.

An important policy problem for governments is how to stimulate economic activity without causing inflation. The rise in inflation during boom times often leads policymakers to tighten their policies in order to bring inflation under control. When inflation falls after a recession, policymakers often feel that they have the leeway to stimulate the economy again. Hence they have to tread carefully to achieve a suitable balance between stimulus and contraction, and we will learn below that timing policy interventions in order to achieve a desired outcome is not a simple matter.

Unemployment

A downturn in economic activity causes an increase in unemployment. Indeed, it was the high unemployment of the 1930s that led to the establishment of the subject now known as macroeconomics, and unemployment is still a central concern of economics. During the Great

Depression of the 1930s UK unemployment rose to nearly 20 per cent of the labour force, and even higher levels were reached in some other countries. Although in the 1950s and 1960s unemployment was consistently very low in most industrial countries, higher unemployment returned in the 1980s and 1990s. UK unemployment reached peaks of 12.2 per cent in 1986 and of 10.8 per cent in 1993 in the two recessions, while unemployment in France and Germany reached post-war highs of 12.5 and 11.7 per cent, respectively, in 1997, and Japanese unemployment was rising rapidly in 1998 to reach levels not seen there since the Second World War. By the late 1990s unemployment had fallen in Britain and the United States, but it was still high in several European countries, such as Spain, Germany, and France. Accordingly, the analysis of the causes of, and potential cures for, unemployment is still very high on the agenda of macroeconomics today, especially in the EU, and a new bout of high unemployment can never be ruled out even for those countries where it has been low for some time.

The solution for unemployment that economists came up with in the 1930s was for governments to increase their spending or reduce taxes. However, the applicability of this solution is thought to be much more restricted today. In Chapter 31 we will discuss why this early solution for unemployment does not seem so promising today.

Government budget deficits

With the exception of two brief periods (1970 and 1988–9) the British government has had a *budget deficit* since the Second World War—it was spending more than it was raising in taxation. In the mid-1970s the budget deficit rose to around 8 per cent of the national product (GDP). In the mid-1990s the budget was again in deficit, but a surplus was projected by the end of the decade. Deficits have to be financed by government borrowing, which raises the national debt.

At one time it was thought that budget deficits might be good for the economy because government spending creates jobs. Nowadays there is much concern about the potential burden of debt, in the form of interest, which has to be paid by taxpayers and which, therefore, keeps taxes high. In later chapters we will discuss how the budget deficit affects the economy and the conflict over the role of the government budget that is central to macroeconomics. We will also discuss the implications of the limitations on budget deficits imposed on EU member states by the Maastricht Treaty and by the Stability and Growth Pact. Deliberate use of government spending and taxes to influence the economy is known as **fiscal policy.**

Interest rates

In addition to fiscal policy, government (or the monetary authority where this is independent of government) has available the tools of monetary policy. **Monetary policy** involves changing interest rates, or the money supply, in order to influence the economy.

High interest rates are a symptom of a tight monetary policy. When interest rates are high, firms find it more costly to borrow, and this makes them more reluctant to invest in expanding their business. Individuals with mortgages or bank loans are also hit by high interest rates since it costs more to make their loan repayments. Hence high interest rates tend to reduce demand in the economy—firms invest less and those with mortgages have less to spend. Low interest rates tend to stimulate demand.

Another important channel of monetary policy is via the exchange rate, at least for countries whose exchange rates are flexible. Exchange rate changes can affect the relative prices, and thereby the competitiveness, of domestic and foreign producers. A significant appreciation of the domestic currency makes domestic goods expensive relative to foreign goods. This may lead to a shift of demand away from domestic goods towards foreign goods. Such shifts have an important influence on domestic economic activity.

Targets and instruments

The issues that we have just discussed fall into two types. First, there are the things that really matter for their own sake. These are the things that affect living conditions and the state of the economic environment. Living standards, unemployment, business cycles, and inflation are outcomes that matter. Almost everyone wants growing living standards, high employment and low unemployment, as well as avoidance of recessions and inflation. These things are known as the **targets** of policy. 'Good' values of these variables are what governments would like to achieve.

Fiscal and monetary policies (government spending, taxes, interest rates, and the money supply) are not so much valued for their own sake. Rather, they are the **instruments** of policy and are valued more for the effect they have on the targets. *Instruments* are the variables that the government can change directly, whereas *targets* are the things that it would like to change.

The macroeconomic policy problem is to choose appropriate values of the policy instruments in order to achieve the best possible combination of the outcomes of the targets. This is a continually changing problem because the targets are perpetually being affected by shocks from various parts of the world economy.

We now turn to a discussion of the measurement of aggregate economic activity before returning to explanations of how that activity is determined.

National output concepts

Macroeconomics has as its central goal the explanation of the determinants of national income and output. Indeed, from Chapter 21 onwards we spend a great deal of our time building up an analytical framework that helps us to understand the forces which influence national income and output. First, however, we have to understand what it is we are talking about. What exactly do we mean by national income and the national product? What do people mean when they refer to GDP, and how does it differ from GNI (or GNP)?

We start by discussing the measurement of national output, and find that by summing the *value added* for each industry or sector we arrive at a standard measure of national product. We then discuss how it is that we can arrive at the same measure of national product both from the expenditure side of the economy and from adding up factor (inputs) incomes. An explicit result of this discussion is a demonstration of the equivalence of the concepts of national income and national product.

The national output or the national product is related to the sum of all the outputs produced in the economy by individuals, firms, and governmental organizations. To obtain it, however, we cannot just add up all of the outputs of individual production units.

Value added as output

The reason that getting a total for the nation's output is not quite so straightforward as it may seem at first sight is that one firm's output may be another firm's input. A maker of clothing buys cloth from a textile manufacturer and buttons, zips, thread, pins, hangers, etc. from a range of other producers. Most modern manufactured products have many ready-made inputs. A car or aircraft manufacturer, for example, has hundreds of component suppliers.

Production occurs in stages: some firms produce outputs that are used as inputs by other firms, and these other firms in turn produce outputs that are used as inputs by yet other firms.

If we merely added up the market values of all outputs of all firms, we would obtain a total that was greatly in excess of the value of the economy's actual output. The error that would arise in estimating the nation's output by adding all sales of all firms is called **double counting**. 'Multiple counting' would be a better term, since if we added up the values of all sales, the same output would be counted every time that it was sold from one firm to another.

The problem of double counting is solved by distin-guishing between two types of output. **Intermediate goods and services** are the outputs of some firms that are in turn inputs for other firms. **Final goods and services** are goods that are not used as inputs by other firms in the period of time under consideration. The term **final demand** refers to the purchase of final goods and services for consumption, for investment (including inventory accumulation), for use by governments, and for export. It does not include goods and services that are purchased by firms and used as inputs for producing other goods and services.

If the sales of firms could be readily separated into sales for final use and sales for further processing by other firms, measuring total output would still be straightforward. Total output would equal the value of all *final goods and services* produced by firms, excluding all intermediate goods and services. However, when British Steel sells steel to Ford UK, it does not care, and usually does not know, whether the steel is for final use (say, construction of a new warehouse) or for use as an intermediate good in the production of cars. The problem of double counting must therefore be resolved in some other manner.

To avoid double counting, statisticians use the important concept of **value added.** Each firm's value added is the value of its output minus the value of the inputs that it purchases from other firms (which were in turn the outputs of those other firms). Thus a steel mill's value added is the value of its output minus the value of the ore that it buys from the mining company, the value of the electricity and fuel oil that it uses, and the values of all other inputs that it buys from other firms. A bakery's value added is the value of the bread and cakes it produces minus the value of the flour and other inputs that it buys from other firms.

The total value of a firm's output is the *gross* value of its output. The firm's value added is the *net* value of its output. It is this latter figure that is the firm's contribution to the nation's total output. It is what its own efforts add to the value of what it takes in as inputs.

Value added measures each firm's own contribution to total output, the amount of market value that is produced by that firm. Its use avoids the statistical problem of double counting.

The concept of value added is further illustrated in Box 20.2. In this simple example, as in all more complex cases, the value of total output of final goods is obtained by summing all the individual values added.

The sum of all values added in an economy is a measure of the economy's total output. This measure of total output is called gross value added. It is a measure of all

Box 20.2   Value added through stages of production

Because the output of one firm often becomes the input of other firms, the total value of goods sold by all firms greatly exceeds the value of the output of final goods. This general principle is illustrated by a simple example in which firm R starts from scratch and produces goods (raw materials) valued at £100; the firm's value added is £100. Firm I purchases these raw materials valued at £100 and produces semi-manufactured goods that it sells for £130. Its value added is £30 because the value of the

goods is increased by £30 as a result of the firm's activities. Firm F purchases the semi-manufactured goods for £130 and works them into a finished state, selling them for £180. Firm F's value added is £50. The value of final goods, £180, is found either by counting the sales of firm F or by taking the sum of the values added by each firm. This value is less than the £410 that we obtain by adding up the market value of the commodities sold by each firm. The table summarizes the example.

Transactions between firms at three different stages of production

	Firm R	Firm I	Firm F	All firms
A: Purchases from other firms	£0	£100	£130	£230 = Total interfirm sales
B: Purchase of factors of production (wages, rent, interest, profits)	100	30	50	180 = Value added
Total A + B = value of product	100	130	180 = Value of final goods and services	410 = Total value of all sales

Table 20.1 Gross value added at current basic prices, by sector, UK, 1997

Sector	£ million	% of GDP
Agriculture, hunting, forestry, and fisheries	10,820	1.3
Mining and quarrying	18,137	2.3
Manufacturing	146,522	18.3
Electricity, gas, and water supply	16,227	2.0
Construction	36,491	4.6
Wholesale and retail trade	83,316	10.4
Hotels and restaurants	22,752	2.8
Transport and communications	59,694	7.4
Financial intermediation and real estate	140,078	17.5
Public administration and defence	38,940	4.9
Education	38,653	4.8
Health and social work	46,476	5.8
Other services	33,955	4.2
Statistical discrepancy (unallocated)	19,209	2.4
Gross value added at current basic prices	711,270	
plus adjustment to current basic prices (taxes minus subsidies on products)	90,702	11.3
= GDP at market prices	**801,972**	**100.0**

The table shows gross value added by industrial sector in the United Kingdom for 1997 at current basic prices. The sector values added combine to make gross value added. Gross value added is equal to the total output of goods and services minus the purchase of intermediate goods. It is also the sum of the factor rewards attributable to each sector. Notice that manufacturing is the largest sector, but it produces only about 18 per cent of GDP.

Source: ONS, UK national accounts (*The Blue Book*), 1998.

final output that is produced by all productive activity in the economy.

Table 20.1 gives the gross value added by major industrial sectors for the UK economy in 1997. You will see from this table that gross value added becomes GDP by the addition of a further term (taxes on products minus subsidies). We will explain this step in moving from value added to GDP below.[1]

Notice that we have used 'gross' in two different senses above—first in comparing the gross and net values of a firm's output and then in the term 'gross value added'. The first usage relies on the common meanings of 'gross' and 'net'. The gross value of the firm's output is the total output before making any deductions, while the net value deducts inputs made by other firms. In 'gross value added' the usage is different. Value added is already defined as firms' net output; the word 'gross' is added because of its specific meaning in national accounts statistics. This is important to understand as we will be using it from here on in terms such as *gross* domestic product and *gross* national income.

'Gross' in national accounts aggregates refers to the fact that we are measuring currently produced outputs or incomes without taking into account the wearing out, or *depreciation*, of capital goods during their production. Thus gross value added is the value added of the economy as a whole *before* any allowance for depreciation, and gross domestic product is the nation's output before allowing for depreciation.

---

[1] Gross value added at basic prices is similar to what used to be called GDP at factor cost, but the latter term fell out of the national accounts in 1998.

GDP, GNI, and GNP

The measures of national income and national product that are used in Britain derive from an accounting system that has recently been standardized by international agreement and is thus common to most major countries. It is known as the System of National Accounts. A more detailed specification of this accounting system applies to all EU member states under the European System of Accounts 1995 (which was to be applied by all EU countries by April 1999 but was introduced into UK accounts in 1998). These accounts have a logical structure, based on the simple yet important idea that all output must be owned by someone. So whenever national output is produced, it must generate an equivalent amount of claims to that output in the form of national income.

Box 20.3 explains how the process that determines national income and national output simultaneously can be represented by a diagram illustrating the circular flow of expenditure and income. The right half of the figure in that box focuses on expenditure to purchase the nation's output in product markets, and the left half focuses on factor markets through which the receipts of producers

are distributed to factors of production, such as workers and the owners of capital and land.

Corresponding to the two halves of the circular flow are two ways of measuring national income: by determining the value of what is produced and by determining the value of the income claims generated by production. Both measures yield the same total, which is called **gross domestic product (GDP)**. When it is calculated by adding up the total expenditure for each of the main components of final output, the result is called *GDP expenditure-based.* When it is calculated by adding up all the incomes generated by the act of production, it is called *GDP income-based.*

All value produced must be accounted for by a claim that someone has to that value. For example, any expenditure you make when you buy a TV set must also be received by the supplier of that set. The value of what you spend is the expenditure; the value of the product sold to you is the output. Thus, the two values calculated on income and expenditure bases are identical conceptually and differ in practice only because of errors of measurement.

Box 20.3 The circular flow of income, output, and expenditure

Consider an economy that is made up of domestic individuals and domestic firms. For a moment we assume that the economy has no imports or exports and no government. The individuals provide labour for the firms and they buy the firms' output. The income that flows to individuals is represented by the black line running up the left-hand side of the diagram and the expenditure on the final output of firms is represented by the black line running down the right-hand side. National output (or national income) can be measured either from the expenditure side in terms of spending on final goods produced, or on the income side. These factor incomes can be measured either as the sum of values added in the economy or as the sum of individual incomes.

In practice final expenditure is not made up just of individuals' consumption expenditure, so when we approach the explanation of GDP from the expenditure side we need to add in investment spending, government consumption, and exports (the green lines). However, it is still true that the national product is equal to the sum of these total final expenditures. It is also true that these final expenditures create incomes that can be added up to generate the equivalence between national income and national output. The flows on the left side of the diagram have to be equal to the flows on the right. Any flow that generates an expenditure also generates income.

We will refer back to this diagram several times in future chapters. When we do so we will point out that for the level of income and output to be constant (rather than rising or falling) the injections of spending from outside the circular flow must just equal the withdrawals (or leakages) from the circular flow. In the model to be developed in subsequent chapters, we call

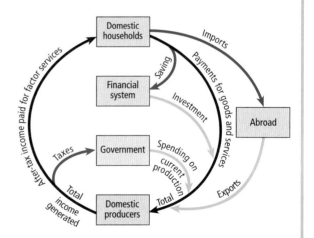

the injections *exogenous* or *autonomous* expenditures. These are investment, government consumption, and exports, and are shown in the diagram in green. The leakages are taxes, saving, and imports, shown in blue.

For present purposes the key point is that

Domestic production creates an income claim on the value of that production, and when all of the claims are added up, they must be equal to the value of all the production.

Any discrepancy arising from such errors is then reconciled so that one common total is given as *the* measure of GDP. Both calculations are of interest, however, because each gives a different and useful breakdown. Also, having two independent ways of measuring the same quantity provides a useful check on statistical procedures and on unavoidable errors in measurement.

GDP expenditure-based

GDP expenditure-based for a given year is calculated by adding up the expenditures going to purchase the final output produced in that year. Total expenditure on final output is expressed in the national accounts as the sum of three broad categories of expenditure: consumption, investment, and net exports. However, consumption is further divided into the consumption expenditures of government and those of private individuals (and non-profit organizations serving households). So there are four important categories of expenditure that we will discuss in considerable detail: private consumption, government consumption, investment, and net exports. In Chapter 21 we explain why these particular categories have received more attention in macroeconomics than have the net sector outputs listed in Table 20.1 and the income categories discussed below (Table 20.3). Here we define what these expenditure categories are and how they are measured. Throughout it is important to remember that they are exhaustive: they are defined in such a way that *all* expenditures on final output fall into one of the four categories.

Private consumption expenditure

Private consumption expenditure includes expenditure by individuals on goods and services produced and sold to their final users during the year. It includes services, such as haircuts, medical care, and legal advice; nondurable goods, such as fresh meat, clothing, cut flowers, and fresh vegetables; and durable goods, such as cars, television sets, and microwave ovens. However, it excludes purchases of newly built houses as these are counted as investment.[2] Also measured in the national accounts as part of private consumption is the final consumption expenditure of non-profit-making institutions serving households (NPISH). These are institutions, such as charities, that are neither firms nor governmental organizations but do contribute some spending and so have to be included somewhere in the national accounts. We denote actual, measured, private consumption expenditure by the symbol C^a.

Government consumption expenditure

When governments provide goods and services that their citizens want, such as health care and street lighting, it is obvious that they are adding to the sum total of valuable

output in the same way as do private firms that produce cars and video cassettes. With other government activities the case may not seem so clear. Should expenditures by the UK government to negotiate over the political situation in Northern Ireland, or to pay a civil servant to help draft legislation, be regarded as contributions to the national product? Some people believe that many (or even most) activities in Whitehall and in town halls are wasteful, if not downright harmful. Others believe that governments produce many of the important things of life, such as education, law and order, and pollution control.

National income statisticians do not speculate about which government expenditures are worthwhile. Instead they include all government purchases of goods and services as part of national income and output. (Government expenditure on investment goods appears as public sector capital formation, which is a part of total investment expenditure.) Just as the national product includes, without distinction, the outputs of both gin and Bibles, it also includes refuse collection and the upkeep of parks, along with the services of judges, Members of Parliament, and even Inland Revenue inspectors.

However, the UK national accounts (since 1998) do distinguish two different categories of government consumption. When government pays for the goods and services that are consumed by private individuals, this is referred to as *individual government final consumption*. This applies to health expenditure and education. If, for example, National Health Service doctors perform an operation, it is paid for by the government but the service is received by an identifiable individual. In contrast, the government also pays for street lighting, national defence, and law and order, but the benefit is consumed by the population at large rather than some specific individual. This is expenditure on *public goods*, which we discussed in Chapter 18. Expenditures that are made by the government but where the consumption cannot be assigned to specific individuals are called in the national accounts *collective government final consumption*. As a simplification (which we explain further in Chapter 21) in macroeconomics we lump together individual government final consumption and collective government final consumption into one term: government consumption, sometimes just called government spending. Actual government consumption spending is denoted by the symbol G^a.

Government output is typically valued at cost rather than at the market value. In most cases there is really no choice. The output of public services is not (generally) sold in the marketplace, so government output is not observed independently of the expenditures that produce it. What, for example, is the market value of the services of a

---

[2] Private consumption does not include purchases of existing houses as these are not part of current production. Rather this involves a transfer of an existing asset.

court of law? No one knows. We do know, however, what it costs the government to provide these services, so we value them at their cost of production.

Although valuing at cost is the only possible way to measure many government activities, it does have one curious consequence. If, owing to an increase in productivity, one civil servant now does what two used to do, and the displaced worker shifts to the private sector, the government's measured contribution to the national product will register a decline. On the other hand, if two workers now do what one worker used to do, the government's measured contribution will rise. Both changes could occur even though the services the government actually provides have not changed. This is an inevitable consequence of measuring the value of the government's output by the cost of the inputs, mainly labour, that are used to produce it, rather than by the value of outputs.[3]

It is important to recognize that only government expenditures *on currently produced goods and services* are included as part of GDP. A great deal of government expenditure is not a part of GDP. For example, when the Department of Health and Social Security (DHSS) makes a payment to an old-age pensioner, the government is not purchasing any currently produced goods or services from the retired. The payment itself adds neither to employment nor to total output. The same is true of payments on account of unemployment benefit, income support, student grants, and interest on the national debt (which transfers income from taxpayers to holders of government bonds). All such payments are examples of **transfer payments,** which are government expenditures that are not made in return for currently produced goods and services. They are not a part of expenditure on the nation's total output and, therefore, are not included in GDP.[4]

Thus when we refer to government expenditure as part of GDP or use the symbol G^a, we include all government expenditure on currently produced goods and services, and we *exclude* all government transfer payments. (The term *total government spending* is often used to describe all government spending, including transfer payments.)

Investment expenditure

Investment expenditure is defined as expenditure on the production of goods not for present consumption but rather for future use. The goods that are created by this expenditure are called **investment** (or **capital**) **goods.** Investment expenditures can be divided into three categories: changes in inventories, **fixed capital formation,** and the net acquisition of valuables.

Changes in inventories Almost all firms hold stocks of their inputs and their own outputs. These stocks are known as inventories. Inventories of inputs and unfinished materials allow firms to maintain a steady stream of production in spite of short-term fluctuations in the deliveries

of inputs bought from other firms. Inventories of outputs allow firms to meet orders in spite of temporary fluctuations in the rate of output or sales. Modern 'just-in-time' methods of production pioneered by the Japanese aim to reduce inventories held by manufacturing plants to nearly zero by delivering inputs just as they are needed. Most of the economy, however, does not achieve this level of efficiency and never will. Retailing, for example, would certainly not be improved if shops held no stocks.

An accumulation of stocks and unfinished goods in the production process counts as current investment because it represents goods produced (even if only half-finished) but not used for current consumption. A drawing down of inventories, also called *de-stocking*, counts as negative investment because it represents a reduction in the stocks of finished goods (produced in the current period) that are available for future use. Inventories are valued at what they will be worth on the market, rather than at what they have cost the firm so far. This is because the expenditure-based measure of GDP includes the value of what final expenditures on these goods would be if they were sold, even though they have not been sold yet.

Fixed capital formation All production uses capital goods. These are manufactured aids to production, such as machines, computers, and factory buildings. Creating new capital goods is an act of investment and is called *fixed investment* or **fixed capital formation.** The economy's total quantity of capital goods is called the **capital stock.** Much of the capital stock is in the form of equipment or buildings used by firms or government agencies in the production of goods and services. This includes not just factories and machines, but also hospitals, schools, and offices. A house or a flat is also a durable asset that yields its utility (housing services) over a long period of time. This meets the definition of fixed capital formation, so (as we pointed out above) housing *construction* is counted as investment expenditure rather than as consumption expenditure. When a family purchases a house from a builder or another owner, the ownership of an already produced asset is transferred, and that transaction is not a part of current GDP.

Net acquisition of valuables Some productive activity creates goods that are neither consumed nor used in the production process. Rather they are held for their intrinsic beauty or for their expected appreciation in value. Examples are jewellery and works of art. Such works are

---

[3] Since 1998 national income statisticians have been trying to incorporate some productivity measures into the output of government, but this exercise is in its infancy.

[4] When the recipients of transfer payments spend these on buying goods and services, their spending is measured as consumption expenditure, and thus as part of GDP, in the same way as any other consumption expenditure. We do not want to measure it twice, which we would be doing if we included in GDP both the government transfer and the spending by the recipient.

known as *valuables*. Acquisitions less disposals of valuables are treated as investments in the national accounts.

Gross and net investment Total investment expenditure is called **gross investment** or **gross capital formation.** Gross investment is divided into two parts: replacement investment and net investment. **Replacement investment** is the amount of investment that just maintains the level of existing capital stock; in other words it replaces the bits that have worn out. Replacement investment is classified as the **capital consumption allowance,** or simply **depreciation.** Gross investment minus replacement investment is **net investment.** Positive net investment increases the economy's total stock of capital, while replacement investment keeps the existing stock intact by replacing what has been used up or worn out.

All of gross investment is included in the calculation of GDP. This is because all investment goods are part of the nation's total output, and their production creates income (and employment) whether the goods produced are a part of net investment or are merely replacement investment. Actual total investment expenditure is denoted by the symbol I^a.

Net exports

The fourth category of aggregate expenditure, one that is very important to the UK economy, arises from foreign trade. How do imports and exports affect the calculation of GDP?

Imports A country's GDP is the total value of final goods and services produced *in that country.* If you spend £15,000 on a car that was made in Germany, only a small part of that value will represent expenditure on UK production. Some of it represents payment for the services of the UK dealer and for transportation within this country; much of the rest is the output of German firms and expenditure on German products, though there may be component suppliers from several countries. If you take your next vacation in Italy, much of your expenditure will be on goods and services produced in Italy and thus will contribute to Italian GDP.

Similarly, when a UK firm makes an investment expenditure on a UK-produced machine tool that was made partly with imported materials, only part of the expenditure is on British production; the rest is expenditure on production by the countries supplying the materials. The same is true for government expenditure on such things as roads and dams; some of the expenditure is for imported materials, and only part of it is for domestically produced goods and services.

Private consumption, government consumption, and investment all have an import content. To arrive at total expenditure on UK output, we need to subtract from total UK residents' expenditure actual expenditure on imports of goods and services, which is represented below by the symbol IM^a.

Exports If UK firms sell goods or services to German consumers, the goods and services are a part of German consumption expenditure but also constitute expenditure on UK output. Indeed, all goods and services that are produced in the United Kingdom and sold to foreigners must be counted as part of UK GDP; they are produced in the United Kingdom, and they create incomes for the UK residents who produce them. They are not purchased by UK residents, however, so they are not included as part of C^a, I^a, or G^a. Therefore, to arrive at the total value of expenditure on the domestic product, it is necessary to add in the value of UK exports. Actual exports of goods and services are denoted by the symbol X^a.

It is convenient to group actual imports and actual exports together as **net exports.** Net exports are defined as total exports of goods and services minus total imports of goods and services ($X^a - IM^a$), which will also be denoted by NX^a. When the value of exports exceeds the value of imports, the net export term is positive. When the value of imports exceeds the value of exports, the net export term becomes negative.

Market prices and basic prices

There is one important difference that arises when calculating the level of GDP from the expenditure side of the economy as compared to calculating it by summing the value added in production. This difference arises because the price paid by consumers for many goods and services is not the same as the sales revenue received by the producer. There are taxes that have to be paid that place a wedge between what consumers pay and producers receive. Taxes attached to transactions are known as *indirect taxes.* Examples of UK indirect taxes include VAT and excise duties.[5] Thus if you pay £100 for a meal in a restaurant, the restaurateur will receive only £82.50, and £17.50 will go to the government in the form of VAT.

In cases where products are subsidized by the government, the producer receives more than the consumer pays. In 1997 subsidies on UK products were minimal, amounting to only 1 per cent of GDP.

The term **basic prices** is used in the national accounts to refer to the prices of products as received by producers. **Market prices** are the prices as paid by consumers. Thus basic prices are equal to market prices *minus* taxes on products *plus* subsidies on products. In the example of the meal bill above, the market price was £100 but the basic price was £82.50.

If you look again at Table 20.1, you will see that the sum

---

[5] The rate of VAT was 17.5% in the UK in 1998 and applied to a wide range of goods and services. Excise duties applied mainly to tobacco, alcohol, and petrol.

of sectoral values added that we presented there is referred to as gross value added at *basic prices*. You should also notice that by adding to gross value added at basic prices a term labelled 'adjustment to current basic prices' we arrived at the total for GDP at market prices. This adjustment to current basic prices is made up of taxes minus subsidies on products.

Since our final expenditure categories are all measured at market prices—as they measure what is spent by purchasers rather than what is received by producers—we can proceed by adding up these final expenditures to arrive at GDP *at market prices* directly.

Total expenditures

The expenditure-based measure of gross domestic product at market prices is the sum of the four expenditure categories that we have discussed above, or in symbols:

$$GDP = C^a + I^a + G^a + (X^a - IM^a).$$

The actual expenditure components of GDP for the United Kingdom in 1997 are shown in Table 20.2.

GDP expenditure-based is the sum of private consumption, government consumption, investment, and net export expenditures on currently produced goods and services. It is GDP at market prices.

GDP income-based

The production of a nation's output generates income. Labour must be employed, land must be rented, and capital must be used. The calculation of GDP from the income side involves adding up factor incomes so that all of that value is accounted for. In essence we are taking the value added displayed for the economy as a whole in Table 20.1 and dividing this up by types of income rather than by industrial sector. We have already noted that because all value produced must be owned by someone, the value of production must equal the value of income claims generated by that production.

National income accountants distinguish three main categories of factor incomes: operating surplus, mixed incomes, and compensation of employees.

Operating surplus   Operating surpluses are net business incomes after payment has been made to hired labour and for material inputs but before *direct taxes* (such as corporation tax) have been paid. Direct taxes are those taxes levied on individuals or firms, usually in relation to their income. Operating surpluses are in large part the profits of firms, but also included is the financial surplus of organizations other than companies, such as universities. Some profits are paid out as **dividends** to owners of firms; the rest are retained for use by firms. The former are called

Table 20.2 Expenditure-based GDP and its components, UK, 1997

Expenditure categories	£ million	% of GDP
Individual consumption		
Household final consumption	500,616	62.4
Final consumption of non-profit institutions serving households	18,484	2.3
Individual government final consumption	86,706	10.8
Total actual individual consumption	605,806	75.5
Collective government final consumption	60,700	7.6
Total final consumption	**666,506**	**83.1**
Gross capital formation		
Gross fixed capital formation	133,710	16.7
Change in inventories	3,101	0.3
Acquisition less disposals of valuables	−219	−0.0
Total gross capital formation	**136,592**	**17.0**
Exports of goods and services	228,702	28.5
less imports of goods and services	−229,334	−28.6
External balance of goods and services (net exports)	**−632**	**−0.1**
Statistical discrepancy	−494	
Gross domestic product at market prices (money GDP)	**801,972**	**100.0**

Expenditure-based GDP is made up of consumption, investment, and net exports. Consumption is by far the largest expenditure category, equal to about 83 per cent of GDP. Private consumption makes up most of this, around 65 per cent of GDP, and government consumption makes up the rest. Investment accounts for about 17 per cent of GDP. Whereas exports and imports are both quite large (each over 25 per cent of GDP), net exports are small; in 1997 they represented a mere (negative) 0.1 per cent of GDP. Government consumption is reported in two parts—that which is paid for by government but is consumed by individuals, such as health services and education, and that which is consumed collectively, such as defence and the legal system.

Source: ONS, UK national accounts (*The Blue Book*), 1998.

distributed profits, and the latter are called *undistributed profits* or *retained earnings*. Both distributed and undistributed profits are included in the calculation of GDP.

Mixed incomes   This category covers the many people who are earning a living by selling their services or output but who are not employed by any organization. It includes some consultants and those who work on short contracts but are not formally employees of an incorporated business. They are self-employed individuals who are running sole-trader businesses. Also included are some partnerships where the partners own the business. The reason why the incomes of this group are referred to as *mixed incomes* is that it is not clear what proportion of their earnings is equivalent to a wage or salary and what proportion is the profit or surplus of the business. They are a mixture of the two.

Compensation of employees This is wages and salaries (usually just referred to as *wages*). It is the payment for the services of labour. Wages include take-home pay, taxes withheld, National Insurance contributions, pension fund contributions, and any other fringe benefits. In other words wages are measured gross. In total, wages represent that part of the value of production that is attributable to hired labour.

The various components of UK income-based GDP in 1997 are shown in Table 20.3. Notice that the three income categories in Table 20.3 add up to gross value added at basic prices, as shown in Table 20.1. These income-based and output- or value-added-based measures are showing the same thing—the sum of factor incomes for the whole economy. In both cases we add taxes on production less subsidies to arrive at GDP at market prices.

Table 20.3 Income-based GDP and its components, UK, 1997

Income type	£ million	% of GDP
Operating surplus, gross (profits)	218,539	27.3
Mixed incomes	42,623	5.3
Compensation of employees	432,280	53.9
Taxes on production and imports	115,572	14.4
less subsidies	−8,035	−1.0
Statistical discrepancy	993	0.1
GDP at market prices	**801,972**	**100.0**
Employees' compensation		
Receipts from rest of world	1,007	
less payments to rest of world	−924	
Total	**83**	
less taxes on production paid to rest of world *plus* subsidies received from rest of world	**−2,605**	
Property and entrepreneurial income		
Receipts from rest of world	108,420	
less payments to rest of world	−96,335	
Total	**12,085**	
Gross national income (GNI) at market prices	**811,535**	

The income-based measure of GDP is made up of gross operating surplus (profit), mixed incomes, compensation of employees, and net taxes on goods. Mixed incomes are largely incomes of the self-employed or non-incorporated businesses, where it is hard to distinguish profits from employee compensation. By far the largest income category is compensation of employees, which makes up about 54 per cent of GDP. GNI is GDP at market prices plus various net income receipts from the rest of the world.

Source: ONS, UK national accounts (*The Blue Book*), 1998.

Note also that one of the terms in the table is a 'statistical discrepancy'. This is a small 'fudge factor' (which also appears with a different value in Tables 20.1 and 20.2). It is there to make sure that the independent measures of income and product come to the same total. The statistical discrepancy is a clear indication that national accounting is not error-free.

Income produced and income received

GDP at market prices provides a measure of total output produced in the United Kingdom and of the total income generated as a result of that production. However, the total income received by UK residents differs from GDP for two reasons. First, some domestic production creates factor earnings for non-residents who either do some paid work for UK residents or have previously invested in the United Kingdom; on this account, income received by UK residents will be less than UK GDP. Second, many UK residents earn income from work for overseas residents or on overseas investments; on this account, income received by UK residents will be greater than GDP.

While GDP measures the output, and hence the income, that is *produced in* this country, the **gross national income (GNI)** measures the income that is *received by* this country. To convert GDP into GNI, it is necessary to add three terms which combine to account for the difference between the income received by this country and the income produced in this country. The first term is employees' compensation receipts from the rest of the world minus payments to the rest of the world. Thus if a London-based consultant sells her services to a French firm, the income received will contribute to UK GNI but will be part of French GDP.

The second term is (minus) net taxes on production paid to the rest of the world plus subsidies received from the rest of the world. The logic of this is that we are measuring GNI (as with GDP) at market prices. If some element of the market prices paid is an indirect tax that generates revenue for a foreign government, then that tax represents a loss of income for the domestic economy as a whole and reduces domestic gross national income. Equally, if the product is subsidized by a foreign government, then this raises domestic incomes by enabling us to consume a given amount of goods at lower prices.

The third component of the difference between GDP and GNI is property and entrepreneurial income receipts from the rest of the world minus payments to the rest of the world. If, for example, you live in Manchester and own a holiday home in Spain that you rent out for part of the year, the revenue earned will count as part of GDP in Spain (as it is produced there), but the income accrues to a UK resident so it adds to UK GNI. Similarly, many UK firms have subsidiaries located in other countries. The value added of those subsidiaries counts as part of GDP in the host country, but, if remitted to the parent, counts as part of GNI in the UK. Conversely, a Japanese firm located in the UK contributes all its value added to UK GDP but profits remitted back to Japan are deducted from GDP in order to arrive at GNI (as they are not part of UK income).

Total output produced in the economy, measured by GDP, differs from total income received, measured by GNI, owing to net income from abroad.

It is important to note that the term gross national income was introduced as recently as 1998 to replace the term gross national product or GNP. GNI and GNP are conceptually identical. The latter has, however, been in use for several decades all over the world, so readers will continue to come across it for many years to come even if it is replaced by GNI in many new publications. This minor difference in terminology is not important for understanding macroeconomics, since this is concerned primarily with GDP, but it is important not to be confused when these terms are encountered.

GDP and GNI (or GNP) at market prices are the most commonly used concepts of national output and national income. Once we move on to theory in the next chapter, we ignore the small difference between GDP and GNI and refer to GDP at all times unless stated otherwise. This is true even though we sometimes talk about 'national income' and sometimes about the 'national product', depending on the context. For analytical purposes they are the same thing.

Reconciling GDP with GNI Table 20.3 shows the reconciliation of GDP with GNI. UK GNI was greater than GDP in 1997, but only by just over 1 per cent. This reflects slightly greater income from abroad for UK residents than is being paid out to foreigners. Clearly, GNI could be smaller than GDP if outward payments were greater than income earned from abroad.

Figure 20.1 on the following page provides a visual representation of the information in Tables 20.1–3. It shows both the relations between gross value added at basic prices and GDP at market prices, and the difference between GDP and GNI (at market prices). Components of the three possible decompositions of GDP are also displayed.

Other income concepts **Personal income** is income that is earned by or paid to individuals, before allowing for personal income taxes on that income. Some personal income goes for taxes, some goes for savings, and the rest goes for consumption. **Personal disposable income** is the amount of current income that individuals have available for spending and saving; it is personal income minus personal income taxes and National Insurance contributions.

Personal disposable income is GNI *minus* any part of it that is not actually paid to persons (such as retained profits of companies) minus personal income taxes plus transfer payments received by individuals.

Interpreting national income and output measures

The information provided by national accounts data is useful, but unless it is carefully interpreted, it can be misleading. Furthermore, each of the specific measures gives different information. Each may be the best statistic for studying a particular range of problems, but it is important to understand these differences if you are going to use these data for analytical purposes. Here we discuss some of the caveats to bear in mind.

Real and nominal measures

It is important to distinguish between *real* and *nominal* measures of national income and output. When we add up money values of outputs, expenditures, or incomes, we end up with what are called *nominal values*. Suppose that we found that a measure of nominal GDP had risen by 70 per cent between 1990 and 2000. If we wanted to compare real GDP in 2000 with that in 1990, we would need to determine how much of that 70 per cent nominal increase was due to increases in the general level of prices and how much was due to increases in quantities of goods and services produced. Although there are many possible ways of doing this, the basic principle is always the same. It is to compute the value of output, expenditure, and income in each period by using a common set of *base-period prices*. When this is done, we speak of real output, expenditure, or income as being measured in *constant pounds* or, say, *1995 prices*.

GDP valued at current prices (i.e. money GDP) is a nominal measure. GDP valued at base-period prices is a real measure of the volume of national output and national income.

Any *change* in nominal GDP reflects the combined effects of changes in quantities and changes in prices.

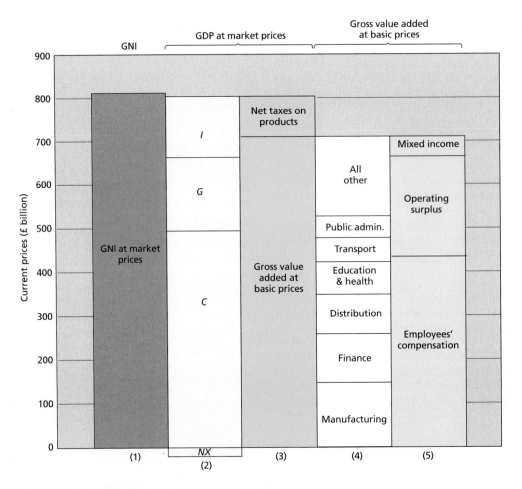

Figure 20.1 UK national income and output measures, 1997

Measurement of national income and output can be approached in three different ways, but they are all related. The figure shows the actual UK aggregates GNI at market prices, GDP at market prices, and gross value added at basic prices for 1997. Column (1) is GNI at market prices. Columns (2) and (3) add up to GDP at market prices. Columns (4) and (5) add up to gross value added at basic prices (or what used to be called GDP at factor cost).

Column (1) exceeds column (2) by about 1.0 per cent. This difference is net income from abroad. In 1997 this was positive but small. Column (2) shows that GDP is made up of the expenditure components: consumption (C), investment (I), government spending (G), and net exports (NX). Notice that in 1997 net exports were negative, so NX has to be subtracted from the sum of $C + I + G$ to arrive at GDP. Columns (3) and (4) show that gross value added at basic prices is equal to GDP at market prices minus net taxes on production.

Column (4) shows that gross value added is made up of the sum of the values added of each of the production sectors of the economy; manufacturing, for example, produces about 18 per cent of gross value added. Column (5) shows that gross value added can also be broken down by income type. Employees' compensation amounts to about 54 per cent of GDP at market prices.

Source: ONS, UK national accounts (*The Blue Book*), 1998.

However, when real income is measured over different periods by using a common set of base-period prices, changes in real income reflect only changes in real output.

The implicit deflator

If nominal and real GDP change by different amounts over some time-period, this must be because prices have changed over that period. Comparing what has happened to nominal and real GDP over the same period implies the existence of a price index measuring the change in prices over that period. We say 'implies' because no price index was used in calculating real and nominal GDP. However, an index can be inferred by comparing these two values.

Box 20.4 Calculation of nominal and real GDP

To see what is involved in calculating nominal GDP, real GDP, and the implicit deflator, an example may be helpful. Consider a simple hypothetical economy that produces only two commodities, wheat and steel. Table I gives the basic data for output and prices in the economy for two years.

Table I

	Quantity produced		Prices	
	Wheat (bushels)	Steel (tons)	Wheat (£ per bu.)	Steel (£ per ton)
Year 1	100	20	10	50
Year 2	110	16	12	55

Table II shows nominal GDP, calculated by adding the money values of wheat output and of steel output for each year. In year 1 the value of both wheat and steel production was £1,000, so nominal income was £2,000. In year 2 wheat output rose, and steel output fell; the value of wheat output rose to £1,320, and that of steel fell to £880. Since the rise in value of wheat was greater than the fall in value of steel, nominal GDP rose by £200.

Table II

Year 1	$(100 \times 10) + (20 \times 50) = £2,000$
Year 2	$(110 \times 12) + (16 \times 55) = £2,200$

Table III shows real GDP, calculated by valuing output in each year by year

2 prices; that is, year 2 becomes the base year for weighting purposes. Using year 2 prices, the value of the fall in steel output between years 1 and 2 exceeded the value of the rise in wheat output, and real GDP fell.

Table III

Year 1	$(100 \times 12) + (20 \times 55) = £2,300$
Year 2	$(110 \times 12) + (16 \times 55) = £2,200$

In Table IV the ratio of nominal to real GDP is calculated for each year and multiplied by 100. This ratio implicitly measures the change in prices over the period in question and is called the *implicit deflator* or *implicit price index*. The implicit deflator shows that the price level increased by 15 per cent between year 1 and year 2 (calculated as $(13.04/86.96) \times 100$, where 13.04 is $(100 - 86.96)$).

Table IV

Year 1	$(2,000/2,300) \times 100 = 86.96$
Year 2	$(2,200/2,200) \times 100 = 100.00$

In Table IV we used year 2 as the base year for comparison purposes, but we could have used year 1. The implicit deflator would then have been 100 in year 1 and 115 in year 2, and the increase in price level would still have been 15 per cent. Or the base year could be some earlier year. No matter what year is picked as the year in which the index had a value of 100, the change in the implicit deflator between year 1 and year 2 is 15 per cent.

Such an index is called an *implicit price index* or an *implicit deflator*. It is defined as follows:

$$\text{Implicit deflator} = \frac{\text{GDP at current prices}}{\text{GDP at base-period prices}} \times 100\%.$$

The implicit GDP deflator is the most comprehensive index of the price level because it covers all the goods and services that are produced by the entire economy. Although some other indexes use fixed weights, or weights that change only periodically, implicit deflators are variable-weight indexes. They use the current year's 'bundle' of production to compare the current year's prices with those prevailing in the base period. Thus the 1997 deflator uses 1997 output weights, and the 2000 deflator uses 2000 output weights. Box 20.4 illustrates the calculation of real and nominal GDP and an implicit deflator for a simple hypothetical economy that produces only wheat and steel. See the appendix to this chapter for a discussion of the construction of the retail price index.

A change in any nominal measure of GDP can be split

into a change due to prices and a change due to quantities. For example, in 1997 UK nominal GDP ('money' GDP) was 6.2 per cent higher than in 1996. This increase was due to a 2.7 per cent increase in prices and a 3.5 per cent increase in real GDP. Table 20.4 gives nominal and real GDP and the implicit deflator for selected years since 1900.

International comparisons of GDP

One purpose to which GDP measures are often put is international comparison of living standards or real income. It is natural to want to know if people have higher living standards in Britain or in, say, Germany or France. However, comparisons using measures such as GDP must be conducted with great care. There are many dimensions to living standards which are not measured by GDP or GNI.

For some purposes we may want to compare the absolute

Table 20.4 Nominal and real GDP at market prices, 1900–1997

	Money GDP (£ billion)	Real GDP (1990 prices) (£ billion)	Implicit GDP deflator (1990 = 100)
1900	1.9	109.5	1.7
1930	4.7	138.6	3.4
1950	13.1	200.4	6.5
1970	51.6	350.9	14.7
1980	231.2	426.8	54.2
1997	802.0	639.4	125.4

The data in the table are money GDP, real GDP, and the implicit GDP price deflator for selected years. The first column shows that money (nominal) GDP increased 422-fold between 1900 and 1997. However, the second column shows that there was only a 5.8-fold increase in real GDP over the same period. The difference between the two is accounted for by the final column, which shows that the implicit price deflator for GDP rose 73.8-fold in this period. Since 1950 real GDP has seen a just-over-3-fold increase, while the GDP price deflator has increased nearly 20-fold.

Sources: *Economic Trends* and *100 Years of Economic Statistics*, Economist, 1989.

size of one economy relative to another, but normally we are interested in how well off the average individual is in each country. For this purpose we want to look at GDP per head or per capita (or perhaps GNI per capita). To get this figure we divide GDP by the total population of the coun-

try. This tells us the share of total GDP that is available for the average citizen.

GDP in each country is measured in the local currency. So, to make comparisons, we have to convert different countries' nominal GDP into the same currency. To do this, we have to use an exchange rate. This is problematic because exchange rates fluctuate, sometimes dramatically. Between 1996 and 1998, for example, the exchange rate between the US dollar and the Japanese yen moved from nearly 80 yen per dollar to around 140 yen per dollar. Would we be happy to conclude that real incomes in Japan had fallen relative to real incomes in the USA by 75 per cent in two years? Even in normal conditions it is not unusual for exchange rates to move by 10 per cent in a few days, but the move could easily be reversed a little later.

To solve the problem of making comparisons using unreliable or atypical exchange rates, economists make comparisons of GDP using the exchange rate that equates the prices of a representative bundle of goods in two countries. This is known as the *purchasing power parity (PPP)* rate. We will discuss this concept more fully in Chapter 28.

Some comparisons of GNI per capita in thirteen different countries (using PPP exchange rates) are given in Table 20.5. Figures are all expressed in US dollars. Several other indicators of material well-being are included in the table. Broadly speaking they tell the same story as the GNI figures—the inhabitants of the richer countries can purchase more goods and services and tend to have longer life-

Table 20.5 International comparisons of living standards

	GNI per capita 1996 (US$)	Real GNI growth per capita 1985–95 (%)	Telephones per 1,000 pop. 1996	Infant mortality per 1,000 live births 1996	Personal computers per 1,000 pop. 1996	Life-expectancy at birth 1996	Cars per 1,000 pop. 1990	Doctors per 100,000 pop. 1990
USA	28,020	1.4	640	7	362.4	77	589	238
Japan	23,420	2.9	489	4	128.0	80	285	164
France	21,510	1.5	564	5	150.7	78	418	286
Canada	21,380	0.4	602	6	192.5	79	473	222
Germany	21,110	1.8	538	5	233.2	76	490	270
UK	19,960	1.4	528	6	192.6	77	403	164
Australia	19,870	1.4	519	6	311.3	78	435	229
Spain	15,290	2.6	392	7	94.2	77	308	357
Mexico	7,660	0.1	95	32	29.0	72	65	81
Brazil	6,340	−0.7	96	36	18.4	67	104	93
Russia	4,190	−5.1	175	17	23.7	66	50	476
China	3,330	8.0	45	33	3.0	70	2	99
India	1,580	3.1	15	65	1.5	63	2	41

The table shows eight different indicators of living standards for thirteen countries. Most of the indicators tell the same story—wealthy countries have more goods and better life expectations. However, there are some interesting anomalies. Russia has more doctors per 100,000 people than any other country in the table, yet life-expectancy is lower than in China, which has one-fifth as many doctors per person.

Sources: *World Bank Atlas*, 1998 and *The Economist*.

expectancy. However, the rankings would be different for each possible indicator of well-being. The significance of this is that GNI per capita contains some useful information but other important indicators sometimes tell a slightly different story.

What GDP does not measure

GDP measures the flow of economic activity in organized markets in a given year. But much economic activity takes place outside of the market economy. Although these activities are not typically included in GDP or GNI, they nevertheless use real resources and satisfy real wants and needs.

Unreported activities A significant omission from measured GDP is the so-called underground or black economy. The transactions that occur in the underground economy are perfectly legal in themselves; the only illegality involved is that such transactions are not reported for tax purposes. One example of this is the carpenter who repairs a leak in your roof and takes payment in cash or in kind in order to avoid taxation. Because such transactions go unreported, they are omitted from GDP.

The growth of the underground economy could be encouraged by high rates of taxation and is facilitated by the rising importance of services in the nation's total output. The higher the tax rates, the more there is to be gained by 'going underground'. It is also much easier for a carpenter or plumber to pass unnoticed by government authorities than it is for a manufacturing establishment.

Studies of the scale of the underground economy show its importance growing in recent years. Estimates have put the underground economy in Britain at about 7 per cent of GDP. A Canadian study concluded that 15 per cent of Canadian GDP went unreported because it was in the underground economy. In other countries the figures are even higher. The Italian underground economy, for example, has been estimated at about 20 per cent of GDP; for Spain estimates are close to 25 per cent, and for Greece 30 per cent!

Non-marketed activities If homeowners hire a firm to do some landscaping, the value of the landscaping enters into GDP; if they do the landscaping themselves, the value of the landscaping is omitted from GDP. Other non-marketed activities include, for example, the services of those who do housework at home, any do-it-yourself activity, and voluntary work such as canvassing for a political party, helping to run a volunteer day-care centre, or coaching an amateur football team.

One important non-marketed activity is leisure itself. If a lawyer voluntarily chooses to work 2,200 hours a year instead of 2,400 hours, measured GDP will fall by the lawyer's hourly wage rate times 200 hours. Yet the value to the lawyer of the 200 hours of new leisure, which is enjoyed outside of the marketplace, must exceed the lost wages (because the leisure has been voluntarily chosen in preference to the extra work), so total economic welfare has risen rather than fallen. Until recently one of the most important ways in which economic growth benefited people was by permitting increased amounts of time off work. Because the time off is not marketed, its value does not show up in measures of GDP.

Economic bads When a coal-fired electricity generator sends sulphur dioxide into the atmosphere, leading to acid rain and environmental damage, the value of the electricity sold is included as part of GDP, but the value of the damage done by the acid rain is not deducted. Similarly, the petrol that we use in our cars is part of GDP, but the damage done by burning that petrol is not deducted. To the extent that economic growth brings with it increases in pollution, congestion, and other disamenities of modern living, GDP measures will overstate the value of the growth. They measure the increased economic output and income, but they fail to deduct the increased 'bads', or negative outputs, that generally accompany economic growth.

Do the omissions matter?

GDP does a reasonable job of measuring the flow of goods and services through the market sector of the economy. Usually an increase in GDP implies greater opportunities for employment for those households that sell their labour services in the market. Unless the importance of unmeasured economic activity changes rapidly, *changes* in GDP will do an excellent job of measuring *changes* in economic activity and well-being. However, when the task at hand is measurement of the overall flow of goods and services available to satisfy people's wants, regardless of the source of the goods and services, then the omissions that we have discussed above become undesirable and potentially serious. Still, in the relatively short term changes in GDP will usually be good measures of the direction, if not the exact magnitude, of changes in economic welfare.

The omissions cause serious problems when GDP measures are used to compare living standards in structurally different economies, as was discussed above. Generally the non-market sector of the economy is larger in rural than in urban settings and in less-developed than in more-developed economies. Be cautious, then, when interpreting data from a country with a very different climate and culture. When you hear that the per capita GNI of India is about US$1,580 per year, you should not imagine living in Manchester on that income. The average Indian is undoubtedly poorer than the average Briton, but perhaps not twelve times poorer as the GNI figures suggest.

Summary

What is macroeconomics

■ Macroeconomics is about the economy as a whole. It studies aggregate phenomena, such as business cycles, living standards, inflation, unemployment, and the balance of payments. It also asks how governments can use their monetary and fiscal policy instruments to help stabilize the economy.

Why do we need macroeconomics?

■ Macroeconomics is useful because it enables us to study events that affect the economy as a whole without getting into too much detail about specific products and sectors.

National output concepts

■ Each firm's contribution to total output is equal to its value added, which is the gross value of the firm's output minus the value of all intermediate goods and services—that is, the outputs of other firms—that it uses. Goods that count as part of the economy's output are called final goods; all others are called intermediate goods. The sum of all the values added produced in an economy is called gross value added at basic prices. Basic prices are the prices received by producers net of taxes on products (plus subsidies).

GDP, GNI, and GNP

■ Gross domestic product (GDP) can be calculated in three different ways: (1) as the sum of all values added by all producers of both intermediate and final goods; (2) as the income claims generated by the total production of goods and services; and (3) as the expenditure needed to purchase all final goods and services produced during the period. By standard accounting conventions these three aggregations define the same total, so long as we add taxes on products (minus subsidies) to the first two in order to measure GDP at market prices. Market prices are the prices paid by consumers.

■ From the expenditure side of the national accounts GDP = $C^a + I^a + G^a + (X^a - IM^a)$. C^a comprises private consumption expenditures. I^a is investment in fixed capital (including residential construction), inventories, and valuables. Gross investment can be split into replacement investment (necessary to keep the stock of capital intact) and net investment (net additions to the stock of capital). G^a is government consumption. $(X^a - IM^a)$ represents net exports, or exports minus imports; it will be negative if imports exceed exports.

■ GDP income-based adds up all factor rewards in production. The main income categories making up GDP are operating surpluses, mixed incomes, and compensation of employees.

■ UK GDP measures production that is located in the United Kingdom, and UK gross national income (GNI) measures income accruing to UK residents. The difference is due to net income from overseas. GNI is the same thing as what used to be called gross national product (GNP).

■ Real GDP is calculated to reflect changes in real volumes of output and real income. Nominal GDP reflects changes in both prices and quantities. Any change in nominal GDP (or GNI) can be split into a change in real GDP and a change due to prices. Appropriate comparisons of nominal and real measures yield implicit deflators.

■ Personal income is income received by individuals before any allowance for personal taxes. Personal disposable income is the amount actually available for individuals to spend or to save, that is, income minus taxes.

Interpreting national income and output measures

■ GDP and related measures of national income and output must be interpreted with their limitations in mind. GDP excludes production that takes place in the underground economy or that does not pass through markets. Moreover, GDP does not measure everything that contributes to human welfare.

■ GDP is one of the best measures available of the total economic activity within a country. It is particularly valuable when changes in GDP are used to indicate how economic activity has changed over time.

Topics for review

- Targets and instruments of macroeconomic policy
- Value added
- Intermediate and final goods
- Expenditure-based and income-based GDP
- GNI and GNP
- Personal disposable income
- Implicit deflator
- What GDP does and does not measure

Questions for discussion

1 Discuss which of the following are microeconomic and which macroeconomic issues: house prices; unemployment in East Anglia; food prices; pensions; the EU single currency; the Common Agricultural Policy; high street spending; income tax rates; mortgage interest rates.

2 Which of the following are instruments of macroeconomic policy and which are targets: the exchange rate; real wages; VAT rates; VAT revenue; government spending on road building; exports; private gross fixed

capital formation; US dollar interest rates; personal consumption?

3 Using the expenditure-based definition (C + I + G + NX), explain where each of the following expenditures appears in the national income accounts measure of GDP, if at all: state pensions; company pensions; student grants; theatre receipts; judges' salaries; unsold cars in showrooms; receipts from beer sales in a students' union bar; receipts from purchases of new copies of this book; receipts from purchases of second-hand copies of this book.

4 Suppose there are only three companies in an economy. Company A grows crops and extracts minerals from its land with no inputs from other companies. Its sales are £100m

per year, half of which goes to consumers and half to companies B and C in equal amounts. Company B buys inputs from A and sells its entire output of £200m to company C. Company C buys inputs from A and B and sells its £450m output directly to consumers (though 20 per cent of this is overseas). What is gross value added at basic prices? If there is only one indirect tax, value added tax, levied at 10 per cent, what is the value of GDP at market prices?

5 Discuss the strengths and weaknesses of using GDP as a measure of national well-being.

6 What would it mean to be told that a country's GNI was greater than its GDP? Is GNI or GDP the more appropriate target for government policy?

Appendix How the RPI is constructed

Two important questions must be answered when any price index is constructed. First, what group of prices should be used? This depends on what the index is intended to measure. The Retail Price Index (RPI), which is calculated by the Office for National Statistics (ONS), covers prices of goods and services that are commonly bought by households. Changes in the RPI are meant to measure changes in the typical household's *cost of living*. (Other indexes, such as the wholesale price index or the producer price index, cover the prices of different baskets of commodities. The implicit deflator for GDP covers all of the nation's output, not just consumer prices.)

Second, how should the movements in consumer prices be added up and summarized in one price index? If all prices changed in the same proportion, this would not matter: a 10 per cent rise in every price would mean a 10 per cent rise in the average of all prices, no matter how the average was constructed. However, different prices usually change in different propor-

tions. It then matters how much importance we give to each price change. Changes in the price of bread, for example, are much more important to the average consumer than changes in the price of caviar. In calculating a price index, each price is given a *weight* that reflects its importance.

Let us see how this is done for the RPI. Government statisticians periodically survey a representative group of households in what is called the Family Expenditure Survey. This shows how consumers spend their incomes. The average bundle of goods that is bought is determined, along with the proportion of expenditure that is devoted to each good. These proportions become the weights attached to the individual prices in calculating the RPI. As a result, the RPI weights rather heavily the prices of commodities on which consumers spend much of their income, and weights rather lightly the prices of commodities on which consumers spend only a little of their income. Table 20A.1 provides a simple example of how these weights are calculated.

Once the weights are chosen, the average price can be calculated for each period. This is done, as shown in Table 20A.2, by multiplying each price by its weight and summing the resulting figures. However, a single average price is not informative. Suppose, for example, you were told that the average price of all goods that were bought by consumers last year was £89.35. 'So what?' you might well ask, and the answer would be: 'So, not very much. By itself, this tells you nothing useful.' Now suppose you are told that this year's average price for the same set of consumers' purchases is £107.22. Now you know that, on average, prices paid by consumers have risen sharply over the year—in fact, the increase is 20 per cent.[6]

The average for each period is divided by the value of the average for the base period and multiplied by 100. The resulting series is called an index number series. By construction the base-period value in this series equals 100; if prices in the next period average 20 per cent higher, the index number for that period will

Table 20A.1 Calculation of weights for a price index

Commodity	Price (£)	Quantity	Expenditure (£) (price × quantity)	Proportional weight
A	5	60	300	0.50
B	1	200	200	0.33
C	4	25	100	0.17
Total			600	1.00

The weights are the proportions of total expenditure that are devoted to each commodity. This simple example lists the prices of three commodities and the quantities bought by a typical household. Multiplying price by quantity gives expenditure on each, and summing these gives the total expenditure on all commodities. Dividing expenditure on each good by total expenditure gives the proportion of total expenditure that is devoted to each commodity, as shown in the last column. These proportions become the weights for the price indexes that are calculated in Table 20A.2.

---

6 The change is £17.87, which is 20 per cent of the initial average price of £89.35.

Table 20A.2 Calculation of a price index

Commodity	Weight	Price (£)			Price × weight (£)		
		1980	1985	1990	1980	1985	1990
A	0.50	5.00	6.00	14.00	2.50	3.00	7.00
B	0.33	1.00	1.50	2.00	0.33	0.495	0.66
C	0.17	4.00	8.00	9.00	0.68	1.36	1.53
Total	1.00				3.51	4.855	9.19

Index	1980	$\dfrac{3.51}{3.51} \times 100 = 100$	
	1985	$\dfrac{4.855}{3.51} \times 100 = 138.3$	
	1990	$\dfrac{9.19}{3.51} \times 100 = 261.8$	

A price index expresses the weighted average of prices in the given year as a percentage of the weighted average of prices in the base year. The prices of the three commodities in each year are multiplied by the weights from Table 20A.1. Summing the weighted prices for each year gives the average price in that year. Dividing the average price in the given year by the average price in the base year and multiplying by 100 gives the price index for the given year. The index is, of course, 100 when the base year is also taken as the given year, as is the case for 1980 in this example.

be 120. A simple example of how these calculations are carried out is given in Table 20A.2.

Price indexes are constructed by assigning weights to reflect the importance of the individual items being combined. The value is set equal to 100 in the base period.

Table 20A.2 shows the calculation of what is called a *fixed-weight index*. The weights are the proportion of income that is spent on each of the three goods in the base year. These weights are then applied to the prices in each subsequent year. The value of the index in each year measures exactly how much the base-year bundle of goods would cost at that year's prices.[7] Fixed-weight indexes are easy to interpret, but problems arise because consumption patterns change over the years; the fixed weights represent with decreasing accuracy the importance that consumers *currently* place on each of the commodities.

The RPI used to be calculated using fixed weights that were changed only every decade or so. Now they are revised annually. This avoids the problem of the fixed-weight index becoming steadily less representative of current expenditure patterns.

Measuring the rate of inflation

At the end of April 1998 the RPI was 162.6. (The average of the monthly values for 1987 equals 100.) This means that at the end of April 1998 it cost just under 63 per cent more to buy a representative bundle of goods than it did in the base period, which in this case is taken as the average of prices prevailing in the year 1987.[8] In other words, there was a 62.6 per cent *increase* in the price level over that period as measured by the RPI. The *per-*

centage change in the cost of purchasing the bundle of goods that is covered by any index is thus the level of the index minus 100.

The *inflation rate* between any two periods of time is measured by the percentage increase in the relevant price index from the first period to the second period. In the rare event of a drop in the price level, we speak of a *deflation*. When the amount of the rise in the price level is being measured from the base period, all that needs to be done is to subtract the base-period index (100) from the later index, as we have just done. When two other periods are being compared, we must be careful to express the change as a percentage of the index in the first period.

If we let P_1 indicate the value of the price index in the first period and P_2 its value in the second period, the inflation rate is merely the difference between the two, expressed as a percentage of the value of the index in the first period.

$$\text{Inflation rate} = \frac{(P_2 - P_1)}{P_1} \times 100.$$

When P_1 is the base period, its value is 100, and the expression shown above reduces to $P_2 - 100$. In other cases the full calculation must be made. For example, suppose the index went to 144.7 in June 2000 from 141.0 in June 1999 (using a hypothetical base year later than 1987). The rise of 3.7 points in the index is a 2.6 per cent rise over its initial value of 141.0, indicating a rate of inflation of 2.6 per cent over the year.

If the two values being compared are not a year apart, it is common to convert the result to an *annual rate*. For example, suppose the RPI is 135.2 in January 2000 and 135.6 in February 2000 (on a base of, say, 1995 = 100). This is an increase of 0.296 per cent over the month [(0.4/135.2) × 100]. It is also an *annual rate* of approximately 3.55 per cent (0.296 per cent × 12) over the year.[9] This means that if the rate of increase that occurred between January and February 2000 did persist for a year, the price level would rise by approximately 3.55 per cent over the year.

Variations on RPI

There are three additional, often-quoted variations on RPI in use in the United Kingdom:

1. RPIX is an index calculated using the same components as RPI except that it excludes mortgage interest payments. This is the index that is used as the basis for the inflation target set by the government for the Bank of England's Monetary Policy Committee. (Chapter 25 discusses the Committee in some detail.)

---

[7] To verify this, calculate the total expenditure required to buy 60 units of commodity A, 200 units of commodity B, and 25 units of commodity C in each of the three years for which price data are given in Table 20A.2. Divide the resulting amounts by £600, multiply by 100, and you will get exactly the index values shown in the table.

[8] Notice that the base year on which the RPI is calculated is changed periodically, so it is likely that the base year in current use will be more recent than 1987. The latter was the base year in use up to 1998 for RPI calculations.

[9] We say *approximately* because a 0.296 per cent rise each month that is *compounded* for twelve months will give rise to an increase over the year that is greater than 3.55 per cent. The appropriate procedure is to increase the index in January by 0.296 per cent twelve times (calculate $[(1.00296)^{12} - 1] \times 100$) rather than just to multiply it by 12. The two results are the difference between simple and compound interest rates.

2. RPIY is RPIX but with the further modification that it excludes the effects of indirect tax changes on prices. RPIY is sometimes referred to as 'underlying inflation' because it excludes the effects on inflation induced by changes in monetary *and* fiscal policies.

3. HICP is yet another measure of UK retail price inflation calculated on a different basis from the RPI in order to conform with EU statistical practices. It is the harmonized index of consumer prices. (This includes some differences in components and is calculated as a geometric rather than arithmetic average. The details of these differences are somewhat arcane and not important to understand at this stage.)

In April 1998 the annual inflation rate according to each of these measures was:

- RPI = 4.0
- RPIX = 3.0
- RPIY = 2.2
- HICP = 1.6

Thus these different measures can diverge by non-trivial amounts.

The European Central Bank uses the HICP for the euro zone as a whole to judge whether it is meeting its objective of price stability.

Chapter 21
A Basic Model of the Determination of GDP

We now embark on the central task of macroeconomics, building a model of the economy as a whole. In Chapter 20 we encountered a number of important macroeconomic variables. We now turn to a more detailed study of what *causes* these variables to behave as they do, and how they are interrelated. In particular we study the forces that determine GDP and the price level.

It is important to realize that we are about to discuss *theory*. In this process we will build up a conceptual model of the economy. This model will be simple. It needs to be simple so that we can understand how it works. In particular we seek to answer questions like 'What happens to GDP when government spending is increased?' and 'Under what conditions do we get inflation?'

Macroeconomics has been around, as a branch of economics, for over half a century. It has developed and changed a great deal in this time. It is going to take several chapters before we get close to understanding contemporary macroeconomics. Hence the reader should be patient and not rush to draw policy conclusions too soon.

We will proceed by starting from a very simple structure and then adding features to it as we go along. Some clearly stated *assumptions* will define our macroeconomic model. Some of these assumptions will be relaxed as we go along, others will remain throughout. The permanent or temporary nature of individual assumptions will be indicated as they are introduced.

In this chapter we set out some of the conceptual foundations of macroeconomics. We then build the simplest possible model of GDP determination, under some very special assumptions. Later chapters make our model increasingly realistic.

Potential GDP and the GDP gap

In macroeconomics it is useful to distinguish between the long-term trend in GDP and the cycle about the trend. In order to facilitate this separation we use the concepts *actual* and *potential GDP*, and we refer to the difference between them as the *GDP gap*.

Actual GDP represents what the economy does in fact produce. An important related concept is **potential GDP**, which measures what the economy could produce if all resources—land, labour, and productive capacity—were fully employed at their normal levels of utilization. This concept is also referred to as *potential income* and is sometimes called *full-employment income* (or *high-employment income*).[1] We give it the symbol Y^* to distinguish it from actual GDP (or national income), which is indicated by just Y.

What is variously called the **output gap** or the **GDP gap** measures the difference between what would have been produced if potential, or full-employment, GDP had been produced and what is actually produced, as measured by the current GDP. The gap is calculated by subtracting actual GDP from potential GDP ($Y^* - Y$).

When potential GDP exceeds actual GDP, the gap measures the market value of goods and services that *could have been produced* if the economy's resources had been fully employed but that actually went unproduced. The goods and services that are not produced when the economy is operating below Y^* are permanently lost to the economy. Because these losses occur when employable resources are unused, they are often called the *deadweight loss* of unemployment. When the economy is operating below its potential level of output—that is, when Y is less than Y^*—the output gap is called a **recessionary gap**.

---

[1] In everyday usage the words *real* and *actual* have similar meanings. In the national accounts, however, their meanings are distinct. *Real* GDP is distinguished from *nominal* GDP, and *actual* GDP is distinguished from *potential* GDP. The latter two refer to real measures, so that the full descriptions are actual real GDP and potential real GDP.

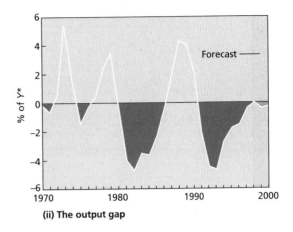

(i) Potential and actual GDP

(ii) The output gap

Figure 21.1 UK potential GDP and the output gap, 1970–2000

Potential and actual GDP have both displayed an upward trend in recent years, but actual GDP fluctuates around its potential level.

(i) Growth in the economy has been such that both potential and actual GDP have nearly doubled since 1970. Both series are in real terms and are measured in 1990 pounds sterling. Measurement of potential GDP is controversial and there is no official UK series at present. These figures were calculated by the IMF. The data for 1998–2000 are IMF forecasts.

(ii) The cycles in the economy are apparent from the behaviour of the output gap. Slumps in economic activity produce large recessionary gaps, and booms produce inflationary gaps. The zero line indicates where actual and potential GDP are the same. The shaded areas below the zero line indicate the deadweight loss that arises from unemployment during periods when there is a recessionary output gap. Notice the large recessionary gaps in the early 1980s and the early 1990s.

Source: International Monetary Fund.

In booms actual GDP may *exceed* potential GDP, causing the output gap to become negative. Actual output can exceed potential output because potential GDP is defined for a *normal rate of utilization* of factors of production, and these normal rates can be exceeded temporarily. Labour may work longer hours than normal; factories may operate an extra shift or not close for routine repairs and maintenance. Although many of these expedients are only temporary, they are effective in the short term. When actual GDP exceeds potential GDP, there is generally upward pressure on prices. For this reason, when Y exceeds Y^*, the output gap is called an **inflationary gap.**

Figure 21.1(i) shows one estimate of UK potential GDP for the years 1970–2000.[2] The rising trend reflects the growth in productive capacity of the UK economy over this period. The figure also shows actual real GDP, which has kept approximately in step with potential GDP. The distance between the two, which is the GDP gap, is plotted in Figure 21.1(ii). Fluctuations in economic activity are apparent from fluctuations in the size of the gap. The deadweight loss from unemployment over any time-span is indicated by the overall amount of the gap over that time-span. It is shown in part (ii) of Figure 21.1 by the shaded area between the curve and the zero line, which represents the level at which actual output equals potential output.

Macroeconomics usually focuses on explaining the GDP gap, while growth theory aims to explain the long-term trend in potential GDP.

Key assumptions

In the previous chapter we learned that 'national income' and 'national output' are the same thing, and can be measured by 'GDP'. From now on we will use these three terms equivalently. However, we refer to national income most frequently when discussing the determinants of domestic spending, as incomes are one of the most important determinants of consumers' expenditure. We refer to national output, or GDP, more commonly when discussing the responses of producers to changes in spending. Remember,

[2] Note that in both parts of Figure 21.1 the data for 1998–2000 are IMF projections rather than actual outturns.

though, that the actual values of these three concepts are identical.[3]

We also saw in Chapter 20 that we could arrive at a measure of GDP by three different routes. We could add up incomes of factors of production, we could add up the values added of each industrial sector, or we could add up total final expenditures. Now that we want to *explain* GDP determination rather than just describe it, we have to decide which of these three classifications we are going to rely on to structure our theories. We will learn very shortly that macroeconomics, as a subject, has developed by attempting to explain the major categories of final expenditure in the economy. We need to understand why this approach was adopted.

Suppose that we were to start our theory of GDP by trying to explain the net output (value added) of each major industrial sector, such as manufacturing, agriculture, etc., as listed in Table 20.1. We could establish the capital stock and employment in each sector and we could analyse demand forces for the output of each sector. In essence we would be building a theory around demand and supply forces in each industry in the economy and then we would add up the results to get total output.

One reason we do not do this in macroeconomics is that such an approach would not really be dealing with the aggregate economy at all. Models that explain output industry by industry do exist in economics, but they are microeconomic and not generally regarded as part of macroeconomics. Such models require so much detail that they make it difficult to handle many important issues that affect the whole economy simultaneously.

A second reason why we do not apply the tools of demand and supply on an industry-by-industry basis in macroeconomics is that the founders of macroeconomic theory thought that those tools were not appropriate for handling the most important macro problems. In particular, macroeconomics as a subject was originally invented to explain why an economy might have unemployment and excess capacity for some time. In contrast, the microeconomic analysis of markets suggests that prices will move to clear markets. Macroeconomists also want to be able to study simultaneous (or near simultaneous) movements in output that are common to all sectors—the business cycle. An important question in macroeconomics is 'What causes the cycle in GDP and can government policy stabilize it, that is, smooth out the cycles?'

Aggregation across industries

In macroeconomics we take the industrial structure of the economy as fixed. When national output expands or contracts, all sectors expand and contract together. There is no consideration given to relative prices of different goods or services. In this respect the economy is best thought of as being made up of many competitive firms, all producing

the same type of product. These firms are all aggregated into a single productive sector. It is the behaviour of this sector that will determine national output and national income.

In macroeconomics we assume the existence of a single productive sector producing a homogeneous output.

This assumption will remain throughout our study of macroeconomics. We will also analyse the behaviour of this single sector as if it were a manufacturing industry, though this is only a matter of convenience.

The fact that we assume a single production sector explains why we approach the determination of GDP by focusing on expenditure categories: there are no subdivisions of output by type of product. However, an important implication for final expenditures is that *in our model* they are all spent on the same final good—the product of United Kingdom PLC. This means that while different categories of expenditures may be differently motivated, they all have the same effect once implemented.

From time to time we use concrete examples, such as 'suppose the government increases spending on road building' or 'suppose firms decide to buy more machines (invest)'. The point to bear in mind is that all expenditures in the model have the same effect, once made, because they are all assumed in our model to be demands for the output of the single-product industrial sector.

The government sector Confusion can arise out of the assumption of a single sector when we come to discuss the role of government. In reality part of government activity involves producing goods and services, such as health and education. However, in order to maintain the simplicity of the assumption that there is only one sector, in macroeconomics we ignore the fact that government is a producer and treat government as a purchaser of the output of the private industrial sector. In other words we make no exceptions to our assumption about the homogeneity of productive activity. Such exceptions can be accommodated, but we do not do so in this book.

Justification The extreme assumption that there is only one output is of course not meant as a description of reality. It is a theoretical abstraction meant to simplify our study without losing the essence of the problem in which we are interested. In this case the one-product model captures the assumption that for what we are interested in the similarities between the effects of £1 spent in each sector of the real-world economy are more important than the differences. Note that it is only similarities with

[3] As we have seen, there is a small difference between GDP and GNI; however, we are now assuming that this difference can be ignored. Recall also that GNI used to be called GNP, but GNI became standard in the UK national accounts in 1998. You will no doubt see references to GNP in the economics literature for many years to come.

respect to the effects of expenditures that are in question. Causes of expenditures are not assumed to be the same. Indeed, much of our effort is directed to developing consumption, investment, and net export functions that explain the *different* motives that determine the various expenditure flows.

Time-scale

Macroeconomics has traditionally been concerned with the short-run behaviour of an economy, while growth theory has been concerned with long-run trends. It is important to note, however, that the concepts of 'short run' and 'long run' have a different meaning in macroeconomics from the usage in microeconomics. Indeed, 'long run' itself will be used in two different senses even within macroeconomics.

Short run   In microeconomics 'short run' is used to analyse the behaviour of firms during the period in which their capital stock is taken as given and they can only change their variable inputs (labour and materials). In other words the short run is a period during which the capital stock is fixed; none the less, firms are in equilibrium because they are producing their optimal output given their capital stock. In macroeconomics the short run is the period during which the economy maintains a deviation of actual from potential output, or a GDP gap. This deviation is associated either with the existence of excess capacity and unemployment, in the case of recession, or unsustainable output and inflation, in the case of a boom. In practice the short run may be measured in terms of several years, so it is not really short in the commonsense meaning of the term.

In its early days as a discipline macroeconomics concentrated entirely on the short run as we have just defined it. Recent developments, however, have increasingly emphasized longer-run considerations.

Analysis of the short run in macroeconomics is concerned with explaining why national output can deviate from its potential level. It is about the GDP gap and how to reduce it.

Long run   The long run is a period sufficient to allow time for the automatic adjustment mechanisms (discussed below) to return economic activity to equilibrium after it has been disturbed by an exogenous shock. This equilibrium is reached when the economy returns to producing the level of potential (or full-employment) output. For analytical purposes we will assume that the long-run level of output is constant and is associated with a fixed capital stock and a fixed level of technical knowledge. This contrasts markedly with the usage of 'long run' in microeconomics, where it relates to a period within which capital stock can vary. Even in macroeconomics there is

really a 'long run' and a 'longer run', where the latter permits growth in productive capacity and, therefore, growth in potential output. For the most part we use the static concept of long run, unless we are explicitly discussing growth, as in Chapters 32 and 33.

The long run in macroeconomics is the period it takes the economy to return to the level of potential GDP once it has been disturbed.

Temporary assumptions

In order to get us started in building a theory of macroeconomics, we need to make a few additional assumptions, but these will be relaxed in succeeding chapters.

The price level   At the outset we will assume that the price level, that is the money price of the output good produced by the economy, is fixed. All input prices are also fixed. Permitting the price level to vary simultaneously with output will be the main task addressed in Chapters 23 and 24. While the price level is held constant, all variables must necessarily be measured in real terms. But it is important to notice for the future that all expenditures (consumption, investment, government spending, and net exports) will continue to be defined in real terms even when the price level is permitted to vary.

Excess capacity   Initially we will think of the economy as having excess capacity; it is not constrained from producing more output by shortages of capital stock or labour. One reason we make this assumption is that this is the context in which macroeconomics as a subject got started. It was trying to explain how an economy could get stuck (for some time at least) with high unemployment and excess capacity. When unemployment is approaching 20 per cent and GDP has fallen sharply, as in the early 1930s, this is a reasonable assumption to make. This would not be regarded as a reasonable assumption for analysing an economy at potential GDP and full employment.

Another reason we start with the twin assumptions of a fixed price level and excess capacity is that it is helpful to begin in an environment where all changes in GDP are changes in real GDP. Explaining how changes in money GDP are divided between changes in the price level and changes in real GDP requires a more complicated model, which we come to in Chapter 23.

Closed economy   In this chapter alone we will ignore the fact that the output of our economy could be sold overseas and that domestic consumers could buy foreign-produced goods. We assume an economy with no foreign trade, so domestic expenditure and domestic output are the same thing. This is not an assumption we will need very long. It will be dropped in the next chapter.

No government   A final simplifying assumption is that

there is no government sector either demanding goods or raising money through taxes. Again, we will drop this assumption in the next chapter.

It is worth summarizing all these assumptions. We have a closed economy with a single industrial sector, producing a homogeneous output, at a fixed price, with no government. There is also excess capacity, so there are no resource constraints preventing the expansion of national output. By now the reader may be wondering what is left after we have assumed away so many potentially important things. The answer is final demand or expenditure on the output of the economy. Explaining final expenditure will explain what determines the national product and national income, that is, GDP.

There is a good reason for starting with an explanation of expenditures. This is that the original inventors of macroeconomics believed that the explanation of recessions was to be found in *demand failure*. Hence they focused explicitly on expenditure categories. The theory was not developed to explain the measured values of expenditure. Rather, the way in which we now measure these expenditure categories (see Table 20.2 on page 345) was influenced by the theory.

Accordingly we now turn to the task of explaining aggregate expenditure.

What determines aggregate expenditure?

Before we can answer the question posed in the heading we must deal with a few more important preliminaries.

Some important preliminaries

From actual to desired expenditure In Chapter 20 we discussed how statisticians divide actual GDP, calculated from the expenditure side, into its components: private consumption, investment, government consumption, and net exports.

In this chapter and the next we are concerned with a different concept. It is variously called *desired, planned,* or *intended* expenditure. Of course, all people would like to spend virtually unlimited amounts, if only they had the resources. Desired expenditure does not refer, however, to what people would like to do under imaginary circumstances; it refers to what people want to spend out of the resources that are at their command. The *actual* values of the various categories of expenditure are indicated by C^a, I^a, G^a, and $(X^a - IM^a)$. We use the same letters without the superscript a to indicate the *desired* expenditure in the same categories: C, I, G, and $(X - IM)$.

Everyone with income to spend makes expenditure decisions. Fortunately it is unnecessary for our purposes to look at each of the millions of such individual decisions. Instead, it is sufficient to consider four main groups of decision-makers: individual consumers (or households), firms, governments, and foreign purchasers of domestic output. The actual purchases made by these four groups account for the four main categories of expenditure that we studied in the previous chapter: private consumption, investment, government consumption, and net exports. These groups' desired expenditures—desired private consumption, desired investment, desired government consumption, and desired exports—account for total desired expenditure. (To allow for the fact that many of the commodities desired by each group will have an import content, we subtract expenditure on imports to arrive at the value of spending on domestic output.) The result is total desired expenditure on domestically produced goods and services, called **aggregate expenditure,** or *AE*:

$$AE = C + I + G + (X - IM).$$

Desired expenditure need not equal actual expenditure, either in total or in any individual category. For example, firms may not plan to invest in the accumulation of unsold stock this year but may do so unintentionally. If they produce goods to meet estimated sales but demand is unexpectedly low, the unsold goods that pile up on their shelves are undesired, and unintended, inventory accumulation. In this case actual investment expenditure, I^a, will exceed desired investment expenditure, I.

The national accounts measure actual expenditures in each of the four categories: private consumption, investment, government consumption, and net exports. The theory of GDP determination deals with desired expenditures in each of these four categories.

Recall, however, that these expenditure categories differ because different agents are doing the spending and have different motivations for that spending. They are not different in the effects of their spending because they all generate spending on the final output of the single productive sector.

Autonomous and induced expenditure In what follows it will be useful to distinguish between *autonomous* and *induced* expenditure. Components of aggregate expenditure that *do not* depend on current domestic incomes are called **autonomous expenditures,** or sometimes *exogenous* expenditures.[4] Autonomous expenditures can and do change, but such changes do not occur systematically in response to changes in income. Components of aggregate expenditure that *do* change in response to changes in income are called **induced expenditures,** or *endogenous* expenditures. As we will see, the induced response of aggregate expenditure to a change in income plays a key role in the determination of equilibrium GDP.

A simple model To develop a theory of GDP determination, we need to examine the determinants of each component of desired aggregate expenditure. In this chapter we focus on desired consumption and desired investment. Private consumption is the largest single component of aggregate expenditure (over 60 per cent of UK GDP in 1997), and as we will see, it provides the single most important link between desired aggregate expenditure and actual GDP. Investment is national output that is not used either for current consumption or by governments, and it is motivated by firms' desire to increase the capital stock.[5]

Desired private consumption expenditure

We are now ready to study the determinants of desired expenditure flows. We start with private consumption.

People can do one of two things with their disposable income: spend it on consumption or save it. **Saving** is all disposable income that is not consumed.

By definition there are only two possible uses of disposable income, consumption and saving. So when each individual decides how much to put to one use, he or she has automatically decided how much to put to the other use.

What determines the division between the amount that people decide to spend on goods and services for consumption and the amount that they decide to save? The factors that influence this decision are summarized in the consumption function and the saving function.

The consumption function

The **consumption function** relates the total desired consumption expenditure of the personal sector to the factors that determine it. It is, as we will see, one of the central relationships in macroeconomics.

Although we are ultimately interested in the relationship between consumption and *national* income (GDP), the underlying behaviour of consumers depends on the income that they actually have to spend—their disposable income. Under the simplifying assumptions that we have made in this chapter, there are no taxes. All income that is

generated is received by individuals.[6] Therefore, disposable income, which we denote by Y_d, is equal to national income, Y. (Later in our discussion Y and Y_d will diverge, because taxes are a part of national income that is not at the disposal of individuals.)

Consumption and disposable income

It should not surprise us to hear that a consumer's expenditure is related to the amount of income available. There is, however, more than one way in which this relationship could work. To see what is involved, consider two quite different types of individual.

The first behaves like the proverbial prodigal son. He spends everything he receives and puts nothing aside for a rainy day. When overtime results in a large pay cheque, he goes on a binge. When it is hard to find work during periods of slack demand, his pay cheque is small and expenditures have to be cut correspondingly. This person's expenditure each week is thus directly linked to each week's take-home pay, that is, to his current disposable income.

The second individual is a prudent planner. She thinks about the future as much as the present, and makes plans that stretch over her lifetime. She puts money aside for retirement and for the occasional rainy day when disposable income may fall temporarily—she knows that she must expect some hard times as well as good times. She also knows that she will need to spend extra money while her children are being raised and educated and that her disposable income will probably be highest later in life when the children have left home and she has finally reached the peak of her career. This person may borrow to meet higher expenses earlier in life, paying back out of the higher income that she expects to attain later in life. A temporary, unexpected windfall of income may be saved. A temporary, unexpected shortfall may be cushioned by spending the savings that were put aside for just such a rainy day. In short this person's current expenditure will be closely related to her expected average *lifetime income.* Fluctuations in her *current income* will have little effect on her current expenditure, unless such fluctuations also cause her to change her expectations of lifetime income, as would be the case, for example, if an unexpected promotion came along.

John Maynard Keynes (1883–1946), the famous English economist who developed the basic theory of macroeconomics—and, incidentally, gave his name to 'Keynesian

[4] 'Autonomous' means self-motivated, or independent. 'Exogenous' means determined outside the model.
[5] In practice some of the nation's investment is done by government and consumers, but we focus mainly on the investment behaviour of firms for simplicity. The principles involved can be generalized.
[6] We are assuming here that all firms pass on all their profits to the people who own them, so there is no retained profit.

economics'—populated his theory with prodigal sons. For them current consumption expenditure depended only on current income. To this day a consumption function based on this assumption is called a *Keynesian consumption function*.

Later two US economists, Franco Modigliani and Milton Friedman, both of whom were subsequently awarded the Nobel Prize in economics, analysed the behaviour of prudent consumers who take a longer-term view in determining their consumption. Their theories, which Modigliani called the *life-cycle theory* and which Friedman called *the permanent-income theory*, explain some observed consumer behaviour that cannot be explained by the Keynesian consumption function. Most modern approaches to private consumption behaviour are based upon the life-cycle or permanent-income approaches in which rational consumers plan their consumption over a broad time-horizon, and may even build in plans to leave money to their children (thus planning consumption *beyond* their own lifetimes).

However, the differences between the modern theories and the Keynesian consumption function are not as great as they might seem at first sight. To see why this is so, let us return to our two imaginary individuals and see why their actual behaviour may not be quite so divergent as we have described it.

Even the prodigal son may be able to do some smooth-

ing of expenditures in the face of income fluctuations. Most people have some money in the bank and some ability to borrow, even if it is just from friends and relatives. As a result not every income fluctuation will be matched by an equivalent expenditure fluctuation.

In contrast, although the prudent person wants to smooth her pattern of consumption completely, she may not have the borrowing capacity to do so. Her bank may not be willing to lend money for consumption when the security consists of nothing more than the expectation that income will be much higher in later years. This may mean that in practice her consumption expenditure fluctuates more with her current income than she would wish.

This suggests that the consumption expenditure of both types of individual will fluctuate to some extent with their current disposable incomes and to some extent with their expectations of future disposable income. Moreover, in any economy there will be some people of both extremes, spendthrifts and planners, and aggregate consumption will be determined by a mix of the two types. As we develop our basic theory, we will often find it useful to make the simplifying assumption that consumption expenditure is primarily determined by current disposable income. That is, we will often use a Keynesian consumption function and then indicate how things change if we consider more sophisticated theories of consumer spending. Figure 21.2 shows real personal disposable in-

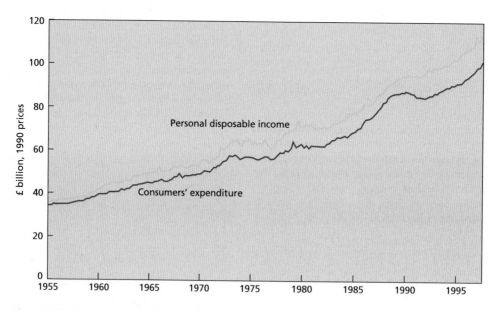

Figure 21.2 Consumers' expenditure and personal disposable income, UK, 1955–1997 (£ billion at constant prices, seasonally adjusted)
Consumer spending and income are closely related over time.
Source: Datastream.

Table 21.1 The calculation of average and marginal propensity to consume (*APC* and *MPC*) (£ million)

Disposable income (Y_d) (1)	Desired consumption (C) (2)	$APC = C/Y_d$ (3)	Change in Y_d (ΔY_d) (4)	Change in C (ΔC) (5)	$MPC = \Delta C/\Delta Y_d$ (6)
0	100	—			
			100	80	0.80
100	180	1.800			
			300	240	0.80
400	420	1.050			
			100	80	0.80
500	500	1.000			
			500	400	0.80
1,000	900	0.900			
			500	400	0.80
1,500	1,300	0.867			
			250	200	0.80
1,750	1,500	0.857			
			250	200	0.80
2,000	1,700	0.850			
			1,000	800	0.80
3,000	2,500	0.833			

APC measures the proportion of disposable income that households desire to spend on consumption; *MPC* measures the proportion of any increment to disposable income that households desire to spend on consumption. The data are hypothetical. We call the level of income at which desired consumption equals disposable income the break-even level; in this example it is £500 million. *APC*, calculated in the third column, exceeds unity—that is, consumption exceeds income—below the break-even level; above the break-even level *APC* is less than unity. It is negatively related to income at all levels of income. The last three columns are set between the lines of the first three columns to indicate that they refer to *changes* in the levels of income and consumption. *MPC*, calculated in the last column, is constant at 0.80 at all levels of Y_d. This indicates that, in this example, £0.80 of every additional £1.00 of disposable income is spent on consumption, and £0.20 is used to increase saving.

come and real consumers' expenditure in the UK from 1955 to 1997. It is clear that the two series are closely related.

The term 'consumption function' describes the relationship between private consumption and the variables that influence it. In the simplest theory consumption is primarily determined by current personal disposable income.

When income is zero, a typical individual will still (via borrowing, or drawing down savings) consume some minimal amount.[7] This level of consumption expenditure is *autonomous* because it persists even when there is no income. The higher a person's income, the more he or she will want to consume. This part of consumption is *induced*; that is, it varies with disposable income and hence, in our simple model, with national income (GDP).

Consider the schedule relating personal disposable income to desired private consumption expenditure for a hypothetical economy that appears in the first two columns of Table 21.1. In this example autonomous consumption expenditure is £100 million, whereas induced consumption expenditure is 80 per cent of disposable income. In what follows we use this hypothetical example to illustrate the various properties of the consumption function.

Average and marginal propensities to consume To discuss the consumption function concisely, economists use two technical expressions.

The **average propensity to consume** (*APC*) is total consumption expenditure divided by total disposable income: $APC = C/Y_d$. The third column of Table 21.1 shows the *APC* calculated from the data in the table. Note that *APC* falls as disposable income rises.

The **marginal propensity to consume** (*MPC*) relates the *change* in consumption to the *change* in disposable income that brought it about. *MPC* is the change in disposable income divided into the resulting consumption change: $MPC = \Delta C/\Delta Y_d$ (where the capital Greek letter delta, Δ, means 'a change in'). The last column of Table 21.1 shows the *MPC* that corresponds to the data in the table. Note that, by construction, *MPC* is constant.

The slope of the consumption function Part (i) of Figure 21.3 shows a graph of the consumption function, derived by plotting consumption against income using data from the first two columns of Table 21.1. The consumption function has a slope of $\Delta C/\Delta Y_d$, which is by definition the marginal propensity to consume. The positive slope of the consumption function shows that the *MPC* is positive; increases in income lead to increases in expenditure.

Using the concepts of the average and marginal propensities to consume, we can summarize the assumed

---

[7] Many individuals have no income but continue to consume, such as dependent children or non-working partners. In this case there is normally at least one earner in a household and it is the household income that is relevant. The household would be the decision unit in that context. Such distinctions are important if we want to study the behaviour of individual spending units, but they are not critical in macroeconomics, which studies the aggregate behaviour of all consumers and relates their total spending to their total income.

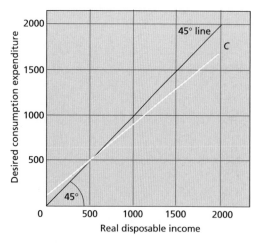

(i) Consumption function (£ million)

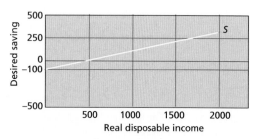

(ii) Saving function (£ million)

Figure 21.3 The consumption and saving functions

Both consumption and saving rise as disposable income rises. Line C in part (i) relates desired consumption expenditure to disposable income by using the hypothetical data from Table 21.1. Its slope, $\Delta C / \Delta Y_d$, is the marginal propensity to consume (MPC). The consumption line cuts the 45° line at the break-even level of disposable income, £500 million in this case. Note that the level of autonomous consumption is £100 million.

Saving is all disposable income that is not spent on consumption ($S = Y_d - C$). The relationship between desired saving and disposable income is derived in Table 21.2, and it is shown in part (ii) by line S. Its slope, $\Delta S / \Delta Y_d$, is the marginal propensity to save (MPS). The saving line cuts the horizontal axis at the break-even level of income. The vertical distance between C and the 45° line in part (i) is by definition the height of S in part (ii); that is, any given level of disposable income must be accounted for by the amount consumed plus the amount saved. Note that the level of autonomous saving is –£100 million. This means that at zero income consumers will draw down existing assets by £100 million a year or borrow this amount.

properties of the short-term consumption function as follows:

1. There is a break-even level of income at which *APC* equals unity. Below this level *APC* is greater than unity; above it *APC* is less than unity. Below the break-even level consumption exceeds income, so consumers run down

savings or borrow. Above the break-even level income exceeds consumption, so there is positive saving.

2. *MPC* is greater than zero but less than unity for all levels of income. This means that for each additional £1 of income, less than £1 is spent on consumption and the rest is saved. For a straight-line consumption function, the *MPC* is constant at all levels of income.

The 45° line Figure 21.3(i) contains a line that is constructed by connecting all points where desired consumption (measured on the vertical axis) equals disposable income (measured on the horizontal axis). Because both axes are given in the same units, this line has a positive slope of unity; that is, it forms an angle of 45° with the axes. The line is therefore called the **45° line.**

The 45° line makes a handy reference line. In part (i) of Figure 21.3 it helps to locate the break-even level of income at which consumption expenditure equals disposable income. The consumption function cuts the 45° line at the break-even level of income, in this instance £500 million. (The 45° line is steeper than the consumption function because *MPC* is less than unity.)

The saving function

Individuals decide how much to consume and how much to save. As we have said, this is a single decision: how to divide disposable income between consumption and saving. It follows that once we know the dependence of consumption on disposable income, we also automatically know the dependence of saving on disposable income. (This is illustrated in Table 21.2.)

Table 21.2 Consumption and saving schedules (£ million)

Disposable income	Desired consumption	Desired saving
0	100	–100
100	180	–80
400	420	–20
500	500	0
1,000	900	+100
1,500	1,300	+200
1,750	1,500	+250
2,000	1,700	+300
3,000	2,500	+500
4,000	3,300	+700

Saving and consumption account for all household disposable income. The first two columns repeat the data from Table 21.1. The third column, desired saving, is disposable income minus desired consumption. Consumption and saving both increase steadily as disposable income rises. In this example the break-even level of income is £500 million. At this level all income is consumed.

There are two saving concepts that are exactly parallel to the consumption concepts of *APC* and *MPC*. The **average propensity to save** (*APS*) is the proportion of disposable income that households want to save, derived by dividing total desired saving by total disposable income: $APS = S/Y_d$. The **marginal propensity to save** (*MPS*) relates the *change* in total desired saving to the *change* in disposable income that brought it about: $MPS = \Delta S/\Delta Y_d$.

There is a simple relationship between the saving and consumption propensities. *APC* and *APS* must sum to unity, and so must *MPC* and *MPS*. Because income is either spent or saved, it follows that the fractions of incomes consumed and saved must account for all income ($APC + APS = 1$). It also follows that the fractions of any increment to income consumed and saved must account for all of that increment ($MPC + MPS = 1$). Calculations from Table 21.2 will allow you to confirm these relationships in the case of the example given. *MPC* is 0.80 and *MPS* is 0.20 at all levels of income, while, for example, at an income of £2,000 million *APC* is 0.85 and *APS* is 0.15.

Figure 21.3(ii) shows the saving schedule given in Table 21.2. At the break-even level of income, where desired consumption equals disposable income, desired saving is zero. The slope of the saving line $\Delta S/\Delta Y_d$ is equal to the *MPS*.

Wealth and the consumption function

The Keynesian consumption function that we have been analysing can easily be combined with the permanent-income or life-cycle theories of consumption. According to these theories households save in order to accumulate wealth that they can use during their retirement (or pass on to their heirs[8]). Suppose that there is an unexpected rise in wealth. This will mean that less of current disposable income needs to be saved for the future, and it will tend to cause a larger fraction of disposable income to be spent on consumption and a smaller fraction to be saved. Thus the consumption function will be shifted upward and the saving function downward, as shown in Figure 21.4. A fall in wealth increases the incentive to save in order to restore wealth. This shifts the consumption function downward and the saving function upward.

Desired investment expenditure

Investment expenditure is the most volatile component of GDP, and changes in investment expenditure are strongly associated with economic fluctuations. For example, the Great Depression witnessed a major fall in investment. Total investment fell by nearly a quarter between 1929 and 1932. A little less dramatically, at the trough of the UK recession of the early 1990s (in 1992), investment expenditure was 13 per cent less than the level two years earlier.

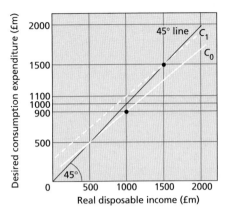

(i) The consumption function shifts upward with an increase in wealth

(ii) The saving function shifts downward

Figure 21.4 Wealth and the consumption function
Changes in wealth shift the consumption function. In part (i) line C_0 reproduces the consumption function from Figure 21.3(i). An increase in the level of wealth raises desired consumption at each level of disposable income, thus shifting the consumption line up to C_1. In the figure the consumption function shifts up by £200 million, so with disposable income of £1,000 million, for example, desired consumption rises from £900 million to £1,100 million. As a result of the rise in wealth the break-even level of income rises to £1,500 million.

The saving function in part (ii) shifts down by £200 million from S_0 to S_1. Thus, for example, at a disposable income of £1,000 million, saving *falls* from +£100 million to −£100 million.

Investment and the real interest rate

Other things being equal, the higher is the real interest rate,[9] the higher is the cost of borrowing money for investment purposes and the less is the amount of desired investment expenditure. This relationship is most easily understood if we disaggregate investment into three

[8] Empirical evidence suggests that there is a significant 'bequest motive' for saving. This means that some individuals plan even further ahead than their own lifetime, because they want to leave money to their children.
[9] The *real* rate of interest is approximately equal to the nominal (money) rate of interest minus the expected rate of inflation.

parts: inventory accumulation, residential house building, and business fixed capital formation.[10]

Inventory accumulation Changes in inventories of finished goods, work in progress, or raw materials represent only a small percentage of private investment in a typical year, but their average size is not an adequate measure of their importance. They are one of the more volatile elements of total investment and therefore have a major influence on shifts in investment expenditure.

When a firm ties up funds by holding bigger inventories of inputs or outputs, those same funds cannot be used elsewhere to earn income. As an alternative to investing in inventories, the firm could lend the money out at the going rate of interest. Thus the higher the rate of interest, the higher will be the opportunity cost of holding inventories of a given size; the higher that opportunity cost, the smaller are the inventories that will be desired.

The higher the real rate of interest, the lower is the desired inventory of goods and materials. Changes in the rate of interest cause temporary bouts of investment (or disinvestment) in inventories.

Residential housing construction Expenditure on new houses is also volatile. Between 1970 and 1997 it varied between 3.7 and 6.0 per cent of UK GDP, and between 20 and 25 per cent of total investment. Because expenditures for housing construction are both large and variable, they exert a major impact on the economy. Notice that what matters for investment is the demand for new housing. House purchases that involve the exchange of ownership of an existing house do not affect the demand for currently produced output and are, therefore, not relevant to determining current GDP.

Most houses are purchased with money that is borrowed by means of a mortgage. Interest on the borrowed money typically accounts for over half of the purchaser's annual mortgage payments; the rest is repayment of the original loan, called the principal. Because interest payments are so large a part of mortgage payments, variations in interest rates exert a substantial effect on the demand for housing. During the mid-1980s UK interest rates fell sharply, and there was a boom in the demand for housing; that boom persisted until late 1988, when interest rates started to rise again. The housing market collapsed and house prices fell. The lower interest rates which arrived in 1992 and 1993 permitted the beginning of a recovery in the housing market; however, this recovery was very slow and house prices did not pick up until the second half of the 1990s.

Expenditure for residential construction tends to vary negatively with interest rates.

Business fixed capital formation Investment by firms in fixed capital (factories, offices, and machines) is the largest component of domestic investment. Over one-half is financed by firms' retained profits (profits that are not paid out to their shareholders). This means that current profits are an important determinant of investment.

The rate of interest is also a major determinant of investment. In the United Kingdom, both during the early 1980s and during 1989–92, high interest rates greatly reduced the volume of investment, as more and more firms found that their expected profits from investment did not cover the interest on borrowed investment funds. Other firms who had cash on hand found that purchasing interest-earning assets provided a better return than investment in factories and machinery. For them the increase in real interest rates meant that the opportunity cost of investing in fixed capital had risen. Interest rates are determined in the monetary sector, so we do not fully incorporate interest rate effects until we have studied money in Chapter 25.

Expectations and business confidence

Investment takes time. When a firm invests, it increases its future capacity to produce output. If the new output can be sold profitably, the investment will prove to be a good one. If the new output does not generate profits, the investment will be a bad one. When the investment is undertaken, the firm does not know if it will turn out well or badly—it is betting on a favourable future that cannot be known with certainty.

When firms expect good times ahead, they will want to invest so as to reap future profits. When they expect bad times, they will not invest, because, given their expectations, there will be no payoff from doing so.

Business investment depends in part on firms' forecasts of the future state of the economy.

Investment as autonomous expenditure

We have seen that investment is influenced by many things. For the moment we treat investment as autonomous, meaning only that it is not influenced by changes in GDP. This allows us to study, first, how GDP is determined when there is an unchanged amount of desired investment expenditure and, second, how alterations in the amount of desired investment cause changes in equilibrium GDP. (In Chapter 26 we will link changes in GDP to changes in investment via induced changes in interest rates.)

---

[10] These represent different motives for investment, and in practice would create demand for different kinds of goods. However, recall that they will all end up creating demand for the output of the single production sector. Thus the impact, in our model, of £1 worth of inventory accumulation is the same as £1 worth of fixed capital formation and, indeed, of £1 worth of consumption. The reason we distinguish investment from consumption is that it is affected by different factors, the most important of which will be the interest rate. Note also that house building is part of gross fixed capital formation in the national accounts. We ignore here the net acquisition of valuables as this is very small.

The aggregate expenditure function

The aggregate expenditure function relates the level of desired real expenditure to the level of real national income, that is, real GDP. Generally, total desired expenditure on the nation's output is the sum of desired private consumption, investment, government consumption, and net export expenditures. In the simplified economy of this chapter aggregate expenditure is just equal to $C + I$:

$$AE = C + I.$$

Table 21.3 shows how the AE function is calculated, given the consumption function of Tables 21.1 and 21.2 and a constant level of desired investment of £250 million. In this specific case all of investment expenditure is autonomous, as is the £100 million of consumption that would be desired when national income is zero (see Table 21.1). Total autonomous expenditure is thus £350 million—induced expenditures are just equal to induced consumption, which is equal to $0.8Y$. Thus desired aggregate expenditure, whether thought of as $C + I$ or as autonomous plus induced expenditure, can be written as

Figure 21.5 An aggregate expenditure function
The aggregate expenditure function relates total desired expenditure to national income. The AE curve in the figure plots the data from the first and the last columns of Table 21.3, which are repeated in Table 21.4. Its intercept (which in this case is £350 million) shows autonomous expenditure, which in this case is the sum of autonomous consumption of £100 million and investment of £250 million. Its slope (which in this case is 0.8) shows the marginal propensity to spend.

Table 21.3 The aggregate expenditure function in a closed economy with no government (£ million)

GDP (national income) (Y)	Desired consumption expenditure ($C = 100 + 0.8Y$)	Desired investment expenditure ($I = 250$)	Desired aggregate expenditure ($AE = C + I$)
100	180	250	430
400	420	250	670
500	500	250	750
1,000	900	250	1,150
1,500	1,300	250	1,550
1,750	1,500	250	1,750
2,000	1,700	250	1,950
3,000	2,500	250	2,750
4,000	3,300	250	3,550

The aggregate expenditure function is the sum of desired consumption, investment, government, and net export expenditures. In this table government and net exports are assumed to be zero, investment is assumed to be constant at £250 million, and desired consumption is based on the hypothetical data given in Table 21.2. The autonomous components of desired aggregate expenditure are desired investment and the constant term in desired consumption expenditure (£100 million). The induced component is the second term in desired consumption expenditure (0.8 Y).

The marginal response of consumption to a change in national income is 0.8, the marginal propensity to consume. The marginal response of desired aggregate expenditure to a change in national income, $\Delta AE/\Delta Y$, is also 0.8, because all induced expenditure in the economy is consumption expenditure.

$AE = $ £350 million $+ 0.8Y$. This aggregate expenditure function is illustrated in Figure 21.5.

The propensity to spend out of national income The fraction of any increment to national income (GDP) that will be spent on purchasing domestic output is called the economy's **marginal propensity to spend.** It is measured by the change in aggregate expenditure divided by the change in income, or $\Delta AE/\Delta Y$, the slope of the aggregate expenditure function. In this book we will denote the marginal propensity to spend by the symbol z, which will typically be a number greater than zero and less than one.

Similarly, the **marginal propensity not to spend** is the fraction of any increment to national income that does not add to desired aggregate expenditure. This is denoted $(1 - z)$—if z is the part of any £1 of incremental income that is spent, $(1 - z)$ is the part that is not spent.[11] In the example given in Table 21.3, z, the marginal propensity to spend, is 0.8. If national income increases by £1, then 80p will go into increased spending. Twenty pence (£1 times 0.2, the value of $(1 - z)$) will go into increased saving and will not be spent.

The marginal propensity to spend, which we have just defined, should not be confused with the marginal propensity to consume, which we defined earlier in the

[11] More fully these terms would be called the marginal propensity to spend *on the national product* and the marginal propensity not to spend *on the national product*. The marginal propensity not to spend, $(1 - z)$, is sometimes referred to as the *marginal propensity to withdraw*. Not spending some part of income amounts to a *withdrawal* or a *leakage* from the circular flow of income, as illustrated in Box 20.3 on page 341.

chapter. The marginal propensity to spend is the amount of extra total expenditure induced when *national* income rises by £1, while the marginal propensity to consume is the amount of extra consumption expenditure induced when *personal disposable income* rises by £1. In the simple model of this chapter the marginal propensity to spend is equal to the marginal propensity to consume, and the

marginal propensity not to spend is equal to the marginal propensity to save. In later chapters, when we add government and the international sector, the marginal propensity to spend differs from the marginal propensity to consume. Both here and in later chapters it is the more general measures z and $(1 - z)$ that are important for determining equilibrium GDP.

Equilibrium GDP

We are now ready to see what determines the *equilibrium* level of national income and output, that is, GDP. When something is in equilibrium, there is no tendency for it to change; forces are acting on it, but they balance out, and the net result is *no change*. Any conditions that are required for something to be in equilibrium are called *equilibrium conditions*.

Table 21.4 illustrates the determination of equilibrium GDP for our simple hypothetical economy. Suppose that firms are producing a final output of £1,000 million, and thus GDP is £1,000 million. According to the table, at this level of national income aggregate desired expenditure is £1,150 million. If firms persist in producing a current output of only £1,000 million in the face of an aggregate

desired expenditure of £1,150 million, one of two things must happen.[12]

One possibility is that consumers and investors will be unable to spend the extra £150 million that they would like to spend, so queues and unfulfilled order books will appear. These will send a signal to firms that they can increase their sales if they increase their production. When the firms increase production, GDP rises. Of course, the individual firms are interested only in their own sales and profits, but their individual actions have as their inevitable consequence an increase in GDP.

The second possibility is that consumers and investors will spend everything that they wanted to spend. Then, however, expenditure will exceed current output, which can happen only when some expenditure plans are fulfilled by purchasing stocks of goods that were produced in the past. In our example, the fulfilment of plans to purchase £1,150 million worth of commodities in the face of a current output of only £1,000 million will reduce inventories by £150 million. As long as stocks last, more goods can be sold than are currently being produced.[13]

Eventually stocks will run out. But before this happens, firms will increase their output as they see their sales increase. Extra sales can then be made without a further depletion of inventories. Once again the consequence of each individual firm's behaviour, in search of its own individual profits, is an increase in the national product and national income. Thus the final response to an excess of aggregate desired expenditure over current output is a rise in GDP.

At any level of GDP at which aggregate desired expenditure exceeds total output, there will be pressure for GDP to rise.

Table 21.4 The determination of equilibrium GDP (£ million)

GDP (national income) (Y)	Desired aggregate expenditure ($AE = C + I$)	
100	430	
400	670	
500	750	Pressure on Y
1,000	1,150	to rise
1,500	1,550	↓
1,750	**1,750**	**Equilibrium Y**
2,000	1,950	↑
3,000	2,750	Pressure on Y
4,000	3,550	to fall

GDP is in equilibrium where aggregate desired expenditure equals national output. The data are copied from Table 21.3. When GDP is below its equilibrium level, aggregate desired expenditure exceeds the value of current output. This creates an incentive for firms to increase output and hence for GDP to rise. When GDP is above its equilibrium level, aggregate desired expenditure is less than the value of current output. This creates an incentive for firms to reduce output and hence for GDP to fall. Only at the equilibrium level of GDP is aggregate desired expenditure equal to the value of current output.

---

[12] A third possibility, that prices could rise, is ruled out by assumption in this chapter.

[13] Notice that in this example actual national income (GDP) is equal to £1,000 million. Desired consumption is £900 million and desired investment is £250 million, but the reduction of inventories by £150 million is unplanned negative investment; thus actual investment is only £100 million.

Next consider the £4,000 million level of GDP in Table 21.4. At this level desired expenditure on domestically produced goods is only £3,550 million. If firms persist in producing £4,000 million worth of goods, £450 million worth must remain unsold. Therefore, stocks of unsold goods must rise. However, firms will not allow unsold goods to accumulate indefinitely; sooner or later they will reduce the level of output to the level of sales. When they do, GDP will fall.

At any level of GDP for which aggregate desired expenditure is less than total output, there will be pressure for GDP to fall.

Finally, look at the GDP level of £1,750 million in Table 21.4. At this level, and only at this level, aggregate desired expenditure is equal to national output (GDP). Purchasers can fulfil their spending plans without causing inventories to change. There is no incentive for firms to alter output. Because everyone wishes to purchase an amount equal to what is being produced, output and income will remain steady; GDP is in equilibrium.

The equilibrium level of GDP occurs where aggregate desired expenditure equals total output.

This conclusion is quite general and does not depend on the numbers that are used in the specific example.

Figure 21.6 shows the determination of the equilibrium level of GDP. In the figure the line labelled 'AE' graphs the aggregate expenditure function given by the first and last columns of Table 21.3, also shown in Table 21.4. The line labelled '45° line (AE = Y)' graphs the equilibrium condition that aggregate desired expenditure equals national output. Since in equilibrium the variables measured on the two axes must be equal, the line showing this equality is a 45° line. Anywhere along that line the value of desired expenditure, which is measured on the vertical axis, is equal to the value of national output, which is measured on the horizontal axis.[14]

Graphically, equilibrium occurs at the level of GDP at which the aggregate desired expenditure line intersects the 45° line. This is the level of GDP where desired expenditure is just equal to total national output and therefore is just sufficient to purchase that output.

Exactly the same equilibrium is illustrated in panel (ii), but in terms of the saving–investment balance. The line labelled 'S' is equal to aggregate saving. In an economy without government and without international trade— the case we are studying here—aggregate saving is just equal to $Y - C$, the difference between national income and consumption. The line labelled 'I' is investment, in this case assumed to be constant at all levels of income.

Notice that the vertical distance between S and I is just equal to the distance between the 45° line and AE. When desired investment exceeds desired saving, desired aggregate expenditure exceeds national output by the

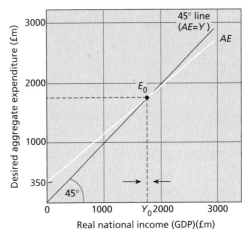

(i) Aggregate expenditure function (AE = Y)

(ii) Saving function (S = I)

Figure 21.6 Equilibrium GDP

Equilibrium GDP occurs at E_0, where the desired aggregate expenditure line intersects the 45° line. If real GDP is below Y_0, desired aggregate expenditure will exceed national output, and production will rise. This is shown in part (i) by the arrow to the left of Y_0. If GDP is above Y_0, desired aggregate expenditure will be less than national output, and production will fall. This is shown by the arrow to the right of Y_0. Only when real GDP is Y_0 will desired aggregate expenditure equal real national output.

When saving is the only withdrawal and investment is the only injection, the equilibrium Y_0 is also the level of GDP at which saving equals investment, shown in part (ii). At levels of GDP greater than Y_0 saving exceeds investment (withdrawals exceed injections), so aggregate spending is less than output and the economy contracts. At levels of GDP below Y_0, investment exceeds saving (injections exceed withdrawals) so spending exceeds output and the level of GDP increases. Part (i) and (ii) are just two different ways of looking at the same phenomena.

---

[14] Because it turns up in many different guises, the 45° line can cause a bit of confusion until one gets used to it. The main thing about it is that it can be used whenever the variables plotted on the two axes are measured in the same units, such as pounds, and are plotted on the same scale. In that case equal distances on the two axes measure the same amounts. One centimetre may, for example, correspond to £1,000 on each axis. In such circumstances the 45° line joins all points where the values of the two variables are the same. In Figures 21.3 and 21.4 the 45° line shows all points where *desired consumption expenditure in real terms* equals *real disposable income*, because these are the two variables that are plotted on the two axes. In Figure 21.6 and all those that follow it the 45° line shows all points at which *desired total expenditure in real terms* equals *real national output (GDP)*, because those are the variables that are measured on the two axes of these figures.

Box 21.1 A hydraulic analogue of GDP determination

The key concept to understand in this chapter is how it is that GDP achieves its equilibrium level (for given values of exogenous expenditures). This is one of the most important ideas in macroeconomics, because it explains how GDP can be in equilibrium even when there is excess capacity in the economy.

Think of the economy as a water container, say a basin, which has inflows and outflows on a continuous basis—the tap is turned on and there is no plug in the plug hole. Although the water is always changing, there is some condition under which the level of water in the basin will remain unchanged. This is when the volume of the inflow and the volume of the outflow are exactly equal.

Call the inflow 'investment', the outflow 'saving', and the level of water in the basin 'GDP'. GDP will stay at one level so long as the volume of investment just equals the volume of saving. (The same principle can be viewed in terms of the circular flow diagram in Box 20.3 on page 341 when there is no foreign trade and no government. Only when $I = S$ will the level of the circular flow be stable.)

What happens if the basin fills up to overflowing? That is the problem of capacity constraints and full employment which we discuss in later chapters. Hopefully, the basin will never run empty, because that means national income and output fall to zero—though the problem of the water getting undesirably low is what macroeconomics was invented to study.

Note also that in later chapters we will see that investment is not the only inflow, or injection (government expenditure and exports will be added), and saving is not the only leakage, or withdrawal (taxes and imports are also leakages).

same amount. When desired investment is less than desired saving, desired aggregate expenditure is less than national output by the same amount.

Now we have explained the determinants of the equilibrium level of GDP at a *given price level*. A simple analogue, which will help us to understand why it is that equilibrium GDP is associated with equality of desired investment and saving, is set out in Box 21.1. In the next section we will study the forces that cause equilibrium income to change. We will see that shifts in autonomous consumption and investment expenditure cause changes in equilibrium GDP.

Changes in GDP

Because the *AE* function plays a central role in our explanation of the determination of the equilibrium value of GDP, you should not be surprised to hear that shifts in the *AE* function play a central role in explaining why GDP changes. (Remember that we continue to assume for the moment that the price level is constant.) To understand this influence, we must recall an important distinction first encountered in Chapter 3—the distinction between *shifts* in a curve and *movements along* a curve.

Suppose desired aggregate expenditure rises. This may be a response to a change in GDP (and therefore in incomes), or it may be the result of an increased desire to spend at each level of GDP. A change in GDP causes a *movement along* the aggregate expenditure function. An increased desire to spend at each level of GDP causes a *shift* in the aggregate expenditure function. Figure 21.7 illustrates this important distinction.

Shifts in the aggregate expenditure function

For any specific aggregate expenditure function there is a unique level of equilibrium GDP. If the aggregate expenditure function shifts, the equilibrium will be disturbed and GDP will change. Thus if we wish to find the causes of changes in GDP, we must understand the causes of shifts in the *AE* function.

The aggregate expenditure function shifts when one of

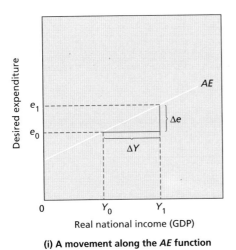

(i) A movement along the *AE* function

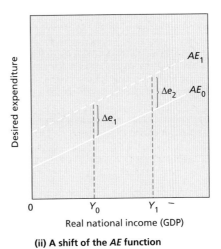

(ii) A shift of the *AE* function

Figure 21.7 Movements along and shifts of the *AE* function

A movement along the aggregate expenditure function occurs in response to a change in income; a shift of the *AE* function indicates a different level of desired expenditure at each level of income. In part (i) a change in income of ΔY, from Y_0 to Y_1, changes desired expenditure by Δe, from e_0 to e_1. In part (ii) a shift in the expenditure function from AE_0 to AE_1 raises the amount of expenditure associated with *each level* of income. At Y_0, for example, desired aggregate expenditure is increased by Δe_1; at Y_1 it is increased by Δe_2. (If the aggregate expenditure line shifts parallel to itself, $\Delta e_1 = \Delta e_2$.) (Notice that from here on we drop 'aggregate' from the vertical axis label and write 'Desired expenditure'. The term 'aggregate' is always understood, even when we omit it to save space.)

its components shifts, that is, when there is a shift in the consumption function, in desired investment expenditure, in desired government expenditure on goods and services, or in desired net exports. In this chapter we consider only shifts in the consumption function and in desired investment expenditure. Both of these are changes in desired aggregate expenditure at every level of income.

Upward shifts What will happen if individuals permanently increase their levels of consumption spending at each level of disposable income, or if ICI invests in more fixed capital because of improved confidence about the future health of the economy? (Recall that an increase in any component of expenditure has the same effect, because it is an increase in demand for the output of the single production sector.) In considering these questions, remember that we are dealing with continuous flows measured as so much per period of time. An upward shift in any expenditure function means that the desired expenditure associated with each level of national income rises to and stays at a higher amount.

Because any such increase in desired expenditure shifts the entire aggregate expenditure function upward, the same analysis applies to each of the changes mentioned. Two important types of shift in *AE* need to be distinguished. First, if the same addition to expenditure occurs at all levels of income, the *AE* curve shifts parallel to itself, as shown in part (i) of Figure 21.8. Second, if there is a change in the propensity to spend out of national income, the slope of the *AE* curve changes, as shown in part (ii) of Figure 21.8. (Recall that the slope of the *AE* curve is z, the marginal propensity to spend.) A change such as the one illustrated would occur if consumers decided to spend more of every £1 of disposable income, that is, if *MPC* rose.

Figure 21.8 shows that upward shifts in the aggregate expenditure function increase equilibrium GDP. After the shift in the *AE* curve, output is no longer in equilibrium at its original level, because at that level desired expenditure exceeds national output. Equilibrium GDP now occurs at the higher level indicated by the intersection of the new *AE* curve with the 45° line, along which aggregate expenditure equals national output.

Downward shifts What happens to GDP if there is a decrease in the amount of consumption or investment expenditure desired at each level of income? These changes shift the aggregate expenditure function downward. A constant reduction in desired expenditure at all levels of income shifts *AE* parallel to itself. A fall in the marginal propensity to spend out of national income reduces the slope of the *AE* function. When we use the saving–investment relation, we must note that a downward shift in the consumption function causes an upward shift in the saving function, reducing the equilibrium level of income and output, at which saving equals investment.

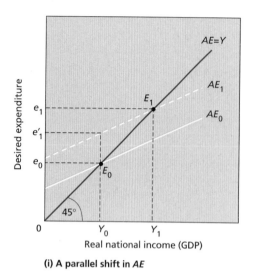

(i) A parallel shift in *AE*

(ii) A change in the slope of *AE*

Figure 21.8 Shifts in the *AE* curve

Upward shifts in the *AE* curve increase equilibrium income and output; downward shifts decrease equilibrium income and output.
In parts (i) and (ii) the aggregate expenditure curve is initially AE_0 with national income Y_0. In part (i) a parallel upward *shift* in the *AE* curve from AE_0 to AE_1 means that desired expenditure has increased by the same amount at each level of national income. For example, at Y_0 desired expenditure rises from e_0 to e'_1 and therefore exceeds national output. Equilibrium is reached at E_1, where output is Y_1 and expenditure is e_1. The increase in desired expenditure from e'_1 to e_1, represented by a *movement along AE_1*, is an induced response to the increase in GDP from Y_0 to Y_1.

In part (ii) a non-parallel upward shift in the *AE* curve, say from AE_0 to AE_2, means that the marginal propensity to spend at each level of national income has increased. This leads to an increase in equilibrium GDP. Equilibrium is reached at E_2, where the new level of expenditure e_2 is equal to output Y_2. Again, the initial *shift* in the *AE* curve induces a *movement along* the new *AE* curve. Downward shifts in the *AE* curve, from AE_1 to AE_0 or from AE_2 to AE_0, lead to a fall in equilibrium GDP to Y_0.

The results restated We have derived two important general propositions of the theory of GDP determination.

1. A rise in the amount of desired aggregate expenditure that is associated with each level of national income will increase equilibrium national output (GDP).

2. A fall in the amount of desired aggregate expenditure that is associated with each level of national income will lower equilibrium national output (GDP).

The multiplier

We have learned how to predict the direction of the changes in GDP that will occur in response to various shifts in the aggregate expenditure function. We would like also to predict the *magnitude* of these changes.

During a recession the government sometimes takes measures to stimulate the economy. If these measures have a larger effect than estimated, demand may rise too much and full employment may be reached with demand still rising. (We will see in Chapter 23 that this outcome will have an inflationary impact on the economy.) If the government greatly overestimates the effect of its measures,

the recession will persist longer than is necessary. In this case there is a danger that the policy will be discredited as ineffective, even though the correct diagnosis is that too little of the right thing was done.

Definition A measure of the magnitude of changes in GDP is provided by the *multiplier*. We have just seen that a shift in the aggregate expenditure curve will cause a change in equilibrium GDP. Such a shift could be caused by a change in any autonomous component of aggregate expenditure, for example an increase or decrease in desired investment. We will soon see that an increase in desired aggregate expenditure increases equilibrium GDP by a multiple of the initial increase in autonomous expenditure. The **multiplier** is the ratio of the change in GDP to the change in expenditure, that is, the change in GDP *divided by* the change in autonomous expenditure that brought it about.

Why the multiplier is greater than unity What will happen to GDP if Glaxo Wellcome PLC spends £100 million per year on new factories? Initially the construction of the factories will create £100m worth of new demand for the output of the production sector (recall that there is only one type of output) and £100m of new national income, and a corresponding amount of extra wages for workers and profits for firms (the income components of GDP). But this is not the end of the story. The increase in national income of £100m will cause an increase in disposable income, which in turn will cause an induced rise in consumption expenditure.

Workers who gain new income directly from the building of the factory will spend some of it on consumer goods. (In reality they will spend it on many different goods, such as beer and cinema visits. In the simplified world of our model all spending is on the final output of the single industrial sector.) When output and employment expand to meet this demand, further new incomes will then be created for workers and firms. When they then spend their newly earned incomes, output and employment will rise further. More income will be created, and more expenditure will be induced. Indeed at this stage we might wonder whether the increases in income will ever come to an end. To deal with this concern, we need to consider the multiplier in somewhat more precise terms.

The simple multiplier defined Consider an increase in autonomous expenditure of ΔA, which might be, say, £100m per year. Remember that ΔA stands for any increase in autonomous expenditure; this could be an increase in investment or in the autonomous component of consumption. The new autonomous expenditure shifts the aggregate expenditure function upward by that amount. GDP is no longer in equilibrium at its original level, because desired aggregate expenditure now exceeds output. Equilibrium is restored by a movement along the new AE curve.

The **simple multiplier** measures the change in equilibrium GDP that occurs in response to a change in autonomous expenditure *at a constant price level*.[15] We refer to it as 'simple' because we have simplified the situation by assuming that the price level is fixed. Figure 21.9 illustrates the simple multiplier. Box 21.2 provides a numerical example.

The size of the simple multiplier

The size of the simple multiplier depends on the slope of the AE function, that is, on the marginal propensity to spend, z. This is illustrated in Figure 21.10.

A high marginal propensity to spend means a steep AE curve. The expenditure induced by any initial increase in income is large, with the result that the final rise in GDP is correspondingly large. By contrast, a low marginal propensity to spend means a relatively flat AE curve. The expenditure induced by the initial increase in income is small, and the final rise in GDP is not much larger than the initial rise in autonomous expenditure that brought it about.

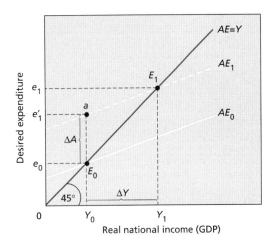

Figure 21.9 The simple multiplier

An increase in the autonomous component of desired aggregate expenditure increases equilibrium GDP by a multiple of the initial increase. The initial equilibrium is at E_0, where AE_0 intersects the 45° line. At this point desired expenditure, e_0, is equal to national output, Y_0. An increase in autonomous expenditure of ΔA then shifts the desired expenditure function upward to AE_1. If GDP stays at Y_0, desired expenditure rises to e_1'. (The coordinates of point a are Y_0 and e_1'.) Because this level of desired expenditure is greater than national output, GDP will rise.

Equilibrium occurs when GDP rises to Y_1. Here desired expenditure, e_1, equals output, Y_1. The extra expenditure of e_1 represents the induced increases in expenditure. It is the amount by which the final increase in income and output, ΔY, exceeds the initial increase in autonomous expenditure, ΔA. Because ΔY is greater than ΔA, the multiplier is greater than unity.

The larger the marginal propensity to spend, the steeper is the aggregate expenditure function and the larger is the multiplier.

The precise value of the simple multiplier can be derived by using elementary algebra. (The derivation is given in the appendix to this chapter.) The result is that the simple multiplier, which we call K, is

$$K = \frac{\Delta Y}{\Delta A} = \frac{1}{1-z},$$

where z is the marginal propensity to spend out of national income. (Recall that z is the slope of the aggregate expenditure function.)

As we saw earlier, the term $(1-z)$ stands for the marginal propensity not to spend out of national income. For example, if £0.80 of every £1.00 of new national income is

---

[15] Recall that we have assumed that there is excess capacity in the economy, so an increase in expenditure *can* lead to extra real activity. The situation is very different when we begin with resources already fully employed. We consider this situation in later chapters.

Box 21.2   The multiplier: a numerical example

Consider an economy that has a marginal propensity to spend out of national income of 0.80. Suppose that autonomous expenditure increases by £100m per year because a large company spends an extra £100m per year on new factories. National income (and output) initially rises by £100m, but that is not the end of it. The factors of production involved in factory building that received the first £100m spend £80m. This second round of spending generates £80m of new income. This new income, in turn, induces £64m of third-round spending, and so it continues, with each successive round of new income generating 80 per cent as much in new expenditure. Each additional round of expenditure creates new income (and output) and yet another round of expenditure.

The table carries the process through ten rounds. Students with sufficient patience (and no faith in mathematics) may compute as many rounds in the process as they wish; they will find that the sum of the rounds of expend-

itures approaches a limit of £500 million, which is five times the initial increase in expenditure.

The graph of the cumulative expenditure increases shows how quickly this limit is approached. The multiplier is thus 5, given that the marginal propensity to spend is 0.8. Had the marginal propensity to spend been lower, say 0.667, the process would have been similar, but it would have approached a limit of three, instead of five times the initial increase in expenditure. Notice that since our model has only a single productive sector, it makes no difference what the initial spending goes on. That, and all subsequent spending, is on the output of this single industry. In reality the impact of spending increases may vary slightly depending on the product first demanded.

Round of spending	Increase in expenditure (£m)	Cumulative total (£m)
Initial increase	100.0	100.0
2	80.0	180.0
3	64.0	244.0
4	51.2	295.2
5	41.0	336.2
6	32.8	369.0
7	26.2	395.2
8	21.0	416.2
9	16.8	433.0
10	13.4	446.4
11–20 combined	47.9	494.3
All others	5.7	500.0

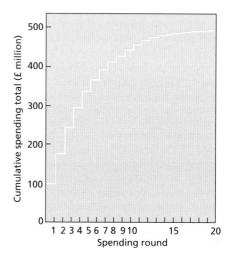

spent ($z = 0.80$), then £0.20 is the amount not spent. The value of the multiplier is then calculated as $K = 1/(0.20) = 5$.

The simple multiplier equals the reciprocal of the marginal propensity not to spend.

From this we see that if $(1 - z)$ is small (that is, if z is large), the multiplier will be large (because extra income induces much extra spending). What if $(1 - z)$ is large? The largest possible value of $(1 - z)$ is unity, which arises when z equals zero, indicating that none of any additional national income is spent. In this case the multiplier itself has a value of unity; the increase in equilibrium GDP is confined to the initial increase in autonomous expenditure. There are no induced additional effects on spending, so GDP only increases by the original increase in autonomous expenditure. The relation between $(1 - z)$ and the size of the multiplier is illustrated in Figure 21.10.

To estimate the size of the multiplier in an actual economy, we need to estimate the value of the marginal propensity not to spend out of national income in that

economy, that is, $(1 - z)$. Evidence suggests that in the United Kingdom the value of the marginal propensity not to spend is much larger than the 0.2 used in the above example. This is because there are 'leakages' from the circular flow of income other than saving—income taxes and import expenditures (which will be added to our model in the next chapter). Allowing for these extra withdrawals leads to a realistic estimate of something around 0.65 for $(1 - z)$.[16] Thus the simple multiplier for the United Kingdom is just over 1.4, rather than 5 as in the above example.

The simple multiplier is a useful starting-point for understanding the effects of expenditure shifts on GDP. However, as we will see in subsequent chapters, many qualifications will arise, so the reader should not place too much policy significance on its value at this stage.

---

[16] This 0.65 is calculated using a marginal propensity to save of 0.2, a marginal propensity to import of 0.25, and an income tax rate of 0.25 (25p in the pound).

Figure 21.10 The size of the simple multiplier

The larger the marginal propensity to spend out of national income (z), the steeper is the AE curve and the larger is the multiplier. In each part of the figure the initial aggregate expenditure function is AE_0, equilibrium is at E_0, with income Y_0. The AE curve then shifts upward to AE_1 as a result of an increase in autonomous expenditure of ΔA. ΔA is the same in each part. The new equilibrium is at E_1. In part (i) the AE function is horizontal, indicating a marginal propensity to spend of zero ($z = 0$). The change in GDP, ΔY, is only the increase in autonomous expenditure, because there is no induced expenditure by those who receive the initial increase in income. The simple multiplier is then unity, its minimum possible value.

In part (ii) the AE curve slopes upward but is still relatively flat (z is low). The increase in GDP to Y_2 is only slightly greater than the increase in autonomous expenditure that brought it about.

In part (iii) the AE function is quite steep (z is high). Now the increase in GDP to Y_3 is much larger than the increase in autonomous expenditure that brought it about. The simple multiplier is quite large.

Summary

Potential GDP and the GDP gap

■ Macroeconomics builds simple models of the economy as a whole to explain the determination of real GDP and the deviations of actual GDP from its potential or long-term equilibrium level.

■ The GDP gap is the difference between actual GDP and potential GDP. Macroeconomics explains deviations of actual from potential GDP. Growth theory explains the long-term trends in potential GDP.

Key assumptions

■ For simplicity we aggregate all industrial sectors into one, so the economy produces only one type of output good. We explain GDP determination through the major expenditure categories: private consumption, investment, government consumption, and net exports.

What determines aggregate expenditure?

■ Desired aggregate expenditure includes desired

consumption, desired investment, and desired government expenditures, plus desired net exports. It is the amount that economic agents want to spend on purchasing the national product. In this chapter we consider only consumption and investment.

■ A change in personal disposable income leads to a change in private consumption and saving. The responsiveness of these changes is measured by the marginal propensity to consume (*MPC*) and the marginal propensity to save (*MPS*), which are both positive and sum to one. This indicates that, by definition, all disposable income is either spent on consumption or saved.

■ A change in wealth tends to cause a change in the allocation of disposable income between consumption and saving. The change in consumption is positively related to the change in wealth, while the change in saving is negatively related to this change.

■ Investment depends, among other things, on real interest rates and business confidence. In our simple theory investment is treated as *autonomous*, or exogenous, as is the constant term in the consumption function, called *autonomous* consumption.

■ The part of consumption that responds to changes in income is called *induced* expenditure.

Equilibrium GDP

■ At the equilibrium level of GDP, purchasers wish to buy exactly the amount of national output that is being produced. At GDP above equilibrium, desired expenditure falls short of national output, and output will sooner or later be curtailed. At GDP below equilibrium, desired expenditure exceeds national output, and output will sooner or later be increased.

■ In a closed economy with no government, desired saving equals desired investment at equilibrium GDP.

■ Equilibrium GDP is represented graphically by the point at which the aggregate expenditure curve cuts the 45° line, that is, where total desired expenditure equals total output. This is the same level of GDP at which the saving function intersects the investment function.

Changes in GDP

■ With a constant price level, equilibrium GDP is increased by a rise in the desired consumption or investment expenditure that is associated with each level of national income. Equilibrium GDP is decreased by a fall in these desired expenditures.

■ The magnitude of the effect on GDP of shifts in autonomous expenditure is given by the multiplier. It is defined as $K = \Delta Y/\Delta A$, where ΔA is the change in autonomous expenditure.

■ The simple multiplier is the multiplier when the price level is constant. It is equal to $1/(1 - z)$, where z is the marginal propensity to spend out of national income. Thus the larger z is, the larger is the multiplier. It is a basic prediction of macroeconomics that the simple multiplier, relating £1 worth of increased spending on domestic output to the resulting increase in GDP, is greater than unity.

Topics for review

■ Aggregation across sectors
■ Actual and potential GDP
■ The GDP gap
■ Desired expenditure
■ Consumption function
■ Average and marginal propensities to consume and to save
■ Aggregate expenditure function
■ Marginal propensities to spend and not to spend
■ Equilibrium GDP at a given price level
■ Saving–investment balance
■ Shifts of, and movements along, expenditure curves
■ The effect on GDP of changes in desired expenditures
■ The simple multiplier
■ The size of the multiplier and slope of the *AE* curve

Questions for discussion

1 What do you understand by the term 'potential GDP'? What evidence would help to decide whether the current level of GDP is above or below its potential level?

2 Recalculate the data in Table 21.1 (after column 1) assuming that the consumption function is given by $C = 100 + 0.6Y$.

3 Work out the implications of the changes made in Question 2 for the *AE* function, and then determine the new equilibrium level of GDP.

4 What factors in addition to real interest rates are likely to be important determinants of investment by firms?

5 The consumption function is usually estimated using what are called *seasonally adjusted* data. What seasonal factors do you think would alter the relationship between disposable income and consumption at different times of the year?

6 Table 21.4 shows an equilibrium level of GDP of £1,750 million. Explain why there are no forces tending to move the economy from that level of GDP even though there is excess capacity in the economy. What could bring about an increase in that equilibrium level of GDP?

7 What would be the value of the multiplier for the following values of the *MPC* (assuming no government or foreign trade): (*a*) 0.4, (*b*) 0.75, (*c*) 0.95?

Appendix The multiplier: an algebraic approach

Basic algebra is all that is needed to derive the exact expression for the multiplier. Readers who feel at home with algebra may want to follow this derivation. Others can skip it and rely on the graphical and numerical arguments that have been given in the text.

First, we derive the equation for the AE curve. Aggregate expenditure is divided into autonomous expenditure, A, and induced expenditure, N. In the simple model of this chapter A is just equal to investment plus autonomous consumption. N is just equal to induced consumption.[17]

Thus we can write

$$AE = N + A. \qquad \text{(i)}$$

Because N is expenditure on domestically produced output that varies with income, we can write

$$N = zY, \qquad \text{(ii)}$$

where z is the marginal propensity to spend out of national income. (z is a positive number between zero and unity. In the simple model of this chapter, with no government and no foreign sector, it is equal to the marginal propensity to consume.) Substituting equation (ii) into equation (i) yields the equation of the AE curve:

$$AE = zY + A. \qquad \text{(iii)}$$

Now we write the equation of the 45° line,

$$AE = Y, \qquad \text{(iv)}$$

which states the equilibrium condition that desired aggregate expenditure equals national income. Equations (iii) and (iv) are two equations with two unknowns, AE and Y. To solve them, we substitute equation (iii) into equation (iv) to obtain

$$Y = zY + A. \qquad \text{(v)}$$

Subtracting zY from both sides yields

$$Y - zY = A. \qquad \text{(vi)}$$

Factoring out Y yields

$$Y(1 - z) = A. \qquad \text{(vii)}$$

Dividing through by $1 - z$ yields

$$Y = \frac{A}{1 - z}. \qquad \text{(viii)}$$

This tells us the equilibrium value of Y in terms of autonomous expenditures A and the propensity not to spend out of national income $(1 - z)$. Now consider a £1 increase in A. The expression $Y = A/(1 - z)$ tells us that if A changes by £1, the change in Y will be £$(1/(1 - z))$. Generally, for a change in autonomous spending of ΔA, the change in Y, which we call ΔY, will be

$$\Delta Y = \frac{\Delta A}{1 - z}. \qquad \text{(ix)}$$

Dividing through by ΔA gives the value of the multiplier, which we designate by K:

$$K = \frac{\Delta Y}{\Delta A} = \frac{1}{1 - z}. \qquad \text{(x)}$$

---

[17] When we add imports and government in the next chapter, N will include induced imports, and A will include government spending and exports. The derivation here is quite general, however. All that matters is that desired aggregate expenditure can be divided into one class of expenditure, N, that varies with income and another class, A, that does not.

Chapter 22
GDP in an Open Economy with Government

In this chapter we continue building a model of the determination of GDP. In building our model in Chapter 21, we maintained four simplifying, but temporary, assumptions —no government, no foreign trade, a fixed price level, and excess capacity. The current chapter relaxes the first two of these. The following chapter relaxes the last two.

Our task in this chapter, then, is to add first a government and then a foreign sector to our simple model. Adding the government sector allows us to study *fiscal policy*, the ability of the government to use its taxing and spending powers to affect the level of GDP. In an open economy net foreign demand for domestic output is an important source of final expenditure, so it has to be included in any complete treatment of the expenditure components of GDP. After adding the government and the foreign trade sector, we examine how these additions change both the structure of the model and its behaviour in response to changes in autonomous expenditures.

As we proceed, it is important to remember that the key elements of our theory of GDP determination are unchanged. The most important of these, which will remain true even after incorporating government and the foreign sector, are restated here.

1. Aggregate desired expenditure can be divided into autonomous expenditure and induced expenditure. Induced expenditure is expenditure that depends on the level of national income and, thus, on GDP.

2. The equilibrium level of GDP (national income and output) is the level at which the sum of autonomous and induced desired expenditures is equal to the level of output. Graphically, this is where the aggregate expenditure line intersects the 45° line.

3. The simple multiplier measures the change in equilibrium GDP that takes place in response to a unit change in autonomous domestic expenditure, with the price level held constant.

Recall that the expenditure-based measure of GDP is made up of private consumption, investment, government consumption expenditure, and net exports. We have built a model of GDP determination which includes private consumption and investment. We are about to extend this model to include government consumption and net exports. Recall also that 'national income', 'national output', and 'GDP' are all equivalent terms for our purposes.

Government spending and taxes

Government spending and taxation policies affect equilibrium GDP in two important ways. First, government expenditure is part of autonomous expenditure in our model; that is, it is an exogenous element of spending in the economy. Second, in deriving disposable income, taxes must be subtracted from national income, and government transfer payments must be added. Because disposable income determines private consumption expenditure, the relationship between desired private consumption and national income becomes more complicated when a government is added. A government's plans for taxes and spending define its *fiscal policy*, which has important

effects on the level of GDP in both the short and the long runs.

Government spending

In Chapter 20 we distinguished between *government consumption expenditure on goods and services* and government *transfer payments*. The distinction bears repeating here. Government consumption is part of GDP. When the government hires a civil servant, buys a paper clip, or purchases fuel for the navy, it is directly adding to the demands on the economy's current output of goods and services. Thus, desired government purchases, *G*, are part of aggregate expenditure. As explained in Chapter 21, in our model we assume government consumption spending buys the output from the single industrial sector. This makes government spending have the same effect on GDP as any other component of autonomous expenditures.

The other part of government spending, transfer payments, also affects desired aggregate expenditure, but only indirectly. Consider, for example, state pensions or unemployment benefit. These are payments (transfers) made by government to individuals, who will spend at least some of the money. Since that expenditure is recorded as personal consumption, we do not want to count it twice by recording it under *G* as well. Government transfer payments affect aggregate expenditure only through the effect that these payments have on personal *disposable* income. Transfer payments increase disposable income, and increases in disposable income, via the consumption function, increase desired consumption expenditure.

This distinction (between transfers and government consumption) is important when it comes to issues such as determining the amount of GDP that is accounted for by government. Measuring the size of government to include transfers makes it look as though government's share of GDP is much bigger than it really is. However, looking only at *G* makes the government's revenue needs look smaller than they are, since transfers must be financed by taxes or borrowing, just as expenditures on goods and services must be. In what follows government spending always excludes transfers, unless the contrary is clearly stated.

Tax revenues

Tax revenues may be thought of as negative transfer payments in their effect on desired aggregate expenditure. Tax payments reduce disposable income relative to national income; transfers raise disposable income relative to national income. For the purpose of calculating the effect of government policy on desired consumption expenditure, it is the net effect of the two that matters.

We define **net taxes** to be total tax revenues received by the government minus total transfer payments made by the government, and we denote net taxes as *T*. (For convenience, when we use the term 'taxes', we will mean *net* taxes unless we explicitly state otherwise.) Since transfer payments are smaller than total taxes, net taxes are positive, and personal disposable income is less than national income. Personal disposable income was 69 per cent of GDP at market prices in 1997.

The budget balance

The **budget balance** is the difference between total government revenue and total government expenditure, or equivalently net taxes minus government spending, *T*– *G*. When revenues exceed expenditure, the government is running a **budget surplus.** The government will then reduce the national debt, since the surplus funds will be used to pay off old debt. When expenditures exceed revenues, as they have for most of the period since the Second World War (1969–70 and 1988–9 were the only exceptions in the United Kingdom), the government is running a **budget deficit.** The government must then add to the national debt, since it must borrow to cover its deficit.[1] When the budget surplus (and deficit) is zero, the government has a **balanced budget.** Since the budget deficit is simply a negative budget surplus, we generally use 'budget surplus' to cover both cases, so bear in mind that the budget surplus can be negative.

Tax and expenditure functions

We treat government expenditure as autonomous. The government is assumed to decide on how much it wishes to spend in real terms and to hold to these plans whatever the level of GDP. We also treat *tax rates* as autonomous. The government sets its tax rates and does not vary them as GDP varies. This makes *tax revenues* endogenous. As GDP rises with given tax rates, the tax revenue will rise. For example, when incomes rise, people pay more total tax, even though tax rates are unchanged.

Table 22.1 and Figure 22.1 illustrate these assumptions with a specific example. They show the size of the government's surplus when its desired purchases (*G*) are constant at £170 million and its net tax revenues are equal to 10 per

Table 22.1 The budget surplus function (£ million)

GDP (*Y*)	Government expenditure (*G*)	Net taxes (*T* = 0.1*Y*)	Government surplus (*T* – *G*)
500	170	50	−120
1,000	170	100	−70
1,750	170	175	5
2,000	170	200	30
3,000	170	300	130
4,000	170	400	230

The budget surplus is negative at low levels of GDP and becomes positive at high levels of GDP. The table shows that the size of the budget surplus increases with GDP, given constant expenditure and constant tax rates. For example, when GDP rises by £1,000 million, the deficit falls or the surplus rises by £100 million.

[1] It does this by selling government bonds (known as 'gilts' in the UK). When the government runs a surplus, it uses the excess revenue to purchase outstanding government bonds. The stock of outstanding bonds is termed the *national* or *public debt* (public debt is the debt of the entire public sector, which includes local authorities and nationalized industries; national debt is the debt of the central government only).

Figure 22.1 Budget surplus function

The budget surplus function increases as GDP increases. This figure plots the *T – G* column from Table 22.1. Notice that the slope of the surplus function is equal to the income tax rate of 0.1.

cent of GDP (national income). Notice that the government budget surplus (or public saving) increases with GDP. This relationship occurs because net tax revenues rise with GDP but, by assumption, government expenditure does not. The slope of the budget surplus function is just equal to the income tax rate. The *position* of the function is determined by fiscal policy, as we discuss later in this chapter.[2]

For given tax rates the government budget surplus (public saving) increases as GDP rises and falls as GDP falls.

[2] The numerical example used here is designed only to illustrate the principles of GDP determination developed in this chapter. To avoid the appearance of direct applicability of overly simplified models, we have deliberately chosen not to use 'realistic' numbers. The example produces GDP of £2,000 million, whereas UK money GDP in 1997 was around £800,000 million.

Net exports

The UK's foreign trade sector is significant in relation to its GDP. Exports of goods and services in 1997 were just over 28 per cent of GDP at market prices. Although the total volume of trade is important for many purposes, such as determining the amount by which a country gains from trade (see Chapter 34), the balance between exports and imports (the current account balance) is particularly important in determining GDP.

The net export function

In macroeconomics we are interested in how the balance of trade responds to changes in GDP, the price level, and the exchange rate. Our theory covers trade in goods *and services*. The effects on GDP of selling a service to a foreigner are identical to those of selling a physical commodity (recall that we have only one type of product in our economy, and that all desired expenditures are treated as demands for this product).

Exports depend on spending decisions made by foreign consumers or overseas firms that purchase domestic goods and services. We assume, therefore, that exports are determined by factors outside of the home economy. They are autonomous, or exogenous, expenditures from the point of view of the determination of domestic GDP.

Imports, however, depend on the spending decisions of domestic residents. Most categories of expenditure have an import content; British-made cars, for example, use large quantities of imported components and raw materials in their manufacture. Thus imports rise when the other categories of expenditure rise. Because consump-

tion rises when the income of domestic consumers rises, imports of foreign-produced consumption goods, and of materials that go into the production of domestically produced consumption goods, also rise with domestic income. Total domestic (national) income, of course, rises identically with GDP.

Desired net exports are negatively related to GDP because of the positive relationship between desired imports and GDP.

This negative relationship between net exports and GDP is called the *net export function*. Data for a hypothetical economy with constant exports and with imports that are 25 per cent of GDP are given in Table 22.2 and illustrated in Figure 22.2. In this example exports form the autonomous component and imports form the induced component of the desired net export function. The formulation in the table implicitly assumes that all imports are for final consumption. Imports rise when income rises, but imports do not change when *other* categories of autonomous expenditure change, so there is no direct import content of *G*, *I*, and *X*. This simplification will prove useful in our development of the determination of equilibrium income and does not affect the essentials of the theory.

Shifts in the net export function

We have seen that the net export function relates net exports $(X - IM)$, which we also denote by *NX*, to GDP. It is drawn on the assumption that everything that affects net

Table 22.2 The net export function (£ million)

GDP (Y)	Exports (X)	Imports (IM = 0.25 Y)	Net exports
0	540	0	540
1,000	540	250	190
2,160	540	540	0
3,000	540	750	−210
4,000	540	1,000	−460
5,000	540	1,250	−710

Net exports fall as GDP rises. We assume that exports are constant and that imports are 25 per cent of GDP. In this case net exports are positive at low levels of GDP and negative at high levels of GDP.

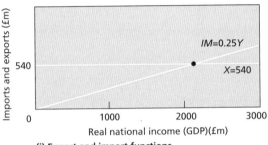

(i) Export and import functions

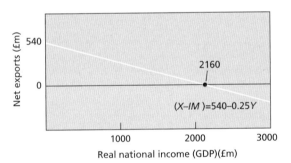

(ii) Net export function

Figure 22.2 The net export function

Net exports, defined as the difference between exports and imports, are inversely related to the level of GDP. In part (i) exports are constant at £540 million, while imports rise with GDP. Therefore net exports, shown in part (ii), decline with GDP. The figure is based on hypothetical data in Table 22.2. With GDP equal to £2,160 million, imports are equal to exports at £540 million and net exports are zero. For levels of GDP below £2,160 million, imports are less than exports, and hence net exports are positive. For levels of GDP above £2,160 million, imports are greater than exports, and hence net exports are negative.

exports, except domestic GDP, remains constant. The major factors that must be held constant are foreign GDP, relative international price levels, and the exchange rate. A change in any of these factors will affect the amount of net exports that will occur at each level of GDP and hence will shift the net export function.

Notice that anything that affects domestic exports will change the values in the 'Exports' column in Table 22.2 and so will shift the net export function parallel to itself, upward if exports increase and downward if exports decrease. Also notice that anything that affects the proportion of income that home consumers wish to spend on imports will change the values in the 'Imports' column in the table and thus will change the slope of the net export function by making imports more or less responsive to changes in domestic income. What factors will cause such shifts?

Foreign GDP An increase in foreign GDP, other things being equal, will lead to an increase in the quantity of domestic-produced goods demanded by foreign countries, that is, to an increase in our exports. This is because as foreign GDP rises, foreign residents will receive higher incomes and they will buy more of all goods, including imports. But foreign imports are domestic exports. Because the same amount more is sold at each level of domestic GDP, the increase is in the constant of the domestic net export function, X. This causes NX to shift upward, parallel to its original position. A fall in foreign GDP leads to a parallel downward shift in the net export function.

Relative international prices Any change in the prices of home-produced goods relative to those of foreign goods will cause both imports and exports to change. This will shift the net export function.

Consider first a rise in domestic prices relative to prices in foreign countries. On the one hand foreigners will now see domestic-produced goods as more expensive relative both to goods produced in their own country and to goods imported from other countries. As a result domestic exports will fall. On the other hand domestic residents will see imports from foreign countries become cheaper relative to the prices of home-produced goods. As a result they will buy more foreign goods, and imports will rise. Both of these responses will cause the net export function to shift downwards and change its slope, as shown in Figure 22.3.

Second, consider the opposite case of a fall in UK prices relative to prices of foreign-made goods. On the one hand potential UK exports will now look cheaper in foreign markets relative both to their home-produced goods and to goods imported from third countries. As a result UK exports will rise. On the other hand the same change in relative prices—British-made goods become cheaper relative to foreign-made goods—will cause UK imports to fall. Thus the net export function will shift upwards, in exactly the opposite way to the movement in Figure 22.3.

What circumstances will cause relative international prices to change? Two important causes of changes in competitiveness, for a country as a whole, are international differences in inflation rates and changes in exchange rates.

Consider inflation rates first, and assume that the UK is

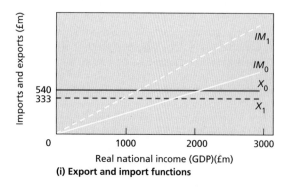

(i) Export and import functions

(ii) Net export function

Figure 22.3 Shifts in the net export function

An upward shift in imports and/or a downward shift in exports shifts the net export function downward. A rise in the domestic price level relative to foreign price levels, or a rise in the exchange rate, lowers exports from X_0 to X_1 and raises the import function from IM_0 to IM_1. This shifts the net export function downward from $(X-IM)_0$ to $(X-IM)_1$. (In the figure imports are 25 per cent of Y along IM_0 and are assumed to rise to a third of Y when domestic goods become more expensive relative to foreign goods, while exports fall from £540 million to £333 million.)

the home country. If the sterling exchange rate remains constant, UK prices will rise relative to foreign prices if the UK inflation rate is higher than the inflation rates in other major trading countries. In contrast, UK prices will fall relative to foreign prices if the UK inflation rate is lower than the rates in other major trading countries.

Now consider the exchange rate. Holding domestic and foreign price levels constant, a depreciation of sterling will make imports more expensive for domestic residents and UK exports cheaper for foreigners. This is because UK residents will get less foreign currency for each pound sterling and foreigners will get more pounds for each unit of their own currency. Both foreigners and domestic consumers will shift expenditure towards the UK-produced goods, which have become cheaper relative to foreign goods. The net export function will thus shift upward.

An appreciation of sterling (holding price levels constant) has the opposite effect. It makes UK goods relatively expensive, thus shifting the net export function downward.[3]

The results of this important chain of reasoning are summarized below (continuing with the UK home country example).

1. UK prices rise relative to foreign prices if either the UK inflation rate exceeds the rate in other major trading countries (with exchange rates fixed) or the pound sterling appreciates (with price levels constant). This discourages exports and encourages imports, causing the net export function to shift downwards.

2. UK prices fall relative to foreign prices if either the UK inflation rate is less than the rates in competitor countries (with exchange rates fixed) or the pound sterling depreciates (with price levels constant). This encourages exports and discourages imports, causing the net export function to shift upwards.

Equilibrium GDP

We are now ready to see how equilibrium GDP is determined in our new model that includes a government and a foreign sector. As in Chapter 21 we can determine the equilibrium in two ways which come to the same thing in the end: by relating output and expenditure, and by relating saving and investment.

The income–expenditure approach

In Chapter 21 we determined equilibrium GDP by finding the level of GDP where desired aggregate expenditure is

equal to national output. The addition of government and the foreign sector changes the calculations that we must make but does not alter the basic principles that are involved. Our first step is to derive a new aggregate ex-

---

[3] A depreciation of sterling which is exactly proportional to the excess of UK inflation over foreign inflation will leave the relative price of UK exports and imports unchanged. This would be referred to as a constant *real exchange rate*, or as preserving purchasing power parity (PPP). The real exchange rate is the relative price of home- and foreign-produced goods. It is also referred to as 'competitiveness' or the 'terms of trade'. A rise in the real exchange rate (fall in competitiveness) shifts the net export function down because it lowers exports and increases imports at each level of GDP. These concepts are discussed more fully in Chapter 28.

penditure function that incorporates the effects of government consumption and foreign trade.

Relating desired consumption to national income

Our theory of GDP determination requires that we relate each of the components of aggregate expenditure to national income, Y. Personal income taxes cause personal disposable income to differ from national income (by the proportion of income taxation net of transfers). We simply assume that disposable income is always 90 per cent of national income.[4] Thus whatever the relationship between C and Y_d, we can always substitute $0.9Y$ for Y_d. For example, if changes in consumption were always 80 per cent of changes in Y_d, changes in consumption would always be 72 per cent (80 per cent of 90 per cent) of changes in Y.

Table 22.3 illustrates how we can write desired consumption as a function of Y as well as of Y_d. We can then derive the marginal response of consumption to changes in Y by determining the proportion of any change in *national income (GDP)* that goes to a change in desired consumption.

The marginal response of consumption to changes in national income ($\Delta C/\Delta Y$) is equal to the marginal propensity to consume out of disposable income ($\Delta C/\Delta Y_d$) multiplied by the fraction of national income (GDP) that becomes personal disposable income ($\Delta Y_d/\Delta Y$).

Table 22.3 Consumption as a function of disposable income and national income (GDP) (£ million)

National income (GDP) (Y)	Disposable income ($Y_d = 0.9Y$)	Desired private consumption ($C = 100 + 0.8Y_d$)
100	90	172
1,000	900	820
2,000	1,800	1,540
3,000	2,700	2,260
4,000	3,600	2,980

If desired private consumption depends on disposable income, which in turn depends on national income, desired consumption can be written as a function of either income concept. The second column shows deductions of 10 per cent of any level of national income to arrive at disposable income. Deductions of 10 per cent of Y imply that the remaining 90 per cent of Y becomes disposable income. The third column shows consumption as £100 million plus 80 per cent of disposable income.

By relating the second and third columns, one sees consumption as a function of disposable income. By relating the first and third columns, one sees the derived relationship between consumption and national income. In this example the change in consumption in response to a change in disposable income (i.e. *MPC*) is 0.8, and the change in consumption in response to a change in national income is 0.72.

This table shows how desired consumption expenditure varies as national income varies, including the effects of taxes and transfer payments ($C = 100 + 0.72Y$; arrived at from $C = 100 + 0.8Y_d$ by substituting $0.9Y$ for Y_d). This equation is part of the aggregate expenditure function.

The aggregate expenditure function

In order to determine the equilibrium level of GDP, we start by defining the aggregate expenditure function,

$$AE = C + I + G + NX.$$

Table 22.4 illustrates the calculation of this function. It shows a schedule of desired expenditure for each of the components of aggregate expenditure, and it shows total desired *aggregate* expenditure at each level of national income (GDP). Figure 22.4 shows this aggregate expenditure function in graphical form.

The marginal propensity to spend

The slope of the aggregate expenditure function is the *marginal propensity to spend* on national output (z). With the addition of taxes and net exports, however, the marginal propensity to spend is no longer equal to the marginal propensity to consume.

Suppose that the economy produces £1 of extra income (and output) and that the response to this is governed by the relationships in Tables 22.1 and 22.2, as summarized in Table 22.4. Since £0.10 is collected by the government as net taxes, £0.90 is converted into disposable income, and 80 per cent of this amount (£0.72) becomes consumption expenditure. However, import expenditure also rises by £0.25, so expenditure on domestic goods, that is, aggregate expenditure, rises by only £0.47. Thus z, the marginal propensity to spend out of national income (GDP), is 0.47. What is not spent on domestic output includes the £0.10 in taxes, the £0.18 of disposable income that is saved, and the £0.25 of import expenditure, for a total of £0.53. Hence the marginal propensity not to spend, $(1 - z)$, is $1 - 0.47 = 0.53$.

Determining equilibrium GDP

The logic of GDP determination in our (now more complicated) hypothetical economy is exactly the same as in the closed economy without government discussed in Chapter 21. We have added two new components of aggregate expenditure, G and $(X - IM)$. We have also made the calculation of desired private consumption expenditure more complicated: taxes must be subtracted from national income in order to determine personal disposable income. However, *equilibrium GDP is still the level of*

---

[4] In this case T, desired net taxes, would be given by the function $T = 0.1Y$. Recall that for simplicity we ignore indirect taxes.

Table 22.4 The aggregate expenditure function (£ million)

National income (GDP) (Y)	Desired private consumption expenditure ($C = 100 + 0.72Y$)	Desired investment expenditure ($I = 250$)	Desired government expenditure ($G = 170$)	Desired net export expenditure ($IM = 540 - 0.25Y$)	Desired aggregate expenditure ($AE = C + I + G + (X - IM)$)
0	100	250	170	540	1,060
100	172	250	170	515	1,107
500	460	250	170	315	1,195
1,000	820	250	170	290	1,530
2,000	1,540	250	170	40	**2,000**
3,000	2,260	250	170	−210	2,470
4,000	2,980	250	170	−460	2,940
5,000	3,700	250	170	−710	3,410

The aggregate expenditure function is the sum of desired private consumption, investment, government, and net export expenditures. The autonomous components of desired aggregate expenditure are desired investment, desired government spending, desired export expenditure, and the constant term in desired consumption (first row). These sum to £1,060 million in the above example. The induced components are the second terms in desired consumption expenditure ($0.72Y$) and desired imports ($0.25Y$).

The marginal response of consumption to a change in national income is 0.72, calculated as the product of the marginal propensity to consume (0.8) and the fraction of national income that becomes disposable income (0.9). The marginal response of desired aggregate expenditure to a change in national income, $\Delta AE/\Delta Y$, is 0.47.

GDP at which desired aggregate expenditure equals national output (and income).

The aggregate expenditure function can be used directly to determine equilibrium GDP. In Table 22.4 the equilibrium is £2,000 billion. When GDP is equal to £2,000 billion, it is also equal to desired aggregate expenditure.

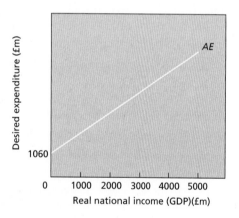

Figure 22.4 An aggregate expenditure curve

The aggregate expenditure curve relates total desired expenditure to national income. The *AE* curve in the figure plots the data from the first and last columns of Table 22.4. Its intercept shows £1,060 million of autonomous expenditure (£100 million autonomous consumption plus £250 million investment plus £170 million government spending plus £540 million autonomous net exports). Its slope is the marginal propensity to spend (which, following the calculations in Table 22.4, is 0.47 in this case).

Suppose that GDP is less than its equilibrium amount. The forces leading back to equilibrium are exactly the same as those described on pages 368–70 of Chapter 21. When domestic consumers, firms, foreign consumers, and governments try to spend at their desired amounts, they will try to purchase more goods and services than the economy is currently producing. Thus some of the desired expenditure must either be frustrated or take the form of purchases of inventories of goods that were produced in the past. As firms see that they are (or could be) selling more than they are producing, they will increase production, thereby increasing the level of national output (and income).

The opposite sequence of events occurs when national output is greater than the level of aggregate desired expenditure at that level of GDP. Now the total of personal consumption, investment, government spending, and net foreign demand for the economy's output is less than the national product. Firms will be unable to sell all of their output. Their unsold stocks will be rising, and they will not let this happen indefinitely. They will seek to reduce the level of output until it equals the level of sales, and GDP (national output and income) will fall.

Finally, when national output is just equal to desired aggregate expenditure (£2,000 billion in Table 22.4), there is no pressure for output to change. Private consumption, investment, government consumption, and net exports just add up to the national product. Firms are producing exactly the quantity of goods and services that purchasers want to buy, given the level of income.

Equilibrium GDP is determined where desired aggregate

expenditure equals national output. In our extended model aggregate expenditure includes private consumption, investment, government consumption, and net exports.

Graphical exposition Figure 22.5 illustrates the determination of equilibrium GDP and the behaviour of the economy when it is not in equilibrium. The line labelled '*AE*' is simply the aggregate expenditure function shown in Figure 22.4. The slope of *AE* is the marginal propensity to spend out of national income (0.47 in our example). Recall that *AE* plots the behaviour of desired purchases. It shows demand for the domestic product at each level of national income (GDP). (The *AE* curve is sometimes referred to as the 'aggregate demand curve' in this context. However, we reserve this term for another, related construct that we use in the next chapter, once we have permitted the price level to be variable.)

The line labelled '*AE = Y*' (the 45° line) depicts the equilibrium condition that desired aggregate expenditure be equal to actual national output (and income). Any point on this line *could* be an equilibrium, but only one is. Equilibrium occurs where behaviour (as depicted by the *AE* function) is consistent with equilibrium (as depicted by *AE = Y*). At the equilibrium level of GDP desired ex-

penditure is just equal to national output (GDP) and is, therefore, just sufficient to purchase the total domestic product.

The augmented saving–investment approach

An equivalent way of determining equilibrium GDP is analogous to finding the point where desired saving equals desired investment. Finding the level of income where $S = I$ was appropriate in Chapter 21, where we were dealing with a closed economy with no government. Now we have to take account of government as well as private saving, and net exports that provide an injection of spending which plays a similar role to investment.

Additional injections and leakages Saving and investment must be equal for GDP to be in equilibrium, as this provides a balance of inflows and outflows (injections and leakages). It may be helpful to review both the hydraulic analogue in Box 21.1 on page 370 and the circular flow of income and expenditure, illustrated in Box 20.3 on page 341, at this stage. The principles involved are unchanged. Now, however, we have two additional sources of leakages and two additional sources of injections.

In Chapter 21 saving was the only leakage of expenditure from the circular flow. The marginal propensity to save told us how much was not spent out of each additional £1 of income received. Now we add personal income taxes. These are levied on individuals' gross incomes, and so they also represent a proportion of income earned that cannot be spent. The second additional leakage is imports. Imports are a leakage because they create demand for foreign output. This does not generate domestic income.

Investment was the only injection in our model in Chapter 21. In this chapter we have added government spending. This is received as income by the private sector, and this extra income leads to further spending as before. Similarly, export demand comes from other countries, but it generates domestic incomes. Hence, export demand is our second new injection.

The condition for GDP to be in equilibrium is now that the sum of desired injections should equal the sum of desired leakages. We can write this condition as an equation, with the sum of all leakages (saving, S, plus taxes, T, plus imports, IM) equal to the sum of all injections (investment, I, plus government spending, G, plus exports, X):

$$S + T + IM = I + G + X.$$

An equivalent equilibrium condition to $AE = Y$ for the determination of equilibrium GDP is that injections (investment plus government spending plus exports) must equal leakages (saving plus income taxes plus imports).

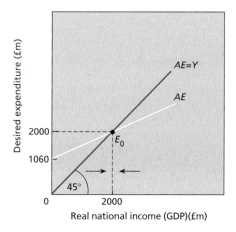

Figure 22.5 Equilibrium GDP

Equilibrium GDP occurs at E_0, where the desired aggregate expenditure line intersects the 45° line. Here the aggregate expenditure line is taken from Table 22.4; autonomous expenditure is £1,060 million, and the slope of *AE* is 0.47. If real GDP is below £2,000 million, desired aggregate expenditure will exceed national output, and production will rise. This is shown by the arrow to the left of $Y = £2,000$ million. If GDP is above £2,000 million, desired aggregate expenditure will be less than national output, and production will fall. This is shown by the arrow to the right of $Y = £2,000$ million. Only when real GDP is £2,000 million will desired aggregate expenditure equal real national output.

Graphical exposition In order to illustrate the determination of GDP via the equality of injections and leakages, it is convenient to rearrange the above equation. The graphical expression is made simpler, and the economic explanation more intuitive.

Subtracting G and IM from both sides of the above equation gives

$$S + (T - G) = I + (X - IM).$$

The brackets do not change the meaning of anything, but they do identify two terms we are already familiar with. $(T - G)$ is the government budget surplus. In this context it can be thought of as public sector (government) saving. Since S is private saving, $S + (T - G)$ is total domestic saving, or national saving. $(X - IM)$ is our old friend net exports. When there is no net income from abroad—that is, when GNI (or GNP) and GDP are equal (as was approximately true in the United Kingdom in 1997)—net exports equal the net accumulation of claims on foreigners. This is because if we sell to foreigners more than we buy from them, we must either acquire a new foreign asset or reduce some foreign liability. Hence net exports cause the net acquisition of foreign assets, or overseas investment. I is domestic investment, so $I + (X - IM)$ is domestic plus overseas investment, or national asset formation. Thus, the equation $S + (T - G) = I + (X - IM)$ can be interpreted as a generalization of the condition that saving equals investment, since it says that national saving equals national asset formation.

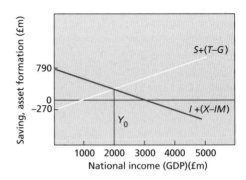

Figure 22.6   National saving and national asset formation
The economy is in equilibrium at Y_0, where desired national saving, $S + (T - G)$, equals desired national asset formation, $I + (X - IM)$. To the left of Y_0 desired national asset formation exceeds desired national saving. This implies that desired aggregate expenditure exceeds national output. Firms will respond to the imbalance by producing more, moving the economy towards equilibrium. To the right of Y_0 desired national asset formation is less than desired national saving, and aggregate expenditure is less than national output. Firms will cut back on output in order to avoid accumulating excess inventories, and the economy will move towards equilibrium.

Figure 22.6 illustrates how GDP is determined by the intersection of the national saving and national asset formation schedules. Notice that this is exactly the same level of GDP at which $AE = Y$.

Changes in aggregate expenditure

Changes in any of the autonomous components of planned aggregate expenditure will cause changes in equilibrium GDP. In Chapter 21 we investigated the consequences of shifts in the consumption function and in the investment function. Here we discuss fiscal policy—the effects of government spending and taxes. We also consider shifts in the net export function. First, we show that the simple multiplier is reduced by the presence of taxes and the marginal propensity to import.

The simple multiplier revisited In Chapter 21 we saw that the *simple multiplier*, the amount by which equilibrium GDP changes when autonomous expenditure changes by £1, was equal to $1/(1 - z)$. In the example considered throughout Chapter 21, z, the marginal propensity to spend, was equal to 0.8, and the multiplier was equal to 5, or $1/(0.2)$. In the example that we have developed in this chapter, with a marginal propensity to import of 0.25 and a marginal (net) income tax rate of 0.1, the marginal pro-

pensity to spend is 0.47. (Ten per cent of a £1 increase in autonomous spending goes to taxes, leaving 90p of disposable income. With a marginal propensity to consume of 0.8, 72p is spent. Of this, 25p is spent on imports, leaving a total of 47p to be spent on domestically produced consumption goods.) Thus $(1 - z)$ is (0.53), and the simple multiplier is $1/(0.53) = 1.89$.

Fiscal policy

Fiscal Policy involves the use of government spending and tax policies to influence total desired expenditure in order to achieve any specific goal set by the government.

Since government expenditure increases aggregate desired expenditure and taxation decreases it, the *directions* of the required changes in spending and taxation are generally easy to determine once we know the direction of the desired change in GDP. But the *timing*, *magnitude*, and *mixture* of the changes pose more difficult issues.

Any policy that attempts to stabilize GDP at or near any desired level (usually potential GDP) is called **stabilization policy.** Here we deal only with the basic ideas of stabilization through fiscal policy. We will return to a more detailed discussion of fiscal policy, along with monetary policy, in Chapter 27, after we have added a monetary sector to our model.

The basic idea of stabilization policy follows from what we have already learned. A reduction in tax rates or an increase in government expenditure shifts the *AE* curve upward, causing an increase in equilibrium GDP. An increase in tax rates or a decrease in government expenditure shifts the *AE* curve downward, causing a decrease in equilibrium GDP.

If the government has some target level of GDP, it can use its taxation and expenditures as instruments to push the economy towards that target. First, suppose the economy is in a serious recession. The government would like to increase GDP. The appropriate fiscal tools are to raise expenditures and/or to lower tax rates. Second, suppose the economy is 'overheated'. In the next two chapters we will study what this means in detail. In the meantime we observe that an 'overheated' economy has such a high level of GDP (relative to potential) that shortages are pushing up prices and causing inflation. Without worrying too much about the details, just assume that the current level of GDP is higher than the target level that the government judges to be appropriate. What should the government do? The fiscal tools at its command are to lower government expenditure and to raise tax rates, both of which have a depressing effect on GDP.

The proposition that governments can avoid recessions by deliberately stimulating aggregate demand created a major revolution in economic thought. This is still known as the Keynesian revolution. We have already done enough macroeconomics to understand what this was all about. According to the theory we have developed so far, an economy can reach an equilibrium level of GDP well below its full-employment or potential level. According to Keynesian theory, governments could use fiscal policy to increase aggregate expenditure by increasing government spending or reducing taxes (or both).

The expenditure model of national income and output determination predicts that GDP can get stuck at a level below its full potential. It also suggests how fiscal policy might be used to return an economy to its potential level of GDP.

Now let us look in a little more detail at how this might work out. Bear in mind, however, that we are still dealing with a special case in which prices are fixed and there is excess capacity, so we are just looking at how our present model works, not yet at how the real world works.

Changes in government spending

Suppose the government decides to increase its road-building programme by £10 million a year.[5] Desired government spending (*G*) would rise by £10 million at every level of income, shifting *AE* upwards by the same amount. By how much would equilibrium GDP change? This can be calculated, in our simple model, using the multiplier. Government purchases are part of autonomous expenditure, so a *change* in government consumption of ΔG will lead to a *change* in equilibrium GDP of the multiplier times ΔG. In this numerical example equilibrium GDP would rise by £10 million times the simple multiplier, or £18.9 million. Figure 22.7 shows the effect on GDP of an

---

[5] It does not matter what we assume the extra expenditure goes on. In our model it is always spent on the output of the single homogeneous industrial sector. Notice also that the value of the multiplier used in this section is hypothetical and based on the numerical example in Table 22.4.

Figure 22.7 The effect of a change in government spending

A change in government spending changes GDP by shifting the *AE* line parallel to its initial position. The figure shows the effect of an increase in government spending. The initial level of aggregate expenditure is AE_0, and the equilibrium level of GDP is Y_0, with desired expenditures e_0. An increase in government spending shifts aggregate expenditure upwards to AE_1. As a result GDP rises to Y_1, at which level desired expenditures are e_1. The increase in GDP from Y_0 to Y_1 is equal to the increase in government spending times the multiplier.

A reduction in government spending can be analysed in the same figure if we start with aggregate expenditure function AE_1 and GDP Y_1. A reduction in government spending shifts the *AE* function downwards from AE_1 to AE_0 and, as a result, equilibrium GDP falls from Y_1 to Y_0. The fall is equal to the change in government spending times the multiplier.

increase in government spending. It shows an upward parallel shift of the aggregate expenditure function, and a resulting increase in GDP. The same analysis could be applied equally to an increase in any other autonomous expenditure, such as investment or exports.

Reducing government expenditure has the opposite effect of shifting the AE function downwards, parallel to itself, and reducing equilibrium GDP. For example, if the government were to spend £2 million less on new roads, equilibrium GDP would fall by £2 million times the simple multiplier, or £3.78 million.

A change in government spending, in this model, changes the equilibrium level of GDP by the size of the spending change times the simple multiplier.

Changes in tax rates

If tax rates change, the relationship between disposable income and national income changes. As a result the relationship between desired consumption expenditure and national income also changes. For any given level of national income there will be a different level of disposable income and thus a different level of consumption. Consequently, a change in tax rates will also cause a change in z, the marginal propensity to spend out of national income.

Consider a decrease in the tax rate. If the government decreases its rate of income tax so that it collects 5p less out of every £1 of national income, then disposable income rises in relation to national income. Thus consumption, which depends on disposable income, will also rise at every level of national income. This results in a non-parallel upward shift of the AE curve, that is, an increase in the slope of the curve, as shown in Figure 22.8. The result of this shift will be a rise in equilibrium GDP.

A rise in the tax rate has the opposite effect. It causes a given percentage decrease in disposable income, and hence consumption expenditure, at each level of national income. This results in a (non-parallel) downward shift of the AE curve and thus decreases the level of equilibrium GDP.

Tax rates and the multiplier We have seen that the *simple multiplier* is equal to the reciprocal of one minus the marginal propensity to spend out of national income. That is, the multiplier equals $1/(1 - z)$. The simple multiplier tells us how much equilibrium GDP changes when autonomous expenditure changes by £1 and there is no change in prices.

When tax rates change, the multiplier also changes. Suppose that *MPC* is 0.8 and the tax rate *falls* by 5p per pound of national income. This would increase the marginal propensity to spend by 4p per pound of national income. (Disposable income would rise by 5p per pound at each level of national income, and consumption would

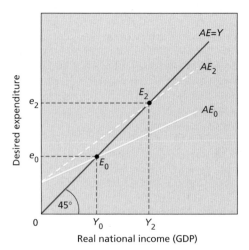

Figure 22.8 The effect of changing the tax rate
Changing the tax rate changes equilibrium GDP by changing the slope of the AE curve. A reduction in the tax rate pivots the AE curve from AE_0 to AE_2. The new curve has a steeper slope, because the lower tax rate withdraws a smaller amount of national income from the desired consumption flow. Equilibrium GDP rises from Y_0 to Y_2, because at every level of national income desired consumption, and hence aggregate expenditure, is higher. If we take AE_2 and Y_2 to be the initial equilibrium, an increase in tax rates will reduce the slope of the AE curve, thereby reducing equilibrium GDP, as shown by AE_0 and Y_0.

rise by the marginal propensity to consume, 0.8, times 5p, which is 4p.) The increase in the value of z, the marginal propensity to spend, would cause the multiplier to rise, making equilibrium GDP more responsive to changes in autonomous expenditure from any source. In our example the multiplier has gone up from 1.89 to 1.96 ($(1 - z)$ has fallen from 0.53 to 0.51).

The lower is the income tax rate, the larger is the simple multiplier.

GDP may change as a result of a shift in any of the other exogenous components of expenditure—net exports, investment, and autonomous consumption. An increase in any of these would increase GDP by the shift times the multiplier, as illustrated (for the case of a government spending increase) in Figure 22.7. An increase in any exogenous expenditure shifts the AE line vertically upwards by the amount of the expenditure increase. The new intersection with the 45° line determines the new level of GDP, and its increase is measured relative to the original position on the horizontal axis. A reduction in any of these exogenous expenditures would shift the AE line downwards by the amount of the fall in spending.

Changes that would alter the slope of the AE line are a shift in the marginal propensity to consume, a shift in the rate of income tax, and a shift in the propensity to import. A fall in the marginal propensity to save (hence a rise in *MPC*, the marginal propensity to consume), a fall in the income tax rate, and a fall in the propensity to import all make the *AE* line steeper and increase the multiplier, as illustrated in Figure 22.8. A rise in any of these three has the opposite effect.

Balanced budget changes

Another policy available to the government is to make a balanced budget change by altering spending and taxes equally. Say the government increases tax rates enough to raise an extra £100 million that it then uses to purchase goods and services. Aggregate expenditure would remain unchanged if, and only if, the £100 million that the government takes from the private sector would otherwise have been spent by that sector. If so, the government's policy would reduce private expenditure by £100 million and raise its own spending by £100 million. Aggregate demand, and hence national income and employment, would remain unchanged.

But this is not the case in our model. When an extra £100 million in taxes is taken away from households, they reduce their spending on domestically produced goods by less than £100 million. If the marginal propensity to consume out of disposable income is, say, 0.75, consumption expenditure will fall by only £75 million. If the government spends the entire £100 million on domestically produced goods, aggregate expenditure will increase by £25 million. In this case the balanced budget increase in government expenditure has an expansionary effect because it shifts the aggregate expenditure function upwards and thus increases GDP.

A balanced budget increase in government expenditure will have a mild expansionary effect on GDP, and a balanced budget decrease will have a mild contractionary effect.

The **balanced budget multiplier** measures these effects. It is the change in GDP divided by the balanced budget change in government expenditure that brought it about. Thus if the extra £100 million of expenditure (combined with the tax increases to finance it) causes GDP to rise by £50 million, the balanced budget multiplier is 0.5; if GDP rises by £100 million, it is 1.0.

When government expenditure is increased with no corresponding increase in tax rates, we say it is deficit-financed. Because there is no increase in tax rates, there is no consequent decrease in consumption to offset the increase in government spending. With a balanced budget increase in expenditure, however, an offsetting increase in the tax rate and decrease in consumption does occur. Thus the balanced budget multiplier is much lower than the multiplier that relates the change in GDP to a deficit-financed increase in government expenditure (with the tax rate constant).

Net exports and equilibrium GDP

As with the other elements of desired aggregate expenditure, if the net export function shifts upward, equilibrium GDP will rise; if the net export function shifts downward, equilibrium GDP will fall. Again we take the UK as the home country.

Autonomous net exports Net exports have both an autonomous component and an induced component. We have assumed that exports themselves are autonomous (exogenous) with respect to domestic GDP. Foreign demand for UK goods and services depends on foreign income, on foreign and UK prices, and on the exchange rate, but it does not depend on UK domestic income. Export demand could also change because of a change in tastes. Suppose that foreign consumers develop a taste for British-made goods (perhaps in reality Jaguars or Land Rovers, but in the model it is for the output of the single sector) and desire to purchase £500 million more per year of such goods than they had in the past. The net export function (and the aggregate expenditure function) will shift up by £500 million, and equilibrium GDP will increase by £500 million times the multiplier.

Induced net exports The domestic demand for imports depends in part on domestic income. The greater is domestic income, the greater will be UK residents' demand for goods and services in general, including those produced abroad. Because imports are subtracted to obtain net exports (net exports equal $X - IM$), the greater is the marginal propensity to import, the lower will be the marginal propensity to spend on the domestic product, and the lower will be the multiplier, $1/(1 - z)$.

The exchange rate regime We have noted above that foreign demand for domestic exports will depend upon the exchange rate. The way in which the exchange rate interacts with net exports will vary according to the exchange rate regime in operation at the time. For example, the adjustment of net exports will be different if the exchange rate is floating (determined by market forces) rather than pegged. It may be different again for countries that share a common currency, such as in the euro zone. We discuss the implication of various exchange rate regimes for external adjustment in some detail in Chapter 28, once we have added money to the model. For now we assume that there are no endogenous exchange rate changes affecting net exports, so our economy can best be thought of as one with a fixed exchange rate regime. The importance of this assumption will become apparent later.

Lessons and limitations of the income–expenditure approach

In this and the preceding chapter we have discussed the determination of the four categories of aggregate expenditure and seen how they simultaneously determine equilibrium national income and output (GDP). The basic approach, which is the same no matter how many categories are considered, was first presented in Chapter 21 and has been restated and extended in this chapter.

Any factor that shifts one or more of the components of desired aggregate expenditure will change equilibrium GDP, *at a given price level*.

In the following chapters we augment the income–expenditure model by allowing the price level to change, in both the short run and the long run. When prices change, real GDP will change by amounts different from those predicted by the simple multiplier. We will see that changes in desired aggregate expenditure generally change both prices *and* real GDP. This is why the simple multiplier, derived under the assumption that prices do not change, is too simple.

However, there are three ways in which the simple income–aggregate expenditure model developed here remains useful, even when prices are incorporated. First, the simple multiplier will continue to be a valuable starting-place in calculating actual changes in GDP in response to changes in autonomous expenditure. Second, no matter what the price level, the components of aggregate expenditure add up to GDP in equilibrium. Third, no matter what the price level, equilibrium requires that desired aggregate expenditure must equal output (GDP) in equilibrium, or equivalently that injections equal leakages.

Summary

Government spending and taxes

■ Government consumption is part of autonomous aggregate expenditure. Taxes minus transfer payments are called net taxes and affect aggregate expenditure indirectly. Taxes reduce disposable income, whereas transfers increase disposable income. Disposable income, in turn, determines desired private consumption, according to the consumption function.

■ The budget balance is defined as government revenues minus government expenditures. When this difference is positive, the budget is in surplus; when it is negative, the budget is in deficit.

■ When the budget is in surplus, there is positive public saving, because the government is spending less on the national product than the amount of income that it is withdrawing from the circular flow of income and expenditure. When the government budget is in deficit, public saving is negative.

Net exports

■ Since desired imports increase as national income increases, desired net exports decrease as national income (GDP) increases, other things being equal. Hence the net export function is negatively sloped (net exports fall as GDP rises).

Equilibrium GDP

■ GDP is in equilibrium when desired aggregate expenditure, $C + I + G + (X - IM)$, equals national output.

■ The sum of investment and net exports is called national asset formation because investment is the increase in the domestic capital stock and net exports result in investment in foreign assets. At the equilibrium level of GDP, desired national saving, $S + T - G$, is just equal to national asset formation, $I + X - IM$.

Changes in aggregate expenditure

■ The size of the multiplier is negatively related to the income tax rate.

■ A shift in exogenous expenditures changes GDP by the value of the shift times the simple multiplier.

Topics for review

■ Taxes and net taxes
■ The budget balance
■ Public saving
■ The net export function
■ The marginal propensity to spend
■ National asset formation
■ National saving
■ Calculation of the simple multiplier
■ Fiscal policy and equilibrium GDP

Questions for discussion

1 Which of the following categories of expenditure are part of government consumption spending, *G*, in the macro model: (*a*) pensioners' cold-weather payments; (*b*) state subsidies to loss-making public enterprises; (*c*) the costs of the BBC World Service; (*d*) the salaries of the Guards Regiment at Buckingham Palace; (*e*) drugs distributed to those entitled to free prescriptions; (*f*) expenditure on new road building?

2 Explain why an increase in tax revenue accompanied by an equal increase in government spending will not have a neutral effect on GDP.

3 If there is an autonomous rise of both imports and exports of the same amount, what effect does this have on equilibrium GDP?

4 Compare and contrast the results in questions 2 and 3. What do these results say about the differences between the balanced budget multiplier and the 'balanced trade multiplier'?

5 Explain how governments might try to use their fiscal policy instruments to end a recession. What practical difficulties might be encountered in implementing such a policy?

6 Calculate the multiplier for a model in which the marginal (net) tax rate is 0.2, the propensity to import is 0.28, and the marginal propensity to consume is 0.9.

Chapter 23
GDP and the Price Level in the Short Run

In this chapter we drop the assumption that the price level is constant. Virtually all shocks to the economy affect *both* real GDP *and* the price level; that is, they affect both the volume of goods and services produced and the money values of those goods and services, at least initially. Economists talk about such shocks as having both *real* and *nominal* effects. To understand these effects, we need to develop some further tools, called the *aggregate demand curve* and the *aggregate supply curve.*

Making the price level endogenous requires an explicit description of the supply side of our macroeconomic model. No longer will we maintain the assumption that

national output is purely demand-determined. As a result, we will be able to analyse more realistic situations where an economy operates close to potential GDP.[1]

We make the transition to a variable price level in two steps. First, we study the consequences for GDP of *exogenous* changes in the price level—changes that happen for reasons that are not explained by our present model of the economy. This gives us what we call the aggregate demand curve. Then we develop a theory of aggregate supply which, when combined with aggregate demand to expand our model, *explains* simultaneous movements in both GDP *and* the price level.

Aggregate demand

What happens to equilibrium GDP when all money prices change for some exogenous reason? To find out, we need to understand how the change affects desired aggregate expenditure.

Shifts in the *AE* curve

There is one key result that we need to establish: a rise in the price level *shifts* the aggregate expenditure curve downward, while a fall in the price level *shifts* it upward. In other words the price level and desired aggregate expenditure are negatively related to each other. A major part of the explanation lies in the way the change in the price level affects desired private consumption expenditure and desired net exports.

Changes in private consumption

The link between a change in the price level and changes in desired consumption is provided by wealth. This link is in two parts.

The first part is provided by the effect of changes in the

price level on the wealth of the private sector. Much of this wealth is held in the form of assets with a fixed nominal money value. One obvious example is money itself—cash and bank deposits. Other examples include many kinds of financial instruments, such as government bonds (gilts) and bills. When a bill or a bond matures, the owner is repaid a stated sum of money. What that money can buy—its real value—depends on the price level. The higher the price level, the less that sum of money can purchase. For this reason a rise in the domestic price level lowers the real value of all assets that are denominated in money units.

How does this affect individuals? An individual who holds a bond has loaned money to the agent that issued it. When the real value of the asset falls the holder has his or her wealth reduced. However, the real wealth of the issuer of the bond has increased. This is because the money value of the bond buys fewer real goods and services as a result

---

[1] Recall that potential GDP may sometimes be referred to as *full-employment* or *capacity output.* Each of these concepts may have slightly different meanings in different contexts. The key feature for present purposes, however, is that we are talking about the maximum level of GDP that is currently sustainable without generating inflation.

of the rise in the price level. So the agent that has to repay the bond will part with less purchasing power to do so, and so has more wealth. For example, if you are owed £100 in one year's time this will be worth less to you if prices rise by 20 per cent over the year than if they remain unchanged. However, the person who owes you the £100 will be better off by an amount equal to your loss if prices rise rather than remain unchanged, in that he or she will have to give up fewer goods to repay you.

A change in the price level affects the wealth of holders of assets denominated in money terms in exactly the opposite way to how it affects the wealth of those who issued the asset.

Inside assets An *inside asset* is one that is issued by someone (an individual or a firm) in the private sector and held by someone else in the private sector. It follows that for inside assets, a rise in the price level lowers the real wealth of a bond-holder but raises the real wealth of the bond-issuer, who will have to part with less purchasing power when the bond is redeemed. With inside assets, therefore, the wealth changes are exactly offsetting. A rise in the price level lowers the real wealth of the person who owns any asset that is denominated in money but it raises the real wealth of the person who must redeem the asset. So with inside assets a change in the price level has no net effect on private sector wealth.

Outside assets *Outside assets* are those held by someone in the domestic private sector but issued by some agent outside that sector. In practice this usually means the government or any foreign issuer. In this case the only private sector wealth-holders to experience wealth changes when the price level changes are the holders of the outside assets. There are no offsetting private sector wealth changes for the issuers of the assets since they are not in the private sector. It follows that a change in the price level does cause a change in net private wealth held in outside assets denominated in nominal money units. A rise in the price level lowers the real wealth of holders of these assets.[2]

A change in the price level causes no net change in the wealth of the private sector with respect to inside assets, but it does cause a change with respect to outside assets since the issuers are not in the private sector.

The second link in the chain running from changes in the price level to changes in desired consumption is provided by the relationship between wealth and consumption that we stressed in Chapter 21 (see Figure 21.4 on page 365). Whenever individuals suffer a decrease in their wealth, they increase their saving so as to restore their wealth to the level that they desire for such purposes as retirement. At any level of income, of course, an increase in desired saving implies a reduction in desired consump-

tion. Conversely, whenever individuals get an increase in their wealth, they reduce their saving and consume more, causing an upward shift in the line that relates desired consumption expenditure and national income.

A rise in the domestic price level lowers the real value of total private sector wealth by lowering the real value of outside assets denominated in money units; this leads to a fall in desired private consumption; this in turn implies a downward shift in the aggregate expenditure curve. A fall in the domestic price level leads to a rise in wealth and desired private consumption, and thus to an upward shift in the aggregate expenditure curve, AE.

We have concentrated here on the direct effect of a change in wealth on desired private consumption expenditure. There is also an indirect effect that operates through the interest rate. Although this effect is potentially very powerful, we cannot study it until we have studied the macroeconomic role of money and interest rates. Further discussion of this point must therefore be postponed until Chapter 26.

Changes in net exports

When the domestic price level rises, domestically produced goods become more expensive relative to foreign goods. This change in relative prices causes domestic consumers to reduce their purchases of domestically produced goods (which have now become relatively more expensive) and to increase their purchases of foreign goods (which have now become relatively less expensive). At the same time consumers in other countries reduce their purchases of the now relatively expensive domestic goods. We saw in Chapter 22 that these changes can be summarized as a downward shift in the net export function.

A rise in the domestic price level shifts the net export function downward, which shifts the aggregate expenditure curve downward. A fall in the domestic price level shifts the net export function and the aggregate expenditure curve upward.

To summarize, if home-produced goods and services become more expensive, fewer of them will be bought, so total desired expenditure on UK output will fall; if home-produced goods and services become cheaper, more will be bought, and total desired expenditure on them will rise.[3]

---

[2] We are assuming that taxpayers do not include in their wealth calculations the real value of future tax liabilities. Taxpayers must pay taxes to service the national debt, and when a rise in the price level lowers its real value, it also lowers the real value of future tax liabilities by exactly the same amount. We ignore this possible offsetting change.

[3] This assumes that the price elasticity of demand for traded goods exceeds unity, so that a fall in price leads to both a greater volume and a greater value being bought.

Changes in equilibrium GDP

Because it shifts both the net export function and the consumption function downwards, a rise in the price level also shifts the aggregate desired expenditure curve downwards, as shown in Figure 23.1. This figure also allows us to reconfirm what we already know from Chapter 22: when the AE curve shifts downward, the equilibrium level of GDP falls.

A rise in the domestic price level reduces equilibrium GDP because it causes the aggregate expenditure curve to shift downward—all other exogenous variables being held constant.

Since a fall in the domestic price level is the opposite of the case that we have just studied, we can quickly summarize the two key effects. First, domestic goods become relatively cheaper internationally, so net exports rise. Second, the real value of some money assets increases, so consumers spend more. The resulting increase in desired expenditure is represented by an upward shift of the AE curve which raises equilibrium GDP, as shown in Figure 23.1.

A fall in the domestic price level increases equilibrium real GDP because it shifts the aggregate expenditure curve upward—all other exogenous variables being held constant.

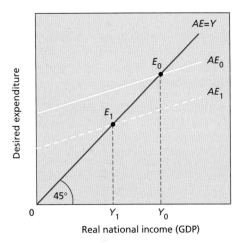

Figure 23.1 Aggregate expenditure and the price level

Changes in the price level cause the AE curve to shift and equilibrium GDP to change. At the initial price level the AE curve is given by the solid line AE_0, and hence equilibrium GDP is Y_0. An increase in the price level reduces desired aggregate expenditure and thus causes the AE curve to shift downward to the dashed line AE_1. As a result equilibrium GDP falls to Y_1. Starting with the dashed line AE_1, a fall in the price level increases desired aggregate expenditure, shifting the AE curve up to AE_0 and raising equilibrium GDP to Y_0.

The aggregate demand curve

We now know from the behaviour underlying the aggregate expenditure curve that the price level and real GDP are negatively related to each other; that is, a change in the price level changes equilibrium GDP in the opposite direction, holding all other exogenous variables (such as government consumption, tax rates, exports, and investment) constant. This negative relationship can be shown in an important new construct called the *aggregate demand curve.*

Recall that the AE curve relates national income to desired expenditure for a given price level, plotting income on the horizontal axis. The **aggregate demand (AD) curve** relates equilibrium GDP to the price level, again plotting GDP on the horizontal axis. Because the horizontal axes of both the AE and the AD curves measure real GDP (national income), the two curves can be placed one above the other so that the level of GDP on each can be compared directly. This is shown in Figure 23.2.

Now let us see how the AD curve is derived. Given a value of the price level, equilibrium GDP is determined in part (i) of Figure 23.2 at the point where the AE curve crosses the 45° line. In part (ii) of Figure 23.2 the combination of the equilibrium level of GDP and the corresponding value of the price level is plotted, giving one point on the AD curve.

When the price level changes, the AE curve shifts, for the reasons just seen. The new position of the AE curve gives rise to a new equilibrium level of GDP that is associated with the new price level. This determines a second point on the AD curve, as shown in Figure 23.2(ii).

Any change in the price level leads to a new AE curve and hence to a new equilibrium GDP. Each combination of equilibrium GDP and its associated price level defines a particular point on the AD curve.

Note that because the AD curve relates equilibrium GDP to the price level, changes in the price level that cause *shifts in* the AE curve cause *movements along* the AD curve. A movement along the AD curve thus traces out the response of equilibrium GDP to a change in the price level. Notice also that the only exogenous change we are permitting at present is a change in the price level. All other exogenous expenditures are held constant along a given AD curve.

The aggregate demand curve shows, for each price level, the associated level of equilibrium GDP for which aggregate desired expenditure equals total output.

In Chapter 22 we showed that points for which aggregate desired expenditure is equal to output are equivalent to points for which injections equal leakages (or in the model of Chapter 21, for which investment equals saving). This

(i) Aggregate expenditure

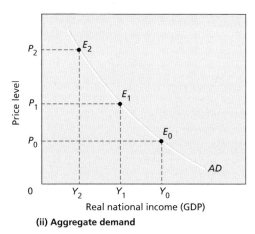

(ii) Aggregate demand

Figure 23.2 The *AD* curve and the *AE* curve

Equilibrium GDP is determined by the *AE* curve for each given price level; the level of GDP and its associated price level are then plotted to yield a point on the *AD* curve. When the price level is P_0, the *AE* curve is AE_0, and hence equilibrium GDP is Y_0, as shown in part (i). (This reproduces the initial equilibrium from Figure 23.1.) Plotting Y_0 against P_0 yields the point E_0 on the *AD* curve in part (ii).

An increase in the price level to P_1 causes AE_0 in part (i) to shift downward to AE_1 and thus causes equilibrium GDP to fall to Y_1. Plotting this new, lower level of GDP Y_1 against the higher price level, P_1, yields a second point, E_1, on the *AD* curve in part (ii). A further increase in the price level to P_2 causes the *AE* curve in part (i) to shift downward further, to AE_2, and thus causes equilibrium GDP to fall further, to Y_2. Plotting Y_2 against P_2 yields a third point, E_2, on the *AD* curve in part (ii).

Thus a change in the price level causes a shift in the *AE* curve in part (i) and a movement along the *AD* curve in part (ii).

equivalence carries through to the *AD* curve. Hence points on the *AD* curve can be thought of as combinations of real GDP and the price level (for given values of all exogenous expenditures) for which injections equal leakages, that is, for which $I + G + X = S + T + IM$. Recall that this equation can be rearranged to make clear the further equivalence to

the condition that national saving is equal to national asset formation: $S + (T - G) = I + (X - IM)$.

The slope of the *AD* curve

Figure 23.2 shows that the *AD* curve is negatively sloped. Starting from some specific point on the *AD* curve:

1. A rise in the price level causes the aggregate expenditure curve, *AE*, to shift downward and hence leads to a movement upward and to the left along the *AD* curve, reflecting a fall in the equilibrium level of GDP.

2. A fall in the price level causes the aggregate expenditure curve, *AE*, to shift upward and hence leads to a movement downward and to the right along the *AD* curve, reflecting a rise in the equilibrium level of GDP.

In Chapter 3 we saw that demand curves for individual goods such as carrots and cars are negatively sloped. However, the reasons for the negative slope of the *AD* curve are different from the reasons for the negative slope of the individual demand curves that are used in microeconomics. This important point is discussed further in Box 23.1.

Points off the *AD* curve

The *AD* curve depicts combinations of GDP and the price level at which aggregate desired expenditure is equal to actual output. These points are said to be *consistent* with expenditure decisions.

The level of GDP given by any point on the aggregate demand curve is such that *if* that level of output is produced, aggregate desired expenditure at the *given price level* will exactly equal total output.

Points to the left of the *AD* curve show combinations of GDP and the price level that cause aggregate desired expenditure to exceed output. There is thus pressure for output to rise because firms could sell more than current output. Points to the right of the *AD* curve show combinations of GDP and the price level for which aggregate desired expenditure is less than current output. There is thus pressure for output to fall because firms will not be able to sell all of their current output. These relationships are illustrated in Figure 23.3.

Shifts in the *AD* curve

Because the *AD* curve plots equilibrium GDP as a function of the price level, anything that alters equilibrium GDP *at any specific price level* must shift the *AD* curve. In other words any change in exogenous expenditures that we have been holding constant causes the aggregate expenditure curve to shift, and will also cause the *AD* curve to shift. (Recall that a change in the price level causes a *movement*

Box 23.1 The shape of the aggregate demand curve

In Chapter 3 we studied the demand curves for individual products. It is tempting to think that the properties of the aggregate demand curve arise from the same behaviour that gives rise to those individual demand curves. However, this would involve committing the fallacy of composition; that is, to assume that what is correct for the parts must be correct for the whole.

Consider a simple example of the fallacy. An art collector can go into the market and add to her private collection of nineteenth-century French paintings provided only that she has enough money. However, the fact that any one person can do this does not mean that everyone could do so simultaneously. The world's stock of nineteenth-century French paintings is fixed. It is not possible for *all* of us to do what any *one* of us with enough money can do.

How does the fallacy of composition relate to demand curves? An individual demand curve describes a situation in which the price of one commodity changes while the prices of all other commodities and consumers' money incomes are constant. Such an individual demand curve is negatively sloped for two reasons. First, as the price of the commodity rises, each consumer's given money income will buy a smaller *total* amount of goods, so a smaller quantity of each commodity will be bought, other things being equal. Second, as the price of the commodity rises, consumers buy less of it and more of the now relatively cheaper substitutes.

The first reason has no application to the aggregate demand curve, which relates the total demand for all output to the price level. All prices and total output are changing as we move along the *AD* curve. Because the value of output determines income, consumers' money incomes will also be changing along this curve.

The second reason does apply to the aggregate demand curve, but in a limited way. A rise in the price level entails a rise in *all* domestic commodity prices. Thus, there is no incentive to substitute among domestic commodities whose prices do not change relative to each other. However, it does give rise, as we saw earlier in this chapter, to some substitution between domestic and foreign goods and services. Domestic goods and services rise in price relative to imported goods and services, and the switch in expenditure will lower desired aggregate expenditure on domestic output and hence will lower equilibrium GDP.

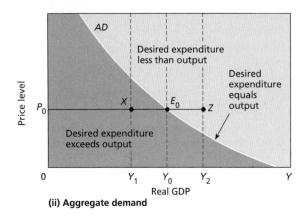

(i) Aggregate expenditure

(ii) Aggregate demand

Figure 23.3 The relationship between the *AE* and *AD* curves

The *AD* curve plots the price level against the level of GDP consistent with expenditure decisions at that price level. With the price level P_0 equilibrium GDP is Y_0, shown by the intersection of *AE* and the 45° line at E_0 in part (i) and by the point E_0 on the *AD* curve in part (ii).

With the price level constant at P_0, consider a level of GDP of Y_1, which is less than Y_0. As can be seen in part (i), if GDP were equal to Y_1, desired aggregate expenditure would be e_1, which is greater than Y_1. Hence Y_1 is not an equilibrium level of GDP when the price level is P_0, and the combination (P_0, Y_1) is not a point on the *AD* curve in part (ii), as shown by point X. Now consider a level of GDP of Y_2, which is greater than Y_0. As can be seen in part (i), if GDP were equal to Y_2, desired aggregate expenditure would be e_2, which is less than Y_2. Hence Y_2 is not an equilibrium level of GDP when the price level is P_0, and the combination (P_0, Y_2) is not a point on the *AD* curve in part (ii), as shown by point Z.

Repeating the same analysis for each given price level tells us that for all points to the left of the *AD* curve (dark blue shaded area), output is tending to rise, because desired expenditure exceeds output, whereas for all points to the right of the *AD* curve (light blue shaded area), output is tending to fall, because desired aggregate expenditure is less than output.

along the *AD* curve.) Such a shift is called an *aggregate demand shock*.

One example of a *positive* aggregate demand shock comes from the United Kingdom. A lowering of tax rates in the 1987 Budget led to an increase in the amount of UK consumption expenditure associated with each level of UK national income. This was an expansionary demand shock that shifted the UK *AD* curve to the right. This stimulated a boom in the domestic economy. The extra domestic demand also spilled over into the balance of payments. Some of the increased domestic demand went onto imports and the balance of payments went into deficit. In the context of our model the net export function shifted downwards. Later, policy was aimed at shifting the *AD* curve down again. This was a contributory factor in the 1990–2 recession.

An example of a *negative* aggregate demand shock can be found in Germany in the early 1990s. The high costs for the German government associated with reunification of East and West Germany required a sharp rise in German income tax rates. Although this was associated with higher spending in East Germany, there was a downward shift of the *AD* curve for West Germany that led to a downturn in output and a substantial rise in unemployment. The situation was made worse by a simultaneous fiscal tightening in several other European countries, such as France,

Belgium, and Italy, as they attempted to reduce their budget deficits to below 3 per cent of GDP to satisfy the Maastricht criteria for entry into the single European currency system in 1999. A simultaneous negative *AD* shock in, say, France would reinforce the fiscally generated *AD* shock in Germany, because it would lead to a downward shift in the German net export function, causing a further downward shift in Germany's *AD* curve.

We now summarize the factors that shift the *AD* curves as follows:

A rise in the amount of (autonomous) desired private consumption, investment, government consumption, or net export expenditure that is associated with each level of national income (GDP) shifts the *AD* curve to the right. A fall in any of these expenditures shifts the *AD* curve to the left.

The simple multiplier and the *AD* curve

We saw in Chapter 22 that the simple multiplier measures the magnitude of the *change* in equilibrium GDP in response to a change in autonomous expenditure when the price level is constant. It follows that this multiplier gives the magnitude of the *horizontal* shift in the *AD* curve in response to a change in autonomous expenditure. This is shown in Figure 23.4.

(i) Aggregate expenditure

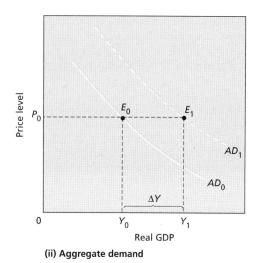

(ii) Aggregate demand

Figure 23.4 The simple multiplier and shifts in the *AD* curve

A change in autonomous expenditure changes equilibrium GDP for any given price level, and the simple multiplier measures the resulting horizontal shift in the aggregate demand curve. The original desired expenditure curve is AE_0 in part (i). Equilibrium is at E_0, with GDP Y_0 at price level P_0. This yields point E_0 on the curve AD_0 in part (ii).

The *AE* curve in part (i) then shifts upwards from AE_0 to AE_1 because of an increase in autonomous expenditure of ΔA. Equilibrium output now rises to Y_1, with the price level still constant at P_0. Thus the *AD* curve in part (ii) shifts to the right to point E_1, indicating the higher equilibrium output Y_1 associated with the same price level P_0. The magnitude of the shift, ΔY, is given by the simple multiplier.

A fall in autonomous expenditure can be analysed by shifting the *AE* curve from AE_1 to AE_0, which shifts the *AD* curve from AD_1 to AD_0 at the price level of P_0. The equilibrium value of GDP falls from Y_1 to Y_0.

The simple multiplier measures the horizontal shift in the AD curve in response to a change in autonomous expenditure.

If the price level were to remain constant and firms were willing to supply everything that was demanded at that price level, the simple multiplier would still show the change in equilibrium GDP that would occur in response to a change in autonomous expenditure. However, this will not normally be the case. To see how producers will actually respond to a shift in aggregate demand, we need to model supply responses.

Aggregate supply and macroeconomic equilibrium

So far we have explained how the equilibrium level of GDP is determined *when the price level is given* and how that equilibrium changes as the price level is changed exogenously. We are now ready to take an important further step: to take account of the supply decisions of producers. Once we have done this, we will be able to combine aggregate demand and supply to provide an *explanation* for the simultaneous determination of the price level and real GDP.

The aggregate supply curve

Aggregate supply is the total output of goods and services that firms wish to produce, assuming that they can sell all that they wish to sell at the going price level. Recall, however, that in our simple model there is only one type of output, so *in our model* aggregate supply is the final output of the single good produced by all the firms in the economy. In the real world the national output is made up of thousands of different types of goods and services. In both our model and the real world, aggregate supply is the outcome of the decisions of all producers in the economy to hire workers and buy other inputs in order to produce goods (and services) to sell to consumers, governments, and other producers, as well as for export.

The *aggregate supply curve* relates the quantity of output supplied to the price level. It is useful to define two types of such curve, in order to allow for different stages of adjustment of the production sector to external shocks. The **short-run aggregate supply (*SRAS*) curve** shows the quantity of output that firms would like to produce and to sell at each price level *on the assumption that the prices of all factors of production (inputs) remain constant*. The **long-run aggregate supply (*LRAS*) curve** plots the desired quantity of output that firms would like to produce after the price level and input prices have fully adjusted to any exogenous shift of aggregate demand. For the remainder of this chapter we confine our attention to the *SRAS* curve.

The slope of the short-run aggregate supply curve

The slope of the *SRAS* curve depends on how production costs are related to output and on how goods prices and output are related.

Costs and output Suppose that firms wish to increase their outputs above current levels. What will this do to their costs per unit of output—often called their **unit costs**? The short-run aggregate supply curve is drawn on the assumption that the prices of all factors of production that firms use, such as labour, remain constant. This does not, however, mean that unit costs will be constant. As output increases, less efficient standby machinery may have to be used, and less efficient workers may have to be hired, while existing workers may have to be paid overtime rates for additional work. For these reasons unit costs will tend to rise as output rises, even when input prices are constant.[4]

Unit costs and output are positively related in the short run.

Prices and output To consider the relationship between price and output, we need to consider firms that sell in two distinct types of markets: those in which firms are price-takers and those in which firms are price-setters. Some industries contain many individual firms selling a homogeneous product. In these cases each one is too small to influence the market price, which is set by the overall forces of demand and supply. So each firm must accept whatever price is set on the open market and adjust its output to that price. The firms are said to be *price-takers* and *quantity-adjusters*. When the market price changes, these firms will react by altering their production.

Price-taking firms only produce more if price rises and will produce less if price falls. This is because their unit costs rise with output.

---

[4] The law of diminishing returns (see Chapter 8) is one reason why costs rise in the short run, as firms try to produce more output with a fixed stock of capital equipment.

Many other industries, including most of those that produce manufactured goods, are not price-takers. Whether there are few large firms or many small ones, each can influence the market price of its output. Most such firms sell differentiated products, although all are similar enough to be thought of as the product of one industry. For example, no two makes of car are identical, but all cars are sufficiently alike that we can talk about 'the car industry' and the commodity 'cars'. In such cases each firm typically sets the price at which it is prepared to sell its products; that is, the firm is a *price-setter*.

Over some (small) range of output price-setting firms will keep their prices constant and satisfy changes in demand by running down or building up inventories, such as numbers of cars in the showroom. However, if the demand for the output of price-setting firms increases sufficiently to take their production level into the range at which their unit costs start to rise (for example, because overtime is worked and standby equipment is brought into production), profit-maximizing firms will not want to increase production further unless they can pass on at least some of these extra costs through higher prices. When demand falls, they will reduce output, and competition among them will tend to cause a reduction in prices whenever unit costs fall.

Price-setting firms will increase their prices when they expand production into the range where unit costs are rising.

This is the basic behaviour of firms in response to changes in demand and prices when input prices are constant, and it explains the slope of the *SRAS* curve, such as the one shown in Figure 23.5.[5]

The actions of both price-taking and price-setting firms cause the price level and the desired supply of output to be positively related—the short-run aggregate supply curve is positively sloped.

Real and nominal wages Another way of explaining why the *SRAS* curve is positively sloped involves real wages. Consider price-taking firms, selling in competitive markets. With given money prices of their inputs—we will concentrate on the labour input—and a given price at which they can sell their output, each firm will produce output at the level where its marginal cost equals its marginal revenue (and average revenue, which is also equal to the market price of its output, as shown in Chapter 9).

Now what happens if an increase in total demand for final output leads to a rise in the output price? Firms will find that their marginal revenue curves (and average revenue) have shifted upwards. They will increase profits by expanding output up to the point where their new marginal revenue curve cuts their marginal cost curve. In the process they will also increase employment. Thus as the price level rises, output increases. This is the positively sloped *SRAS* curve.

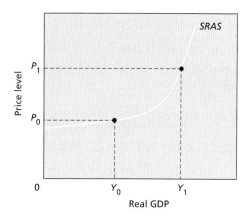

Figure 23.5 A short-run aggregate supply curve
The *SRAS* curve is positively sloped. The positive slope of the *SRAS* curve shows that with the prices of labour and other inputs given, total desired output and the price level will be positively associated. Thus a rise in the price level from P_0 to P_1 will be associated with a rise in the quantity of total output supplied from Y_0 to Y_1. The slope of the *SRAS* curve is fairly flat at low levels of output and very steep at higher levels.

Notice, however, what is happening to the real wage rate. Money wages are fixed (by assumption, in the short run) in money terms. As the price of final output goes up, workers' money wages will buy fewer goods. The *real wage* has fallen. This is why firms choose to hire more labour and expand output. The relative price of their inputs has fallen in comparison with the price of their output.

Of course, this will not be the end of the story. Workers will resist a permanent fall in their real wage, and their representatives will bargain for higher wage rates. Money wages will eventually start to rise, and as they do, the relative input and output prices faced by firms will tend to return to their initial level. So firms' output and employment will return to their original level. But this is the long-run story, to which we return in Chapter 24.

As we move upwards along a given *SRAS* curve, the rise in the price level and output is associated with a fall in the real wage—that is, a rise in output prices relative to input prices.

Shifts in the *SRAS* curve

Shifts in the *SRAS* curve, which are shown in Figure 23.6, are called *aggregate supply shocks*. Two sources of aggregate

---

[5] Notice that our argument here relating to two different types of firm is not really consistent with our assumption that there is only one type of output. However, since both price-takers and price-setters generate a positively sloped supply curve, for the purpose of building our macro model this does not cause any difficulties. It is worth bearing in mind, however, that in reality price-setting behaviour varies with product type and market structure.

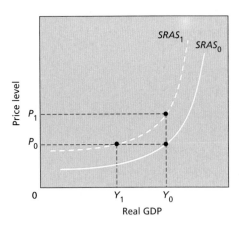

Figure 23.6 Shifts in the *SRAS* curve
A shift to the left of the *SRAS* curve reflects a decrease in supply; a shift to the right reflects an increase in supply. Starting from (P_0, Y_0) on $SRAS_0$, suppose there is an increase in input prices. At price level P_0 only Y_1 would be produced. Alternatively, to get output Y_0 would require a rise to price level P_1. The new supply curve is $SRAS_1$, which may be viewed as being above and to the left of $SRAS_0$. An increase in supply, caused, say, by a decrease in input prices, would shift the *SRAS* curve downward and to the right, from $SRAS_1$ to $SRAS_0$.

supply shocks are of particular importance: changes in the price of inputs, and increases in productivity.

Changes in input prices Input prices are held constant along the *SRAS* curve; when they change, the curve shifts. If input prices rise, firms will find the profitability of their current production reduced. If output prices do not rise, firms will react by decreasing production. For the economy as a whole this means that there will be less output at each price level than before the increase in input prices. Thus if input prices rise, the *SRAS* curve shifts upward. (Notice that when a positively sloped curve shifts upward, indicating that any given quantity is associated with a higher price level, it also shifts to the left, indicating that any given price level is associated with a lower quantity.)

Similarly, a fall in input prices causes the *SRAS* curve to shift downward (and to the right). More will be produced and offered for sale at each price level.[6]

Increases in productivity If labour productivity rises, meaning that each worker can produce more per hour, the unit costs of production will fall, as long as wage rates do not rise sufficiently to offset fully the productivity rise. Lower costs generally lead to lower prices. Competing firms cut prices in an attempt to raise their market shares, and the net result of such competition is that the fall in production costs is accompanied by a fall in prices. Because the same output is sold at a lower price, the increased productivity causes a downward shift in the *SRAS* curve. This shift is an increase in supply, as illustrated in Figure 23.6.

A rightward shift in the *SRAS* curve, brought about, for example, by an increase in productivity with no increase in input prices, implies that firms will be willing to produce more output with no increase in the price level.

A change in either input prices or productivity will shift the *SRAS* curve, because any given output will be supplied at a different price level than previously. An increase in input prices or a decrease in productivity shifts the *SRAS* curve to the left; an increase in productivity or a decrease in input prices shifts it to the right.

Macroeconomic equilibrium

We have now added the *SRAS* curve to our model, and we are ready to see how both real GDP and the price level are simultaneously determined by the interaction of aggregate demand and aggregate supply.

The equilibrium values of real GDP and the price level occur at the intersection of the *AD* and *SRAS* curves, as shown by the pair Y_0 and P_0 at point E_0 in Figure 23.7. We call the combination of real GDP and price level at the intersection of the *AD* and *SRAS* curves a *macroeconomic equilibrium*.

To see why the pair of points (Y_0, P_0) is the only macroeconomic equilibrium, first consider what Figure 23.7 shows would happen if the price level were below P_0. At this lower price level the desired output of firms, as given by the *SRAS* curve, is less than desired aggregate expenditure at that level of GDP. The excess desired aggregate expenditure will cause prices to be bid up, and output will increase along the *SRAS* curve. Hence there can be no macroeconomic *equilibrium* when the price level is below P_0.

Similarly, Figure 23.7 shows that when the price level is above P_0, the behaviour underlying the *SRAS* and *AD* curves is not consistent. In this case producers will wish to supply more than the output that is demanded at that price level. Desired expenditure will not be large enough to purchase everything that firms wish to produce at that price level.

Only at the combination of GDP and price level given by the intersection of the *SRAS* and *AD* curves are spending (demand) behaviour and production (supply) activity consistent.

When the price level is less than its equilibrium value, expenditure behaviour is consistent with a level of GDP that is greater than the desired output of firms. When the

---

[6] Note that for either the *AD* or the *SRAS* curve a shift to the right means an increase, and a shift to the left means a decrease. Upward and downward shifts, however, have different meanings for the two curves. An upward shift of the *AD* curve reflects an increase in aggregate demand, but an upward shift in the *SRAS* curve reflects a decrease in aggregate supply.

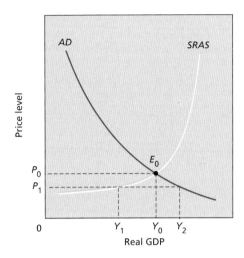

Figure 23.7 Macroeconomic equilibrium

Macroeconomic equilibrium occurs at the intersection of the *AD* and *SRAS* curves and determines the equilibrium values for GDP and the price level. Given the *AD* and *SRAS* curves in the figure, macroeconomic equilibrium occurs at E_0, with GDP equal to Y_0 and the price level equal to P_0. At P_0 the desired output of firms, as given by the *SRAS* curve, is equal to the level of GDP that is consistent with expenditure decisions, as given by the *AD* curve.

If the price level were equal to P_1, less than P_0, the desired output of firms, given by the *SRAS* curve, would be Y_1. However, at P_1 the level of output that is consistent with expenditure decisions, given by the *AD* curve, would be Y_2, greater than Y_1. Hence when the price level is P_1, or any other level less than P_0, the desired output of firms will be less than the level of output that is consistent with expenditure decisions.

Similarly, for any price level above P_0, the desired output of firms, given by the *SRAS* curve, would exceed the level of output that is consistent with expenditure decisions, given by the *AD* curve.

price level is greater than its equilibrium value, expenditure behaviour is consistent with a level of GDP that is less than the desired output of firms.

Macroeconomic equilibrium thus requires that two conditions be satisfied. The first is familiar to us because it comes from Chapters 21 and 22: at the prevailing price level, desired aggregate expenditure must be equal to national output, which means that agents are just willing to buy all that is produced. The *AD* curve is constructed in such a way that this condition holds everywhere on it. The second requirement for equilibrium is introduced by consideration of aggregate supply: at the prevailing price level, firms must wish to produce the prevailing level of national output, no more and no less. This condition is fulfilled everywhere on the *SRAS* curve. Only where the two curves intersect are both conditions fulfilled simultaneously.

Changes in GDP and the price level

The aggregate demand and aggregate supply curves can now be used to understand how various shocks to the economy change both real GDP and the price level.

A shift in the *AD* curve is called an **aggregate demand shock**. A *rightward* shift in the *AD* curve results from an *increase* in aggregate demand; it means that at all price levels expenditure decisions will now be consistent with a *higher* level of real GDP. Similarly, a *leftward* shift in the *AD* curve indicates a *decrease* in aggregate demand; it means that at all price levels expenditure decisions will now be consistent with a *lower* level of real GDP.[7]

A shift in the *SRAS* curve is called an **aggregate supply shock**. A *rightward* shift in the *SRAS* curve represents an *increase* in aggregate supply: at any given price level *more* real national output will be supplied. A *leftward* shift in the *SRAS* curve is a *decrease* in aggregate supply: at any given price level *less* real national output will be supplied.[8]

What happens to real GDP and to the price level when either the aggregate demand or aggregate supply curve shifts?

A shift in either the *AD* or the *SRAS* curve leads to changes in the equilibrium values of the price level and real GDP.

Box 23.2 deals with the special case of a perfectly elastic *SRAS* curve. In that case, the aggregate supply curve determines the price level, while the aggregate demand curve determines real GDP. This is a special case that is unlikely to arise in practice, but it is the only case where the model of Chapter 22 (with a fixed price level) would be adequate to determine real GDP.

---

[7] The factors that could shift *AD* are the same as those that could shift *AE* (*apart from the price level*). An autonomous increase in private consumption, government consumption, investment, or net exports, or a reduction in tax rates, will all shift *AD* upwards to the right. The opposite shift in any of these will move *AD* downwards to the left.

[8] The distinction between movements along and shifts of curves that we encountered in studying demand and supply in Chapter 3 is also relevant here. A *movement along* an aggregate demand curve indicates a change in the quantity demanded, whereas a *shift* in an aggregate demand curve indicates a 'change in demand'. A similar distinction applies to the supply curve.

Box 23.2 The Keynesian *SRAS* curve

One extreme version of the *SRAS* curve, which is horizontal over some range of GDP, is called the Keynesian short-run aggregate supply curve. The reference is to John Maynard Keynes, who in his famous book *The General Theory of Employment, Interest and Money* (1936) pioneered the study of the behaviour of economies under conditions of high unemployment.

The following behaviour gives rise to the Keynesian *SRAS* curve. When real GDP is below potential GDP, individual firms are operating at less than normal-capacity output, and they hold their prices constant at the level that would maximize profits if production were at normal capacity. They then respond to demand variations below that capacity by altering output. In other words, firms will supply whatever they can sell at their existing prices as long as they are producing below their normal capacity. This means that the firms have horizontal supply curves and that their output is *demand-determined.**

Under these circumstances, the economy has a horizontal aggregate supply curve, indicating that any output up to potential will be supplied at the going price level. The amount that is actually produced is then determined by the position of the aggregate demand curve, as shown in the figure. Thus, we say that real GDP is demand-determined. If demand rises enough so that firms are trying to squeeze more than normal output out of their plants, their costs will rise, and so will their prices. Thus, the horizontal Keynesian *SRAS* curve applies only to situations below potential GDP.

* The evidence is strong that firms, particularly in the manufacturing sector, do behave like this in the short run. One possible explanation for this is that changing prices frequently is too costly, so firms set the best possible (profit-maximizing) prices when output is at normal capacity and then do not change prices in the face of short-term fluctuations in demand (see Chapter 11).

Aggregate demand shocks

Figure 23.8 shows the effects of an increase in aggregate demand. This increase could have occurred because of, say, increased investment or government spending; it means that more national output will be demanded at any given price level. For now we are not concerned with the source of the shock; we are interested in its implications for the price level and real GDP. As is shown in the figure, following an increase in aggregate demand, both the price level and real GDP rise.

Figure 23.8 also shows that both the price level and real GDP fall as the result of a decrease in aggregate demand.

Aggregate demand shocks cause the price level and real GDP to change in the same direction; both rise with an increase in aggregate demand, and both fall with a decrease in aggregate demand.

An aggregate demand shock means that there is a shift in the *AD* curve (for example, from AD_0 to AD_1 in Figure 23.8). Adjustment to the new equilibrium following an aggregate demand shock involves a movement along the *SRAS* curve (for example, from point E_0 to point E_1).

The multiplier when the price level varies

We saw earlier in this chapter that the simple multiplier gives the extent of the horizontal shift in the *AD* curve in response to a change in autonomous expenditure. If the price level remains constant and *if* firms are willing to supply all that is demanded at the existing price level (that is, the aggregate supply curve is horizontal), then the simple multiplier gives the increase in equilibrium GDP.

Now that we can use aggregate demand and aggregate supply curves, we can answer a more interesting question:

Figure 23.8 Aggregate demand shocks

Shifts in aggregate demand cause the price level and real GDP to move in the same direction. An increase in aggregate demand shifts the *AD* curve to the right—say, from AD_0 to AD_1. Macroeconomic equilibrium moves from E_0 to E_1. The price level rises from P_0 to P_1 and real GDP rises from Y_0 to Y_1, reflecting a movement along the *SRAS* curve.

A decrease in aggregate demand shifts the *AD* curve to the left—say, from AD_1 to AD_0. Equilibrium moves from E_1 to E_0. Prices fall from P_1 to P_0, and real GDP falls from Y_1 to Y_0.

what happens in the more usual case where the aggregate supply curve slopes upward?

Figure 23.8 shows that when the *SRAS* curve is positively sloped, the change in GDP that is caused by a change in autonomous expenditure is no longer equal to the size of the horizontal shift in the *AD* curve. A rightward shift of the *AD* curve causes the price level to rise, which in turn causes the rise in GDP to be less than the horizontal shift of the *AD* curve. Part of the expansionary impact of an increase in demand is dissipated by a rise in the price level, and only part is transmitted to a rise in real output. Of course, there is still an increase in output, so there is still a positive multiplier effect, but its value is not the same as that of the simple multiplier.

When the *SRAS* curve is positively sloped, the multiplier is smaller than the simple multiplier.

Why is the multiplier smaller when the *SRAS* curve is positively sloped? The answer lies in the behaviour that is summarized by the *AE* curve. To understand this, it is useful to think of the final change in GDP as occurring in two stages, as shown in Figure 23.9.

First, with prices remaining constant, an increase in autonomous expenditure shifts the *AE* curve upward (part (i) of the figure) and therefore shifts the *AD* curve to the right (part (ii)). The horizontal shift in the *AD* curve is measured by the simple multiplier, but this cannot be the final equilibrium position because firms are unwilling to produce enough to satisfy the extra demand at the existing price level.

Second, we take account of the rise in the price level that occurs owing to the positive slope of the *SRAS* curve. A rise in the price level, via its negative effect on net exports and on wealth, leads to a downward shift in the *AE* curve. This second shift of the *AE* curve partially counteracts the initial rise in GDP and so reduces the size of the multiplier. The second stage shows up as a downward shift of the *AE* curve in part (i) of Figure 23.9 and a movement upward and to the left along the *AD* curve in part (ii).

The importance of the shape of the *SRAS* curve

The shape of the *SRAS* curve has important implications for how the effects of an aggregate demand shock are divided between changes in real GDP and changes in the price level. Figure 23.10 highlights this point by considering *AD* shocks in the presence of an *SRAS* curve that exhibits three distinct ranges. Box 23.3 explores some possible reasons for such an increasing slope of the *SRAS* curve.

Over the *flat* range in Figure 23.10, from 0 to Y_0, any change in aggregate demand leads to no change in prices and a response of output equal to that predicted by the simple multiplier.

Over the *intermediate* range along which the *SRAS* curve

(i) Aggregate expenditure

(ii) Aggregate demand

Figure 23.9 The *AE* curve and the multiplier when the price level varies

An increase in autonomous expenditure causes the *AE* curve to shift upward, but the rise in the price level causes it to shift part of the way down again. Hence the multiplier effect on GDP is smaller than when the price level is constant. Originally equilibrium is at point E_0 in both part (i) and part (ii), with real GDP at Y_0 and price level at P_0. Desired aggregate expenditure then shifts by ΔA to AE_1', taking the aggregate demand curve to AD_1. These shifts are shown by arrow 1 in both parts. If the price level had remained constant at P_0, the new equilibrium would have been E_1' and real GDP would have risen to Y_1'. The amount $Y_0 Y_1'$ is the change called for by the simple multiplier.

Instead, however, the shift in the *AD* curve raises the price level to P_1 and shifts the aggregate expenditure curve down to AE_1, as shown by arrow 2 in part (i). This is shown as a movement along the *AD* curve, as indicated by arrow 2 in part (ii). The new equilibrium is thus at E_1. The amount $Y_0 Y_1$ is ΔY, the actual increase in real GDP, whereas the amount $Y_1 Y_1'$ is the shortfall relative to the simple multiplier owing to the rise in the price level.

The multiplier is the ratio $\Delta Y/\Delta A$ in part (i).

is positively sloped, from Y_1 to Y_4, a shift in the *AD* curve gives rise to appreciable changes in both real GDP and the price level. As we saw earlier in this chapter, the change in the price level reduces the response of GDP to a change in autonomous expenditure.

Box 23.3 More on the shape of the *SRAS* curve

The *SRAS* curve relates the price level to the quantity of output that producers are willing to sell. Notice two things about the shape of the *SRAS* curve that is reproduced in Figure 23.8: it has a positive slope, and the slope increases as output rises.

Positive slope

The most obvious feature of the *SRAS* curve is its positive slope, indicating that a higher price level is associated with a higher volume of real output, other things being equal. Because the prices of all of the inputs to production are being held constant along the *SRAS* curve, why is the curve not horizontal, indicating that firms would be willing to supply as much output as might be demanded with no increase in the price level?

The answer is that, even though *input prices* are constant, *unit costs of production* eventually rise as output increases. Thus, a higher price level for increasing output—rising short-run aggregate supply—is necessary to compensate firms for rising costs.

The preceding paragraph addresses the question of what has to happen to the price level if national output increases, with the price of inputs remaining constant. Alternatively, one could ask what will happen to firms' willingness to supply output if product prices rise with no increase in input prices. Production becomes more profitable, and since firms are interested in making profits, they will usually produce more. Thus, when the price level of final output rises while input prices are held constant, firms are motivated to increase their outputs. This is true for the individual firm and also for firms in the aggregate. This increase in the amount produced leads to an upward slope of the *SRAS* curve.

Thus, whether we look at how the price level responds in the short run to increases in output or how the level of output responds to an increase in the price level with input prices being held constant, we find that the *SRAS* curve has a positive slope.

Increasing slope

A less obvious but in many ways more important property of a typical *SRAS* curve is that its slope *increases* as output rises. It is rather flat to the left of potential output and rather steep to the right. Why? Below potential output, firms typically have unused capacity—some plant and equipment are idle. When firms are faced with unused capacity, only a small increase in the price of their output may be needed to induce them to expand production—at least up to normal capacity.

Once output is pushed far beyond normal capacity, however, unit costs tend to rise quite rapidly. Many higher-cost expedients may have to be adopted. Standby capacity, overtime, and extra shifts may have to be used. Such expedients raise the cost of producing a unit of output. These higher-cost methods will not be used unless the selling price of the output has risen enough to cover them. The further output is expanded beyond normal capacity, the more rapidly unit costs rise and hence the larger is the rise in price that is needed to induce firms to increase output even further.

This increasing slope is sometimes called the *first important asymmetry* in the behaviour of aggregate supply. (The second, 'sticky wages', will be discussed in the next chapter.)

The analysis of Chapter 9 shows how a firm in a perfectly competitive market, when faced with a higher output price, expands output *along* its marginal cost curve until marginal cost is once again equal to price.

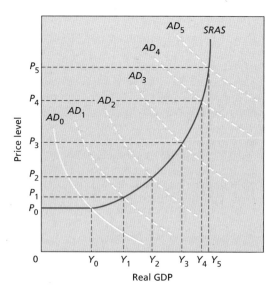

Figure 23.10 The effects of increases in aggregate demand

The effects of increases in aggregate demand are divided between increases in real output and increases in prices, depending on the shape of the *SRAS* curve. Increases in aggregate demand up to AD_0 have virtually no impact on the price level. When aggregate demand increases from AD_0 to AD_1, there is a relatively small increase in the price level, from P_0 to P_1, and a relatively large increase in output, from Y_0 to Y_1. Successive further increases bring larger price increases and relatively smaller output increases. By the time aggregate demand is at AD_5, virtually all of the effect is on the price level.

Over the *steep* range, for GDP above Y_4, the economy is near its capacity constraint. Any change in aggregate demand leads to a sharp change in the price level and to little change in real GDP. The multiplier in this case is nearly zero.

How do we reconcile what we have just discovered with the analysis of Chapters 21 and 22, where shifts in *AE* *always* change real GDP? The answer is that each *AE* curve is drawn on the assumption that there is a constant price level and plenty of excess capacity. A rise in *AE* shifts the *AD* curve to the right. However, a steep *SRAS* curve means that the price level rises significantly (because there is little excess capacity), and this shifts the *AE* curve downward, offsetting some of its initial rise.

This interaction is seen most easily if we study the extreme case, shown in Figure 23.11, in which the *SRAS* curve is vertical. An increase in autonomous expenditure shifts the *AE* curve upward, thus raising the amount demanded. However, a vertical *SRAS* curve means that output cannot be expanded to satisfy the increased demand. Instead, the extra demand merely forces prices up, and as prices rise, the *AE* curve shifts downward once again. The rise in prices continues until the *AE* curve is back to where

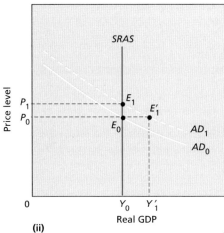

Figure 23.11 Demand shocks when the *SRAS* curve is vertical

If the *SRAS* curve were vertical, the effect of an increase in autonomous expenditure would be solely a rise in the price level. An increase in autonomous expenditure shifts the *AE* curve upwards from AE_0 to AE_1, as shown by arrow 1 in part (i). Given the initial price level P_0, equilibrium would shift from E_0 to E_1' and real GDP would rise from Y_0 to Y_1'. However, the price level does not remain constant. This is shown by the *SRAS* curve in part (ii). Instead, the price level rises to P_1. This causes the *AE* curve to shift back down all the way to AE_0, as shown by arrow 2 in part (i), and equilibrium output stays at Y_0. In part (ii) the new equilibrium is at E_1, with GDP at Y_0 and price level P_1.

it started. Thus the rise in prices offsets the expansionary effect of the original shift and, as a result, leaves both real aggregate expenditure and equilibrium real GDP unchanged.

The discussion of Figures 23.10 and 23.11 illustrates a general proposition:

The effect of any given shift in aggregate demand will be

divided between a change in real output and a change in the price level, depending on the conditions of aggregate supply. The steeper the *SRAS* curve, the greater is the price effect, and the smaller is the output effect.

For reasons discussed in Boxes 23.2 and 23.3, the *SRAS* curve probably has the shape shown in Figure 23.10, that is, relatively flat for low levels of output and becoming steeper as the level of GDP increases (relative to potential GDP). This shape of the *SRAS* curve implies that at low levels of GDP (well below potential), shifts in aggregate demand primarily affect output, and at high levels of GDP (above potential), shifts in aggregate demand primarily affect prices.

Of course, as we have noted already, treating wages and other input prices as constant is appropriate only when the time-period under consideration is short. Hence the *SRAS* curve is used only to analyse short-run, or *impact*, effects. In the next chapter we will see what happens in the *long run* when input prices (especially wages) respond to changes in GDP and the price level. First, however, our analysis of the short run needs to be completed with a discussion of aggregate supply shocks.

Aggregate supply shocks

A decrease in aggregate supply is shown by a shift to the left of the *SRAS* curve and means that less national output will be supplied at any given price level. An increase in aggregate supply is shown by a shift to the right of the *SRAS* curve and means that more national output will be produced at any given price level.

Figure 23.12 illustrates the effects on the price level and real GDP of aggregate supply shocks. Following a decrease in aggregate supply, the price level rises and real GDP falls. This combination of events is called *stagflation*, a rather inelegant word that has been derived by combining *stagnation* (a term that is sometimes used to mean slow growth or even falling output) and *inflation*.

Figure 23.12 also shows that an increase in aggregate supply leads to an increase in real GDP and a decrease in the price level.

Aggregate supply shocks cause the price level and real GDP to change in opposite directions: with an increase in supply the price level falls and output rises; with a decrease in supply the price level rises and output falls.

An aggregate supply shock means that there is a shift in the *SRAS* curve (for example, from $SRAS_0$ to $SRAS_1$ in Figure 23.12). Adjustment to the new equilibrium following the shock involves a movement along the *AD* curve (for example, from E_0 to E_1).

Oil prices have provided three major examples of aggregate supply shocks in recent decades. The major industrial

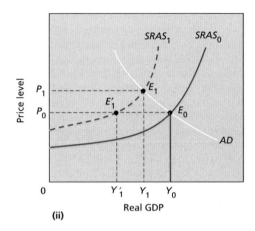

Figure 23.12 Aggregate supply shocks

Shifts in aggregate supply cause the price level and real GDP to move in opposite directions. The original equilibrium is at E_0 with GDP of Y_0 in both parts of the figure. The price level is P_0 in part (ii), and at that price level the desired aggregate expenditure curve is AE_0 in part (i).

   An aggregate supply shock now shifts the *SRAS* curve in part (ii) to $SRAS_1$. At the original price level of P_0, firms are now willing to supply only Y_1'. The fall in supply, with no corresponding fall in demand, causes a shortage that leads to a rise in the price level along $SRAS_1$. The new equilibrium is reached at E_1, where the *AD* curve intersects $SRAS_1$. At the new, and higher, equilibrium price level of P_1, the *AE* curve has fallen to AE_1, as shown in part (i), which is consistent with equilibrium GDP of Y_1.

economies have been especially responsive to changes in the market for oil, because, in addition to being used to produce energy, oil is an input into plastics and many other materials that are widely used in production. Massive increases in oil prices during 1973–4 and 1979–80 caused leftward shifts in the *SRAS* curve for virtually all major economies. GDP fell while the price level rose, causing stagflation. During the mid-1980s oil prices fell substantially. This shifted the *SRAS* curve to the right, increasing GDP and putting downward pressure on the price level. We can see now how a rightward shift in the *SRAS* curve, which is brought about by an increase in productivity or a fall in input prices, raises real GDP and lowers the price level.

Summary

Aggregate demand

■ A change in the price level shifts the *AE* curve upward when the price level falls and downward when the price level rises. A new equilibrium level of GDP results.

■ The *AD* curve plots the equilibrium level of GDP that corresponds to each possible price level. A change in equilibrium GDP following a change in the price level is shown by a *movement along* the *AD* curve.

■ A rise in the price level lowers exports and lowers private consumption spending (because it decreases consumers' wealth). Both of these changes lower equilibrium GDP and cause the aggregate demand curve to have a negative slope.

■ The *AD* curve shifts when any element of autonomous expenditure changes, and the simple multiplier measures the magnitude of the shift. This multiplier also measures

the size of the change in equilibrium GDP when the price level remains constant *and* firms produce everything that is demanded at that price level.

Aggregate supply and macroeconomic equilibrium

■ The short-run aggregate supply (*SRAS*) curve, drawn for given input prices, is positively sloped because unit costs rise with increasing output and because rising product prices make it profitable to increase output. An increase in productivity or a decrease in input prices shifts the curve to the right. A decrease in productivity or an increase in input prices has the opposite effect.

■ Macroeconomic equilibrium refers to equilibrium values of real GDP and the price level, as determined by the intersection of the *AD* and *SRAS* curves. Shifts in the *AD* and *SRAS* curves, called aggregate demand shocks and aggregate supply shocks, change the equilibrium values of real GDP and the price level.

Changes in GDP and the price level

■ When the *SRAS* curve is positively sloped, an aggregate demand shock causes the price level and real GDP to move in the same direction, the division between these effects depending on the shape of the *SRAS* curve. The main effect is on real GDP when the *SRAS* curve is flat and on the price level when it is steep.

■ An aggregate supply shock moves equilibrium real GDP along the *AD* curve, causing the price level and output to move in opposite directions. A leftward shift in the *SRAS* curve causes a stagflation—rising prices and falling output. A rightward shift causes an increase in real GDP and a fall in the price level. The division of the effects of a shift in *SRAS* between a change in real GDP and a change in the price level depends on the shape of the *AD* curve.

Topics for review

- Effects of a change in the price level
- Relationship between the *AE* and *AD* curves
- Negative slope of the *AD* curve
- Positive slope of the *SRAS* curve
- Macroeconomic equilibrium
- Aggregate demand shocks
- The multiplier when the price level varies
- Aggregate supply shocks
- Stagflation

Questions for discussion

1 Explain why it is that changes in the price level lead to changes in desired aggregate expenditure for each level of GDP.

2 Explain what happens to the UK *AD* curve in response to each of the following exogenous changes: (*a*) a rise in optimism leads to higher investment, (*b*) the government decides to build some new schools, (*c*) there is a recession in the United States, (*d*) consumers become cautious about the future and decide to save more, (*e*) GDP in France and Germany rises, (*f*) new computer technology increases productivity in manufacturing industry.

3 Show what would happen to the *SRAS* curve if (*a*) investment in transport infrastructure lowers costs of shipping goods and raw materials, (*b*) oil prices rise, (*c*) workers agree to work for lower wages, (*d*) there is an increase in export demand, (*e*) there is technical innovation in manufacturing industry.

4 Outline how the interaction of the *AD* and *SRAS* curves determines the course of GDP and the price level in response to (*a*) a rise in wage rates, (*b*) an increase in investment, (*c*) a reduction in government consumption, (*d*) a boom in demand in neighbouring economies.

5 Explain why the change in GDP in response to an increase in export demand is smaller than that suggested by the simple multiplier. What happens to the size of this effect as GDP gets above its potential level?

6 Explain how it is that the shifts in *AD* set out in question 2 are consistent with the condition that injections equal leakages.

Chapter 24
GDP and the Price Level in the Long Run

Every employee knows that the best time to ask for a pay rise is during a boom, when the demand for labour is high. Every employee also knows that it is difficult to get significant wage increases during a recession, when high unemployment signals a low demand for labour. Every manager in industry knows that the cost of many materials tends to rise rapidly during business expansions and to fall—often dramatically—during recessions. In short, input prices change with economic conditions, and we need to allow for these effects.

It is necessary, therefore, to go beyond the assumption of fixed input prices that we used in Chapter 23 to study the initial effects of aggregate demand and aggregate supply shocks. To do this we need to see what happens in a longer-term setting, when changes in GDP *induce* changes in input prices. Once we have completed this task, we can use our model of the macroeconomy to investigate the causes and consequences of business cycles and further our analysis of fiscal policy.

Induced changes in input prices

We begin by revising two key concepts that we first encountered in Chapter 21: potential output and the GDP gap.

Another look at potential output and the GDP gap

Recall that potential output is the total output that can be produced when all productive resources are being used at their *normal rates of utilization*. When a nation's actual output diverges from its potential output, the difference is called the GDP gap or output gap. (See Figure 21.1 on page 357.)

Although growth in potential output has powerful effects from one decade to the next, its change from one year to the next is small enough to be ignored when studying the year-to-year behaviour of GDP and the price level. (See Chapter 32 for a discussion of the determinants of the growth of potential output.) Therefore, in this discussion we will continue with the convention, first adopted in Chapter 21, of ignoring the small changes in potential GDP caused by year-to-year changes in productivity. This means that variations in the output gap are determined solely by variations in actual GDP around a given potential GDP.

Figure 24.1 shows actual GDP being determined by the intersection of the *AD* and *SRAS* curves. Potential GDP is constant, and it is shown by identical vertical lines in the two parts of the figure. In part (i), the *AD* and *SRAS* curves intersect to produce an equilibrium GDP that falls short of potential GDP. The result is called a *recessionary gap* because recessions often begin when actual output falls below potential output. In part (ii) the *AD* and *SRAS* curves intersect to produce an equilibrium GDP that exceeds potential output, resulting in an *inflationary gap*. The way in which an inflationary output gap puts upward pressure on prices will become clear in the following discussion.

Input prices and the output gap

The output gap provides a convenient measure of the pressure of demand on input prices. When actual GDP is high relative to potential GDP, demand for inputs will also be high. When actual GDP is low relative to potential GDP, demand for inputs will be relatively low. This relationship is true of all inputs. The discussion that follows is simplified, however, by focusing on one key input, labour, and on its price, the wage rate.

When there is an inflationary gap, actual output exceeds

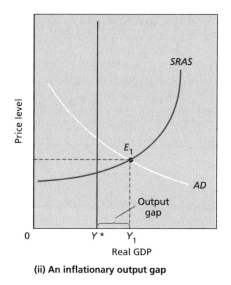

(i) A recessionary output gap   (ii) An inflationary output gap

Figure 24.1 Actual GDP, potential GDP, and the output gap
The output gap is the difference between potential GDP, Y^*, and actual GDP, Y. Potential GDP is shown by a vertical line because it refers to a given, constant level of real GDP. Actual GDP is determined by the intersection of the aggregate demand (AD) and short-run aggregate supply ($SRAS$) curves.

In part (i) the positions of the AD and $SRAS$ curves result in a recessionary gap: equilibrium is at E_0, so actual GDP is given by Y_0, which is less than potential output. The output gap is thus $Y^* - Y_0$. In part (ii) the positions of the AD and $SRAS$ curves result in an inflationary gap. Although potential output is unchanged at Y^*, equilibrium is now at E_1, so actual GDP is given by Y_1, which is greater than potential output. The output gap is $Y_1 - Y^*$.

potential, and the demand for labour services will be relatively high. When there is a recessionary gap, actual output is below potential, and the demand for labour services will be relatively low.

Each of these situations has implications for wages. Before turning to a detailed analysis, we first consider a benchmark for the behaviour of wages. Earlier we referred to average costs per unit of output as *unit costs*; to focus on labour costs, we now use average wage costs per unit of output, which we refer to as *unit labour costs*.

Upward and downward wage pressures In this section we consider the *upward* and *downward* pressures on wages that are associated with various output gaps. Most wage bargaining starts from the assumption that, other things being equal, workers will get the benefit of increases in their own productivity by receiving higher wages. Thus when GDP is at its potential level, wages will tend to be rising at the same rate as productivity is rising.[1] When wages and productivity change proportionately, *unit labour costs* remain unchanged. For example, if each worker produces 4 per cent more and earns 4 per cent more, unit labour costs will remain constant. This, then, is the benchmark:

When there is neither excess demand nor excess supply in

the labour market, wages will tend to be rising at the same rate as labour productivity; as a result unit labour costs will remain constant.

Note that with unit labour costs remaining constant, there is no pressure coming from the labour market for the $SRAS$ curve to shift. Hence there is no pressure for the price level to change. (Notice also our implicit assumption that at potential GDP the labour market is in equilibrium.) Indeed, a key characteristic of the definition of potential GDP is that there is no pressure for unit labour costs to rise or fall. So the state of the labour market and the level of potential GDP are inextricably connected.

In comparison with this benchmark of constant unit labour costs, *upward pressure on wages* means that there is pressure for wages to rise faster than productivity is rising. Thus unit labour costs will also be rising. For example, if money wages rise by 8 per cent while productivity rises by

[1] Ongoing inflation would also influence the normal pattern of wage changes. Wage contracts often allow for changes in prices that are expected to occur during the life of the contract. For now we make the simplifying assumption that the price level is expected to be constant; hence changes in money wages also are expected to be changes in real wages. The distinction between changes in money wages and real wages, and the important role played by expectations of price level changes, will be discussed later.

only 4 per cent, labour costs per unit of output will be rising by about 4 per cent. In this case the *SRAS* curve will be shifting to the left, reflecting upward pressure on wage costs coming from the labour market.

Downward pressure on wages means that there is pressure for wages to rise more slowly than productivity is rising. When this occurs, unit labour costs will be falling. For example, if productivity rises by 4 per cent while money wages rise by only 2 per cent, labour costs per unit of output will be falling by about 2 per cent. In this case the *SRAS* curve will be shifting to the right, reflecting downward pressure on wage costs coming from the labour market.

Actual GDP exceeds potential GDP Sometimes the *AD* and *SRAS* curves intersect where actual output exceeds potential, as illustrated in part (ii) of Figure 24.1. Firms are producing beyond their normal-capacity output, so there is an unusually large demand for all inputs, including labour. Labour shortages will emerge in some industries and among many groups of workers, particularly skilled workers. Firms will try to bid workers away from other firms in order to maintain the high levels of output and sales made possible by the boom conditions.

As a result of these tight labour market conditions, workers will find that they have considerable bargaining power with their employers, and they will put upward pressure on wages relative to productivity. Firms, recognizing that demand for their goods is strong, will be anxious to maintain a high level of output. Thus, to prevent their workers from either striking or quitting and moving to other employers, firms will be willing to accede to some of these upward pressures.

The boom that is associated with an inflationary gap generates a set of conditions—high profits for firms and unusually large demand for labour—that exerts upward pressure on wages.

Actual GDP is less than potential GDP Sometimes the *AD* and *SRAS* curves intersect where actual output is less than potential, as illustrated in part (i) of Figure 24.1. In this situation firms are producing below their normal-capacity output, so the demands for all inputs, including labour, are unusually low. The general conditions in the market for labour will be the opposite of those that occur when actual output exceeds potential. There will be labour surpluses in some industries and among some groups of workers. Firms will have below-normal sales, and will not only resist upward pressures on wages, but also tend to offer wage increases below productivity increases. They may even seek reductions in money wages.

The slump that is associated with a recessionary gap generates a set of conditions—low profits for firms, unusually low demand for labour, and a desire on the part of firms to resist wage demands and even to push for wage

concessions—that exerts downward pressure on wages and unit labour costs.

Adjustment asymmetry There is an asymmetry in the economy's aggregate supply behaviour. Boom conditions, along with severe labour shortages, cause wages, unit labour costs, and the price level to rise rapidly. When there is a large excess demand for labour, wage (and price) increases may well run ahead of productivity increases. Money wages might be rising by, say, 6 per cent, while productivity is rising at only 2 per cent, so that unit labour costs would be rising by around 4 per cent.

The experience of most European economies (and other industrial economies, such as the United States and Canada) suggests, however, that the downward pressures on wages during slumps often do not operate as quickly as do the upward pressures during booms. Even in quite severe recessions, when the price level is fairly stable, money wages may continue to rise, although their rate of increase tends to fall below that of productivity. For example, productivity might be rising at, say, 1.5 per cent per year while money wages are rising at 0.5 per cent. In this case unit labour costs are falling, but only by about 1 per cent per year. The rightward shift in the *SRAS* curve and the downward pressure on the price level are correspondingly slight. Money wages may actually fall, reducing unit wage costs even more, but the reduction in unit labour costs in the times of deepest recession has not been as fast as the increases that have occurred during several of the strongest booms.

Both upward and downward adjustments to unit labour costs do occur, but there is a difference in the speed at which they typically operate. Excess demand can cause unit labour costs to rise very rapidly; excess supply normally causes unit labour costs to fall only slowly.[2]

Inflationary and recessionary gaps Now it should be clear why the output gaps are named as they are. When actual GDP exceeds potential GDP, there will normally be rising unit costs, and the *SRAS* curve will be shifting upward. This in turn will push the price level up. Indeed, the most obvious event accompanying these conditions is likely to be a significant inflation. The larger is the excess of actual output over potential output, the greater will be the inflationary pressure. The term *inflationary gap* emphasizes this salient feature.

When actual output is less than potential output, as we have seen, there will be unemployment of labour and other productive resources. Unit labour costs will fall only slowly, leading to a slow downward shift in the *SRAS* curve. Hence the price level will be falling only slowly, so

---

[2] This is the second asymmetry in aggregate supply that we have encountered. The first refers to the variable slope of the *SRAS* curve, as discussed in Box 23.3.

that *unemployment* will be the output gap's most obvious result. The term *recessionary gap* emphasizes this salient feature that high rates of unemployment occur when actual output falls short of potential output.

The induced effects of output gaps on unit labour costs and the consequent shifts in the *SRAS* curve play an important role in our analysis of the long-run consequences of aggregate demand shocks, to which we now turn.

The long-run consequences of aggregate demand shocks

We can now extend our study to cover the longer-run consequences of aggregate demand shocks, by incorporating changes in input prices. We need to examine separately the effects of aggregate demand shocks on input prices for expansionary and for contractionary shocks, since the behaviour of unit costs is not symmetrical for the two cases.

Expansionary shocks

Suppose that the economy starts with a stable price level at full employment, so actual GDP equals potential GDP,

as shown by the initial equilibrium in part (i) of Figure 24.2.

Now suppose that this happy situation is disturbed by an increase in autonomous expenditure, perhaps caused by a sudden boom in investment spending. Figure 24.2(i) shows the effects of this aggregate demand shock in raising both the price level and GDP. Now actual GDP exceeds potential GDP, and there is an inflationary gap.

We have seen that an inflationary gap leads wages to rise faster than productivity, which causes unit costs to rise. The *SRAS* curve shifts to the left as firms seek to pass on their increases in input costs by increasing their output

(i) Autonomous increase in aggregate demand   **(ii) Induced shift in aggregate supply**

Figure 24.2 Demand-shock inflation
A rightward shift of the *AD* curve first raises prices and output along the *SRAS* curve. It then induces a shift of the *SRAS* curve that further raises prices but lowers output along the *AD* curve. In part (i) the economy is in equilibrium at E_0, at its level of potential output Y^* and price level P_0. The *AD* curve then shifts to AD_1. This moves equilibrium to E_1, with GDP Y_1 and price level P_1, and opens up an inflationary gap of $Y^* - Y_1$.

In part (ii) the inflationary gap results in an increase in wages and other input costs, shifting the *SRAS* curve leftward. As this happens, output falls and the price level rises along AD_1. Eventually, when the *SRAS* curve has shifted to $SRAS_1$, output is back to Y^* and the inflationary gap has been eliminated. However, the price level has risen to P_2.

prices. For this reason the initial increases in the price level and in real GDP shown in part (i) of Figure 24.2 are *not* the final effects of the demand shock. As seen in part (ii) of the figure, the upward shift of the *SRAS* curve causes a further rise in the price level, but this time the price rise is associated with a fall in output.

The cost increases (and the consequent upward shifts of the *SRAS* curve) continue until the inflationary gap has been removed, that is, until output returns to Y^*, its potential level. Only then is there no abnormal demand for labour, and only then do wages and unit costs, and hence the *SRAS* curve, stabilize.

This important expansionary demand-shock sequence can be summarized as follows:

1. Starting from full employment, a rise in aggregate demand raises the price level and raises output above its potential level as the economy expands along a given *SRAS* curve.

2. The expansion of output beyond its normal-capacity level puts pressure on input (especially labour) markets; input prices begin to increase faster than productivity, shifting the *SRAS* curve upward, such that prices are higher at every level of output.

3. The shift of the *SRAS* curve causes GDP to fall along the *AD* curve. This process continues *as long as* actual output exceeds potential output. Therefore, actual output eventually falls back to its potential level. The price level is, however, now higher than it was after the initial impact of the increased aggregate demand, but inflation will have come to a halt.

The ability to wring more output (and income) from the economy than its underlying potential output (as in point 2 above) is only a short-term possibility. GDP greater than Y^* sets into motion inflationary pressures that tend to push GDP back to Y^*.

A once-and-for-all demand shock sets off an adjustment process that eventually returns GDP to its potential level but (normally) at a different price level.

Contractionary shocks

Let us return to that fortunate economy with full employment and stable prices. It appears again in part (i) of Figure 24.3, which is similar to part (i) of Figure 24.2. Now assume that there is a *decline* in aggregate demand,

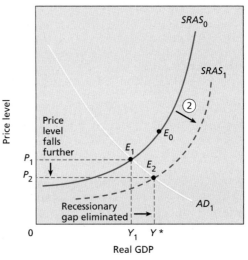

(i) Autonomous falls in aggregate demand   **(ii) Induced shift in aggregate supply**

Figure 24.3 Demand-shock deflation with flexible wages
A leftward shift of the *AD* curve first lowers prices and output along the *SRAS* curve and then induces a (slow) shift of the *SRAS* curve that further lowers prices but raises output along the *AD* curve. In part (i) the economy is in equilibrium at E_0, at its level of potential output Y^* and price level P_0. The *AD* curve then shifts to AD_1, moving equilibrium to E_1, with output Y_1 and price level P_1, and opens up a recessionary gap of $Y^* - Y_1$.

Part (ii) shows the adjustment back to full employment that occurs from the supply side of the economy. The fall in wages shifts the *SRAS* curve to the right. Real GDP rises, and the price level falls further along the *AD* curve. Eventually the *SRAS* curve reaches $SRAS_1$, with equilibrium at E_2. The price level stabilizes at P_2 when GDP returns to Y^*, eliminating the recessionary gap.

perhaps owing to a major reduction in investment expenditure, or to a fall in exports as a result of a fall in overseas demand.

The first effects of the decline are a fall in output and some downward adjustment of the price level, as shown in part (i) of the figure. As output falls, unemployment rises. The difference between potential GDP and actual GDP is the recessionary gap that is shown in the figure.

Flexible wages What would happen if severe unemployment caused wage rates to fall rapidly relative to productivity? For example, with productivity rising by 1 per cent per year, suppose that money wages fell by 4 per cent. Unit costs would then *fall* by 5 per cent. Falling wage rates would lower unit costs, causing a rightward shift of the *SRAS* curve. As shown in part (ii) of Figure 24.3, the economy would move along AD_1, with falling prices and rising output, until full employment was restored at potential GDP, Y^*. We conclude that if wages were to fall whenever there was unemployment, the resulting fall in the *SRAS* curve would restore full employment.

Flexible wages that fell during periods of unemployment would provide an automatic adjustment mechanism that would push the economy back towards full employment whenever output fell below potential.

Sticky wages Boom conditions, along with severe labour shortages, do cause wages to rise rapidly, shifting the *SRAS* curve upward. However, as we noted earlier when we encountered the second asymmetry of aggregate supply behaviour, the experience of many economies suggests that wages typically do not fall rapidly in response to recessionary gaps and their accompanying unemployment. It is sometimes said that wages are 'sticky' in a downward direction. This does not mean that wages never fall. In recession money wages often rise more slowly than productivity and some money wages even fall. But the gap between money wages changes and productivity changes is typically quite small during recessions. This means that unit labour costs will fall only slowly. This in turn means that the downward shifts in the *SRAS* curve occur slowly, and the adjustment mechanism that depends on these shifts will act sluggishly.

One reason why wage rates do not adjust quickly to clear labour markets will be discussed in Chapter 31. This explanation is associated with the idea of *efficiency wages*, which we first encountered in Chapter 15 (pages 253–4). Because labour is not a standardized commodity, employers face both a problem of attracting the best workers and a problem of motivating those workers who have been hired. Employers are reluctant to lower wages for their workforce, even when there is an excess supply of potential new workers, because lower wages are more likely to attract lower-quality workers at the margin, and existing staff would be demotivated by such actions.

The weakness of the adjustment mechanism does not mean that slumps must always be prolonged. Rather, this weakness means that speedy recovery back to full employment must be generated mainly from the demand side. If the economy is to avoid a lengthy period of recession or stagnation, the force leading to recovery must usually be a rightward shift of the *AD* curve rather than a downward drift of the *SRAS* curve. Could government *stabilization policy* accomplish the needed shift in *AD*? This is one of the more important and contentious issues in macroeconomics, one that we will return to later in this book.

The SRAS curve shifts to the left fairly rapidly when GDP exceeds Y*, but it shifts to the right only slowly when GDP is less than Y*.

The asymmetry This difference in speed of adjustment is a consequence of the important asymmetry in the behaviour of aggregate supply that was noted earlier in this chapter. This asymmetry helps to explain two key facts about our economy. First, unemployment can persist for quite long periods without causing decreases in unit costs and prices of sufficient magnitude to remove the unemployment. Second, booms, along with labour shortages and production beyond normal capacity, do not persist for long periods without causing increases in unit costs and the price level.

The long-run aggregate supply (*LRAS*) curve

The adjustment mechanism leads us to an important construct called the **long-run aggregate supply (*LRAS*) curve.** This curve relates the price level to real GDP after wage rates and all other input costs have been fully adjusted to eliminate any unemployment or overall labour shortages.

Shape of the *LRAS* curve Once all the adjustments that are required have occurred, the economy will have eliminated any excess demand or excess supply of labour. In other words full employment will prevail, and output will necessarily be at its potential level, Y^*. It follows that the aggregate supply curve becomes a vertical line at Y^*, as shown in Figure 24.4. The *LRAS* curve is sometimes called the classical aggregate supply curve because the classical economists were concerned mainly with the behaviour of the economy in long-run equilibrium.

Notice that the vertical *LRAS* curve does not represent the same thing as the vertical portion of the *SRAS* curve (see Figure 23.10). Over the vertical range of the *SRAS* curve, the economy is at the utmost limit of its existing productive capacity, as might occur in an all-out war effort. No more can be squeezed out. The vertical shape of the *LRAS* curve is due to the workings of an adjustment mechanism that brings the economy back to its potential

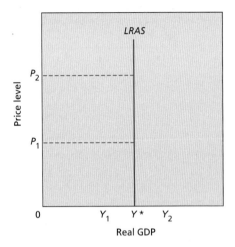

Figure 24.4 The long-run aggregate supply (*LRAS*) curve
The long-run aggregate supply curve is a vertical line drawn at the level of GDP that is equal to potential GDP, Y^*. It is a vertical line because the total amount of goods that the economy produces when all factors are efficiently used at their normal rate of utilization does not vary with the price level. If the price level were to rise from P_1 to P_2 and wages and all other factor prices were to rise by the same proportion, the total desired output of firms would remain at Y^*.

If output were Y_1, which is less than Y^*, wages would be falling and the *SRAS* curve would be shifting rightward; hence the economy would not be on its *LRAS* curve. If output were Y_2, which is greater than Y^*, wages would be rising and the *SRAS* curve would be shifting leftward; hence, again, the economy would not be on its *LRAS* curve.

output, even though actual output may differ from its potential level for considerable periods of time. It is called the long-run aggregate supply curve because it arises as a result of adjustments that take a significant amount of time.

Along the *LRAS* curve all the prices of all outputs and all inputs have been fully adjusted to eliminate any excess demands or supplies. Proportionate changes in money wages and the price level (which, by definition, will leave real wages unaltered) will also leave equilibrium employment and total output unchanged. In the next section we will ask what does change when we move from one point on the *LRAS* curve to another.

Long-run equilibrium

Figure 24.5 shows equilibrium GDP and the price level as they are determined by the intersection of the *AD* curve and the vertical *LRAS* curve. Because the *LRAS* curve is vertical, shifts in aggregate demand change the price level but not the level of equilibrium GDP, as shown in part (i). By contrast, a shift in aggregate supply changes both GDP and the price level, as shown in part (ii). For example, a

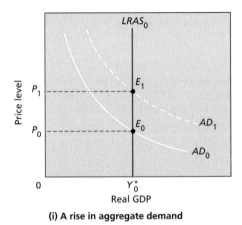

(i) A rise in aggregate demand

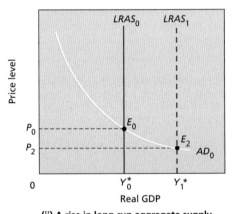

(ii) A rise in long-run aggregate supply

Figure 24.5 Long-run equilibrium and aggregate supply
When the *LRAS* curve is vertical, aggregate supply determines the long-run equilibrium value of GDP at Y^*. Given Y^*, aggregate demand determines the long-run equilibrium value of the price level. In both parts of the figure the initial long-run equilibrium is at E_0, so the price level is P_0 and GDP is Y_0^*.

In part (i) a shift in the *AD* curve from AD_0 to AD_1, with the *LRAS* curve remaining unchanged, moves the long-run equilibrium from E_0 to E_1. This raises the price level from P_0 to P_1 but leaves GDP unchanged at Y_0^* in the long run.

In part (ii) a shift in the *LRAS* curve from $LRAS_0$ to $LRAS_1$, with the aggregate demand curve remaining constant at AD_0, moves the long-run equilibrium from E_0 to E_2. This raises GDP from Y_0^* to Y_1^* but lowers the price level from P_0 to P_2.

rightward shift of the *LRAS* curve increases real GDP and leads to a fall in the price level.

With a vertical *LRAS* curve, in the long run total output is determined solely by conditions of supply, and the role of aggregate demand is simply to determine the price level.

What does change when the economy moves from one point on the *LRAS* curve, such as E_0 in part (i) of Figure

24.5, to another point, such as E_1? Although total output and total desired expenditure do not change, their *compositions* do change. The higher the price level, the lower is personal wealth (for a given nominal stock of assets) and hence the lower is private consumption. (Recall from Chapter 21 that private consumption is positively related to wealth.) Also the higher the price level, the lower are exports and the higher are imports, and hence the lower are net exports.

Suppose the economy starts at a point on the *SRAS* curve and an increase in government expenditure then creates an inflationary gap. Money wages and the price level rise until the gap is removed. At the new long-run equilibrium, the higher level of government spending is exactly offset by lower private consumption and net exports, leaving total output unchanged. A similar analysis holds for an increase in investment. In the new long-run equilibrium, the higher level of investment spending will be exactly offset by lower consumption spending and net exports.

The vertical *LRAS* curve shows that, given full adjustment of input prices, potential GDP, Y^*, is compatible with any price level although its composition among private consumption, investment, government consumption, and net exports may vary with different price levels.

In Chapter 26 we will discover circumstances under which a rise in the price level has *no real effects*, so that not only are real GDP and total expenditure the same at all points on the *LRAS* curve, but also the composition of expenditure among C, I, G, and $(X - IM)$ is also the same. We will also learn, once we have added a monetary sector, that interest rate changes have important effects on the composition of expenditure.

Real GDP in the short and long runs

We have now identified two distinct equilibrium conditions for the economy:

1. In the short run the economy is in equilibrium at the level of GDP and the price level where the *SRAS* curve intersects the *AD* curve.

2. In the long run the economy is in equilibrium at potential GDP, the position of the vertical *LRAS* curve. The price level is that at which the *AD* curve intersects the *LRAS* curve.

The *position* of the *LRAS* curve is at Y^*, which is determined by past economic growth. Deviations of actual output from potential output—GDP gaps—are generally associated with business cycles. Changes in total real output (and hence in employment, unemployment, and living standards) may take place as a result of either growth or the business cycle.

This discussion suggests a need to distinguish three ways in which GDP can be increased. These are illustrated in Figure 24.6.

Increases in aggregate demand As shown in part (i) of Figure 24.6, an increase in aggregate demand will yield a one-time increase in real GDP. If that increase occurs when there is a recessionary gap, it pushes GDP towards its potential level. It thus short-circuits the working of the automatic adjustment mechanism that would eventually have achieved the same outcome by depressing unit costs, as discussed earlier in this chapter.

If the demand shock pushes GDP beyond its potential level, the rise in GDP will be only temporary; the inflationary gap will cause wages and other costs to rise, shifting the *SRAS* curve to the left. This drives GDP back towards its potential level, so that the only lasting effect is on the price level. Box 24.1 gives a number of reasons why we might expect the effect of demand shocks on GDP to be cyclical, that is, to cause GDP to move first one way, then the other.

Increases in aggregate supply Increases in aggregate supply will also lead to increases in GDP. Here it is useful to distinguish between two possible kinds of increase that might occur—those that leave the *LRAS* curve unchanged and those that shift it.

Part (ii) of Figure 24.6 shows the effects of a positive shock to short-run aggregate supply that leaves potential GDP unchanged. This will shift the *SRAS* curve to the right but will have no effect on the *LRAS* curve. The shock will thus cause GDP to rise towards potential if it starts out below, but an increase that takes GDP beyond potential will eventually be reversed.

Part (iii) of Figure 24.6 shows the effects of permanent increases in aggregate supply that shift the *LRAS* curve. A once-and-for-all increase due, say, to a labour market policy that reduces the level of structural unemployment will lead to a one-time increase in potential GDP. A recurring increase that is due, say, to population growth, capital accumulation, or ongoing improvements in productivity causes a continual rightward shift in the *LRAS* curve,

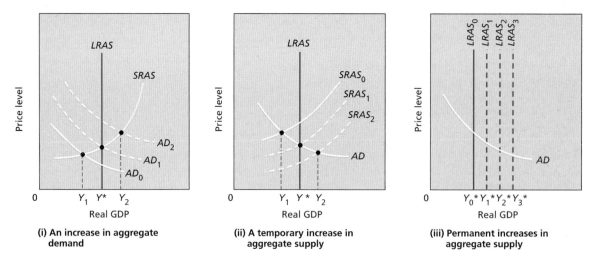

(i) An increase in aggregate demand

(ii) A temporary increase in aggregate supply

(iii) Permanent increases in aggregate supply

Figure 24.6 Three ways of increasing GDP

GDP will increase in response to an increase in aggregate demand or an increase in aggregate supply. The increase will be permanent if the *LRAS* curve shifts, but if the *LRAS* curve does not shift, any divergences of GDP from potential will be only temporary; the output gap that is created will set in motion the wage adjustments that we studied earlier in this chapter. In part (i) of the figure the *AD* curve shifts to the right. If the initial level of output is Y_1, then the shift from AD_0 to AD_1 eliminates the recessionary gap and raises GDP to Y^*. If the initial level of GDP is Y^*, then the shift from AD_1 to AD_2 raises GDP to Y_2 and thereby opens up an inflationary gap.

In part (ii) the *SRAS* curve shifts to the right. If the initial level of output is Y_1, then the shift from $SRAS_0$ to $SRAS_1$ eliminates the recessionary gap and raises GDP to Y^*. If the initial level of output is Y^*, then the shift from $SRAS_1$ to $SRAS_2$ raises GDP to Y_2 and thereby opens up an inflationary gap.

In the cases shown in parts (i) and (ii) any increase in output beyond potential is temporary, since, in the absence of any additional shocks, the inflationary gap will cause wages and other factor prices to rise; this will cause the *SRAS* curve to shift upward and, hence, GDP to converge to Y^*.

In part (iii) the *LRAS* curve shifts to the right, causing potential GDP to increase. Whether or not actual output increases immediately depends on what happens to the *AD* and *SRAS* curves. Since, in the absence of other shocks, actual GDP eventually converges to potential GDP, a rightward shift in the *LRAS* curve eventually leads to an increase in actual GDP. If the shift in the *LRAS* curve is recurring, then GDP will grow continually.

Box 24.1 Demand shocks and business cycles

Aggregate demand shocks are a major source of fluctuations in GDP around Y^*. As we have seen, an expansionary demand shock, starting from a position of full employment, will lead to an increase in output, followed by a fall in output accompanied by an increase in prices as the adjustment mechanism restores the economy to equilibrium. Depending on the nature and magnitude of the shock, the adjustment will take many months, often stretching into one or two years.

Suppose that the government increases spending on roads or that economic growth in Germany leads to an increase in demand for UK exports. No matter what the source of growth in demand, the economy will not respond instantaneously. In many industries it takes weeks or months, or even longer, to bring new or mothballed capacity into production and to hire and train new workers. The multiplier process itself also takes time, as people and firms respond to the change in income that results from an initial increase in autonomous spending.

Because of these lags in the economy's response, changes in demand give rise to changes in output that are spread out over a substantial period of time. An increase in demand may lead to a gradual increase in output that builds up over several months. Then, as output does change, the adjustment mechanism comes into play. As an inflationary gap opens up, wages and costs start to rise, shifting the *SRAS* curve to the left.

Thus a once-and-for-all positive demand shock gives rise to a *cyclical* output response, with GDP first rising because of the rightward shift in the *AD* curve, and then falling because of the upward shift in the *SRAS* curve. A negative demand shock is likely to play out even more slowly because of the asymmetry of response. Again, however, the behaviour of output will be cyclical: starting from potential output, GDP will fall over a period of time, because of a leftward shift in the *AD* curve, and then rise slowly as the adjustment mechanism shifts *SRAS* to the right.

Each major component of aggregate expenditure—private consumption, investment, net exports, and government consumption—is subject to continual random shifts, which are sometimes large enough to disturb the economy significantly. Adjustment lags convert such shifts into cyclical oscillations in GDP.

giving rise to a continual increase in the level of potential GDP.

Economic growth

A gradual but continual rise in potential GDP, or what we have called *economic growth*, is the main source of improvements in the standard of living over the long term.

Eliminating a severe recessionary gap could cause a once-and-for-all increase in GDP of, say, 4 per cent, while eliminating structural unemployment will raise it by somewhat less. However, a growth rate of 3 per cent per year raises GDP by 10 per cent in 3 years, *doubles* it in 24 years, and *quadruples* it in 48 years.

In any given year the position of the *LRAS* curve is at potential GDP, Y^*. The 'long run' to which the *LRAS* curve refers is thus one in which the resources available to the economy do not change, but in which all markets reach equilibrium. Economic growth moves the *LRAS* curve to the right, year by year. Here the 'long run' is not a period in which everything settles down, because growth is a continuing process. Rather, the movement in *LRAS* causes a continuing movement in Y^*.

Determinants of long-run shifts in potential GDP, or economic growth, used to be regarded as beyond the scope of macroeconomics. However, it is clearly one of the most important factors in determining living standards. There is now a much stronger case for treating growth as an integral part of macroeconomics. This is that the forces of growth may be endogenous; that is, apparently short-term policies may have implications for long-term growth. No longer is it safe to assume that the determinants of growth are independent of the determinants of the short-term cycle. We discuss the determinants of economic growth further in Chapters 32 and 33.

Cyclical fluctuations

Figure 24.6 allows us to distinguish the causes of trend growth in potential GDP, which is the gradual rightward shifting of the *LRAS* curve, from the causes of cyclical fluctuations, which are deviations from that trend.

Cyclical fluctuations in GDP are caused by shifts in the *AD* and *SRAS* curves that cause actual GDP to deviate temporarily from potential GDP.

These shifts in turn are caused by changes in a variety of factors, including interest rates, exchange rates, consumer and business confidence, and government policy. Although the resulting deviations of actual from potential GDP are described as 'temporary', recall from the discussion above that the automatic adjustment mechanism may work slowly enough that the deviations can persist for some time, perhaps several years.

Figure 24.7(i) shows the level of UK real GDP since 1885. The dominant feature of this graph is the continued

(i) Real GDP, United Kingdom, 1885–1997 (annual data, 1985 prices)

(ii) Annual growth rate of real GDP, United Kingdom, 1886–1997

Figure 24.7 UK real GDP and growth rate

Real GDP, which measures the total production of goods and services for the whole economy over a year, has grown steadily over the last century.

(i) Long-term growth is reflected in the upward trend of real GDP. There were significant declines in real GDP after each of the world wars, there was a recession in the 1930s, and there have been three noticeable recessions since 1970. Otherwise the trend dominates the cycle in the long term.

(ii) Real growth is measured by the annual rate of change of GDP. This has fluctuated sharply, but has generally been positive.

Sources: 100 Years of Economic Statistics, The Economist, 1989, and Economic Trends.

upward trend that has led to a more than sixfold increase in real GDP in just over 100 years. The average year-to-year increase is only about 2.25 per cent, but the cumulative effect of this slow but steady growth has been spectacular. This long-term trend reflects the steady rightward shift in the *LRAS* curve associated with sustained increases in potential GDP.

Part (ii) of Figure 24.7 shows the year-to-year percentage changes in UK real GDP. Fluctuations in the annual rate of growth reflect the effects of aggregate demand and supply shocks. The two largest positive shocks derive from the increases in aggregate demand associated with the First and Second World Wars. The two largest negative demand shocks appear to be associated with the ends of those two wars, though there were sharp recessions in the early 1920s and early 1930s. The three post-1970 recessions look trivial in comparison with these earlier events, even though many who lived through them suffered severe loss of income and/or employment.

Government policy and the business cycle

Macroeconomics, as a formal discipline, was developed not just to explain business cycles, but also to suggest policies that could be used to avoid the worst occurrences of recessions—where there is persistent high unemployment and excess capacity. Central to the so-called Keynesian revolution in economic policymaking was the idea that government policy could be used in a countercyclical manner to stabilize the economy. Accordingly, in the remainder of this chapter we discuss how changes in governments' taxing and spending policies might be used as tools of stabilization policy. The use of taxes and spending by the government in an attempt to control the economy is known as discretionary *fiscal stabilization policy*, which is defined as *deliberate* changes in tax rates or government expenditure that are targeted at stabilizing the economy. In Chapter 27 we will return to the subject of stabilization policy, because by then we will also be able to discuss the role of *monetary policy*.

Since increases in government expenditure increase aggregate demand and increases in taxation decrease it, the *directions* of the required changes in spending and taxation are generally easy to determine, once we know the direction of the desired change in GDP. However, the *timing, magnitude*, and *mixture* of the changes pose more difficult issues.

There is no doubt that the government can exert a major influence on GDP. Prime examples are the massive increases in military spending during major wars. British government expenditure during the Second World War rose from 13.4 per cent of GDP in 1938 to 49.2 per cent of GDP in 1944. At the same time the unemployment rate fell from 9.2 per cent to 0.3 per cent. Most observers agree that the increase in government spending helped to bring about the rise in GDP and the associated fall in unemployment. Similar experiences occurred during the rearmament of most European countries before, or just following, the outbreak of the Second World War in 1939 and in the United States during the Vietnam War in the late 1960s and early 1970s.

It might seem from what we have just said that fiscal policy can be an important tool for stabilizing the economy. In the heyday of fiscal policy activism, from about 1945 to about 1970, many economists were convinced that the economy could be stabilized adequately just by varying the size of the government's taxes and expenditures. That day is past. Today most economists are aware of the many limitations of fiscal policy.

The basic theory of fiscal stabilization

A reduction in tax rates or an increase in government expenditure will shift the *AD* curve to the right, causing an increase in GDP. An increase in tax rates or a cut in government expenditure will shift the *AD* curve to the left, causing a decrease in GDP.

A more detailed look at how fiscal stabilization works will provide a useful review. It will also help to show some of the complications that arise in making fiscal policy.

A recessionary gap The removal of a recessionary gap is illustrated in Figure 24.8. There are two possible ways in which the gap may be removed.

First, the recessionary gap may eventually drive wages and other factor prices down by enough to shift the *SRAS* curve to the right and thereby reinstate full employment and potential GDP (at a lower price level). The evidence, however, is that this process takes a substantial period of time.

Second, the *AD* curve could shift to the right, restoring the economy to full employment and potential GDP (at a higher price level). The government can cause such a shift by using expansionary fiscal policy, lowering taxes or raising spending. The advantage of using fiscal policy is that it may substantially shorten what would otherwise be a long recession. One disadvantage is that the use of fiscal policy may stimulate the economy just before private sector spending recovers on its own. As a result the economy may overshoot its potential output, and an inflationary gap may open up. In this case fiscal policy that is intended to promote economic stability can actually cause instability.

An inflationary gap Figure 24.9 shows the ways in which an inflationary gap can be removed.

First, wages and other factor prices may be pushed up by

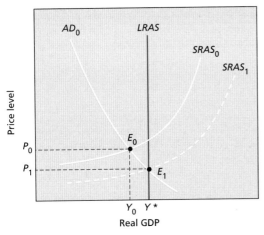

(i) A recessionary gap removed by a rightward shift in SRAS

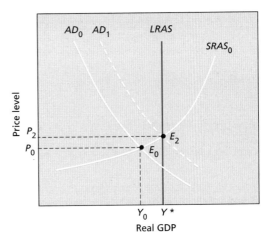

(ii) A recessionary gap removed by a rightward shift in AD

Figure 24.8 Removal of a recessionary gap

A recessionary gap may be removed by a (slow) rightward shift of the SRAS curve, a natural revival of private sector demand, or a fiscal-policy-induced increase in aggregate demand. Initially equilibrium is at E_0, with GDP at Y_0 and the price level at P_0. The recessionary gap is $Y^* - Y_0$.

In part (i) the gap might be removed by a shift in the SRAS curve to $SRAS_1$, as a result of reductions in wage rates and other input prices. The shift in the SRAS curve causes a movement down and to the right along AD_0 and establishes a new equilibrium at E_1, achieving potential GDP, Y^*, and lowering the price level to P_1.

In part (ii) the gap might also be removed by a shift of the AD curve to AD_1. That occurs either because of a natural revival of private sector expenditure or because of a fiscal-policy-induced increase in expenditure. The shift in the AD curve causes a movement up and to the right along $SRAS_0$ and shifts the equilibrium to E_2, raising GDP to Y^* and the price level to P_2.

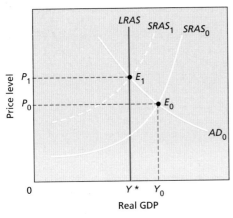

(i) An inflationary gap removed by a leftward shift in SRAS

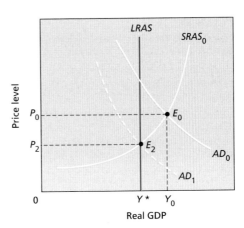

(ii) An inflationary gap removed by a leftward shift in AD

Figure 24.9 Removal of an inflationary gap

An inflationary gap may be removed by a leftward shift of the SRAS curve, a reduction in private sector demand, or a fiscal-policy-induced reduction in aggregate demand. Initially equilibrium is at E_0, with GDP at Y_0 and the price level at P_0. The inflationary gap is $Y^* - Y_0$.

In part (i) the gap might be removed by a shift in the SRAS curve to $SRAS_1$ that occurs as a result of increases in wage rates and other input prices. The shift in the SRAS curve causes a movement up and to the left along AD_0 and establishes a new equilibrium at E_1, reducing GDP to its potential level, Y^*, and raising the price level to P_1.

In part (ii) the gap might also be removed by a shift of the AD curve to AD_1 that occurs either because of a fall in private spending or because of contractionary fiscal policy. The shift in the AD curve causes a movement down and to the left along $SRAS_0$. This movement shifts the equilibrium to E_2, lowering GDP to Y^* and the price level to P_2.

the excess demand. The *SRAS* curve will therefore shift to the left, eventually eliminating the gap, reducing GDP to its potential level, and raising the price level.

Second, the *AD* curve could shift to the left, restoring equilibrium GDP. The government, by raising taxes or cutting spending, can induce such a shift, reducing aggregate demand sufficiently to remove the inflationary gap. The advantage of this approach is that it avoids the inflationary increase in prices that accompanies the first method. One disadvantage is that if private sector expenditure falls, GDP may be pushed below potential, thus opening up a recessionary gap.

A key proposition This discussion suggests that in circumstances in which the automatic adjustment mechanisms either fail to operate quickly enough, or give rise to undesirable side-effects such as rising prices, there is a potential stabilizing role for fiscal policy.

Government taxes and expenditure shift the *AD* curve and hence can be used to remove persistent GDP gaps.

Automatic stabilizers

The government budget surplus increases as GDP increases because tax revenues rise, and some transfer payments, especially unemployment-related benefits, fall. Thus net taxes move in the same direction as GDP. (Unless there are changes in policy, government consumption is generally unaffected by cyclical movements in the economy.) With procyclical net tax revenues, personal disposable income moves in the same direction as national income but does not move by as much. The government keeps a share of the increased GDP when it rises. When GDP falls, the fall in net taxes makes disposable income fall by less.

For example, in Chapter 22 we assumed that the net income tax rate was 10 per cent. This implies that a £1 rise in autonomous spending would increase disposable income by only 90p, dampening the multiplier effect of the initial increase. Generally, the wedge that income taxes place between national income and disposable income reduces the marginal propensity to spend out of national income, thereby reducing the size of the multiplier. The lower the multiplier, the less will equilibrium GDP tend to change for a given change in autonomous expenditure. The effect is to stabilize the economy, reducing the fluctuations in GDP that are caused by changes in autonomous expenditure. Because no policies need to be changed in order to achieve this result, the properties of the government budget that cause the multiplier to be reduced are called **automatic fiscal stabilizers.**

Even when the government does not undertake to stabilize the economy via discretionary fiscal policy, the fact that net tax revenues rise with GDP means that there are fiscal effects that cause the budget to act as an *automatic stabilizer* for the economy.

Of course, it is possible that a government might try to tie its spending in each period to the tax revenue it raises. This would change the impact of fiscal policy in a major way. Thus if a government follows a balanced budget policy in every period, its fiscal policy becomes *procyclical*. It will restrict its spending during a recession because its tax revenue is low, and it will increase its spending during a recovery when its tax revenue is rising. In other words it moves with the economy, raising and lowering its spending in step with everyone else, exactly counter to the theory of fiscal stabilization that we just discussed. Some politicians have proposed changing the law so that governments must balance their budget in every year. However, most economists rarely call for anything more restrictive than a policy whereby governments aim to balance their budget on average over the course of the business cycle. A budget that was balanced on average would still permit the automatic stabilizer that is built into fiscal policy to work.

Limitations of discretionary fiscal policy

The discussion of the previous few pages might suggest that returning the economy to potential is simply a matter of changing taxes and government spending, in some combination. However, many economists argue that such policies would be as likely to harm as help. Part of their reasoning is that the execution of successful discretionary fiscal policy is anything but simple.[3]

Lags Changing fiscal policy requires changing taxes and government expenditures. In the UK case the changes must be agreed upon by the Cabinet and passed by Parliament. Major changes in taxes are normally announced only once a year, in the spring Budget Statement, although 'mini-budgets' are possible if 'crisis' measures need to be taken at other times of year. In the United States and most European countries, the budgetary process also involves an annual round of policy proposals and legislation.

The political stakes in such changes are generally very large. Taxes and spending are called 'bread-and-butter issues' precisely because they affect the economic well-being of almost everyone. Thus even if experts agreed that the economy would be helped by a tax cut, politicians may spend a good deal of time debating *whose* taxes should be cut and *by how much.* The delay between the initial recognition of a recession or inflation and the enactment of legislation to change fiscal policy is called a **decision lag.** Even prior to this lag there is an inevitable delay because

---

[3] Another part has to do with the long-term consequences of budget deficits. Governments that run deficits for long periods build up substantial debts. These debts require significant tax revenues just to pay the interest, and this limits the ability of governments to spend on other programmes. Also, depending on the exchange rate regime, international considerations may reduce (but not eliminate) fiscal policy's effectiveness as a stabilization tool.

statistics take time to collect and process; this is known as an **information lag.**

Once policy changes are agreed upon, there is still an **execution lag,** adding time between the enactment and the implementation of the change. Furthermore, once policies are in place, it will usually take still more time for their economic consequences to be felt.

Because of these lags, it is quite possible that by the time a given policy decision has any impact on the economy, circumstances will have changed such that the policy is no longer appropriate.

Figure 24.10 illustrates the problems that can arise in these circumstances.

To make matters even more frustrating, tax measures that are known to be temporary are generally less effective than measures that are expected to be permanent. If consumers know that a given tax cut will last for only a year, they may recognize that the effect on their long-run consumption possibilities is small and may adjust their short-run consumption relatively little. The more closely

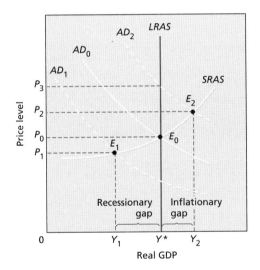

Figure 24.10 Effects of fiscal policies that are not reversed

Fiscal policies that are initially appropriate may become inappropriate when private expenditure shifts. The initial position is on AD_0, at Y^* and price level P_0. Suppose a slump in private investment shifts aggregate demand to AD_1, lowering GDP to Y_1 and causing a recessionary gap of $Y^* - Y_1$.

The government now introduces fiscal expansion to restore aggregate demand to AD_0. But private investment then recovers, raising aggregate demand to AD_2. If fiscal policy can be quickly reversed, aggregate demand can be returned to AD_0 and GDP stabilized at Y^*. If the policy is not quickly reversed, the economy is at E_2 with an inflationary gap $Y^* - Y_2$. This gap will cause wages to rise and thus will shift the $SRAS$ curve leftward and eventually restore Y^* at price level P_3.

household consumption expenditure is related to lifetime (or 'permanent') income rather than to current income, the smaller will be the effects on current consumption of tax changes that are known to be of short duration.

The role of discretionary fiscal policy All of the above-mentioned difficulties suggest that attempts to use discretionary fiscal policy to fine-tune the economy are fraught with difficulties. **Fine-tuning** refers to the use of fiscal and monetary policy to offset virtually all fluctuations in private sector spending and so hold GDP at, or very near, its potential level at all times. Unfortunately neither economic nor political science has yet advanced far enough to allow policymakers to undo the consequences of every aggregate demand shock.

On the other hand many economists would still argue that when a recessionary gap is large enough and persists for long enough, gross-tuning may be appropriate. **Gross-tuning** refers to the occasional use of fiscal and monetary policy to remove large and persistent GDP gaps. Advocates of gross-tuning hold that fiscal policy can and should be used to push the economy towards full employment when a GDP gap is large and has persisted for a long time. Other economists believe that fiscal policy should not be used for economic stabilization under any circumstances. They argue that tax and spending behaviour should be the outcome of public choices regarding the long-term size and financing of the public sector and should not be altered for short-term considerations.

Economic policy, economic stability, and economic growth

The desirability of using fiscal policy to stabilize the economy depends a great deal on the speed with which the adjustment mechanism returns the economy to potential GDP. If the adjustment mechanism works quickly, there is no role for discretionary fiscal policy. If the adjustment mechanism works slowly, there may well be a role for policies that can be used to shift aggregate demand. Fiscal policy is one such policy. Monetary policy, which we take up in Chapter 26, is another. Only when we have completed our study of the way in which money fits into the overall macroeconomy can we fully outline the choices available to governments wishing to stabilize their economies.

EU fiscal policy and the single currency

Since the 1992 Maastricht Treaty, which established limits on fiscal deficits and public debt for EU member states that wished to join the euro single-currency zone, those member states' governments have operated fiscal policy under severe constraints. This meant that almost all EU member states initiated tight fiscal polices even though many of their economies were in recession. This extra negative shock to aggregate demand made the resulting recession worse and drove EU unemployment up to levels not seen since the Second World War.

After the implementation of the euro in 1999, fiscal constraints on member states remained in place in the form of the so-called Stability and Growth Pact. This puts limitations on fiscal deficits similar to those imposed by the Maastricht criteria. The limits ensure that fiscal policy at the level of individual member states will have only a minor role in the control of their national aggregate demand. A fiscal policy role may develop for the EU central budget. However, that (up to 1999) was very small in comparison with the budgets of governments of member states, making it unlikely that the EU will exert significant fiscal leverage in the near future. This could be a severe problem for members of the euro zone. The creation of the euro itself takes away monetary policy power, and the Stability and Growth Pact limits fiscal freedom. Accordingly, governments appear to have very few tools left with which to influence the business cycle in their own countries. This will be an especially severe problem for member states who find their economies out of phase with the cycle in the majority of other states. We will return to this issue in Chapter 35.

Business cycles, and the effects of economic policy on them, are among the key subjects of this book. With the tools that we have developed thus far, we have been able to begin to see how they fit together. Once we add a better understanding of money and monetary policy we will be able to complete the story of stabilization policy.

Summary

- Potential GDP is represented by a vertical line at Y^*. The output gap is equal to the horizontal distance between Y^* and the actual level of GDP, as determined by the intersection of the AD and SRAS curves.

Induced changes in input prices

- An inflationary gap means that actual GDP, Y, is greater than Y^*, and hence excess demand in the labour market. As a result wages rise faster than productivity, causing unit labour costs to rise. The SRAS curve shifts leftward, and the price level rises.

- A recessionary gap means that Y is less than Y^*, and hence demand in the labour market is relatively low. Although there is some resulting tendency for wages to fall relative to productivity, asymmetrical behaviour means that this force will be much weaker than in the case of an inflationary gap. Unit labour costs will fall only slowly, so the output gap will persist for some time.

- An expansionary demand shock creates an inflationary gap.

- A contractionary demand shock works in the opposite direction by creating a recessionary gap.

The long-run consequences of aggregate demand shocks

- The long-run aggregate supply (LRAS) curve relates the price level and real GDP after all wages and other costs have been adjusted fully to long-run equilibrium. The LRAS curve is vertical at the level of potential GDP, Y^*.

- Because the LRAS curve is vertical, output in the long run is determined by the position of the LRAS curve, and the only long-run role of the AD curve is to determine the price level. Economic growth determines the position of the LRAS curve.

Real GDP in the short and long runs

- GDP can increase (or decrease) for any of three reasons: a change in aggregate demand, a change in short-run aggregate supply, or a change in long-run aggregate supply (which is called economic growth). The first two changes are typically associated with business cycles.

Government policy and the business cycle

- In principle, fiscal policy can be used to stabilize the position of the AD curve at or near potential GDP. To remove a recessionary gap, governments can shift AD to the right by cutting taxes and increasing spending. To remove an inflationary gap, governments can pursue the opposite policies.

- Because government tax and transfer programmes tend to reduce the size of the multiplier, they act as automatic stabilizers. When national income changes, in either direction, disposable income changes by less because of taxes and transfers.

- Discretionary fiscal policy is subject to information, decision, and execution lags that limit its ability to take effect quickly.

Topics for review

- The GDP gap and the labour market
- Inflationary gaps
- Recessionary gaps
- Asymmetry of wage adjustment
- Changes in aggregate demand and induced wage changes
- Wages, productivity, and unit costs
- Adjustment mechanism
- Long-run aggregate supply (*LRAS*) curve
- Economic stabilization
- Information, decision, and execution lags
- Automatic stabilizers

Questions for discussion

1 Explain carefully the differences between the adjustment of the economy in a recessionary gap and an inflationary gap.

2 Why is the *LRAS* curve vertical?

3 Starting with the economy at Y^*, explain what happens to the price level and real GDP in response to (*a*) an increase in export demand, (*b*) an increase in oil prices (assuming that oil is an input into production), (*c*) a permanent increase in productivity, (*d*) an increase in income tax rates.

4 Set out the reasons why fiscal policy was once thought to be able to offset shocks to the economy. Why is the effectiveness of fiscal policy now thought to be much more limited?

5 Outline the reasons for asymmetry in the adjustment mechanism to external shocks. How would the response to a positive demand shock differ from the response to a negative demand shock?

6 Explain what is meant by 'automatic stabilizers'. How do these help to reduce the amplitude of the business cycle?

Part Six
Macro Policy in a Monetary Economy

Chapter 25
Money and Monetary Institutions

In this chapter we start on the process of understanding the role of money and monetary policy in the economy. Here we concentrate on understanding important aspects of the institutional framework of the monetary system. We start with an examination of money itself: why do we have it and how did it evolve? We then ask how money gets into the economy and how the money stock is determined. Finally, we look at the functions of central banks in the United Kingdom and Europe and ask, in particular, how their operations enable them to set interest rates. In the following two chapters we add a monetary sector to our macro model and analyse how monetary policy works in that model.

Many people believe that money is one of the more important things in life, and that there is never enough of it. Yet economists argue that increasing the world's money supply would not make the average person better off. Although money allows those who have it to buy someone else's output, the total amount of goods and services available for everyone to buy depends on the total output produced, not on the total amount of money that people possess. In the terminology of Chapter 24, an increase in the quantity of money will not increase $Y^\star$, the level of potential GDP. However, money's role in the economy has been a controversial topic.

The classical view

In the eighteenth century economists explained the independence of $Y^\star$ from monetary factors in terms of an economic theory that distinguished sharply between the 'real sector of the economy' and the 'monetary sector'. This approach led to a view of the economy that is now referred to as the *classical dichotomy*, which meant that the real sector of the economy (the production and consumption of real goods and services) could be analysed separately from the monetary sector. In other words economic forces originating in the monetary sector did not affect real activity.

According to these so-called classical economists, the allocation of resources, and hence the determination of real GDP, is fully determined in the real sector. Further,

they argued that it is *relative prices*, including the level of wages relative to the price of commodities, rather than money (nominal) prices, that matter for this process.

These early economists argued that the price *level* is determined in the monetary sector of the economy. If the quantity of money were doubled, other things being equal, the prices of all commodities and money incomes would double. Relative prices would remain unchanged, and the real sector would be unaffected.

According to the classical economists, an increase in the money supply leads to a proportionate increase in all money prices, with no change in the allocation of resources or the level of real GDP.

The doctrine that the quantity of money influences the level of money prices but has no effect on the real part of the economy is called the **neutrality of money.** Because early economists believed that the most important questions—How much does the economy produce? What share of it does each group in society get?—were answered in the real sector, they spoke of money as a 'veil' behind which occurred the real events that affected material well-being. Of course, if the classical view were correct, we would not need to study monetary factors in trying to explain the determination of real national income.

The modern view

Most modern economists still accept the insights of the early economists that relative prices are a major determinant of the allocation of resources and that the quantity of money has a lot to do with determining the absolute level of prices. They accept the neutrality of money in long-run equilibrium when all the forces causing change have fully worked themselves out. However, they do not accept the neutrality of money when the economy is adjusting to shocks, that is, when the economy is not in a state of long-run equilibrium. Thus they reject the classical dichotomy.

Money and the price level Modern economists stress that there is a strong link between money and the price level, especially over long periods of time, when the conditions of long-run equilibrium are apt to be most relevant. In Chapter 30 we will discuss inflation explicitly and present some evidence from the United Kingdom and other countries over the recent past. In the post-Second World War period prices have shown a strong upward trend. Table 20.4 on page 350, for example, shows that UK prices rose nearly twentyfold between 1950 and 1997. Since 1970 alone the UK price level has increased over eightfold.

The nature of money

There is probably more widespread misunderstanding of money and the monetary system than of any other aspect of the economy. In this section we describe the functions of money and briefly outline its history.

What is money?

Money is defined as any generally accepted medium of exchange. A *medium of exchange* is anything that will be widely accepted in a society in exchange for goods and services. Although being a medium of exchange is usually regarded as money's defining function, money can also serve other roles:

Money acts as a medium of exchange and can also serve as a store of value and a unit of account.

A medium of exchange As we saw in Chapter 1, if there were no money, goods would have to be exchanged by barter (one good being swapped directly for another). The major difficulty with barter is that each transaction requires a double coincidence of wants; anyone who specialized in producing one commodity would have to spend a great deal of time searching for satisfactory transactions. Thus a thirsty economics lecturer would have to find a brewer who wanted to learn economics before he could swap a lesson in economics for a pint of beer.

The use of money as a medium of exchange alleviates this problem. People can sell their output for money and subsequently use the money to buy what they wish from others. So a monetary economy typically involves exchanges of goods and services for money and of money for goods, but not of goods for goods.

The double coincidence of wants, which is required for barter, is unnecessary when a medium of exchange is used.

By facilitating transactions, money makes possible the benefits of specialization and the division of labour, which in turn contribute to the efficiency of the economic system. It is not without justification that money has been called one of the great inventions contributing to human freedom and well-being.

To serve as an efficient medium of exchange, money must have a number of characteristics. It must be readily acceptable and therefore of known value. It must have a high value relative to its weight (otherwise it would be a nuisance to carry around). It must be divisible, because money that comes only in large denominations is useless for transactions having only a small value. Finally, it must be difficult, if not impossible, to counterfeit.

A store of value Money is a convenient way to store purchasing power; goods may be sold today, and the money taken in exchange for them may be stored until it is needed. To be a satisfactory store of value, however, money must have a relatively stable value. A rise in the price level leads to a decrease in the purchasing power of money, because more money is required to buy a typical basket of goods. When the price level is stable, the purchasing power of a given sum of money is also stable; when the price level is highly variable, this is not so, and the usefulness of money as a store of value is undermined.

Although in a non-inflationary environment money can serve as a satisfactory store of accumulated purchasing power for a single individual, even in those circumstances it cannot do so for society as a whole. A single individual can accumulate money and, when the time comes to spend it, can command the current output of some other individual. However, if all individuals in a society were to save their money and then retire simultaneously to live on their savings, there would be no current production to purchase and consume. Society's ability to satisfy wants depends on goods and services being available. If some of this want-satisfying capacity is to be stored up for society as a whole, some goods that are produced today must be saved for future periods. In other words money may be accumulated as savings to help individuals buy future goods, but it is the future real capital stock and labour resources that will determine future real output. Money and real wealth should not be confused.

Money is a store of value for individuals but not for society as a whole.

A unit of account Money also may be used purely for accounting purposes, without having a physical existence of its own. For instance, a government store in an imaginary centrally planned society might say that everyone had so many 'pounds' to spend or save each month. Goods could then be assigned prices and each consumer's purchases recorded, the consumer being allowed to buy until his or her allocated supply of pounds was exhausted. These pounds need have no existence other than as entries in the store's books, yet they would serve as a perfectly satisfactory unit of account.

Whether they could also serve as a medium of exchange between individuals depends on whether the store would agree to transfer credits from one customer to another at the customer's request. Banks will transfer pounds credited to current account deposits in this way, and so a bank deposit can serve as both a unit of account and a medium of exchange. Notice that the use of 'pounds' in this context suggests a further sense in which money is a unit of account. People think about values in terms of the monetary unit with which they are familiar.

A related function of money is that it can be used as a standard of deferred payments. Payments that are to be made in the future, on account of debts and so on, are reckoned in money. Money's ability to serve as a unit of account over time in this manner can be diminished if there is significant inflation.

The origins of money

The origins of money go far back in antiquity. Many primitive tribes seem to have made some use of it.

Metallic money

All sorts of commodities have been used as money at one time or another, but gold and silver proved to have great advantages. They were precious because their supplies were relatively limited, and they were in constant demand by the wealthy for ornament and decoration. Thus these metals tended to have a high and stable price. Further, they were easily recognized, they were divisible into extremely small units, and they did not easily wear out.

Before the invention of coins, it was necessary to carry the metals in bulk. When a purchase was made, the requisite quantity of the metal was carefully weighed on a scale. The invention of coinage eliminated the need to weigh the metal at each transaction, but it created an important role for an authority, usually a monarch, who made the coins by mixing gold or silver with base metals to create convenient size and durability, and affixed his or her seal, guaranteeing the amount of precious metal that the coin contained. This was clearly a great convenience, as long as traders knew that they could accept the coin at its 'face value'. The face value was nothing more than a statement that a certain weight of gold or silver was contained therein.

However, coins often could not be taken at their face value. A form of counterfeiting—clipping a thin slice off the edge of the coin and keeping the valuable metal—became common. This, of course, served to undermine the acceptability of coins—even if they were stamped. To get around this problem, the idea arose of minting the coins with a rough edge; the absence of the rough edge would immediately indicate that the coin had been clipped. This practice, called milling, survives on some coins (such as the current UK 5p, 10p, £1, and £2 coins) as an interesting anachronism to remind us that there were days when the market value of the metal in the coin was equal to the face value of the coin.

Not to be outdone by the cunning of their subjects, some rulers were quick to seize the chance of getting something for nothing. The power to mint placed rulers in a position to work a really profitable fraud. They often used some suitable occasion—a marriage, an anniversary, an alliance—to re-mint the coinage. Subjects would be ordered to bring their coins into the mint to be melted down and coined afresh with a new stamp. Between the melting down and the recoining, however, the rulers had only to toss some further inexpensive base metal in with the molten coins. This debasing of the coinage allowed the ruler to earn a handsome profit by minting more new coins than the number of old ones collected, and putting the extras in the royal vault.

The result of debasement was inflation. The subjects had the same number of coins as before, and hence could demand the same quantity of goods. When rulers paid their bills, however, the recipients of the extra coins could be expected to spend them. This caused a net increase in demand, which in turn bid up prices.

Debasing the coinage was a common cause of increases in prices.

It was the experience of such inflations that led early economists to stress the link between the quantity of money and the price level. The relationship, known as the 'quantity theory of money', will be discussed in Chapter 26. A famous law in economics that owes its origins to the era of metallic money is set out in Box 25.1.

To this day the revenue generated from the power to create currency is known as *seigniorage*. Seigniorage was not normally revenue generated by debasement; originally it was an explicit duty, or tax, levied on the mint. In the modern context the possibility of debasement does not enter, so the term applies to the revenue that accrues from the power to print banknotes (which have very low production costs relative to their face value) and from the fact that many central banks force commercial banks to place non-interest-bearing deposits at the central bank (both of which finance the holding of interest-bearing securities). In the United Kingdom most of the revenue from seigniorage is returned to HM Treasury by the Bank

Box 25.1   Gresham's Law

The early experience of currency debasement led to the observation known as Gresham's Law, after Sir Thomas Gresham, an adviser to the Elizabethan court, who stated that 'bad money drives out good'.

When Queen Elizabeth I came to the throne of England in the middle of the sixteenth century, the coinage had been severely debased. Seeking to help trade, Elizabeth minted new coins that contained their full face value in gold. However, as fast as she fed these new coins into circulation, they disappeared. Why?

Suppose that you possessed one new and one old coin, each with the same face value, and had a bill to pay. What would you do? Clearly, you would use the debased coin to pay the bill and keep the undebased one. (You part with less gold that way.) Again suppose that you wanted to obtain a certain amount of gold bullion by melting down the gold coins (as was frequently done). Which coins would you use? Clearly, you would use new, undebased coins because you would part with less 'face value' that way. For these reasons, the debased coins would remain in circulation, and the undebased coins would disappear.

Gresham's insights have proven helpful in explaining the experience of a number of modern high-inflation economies. For example, in the 1970s, inflation in Chile raised the value of the metallic content in coins above their face value. Coins quickly disappeared from circulation as private citizens sold them to entrepreneurs who melted them down for their metal. Only paper currency remained in circulation and was used even for tiny transactions such as purchasing a box of matches. Gresham's Law is one reason why modern coins, unlike their historical counterparts, are merely tokens that contain a metallic value that is only a minute fraction of their face value.

Gresham's Law has had another modern interpretation, in regimes of pegged exchange rates, where the values of two currencies are pegged together artificially. If one currency is overvalued and widely expected to have to be devalued, this causes people to spend it fast, while building up their holdings of the undervalued currency. The combination of hoarding one currency and running down balances of the other often brings about the devaluation that was feared—as when the pound sterling was forced to leave the European Exchange Rate Mechanism (ERM) in September 1992.

of England; only an amount to cover the Bank's running costs is retained.[1]

Paper money

The next important step in the history of money was the evolution of paper currency, one source of which was goldsmiths. Since goldsmiths had secure safes, the public began to deposit their gold with them for safekeeping. Goldsmiths would give their depositors receipts promising to hand over the gold on demand. When any depositor wished to make a large purchase, she could go to her goldsmith, reclaim some of her gold, and hand it over to the seller of the goods. If the seller had no immediate need for the gold, he would carry it back to the goldsmith for safekeeping on his behalf.

If people knew the goldsmith to be reliable, there was no need to go through the cumbersome and risky business of physically transferring the gold. The buyer needed only to transfer the goldsmith's receipt to the seller, who would accept it as long as he was confident that the goldsmith would pay over the gold whenever it was needed. If the seller wished to buy a good from a third party who also knew the goldsmith to be reliable, this transaction too could be effected by passing the goldsmith's receipt from the buyer to the seller. The deposit receipt was 'as good as gold'. The convenience of using pieces of paper instead of gold is obvious.

When it came into being in this way, paper money represented a promise to pay so much gold on demand. In this case the promise was made first by goldsmiths and later by banks.[2] Such paper money, which became banknotes, was backed by precious metal and was convertible on demand into this metal.[3]

Fractionally backed paper money   Early on many goldsmiths and banks discovered that it was not necessary to keep a full ounce of gold in the vaults for every claim to an ounce circulating as paper money. At any one time, some of the bank's customers would be withdrawing gold, others would be depositing it, and most would be trading in the bank's paper notes without indicating any need or desire to convert them into gold.

As a result the bank was able to issue more money (initially notes, but later deposits) redeemable in gold than the amount of gold that it held in its vaults. This was good business, because the money could be invested profitably in interest-earning loans (often called advances) to individuals and firms. The demand for loans arose, as it does today, because some customers wanted credit to help them over hard times or to buy equipment for their businesses. To this day banks have many more claims outstanding against them than they actually have in reserves available to pay those claims. We say that the currency issued in such a situation is *fractionally backed* by the reserves.

The major problem with a fractionally backed, convert-

---

[1] In 1998 the Bank of England paid over £1.5 billion to HM Treasury from this source.

[2] Banks grew out of at least two other trades in addition to that of the goldsmiths. There were scriveners, who had writing skills and sold their services managing other people's financial affairs; there were also merchant bankers, who started trading in commodities but ended up specializing in trade finance—Barings and Rothschilds started this way, and are still referred to as 'merchant banks' today. (In US terminology they would be called 'investment banks'.)

[3] One of the earliest issuers of formal banknotes was the Riksbank of Sweden, established in 1668. It is thus twenty-six years older than the Bank of England, which was established in 1694. The Riksbank, which is now the central bank of Sweden, instituted the Nobel Prize for economics in 1968 to commemorate its tercentenary.

ible currency was maintaining its convertibility into the precious metal by which it was backed. The imprudent bank that issued too much paper money would find itself unable to redeem its currency in gold when the demand for gold was even slightly higher than usual. It would then have to suspend payments, and all holders of its notes would suddenly find that the notes were worthless. However, the prudent bank that kept a reasonable relationship between its note issue and its gold reserve would find that it could meet a normal range of demand for gold without any trouble.

If the public lost confidence and demanded redemption of its currency *en masse*, however, the banks would be unable to honour their pledges. The history of nineteenth- and early-twentieth-century banking around the world is full of examples of banks that were ruined by 'panics', or sudden runs on their gold reserves. When this happened, the banks' depositors and the holders of their notes would find themselves with worthless pieces of paper.[4]

Fiat money

As time went on, note issue by private banks became less common, and **central banks,** which are (usually) state-owned institutions, took control of the currency. Over time central banks have assumed a monopoly in the provision of money (cash) to the economy.[5] As a result they have the job of controlling monetary conditions and are ultimately responsible for determining the value of a nation's (or group of nations') currency.

Originally the central banks issued paper currency that was fully convertible into gold. In those days gold would be brought to the central bank, which would issue currency in the form of 'gold certificates' that asserted that the gold was available on demand. The gold supply thus set some upper limit on the amount of currency. However, central banks, like private banks before them, could issue more currency than they had in gold, because in normal times only a small fraction of the currency was presented for payment at any one time. Thus even though the need to maintain convertibility under a **gold standard** put an upper limit on note issue, central banks had substantial discretionary control over the quantity of currency outstanding.

During the period between the two world wars almost all of the countries of the world abandoned the gold standard; their currencies were thus no longer convertible into gold. Money that is not convertible by law into anything else derives its value from its acceptability in exchange. *Fiat money* is widely acceptable because it is declared by government order, or fiat,[6] to be legal tender. Legal tender is anything that by law must be accepted when offered either for the purchase of goods or services or to discharge a debt. Bank of England notes have been legal tender in England and Wales since 1833.

Today almost all currency is fiat money.

Bank of England notes still say on them 'I promise to pay the bearer on demand the sum of *x* pounds', and they are signed by the chief cashier. Until 1931 (apart from suspensions of convertibility for the Napoleonic (1797–1821) and First World Wars (1914–25), and temporary crises in the nineteenth century—1847, 1857, and 1866) you could take these notes into the Bank of England and demand gold of equivalent value in return for your notes. Today, however, the promise is a quaint tradition rather than a real contract. The pound sterling, like all major currencies, is a fiat currency which is not backed by gold or any other commodity (though some people still argue for the return to a gold standard).

Fiat money is valuable because it is accepted by convention and in law in payment for the purchase of goods or services and for the discharge of debts.

Many people are disturbed to learn that present-day paper money is neither backed by nor convertible into anything more valuable—that it consists of nothing but pieces of paper whose value derives from common acceptance. Many people believe that their money should be more substantial than this. Yet money is, in fact, nothing more than pieces of paper.

If fiat money is acceptable, it is a medium of exchange. Further, if its purchasing power remains stable, it is a satisfactory store of value. And if both of these things are true, it will also serve as a satisfactory unit of account.

How does fiat money get into the economy?

When gold was the basis of money, it was not too difficult to see how more gold got into circulation. It was either produced from gold mines, converted from non-monetary uses (such as jewellery), or imported from other countries. In effect it was received in payment for some transaction from the owners of gold mines, or from the previous owner of the gold, wherever in the world they happened to be. However, it is not so obvious how fiat money gets into the economic system. In fact, as suggested above, it comes from the central bank—in the UK the Bank of England, in

---

[4] In the early 1930s about 10,000 banks, or a third of the total, went bust in the United States. The personal and corporate losses involved were a major contributor to the Great Depression.

[5] In England and Wales no new banks have been permitted to issue notes since the 1844 Bank Charter Act, though in Scotland banks such as the Bank of Scotland, the Royal Bank of Scotland, and the Clydesdale Bank still issue the main notes in circulation. (Since 1845, however, the Scottish note issue has had 100 per cent backing with Bank of England liabilities, and hence has been fully under Bank of England direction.) It is planned that by 2002 the euro notes circulating in eleven EU countries will be issued by the European Central Bank (see pages 441–2 below).

[6] Fiat means 'let there be' in Latin, and hence 'by decree'.

the USA the Federal Reserve, in the euro area the European Central Bank (ECB).[7]

The central bank does not just drop money from the sky, or even just give it to the government to spend. What the central bank has direct control over is referred to as *high-powered money, the cash base,* or *the monetary base.* (In the United Kingdom it is also defined as M0; see Box 25.2 below.) This consists of currency (banknotes and coin) held by the public and the banks, and of deposits held by the banks with the central bank. The monetary base is referred to as high-powered money because it is the basis upon which a much bigger stock of monetary assets is built (including the biggest component of the money stock, bank deposits). High-powered money is an asset to anyone in the private sector who holds it, but to the central bank it is a liability.

The central bank gets high-powered money into the economic system simply by buying securities (usually government debt instruments). It pays for these purchases with newly issued high-powered money.

Hence, in creating new high-powered money, the central bank is expanding both sides of its own balance sheet. At the same time as it increases its liabilities, it purchases assets of equal value. Of the two components of high-powered money, in the UK case bankers' deposits are the liability of the Banking Department of the Bank of England and currency is the liability of the Issue Department. The balance sheets of these two departments are shown in Table 25.1.

It is simplest to think of the process of high-powered money creation in two steps. First, we will discuss, using the UK example, how the purchase of securities by the Bank of England creates bankers' deposits. Then we will see how currency gets into circulation.

Bankers' deposits Consider a situation in which there are initially no net transactions between the Bank of England and the rest of the economy. The Bank now buys £1m worth of securities from an agent in the private sector. The seller receives a cheque for £1m from the Bank of England which is paid into the recipient's bank account at, say, Lloyds Bank. Lloyds' deposits rise by £1m, but at the same time Lloyds receives an increase of £1m in its deposits at the Bank of England. The balance in Lloyds' account at the Bank of England is an example of what are called *bankers' deposits.* This increase in its bankers' deposits at the Bank of England arises when Lloyds clears the cheque drawn on the Bank of England. (A cheque deposited in Lloyds drawn on the Midland Bank would simply transfer bankers' deposits from Midland to Lloyds, but a cheque drawn on the Bank of England creates new bankers' deposits at the central bank.)

This will not be the end of the story so far as Lloyds is concerned, because it has now increased its reserves. We will explain how the banking system can increase its de-

Table 25.1 Bank of England balance sheet, 25 Feb. 1998

Assets	(£m)	Liabilities	(£m)
(i) *Balance sheet of Issue Dept.*			
Government securities	3,090	Notes in circulation	22,103
Other securities	19,020	Notes in Banking Dept.	7
Total assets	22,110	Total liabilities	22,110
(ii) *Balance sheet of Banking Dept.*			
Government securities	1,366	Public deposits	1,153
Advances	8,650	Bankers' deposits	2,865
Premises	452	Reserves and other acs.	6,457
Notes and coin	7		
Total assets	10,475		10,475

The Bank of England is divided into the Issue Department and the Banking Department. The table shows the balance sheets of these two departments on 25 February 1998. The only function of the Issue Department is to issue currency (banknotes and coins). It does this in exchange for purchases of securities, normally through a transaction with the Banking Department. The Banking Department acts as banker to the government and also holds deposits from the banks. In February 1998 the value of notes in circulation was £22,103 million.

Source: Bank of England, *Monetary and Financial Statistics.*

posits on the basis of larger reserves below. However, this is most of what we need to know about how the Bank of England expands the monetary base, though we will look more closely below at how the Bank of England uses its money market operations to set interest rates. Contraction of the monetary base simply reverses the process—the Bank sells securities. A member of the public then writes a cheque drawn on, say, Barclays Bank, payable to the Bank of England, and Barclays transfers bankers' deposits to the Bank of an equivalent amount. The monetary base falls.

We assumed above that the Bank purchased a security from a member of the public. However, what would happen if the Bank purchased a new security issued by the government? In this case the government would acquire an increase in its deposits[8] in the Banking Department of the Bank (which would acquire a matching security). As soon as the government writes a cheque (perhaps to pay civil service salaries), it transfers deposits to private individuals and banks acquire a corresponding increase in bankers' deposits at the Bank. Thus when the central bank lends money to the government, by buying new government securities and creating new government deposits, it

---

[7] Transition arrangements are in place for the ECB between 1999 and 2002. During this period the old notes of existing member central banks will still circulate, but after 2002 there will be euro banknotes that are the liability of the ECB.

[8] The government and the main commercial banks have bank accounts with the Bank of England; indeed, the Bank of England is the main banker to the government.

is increasing the monetary base. This is the nearest that governments can come to 'printing money' in the modern institutional environment. It is also known as monetizing the government debt, a process often associated with inflation (see Chapter 30).

Currency   The above discussion explains how central banks, such as the Bank of England, create or destroy high-powered money. The composition of high-powered money between bankers' deposits and currency is determined by the demand for currency on the part of the general public. If private individuals (or firms) choose to increase their currency holding, relative to bank deposits, they simply go to their bank and withdraw deposits in cash. The bank (if it did not have enough cash in its tills) would go to the Bank of England and withdraw some bankers' deposits in cash from the Banking Department. The Banking Department, in turn, would replenish its own stock of cash by selling securities to the Issue Department. The Issue Department prints the new currency. Currency is made available on demand to the economy in this way and is not restricted in supply by the Bank of England.

The stock of currency in circulation is determined entirely by the demands of the economy and is not set by any policymakers.

In the current UK financial system the total stock of high-powered money is also demand-determined. This is because the authorities choose to set short-term interest rates and supply whatever high-powered money is demanded at those rates. A discussion of the implementation of monetary policy follows later in this chapter.

Modern money

The creation of high-powered money is only part of the story of how the money supply is created, because most measures of the money supply include a wider range of assets than just the monetary base. In particular, money is usually defined to include bank deposits.

Deposit money

Today's bank customers frequently deposit coins and paper money with the banks for safekeeping, just as in former times they deposited gold. Such a deposit is recorded as a credit to the customer's account. A customer who wishes to pay a debt may come to the bank, claim the money in currency, and then pay the money to other persons, who may themselves redeposit the money in a bank.

As with gold transfers, this is a tedious procedure. It is more convenient to have the bank transfer claims to money on deposit. As soon as cheques, which are written instructions to the bank to make a transfer, became widely accepted in payment for commodities and debts, bank deposits became a form of money called 'deposit money'. Deposit money is defined as money held by the public in the form of deposits in commercial banks that can be withdrawn on demand. Cheques, unlike banknotes, do not circulate freely from hand to hand; thus cheques themselves are not currency. However, a balance in a current account deposit is money; the cheque simply transfers that money from one person to another. Because cheques are easily drawn and deposited, and because they are relatively safe from theft, they have been widely used. New technology has recently replaced many cheque transactions by computer transfer. Plastic cards, such as Visa, Mastercard, and Switch, enable holders of bank accounts to transfer money to another person's account in new ways.[9] The principle is the same, however: the balance in the bank account is the money that is to be transferred between customers, not the cheque or the plastic card.

When commercial banks lost the right to issue notes of their own, the form of bank money changed, but the substance did not. Today banks have money in their vaults (or on deposit with the central bank) just as they always did. Once it was gold; today it is the legal tender of the times—fiat money. It is true today, just as in the past, that most of the banks' customers are content to pay their bills by passing among themselves the banks' promises to pay money on demand. Only a small proportion of the value of the transactions made by the banks' customers involves the use of cash.

Bank deposits are money. Today, just as in the past, banks can create money by issuing more promises to pay (deposits) than they have cash reserves available to pay out.

Box 25.2 shows the various measures of the money stock that were in standard use in the United Kingdom in 1998. The main aggregates are M0, a narrow measure that excludes all private sector bank and building society deposits, and M4, a broad measure that includes all such bank and building society deposits. Notice also that there is now an EU harmonized measure of broad money known in the UK as M3H. This is slightly larger than M4 because it adds residents' foreign currency deposits (and some public sector deposits) to M4. The only other monetary aggregate current in the UK is M2, which is also known as 'retail M4' as it excludes the wholesale deposits in M4.

We now turn to a discussion of the role of banks in determining the broad money supply and in transmitting policy-determined interest rate changes to the economy.

---

[9] With credit cards such as Visa or Mastercard, if you buy, say, petrol today, the petrol company will receive a credit in its bank account after a few days and you will have to settle with the credit card company once a month. With so-called EFTPOS (electronic funds transfer at the point of sale) cards like Switch, however, the funds are transferred directly from your account to the account of the petrol company very quickly. The technology is likely to keep changing, but it does not fundamentally alter the nature of the bank account transfer that is involved.

Box 25.2 Definitions of UK monetary aggregates

The way in which 'money' is defined has changed a great deal over time and is likely to change again in future. In 1750 money would almost certainly have been defined as the stock of gold in circulation (specie). By 1850 it would probably have been defined as gold in the hands of the non-bank public plus banknotes in circulation. In 1950 the most likely definition would have been currency held by the public plus current account bank deposits. In 1998 money was usually defined to include currency held by the public plus all deposits (current and savings) in banks and building societies. By 2050, who knows? Perhaps money on the Internet will be included.

There have been many changes in the definition of money even in the last few years. Many of these are the result of the financial innovations of the 1980s. We should not expect this to be the end of the story. UK money measures such as M1 and £M3 (sterling M3), which were at the centre of monetary policy debates into the first half of the 1980s, have disappeared. These had to be dropped after 1989, when the Abbey National Building Society converted into a bank (and other conversions followed later). Thereafter, any monetary aggregate that contained bank deposits but not building society deposits became distorted. M0 contains neither; M2 and M4 contain both.

The money measures current in 1998 were as follows:

■ **M0 (the monetary base).** This measure refers to all the currency in circulation outside the Bank of England plus bankers' deposits (in excess of their cash ratio deposits) with the Bank of England.
■ **M2.** This encompasses UK non-bank and non-building society holdings of notes and coins, plus sterling retail deposits with UK banks and building societies. The definition of M2 was changed in 1992 to make it a subset of M4, and it is now referred to in official statistics as 'retail M4'.
■ **M4.** M4 is M2 plus all other private sector sterling interest-bearing deposits at banks and building societies, plus sterling certificates of deposit (and other paper issued by banks and building societies of not more than five years' original maturity). (£M3 was effectively M4 minus building society deposits.)

■ **M3H.** This is a new harmonized measure created to have standard money definitions throughout the EU. It is equal to M4 plus residents' foreign currency deposits in UK banks and building societies plus public corporations' sterling and foreign currency deposits in UK banks and building societies.

The accompanying table presents data for these monetary aggregates for February 1998.

**UK money supply, Feb. 1998
(£ million, not seasonally adjusted)**

Notes and coin outside Bank of England	25,891	
Bankers' deposits at Bank of England	180	
M0	26,071	
Notes and coin with public (part of M0)		21,648
Non-interest-bearing bank deposits		34,295
Other retail bank deposits		331,783
Building society retail shares and deposits		96,747
M2 (retail M4)		484,473
Wholesale bank deposits + CDs		234,660
Wholesale building society deposits + CDs		6,868
M4		726,001
M3H		848,277

Note: M0 is not a subset of M2 and M4 because it includes notes and coin held by banks, which are excluded from M2 and M4. If notes and coin held by banks were included in the latter, there would be double counting, because notes and coin held by banks are assets, and the deposits (liabilities) that are counterparts to those assets are included in M2 and M4 already. CDs are certificates of deposit.

Source: ONS *Financial Statistics*.

Two models of banking

Banks are firms that operate within a market-determined environment. We have already seen in the first half of this book that we need different models to understand how firms behave in different market environments—for example, monopolists behave differently from firms in perfectly competitive industries even though they are all profit-maximizers. So also is it useful to apply different models to explain different aspects of banks' behaviour. First, we will explain a traditional analysis of banks that is useful for understanding the process of deposit creation on the basis of a given base of high-powered money (as, for example, in the case of goldsmiths mentioned above). However, this traditional model is insufficient for under-

standing other aspects of modern banking. Our second model is more suited to understanding both the forces of competition between banks themselves and the competition between banks and other channels of financial intermediation (such as securities markets).

The first model would be most helpful for understanding the process of money creation if monetary policy operated by fixing the monetary base. However, it does not operate this way in the United Kingdom or in any other major country. Rather, central banks set a particular interest rate and permit the monetary base to be whatever is demanded at that interest rate. The second model is needed to help understand this modern monetary policy environment, and we will also see that it has important applications to the understanding of contemporary monetary policy in the United Kingdom and the EU.

The ratios approach to the creation of deposit money

If you deposit cash with a bank, that deposit is an asset to you and a liability to the bank. The bank holds the cash as an asset, so its assets equal its liabilities. If it extends a loan to someone else on the basis of your cash, that will be an asset to the bank, but any deposit created will be a liability. If a bank gives you a loan, it writes an extra balance into your account. This creates a deposit for you, but it is also a loan which you have to repay. So the process of overdraft or loan creation creates both deposits and loans simultaneously. In general, banks' deposits are their liabilities, and whatever loans they make or securities they purchase constitute their assets. We will now see how banks can create deposits (and loans) that are some multiple of their cash reserves. This *fractional reserve* banking is analogous to the fractional backing of the note issue discussed above. Notice that 'cash' held by the banks can be currency or deposits at the central bank, but 'cash' for the public means currency.

Suppose that, in a system with many banks, each bank obtains new deposits in cash. Say, for example, that there are ten banks of equal size and that each receives a new deposit of £100 in cash. Each bank now has on its books the new entries shown in Table 25.2. The banks are on a fractional reserve system, and we assume for purposes of this illustration that they wish to hold 10 per cent reserves against all deposits. The new deposits put the banks into disequilibrium, since they each have 100 per cent reserves against these new deposits.

First, suppose that only one of the ten banks begins to expand deposits by making new loans (advances). When a bank makes a loan to a customer, it simply writes a larger balance into the customer's account, thereby increasing the size of its deposits. Now when cheques are written on these deposits, the majority will be deposited in other banks. If, for example, this one bank has only 10 per cent

Table 25.2 A new cash deposit

Liabilities	(£)	Assets	(£)
Deposit	100	Cash	100

A new cash deposit has 100 per cent backing. The balance sheet shows the changes in assets and liabilities resulting from a new cash deposit. Both cash assets and deposit liabilities rise by the same amount.

Table 25.3 Deposit expansion in expectation of a cash drain

Liabilities	(£)	Assets	(£)
Deposit	190	Cash	100
		Loans	90
	—		—
	190		190

If a bank expands deposits in the expectation of a cash drain, it will end up with excess reserves. The table shows the position if a bank expands deposits on the basis of receiving £100 in new cash deposits and in the expectation that 90 per cent of any new deposits will drain out of the bank in a cash flow. The bank obtains new assets of loans and bonds of £90 by creating new deposits of that amount. It expects £81 of these to be withdrawn in cash, leaving it with £19 to provide a 10 per cent reserve against £190 of deposits.

of the total deposits held by the community, then, on average, 90 per cent of any new deposits it creates for its customers—and thus much of its £100 in cash—will drain away to other banks. On this basis the bank will make loans of £90, expecting that it will suffer a cash drain of £81 on account of these loans, leaving it with a £19 cash reserve (£100 new deposit minus the £81 cash drain). This is the position shown in Table 25.3.

One bank in a multi-bank system cannot produce a large multiple expansion of deposits based on an original accretion of cash when other banks do not also expand their deposits.

Now assume, however, that all ten banks begin to expand their deposits based on the £100 of new reserves that each received. On the one hand, since each bank does one-tenth of the total banking business, 90 per cent of the value of any newly created deposits will find its way into other banks as customers make payments by cheque to various members of the community. This represents a cash drain to these other banks. On the other hand, 10 per cent of the new deposits created by each other bank should find its way into this bank. Thus, if all banks receive new cash, and all start creating deposits simultaneously, no bank should suffer a significant cash drain to any other bank. Instead of finding itself with its surplus cash drained away, a bank with the balance sheet shown in Table 25.3 would have cash reserves of close to 53 per cent (£100 reserves against £190 deposits) rather than only 10 per cent as desired.

When all banks can go on expanding deposits without losing cash to each other, they need only worry about keeping enough cash to satisfy those depositors who occasionally require cash. Thus the expansion can go on, with each bank watching its own ratio of cash reserves to deposits, expanding its deposits as long as the ratio exceeds 1:10 and ceasing to do so when it reaches that figure.

Table 25.4 Restoration of a 10 per cent reserve ratio

Liabilities	(£)	Assets	(£)
Deposit	1,000	Cash	100
		Loans	900
	1,000		1,000

With no cash drain, a new cash deposit will support a multiple expansion of deposit liabilities. The table shows the changes in assets and liabilities when all banks engage in deposit expansion after each has received a new cash deposit of £100. New assets are £900 and new deposits are £900. The accretion of £100 in cash now supports £1,000 in deposits, thus restoring the 10 per cent reserve ratio.

Assuming no cash drain to the public, the process will not come to a halt until each bank has created £900 in additional deposits, so that, for each initial £100 cash deposit, there is now £1,000 in deposits backed by £100 in cash. Now each of the banks will have new entries in its books similar to those shown in Table 25.4.

A multi-bank system creates a multiple increase in deposit money when all banks with excess reserves expand their deposits in step with each other.

A complication: cash drain to the public

So far we have ignored the fact that the public actually divides its money holdings in a fairly stable proportion between cash and deposits. This means that when the banking system as a whole creates significant amounts of new deposit money, the system will suffer a cash drain as the public withdraws enough cash from the banks to maintain its desired ratio of cash to deposits.

An example Assume that the public wishes to hold a proportion of cash equal to 10 per cent of the size of its bank deposits. This means that for a given stock of cash in the system, the amount that will be held in bank reserves is reduced, so the maximum amount of deposit creation is also reduced. In this special case in which banks have a reserve ratio of 10 per cent and the public holds cash to the value of 10 per cent of the size of its bank deposits, the outcome will be as in Table 25.5. Half of the cash in existence (assumed to be £100 in total) will be held in banks' reserves and the other half will be held by the public. On the basis of their £50 reserves, banks will extend £450 of loans, so total deposits will be £500. This is only half of the value of deposits which were created when the entire £100 of cash was held in bank reserves (as shown in Table 25.3).

A cash drain to the public reduces the expansion of deposit money that can be supported by the banking system.

Table 25.5 Deposit creation with a cash drain to the public

Liabilities	(£)	Assets	(£)
Deposit	500	Cash	50
		Loans	450
	500		500

A cash drain to the public greatly reduces the amount of new deposits that can be created on the basis of a given amount of cash. The table shows the balance sheet of the banking system on the assumption that there is £100 of cash in the system but the public desires cash holdings equal to 10 per cent of their bank deposits. The outcome which satisfies both banks' desired reserve ratio and the public's cash to deposit ratio is such that the banks hold £50 in reserves and issue £450 worth of loans. Total deposits are £500, and £50 is held in cash by the public. The total money stock is £550 (deposits plus cash held by the public). An example in which the banks' reserve ratio differs from the public's cash to deposits ratio is given in Table 25.6.

The general case of deposit creation The two ratios that we have discussed (the banks' reserve ratio and public's ratio of cash to deposits) can now be used to determine the total level of deposit creation in a formal way. Let R be the cash held in bank reserves, C be the cash held by the non-bank public, H (for high-powered money) be the total cash in the economy, and D be the size of bank deposits. Thus

$$C + R = H. \qquad (1)$$

This says that the total cash in the economy is held either by the banks or by the public. Let the desired reserve ratio of banks be x. This allows us to write

$$R = xD. \qquad (2)$$

Finally, let the public hold a fraction, b, of its bank deposits in cash:

$$C = bD. \qquad (3)$$

Substituting the second and third equations into the first gives

$$bD + xD = H,$$

and solving for D yields

$$D = \frac{H}{(b + x)}. \qquad (4)$$

Equation (4) shows that if the public's desired cash ratio is zero, deposits rise by the reciprocal of the cash reserve ratio. (If the banks' reserve ratio were 0.1 (10 per cent), then deposits would be ten times the cash in the economy.) A positive value of b, however, means that the resulting cash drain lowers the increase in deposits since it raises the value of the denominator in (4).

The money multiplier The total money supply in an economy with a banking system is defined as $D + C$. (It does not include R because the deposit that created the original bank reserves is already counted in with deposits, D, and should not be counted twice.) Hence the money supply, M, is

$$M = C + D. \qquad (5)$$

We can arrive at an expression that links M and H by substituting (2) into (5) for C and then (4) into (5) for D. This gives

$$M = \frac{b+1}{b+x} H. \qquad (6)$$

Expression (6) is known as the money multiplier, because it tells us how much bigger is the money supply than the cash base of the system. In the modern UK banking system, where reserve ratios and cash ratios are very small, the money multiplier could be of the order of 28, since M4 was 28 times greater than M0 in February 1998.

The money multiplier should not be confused with the multiplier that links changes in exogenous spending with changes in GDP. The same term is used for two different concepts.

The size of the money multiplier is greater, the smaller is the banks' desired reserve ratio x and the smaller is the public's desired cash ratio b.

A diagrammatic exposition of the above algebra is given in Figure 25.1. It shows that the two ratios, combined with a given cash base, can be used to determine the level of deposits that result and also the money supply. A numerical example of the same ideas is given in Table 25.6.

A competitive banking system

The ratios approach to bank behaviour gives us important insights into how deposit money is created as some multiple of high-powered money, but it provides an inaccurate picture of how modern banks work. They do not just sit around waiting for cash deposits to be made and then, when a deposit is made, go out and lend some multiple of the deposit (though it is certainly true that their deposits are some multiple of their reserves, and equation (6) above is an identity so it cannot be 'wrong'). On the contrary, modern bankers usually start from the other end. They wait until they have found a profitable lending opportunity, and they then take steps to make sure that funds are available to make the loan. This they can do either by offering higher interest on deposits, or by borrowing from other banks.

In the ratios world, banks passively receive deposits and then use these to make loans. In the modern world, however, banks are trading in highly competitive markets for both deposits and loans. In a competitive market there will

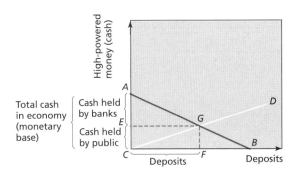

Figure 25.1 The ratios approach to the determination of the money supply

The money supply is determined by the stock of high-powered money (monetary base), the reserve ratio of the banks, and the cash–deposit ratio of the non-bank public. The diagram illustrates the size of deposit creation, given the banks' reserve ratio x (= AC/CB), the public's cash–deposit ratio b (= EC/CF), and the total cash in the economy AC. Deposits plus cash held by the public make up the total money supply. The total stock of high-powered money, or cash, in the economy has to be held by either the banks or the public. At point A the public holds all the cash available so there are no bank deposits, and the total money supply is just AC, which is all cash. At point C the banks hold all the cash and on that reserve base they create deposits of CB. The line AB thus plots the level of deposit creation resulting from each level of cash reserves (where point A represents the point where banks have no cash or deposits and point C represents the point where all the cash in the economy is held in bank reserves and CB is the value of bank deposits created on that reserve base). The banks' reserve ratio AC/CB is thus equal to (minus) the slope of AB.

The line CD represents the cash–deposit ratio for the non-bank public. Its slope, measured by EC/CF, is equal to that cash–deposit ratio. For a given base of high-powered money (cash), deposit creation will be determined at the point where these two ratios are both satisfied. This will be where CD and AB intersect. So the actual outcome is at point G, where banks have AE cash in reserves and create CF of deposits. The public holds EC of cash and CF of deposits. The total money supply at G is given by CF plus EC.

be a market-clearing interest rate for both deposit money and loans. Banks cannot expand their activity in either of these markets without taking into account the supply curve of deposits and the demand curve for loans that they face.

The market for bank loans is illustrated in Figure 25.2. This shows a positively sloped supply curve of loans and a negatively sloped demand curve for loans. The supply curve of loans is determined by two factors: the supply curve of deposits, and the spread. The **spread** is the difference between what the banks have to pay to borrow money and what they get by lending it (which has to provide a margin to cover staff costs, return on capital employed, and default risk). Remember that banks have to take in deposits in order to make loans. They borrow from one set of people or firms and lend to another.

The supply curve of deposits is positively sloped because

Table 25.6 High-powered money, deposits, and the money supply

Banks		Non-bank public		High-powered money ($H = C + R$)	Money supply ($M = C + D$)
Reserves (R)	Deposits (D) ($R \times 20$)	Cash (C) ($1,000 - R$)	Deposits (D) ($C \times 10$)		
(1)	(2)	(3)	(4)	(5)	(6)
1,000	20,000	0	0	1,000	
600	12,000	400	4,000	1,000	
400	8,000	600	6,000	1,000	
333.3	**6,666.6**	**666.6**	**6,666.6**	**1,000**	**7,333.3**
200	4,000	800	8,000	1,000	
100	2,000	900	9,000	1,000	
0	0	1,000	10,000	1,000	

For a given stock of high-powered money the amount of bank deposits created will be the amount which is consistent with the banks' reserve ratio and the non-bank public's cash–deposit ratio. The table sets out a range of desired positions for banks and the non-bank public independently. Only one of these positions satisfies the desired positions for both the banks and the public, such that the deposits the banks wish to create are the same as the deposits the public wishes to hold.

The example assumes that high-powered money (the cash base or monetary base) is fixed at £1,000. This can be held in some proportion between the banks and the public, but it cannot be changed other than by the monetary authorities. Banks are assumed to have a reserve ratio of 5 per cent, and the non-bank public is assumed to wish to hold cash at a level 10 per cent of their holding of bank deposits. Column (1) shows a range of possible levels of reserve holding for the banks, ranging from all of the £1,000 to none of it. Column (2) shows the level of deposits they would like to create (by making loans) in order to satisfy their desired reserve ratio for each level of reserve holding in column (1). Column (3) shows the cash holding by the public that is implied for each level of banks' reserves in column (1), so it is equal to £1,000 minus the number in column (1). Column (4) shows the level of deposits that the public would like to hold given their cash holdings in column (3). Column (5) reminds us that the stock of high-powered money is fixed at £1,000 throughout. Column (6) shows the value of the money supply for the unique position that satisfies the desires of both the banks and the public.

The actual outcome is the single position where the deposits that the banks wish to create are exactly equal to the deposits the public wishes to hold. This is where the level of deposits is £6,666.6. At this point the banks hold £333.3 in reserves and the public holds £666.6 in cash. The money supply is £7,333.3 (deposits plus cash held by the public) and the money multiplier is 7.333 (M/H). We could also calculate this from equation (6) on p. 437: $(b + 1)/(b + x)$ is 1.1/0.15 (where $b = 0.1$ and $x = 0.05$); this is 7.333.

for given interest rates elsewhere in the economy, banks can attract more deposits by offering higher interest rates. (Not all deposits in banks pay interest, but the deposits that banks can increase by offering high interest rates—their marginal deposits—do.) The spread is assumed, for simplicity, to be of a constant absolute size, so that the supply curve of loans is drawn parallel to the supply curve of deposits, but above it by the constant size of the spread. This is a reasonable assumption to apply to the total market for loans; in reality for each specific loan the percentage spread will be inversely related to the size of the loan, other things being equal. In other words the percentage spread on small loans is bigger than the percentage spread on large loans. Competition in banking drives the spread to the point where it is just enough to cover costs and return on capital, but does not involve any pure profit.

The demand curve for loans is negatively sloped because as banks charge higher interest rates on loans, customers will opt to borrow less. At lower interest rates customers will opt to borrow more. Equilibrium in the market for bank loans occurs where the demand and supply curves intersect. We will find this analysis of the market for bank loans very important below, when we discuss monetary

policy. The way in which the Bank of England seeks to control the UK money supply is via its ability to set interest rates. In effect the Bank shifts the supply curve of deposits and this alters the interest rate in the loan market. By forcing up interest rates, the Bank lowers the demand for loans; and by lowering interest rates, the Bank increases the demand for loans.

Money supply and competitive banking

The ratios approach to money supply creation and the competitive model of banking present two rather different ways of looking at the banking system, but they are compatible. Indeed, each helps us understand the other better, and both are necessary for a complete understanding of modern monetary control techniques.

The ratios approach tells us that the total money supply is related to the stock of high-powered money, this relationship being determined by the reserve ratio of banks and the cash–deposits ratio of the public. For given reserve ratios the total money supply would be determined if the authorities fixed the supply of high-powered money. However, the UK monetary authorities (and most other

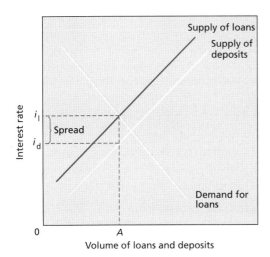

Figure 25.2 Competitive banking: supply of and demand for loans

The volume of bank loans is determined by the intersection of the supply curve of loans and the demand curve for loans. The diagram shows the positively sloped supply curve of loans and the negatively sloped demand curve for loans. The supply curve of loans is determined by the supply curve of deposits and the spread, or the interest margin that banks require to cover costs and risk. For given interest rates elsewhere in the economy, the supply curve of deposits is positively sloped because higher interest will attract more savings. The demand curve for loans is negatively sloped—high interest rates discourage borrowing and low rates encourage borrowing. Competition in banking drives the margin between deposit and loan rates to a level like i_l–i_d, where the spread is just enough to allow banks to cover costs and make a normal return on capital. With the demand and supply curves shown there will be $0A$ deposits and loans, and depositors will receive an interest rate of i_d while borrowers pay the loan rate i_l.

central banks, including the ECB) do not operate this way. Rather, they aim to control total deposits via the demand for bank loans. If they wish to lower deposits (and loans), they force up short-term interest rates, as shown in Figure 25.2. In other words the authorities use the knowledge of the market demand curve for loans in order to influence the total stock of deposits and, therefore, also the money supply.

Having chosen what they think is the correct interest rate to generate the desired demand for loans, the UK monetary authorities supply whatever high-powered money is demanded at that going interest rate. So the authorities do not fix the supply of high-powered money; rather, this is demand-determined at the interest rate that policymakers have set. The competitive model of banking helps us to see how this can be done by moving up or down the market demand curve for bank loans. We will return to this issue in more detail below.

Before moving on, however, there are two other important insights provided by the competitive model of banking. First, in the absence of reserve requirements imposed on the banking system by the monetary authorities,[10] we can see that the reserve ratio that banks will choose will be the outcome of an internal optimization process. Banks will try to keep the level of reserves as low as possible, subject to the need to supply cash on demand when customers wish to withdraw deposits. This is because reserves earn no interest and banks would like to devote as much of their capital as possible to profitable uses. This means that in the absence of high legal reserve requirements, banks' chosen reserve ratios tend to be very small, especially where they can access liquid funds very quickly by borrowing in the interbank market. The money multiplier has, as a result, become quite large (as mentioned above).

Second, the competitive model helps us to understand that the banking system as a whole is in competition with other financial channels in the economy for the available amount of borrowing and lending (intermediation) business at any point in time. The real size of the banking sector, relative to other channels of finance (and, indeed, other industries), is determined by how efficient it is in supplying the intermediation services that the economy requires. Issues relating to the nominal size of bank deposits and the money supply should be kept separate from the question of the real relative size of the banking system.

Implementation of monetary policy

We now conclude this chapter with an explanation of how monetary policy is implemented by the Bank of England in the United Kingdom, and by the European Central Bank (ECB) for the eleven members of the euro zone. In both cases the main objective of monetary policy is to maintain price stability, that is, to control inflation, and in both cases the chosen monetary stance is implemented via setting a specific short-term interest rate that then influences other local-currency interest rates. The same is also generally true of other central banks in the major industrial countries. The institutional details vary from place to place. They are also likely to change over time. Indeed, the arrangements

---

[10] In the United Kingdom in June 1998 reserves (known as the cash-ratio deposit, or CRD) held with the Bank of England were required to be around 0.20 per cent of deposits.

we describe were only introduced in the UK in 1997 and were to be implemented by the ECB in January 1999.

The Bank of England

The Bank of England started life as a privately owned joint-stock company, but in 1946 it was nationalized. From 1946 to 1997 the Bank had a key role in implementing monetary policy, but the decisions about policy were all taken by the elected government of the day, in the person of the Chancellor of the Exchequer. However, in May 1997 the incoming Labour government decided to delegate the power to set interest rates to the Bank of England with effect from June 1997, and the new arrangements were embodied in the Bank of England Act of 1998. This formally established the Monetary Policy Committee and the framework within which it operates. First, we outline the make-up and procedures of this committee; then we will explain what it tries to achieve; and finally, we describe how its interest rate decisions are transmitted to the financial markets.

The Monetary Policy Committee

The Monetary Policy Committee (MPC) is made up of nine members. Five of these are senior Bank of England officials and four are outsiders appointed by the Chancellor of the Exchequer. The committee is chaired by the Governor of the Bank of England. The outside members are each appointed for a three-year period, while the term of the Bank insiders depends upon the length of their Bank contract.

The MPC meets formally to set interest rates once every month, with announcements coming at noon on the first Thursday after the first Monday of each month. Decisions are made by a simple majority vote, with the Governor having a casting vote in the event of a tie. Prior to making this decision the MPC has three days of meetings to evaluate the latest data on the state of the economy and debate among themselves the appropriate course of action. A record of debate is published two weeks later in the form of the minutes of the meeting.

Four times a year the Bank also publishes its *Inflation Report*, which gives an in-depth assessment of the state of the economy. It contains the Bank's forecast of inflation and GDP growth over the succeeding two-year period. Members of the MPC are also summoned from time to time by the Treasury Select Committee of the House of Commons (the elected parliament) to answer questions about how and why they reached the decisions they did on monetary policy in the past.

Policy goals The MPC does not get to decide what goal it is aiming to achieve; rather, the goal has been set for it by the government. The goal set originally in 1997 was to keep inflation at 2.5 per cent using RPIX as the measure of

inflation targeted. RPIX is constructed by removing mortgage interest payments from the standard RPI (see the appendix to Chapter 20). The logic of using this measure is that if inflation were expected to rise and the MPC tightened monetary policy in order to control it, this rise in interest rates would itself raise RPI but not RPIX.

It is clearly understood by all concerned that it is impossible to hit an inflation target exactly, so the MPC has been given a band of plus or minus 1 per cent. If RPIX inflation turns out at more than 3.5 per cent or less than 1.5 per cent, the MPC has to write an open letter to the Chancellor of the Exchequer explaining why this deviation has happened and setting out what it intends to do about it. This covers the possibility that there will be unavoidable external shocks affecting inflation, for example an oil price rise, such that the return to low inflation will have to be managed over some time.

The MPC has been given *instrument independence* in that it can set the interest rate at whatever level it thinks appropriate, but it does not have *goal independence* as the inflation target is set by the government.

Choosing an interest rate to achieve an inflation target is not a simple matter. It requires a detailed and quantitative understanding of the transmission mechanism in the economy that we will discuss extensively in the following chapters. There are time-lags involved which mean that any policy change today may take many months to have its full effect. This means that policy has to be forward-looking. In effect the policymakers are targeting an inflation forecast rather than current inflation, because there is nothing they can do about inflation already reported, but they can take actions that will influence inflation in the future.

Figure 25.3 shows a 'fan chart' for inflation as published in the Bank of England *Inflation Report*. This shows a probability distribution of future inflation over a two-year period looking forward. Each shaded band represents 10 per cent probability and the shaded area represents 90 per cent of the potential possibilities. Clearly, an important piece of information in the policy process is the mean of this probability distribution, which expresses the most likely outcome for the inflation rate. If the mean forecast inflation rate is well above the target of 2.5 per cent, the MPC will be likely to raise interest rates in order to bring inflation down. If the mean forecast inflation rate is well below 2.5 per cent, it will be likely to bring interest rates down because inflation is well under control. If the mean forecast is very close to target, there is likely to be a fine balance between raising and lowering interest rates, with a bias towards unchanged policy.

The monetary regime in the United Kingdom is one where interest rates are adjusted in order to hit an inflation target looking up to about two years forward. A key

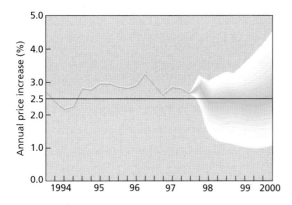

Figure 25.3 Bank of England RPIX inflation forecast
The Bank of England forecasts the probability distribution of inflation up to a two-year horizon. Each level of shading represents 10 per cent of the probability distribution. There are nine bands, so the bank is 90 per cent sure that inflation will lie somewhere in the shaded area. The mean of the forecast is in the dark area at the centre of the distribution. The target inflation rate is 2.5 per cent.

Source: Bank of England, *The Inflation Report*, May 1998.

intermediate target is the inflation forecast, which determines whether monetary policy needs to be tightened or loosened.

Implementation Suppose that the MPC has decided to change interest rates. How does it act in order to make this change stick? In practice it announces the new rate to the media and it appears on Reuters and Bloomberg screens around the City at noon on the announcement day. Banks then change their base rates[11] more or less immediately. Why do money markets have to adjust their interest rates in this way?

The reason is that they know that the Bank of England has raised the interest rate at which it will lend high-powered money (M0) to the banks. And they also know that *the Bank of England can force them to borrow from it on a regular basis*. Thus the general level of money market rates is set by the rate at which the central bank will provide base money (cash plus bankers' deposits at the Bank of England in the UK case) to the participants in the money markets.

The Bank of England can force other banks to borrow from it because it is the monopoly supplier of high-powered money and it can conduct security sales or purchases (open-market operations) to ensure that the banks are short of cash.

The standard instrument through which the Bank of England now lends money to the banks is known as a **repo** or **reverse repo**. 'Repo' is short for 'sale and repurchase agreement'. It sounds complicated, but it is actually very simple. The basic problem is that the Bank of England

needs to be able to lend high-powered money to private banks, but it does not want to take on any credit risk—it does not want the risk that some counterparty (some institution to which it has lent money) may go bust and not be able to repay. Accordingly it makes only secured loans. 'Secured' means that the borrower gives up the claim to some asset as security for the loan. (A mortgage on a house is a secured loan—if you do not repay the loan, the lender can take your house.) A repo is a loan secured upon a government security.

A repo has two parts. Suppose the Bank of England does a repo transaction with NatWest for £100 million. NatWest needs cash but it starts with some government securities (gilts) on its balance sheet. It is going to borrow money from the Bank using the gilts as security. Step one: it sells £100 million of gilts to the Bank of England in exchange for a credit in NatWest's account at the Bank. Step two: it agrees to buy back the gilts on some future date. But it will not pay back £100 million; rather, it will pay back a bit more—the extra representing the interest rate for the loan over that period. This interest rate is known as the repo rate, *and this is the interest rate that the Bank of England sets*. The two steps in the repo deal are both agreed at the outset, so the sale and repurchase are structured as part of a single contract. A reverse repo would involve a bank lending, rather than borrowing, in the same way. In practice it is the two-week repo rate that is set by the Bank of England.

Interest rate decisions of the MPC are implemented by the Bank of England fixing the interest rate at which it will do two-week repos. In effect this is just the rate at which the Bank will lend high-powered money to private banks.

The European Central Bank

At the time of writing the European Central Bank (ECB) has been formally established and starts its full operations in January 1999. From then on the ECB will be running monetary policy for eleven EU countries.[12] As with all institutions, the working of the ECB will evolve over time, but much is already known about its operations.

The ECB is at the centre of the European System of Central Banks (ESCB), which includes also the central banks of EU member countries. For monetary policy purposes only central banks of euro zone members have a say in ECB monetary policy. The ECB has an Executive Board of six members responsible for implementation of

---

[11] The base rate is an interest rate set by each bank as a reference point for the loan rates charged to customers. For example, a large corporate client may be charged interest at the base rate plus 1 per cent, while a (more risky) smaller business may be charged base rate plus 4 per cent.

[12] The eleven countries are France, Germany, Italy, Spain, Portugal, Belgium, the Netherlands, Luxembourg, Austria, Finland, and the Republic of Ireland.

monetary policy decisions. The Governing Council of the ECB is responsible for taking monetary policy decisions, and it is made up of the Executive Board plus the governors of the member central banks (of the euro zone).

The Maastricht Treaty defined the primary objective of the ESCB to be 'to maintain price stability'. But 'without prejudice to the primary objective of price stability' the ESCB has to support the general economic policies of the European Union. In October 1998 the Governing Council of the ECB decided that 'price stability shall be defined as a year-on-year increase in the Harmonized Index of Consumer Prices (HICP) for the euro area of below 2 per cent' and that the goal would be to maintain price stability according to this criterion over the medium term.

In order to achieve its goal of price stability the ECB announced in December 1998 a reference value for the growth rate of broad money of 4.5 per cent per annum. It also defined the monetary aggregate that it would monitor as M3 for the euro area as a whole. (See Box 25.2 on page 434 for the European harmonized definition of M3. Note that definitions may vary slightly for each member of the euro area.) However, in addition to this explicit reference rate for monetary growth, 'a broadly based assessment of the outlook for price developments and the risks to price stability in the euro area will play a major role in the ECB's strategy'.

The ECB has both target and instrument independence but with a general objective to maintain price stability.

Implementation

In preparing the ground for how monetary policy will be conducted, the European Monetary Institute (the precursor of the ECB) set out the instruments that will be used. The general principles are very similar to those set out for the Bank of England, though the ECB will operate initially at least through its member central banks (just as the US Federal Reserve Board operates mainly through the Federal Reserve Bank of New York). There are three main elements to the operating procedures.

Open-market operations This involves repo-style secured lending and borrowing operations *vis-à-vis* the money markets. This will be the main day-to-day operating procedure, and it will be the rate at which the ECB will lend to the money markets (on secured terms) that determines the general level of short-term interest rates within the euro area. As with the Bank of England, repo operations at about two-week maturity are thought to be the most likely point of official participation, and this is similar to the way that many other central banks already operate.

Standing facilities The ECB will offer a standing facility for participating banks to make deposits with and take loans from the ECB for overnight duration. The deposit and loan rates so specified will in effect put upper and lower bands around the short-term interest rate that can rule in the market for overnight money, and would in themselves be an adequate instrument for setting very-short-term market rates even without participation in the repo market. The lending facility must be secured on eligible assets (such as government securities). These facilities will be open on a daily basis and will provide and absorb overnight liquidity as well as providing a tool for signalling monetary policy stance.

Minimum reserves The ECB has the power to set minimum reserves required from private banks within the system. In October 1998 the ECB announced that the required reserve would initially be 2 per cent of bank deposits. This is much larger than the scale of the cash-ratio deposits required in the United Kingdom. However, the ECB will pay interest on these reserves at a level determined by its repo rate. A change in reserve requirements will be used to influence the money supply, as we explained in our discussion of the money multiplier earlier in this chapter.

Transition

It is likely that there will be a lengthy period of transition for the ECB, during which the targets and instruments of monetary policy evolve. But the target of maintaining euro zone inflation at less than 2 per cent over the medium term is likely to endure for the foreseeable future. The reference rate for monetary growth will no doubt be adjusted from time to time, and the ECB will use other information about the state of the economy, including economic forecasts, in order to inform its decisions.[13]

The final symbolic step in the introduction of the new currency, the introduction of new euro notes, will be completed only in 2002. Until this time the old currencies will continue to circulate even though they have exact mutual conversion values.

The success of both the new monetary arrangements in the United Kingdom and the new system in Europe will be judged by how well the respective monetary authorities do in controlling inflation, as well as by the price that has to be paid, if any, in terms of lost output and employment. In order to understand these important issues we have to incorporate money into our macro model, and it is to this task that we now turn.

---

[13] The latest information about policy statements from the Bank of England can be found via the Internet at www.bankofengland.co.uk, and at www.ecb.int for the ECB.

Summary

The nature of money

- Money is a medium of exchange, a unit of account, and a store of value.

- Money has evolved from being based primarily on a precious metal to being mainly in the form of bank deposits.

- The existence of money frees the process of exchange from the constraint of the mutual coincidence of wants.

Two models of banking

- Banks create deposits to some multiple of their cash reserves.

- In a competitive market in which banks pay interest on deposits and charge interest on loans, banks' behaviour is best understood in terms of demand and supply curves of deposits and loans. Banks must pay competitive interest rates to attract deposits, and they must charge competitive rates on their loans.

Implementation of monetary policy

- Central banks are the ultimate suppliers of cash to the monetary system, and they have the power to set short-term interest rates in the money markets.

- The Bank of England uses the two-week repo rate as its policy instrument.

- The UK inflation target is set by the government, and the Monetary Policy Committee has been delegated the responsibility to keep inflation close to target.

- The European Central Bank has the objective of maintaining price stability, but it has the freedom to set its own quantitative targets.

- The ECB sets short-term interest rates for all the members of the euro area.

Topics for review

- Functions of money
- Money multiplier
- Competitive banking systems
- The role of central banks
- Bank of England
- Monetary Policy Committee
- Repo and reverse repo
- European Central Bank
- Open-market operations
- Standing facilities
- Reserve requirements

Questions for discussion

1 What difference would it make to the economy if there were no money? What types of commodity might serve as money instead?

2 Explain carefully what would happen to the money supply, for a given monetary base, if there were a rise in (a) the banks' reserve ratio, (b) the general public's ratio of cash to bank deposits.

3 What would happen to the money supply if the general public chose to hold (a) no cash, (b) no bank deposits?

4 Explain how a tightening of monetary policy (higher repo rate) leads to a fall in the money stock.

5 What are the main differences between the operating procedures of the Bank of England and those of the European Central Bank?

Chapter 26
The Role of Money in Macroeconomics

In this chapter we return to the task of adding money to our model of the determination of GDP and the price level. In particular we want to know how monetary forces affect economic activity. We approach this issue in a number of steps. First, we discuss the factors that influence the demand for and supply of money balances in the economy. Second, we ask how monetary factors spill over into real activity. We are then able to accomplish the final task of integrating money and monetary policy into the aggregate demand and aggregate supply framework that we built up in Chapters 21–24.

In previous macro chapters we have discussed the determinants of *flows* of output and expenditures. Once we incorporate money and financial markets we are also talking about *stocks* of assets and financial instruments. The central question we need to understand is how markets for financial assets and liabilities interact with goods markets. We will discover that financial markets influence goods markets through two important prices—the interest rate, which is the price we pay to borrow money, and the exchange rate—and through wealth effects that arise when the real value of assets changes. We start with an introductory discussion of some important characteristics of financial assets and interest rates.

Financial assets

At any particular moment people have a stock of wealth that they hold in many forms. Some of it may be money in the bank or building society; some may be cash in hand or under the mattress; some may be in shares; and some of it may be in property, such as a house.

To simplify our discussion, we group wealth into just two categories, which we call *money* and *bonds*. By 'money' we mean the assets that serve as a medium of exchange, that is, paper money, coins, and deposits on which cheques may be drawn. We outlined the various definitions of money in Chapter 25 (see Box 25.2 on page 434). For present purposes it is adequate to think of money as including cash held by the public plus deposits in banks and building societies. By 'bonds' we mean all other forms

of financial wealth; these include interest-earning financial assets *plus* claims on real capital. For simplicity, however, our analysis of bonds will assume an asset that is exactly like the debt of the central government (known in the UK as a *gilt*), rather than having the characteristics of corporate bonds or equities.[1]

Money and bonds have different characteristics as assets. The market price of bonds can rise or fall, but the price of money is fixed in money terms (obviously £1 is always worth £1). The price of bonds is related to market interest rates, so our first task is to understand this relationship.

The rate of interest and present value

A bond is a financial asset that promises to make one or more interest payments and to repay a capital sum at a specified date in the future. The **present value** (*PV*) of a bond, or of any asset, refers to the value now of the future payment or payments to which the asset represents a claim. The concept of present value was discussed in more detail in Chapter 16 on pages 260–1. For those of you who have read Chapter 16 what follows is a review; for the rest it is essential reading.

Present value depends on the rate of interest, because when we calculate present value, the interest rate is used to *discount* the future payments. This relationship between the rate of interest and present value can be seen by considering two extreme examples.

A single payment one year hence We start with the simplest case. How much would someone be prepared to pay *now* to purchase a bond that will produce a single payment of £100 in one year's time?

Suppose that the interest rate is 5 per cent, which means that £1.00 invested today will be worth £1.05 in one year's time. Now ask how much someone would have to lend out in order to have £100 a year from now. If we use *PV* to stand for this unknown amount, we can write *PV*(1.05) [which means *PV multiplied by* 1.05] = £100. Thus *PV* =

---

[1] This simplification can take us quite a long way and is necessary in order to keep our model straightforward.

£100/1.05 = £95.24.[2] This tells us that the present value of £100 receivable in one year's time is £95.24; anyone who lends out £95.24 for one year at 5 per cent interest will get back the £95.24 plus £4.76 in interest, which makes £100.

What if the interest rate had been 7 per cent? At that interest rate the present value of the £100 receivable in one year's time would be £100/1.07 = £93.46, which is less than the present value when the interest rate was 5 per cent.

A perpetuity Now consider another extreme case—a perpetuity that promises to pay £100 per year to its holder *for ever*. The *present value* of the perpetuity depends on how much £100 per year is worth, and this again depends on the rate of interest.

A bond that will produce a stream of income of £100 per year for ever is worth £1,000 at 10 per cent interest, because £1,000 invested at 10 per cent per year will yield £100 interest per year for ever. However, the same bond is worth £2,000 when the interest rate is 5 per cent per year, because it takes £2,000 invested at 5 per cent per year to yield £100 interest per year. The lower the rate of interest obtainable on the market, the more valuable is a bond paying a fixed amount of interest.

Similar relations apply to bonds that are more complicated than single payments but that are not perpetuities. Although in such cases the calculation of present value is more complicated, the same negative relationship between the interest rate and present value still holds.

The present value of any asset that yields a given stream of money over time is negatively related to the interest rate.

Present value and market price

Present value is important because it establishes the market price for an asset.

The present value of an asset is the amount that someone would be willing to pay now to secure the right to the future stream of payments conferred by ownership of the asset.

To see this, return to our example of a bond that promises to pay £100 one year hence. When the interest rate is 5 per cent, the present value is £95.24. To see why this is the maximum that anyone would pay for this bond, suppose that some sellers offer to sell the bond at some other price, say £98. If, instead of paying this amount for the bond, a potential buyer lends her £98 out at 5 per cent interest, she would have at the end of one year more than the £100 that the bond will produce: at 5 per cent interest, £98 yields £4.90 in interest, which when added to the principal makes £102.90. Clearly, no well-informed individual would pay £98—or by the same reasoning any sum in excess of £95.24 —for the bond.

Now suppose that the bond is offered for sale at a price less than £95.24, say £90. A potential buyer could borrow £90 to buy the bond and would pay £4.50 in interest on the loan. At the end of the year the bond yields £100. When this is used to repay the £90 loan and the £4.50 in interest, £5.50 is left as profit. Clearly, it would be worthwhile for someone to buy the bond at the price of £90—or by the same argument at any price less than £95.24. But at £90 no holder would want to sell the bond. If she needed £90 she could borrow it for a year then cash in the bond at the end of the year, pay back the £90 plus £4.50 interest, and be £5.50 better off than if she had sold the bond at the beginning of the year.

Thus *all* bond-holders would want to sell at £98 and *none* would want to sell at £90, so £95.24 is the only price at which there are buyers and sellers—it is the market price.

This discussion should make clear that the present value of an asset determines its market price. If the market price of any asset is greater than the present value of the income stream that it produces, no one will want to buy it, and the market price will fall. If the market value is below its present value, there will be a rush to buy it, and the market price will rise. These facts lead to the following conclusion:

In a free market the equilibrium price of any asset will be the present value of the income stream that it produces.

The rate of interest and market price

The discussion above leads us to three important propositions. The first two stress the negative relationship between interest rates and asset prices:

1. If the rate of interest falls, the value of an asset producing a given income stream will rise.

2. A rise in the market price of an asset producing a given income stream is equivalent to a decrease in the rate of interest earned by the asset.

Thus a promise to pay £100 one year from now is worth £92.59 when the interest rate is 8 per cent and only £89.29 when the interest rate is 12 per cent: £92.59 at 8 per cent interest (£92.59 × 1.08) and £89.29 at 12 per cent interest (£89.29 × 1.12) are both worth £100 in one year's time.

The third proposition focuses on the term to maturity of the bond:

3. The sooner the maturity date of a bond, the less the bond's value will change with a change in the rate of interest.

To see this, consider an extreme case. The present value of a bond that is redeemable for £1,000 in one week's time

---

[2] Notice that in this type of formula the interest rate, i, is expressed as a decimal fraction. For example, 5 per cent is expressed as 0.05, so $(1 + i)$ equals 1.05.

will be very close to £1,000 no matter what the interest rate is. Thus its value will not change much even if the rate of interest leaps from 5 per cent to 10 per cent during that week. Note that any interest-earning components of *money* are so short-term that their values remain unchanged when the interest rate changes.

As a second example consider two bonds, one that promises to pay £100 next year and one that promises to pay £100 in ten years. A rise in the interest rate from 8 to 12 per cent will lower the value of £100 payable in one year's time by 3.6 per cent, but it will lower the value of £100 payable in ten years' time by 37.9 per cent.[3]

The supply of money and the demand for money

We now return to our central task of adding a monetary sector to the macro model built up over Chapters 21–24. This task cannot be completed immediately. Rather, we proceed in several small steps. In this chapter and the next we make some restrictive assumptions about the international financial environment in which our economy operates. In effect we assume that the exchange rate is fixed, and that there is some segmentation of domestic and international financial markets. This will enable us to analyse domestic monetary equilibrium without fully incorporating international influences. In Chapter 28 we introduce international transactions explicitly, and in Chapter 29 we incorporate the influences of international financial markets and the exchange rate regime.

The supply of money

The money supply is a *stock* (in the UK it is so many billions of pounds), not a *flow* of so many pounds per unit of time. It is important to notice that the money supply is a nominal variable measured in money units, whereas the other variables in our macro model are real variables measured in purchasing power units. In a modern economy the supply of money is determined by the interaction of the banking system and the non-bank private sector. We have already discussed the variety of definitions of the money stock and the way in which the money supply is determined in detail in Chapter 25. For present purposes we use the broad definition of money, M4 (see page 434).

In most major countries the authorities implement monetary policy by setting interest rates and letting the money stock be determined by how much is demanded at that interest rate. We have already explained some aspects of how this works in Chapter 25. But to complete the story we need to understand demand for money and how policy-determined changes in interest rates affect the real economy. Our analysis, therefore, now focuses on the factors influencing money demand.

The demand for money

The amount of wealth that everyone in the economy wishes to hold in the form of money balances is called the **demand for money**. Because people are choosing how to divide their given stock of wealth between money and bonds, it follows that if we know the demand for money, we also know the demand for bonds. With a *given level of wealth*, a rise in the demand for money necessarily implies a fall in the demand for bonds; if people wish to hold £1 billion more money, they must wish to hold £1 billion less of bonds. It also follows that if households are in equilibrium with respect to their money holdings, they are in equilibrium with respect to their bond holdings.

When we say that in February 1998 the quantity of money demanded was £726 billion (the approximate value of the broad money stock, M4, at that time), we mean that at that time the public wished to hold money balances that totalled £726 billion. But why do firms and individuals wish to hold money balances at all? There is a cost to holding any money balance. The money could have been used to purchase bonds, which earn higher interest than does money.[4] For the present we assume no ongoing inflation, so there is no difference between real and nominal interest rates.

---

[3] The example assumes annual compounding. The first case is calculated from the numbers of the previous example: (92.58 − 89.29)/92.58. The ten-year case uses the formula

$$\text{Present value} = \text{principal}/(1 + i)^n,$$

which gives £46.30 at 8 per cent and £28.75 at 12 per cent. The percentage fall in value is thus (46.30 − 28.75)/46.30 = 0.379, or 37.9 per cent.

[4] Many of the bank and building society deposits that are included in M4 now yield interest. This complicates, but does not fundamentally alter, the analysis of the demand for money. In particular it means that the opportunity cost of holding those interest-bearing components of money is not the *level* of interest rates paid on bonds but the *difference* between that rate and the rate paid on money. Because the interest earned on deposits tends to fluctuate less than rates on marketable securities, the difference tends to move with the level of interest rates in the economy, rising when rates rise and falling when rates fall. For simplicity we talk of the demand for money responding to the *level* of interest rates, although in reality it is the *difference* that is the opportunity cost of money.

The opportunity cost of holding any money balance is the extra interest that could have been earned if the money had been used instead to purchase bonds.

Clearly, money will be held only when it provides services that are valued at least as highly as the opportunity cost of holding it. Three important services that are provided by money balances give rise to three motives for holding money: the transactions, precautionary, and speculative motives. We examine each of these in detail.

The transactions motive

Most transactions require money. Money passes from consumers to firms to pay for the goods and services produced by firms; money passes from firms to employees to pay for the labour services supplied by workers to firms. Money balances that are held to finance such flows are called **transactions balances.**

In an imaginary world in which the receipts and disbursements of consumers and firms were perfectly synchronized, it would be unnecessary to hold transactions balances. If every time a consumer spent £10 she received £10 as part payment of her wages, no transactions balances would be needed. In the real world, however, receipts and payments are not perfectly synchronized.

Consider the balances that are held because of wage payments. Suppose, for purposes of illustration, that firms pay wages every Friday and that employees spend all their wages on goods and services, with the expenditure spread out evenly over the week. Thus on Friday morning firms must hold balances equal to the weekly wage bill; on Friday afternoon the employees will hold these balances.

Over the week workers' balances will be drawn down as a result of purchasing goods and services. Over the same period the balances held by firms will build up as a result of selling goods and services until, on the following Friday morning, firms will again have amassed balances equal to the wage bill that must be met on that day.

The transactions motive arises because payments and receipts are not synchronized.

What determines the size of the transactions balances to be held? It is clear that in our example total transactions balances vary with the value of the wage bill. If the wage bill doubles for any reason, the transactions balances held by firms and households for this purpose will also double, on average. As it is with wages, so it is with all other transactions: the size of the balances held is positively related to the value of the transactions.

It is the average value of money balances that people choose to hold over a particular period that is relevant for macroeconomics, but we need to know how money demand relates to GDP rather than to total transactions. In fact the value of all transactions exceeds the value of the economy's final output. When the miller buys wheat from

the farmer and when the baker buys flour from the miller, both are transactions against which money balances must be held, although only the value added at each stage is part of GDP.

Generally there will be a stable, positive relationship between transactions and GDP. A rise in GDP also leads to a rise in the total value of all transactions and hence to an associated rise in the demand for transactions balances. This allows us to relate transactions balances to GDP.

The larger the value of GDP, the larger is the value of transactions balances that will be held.

The precautionary motive

Many expenditures arise unexpectedly, such as when your car breaks down, or when you have to make an unplanned journey to visit a sick relative. As a precaution against cash crises, when receipts are abnormally low or disbursements are abnormally high, firms and individuals carry money balances. **Precautionary balances** provide a cushion against uncertainty about the timing of cash flows. The larger such balances are, the greater is the protection against running out of money because of temporary fluctuations in cash flows.

The seriousness of the risk of a cash crisis depends on the penalties that are inflicted for being caught without sufficient money balances. A firm is unlikely to be pushed into insolvency, but it may incur considerable costs if it is forced to borrow money at high interest rates in order to meet a temporary cash crisis.

The precautionary motive arises because individuals and firms are uncertain about the degree to which payments and receipts will be synchronized.

The protection provided by a given quantity of precautionary balances depends on the volume of payments and receipts. A £100 precautionary balance provides a large cushion for a person whose volume of payments per month is £800 and a small cushion for a firm whose monthly volume is £250,000. To provide the same degree of protection as the value of transactions rises, more money is necessary.

The precautionary motive, like the transactions motive, causes the demand for money to vary positively with the money value of GDP.

For most purposes the transactions and precautionary motives can be merged, as they both show that desired money holdings are positively related to GDP. Indeed, they both show money being held in relation to transactions, either planned or potential.

The speculative motive

Money can be held for its characteristics as an asset. Firms and individuals may hold some money in order to provide a hedge against the uncertainty inherent in fluctuating prices of other financial assets. Money balances held for this purpose are called **speculative balances.** This motive was first analysed by Keynes, and the classic modern analysis was developed by Professor James Tobin, the 1981 Nobel Laureate in economics.

Any holder of money balances forgoes the extra interest income that could be earned if bonds were held instead. However, market interest rates fluctuate, and so do the market prices of existing bonds (their present values depend on the interest rate). Because their prices fluctuate, bonds are a risky asset. Many individuals and firms do not like risk; they are said to be *risk-averse.*[5]

In choosing between holding money and holding bonds, wealth-holders must balance the extra interest income that they could earn by holding bonds against the risk that bonds carry. At one extreme if individuals hold all their wealth in the form of bonds, they earn extra interest on their entire wealth, but they also expose their entire wealth to the risk of changes in the price of bonds. At the other extreme if people hold all their wealth in the form of money, they earn less interest income, but they do not face the risk of unexpected changes in the price of bonds. Wealth-holders usually do not take either extreme position. They hold part of their wealth as money and part of it as bonds; that is, they *diversify* their holdings. The fact that some proportion of wealth is held in money and some in bonds suggests that, as wealth rises, so will desired money holdings.

The speculative motive implies that the demand for money varies positively with wealth.

Although one individual's wealth may rise or fall rapidly, the total wealth of a society changes only slowly. For the analysis of short-term fluctuations in GDP, the effects of changes in wealth are fairly small, and we will ignore them for the present. Specific individuals may undergo large wealth changes in response to bond price changes, but with inside wealth the total effect is negligible.[6] When lenders gain, borrowers lose; and when lenders lose, borrowers gain. Over the long term, however, variations in aggregate wealth can have a major effect on the demand for money.

Wealth that is held in cash or deposits earns less interest than could be earned by holding bonds; hence the reduction in risk involved in holding money carries an opportunity cost in terms of forgone interest earnings. The speculative motive leads individuals and firms to add to their money holdings until the reduction in risk obtained by the last pound added is just balanced (in each wealth-holder's view) by the cost in terms of the interest forgone on that pound. A fall in the rate of return on bonds for the same level of risk will encourage people to hold more of their wealth as money and less in bonds. A rise in their rate of return for a given level of risk will cause people to hold more bonds and less money.

The speculative motive implies that the demand for money will be negatively related to the rate of interest.

The precautionary and transactions motives may also be negatively related to interest rates at the margin, because higher returns on bonds encourage people to economize on their money-holding. However, in practice we only observe total money holdings, so we cannot distinguish the components held for different motives. Hence demand for money as a whole is likely to be positively related to GDP and wealth, and negatively related to the interest rate.

Real and nominal money balances

The money supply is a nominal quantity, but it is important to distinguish *demand* for real money balances from nominal money demand. Real money demand is the number of units of purchasing power that the public wishes to hold in the form of money balances. For example, in an imaginary one-product (wheat) economy, this would be measured by the number of bushels of wheat that could be purchased with the money balances held. In a more complex economy it could be measured in terms of the number of 'baskets of goods', represented by a price index such as the RPI, that could be purchased with the money balances held. When we speak of the demand for money in real terms, we speak of the amount demanded in constant pounds (that is, with a constant price level):

The real demand for money (or the demand for real money balances) is the nominal quantity demanded divided by the price level.

In the sixteen years from March 1982 to March 1998, on the M4 definition, the nominal quantity of money balances held in the United Kingdom increased more than fivefold, from just over £140 billion to around £734 billion. Over the same period, however, the price level, as measured by the RPI, rose by about 104 per cent (that is, it slightly more than doubled). This tells us that the real quantity of money rose from £140 billion to about £360 billion, measured in constant 1982 prices, a nearly 2.6-fold increase.

So far we have held the price level constant, and so we have identified the determinants of the demand for real money balances as real GDP, real wealth, and the interest rate. Now suppose that with the interest rate, real wealth, and real GDP being held constant, the price level doubles. Because the demand for real money balances will be unchanged, the demand for nominal balances must double. If the public previously demanded £300 billion in nominal money balances, it will now demand £600 billion. This

---

[5] A person is risk-averse when he or she prefers a certain sum of money to an uncertain outcome for which the expected value is the same. See Chapter 12 for a discussion of risk-aversion.

[6] 'Inside wealth' is not net wealth for the economy *as a whole*—one agent's assets are another agent's liabilities.

Box 26.1 The quantity theory of money

The quantity theory of money can be set out in terms of four equations. Equation (i) states that the demand for money balances depends on the value of transactions as measured by nominal GDP, which is real GDP multiplied by the price level:

$$M^D = kPY. \qquad \text{(i)}$$

Equation (ii) states that the supply of money, M, is exogenously determined:

$$M^S = M. \qquad \text{(ii)}$$

Equation (iii) states the equilibrium condition that the demand for money must equal the supply:

$$M^D = M^S. \qquad \text{(iii)}$$

Substitution from (ii) and (iii) into equation (i) yields

$$M = kPY. \qquad \text{(iv)}$$

The original classical quantity theory assumes that k is a constant given by the transactions demand for money and that Y is constant because full employment (equilibrium GDP) is maintained. Thus increases or decreases in the money supply lead to proportional increases or decreases in prices.

Often the quantity theory is presented by using the *equation of exchange*:

$$MV = PY, \qquad \text{(v)}$$

where V is the **velocity of circulation,** defined as nominal GDP divided by the quantity of money:

$$V = PY/M. \qquad \text{(vi)}$$

Velocity may be interpreted as showing the average amount of 'work' done by a unit of money. If annual money GDP is £600 billion and the stock of money is £200 billion, on average each pound's worth of money is used three times to create the values added that compose GDP.

There is a simple relationship between k and V. One is the reciprocal of the other, as may be seen immediately by comparing (iv) and (vi). Thus it makes no difference whether we choose to work with k or V. Further, if k is assumed to be constant, this implies that V must also be treated as being constant.

An example may help to illustrate the interpretation of each. Suppose the stock of money that people wish to hold equals one-fifth of the value of total transactions. Thus k is 0.2 and V, the reciprocal of k, is 5. If the money supply is to be one-fifth of the value of annual transactions, each pound must be 'used' on average five times.

The modern version of the quantity theory does not assume that k and V are exogenously fixed. However, it does argue that they will not change in response to a change in the quantity of money.

keeps the real demand unchanged at £600/2 = £300 billion. The money balances of £600 billion at the new, higher price level represent exactly the same purchasing power as £300 billion at the old price level.

Other things being equal, the nominal demand for money balances varies in proportion to the price level; when the price level doubles, desired nominal money balances also double.

This is a central proposition of the quantity theory of money, which is discussed further in Box 26.1.

Total demand for money

Figure 26.1 summarizes the influences of the nominal rate of interest, real GDP, and the price level, the three variables that account for most of the short-term variations in the nominal quantity of money demanded. The function

Figure 26.1 The demand for money as a function of interest rates, GDP, and the price level
The quantity of money demanded varies negatively with the nominal rate of interest and positively with both real GDP and the price level. In part (i) the quantity of money demanded varies negatively with the interest rate. When the interest rate rises from i_0 to i_1, the quantity of money demanded falls from M_0 to M_1. In part (ii) the quantity of money demanded is positively related to real GDP. When GDP rises from Y_0 to Y_1, the quantity demanded rises from M_2 to M_3. In part (iii) the quantity of money demanded is proportional to the price level. When the price level doubles from P_0 to P_1, the quantity demanded doubles from M_4 to M_5. In the text we refer to the M^D curve in (i) as the money demand function. It is drawn for given values of real GDP, wealth, and the price level.

relating money demanded to the rate of interest is often called the **demand for money function,** even though the demand for nominal money depends also on GDP, wealth, and prices.

We have seen that the public has a fixed stock of wealth at any point in time. When it decides how much money to hold, for the reasons just mentioned, it is also deciding

how many bonds to hold. So the public can be seen as adjusting the balance of its portfolio of wealth between the two assets money and bonds. When it is in disequilibrium, it is trying to alter that balance either by selling bonds and getting money, or by buying bonds and giving up money. When it is in equilibrium, it has the desired balance between the two assets.

Monetary forces and aggregate demand

We are now in a position to examine the relationship between monetary forces, on the one hand, and the equilibrium values of GDP and the price level, on the other. The first step in explaining this relationship is a new one: the link between monetary equilibrium and aggregate demand. The second is familiar from earlier chapters: the effects of shifts in aggregate demand on equilibrium values of GDP and the price level. The first step we set out in this chapter and the second we analyse in the next chapter, where we compare monetary and fiscal polices as tools for controlling the economy.

Monetary equilibrium and the interest rate

Monetary equilibrium occurs when the demand for money equals the supply of money. In Chapter 3 we saw that in competitive markets the price will adjust so as to ensure equilibrium. The rate of interest is the relevant price in the money markets. However, in UK and European money markets (as well as those of most major countries) the monetary authorities set the level of interest rates and the money supply adjusts to become equal to the quantity of money demanded at the policy-determined rate of interest.[7]

The easiest way to understand how this works is to start by showing how interest rates would adjust to clear the money market (equate demand and supply) if there were a given money supply. We then show how the money stock adjusts to equate demand and supply when the authorities choose to change the interest rate for macro policy reasons.

Equilibrium interest rate

Figure 26.2 shows supply and demand curves for money. The supply of money that is in existence at the initial point in time is shown as a vertical line, indicating that the money supply is a given nominal quantity. The money demand curve is based upon the speculative demand illustrated in Figure 26.1(i). It is negatively sloped because people desire

to hold less money as interest rates rise. The money demand curve is drawn for given levels of real GDP, the price level, and wealth, and will shift to the right if any of these variables increases.

Figure 26.2 also shows how the interest rate would move in order to equate the demand for money with its supply, given the initial money stock and the existing stock of bonds. When a few people find that they have less money than they wish to hold, they can sell some bonds and add the proceeds to their money holdings. This transaction simply redistributes given supplies of bonds and money among individuals; it does not change the total supply of either money or bonds.

Now suppose that all of the firms and households in the economy have excess demands for money balances. They all try to sell bonds to add to their money balances, but what one person can do, all cannot necessarily do. At any moment the economy's total supply of money and bonds is fixed; there is just so much money and there are just so many bonds in existence. If everyone tries to sell bonds, there will be no one to buy them, and the price of bonds will fall.

We saw earlier in this chapter that a fall in the price of bonds means a rise in the rate of interest. As the interest rate rises, people economize on money balances, because the opportunity cost of holding such balances is rising. This is what we saw in Figure 26.1(i), where the quantity of money demanded falls along the demand curve in response to a rise in the rate of interest. Eventually the interest rate will rise enough that people will no longer be trying to add to their money balances by selling bonds. At that point there is no longer an excess supply of bonds, and the interest rate will stop rising. The demand for money again equals the supply.

Suppose now that all firms and households hold larger money balances than they would like. A single household

---

[7] The authorities actually set a specific rate at which they trade with the wholesale money markets. All other rates are determined relative to this policy rate by market forces. We will talk as if there is only one interest rate and this is the one the authorities set. More institutional detail on the process of interest rate setting was set out in Chapter 25.

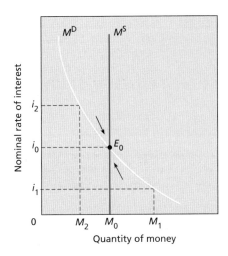

Figure 26.2 The equilibrium interest rate

The equilibrium interest rate arises where demand for money equals the supply of money. A given quantity of money, M_0, is shown by the vertical supply curve M^S. The demand for money is M^D; its negative slope indicates that a fall in the rate of interest causes the quantity of money demanded to increase. Equilibrium is at E_0, with a rate of interest i_0.

If the interest rate is i_1, there will be an excess demand for money of $M_1 - M_0$. Bonds will be offered for sale in an attempt to increase money holdings. This will force the rate of interest up to i_0 (the price of bonds falls), at which point the quantity of money demanded is equal to the fixed supply, M_0. If the interest rate is i_2, there will be an excess supply of money $M_0 - M_2$. Bonds will be demanded in return for excess money balances. This will force the rate of interest down to i_0 (the price of bonds rises), at which point the quantity of money demanded has risen to equal the fixed money supply, M_0.

or firm would purchase bonds with its excess balances, achieving monetary equilibrium by reducing its money holdings and by increasing its bond holdings. However, just as in the previous example, what one individual can do, all cannot do. At any moment the total quantity of bonds is fixed, so everyone cannot simultaneously add to personal bond-holdings. When all agents enter the bond market and try to purchase bonds with unwanted money balances, they bid up the price of existing bonds, and the interest rate falls. Individuals and firms then become willing to hold larger quantities of money; that is, the quantity of money demanded increases along the money demand curve in response to a fall in the rate of interest. The rise in the price of bonds continues until firms and households stop trying to convert bonds into money. In other words, it continues until everyone is content to hold the existing supply of money and bonds.

Monetary equilibrium occurs when the rate of interest is such that the demand for money equals its supply, and hence the demand for bonds equals their supply.

The determination of the interest rate depicted in

Figure 26.2 is often called the *liquidity preference theory* of interest and sometimes the *portfolio balance theory*.

As we will see, a monetary disturbance—a change in either the demand for money or the policy-determined interest rate—will lead to an adjustment in the money supply. However, the critical factor is that aggregate expenditure, especially investment (as we saw in Chapter 21), is sensitive to changes in the interest rate. Here, then, is a link between monetary factors and real expenditure flows.

Interest rates as the monetary policy instrument

In the section above we have seen how the interest rate would adjust to clear the money market for a given level of the money stock and a given money demand curve. In most industrial countries, including the UK and the euro zone, the monetary authorities set the interest rate and then let the money supply adjust to whatever interest rate is set.

Figure 26.3 illustrates how this works. Suppose the economy were to start at E_0 with interest rate i_0 and money supply M_0. If the authorities wished to relax monetary

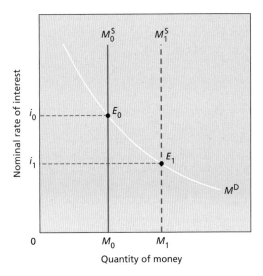

Figure 26.3 Interest rates and money supply changes

A change in the policy-determined interest rate requires the money supply to change. In the figure the initial money supply is shown by the vertical line M_0^S, and the demand for money is shown by the negatively sloped curve M^D. The initial equilibrium is at E_0, with corresponding interest rate i_0. The monetary authorities choose to lower the interest rate from i_0 to i_1. In order to achieve this they must generate an increase in the money supply, from M_0^S to M_1^S. The new equilibrium is at E_1. Starting at E_1, with M_1^S and i_1, it can be seen that a decrease in the money supply to M_0^S would be required to achieve an increase in the interest rate from i_1 to i_0.

policy they *could do so* by increasing the money supply to, say, M_1. If they did this, there would initially be an excess supply of money. Holders of this money would demand more bonds, and via the process discussed above this would raise the price of bonds and lower the interest rate to i_1.

However, in reality this is not what happens. Rather than setting a level of the money supply, the authorities set the level of the interest rate. In the figure the initial equilibrium is at i_0. The Bank now decides to loosen monetary policy and lowers the interest rate to i_1. At this lower interest rate, the public wishes to hold M_1 of money, but only M_0 is available. So there is excess demand for money. In order to achieve portfolio balance (that is, the desired composition of asset holding), the public tries to sell bonds for money. If the Bank did nothing, the sales of bonds would raise the interest rate. However, the Bank is setting the interest rate, so, in order to maintain that rate, it accommodates the public's desire to switch from bonds to money by buying bonds and supplying money. The money supply increases from M_0 to M_1.[8]

Notice that the outcome in Figure 26.3 is exactly the same when the authorities fix interest rates and let the money supply adjust as it is when they set the money supply and let interest rates adjust. It is not generally true, when analysing the impact of exogenous shocks on the economy, that a policy of fixing interest rates leads to identical adjustment paths to those of a policy of setting the money stock (or the monetary base). However, it is true that it makes no difference to the equilibrium of our macro model which way it is done.

The monetary authorities in most industrial countries (or currency zones) set the interest rate and let the money stock adjust to demand.

The transmission mechanism

The mechanism by which changes in monetary policy affect aggregate demand is called the **transmission mechanism.** The transmission mechanism operates in two stages: the first is the link between the interest rate and investment expenditure, and the second is the link between investment expenditure and aggregate demand. For this discussion we assume that the authorities are setting the interest rate. The case where the authorities set the exchange rate is discussed in Chapter 29.

From changes in the interest rate to shifts in investment
The first step in the transmission mechanism relates

[8]   In practice it is the monetary base, M0, that the authorities supply in order to maintain interest rates. Broader monetary aggregates are then determined by demand at whatever level the set interest rate determines (as a result of the public's demand for loans and deposits). This complication does not change the principles involved. The process was explained in Chapter 25.

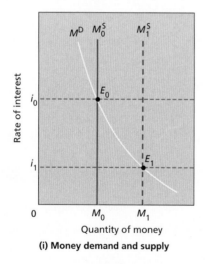

(i) Money demand and supply

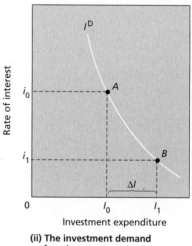

(ii) The investment demand function

Figure 26.4 The effect of changes in the interest rate on investment expenditure

A reduction in the rate of interest increases desired investment expenditure. Initial equilibrium is at E_0, with a quantity of money M_0 (shown by the vertical money supply curve M_0^S), an interest rate of i_0, and an investment expenditure of I_0 (point A in part (ii)). The monetary authorities then lower the rate of interest to i_1 (and increase the money supply to M_1), and this increases investment expenditure by ΔI to I_1 (point B). A policy-induced rise in the interest rate from i_1 to i_0 is accompanied by a fall in the money stock from M_1 to M_0 and leads investment to fall by ΔI from I_1 to I_0.

interest rates to aggregate expenditure via changes in investment. We saw in Chapter 21 that investment, which includes expenditure on inventory accumulation, residential construction, and business fixed investment, responds to changes in the real rate of interest. Other things being equal, a decrease in the real rate of interest makes borrowing cheaper and generates new investment expenditure.[9] This negative relationship between investment and the rate of interest is called the **investment demand function.**

This link between the interest rate and investment is shown in Figure 26.4. In part (i) we see that if the authorities wish to lower the interest rate from i_0 to i_1, they can do so (as discussed above) by buying all the extra bonds offered for sale at the new interest rate and thereby increasing the money supply from M_0 to M_1. In part (ii) we see that a change in the interest rate causes the level of investment expenditure to change in the opposite direction.[10] A fall in the interest rate causes investment to rise, and a rise in the interest rate causes investment to fall.

A fall in the interest rate leads to an increase in investment expenditure. A rise in the interest rate leads to a decrease in investment expenditure.

The change in investment expenditure shifts the aggregate expenditure curve, AE, as shown in Chapters 21 and 22.

From shifts in aggregate expenditure to shifts in aggregate demand Now we are back on familiar ground. In Chapter 23 we saw that a shift in the aggregate expenditure curve leads to a shift in the AD curve. This is shown again in Figure 26.5.

A change in the interest rate, by causing a change in desired investment expenditure (which in previous chapters was assumed to be exogenous) and hence a shift in the AE curve, causes the AD curve to shift. A fall in the interest rate causes an increase in investment expenditure and hence an increase in aggregate demand. A rise in the interest rate causes a decrease in investment expenditure and therefore a decrease in aggregate demand.

The transmission mechanism connects monetary forces and real expenditure flows. A change in the interest rate causes a change in investment expenditure, which in turn leads to a shift in the aggregate demand curve.

Thus a lowering of the interest rate increases investment and this shifts the AD curve to the right. A raising of interest rates lowers investment and this shifts AD to the left.

Later we will see that another important channel of the transmission mechanism is provided by the exchange rate. A preliminary discussion of how the openness of the economy affects the transmission mechanism is presented in Box 26.2. This discussion is extended in Chapters 28 and 29.

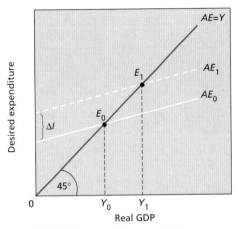

(i) Shift in aggregate expenditure

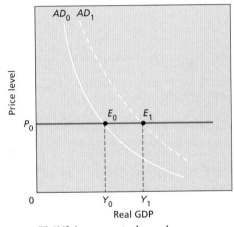

(ii) Shift in aggregate demand

Figure 26.5 The effects of changes in the interest rate on aggregate demand

Changes in the interest rate cause shifts in the aggregate expenditure and aggregate demand functions. In Figure 26.4 a fall in the interest rate increased desired investment expenditure by ΔI. Here, in part (i) the aggregate expenditure function shifts up by ΔI, from AE_0 to AE_1. At the fixed price level P_0, equilibrium GDP rises from Y_0 to Y_1, shifting the aggregate demand curve horizontally from AD_0 to AD_1 in part (ii).

When the interest rate rises (as from i_1 to i_0 in Figure 26.4), investment falls by ΔI, thereby shifting aggregate expenditure from AE_1 to AE_0. At the fixed price level P_0 this reduces equilibrium income from Y_1 to Y_0 and shifts the AD curve from AD_1 to AD_0.

---

[9] Purchases of durable consumer goods may also respond to changes in the real interest rate. In this chapter we concentrate on investment expenditure, which may be taken to stand for *all* interest-sensitive expenditure, and we maintain our simplifying assumption that expected inflation is zero so that the real and nominal interest rates are equal.

[10] Recall that we have assumed that real and nominal interest rates are the same. Generally, as long as inflation expectations are constant, the change in the nominal interest rate determined in part (i) of Figure 26.4 is equal to the change in the real interest rate in part (ii).

Box 26.2 The transmission mechanism in an open economy

The text focuses on the interest rate as the channel through which the effects of monetary policy are transmitted to the economy. However, as we have observed in earlier chapters, the 'openness' of the economy to international trade and to capital flows means that one additional complication must be allowed for. There is an added channel through which the effects of monetary policy are transmitted to real aggregate demand. This is through changes in the external value of the domestic currency on the foreign exchange market. (This effect applies almost exclusively to a floating exchange rate regime.) We use the UK situation as an example.

The link between interest rates and the external value of the pound

If UK interest rates are raised relative to those in other countries, the demand for sterling-denominated assets will also rise. UK residents will be less inclined to invest in assets of other countries, and foreign demand for high-yielding UK assets will increase. In order to invest in these assets, foreigners need to buy pounds, and their demand for these pounds on the foreign exchange market will cause the pound to appreciate.

Low UK interest rates have the opposite effect. UK residents will want to invest in foreign assets, and foreigners will be less anxious to invest in UK assets. Foreigners will demand fewer pounds, and people in the United Kingdom will be selling more pounds in order to obtain foreign currencies to invest in higher-yielding foreign assets. This will cause a depreciation of the pound on the foreign exchange market.

Other things being equal, the higher UK interest rates are, the higher will be the external value of the pound, and the lower UK interest rates are, the lower will be the external value of the pound.

The transmission mechanism

How are changes in the interest rate and the external value of the pound transmitted into changes in the level of economic activity? The induced changes in the value of the pound add a new channel by which monetary policy is transmitted to the economy, though clearly this applies only when the exchange rate is floating. A depreciation of the pound, other things being equal, makes UK-produced goods more competitive on world markets and thus increases exports and decreases imports.

Because a relaxation of monetary policy leads to a depreciation of the pound sterling, it stimulates net exports and thereby raises aggregate demand. Similarly, a tightening of monetary policy will lower aggregate demand because it leads to an appreciation of the pound and hence to a fall in net exports.

The operation of this channel of the transmission mechanism can be seen in terms of the definition of aggregate demand:

$$AD = C + I + G + (X - IM).$$

In a closed economy monetary policy operates through changes in the interest rate influencing investment expenditure (I) as well as any interest-sensitive consumption expenditures (C); in the open economy the effects on aggregate demand are reinforced through the effects of changes in the exchange rate on net exports ($X - IM$).

Although the channels are different, the ability of monetary policy to affect GDP remains. We maintain the assumption of a given exchange rate and limited international capital flows for simplicity in this and the next chapter; and we return to the open economy issues in Chapters 28 and 29.

An alternative derivation of the *AD* curve: *IS/LM*

We have now added a monetary sector to our macro model. In the next chapter we will use the model we have built to discuss the role of monetary and fiscal policies in stabilizing the economy. For the remainder of this chapter we show how our new-found knowledge of the monetary sector helps us derive the aggregate demand curve. There are no new economic relationships or even different assumptions involved here. This particular diagrammatic exposition was devised by the English Nobel Laureate Sir John Hicks (1904–89). It is so familiar to economists who have trained since the Second World War that it is frequently quoted. Students who have followed the macroeconomics chapters this far already know the economics behind the *IS/LM* model, but it is also helpful to know what specific bit of analysis '*IS/LM*' refers to. The diagrammatic apparatus has one important additional payoff. It makes clear differences in the transmission mechanism between monetary and fiscal policy.

For purposes of the present analysis we assume that real wealth is constant and that there are no relative price changes between domestic and foreign goods—these were the factors which gave us a negatively sloped aggregate demand curve in Chapters 23 and 24. By eliminating them, we focus on the way in which money markets, acting through interest rates on to expenditure, contribute to the negative slope of the *AD* curve.

The *IS* curve

Figure 26.4(ii) above plots the negative relationship between interest rates and investment, called the investment demand function. We have also seen (in Figure 26.5) that an increase in investment shifts the *AE* curve upwards and that this is associated with an increase in equilibrium GDP (a rightward shift of *AD*).

The *IS* curve plots the relationship between the interest

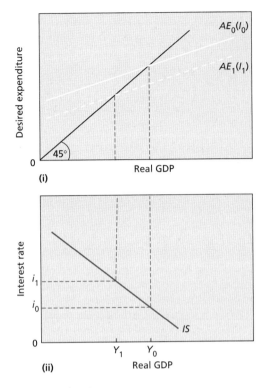

(i)

(ii)

Figure 26.6 The *IS* curve

The *IS* curve shows the equilibrium level of GDP associated with each given rate of interest. It shows combinations of the interest rate and GDP for which desired expenditures equal actual national output, and for which injections equal withdrawals. Part (i) shows a fall in *AE* resulting from a fall in investment from I_0 to I_1. This fall in *I* is caused by a rise in the interest rate from i_0 to i_1. The fall in investment produces a fall in GDP from Y_0 to Y_1.

Part (ii) shows the resulting combinations of the interest rate and real GDP. For given values of exogenous expenditures, i_0 leads to a level of GDP Y_0, and i_1 leads to level of GDP Y_1. Choosing any other level of the interest rate and following through its effect on GDP via investment produces another point on the *IS* curve.

rate and the equilibrium level of GDP, via the aggregate expenditure line *AE*. It is telling us the level of final expenditures, and therefore the equilibrium level of GDP, for each rate of interest. The relationship is negative, because higher interest rates cause investment to fall, which shifts *AE* down and lowers equilibrium GDP. Lower interest rates cause investment to rise, which shifts *AE* up and raises equilibrium GDP. This relationship is plotted in Figure 26.6.

In a closed economy with no government the *IS* curve plots the combinations of the interest rate and GDP for which saving and investment are equal. In an open economy with a government it plots the combinations of the interest rate and GDP for which desired expenditure (*AE*) equals output, or for which injections equal withdrawals

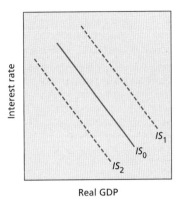

Figure 26.7 Shifts in the *IS* curve

An increase in exogenous expenditures shifts the *IS* curve to the right, while a decrease shifts it to the left. The initial *IS* curve is IS_0. Suppose there is an autonomous increase in government consumption. The *IS* curve shifts right to IS_1. This means that for each level of the interest rate there is a higher level of GDP consistent with injections being equal to withdrawals. Increases in any other autonomous expenditures give the same shift. In contrast, if the change is a fall in autonomous expenditures the *IS* curve shifts left to IS_2.

$(S + T + IM = I + G + X)$. The *IS* curve is drawn for given values of exogenous expenditures such as government consumption, exports, tax rates, and autonomous consumption.

The *IS* curve is the locus of interest rates and equilibrium levels of GDP which are consistent with equilibrium between desired expenditures and output. It is drawn for given values of all other exogenous expenditures, such as *G* and *X*, and for a given price level.

Now let us see what shifts the *IS* curve. In particular we are interested in the effects of shifts in exogenous expenditures. An increase in exogenous expenditures shifts the *AE* curve up in Figure 26.6(i), so it shifts the *IS* curve to the right (by the initial increase in expenditure times the multiplier). A fall in exogenous expenditures shifts the *AE* curve down, so it shifts the *IS* curve to the left. These shifts in the *IS* curve are illustrated in Figure 26.7.

The *LM* curve

To understand the *LM* curve it is simpler to assume initially that there is a given money supply. Later we explain how the fact that the monetary authorities set interest rates can be handled in this framework. Figure 26.2 on page 451 illustrates equilibrium in the money market at the point where the money demand curve intersects the money supply curve. The money demand curve is plotted for given levels of real GDP, the price level, and wealth. We continue to assume that wealth and the price level are constant, but what happens in that figure if real GDP were to increase?

The answer is shown in Figure 26.8(i). As GDP increases, transactions and precautionary demands for money both increase, and so the money demand curve shifts to the right. At higher GDP levels, and with a given money supply, the equilibrium interest rate will rise. This is because while the actual money supply is fixed, higher GDP has increased money demand. People will try to sell bonds (to get more money) until the price of bonds falls and interest rates, therefore, rise. The required rise in the interest rate is the amount that is just sufficient to cause a fall in speculative demand that exactly offsets the rise in transactions demand.

The *LM* curve is shown in Figure 26.8(ii). It shows the combinations of GDP and the interest rate consistent with money market equilibrium. From the way it is constructed it is clear that the *LM* curve is drawn for given values of the price level, wealth, and the money supply.

Now let us see how the curve shifts. As with any other curve, a change in any of the variables held constant along the curve will cause the curve to shift. We focus here on the effect of a change in the money supply. An increase in the money supply shifts the *LM* curve to the right, while a decrease in the money supply shifts the *LM* curve to the left. To see this, shift the vertical money supply curve in part (i) of the figure.

An increase in the money supply produces a lower equilibrium interest rate for each level of Y (and therefore for each M^D curve). This is shown as a shift of the *LM* curve from LM_0 to LM_1 in Figure 26.8(ii). A decrease in the money supply produces a higher equilibrium interest rate for each level of real GDP, as shown by a shift of the *LM* curve from LM_0 to LM_2.

The *LM* curve plots combinations of GDP and the interest rate, for a given money supply and given price level, that are consistent with the equality of money demand and money supply.

IS/LM and aggregate demand

The *IS* and *LM* curves each tell part of the story of the determination of aggregate demand. The *IS* curve determines GDP for given interest rates, while the *LM* curve determines the interest rate for given levels of GDP. In effect they are two simultaneous equations in GDP and the interest rate. One (*IS*) represents the set of equilibrium points for which desired expenditures equal national output (and injections equal leakages). The other (*LM*) represents the set of equilibrium points for which money demand equals money supply. Equilibrium for the whole economy (but still excluding the aggregate supply side) must be on both the *IS* and *LM* curves. This will be where they intersect. This is shown in Figure 26.9.

In the past the *IS/LM* model was widely used to analyse the effects of either changes in monetary policy (shifts in *LM*) or changes in fiscal policy (shifts in *IS*) on GDP. However, this framework has the limitation that it can only be

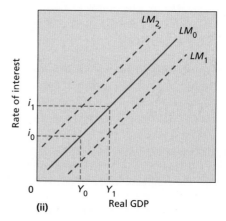

Figure 26.8 The *LM* curve

The *LM* curve shows the combinations of real GDP and the interest rate that are consistent with the equality of money demand and supply for a given nominal money supply and given price level. Part (i) shows equilibrium in the money market with a given money supply and an M^D function that is negatively sloped. At an initial level of GDP Y_0 the demand curve for money is given by M_0^D and the equilibrium interest rate is i_0. At higher levels of GDP the M^D curve shifts to the right (higher levels of GDP cause higher transactions demand for money). When GDP increases to Y_1, the money demand curve shifts to M_1^D and the associated equilibrium interest rate rises to i_1.

In part (ii) the *LM* curve LM_0 plots out the equilibrium interest rate associated with each possible Y and the given money stock M^S. This is a positively sloped curve. An increase in the nominal money supply shifts the *LM* curve parallel to the right, such as to LM_1, and a decrease in the nominal money supply shifts the *LM* curve to the left, such as to LM_2.

Figure 26.9 *IS/LM* **and aggregate demand**

The *AD* curve plots the *IS/LM* equilibrium level of GDP for each given price level (holding all exogenous expenditures and the nominal money supply constant). Part (i) has the initial position as the intersection of LM_0 (which is drawn with price level P_0) with the *IS* curve. This gives the overall equilibrium levels of real GDP and the interest rate as Y_0 and i_0. At higher price levels the *LM* curve shifts to the left (because the real money supply falls). At price level P_1 the *LM* curve is given by LM_1, and this leads to equilibrium GDP and interest rate of Y_1 and i_1. Part (ii) plots out the resulting combinations of the price level and GDP. This is the aggregate demand curve, *AD*.

used (on its own) for cases where either the price level is fixed and real GDP is variable, or where real GDP is fixed and the price level is variable. When output and prices are simultaneously variable we need to move to the *AS/AD* framework to handle the analysis.

There is nothing wrong in the *IS/LM* model, it is just incomplete. Indeed, it can be used to derive the *AD* curve (thereby illustrating that the *IS/LM* model is consistent with our approach to *AD*). The *AD* curve implied by our *IS/LM* model is derived in Figure 26.9(ii).

To derive *AD* we take a given *IS* and *LM* curve and ask what happens to the level of GDP (determined by their intersection) as the price level rises. The answer is that a higher price level shifts the *LM* curve to the left and, for a given nominal money supply and given all exogenous expenditures, leads to a lower level of equilibrium GDP.

The reason why an increase in the price level shifts the *LM* curve to the left is that the given money supply is *nominal* but money is demanded in relation to its *real* purchasing power. This means that, as the price level rises, there is an increase in the nominal quantity of money demanded to finance a given volume of real transactions. This leads to an upward shift in the M^D curves in Figure 26.8(i) and so leads to a higher equilibrium interest rate for each level of real GDP. This shifts the *LM* curve (upwards) to the left. An alternative way of making the same point (that a higher price level shifts the *LM* curve to the left) is to draw Figure 26.8(i) with the *real* money stock on the horizontal axis. Then, an increase in the price level simply reduces the real money supply and shifts the money supply curve to the left. These two different ways of expressing the point are equivalent and lead to the same impact of price level changes on the *LM* curve.

By taking different values of the price level we plot out the aggregate demand curve. Notice that the *AD* curve is drawn for given levels of the money supply and exogenous expenditures, but *not* for given levels of endogenous variables like the interest rate (for the moment), consumption, investment, net exports, and GDP.

This derivation also helps us to understand the determinants of the slope of the *AD* curve. Since it is determined by the intersection of the *IS* and *LM* curves, it depends upon the slopes of both. These in turn depend on four factors: the interest and income elasticities of demand for money, the interest elasticity of investment, and the size of the multiplier.

This reinforces our earlier argument that the reasons for the slope of the *AD* curve are not logically the same as those for the slope of any micro demand curve. The logic here is more tortuous—a higher price level lowers real money supply; this raises equilibrium interest rates; this lowers investment; this lowers GDP via the multiplier. In addition there is the wealth effect and the effect of relative prices (domestic and foreign) on net exports, which we explained in Chapter 22.

We now show that an increase in the money supply will shift the *AD* curve to the right while a decrease in the money supply will shift the *AD* curve to the left. This is done in Figure 26.10 simply by shifting the *LM* curve. With a given *IS* curve, each level of the money supply will be associated with a different equilibrium level of GDP for any given price level. A reduction in the money supply is represented by a leftward shift of the *LM* curve, and this leads to a leftward shift of the *AD* curve. Hence an exogenous fall in the nominal money supply shifts the *AD* curve to the left. An exogenous increase in the nominal money supply shifts the *AD* curve to the right.

It follows from this analysis that where the monetary authorities are setting interest rates rather than fixing the money stock, a rise in the policy-determined interest rate will shift the *AD* curve to the left, while a fall in the policy-

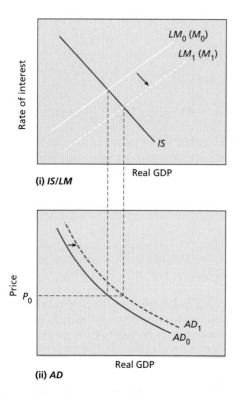

(i) IS/LM

(ii) AD

Figure 26.10 Shifts in the AD curve
A change in the money supply leads to a shift in the AD curve. The curves are drawn with an initial money stock M_0 leading to LM curve LM_0 and AD curve AD_0. An increase in the money stock to M_1 shifts the LM curve right to LM_1 and with a given IS curve produces AD curve AD_1. Thus a higher GDP is associated with each level of P. The reverse happens for a fall in the money stock—LM and AD shift left.

determined interest rate will shift the AD curve to the right. This follows because for policymakers to lower interest rates they need to permit the money stock to increase, and to raise interest rates they need to force the money stock to fall. Thus changes of monetary policy can be interpreted as shifts of the LM curve irrespective of whether the authorities are fixing the interest rate or the money supply. Hence once we are in the IS/LM framework we have an analytical tool which is just as suitable for either policy environment. The reason that this is true is that the LM curve represents equilibrium states in the money market: it does not matter whether that equilibrium is achieved by the interest rate adjusting to the money stock or by the money stock adjusting to the interest rate—the outcome is the same either way. A relaxation of monetary policy involves the LM curve shifting to the right, while a tightening of monetary policy involves the LM curve shifting to the left. We use this analysis further below.

In the next chapter we look more closely at how we can use our macro model to understand business cycles and the role of monetary and fiscal policies in stabilizing activity.

Summary

■ For simplicity we group all forms in which wealth is held into money, which is a medium of exchange, and bonds, which earn a higher interest return than money and can be turned into money by being sold at a price that is determined on the open market.

■ The price of existing bonds varies negatively with the rate of interest. A rise in the interest rate lowers the prices of all outstanding bonds. The longer a bond's term to maturity, the greater the change in its price will be for a given change in the interest rate.

The supply of money and the demand for money

■ The value of money balances that the public wishes to

hold is called the *demand for money*. It is a stock (not a flow), measured in the United Kingdom as so many billions of pounds.

■ Money balances are held, despite the opportunity cost of bond interest forgone, because of the transactions, precautionary, and speculative motives. They have the effect of making the demand for money vary positively with real GDP, the price level, and wealth, and negatively with the nominal rate of interest. The nominal demand for money varies proportionally with the price level.

■ When there is an excess demand for money balances, people try to sell bonds. This pushes the price of bonds down and the interest rate up. When there is an excess supply of money balances, people try to buy bonds. This pushes the price of bonds up and the rate of interest down. Monetary equilibrium is established when people are willing to hold the existing stocks of money and bonds at the current rate of interest.

Monetary forces and aggregate demand

■ With given inflationary expectations, changes in the nominal interest rate translate into changes in the real interest rate. A change in the real interest rate causes desired investment to change along the investment demand function. This shifts the aggregate desired expenditure function and causes equilibrium GDP to change.

■ A rise in interest rates (or a decrease in the supply of money) reduces aggregate demand; that is, it shifts *AD* to the left. A cut in interest rates (or an increase in the money supply) increases aggregate demand; that is, it shifts *AD* to the right.

■ The negatively sloped aggregate demand curve indicates that the higher the price level, the lower the equilibrium GDP. The explanation lies in part with the effect of money on the adjustment mechanism: other things being equal (for a given money stock), the higher the price level, the higher the demand for money and the rate of interest, the lower the level of investment and therefore the lower the aggregate expenditure function, and thus the lower the equilibrium level of GDP.

An alternative derivation of the *AD* curve: *IS/LM*

■ Combinations of the interest rate and equilibrium GDP for which desired expenditure equals actual real national output can be represented by the *IS* curve, which is negatively sloped. Combinations of real GDP and the equilibrium interest rate for which money demand equals money supply can be represented by the *LM* curve, which is positively sloped.

■ The *AD* curve can be derived from the *IS/LM* model, holding all exogenous expenditures and the nominal money supply constant. A rise in the price level lowers the real money supply, leading to higher interest rates and lower GDP. A fall in the price level leads to an increase in the *real* money supply, which lowers interest rates and increases GDP. Hence the *AD* curve is negatively sloped. This reinforces our earlier discussion of why *AD* has a negative slope.

Topics for review

■ Interest rates and bond prices
■ Transactions, precautionary, and speculative motives for holding money
■ Negative relationship between the quantity of money demanded and the interest rate
■ Monetary equilibrium
■ Transmission mechanism
■ Investment demand function
■ The *IS* and *LM* curves
■ The slope of the *AD* curve

Questions for discussion

1 Under what conditions will individuals be happy to hold the existing stock of money and bonds? Since bonds yield more interest than money does, what compensates money-holders at the margin for the loss of interest on the last £1 of money they choose to hold?

2 For a given initial money supply, explain what happens to the equilibrium interest rates in money markets (in the absence of intervention by the monetary authorities) if (a) the introduction of electronic money reduces demand for traditional forms of money; (b) better bank service increases demand for money; (c) domestic residents start using foreign money for some of their transactions.

3 Explain what happens to the *IS* and *LM* curves if (a) a productivity improvement increases the yield on investments; (b) there is an increase in export demand; (c) there is an autonomous increase in money demand.

4 Explain how changes in monetary and fiscal polices shift the *AD* curve, using the *IS/LM* framework.

5 Why does the *AD* curve have a negative slope and what factors determine this slope?

Chapter 27
Monetary and Fiscal Policy and the Business Cycle

In the previous chapters we have built up a model of the macroeconomy. Macroeconomics as a subject was invented in order to provide insights into how governments could use their policy tools to avoid the booms and slumps that have been observed in most modern economies from time to time. The role of monetary and fiscal policies in stabilizing the economy is the central topic of this chapter.

Business cycles have been observed for almost as long as recorded history. The Old Testament, for example, talks about a pattern in which seven good years are followed by seven lean years. In modern industrial economies the good and bad times are less evenly spread, with recessions tending to be shorter than recoveries. A *recession* is defined as more than two successive quarters of negative GDP growth. The UK, for example, had a recession from 1979Q3

to 1981Q1, which was followed by a recovery lasting from 1981Q2 to 1990Q1. Thus the recession lasted less than two years while the recovery was of nine years' duration. Similarly, the recession in the UK in the early 1990s ran from 1990Q2 to 1992Q1 (another period of around two years) while the recovery that started in 1992Q2 was still going at the time of writing (spring of 1998), six years later.

Figure 21.1 on page 357 shows the cycle of real GDP in the UK around its potential level. Figure 27.1 shows the cycle in the growth rates of GDP in the UK, the USA, and Germany during the period 1970–1997. This shows that all countries exhibit cyclical patterns in their growth rates. Indeed, the cycles in different countries are often related, because when one country goes into recession its citizens

Figure 27.1 The growth rate of GDP in the UK, the USA, and Germany
All countries experience business cycles, and these cycles are often correlated.
Source: Datastream.

demand less imports and this leads to a fall in aggregate demand in other countries.

We start by discussing some of the reasons why there are cycles in the economy before using our macro model to

analyse how monetary and fiscal policies can be used to help moderate fluctuations in activity. Finally, we discuss some of the controversies over the causes of and cures for business cycles.

Theories of the cycle

There are two components to any theory of cycles. The first is a pattern of shocks or disturbances that hits the economy. The second is a model of the dynamic behaviour of the endogenous variables (GDP, consumption, investment, etc.) that generate cycles over time. Let us look at each of these components in turn.

Systematic or random shocks?

One way in which cycles can be generated is from cycles in the exogenous shocks hitting the economy. Before the industrial revolution, when agriculture was the main activity, cycles were sometimes caused by weather patterns, overplanting followed by underplanting ('hog-cycles'), and even incidences of crop disease. In industrial economies cycles can result from patterns of innovation (product cycles) and waves of productivity improvements. There are also cycles in demand for the exports of open economies resulting from cycles in the rest of the world.

For a small open economy such as the UK there are undoubtedly systematic movements in exogenous variables, notably world demand. None the less, most effort in the economic analysis of cycles has been directed towards understanding the generation of cycles from random external shocks (or discrete changes in exogenous variables) which then trigger some cyclical internal adjustment mechanism.

Most theories of this type rely on time-lags in responses. Many empirical macro models that are designed to fit the data have quite long lags in their behavioural relations. For example, if a fall in the rate of interest makes a new investment programme profitable, it may take six months to plan it, three months to let contracts, six more months before spending builds up to its top rate, and another two years to complete the project. Such long adjustment lags can cause random or erratic shocks to the economy to generate a cyclical path for GDP and the other endogenous macro variables.

Each of the major components of aggregate expenditure is sometimes subject to exogenous shocks. The long lags in responses to these shocks can then convert them into cyclical oscillations in GDP.

Cyclical adjustment mechanisms

There are many ways of formulating a dynamic model of

the economy so that it generates cycles. Here we outline one simple mechanism that can generate cycles in response to discrete changes in exogenous variables. It is called the multiplier–accelerator mechanism. No one believes any longer that it provides *the* explanation of cycles; many economists still accept, however, that it captures one major element of cyclical fluctuations. To understand it, we need to return to a discussion of the causes of variations in investment.

The accelerator theory of investment In our macroeconomic model above investment changes in response to changes in interest rates. The **accelerator theory of investment** relies on another determinant of investment that can be formalized only in a dynamic model. This theory relates investment to GDP. The possibility of systematic fluctuations arises because the *level* of investment is related to *changes* in GDP.

The demand for machinery and factories is obviously derived from the demand for the goods that the capital equipment is designed to produce. If there is a demand that is expected to persist, and that cannot be met by increasing production with existing industrial capacity, then new plant and equipment will be needed.

Investment expenditure occurs while the new capital equipment is being built and installed. If the desired stock of capital goods increases, there will be an investment boom while the new capital is being produced. But if nothing else changes, and even though business conditions continue to look rosy enough to justify the increased stock of capital, investment in new plant and equipment will cease once the larger capital stock is achieved. This makes investment depend on changes in final demand, and hence on changes in GDP, as illustrated in Table 27.1.[1]

---

[1] A more formal derivation is: let the relationship between the GDP level and the amount of capital needed to produce it be

$$K = \alpha Y, \tag{1}$$

where K is the required capital stock. The coefficient α is the capital–output ratio; $\alpha = K/Y$ and is also called the accelerator coefficient. Taking changes in (1), and noticing that investment is, by definition, the change in the capital stock, yields

$$I = \Delta K = \alpha \Delta Y$$

This says that investment is some constant times *the change* in GDP. This is called the 'simple', or sometimes the 'naïve', accelerator.

Table 27.1 An illustration of the accelerator theory of investment

Year	Annual sales	Change in sales	Required stock of capital[a]	Net investment increase in required capital stock
(1)	(2)	(3)	(4)	(5)
1	£10	£0	£50	£0
2	10	0	50	0
3	11	1	55	5
4	13	2	65	10
5	16	3	80	15
6	19	3	95	15
7	22	3	110	15
8	24	2	120	10
9	25	1	125	5
10	25	0	125	0

With a fixed capital–output ratio, net investment occurs only when it is necessary to increase the stock of capital in order to change output. Assume that it takes £5 of capital to produce £1 of output per year. In years 1 and 2 there is no need for investment. In year 3 a rise in sales of £1 requires investment of £5 to provide the needed capital stock. In year 4 a further rise of £2 in sales requires an additional investment of £10 to provide the needed capital stock. As columns (3) and (5) show, the amount of net investment is proportional to the *change* in sales. When the increase in sales tapers off in years 7–9, investment declines. When sales no longer increase in year 10, net investment falls to zero because the capital stock of year 9 is adequate to provide output for year 10's sales.

[a] Assuming a capital–output ratio of 5:1.

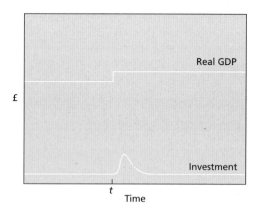

Figure 27.2 The accelerator and investment
When there is a change in the level of final output, there is a much bigger percentage change in the rate of investment. The figure illustrates the path over time of GDP and investment. We assume that GDP is constant but that at time *t* it jumps to a new, higher level and then continues at this level. Replacement investment carries on at some constant level, but the increase in output requires a higher capital stock. This in turn requires a burst of *new investment*. Once this burst of new investment is over (shown as being spread out over time), the level of new investment returns to zero.

Figure 27.2 illustrates what happens to investment under the accelerator theory when GDP rises from one constant level to another.

The main insight that the accelerator theory provides is its emphasis on the role of net investment as a *disequilibrium* phenomenon—something that occurs when the stock of capital goods differs from what firms and households would like it to be. This makes the accelerator a possible explanation of *fluctuations* in GDP. As we will see, it can itself contribute to those fluctuations.

Taken literally, the simple accelerator assumes a mechanical and rigid response of investment to changes in sales (and thus, in the aggregate, to changes in GDP). It does this by assuming a proportional relationship between changes in output and changes in the desired capital stock. It also assumes that there is a fixed ratio between the level of output and the level of the capital stock. This ratio is called the *capital–output ratio*. Both assumptions are to some degree questionable.

The accelerator does not by itself give anything like a complete explanation of variations in investment in capital goods, and it should not be surprising that a simple accelerator theory provides a relatively poor overall expla-

nation of changes in investment. Yet accelerator-like influences do exist, and they play a role in the cyclical variability of investment. Modern investment theories often include a flexible version of the accelerator, in which the capital–output ratio (coefficient α of footnote 1) varies with other factors such as interest rates.

Multiplier–accelerator interaction The theory linking systematic fluctuations in GDP to systematic fluctuations in investment expenditure combines the accelerator theory just discussed with the multiplier.

This **multiplier–accelerator theory** of the cycle is divided into three steps. First, a theory of cumulative upswings and downswings explains why, once started, movements tend to carry on in the same direction. Second, a theory of floors and ceilings explains why upward and downward movements are eventually brought to a halt. And third, a theory of instability explains how, once a process of upward or downward movement is brought to a halt, it tends to reverse itself.

Why does a period of expansion or contraction, once begun, tend to develop its own momentum? First, the multiplier process tends to cause cumulative movements. As soon as a revival begins, some unemployed people find work again. These people, with their newly acquired income, can afford to make much-needed consumption expenditures. This new demand causes an increase in production and creates new jobs for others. As incomes rise, demand rises; as demand rises, incomes rise. Just the reverse happens in a downswing. Unemployment in one sector causes a fall in demand for the products of other sectors, which leads to a further fall in employment and a further fall in demand.

A second major factor is the accelerator theory. New investment is needed to expand existing productive capacity and to introduce new methods of production. When consumer demand is low and there is excess capacity, investment is likely to fall to a very low level; once demand and output start to rise and entrepreneurs come to expect further rises, investment expenditure may rise very rapidly. Furthermore, when full employment of existing capacity is reached, new investment becomes one of the few ways available for firms to increase their output.

A third major explanation for cumulative movements is expectations. All production plans take time to fulfil. Current decisions to produce consumer goods and investment goods are very strongly influenced by business expectations. Such expectations can sometimes be volatile, and sometimes self-fulfilling. If enough people think, for example, that equity prices are going to rise, they will all buy equities in anticipation of the price rise, and these purchases will themselves cause prices to rise. If, on the other hand, enough people think that equity prices are going to fall, they will sell quickly at what they regard as a high price, and thereby actually cause prices to fall. This is the phenomenon of *self-realizing expectations*. It applies to many parts of the economy. If enough managers think the future looks rosy and begin to invest in increasing capacity, this will create new employment and income in the capital goods industries, and the resulting increase in demand will help to create the rosy conditions whose vision started the whole process. There is a bandwagon effect. Once things begin to improve, people expect further improvements, and their actions, based on this expectation, help to cause further improvements. On the other hand, once things begin to worsen, people often expect further worsening, and then their actions, based on this expectation, help to make things worse.

The multiplier–accelerator process, combined with changes in expectations that cause autonomous shifts of expenditure, can explain the cumulative tendencies of recessions and recoveries.

The next question that arises is why these upward and downward processes ever come to an end.

A very rapid expansion can continue for some time, but it cannot go on for ever because eventually the economy will run into bottlenecks (or ceilings) in terms of some re-

sources. This will happen when firms cannot take on more workers without paying much higher wages to attract them from other firms. Inflation will pick up, and either the monetary authorities will put interest rates up or firms will cut investment in anticipation of a downturn. This expectation itself may become self-fulfilling.

A rapid contraction, too, is eventually brought to an end. Firms can postpone investment and run down stocks, and consumers can put off buying new clothes and new cars. Eventually some kinds of spending can be postponed no longer. Even a modest increase in sales can cause confidence to return. The small upturn in spending then leads to further spending and the start of an upswing of the cycle, through the interaction of the multiplier and accelerator together.

Indeed, the accelerator can explain how expansions and contractions reverse direction. We have seen that the accelerator causes the desired level of *new* (not replacement) investment to depend upon the rate of change of GDP. If GDP is rising at a constant rate, then investment will be at a constant *level*; if there is a slackening in the speed at which GDP is rising, the level of investment will decline. This means that a *levelling-off* in GDP at the top of a cycle may lead to a *decline* in the amount of investment. The decline in investment at the upper turning-point will cause a decline in the level of GDP. This will be intensified through the multiplier process.

The accelerator theory explains why a slowdown in the growth of GDP can lead to negative growth in subsequent periods, via a fall in investment spending.

Recessions do not go on for ever. Investment theory predicts that sooner or later an upturn will begin. If nothing else causes an expansion of business activity, eventually there will be a revival of replacement investment. As existing capital wears out, the capital stock will fall below the level required to produce current output. At this stage new machines will have to be bought to replace those that are wearing out. The rise in the level of activity in the capital goods industries will then cause, by way of the multiplier, a further rise in incomes and output. The economy will have turned the corner. An expansion, once started, may trigger the sort of cumulative upward movement already discussed.

We now outline how the course of business cycles is worked out within the framework of our macro model, and we then discuss how monetary and fiscal policies can be used to speed up adjustment of the economy back towards equilibrium.

Macroeconomic cycles and aggregate shocks

In Chapter 24 we discussed how fiscal policy could be used to return GDP to its potential level following an inflationary or deflationary shock. Now that we have added a monetary sector to our model we are able to tell a much more detailed story about how shocks work their way through the economy and about the policy options available to the authorities to respond to those shocks.

Before looking at the economy as a whole, however, we first spend a little time thinking about how changes in both monetary policy and fiscal policy work through into our aggregate demand and aggregate supply framework. We then see how fiscal and monetary policies interact. This latter exercise is important because it turns out that the short-run effect of fiscal policy changes is different when the monetary authorities peg the interest rate than it would be if they fixed the money stock.

Monetary policy and aggregate demand

We have already explained in Chapter 26 that the aggregate demand curve is drawn for a given money stock. However, since most monetary authorities set the interest rate and not the money supply, we need to understand how monetary policy changes work in our model.

We saw in Figure 26.9 on page 457 how the AD curve can be derived from the intersection of the IS and LM curves as we vary the price level. And we also saw in Figure 26.10 that a change in the money stock shifts the AD curve. We now want to make the connection between shifts of the AD curve and changes in monetary policy, that is, changes in the interest rate. This is shown in Figure 27.3.

The initial position is shown in part (i) by the intersection of IS and LM_0 and in part (ii) by the aggregate demand curve AD_0. Suppose now the monetary authorities decide to relax monetary policy and lower interest rates from i_0 to i_1. They enter the bond market and buy bonds. This raises the price of bonds and, what is the same thing, lowers the rate of interest. Their purchases provide the extra money supply that will be demanded at the lower interest rate. In providing this they shift the LM curve to the right. At each price level, such as at the initial level P_0, this gives us a point on the new AD curve. This has shifted to the right by the horizontal distance $Y_0 - Y_1$. Notice that the size of the horizontal shift in AD depends not only on the size of the shift in LM (necessary to equate demand and supply of money at the new lower interest rate) but also on the slope of the IS curve. The slope of the IS curve is important because it is determined by how much investment has increased as a result of the fall in the interest rate, and by the multiplier. And it is the change in investment times the multiplier that determines how much real GDP increases.

(This will not be the actual increase in GDP as we do not have the aggregate supply curves in this figure.)

A monetary policy loosening that involves a policy-induced lowering of interest rates shifts the AD curve to the right. A monetary policy tightening involves raising interest rates and shifts the AD curve to the left.

Fiscal policy and aggregate demand

We have seen in Chapter 24 how fiscal policy can be used to shift the aggregate demand curve. However, now that we have added a monetary sector to our model, we can see more clearly how the size of that shift is determined. In particular it turns out that the effects of a fiscal policy

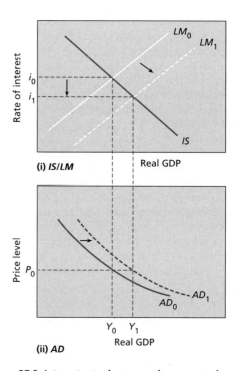

Figure 27.3 Interest rate changes and aggregate demand

A policy-induced fall in the interest rate shifts the AD curve to the right. In part (i) from an initial position with interest rate i_0 at the intersection of IS and LM_0, which is associated with aggregate demand curve AD_0 in part (ii), a fall in the interest rate to i_1 requires an increase in the money stock, which shifts the LM curve rightward to LM_1. In part (ii) this implies that the AD curve has shifted from AD_0 to AD_1 and at a price level such as P_0 there has been an increase in GDP from Y_0 to Y_1. A rise in interest rates would have the reverse effect, requiring a lowering of the money stock and a leftward shift of AD.

change depend in part on what the monetary authorities are doing.

The initial position is shown in Figure 27.4 part (i) by the intersection of IS_0 and LM_0 and in part (ii) by the aggregate demand curve AD_0. An expansionary fiscal policy, for example an increase in government spending, shifts the IS curve to the right in part (i). With a given LM curve associated with a fixed money supply, interest rates would rise, and this rise in interest rates would *crowd out* some investment expenditure. The AD curve would shift from AD_0 to AD_1 and GDP would increase from Y_0 to Y_1 for a price level such as P_0.

However, if the monetary authorities are pegging the interest rate at i_0, this will not be the outcome. Once the IS curve starts to shift to the right, this will put upward pressure on interest rates (because the increase in spending increases GDP and this increases demand for money). To obtain the extra money people sell bonds. The monetary authority purchases the bonds, thus stabilizing the interest rate and supplying the extra money people require. Accordingly, the LM curve will also shift to the right and so the AD curve shifts to AD_2, which involves a horizontal shift of $Y_0 - Y_2$. This is clearly a greater horizontal shift than would have obtained in the case where the money stock is unchanged.

Notice that when the monetary authorities peg the interest rate the effect of a given fiscal policy change on GDP is larger than when they fix the money supply. With a fixed money stock a rise in the interest rate would have offset some of the expansionary effect of the fiscal stimulus. But with a pegged interest rate this offsetting effect is eliminated. Of course, the monetary authorities could *choose* to raise interest rates in response to a fiscal policy relaxation, but this would be an independent policy choice rather than something that happens automatically within the economy. Notice also that the shift in *AD when interest rates are held constant* is equal to the direct change in spending times the simple multiplier. In effect the monetary sector is passive to the changes in fiscal policy, and the analysis we set out in Chapters 21–24 is adequate to understand the determinants of GDP. In reality, of course, although the monetary authorities are setting interest rates, they do not hold them constant for ever. Rather, they change them in an attempt to control inflation and (perhaps) to avoid large deviations of GDP from its potential level.

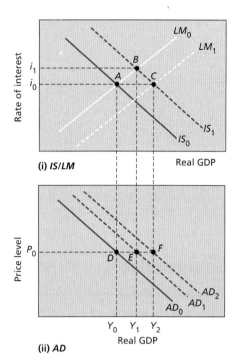

Figure 27.4 Fiscal policy changes and aggregate demand

An expansionary fiscal policy shifts the *AD* curve to the right, but the shift is greater if the monetary authorities peg interest rates than if they fix the money stock. The initial position is shown in part (i) by point *A* and in part (ii) by point *D*, with a given price level of P_0 and initial values of the interest rate of i_0 and of GDP of Y_0. The introduction of an expansionary fiscal policy shifts the *IS* curve to the right from IS_0 to IS_1. With a given money stock the *LM* curve would stay put at LM_0 and the interest rate would rise to i_1, illustrated by point *B*. Accordingly, the new *AD* curve would now pass through point *E*, reflecting an increase in GDP from Y_0 to Y_1.

However, if the monetary authorities act to prevent interest rates rising, they will permit an increase in the money supply, represented by a shift of the *LM* curve to LM_1 where it intersects IS_1 at point *C*. The associated *AD* curve passes through point *F*, so the new *AD* curve is AD_2. At the given price level P_0 GDP has increased to Y_2. This shift in *AD* is equal to the change in government spending that triggered it times the simple multiplier. A contractionary fiscal policy change would lead to a symmetrical leftward shift in *AD*.

Aggregate demand and supply shocks

Let us now return to our complete model in which we add the long-run and short-run aggregate supply curves developed in Chapters 23 and 24 to the aggregate demand curve. We want, first, to study how the economy responds to shocks to aggregate demand and supply and, second, to discuss what monetary and fiscal policy can do to 'improve' the response.

Aggregate demand shocks

How does the economy respond to an aggregate demand shock? Such shocks could come from a change in world demand for domestic exports, or from an autonomous shift in investment or consumption coming, perhaps, from a wave of optimism or a wave of pessimism. Some of the detail of the resulting changes will depend upon the precise nature of the shock, but the general principles will be the same. For simplicity we assume that the shock is an autonomous shift in domestic investment.

Positive demand shock Figure 27.5 shows how the economy responds to an autonomous increase in investment. Starting at point A, the AD curve shifts to the right. This rightward shift of AD has two components. First, the rise in investment shifts the IS curve to the right (not shown) and this in itself shifts AD to the right. With a given money supply, that would be the end of the story. However, the increase in GDP brought about by the increase in investment increases the transactions demand for money and this puts upward pressure on interest rates. If the monetary authorities are to hold the initial level of the interest rate, they must buy bonds and so permit the money stock to rise. This increase in the money stock imparts a further

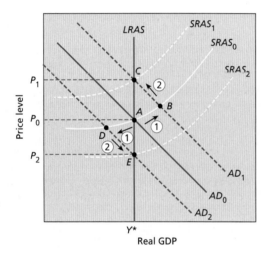

Figure 27.5 Aggregate demand shocks

A positive demand shock leads to a temporary boom in GDP and a permanent rise in the price level, while a negative demand shock leads to a temporary fall in output and (ultimately) lower prices. Consider an initial position at point A with the economy at Y^* with an initial price level P_0. A positive demand shock shifts the AD curve from AD_0 to AD_1. This shift will be greater with a pegged interest rate than with a fixed money stock, as the money supply will increase, reinforcing the rightward shift. The economy will move from point A to a point such as B. The inflationary gap will now lead to upward pressure on money wages. As wages rise, the rise is partly passed on in higher prices, and the SRAS curve shifts leftward from $SRAS_0$ to $SRAS_1$. At the equilibrium, point C, the economy has returned to the initial level of potential GDP, Y^*, but at a higher price level.

A negative demand shock shifts the AD curve from AD_0 to AD_2, and the economy moves from point A to a point such as D. The recessionary gap eventually leads to wage cuts, and, as these are passed on into prices, output recovers and the economy moves to a point such as E with price level P_2.

rightward shift to AD (such that the total horizontal shift is equal to the initial shift in investment times the simple multiplier).

With given initial input prices, the economy expands from point A to point B along the short-run aggregate supply curve $SRAS_0$. The economy is in a boom. In the first phase of this boom prices may be slow to respond, but as GDP moves further above its potential level, the price level will start to rise. Real wages fall because money wages are assumed to be fixed, at least initially. However, workers will not for long be happy to see their real wages fall while the economy is booming. Also unemployment will be falling and excess demand for certain types of labour will develop. Soon workers will demand, and employers will concede, increases in money wage rates. Once money wages start to rise, the SRAS curve starts to shift upwards to the left, the wage rises are partly passed on in the form of higher prices, and output starts to fall. The economy moves from B to C in the figure.

Once the economy has returned to point C it is back in equilibrium, with GDP returned to its potential level but at a higher price level. This price level will be higher in the case where interest rates are pegged than it would be if the money stock were fixed, because the authorities have permitted an increase in the money stock to prevent interest rates from rising.

We have talked here as if the adjustment to the shock is a smooth process that moves in two steps from A to B and then returns to C. Indeed, this is the logic of our macro model. However, the accelerator mechanism discussed above could make it a far from smooth ride. While the economy is expanding from A to B, the growth in output will tend to increase investment still further and give even more upward momentum to the boom. Once the turning-point has been reached, even a slowing of output growth will lead to a downward adjustment of investment, reinforcing the slowdown. The fall in output from point B to point C may not stop there, as declining investment may take the economy into recession. Indeed the economy may oscillate around its potential output level for some time (even though a discrete shock triggered the process).

Negative demand shock Suppose instead there was an autonomous fall in investment, starting from the same initial position as above. This is shown in Figure 27.5 as a leftward shift in the AD curve from AD_0 to AD_2. The economy now moves into recession as GDP falls along the path from A to D. As GDP falls, the transactions demand for money will also fall, and with a fixed money stock this would lead to a fall in interest rates. However, if the monetary authorities are pegging interest rates, they will reduce the money supply in order to stop interest rates falling. This imparts two steps to the leftward shift in AD (as above but in reverse).

The major difference in this case (apart from the direction of change) is that because the *SRAS* curve is flatter to the left of Y^* than to the right, more of the initial adjustment falls on GDP and less on the price level. Indeed, if prices and money wages are slow to adjust downwards as is often claimed, in the absence of a policy response the economy may get stuck for some time in the neighbourhood of point *D*. Only as higher unemployment leads to *falling* money wages and these falls get passed on into lower prices, so that the *SRAS* curve shifts down to $SRAS_2$ along the path *D* to *E*, will the economy return to its potential level of output at a point like *E*. Again the accelerator mechanism may initially worsen the downturn and later speed the recovery, as well as contributing to a further cycle around potential GDP.

The ultimate fall in the price level from point *A* to point *E* (assuming the economy returns smoothly to this point) will be greater in the case where interest rates are held constant than in the case where the money stock is fixed, because in the former case the money stock has been allowed to fall relative to its initial level. What then could policymakers have done to moderate these responses to demand shocks?

Policy responses In order to understand the problem faced by policymakers, we have to be clear that the economy is being hit by various shocks of differing strength more or less continuously. Also the economy is continuing to respond in complex ways to past shocks, through mechanisms such as the multiplier and accelerator that we discussed above. However, in order to get some insights into the nature of the policy problem, we study single discrete shocks, even though we know that in reality the authorities have to cope with a continually changing situation.

Let us consider first what could be done to offset the effects of a positive demand shock. Again we refer to Figure 27.5 and we ignore for simplicity the complications caused by the accelerator. If the authorities had known that investment was about to rise and could have implemented a policy change that had immediate effect (a very big IF), they could have acted to shift the *AD* curve straight back down again so that it never shifted from AD_0 and the economy stayed put at point *A*. The monetary authorities could do this by raising interest rates and the fiscal authorities could do this by increasing taxes or cutting government spending.

Even here there would still be a slight difference depending upon whether it was the monetary or fiscal authorities who acted. With higher interest rates the reversal of the *AD* shift would be achieved by lowering investment (or other interest-sensitive spending) relative to the level it would otherwise have achieved. Higher taxes shift *AD* down to the left via a fall in personal consumption, while lower government spending obviously leads to a fall in *G*. Thus, although monetary and fiscal policies have identical effects on the price level and aggregate GDP, they have different effects on the composition of GDP. We will learn in Chapter 29 that once exchange rate adjustments are incorporated, changes in net exports are also part of this story.

Of course, it is not realistic to think that policymakers can react at the same time as shocks occur or that they can implement policy changes immediately. We discussed the problems created by information lags and policy lags for fiscal policy in Chapter 24. These problems also apply to monetary policy. Indeed, Milton Friedman said many years ago that the impact of monetary policy was subject to 'long and variable lags'.

If the monetary authorities respond to the positive demand shock in a timely way, they may be able to improve the outcome. This could be by helping the economy return from point *B* to point *A*, or at least some point between *A* and *C*, thereby reducing the inflation that results from the positive demand shock. However, the danger of mistimed policy interventions is a serious one. Suppose, for example, the impact of a monetary tightening only starts to bite just as the economy is arriving at point *C*. This tightening will force the economy to the left of point *C* and will *cause* a recession that would not otherwise have occurred. The same error could obviously arise from badly timed fiscal policy, and this is the main case against attempts to use active monetary or fiscal fine-tuning of the economy.

The case for an active policy response may be much stronger in the event of a negative demand shock than in the above case. This is because there is good reason to believe that the automatic adjustment processes are much slower working in a downward than an upward direction —because of the asymmetry in the aggregate supply curve and the (possible) fact that money wages are slower to adjust down than up. If this is true, with the economy stuck for some time around point *D* in Figure 27.5, a lowering of interest rates would help shift production back towards point *A*, as would a cut in taxes or an increase in government spending. Again there would be differences in the composition of GDP but not the level (in equilibrium).

Aggregate supply shocks

Let us now consider shocks to aggregate supply instead of shocks to demand. For the purpose of this analysis we will assume that the supply shock affects only the *SRAS* curve and does not affect Y^*, the level of potential output. In many cases supply shocks will have long-run effects so that Y^* changes—a productivity shock, for example, will increase aggregate supply in both the short and long runs. Where there are long-run effects, there is no potential for monetary and fiscal policies to influence the long-run outcome, as these policy tools only influence aggregate demand. It is for this reason that nothing is lost if we assume that the position of the *LRAS* curve is unchanged. This is equivalent to assuming that the position of *LRAS* is invariant to monetary and fiscal policy; but bear in mind that this assumption will not generally be true.[2]

Positive supply shock Figure 27.6 illustrates the effect of a positive supply shock. Starting at the initial point A at Y^* and on $SRAS_0$, the supply shock, such as a fall in world raw material prices, shifts the $SRAS$ curve down to the right. The economy will experience a rise in GDP and falling prices as it starts to move from A to E. Both of these would be not unwelcome events, but a move to point E would not be the end of the story.

First, as the price level falls below P_0 the real money supply starts to rise (for a given nominal money stock), and this in turn leads to lower interest rates. It is this fall in interest rates causing an increase in investment that tends to increase real GDP. However, if the monetary authorities were pegging interest rates they would tend to reduce the money stock rather than let interest rates fall, and this

would make the economy follow a path closer to $A \rightarrow D$ rather than $A \rightarrow E$.

Second, to the extent that the economy did move to the right of Y^*, this would set up inflationary pressure (and a positive accelerator effect in investment) which would tend to make prices rise again until $SRAS$ had shifted back up to its initial position at point A. Thus, with a fixed money stock, the economy would tend to move from A to E and back again to A, while with a fixed interest rate it would tend to move from A to D and then stop. (Here the assumption of unchanged Y^* is important, as it is quite likely that the ultimate effect of a positive supply shock would be a new level of potential output to the right of Y^*.)

Negative supply shock Suppose we start from the same initial equilibrium at point A and there is now a rise in raw material prices, such as a rise in the price of oil. Here the short-run aggregate supply curve shifts upward to the left from $SRAS_0$ to $SRAS_1$. With the given initial aggregate demand curve AD_0, the economy will tend to move from point A to point B (though the fall in output will induce a negative accelerator effect on investment—tending to shift AD down to the left, not shown). This situation is characterized by both a rising price level and falling output—known (when it occurred in the 1970s) as *stagflation*. In practice the move from A to B along a given AD curve will only occur if the money stock is held constant. Then the logic would be that the rising price level reduces the real money supply, forcing up interest rates, and thus leading to lower investment, which in turn lowers GDP. However, if the monetary authorities peg the interest rate, they will resist the rise in interest rates by increasing the money supply, and this will shift the AD curve to the right, causing the economy to move along a path more like $A \rightarrow C$ than $A \rightarrow B$.

The contrast between the effects of supply shocks and demand shocks is worth emphasizing. The outcomes also differ depending on whether the monetary authorities are setting interest rates or fixing the money supply.

A monetary policy that sets the interest rate stabilizes the effects of supply shocks on real GDP but it amplifies the effects of demand shocks.

Notice that this applies to the automatic effects of the policy and *not* to discretionary policy changes, which could have quite different effects.

Policy responses The optimal policy response to supply shocks is far from clear, especially if mistiming is possible. With a fixed interest rate there will automatically be a stabilizing change in the money supply, although if policy-

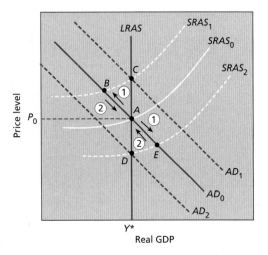

Figure 27.6 Supply shocks
A positive supply shock increases output and lowers prices temporarily, while a negative supply shock lowers output and raises prices temporarily. The economy starts at point A as in Figure 27.5. A positive supply shock shifts the $SRAS$ curve from $SRAS_0$ to $SRAS_2$. This stimulates output and lowers the price level as the economy moves from A to E. However, if the monetary authorities peg the interest rate, they will resist the interest rate fall necessary to increase investment and instead will reduce the money supply, taking the economy from A to D. With a fixed money stock the move from A to E will eventually be reversed as the inflationary gap leads to money wage rises and $SRAS_2$ shifts back to its original position.

A negative supply shock shifts the $SRAS$ curve from $SRAS_0$ to $SRAS_1$. This raises prices and lowers output as the economy moves from A to B. With a fixed money stock the recessionary gap will eventually lead to lower wages and prices, $SRAS$ will shift back to $SRAS_0$, and the economy will return to point A. However, with pegged interest rates the money stock will increase (as the authorities accommodate the supply shock) and the economy will move from A to C.

---

[2] Indeed, some economists have proposed distinguishing supply shocks from demand shocks by the condition that demand shocks have no long-run effect on output while supply shocks do.

makers are fixing the money stock there may be a role for temporary countercyclical monetary or fiscal changes to aid the return to equilibrium. However, these will have to be reversed rapidly as the economy returns to equilibrium. Otherwise policy action could lead to deviations from Y^* that could have been avoided. That is, policy intended to return the economy to equilibrium could end up leading it to overshoot in the opposite direction. Indeed, the possibility that policymakers might do more harm than good is much debated.

As we have discussed above, getting macro policy right is a difficult task in a complex world. Often, for example, the authorities do not know what shocks are hitting the economy until some time after the event, and even then they are uncertain about the quantitative significance of specific shocks. Stabilization policy is therefore an imperfect art, and the correct role of policy has been (and continues to be) a source of great controversy. We now outline the ideas of some of the diverse schools of thought that have contributed to these controversies about the causes of business cycles, and the potential role for policymakers in controlling them.

Cyclical controversies

Many of the different schools of thought in economics have had their own approach to explaining business cycles; indeed, attempts to document and explain the cycle in economic activity predate modern macroeconomics. We concentrate here on the views of the major schools of thought that have existed within macroeconomics over the last quarter century or so.

The monetarist approach

Monetarists believe that the economy is inherently stable because private sector expenditure functions are relatively stable and price adjustment will bring the economy back to potential output. In addition, they believe that shifts in the aggregate demand curve are due mainly to policy-induced changes in the money supply.[3]

The view that business cycles have mainly monetary causes originally relied partly on the evidence advanced by Milton Friedman and Anna Schwartz in their classic study *A Monetary History of the United States, 1867–1960*. They purported to have established a strong correlation between changes in the money supply and changes in economic activity. Major recessions have been associated with absolute declines in the money supply and minor recessions with the slowing of the rate of increase in the money supply below its long-term trend.

More recent work has shown that the Friedman–Schwartz relations are not as close, even in the United States, as these authors tried to show. Attempts to establish a similar close relation for the United Kingdom have not been successful. None the less, there is a broad association —even if a loose one—between changes in the money supply and changes in money GDP. The sustained increases in the price level that result from a major inflation are invariably accompanied by a sustained increase in the money stock.

The rough correlation between changes in the money supply and changes in the level of economic activity is accepted by many economists. But there is controversy over how this correlation is to be interpreted. Do changes in money supply cause changes in the level of aggregate demand and hence of business activity, or vice versa?

Friedman and Schwartz maintained that changes in the money supply cause changes in business activity. They argued, for example, that the severity of the Great Depression was due to a major contraction in the money supply, which shifted the aggregate demand curve far to the left.

According to monetarists, fluctuations in the money supply cause fluctuations in GDP.

This leads the monetarists to advocate a policy of stabilizing the growth of the money supply. In their view this would avoid policy-induced instability of the aggregate demand curve.

The Keynesian approach

The traditional Keynesian explanation of cyclical fluctuations in the economy has two parts. First, it emphasizes variations in investment as a cause of business cycles and stresses the non-monetary causes of such variations, such as expectations or, as Keynes put it, 'animal spirits'.[4]

---

[3] The view that fluctuations often have monetary causes is not new. The English economist R. G. Hawtrey (1879–1971), the Austrian Nobel Laureate F. A. von Hayek (1899–1991), and the Swedish economist Knut Wicksell (1851–1926) were prominent among those who have given monetary factors an important role in explaining the turning-points in cycles and/or the tendency for expansions and contractions, once begun, to become cumulative and self-reinforcing. Modern monetarists carry on this tradition.

[4] Like the monetarists, the Keynesians are modern advocates of views that have a long history. The great Austrian (and later American) economist Joseph Schumpeter (1883–1950) stressed such explanations early in the present century. Knut Wicksell and the German Arthur Spiethoff (1873–1957) both stressed this aspect of economic fluctuations before the emergence of the Keynesian school of thought.

Keynesians reject what they regard as the extreme monetarist view that only money matters in explaining cyclical fluctuations. Many Keynesians believe that both monetary and non-monetary forces are important in explaining cycles. Although they accept serious monetary mismanagement as one potential source of economic fluctuations, they do not believe that it is the only, or even the major, source of such fluctuations. Thus they deny the monetary interpretation of business cycle history given by Friedman and Schwartz. They believe that most fluctuations in the aggregate demand curve are due to variations in the desire to spend on the part of the private sector and are not induced by government policy.

Keynesians also believe that the economy lacks strong natural corrective mechanisms that will always force it easily and quickly back to full employment. They believe that while the price level rises fairly quickly to eliminate *inflationary* gaps, prices and wages fall only slowly in response to recessionary gaps. As a result Keynesians believe that recessionary gaps can sometimes persist for long periods of time unless they are eliminated by an active stabilization policy.

The second part of the Keynesian view on cyclical fluctuations concerns the alleged correlation between changes in the money supply and changes in the level of economic activity. In so far as this correlation exists, the Keynesian explanation reverses the causality suggested by the monetarists. Keynesians argue that changes in the level of economic activity often cause changes in the money supply.

Certainly, Keynesians are on strong ground when the monetary authorities are setting interest rates (or when there is a fixed exchange rate regime, as we will see in Chapter 29) as the money stock is endogenously determined by demand under this regime. For a given interest rate, changes in GDP will cause changes in the money stock, rather than vice versa.

According to Keynesians, fluctuations in GDP are often caused by fluctuations in autonomous expenditures. Further, they believe that fluctuations in GDP usually cause fluctuations in the money supply.

Nevertheless, most Keynesians also agree that deliberate changes in monetary policy can cause GDP to change, via induced changes in aggregate demand. However, notice that the monetarist approach makes the monetary authorities the main cause of cycles—hence the recommendation that they should be constrained to follow a rigid policy rule. For many Keynesians it is fluctuations in private sector investment behaviour (and perhaps exports) that matter, and the authorities are the 'good guys' who can offset this privately generated instability. It is for this reason that Keynesians are often interventionist and monetarists are usually non-interventionist.

A shift of emphasis within the Keynesian school has come out of the New Keynesian research agenda (to be discussed in Chapter 31). Early Keynesians focused mainly on the use of aggregate demand (especially fiscal) policies to stabilize the cycle; New Keynesians hope to see GDP kept close to its potential level by whatever means possible, but place more stress on supply-side (labour market) policies to eliminate persistent (equilibrium) unemployment than did their Keynesian predecessors.

The New Classical approach

The New Classical approach to explaining business cycles has something in common with the monetarists, in that the shock that sets off the cycle is a change in the money supply. However, what happens next in the New Classical story is quite different from traditional (monetarist or Keynesian) business cycle theory, because the New Classical school wanted a model in which markets were always in equilibrium. An alternative approach to modelling business cycles in 'equilibrium' models, which does not rely on monetary shocks, is discussed below.

The Lucas aggregate supply function The key element in the New Classical approach is a particular specification of the aggregate supply function which was formulated by US economist Robert Lucas.

In Chapter 23, where we first set out the *SRAS* curve, we assumed that in the short run output prices are variable (they can respond to changes in demand in the current period) while input prices (we will concentrate here on wages) are fixed. In the long run, if output prices rise, wages get negotiated upwards to catch up with prices. This is what makes the *LRAS* curve vertical.

In the Lucas approach wages are not just given on the basis of last period's equilibrium; rather, they are set at the beginning of the current period at the market-clearing level for *given expectations of what output prices in the current period will be*. In other words they are set on the basis of forward-looking expectations of what the market outcome will be.

This may seem like a harmless modification of our original assumption, but it turns out to have fundamental implications. Figure 27.7 illustrates the implications for aggregate supply behaviour. The key point is that any shift in aggregate demand that is expected at the time wages are set, such as an announced (or anticipated) increase in the money supply, will cause the *SRAS* curve to shift up immediately. The economy will therefore experience an immediate increase in the price level and no increase in GDP. Only an *unexpected* increase in *AD* will lead to an increase in GDP in the short run. Lucas assumed that this shock to *AD* would be an unexpected increase in the money supply.

In the New Classical approach cycles in real economic activity are triggered by unexpected increases in the money supply.

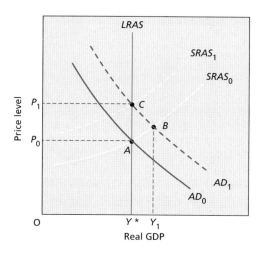

Figure 27.7 The Lucas aggregate supply curve
In the new classical approach a given *SRAS* curve applies only to unexpected shifts in *AD*. Suppose there is a shift in aggregate demand
from AD_0 to AD_1. If the shift is unexpected, the economy will move from
the initial position at point *A* to point *B*, at the intersection of $SRAS_0$ and
AD_1. However, if the shift in *AD* is expected, agents will negotiate higher
wages immediately on the basis of this expectation, and the *SRAS* curve
will shift up to $SRAS_1$. The price level will go straight from P_0 to P_1, and
the economy will move from *A* to *C*, with no increase in GDP.
  Policy ineffectiveness follows from the same analysis. Any predictable
change in monetary or fiscal policy causing a change in aggregate demand, such as the shift in *AD* from AD_0 to AD_1, will lead to an immediate
rise in prices from P_0 to P_1 and will have no effect on real GDP. An
unexpected policy change of the same magnitude, however, would take
the economy from point *A* to point *B* in the short run, and to *C* only in the
long run.

New Classical economists assume that the actors in the
private sector of the economy have **rational expectations.**
This assumes that agents form expectations based upon all
available information about the future at the time they
take the decision. So agents make only random errors in
forecasting the future course of economic variables. This
means that the expectational errors that trigger cycles
cannot be systematic. (If they were systematic, agents
could learn from the pattern of mistakes and improve
their forecasts.) It would be tempting to conclude from
this that deviations from potential output must, therefore,
be random—which is clearly contradicted by evidence.
However, to avoid this erroneous implication, Lucas
added a lagged adjustment process to his model. This
meant that, once shocked, it behaved like any of the other
cycle models described above. Hence it is difficult to distinguish this approach from others on the basis of
observations of real-world cycles.

Policy invariance A perhaps surprising implication of the
New Classical approach is that changes in monetary or
fiscal policy, which may be intended to influence economic

activity by shifting the *AD* curve, will have real effects only
if they are unexpected. For example, a stimulus to demand
involving an announced reduction in interest rates (and
consequent increase in the money supply) will create
expectations of rising prices. These expectations will
influence wage-setting, so the *SRAS* curve will shift up
immediately and prices will rise straight away with no
temporary increase in output. This outcome is illustrated
in Figure 27.7 by the fact that an anticipated interest rate
reduction shifts the *AD* curve to the right and the *SRAS*
curve to the left, the net effect being that the economy
moves straight up the *LRAS* curve, the price level rising but
real GDP remaining unchanged.

According to the New Classical approach, only unanticipated policy changes lead to changes in real national income. Systematic policy changes will be predictable and
will have no real effects.

  Most economists do not accept the proposition that
only unexpected policy changes will have real effects. One
reason is that there is so much inertia in price- and wage-
setting behaviour that very few contracts can be renegoti-
ated as soon as a policy change is announced. Hence the
policymakers certainly have some leverage over real activity, even when making policy changes that are predictable.
  A second reason is that the massive complexity of the
economy makes it impossible for individual agents to
know how some shock will affect all the relevant prices and
quantities that matter to them over any specified period of
time. The idea of everyone knowing the exact nature of
some policy disturbance and solving the equations of the
economy to determine the exact outcome, and of their acting to anticipate these outcomes, is far-fetched. After all,
the great virtue of the price system is that it co-ordinates
activity without the need for anyone to have knowledge of
all the prices and quantities that exist.
  However, the New Classical presumption that private
agents have expectations of what policymakers are going
to do, and that this influences private behaviour, is important. Without assuming omniscience, just reasonable
approximate expectations, private anticipation of government action can affect the outcome of policies. This
realization has had a fundamental impact on macroeconomic policy analysis. In both Keynesian and monetarist models the government was exogenous to the model.
However, in the New Classical framework the government
and the private sector interact by trying to guess what the
other is going to do. The conduct of policy becomes more
like a 'game', where strategy and perception of the other
players matter.
  This change in perception of policy as interactive rather
than exogenous has two important implications.

Policy credibility If private agents are watching the government (and the monetary authorities where these are

different) and trying to form expectations of its future behaviour, not only does it matter what the government does, but it also matters what agents think it will do in future. This means that a government needs more than just the correct current policies. It also needs to establish **credibility** that it will follow the correct policies in future.

Suppose, for example, that a government enters office with a commitment to control inflation. It introduces tight monetary and fiscal policies, which in due course succeed in bringing down inflation. Now, however, there is an election approaching, and the government would like to increase real GDP to improve its chances of re-election. It may be tempted to break its original commitment to anti-inflationary policies.[5] However, private agents know that this incentive exists, so it matters to the outcome whether the private agents anticipate the government breaking its word or not. In other words the government's credibility actually affects private behaviour. Of course, once the government has broken its commitments, it will be very hard for it to establish credibility again—at least without a change in personnel.

The Lucas critique The assumption that private agents are forming expectations of government behaviour has important implications for how economic models can be used to predict the effects of changes in policy.

A great deal of effort over the last thirty years has gone into building empirical econometric macroeconomic models of the economy for forecasting purposes (such as the National Institute model and the London Business School model). Lucas pointed out that such models contain estimates of key behavioural parameters that were derived from past data. These data were collected under particular policy regimes.

Any attempt to use such a model to predict the consequences of significant policy changes may be erroneous. This is because the behaviour of private agents may change when the behaviour of policymakers changes, as they are interdependent in some areas.

One example is the failure of the government to understand (and the forecasters to forecast) the buildup of inflationary pressures in the UK economy in the late 1980s, following the financial innovations of the mid-1980s. Another is the difficulty of forecasting behaviour of agents in the EU following the introduction in January 1999 of the new single currency, the euro.

The Lucas critique suggests that there will be shifts in many private sector behaviour functions when there are significant changes in the policy regime. Hence the effects of such regime changes will be impossible to forecast accurately using traditional macro models.

The New Classical approach to business cycles clearly supports a non-interventionist approach to macroeconomic policy. Governments can initiate shocks, but systematic attempts to stabilize cycles will be frustrated by their very predictability.

Real business cycles

Another group has taken up the task of explaining business cycles in the context of equilibrium models of the economy. Real business cycle (RBC) research has evolved from the New Classical attempt to explain cyclical fluctuations in the context of models in which equilibrium prevails at all times. In this sense the models can be seen as an extension of the New Classical approach.

The view of the business cycle found in RBC models is that fluctuations in national income are caused by fluctuations in the vertical *LRAS* curve arising from *technology shocks*. In contrast, the previous three approaches to fluctuations were based on fluctuations in the *AD* curve.

The explanation of cyclical fluctuations that arises in RBC models is based on the role of supply (productivity) shocks originating from sources such as oil price changes, technical progress, and changes in tastes.

In this view output is always equal to potential GDP, but it is potential GDP itself that fluctuates.

Policy implications Because the approach gives no role to aggregate demand in influencing business cycles, it provides no role for stabilization operating through monetary and fiscal policies. Indeed, the models used by this school to date predict that the use of such demand management policies can be harmful.[6]

The basis for this prediction is the proposition in RBC models that cycles represent *efficient* responses to the shocks that are hitting the economy. Policymakers may mistakenly interpret cyclical fluctuations as deviations from full-employment equilibrium that are caused by fluctuations in aggregate demand. The policymakers may try to stabilize output and thereby distort the maximizing decisions made by households and firms. In turn this distortion will cause the responses to the real shocks (as opposed to nominal, monetary shocks) to be inefficient.

Although only a minority of economists espouse these models as complete or even reasonable descriptions of the business cycle, and thus only a minority take seriously the strict implications for policy, many accept the view that real disturbances can play an important role in business cycles. It is, of course, highly controversial to argue that

---

[5] The fact that it may now be rational for the government to renege on its commitments was labelled *time inconsistency* by US economists F. Kydland and E. Prescott.

[6] In reality it is more of an assumption than a prediction because it is implicit in the assumption of continuous market-clearing. This makes whatever happens to the economy, in response to real shocks, an optimal (equilibrium) adjustment, with which policy changes can only interfere. This is not a result of analysis of actual policy, but it is a result of the assumption of equilibrium.

whatever the cycles in the economy, they are an optimal response to shocks, upon which no policy actions can improve. Indeed, if this were the case, macroeconomics as a subject would have no purpose—invented as it was to help policymakers cure recessions and alleviate unemployment—and Europe's 30 million unemployed (in 1998) have been voluntarily idle, either because they have preferred leisure to work at correctly perceived real wage rates, or because, in contradiction of rational expectations, they have been systematically underpredicting the real wage rate for many years in succession.

The political business cycle

As early as 1944 the Polish-born Keynesian economist Michal Kalecki (1899–1970) warned that once governments had learned to manipulate the economy, they might engineer an election-geared business cycle. In pre-election periods they would raise spending and cut taxes. The resulting expansionary demand shock would create high employment and good business conditions, which would gain voters' support for the government. But the resulting inflationary gap would lead to a rising price level. So, after the election was won, the government would depress demand to remove the inflationary gap, also providing some slack for expansion before the next election.

This theory invokes the image of a vote-maximizing government manipulating employment and GDP solely for electoral purposes. Few people believe that governments deliberately do this all the time, but the temptation to do it some of the time, particularly before close elections, may prove irresistible. In the UK electoral system, where the length of parliaments is flexible, it is also natural for the government to seek a general election at a time favourable to itself, within the maximum five-year horizon.

A naïve political business cycle, in which private agents never learn to anticipate that politicians are going to boost the economy before a general election, is impossible to justify in a world of rational expectations, or almost any theory of expectations in which agents learn. This is because there is no reason for voters to be fooled, certainly not repeatedly. Just as they form inflation expectations in relation to their wage-setting behaviour (as we explain in Chapter 30), so they can use those same expectations to inform their voting behaviour, and to punish a government that deliberately creates an inflationary gap, even though the full effects of the inflation may be still to come. Credibility now matters, and probably always did. (Indeed, this is why the UK government gave its power to set interest rates to a newly formed Monetary Policy Committee of the Bank of England in May 1997.)

However, a politically induced cycle can follow from electoral considerations, even where expectations are rational, so long as the rival political parties have different policy agendas. The approach of an election, combined with a changing probability that a different party will come to power, influences expectations of what future policy will be and thereby changes behaviour even before the election has happened. This *partisanship* approach does not predict a simple pattern of pre-election boom and post-election slump (which is not supported by evidence anyway[7]). Rather, it merely says that expectations of electoral outcomes matter and that they may cause shocks to the system at almost any time, via changes in the expectations of firms and consumers relating to the future.

Supply shocks

Monetarist, Keynesian, and New Classical approaches to the business cycle all assume that cycles are triggered by demand shocks—changes in the money supply, changes in autonomous investment, and money surprises. Only the real business cycle school, of the approaches we have discussed, emphasizes shocks coming from the supply side of the economy. As we saw above, any shock that disturbs the equilibrium of the economy can generate a cyclical response so long as there is some lagged adjustment process within the economy.

The idea that supply shocks can cause cycles in real activity has a long pedigree in economics. In the nineteenth century, for example, serious credence was given to the theory that 'sun spots' triggered business cycles on Earth. The logic of this was that changes in the intensity of the sun's rays, associated with the observation of spots on the sun, affected the quality of the harvest on earth. Variations in the harvest would provide a shock to the real incomes of farmers, and variations in food prices would affect real wages in other sectors. Such shocks could take several seasons to work through the system.

Notice also, as is clear from part (ii) of Figure 24.7 on page 417, that the two most extreme cycles in economic activity in this century were associated with the First and Second World Wars. The impact of a war on the economy is complex, but it has both demand- and supply-shock elements. There were also lesser shocks to the world economy caused by the Korean War in the early 1950s and the Vietnam War in the late 1960s and early 1970s.

Since 1970 the most important supply shocks have been changes in energy prices associated with the 1973 and 1979 OPEC oil price rises. The fact that all major countries

[7] There have been nine general elections in the United Kingdom since 1960. (The two in 1974 are counted as one.) Four took place in relative boom conditions, but in three of these (1964, 1979, and 1997) the incumbent government was defeated. This leaves 1987 as the only clear case of a 'successful' pre-election boom that was followed just over a year later by severe policy tightening. In 1983 and 1992 the government was returned to power despite recessions and high unemployment. In 1970 and 1974 (Feb.) governments called elections in recessions (1970 was the tail end of a recession, 1974 was during the onset of recession) and lost. In 1966 there was a relative slowdown and a balance of payments crisis, but the incumbent government won.

were affected by these energy price shocks simultaneously did much to ensure that the 1974–5 and 1979–81 recessions were worldwide phenomena which could not be explained by domestic demand shocks alone. The economic cycle in Germany (and perhaps in much of Europe) has been affected by the fall of the Berlin Wall in 1989 and the massive costs of reconstruction that followed. (This is both a demand and a supply shock.)

Most economists now agree that both supply shocks and demand shocks can be important, that most of the factors we have discussed can contribute to cycles, but that no two economic cycles are ever quite the same. This means that explanations based upon a single key causal factor will never be adequate for every case. The long-term trend in real GDP is upwards, but despite over half a century of macroeconomic analysis of stabilization policy, cycles about the trend appear to be endemic. In principle policymakers have the tools to reduce fluctuations in the economy, but in practice they frequently make things worse.

Summary

Theories of the cycle

■ Cycles in the economy may result from random exogenous shocks or from discrete changes in exogenous variables combined with the dynamic interaction of the multiplier and the accelerator (or many other possible lagged adjustment mechanisms).

Macroeconomic cycles and aggregate shocks

■ A positive demand shock (starting at potential GDP) will trigger a temporary boom in output and lead to a permanent increase in the price level. The latter will be greater if interest rates are pegged than if the money stock is fixed.

■ A negative demand shock will cause a recession, and the automatic adjustment mechanisms may be slow to return the economy to equilibrium.

■ A positive supply shock will increase output and reduce the price level temporarily, but inflationary pressure will eventually return the economy close to its initial position (where there is no permanent impact on potential GDP).

■ A negative supply shock is associated with rising prices and falling output—a situation known as stagflation.

■ Monetary and fiscal policies can assist the return of the economy to equilibrium, but inappropriate policies can also make things worse.

Cyclical controversies

■ Monetarists think that the dominant cause of business cycles is changes in the money supply. Many Keynesians think that it is swings in autonomous expenditures (investment and exports).

■ The New Classical school emphasizes that only unexpected shifts in aggregate demand will have real effects. Real business cycle theorists assume that supply-side shocks trigger the cycle in a market-clearing model.

■ Policy credibility is important once it is perceived that private agents' behaviour is influenced by their expectations of the government's future policy actions.

■ Both demand and supply shocks can trigger cycles, but no two cycles are ever exactly the same.

Topics for review

- The accelerator
- Multiplier–accelerator interaction
- Demand and supply shocks
- Monetary and fiscal policy reactions
- Lucas aggregate supply curve
- Money surprises
- Policy invariance
- Credibility
- The political business cycle

Questions for discussion

1 Explain why it is that a once-and-for-all shift in an exogenous variable can generate a cyclical outcome for real GDP.

2 Using appropriate *AS/AD* diagrams, trace out how the economy responds (starting from equilibrium at *Y**) to each of the following: (a) an earthquake that destroys a significant portion of the factory capacity in the home economy; (b) the invention of a new process that dramatically reduces the cost of making steel; (c) a rise in incomes in a large neighbouring economy that boosts demand for home exports; (d) concern for the future that leads to a sharp upward shift in precautionary savings behaviour.

3 Discuss how the New Classical 'surprise' aggregate supply theory affects the potential for monetary and fiscal policies to stabilize the economy.

4 What difference does it make to the course of the business cycle if the monetary authorities set interest rates rather than the money stock (in the absence of discretionary policy changes)?

5 Why might governments attempt to create boom conditions prior to elections? What institutional arrangements would help to eliminate this temptation?

Chapter 28
The Balance of Payments and Exchange Rates

This chapter focuses on the linkages between the macro-economy and the rest of the world. We have mentioned these linkages many times before, but here they become the main concern. There are financial (or monetary) linkages, through the international money and capital markets, and there are 'real' dimensions, through international trade and travel. The real and the monetary factors are not independent of each other. Real transactions cannot take place without money and finance, and are influenced by monetary forces; equally, money markets are influenced by the fundamentals of the real economy.

The discussion of these issues will bring together much material from elsewhere in this book: the theory of supply and demand (Chapter 3), the nature of money (Chapter 25), international trade (yet to come in Chapter 34), and macroeconomics (Chapters 21–27). Indeed, we have had

the balance of payments (net exports of goods and services, *NX*) explicitly in our macroeconomic model since Chapter 22. Also we have seen in Box 26.2 that external linkages can have a critical effect on the transmission mechanism of macro policy. We now need to look at these issues in much greater detail, to prepare the ground for our policy discussions in the next chapter.

In the first part of this chapter we discuss the balance of payments. This is an important concept concerned with net transactions between one country and the rest of the world. We ask what the 'balance of payments' means, how it is measured, and why it matters. In the second part we discuss the exchange rate—what role it plays in connecting the domestic economy with foreign economies, and what economic forces determine its value.

The balance of payments

The economy's balance of payments has had a high profile in political arguments over economic policy throughout this century, especially in countries like the United Kingdom that have recurrent balance of payments problems. We will first explain how the balance of payments is recorded, using the United Kingdom as an example, and we will then ask in what ways the balance of payments matters.

Balance of payments accounts

In order to know what is happening to the course of international trade, governments keep track of the transactions between countries. The record of such transactions is made in the *balance of payments accounts*. Each transaction, such as a shipment of exports or the arrival of imported goods, is classified according to the payments or receipts that would typically arise from it.

Transactions that lead to a receipt of payment from foreigners, such as a commodity export or a sale of an asset abroad, are recorded in the balance of payments accounts as a *credit*. In terms of our later objective of analysing the market for foreign exchange, these transactions represent the supply of foreign exchange and the demand for sterling on the foreign exchange market, because foreigners have to buy our currency in order to pay us in sterling for the goods or assets they have bought. Transactions that lead to a payment to foreigners, such as a commodity import or the purchase of a foreign asset, are recorded as a *debit*. These transactions represent the demand for foreign exchange and the supply of sterling on the foreign exchange market, because we have to buy foreign currency with sterling in order to pay for our overseas purchases. In calculating the *balance*, credits are positive and debits are negative, so the overall balance is simply credits minus debits.

Balance of payments accounts are divided into two broad parts. One part deals with payments for goods and

Table 28.1 UK balance of payments, 1997 (£ million)

	Credits	Debits	Balances
1 Current account	**354,179**	**346,173**	**8,006**
A Goods and services	228,702	229,334	−632
1 Goods	171,798	183,590	−11,792
2 Services	56,904	45,744	11,160
B Income	109,427	97,259	12,168
1 Compensation of employees	1,007	924	83
2 Investment income	108,420	96,335	12,085
2.1 Direct investment	32,715	18,365	14,350
2.2 Portfolio investment	26,002	23,454	2,548
2.3 Other investment (including earnings on reserve assets)	49,703	54,516	−4,813
C Current transfers	16,050	19,580	−3,530
1 Central government	6,358	5,071	1,287
2 Other sectors	9,692	14,509	−4,817
2 Capital and financial accounts	**249,187**	**257,037**	**−7,850**
A Capital account	1,052	790	262
1 Capital transfers	982	686	296
2 Acquisition/disposal of non-produced, non-financial assets	70	104	−34
B Financial account	248,135	256,247	−8,112
1 Direct investment	23,257	36,344	−13,087
2 Portfolio investment	29,621	51,989	−22,368
3 Other investment	195,257	170,271	24,986
4 Reserve assets		−2,357	2,357
Total	**603,366**	**603,210**	**156**
Net errors and omissions	−156		−156

services, income, and transfers. This is known as the **current account**. The other part records transactions in assets and is, accordingly, known as the **capital and financial account**. A summary of the balance of payments accounts of the United Kingdom for 1997 is given in Table 28.1. This is the format for balance of payments accounts introduced in 1998, and as this is now an international standard format, balance of payments accounts for other countries have a similar structure.

Current account

The current account records transactions arising from trade in goods and services, from income accruing to residents of one country from another, and from transfers by residents of one country to residents of another. The current account is divided into three main sections.

The first of these is the *goods and services* account. This has two parts. The component of this relating to 'goods' trade is often called the **visible account**, the **trade account**, or the **merchandise account**. It records payments and receipts arising from the import and export of tangible goods, such as computers, cars, wheat, and shoes. UK imports require payments to be made to foreign residents in

foreign exchange, and hence are entered as debit items on the visible account. In 1997 UK residents spent just over £183 billion on buying goods imported from overseas. UK exports earn payments from foreign residents in foreign exchange (though the foreign exchange will be converted into sterling through the foreign exchange market), and hence are recorded as credit items. In 1997 UK exports amounted to about £172 billion. Exports represent goods leaving the country, but payment for those goods passes in the opposite direction. With imports, goods enter the country and payment has to be made to the foreign manufacturers. We can see that in 1997 there was a goods trade deficit of a little under £12 billion, which is the difference between the value of exports and imports.

The second part of the goods and services account is services. Trade in services involves transactions that do not involve a physical commodity (or asset) changing hands, such as insurance, banking, shipping, and tourism.[1] Trade in services showed a surplus of just over £11 billion in 1997; however, this was smaller than the deficit in goods

---

[1] The symbols X and IM as used in this book refer to exports and imports of both tangible goods *and* services, but do not include payments of interest, dividends and profits, or transfers.

trade, so that trade in goods and services had a (negative) balance of –£0.6 billion.

The second element of the current account is the *income account*. This again has two components. The first is employee compensation. Credit items involve UK residents being paid for working for non-residents, while the debit items result from UK residents employing non-residents. The second component is investment income. Credit items involve interest and dividend income received by UK residents from assets overseas, while debits reflect similar payments to non-resident owners of assets in the UK. The income component of the current account showed a surplus of £12.2 billion in 1997.

The third element in the current account is *current transfers*. This is subdivided into central government and other transfers. An example of a central government transfer is payment of a UK old-age pension to a former UK resident now living in Spain. An Italian waiter in London sending money to his mother in Milan is an example of an 'other' transfer. Current transfers contributed a deficit of –£3.5 billion to the UK current account in 1997.

All components of the current account *other than trade in goods* are sometimes referred to as **invisibles** because you can see goods entering the country but you cannot see, for example, the services of a consultant crossing borders.

Overall the current account of the UK balance of payments showed a balance (or surplus) of £8 billion in 1997.

Capital and financial accounts

The other major component in the balance of payments is the capital and financial accounts, which record transactions related to international movements of ownership of financial assets. It is important to notice right away that the 'capital' and financial accounts do not relate to imports and exports of physical capital: trade in such things as machine tools and construction equipment is part of the *goods trade account*. Rather, the capital and financial accounts of the balance of payments relate only to cross-border movements in ownership of assets, a large part of which involves financial instruments such as ownership of company shares, bank loans, or government securities.

The entire capital and financial accounts used to be referred to just as the 'capital account', and we will continue this usage below. However, in the UK accounts shown in Table 28.1, the 'capital account' and 'financial account' are itemized separately. In the new accounting conventions the item labelled 'capital account' is a relatively insignificant one. It is made up of 'capital transfers' and 'acquisition/disposal of non-produced, non-financial assets'. Included in the former are items such as a government investment grant to build a hospital overseas, and debt forgiveness between the UK government and an overseas government. The latter includes overseas sales or purchases of patents, trade marks, or copyrights.

The second component of the capital and financial accounts is the financial account. This is made up of four elements: direct investment, portfolio investment, other investment, and reserve assets. **Direct investment** relates to changes in non-resident ownership of domestic firms and resident ownership of foreign firms. One form of direct investment, called greenfield investment, is the building of a factory in the United Kingdom by a foreign firm—for example, the Toyota car factory near Derby. Another form of direct investment, called brownfield investment, is a takeover in which a controlling interest in a firm previously controlled by residents is acquired by foreigners—such as when BMW acquired a majority interest in the Rover Group from British Aerospace. **Portfolio investment,** on the other hand, is investment in bonds or a minority holding of shares that does not involve legal control. Direct and portfolio investment combined is sometimes referred to as the *long-term capital* element of the capital and financial accounts.

'Other investments' is made up mainly of what are called *short-term capital flows*. These include transfers into overseas banks, and sales or purchases of short-term financial instruments, such as Treasury Bills or commercial bills. The large size of these other investment flows in the UK balance of payments accounts reflects in part the role of the City of London as an international financial centre. 'Reserve assets' reflects changes in the official foreign exchange reserves that are held by the Bank of England.

From now on we adopt the convention that the terms 'capital flows' and 'capital account' refer to all items in the 'capital and financial accounts' of the balance of payments. UK purchases of foreign investments (which then become assets to the UK) are called a *capital outflow*. They use foreign exchange in order to buy the foreign investment, and so they are entered as a debit item in the UK payments accounts.[2] Foreign investment in the United Kingdom (which thereby increases UK liabilities to foreigners) is called a *capital inflow*. It earns foreign exchange and so is entered as a credit (positive) item.

As shown in Table 28.1, in 1997 UK residents increased their investments abroad by nearly £260 billion, while foreigners increased their investments in the United Kingdom by just under £250 billion. These may seem like very large amounts, and indeed they are. However, as already mentioned, a high proportion of this activity is the international borrowing and lending of the financial institutions in the City of London. The net capital outflow

---

[2] Capital outflows are sometimes also referred to as *capital exports*. It may seem odd that whereas a merchandise export is a credit item on current account, a capital export is a debit item on capital account. To understand this terminology, consider the export of UK funds for investment in a German bond. The capital transaction involves the purchase, and hence the *import*, of a German bond, and this has the same effect on the balance of payments as the purchase, and hence the import, of a German good. Both items involve payments to foreigners, and both use foreign exchange. Both are thus debit items in UK balance of payments accounts.

resulted in a deficit in the capital account of only about £7.8 billion. This means that there was a net increase in foreign assets of £7.8 billion.[3]

The meaning of payments balances and imbalances

We have seen that the payments accounts show the total of receipts of foreign exchange (credit items) and payments of foreign exchange (debit items) on account of each category of payment. It is also common to calculate the *balance* on separate items or groups of items. The concept of the balance of payments is used in a number of different ways, so we must approach this issue in a series of steps.

The balance of payments must balance overall

The notion that the balance of payments accounts must balance should present no great mystery. The accounts are constructed so that this has to be true. The idea behind this proposition is quite general. Take your own personal income and expenditure. Suppose you earn £100 by selling your services (labour) and you buy £90 worth of clothing. You have exports (of services/labour) worth £100, and imports (of clothing) worth £90. Your current account surplus is £10. However, that £10 surplus must be invested in holding a financial claim on someone else—if you hold cash, it is a claim on the Bank of England; if you deposit the money in a building society, it becomes a claim on the building society; and so on.

Whichever way you look at it, the £10 you have acquired is the acquisition of an asset. It represents a capital outflow from your personal economy which is the inevitable consequence of your current account surplus. So you have a current account surplus of £10 and a capital account deficit (outflow) of £10. The only difference between your accounts and those for the economy as a whole is that with the latter, payments across the foreign exchange markets are involved. A country with a current account surplus in its balance of payments must, at the same time, have acquired net claims on foreigners to the same value.

The current and capital account balances are necessarily of equal and opposite size. When added together, they equal zero.

There is one important caveat to the above statement with regard to actual official accounts. This is that while conceptually the current and capital account are defined to be equal and opposite, in practice the national income statisticians are not able to keep accurate records of all transactions, and hence there are always errors in measurement. This means that a balancing item, called 'net errors and omissions', is included in the balance of payments

table. The balancing item stands for all unrecorded transactions and is defined to be equal to the difference between the measured current account and the measured capital and financial account. So actually it is the sum of the current account, the capital and financial accounts, and net errors and omissions that is always zero by construction.

Does the balance of payments matter?

The *balance of payments on current account* is the sum of the balances on the visible and invisible accounts. As a carry-over from a long-discredited eighteenth-century economic doctrine called *mercantilism*, a credit balance on current account (where receipts exceed payments) is often called a *favourable balance*, and a debit balance (where payments exceed receipts) is often called an *unfavourable balance*. Mercantilists, both ancient and modern, hold that the gains from trade arise only from having a favourable balance of trade. This misses the point of the doctrine of comparative advantage, first introduced in Box 1.4. It states that countries can gain from a *balanced increase* in trade because this allows each country to specialize according to its comparative advantage. The modern resurgence of mercantilism is discussed in Box 28.1.

It would be tempting to refer to a deficit on capital account as an unfavourable balance as well. However, by now it should be clear that this would be a nonsense, because a current account surplus is the same thing as a capital account deficit. Hence it is impossible for one to be 'good' and the other 'bad'. However, this discussion does have one important implication.

The terms balance of payments *deficit* and balance of payments *surplus* must refer to the balance on some part of the payments accounts. In the United Kingdom these terms almost always apply to the current account.

A current account deficit is just as likely to be the product of a healthy growing economy as it is of an unhealthy economy. Suppose, for example, that an economy has rapidly growing domestic industries which offer a high rate of return on domestic investment. Such an economy would be attracting investment from the rest of the world, and as a result it would have a capital account surplus (capital inflows) and a current account deficit. Far from being a sign of weakness, the current account deficit would indicate economic health. True, the economy is acquiring external debt; but if this debt is being used to finance rapid real growth, it can be repaid out of higher future output.[4]

---

[3] Note that this figure relates only to transactions in assets. It does not account for capital gains or losses resulting from valuation changes of existing asset holdings. Thus the capital and financial accounts balance is *not* a measure of the total change in indebtedness between the United Kingdom and the rest of the world.

[4] 'Debt' is used here in its general sense to refer to foreign liabilities rather than in the context of debt versus equity. These external debts could be in any specific form, including equity, bonds, or bank loans.

Box 28.1 Trade and the new mercantilism

Media commentators, political figures, and much of the general public often judge the national balance of payments as they would the accounts of a single firm. Just as a firm is supposed to show a profit, the nation is supposed to secure a balance of payments surplus on current account, with the benefits derived from international trade measured by the size of that surplus.

This view is related to the exploitation doctrine of international trade: one country's surplus is another country's deficit. Thus, one country's gain, judged by its surplus, must be another country's loss, judged by its deficit.

People who hold such views today are echoing an ancient economic doctrine called *mercantilism*. The mercantilists were a group of economists who preceded Adam Smith. They judged the success of trade by the size of the trade balance. In many cases, this doctrine made sense in terms of their objective, which was to use international trade as a means of building up the political and military power of the state, rather than as a means of raising the living standards of its citizens. A balance of payments surplus allowed the nation (then and now) to acquire foreign exchange reserves. (In those days the reserves took the form of gold. Today they are a mixture of gold and claims on the currencies of other countries.) These reserves could then be used to pay armies, to purchase weapons from abroad, and generally to finance colonial expansions.

People who advocate this view in modern times are called *neo-mercantilists*. In so far as their object is to increase the military power of the state, they are choosing means that could achieve their ends. In so far as

they are drawing an analogy between what is a sensible objective for a business, interested in its own material welfare, and what is a sensible objective for a society, interested in the material welfare of its citizens, their views are erroneous, because their analogy is false.

If the object of economic activity is to promote the welfare and living standards of ordinary citizens, rather than the power of governments, then the mercantilist focus on the balance of trade makes no sense. The law of comparative advantage shows that average living standards are maximized by having individuals, regions, and countries specialize in the things that they can produce comparatively best and then trading to obtain the things that they can produce comparatively worst. The more specialization there is, the more trade occurs.

On this view the gains from trade are to be judged by the volume of trade. A situation in which there is a *large volume* of trade but in which each country has a *zero balance* of trade can thus be regarded as quite satisfactory. Furthermore, a change in commercial policy that results in a balanced increase in trade between two countries will bring gain, because it allows for specialization according to comparative advantage, even though it causes no change in either country's trade balance.

To the business interested in private profit, and to the government interested in the power of the state, it is the *balance* of trade that matters. To the person interested in the welfare of ordinary citizens, it is the *volume* of trade that matters.

In contrast, another economy may indeed have inefficient and unproductive domestic industry, and may be in a situation where domestic spending exceeds domestic output. (Recall from Chapter 20 that the balance of trade in goods and services is equal to the difference between total domestic expenditure and total domestic production.) Therefore, it will have a trade deficit and will be borrowing from abroad to finance the extra consumption.[5]

The existence of a current account balance of payments deficit tells us only that an economy's total spending exceeds its total income and that it has a capital inflow. The existence of such a deficit is consistent both with healthy, growing economies and with unhealthy, inefficient economies.

Actual and desired transactions The discussion in this section has focused on *actual* transactions as measured in the balance of payments accounts. It is the actual capital inflow that must equal the actual current account deficit. There is no reason at all, however, why *desired* (or planned) current account transactions should equal desired capital account transactions. In practice it is movements in the exchange rate that play a key role in reconciling actual and desired transactions. We now turn to a discussion of the exchange rate and how it is determined.

---

[5] It is assumed here that the balance of trade and current account balance are the same. The balance of trade is the difference between domestic spending and GDP while the current account is the difference between domestic spending and GNI.

The market for foreign exchange

The foreign exchange markets are the markets in which one currency can be traded for another. We are used to thinking about markets in which goods are exchanged for money. In a foreign exchange market, it is one country's money that is exchanged for another country's money. As with all markets, the foreign exchange market can be

analysed with the tools of demand and supply developed earlier in this book. Before proceeding with this exercise, it is helpful to remind ourselves why we need such markets.

Money is central to the efficient working of any modern economy that relies on specialization and exchange. Yet fiat money as we know it is a *national* matter, one that is closely controlled by national governments. Until recently each nation-state had its own currency, though in 1999 eleven EU nations adopted a common currency, the euro. For purposes of the following discussion we treat the euro zone countries as if they were a single country, as they have a single external exchange rate. Other nation-states each have their own currency. If you live in Sweden, you earn kronor and spend kronor; if you run a business in Australia, you borrow Australian dollars and meet your wage bill with Australian dollars. The currency of a country is acceptable within the bounds of that country, but usually it will not be accepted by people and firms in another country. The Stockholm buses will accept kronor for a fare, but not Australian dollars; the Australian worker will not take Swedish kronor for wages, but insists on being paid in Australian dollars.

UK producers require payment in pounds sterling for their products. They need pounds to meet their wage bills, to pay for their raw materials, and to reinvest or distribute their profits. There is no problem when they sell to UK-based purchasers. However, if they sell their goods to, say, Indian importers, either the Indians must exchange their rupees to acquire pounds to pay for the goods, or the UK producers must accept rupees;[6] and they will accept rupees only if they know that they can exchange the rupees for pounds. The same holds true for producers in all countries; they must eventually receive payment in the currency of their own country.

Trade between nations typically requires the exchange of one nation's currency for that of another. The major exception is the euro zone, where member states have a common currency.

International payments involve the exchange of currencies between people who have one currency and require another. Suppose that a UK firm wishes to acquire ¥3 million for some purpose. (¥ is the currency symbol for the Japanese yen.) The firm can go to its bank and buy a cheque, or money order, that will be accepted in Japan as ¥3 million. How many *pounds* the firm must pay to purchase this cheque will depend on the value of the yen in terms of pounds.

The exchange of one currency for another is a *foreign exchange transaction*. The term 'foreign exchange' refers to the actual foreign currency or various claims on it, such as bank deposits or promises to pay, that are traded for each other. The *exchange rate* is the value of the domestic currency in terms of foreign currency; it is the amount of foreign currency that can be obtained with one unit of the domestic currency. For example, if £1 will buy ¥150, the yen–pound exchange rate is 150.

A rise in the external value of the pound (that is, a rise in the exchange rate) is called an **appreciation** of the pound; for example, if one can now obtain ¥175 for £1, the pound has *appreciated*. A fall in the external value of

the pound (that is, a fall in the exchange rate) is called a **depreciation** of the pound; for example, if one can now obtain only ¥125 for £1, the pound has *depreciated*.[7]

Because the exchange rate expresses the value of one currency in terms of another, when one currency appreciates, the other must depreciate.

The demand for and supply of pounds

The exchange rate is just a price, albeit a very important price. As with other prices, we will approach the explanation of exchange rates from the perspective of demand and supply. However, the exchange rate is potentially influenced by (and influences) all payments into and out of the national economy from abroad. Hence we must first be clear about what those payments are.

For the sake of simplicity we use an example involving trade between the United Kingdom and the United States and the determination of the exchange rate between their two currencies, the pound sterling and the US dollar, for which we use the shorthand forms 'pound' and 'dollar'. The two-country example simplifies things, but the principles apply to all foreign transactions. Thus 'dollar' stands for foreign exchange in general, and the value of the pound in terms of dollars stands for the foreign exchange rate in general.[8]

When £1 = $1.50, a US importer who offers to buy £1 million with dollars must be offering to sell $1.5 million. Similarly, a UK importer who offers to sell £1 million for dollars must be offering to buy $1.5 million.

Because one currency is traded for another in the foreign exchange market, it follows that a demand for foreign exchange (dollars) implies a supply of pounds, while a supply of foreign exchange (dollars) implies a demand for pounds.

For this reason a theory of the exchange rate between the pound and the dollar can deal either with the demand for and the supply of pounds or with the demand for and the supply of dollars: both need not be considered. We will concentrate on the demand, supply, and price of the pound (quoted in dollars).

We develop our example in terms of the demand-and-

---

[6] Some trade, especially in primary commodities such as wheat and oil, is conducted in US dollars, even when US residents are not involved. In this respect the US dollar has a special role as an international medium of exchange or unit of account.

[7] When the external value of the currency changes as a result of an explicit policy of the central bank, it is often said to have been *devalued* when it falls and *revalued* when it rises.

[8] The foreign exchange market between the pound and the dollar is referred to in the market as 'cable', because it grew to its present structure by use of one of the first transatlantic telephone cables.

supply analysis first encountered in Chapter 3. To do so, we need only recall that *in the market for foreign exchange*, transactions that generate a receipt of foreign exchange (a credit in the balance of payments) represent a demand for pounds, and transactions that require a payment of foreign exchange represent a supply of pounds. We focus on the demand and supply of pounds arising from both the current and capital accounts. Later we turn to the important role of official intervention by the domestic government.

The demand for pounds

The demand for pounds arises from all international transactions that generate a receipt of foreign exchange, that is, credits in the balance of payments.

UK exports One important source of demand for pounds in foreign exchange markets is foreigners who do not currently hold pounds but who wish to buy UK-made goods and services. A German importer of Scotch whisky is such a purchaser; an Austrian couple planning to take a holiday in Cornwall is another; the Chinese national airline seeking to buy Rolls Royce engines for its passenger aircraft is yet another. All are sources of demand for pounds, arising out of international trade. Each potential buyer wants to sell their own currency and buy pounds for the purpose of purchasing UK exports.

Income payments and transfers A UK resident who owns shares in, say, General Motors receives dividend payments on those shares. The dividend is paid by GM in dollars. But the UK resident wants to use the money for a meal out in London, so converts the dollars into pounds, thereby creating a demand for pounds. Thus credit items in the balance of payments accounts for income or transfers create demand for pounds.

Capital inflows A third source of a demand for pounds comes from foreigners who wish to purchase UK assets. In order to buy UK assets, holders of foreign currencies must first buy pounds in foreign exchange markets.[9]

Reserve currency Governments often accumulate and hold foreign exchange reserves, just as individuals maintain savings accounts. The government of Nigeria, for example, may decide to increase its reserve holdings of pounds and reduce its reserve holdings of dollars; if it does so, it will be a demander of pounds (and a supplier of dollars) in foreign exchange markets. The pound sterling used to be a very important reserve currency, particularly for countries that were formerly British colonies. This role has been greatly reduced (relative to the US dollar and euro), but it still creates a significant overseas demand for pounds. Currency reserves are almost always held in an interest-bearing asset, so it is the expected return on these assets that is likely to influence the choice, just as with private sector capital flows.

The total demand for pounds

The demand for pounds by holders of foreign currencies is the sum of the demands for all of the purposes just discussed—for purchases of UK exports of goods and services, for income payments and transfers, for capital movements, or for adding to currency reserves.

Furthermore, because people, firms, and governments in all countries purchase goods from, and invest in, many other countries, the demand for any one currency will be the aggregate demand of individuals, firms, and governments in a number of different countries. Thus the total demand for pounds, for example, may include Germans who are offering euros, Japanese who are offering yen, Greeks who are offering drachmas, and so on. For simplicity, however, we continue with our two-country example and use only the United Kingdom and the United States.

The demand curve for pounds

The demand for pounds in terms of dollars is represented by a negatively sloped curve, such as the one shown in Figure 28.1. This figure plots the price of the pound (measured in dollars) on the vertical axis and the quantity of pounds on the horizontal axis. Moving down the vertical scale, the pound is worth fewer dollars and hence is depreciating in the foreign exchange market. Moving up the scale, the pound is appreciating.

Why is the demand curve for pounds negatively sloped? Consider the demand for pounds for foreign purchases of UK exports. If the pound depreciates, the dollar price of UK exports will fall because holders of dollars require fewer of them to buy £1. US citizens will buy more of the cheaper UK goods and will require more pounds for this purpose. The quantity of pounds demanded will therefore rise. In the opposite case, when the pound appreciates, more dollars are required to buy £1, and so the price of UK exports rises in terms of dollars. US citizens will buy fewer UK goods and thus will demand fewer pounds.

Similar considerations affect other sources of demand for pounds. When the pound is cheaper, UK assets become attractive purchases, and the quantity purchased will rise. As it does, the quantity of pounds demanded to pay for the purchases will increase.

The demand curve for pounds in the foreign exchange market is negatively sloped when it is plotted against the dollar price of £1.

The supply of pounds

The sources of supply of pounds in the foreign exchange market are merely the opposite side of the demand for

---

[9] Capital inflows also arise when UK citizens sell foreign assets, because they enter the foreign exchange market and sell the foreign currency received for the assets and buy pounds.

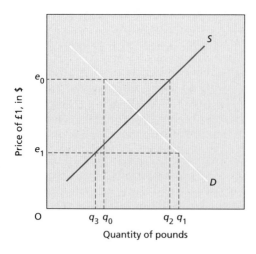

Figure 28.1 The market for foreign exchange

The demand curve for pounds is negatively sloped, and the supply curve of pounds is positively sloped. The demand for pounds is D. It represents the sum of transactions giving rise to receipts of foreign exchange. When the exchange rate is e_0, the quantity of pounds demanded is q_0. A depreciation of the pound is indicated by a fall in the exchange rate to e_1; foreign demand for UK goods and assets rises, and hence the quantity of pounds demanded also rises, from q_0 to q_1. An appreciation has the opposite effect; a rise in the exchange rate from e_1 to e_0 causes the quantity of pounds demanded to fall from q_1 to q_0.

The supply of pounds is given by line S. It represents the sum of transactions that require payments of foreign exchange. When the exchange rate is e_0, the quantity of pounds supplied is q_2. If the exchange rate falls to e_1, UK demand for foreign goods and assets falls, and hence the quantity of pounds supplied also falls, from q_2 to q_3. An appreciation has the opposite effect; a rise in the exchange rate from e_1 to e_0 causes the quantity of pounds supplied to rise from q_3 to q_2.

dollars. (Recall that the *supply* of pounds by people who are seeking dollars is the same as the *demand* for dollars by holders of pounds.)

Who wants to sell pounds? UK residents seeking to purchase foreign goods and services or assets will be supplying pounds and purchasing foreign exchange for this purpose. In addition, holders of UK assets may decide to sell their UK holdings and shift them into foreign assets, and if they do they will sell pounds; that is, they will be supplying pounds to the foreign exchange market. Similarly, a country with some sterling reserves of foreign exchange may decide that the sterling-denominated assets offer a poor return and that it should sell pounds in order to buy another currency.

The supply curve of pounds

When the pound sterling depreciates, the sterling price of

US exports to the UK rises. It takes more pounds to buy the same US goods, so UK residents will buy fewer of the now more expensive US goods. The quantity of pounds being offered in exchange for dollars in order to pay for US exports to the UK (UK imports) will therefore fall.[10]

In the opposite case, when the pound appreciates, US exports to the United Kingdom become cheaper, more are sold, and a greater quantity of pounds is spent on them. Thus, more pounds will be offered in exchange for dollars to obtain the foreign exchange needed to pay for the extra imports. The argument also applies to purchases and sales of assets.

The supply curve of pounds in the foreign exchange market is positively sloped when it is plotted against the dollar price of £1.

This too is illustrated in Figure 28.1.

The determination of exchange rates

The demand and supply curves in Figure 28.1 do not include official foreign exchange market intervention by the domestic government (or by the monetary authorities,[11] depending on the institutional arrangements in the country concerned), though they do include any transactions in pounds by foreign monetary authorities. In order to complete our analysis, we need to incorporate the role of domestic official intervention.[12] Three important cases need to be considered:

1. When there is no official intervention by the monetary authorities or the government, the exchange rate is determined by the equality between the supply and demand for

[10] As long as the demand for imports is elastic (price elasticity greater than 1 (in absolute terms)), the fall in the volume of imports will swamp the rise in price, and hence fewer pounds will be spent on imports. If the elasticity of demand for imports is less than 1 (in absolute terms), the volume of imports will fall but the amount of domestic money spent on them will still rise. In what follows, we adopt the case of elastic demand, which is usual in this area. In a more general form this is called the *Marshall–Lerner condition*, after two famous British economists who first studied the problem.

[11] In the UK the official reserves used to be entirely owned by the government but managed by the Bank of England. However, following the 1998 Bank of England Act, the Bank was given some of the UK reserves, so foreign exchange market intervention could be performed with either the Treasury's or the Bank's reserves. The European Central Bank can also intervene in foreign exchange markets as it has its own foreign exchange reserves.

[12] Official intervention is included in the balance of payments accounts in Table 28.1 under 'reserve assets'.

pounds arising from the capital and current accounts. This is called a *flexible* or *floating exchange rate regime*.

2. When official intervention is used to maintain the exchange rate at (or close to) a particular value, there is said to be a *fixed* or *pegged exchange rate regime*.

3. Between these two 'pure' regimes are many possible intermediate cases, including the *adjustable peg* and the *managed float*. Under an adjustable peg governments set and attempt to maintain par values for their exchange rates, but they explicitly recognize that circumstances may arise in which they will change the par value. In a managed float the authorities seek to have some stabilizing influence on the exchange rate but do not try to fix it at some publicly announced par value.

Flexible exchange rates

Consider an exchange rate that is set in a freely competitive market, with no intervention by the authorities. Like any competitive price, this rate fluctuates according to the conditions of demand and supply.

Suppose that the current price of the pound is so low (say, at e_1 in Figure 28.1) that the quantity of pounds demanded exceeds the quantity supplied. Pounds will be in scarce supply in the foreign exchange market; some people who require pounds to make payments to the United Kingdom will be unable to obtain them; and the price of the pound will be bid up. The value of the pound *vis-à-vis* the dollar will appreciate. As the price of the pound rises, the dollar price of UK exports to the United States rises and the quantity of pounds demanded to buy UK goods decreases. At the same time as the sterling price of imports from the United States falls, a larger quantity will be purchased and the quantity of pounds supplied will rise. Thus a rise in the price of the pound reduces the quantity demanded and increases the quantity supplied. Where the two curves intersect, quantity demanded equals quantity supplied and the exchange rate is in equilibrium.

What happens when the price of the pound is above its equilibrium value? The quantity of pounds demanded will be less than the quantity supplied. With pounds in excess supply, some people who wish to convert pounds into dollars will be unable to do so. (Equivalently, we could say that there is an excess demand for dollars.) The price of the pound will fall, fewer pounds will be supplied, more will be demanded, and an equilibrium will be re-established.

A foreign exchange market is like other competitive markets in that the forces of demand and supply lead to an equilibrium price at which quantity demanded equals quantity supplied.

In a floating exchange rate regime it is exchange rate adjustment that determines the actual current and capital account transactions, even though planned, or desired, trade and investment decisions may have been inconsistent. Suppose that at the beginning of some period importers and exporters had plans that would have created a current account deficit and domestic investors had plans to buy foreign securities (while foreigners had no such plans). The attempt to implement these plans would create a massive excess supply of pounds (demand for dollars). This would force a sterling depreciation, which would continue until it moved far enough to force changes in plans. Indeed, it would depreciate just far enough so that any supply of pounds generated by a current account deficit was just balanced by a capital inflow (or any current account surplus was just balanced by a capital outflow).

Fixed exchange rates

When there is official intervention in the foreign exchange market to maintain a particular exchange rate, this stops some movement in the exchange rate that would otherwise have happened. In this way it may prevent the exchange rate from adjusting sufficiently to guarantee that the current account balance and the (private sector) capital account balance are equal and opposite. In this situation any desired excess demand or supply of pounds by the private sector must be met by the authorities. In the process of intervention the authorities will be building up or running down their foreign exchange reserves.

The official foreign exchange reserves are the stock of foreign-currency-denominated assets that the monetary authorities hold in order to be able to intervene in the foreign exchange markets.

When the authorities peg the exchange rate, they do not do so at one specific rate, but rather within some range. In the post-war exchange regime that existed until 1972 (in the UK case) exchange rates were pegged within one percentage point on either side of a central (or 'par') rate. This was known as the Bretton Woods regime, after the town in the United States where the agreement was drawn up. In the European Exchange Rate Mechanism (ERM) of the 1980s and early 1990s, the range of permitted fluctuation was 2.25 per cent for some countries and 6 per cent for others (including the United Kingdom from October 1990 to September 1992), though the band was widened to 15 per cent after a crisis in 1993.

Let us consider a simplified analysis of how such pegged exchange rate regimes operate. Assume for simplicity that the domestic authorities peg the UK exchange rate between, say, $1.50 and $1.60. This case is illustrated in Figure 28.2. The authorities would then enter the market to prevent the rate from going outside this range. At the price of $1.50 the authorities offer to buy pounds (in exchange for dollars) in unlimited amounts. At the price

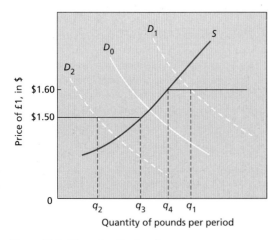

Figure 28.2　Managing fixed exchange rates
Under a fixed exchange rate regime the authorities intervene in the foreign exchange market to ensure that the exchange rate stays within specified bands. The supply curve is S, and the exchange rate is pegged within the range $1.50–$1.60. If the demand curve is given by D_0, the equilibrium exchange rate is within the bands so no intervention by the authorities is required. With demand curve D_1 the equilibrium exchange rate would be above $1.60. To stop the exchange rate rising above $1.60, the authorities have to sell $q_4 q_1$ pounds per period and buy dollars of equivalent value. (For every £100 sold, they will acquire $160.) If the demand curve were D_2, the exchange rate would fall below $1.50 in a free market, so the authorities have to buy $q_2 q_3$ pounds per period with dollars.

$1.60 the authorities offer to sell pounds (in exchange for dollars) in unlimited amounts. When the authorities buy dollars (sell pounds) their exchange reserves rise, but when they sell dollars (buy pounds) their foreign exchange reserves fall.

If on average the demand and supply curves intersect in the range $1.50–$1.60, then exchange reserves will be relatively stable. However, if demand for pounds intersects the supply curve below $1.50, the authorities will find themselves losing reserves each period, and such a situation cannot be sustained indefinitely (because the authorities will run out of reserves). They must then either move the bands of fluctuation (devalue), or take action to shift the demand or supply curves. This could be done, for example, by trade restrictions, or by raising interest rates to attract short-term capital inflows.

In a fixed exchange rate regime with an overvalued currency the balance of payments becomes a problem. In this case it is not necessarily a current account deficit that is the problem; rather, it is the overall excess supply of domestic currency (excess demand for foreign currency) in the foreign exchange market, which could arise from any of the components of the balance of payments.

With fixed exchange rates and an overvalued currency,

the monetary authorities will be suffering a loss of reserves. It is this that causes balance of payments crises for governments operating under fixed exchange rate regimes.

The problems associated with fixing the exchange rate provide a further example of the difficulties of price intervention listed in Chapter 5. In the remainder of this chapter we focus on flexible exchange rates.

Changes in exchange rates

What causes flexible exchange rates to move? The simplest answer to this question is changes in demand or supply in the foreign exchange market. Anything that shifts the demand curve for pounds to the right or the supply curve of pounds to the left leads to an appreciation of the pound; anything that shifts the demand curve for pounds to the left or the supply curve of pounds to the right leads to a depreciation of the pound. This is nothing more than a restatement of the laws of supply and demand, applied now to the market for foreign currencies; it is illustrated in Figure 28.3.

What causes the shifts in demand and supply that lead to changes in exchange rates? There are many causes, some of which are transitory and some of which are persistent. We will discuss some of the most important ones.

A rise in the domestic price of exports

Suppose that the sterling price of UK-produced telephone equipment rises. The effect on the demand for pounds depends on the price elasticity of foreign demand for the UK products.

If the demand is inelastic (say, because the United Kingdom is uniquely able to supply the product for which there are no close substitutes), then more will be spent; the demand for pounds to pay the bigger bill will shift the demand curve to the right, and the pound will appreciate. This is illustrated in Figure 28.3(i).

If the demand is elastic, perhaps because other countries supply the same product to competitive world markets, the total amount spent will decrease and thus fewer pounds will be demanded; that is, the demand curve for pounds will shift to the left, and the pound will depreciate. This too is illustrated in Figure 28.3(i), by a reverse of the previous shift.

A rise in the foreign price of imports

Suppose that the dollar price of US-produced videos increases sharply. Suppose also that UK consumers have an elastic demand for US videos because they can easily switch to UK substitutes. In this case they will spend fewer dollars for US videos than they did before. Hence they will supply fewer pounds to the foreign exchange market. The supply curve of pounds shifts to the left, and the pound will appreciate. If the demand for US videos were inelastic, spending on them would rise and the supply of pounds would shift to the right, leading to a depreciation of the pound. This is illustrated in Figure 28.3(ii).

Changes in price levels

Suppose that instead of a change in the price of a specific exported product, there is a change in *all* prices because of inflation. What matters here is the change in the UK price level *relative to* the price levels of its trading partners. (Recall that in our two-country example the United States stands for the rest of the world.)

If UK inflation is higher than that in the United States, UK exports are becoming relatively expensive in US markets while imports from the United States are becoming relatively cheap in the United Kingdom. This will shift the demand curve for pounds to the left and the supply curve to the right. Each change causes the dollar price of £1 to fall, that is, causes the pound to depreciate.

If the price level of one country is rising relative to that of another country, the equilibrium value of its currency will be falling relative to that of the other country.

Indeed, the price level and the exchange rate are both measures of a currency's value. The price level is the value of a currency measured against a typical basket of goods, while the exchange rate values a currency against other currencies.

Capital movements

Major capital flows can exert a strong influence on exchange rates, especially as the size of capital flows (in the modern globalized financial system) can swamp trade payments on any particular day. An increased desire by UK residents to invest in US assets will shift the supply curve for pounds to the right, and the pound will depreciate. This is illustrated in Figure 28.3(ii).

A significant movement of investment funds has the effect of appreciating the currency of the capital-importing country and depreciating the currency of the capital-exporting country.

This statement is true for all capital movements—short-term and long-term. Because the motives that lead to large capital movements are likely to be different in the short and long terms, however, it is worth considering each separately.

Short-term capital movements   A major motive for short-

(i) Demand shifts

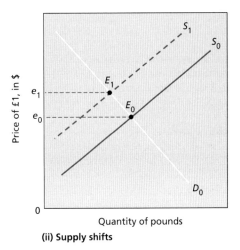

(ii) Supply shifts

Figure 28.3 Changes in exchange rates

An increase in the demand for pounds or a decrease in the supply will cause the pound to appreciate; a decrease in the demand or an increase in supply will cause it to depreciate. The initial demand and supply curves, D_0 and S_0, are shown as solid lines. Equilibrium is at E_0 with an exchange rate of e_0. An increase in the demand for pounds, as shown by a rightward shift in the demand curve from D_0 to D_1 in part (i), or a decrease in the supply of pounds, as shown by a leftward shift in the supply curve from S_0 to S_1 in part (ii), will cause the pound to appreciate. In both parts the new equilibrium is at E_1, and the appreciation is shown by the rise in the exchange rate from e_0 to e_1.

A decrease in the demand for pounds, as shown by a leftward shift in the demand curve from D_1 to D_0 in part (i), or an increase in the supply of pounds, as shown by a rightward shift in the supply curve from S_1 to S_0 in part (ii), will cause the pound to depreciate. The equilibrium will shift from E_1 to E_0, and the depreciation is shown by the fall in the exchange rate from e_1 to e_0 in both parts.

term capital flows is a change in interest rates. International traders hold transactions balances just as domestic traders do. These balances are usually lent out on a short-term basis rather than being left in a non-interest-bearing deposit. Naturally, other things being equal, the holders of these balances will tend to lend them in those markets where interest rates are highest. Thus if one major country's short-term rate of interest rises above the rates in most other countries, there will tend to be an inflow of short-term capital into that country (or at least of deposits in major financial centres denominated in that country's currency) in an effort to take advantage of the high rate, and this will tend to appreciate the currency. If these short-term interest rates should fall, there will most likely be a sudden shift away from that country as a location for short-term funds, and its currency will tend to depreciate.

A second motive for short-term capital movements is speculation about a country's exchange rate. If foreigners expect the pound to appreciate, they will rush to buy assets denominated in pounds; if they expect the pound to depreciate, they will be reluctant to buy or to hold UK financial assets.

Long-term capital movements Long-term capital movements are largely influenced by long-term expectations about another country's profit opportunities and the long-run value of its currency. A US firm would be more willing to purchase a UK firm if it expected that the profits in pounds would buy more dollars in future years than the profits from investment in a US factory. This could happen if the UK business earned greater profits than the US alternative, with exchange rates remaining unchanged. It could also happen if the profits were the same but the US firm expected the pound to appreciate relative to the dollar.

Structural changes

An economy can undergo structural changes that alter the equilibrium exchange rate. 'Structural change' is an all-purpose term for a change in technology, the invention of new products, or anything else that affects the pattern of comparative advantage. For example, when a country's products do not improve in quality as rapidly as those of some other countries, that country's consumers' demand (at fixed prices) shifts slowly away from its own products and towards those of its foreign competitors. This causes a slow depreciation in the first country's currency, because the demand for its currency is shifting slowly leftward as illustrated in Figure 28.3(i).

An important example of a structural change in recent UK history was the production of oil and gas from the North Sea in the 1970s. This reduced UK demand for imported oil, leading to a reduced supply of pounds in the foreign exchange market and an appreciation of the UK exchange rate.

The behaviour of exchange rates

The degree of exchange rate variability experienced since the advent of floating in the early 1970s has been bigger than was expected.

Why have exchange rates been volatile? This question remains at the centre of debate and controversy among researchers and policy commentators. In this section we provide only a cursory view of this and related questions about the behaviour of exchange rates.

First, we look at one measure of the value that the exchange rate would take on if it were subject to the influence of what might be called the underlying, or fundamental, market determinants. We can then compare this with the actual value of the exchange rate. Second, we provide one explanation for the divergence of the exchange rate from the path determined by these fundamentals.

Purchasing power parity

Purchasing power parity (PPP) theory holds that over the long term the average value of the exchange rate between two currencies depends on their relative purchasing power. The theory holds that a currency will tend to have the same purchasing power when it is spent in its home country as it would have if it were converted to foreign exchange and spent in the foreign country.

If at existing values of relative price levels and the existing exchange rate a currency has a higher purchasing power in its own country, it is said to be undervalued; there is then an incentive to sell foreign exchange and buy the domestic currency in order to take advantage of this higher purchasing power (that is, the fact that goods seem cheaper) in the domestic economy. This will put upward pressure on the domestic currency.

Similarly, if a currency has a lower purchasing power in its own country, it is said to be overvalued; there is then an incentive to sell the domestic currency and buy foreign exchange in order to take advantage of the higher purchasing power (cheaper goods) abroad. This will put downward pressure on the domestic currency.

The PPP exchange rate is determined by relative price levels in the two countries.

For example, assume that the UK price level rises by 20 per cent, while the US price level rises by only 5 per cent over the same period. The PPP value of the dollar then appreciates by approximately 15 per cent against sterling. This means that in the United States the prices of all goods (both US-produced and imported UK goods) will rise by 5 per cent, measured in dollars, while in the United Kingdom the prices of all goods (both UK-produced and imported US goods) will rise by 20 per cent, measured in pounds.

Box 28.2 Exchange rates and the quantity theory of money

A simple expression for the exchange rate can be derived from the quantity theory of money (as set out in Box 26.1) when there are two countries and an exchange rate that follows its PPP value.

Let the foreign country be denoted by an asterisk (*), so that it has an equation linking money, prices, income, and velocity:

$$M^*V^* = P^*Y^*. \qquad \text{(i)}$$

Using values for home money supply, prices, velocity, and income, we already had:

$$MV = PY. \qquad \text{(ii)}$$

All we need to add is the relationship implied by PPP. This is that prices will be the same in both economies when converted at the current exchange rate:

$$PE = P^*, \qquad \text{(iii)}$$

where P is the home country price level, P^* is the foreign country price level, and E is the exchange rate (number of units of foreign currency per unit of home currency). Now all we do is rearrange (i) and (ii) as expressions for P and P^*, then substitute into (iii) and arrange as an expression for E. This gives[†]

$$E = \frac{M^*}{M} \cdot \frac{Y}{Y^*} \cdot \frac{V^*}{V}. \qquad \text{(iv)}$$

This is an important equation which gives us some new insights into the exchange rate. The first term is the ratio of the home and foreign money supplies. E falls in proportion to the home money supply and rises in proportion to the foreign money supply. This means that, when the home money supply rises, the exchange rate depreciates in the same proportion. The logic of this has two steps. First, a rise in home money supply leads to a proportional increase in the home price level (for given levels of Y and V). Second, a rise in the home price level leads to a proportional depreciation of the home currency to preserve PPP.

The second term in (iv) has a very important implication. Domestic real national income is positively related to E. This means that, other things being equal, a rise in domestic national income leads to an appreciation of the home currency. The reason for this is that an increase in Y leads to an increased transactions demand for the home currency. As we have learned in this chapter, anything that increases demand for the home currency will tend to appreciate its exchange rate.

This simple model of exchange rates gives important insights, but it is only a beginning. Many more complicated factors affecting interest rates and expectations can easily be incorporated by a more detailed specification of the determinants of V. However, the main elements of (iv) are recognizable in many of the empirical exchange rate models of the last two decades.

[†] The steps are as follows:

1. $P^* = M^*V^*/Y^*$ and $P = MV/Y$.
2. Substituting into (iii), $E(MV/Y) = M^*V^*/Y^*$.
3. Rearranging gives (iv).

The PPP exchange rate adjusts so that the relative prices of the two nations' goods (measured in the same currency) are unchanged, because the change in the relative values of two currencies compensates exactly for differences in national inflation rates.

If the actual exchange rate changes along with the PPP rate, the competitive positions of producers in the two countries will be unchanged. Firms that are located in countries with high inflation rates will still be able to sell their outputs on international markets, because the exchange rate will adjust to offset the effect of the rising domestic prices. An exchange rate that adjusts in line with the PPP exchange rate is also referred to as a constant *real exchange rate*.[13] A simple model of the exchange rate implied by the quantity theory of money and PPP is set out in Box 28.2.

Figure 28.4 shows an index of the real exchange rate for the United Kingdom, the United States, and Germany for 1980–98. PPP requires that the real exchange rate should be constant in the long term. This is broadly true. Notice also, however, the large fluctuations around the PPP rate. The United Kingdom had a high real exchange rate in the early 1980s, associated with its emergence as an oil producer. This led to a sharp loss of competitiveness of the non-oil sectors of the economy (especially manufactur-

ing), causing a sharp decline in UK manufacturing output which in turn contributed to the 1979–81 recession. The UK real exchange rate fell significantly between 1981 and 1986. The most dramatic swing in the 1980s, however, was in the US real exchange rate, which increased 50 per cent between 1980 and 1985, and then fell back to its 1980 level by 1987.

PPP governs exchange rate behaviour in the long term, but there often are significant deviations from PPP in the short to medium term.

Why have these wide fluctuations occurred? One of the most important reasons is associated with international differences in interest rates. Another, related reason— responses to new information—is discussed in Box 28.3.

Exchange rate overshooting

Differences in interest rates between countries, arising from differences in monetary and fiscal policies, among other factors, can trigger large capital flows as investors

[13] The real exchange rate is the inverse of competitiveness. A country whose goods were becoming relatively cheap in world markets would be said to be improving its competitiveness but to be having a falling real exchange rate, and vice versa. The real exchange rate is not an actual price of currency: it is an index number of the relative prices of home and foreign goods.

Figure 28.4 Real exchange rates for the USA, Germany, and the UK, 1980–1998

Deviations from PPP can be substantial in the short run, but over the long run exchange rates tend to converge to their PPP values. At the PPP exchange rate the real exchange rate would be constant. The chart shows real exchange rates for three countries, calculated by adjusting actual exchange rates by indexes of consumer prices, and set to a value of 100 in the first quarter of 1980.

The UK real exchange rate rose between 1980 and early 1981. It then fell in stages. It rose again at the end of the 1980s but fell sharply after September 1992, when Britain left the ERM. The United States experienced a dramatic appreciation of its real exchange rate from 1980 to 1985, after which time it fell back; at the end of 1996 the US real exchange rate was roughly the same as in 1980. The real exchange rate of Germany fell in the early 1980s but then cycled about a fairly constant level.

Source: Datastream.

Box 28.3 'News' and the exchange rate

Foreign exchange markets are different from markets for consumer goods in that the vast bulk of trading takes place between professional foreign exchange dealers of banks. These dealers do not meet each other face to face. Rather, they do their transactions over the telephone, and the other party to the deal could be anywhere in the world. The structure of this market has one interesting implication: exchange rates respond to news. Let us see why this is and what it means.

Deals done by the professional dealers are all on a large scale, typically involving sums no smaller than £1 million and often very much larger. Each dealer tends to specialize in deals between a small number of currencies, say the pound sterling and the euro. But the dealers in all currencies for each bank sit close together, in a dealing room, so that they can hear what is going on in other markets. When a big news event breaks, anywhere in the world, this will be shouted out to all dealers in the room simultaneously.

Each dealer is also faced with several computer screens and many buttons which will connect him or her very quickly by telephone to other dealers. Speed of transaction can be very important if you are dealing with large volumes of money in a market that is continuously changing the prices quoted. Latest price quotes from around the world appear on the screens. However, contracts are agreed over the telephone (and nowadays are recorded in case of disagreement) and the paperwork follows within two days.

As exchange rates are closely related to expectations and to interest rates, the foreign exchange dealers have to keep an eye on all major news events affecting the economic environment. Since all the players in the

foreign exchange markets are professionals, they are all well informed, not just about what has happened but also about forecasts of what is likely to happen. Accordingly, the exchange rate, at any point in time, reflects not just history but also current expectations of what is going to happen in future.

As soon as some future event comes to be expected, it will be reflected in the current exchange rate. Events expected to happen soon will usually be given more weight than distant events. The only component in today's news that will cause the exchange rate to change is what was *not* expected to happen. Economists attribute the unforecastable component of news to a random error. It is random in the sense that it has no detectable pattern to it and it is unrelated to the information available before it happened.

Some events are clearly unforecastable, like an earthquake in Japan or a head of state having a heart attack. Others are the production of economic statistics for which forecasts have generally been published. In the latter case it is the deviation of announced figures from their forecast value which, if large, tends to move exchange rates.

Exchange rates are moved by news. Since news is random and unpredictable, changes in exchange rates will tend to be random.

Some people, observing the volatility of exchange rates, conclude that foreign exchange markets are inefficient. However, with well-informed professional players who have forward-looking expectations, new information is rapidly transmitted into prices. Volatility of exchange rates may, therefore, reflect the volatility of relevant, but unexpected, events around the world.

seek to place their funds where returns are highest. These capital flows will in turn result in swings in the exchange rate between the two countries. Some economists argue that this is the fundamental reason for the wide fluctuations in exchange rates that have been observed.

To illustrate, suppose that an exogenous change in monetary policy causes UK interest rates to rise 4 percentage points above those in New York. The interest rate differential will lead to a capital inflow into the United Kingdom. UK and foreign investors alike will sell assets denominated in US dollars and will buy UK assets that earn higher interest. These capital inflows will lead to an increased demand for pounds on the foreign exchange market as investors exchange dollars for pounds to buy UK assets. The increased demand will in turn lead to an appreciation of sterling.

A relative rise in domestic interest rates will cause a capital inflow and an appreciation of the home currency.

When will the process stop? It will stop only when expected returns on UK and foreign assets are again roughly equalized; as long as the return on UK assets is above that on foreign assets, the capital inflows will continue, and the upward pressure on the pound will continue. The key is that the expected return includes not only the interest earnings, but also the expected gains or losses that might arise because of changes in the exchange rate during the period of the investment. A foreign investor holding a UK asset will receive pounds when the asset is sold, and will at that time want to exchange pounds for foreign exchange. If the value of the pound has fallen, that will be a source of loss that has to be balanced against the interest income in assessing the net return on holding the asset.

Equilibrium in the above example occurs when the rise in value of the pound sterling in foreign exchange markets is large enough that investors will expect a future depreciation which just offsets the interest premium from investing funds in sterling-denominated assets.

Suppose investors believe that the PPP rate is £1 = $1.50, but as they rush to buy pounds to take advantage of higher UK interest rates, they drive the rate to, say, £1 = $1.75. (Because £1 now buys more dollars, the pound has appreciated, and because it takes more dollars to buy £1, the dollar has depreciated.) They do not believe that this rate will be sustained and instead expect the pound to lose value in future periods. If foreign investors expect the pound to depreciate by 4 per cent per year, they will be indifferent between lending money in London and doing so in New York. The extra 4 per cent per year of interest that they earn in London is exactly offset by the 4 per cent that they expect to lose when they turn their money back into their own currency.

A policy that raises domestic interest rates above world

levels will cause the external value of the domestic currency to appreciate enough to create an expected future depreciation that will be sufficient to offset the interest differential.

While interest differentials persist, the exchange rate must deviate from its equilibrium or PPP value; this is often referred to as exchange rate *overshooting*, because at the time interest rates are raised, the exchange rate will jump beyond its long-run equilibrium level. This is illustrated in Figure 28.5.

The argument that a rise in domestic interest rates will cause an appreciation of the home currency requires an important proviso. The interest rate rise has to occur with all other factors—especially long-run inflation expectations—held constant. If, for example, it was a rise in expectations of future inflation that triggered off events, the story would be quite different. In this case the interest rate rise would be responding to these expectations and to the consequent expectation of a long-run *depreciation* in the home currency. Now the change in the exchange rate would depend upon the size of the interest rate rise relative to the size of the expected long-run depreciation. In short we need to be careful when applying economic analysis that works *holding other things constant* to a world where many things are changing simultaneously.

Implications of overshooting One policy implication of exchange rate theory is that a central bank that is seeking to use its monetary policy to attain its domestic policy targets may have to put up with large fluctuations in the

Figure 28.5 Exchange rate overshooting
The adjustment of exchange rates to policy changes often involves overshooting the long-run equilibrium. The figure illustrates how the exchange rate may move over time after a monetary policy tightening. The initial exchange rate is e_0. At time t_1 the central bank raises domestic interest rates and the exchange rate appreciates to e_1. Over time it then depreciates back towards the new long-run equilibrium level of e_2.

exchange rate. Indeed, overshooting of the exchange rate in response to interest rate changes may be one of the most important elements of the monetary transmission mechanism.

In the case of a tightening of monetary policy which raises interest rates, the overshooting (appreciation) of the pound beyond its PPP rate would put export- and import-competing industries under temporary but severe pressure from foreign competition, because UK goods would become expensive relative to imported goods. The resulting fall in demand for UK goods would open up a recessionary gap, thus providing a further mechanism by which the restrictive monetary policy was transmitted to the rest of the economy. This is discussed further in Chapter 29.

The two recessions in the United Kingdom in the early 1980s and early 1990s both illustrate this mechanism at work. Both were associated with tight monetary policy and an overvalued exchange rate, although, as there were worldwide recessions at roughly the same time, domestic factors cannot be the whole story.

In the run-up to the 1979–81 recession the pound had appreciated strongly. In 1979 interest rates were raised sharply and the pound appreciated further, as the Thatcher government implemented its commitment to control inflation by tight monetary policy. The high exchange rate meant that domestic producers became very uncompetitive, and so imports of cheaper foreign goods rose. Between late 1979 and early 1981, domestic manufacturing output fell by nearly 20 per cent and unemployment subsequently rose to over 3 million.

The high exchange rate cannot be blamed on tight monetary policy alone, because this was also the time when the United Kingdom was emerging as an oil producer (and the price of oil had doubled in 1979). However, monetary policy (especially the sharp rise in interest rates in 1979) certainly contributed to the overshooting of sterling, and the extremely high exchange rate was undoubtedly a central element in the transmission mechanism between the monetary sector and the real economy.

The recession of 1990–2 was made worse by an attempt to maintain an overvalued exchange rate. From 1981 to 1988 the economy had seen a sustained recovery, and by 1988 inflationary pressures had built up. The government

tightened monetary policy in the autumn of 1988 by raising interest rates. Higher interest rates created a higher foreign exchange value of the pound than would otherwise have happened. Then in October 1990 the pound was pegged in the European Exchange Rate Mechanism (ERM). The onset of recession and fall of inflation, which was evident from 1991, would normally have permitted a reduction in interest rates (and a subsequent decline in the foreign exchange value of sterling), but ERM membership prevented this. This was because of the need to keep interest rates consistent with those of other ERM members, notably Germany, in order to defend the exchange rate. In September 1992 sterling was forced to leave the ERM by speculative pressure which caused reserve losses (as illustrated in Figure 28.2). This permitted a sharp fall in UK interest rates, which was associated with a fall in the exchange rate. (Sterling fell from nearly $2.00 per pound in the summer of 1992 to around $1.50 after September, and stayed around that level for the next couple of years.) The fall in interest rates and in the exchange rate led fairly quickly to economic recovery by the spring of 1993.

The UK exchange rate experienced another period of overvaluation from mid-1996 until (at least) the summer of 1998. Initially it is likely that the strength of sterling was due to the uncertainty affecting other EU currencies (especially the Deutschmark) over prospects for creation of a single currency. Sterling was regarded as something of a 'safe haven' for investors of funds. This was reinforced by the extra credibility attached to the UK monetary policy regime once the Bank of England was given monetary policy independence in May 1997 (see Chapter 25). The strength of the pound in this period made UK exporters (and producers of import-competing goods) less competitive, and was expected to lead to a significant slowdown of domestic output growth in 1998 (of which there were some early signs at the time of writing).

A more detailed analysis of the role of the exchange rate in macroeconomic adjustment follows in the next chapter. What we have learned in this chapter is that the exchange rate is an essential element of the transmission mechanism that turns monetary policy shocks into real shocks in an open economy under flexible exchange rates.

Summary

■ International trade normally requires the exchange of the currency of one country for that of another. The major exception is trade within the euro zone. The exchange rate between two currencies is the amount of one currency that must be paid in order to obtain one unit of another currency.

The balance of payments

■ Actual transactions among the firms, consumers, and governments of various countries are recorded in the balance of payments accounts. In these accounts any transaction that uses foreign exchange is recorded as a debit item, and any transaction that produces foreign exchange is recorded as a credit item. If all transactions are recorded, the sum of all credit items necessarily equals the sum of all debit items, because the foreign exchange that is bought must also have been sold.

■ The two major categories in the balance of payments accounts are the current account and the capital and financial accounts. When we talk about a balance of payments surplus or deficit, we are normally referring to the current account balance alone. A balance on the current account must be matched by a balance on the capital and financial accounts of equal magnitude but opposite sign.

■ There is nothing inherently good or bad about deficits or surpluses on the current account. Persistent deficits or surpluses involve a buildup or run-down of a country's net foreign assets.

The market for foreign exchange

■ The demand for pounds arises from UK exports of goods and services, income payments from overseas, capital inflows, and the desire of foreign governments to use sterling assets as part of their reserves.

■ The supply of pounds to purchase foreign currencies arises from UK imports of goods and services, income payments to overseas, capital outflows, and the desire of holders of sterling assets to decrease the size of their holdings.

■ The demand curve for pounds is negatively sloped and the supply curve of pounds is positively sloped when the quantities demanded and supplied are plotted against the price of pounds, measured in terms of a foreign currency.

The determination of exchange rates

■ When the authorities do not intervene in the foreign exchange market, there is a flexible exchange rate. Under fixed exchange rates the authorities intervene in the foreign exchange market to maintain the exchange rate within a specified range. To do this, they must hold sufficient stocks of foreign exchange reserves.

■ Under a flexible (or floating) exchange rate regime the exchange rate is market-determined by supply and demand for the currency.

■ Fluctuations in exchange rates can be understood as fluctuations around a trend value that is determined by the purchasing power parity (PPP) rate. The PPP rate adjusts in response to differences in national inflation rates. Deviations from the PPP rate are related, among other things, to international differences in interest rates.

■ Exchange rates tend to overshoot their long-run equilibrium in response to shocks. A relaxation of monetary policy which lowers domestic interest rates will cause the exchange rate to depreciate. However, it will tend to depreciate to a point from which it can then appreciate at a rate sufficient to compensate for the interest rate fall. A rise in domestic interest rates will tend to make the exchange rate overshoot in the opposite direction (upwards).

Topics for review

■ Balance of trade in goods and services
■ Balance of income payments and transfers
■ Current and capital accounts
■ Mercantilist views on the balance of trade and volume of trade
■ Foreign exchange and exchange rates
■ Appreciation and depreciation
■ Sources of the demand for and supply of foreign exchange
■ Effects on exchange rates of capital flows, inflation, interest rates, and expectations about exchange rates
■ Fixed and flexible exchange rates
■ Adjustable pegs and managed floats
■ Purchasing power parity
■ Exchange rate overshooting

Questions for discussion

1 If the balance of payments accounts always balance, how can the balance of payments ever be a problem?

2 What is measured by the current account of the balance of payments? A current account deficit is sometimes considered to be a sign of weakness of the domestic economy. Is this really a sign of weakness, and, if not, what is it a sign of?

3 'Capital outflows are a bad thing for the home economy as they mean that we are investing in jobs overseas.' Critically evaluate this statement.

4 Where would each of the following items appear in the UK balance of payments accounts (if at all): (a) Martina Hingis (a Swiss national) wins the Wimbledon Ladies' Championship (including a cheque for £450,000); (b) the UK government buys a new software system from Sun Microsystems of California; (c) the university teachers' pension fund sells shares in IBM and buys an equivalent amount in BMW; (d) Arsenal football club hires a Lufthansa plane to fly the team to a match in Germany in the European Champions' League; (e) a UK resident attends the 1998 World Cup finals in Paris; (f) a resident of Florence buys a life insurance policy from Norwich Union; (g) a UK resident buys a Toyota car assembled in the UK.

5 Explain what factors determine exchange rates in the long run and explain why they tend to overshoot in response to shocks in the short run.

Chapter 29
Macroeconomic Policy in an Open Economy

In this chapter we study how the exchange rate regime and the explicit incorporation of international financial capital flows affect the impact of fiscal and monetary policies. This will give us a much better grasp of how the transmission mechanism works in a world of globalized finance. It will also be helpful in understanding the macroeconomies of those EU countries that have become members of the euro currency system.

In Chapters 26 and 27 we expanded our model of the economy to incorporate monetary forces in the determination of aggregate demand. In that analysis we did make some allowances for openness, as net exports were a component of aggregate demand, and Box 26.2 discussed the topic of financial openness. Chapter 28 discussed the determinants of the exchange rate, and capital flows were

an important part of that analysis. In this chapter we incorporate financial capital flows explicitly into our model and then go on to reconsider the impact of monetary and fiscal policies, under the alternative regimes of fixed and floating exchange rates.

Before proceeding, you should revise the middle section of Chapter 27 on pages 464–9, in which we set out the steps in the chain of causation from exogenous shocks to GDP and price level changes in the short run and the long run. In that chapter we neglected the role of external influences, such as capital flows and the exchange rate, in the adjustment process. Now they must be incorporated in order to complete our formal development of the model of the macroeconomy.

Why does openness matter?

There are three reasons why we have to take a much closer look at the interactions between our macro model and the rest of the world. First, while we have always had net exports in our model, we have not paid attention to all the possible implications of trade imbalances. Second, we have mentioned several times in earlier chapters the fact that financial markets have become more integrated around the world. We refer to this as globalization of financial markets, and Box 29.1 discusses some of the reasons why this has happened. The high international mobility of financial capital implies that money markets in one country are not independent of world financial markets. Third, the exchange rate regime matters for the conduct of monetary policy because it affects the possibilities for *arbitrage* between domestic and overseas financial markets (and therefore the link between domestic and overseas interest rates). **Arbitrage** involves buying where a price is low and selling where it is high, in order to make profit. The process of arbitrage tends to drive prices together in different locations.

Let us expand a little on each of these three factors before we proceed to an explicit analysis of the macro model in which capital flows are included and explicit attention is paid to the trade balance.

Net exports

Our macro model, from Chapter 22 onwards, included net exports, *NX*. The first thing we learned about the *NX* function was that it is negatively sloped. This means that net exports fall as GDP rises—because induced imports rise while autonomous exports are constant.

We also discovered that the net export function will shift if there is an exogenous (autonomous) change in export demand, and if there is a change in the domestic price level relative to foreign prices (caused either by an exchange rate change with given price levels, or a price level change with given exchange rates). An autonomous rise in exports increases net exports (shifts the *NX* function upwards for each level of GDP—see Figures 22.2 and 22.3 on pages

Box 29.1 The globalization of financial markets

Technological innovations in communication and financial liberalization have led to a globalization of the financial services industry over the past few decades. Computers, satellite communication systems, reliable telephones with direct worldwide dialling, electronic mail, and fax machines have put people in instantaneous contact anywhere in the world.

As a result of these new technologies, borrowers and lenders can learn about market conditions anywhere in the world and then move their funds instantly in search of the best loan rates. Large firms need transaction balances only while banks in their area are open. Once banks close for the day in each area, the firms will not need these balances until the following day's reopening. Thus the funds can be moved to another market, where they are used until it closes, and then moved to yet another market. Funds are thus free to move from, say, London to New York to Tokyo and back to London on a daily rotation. This is a degree of global sophistication that was inconceivable before the advent of the computer, when international communication was much slower and costlier than it now is. To facilitate the movement in and out of various national currencies, increasing amounts of bank deposits are denominated in foreign rather than domestic currencies.

One of the first developments in this movement towards globalization was the growth of the foreign currency markets in Europe in the 1960s. At first the main currency involved was the US dollar. (The market for dollar-denominated bank deposits and loans outside the United States is known as the Eurodollar market—not to be confused with the foreign exchange market in the which the euro exchanges for the dollar today.) The progressive worldwide lifting of domestic interest rate ceilings and other capital market restrictions that occurred in the 1980s led to a further globalization of financial markets. Particularly important was the abolition

of exchange controls in country after country. The United Kingdom abolished its exchange controls in 1979, Japan did so in 1980, France and Italy in 1989, Spain in 1991, Portugal and Ireland in 1992, and Greece in 1994. Once such restrictions were abolished, the wholesale money markets integrated with the international money markets very quickly. This is because sophisticated borrowers and lenders dealing with large amounts of money have an incentive to shop around for the best terms.

The increasing sophistication of information transfer has also led to a breakdown of the high degree of specialization that had characterized financial markets in earlier decades. When information was difficult to obtain and analyse, an efficient division of labour called for a host of specialist institutions, each with expertise in a narrow range of transactions. New developments in communications technology created economies of scale which led to the integration of various financial operations within one firm. For example, in many countries banks have moved into the markets where securities are traded, while many security-trading firms have begun to offer a range of banking services. As the scale of such integrated firms increases, they find it easier to extend their operations geographically as well as functionally. The introduction of the euro in 1999 added further impetus to globalization as it increased the integration of EU financial markets and created a currency that has become an important international instrument.

The heavy government intervention in domestic capital markets and government control over international capital flows that characterized the 1950s and 1960s is no longer possible. International markets are just too sophisticated. Globalization is here to stay, and, by removing domestic restrictions and exchange controls, governments in advanced countries were only bowing to the inevitable.

381–2). A rise in domestic relative prices reduces net exports (shifts the *NX* function down and changes its slope).

When we studied how fiscal and monetary policy can be used to speed up the adjustment of GDP back to equilibrium (see pages 464–9), we ignored any repercussions that might be induced by changes in the balance of trade. We can no longer do so. We now analyse the impacts of monetary and fiscal policies taking explicit account of the forces that are put in play by the change in the trade balance as GDP changes. The nature of these effects is influenced by the degree of mobility of financial capital and by the exchange rate regime. We will focus on the case of highly mobile financial capital, because this conforms most closely to the modern world.

Mobile capital

Recall that when we talk about capital flows in the context of the balance of payments, we are *not* talking about imports and exports of capital goods, such as machine tools and heavy equipment; rather, we are talking about trade in assets and liabilities, such as shares and bonds, or lending by banks in one country to customers in another.

Capital flows matter for two reasons. First, as we saw in

Chapter 28, net capital flows must equal (with opposite sign) the current account balance. This relationship is true by definition, so it must always hold. It is important to realize, however, that the economic causation between goods trade and capital flows is not unidirectional. Changes affecting capital flows will have implications for net exports (possibly via exchange rate changes), just as shifts affecting net exports will have implications for the capital account. We will be more specific about these linkages below.

The second reason why capital flows matter for the macro model is that they influence the domestic interest rate. If everyone is free to borrow and lend both domestically and internationally, they will borrow where the interest rate is lowest and lend where it is highest. Mobile capital tends to drive the domestic interest rate towards the level of interest rates in world markets. In effect the domestic economy is close to a price-taker in world financial markets. The price involved in our model is the interest rate on bonds.

We will examine how capital mobility affects our model below. The key point to notice now is that in an open economy with mobile financial capital, we cannot analyse the determination of the domestic interest rate using domestic demand and supply factors alone. Changes in the domestic interest rate brought about by domestic shocks and policy responses will generate reactions through international capital flows and net exports, which will inevitably complicate the picture.

The exchange rate regime

The exchange rate regime matters because it determines which variables are free to adjust. Clearly, under fixed exchange rates, the exchange rate is not free to adjust. But fixing the exchange rate ties down other variables as well. Fixed exchange rates tie together the value of domestic and foreign money. This means that the domestic price level cannot deviate from the foreign price level in the long run.

Fixed exchange rates, with mobile capital, also tie domestic and foreign interest rates together because there is no exchange rate uncertainty. In such circumstances the domestic monetary authorities have no discretion in setting the domestic interest rates. The money supply is endogenously determined by demand, at whatever interest rate is dictated by world money markets. This explains why the UK authorities had no discretion to lower interest rates (as would have been dictated by internal considerations alone) during October 1990–September 1992, when the UK was a member of the ERM. It is also relevant to understanding the behaviour of the economies of the eleven members of the euro zone after January 1999. For these countries there is only one interest rate, set by the European Central Bank, so monetary policy is the same for all.

In general the monetary authorities of nations with independent currencies can fix any one (but only one) of the interest rate, the exchange rate, and the money supply. Once they choose one of these, the other two become endogenous. Fixing the exchange rate is one possible monetary policy, but, having done this, the authorities cannot also control either the interest rate or the money supply. Most major countries (outside the euro zone) set short-term interest rates and let the money supply and the exchange rate adjust.

Under floating exchange rates much of the adjustment to shocks comes through exchange rate changes and the resulting effect on the relative prices of domestic and foreign goods (and assets). In contrast, under fixed exchange rates much more of the adjustment to shocks is worked out via aggregate demand, money stock, and output changes at given relative prices. These differences will become clearer as we work through specific examples below.

We now turn to a discussion of how the macro model is modified by the inclusion of capital flows, and how the presence of capital flows alters the impact of monetary and fiscal policies.

Macro policy in a world with perfect capital mobility

As we have seen, capital flows in the balance of payments accounts include net cross-border sales of a wide variety of domestic and foreign assets—shares and bonds, etc. To keep things as simple as possible, we assume that there are just two types of asset: domestic bonds and foreign bonds. Domestic bonds are denominated in pounds sterling and foreign bonds are denominated in US dollars. (Which foreign currency we select is not critical; in our model it represents the rest of the world.)

Capital flows into the home economy when asset-holders switch from foreign bonds to domestic bonds. Capital flows out of the home economy when asset-holders switch from domestic bonds to foreign bonds. The process of switching involves sales of one currency for the other, so it creates a demand or supply of foreign exchange in the foreign exchange market.

An important assumption we make throughout is that net exports (the goods and services balance) and the current account of the balance of payments are identical. In effect this means that we are ignoring the net income and transfers components of the current account.[1] This is a reasonable assumption for the United Kingdom in 1997; as Table 28.1 on page 476 shows, the balance of these was around 1 per cent of GDP in that year. Even if this item were not so small, it could be ignored for analytical purposes, because it does not vary much in response to short-run changes in exchange rates or GDP.

In order to incorporate capital flows into the macro model, we need to use the *IS* and *LM* curves discussed on pages 454–8, so it is worth reviewing the derivation of those curves. Recall that the *IS* and *LM* curves are just a convenient way of showing how the monetary sector interacts with the determinants of aggregate expenditures to determine the position of the aggregate demand curve.

The macro model with capital flows

Two relationships must be kept in mind when incorpor-

---

[1] This assumption is equivalent to assuming that GNI is equal to GDP.

ating capital flows into our model. First, since net capital flows must be of equal size and opposite sign to the current account balance of payments surplus or deficit, a capital inflow implies a current account deficit of equal size. Second, the foreign demand for domestic bonds depends upon the differential in interest rates between domestic and foreign bonds.

We need to make some assumption about how sensitive demand for domestic bonds will be to this interest differential. The analysis of Chapter 27 implicitly assumed immobile financial capital, so that there would be no switching between domestic and foreign bonds at any feasible interest rate. Now we make the opposite assumption that foreign demand for domestic bonds is perfectly elastic with respect to the interest differential. In effect we are assuming that domestic and foreign bonds are perfect substitutes.[2] This is only one of several possible assumptions, but it is close to the realities of the modern world of globalized finance and highly mobile international capital. Hence it is a reasonable simplifying assumption to make in the UK context, and for most other major countries, though it will be inappropriate for economies that still have official exchange controls affecting capital flows.

Perfect substitutability between domestic bonds and foreign bonds is called perfect capital mobility. Its implications are illustrated in Figure 29.1, which shows the IS/LM diagram used in Chapters 26 and 27, with the addition of a horizontal line labelled BB. Points on the BB line represent combinations of the interest rate and GDP for which there is an equality between the current account balance of payments and capital flows. It joins short-run balance of payments equilibrium points. Its horizontal slope reflects the assumption that capital is perfectly mobile. If the return on domestic bonds were slightly higher than that on foreign bonds, there would be immediate huge demand for them. This would drive up the price of domestic bonds and drive down their yield. Similarly, if domestic bonds had a yield below foreign bonds, holders would sell them to buy foreign bonds. This would drive their price down and their yield up. The result is that the domestic interest rate must equal the world interest rate i^*.[3] The intuition is that any two commodities that are perfect substitutes must have a common price (because they are, in effect, one commodity).

It is important to notice that the BB curve does not represent points for which the current account balance is zero. Indeed, for a given net export function, the current account balance deteriorates as we move to the right (GDP increases). If this involves a deficit, however, this can be financed by borrowing from abroad at the going world rate of interest. Thus, any point on BB for which there is a current account imbalance will also be associated with an equal and opposite capital account imbalance. The horizontal shape of BB reflects the perfectly elastic supply curve of capital, as discussed above.

How can we be sure that the BB line cuts the IS and LM curves at their intersection? The answer is that initially it may not do so; but if it does not, there will be endogenous adjustments of exchange rates and/or money supply. These will shift either the IS or the LM curve (or both) until all three have a common intersection. We will shortly be discussing cases where policy changes create such non-intersections, and we will then see in detail how such adjustment works. The exact process depends upon the exchange rate regime in operation as well as the monetary policy regime.

The implication that domestic and foreign interest rates are equal requires further comment. Recall that domestic and foreign bonds are denominated in different currencies. When exchange rates are fixed (and expected to remain fixed), this causes no complications. The comparative yield is given by the interest differential. Perfect capital mobility does indeed require exact equality of domestic and foreign interest rates at all times—as it would also do for risk-free bonds within the euro zone.

However, under floating exchange rates, where exchange

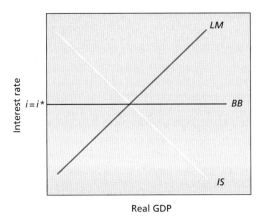

Figure 29.1 The macroeconomic implications of perfect capital mobility

With perfect capital mobility the domestic interest rate must be equal to the foreign interest rate in equilibrium. The BB line shows the combinations of interest rates and GDP for which a current account surplus (deficit) equals the associated capital outflow (inflow). The BB line is drawn horizontally at the point where the domestic interest rate is equal to the foreign rate i^*. The shape of BB means that any size of current account deficit can be financed by borrowing at the going interest rate on world capital markets.

[2] Since corporate bonds vary in riskiness, at best there will be perfect substitutability only between the bonds issued by governments of major industrial countries, as these have virtually no default risk.

[3] If capital flows were imperfect, the BB line would be positively sloped because net exports decrease as GDP increases, and the higher capital flows required to finance an increasing current account deficit could be attracted only at increasing interest rates.

rates are expected to change, the position is more complicated. Here there can be a differential in nominal interest rates which will be equal to the expected rate of change of the exchange rate. This effect is associated with exchange rate overshooting, and was discussed in Chapter 28 and illustrated in Figure 28.5 on page 489. Suppose, for example, that holders of bonds expect sterling to depreciate against the US dollar by 5 per cent over the next year. If the yield on US bonds is 10 per cent per year, they will need a yield of about 15 per cent per year on sterling bonds to compensate for the expected currency depreciation. In this case the expected returns would be equal, but the nominal interest rates would not.[4]

This means that when we discuss floating exchange rates, points on the horizontal *BB* line represent the full equilibrium, when there are no further expectations of exchange rate changes—but we can deviate from it during the adjustment process. With fixed exchange rates, on the other hand, we must be on it all the time.

Perfect capital mobility means that with fixed exchange rates the domestic interest rate must always equal the foreign interest rate. With floating exchange rates any interest differential must equal the expected exchange rate change. This will be zero in full equilibrium.

The explicit addition of capital flows to our model introduces a new adjustment mechanism which reconciles differences in the desired trade surplus and desired net capital flows via either official reserve changes (under fixed exchange rates) or exchange rate changes (under floating rates). This we will explain using specific examples.

Policy changes with fixed exchange rates

Now we can trace through the effects of monetary and fiscal policy changes in a model that allows for perfect capital mobility. Of particular interest will be the new predictions that follow from the addition of capital flows to the model.

To make it easier to understand how the adjustment mechanism works with capital flows included, initially we consider the effects of policy changes starting from a position of full equilibrium, where $Y = Y^*$. Of course, policy changes would normally be made to correct a disequilibrium that had been caused by some exogenous shock. If we start our analysis from disequilibrium, however, there can be many different reasons for disequilibrium (that is, shocks from many different sources), and the effect of policy changes may depend upon what has caused the deviation of Y from Y^*. When we start at Y^*, there should be no surprise to find that eventually we return to Y^*. What matters is to understand how the adjustment mechanism of the economy works when perfect capital mobility is

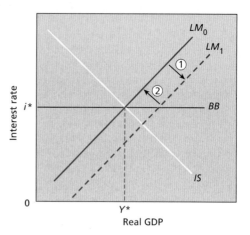

Figure 29.2 Monetary policy with fixed exchange rates and perfect capital mobility

Monetary policy is powerless to influence economic activity under fixed exchange rates and perfect capital mobility. An attempted cut in domestic interest rates increases the money supply and shifts the *LM* curve to the right from LM_0 to LM_1. However, the smallest fall in domestic interest rates causes a massive desired capital outflow. This puts downward pressure on the exchange rate. The monetary authorities are forced to buy sterling immediately in order to stop the exchange rate falling, and the *LM* curve shifts back to its original position, LM_0.

assumed, and how the exchange rate regime affects this. We will discuss how the result might change if we start with disequilibrium later. We first discuss a fixed exchange rate regime.

Monetary policy

Starting with an economy in full equilibrium, we assume that the monetary authorities relax the monetary policy stance by reducing the domestic interest rate. The analysis, which is shown in Figure 29.2, is simple under a fixed exchange rate regime.

The policy change, if it could be made to stick, would shift the *LM* curve to the right (because a lower interest rate would lead to a higher money stock, as discussed in Chapter 26), which in turn would shift the *AD* curve to the right. However, we do not bother to translate this shift into an aggregate demand shift, because it will have to be reversed immediately. As soon as domestic interest rates dip slightly below world rates, there will be a massive sale of domestic bonds. This will create an excess supply of sterling in the foreign exchange market (because holders

---

[4] The exact expression that must hold for expected yields on the two bonds denominated in different currencies to be equal is: $(1 + i) = (1 + i^*)(e_t/e_{t+1})$, where i is the yield on UK bonds (expressed as a decimal, so 10 per cent is 0.1), i^* is the yield on foreign bonds, e_t is the exchange rate (\$ per £) at the beginning of the holding period, and e_{t+1} is the exchange rate expected to obtain at the end of the holding period.

are selling sterling bonds and converting the proceeds into dollars to buy dollar bonds), and the authorities will have to buy sterling (and sell reserves) in order to stop the exchange rate from falling.

As they buy back sterling, just as when they sell bonds in Chapter 26 and 27 (here they are selling dollars), the domestic money supply is reduced, and the *LM* curve shifts back to its initial position. In effect the domestic monetary authorities are forced to abandon their attempt to lower domestic interest rates by the massive capital outflows (and loss of foreign exchange reserves) that follow. The conclusion is that with perfect capital mobility and fixed exchange rates the monetary authorities have control over neither domestic interest rates nor the stock of money. If they do not set the domestic interest rates at the ruling world interest rate, they are swamped with massive inflows or outflows of financial capital (bond sales or purchases). Thus perfect capital mobility means that it is impossible to

use monetary policy to influence real economic activity under fixed exchange rates. For exactly the same reasons there cannot be independent monetary policies in the member states of the euro zone—the ECB can change the interest rate for all member countries, but no single country can change its own interest rate (indeed, there is only one interest rate for all member countries).

Monetary policy under fixed exchange rates and perfect capital mobility cannot exert any independent influence over real economic activity.

Fiscal policy

The analysis of what happens when fiscal policy changes is more complicated than in the case of a monetary policy change. It is also very different from events in the absence of capital flows. The course of events is illustrated in Figure 29.3.

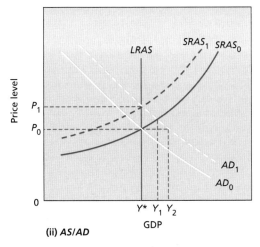

Figure 29.3 Fiscal policy with fixed exchange rates and perfect capital mobility

Starting from full equilibrium, an increase in government spending creates a significant stimulus to real activity in the short run, but in the long run it leads to a higher price level and a current account deficit. The increase in government spending shifts the *IS* curve from IS_0 to IS_1 in part (i). With a given money supply this puts upward pressure on domestic interest rates. The slightest rise in domestic interest rates causes a massive capital inflow, which puts upward pressure on the exchange rate. To stop the exchange rate rising, the monetary authorities sell sterling in the foreign exchange market. This increases the money supply and shifts the *LM* curve to the right, from LM_0 to LM_1. The combined effect of the *IS* and *LM* curves shifting is that *AD* shifts right, from AD_0 to AD_1, as shown in part (ii).

The increase in aggregate demand causes GDP to increase from Y^* to Y_1 in the short run, and there is a small initial increase in the price level. (This price level rise shifts the *IS* and *LM* curves slightly leftward to IS_2 and LM_2 so that they intersect at Y_1 rather than Y_2.) Net exports become negative. In the long run inflationary pressure causes the price level to rise to P_1 as the *SRAS* curve shifts up to $SRAS_1$ and GDP returns to Y^*. However, the sustained rise in the price level (for given foreign prices) causes a permanent trade deficit, which is equal to the budget deficit. At price level P_1 the real money supply has fallen, so the *LM* curve shifts back to LM_0. The higher price of domestic goods causes net exports to shift downwards, so *IS* also shifts back to its original position, IS_0.

Again, we start with the economy in full equilibrium. We need also to clarify what the monetary authorities are doing. As we explained above, the monetary authorities cannot set *both* the domestic interest rate *and* the exchange rate. Since we are studying the fixed exchange rate case here, we must temporarily drop the assumption that the monetary authorities are fixing the domestic interest rate. Rather, the monetary policy is pegging the exchange rate, and the interest rate is determined by world interest rates.

The assumed fiscal policy change is an increase in government spending. The initial effect of this increase is to shift the IS curve to the right. With a given initial nominal money stock (given LM curve), this will put upward pressure on domestic interest rates. However, even the smallest rise in domestic interest rates generates a capital inflow (foreign demand for domestic bonds) and creates excess demand for sterling in the foreign exchange markets. To stop the exchange rate rising, the monetary authorities have to sell sterling and buy foreign currency. These sales of sterling increase the supply of money and shift the LM curve to the right.

Thus the initial rightward shift of the IS curve has been reinforced by a rightward shift of the LM curve. The AD curve shifts to the right as a result of each of these shifts. The combined effect is shown in part (ii) of the figure. This is a bigger shift of AD than would have resulted from a shift in the IS curve alone. Indeed, the size of the horizontal shift of AD is equal to the full value of the simple (open economy) multiplier, because there is no negative feedback (via higher interest rates) from the monetary sector. This comes about because interest rates cannot rise, so the authorities have to increase the money supply to avoid an exchange rate appreciation.

This is not the end of the story. The increase in aggregate demand shifts the aggregate demand curve to intersect the initial short-run aggregate supply curve at a level of GDP well above its potential level. The resulting inflationary gap causes a short-term boom in the economy, and real GDP rises temporarily above its potential level.

The inflationary gap, once created, puts upward pressure on the domestic price level. Initially this is felt only in output prices. The increase in output prices, combined with the increase in real GDP, creates a trade deficit. The current account balance deteriorates because (induced) imports increase with domestic income. The price level rise reinforces this increase because (with a fixed exchange rate and given foreign prices) domestic goods become more expensive relative to foreign goods. Thus there is a change in the import propensity and a fall in net exports. Indeed, it is this price level rise that moves the economy back up the AD curve and reduces the impact on GDP, compared with the full impact of the simple multiplier (as measured by the horizontal shift in AD).

In the longer term inflationary forces pass through to input prices, and the short-run aggregate supply curve shifts up to the left. This raises the price level further, as the economy moves back up the AD curve and GDP returns to its potential level. The higher price level reduces the real money supply, and so the LM curve shifts back leftwards to its initial position. It also further increases the trade deficit, and this downward shift in net exports also shifts the IS curve back leftwards to its original position.

Thus instead of crowding out investment (as would happen in the absence of capital flows), the increase in government spending has led to a trade deficit of equal value. (Real GDP returns to its original level but real national expenditure has risen by the amount of extra government spending. The excess of national expenditure over national output is equal to the trade deficit.)

An increase in government spending (starting at full equilibrium), with fixed exchange rates and perfect capital mobility, creates a short-run economic boom, but the long-run effect is an increase in the domestic price level and a trade deficit.

This trade deficit will be equal to the government budget deficit if the initial position was one of budget balance and trade balance. Notice also that the mechanism that brought about the trade deficit was a rise in domestic prices (relative to foreign prices). This is equivalent to a rise in the real exchange rate, even though the nominal exchange rate is fixed. However, in this case there has been no crowding out of investment because fiscal policy is powerless to influence interest rates. In effect domestic investment can be financed at the going world interest rate. The trade deficit is matched by a capital inflow (foreign purchases of domestic bonds) of equal size.

This is the end of the story in our model, but it cannot be the end of the story in reality. We have an equilibrium in which there is a current account deficit on the balance of payments and, therefore, continuing capital inflows. The domestic economy is borrowing from the rest of the world to finance the excess of spending over output.

If this borrowing finances current consumption (government consumption in this case), the wealth of the economy will be falling (relative to the initial trend position), and this cannot go on for ever. At some point the wealth effects will lead to either a shift in domestic expenditures (downward) or a reversal of government policy. (The government cannot build up infinite debt, and any financing problems may cause reserve losses.) The modelling of such wealth effects is beyond the scope of this book. Readers should merely note that some further adjustment must happen.

However, if the borrowing finances real investment (or if an equivalent amount of real investment takes place anyway), the story could be quite different. If the return on real investment were greater than the interest rate on foreign borrowing, this economy would be increasing its wealth over time. So long as investment returns continued to exceed interest costs, this position could be sustained and potential GDP would be growing over time. Therefore, one cannot assume that a current account balance of payments deficit is always undesirable. This reinforces the point first stated in Chapter 28.

Policy changes with floating exchange rates

We now turn to the analysis of policy changes under a regime of floating exchange rates. This is the current regime in the United Kingdom, as it is for most major countries (where the euro zone is counted as one country), so this analysis is the one that is appropriate for analysing the effects of macroeconomic policy in the major economies today. It represents the culmination of all our efforts to build a macroeconomic model. We return to a framework in which the monetary authorities set the interest rate (as the exchange rate is set by market forces in a floating exchange rate regime).

Monetary policy

Again, we start with a relaxation of domestic monetary policy in the form of a reduction in the interest rate initiated by the domestic monetary authorities from a position of full equilibrium, as illustrated in Figure 29.4. This shifts the LM curve downward to the right (because the authorities buy bonds and increase the money stock in order to lower the market interest rate).

The fall in domestic interest rates, with perfect capital mobility, would normally cause a massive capital outflow. However, since the exchange rate is floating, the emergence of an excess supply of sterling causes an immediate drop in the exchange rate. It drops to the point where it is expected to appreciate at a rate sufficient to compensate for the lower domestic interest rate; in other words it overshoots its long-run equilibrium in a downward direction. We discussed this notion of overshooting in Chapter 28, pages 487–90.

The fall in the nominal exchange rate also represents a fall in the real exchange rate, because the domestic price level does not change quickly, while the exchange rate has

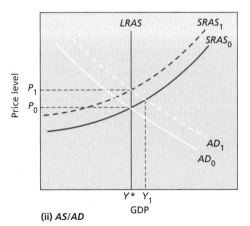

Figure 29.4 Monetary policy with floating exchange rates and perfect capital mobility

Starting at full equilibrium, a monetary loosening causes an output boom in the short run but in the long run causes only higher prices and currency depreciation. The LM curve shifts to the right. Any fall in the domestic interest rate causes the exchange rate to depreciate to a point from which it is expected to appreciate. This involves overshooting and a fall in the real exchange rate. This fall in the real exchange rate shifts the net export function upwards, so, as part (i) shows, there is a shift in the IS curve from IS_0 to IS_1 accompanying the initial shift in the LM curve from LM_0 to LM_1. The combined effect of these two shifts on aggregate demand is shown in part (ii) as the shift from AD_0 to AD_1.

The increase in aggregate demand creates an inflationary gap. GDP increases from Y^* to Y_1 in the short run, and the price level starts to rise to the level indicated by the intersection of AD_1 and $SRAS_0$. Eventually inflationary pressure works through to input prices, and the short-run aggregate supply curve shifts upwards to $SRAS_1$. The price level rises to P_1, and GDP falls back to Y^*. The LM curve shifts back to LM_0 as the rise in price level reduces the real money supply. The IS curve shifts back to IS_0 as higher domestic prices raise the relative price of domestic goods and the net export function shifts downwards. The long-run outcome is an increase in prices but the same real GDP.

fallen instantaneously. So the relative price of domestic goods has fallen. This leads to an upward shift in the net export function, which causes a shift of the IS curve to the right. The combined effect of the rightward shifts of the LM and IS curves causes a rightward shift in the AD curve.

The increase in aggregate demand takes GDP beyond its potential level and creates an inflationary gap. In the short run the economy experiences a boom in output and a small increase in the domestic price level. This increase in prices reduces the real money supply slightly and also offsets a little the upward shift in net exports; so both the IS and LM curves shift back a fraction relative to their new positions. However, the full adjustment takes place in the longer term, when inflationary pressure works through into input costs and the short-run aggregate supply curve shifts upwards.

As the price level rises to its long-run equilibrium, the real money supply returns to its original level, so the LM curve shifts back to its initial position, reversing the initial interest rate fall. Also the real exchange rate returns to its initial position (the price level rises in proportion to the long-run currency depreciation), so net exports shift back to where they started. Notice, however, that during the adjustment period the current account has been in surplus because of the lower real exchange rate (and therefore there have been capital outflows), and so there has been an accumulation of net foreign assets (or a rundown of foreign liabilities). This accumulation has occurred because national expenditure has been less than national output during the adjustment process (i.e. there has been a trade surplus). The current account is back in balance at the long-run equilibrium.

An expansionary monetary policy under floating exchange rates with perfect capital mobility causes a boom in real economic activity in the short run, but the long-run effect is a higher price level and a depreciation of the nominal exchange rate, with no permanent gain in real output and an unchanged real exchange rate.

Although we assume in the context of our model that GDP returns to its potential level, in practice there may be some long-run real effects. During the transition period national wealth has increased. Lower interest rates cause a temporary rise in investment which creates domestic assets, and the temporary trade surplus causes an accumulation of foreign assets. These effects are ignored in our model, but in reality they may be significant.

Notice also the change in the monetary adjustment mechanism when there is perfect capital mobility. In the absence of capital flows the monetary expansion creates a desired current account deficit, whereas in the presence of capital flows it creates an exchange rate depreciation, which results in an actual current account surplus and a capital outflow. In the long run the outcome is the same (a

higher price level and proportional depreciation of the currency with the same real national income), but external payments adjustment during the transition to full equilibrium is quite different.

Fiscal policy

The case of a fiscal policy expansion under floating exchange rates with perfect capital mobility is illustrated in Figure 29.5. Again, we take as our policy change an increase in government spending at full equilibrium.

The increase in government spending shifts the IS curve to the right. What happens next depends on what the monetary authorities do. We examine two cases. In the first the authorities adjust the domestic interest rate upwards in order to maintain a constant money stock; and in the second case the authorities hold the domestic interest rate fixed by buying bonds and increasing the money stock.

Fixed money stock With a given money supply (fixed LM curve), a rightward shift of the IS curve, resulting from the expansionary fiscal policy, puts upward pressure on domestic interest rates. Any rise in domestic interest rates creates massive desired capital inflows and thereby puts upward pressure on the exchange rate. The exchange rate immediately appreciates to a point from which it can be expected to depreciate at a rate equal to the interest differential.

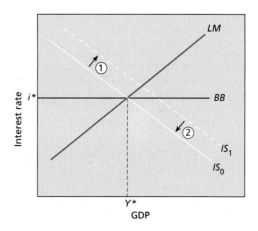

Figure 29.5 Fiscal policy with floating exchange rates and perfect capital mobility

Starting at full equilibrium, a fiscal expansion leads to a currency appreciation which crowds out an equivalent volume of net exports, causing a current account deficit but little or no stimulus to GDP. The initial increase in government spending shifts the IS curve to the right from IS_0 to IS_1. But the resulting appreciation of the exchange rate (real and nominal) shifts the net export function downwards, which shifts the IS curve back to the left.

The exchange rate appreciation, for a given initial price level, also appreciates the real exchange rate, which means that domestic goods become more expensive than foreign goods. This rise in the relative price of domestic goods shifts the net export function downwards, and therefore also shifts the *IS* curve back towards its original position. A current account balance of payments deficit results, which is matched by net capital inflows.

There is ambiguity about the precise course of aggregate demand in the short run. The increase in government spending shifts *AD* to the right, but the downward shift in net exports shifts it back to the left. On balance the likely outcome is that it will remain roughly at its initial position. The factors affecting the adjustment of net exports to an exchange rate change are discussed in Box 29.2. In any event the effect on real GDP, even in the short run, may well be negligible.

The long-run outcome is that there is a trade deficit that matches the government budget deficit. There is also a permanent increase in the real exchange rate, brought about by a sustained appreciation of the nominal exchange rate, though less than the appreciation achieved during the overshooting phase. There is a significant difference between short-run adjustment to a fiscal policy expansion under floating exchange rates with perfect capital mobility compared to the case with no capital flows. With no capital

flows the increase in *G* creates an inflationary gap and a currency depreciation, the domestic price level rises, and interest rates rise, thereby crowding out investment. With capital flows the same increase in the relative price of domestic output is brought about by exchange rate appreciation, but there is no interest rate rise, and no sustained crowding-out of investment. There is, however, a trade deficit which matches the budget deficit.

Again, this cannot be the end of the story, because there is ongoing borrowing by the government and increasing indebtedness to foreigners. Thus similar wealth effects arise to those we discussed in the context of fiscal policy under fixed exchange rates. The big difference, however, is that under floating exchange rates a fiscal expansion, holding *M* constant, creates a minimal stimulus to real GDP, whereas under fixed rates a fiscal expansion leads to a short-run boom.

An expansionary fiscal policy, under floating exchange rates, has little impact on real GDP in the short run when the money stock is fixed; rather, it causes an exchange rate appreciation and a trade deficit. In the long run there is a permanent appreciation of the real exchange rate, and the government budget deficit is equal to the trade deficit.

Fixed interest rate The response to a fiscal policy change is somewhat different if the monetary authorities maintain

Box 29.2 The J-curve

In this chapter we consider what happens when there is a change in monetary or fiscal policy under fixed or floating exchange rates. We do not ask what happens under a fixed exchange rate regime if there is a discrete devaluation. In such a devaluation there is a sudden fall in the exchange rate at which the currency is pegged.

Devaluations usually occur when a persistent current account deficit is causing a serious drain on official reserves. Their purpose is to reduce the deficit and, thereby, reduce outflows of official international reserves. However, the effect on the current account is often not immediately positive.

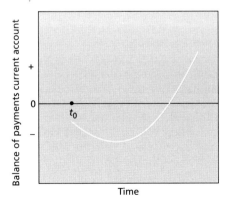

A common pattern is for the current account first to deteriorate further but later to improve. This pattern is known as the J-curve because of the shape of the curve the current account traces over time. The figure plots the path of the current account over time, starting in deficit. A devaluation at time t_0 initially makes the deficit worse, but eventually it leads to a surplus after a lag of perhaps two years.

The reason for the initial deterioration in the current account is that volumes of imports and exports take time to adjust to the new relative prices. Devaluation makes domestic goods cheaper than foreign goods and if volumes did not change at all, the domestic currency value of exports would stay the same but the domestic currency value of imports would rise (because their price has gone up in domestic currency terms).

It is only when the volumes of imports and exports adjust more than in proportion to the change in relative goods prices that the current account of the balance of payments improves. After the 1967 devaluation of sterling, it took between eighteen months and two years for the current account to move into surplus.

The J-curve is also applicable to a world of floating exchange rates after a sudden sustained exchange rate change. It helps us to understand that it takes many months, if not years, for the trade account fully to adjust to such exchange rate changes. Thus when the UK left the ERM in September 1992 its currency devalued by about 20 per cent against the US dollar and the effects of this took several years to work through. When exchange rates change in small steps, the economic adjustments are still there, but they are harder to detect.

a fixed interest rate, rather than raising rates in order to keep the money supply constant. Indeed, the outcome is initially similar to that illustrated in Figure 29.4. The fiscal policy expansion shifts the *IS* curve to the right, and the money supply increase that results from the authorities' attempts to keep the interest rate from rising shifts the *LM* curve to the right. Thus the *AD* curve shifts to the right and GDP goes from Y^* to Y_1, as shown in Figure 29.4(ii). This creates an inflationary gap, and wage rises eventually shift the *SRAS* curve to the left, returning the economy to equilibrium at the original level of GDP but with a higher price level.

This is different from the case where the money stock is fixed because the fiscal expansion has given a temporary stimulus to real output. The increase in aggregate spending coming from higher government consumption does not crowd out net exports via a rapid rise in the real exchange rate. Rather, an expansion of the money stock acts to keep the real exchange rate down. Thus the money stock expansion created by the monetary authorities reinforces the expansionary effect of fiscal policy in the short run. However, this expansion of the money stock must eventually lead to a higher price level, and this rise in the price level will eventually crowd out net exports. Investment is not crowded out because interest rates do not change. But something has to be crowded out once the level of GDP returns to its potential level, Y^*: because *G* is bigger, some other component of $C + I + G + NX$ must be smaller. Thus the economy returns to equilibrium with a current account deficit. This will be financed by borrowing from abroad.

A fiscal policy expansion does have a short-run expansionary effect on the economy if the monetary authorities increase the money supply to accommodate the increase in GDP at a constant interest rate. But net exports are crowded out in the long run by a higher domestic price level that raises the real exchange rate.

Again this cannot be the end of the story, as the current account deficit will lead to declining national wealth. This decline in wealth will eventually lead to an expenditure fall that will correct the imbalance in external payments; however, this is where our analysis stops.

Let us now summarize what we have learned about the adjustment to monetary and fiscal policy changes in the presence of perfect capital mobility, assuming that we start in full equilibrium. We will then see whether starting in disequilibrium makes any difference.

1. *Under fixed exchange rates* monetary policy is powerless to influence real economic activity. The money supply is demand-determined, and the authorities have no discretion over interest rates. A fiscal policy expansion under fixed exchange rates causes a short-run boom in real activity, but this leads to inflation. The long-run effect is a permanent rise in the domestic price level and the real exchange rate, a budget deficit, and a trade deficit financed by capital inflows.

2. *Under floating exchange rates* an expansionary monetary policy creates an inflationary boom in real activity in the short run; in the long run the price level rises in proportion to the money stock increase, and the nominal exchange rate depreciates in the same proportion. A fiscal policy expansion under floating exchange rates creates little or no increase in real GDP if the money stock is held fixed, even in the short run. In the long run there is a sustained real and nominal exchange rate appreciation, and the government budget deficit is matched by a trade deficit and capital account surplus. In contrast, if the monetary authorities maintain a fixed interest rate, and therefore increase the money stock to accompany the fiscal policy expansion, there will be a short-term stimulus to real GDP. In the long run the price level will rise and net exports will be crowded out, via a real exchange rate rise as before.

Policy changes to correct disequilibrium

We now need to check if our conclusions are specific to the case in which the economy is initially in equilibrium. In reality policymakers will want to use monetary and fiscal policies as tools for returning the economy to equilibrium, not for moving it away. There are many possible examples, but we can get a feel for the significance of the equilibrium assumption by studying a few illustrative cases in depth. We will look closely only at flexible exchange rates, as that is the current situation for most major economies, and we will consider only the response to a negative aggregate demand shock. However, the fixed exchange rate case is easy to summarize, and we will now do that before proceeding.

Let us suppose that the economy is in a situation where *Y* is less than Y^*, and that this has come about because of an autonomous fall in domestic investment. Under a fixed exchange rate regime with perfect capital mobility, monetary policy can do nothing to change this situation. The monetary authorities cannot lower interest rates (because of the horizontal *BB* curve), nor can they increase the money supply. Hence the conclusion about the impotence of monetary policy under fixed exchange rates is robust, even when we start in disequilibrium. This result carries over to the economies of those EU countries that are members of the euro zone. Essentially the national monetary authorities have no power to affect monetary conditions in their own country. Only the ECB can change the monetary stance (for all eleven member countries at once).

Fiscal policy, however, can have a beneficial effect. The fall in investment shifts the *IS* and *AD* curves to the left. An increase in government spending can shift these two curves back to their initial position without any of the longer-term harmful effects that arise when *G* is increased starting from full equilibrium.[5] There is no real exchange rate appreciation or crowding-out of the balance of payments, though there is a budget deficit. Certainly, government spending has replaced investment expenditure in equilibrium GDP, but this is not crowding-out since the causation is reversed—*G* is filling the gap left by an autonomous fall in *I*. Crowding-out involves higher *G* causing lower *I* through higher interest rates.

Now let the initial negative demand shock be an exogenous fall in export demand, rather than an autonomous fall in investment. The offsetting increase in *G* and the accompanying budget deficit will be matched by a current account balance of payments deficit in equilibrium. But again this is not crowding-out, because of the reversed causality. Also the increase in *G* will only improve the outcome if it is timed correctly. This point also arises under a floating exchange rate, so let us now look more closely at policy responses to a negative demand shock under floating exchange rates.

Monetary policy

Let us suppose, again, that a negative demand shock results from an autonomous fall in investment with a given initial money stock. The situation created by this investment fall is illustrated in Figure 29.6. The fall in investment shifts the *IS* curve to the left. This is associated with a shift to the left of the *AD* curve. The leftward shift of *AD* leads to a small fall in the price level, given an upward-sloping *SRAS* curve; so with a constant nominal money stock the *LM* curve shifts slightly to the right, because the

---

[5] Notice, however, that some restrictions are imposed on the size of budget deficits for euro member countries by the Stability and Growth Pact. These are discussed in Chapter 35.

(i) *IS/LM*

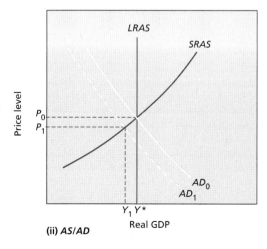

(ii) *AS/AD*

Figure 29.6 Macro policies to correct a disequilibrium

Monetary and fiscal policy can help the economy recover from a negative demand shock, so long as they are appropriately timed. The negative demand shock is assumed to be an autonomous fall in investment. The economy is initially in full equilibrium at Y^*. The fall in investment shifts the *IS* curve from IS_0 to IS_1 in part (i), and it shifts the *AD* curve from AD_0 to AD_1 in part (ii). The resulting fall in the price level from P_0 to P_1 increases the real money supply (assuming the authorities adjust interest rates to hold the money stock constant), which shifts the *LM* curve to LM_1. The economy thus goes to GDP level Y_1, where there is a recessionary gap.

In the absence of policy changes the automatic adjustment mechanism will eventually bring GDP back to Y^*. Monetary policy can speed up this adjustment process by lowering domestic interest rates and causing a currency depreciation. Fiscal policy can shift the *IS* and *AD* curves back to their original positions.

real money stock has risen. Hence the effect of the fall in investment is to lower GDP from Y^* to Y_1 in the figure.[6]

With the economy at Y_1, if the monetary authorities permit interest rates to fall in order to keep the nominal money stock fixed, desired capital outflows will cause the exchange rate to depreciate. It will fall to the point where it is expected to appreciate at just the right rate to compensate for the lower domestic interest rate. The currency depreciation, combined with the lower price level, means that domestic goods have fallen in price relative to foreign goods. There has been a real exchange rate depreciation. This causes an upward shift in the net export function and an associated current account balance of payments surplus.

The upward shift in the net export function shifts the *IS* curve back to the right, and this could be sufficient to return the economy to equilibrium at Y^*. However, it is possible that the initial recessionary gap may also cause the *SRAS* curve to shift to the right, via a reduction in money wage rates. Both of these responses, however, take some time, so the monetary authorities could, in principle, speed up the return to Y^* by increasing the nominal money supply, which would shift the *LM* curve to the right.

The advisability of such a monetary response depends upon the authorities being able to achieve their effects quickly. Recall from Chapter 27 that some economists believe that monetary policy works with 'long and variable lags'. If the effects of this monetary stimulus are not felt until GDP has already returned to a level close to potential, then, rather than help end the recession, it could cause the economy to overshoot into an inflationary boom. In any event the monetary stimulus would have to be reversed at some stage if inflation is to be avoided in the longer term.

Thus monetary policy can be used in the short term to offset the recessionary effects of a negative demand shock, but whether this can be done with enough accuracy to improve on the automatic adjustment mechanisms is controversial.

Monetary policy affects the real economy via the effects of the exchange rate on net exports, and via the effects of interest rate changes on investment, but timing this response correctly is difficult.

Fiscal policy

Now let us consider the possibilities of a fiscal reaction to the same negative demand shock that is illustrated in Figure 29.6. As a result of the fall in investment, GDP has fallen from Y^* to Y_1, assuming that the authorities have adjusted interest rates downward to maintain a constant money stock.

An appropriate increase in government spending would shift the *IS* and *AD* curves back to their initial positions

and thereby restore GDP to Y^*. If this could be timed exactly to coincide with the fall in investment, there would be no need for a fall in interest rates and no exchange rate depreciation, and so there would be no shift in the net export function. The only change at full equilibrium would be lower investment and a budget deficit (assuming that the budget was in balance before the increase in government spending).[7]

However, as with monetary policy, there is the problem of getting the timing right. If the increase in government expenditure takes effect after the automatic adjustment process does its job, then the increased spending could create an inflationary gap (as happens when *G* is increased with the economy starting at Y^* as above).

There is, however, an important difference between fiscal and monetary stabilization in response to this same negative demand shock. Monetary stabilization policy speeds up the automatic response mechanism by lowering the interest rate and exchange rate further than they would otherwise go. If monetary policy is timed accurately, the long-run outcome is the same as if automatic stabilizing forces did the work. Monetary policy just helps to get the economy to full equilibrium more quickly.

By contrast, fiscal policy cuts out the automatic adjustment mechanism and leads to a different composition of final demand in equilibrium. The increased budget deficit crowds out an equivalent volume of net exports, relative to what would have happened if the automatic adjustment had been left alone. This is because the fiscal stimulus stops the fall in the nominal and real exchange rate which would otherwise have shifted the net export function upwards.

In the case of an initial fall in investment the automatic adjustment mechanism creates a current account balance of payments surplus at full equilibrium. A fiscal stimulus replaces this with a budget deficit (and a current account balance at full equilibrium). If the initial negative demand shock had been caused by a fall in net exports, the automatic adjustment mechanism would have restored current account balance at full equilibrium. But an offsetting fiscal stimulus would mean that there was both a current account deficit and a budget deficit at full employment.

In short, when the economy starts at less than potential GDP and has a flexible exchange rate, both monetary and fiscal policies can speed up the adjustment of GDP back to its potential level.

However, whether actual fiscal and monetary policies

[6] The initial fall in GDP would be much greater if the monetary authorities were pegging the interest rate rather than the nominal money stock. In that case GDP would initially fall to Y_2 in the figure. The authorities would have to abandon this pegged interest rate policy in order to use monetary policy to stimulate the economy, so we revert to the assumption of an initially fixed nominal money supply.

[7] If the negative demand shock had been caused by an exogenous fall in net exports, rather than investment, the net effect would be a sustained budget deficit and a balance of payments deficit in full equilibrium.

improve on the automatic adjustment mechanism in practice depends crucially on timing. If the impact of policy is felt too late, it will push the recovery of GDP beyond potential GDP and into an inflationary boom, even though it was conceived as a response to an earlier recessionary gap.

Some implications

Readers will probably have found the material in this chapter hard going, on first reading. However, the effort is worthwhile because we have now reached a very advanced level of understanding of a coherent model of the macroeconomy. In the following chapters we will discuss a number of important policy issues. Before doing so it is worth drawing together some of the implications of what we have already learned.

The transmission of monetary policy

When we first introduced a monetary sector into our macro model in Chapter 26, we discussed the way in which changes in monetary policy are transmitted to the real economy via changes in domestic interest rates.

The transmission mechanism was set out as follows: the monetary authorities decide to stimulate the economy by lowering the interest rate. In order to lower the interest rate they buy bonds, and this leads to an increase in the money supply. The lower interest rate increases investment, which, via the multiplier, increases desired aggregate expenditure. This increase in desired aggregate expenditure means that there is an increase in aggregate demand. The increase in aggregate demand then leads to an increase in real GDP and a rise in the price level. As the price level rises further, in response to inflationary pressure, the real money stock falls and GDP returns to its potential level at a higher price level.

We have now learned that the transmission of monetary policy does not work quite like this in most forms of open economy. With fixed exchange rates monetary policy is powerless to influence the real economy, because excess supply of the home currency in the foreign exchange market will rapidly force a policy reversal. This happens especially quickly in the modern world of highly mobile financial capital.

Under floating exchange rates with perfect capital mobility monetary policy is able to stimulate real activity in the short run. It does so largely because a monetary policy expansion depreciates the real exchange rate, which stimulates net exports. Deliberate use of monetary policy can be helpful in speeding the adjustment to a negative demand shock. In our model nominal interest rates fall temporarily and this stimulates investment. However, in practice the effect on investment may be small. Hence it is likely that the principal link in the transmission mechanism from the monetary sector to real activity in an open economy, with floating exchange rates, is through the exchange rate to net exports.

The efficacy of fiscal policy

We have found that fiscal policy is a very powerful tool for stimulating real activity in the short run in an economy with fixed exchange rates and mobile international capital. In that case the monetary authorities are forced by capital inflows to reinforce the fiscal expansion with an increase in the money supply.

Under floating exchange rates with mobile capital and a fixed money supply, however, the expansionary fiscal policy creates a currency appreciation, which neutralizes the stimulation to real activity. A fiscal stimulus would give a temporary boost to the real economy where the monetary authorities peg the interest rate—and thus create an accommodatory rise in the money stock. The long-run effect of a fiscal expansion, with no capital flows, is to crowd out investment. But with mobile capital a fiscal expansion crowds out net exports via an appreciation of the real exchange rate.

There is a potential role for fiscal policy in offsetting the negative demand shocks that cause recessionary gaps. In such cases, at best, fiscal adjustment would replace the automatic adjustment mechanism of the economy and would lead to a deterioration of the budget balance in equilibrium. However, there may be situations in which this is preferable to waiting for recovery.

In general the role of fiscal policy in influencing macroeconomic activity is much more limited in a world of floating exchange rates and mobile international capital than it is under a fixed exchange rate regime, or in the world of restricted capital flows.

Global transmission of cycles

Small countries may be price-takers in globalized financial markets, so that they have only limited freedom to influence domestic nominal interest rates, and even less freedom to influence domestic real interest rates. But this does not mean that the world interest rates will not move. Rather, it means that interest rates will tend to move up

Box 29.3 International policy co-ordination?

The analyses of macroeconomic policy in this chapter have taken place in the context of a single economy. However, openness to foreign trade and the globalization of financial markets have caused all major countries in the world to be influenced at least as much by global economic forces as by local conditions. No country has been able to insulate itself from the effects of a worldwide recession, of which there have been three since 1970 (1974–5, 1980–2, and 1990–2). Chart (i) shows the growth rate of GDP for the world, illustrating the three periods of slowdown.

The two parts of chart (ii) show the GDP gaps of the G7 countries since 1982; that is, the difference between actual and potential GDP. Clearly the cycles in all these countries are closely related, though the USA, the UK, and Canada peaked earlier and started to recover earlier than Germany, France, Italy, and Japan.

Open economies are ultimately constrained by world aggregate demand and appear unable significantly to offset swings in world demand by local monetary or fiscal policy changes. No one country acting alone (except perhaps the United States, or the EU countries acting together) can influence world aggregate demand substantially. So perhaps the only possibility of stabilizing world aggregate demand is for countries to co-ordinate their macroeconomic policies.

However, the realities of the politics of policy-formation create formidable obstacles to co-ordinated action. There are already decision lags and implementation lags in the policy-formation process in each country. These would be magnified if policy were to be determined at the supranational level. Realistically, explicit co-ordination of macroeconomic policies is not going to happen in the foreseeable future. This may mean that the global business cycle is a phenomenon countries will have to continue to live with.

(i) Growth and world real GDP

(ii) Major industrial countries: output gaps

Note: Shaded areas indicate IMF staff projections.

Source: IMF, *World Economic Outlook*, October 1997.

and down together as the demand and supply of savings and loans moves up and down at the world level.

World interest rate movements will be transmitted to real activity through our original transmission mechanism. Correlation of interest rate movements around the world also causes correlation of the cycles in real activity. Chart (i) in Box 29.3 shows the growth rate of world GDP since 1970. Also shown, in the two parts of charts (ii), are the GDP gaps over the most recent economic cycle for several of the major economies. Clearly, there is a very high level of correlation of the cycles about trend GDP in most of the industrial countries of the world. This suggests that one country acting alone cannot do much to stabilize its economic cycle, as it will still be subject to fluctuations in world demand (and supply). The world cycle may only be

controllable, if at all, by co-ordinated stabilization policy among groups of countries, or at the world level.

This argument should not be taken to mean that domestic macro policies do not matter. Rather, the point is that they are not the only things that matter. External influences are much more important today than they were, say, in the 1950s. But there are, certainly, many things that domestic policymakers can do that affect the performance of their home economy for better or worse. Despite the clear existence of a global business cycle, there have been widely differing experiences with regard to inflation and unemployment among economies more or less equally exposed to external forces. It is to the causes and cures of inflation and unemployment that we turn in Chapters 30 and 31.

Summary

cycles in one country are often closely related to cycles in other important economies.

Why does openness matter?

■ Openness of the economy matters because trade and capital flows influence real activity, international financial markets influence domestic money markets, and the exchange rate regime determines which monetary instruments are available to the authorities.

Macro policy in a world with perfect capital mobility

■ Perfect capital mobility can be represented by a horizontal *BB* line in the *IS/LM* diagram.

■ Under fixed exchange rates and perfect capital mobility an expansionary monetary policy is rapidly reversed through losses of foreign exchange reserves. It has no real impact.

■ Starting from equilibrium GDP, an increase in government spending, under fixed exchange rates and perfect capital mobility, creates an inflationary gap and a significant stimulus to real GDP in the short run. In the long run there is a rise in the relative price of domestic goods, a budget deficit, and a trade deficit.

■ Starting from equilibrium, a monetary policy expansion, under floating exchange rates and perfect capital mobility, leads to a currency depreciation and creates an inflationary gap. In the long run the price level rises in proportion to the money supply increase and the exchange rate depreciates in the same proportion.

■ Starting from equilibrium, an increase in government spending, with floating exchange rates and perfect capital mobility, creates little or no stimulus to real GDP if the money stock is held constant; but it does create a temporary stimulus if the interest rate is held constant. In the long run in both cases it leads to a real exchange rate appreciation and a trade deficit. The budget deficit and the trade deficit are of equal size.

■ Starting with a recessionary gap, both monetary and fiscal policies can speed up the return to potential GDP if they are timed correctly. Fiscal policy can be used to increase final demand, while monetary policy can lower interest rates and/or the exchange rate.

Some implications

■ The transmission mechanism of monetary policy and the efficacy of fiscal policy are both affected by openness and capital mobility.

■ Financial and expenditure linkages between economies mean that business cycles are a global phenomenon, and

Topics for review

■ Monetary policy
■ Fiscal policy
■ Fixed exchange rates
■ Floating exchange rates
■ Capital mobility
■ Overshooting
■ Crowding-out

Questions for discussion

1 Explain why it is that the *BB* line in Figure 29.1 is horizontal.

2 Outline carefully what would happen to the domestic economy if, starting from equilibrium with a zero current account deficit and the economy at potential GDP, there was an exogenous increase in export demand coming from a rise in incomes in the rest of the world. Assume that the home economy is operating under a fixed exchange rate regime.

3 Repeat question 2 for a floating exchange rate regime.

4 Suppose that the Netherlands, a member of the euro zone, suffered a negative demand shock that did not affect directly any other euro zone countries (caused perhaps by a collapse of world demand for a product made by Dutch firms). Explain how the economy of the Netherlands would adjust over time to this shock and then discuss what monetary and/or fiscal measures the Dutch authorities might take in order to speed up adjustment back to potential GDP.

5 Can the European Central Bank help to stabilize the business cycle in the member countries of the euro zone? Under what circumstances should it change its interest rate?

6 Discuss the most recent statements by monetary and fiscal policymakers in your home country (as could be found for the UK in the *Inflation Report* and *Budget Statement*). To what extent can recent policies be understood as an attempt to reduce a GDP gap?

Part Seven
Global Economic Issues

Chapter 30
Inflation

Inflation, unemployment, and growth are the big macro-economic issues of our time. In this chapter we focus on inflation, while the following chapters concentrate on unemployment and growth. But it is important to know right away that inflation and unemployment are closely related, at least in the short run. Attempts to reduce unemployment have often been accompanied by a rise in inflation, and attempts to reduce inflation have usually led to episodes of increased unemployment, which although temporary are often severe. Macroeconomic policymakers must walk a tightrope with inflation on one side and un-employment on the other.

Inflation is bad, especially when unexpected, because it distorts the working of the price system, creates arbitrary redistribution from debtors to creditors, creates incentives for speculative as opposed to productive investment activity, and is usually costly to eliminate. Unemployment is bad because it disrupts lives and is associated with an irrecoverable loss of real output.

The recent history of inflation and unemployment in the United Kingdom is set out in Figure 30.1(i). In the 1950s and 1960s both were low. Inflation averaged about 3.5 per cent and unemployment was always below 750,000, averaging about 1.5 per cent of the workforce. However, this picture changed dramatically in the 1970s. Inflation rose to over 25 per cent in 1975 (the highest peace-time inflation rate in the United Kingdom for at least 300 years) and unemployment fluctuated about a rising trend, reaching 1.5 million in 1977, and over 3 million by 1983. Inflation fell to under 5 per cent by the mid-1980s, but it rose again to around 10 per cent as a result of the late-1980s boom. This boom also brought unemployment down to around 1.5 million. However, it rose again to around 3 million in the recession of the early 1990s; at the same time inflation fell to around 2 per cent. The negative relationship between inflation and unemployment, at least since the end of the 1970s, is evident from the figure.

Figure 30.1(ii) shows average inflation in developing and advanced economies since 1970. Inflation rose worldwide in the early 1970s. It fluctuated at a historically high level through the 1970s and fell sharply in the advanced economies in the 1980s; but the fall in developing economies only came in the early 1990s. The IMF projects that inflation will remain low into the twenty-first century.

We want to understand the forces that caused inflation in the 1970s and 1980s so that the mistakes of the past are not repeated. Inflation may finally be under control around the world, but it could easily return.

In this chapter we will first use the macroeconomic model we have built up to investigate how inflation can arise. We will then set out a theoretical framework for analysing the trade-off between inflation and unemployment. Finally, we will discuss the implications of our analysis for counterinflationary policymaking.

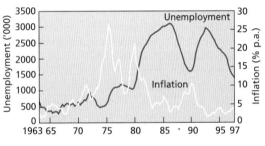

(i) Inflation and unemployment in the United Kingdom, 1963–1997

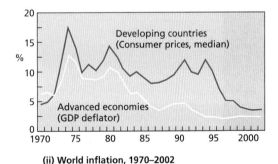

(ii) World inflation, 1970–2002

Figure 30.1 UK and world inflation

Much of the world has had similar inflation experience. Part (i) shows that UK inflation was high in the 1970s and unemployment was high in the 1980s. Part (ii) shows that inflation was a worldwide problem in the 1970s, but by the late 1990s it was low in both advanced and developing countries. The shaded areas indicate IMF staff projections.

Sources: part (i): Datastream and ONS, *Economic Trends*; part (ii): IMF, *World Economic Outlook*, Oct. 1997.

Inflation in the macro model

Although any increase in the price level is called inflation, we need to distinguish between the forces that cause a once-and-for-all increase in the price level and those that cause a continuing, or sustained, increase. Any event that tends to drive the price level upwards is called an *inflationary shock*. To examine such shocks, we begin with an economy in long-run macroeconomic equilibrium operating under a flexible exchange rate regime. The price level is stable, and GDP is at its potential level. We then study the economy as it is buffeted by different types of inflationary shock.

Supply shocks

Suppose there is a negative supply shock that shifts the *SRAS* curve upwards. This might be caused by a rise in the costs of imported raw materials or by a rise in domestic wage costs per unit of output, such as from the introduction of a high minimum wage. With a given *AD* curve the impact effect is for output to fall and the price level to rise. That is, GDP falls while inflation picks up. What happens next depends on how the monetary authorities react. The authorities now have two alternatives.

First, they can lower the interest rate sufficiently to shift the *AD* curve rightwards, so that it intersects the new *SRAS* curve at potential GDP. To achieve this, they must buy bonds and supply money in return. This injects new money into the system, thereby shifting *AD* rightwards. The supply shock is then said to be 'accommodated' by an increase in the money supply. This is a case of *monetary accommodation*.

Second, the authorities can adopt an interest rate policy

that keeps the money supply constant and the *AD* curve in its initial position.[1] We then say that the supply shock is 'not accommodated' by an increase in the money supply. This is the case of *no monetary accommodation*.

What happens also depends on whether the supply shock is an isolated event or one of a series of continued shocks. We take these two cases in turn.

Isolated supply shocks

Suppose that the leftward shift in the *SRAS* curve is an isolated event. It might, for example, be caused by a once-and-for-all increase in the cost of imported raw materials.

No monetary accommodation The leftward shift in the *SRAS* curve causes the price level to rise and pushes GDP below its potential level, opening up a recessionary gap. As a result of this recessionary gap, market pressures tend to cause wages and other factor costs to fall relative to productivity. When this happens, the *SRAS* curve shifts downward, causing a return of GDP to its potential level, and a fall in the price level. The period of inflation accompanying the original supply shock is followed by a period of deflation, which continues until long-run equilibrium is re-established. This sequence is illustrated in Figure 30.2. Since money wages tend to react only sluggishly to

[1] Whether this requires higher, constant (or even lower) interest rates depends on what happens to demand for money. Output has fallen, lowering money demand; but prices have risen, raising money demand. If there is a net increase in money demand following the supply shock, interest rates will have to rise to maintain a constant money supply. If money demand is unchanged, constant interest rates will be consistent with a constant money stock.

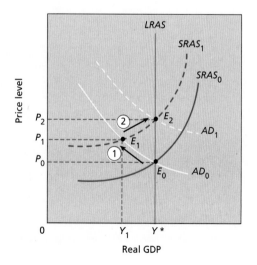

Figure 30.2 A single supply shock
The final effect of a single supply shock depends on whether or not it is accommodated by monetary expansion. A supply shock causes the *SRAS* curve to shift leftward from $SRAS_0$ to $SRAS_1$, as shown by arrow 1. Short-run equilibrium is established at E_1. If there is no monetary accommodation, the unemployment would exert a downward pressure on wage costs, causing the *SRAS* curve to shift slowly back to the right to $SRAS_0$. Prices would fall, and output would rise, until the original equilibrium was restored at E_0. If there is monetary accommodation, the *AD* curve shifts from AD_0 to AD_1, as shown by arrow 2. This re-establishes full-employment equilibrium at E_2, but with a higher price level, P_2.

excess supply in the labour market, unit costs of production fall only slowly, so the recovery to full equilibrium at Y^* may take a long time.

Monetary accommodation Now suppose that the monetary authorities react by loosening their monetary stance, buying bonds and generating an increase in the money supply. This shifts the AD curve to the right, causing both the price level and output to rise. (Part of this adjustment may come from a currency depreciation, causing an upward shift of the net export function.) When the recessionary gap is eliminated, the price level, rather than falling back to its original value, will have risen further. These effects are also shown in Figure 30.2.

The monetary authorities might decide to accommodate the supply shock because relying on cost deflation to restore activity to its potential level forces the economy to suffer an extended slump.

Monetary accommodation can return the economy to potential GDP relatively quickly, but at the cost of a once-and-for-all increase in the price level.

Repeated supply shocks

As an example of a repeated supply shock, assume that powerful unions are able to raise money wages faster than productivity is increasing, even in the face of a significant excess supply of labour. Firms then pass these higher wages on in the form of higher prices. This type of supply shock causes what is called a wage-cost push inflation—an increase in the price level due to increases in money wages that are not associated with an excess demand for labour.

No monetary accommodation Suppose the monetary authorities do not accommodate these supply shocks. The initial effect of the leftward shift in the $SRAS$ curve is to open up a recessionary gap, as shown in Figure 30.2. If unions continue to negotiate increases in wages, subjecting the economy to further supply shocks, prices continue to rise while output and employment continue to fall. Eventually the trade-off between higher wages and unemployment will become obvious to everyone. Long before everyone is unemployed, unions will cease forcing up wages in order to maintain jobs for those who are still employed.

Once the wage-cost push ceases, there are two possibilities. First, the unions may succeed in holding on to their high real wages, but not push for further increases of money wages in excess of productivity increases. The economy will then come to rest with a stable price level and a large recessionary gap. Second, the persistent unemployment may eventually erode the power of the unions, so that real wages and hence unit costs begin to fall, because money wages rise more slowly than productivity is rising. In this case the supply shock is reversed, and the $SRAS$ curve

will shift downward until full employment is eventually restored.

A non-accommodated wage-cost push tends to be self-limiting because the rising unemployment that it causes tends to restrain further wage increases.

Monetary accommodation Now suppose that the monetary authorities accommodate the shock by relaxing their monetary policy stance, lowering interest rates relative to where they would otherwise be by buying bonds and increasing the money supply. This shifts the AD curve to the right, as shown in Figure 30.3. In the new full-employment equilibrium, where GDP is at its potential level, both money wages and prices have risen. The rise in wages has been offset by a rise in prices. Workers are no better off than they were originally, although those who remained in jobs were temporarily better off in the transition period when wages had risen (taking equilibrium to E_1 in Figure 30.2) but before the price level had risen enough to restore full employment (taking equilibrium to E_2).

The stage is now set for the unions to try again. If they succeed in negotiating further increases in money wages, they hit the economy with another supply shock. If the monetary authorities again accommodate the shock, full employment is maintained, but at the cost of a further

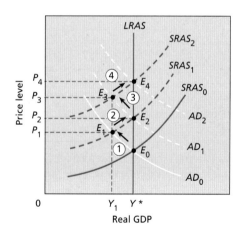

Figure 30.3 Monetary accommodation of a repeated supply shock

Monetary accommodation of a repeated supply shock causes a continuous inflation in the absence of excess demand. The initial equilibrium is at E_0. A supply shock then takes equilibrium to E_1, just as in Figure 30.2. This is the stagflation phase of rising prices and falling output; it is indicated by arrow 1. If the monetary authorities then accommodate the supply shock, the AD curve shifts to AD_1, taking equilibrium to E_2. This is the expansionary phase of rising prices and rising output (arrow 2). A second supply shock takes equilibrium to E_3 (arrow 3), and a second round of monetary accommodation takes it to E_4 (arrow 4). As long as the supply shocks and the monetary accommodation continue, the inflation continues.

round of inflation. If this process goes on repeatedly, it can give rise to a continual wage-cost push inflation as shown in Figure 30.3. The wage-cost push tends to cause a stagflation, with rising prices and falling output. Monetary accommodation tends to reinforce the rise in prices and to offset the fall in output. It will also be associated with repeated currency depreciation.

There are two requirements for continuing wage-cost push inflation. First, powerful groups, such as industrial unions or government employees, must press for, and employers must grant, increases in money wages in excess of productivity growth, even in the absence of excess demand for labour and goods. Second, the monetary authorities must accommodate the resulting inflation by loosening their monetary stance, in order to prevent the rising unemployment that would otherwise occur. The process set up by this sequence of wage-cost push and monetary accommodation is often called a wage–price spiral.

Is monetary accommodation desirable? Once started, a wage–price spiral can be halted only if the monetary authorities stop accommodating the supply shocks that are causing the inflation. The longer they wait to do so, the more entrenched will become the expectations of continuing inflation. These entrenched expectations may cause wages to continue to rise after accommodation has ceased. Because employers expect prices to rise, they go on granting wage increases. If expectations are firmly enough entrenched, the wage push can continue for quite some time, in spite of the downward pressure caused by the rising unemployment associated with the growing recessionary gap.

Evidence suggests that when politicians run monetary policy, they typically accommodate supply shocks to avoid the short-term unpopularity that is generated by rising unemployment. For this reason many economists have recommended that central banks be given the clear objective of maintaining a stable price level and then insulated from further political direction. This is what has been done in the United Kingdom since May 1997.[2] Although the Bank of England's Monetary Policy Committee may elect to accommodate some isolated supply shocks, the Bank's independence makes it unlikely that persistent wage–price spirals will be permitted to develop through continued monetary accommodation. The same applies in the euro zone, where the ECB has been given the goal of achieving price stability and has been insulated from short-term political pressures.

Accommodating a negative supply shock risks setting off a wage–price spiral, but accommodating the first-round effects of shocks may limit the output and employment losses that are otherwise inevitable.

This may not seem like a big issue in the early twenty-first century, but it certainly was important in the 1970s

and 1980s, and may be again in the future. Notice also that wage shocks are not the only type of possible supply shock. The energy price rises of 1973 and 1979 (oil shocks) were very important, and their effects can be analysed just as above. Equally, a price rise in any imported materials would have a similar effect. Exchange rate depreciations contribute to input price shocks because the price of imported materials rises, but exchange rate changes have demand dimensions as well, as they shift the net export function.

Demand shocks

Now suppose that an initial equilibrium is disturbed by a rightward shift in the aggregate demand curve, a shift that could have been caused by either an increase in some category of autonomous expenditure or a relaxation of monetary policy. This causes the price level and output to rise. If the monetary authorities react to the increase in the demand for money that accompanies an increase in autonomous expenditure by permitting the money supply to rise, they are said to be *validating* the shock. (Notice that this terminology distinguishes between the response to a supply shock, which is described as 'accommodating' the shock, and the response to a demand shock, which is described as 'validating' the shock.)

No monetary validation This is the standard case of a once-and-for-all increase in aggregate demand, such as shown in Figure 27.5 on page 466. Because the initial *AD* shock takes output above the full-employment level, an inflationary gap opens up. The pressure of excess demand soon causes wages to rise faster than productivity, shifting the *SRAS* curve upwards. As output and prices are higher, money demand increases. In order to hold the money supply constant in the face of a higher money demand, the monetary authorities will have to sell bonds and raise interest rates, thus choking off the excess demand for money. As long as the authorities follow an interest rate policy that holds the money supply constant, the rise in the price level moves the economy upwards along its fixed *AD* curve. The rise in the price level thus eventually eliminates the inflationary gap. In this case the initial period of inflation is followed by further inflation, which continues until the new long-run equilibrium is reached. The potential level of GDP and a stable price level are then restored.

Monetary validation Next suppose that once the initial demand shock has created an inflationary gap, the monetary authorities frustrate the forces that would return GDP to its potential level by relaxing monetary policy, thereby

---

[2] The framework for setting and implementing monetary policy in the Bank of England and the ECB is discussed in Chapter 25.

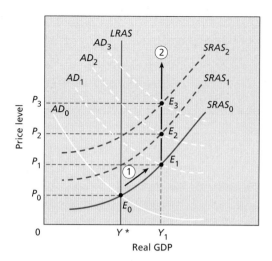

Figure 30.4 A validated demand-shock inflation

Monetary validation will cause the *AD* curve to shift, offsetting the leftward shift in the *SRAS* curve and maintaining an inflationary gap in spite of the ever-rising price level. An initial demand shock shifts equilibrium from E_0 to E_1 (along the path indicated by arrow 1), taking GDP to Y_1 and the price level to P_1. The resulting inflationary gap then causes the *SRAS* curve to shift to the left. This time, however, the money supply increases, shifting the *AD* curve to the right. By the time the aggregate supply curve has reached $SRAS_1$, the aggregate demand curve has reached AD_2, taking equilibrium to E_2. GDP remains constant at Y_1, while the price level rises to P_2.

The persistent inflationary gap continues to push the *SRAS* curve to the left, while the continued monetary validation continues to push the *AD* curve to the right. By the time aggregate supply reaches $SRAS_2$, aggregate demand has reached AD_3. The price level has risen still further to P_3, but the inflationary gap remains unchanged at $Y_1 - Y^*$. As long as this monetary validation continues, the economy moves along the vertical path of arrow 2.

permitting the nominal money supply to rise when output starts to fall. This is the case illustrated in Figure 30.4. Two forces are now brought into play. Spurred by the inflationary gap, the wage increases cause the *SRAS* curve to shift to the left. Fuelled by the expansionary monetary policy, the *AD* curve shifts to the right. As a result of both of these shifts, the price level rises. But if the shift in the *AD* curve offsets the shift in the *SRAS* curve, the inflationary gap does not diminish. The validation of an isolated demand shock thus creates a series of repeated demand shocks that permit the inflation to continue.

Validation of a demand shock turns what would have been a transitory inflation into a sustained inflation fuelled by monetary expansion.

We can now see why a rise in the price level may not remove an inflationary gap. Because the money supply may expand endogenously to meet any demand for it, when the monetary authorities are pegging nominal interest rates,

there is no automatic adjustment mechanism to eliminate the inflationary gap. As the price level rises, the nominal money supply rises sufficiently to keep the real money supply constant, and the inflationary gap is not reduced. This sequence requires either that the monetary authorities do not pick up the warnings of impending inflation coming from the rising money supply figures, or that they decide on an inflationary policy.

Although there is controversy over how much control the monetary authorities can have over the money supply, few economists doubt that a determined enough anti-inflationary policy can stop the nominal money supply from expanding as fast as prices are rising. Most monetary authorities have pursued such a policy at one time or another over the past few decades, thereby ending an inflation in their own country. Thus, in the world in which we live, inflations cannot go on indefinitely unless they are validated by policy decisions taken by the monetary authorities.

Figure 30.5 summarizes all the cases of supply and demand shock with or without accommodation or validation.

Inflation as a monetary phenomenon

Economists have debated the extent to which inflation is a monetary phenomenon. Does it have purely monetary causes—increases in the supply of money? Does it have purely monetary consequences—only the price level is affected? One slogan stating an extreme position on this issue was made popular by the US economist Milton Friedman: 'Inflation is everywhere and always a monetary phenomenon.' This could be a mere tautology, since inflation is by definition a fall in the purchasing power of money. However, avoiding semantics, let us summarize what we have already learned about the causes of inflation.

1. Many forces can cause the price level to rise. On the demand side anything that shifts the *AD* curve to the right will have this result—*ceteris paribus*, increases in desired expenditure on exports, government spending, investment, and consumption, as well as relaxation of monetary policy or decreases in money demand. On the supply side anything that increases unit costs of production will shift the *SRAS* curve to the left and cause the price level to rise.

2. Such inflations can continue for some time without any increases in the money supply.

3. The rise in prices must eventually come to a halt, unless monetary expansion occurs.

Points 1 and 2 indicate that a temporary burst of inflation may or may not be a monetary phenomenon; it need not have monetary causes, and it need not be accompanied by monetary expansion. Point 3 implies that a sustained inflation must be a monetary phenomenon. If a rise in prices is to continue, it must be accompanied by continuing

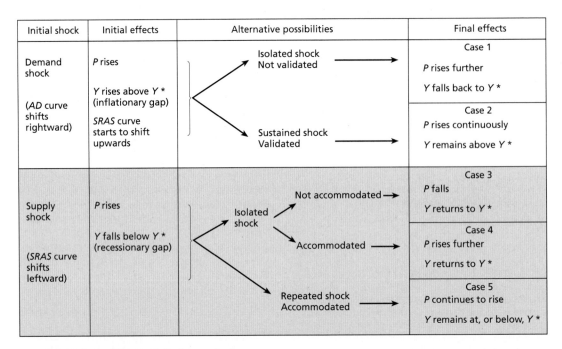

Figure 30.5 The effects of inflationary shocks

Demand and supply shocks have different final effects, depending on whether or not they are isolated or sustained and are validated or accommodated. This figure summarizes the analysis of each of the five cases given in the text. It should be referred to after reading the text discussion of each of the cases. All comparisons assume that GDP starts at its potential level and that initially the price level is stable.

The initial effects of a demand shock are to raise GDP and the price level. If the shock is isolated, the price level continues to rise until GDP falls back to its potential level (case 1). If the shock is sustained and validated (validation turns an isolated shock into a sustained shock), the price level continues to rise while GDP stays above its potential level (case 2).

The initial effects of a supply shock are to raise the price level but to reduce GDP. Once the shock is over, GDP will return to its potential level, with a lowered price level if there is no accommodation (case 3), and with a higher price level if there is accommodation (case 4). If the shock is sustained and accommodated, the price level can continue to rise, with or without a persistent recessionary gap (case 5).

increases in the money supply (or decreases in money demand). This is true regardless of the cause that set the rise in prices in motion. What happens when monetary validation gets out of hand is discussed in Box 30.1.

Now let us summarize what we have learned about the consequences of an inflation, assuming that the economy begins from a situation of full employment and a stable price level.

1. In the short run a demand-shock inflation tends to be accompanied by an increase in GDP.

2. In the short run a supply-shock inflation tends to be accompanied by a decrease in GDP.

3. When all adjustments have been fully made, so that the relevant supply-side curve is the *LRAS* curve, shifts in either the *AD* or *SRAS* curve leave GDP unchanged and affect only the price level.

Points 1 and 2 are saying that inflation is not, in the short

run, a purely monetary phenomenon; it has real consequences for output and employment. Point 3 states that from the point of view of long-run equilibrium inflation is a purely monetary phenomenon.

We have now established three important conclusions:

1. Without monetary accommodation supply shocks cause temporary bursts of inflation accompanied by recessionary gaps. The gaps are removed if, and when, unit costs of production fall, restoring equilibrium at potential GDP and at the initial price level.

2. Without monetary validation demand shocks cause temporary bursts of inflation accompanied by inflationary gaps. The gaps are removed as wages rise, returning GDP to its potential level, but at a higher price level.

3. With an appropriate response from the monetary authorities an inflation initiated by either supply or demand shocks can continue indefinitely; an ever-

Box 30.1 Hyperinflation

Monetary validation of ongoing inflation sometimes gets out of hand. In extreme cases it leads to hyperinflation, in which inflation is so rapid that money ceases to be useful as a medium of exchange and a store of value. However, inflation rates of 50, 100, and even 200 per cent or more per year have occurred year after year in some countries and have proven to be manageable as people adjust their contracts in real terms. Although there are strains and side-effects, the evidence shows such situations to be possible without causing money to become useless.

Does this mean that there is no reason to fear that rapid inflation will turn into a hyperinflation that will destroy the value of money completely? The historical record is not entirely reassuring. There have been a number of cases in which prices began to rise at an ever-accelerating rate until a nation's money ceased to be a satisfactory store of value, even for the short period between receipt and expenditure, and hence ceased also to be useful as a medium of exchange.

The index of wholesale prices in Germany before and after the First World War is given in the table. The index shows that a product purchased with one 100 mark note in July 1923 would have required ten million 100 mark notes for its purchase only four months later! Although Germany had experienced substantial inflation during the war, averaging more than 30 per cent per year, the immediate post-war years of 1920 and 1921 gave no sign of an explosive inflation; indeed, during 1920 price stability was experienced. In 1922 and 1923, however, the price level exploded. On 15 November 1923 the mark was officially repudiated, its value wholly destroyed. How could this happen?

German wholesale price index (1913 = 1)

January 1913	1
January 1920	13
January 1921	14
January 1922	37
July 1922	101
January 1923	2,785
July 1923	74,800
August 1923	944,000
September 1923	23,900,000
October 1923	7,096,000,000
November 1923	750,000,000,000

When an inflation becomes so rapid that people lose confidence in the purchasing power of their currency, they rush to spend it. People who have goods become increasingly reluctant to accept the rapidly depreciating money in exchange. The rush to spend money accelerates the increase in prices until people finally become unwilling to accept money on any terms. What was once money ceases to be money.

The price system can then be restored only by repudiation of the old monetary unit and its replacement by a new unit. This destroys the value of monetary savings and of all contracts specified in terms of the old monetary unit.

There are about a dozen documented hyperinflations in world history, among them the collapses of the continental* during the American War of Independence, the rouble during the Russian Revolution, the drachma during and after the German occupation of Greece in the Second World War, the pengo in Hungary during 1945–6, and the Chinese national currency during 1946–8. Every one of these hyperinflations was accompanied by great increases in the money supply; new money was printed to give governments the purchasing power that they could not or would not obtain by taxation. Further, every one occurred in the midst of a major political upheaval in which grave doubts existed about the stability and the future of the government itself.

Is hyperinflation likely in the absence of civil war, revolution, or collapse of the government? Most economists think not. Further, it is clear that high inflation rates over a period of time do not mean the inevitable or even likely onset of hyperinflation.

However, do not assume that hyperinflation is a curiosity only to be found in the history books. The following is an extract from a newspaper report on events in Serbia in 1993 and 1994:

Worried that Serbian cities might starve during the winter, the government announced [in July 1993] that it would buy a million tons of the wheat harvest from private farmers at guaranteed prices. . . . The entire country, now highly attuned to living with an unstable currency, realised what this would mean. The government could only pay by printing a lot more money, which the peasants would switch into marks the moment they were paid. It would, in short, kill the currency.

Sure enough, three times during July, the dinar/mark exchange rate lurched downwards. Then it spun out of control.

The exponential growth of inflation during these months still astonishes even the Yugoslav economists who had seen it coming. Between July and the end of the year it went from 500 per cent to 2,000 per cent a month, to 20,000 per cent, then 500,000 per cent and onwards. By January, prices were rising faster than 100 per cent an hour.

At the final assessment before the recovery plan was put into effect on January 24th [1994], the monthly inflation rate had reached a mind-blowing 302 million per cent. Compare that with the inflation rate in Germany, which at its height in 1923 reached only 332 per cent per month, while inflation in Latin American countries during the 1980s never went beyond 300 per cent per year.

(*Independent on Sunday*, 9 October 1994, p. 9)

* This is the name given to the notes issued by the American Continental Congress at that time.

increasing money supply is necessary for an ever-continuing inflation.

Fortunately, the lessons from the inflation episodes of the 1970s and 1980s have been learned by policymakers, and in many countries central banks have been told that their job is to maintain low inflation. So sustained periods of rapid inflation are much less likely to occur in the near future. Politicians learned these lessons the hard way, rather than by reading textbooks such as this.

The Phillips curve

Up to now it has been enough to say that an inflationary gap implies excess demand for labour, low unemployment, pressure on wages to rise faster than productivity, and hence an upward-shifting *SRAS* curve. But now we need to look in more detail at the influence of wages on inflation. To do this, we make use of a famous relation called the Phillips curve, which helps us understand how fast the *SRAS* curve shifts. We first present the Phillips curve in its original form and then transform into a form more applicable to the *AD–AS* model. Since the original curve uses unemployment rather than GDP as its indicator of excess demand in labour markets, we must first show the relation between the two.

The NAIRU When current GDP is at its potential level, unemployment is not zero, even though we sometimes refer to this situation as 'full employment'. Instead, there may be a substantial amount of *frictional unemployment*, caused by the movement of people among jobs, and *structural unemployment*, caused by a mismatch between the characteristics of the demand for labour and the characteristics of its supply. The amount of frictional and structural unemployment that exists when GDP is at its potential level is called the **NAIRU** or the **natural rate of unemployment** (U^*).[3] We use the term NAIRU rather than natural rate because the latter term may create the erroneous impression that nothing can be done to reduce unemployment below a rate that is 'natural'.

It follows from the definition of the NAIRU that when GDP exceeds potential GDP ($Y > Y^*$), unemployment will be less than the NAIRU ($U < U^*$). When GDP is less than potential GDP ($Y < Y^*$), unemployment will exceed the NAIRU ($U > U^*$).

We can now use the NAIRU terminology to restate our earlier assumptions about the pressure that is put on wage rates, and through them on the *SRAS* curve, by inflationary and recessionary gaps.

When the unemployment rate is below the NAIRU, demand forces put pressure on wages to rise faster than productivity. When the unemployment rate is above the NAIRU, demand forces put pressure on wages to rise more slowly than productivity, or even to fall. When unemployment is at the NAIRU, demand forces exert neither upward nor downward pressure on wages relative to productivity.

The theory of the Phillips curve

In the 1950s Professor A. W. Phillips (1914–75) was doing research on stabilization policy at the London School of Economics. He was interested in the question of the speed with which input prices responded to excess demand and excess supply. To study this question, he looked at the rate of change of money wage rates in the United Kingdom over a period of 100 years. By relating these wage changes to the level of unemployment, he discovered a remarkable relationship which came to be known as the Phillips curve. This was an empirical relationship which later theoretical work tried to explain. We will incorporate the key elements of Phillips curve theory into the context of our macro model.

The **Phillips curve** relates the percentage rate of change of money wage rates (measured at an annual rate) to the level of unemployment (measured as the percentage of the labour force unemployed). Unemployment is plotted on the horizontal axis, and wage changes on the vertical axis. Thus any point on the curve relates a particular level of unemployment to a particular rate of increase of money wages.

So far in this book we have dealt with the levels of variables. The Phillips curve relates the amount of unemployment to the rate of change of money wages. Letting ΔW stand for the change in money wage rates from one year to the next, and W for the level of wage rates in the first year, the equation of the Phillips curve is

$$(\Delta W/W) = \mathrm{f}(U), \qquad (1)$$

where f stands for a functional relation.

A numerical example of a Phillips curve is shown in Figure 30.6. The numbers on the figure are hypothetical. (The original curve became negative at high rates of unemployment.) We will see that, appropriately interpreted, the Phillips curve can handle all of the causes of inflation. For the moment we will concentrate on the influence of demand forces.

The shape of the Phillips curve

A negative slope Note first that the Phillips curve has a negative slope, showing that the lower is the level of unemployment, the higher is the rate of change of money wages. This should not surprise us. Low rates of unemployment are associated with boom conditions, when excess demand for labour will be causing money wages to rise rapidly. High rates of unemployment, on the other hand, are associated with slump conditions, when the slack

---

[3] 'NAIRU' is an acronym for non-accelerating-inflation rate of unemployment. The reason for this name will become apparent later in the chapter. We talk about the natural rate of unemployment and the NAIRU as if they were the same concept. In reality they are different except when the economy is in full equilibrium.

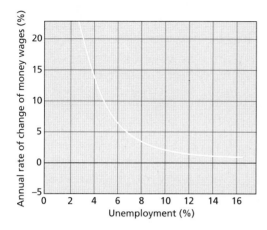

Figure 30.6 A Phillips curve

The Phillips curve relates the level of unemployment to the rate of change of money wage rates. The figure shows a numerical example of a Phillips curve. According to the example, an increase in unemployment by four percentage points, from 8 to 12 per cent, will lower wage inflation from 3 to 2 per cent, while a reduction in unemployment by four percentage points, from 8 to 4 per cent, will raise wage inflation from 3 to 14 per cent.

demand for labour will lead to low increases in money wages, or possibly even to decreases.

A flattening slope Moving along the Phillips curve from left to right, the curve gets flatter. This shape is another way of showing the asymmetry of aggregate supply, namely that input prices change more rapidly upwards than downwards. Let us recall why.

First, assume that a recovery is increasing the excess demand for labour. As a boom develops, the unemployment rate will decrease towards, but will never reach, zero. (There will always be some frictional and structural unemployment.) At the same time the growing excess demand for labour will be bidding up wage rates more and more rapidly. This behaviour causes the Phillips curve to get very steep and to lie far above the horizontal axis at its left-hand end. The further the curve is above the axis, the faster wages are rising.

The steepness of the curve in the range of low unemployment shows that wage inflation is very responsive to changes in unemployment in that range.

Second, consider the onset of a recession that raises unemployment. This recession restrains wage increases. As a result, the Phillips curve comes closer and closer to the horizontal axis, indicating less and less upward pressure on wages the higher the level of unemployment. If the curve fell below the axis, then money wages would actually be falling over some range of high unemployment. We

do not show this case in the figure but instead assume that as unemployment gets very high, the rate of increase in money wages approaches zero but never becomes negative.

The flatness of the Phillips curve in the range of high unemployment shows that the rate of wage inflation is relatively unresponsive to changes in unemployment over that range.

The Phillips curve and the *SRAS* curve

To see what is happening to unit costs of production, we need to relate the increase in wage rates to the increase in labour productivity. For simplicity in the rest of the discussion we will assume that labour is the only variable factor used by firms. This allows us to associate the labour costs of each unit of output with total variable costs per unit of output. (We could equally well have assumed that all input prices change at the same rate as does the price of labour.)

What happens to unit costs of production now depends only on the differences between what labour costs the firm and what labour produces for the firm. To illustrate what is involved, we repeat in part (i) of Figure 30.7 the Phillips curve from Figure 30.6. We then add to it a horizontal line labelled g, for growth in output per unit of labour input, which shows the rate at which labour productivity is growing year by year. In the hypothetical example of the figure we have assumed that productivity is rising at 3 per cent per year. The intersection of the Phillips curve and the productivity line at the point x now divides the graph into an inflationary and a deflationary range described in the numbered points below. Given the assumptions about wage behaviour made earlier, point x must occur at the NAIRU (labelled U^*)—which corresponds to a level of output equal to potential GDP, Y^*.

1. At unemployment rates less than at the intersection point, wages are rising faster than productivity and thus unit costs of production (input costs per unit of output) are rising. If unit costs are rising, the *SRAS* curve must be shifting upwards.

2. At unemployment rates greater than at the intersection point, money wage rates are rising more slowly than productivity is rising. Thus unit costs are falling. If unit costs are falling, the *SRAS* curve must be shifting downwards.

Notice that although we have drawn the Phillips curve to show complete downward inflexibility of money wages, this does not imply complete downward inflexibility of unit costs. As long as money wages rise less than productivity

(i)

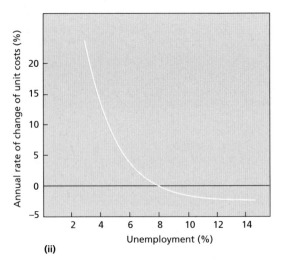

(ii)

(iii)

Figure 30.7 The Phillips curve transformed

The Phillips curve is transformed in two steps into a curve relating GDP to the rate of change of unit costs. Part (i) repeats the numerical example from Figure 30.6. It also adds a straight line labelled 'g', indicating a 3 per cent rate of increase in labour productivity. Part (ii) shows unemployment related to the rate of change of unit costs, which is the rate of change of money wages minus the rate of change of productivity. Part (iii) substitutes Y for U, making use of the negative relation between the two variables. It shows the rate of change of unit costs positively related to GDP.

rises, unit costs of production will be falling, and the *SRAS* curve will be shifting downwards. Complete downward inflexibility of unit costs—and thus the total absence of the equilibrating mechanism that comes from downward shifts in the *SRAS* curve—requires more than the downward inflexibility of money wages: it requires that money wages never rise by less than the increase in productivity.

We will now derive from the Phillips curve a new curve that expresses the verbal argument just given.

Part (ii) of Figure 30.7 shows a new curve which relates the rate of unemployment to the change in unit costs, rather than to the change in money wage rates. The new curve still measures unemployment on the horizontal axis, but now it measures the rate of increase in unit costs on the vertical axis. Since this is merely the rate of increase in money wage rates minus the rate of increase of productivity, the new diagram is the same as part (i) of the figure, except that the origin on the vertical axis has been shifted by the rate of productivity growth.

The new curve tells us the rate at which unit costs of production are changing—and thus the rate at which the *SRAS* curve is shifting upwards or downwards—at each level of unemployment.

So far we have followed Phillips in plotting unemployment on the horizontal axis. The *SRAS* curve, however, plots GDP on its horizontal axis. To get a curve that relates the change in unit costs of production to the level of GDP, we note that unemployment is negatively related to the level of GDP. As GDP rises, unemployment tends to fall.

To make the relation precise, we assume that the labour force remains constant. Now any short-run increase in GDP, which means that more labour is employed, must mean that less labour is unemployed. In this case any increase in GDP must mean a decrease in unemployment.

We can now transform the curve in part (ii) of Figure 30.7, which plots changes in unit costs of production against the unemployment rate, into a new relation, shown in part (iii) of the figure. This curve shows the same rate of change in unit costs of production, but plots it against the level of GDP. Since GDP and unemployment vary negatively with each other, the curve in part (iii) of the figure has the opposite slope to the curve in part (ii) of the same figure.[4] We call this new curve the transformed Phillips curve.

Shifts in the *SRAS* curve explained

Figure 30.8(i) shows the familiar aggregate demand/aggregate supply diagram. Part (ii) shows the transformed Phillips curve (*PC*), relating the rate of change of unit costs to GDP. Both parts have GDP on their horizontal axes, and by lining these up we can compare one with the other. The *AD* and *SRAS* curves in part (i) determine the short-run levels of prices and GDP. Given the GDP so determined, the transformed Phillips curve tells us the rate at which the *SRAS* curve is shifting. Since from now on we will always be working with this transformed curve, we will just call it a Phillips curve. (Notice that to emphasize that we are dealing with rates of change, we place a dot over the variable to indicate its annual percentage rate of change—in this case the symbol is $\dot{c}$.)

The long-run equilibrium of the economy is at potential GDP. All that the curve in part (ii) tells us is how fast the *SRAS* curve in part (i) is shifting, moving the economy towards its long-run equilibrium. The steepness of the curve for Y greater than $Y^{\star}$ (i.e. above equilibrium) shows the rapid adjustment towards equilibrium after a single expansionary shock. The flatness of the curve below equilibrium shows the slowness of adjustment towards equilibrium after a single contractionary shock.

The nonlinearity of the transformed Phillips curve expresses the asymmetry of aggregate supply: that costs, and hence prices, rise rapidly in the face of an inflationary gap, but fall only slowly in the face of a recessionary gap.

The micro underpinnings of the asymmetry

The micro behaviour that lies behind the flat part of the Phillips curve to the left of $Y^{\star}$ is explained in two parts. The first concerns the theory of short-run oligopoly pricing described in Chapter 11—firms tend to absorb cyclical demand fluctuations by varying their outputs rather than their prices. The second concerns the theory that money wage rates do not fall rapidly in the face of an excess supply of labour, although they can rise rapidly in the face of excess demand for labour. This issue of wage inflexibility is central to the modern New Keynesian attempts to understand labour markets, and will be discussed in Chapter 31.

The overall microeconomics of wage behaviour is thought to be as follows. When demand falls, oligopolistic firms reduce their outputs and their demands for labour, holding their mark-ups approximately constant. The unemployment does not force money wage rates down

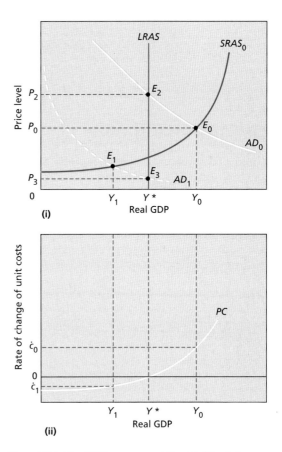

Figure 30.8 The Phillips curve and the *AS–AD* relation

The transformed Phillips curve shows the speed with which the *SRAS* curve is shifting upwards. When the curves are AD_0 and $SRAS_0$ in part (i), they intersect at E_0 to produce equilibrium GDP of Y_0. Part (ii) shows that when GDP is Y_0, the rate of change of unit costs, and hence the rate of increase in the *SRAS* curve, is $\dot{c}_0$ per cent per year. Thus equilibrium GDP is moving rapidly towards $Y^{\star}$ as the point of macroeconomic equilibrium moves up the fixed *AD* curve towards the long-run equilibrium at E_2.

When the curves are AD_1 and $SRAS_0$ in part (i), equilibrium is at E_1, with GDP Y_1. Part (ii) shows that when GDP is Y_1, unit costs, and hence the *SRAS* curve, will be shifting downwards at the rate of $\dot{c}_1$ per cent per year. Thus equilibrium GDP is moving slowly along AD_1 towards a long-run equilibrium at E_3. Each long-run equilibrium has the same level of GDP but a different price level.

significantly, so firms' unit costs, and hence their prices, fall no faster than productivity is rising. There will also be some downward pressure on money wages (particularly in non-unionized markets) and on prices in more competitive markets, and the result will be a slow downward drift

---

[4] We started with the relation $\Delta W/W = \mathrm{f}(U)$, which is the original Phillips curve. We then subtracted productivity growth, g, to get a unit-cost-increase curve: $\Delta c/c = \mathrm{f}(U) - g$. Then we substituted a relation between unemployment and national income, $U = \mathrm{u}(Y)$, to get a curve relating the rate of increase in unit costs to the level of unemployment: $\Delta c/c = \mathrm{f}(\mathrm{u}(Y))$.

of the price level. When demand rises above potential output, firms try to expand output by hiring more labour, and the labour shortages that develop cause wages to rise. As costs rise, firms pass these on in higher prices. This is a continuing process, which goes on as long as excess demand holds GDP above its potential level.

Expectational forces

We must now consider influences on costs and prices other than demand. A second force that can influence wage costs is expectations. Suppose, for example, that both employers and employees expect a 4 per cent inflation next year. Unions will start negotiations from a base of a 4 per cent increase in money wages, which would hold their real wages constant. Firms also may be inclined to begin bargaining by conceding at least a 4 per cent increase in money wages, since they expect that the prices at which they sell their products will rise by 4 per cent. Starting from that base, unions will attempt to obtain some desired increase in their real wages. At this point such factors as profits, productivity, and bargaining power become important.

The general expectation of an *x* per cent inflation creates pressures for wages to rise by *x* per cent more than productivity, and hence for the *SRAS* curve to shift upwards by *x* per cent.

The key point is that the *SRAS* curve can be shifting upwards even if there is no inflationary gap. As long as people expect prices to rise, their behaviour will push money wages and unit costs up. This brings about the rise in prices that was expected. This is an example of the phenomenon of self-fulfilling expectations—if everyone thinks that event X is going to occur, their actions in anticipation of X may make X occur.

Expectations formation

We have already discussed expectations in Chapter 28, in the context of exchange rate determination. Expectations are also important in investment behaviour, since firms invest in the expectation of increasing future profits. Here we consider the importance of inflation expectations in the context of the Phillips curve. This is closely related to the discussion in Chapter 27 of price level expectations that was related to the 'surprise' aggregate supply curve.

Backward-looking theories Keynesian theories of expectations assume that expectations are slow to change. The theory of *extrapolative expectations* says that expectations depend on extrapolations of past behaviour and respond only slowly to what is currently happening to costs. In one simple form of the theory the expected future inflation rate is merely a moving average of past actual rates. The rationale is that unless a deviation from past trends persists, firms and workers will dismiss the deviation as transitory. They do not let it influence their wage- and price-setting behaviour.

The theory of *adaptive expectations* states that the expectation of future inflation rates adjusts to the error in predicting the current rate. Thus if you thought the current rate was going to be 6 per cent and it turned out to be 10 per cent, you might revise your estimate of the next period's inflation rate upwards by, say, half of your error, making the new expectation 8 per cent.

These two theories make expectations about future inflation depend on past actual rates. In an obvious sense such expectations are backward-looking, since the expectation can be calculated using data on what has happened already.

Forward-looking theories **Rational expectations** are forward-looking.[5] The rational expectations hypothesis assumes that people do not continue to make persistent, systematic errors in forming their expectations. Thus if the economic system about which they are forming expectations remains stable, their expectations will be correct *on average*. Any individual's expectations at any time about next year's price level can thus be thought of as the actual price level that will occur next year plus a random error term which has a mean of zero.

Rational expectations have the effect of speeding up the adjustment of expectations. Instead of being based on past inflation rates, expected inflation is based on an informed forecast of the outcome of existing (and expected) policies.

Backward-looking expectations are overly naïve. People do look ahead to the future and assess future possibilities rather than just blindly reacting to what has gone before. Yet the assumption of unbiased forward-looking expectations requires that workers and firms have a degree of understanding of inflation forecasting that few economists would claim to have. It is possible that in reality wage-setting is a mixture of rational, forward-looking behaviour and expectations based on the experience of the recent past. Depending on the circumstances, expectations will sometimes tend to rely more on past experience, and at other times to rely more on present events whose effects are expected to influence the future.

Of course, people will not make the error of consistently underpredicting (or overpredicting) the inflation rate for decades, but it can happen for several years, whenever people do not fully understand the causes of current inflation. Every past period of inflation has led to intense debate among economists about its causes, cures, and probable future course. If professionals are uncertain, it

---

[5] Rational expectations were first discussed in Chapter 27 on page 471.

would be surprising if wage- and price-setters got these matters right even on average. None the less, economists can use assumptions such as rational expectations in their models and then test the predictions to see if they are consistent with the data.

The belief that expectations are at least to some extent rational is one of the reasons that politicians around the world have sought to establish *credible* regimes for the control of inflation. Independent central banks with clearly defined low-inflation objectives have been put in place not just to control inflation directly but also to *make people believe that inflation really will be kept under control.* Once people believe that inflation will be low, it is very much easier (in terms of output and employment costs) for policymakers to keep it low.

Random shocks

Wage changes are also affected by forces other than excess demand and expectations of inflation. These forces can be positive, pushing wages higher than they would otherwise go, or negative, pushing wages lower than they would otherwise go. One such shock occurs when an exceptionally strong union, or an exceptionally weak management, comes to the bargaining table and produces a wage increase that is a percentage point or two higher than would have occurred under more typical bargaining conditions.

One simple approach is to assume that there are many sources of shock, and that they are independent of one another. This means that, overall, they exert a random influence on wages—sometimes speeding wage changes up a bit, sometimes slowing them down a bit, but having a net effect that more or less cancels out when taken over several years. Over the long term they may be regarded as random events and are referred to as random shocks.

Random shocks may have a large positive or negative effect in any one year. Over the period of a sustained inflation, however, positive shocks in some years will tend to be offset by negative shocks in other years, so that overall they contribute little to the long-term trend of the price level.

The overall effect on wages

The overall change in wage costs is a result of the three basic forces just studied. We may express this as follows:

$$\begin{matrix} \text{Percentage} \\ \text{increase} \\ \text{in unit} \\ \text{wage costs} \end{matrix} = \begin{matrix} \text{demand} \\ \text{effect} \end{matrix} + \begin{matrix} \text{expectational} \\ \text{effect} \end{matrix} + \begin{matrix} \text{shock} \\ \text{effect} \end{matrix}. \quad (2)$$

The expectations-augmented Phillips curve

We can now add the forces of expectations and random shocks to the Phillips curve determining the behaviour of unit labour costs. The Phillips curve in Figure 30.7 shows the effects only of demand pressures. It will predict actual inflation only if the expected inflation rate is zero and there are no random shocks.

The relation shown in (2) above defines a whole set of Phillips curves. Each curve is drawn for zero shocks and a given expected rate of inflation, which enters as an additive constant. At Y^* there are no demand pressures on wages, so the height of the Phillips curve above the axis at that point is determined by the expected rate of inflation. The whole Phillips curve then shows how much the rate of change of unit costs varies from the expected inflation rate as a result of excess demand or excess supply in the labour market. Any particular Phillips curve drawn for a given expected rate of inflation is called a **short-run Phillips curve** (*SRPC*) or an **expectations-augmented Phillips curve.**

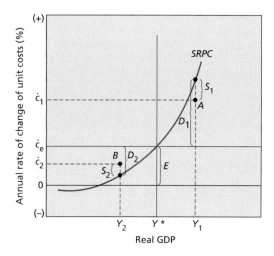

Figure 30.9 The components of cost inflation illustrated
The rate of cost inflation can be separated into three components: expectational inflation, demand inflation, and shock inflation. The Phillips curve is drawn for a given expected rate of inflation and hence is labelled a short-run Phillips curve. The given expected inflation rate, $\dot c_e$, is shown by the height of the horizontal solid blue line. Point A indicates a GDP of Y_1 combined with a rate of cost inflation of $\dot c_1$. This rate is composed of a rate to match expected inflation, shown by the bracket E; a positive demand component, shown by the bracket D_1 (determined by the shape of *SRPC*); and a negative shock component, shown by the bracket S_1. Point B indicates a GDP of Y_2 combined with a rate of cost inflation of $\dot c_2$. This rate is composed of a rate to match expected inflation, once again shown by the bracket E; the demand component, shown by the bracket D_2, which is now negative (since income Y_2 is less than Y^*); and a positive shock component, shown by the bracket S_2.

Figure 30.9 gives an example of one short-run curve and uses it to illustrate the relations shown in equation (2). It shows unit costs rising as a result of increases in wage costs brought about by demand pressures (shown by the Phillips curve), expectations of inflation (which determine the height of the Phillips curve above the axis at Y^*), and random shocks (which are shown as deviations from the Phillips curve).

Rising inflation

Now consider attempts to sustain a steady inflation. Assume that the economy starts out in macro equilibrium at potential GDP and steady prices, as shown in Figure 30.10. The government then increases its expenditure. This shifts the AD curve to the right, raising GDP above its potential level, so that unemployment falls below the NAIRU. Inflation then sets in at a rate determined by the Phillips curve, and by validating that inflation, low unemployment and high output can be achieved.

If that were the end of the story, the outcome might seem like a reasonable bargain. At the cost of some inflation, extra output and extra employment have been obtained. Indeed, this is what many governments thought they could do in the 1960s and 1970s. Governments that wanted lower unemployment could have it, but at the cost of higher inflation.

We now know, however, that there is more to the story. Whatever theory of the formation of inflationary expecta-

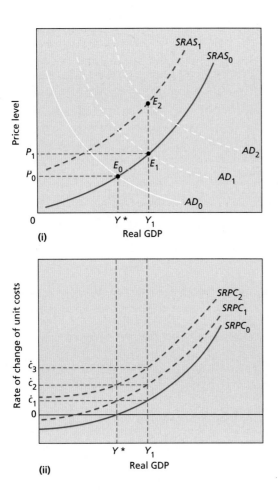

Figure 30.10 Rising inflation
The attempt to hold GDP above its potential level and unemployment below the NAIRU will lead to an ever-rising inflation. Macroeconomic equilibrium is originally at E_0 with income Y^* and a stable price level of P_0. The government then adopts measures to shift the AD curve to AD_1, taking GDP to Y_1 and the price level to P_1. Now, however, unit costs begin to rise at a rate of $\dot{c}_1$. This shifts the $SRAS$ curve to the left and, to offset its effects, the monetary authorities validate the inflation with monetary expansion. As long as the Phillips curve in part (ii) stays constant, inflation proceeds at a constant rate. When the curves in part (i) have reached, say, $SRAS_1$ and AD_2, people come to expect the inflation to continue at the rate $\dot{c}_1$. The short-run Phillips curve now shifts upwards to $SRPC_1$, which passes through the point $(Y^*, \dot{c}_1)$. With income at Y_1 the inflation rate now rises to $\dot{c}_2$. The $SRAS$ curve now shifts upwards more rapidly and, to maintain income at Y_1, the rate of monetary validation must be increased to allow the AD curve to shift more rapidly.

Sooner or later the inflation rate of $\dot{c}_2$ comes to be expected and the Phillips curve shifts to $SRPC_2$, which passes through the point $(Y^*, \dot{c}_2)$. The inflation rate now rises to $\dot{c}_3$, and the rate of monetary expansion must be further increased to hold GDP at Y_1.

tions we adopt, any persistent inflation will come to be expected sooner or later. The expected inflation rate will then rise, and the *SRPC* will shift upward. If the same level of GDP is to be maintained, the monetary authorities will have to relax their policy stance so as to permit a higher rate of monetary expansion to prevent the more rapid inflation rate from shifting the *AD* curve to the left (by lowering the real money supply).

This is not all. Ignoring random inflation shocks, we know that the actual inflation rate is the sum of the expected rate and the demand component. We also know that when GDP is above Y^*, the demand component is positive. It follows that whenever actual GDP exceeds potential GDP, actual inflation must exceed expected inflation. It also follows that the expected rate will itself continue to rise as it adjusts towards the actual rate. This means that the short-run Phillips curve will continue to shift upward.

Upward shifts of the Phillips curve mean that any given level of GDP is associated with higher and higher rates of inflation. To maintain that GDP level, the monetary authorities must then adopt a monetary policy stance that generates a faster and faster rate of monetary expansion.

This gives us what is called *the accelerationist hypothesis*, because when inflation rises the price level accelerates:

If the monetary authorities validate any rate of inflation that results when GDP is held above its potential level, then the inflation rate itself will rise continuously; and the rate of monetary expansion required to sustain that level of GDP will also rise continuously.

The long-run Phillips curve

Is there any level of GDP in this model that is compatible with a constant rate of inflation? The answer is yes: potential GDP. When GDP is at Y^*, the demand component of inflation is zero, as shown in Figure 30.8. This means that

actual inflation equals expected inflation. There are no surprises. No one's plans are upset, so no one has any incentive to alter plans as a result of what actually happens to inflation.

Provided the inflation rate is fully validated, any rate of inflation can persist indefinitely as long as GDP is held at its potential level.[6]

We now define the **long-run Phillips curve (*LRPC*)** as the relation between GDP and stable rates of inflation that neither accelerate nor decelerate. This occurs when the expected and actual inflation rates are equal. On the theory just described, the long-run Phillips curve is vertical, because only at Y^* can the expected and actual rates of inflation be equal. The long-run Phillips curve is shown in Figure 30.11.

Maintaining a point on the *LRPC* leads to steady inflation at the expected rate. This is illustrated in Figure 30.12, which shows a positive expected inflation rate being fully accommodated by the monetary authorities' permissive monetary stance. Because GDP is at its potential level, there is no demand effect on inflation. Thus the actual and the expected inflation rates are equal. As a result the situation is sustainable (as long as the monetary authorities continue to accommodate the inflation). The *SRAS* curve shifts upwards at a constant rate, while the short-run Phillips curve stays stable. Since everyone's expectations are being fulfilled, there is no reason for anyone to change their behaviour.

The long-run Phillips curve is vertical at Y^*; only Y^* is compatible with a stable rate of inflation; and any stable rate is, if fully accommodated, compatible with Y^*.

[6] We now see why the level of unemployment associated with potential GDP is called the non-accelerating-inflation rate of unemployment (NAIRU). At any lower level of unemployment GDP exceeds potential GDP and the inflation rate will tend to rise. At any higher level of unemployment GDP is below potential GDP and inflation will tend to fall. (Money wage increases are lower than the rate of productivity growth.)

Figure 30.11 The vertical long-run Phillips curve
When actual inflation equals expected inflation, there is no trade-off between inflation and unemployment. In long-term equilibrium the actual rate of inflation must remain equal to the expected rate (otherwise expectations would be revised). This can occur only at potential GDP Y^*, that is, along the *LRPC*. At Y^* there is no demand pressure on the price level; hence the only influence on actual inflation is expected inflation. Any stable rate of inflation (provided it is accommodated by the appropriate rate of monetary expansion) is compatible with Y^* and its associated NAIRU.

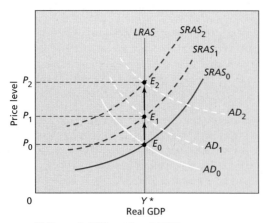

(i) Upward-shifting *AD* and *SRAS* curves

(ii) Steady inflation

Figure 30.12 Monetary accommodation and steady inflation

Positive expected inflation means that unit costs will be rising even when output is only at its potential level; monetary accommodation can then keep GDP constant and sustain the inflation rate. The expected inflation rate is shown in part (ii) by $\dot{c}_e$, which determines the height of the short-run Phillips curve above the axis at Y^*. This translates into an *SRAS* curve that is shifting upward at a constant rate from $SRAS_0$ to $SRAS_1$ to $SRAS_2$ in part (i). Monetary accommodation means that the *AD* curve in (i) also shifts upward, from AD_0 to AD_1 to AD_2. As drawn, the monetary accommodation just keeps GDP constant at Y^*, so inflation persists at the expected rate $\dot{c}_e$. The inflation of unit costs in part (ii) is reflected in a constant rate of price increase, with the price level going from P_0 to P_1 to P_2 in part (i). Since the economy is on its *LRPC*, expected inflation is constant and the *SRPC* is stable.

Is inflation dead?

In Figure 30.1 on page 511 we saw that inflation is projected to stay low in the advanced economies in the early years of the twenty-first century. One should not conclude from this that inflation no longer matters. On the contrary, the correct conclusion is that high inflation is so disruptive to a modern economy—and the costs of eliminating it once it is entrenched are so great—that it is important that the lessons of the recent past be learned and remembered by future generations, so that similar mistakes are not repeated.

It is not an accident that central banks around the world, from New Zealand to the United Kingdom, and within the euro zone, have been given the power to determine monetary policy independently of elected politicians. This is to avoid the inflationary bias created when politicians are tempted to generate pre-election booms in order to aid their re-election. This problem is known as

time-inconsistency, since it is in the self-interest of politicians to promise low inflation, but then also to break their promise at a later date, once inflation expectations are low. This means that leaving the control of inflation to elected politicians can bring into question the credibility of counterinflationary credentials. A central bank with, at least, instrument independence can solve this problem. It is in the interest of the appointed central bankers to deliver on the imposed objective of price stability. Central bankers who do not stand for re-election have less problem in establishing a highly credible low-inflation regime.

This regime change is an important component in the explanation of why inflation has fallen and why it is expected to stay low. However, the underlying cause has been both a public determination to support anti-inflation policies and a realization by the politicians themselves that inflation does not deliver prosperity. Economists have played an important role in the debate about the causes of and cures for inflation, and it was economic analysis that underpinned the case for independent central banks.

While inflation has generally been conquered by the late 1990s, there is no guarantee that it will stay low for ever. After all, it was low throughout the 1950s and 1960s, yet the 1970s followed. Only sound monetary policies can deliver continued low inflation. Monetary policy is made by human beings, as are the institutions within which monetary policies are formulated. Thus it is important that economists continue to study, and increase their understanding of, inflation, so that future generations can learn by our mistakes rather than from their own.

The efforts of the 1980s and 1990s to bring down inflation have not been costless. Many millions of workers have spent time in unemployment, and many owners of businesses have seen their business go bust, in the recessions that followed episodes of sharp monetary tightening. Indeed, in the late 1990s unemployment across Europe was at very high levels by historical standards, and one of the proximate causes was the tight monetary and fiscal policies of the earlier 1990s. The issue then is not just how to control inflation, but rather how to control inflation *and* maintain a high level of employment and economic activity. It is to the issue of employment and unemployment that we now turn.

Summary

Inflation in the macro model

■ A shift in the *SRAS* curve is called a supply shock, while a shift in the *AD* curve is called a demand shock.

■ A single leftward shift in the *SRAS* curve causes a rise in the price level and a fall in GDP. Full employment can be restored either by a fall in unit wage costs, which shifts the *SRAS* curve to the right, or by a monetary expansion, which shifts the *AD* curve to the right.

■ Repeated supply shocks in terms of leftward shifts of the *SRAS* curve carry their own restraining force in terms of ever-rising unemployment if they are not accommodated by monetary expansion. If accommodated, they can give rise to a sustained supply-side inflation.

■ An isolated expansionary demand shock leads to a temporary rise in GDP and a rise in the price level. If it is not validated, output will fall while the price level rises as GDP returns to its potential level.

■ Sustained demand shocks that are validated by monetary expansion lead to sustained inflation with GDP remaining above potential.

The Phillips curve

■ The original Phillips curve relates wage inflation to the level of unemployment; suitably transformed, it relates unit cost inflation to GDP. It thus determines the rate at which the *SRAS* curve is shifting.

■ Unit cost inflation depends on the state of demand—being positive when $Y > Y^*$ and negative when $Y < Y^*$—and on expectations of inflation and random shocks. The expectations-augmented Phillips curve relates GDP to unit cost inflation and is displaced from the point of zero

demand inflation at $Y = Y^*$ by the amount of expectational inflation.

Rising inflation

■ When $Y > Y^*$, actual inflation must exceed expected inflation. If expected inflation adjusts towards actual inflation, then the expectations-augmented Phillips curve must be shifting upwards. Hence if GDP is held above potential by a constant amount, inflation must be rising.

■ A sustained inflation at a constant rate is possible only when $Y = Y^*$ and the monetary authorities accommodate the inflation. Expected inflation is then equal to actual inflation.

Is inflation dead?

■ The establishment of a low-inflation environment at the end of the 1990s was aided by the institutional changes that put monetary policy in the hands of central banks with independent control over the monetary policy instruments (as discussed in Chapter 25).

Topics for review

■ The causes and consequences of demand and supply shocks

■ Once-and-for-all and sustained inflations

■ Wage inflation, productivity growth, and unit costs

■ The NAIRU

■ The original, the transformed, and the expectations-augmented Phillips curves

■ The causes of sustained inflations

■ The credibility of independent central banks

Questions for discussion

1 Starting from equilibrium, explain what happens to inflation when there is a one-off rise in the price of oil but the monetary authorities do not accommodate the shock.

2 Repeat question 1, but now assume that the monetary authorities relax monetary policy in an attempt to avoid any output loss from the supply shock.

3 What is the difference between the short-run and long-run Phillips curves? How do these relate to the short-run

and long-run aggregate supply curves that we studied in Chapters 23 and 24?

4 Using the Phillips curve framework, outline how inflation and unemployment respond (starting from zero inflation and at the NAIRU) to a permanent positive exogenous shock to aggregate demand. Make clear what you are assuming about the monetary policy response.

5 Repeat question 4 but now assume that there has been an exogenous negative supply shock.

6 What factors lay behind the high inflation of the 1970s and what changed by the 1990s to bring about the apparent elimination of inflation?

Chapter 31
Employment and Unemployment

In the previous chapter we learned that inflation was a major problem in the 1970s and 1980s but that it had largely been brought under control by the late 1990s. Part of the price paid for bringing inflation down was higher unemployment, though the high unemployment levels often associated with lowering inflation are usually temporary. Indeed unemployment too has fallen in several countries, such as the United States and the United Kingdom, where in the second half of the 1990s it fell to levels not seen since the 1970s. But unemployment remained a problem in many economies, especially within the European Union. As the 1994 *OECD Jobs Study* put it,

Unemployment is probably the most widely feared phenomenon of our times. It touches all parts of society. There are 35 million people unemployed in OECD countries (about 8.5 per cent of the labour force). Perhaps another 15 million have either given up looking for work or unwillingly accepted a part-time job. As many as a third of young workers in some OECD countries have no job.

Economic growth will play a part in reducing unemployment. But beyond the cyclical component of unemployment is a structural element that persists even into recovery. This is harder to reduce and is even more troubling.

Structural unemployment grows from the gap between the pressure on the economies to adapt to change and their ability to do so. Adaptation is fundamental to progress in a world of new technologies, globalisation and intense national and international competition.

The Keynesian revolution, which established the branch of economics we now call macroeconomics, was stimulated by the need to explain and then solve the high unemployment problems of the 1930s. The proposed solution focused on the use of countercyclical aggregate demand policies to cure unemployment. The simple message that unemployment can be cured by stimulating demand is no longer accepted in its original form. Most unemployment policies did not distinguish between unemployment that arises when the economy is below potential output and the unemployment that would exist even when the economy is in equilibrium at the potential level of GDP. Early Keynesian macroeconomics focused mainly on the former, which is called *cyclical* unemployment. We now know that the latter type of unemployment, called *equilibrium* unemployment, is also important. Hence we need explanations of both cyclical and equilibrium unemployment.

In this chapter we first introduce some definitions and measurement issues relating to unemployment. Next we set out some of the stylized facts. Then we study cyclical unemployment. Finally, we discuss equilibrium unemployment and the NAIRU[1] in much more detail. In particular we ask, 'Why does equilibrium unemployment exist and what makes it change?' and 'Can government policy do anything to reduce the NAIRU?'

Employment and unemployment characteristics

Measurement and definitions

For purposes of study the unemployed can be classified in various ways. They can be grouped by personal characteristics, such as age, sex, degree of skill or education, and ethnic group. They can also be classified by geographical location, by occupation, by the duration of unemployment, or by the reasons for their unemployment. In this chapter we are concerned with explanations of unemploy-ment. Although it is not always possible to say why a particular person does not have a job, it is usually possible to test hypotheses about the causes of aggregate unemployment differences, both over time for one country and between countries at the same point in time.

The recorded figures for unemployment may significantly understate or overstate the numbers who are actually

[1] The non-accelerating-inflation rate of unemployment (NAIRU) was explained in Chapter 30.

willing to work at the existing set of wage rates. Overstatement arises because the measured figure for unemployment includes people who are not interested in work but who say they are in order to collect unemployment benefits. Understatement arises because of the voluntary withdrawal from the labour force of people who would like to work but have ceased to believe that suitable jobs are available. Although these people may not be measured in the unemployment figures, they are unemployed in the sense that they would accept a job if one were available at the going wage rate. People in this category are referred to as *discouraged workers*. They have voluntarily withdrawn from the labour force, not because they do not want to work, but because they believe that they cannot find a job given current labour market conditions.

The ways in which unemployment is measured have changed many times over the years. UK figures used to include only those people actively looking for work and registering for benefits. This is referred to as the *claimant*

count. The claimant count is still published, but it is more common to use a measure of unemployment based upon a survey of the labour force. These two measures of unemployment are explained in Box 31.1.

There are three main types of unemployment that we will refer to in this chapter. **Cyclical** or **demand-deficient unemployment** occurs when aggregate desired expenditures in the economy are insufficient to purchase the output that would be supplied when the economy is at potential GDP. An alternative definition, which focuses on the labour market rather than the goods market, is that this is unemployment in excess of the NAIRU. **Frictional unemployment** is unemployment that arises as part of the normal turnover of labour. For example, in a market economy firms and products are continually changing and workers are moving from one job to another, or from work to training and from training to work. In the course of this dynamic movement there will always be some workers who are between jobs and classified as unemployed. **Struc-**

Box 31.1 How is unemployment measured?

Figure 30.1 on page 511 shows data for the numbers unemployed in the United Kingdom since 1963, and Figure 2.2 on page 21 shows similar data expressed as a percentage of the workforce. Both these figures use the same measure of unemployment, which is known as the *claimant count*. The claimant count gives us the longest available data series on UK unemployment, but it is being replaced as the standard measure of unemployment by a different series. This alternative measure is an international standard defined by the United Nations International Labour Office, and hence it is known as *ILO unemployment*. The European Union and the OECD have adopted the ILO unemployment definition. So what is the difference between the claimant count and ILO unemployment?

The claimant count

The UK claimant count is all those people claiming unemployment-related benefits at Employment Service offices. In 1998 the relevant benefits that could be claimed were the Jobseeker's Allowance and National Insurance credits. Percentage unemployment is then expressed using the numbers of claimants as a percentage of 'workforce jobs' plus claimant unemployment. *Workforce jobs* is a measure of the number of full-time and part-time jobs in the economy.

One big advantage of the claimant count is that it is an accurate measure of *all* those claiming benefits. It gives a correct picture of who is registered for benefits both at national level and at local level, and it is timely in that it does not take long to produce an unemployment figure. But there are several disadvantages. First, as the benefits system changes, so the numbers able to claim benefits change. Second, it does not measure anyone who is unemployed but does not bother to claim benefit. Third, the measure of workforce jobs overestimates the numbers in work because it counts twice anyone with two jobs, so the *percentage* of persons unemployed is underestimated.

ILO unemployment

Under the ILO approach all people aged 16 and over are classified into one

of three states: in employment, ILO unemployed, or economically inactive. ILO unemployed are those who either

- are out of work, want a job, have actively sought work in the last four weeks, and are available to start work in the next two weeks, or
- are out of work, have found a job, and are waiting to start it in the next two weeks.

Anyone who carries out at least one hour's paid work in a week, is on a government-supported training scheme, does unpaid work for a family business, or is away temporarily from a job (such as on vacation) is counted as being in employment. Those who are out of work but do not meet the criteria for ILO unemployment are defined as economically inactive. The unemployment percentage expresses numbers of ILO unemployed as a percentage of the total numbers of economically active.

ILO unemployment is measured by means of a monthly survey, which in the United Kingdom is called the Labour Force Survey (LFS), and hence ILO unemployment is sometimes also referred to as *LFS unemployment*. About 40,000 individuals are interviewed each month, and the unemployment figure announced is the average of data for the last three months.

The advantage of the ILO measure of unemployment is that it is comprehensive—it measures those who say they are unemployed and not just those claiming benefits. The disadvantages are that it is based on a survey and so is subject to sampling error, it takes time to produce, it lumps together as 'employed' anyone who takes even one hour's paid work with those who work much longer hours, and, because of the small numbers involved, it is not accurate at the local level.

In 1998Q2 UK unemployment by the ILO definition was 1.802 million, while the claimant count was 1.361 million. The unemployment percentage was 6.2 by the ILO definition and 4.8 by the claimant count definition. These are by no means insignificant differences; missing half a million people who are looking for work from the unemployment measure is not a trivial matter. In the same period the ILO unemployment percentage was 4.3 in the United States, 11.2 in Germany, and 11.8 in France.

tural unemployment occurs when there is a mismatch between the characteristics and skills of the people looking for work and those desired by potential employers. Jobs may exist in London while the workers available are in Liverpool, or there may be plenty of opportunities for computer programmers while many social workers are looking for jobs. Frictional and structural unemployment make up **equilibrium unemployment,** which is defined as the unemployment that exists when GDP is at its potential level, and hence when there is neither a recessionary nor an inflationary gap. In what follows we assume that equilibrium unemployment and the NAIRU are the same.

UK experience

Figure 30.1 on page 511 shows UK unemployment since 1963. It looks as though there was a rising trend in UK unemployment in successive cycles, through the 1970s and into the 1980s, though the trend may be downward in the 1990s. Indeed, a longer perspective suggests that there is no long-term upward trend. Rather, there is a high degree of persistence. Once unemployment is high it tends to stay high; once low it tends to stay low. In the inter-war period unemployment was consistently high, but in the 1950s and 1960s it was consistently low. In the 1980s and early 1990s it has been high, but not as high as in the 1930s.

Unemployment varies much more between business cycles than within business cycles. For example, in the 1920s and 1930s unemployment cycled about a high average level, but in the 1950s it cycled about a low level. Also, compare the low average unemployment levels of the 1960s and early 1970s with the high levels of the 1980s. This evidence suggests that there are long-term changes in social institutions affecting employment and unemployment, and perhaps that big shocks to the economic system —a major war being the obvious example—have long-lasting effects.

Total employment in the United Kingdom has been remarkably stable in the post-war period. The numbers in employment in 1998 were less than 10 per cent higher than in 1960, nearly four decades earlier. This is partly explained by slow population growth, but there have also been some big structural changes in the pattern of employment. There were, for example, big shifts between sectors, such as a decline in manufacturing employment and a rise in services. Also there have been changes in the composition of the labour force. Increased female participation rates have been offset by declining male employment.

International comparisons

As the *OECD Jobs Study* quoted above makes clear, unemployment has not been a uniquely UK problem. Hence international comparisons are instructive.

(i) Unemployment rates (%)

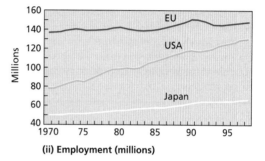

(ii) Employment (millions)

Figure 31.1 Employment and unemployment in the EU, the USA, and Japan, 1970–1998

The behaviour of employment and unemployment has varied considerably within the industrialized world.

Part (i) shows that unemployment was high in the EU in the 1980s and 1990s, but it fell in the USA and remained low in Japan. The chart is based on national definitions.

Part (ii) shows that the US economy created 50 million jobs between 1970 and 1998 whereas the EU created only about 10 million. The shaded areas in both parts indicate IMF staff projections.

Source: IMF, *World Economic Outlook*, Oct. 1997.

There has been a dramatic contrast over the last three decades between employment growth in the United States and employment growth in Europe. Total employment grew by only 10 per cent in EU countries between 1970 and 1998, whereas in the USA employment grew by over 60 per cent in the same period. This is shown in part (ii) of Figure 31.1.

In part this reflects slow population growth in Europe, compared with high levels of immigration into the United States. However, Europe has also found itself with much higher levels of unemployment than the US level in the late 1990s, as shown in Figure 31.1(i), though both had consistently higher unemployment than Japan.[2]

Unemployment varies between countries, even within

---

[2] Japanese unemployment measures differ markedly from European ones and are generally considered to underestimate the true level of unemployment. Note that the projections in Figure 31.1(i) turned out to be wrong as Japanese unemployment exceeded that in the USA by late 1998.

the European Union. In 1998, for example, unemployment in EU member states varied from a low of 3.6 per cent in Luxembourg to a high of 19.9 per cent in Spain. Figure 31.2 shows that unemployment was rising in France, Germany, and Italy in the mid-1990s, but that in Ireland, the Netherlands, Denmark, and the United Kingdom it fell steadily after 1994.

It is dangerous to make comparisons when countries may be at different stages of the business cycle. However, there is one broad generalization that will be helpful in our attempt to understand the causes of equilibrium unemployment. Unemployment is the result of the balance of two continuous flows: the inflow of potential workers into unemployment (leaving employment but seeking work, or joining the labour force but not finding employment) and the outflow of workers from unemployment (finding jobs, or withdrawing from the labour force).

In EU countries the flow into unemployment is quite small and does not change much over time. However, the outflow is also small, so a very high proportion of workers who are unemployed have been unemployed for a long

time. For example, in Belgium, Ireland, and Italy around 60 per cent of the unemployed (in 1994) had been unemployed for more than twelve months, defined as long-term unemployment. The figures for Germany, France, and the United Kingdom were all around 35 per cent. This contrasts with Canada and the United States, where only just over 10 per cent had been unemployed for more than twelve months. In the United States, in particular, flows into unemployment are high, but flows out are just as high, so the level of long-term unemployment is low.

This may give an important clue as to the causes of the higher persistence of unemployment in the European Union. Skills and human capital deteriorate during periods out of employment, so the long-term unemployed are perceived (rightly or wrongly) as being less employable than those who have recently been in work.

A common pattern across countries is that low-skilled workers are four or five times more likely to be unemployed than skilled or professional workers. About 75 per cent of unemployed men are manual workers. This suggests that it is the unemployment of unskilled manual workers that should be the main focus of study.

Older workers are less likely to be unemployed than young workers. Youth unemployment is universally higher than adult unemployment—extreme cases include Spain with 43 per cent youth unemployment, and Italy with 30 per cent; the UK figure was 17 per cent in 1994.

In most EU countries female unemployment is greater than male unemployment. The United Kingdom is the exception, with 5.5 per cent female unemployment compared with around 7.3 per cent for males in 1997 (although a high proportion of female employment is part-time[3]).

Another universal feature of unemployment is that movement into the ranks of the unemployed is predominantly the result of redundancy rather than voluntary job-leaving. This may seem obvious, but it is important from an economic theory perspective because the New Classical school, first discussed in Chapter 27, has attempted to explain unemployment as a voluntary choice made by workers. There is certainly some element of choice involved in deciding whether or not to accept a job offer once one has been located, but this is very different from having chosen to be unemployed in the first place. Hence most economists believe that the majority of those who are recorded as unemployed are involuntarily unemployed. Someone is **involuntarily unemployed** if they would accept an offer of work in a job for which they are trained, at the going wage rate, if such an offer could be found.

Figure 31.2 Unemployment rates in specific EU countries, 1970–1998

Unemployment has reached new peaks in the EU and in Germany, France, and Italy. In the UK, the Netherlands, Denmark, and Ireland, however, unemployment has declined. The charts are based on national definitions of unemployment, and the shaded areas indicate IMF staff projections.

Source: IMF, *World Economic Outlook*, Oct. 1997.

---

[3] A survey of females in part-time jobs in the spring of 1993 found that 80 per cent did not want full-time employment, 10 per cent could not find a full-time job, and most of the rest were studying part-time. Among the much smaller group of males in part-time jobs, 30 per cent would have preferred a full-time job (*source*: CSO, *Social Trends*, 1994, Table 4.13).

Consequences of unemployment

Involuntary unemployment is a social 'bad' just as much as output is a social 'good'. The harm caused by such involuntary unemployment is measured in terms of the output lost to the whole economy and the harm done to the individuals who are affected.

Lost output   Every involuntarily unemployed person is someone willing and able to work but unable to find a job. The unemployed are valuable resources whose potential output is wasted. The material counterpart of unemployment is the recessionary gap—potential GDP that is not produced. The cumulative loss of UK output in the seven years 1991–7 was £120 billion (at 1990 prices);[4] this is about £2,000 for every member of the population, or about £4,600 for each member of the labour force. In a world of scarcity with many unsatisfied wants, this loss is serious. It represents goods and services that could have been produced but are gone for ever.

Personal costs   The social welfare system, designed to alleviate the short-term economic consequences of unemployment, has been extended in the post-war period. Being unemployed in the United Kingdom, even for some substantial period of time, is no longer quite the personal disaster that it once was. But the longer-term effects of high unemployment rates for the disillusioned, who have given up trying to make it within the system and who contribute to social unrest, should be a matter of serious concern to the haves as well as the have-nots. As UK economists Richard Layard, Stephen Nickell, and Richard Jackman put it in *The Unemployment Crisis* (OUP, 1994),

Unemployment matters. It generally reduces output and aggregate income. It increases inequality, since the unemployed lose more than the employed. It erodes human capital. And, finally, it involves psychic costs. People need to be needed. Though unemployment increases leisure, the value of this is largely offset by the pain of rejection.

We now proceed to study the causes of cyclical and structural unemployment before asking what policymakers can do to reduce unemployment.

Cyclical unemployment

Cyclical unemployment, or demand-deficient unemployment, occurs whenever total demand is insufficient to purchase all of the economy's potential output, causing a recessionary gap in which actual output is less than potential output. Cyclical unemployment can be measured as the number of persons who would be employed if the economy were at potential GDP minus the number of persons currently employed. When cyclical unemployment is zero, all existing unemployment is either structural or frictional, and the rate of unemployment is the NAIRU. Notice that cyclical unemployment can be less than zero, because GDP can be above potential GDP, at least temporarily.

Macroeconomic theory has traditionally sought to explain only cyclical unemployment.

Equilibrium unemployment was once presumed to be outside the scope of macroeconomics. However, we will see below that it is unwise to try to establish a simple dichotomy between cyclical unemployment as being due to macro causes and equilibrium unemployment as being due to micro causes. Both micro and macro factors contribute to cyclical unemployment and to equilibrium unemployment. (The microeconomics of labour markets is discussed in Chapter 15.) Indeed, we will find that a

strong case can be made for the view that high cyclical unemployment raises the level of equilibrium unemployment for some time. Hence we must caution against the presumption that cyclical unemployment and equilibrium unemployment have different causes, or, indeed, that they are unrelated. However, it is useful to analyse cyclical unemployment separately, because this is the component of unemployment that can potentially be reduced by monetary and fiscal policies, via their effect in shifting aggregate demand.

Fluctuations in GDP are not sufficient to create fluctuations in involuntary unemployment. Something else is needed. Suppose, for example, that aggregate demand is fluctuating, causing GDP to fluctuate around its potential level. This fluctuation will cause the demand for labour to fluctuate as well, rising in booms and falling in slumps. If the labour market had fully flexible wage rates, then wages would fluctuate to keep quantity demanded equal to quantity supplied. We would observe cyclical fluctuations in employment (and therefore also in voluntary unemployment) and in the wage rate, but no changes

---

[4]   This figure is calculated using the IMF estimates of actual and potential GDP shown in Figure 21.1 on page 357. The loss is just the sum of the gaps between actual and potential output in each of these seven years.

in involuntary unemployment. Employment and wages would vary procyclically (i.e. rising in booms and falling in slumps), but there would be no significant amounts of involuntary unemployment. Such behaviour is shown for a typical labour market in Figure 31.3.

The hypothetical situation we have just described is not what we actually observe. Instead we see cyclical fluctuations not only in employment, but also in involuntary unemployment. Furthermore, the changes in wage rates that do occur are insufficient to equate demand and supply, as is shown in Figure 31.4. Unemployment exceeds the NAIRU in slumps and is below it in booms. Although wages do tend to vary procyclically over the cycle, the fluctuations are not sufficient to remove all cyclical variations in unemployment. Why is this so?

Two types of explanation have been advanced over the years. The line that we consider first is associated with the New Classical school, first discussed in Chapter 27. Their explanation assumes that labour markets are always in equilibrium in the sense that quantity demanded is continually equated with quantity supplied. While the New Classical approach is hard to accept as a description of the causes of unemployment, for reasons already mentioned (such as the assumption of no involuntary lay-offs), the New Classical school set down a challenge which was picked up under the umbrella of what is called the New Keynesian agenda. Also, it is worth noting that the predic-

tions of New Classical models and New Keynesian models, while based on very different assumptions, are difficult to distinguish empirically.

The New Classical approach

The major characteristic of the New Classical approach is that agents continuously optimize and markets continuously clear; hence there can be no involuntary unemployment. They then seek to explain unemployment as the outcome of voluntary decisions made by rational people who are choosing to do what they do, including spending some time out of employment. Notice the contrast with traditional Keynesian (and early monetarist) macroeconomics. Theories in this class assume that unemployment is a sign of market failure, associated with non-market-clearing prices and/or wages, and that a high proportion of unemployment is involuntary.

One New Classical explanation of cyclical fluctuations in employment assumes that they are caused by fluctuations in the willingness of people to supply their labour, as shown in part (ii) of Figure 31.3. If the supply curve of labour fluctuates cyclically, this will lead to cyclical variations in employment. This explanation of cyclical behaviour in the labour market has two problems. First, the wage will tend to rise in slumps and fall in booms,

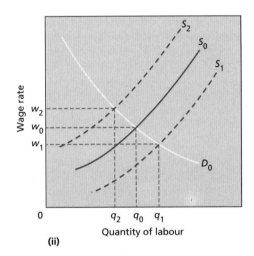

Figure 31.3 Employment and wages in a single competitive labour market

In a perfectly competitive labour market, wages and employment fluctuate in the same direction when demand fluctuates and in opposite directions when supply fluctuates; in both cases there is no involuntary unemployment. The figure shows a single perfectly competitive market for one type of labour. In part (i) the demand curves D_1, D_2, and D_0 are the demands for this market when there is a slump, a boom, and when aggregate GDP is at its potential level. As demand rises from D_1 to D_0 to D_2, wages rise from w_1 to w_0 to w_2, and employment rises from q_1 to q_0 to q_2. At no time, however, is there any involuntary unemployment.

In part (ii) the supply of labour fluctuates from S_1 to S_0 to S_2, and wages fluctuate from w_1 to w_0 to w_2. In this case wages fall when employment rises and vice versa, but again there is no involuntary unemployment.

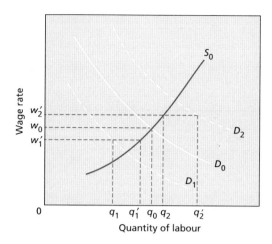

Figure 31.4 Unemployment in a single labour market with sticky wages

When the wage rate does not change enough to equate quantity demanded and quantity supplied at all times, there will be unemployment in slumps and labour shortages in booms in each individual labour market. When demand is at its normal level, D_0, the market is cleared with wage rate w_0, employment is q_0, and there is no unemployment. In a recession demand falls to D_1, but the wage falls only to w_1'. As a result q_1 labour is demanded, but q_1' is supplied. Employment is determined by the quantity demanded at q_1; the remainder of the supply for which there is no demand, $q_1 q_1'$, is unemployed. In a boom demand rises to D_2, but the wage rate rises only to w_2'. As a result the quantity demanded is q_2', whereas only q_2 is supplied. Employment rises to q_2, that is, the amount supplied; the rest of the demand cannot be satisfied, making an excess demand for labour of $q_2 q_2'$.

which is not what we observe. Second, there will still be no systematic cyclical *involuntary unemployment*, since labour markets always clear, leaving everyone who wishes to work actually working. Supply-induced fluctuations in employment form part of the basis of what is called real business cycle theory, which was discussed in Chapter 27. However, the real supply shocks that trigger 'real' business cycles cause changes in the NAIRU, so at best this explains variations in equilibrium but not cyclical unemployment.[5]

A second line of explanation lies in errors on the part of workers and employers in predicting the course of the price level over the business cycle. To understand the argument, start by assuming that each of the economy's markets is in equilibrium, that there is full employment, that prices are stable, and that the actual and the expected rates of inflation are zero. Now suppose that the government relaxes monetary policy to permit the money supply to increase unexpectedly by 5 per cent in such a way that inflation expectations are unaffected. People find themselves with unwanted money balances, which they seek to spend. For simplicity assume that the increased money

supply leads to an increase in desired expenditure on *all* commodities. The demand for each commodity shifts to the right, and all prices, being competitively determined, rise. Individual decision-makers see their selling prices go up and mistakenly interpret the increase as a rise in their own relative price. This is because they expect the overall inflation rate to be zero. Firms will produce more, and workers will work more, because both groups think they are getting an increased *relative* price for what they sell. Thus total output and employment rise.

When both groups eventually realize that their own relative prices are in fact unchanged, output and employment fall back to their initial levels. The extra output and employment occur only while people are being fooled. When they realize that *all* prices have risen by 5 per cent, they revert to their initial behaviour. The only difference is that now the price level has risen by 5 per cent, leaving relative prices unchanged.

A similar argument shows that an unanticipated monetary contraction would cause output to fall below its full-employment level.

All New Classical explanations assume that labour markets clear, and then look for reasons why employment fluctuates. They all imply, therefore, that people who are not working have voluntarily withdrawn from the labour market, either because this is their optimal decision or because they have misinterpreted market signals.

The New Keynesian agenda

Many economists find New Classical explanations implausible. They believe that people correctly read market signals but react in ways that do not cause markets to be in equilibrium at all times. These economists believe that many who are recorded as unemployed are involuntarily unemployed.

However, the New Classical approach has attractions. It assumes rational agents who are always optimizing. In other words it has rigorous microfoundations which are attractive to economists trained to analyse the utility-maximizing behaviour of agents interacting in clearing markets. Economists so trained are uncomfortable with the early Keynesian assumptions of arbitrary price and wage stickiness (in the face of sustained excess supply) and markets that do not clear. Those who are unhappy to assume no involuntary unemployment therefore seek to explain why there could be a labour market *equilibrium* in which there is an excess supply of labour at the going wage. We refer to this as the New Keynesian 'agenda' rather than

[5] The distinction here is semantic if the NAIRU is cyclical. We do not pursue the argument further, because although supply shocks are undoubtedly important, the assumption of continuous market-clearing seems unnecessarily restrictive and implausible.

'theory', because there are many different theories encompassed by it and it is ongoing.[6]

Most attempts to explain involuntary unemployment examine the forces that determine wage-setting and hiring decisions in realistic labour market institutions. They look for reasons (consistent with optimizing behaviour by participants) why wages do not respond quickly to shifts in supply and demand in the labour market. So quantity supplied and quantity demanded may *not* be equated for extended periods of time. Labour markets will then display unemployment during recessions and excess demand during booms. This is shown for one typical labour market in Figure 31.4.

These theories start with the everyday observation that wage rates do not change every time demand or supply shifts. When unemployed workers are looking for jobs, they do not knock on employers' doors and offer to work at lower wages than are being paid to current workers. Instead, they answer job advertisements and hope to get the jobs offered, but often are disappointed. Similarly, employers, seeing an excess of applicants for the few jobs that are available, do not go to their current workers and reduce their wages until there is no one who is looking for a job.[7]

In discussing New Keynesian approaches, it is helpful to divide them into two groups. The first seeks to explain nominal wage and price rigidities that slow the adjustment towards full equilibrium. The second focuses on real wage rigidities which are not eliminated over time, but continue in full equilibrium. We will associate the former approaches with long-term relationships and menu costs; the latter we will discuss in the context of efficiency wages and union bargaining models. Chapter 15 also discusses labour markets and covers some of the same issues in more detail.

Long-term relationships

One set of theories explains the familiar observation that money wages do not adjust to clear labour markets as resulting from the advantages to both workers and employers of relatively long-term, stable employment relationships. Workers want job security in the face of fluctuating demand; employers want workers who understand the firm's organization, production, and marketing plans. Under these circumstances both parties care about things in addition to the wage rate, and wages become somewhat less sensitive to fluctuations in current economic conditions. Wages are in effect regular payments to workers over an extended employment relationship, rather than a device for fine-tuning the current supplies and demands for labour. Given this situation, the tendency is for employers to 'smooth out' the income of employees by paying a steady money wage and letting profits and employment fluctuate to absorb the effects of temporary increases and decreases in demand for the firm's product.

A number of labour market institutions work to achieve these results. Employment contracts provide for a schedule of money wages over a period of several years. Fringe benefits, such as membership of the company pension scheme, a company car, and perhaps private health insurance, tend to bind workers to their employers. A worker's pay tends to rise with years of service, despite the known fact that the output attributable to workers rises rapidly as they gain experience, reaches a peak, and then falls off as they age. Under gradually rising wages, workers who spend a long time in the same firm tend to get less than the value of their marginal product when they are young and more than the value of their marginal product as they near retirement. But over the long haul they are paid, on average, the value of their marginal product, just as microeconomic theory predicts. Such features help to bind the employee to the company, whereas redundancy pay, related to years of service, tends to bind the employer to the long-term worker, who would cost the firm more to dismiss.

In labour markets characterized by long-term relationships, the wage rate does not fluctuate to clear the market. Wages are written over what has been called the long-term 'economic climate' rather than the short-term 'economic weather'. Optimizing firms in such an environment will adjust employment rather than wages during the cycle. However, employees might prefer to accept a lower wage rather than be laid off. So it remains unclear why sticky wages are optimal for both workers and firms.

Menu costs and wage contracts

A typical large manufacturing firm sells differentiated products numbered in the thousands and employs hundreds of different types of labour. Changing prices and wages in response to every minor fluctuation in demand is a costly and time-consuming activity. Firms find it optimal to keep their price lists (*menus*) constant for significant periods of time. Since all manufacturing firms are operating in imperfectly competitive markets, they have some discretion over price. Hence it may be optimal for firms to react to small changes in demand by holding prices constant and responding with changes in output and employment. If many firms are behaving this way, output and employment will respond to changes in aggregate demand.

The UK evidence is consistent with the existence of sluggish price adjustment by manufacturers. This, of

---

[6] Many economists working in this area might not accept the label 'Keynesian'. Indeed, some of the new approaches explain why real wages may be held 'too high' to generate employment for all those seeking work at the going wage. This used to be called 'Classical' unemployment. 'Keynesian' used to be reserved for demand-deficient unemployment. Thus much of the new work makes these old taxonomies irrelevant.

[7] This observation concerns cyclical variations in the demand for labour. It does not conflict with the different observation that when firms get into long-term competitive trouble, workers sometimes renegotiate contracts and agree to wage cuts in order to save the firm, and their jobs.

course, is where Keynesian economics came in (with an assumption of price stickiness). The New Keynesian literature attempts to model it as an optimal response to adjustment costs and adverse customer reactions.

Money wages tend to be inflexible in the short term because wage rates are generally set on an annual basis. In some other countries they are set for longer periods—three years is not uncommon with union contracts in North America. Such short-term inflexibility of wages, particularly in the face of negative supply shocks such as the oil price shocks of 1973 and 1979, will lead to increases in unemployment.

We now turn to a discussion of the New Keynesian approaches that focus on real rigidities in labour markets.

Efficiency wages

The idea of the *efficiency wage* forms the core of a strand of thinking about why it may be optimal for firms to set wages permanently above the level that would clear the labour market. Efficiency wage theory applies to hiring, to productivity on the job, and to worker turnover.

Workers are not homogeneous. There are good workers and bad workers, but there is *asymmetrical information*: firms do not know the characteristics of a specific worker until after they have sunk costs into hiring and training her. Good workers know who they are and are likely to have a higher reservation wage (the wage at which they are prepared to work) than bad workers. By lowering the wage they offer, firms will significantly lower the average ability of the workers who apply to them for jobs, and so they could find that paying lower wages makes them worse off. This is known as *adverse selection*. It is a concept we have already met in the context of insurance (see pages 194–5), but it is also an essential feature of labour markets.

In labour markets with informational asymmetries, where unobserved characteristics of job applicants are correlated with the reservation wage, it may not be optimal for firms to pay the market-clearing wage.

Once in employment, workers are likely to give greater effort if they feel they are being well rewarded and the costs of losing their job are high. If wages are so low that workers are just indifferent between staying and losing their jobs, they are likely to please themselves how hard they work and they will not be afraid of getting the sack. Employers have a problem of monitoring and enforcing efficient work practices—this is another case of the principal–agent problem discussed on page 211. Paying a high wage reduces the problem, both because workers will expect to be much worse off if they lose their current job, and because there will be a queue of good-quality workers prepared to work for the higher wage. The high wage improves efficiency—hence the term *efficiency wages*.

Another way in which higher wages may improve productivity is through the direct effects on worker nutrition and general health. In improving the physical well-being of the worker, the marginal productivity of workers may be increased. This is a very important effect in developing countries, but it may also apply in some sectors of developed economies. However, an effect that clearly does apply in developed countries is that workers who are paid well above their best alternative wage have an incentive to invest in self-education and skill acquisition in order to secure their continued employment prospects.

Finally, firms for which high quit rates are costly will be reluctant to lower the wages of existing workers, even in the face of an excess supply of labour. It is possible for firms to pay lower wages to new workers, but tiered wage structures, in which several people doing the same job get different rates of pay, often cause morale problems. This does not prevent firms from paying experienced workers more than inexperienced ones. But it does restrain firms from responding to job queues by offering new workers a lower lifetime earnings profile than that enjoyed by existing workers.

Efficiency wage theory implies that firms may find it advantageous to pay high enough wages so that working is a clearly superior alternative to being laid off. This will improve the quality of workers' output without firms having to spend heavily to monitor workers' performance.

Efficiency wage theory helps us to understand much about labour markets. It also explains why firms may wish to pay wages above market-clearing levels. This helps to explain why involuntary unemployment can persist in equilibrium when GDP is at its potential level.

Union bargaining

The final theoretical approach to be considered under the New Keynesian agenda assumes that those already in employment ('insiders') have more say in wage bargaining than those out of work ('outsiders'). Typically, those in employment are represented by a union which negotiates the wage rate with firms. The union will generally represent the interests of its members, the bulk of whom will be in employment. It will not necessarily reflect the interests of those excluded from employment.

It is easy to see that insiders will wish to bid up wages even though to do so will harm the employment prospects of outsiders. Hence this framework can generate an outcome to the bargaining process between firms and unions in which the wage is set higher than the market-clearing level, just as with the efficiency wage.

Again, these models help explain the existence of involuntary unemployment even when GDP is at its potential level. However, they do add one important new insight into the causes of international differences in unemployment.

In some countries unions bargain at the level of the firm; in others they bargain at the level of the whole industry or the whole economy. Where bargaining is decentralized, the union can push for higher wages for the insiders without worrying about effects on the rest of the economy or on outsiders. However, where bargaining is centralized, the effects on the rest of the economy become internalized into the bargaining process, because union negotiators are bargaining on behalf of all workers (and potential workers), rather than just those in one firm.

The prediction is that decentralized bargaining with strong unions will lead to higher than market-clearing wages, and the outsiders will be excluded from jobs, whereas centralized bargaining will produce an outcome closer to the market-clearing outcome (because outsider concerns are voiced), so unemployment will be low.

The third alternative to centralized and decentralized union bargaining is no union bargaining at all because unionization is low and unions are weak. This too will produce an outcome close to the free-market rate even in the absence of efficiency wage considerations. This analysis may explain why unemployment is relatively high in EU countries where unions are strong but bargaining is decentralized, but lower in Scandinavia, where unions are also strong but bargaining is centralized, and the United States, where unions are weak.

The basic message of New Keynesian theories of unemployment is that labour markets cannot be relied upon to eliminate involuntary unemployment by equating current demand for labour with current supply.

The New Keynesian theories have concentrated on explaining why wages do not fluctuate to clear labour markets instantaneously. This helps to explain the existence of involuntary cyclical unemployment in the face of fluctuations in aggregate demand. These demand fluctuations are, however, still a necessary part of the explanation of cyclical fluctuations. They leave the emphasis of anticyclical policy on demand-side measures whenever the automatic adjustment mechanism does not work fast enough. To the extent that the theories explain why wages do not clear labour markets even in the long term, they help to explain high *equilibrium unemployment*. It is to this that we now turn.

Equilibrium unemployment: the NAIRU

Equilibrium unemployment, or the NAIRU, is composed of *frictional* and *structural* unemployment.

Frictional unemployment

Frictional unemployment results from the normal turnover of labour. An important source of frictional unemployment is young people who enter the labour force looking for jobs. Another source is people who are in the process of changing their jobs and are caught between one job and the next. Some may quit because they are dissatisfied with the type of work or their working conditions; others may be sacked. Whatever the reason, they must search for new jobs, which takes time. People who are unemployed while searching for jobs are said to be frictionally unemployed or, alternatively, in search unemployment.

The normal turnover of labour would cause some frictional unemployment to persist, even if the economy were at potential GDP and the structure of jobs in terms of skills, industries, occupations, and location were unchanging.

Structural unemployment

Structural adjustments can cause unemployment. When the pattern of demand for goods changes, the pattern of the demand for labour changes. Until labour adjusts fully, structural unemployment develops. Such unemployment may be defined as unemployment caused by a mismatch between the structure of the labour force—in terms of skills, occupations, industries, or geographical locations—and the structure of the demand for labour.

Endogenous change

Changes that accompany economic growth shift the structure of the demand for labour. One of the more dramatic recent structural changes has been in the organization of the firm. Large firms used to be organized much like an army, with a pyramid command structure. Most key strategic decisions were made near the top, with lesser ones concerning implementation made at lower levels. This structure required an array of middle-level managers who passed information upward to the top level and downward to the production level and who made various secondary decisions themselves. Recent changes associated with the IT revolution have led to a much looser organization with much more local autonomy among the subsections of the firm. As a result large numbers of middle managers have been made redundant. They find themselves on the labour market at middle age and with many of their skills rendered obsolete.

Another key structural change in the UK (and in many other economies) has been the decline in manufacturing employment. Employment in this sector has been declining since the late 1950s, but the UK real exchange rate appreciation of the late 1970s and early 1980s (partly associated with another structural change, the emergence of North Sea oil production) accelerated this adjustment in the UK. Many factories closed in the early 1980s or were replaced by capital-intensive rather than labour-intensive plant.

Increases in international competition can have effects similar to those of economic growth and change. As the geographical distribution of world production changes, so does the composition of production and of labour demand in any one country. Labour adapts to such shifts by changing jobs, skills, and locations, but until the transition is complete, structural unemployment exists.

Structural unemployment increases if there is either an increase in the speed at which the structure of the demand for labour is changing or a decrease in the speed at which labour is adapting to these changes.

Policy influences

Government policies can influence the speed with which labour markets adapt to change. Some countries have adopted policies that discourage movement among regions, industries, and occupations. These policies tend to raise structural unemployment, though state subsidies may disguise it for a while. The EU Common Agricultural Policy (CAP), for example, is intended (partly) to resist the decline of incomes and employment in agriculture, even though employment in agriculture has been declining in Europe since the late eighteenth century. Other countries, such as Sweden, have done the reverse and have encouraged workers to adapt to change. Partly for this reason, Sweden's unemployment rates were well below the European average during the 1980s.

Policies that discourage firms from replacing labour with machines may protect employment over the short term. However, if such policies lead to the decline of an industry because it cannot compete effectively with innovative foreign competitors, serious structural unemployment can result in the long run.

High minimum-wage laws may cause structural unemployment by pricing low-skilled labour out of the market. As explained in Chapter 15, minimum-wage laws have two effects when they are imposed on competitive markets: they reduce employment of the unskilled, and they raise the wages of the unskilled who retain their jobs.

Why does the NAIRU change?

We have noted that structural unemployment can increase because the pace of change accelerates or the pace of

adjustment to change slows down. An increase in the rate of growth, for example, usually speeds up the rate at which the structure of the demand for labour is changing. The adaptation of labour to the changing structure of demand may be slowed by such diverse factors as a decline in educational achievement and regulations that make it harder for workers in a given occupation to take new jobs in other areas or occupations. Any of these changes will cause the NAIRU to rise. Changes in the opposite direction will cause the NAIRU to fall.

Demographic changes

Because people usually try several jobs before settling into one for a longer period of time, young or inexperienced workers have higher unemployment rates than experienced workers. The proportion of inexperienced workers in the labour force rose significantly as the post-war baby boom generation entered the labour force in the late 1960s and 1970s, along with an unprecedented number of women who elected to work outside the home. In the 1980s youth unemployment became an even bigger problem, because school-leavers found it hard to get a foothold on the career ladder when unemployment was rising and even experienced workers were being laid off.

Even if youth unemployment should fall in future, many observers worry about the long-term consequences for some individuals. Learning through on-the-job experience is a critical part of developing marketable labour skills, and those who suffered prolonged unemployment during their teens and twenties have been denied that experience early in their working careers. These workers may have little option later in life but to take temporary jobs at low pay and with little future job security, or drop out of the labour force entirely.

The significant increase in female participation rates, and the related increase in the number of households with more than one income-earner, has also affected the NAIRU. When both husband and wife work, it is possible for one to support both while the other looks for 'a really good job', rather than accepting the first job offer that comes along, or spends time in retraining. This can increase recorded unemployment while not inflicting excessive hardship on those involved.

Hysteresis

Recent models of unemployment show that the size of the NAIRU can be influenced by the *size* of the actual current rate of unemployment. Such models get their name from the Greek word **hysteresis,** meaning 'coming late'.[8] In economics it means that the current equilibrium is not independent of what has gone before—it is path-dependent.

---

[8] It was first used in electronics to relate to effects coming after their causes, i.e. lagged effects.

This means that the NAIRU will be higher after periods of high unemployment than after periods of low unemployment. If this is correct, we have to distinguish between the short-run NAIRU and the long-run **natural rate.** The latter is the true long-run equilibrium towards which the short-run NAIRU will adjust slowly over time.

One mechanism that can lead to hysteresis in labour markets has already been noted. It arises from the importance of experience and on-the-job training. Suppose, for example, that a period of recession causes a significant group of new entrants to the labour force to have unusual difficulty in obtaining their first jobs. As a result the unlucky group will be slow to acquire the important skills that workers generally learn in their first jobs. When demand increases again, this group of workers will be at a disadvantage relative to workers with normal histories of job experience, and the unlucky group may have unemployment rates that will be higher than average. Thus the NAIRU will be higher than it would have been had there been no recession.

Another force that can cause such effects is insider–outsider segregation in a heavily unionized labour force with decentralized bargaining, discussed above. In times of high unemployment people who are currently employed (insiders) may use their bargaining power to ensure that their own status is maintained and to prevent new entrants to the labour force (outsiders) from competing effectively. In an insider–outsider model of this type a period of prolonged high unemployment—whatever its initial cause—will tend to become 'locked in'. If outsiders are denied access to the labour market, their unemployment will fail to exert downward pressure on wages, and the NAIRU will tend to rise.

Hysteresis is part of the explanation of the high levels of persistence of unemployment in many EU countries, including the United Kingdom.

Increasing structural change

The amount of industrial restructuring, both locally and internationally, increased in the 1980s and appears to be carrying on through the 1990s. In part this is the result of the increasing integration of the UK economy with the European Union and the rest of the world, and the globalization of world markets. Most observers feel that this integration has been beneficial overall. One less fortunate consequence, however, is that labour markets are increasingly affected by changes in demand and supply conditions anywhere in the world.

The following numerous structural changes have created a continuing need for rapid adjustments:

- the collapse of communism and the conversion of the countries of Eastern Europe to market economies;
- increases in the supply of agricultural products owing to

the green revolution in less developed countries and heavy agricultural subsidization in the European Union;

- enormous OPEC-induced increases in the price of oil in the 1970s and early 1980s, followed by almost equally precipitous declines in the mid-1980s that carried through into the 1990s;
- the emergence of several Asian countries as industrial economies, of which China will, in the long run, be the most important;
- the communications revolution, leading to the decentralization of industry, with components produced in various countries and assembled in others;
- robotization, which increased industrial productivity and reduced the demand for assembly-line workers;
- the growth of knowledge-intensive industries, which require highly educated and geographically mobile workforces;
- the globalization of competition, with fewer and fewer domestic markets that are sheltered by artificial barriers;
- changes in the organization of firms;
- the privatization of large sections of formerly state-owned industries;
- the decline of employment in manufacturing;
- the enormous growth in service employment.

Although evidence is difficult to obtain, some observers argue that the increasing pace and the changing nature of technological change since the mid-1970s have contributed to an increase in the level of structural unemployment.

Mismatch Structural change that creates unemployed workers with the wrong characteristics (skills, experience, location) for the available jobs is known as *mismatch.* As we saw above, the biggest mismatch is likely to be that modern industry requires skilled and flexible workers while the majority of the unemployed are unskilled. Intuitively this makes sense—a metal-worker made redundant in Sheffield in 1980 is unlikely to have found work (quickly) as an advertising executive, even if vacancies existed.

Researchers studying UK unemployment have found mismatch to be important in increasing the NAIRU, but mismatch does not appear to have increased markedly since the early 1970s. Thus it explains the rise in the NAIRU between the 1960s and 1970s but not subsequent rises. Though further studies may produce different evidence.

Unemployment benefits

Workers who lose their jobs receive unemployment benefit. The size of the benefits paid, relative to pay levels in work, is known as the **replacement ratio.** A high replacement ratio raises the NAIRU. It affects the willingness of the unemployed to accept job offers and it affects the intensity with which they search for work.

Changes in the replacement ratio do have significant statistical effects on the NAIRU, but in *The Unemployment Crisis* Layard, Nickell, and Jackman found that it explains only 0.8 percentage points of the 6.2 percentage point rise in equilibrium unemployment between the 1960s and 1980s.

However, differences in benefit systems between countries do seem to play a very important role in explaining international differences in unemployment. It is not just the replacement ratio faced by a newly unemployed worker that matters; also important is the duration for which that benefit is provided (if it is for a short period, the worker has an incentive to find work very quickly) and the degree to which the benefit is conditional on job-seeking activity. Countries with only temporary benefits and both incentives and assistance with finding work tend to have lower equilibrium unemployment rates.

Other effects

Two other factors are often reported to have at least a temporary effect on the NAIRU. The first is the tax wedge. This is the difference between what an employer has to pay to hire a worker and what the worker receives in take-home pay. Increasing the tax wedge for a given quantity of labour demanded reduces take-home pay. This is likely to increase wage-bargaining pressure as a result of workers' reluctance to accept lower real wages. In effect this shifts up the short-run Phillips curve, thereby worsening the inflation–unemployment trade-off in the short run. However, this has no long-run effect on the NAIRU, as the tax wedge cannot keep increasing.

The second factor is associated with a terms of trade loss, or real exchange rate depreciation. This is argued to have a similar effect; because it raises import prices, it also reduces real wages. Real wage resistance shifts the short-run Phillips curve upwards and we get the same result as in the previous paragraph.

Explaining unemployment

By combining the analysis of demand and supply shocks and the Phillips curve of Chapter 30 with what we have learned about labour markets above, we can now produce an explanation for the unemployment experience which we summarized at the beginning of this chapter. This explanation is broadly that set out by Layard, Nickell, and Jackman in *The Unemployment Crisis*.

Supply shocks Most countries were subjected to two major supply shocks associated with the oil price rises of 1973 and 1979. Countries with more centralized wage bargaining suffered less unemployment than others, because wage negotiators were more prepared to accept cuts in real wages. The shock was complicated in the United Kingdom by structural adjustment resulting from the emergence of an oil-producing sector. The pace of technological and organizational change has speeded up and affected unemployment most in those countries with inflexible labour market institutions and regulations.

Demand shocks Governments reacted to high inflation in the 1970s with tight monetary and fiscal policies. Slow downward adjustment of inflation expectations, combined with negative demand shocks, created recessionary gaps and rising unemployment. (The adjustment to negative demand shocks was discussed in Chapter 28, and the adjustment to positive demand and supply shocks was analysed in Chapter 30.) The short-run impact of these demand shocks on unemployment was less, the more flexible were wage contracts. (Policymakers in the United Kingdom probably made the UK business cycle worse than was necessary because of mistimed or inappropriate policy changes.)

Persistence Unemployment became persistent in those countries with open-ended unemployment benefits and, once in place, was sustained by hysteresis effects. Countries that did least to get the long-term unemployed back to work suffered most in terms of rising equilibrium unemployment rates.

Reducing unemployment

Other things being equal, all governments would like to reduce unemployment. The questions are 'Can it be done?' and 'If so, at what cost?' Some commonly aired 'solutions' which will almost certainly not help are discussed in Box 31.2.

In this section we review the policies that governments could use to help lower unemployment once it is high. The simple solution, in view of what we have learned about persistence, is: don't start from here! That is, eliminating unemployment once it has reached high levels may be more difficult than preventing it from arising in the first place.

Demand management

The traditional macroeconomic solution to unemployment is a policy-induced stimulus to aggregate demand. We now know that this will cure the problem, if at all, only if the unemployment is recent and cyclical. This is so whatever the size of the NAIRU. And it suggests that the authorities should act quickly to accommodate the effects of a negative shock to aggregate supply.

With GDP close to its potential level, however, an increase in aggregate demand intended to reduce equilibrium unemployment would rapidly lead to a rise in inflation. By definition inflation will start to accelerate once unemployment falls below the NAIRU.

This means that the most that demand management can do about equilibrium unemployment is to try to make sure that it does not rise as a result of hysteresis effects associated with major deflations. Unfortunately, it was attempts to eliminate inflation rapidly by restrictive aggregate demand policies that contributed to high unemployment in the first place.

Once inflation is low and the unemployment level is close to the NAIRU, aggregate demand policy should be neutral; that is, it should aim to maintain GDP at its potential level.

Reducing persistence

The reduction of persistence and hysteresis effects is a major challenge. It probably requires both a reform of the

---

Box 31.2 False trails: what won't cure unemployment

The existence of high unemployment prompts many well-meaning but ill-considered suggestions for solving the problem. The most common error made when thinking about unemployment is to assume that there is a fixed number of jobs available to be shared out. This leads to proposals for compulsory job sharing and enforced early retirement to divide existing jobs among available workers, proposals to halt new technology 'destroying' jobs, and protectionism to stop 'our jobs' being taken by low-wage foreigners. (In 1998, the French government even proposed a law limiting the length of the working week as a solution for unemployment.)

The following arguments against these false assumptions are all drawn from the 1994 *OECD Jobs Study*, referred to earlier in this chapter.

Job sharing Enforced job sharing and involuntary early retirement reduce potential GDP because they prevent those who are willing and able to work productively from doing so. It makes the individuals so restricted worse off, and it makes society as a whole worse off. Indeed, it is a form of forced unemployment. As the *OECD Jobs Study* puts it (p. 27):

Legislated, across-the-board, work-sharing addresses the unemployment problem not by increasing the number of jobs through more economic activity, but through rationing gainful work. Enforced work-sharing has never succeeded in cutting unemployment significantly, not least because of workers' resistance to reduced income.

This is not to say that flexible working practices, which enable part-time working for those who would otherwise be unable to work, are a bad thing; on the contrary, the key is that each individual should be able to maximize his or her productive activity in the manner most suited to his or her needs and commitments. Anything that limits the opportunities to work is harmful.

Technology In 1811 Nottinghamshire frameworkers (led by the probably mythical Ned Ludd) smashed new machinery. This was because they thought that the new technology of the industrial revolution was doing them out of a livelihood, as indeed it would for those not prepared to learn new skills. Before that time real wages were constant, possibly for centuries. Since that time real wages have multiplied at least tenfold even for manual workers, and job opportunities have multiplied in incalculable ways. To quote the OECD study again (p. 29):

History has shown that when technological progress accelerates,

so do growth, living standards and employment. Technological progress would lead to high unemployment only in a world of saturated wants or perpetual restriction of demand, conditions that have not occurred in the past, and seem unlikely in the foreseeable future. Furthermore, worries about a new era of 'jobless growth' appear unfounded: the current upswing in the United States and a number of other countries has brought job growth in its train, and broadly in line with past relationships between growth and employment.

Protectionism It is an erroneous but widely held view in Europe that competition from low-wage countries, especially in Asia, is responsible for much of the current unemployment. This is an argument that the OECD economists are able to dismiss (p. 28):

The weight of low-wage countries' exports in the overall expenditure of OECD countries on goods and services is only about 1.5 per cent. The number of markets which they contest is greater, and their effect on the intensity of competition is increasing. But the judgement on present evidence is that the overall impact both of imports from these countries and their contestation of OECD markets is too small to account for a significant part of either current unemployment or falling relative wages of the low-skilled. On the other hand, these countries represent a large and growing potential market for OECD exports of goods and services, and hence represent an important source of current and future growth and employment.

On the case for using protectionism to 'keep jobs at home', the OECD has no doubts (p. 29):

Protectionism reduces overall economic welfare; increases costs to consumers, often hurting most those with lowest incomes; penalises successful enterprise; harms exports; encourages tariff factories; harms developing countries' trade; and increases the pressures for international migration. It encourages domestic monopolies, while cutting the economy off from mainstream developments in the world outside. Producers, dependent on protection for their survival, ultimately become prepared to spend large sums to preserve its continuance. Lobbying, and even bribery and corruption, become more widespread.

benefits system and active policies to ensure that those in danger of long-term unemployment get work experience and training. This is the aim of the 'Welfare to Work' programme introduced in the United Kingdom in 1998 (see Box 19.4 on page 327).

The feature of the benefits system that seems to be most harmful (in the sense of creating long-term unemployment) is an indefinite period of benefits payments. This reduces the incentive of the recently unemployed to seek work urgently. Some commentators advocate compulsory public sector work for the unemployed after some period of time; others advocate state subsidies towards private sector employment as a way of getting people back into the labour market. The general point, however, is that whatever the policies are, they have to be targeted on the unemployed directly, rather than in the form of general reflation.

Another aspect of persistence is mismatch. Policies to reduce this must involve making it easier for workers to change occupations by assistance for retraining and re-location. It could be argued that it is the responsibility of individuals or firms to finance retraining. However, individuals may be financially constrained, and firms may feel that it is not worth training a worker who may go elsewhere. The state funds education for the young, so there is no reason, in principle, why those needing retraining should be treated differently.

Labour market reform

A third class of policies that may help to reduce unemployment involves labour market reforms, especially the structure of wage bargaining. We have seen that insiders may hold wage rates high, to the detriment of outsiders. We have also seen that centralized wage bargaining may generate lower unemployment than decentralized bargaining. However, union structures have evolved over decades, and it is no easy matter in a free society to scrap the lot and start again.

Conclusion

Unemployment is a major problem of our time. We have been able to understand, with a combination of the tools provided by the macro model and our new understanding of labour markets, how unemployment came about and why it is characterized by persistence. We have also learned why the traditional macroeconomic approach to reducing unemployment is no longer adequate. The bad news is that reducing equilibrium unemployment is likely to be a slow process. The good news is that persistence does not mean permanence. Normal economic change and new economic policies can make progress against persistence, which need not be accepted as inevitable.

Summary

Employment and unemployment characteristics

■ Employment has grown little in Europe in the last three decades, and unemployment appeared to have an upward trend in the 1970s and 1980s. However, unemployment is untrended in the long run, and there were signs that the prospects for reducing unemployment might be improving at the end of the 1990s.

■ It is useful to distinguish among several kinds of unemployment: (a) cyclical unemployment, which is caused by too low a level of aggregate demand; (b) frictional unemployment, which is caused by the length of time it takes to find a first job and to move from job to job as a result of normal labour turnover; and (c) structural unemployment, which is caused by the need to reallocate resources among occupations, regions, and industries as the structure of demands and supplies changes. Together frictional unemployment and structural unemployment make up equilibrium unemployment, the NAIRU, which is then expressed as a percentage of the total labour force.

Cyclical unemployment

■ New Classical theories look to explanations that allow the labour market to be cleared continuously. Such theories can explain cyclical variations in employment but do not explain involuntary unemployment, that is, the unemployment of workers who would like to work at the going wage rates but for whom jobs are not available.

■ Recent New Keynesian theories have focused on the long-term nature of employer–worker relationships and on the possibility that it is efficient for employers to pay wages that are above the level that would clear the labour market. These explain why wages may be rigid enough for demand fluctuations to produce cyclical fluctuations in unemployment.

Equilibrium unemployment

■ The NAIRU will always be positive because it takes time for labour to move between jobs both in normal turnover and in response to changes in the structure of the demand for labour. Government policies can also influence the NAIRU.

■ Changes in the NAIRU can result from demographic changes, hysteresis effects, structural change in the economy, or from changes in the unemployment benefit system.

Reducing unemployment

■ Cyclical unemployment can be reduced by aggregate demand policies.

■ Equilibrium unemployment can be reduced by lowering benefits (level and duration), imposing active manpower policies, and reforming wage-bargaining institutions.

■ In a growing, changing economy populated by people who wish to change jobs for many reasons, it is neither possible nor desirable to reduce unemployment to zero. Most important is the avoidance of the buildup of long-term unemployment.

Topics for review

■ Cyclical unemployment
■ Frictional unemployment
■ Structural unemployment
■ Efficiency wages
■ Hysteresis
■ Persistence

■ Determinants of the size of the NAIRU
■ Policies to reduce unemployment

Questions for discussion

1 Explain the differences between cyclical, frictional, and structural unemployment.

2 Why does it matter whether unemployment is voluntary or involuntary?

3 Why does the issue of whether or not wage rates are sticky enter into the question of what determines unemployment?

4 How do efficiency wage theories explain why firms are unwilling to adjust wages in response to an excess supply of labour?

5 Outline potential policy solutions to (a) cyclical and (b) structural unemployment.

6 Re-read the analysis of labour markets in Chapter 15 and discuss which parts of the analysis in that chapter help one to understand the determinants of unemployment.

Chapter 32
Economic Growth

In our macro model developed above we have taken the position of the *LRAS* curve, which was first introduced in Chapter 24, as fixed. We have then studied how actual GDP varied around potential GDP as a result of shifts in the *AD* and the *SRAS* curves. This is the theory of how output fluctuates in the short term around a given level of potential output. Now we add to this earlier study of output fluctuations by taking an important new step. We consider changes in potential GDP. These are long-term changes, called economic growth, that typically shift the *LRAS* curve to the right over the years, gradually but continually. The cumulative effects of these changes dominate the effects of fluctuations over any time-span longer than a decade. See for example the data for

UK real GDP over the last century in Figure 24.7 on page 417.

In this chapter we first deal with the distinction between growth and other goals of economic policy. Then we discuss the costs and benefits of economic growth. This leads to a study of how the saving and investment flows that were dealt with in earlier chapters affect growth. After that we outline the theories that economists use to understand the growth process. We deal with these first at a highly aggregated (or macro) level, then at a more disaggregated (or micro) level. Then we briefly consider the relation between a country's economic growth and its international competitiveness. We end with a brief discussion of possible limits to growth.

The nature of economic growth

Economic growth is the economy's most powerful engine for generating long-term increases in living standards. Throughout most of the nineteenth century and the first three-quarters of the twentieth, per capita GDP rose steadily while its distribution became somewhat less unequal. As a result the citizens of the countries in the European Union became materially better off decade by decade, and children typically were substantially better off than their parents were at the same age. In the last quarter of the twentieth century, however, the engine of growth faltered somewhat. Growth rates fell and the distribution of income became somewhat more unequal. As a result the real incomes of many European families grew less fast than in the early post-war years. Although we still live in one of the richest societies in all of human history, some people began to speak of the end of the dream that each generation could expect to be much better off than its predecessors—although the evidence does not suggest a cessation of long-term growth.

These changes in attitudes and perceptions among ordinary, middle-class citizens have been brought about by the mere slowdown of rapid growth. Such changes may also be felt in the countries of Southeast Asia which experi-

enced a slowdown in their previously rapid growth at the end of the 1990s. The changes show how important steady growth has been in people's minds and hearts over the previous decades of the nineteenth and twentieth centuries.

Shifts in aggregate demand and aggregate supply

In earlier chapters we studied how monetary and fiscal policies work via shifts in the aggregate demand curve. A policy-induced shift in this curve can, for example, eliminate a recessionary gap, raising GDP to its potential level. In contrast, economic growth can increase GDP by increasing the level of potential GDP, thus shifting the long-run aggregate supply curve.

Figure 32.1 illustrates the effects of shifts in the long-run aggregate supply curve. Policies that permanently reduce structural unemployment increase potential GDP by causing a once-and-for-all rightward shift in the long-run aggregate supply curve. In this case GDP rises because more people are employed. Similar results come from measures

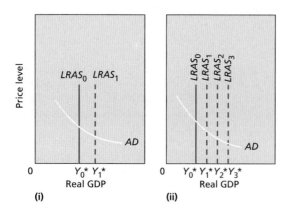

Figure 32.1 Increasing potential output
Permanent reductions in unemployment and increases in efficiency cause once-and-for-all increases in potential output; permanent economic growth causes continual increases in potential output. A reduction in structural unemployment or an increase in the efficiency of resource allocation shifts the long-run aggregate supply curve in part (i) and raises long-run equilibrium GDP from Y_0^* to Y_1^*. Economic growth continually shifts the long-run aggregate supply curve in part (ii), taking long-run equilibrium GDP from Y_0^* to Y_1^* to Y_2^*, and so on.

Table 32.1 How national incomes change when growth rates differ

Year	\multicolumn{5}{l}{Country (rate of growth per year)}
	A (1%)	B (2%)	C (3%)	D (5%)	E (7%)
2000	100	100	100	100	100
2010	110	122	135	165	201
2030	135	182	246	448	817
2050	165	272	448	1,218	3,312
2070	201	406	817	3,312	13,429
2100	272	739	2,009	14,841	109,660

Small differences in growth rates cause enormous differences in national incomes over even a few decades. In the year 2000 all five countries shown in the table have the same level of national income equal to 100 but they have different growth rates. Within ten years there are large differences between the national incomes of the various countries, and by 2070, the span of one lifetime, there are massive differences. By 2070 even the country with a 2 per cent growth rate has twice the income of the country with the 1 per cent rate, while the others have vastly more.

that increase the efficiency of resource allocation. In this case there is a once-and-for-all increase in potential output because the nation's resources are employed more efficiently. These once-and-for-all shifts are illustrated in part (i) of the figure.

In contrast, part (ii) shows the continued increases in GDP that result from **economic growth,** which is defined as an increase in potential output arising from changes in factor supplies (labour and capital) or in the productivity of factors (output per unit of factor input). The removal of a serious recessionary gap, or the elimination of all structural unemployment, or the removal of major allocative inefficiencies might cause a once-and-for-all increase in GDP by, at the very most, 5–10 per cent. However, a growth rate of 3 per cent per year raises potential GDP by 10 per cent in three years, *doubles* it in about 24 years, and quadruples it in 48 years. Even a 1 per cent growth rate doubles potential GDP over a normal lifetime of about 70 years.

Growth is a much more powerful method of raising living standards than is the removal of recessionary gaps, structural unemployment, or allocative inefficiencies, *because growth can go on indefinitely.*

Table 32.1 illustrates the cumulative effect of what seem to be very small differences in growth rates. Notice that if one country grows faster than another, the gap in their respective living standards will widen progressively. If, for example, two countries start from the same level of income, and the first country grows at 2 per cent per year while the second grows at 1 per cent, the first country's per

capita income will be twice that of the second country's in about 70 years. Having started from equality, the citizens of the second country will come within one lifetime to look poor and backward to the citizens of the first country.

Economic growth, efficiency, and redistribution

Observing that economic growth is the most important force for raising living standards over the long term in no way implies that policies designed to reduce unemployment, increase economic efficiency, or redistribute income are unimportant.

Reducing structural unemployment We have seen in Chapter 31 that long-term unemployment is undesirable for many reasons. Reducing it is thus an important social goal even if the effects on potential GDP are small.

Reducing inefficiency Removing allocative inefficiencies increases GDP. Any such increase is welcome in a world where many wants go unsatisfied.

Redistribution Economic growth has made the poor vastly better off than they would have been if they had lived 100 years ago. Yet that is little consolation when they see that they cannot afford many things that are currently available to citizens with higher incomes. People compare themselves with others in their own society, not with their counterparts at other times or in other places. Because many people care about *relative* differences among individuals, governments continue to have policies to redistribute income and to make such basic services as education and hospital care available to everyone, at least to some minimum acceptable degree.

Interrelations among the goals Economists once assumed that the goals of reducing unemployment, increasing efficiency, redistributing income, and ensuring growth could be treated independently of each other. It is now understood, as we first observed in Chapters 18 and 19, that employment, distribution, efficiency, and growth are interrelated. For example, policies that create a distribution of income unrelated to the market value of work can adversely affect the growth rate by reducing incentives. For another example, government support of inefficient firms, which may be criticized on grounds of productive and allocative inefficiency, may also lower growth rates by keeping resources away from innovative firms.

It follows that policies designed to increase employment, reduce allocative inefficiencies, or redistribute income need to be examined carefully for any effects that they may have on growth, while policies designed to affect growth need to be examined for their effects on employment, economic efficiency, and income distribution. A policy that reduces growth *may* be a bad bargain, even if it increases the immediate efficiency of the economy or creates a more equitable distribution of income.

Of course, not all redistribution policies have unfavourable effects on the growth rate. Some may have no effect, and others—by raising the health and educational standards of ordinary workers—may raise the growth rate. The point is that policies have multiple effects and in assessing them it is necessary to look beyond their designed effects to consider the often unintended side-effects on other policy goals.

Benefits and costs of growth

We start by looking at the benefits of growth, and we then consider the costs. Boxes 32.1 and 32.2 outline some of the popular arguments on both sides of the growth debate. Although each makes only one side of the case, each makes some valid points.

Benefits of growth

Growth and living standards For those who share in it, growth is a powerful weapon against poverty. A family that is earning £25,000 today can expect an income of about £30,500 within ten years (in constant pounds and with no promotion) if it shares in a 2 per cent growth rate, and £37,000 if that rate is 4 per cent.

The transformation of the life-style of ordinary workers in advanced industrial nations over the last two centuries shows the massive improvements in living standards and quality of life that growth makes possible. Much of the recent concern over economic problems facing European families stems from the decline of growth that occurred in the mid-1970s, and in the recessions of the early 1980s and early 1990s. Partly because growth slowed in those periods and partly because the distribution of income has changed unfavourably for them, the real incomes of many working families grew little in the 1970s and only modestly in the 1980s and 1990s.

Growth and life-style A family often finds that a big increase in its income can lead to a major change in the pattern of its consumption—that extra money buys important amenities of life. In the same way, members of

society as a whole may change their consumption patterns as their average income rises. Not only do markets in a country that is growing rapidly make it profitable to produce more cars, but also the government is led to construct more roads and to provide more recreational areas for its newly affluent and mobile citizens. At yet a later stage a concern about litter, pollution, and congestion may become important, and their correction may then begin to account for a significant fraction of GDP. Such 'amenities' usually become matters of social concern only when growth has ensured the provision of the basic requirements for food, clothing, and housing of a substantial majority of the population.

More subtle, but in the long term more important, are the effects of technological change on the whole nation's life-style. Today's real incomes are five to ten times those of Victorians who lived 100 years ago. But we do not spend this higher purchasing power on more of what Victorians consumed; instead we buy new and better products made in new and better ways.

The new products created by technological change transform our entire ways of living.

Growth and income redistribution Not everyone benefits equally from growth. Many of the poorest are not even in the labour force and thus are unlikely to share in the higher wages that, along with profits, are the primary means by which the gains from growth are distributed. Others lose their jobs as a result of technical change, and the older ones may find it difficult to retrain for anything like as good a

---

Box 32.1 An election manifesto for the Pro-Growth Party

Dear Voter:

You live in the world's first civilization that is devoted principally to satisfying *your* needs rather than those of a privileged minority. Past civilizations have always been based on leisure and high consumption for a tiny upper class, a reasonable living standard for a small middle class, and hard work with little more than subsistence consumption for the great mass of people.

The continuing industrial revolution is based on mass-produced goods for you, the ordinary citizen. You were born in a period of sustained economic growth that has dramatically raised the consumption standards of ordinary citizens. Reflect on a few examples: travel, live and recorded music, art, good food, inexpensive books, universal literacy, and a genuine chance to be educated. Most important, there is leisure to provide time and energy to enjoy these and thousands of other products of the modern industrial economy.

Would any ordinary family seriously prefer to go back to the world of 150 or 500 years ago in its same relative social and economic position? Surely the answer is no. However, for those with incomes in the top 1 or 2 per cent of the income distribution, economic growth has destroyed much of their privileged consumption position. They must now vie with the masses when they visit the world's beauty spots, and be annoyed, while lounging on the terrace of a palatial mansion, by the sound of charter flights carrying ordinary people to inexpensive holidays in far places. Many of the rich complain

bitterly about the loss of exclusive rights to luxury consumption, and it is not surprising that they find their intellectual apologists. Whether they know it or not, the anti-growth economists are not the social revolutionaries that they think they are. They say that growth has produced pollution and the wasteful consumption of all kinds of frivolous products that add nothing to human happiness. However, the democratic solution to pollution is not to go back to where so few people consumed luxuries that pollution was trivial, but rather to learn to control the pollution that mass consumption tends to create.

It is only through further growth that the average citizen can enjoy consumption standards (of travel, culture, medical and health care, etc.) now available only to people in the top 25 per cent of the income distribution—a group that includes the intellectuals who earn large royalties from the books that they write in which they denounce growth. If you think that extra income confers little real benefit, just ask those in the top 25 per cent to trade incomes with average citizens.

Ordinary citizens, do not be deceived by disguised élitist doctrines. Remember that the very rich and the élite have much to gain by stopping growth, and even more by rolling it back, but you have everything to gain by letting it go forward.

VOTE FOR GROWTH. VOTE FOR US.

---

job as they lost. For this reason, even in a growing economy redistribution policies will be needed if poverty and extreme hardship are to be averted.

If a constant total of national income is redistributed, someone's standard of living will actually have to be lowered. However, when there is economic growth, and when only the increment in income is redistributed (through government intervention), it is possible to reduce income inequalities without actually having to *lower* anyone's income. It is much easier for a rapidly growing

---

Box 32.2 An election manifesto for the Anti-Growth Party

Dear Voter:

You live in a world that is being despoiled by a mindless search for ever-higher levels of material consumption at the cost of all other values. Once upon a time men and women knew how to enjoy creative work and to derive satisfaction from simple activities. Today the ordinary worker is a mindless cog in an assembly line that turns out more and more goods and services that the advertisers must work overtime to persuade the workers to consume.

Statisticians count the increasing flow of material output as a triumph of modern civilization. You arise from your electric-blanketed bed, clean your teeth with an electric toothbrush, and pop into your electric toaster a slice or two of bread baked from super-refined and chemically refortified flour; you climb into your car to sit in vast traffic jams on exhaust-polluted roads.

Television commercials tell you that by consuming more you are happier, but happiness lies not in increasing consumption, but in increasing the ratio of *satisfaction of wants* to *total wants*. Since, the more you consume, the more the advertisers persuade you that you *want* to consume, you are almost certainly less happy than the average citizen in a small town in 1955, whom we can visualize standing at the front gate, chatting with neighbours, and watching the local children skipping with pieces of old clothesline.

Today the landscape is dotted with endless factories that produce the plastic trivia of the modern industrial society. They drown you in a cloud of noise, air, and water pollution. The countryside is despoiled by open-cast mines, petroleum refineries, acid rain, and dangerous nuclear power stations, producing energy that is devoured insatiably by modern factories and motor vehicles. Worse, our precious heritage of natural resources is being rapidly depleted.

Now is the time to stop this madness. We must stabilize production, reduce pollution, conserve our natural resources, and seek justice through a more equitable distribution of existing total income.

A long time ago Malthus taught us that if we do not limit population voluntarily, nature will do it for us in a cruel and savage manner. Today the same is true of output: if we do not halt its growth voluntarily, the halt will be imposed upon us by a disastrous increase in pollution and a rapid exhaustion of natural resources.

Citizens, awake! Shake off the worship of growth, learn to enjoy the bounty that is yours already, and reject the endless, self-defeating search for increased happiness through ever-increasing consumption.

VOTE AGAINST GROWTH. VOTE FOR US.

economy to be generous towards its less fortunate citizens —or neighbours—than it is for a static economy.

Costs of growth

Other things being equal, most people would probably regard a fast rate of growth as preferable to a slow one; but other things are seldom equal.

The opportunity cost of growth In a world of scarcity almost nothing is free. Growth requires heavy investment of resources in capital goods, as well as in activities such as education. Often these investments yield no immediate return in terms of goods and services for consumption; thus they imply that sacrifices have been made by the current generation of consumers.

Growth, which promises more goods tomorrow, is achieved by consuming fewer goods today. For the economy as a whole, this sacrifice of current consumption is the primary cost of growth.

Social and personal costs of growth A growing economy is a changing economy. Innovation renders some machines obsolete and also leaves some people partly obsolete. No matter how well trained workers are at age 25, in another 25 years many will find that their skills are at least partly obsolete. A rapid growth rate requires rapid adjustments, which can cause much upset and misery to the people who are affected by them.

It is often argued that costs of this kind are a small price to pay for the great benefits that growth can bring. Even if this is true in the aggregate, these personal costs are very unevenly borne. Indeed, many of those for whom growth is most costly (in terms of lost jobs) share least in the fruits that growth brings.

Growth creates new jobs and destroys some old jobs. Those who were trained for the jobs that are lost can, and often do, suffer. Box 32.3 deals with a less-well-founded worry, that growth may destroy more jobs than it creates, leading to long-term heavy unemployment for a growing body of structurally unemployed workers.

Time-distribution of costs and benefits The costs of technological change tend to be borne immediately. Jobs are lost, and people trained in the old technologies lose their jobs and find their skills obsolete. The forgone consumption needed to finance the investment that embodies the new technologies happens right away. In contrast the benefits are felt by many in the present generation and by almost everyone in the future. We are all better off for most

Box 32.3 The end of work?

From time immemorial people have observed that technological change destroys particular jobs and have worried that it will destroy jobs in general. Two points are important in assessing this issue.

First, technological change does destroy particular jobs. When waterwheels were used to automate the fulling of cloth in twelfth-century Europe, there were riots and protests among the fullers who lost their jobs. A century ago half of the labour force in North America and Europe was required to produce the required food. (The figure was a little lower in the UK because British manufactured goods were exported in return for imported foodstuffs.) Today less than 5 per cent of the labour force is needed in the high-income countries to feed all their citizens. In other words, out of every 100 jobs that existed in 1900, 50 were in agriculture and 45 of those have been destroyed by technological progress over the course of the last century.

The second point is that new technologies create new jobs just as they destroy old ones. The displaced agricultural workers did not join the ranks of the permanently unemployed—although some of the older ones may have done, their children did not. Instead they, and their children, took jobs in manufacturing and service industries and helped to produce the mass of new goods and services that have raised living standards over the century —such as cars, refrigerators, computers, foreign travel, and so on over a vast list of new things.

New technologies usually require new skills. Those who are unable to retrain may suffer but their children can train appropriately from the outset.

Technological change raises living standards by destroying jobs in existing lines of production and freeing labour to produce new commodities as well as more of some existing commodities.

Modern technologies have two new aspects which worry some observers. First, they tend to be knowledge-intensive. A fairly high degree of literacy and numeracy, as well as familiarity with computers, is needed to work with many but not all of these new technologies. Second, owing to the globalizing of world markets—through falling costs of transporting goods and co-ordinating their production worldwide—unskilled workers in advanced countries have come into competition with unskilled workers everywhere in the world. Both of these forces are decreasing the relative demand for unskilled workers in developed countries and may lead to falling relative wages for the unskilled and, if labour markets are sufficiently inflexible, to some structural unemployment.

For these reasons some people blame the high unemployment rates in Europe on the new technologies. This is hard to reconcile, however, with the fact that the lowest unemployment rates in the industrialized countries are currently being recorded in the United States, which is the most technologically dynamic of all countries and the one where policymakers have worried least about the unemployment effects of new technologies. This suggests that the cause of high European unemployment rates may be not enough technological change and too much government interference rather than too much technological change.

Worries that technological change will cause general unemployment have been recorded for at least 200 years but, so far at least, there is no sign that those displaced by technological change or their children are being forced into the ranks of the permanently unemployed.

Over all of recorded history so far, technological change has created more jobs than it has destroyed.

of the new products that are created by technological change, even though those who made the older competing products probably suffered when the new ones were first introduced. As a result everyone is a beneficiary of past growth-inducing technological change—the costs have

been paid and the benefits are still with us. But not everyone is a beneficiary of current change. Most benefit, but some suffer, and some of those would have been better off if the change that affected them adversely had never happened.

Theories of economic growth

In this section we study some of the theories that economists use to understand economic growth. This is an exciting area. Ideas are changing rapidly as both theoretical and empirical research expands our knowledge. Our first step is to relate savings and investment, which we studied in detail in previous chapters, to economic growth.

Saving, investment, and growth

Saving and investment affect both the level and the rate of growth of real GDP. To understand their influence, it is critical to distinguish between their short-run and long-run effects.

Investment in the short and long runs

The theory of GDP determination that we studied in previous chapters is a short-run theory. It takes potential output as constant and concentrates on the effects of shocks to aggregate demand or *SRAS*. One such demand shock would be an autonomous change in investment. These shocks cause actual GDP to fluctuate around a given potential GDP.

In the long run, by adding to the nation's capital stock, investment raises potential GDP. This effect is shown by the continuing shift of the *LRAS* curve in Figure 32.1(ii).

The theory of economic growth is a long-run theory. It concentrates on the effects of investment in raising potential GDP and ignores short-run fluctuations of actual output around potential output.

In the short run any activity that puts income into people's hands will raise aggregate demand. Thus the short-run effect on GDP is the same whether a firm 'invests' in digging holes and refilling them or in building a new factory. The long-run growth of potential GDP, however, is affected only by the part of investment that adds to a nation's productive capacity—that is, by the factory, but not by the refilled hole.

Similar observations hold for public sector expenditure, *G*. Any expenditure will add to aggregate demand and raise national income and output if there are unemployed resources, but only some expenditure increases potential GDP. Although public investment expenditure on such things as roads and health may increase potential GDP, expenditure that shores up a declining industry in order to create employment may have an adverse effect on the growth of potential output.

Saving in the short and long runs

The short-run effect of an increase in saving is to reduce aggregate demand. If, for example, households or governments elect to save more, then they spend less. The resulting downward shift in the aggregate expenditure function lowers aggregate demand and thus lowers equilibrium GDP. This effect is sometimes referred to as *the paradox of thrift.*

In the longer term, however, higher national saving is necessary for higher investment. Firms usually reinvest their own savings, and the savings of households pass to firms, either directly through the purchase of shares and bonds or indirectly through financial intermediaries. In the long run, *ceteris paribus*, the higher the level of national saving, the higher the level of investment; and owing to the accumulation of more and better capital equipment, the higher the level of investment, the higher the level of real income. *Ceteris paribus*, a high-saving economy accumulates assets faster, and thus grows faster, than does a low-saving economy. We must add the 'other things equal' qualification to the above sentences because they are only strictly true for nations that cannot borrow abroad. Foreign lending breaks the strict equality between domestic savings and domestic investment. So countries can have investment rates that exceed their domestic savings rates—and many developing countries do just that. None the less, a great deal of investment is financed by local funds including the savings of firms and private households; so, other things being equal, high domestic savings tend to be associated with high domestic investment rates.

In the long run there is no paradox of thrift. Savings are needed to finance investment, and, other things being equal, countries with high rates of national saving tend to have high investment rates and high growth rates of real GDP.

Notice that the discussion refers to *national* saving, which is net public sector plus private sector saving. The amount of national saving available for private sector investment is private sector saving plus or minus the government's budget surplus or deficit: $S + (T - G)$, where, as we saw in Chapter 22, T is tax revenues net of transfer payments. This expression tells us that if the government spends more than it raises in taxes, then it diminishes the pool of savings available for private investment. In contrast, if the government spends less than it raises in taxes, then it adds to the pool. It does this by paying off some of its debts and leaving the funds in the hands of private wealth-holders.

Determinants of growth

Research suggests that four of the most important determinants of growth of total output are as follows:

1. *Growth in the labour force*, such as occurs when the population grows or participation rates rise.

2. *Investment in human capital*, such as formal education and on-the-job experience.

3. *Investment in physical capital*, such as factories, machines, transportation, and communications facilities.

4. *Technological change*, brought about by innovation that introduces new products, new ways of producing existing products, and new forms of business organization.

One line of investigation studies how these four forces operate in what is called the **aggregate production function**. This is an expression for the relation between the total amounts of labour (L), physical capital (K), and human capital (H) that are employed[1] and the nation's total output, its GDP:

$$GDP = f(L, K, H).$$

This is an aggregate function because it relates the economy's total output, its GDP, to the total amount of the three main factors that are used to produce that output. (A micro production function, such as is discussed in Chapter 8, relates the output of one firm to the factors of production employed by that firm.) The function, indicated by the letter 'f', shows the relation between the inputs of L, K, and H and the output of GDP. The production function tells us how much GDP will be produced for given amounts of labour and capital employed. For example, the function may tell us that when 200 million units of labour, 400 million units of physical capital, and 100 million units of human capital are used, the GDP will be 4,000 million.[2]

In growth theory we ignore short-term fluctuations of

output around its potential value. Thus the GDP in the above production function can be interpreted as potential GDP.

We may now use this aggregate production function to discuss some theories of economic growth.

Neoclassical growth theory

One branch of neoclassical theory deals with growth when the stock of technological knowledge remains unchanged. There are no innovations—no new ways of making things, and no new products. As a result the relation between inputs and output, as shown by the production function, does not change. The key aspects of what is called the neoclassical model are that the aggregate production function displays *decreasing returns* when any factor is increased on its own, and *constant returns* when all factors are increased together and in the same proportion.

Decreasing returns to a single factor

To start with, suppose that the population of the country grows while the stocks of physical and human capital remain constant. More and more people go to work using the same fixed quantity of physical capital and knowledge. The amount that each new unit of input adds to total output is called its *marginal product*. The operation of the famous **law of diminishing returns** tells us that the successive employment of equal additional amounts (or units) of labour will eventually add less to total output than the immediately previous unit of labour. In other words sooner or later each additional unit of labour will produce a diminishing marginal product. This is referred to as *diminishing returns to a single factor*. We first met it in Chapter 8, and it is illustrated in Figure 32.2.

The law of diminishing returns applies to any factor that is varied while the other factors are held constant. Thus successive amounts of capital added to *a fixed supply of labour* will also eventually add less and less to GDP.

According to the law of diminishing returns, the increment to total production will eventually fall whenever

---

[1] Basic growth theory emphasizes the production of manufactured goods and services, where, in contrast to agriculture, land is rarely a limiting factor. All the relatively small amounts of land that are needed can be obtained, and hence nothing significant is lost by ignoring land in the analysis of an industrialized economy—although this cannot be done for an agricultural economy.

[2] A simple example of a production function is $GDP = z(LKH)^{1/3}$. This equation says that to find the amount of GDP produced, multiply the amount of labour by the amount of physical capital and by the amount of human capital, take the cube root, and multiply the result by the constant z. This production function has positive but diminishing returns to each factor. This can be shown using calculus by evaluating the first and second partial derivatives and showing that the first derivatives are positive while the second derivatives are negative. In the numerical example in the text z is taken as 20, making $20[(200)(400)(100)]^{1/3} = 4,000$.

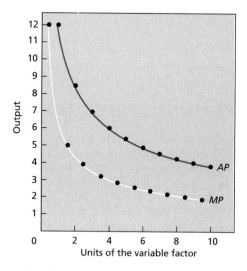

Figure 32.2 The average and marginal products of a variable factor

The average and marginal products of any variable factor decline as successive units of that factor are added to a fixed amount of another factor. This figure shows the marginal and average products of the variable factor declining as more and more units of that factor are used. The marginal products are plotted between the units of the variable factor since they apply to a change from one amount to the next.

equal increases of a variable factor of production are combined with another factor of production whose quantity is fixed.[3]

Constant returns to scale

The other main property of the neoclassical aggregate production function is **constant returns to scale**. This means that if the amounts of labour and physical and human capital are all changed in equal proportion, the total output will also change in that proportion. For example, a 10 per cent increase in the amounts of labour and physical and human capital used will lead to a 10 per cent increase in GDP.

Sources of growth in the neoclassical model

Now consider each of the sources of growth listed above. To begin with, we let each source operate with the others held constant.

Labour force growth In the long term we can associate labour force growth with population growth (although in the short term the labour force can grow if participation rates rise even though the population remains constant). As more labour is used, there will be more output and, consequently, a growth in total GDP. The law of diminishing returns tells us that sooner or later each further unit of

labour to be employed will cause a smaller and smaller addition to GDP. Eventually, not only will the marginal product of labour be falling, but the average product will fall as well. Beyond that point, although economic growth continues in the sense that total output is growing, living standards are falling in the sense that average GDP per head of population is falling. If we are interested in the growth in living standards, we are concerned with increasing GDP *per person*.

Whenever diminishing average returns apply, increases in population on their own are eventually accompanied by falling living standards.[4]

Physical capital Increases in the amount of physical capital on their own affect GDP in a manner similar to population growth alone. Eventually, each successive unit of physical capital will add less to total output than each previous unit of physical capital.

There is, however, a major contrast with the case of labour growth, because it is output per person that determines living standards, not output per unit of capital. Thus, as physical capital increases, living standards increase because output is rising while the population is constant. Indeed, per capita output can be increased by adding more physical capital as long as its marginal product exceeds zero. However, since the increases in output are subject to diminishing returns, successive additions to the economy's capital stock bring smaller and smaller increases in per capita output.

In the neoclassical model the operation of diminishing returns means that physical capital accumulation on its own brings smaller and smaller increases in per capita GDP.

Human capital Human capital has several aspects. One involves improvements in the health and longevity of the population. Of course, these are desired as ends in themselves, but they also have consequences for both the size and the productivity of the labour force. There is no doubt that improvements in the health of workers have increased productivity per worker-hour by cutting down on illness, accidents, and absenteeism.

A second aspect of the quality of human capital concerns technical training—from learning to operate a machine to learning how to be a scientist. This training depends on the current state of knowledge, and advances

[3] In some production functions marginal product may rise at first and begin to decline only after a certain critical amount of the variable factor is used. In the neoclassical, constant-returns production function, however, marginal product declines from the outset, as shown in Figure 32.2.

[4] In the neoclassical model diminishing returns set in from the outset, so that there is no range over which population increases cause rising marginal or average product of labour. The issue of when diminishing returns set in need not concern us here, since all that matters for the text discussion is that increases in any one factor, other things held constant, must eventually encounter diminishing returns.

in knowledge allow us not only to build more productive physical capital, but also to create more effective human capital. Training is clearly required if a person is to operate, repair, manage, or invent complex machines. More subtly, there may be general social advantages to an educated population. Productivity improves with literacy. The longer a person has been educated, the more adaptable, and thus the more productive in the long run, that person is in the face of new and changing challenges.

A third aspect of human capital is its contribution to growth and innovation.

Not only can current human capital embody in people the best current technological knowledge, but, by training potential innovators, it leads to advances in our knowledge and hence contributes to growth.

Balanced growth Now consider what happens if labour and physical and human capital all grow at the same rate. In this case the neoclassical assumption of constant returns to scale means that GDP grows at the same rate. As a result per capita output (GDP/L) remains constant.[5] This is called a **balanced growth path**. It is one in which all inputs and output are growing at the same constant rate. Per capita GDP, however, is unchanged.

This is not the kind of growth that concerns those interested in living standards. It is just more of the same: larger and larger economies, with more capital and more labour, doing exactly what the existing capital and the existing labour were already doing. There is nothing new.

Growth and living standards In this constant-technology neoclassical model the only way for growth to add to living standards is for the per capita stocks of physical and human capital to increase. The law of diminishing returns dictates, however, that the rise in living standards brought about by successive equal increases in capital will inexorably diminish. Raising living standards becomes more and more difficult as capital accumulation continues.

Technological change in the neoclassical growth model

So far we have held technology constant. In fact over the centuries (and even decades) economic growth is dominated by technological changes. As we have already observed, we are not better off than our Victorian ancestors because we have more Victorian factories making more Victorian commodities. We are better off because technological change has provided us with new commodities often made in radically new ways. Box 32.4 discusses some of the many new products that have literally transformed life-styles over the past century. In the neoclassical model technological change can be shown as shifting the production function so that the same amount of labour, physical capital, and human capital produces more GDP. This result is depicted in Figure 32.3 by rightward shifts in the MP

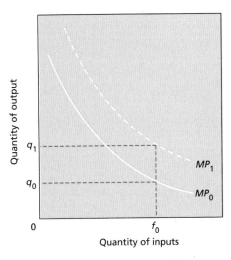

Figure 32.3 Shifts in marginal product curves
Technological change shifts the marginal product curve of each factor so that any given amount will produce more. In this example technological change shifts the marginal product curve of the factor from MP_0 to MP_1. The amount f_0 of the factor formerly produced a marginal product of q_0, but after the change it produces the larger amount q_1.

curves of each input: the same amount of input produces more output.[6]

The neoclassical growth model can accommodate technological change along balanced growth paths if the changes increase the efficiency of labour, making labour grow at a constant exponential rate when measured in *efficiency units*. This is called labour-augmenting technical change. The result is that there is no increase in output per efficiency unit of labour, but there is an increase in output per worker. Along such a balanced growth path labour is constant measured in number of persons employed, while human and physical capital, the efficiency of labour, and total and per capita output are all growing at a constant rate.

Kinds of technological change Increases in productive capacity that are created by installing new and better capital goods are called **embodied technical change**. The historical importance of embodied technical change is clear: the assembly line and automation transformed most manufacturing industries, the aeroplane revolutionized

---

[5] In all of these models a constant fraction of the population is assumed to be in the labour force, so that output per employed person and output per head of population always change in the same direction.

[6] In the neoclassical production function which allows for growth we have GDP = $z(L^\alpha K^\beta H^{1-\alpha-\beta})$, $0 < \alpha, \beta, \alpha + \beta < 1$. The parameter z is a constant that relates given inputs of L, K, and H to a specific GDP. Increases in factor productivity cause z to rise, so the given amounts of L, K, and H are associated with higher GDP. Exogenous technical progress at a constant rate can be shown as GDP$_t = z_t(L^\alpha K^\beta H^{1-\alpha-\beta})$, where z grows at a constant rate as time passes.

Box 32.4 Technical change and living standards

Why are our material living standards higher than those of our Victorian ancestors who lived in the 1890s, and why were they better off than their Georgian ancestors who lived in the 1790s were? We are better off today not because we consume more of the same goods than our predecessors did. We are better off because we have new goods made in different ways.

Today we enjoy five to ten times as much purchasing power as did Victorians (measured in constant pounds), but we consume it largely in terms of new commodities produced with new techniques. We are better off, in largest part, *not* because we have accumulated more polluting Victorian factories that produce yet more horse carriages, penny-farthing bicycles, and other Victorian commodities. We are better off because we have a vast array of new goods and services to choose from, and those goods are produced in much more efficient ways.

Victorians could not have imagined modern dental and medical equipment, penicillin, pain killers, bypass operations, safe births and abortions, personal computers, the Internet, compact discs, TV, cars, aeroplanes, opportunities for cheap, fast, worldwide travel, affordable universities, food of great variety and free of the risk of ptomaine poisoning and botulism, central heating, the elimination of endless domestic drudgery by either wives or masses of servants through the use of detergents, washing machines, vacuum cleaners, and a host of other new household products that their great-grandchildren take for granted.

Nor could they have imagined the modern automated, air-conditioned factory free of noisy, smelly steam engines and unsafe pulleys, belts, and cogs. Nor could they have imagined the modern office dominated by computers and free of Bob Cratchits adding up long columns of figures and recording them with quill pen and bottled ink.

The point is important. Technological advance transforms our lives by inventing new, undreamed-of things and making them in new, undreamed-of ways.

---

transportation, and electronic devices now dominate the information and communications industries. These innovations, plus lesser known but no less profound ones—for example, improvements in the strength of metals, the productivity of seeds, and the techniques for recovering basic raw materials from the ground—create new investment opportunities.

Less obvious but none the less important changes occur through **disembodied technical change,** that is, changes in the organization of production that are not embodied in particular capital goods. Examples are improved techniques of management, design, marketing, organization of business activity, and feedback from user experience to product improvement.

The modern understanding that technological innovation is at the heart of the growth process has led to two important developments in many economists' views on

growth. The first is that technological change is largely endogenous to the economic system. The second is that investment that increases the capital stock may encounter increasing rather than diminishing returns. These insights have led to new growth theories that go far beyond the neoclassical growth model.

Endogenous growth

In the neoclassical model innovation shifts the production function but is itself unexplained. In other words technological change is *exogenous*. It has profound effects on economic variables, such as GDP, but it is not influenced by economic causes. It just happens.

Yet microeconomic research by many scholars over the last several decades has established that technological change *is* responsive to such economic 'signals' as prices and profits. In other words technological change is *endogenous* to the economic system. Much of the earliest work on this issue was done in the United Kingdom by scholars associated with the Science Policy Research Unit (SPRU) at Sussex University. The most influential overall single study, however, was by the American professor Nathan Rosenberg, whose path-breaking book *Inside the Black Box* argued this case in great detail.[7]

Technological change stems from research and development (R&D) and from innovating activities that put the results of R&D into practice. These are costly and highly risky activities, undertaken largely by firms and usually in pursuit of profit. It is not surprising, therefore, that these activities respond to economic incentives.

Rosenberg establishes two key relations. First, R&D designed to apply known basic principles to new problems is responsive to economic signals. For example, if the price of some particular input such as petroleum or skilled labour goes up, R&D and innovating activities will be directed to altering the production function to economize on these inputs. This process does not involve a substitution of less expensive inputs for more expensive ones within the confines of known technologies; rather, it is the development of new technologies in response to changes in relative prices. Second, *basic research* itself is also responsive to economic incentives. One reason for this is that the basic research agenda is strongly influenced by practical issues of the day. For example, basic research in solid-state physics became popular, and was heavily funded, only after the development of the transistor.

There are many important implications of this new understanding that, to a great extent, growth is achieved through costly, risky, innovative activity which occurs to a

---

[7] N. Rosenberg, *Inside the Black Box: Technology and Economics* (Cambridge University Press, 1982). See also the same author's *Exploring the Black Box: Technology, Economics, and History* (Cambridge University Press, 1994).

significant extent in response to economic signals. We will discuss a few of these below.

The complexity of the innovation process

The pioneering theorist of innovation Joseph Schumpeter developed a model in which innovation flowed in one direction, starting from a pure discovery 'upstream', to more applied R&D, then to working machines, and finally to output 'downstream'.

In contrast, modern research shows that innovation involves a large amount of 'learning by doing' at all of its stages. (This phenomenon, whereby costs per unit of output fall steadily over time as firms learn how to manage new technologies, is discussed in more detail in Chapter 34.) What is learned 'downstream' then modifies what must be done 'upstream'. The best innovation-managing systems encourage feedback from the more applied steps to the purer researchers and from users to designers.

This interaction is illustrated by the differences between the Japanese car manufacturers and their European and North American competitors in the handling of new models. European and North American design has traditionally been centralized: design production teams develop the overall design and then tell their production sections what to do, as well as asking for bids from parts manufacturers to produce according to specific blueprints. As a result, defects in the original design are often not discovered until production is under way, causing many costly delays and rejection of parts already supplied. Japanese firms, on the other hand, involve their design and production departments and their parts manufacturers in all stages of the design process. Parts manufacturers are not given specific blueprints for production; rather, they are given general specifications and asked to develop their own detailed designs. As they do so, they learn. They then feed information about the problems they are encountering back to the main designers while the general outlines are still being finalized. As a result, compared with North American and European car firms, the Japanese usually design a new product faster, at less cost, and with far fewer problems when production is finally put into place.[8]

The location of innovation

Innovation typically takes place in different parts of the producer–user chain in different industries—as shown, for example, by the research of Eric von Hippel of the Massachusetts Institute of Technology (MIT) in his book *The Sources of Innovation*. Von Hippel describes how while in some industries manufacturers make most of the product innovations, in other industries it is users who make most of them, and in yet others the innovating is done by those who supply components or materials to the manufacturer.

Unless these differences are appreciated, public policy designed to encourage innovation can go seriously astray. An example is provided by von Hippel:

Consider the current concern of US policymakers that the products of US semiconductor process equipment firms are falling behind the leading edge. The conventional assessment of this problem is that these firms should somehow be strengthened and helped to innovate so that US semiconductor equipment users (makers of semiconductors) will not also fall behind. But investigation shows that most process equipment innovations in this field are, in fact, developed by equipment users. Therefore, the causality is probably reversed: US equipment builders are falling behind because the US user community they deal with is falling behind. If this is so, the policy prescription should change. Perhaps US equipment builders can best be helped by helping US equipment users to innovate at the leading edge once more.[9]

The message for economists and policymakers is important: an understanding of the details of the innovating process in each industry is needed if successful innovation-encouraging policies are to be developed.

Costly diffusion

The *diffusion* of technological knowledge from those who have it to those who want it is not costless (as it was assumed to be in Schumpeter's model). Firms need research capacity just to adopt the technologies developed by others. Some of the knowledge needed to use a new technology can be learned only through experience by plant managers, technicians, and operators. (Such knowledge is called *tacit knowledge*.) We often tend to think that once a production process is developed, it can easily be copied by others. Indeed, some advanced economic theories use the hypothesis of replication, which holds that any known process can be replicated in any new location by using the same factor inputs and management as are used in the old location. In practice, however, the diffusion of new technological knowledge is not so simple.

For example, US economists Richard Nelson and Sidney Winter have argued that most industrial technologies require technology-specific organizational skills that can be 'embodied' neither in the machines themselves, nor in instruction books, nor in blueprints. Acquiring tacit knowledge requires a deliberate process of building up new skills, work practices, knowledge, and experience.

The fact that diffusion is a costly, risky, and time-consuming business explains why new technologies take considerable time to diffuse, first through the economy of the originating country and then through the rest of the

---

[8] A detailed account of this issue can be found in J. Womack, D. Jones, and D. Roos, *The Machine that Changed the World* (New York: Ransom Associates, 1990). North American firms have recently begun to adopt some of these Japanese practices.

[9] Eric von Hippel, *The Sources of Innovation* (New York: Oxford University Press, 1988), pp. 9–10.

world. If diffusion were simple and virtually costless, the puzzle would be why technological knowledge and best industrial practices do not diffuse very quickly. As it is, decades can pass before a new technological process is diffused everywhere that it could be employed.

Market structure and innovation

Because it is highly risky, innovation is encouraged by a strongly competitive environment and is discouraged by monopoly practices. Competition among three or four large firms often produces much innovation, but a single firm, especially if it serves a secure home market protected by trade barriers, seems much less inclined to innovate.[10]

Although the ideas of Joseph Schumpeter lie behind much of modern growth theory, this emphasis on competition seems on the surface to conflict with his ideas. The apparent conflict arises because the theories available to Schumpeter in his time offered only two market structures: perfect competition and monopoly. He chose monopoly as the structure more conducive to growth on the grounds that monopoly profits would provide the incentive to innovate, and innovation itself would provide the mechanism whereby new entrants could compete with established monopolies. (He called this latter process 'creative destruction'.) Modern economists, faced with a richer variety of theoretical market structures, find that competition among oligopolists is usually more conducive to growth-enhancing technological change than is either monopoly or perfect competition.

Government interventions that are designed to encourage innovation often allow the firms in an industry to work together as one. Unless great care is exercised, and unless sufficient foreign competition exists, the result may be a national monopoly that will discourage risk-taking rather than encourage it, as the policy intends.

The United Kingdom provides many examples of this mistaken view of policy. For example:

[UK policy in the 1960s] operated under the faulty theory that encouraging British companies to merge would create world-class competitors. Consolidation of steel, automobiles, machine tools, and computers all led to notable failures. A program of research support for industry . . . proved disastrous. The British government tried to choose promising technologies and gave direct grants to firms to develop them. Most of the choices were failures. . . . [In contrast] unusually low levels of regulation in some service industries have avoided disadvantages faced by other nations and allowed innovation and change . . . in auctioneering . . . trading and insurance. British firms in these industries have been among the most innovative in the world.[11]

Shocks and innovation

One interesting consequence of endogenous technical

change is that shocks that would be unambiguously adverse to an economy operating with fixed technology can sometimes provide a spur to innovation that proves a blessing in disguise. A sharp rise in the price of one input can raise costs and lower the value of output per person for some time. But it may lead to a wave of innovations that reduce the need for this expensive input and, as a side-effect, greatly raise the productivity of labour.[12]

Sometimes individual firms will respond differently to the same economic signal. Those who respond by altering technology may do better than those who concentrate their efforts on substituting within the confines of known technology. For example, in *The Competitive Advantage of Nations*, Michael Porter tells of how US consumer electronics firms decided to move their operations abroad to avoid high, and rigid, labour costs. They continued to use their existing technology and went where labour costs were low enough to make that technology pay. Their Japanese competitors, however, stayed at home. They innovated away most of their labour costs—and then built factories in the United States to replace the factories of US firms that had gone abroad!

Innovation as a competitive strategy

Managing innovation better than one's competitors is one of the most important objectives of any modern firm that wishes to survive. Firms often fail because they do not keep up with their competitors in the race to develop new and improved products and techniques of production and distribution. Success in real-world competition often depends more on success in managing innovation than on success in adopting the right pricing policies or in making the right capacity decisions from already-known technological possibilities.

Increasing returns theories

We saw earlier that neoclassical theories assume that investment is always subject to diminishing returns. New growth theories emphasize the possibility of *historical increasing returns to investment*. This means that as invest-

---

[10] This is an important theme in much contemporary research, supported by evidence from such authors as Alfred D. Chandler, Jr (*Scale and Scope: The Dynamics of Industrial Capitalism*, Cambridge, Mass.: Harvard University Press, 1990), David Mowrey and Nathan Rosenberg (*Technology and the Pursuit of Economic Growth*, Cambridge University Press, 1989), and Michael Porter (*The Competitive Advantage of Nations*, New York: Free Press, 1990).

[11] Porter, *The Competitive Advantage of Nations*, p. 507.

[12] This is why in microeconomics we study three runs: the short run, the long run, and the very long run. Often the very-long-run response to a change in relative prices is much more important than either the short-run response, limited by fixed capital, or the long-run response, limited by existing technology.

ment in some new area, product, power source, or production technology proceeds through time, each new increment of investment is more productive than previous increments. A number of sources of increasing returns have been noted. These fall under the general categories of once-and-for-all costs and ideas.

Fixed costs

Here are three ways in which once-and-for-all costs can cause increasing returns to investment:

1. Investment in the early stages of development of a country or region may create new skills and attitudes in the workforce that are then available to all subsequent investors, whose costs are therefore lower than those encountered by the initial investors. In the language of Chapter 18 the early firms are conferring an externality on those who follow them.

2. Each new investor may find the environment more and more favourable to its investment because of the infrastructure that has been created by those who came before.

3. The first investment in a new product will encounter countless problems, both technical problems of production and problems of product acceptance among customers. Once the technical problems are overcome, they do not exist for subsequent investors. When a new product is developed, customers will often resist adopting it, partly because they may be conservative and partly because they know that new products often have teething troubles. Customers also need time to learn how best to use the new product—they need to do what is called 'learning by using'. The first firms in the field with a truly new idea, such as personal computers, usually meet strong customer resistance, but this resistance is eroded over time.

All of these cases, and many more that could be mentioned, are examples of a single phenomenon:

Many investments require fixed costs, the advantages of which are then available to subsequent investors; hence the investment costs for 'followers' can be substantially less than the investment costs for 'pioneers'.

More generally, many of the sources of increasing returns are variations on the following theme:

Doing something really new is difficult, both technically and in terms of customer acceptance, whereas making further variations on an accepted and developed new idea becomes progressively easier.

The implications of these ideas have been the subject of intense study ever since they were first embedded in modern growth models by Paul Romer of the University of California and Maurice Scott of Oxford University.[13]

Ideas

An even more fundamental change in the new theories is the shift from the economics of goods to the economics of ideas.

Physical goods, such as factories and machines, exist in one place at one time. The nature of this existence has two consequences. First, when physical goods are used by someone, they cannot be used by someone else. Second, if a given labour force is provided with more and more physical objects to use in production, sooner or later diminishing returns will be encountered.

Ideas have different characteristics. First, once someone has an idea and develops it, it is available for use by everyone. Ideas can be used by one person without reducing their use by others. For example, if one firm is using a certain van, another firm cannot use that van at the same time; but one firm's use of a revolutionary design for a new suspension on a van or lorry does not prevent other firms from using that design as well. Ideas are not subject to the same use restrictions as goods. (In the language of Table 18.1 on page 289 physical goods are rivalrous; ideas are non-rivalrous.)

Second, ideas are not necessarily subject to decreasing returns. As our knowledge increases, each increment of new knowledge does *not* inevitably add less to our productive ability than did each previous increment. A year spent improving the operation of semiconductors may be more productive than a year spent improving the operation of vacuum tubes (the technology used before semiconductors).

The evidence from modern research is that new technologies are usually absolutely factor-saving—in other words they use less of all inputs per unit of output. Furthermore, there is no evidence that from decade to decade the factor saving associated with increments of new knowledge is diminishing.

Modern growth theories stress the importance of ideas in producing what can be called knowledge-driven growth. New knowledge provides the input that allows investment to produce increasing rather than diminishing returns. Since there are no practical boundaries to human knowledge, there need be no immediate boundaries to finding new ways to produce more output using less of all inputs.[14]

Classical and neoclassical growth theories gave economics the name 'dismal science' by emphasizing diminishing returns under conditions of given technology. The modern growth theories are more optimistic because they

---

[13] As with so many innovations, these new views have many historical antecedents, including a classic article in the 1960s by Nobel Prize-winner Kenneth Arrow of Stanford University: 'The Economic Implications for Learning by Doing', *Review of Economic Studies*, 29 (1962).

[14] Possibly, at some distant date, we may know everything there is to know, but if that time ever comes, it is clearly going to be a long, long way in the future.

emphasize the unlimited potential of knowledge-driven technological change to economize on all resource inputs, and because they display increasing returns to investment with constant population.

In so far as these new ideas are true, however, they refer to long-term trends. The dynamics of market systems cause growth rates to vary from decade to decade for reasons that are not fully understood. Over the long haul, however, there seems no reason to believe that equal increments of human effort must inevitably be rewarded by ever-diminishing increments to material output.

Further causes of growth

So far we have looked at increases in labour and capital and at technological change as causes of growth. Contemporary studies suggest that other causes of growth are also important. The effects of these other causes appear as shifts in the production function, so that any given number of hours of labour operating with a given amount of capital produces more and more output as time passes.

Institutions

Almost all aspects of a country's institutions can foster or deter the efficient use of a society's natural and human resources. Social and religious habits, legal institutions, and traditional patterns of national and international trade are all important. So, too, is the political climate.

Historians of economic growth, such as Paul David and Nathan Rosenberg, attribute much of the growth of Western economies in the post-medieval world to the development of *new institutions*, such as the joint-stock company and limited liability. Many students of modern growth suggest that institutions are as important today as they were in the past. They suggest that the societies that are most successful in developing the new institutions that are needed in today's knowledge-intensive world of globalized competition will be those that are at the forefront of economic growth.

The role of the government

Governments play an important role in the growth process.

First, the government needs to provide the framework for the market economy that is given by such things as well-defined property rights secure from arbitrary confiscation, security and enforcement of contracts, law and order, a sound money, and the basic rights of the individual to locate, sell, and invest where and how he or she decides.

Second, governments need to provide infrastructure. For example, transportation and communications networks are critical to growth in the modern globalized economy. Some of these facilities, such as roads, bridges, and harbours, are usually provided directly by governments; others, such as telecommunications, rail, and air services, can be provided by private firms, but government regulations and competition policy may be needed to prevent the emergence of growth-inhibiting monopolies in these areas.

Education and health (especially for the disadvantaged) are important forms of government expenditure. Creating the appropriate factors of production is critical to creating comparative advantages in products that can be exported. This requires general education, trade schools, and other appropriate institutions for formal education as well as policies to increase on-the-job training within firms.

Other possible government policies include favourable tax treatment of saving, investment, and capital gains, R&D tax incentives and funding assistance, and policies to encourage some fraction of the large pools of financial capital held by pension funds and insurance companies to be used to finance innovation.

Finally, emphasis can be placed on poverty reduction for at least two reasons. First, poverty can exert powerful anti-growth effects. People living in poverty will not develop the skills to provide a productive labour force, and they may not even respond to incentives that are provided. Malnutrition in early childhood can affect a person's capacities for life. Second, although economic growth tends to reduce the incidence of poverty, it does not eliminate it.

Are there limits to growth?

Many opponents of growth argue that sustained world growth is undesirable; some argue that it is impossible. Of course, all terrestrial things have an ultimate limit. Astronomers predict that the solar system itself will die when the sun burns out in another five billion or so years. To be of practical concern, a limit must be within our planning horizons.

Resource exhaustion

The years since the Second World War have seen a rapid acceleration in the consumption of the world's resources, particularly fossil fuels and basic minerals. World population has increased from under 2.5 billion to nearly 6 billion in that period; this increase alone has intensified the demand for the world's resources. Furthermore, as economic development spreads to more and more countries, living standards are rising, in some cases at a rapid rate. As people attain higher incomes, they consume more resources. So not only are there more people in the world, but many of those people are consuming increasing quantities of resources.

Most (but not all) economists believe that the technology and resources available at the beginning of the twenty-first century could not possibly support the world's population at a standard of living equal to that currently enjoyed by the average European family. To do so, for example, the annual consumption of oil would have to increase more than tenfold. It is evident that resources and our present capacity to cope with pollution and environmental degradation are insufficient to accomplish this rise in living standards with our present technology.

Most economists, however, agree that *absolute* limits to growth, based on the assumptions of constant technology and fixed resources, are not relevant. As modern growth theory stresses, technology changes continually, as do stocks of resources. For example, forty years ago few would have thought that the world could produce enough food to feed its present population of nearly 6 billion people, let alone the 10 billion at which the population is projected to stabilize sometime in the mid-twenty-first century. Yet this task now seems feasible.

At the turn of the century the developed world is struggling, not with a food shortage, but with a food glut. Farm support policies in the European Union have turned the countries of Europe into food exporters rather than food importers, as they had been in the past. A mere 3 per cent of European, US, and Canadian labour applied to limited farmland with modern technology is producing more food than the world markets can consume. The problem in the mid-1990s is how to reduce subsidized production, not how to produce more.

Although globally there is enough food for everyone, severe problems arise when primarily agricultural economies suffer drought and other natural disasters, or wars and other man-made disasters. The problem, then, is not to produce more food worldwide, but to be sure that it is available where it is needed.

It is possible that forty years from now the global energy problem will be as much a thing of the past as the global food shortage problem is today. Technology could by then have produced a cheap, non-polluting energy source (possibly based on solar energy or nuclear fusion).

Furthermore, research into technological change shows that the typical innovation in production processes uses less of all inputs per unit of output. Thus technological change is part of the *solution*, as well as being part of the problem. The problem is too many people aspiring to levels of consumption that cannot be sustained *with existing technologies*.

The future is always uncertain, and it is instructive to recall how many things that we accept as commonplace today would have seemed miraculous a mere twenty-five years ago.

Yet there is surely cause for concern. Although many barriers can be overcome by technological advances, such achievements are not instantaneous and are certainly not automatic. There is a critical problem of timing: how soon can we discover and put into practice the knowledge required to solve the problems that are made ever more imminent by the growth in the population, the affluence of the rich nations, and the aspirations of the billions who now live in poverty? There is no guarantee that a whole generation will not be caught in transition between technologies, with enormous social and political consequences.

Renewable resources

One possible limitation to growth relates to renewable resources. The demands placed on them threaten to destroy their natural recuperative cycle. Throughout history, for example, fishermen were a small part of the predatory process. Now the demands of nearly 6 billion people have made fish a scarce resource, threatening to destroy the fish-generating capacity of many oceans, as we saw in Box 18.2 on page 292.

Pollution

A further problem is how to cope with pollution. Air, water, and earth are polluted by a variety of natural activities, and through billions of years the environment has coped with these. The Earth's natural processes had little trouble dealing with the pollution generated by its 1 billion inhabitants in 1800. But the nearly 6 billion people who now exist put demands on pollution-abatement systems that threaten to become unsustainable. Smoke, sewage, chemical waste, hydrocarbon emissions, spent nuclear fuel, and a host of other pollutants threaten to overwhelm the Earth's natural regenerative processes. Detailed analysis of how these problems may be dealt with was given in Chapters 18 and 19.

Conscious management of pollution and renewable resources was unnecessary when the world's population was 1 billion people, but such management has become a pressing matter of survival now that nearly 6 billion people are seeking to live in the same space and off the world's limited resources.

Conclusion

Growth has raised the average citizens of advanced countries from poverty to plenty in the course of two centuries

—a short time in terms of human history. Yet the world still faces many problems. Starvation and poverty are the common lot of citizens in many countries and are not unknown in the European Union and the United States, where average living standards are high. Further growth is needed if people in less developed countries are to escape material poverty, and further growth would help advanced countries to deal with many of their pressing economic problems.

Rising population and rising per capita consumption, however, put pressure on the world's natural ecosystems, especially through pollution and congestion. Further growth must be sustainable growth, which in turn must be based on idea-driven technological change. Past experi-

ence suggests that new technologies will use less of all resources per unit of output. However, if they are to reduce dramatically the demands placed on the Earth's ecosystems, price and policy incentives will be needed to direct technological change in more 'environmentally friendly' ways. Just as present technologies are much less polluting than the technologies of 100 years ago, the technologies of the twenty-first century must be made much less polluting than today's.

There is no guarantee that the world will solve the problems of sustainable growth, but there is nothing in modern growth theory and existing evidence to suggest that such an achievement is impossible.

Summary

The nature of economic growth

■ Real GDP can be increased on a once-and-for-all basis from the demand side by removing recessionary gaps and from the supply side by reducing structural impediments and economic inefficiencies. Sustained increases, however, are due mainly to economic growth, which continuously pushes the *LRAS* curve outward, thereby increasing potential output.

Benefits and costs of growth

■ The most important benefit of growth lies in its contribution to the long-run struggle to raise living standards and to escape poverty. The cumulative effects of even small differences in growth rates become large over periods of a decade or more. It is also easier to redistribute income in a growing society than in a static one.

■ The opportunity cost of growth is the diversion of resources from current consumption to capital formation. For individuals who are left behind in a rapidly changing world, the costs can be high and more personal.

Theories of economic growth

■ Investment has short-term effects on actual GDP through aggregate demand and long-term effects through growth in potential GDP. Saving reduces consumption and aggregate demand and therefore reduces GDP in the short run, but in the long run saving finances the investment that leads to growth in potential output.

■ The aggregate neoclassical model displays diminishing returns when one factor is increased on its own and constant returns when all factors are increased together. In a balanced growth path, labour, capital, and national output all increase at a constant rate, leaving living standards unchanged. When labour-augmenting

productivity growth occurs, a balanced growth path is consistent with rising per capita output and income.

■ In the long term technological change is the major cause of growth, together with the new capital investment which is needed to embody new technologies. Modern growth theory treats technological change as an endogenous variable that responds to market signals. The diffusion of technology is also endogenous. It is costly and often proceeds at a relatively slow pace.

■ Some modern growth theories display increasing returns as investment increases on its own. This is because investment creates externalities so that successive increments of investment may add constant or even successively *increasing* amounts to total output.

■ The critical importance of increasing knowledge and new technology to the goal of sustaining growth is highlighted by the great drain on existing natural resources that has resulted from the explosive growth of population and output in recent decades. Without continuing technological change, the present needs and aspirations of the world's population cannot come anywhere close to being met.

Are there limits to growth?

■ Rising population and rising real incomes place pressure on resources. Although resources in general will not be exhausted, particular resources, such as petroleum, will be. Furthermore, resources that renewed themselves without help from humans when the world's population was 1 billion people could easily be exhausted unless they are consciously conserved now that the world's population exceeds 5 billion.

■ The enormous increase in population also creates severe problems of pollution. The Earth's environment could cope naturally with most human pollution 200 years ago, but the present population is so large that pollution has outstripped nature's coping mechanisms in many cases. Technological advance is needed to reduce the amount of pollution created by each unit of output.

Topics for review

- Short-run and long-run effects of investment and saving
- The cumulative nature of growth
- Benefits and costs of growth
- The neoclassical aggregate production function
- Balanced growth
- Endogenous technical change
- Increasing returns to investment
- Embodied and disembodied technical change
- The economics of goods and of ideas
- Resource depletion and pollution

Questions for discussion

1 Some environmentalists advocate ending all economic growth. If the UK government decided to follow this advice, would it be possible to do so? Consider your answer in relation to each of the causes of growth identified in this chapter. How would the UK be affected by its attempts to slow or even stop growth if the rest of the EU countries did not follow suit?

2 Discuss the following newspaper headlines in terms of the sources, costs, and benefits of growth: (a) 'Stress addiction: life in the fast lane may have its benefits'; (b) 'Education: an expert urges major curriculum reforms'; (c) 'Industrial radiation: risks higher than previously thought'; (d) 'Middle managers lose jobs as firms go "leaner"'; (e) 'Ozone layer depletion reaching alarming proportions'; (f) 'Study shows health and safety standards much higher than 50 years ago'.

3 Economic growth is often studied in macro models. But in a market economy who makes the decisions that lead to growth? What kinds of decisions and what kinds of actions cause growth to occur? How might a detailed study of individual markets be helpful in understanding growth?

4 List as many products as you can that were not available when your parents were young. Now do the same for your grandparents.

5 In the last years of the twentieth century, the Irish Republic posted phenomenally high growth rates. Look up a source to discover if these rates have persisted until now. What have the fast growth rates done to the relative per capita incomes of Ireland and the UK?

Chapter 33
Growth in Developing Countries

Traditionally in economics the growth of high-income countries has been treated as a separate subject from the growth of lower-income countries (an intercountry distinction which is described in more detail below), and the latter subject is often not included in introductory courses. For this reason this chapter has been made self-contained so that it can be skipped if desired.

We include this material here for two main reasons. First, the deeper understanding that economists are developing of the role that technological change plays in economic growth is blurring the traditional distinction between the forces that cause growth in high-income and in lower-income countries. Second, the growth successes of Japan in the mid-twentieth century and of several Southeast Asian countries later in the century has blurred what earlier seemed to be a clear distinction between the high-income, largely industrialized, countries and all the rest. We now see what looks more like a continuous gradation from the very-highest-income countries, which include the USA, most countries of the EU, and Japan, through South Korea, Hong Kong, Singapore, Taiwan, some of the lower-income countries of the EU (among others), and some of the higher-income countries of Latin America at the upper-middle end of the scale, through countries such as Indonesia and Malaysia a little further down, followed by India and a rapidly growing China, to yet others, particularly many of the countries of sub-Saharan Africa, not only with very low incomes but also with static ones.

For these and other reasons it no longer seems reasonable to assume that the forces that govern growth in rich countries are fundamentally different from the forces that govern growth in middle- and lower-rank countries.

From the outset development economics has had a micro component, concentrating on social and economic structures as influences on growth. While not forgetting the important macro influences of aggregate saving and investment, those economists who study technological change in high-income countries have come to place increasing emphasis on the microeconomic aspects of social and economic structure that encourage the innovation and diffusion of new technologies in the countries that they study. (See for example Box 33.3 later in this chapter, on page 575.)

Probably the most important boundary that divides countries where different explanations of growth are required is between countries that have very low and static incomes and all the rest. A country that has shown no significant economic growth for decades (or even for centuries) probably has economic and social structures, as well as fundamental direction to its economic policies, that are basically unfavourable to growth. If the people of that country wish to grow, they must contemplate fundamental structural changes, as well as major reversals in their economic policies. All the other countries, in which growth is occurring (although sometimes at a rate that is regarded as too low), face many common problems, whether they are low-, middle-, or high-income countries. The importance of individual forces may vary, but overall these countries face problems that have a significant degree of similarity. Of course, their underlying social and economic structures do affect their growth rates, but since they are currently growing, they do not face the same urgent need to consider major alterations of these structures as do the non-growing countries.

The uneven pattern of development

In the civilized and comfortable urban life of today's developed countries most people have lost sight of the fact that a short time ago—very short in terms of the lifespan of the Earth—people were nomadic food-gatherers, existing as best they could from what nature threw their way. It has been only about 10,000 years since the neolithic agricultural revolution, when people changed from food-gatherers to food-producers. Throughout most of subsequent human history civilizations have been based on a comfortable life for a privileged minority and unremitting toil for the vast majority. It has been only within the last two centuries that ordinary people have become able to expect leisure and high consumption standards—and then only in the world's economically developed countries.

Close to 6 billion people are alive today, but the wealthy parts of the world—where people work no more than 40 or 50 hours per week, enjoy substantial leisure, and have a level of consumption at least *half* that attained by the United States (the country with the highest per capita GNI[1])—contain no more than 15 per cent of the world's population. Many of the rest struggle for subsistence. Many exist on a level at or below that endured by peasants in ancient Egypt or Babylon.

The richest countries with the highest per capita incomes are referred to by the United Nations as **developed countries.** These include the United States, Canada, most of the countries of Western Europe, South Africa, Australia, New Zealand, Japan, and a few others. The poorer countries are referred to by the UN as the **developing countries**[2] and include a diverse set of nations. Some, such as Vietnam and China, have grown very rapidly in the 1990s, while others, such as Burundi and Djibouti, actually had negative growth rates of per capita real income. Between these two is another group of nations, variously called newly industrialized economies (NIEs) or **newly industrialized countries (NICs);** they include South Korea, Singapore, Taiwan, Brazil, and Hong Kong. These countries have grown rapidly and typically have per capita incomes that have risen above 50 per cent of those found in the developed nations. Several other countries in Southeast Asia are close behind the NICs, including Malaysia and Thailand. A new group of developing countries has been given a collective label since about 1990. These are the countries of the former Soviet Bloc that used to have centrally planned economies but are now trying to build market economies. These are known as **transition economies.** Examples are Poland, Hungary, the Czech Republic, and Russia.

Data on per capita incomes throughout the world are summarized in Table 33.1.[3] The data reflect enormous real differences in living standards that no statistical inaccuracies can hide. The **development gap**—the discrepancy between the standards of living in countries at either end of the distribution—is real and large.[4]

The consequences of very low income levels can be severe. In a rich country such as the United Kingdom variations in rainfall are reflected in farm output and farm

---

[1] Luxembourg was higher in 1996, but it has special features that make it an unusual economy.

[2] The terminology of development is often confusing. 'Underdeveloped', 'less developed', and 'developing' do not mean the same thing in ordinary English, yet each has been used to describe the same phenomenon. For the most part we will use the term 'developing', which is the term currently used by the United Nations to describe the lower-income countries. Some of these countries are making progress in raising their living standards; that is, they are developing in the ordinary sense of that word. Others are not.

[3] There are many problems when we compare incomes across countries. For example, home-grown food is vitally important to living standards in underdeveloped countries, but it is excluded, or at best imperfectly included, in the national income statistics of most countries. In Norway significant amounts of income go to heating houses during cold winters. Such heating is not necessary in countries that have warm climates.

[4] You will find large differences in international comparisons depending on the exchange rates that are used to convert incomes valued in domestic currencies to a common currency unit. Use of rates based on the relative purchasing powers of national currencies (called purchasing power parity rates and described in Chapter 28) is more satisfactory, while use of current rates causes international standings to vary substantially from one year to the next.

Table 33.1 Income and population differences among groups of countries, 1996

Income groups by GNI per capita (US$)	Number of countries (1)	GNI (US$ million) (2)	Population (millions) (3)	GNI per capita (US$) (4)	World population (%) (5)	World GNI (%) (6)
Low ($785 or less)	63	1,596,837	3,236	490	56.2	5.4
Lower-middle ($786–$3,115)	63	1,962,719	1,125	1,740	19.6	6.6
Upper-middle ($3,116–$9,635)	31	2,178,234	473	4,600	8.2	7.4
High ($9,636 or more)	53	23,771,825	919	25,870	16.0	80.6
World	210	29,509,614	5,754	5,130	100.0	100.0

The unequal distribution of world income is shown in columns (5) and (6). The poorest 56 per cent of the world's population earns only 5 per cent of world income; the richest 16 per cent earns 81 per cent of world income.

Source: World Bank, *World Bank Atlas 1998* (Washington, DC).

income. In very poor countries variations in rainfall are often reflected in the death rate. In these countries many people live so close to a subsistence level that even slight fluctuations in the food supply can bring death by starvation to large numbers. Other, less dramatic, characteristics of poverty include inadequate diet, poor health, short life-expectancy, and illiteracy.

For these reasons reformers in very-low-income countries feel a sense of urgency not felt by their counterparts in higher-income countries. Yet as Table 33.2 shows, some of the poorest countries in the world are among those with very low or negative growth rates of per capita GNI. As a result,

The development gap has been widening for the very poorest countries.

As we will see, this is a problem of both output and population. It is also an international political problem. What are the causes of underdevelopment, and how may they be overcome?

Table 33.2 The relationship between the level and the rate of growth of per capita income, 1990–1996

Growth of GNI per capita, 1990–6 (%)	Number of countries	GNI, 1996 (US$m)	Population, 1996 (millions)	GNI per capita, 1996 (US$)
Less than 0	69	2,152,165	832	2,590
0–0.9	21	6,037,894	342	17,680
1.0–1.9	25	15,772,567	1,043	15,130
2.0–2.9	20	1,399,561	488	2,870
3.0 or more	39	3,899,334	2,896	1,350
No data	36	248,094	153	1,620

Some of the very poorest countries spend much of their increase in income on a rising population. The gap in income between rich and many of the very poor countries is not closing; however, some countries with low per capita GNI were among the faster growing in this period. Notice that there are no consistent growth data for 36 of the poorest countries.

Source: World Bank, *World Bank Atlas 1998* (Washington, DC).

Restraints on economic development

Per capita income grows when aggregate national income grows faster than population. Many forces can impede such growth. Here we study a list of possible restraints that starts with natural resources and ends with infrastructure. These can apply to countries at all income levels, but they tend to be most severe in the poorest countries.

Inadequate natural resources

A country's supply of natural resources is important. A country with infertile land and inadequate supplies of natural resources will find growth in income more difficult to achieve than one that is richly endowed with such resources.

How these resources are managed also matters. When farmland is divided into many small parcels, it may be much more difficult to achieve the advantages of modern agriculture than when the land is available in huge tracts for large-scale farming. Fragmented land-holdings may result from a dowry or inheritance system, or they may be politically imposed. One of the popular policies following the Mexican revolution early in the twentieth century was the redistribution of land from large landowners to ordinary peasants. Today, however, the fragmented land-ownership prevents Mexican agriculture from producing many products at costs low enough to compete in international markets. Since it has joined the North American Free Trade Association (NAFTA), the Mexican govern-

ment can no longer choose to continue to protect a large agricultural sector whose inefficiency has been increasing relative to competing suppliers. Market forces will lead to much larger land-holdings. Although average incomes will rise as a result, many small-holders will suffer in the transition.

Although abundant supplies of natural resources can assist growth, they are neither sufficient to ensure growth nor necessary for it. Some countries with large supplies of natural resources have poor growth performances because the economic structure or political system inhibits growth; prime examples are Russia, Ukraine, and Argentina up until the 1990s. In contrast, other countries have enjoyed rapid rates of economic growth based on human capital and entrepreneurial ability in spite of a dearth of natural resources; prime examples are Japan over the last 100 years, and Singapore, Hong Kong, Israel, and Taiwan in the last 40 years.

Inefficiently used natural resources

Three kinds of economic inefficiency need to be distinguished. *Allocative inefficiency* occurs when factors of production are used to make an inefficient combination of goods. There are too many of some goods and too few of others. This means that the economy is at the 'wrong' point on its production-possibility boundary. If resources are reallocated to produce fewer of some and more of other types of goods, some people can be made better off while no one need be made worse off.

Productive inefficiency occurs when factors of production are used in inefficient combinations. Given the prices of capital and labour, some production processes use too much capital relative to labour, while others use too little. This means that the economy is inside its production-possibility boundary (as illustrated in Figure 1.1 on page 5). If factor combinations are altered, more of all goods can be produced. Monopolistic market structures, as well as taxes, tariffs, and subsidies, are important sources of the distortions that lead to both allocative and productive inefficiencies.

A third kind of inefficiency, called **X-inefficiency**, occurs either when firms do not seek to maximize their profits or when owners of the factors of production do not seek to maximize their material welfare. X-inefficiency also puts the economy inside its production-possibility boundary.

Professor Harvey Leibenstein of the University of California, the economist who developed the concept, has studied X-inefficiency in developing countries. He cites psychological evidence to show that non-maximizing behaviour is typical of situations in which the pressure that has been placed on decision-makers is either very low or very high. If the customary living standard can be obtained with little effort, according to this evidence, people are likely to follow customary behaviour and spend little time trying to make optimal decisions. When pressure builds up, so that making a reasonable income becomes more difficult, optimizing behaviour becomes more common. Under extreme pressure, however, such as very low living standards or a rapidly deteriorating environment, people become disoriented and once again do not adopt optimizing behaviour.

X-inefficiency may be typical of industries, and whole economies, where customary behaviour leads to acceptable living standards or where the challenges become overwhelming.[5]

Inefficient agriculture A developing country whose labour force is mainly devoted to agriculture has little choice but to accept this basic allocation of resources. It can build up its industrial sector, and if its efforts are successful the proportion of the population devoted to urban pursuits will rise. But the change will come slowly, leaving a large portion of the country's resources in rural pursuits for a long time to come.

It follows that policies to help the agricultural sector raise productivity are an important part of the development strategy in any agriculture-based poor country. These policies can fill the dual purposes of raising the incomes of rural workers and reducing the cost of food for urban workers.

A developing country's government may choose to de-

vote a major portion of its resources to stimulating agricultural production, for example by mechanizing farms, irrigating land, using new seeds and fertilizers, and promoting agricultural R&D. If successful, the country will stave off starvation for its current population, and it may even develop an excess over current needs and so have foodstuffs available for export. A food surplus can thereby earn foreign exchange to buy needed imports.

In the last three decades India, Pakistan, Taiwan, and other Asian countries have achieved dramatic increases in food production by the application of new technology and the use of new seed in agricultural production. This has been labelled the *green revolution.*

The gains from this strategy, while large at first, are subject to diminishing returns. Further gains in agricultural production have an ever-higher opportunity cost, measured in terms of the resources needed to irrigate land and to mechanize production. Critics of reliance on agricultural output argue that newly developing economies must start at once to develop other bases for economic growth.

Many developing countries (as well as many developed ones) suffer from misguided government intervention in the agriculture sector. In India, for example, the government has encouraged crops such as oilseeds and sugar cane, in which India has a comparative disadvantage, and discouraged crops such as rice, wheat, and cotton, in which India has a strong comparative advantage. It has subsidized food prices, thus giving large benefits to the urban population. About 8 per cent of all Indian government spending is on subsidies that go to fertilizers, to farmers' debt payments, and to urban food consumption.

Rapid population growth

Population growth is one of the central problems of economic development. For example, in the seven years 1990–6 Algeria, Kenya, and Zambia had growth rates of population of 2.3, 2.6, and 2.8 per cent per year alongside GDP growth rates of 0.9, 2.4, and 2.5 per cent, respectively. Hence they experienced *negative* rates of growth of GDP *per capita* (of −1.4, −0.2, and −0.3 per cent per year). Many less developed countries have rates of population growth that are nearly as large as their rates of growth of GDP. As a result their standards of living are barely higher than they were 100 years ago. They have made appreciable gains in aggregate income, but most of the gains have been literally eaten up by the increasing population. The fact that sixty-nine countries had negative growth rates in national income per head during the 1990–6 period is illustrated in Table 33.2 on page 564.

---

[5] Although such behaviour is no doubt often found in some developing economies, it is also sometimes found in advanced countries. For example, studies of monopolies have often indicated a preference on the part of their managers and workers for the 'quiet life' rather than an active search for profit- and income-maximizing forms of behaviour.

The critical importance of population growth to living standards was perceived early in the nineteenth century by the Reverend Thomas Malthus. He asserted two relations concerning rates of increase. First, food production tends to increase in an arithmetic progression (e.g. 100, 103, 106, 109, 112, where the increments in this example are 3 units per period). Second, population tends to increase in a geometric progression (e.g., 100, 103, 106.09, 109.27, 112.55, where the increase in this example is 3 *per cent per period*). As a result of these relationships Malthus argued that population growth will always tend to outrun the growth in food supply. The difference in the above example may not seem like much after only five periods. But after twenty periods the arithmetic increase in food supply has increased it to 160 while the geometric increase in the population has increased it to 181.

Malthus's prediction gave economics the name of 'the dismal science'. In some poor areas of the world the predictions seem all too accurate, even today. There, agricultural methods are fairly traditional, so that food production increases only slowly while population tends to increase at more rapid rates. The result is subsistence living, with population held in check by low life-expectancies and periodic famines.

Fortunately, over most of the world Malthus's predictions have been proved false. Two reasons are paramount. First, Malthus underestimated the importance of technological change, which has increased productivity in agriculture at a *geometric* rate far higher than the rate at which the demand for food has been growing in most advanced countries. Second, he underestimated the extent of voluntary restrictions of population growth. As a result population has grown more slowly than has the production of food (and most other things) in developed countries. For them living standards have been rising rather than falling.

For the more advanced industrialized countries, Malthusian pressures are not a problem today. However, for many poor countries, where people subsist on what they grow for themselves, the tendency for the growth in population to outstrip the growth in the food supply makes Malthusian pressures a current threat.

Figure 33.1 illustrates actual and projected world population. By now the population problem is almost completely limited to the low-income countries. About 97 per cent of the expected growth in the world's population between now and 2050 will be in the developing countries of Africa, Asia, and Latin America.

Inadequate human resources

Numbers of people matter, and so do their training and experience. A well-developed entrepreneurial class motivated and trained to organize resources for efficient

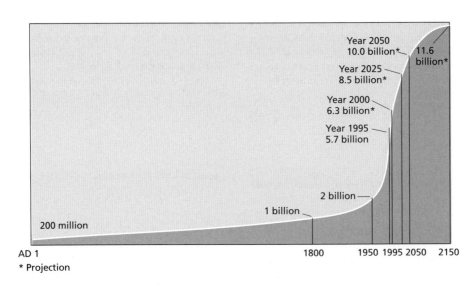

Figure 33.1 World population since AD 1

World population reached 5.7 billion in 1995 and is projected to rise to 10 billion by the middle of the twenty-first century. The population of industrialized countries has nearly stabilized. But in developing countries the population is skyrocketing. Up to 97 per cent of population growth between now and 2050 will occur in developing countries. Birth and death rates among present populations allow estimates to be made up to about the middle of the twenty-first century with reasonable accuracy. The projection of 11.6 billion in 2150 is much more uncertain.

Source: United Nations Population Fund.

production is often missing in poor countries. The cause may be that managerial positions are awarded on the basis of family status or political patronage (leading to *X*-inefficiency); it may be the presence of economic or cultural attitudes that do not favour acquisition of wealth by organizing productive activities; or it may simply be the absence of the quantity or quality of education or training that is required.

In today's world much production is knowledge-intensive. This puts a premium on a well-educated workforce. The abilities to read, do basic calculations, operate electronic equipment, and follow relatively complex instructions are important requirements for much modern labour. Failure to create such essential labour skills can be an important cause of lack of growth.

Poor health is another source of inadequate human resources. When the labour force is healthy, less time is lost and more effective effort is expended.

Cultural barriers

Traditions and habitual ways of doing business vary among societies, and not all are equally conducive to high productivity. Often in developing countries cultural forces are a source of *X*-inefficiency. Sometimes personal considerations of family, past favours, or traditional friendship or enmity are more important than market incentives in motivating behaviour. One may find a firm that is too small struggling to survive against a larger rival, and learn that the owner prefers to remain small because expansion would require use of non-family capital or leadership. To avoid paying too harsh a competitive price for built-in inefficiency, the firm's owners may then attempt to influence the government to prevent larger firms from being formed, or try to secure restrictions on the sale of output —and they may well succeed. Such behaviour will inhibit economic growth.

In a society in which people believe that it is more important who your father is than what you do, it may take a generation to persuade employers to change their attitudes, and another generation to persuade workers that times have changed. It is more difficult for the workforce to change its characteristics and to adapt to the requirements of growth in a traditional society, in which children are expected to follow their parents' occupations, than in a society in which upward mobility is itself a goal.

There has been a lively debate about the importance of differing cultural attitudes. Some analysts believe that traditional considerations dominate peasant societies to the exclusion of economic responses; others suggest that any resulting inefficiency may be relatively small. A country that wants development must accept some alteration in its traditional ways of doing things. However, a trade-off between speed of development and amount of social upheaval can be made. Many critics argue that development

plans, particularly when imposed by economists from advanced countries, pay too little attention to local cultural and religious values. An even more unfavourable possibility is that the social upheaval will occur without achieving even the expected benefits of a rising GDP. If the development policy does not take local values into account, the local population may not respond as predicted by Western economic theories. In this case the results of the development effort may be disappointingly small.

Inadequate financial institutions

The lack of an adequate, trustworthy, and trusted system of financial institutions is often a restraint on development. Investment plays a key role in growth, and an important source of funds for investment is the savings of households and firms. When banks and other financial institutions do not function effectively, the link between private saving and investment may be broken, making it difficult to raise funds for investment.

Many people in poor countries do not trust banks—sometimes with good reason, but often without. Either they do not maintain deposits, or else they panic periodically, withdrawing their balances and seeking security for their money under mattresses, in gold, or in real estate. When banks cannot count on their deposits being left in the banking system, they cannot engage in the kind of long-term loans that are needed to finance investments. When this happens, savings do not become available for investment in productive capacity.

More importantly, a poorly functioning banking system, often one that is nationalized or dominated by a strong government-supported union, can seriously slow growth. India was still in this situation in the late 1990s; although governments have introduced many market-oriented reforms over the last decade, they have so far been unwilling to take on the unions that dominate India's large, inefficient banking system.

Inadequate domestic savings

Although modern development strategies in many instances seek an infusion of foreign capital imported by transnational corporations (TNCs), the rise of domestically owned firms, which will reap some of the externalities created by foreign technology, is one key to sustained development. And a supply of domestic savings is needed to finance the growth of domestic firms.

If more domestic capital is to be created by a country's own efforts, resources must be diverted from the production of goods for current consumption. This means a cut in present living standards. If living standards are already at or near subsistence level, such a diversion will be difficult. At best it will be possible to reallocate only a small proportion of resources to the production of capital goods.

Such a situation is often described as the *vicious circle of poverty*: because a country has little capital per head, it is poor; because it is poor, it can devote few resources to creating new capital rather than to producing goods for consumption; because little new capital can be produced, capital per head remains low; and the country remains poor.

The vicious circle can be made to seem an absolute constraint on growth rates. Of course, it is not; if it were, we would all still be at the level of the early agricultural civilizations. The grain of truth in the vicious-circle argument is that some surplus must be available somewhere in the society to allow saving and investment. In a poor society with an even distribution of income in which nearly everyone is at the subsistence level, saving may be very difficult. But this is not the common experience. Usually there is at least a small middle class that can save and invest if opportunities for the profitable use of funds arise. Also, in most poor societies today the average household is above the physical subsistence level. Even the poorest households will find that they can sacrifice some present living standards for a future gain. For example, presented with a profitable opportunity, villagers in Ghana planted cocoa plants at the start of the twentieth century, even though there was a seven-year growing period before any return could be expected.

Where social attitudes do not sanction the sacrifice of current living standards in order to generate a large volume of domestic saving, a government can impose compulsory saving, or seek to increase the national savings rate through fiscal and monetary policies. Unfortunately, even where the governments of developing countries have succeeded in raising their national savings rate, a large proportion of the savings was wasted in inefficient state-owned enterprises that could never become profitable. If the funds had been invested in the much-needed infrastructure that only a government can create, then government intervention might have been effective in encouraging development.

An important consideration is that in less developed countries one resource that is often *not* scarce is labour. Profitable home or village investment that requires mainly labour inputs may be made with relatively little sacrifice in current living standards. Unfortunately, this kind of investment often does not appeal to local governments, which are too often mesmerized by large and symbolic investments, such as dams, nuclear power stations, and steel mills.

Inadequate infrastructure

Key services, such as transportation and a communications network, called **infrastructure,** are necessary for efficient commerce. Roads, bridges, railways, and harbours are needed to transport people, materials, and finished goods. Phone and postal services, a safe water supply, and sanitation are essential to economic development.

The absence, for whatever reason, of a dependable infrastructure can impose severe barriers to economic development.

Many governments feel that money spent on a new steel mill shows more impressive results than money spent on such infrastructure investments as automating the telephone system. Yet private, growth-creating, entrepreneurial activity will be discouraged more by the absence of good communications than by the lack of domestically produced steel.

Development policies

The past two decades have seen a remarkable change in the views of appropriate policies for industrial development. The views that dominated development policies during the period from 1945 to the early 1980s have given way to a new set of views that reflect the experience of the earlier period.

The older view

The dominant views on appropriate development strategies from 1945 to the early 1980s were inward-looking and interventionist.

They were inward-looking in the sense that local industries were fostered primarily to replace imports. These local industries were usually protected with high tariffs, typically well over 100 per cent, and supported by large subsidies and favourable tax treatment. The exchange rate was almost always pegged, usually at an overvalued rate. As we saw in Chapter 28, fixing the exchange rate above its free-market level raises the prices of exports and lowers the prices of imports, which leads to an excess demand for foreign exchange. The argument for keeping export prices high was that foreign demand for traditional exports was inelastic. As we saw in Chapter 4, raising the prices of goods with inelastic demands raises the amount received by their sellers. The excess demand for foreign exchange caused by the overvaluation of the currency led to a host of import restrictions and exchange controls, such as import licences and quotas issued by government officials.

Many governments were hostile to foreign investment and made it difficult for multinational firms to locate in their countries. For example, many had local ownership rules, requiring that any foreign firm wanting to invest there must set up a subsidiary in which local residents would own at least half of the shares. Much new investment was undertaken by government-owned industries, while subsidization of privately owned, local industries was often heavy and indiscriminate. Industrial activity was often controlled, with a licence being required to set up a firm or to purchase supplies of scarce commodities. Much investment was financed by local savings, sometimes voluntarily and sometimes enforced by the government. One method of enforcement was for a state marketing board to be empowered to buy all the outputs of traditional export industries at very low prices, sell them abroad at high prices, and use the profits so generated to finance government-owned industries. Often, as with cocoa in Ghana, the prices paid to farmers were too low to encourage them to be efficient, and government funds were wasted on grandiose but ultimately unprofitable projects.

The focus of commercial policy is on *import substitution*. Strictly, 'import substitution' refers to the attempt to build local industries behind protectionist walls to replace imports. Often, however, the term is used to refer to the set of related measures just described.

These interventionist measures gave great power to government officials, and not surprisingly corruption was rife. Bribes were needed to obtain many things, including state subsidies, licences, and quotas. As a result many resources were allocated to those who had the most political power and were willing to pay the highest bribes, rather than to those who could use the resources most efficiently.

Heavy subsidization of private firms and state investment in public firms required much money, and the tax structures of many poor countries could not provide sufficient funds. As a result, *inflationary finance* was often used.[6] Persistent inflation was a major problem in many of these countries. It was almost always in the two-digit range, and quite often soared to figures of several hundred per cent per year.

Most of the economies in which these policies were employed fell short of full central planning and full state ownership of resources. As a result there was still some private initiative and some profit-seeking through normal market means. But the overall policy thrust was interventionist and inward-looking.

The rise of the new view

During the 1980s four important events contributed to a reappraisal of this development model. First, developing countries that had followed these policies most faithfully had some of the poorest growth records. Second, the GDP growth rates of the more industrialized countries of Eastern Europe and the Soviet Union that had followed interventionist, non-market approaches to their own growth were visibly falling behind those of the market-based economies. Third, Taiwan, Singapore, South Korea, and Hong Kong, which had departed from the accepted model by adopting more market-based policies, were prospering and growing rapidly. Fourth, the globalization of the world's economy led to an understanding that countries could no longer play a full part in world economic growth without a substantial presence of multinational corporations within their boundaries. Given the size of developing countries, this mainly meant the presence of foreign-owned multinationals. We discuss each of these four events in more detail in the next four sections.

The experience of the developing countries

Highly interventionist economies fared poorly in the 1950s, 1960s, and 1970s. Economies as varied as Argentina, Myanmar, Tanzania, Ethiopia, and Ghana were all interventionist and all grew slowly, if at all. In Ethiopia the emperor was overthrown, and the new government adopted rigid Soviet-style policies. Attempts to collectivize agriculture led, as they had fifty years earlier in the Soviet Union, to widespread famine. Some countries, such as Ghana and Nigeria, started from relatively strong economic positions when they first gained their independence, only to see their GDPs and living standards shrink. Other countries, such as India and Kenya, sought a middle way between capitalism and communism. They fared better than their more highly interventionist neighbours, but their development was still disappointingly slow.

The experience of the communist countries

Underdevelopment is as old as civilization. Concern with it as a remediable condition, however, became a compelling policy issue only within the twentieth century. One incentive behind this new attention to development was the apparent success of planned programmes of 'crash' development, of which the Soviet experience has been the most remarkable, and the Chinese the most recent. Not surprisingly, therefore, the early successes of the growth policies of many communist countries provided role models for many of the early development policies of the poorer countries. Their governments sought to copy the

[6] Under inflationary finance the government sells newly created bonds to the central bank, which pays for them with newly created money. The large increase in money supply creates rapid inflation, as we saw in Box 30.1 on page 517.

planning techniques that appeared to underlie these earlier successes.

In recent decades, however, the more developed communist countries began to discover the limitations of their planning techniques. Highly planned government intervention seems most successful in providing infrastructure and developing basic industries, such as electric power and steel—where these are needed, and where the technology could be copied from more market-oriented economies. It is now seen to be much less successful in providing the entrepreneurial activity, risk-taking, and adaptability to change that are key ingredients to *sustained* economic growth and technological change.

The discrediting of the Soviet approach to development was given added emphasis when the countries of Eastern Europe and the former Soviet Union abandoned their system *en masse* and took the difficult path of rapidly introducing market economies. Many of these countries experienced large negative growth rates in their early years of transition, though some, such as Poland, Romania, Slovakia and the Czech Republic, had moved into positive GDP growth by the second half of the 1990s. Box 33.1 discusses the problems of these transition economies.

Although China, the last major centrally planned economy holdout (apart from Cuba and North Korea), has been posting impressive growth figures, two very 'noncommunist' reasons are important in explaining this performance. First, over 90 per cent of the population is engaged in basically free-market agriculture—because that sector has long been free of the central planning apparatus that so hampered agriculture in the former Soviet Union. Second, while the state-controlled industries suffer increasing inefficiencies and absorb ever-larger proportions of the state budget in subsidies, a major investment boom has gone on in China's southeast coastal provinces. Here foreign investment, largely from Japan and the Asian NIEs, has introduced a rapidly growing, and highly efficient, industrialized market sector.[7]

The experience of the NIEs

Countries such as South Korea, Taiwan, Hong Kong, and Singapore are often called Asian Tigers. All four have turned themselves from poor countries into relatively high-income, industrialized countries in the course of less than forty years.

During the early stages of their development, their governments used import restrictions to build up local industries and to develop labour forces with the requisite skills and experiences. In the 1950s and early 1960s, however, each of the four abandoned many of the interventionist aspects of the older development model. They created market-oriented economies with less direct government intervention than other developing economies, who stuck with the accepted development model.

South Korea and Singapore did not adopt a *laissez-faire* stance. Instead, both followed quite strong policies which targeted specific areas for development and encouraged those areas with various economic incentives. In contrast, Hong Kong had a much more *laissez-faire* attitude towards the direction of industrial development. Taiwan was somewhere between these extremes. In contrast to South Korea it relied on small entrepreneurial firms rather than massive conglomerates. In contrast to Hong Kong it assisted many infant industries. For example, the government initially developed the electronics sector through state-owned firms, which it transferred to private owners after they had become established.

After local industries had been established, all four of these countries adopted outward-looking, market-based, export-oriented policies. This tested the success of various policies to encourage specific industries by their ability to compete in the international marketplace. With industries designed to serve a sheltered home market, it is all too easy to shelter inefficiency more or less indefinitely. With export-oriented policies *not based on subsidies*, the success of targeted firms and industries is tested in international markets, and unprofitable firms fail.

Each country has experienced great successes and some failures of policy. Taiwan was typical in demonstrating the value of the new market-oriented approach when, in the period 1956–60, it abandoned most of the apparatus of the older development model and moved to market-oriented policies. Before long its growth rate increased, and it started on a path that has taken it from a per capita GDP of about 10 per cent of that of the United States in 1955 to one of over 50 per cent in the late 1990s. Today Taiwan has become a major foreign investor as its less skill-intensive industries migrate to mainland China and other locations in Southeast Asia. In Taiwan real wages have risen, making low-skill-intensive manufacturing uneconomic and pushing local industries to higher-value-added lines of production which can support higher wages and hence higher living standards for the workers.

Not far behind the NIEs is a second generation of Asian and Latin American countries that have also adopted more market-oriented policies and have seen substantial growth follow; Thailand, the Philippines, Mexico, Chile, and Argentina are examples. Even Vietnam and Laos are liberalizing their economies as Communist governments come to accept that a market economy is a necessary condition for sustained economic growth.

---

[7] Karl Marx predicted that the state would wither away under communism, whereas it actually became ever more powerful. Ironically, communism may be withering away in China (rather than being swept away in one grand gesture, as it was in Eastern Europe). The Communist government could not eliminate foreign investment and the market-oriented production in its coastal regions because it generates too large a proportion of China's GDP and employment. In contrast, the state-owned industries continue to languish, requiring ever-larger subsidies merely to keep their inefficient operations in existence.

A setback in the success story of rapid growth by the NIEs of Southeast Asia occurred in and after the summer of 1997 with a major financial crisis. This affected all the countries in the region to some degree, but it was especially serious in Thailand, South Korea, and Indonesia. At the time of writing this crisis was still evolving, but it was clearly of great significance. We discuss the events surrounding this crisis more fully in Chapter 35.

Box 33.1 Transition economies: from plan to market

Between 1917 and 1950, countries containing one-third of the world's population seceded from the market economy and launched an experiment in constructing an alternative economic system. First in the former Russian Empire and Mongolia, then, after World War II, in Central and Eastern Europe and the Baltic States, and subsequently in China, northern Korea, and Vietnam (with offshoots and imitators elsewhere), a massive effort was made to centralize control of production and allocate resources through state planning. This vast experiment transformed the political and the economic map of the world and set the course of much of the twentieth century. Now its failure has set in motion just as radical a transformation, as these same countries change course, seeking to rebuild markets and reintegrate themselves into the world economy. . . .

The long-term goal of transition is the same as that of economic reforms elsewhere: to build a thriving market economy capable of delivering long-term growth in living standards. What distinguishes transition from reforms in other countries is the systemic change involved: reform must penetrate to the fundamental rules of the game, to the institutions that shape behavior and guide organizations. This makes it a profound social transition as well as an economic one. Similar changes have been needed in many other countries, and the transition experience is therefore of interest to them as well. But most of their reform programs pale in comparison to the scale and intensity of the transition from plan to market. . . .

The economic challenge of transition is daunting in itself. Planned economies were autarkic . . . none traded extensively with the world at large. Decades of bureaucratic allocation created serious distortions, with some sectors (particularly heavy industry) massively overbuilt and others (light industry and services) severely repressed; perhaps as much as a quarter of the Soviet economy served the military alone. Relative prices diverged greatly from market patterns, and this meant massive explicit or implicit subsidies among sectors. Energy, housing, public transport, and staple foods were extraordinarily cheap, whereas consumer manufactures, if available at all, were often shoddy. Pervasive shortages allowed firms to operate in sellers' markets and reduced incentives to improve quality. With near-complete state ownership, enterprises lacked the defined property rights that spur work effort and profitmaking in market economies. Firms had little reason to use inputs efficiently and strong incentives to hoard both labor and raw materials. Many firms added negative value; at world prices the costs of their inputs would have exceeded the value of their output. The combination of dominant heavy industry, low energy prices, and wasteful use of inputs caused energy intensity to rise to several times its level in market economies and had harsh environmental impacts.

Transition must therefore unleash a complex process of creation, adaptation, and destruction. Queuing gives way to markets. The shortage economy gives way to an economy of vast choice, with repressed sectors and activities growing rapidly and overbuilt sectors

contracting or adjusting. Property rights are formally established and distributed, and large amounts of wealth cease to be state owned and controlled. Old institutions and organizations evolve, or are replaced, requiring new skills and attitudes. And the relationship between citizens and the state changes fundamentally, with greater freedom of choice but also much greater economic risk. True, changes of a similar nature may be needed in many countries around the world. But in the transition economies the magnitudes are exponentially greater. For example, transition economies have privatized more than 30,000 large and medium-size enterprises in five years. In eleven years between 1980 and 1991 the rest of the world privatized fewer than 7,000. Countries will have completed their transition only when their problems and further reforms come to resemble those of long-established market economies at similar levels of income. (World Bank, *From Plan to Market, World Development Report 1996*, New York: Oxford University Press for the World Bank, June 1996)

Change as fundamental as that described above is extremely costly in the short term. The benefits of the market system could not be expected to show up over night. As a result, all of the economies of Eastern Europe and Central Asia exhibited negative rates of GDP growth in the early years of transition, and some of these negative growth rates were large. Of course, there are severe measurement problems involved in comparing output under central planning with output in the market economy, as much of the former output was unwanted or of little value. None the less, there can be little doubt that all suffered income and output losses in the early days. As the chart shows, for some countries such as Poland and Hungary positive GDP growth was achieved quite quickly. In contrast, others such as Ukraine still had declining GDP in 1997. In general, however, from about 1994 onwards there was a positive trend in GDP growth in most of the transition economies, suggesting that the worst of the adjustment costs might be over and the prospects for the future are looking up. Only time will tell if this is true.

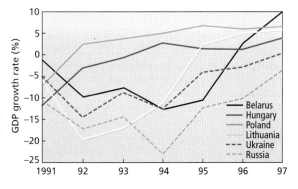

Growth rates of GDP in six transition economies, 1991–1997

Globalization of trade and investment by transnationals

At the heart of globalization lie the rapid reduction in transportation costs and the revolution in information technology that have characterized the last two decades. One consequence has been that the internal organization of firms, whether multinational or not, is changing to become less hierarchical and rigid, and more decentralized and fluid. Another consequence is that the strategies of transnational corporations (TNCs), which span national borders in their organizational structures, are driving globalization and much of economic development. Because most trade, and much investment, is undertaken by TNCs, no country can develop into an integrated part of the world economy without a substantial presence of TNCs within its borders. This is now recognized, and most aspiring developing countries generally put out a welcome mat for TNCs. A few countries, such as India, still put obstacles in the way of foreign investment; but even in these cases the attitudes are softening, so that foreign investment is increasingly tolerated, and even encouraged. Unfortunately, the new Indian government that took power after the 1998 elections has re-adopted many of the long-discredited inward-looking policies, including higher tariffs and heavier restrictions on foreign investment.

In industries that sell undifferentiated products such as steel and paper, and in industries with substantial scale economies such as aircraft, production tends to be concentrated in the home country while the output is exported. In contrast, foreign direct investment (FDI) tends to be high in industries selling differentiated products not subject to major scale economies, which includes many consumer goods. The FDI allows the local market to be served with suitable product variations and often creates multidirectional trade in different varieties of the same basic product, much of which is intra-firm trade.

TNCs increasingly operate in high-tech sectors, in complex manufacturing, and in services. TNCs that produce in these sectors tend to concentrate in countries where the productivity of capital is high, the business environment is favourable, and other investors are present. This FDI is often undertaken by domestic firms that have built up some advantage in the local market, such as patents and know-how, that gives them advantages when they move into foreign markets.

Although some countries, such as Japan and Taiwan, did industrialize without major infusions of FDI, they did so before the globalization of the world's economy. It is doubtful that many (or any) of today's poor countries could achieve sustained, rapid growth paths without a substantial amount of FDI brought in by foreign-owned transnationals. Without such FDI both the transfer of technology and foreign networking would be difficult to achieve.

Box 33.2 The importance of foreign direct investment

Foreign direct investment (FDI) provides a major source of capital which brings with it up-to-date technology. It would be difficult to generate this capital through domestic savings, and even then it would still be difficult to import the necessary technology from abroad, since the transfer of technology to firms with no previous experience of using it is difficult, risky, and expensive.

Over a long period of time FDI creates many externalities in the form of benefits available to the whole economy which the TNCs cannot appropriate as part of their own income. These include transfers of general knowledge and of specific technologies in production and distribution, industrial upgrading, work experience for the labour force, the introduction of modern management and accounting methods, the establishment of finance-related and trading networks, and the upgrading of telecommunications services. FDI in services affects the host country's competitiveness by raising the productivity of capital and enabling the host country to attract new capital on favourable terms. It also does so by creating services that can be used as strategic inputs in the traditional export sector to expand the volume of trade and to upgrade production through product and process innovation.

By altering a country's comparative advantages and improving its competitiveness through technology transfer and the effects of myriad externalities, foreign as well as domestic investment can alter a country's volume and pattern of trade in many income-enhancing directions. .

Developing countries have gradually come to accept the advantages in dropping their traditional hostility to foreign direct investment. First, the FDI often provides somewhat higher-paying jobs than might otherwise be available to local inhabitants. Second, it provides investment that does not have to be financed by local savings. Third, it links the local economy into the world economy in ways that would be hard to accomplish by new firms of a purely local origin. Fourth, it provides training in worker and management skills that come from working with large firms linked into the global market. Fifth, it can provide advanced technology that is not easily transferred outside of the firms that are already familiar with its use.

Today most developing countries encourage foreign TNCs to locate within their borders. Where governments used to worry that their countries had too much FDI, they now worry that there may be too little.

Box 33.2 discusses the place of foreign investment in development.

Elements of the new view

As a result of the above experiences a new consensus on development policy has emerged. The revised model calls for a more *outward-looking, international-trade-oriented, market-incentive-based route to development*. It calls for accepting market prices as an instrument for the allocation of resources. This means abandoning both the heavy subsidization and the pervasive regulations that characterized the older approach.

One of the most important parts of this new consensus is an acceptance of the beneficial role played by competition (in its broadest sense) as a defender of the public interest and as a stimulus to growth-creating innovation. The other side of the coin is a recognition of the harmful role played by monopolies (in the broadest sense), whether of private firms, closed-shop union agreements, communications media, government institutions, or government-owned industries.

Another important part of the consensus is that it is more efficient to locate economic activities in the private rather than the public sector (unless there are compelling reasons for doing otherwise, as there may be with a range of 'social services' such as medical and hospital care). Some of the reasons that lie behind this presumption are: the incentives for efficiency when managers are responsible to owners who are risking their own wealth; the constraint provided by the need to be profitable, which acts as a rapid cut-off device when failure is evident; and the corrective for inefficiency provided by the possibility of a hostile takeover.

A view about the appropriate role of government is another part of the new consensus. Two basic classes of activity are important. First, the government needs to provide a framework for the market economy, which is given by such things as well-defined property rights secure from arbitrary confiscation; security and enforcement of contracts; law and order; a sound money; ensuring the basic rights of the individual to locate, sell, and invest where and how he or she decides; and the provision of infrastructure.

Second, state activity is needed to resolve conflicts of interest, to handle market failures, and to redistribute income in line with currently accepted ideas of social justice. Redistributive policies cannot be judged in isolation (nor can growth policies). Instead, they must be constantly scrutinized for their impacts on growth; where these are significant, trade-offs need to be consciously made.

The Washington Consensus

What John Williamson of the Institute for International Economics in Washington, DC, has called the Washington Consensus describes the conditions that, according to the newer views, are necessary for a poorer country to get itself on a path of sustained development. These views are accepted by a number of international agencies, including the World Bank, the IMF, and several UN organizations. The main elements of this consensus are as follows.

1. Sound fiscal policies are required. Large budget deficits financed by bonds sold to the central bank can lead to rapid inflation and financial instability. For example, Brazil ended an excellent growth performance largely as a result of unsound macro policies.

2. The tax base should be broad, and marginal rates should be moderate.

3. Markets should be allowed to determine prices and the allocation of resources. Policies designed to affect resource allocation should work through price incentives rather than either central planning or price-distorting interventions. Exchange rates should be determined by market forces. Trade liberalization is desirable; in particular, import licensing, with its potential for corruption, should be avoided.

4. The desirability of free trade is, however, subject to the qualification of the infant industry argument discussed in Chapter 34 below. This allows targeted protection for specific industries and a moderate general tariff of, say, 10–20 per cent to provide a bias towards widening the industrial base of a less developed country. Such protection should be for a specified period that is not easily extended.

5. In today's world, however, measures to insulate the home market by domestic protection should be held to the minimum possible level consistent with developing strategic clusters of new industries. Industrial development should rely to an important extent on local firms and on attracting FDI and subjecting it to a minimum of local restrictions that discriminate between local and foreign firms. (Of course, restrictions will be required for such things as environmental policies, but these should apply to all firms, whether foreign-owned or locally owned.)

6. An export-orientation provides a powerful impetus to the development of national capabilities (as long as exports do not rely on permanent subsidies). It provides competitive incentives for the building of skills and technologies geared to world markets; it permits the realization of scale economies; it furnishes the foreign exchange required for needed imports of capital; and it provides access to valuable information flows from buyers and competitors in advanced countries.

7. Education, health (especially for the disadvantaged), and infrastructure investment are desirable forms of public expenditure. Creating the appropriate factors of production is critical to creating comparative advantages in products that can be exported. This means general education, trade schools, and other appropriate institutions for formal education as well as assistance to increase on-the-job training within firms. Because future demands are hard to predict and subject to rapid change, a balance must be struck between training for specific skills and training to develop generalized, and adaptive, abilities.

8. Finally, emphasis needs to be placed on the reduction

of poverty, for at least two reasons. First, poverty can exert powerful anti-growth effects. People living in poverty will not develop the skills to provide an attractive labour force, and they may not even respond to incentives when these are provided; malnutrition in early childhood can affect a person's capacities for life. Second, although economic growth tends to reduce the incidence of poverty, it does not eliminate it. Commonly accepted views of equity call for some of the benefits of growth to be made available to those who do not gain from it through the normal operations of the market. Self-interest calls for avoiding growing inequality in the distribution of income as those who benefit from growth (including employed workers) enjoy rising incomes, while major groups are untouched by the growth process and suffer static or declining incomes.

Debate beyond the Washington Consensus

The basic Washington Consensus on outward-looking, market-oriented, fiscally sound economic policies provides what many people believe are necessary conditions for a country to achieve a sustained growth path in today's world—which in most cases will require that it is able to attract quite a large volume of FDI.

The policies suggested by the Washington Consensus relate primarily to the behaviour of governments themselves.

Sufficient or just necessary?

There has been substantial debate about one crucial issue: are the conditions of the Washington Consensus *sufficient* to encourage the kinds and volumes of both domestic and foreign investments needed to develop dynamic comparative advantages in higher-value-added industries, or are they merely necessary?

Some observers believe that they are sufficient. In their view all a country needs to do is to meet these conditions; then domestic savings will finance domestic investments, FDI will flow in, and a sustained growth path will be established. Other economists worry that many countries may have only limited ability to attract FDI, to benefit from it, and to create sufficient domestic investment, even after fulfilling the necessary conditions of the Washington Consensus. The latter set of economists point to the experience of some African countries in which TNCs operated extractive industries which despoiled the countryside and left little permanent benefit behind them; the corporations merely extracted the available resources and then left. Others point out that there is a major difference between purely extractive enterprises and manufacturing

enterprises, the latter having more potential spillovers to the local economy than the former.

Policies that go beyond the Washington Consensus are directed at *the interactions between governments and the private sector*, particularly as represented by TNCs.

Such policies relate, in British economist John Dunning's words, to the 'interface between the global strategies of TNCs designed to advance corporate profitability and growth, and the strategies of national governments intended to promote the economic and social welfare of their citizens'.

Implications of modern growth theory

The key insight of the new growth theory is that *endogenous* technological innovation is the mainspring of economic growth. Things emphasized by economists for centuries, such as aggregate savings and investment, are still essential, but technological change is now seen to lie at the core of the growth process.

As we saw in Chapter 32, technological change is a costly process, one that is undertaken mainly by firms in pursuit of profit and that responds to economic incentives. Research and development are in their nature highly risky and highly uncertain activities. The technological path followed by firms and industries is evolutionary in the sense that it develops as experiments and errors are made.

For developing countries one of the most important of the many new insights stemming from research into the growth process is that adopting someone else's technology is not a simple, costless task. Substantial R&D capacity is needed to adapt other people's technology to one's own purposes, and to learn how to use it. For one thing, much of the knowledge required to use a technology is tacit; it can be obtained only from learning by doing and learning by using. This creates difficulties in imitating the knowledge, as well as uncertainty regarding which modifications will work in any new situation. This is true even when technology moves from one firm to another in the same industry and the same country. It follows that not all knowledge is freely tradable. Neither a firm nor a government can go out and buy it ready to use. Acquiring *working* technological knowledge requires both investment (sometimes in large, indivisible lumps) and the experience that allows workers and management slowly to acquire the needed tacit knowledge. Box 33.3 further considers the diffusion process.

Usable new knowledge comes to a less developed country through a slow, costly diffusion process.

What may be needed

Some economists argue for active government policies that go beyond the Washington Consensus. Such policies

Box 33.3 The importance of diffusion

In the past one reason for making a clear distinction between the economics of developed and developing countries arose from the belief that advanced countries grew by innovating in new technologies while poorer countries grew by copying technologies from the advanced countries—that is, from the diffusion of technologies that had been fully developed in the advanced countries. If this were so, then the economics of growth in advanced countries would be the economics of innovation, while the economics of growth in poorer countries would be the economics of diffusion. This view was in line with early theories of technological change, which assumed that a new technology was invented and put in place in fully developed form by some innovator and that its use then diffused in more or less unchanged form to other firms, industries, and countries.

Modern research into invention, diffusion, and innovation has shown that this clear line does not exist in reality. A new technology almost always comes into existence in rudimentary form with few uses and high operating costs. As the technology is used, it is developed continually, and its costs of operation fall while the quality of its performance and the range of its application rise.

For example, electronic computers were first developed for military applications during the early 1940s. By modern standards these early computers were extremely limited in what they could do and were both slow and costly in doing it. When the first commercial applications were developed at the end of the Second World War, the world demand was thought to be for about twelve computers! The efficiency of computers was increased slowly over the decades, and it made a quantum leap when transistors were substituted for vacuum tubes as the switching device. At the same time the costs were lowered and the range of applications was increased as computers became more varied and more flexible. These were not small improvements but orders-of-magnitude changes occurring every few years. Today the product that was a technological curiosity fifty years ago is revolutionizing all of production, distribution, design, and just about every other economic activity.

A similar story can be told about the aeroplane. Its modern story began in 1903 with the first heavier-than-air flight (covering less than 100 yards). The aeroplane first became really successful commercially in 1936 with the introduction of the DC3. It improved through slow design changes and discontinuous innovations, such as the replacement of piston engines with jets, until by the 1970s it had become the dominant method of transporting people over long distances.

So the diffusion of technologies is not a flow that goes just from advanced to less advanced nations. Diffusion is a key part of technological change in advanced as well as developing nations and it follows similar patterns in each.

In any one high-income nation most of the technological advances that come into use have been originally developed in other nations. Indeed, a small subset of the advanced nations does most of the development of fundamental new technologies, which then diffuse to other high-income countries, being adapted and improved in the process.

It is true that a country just beginning to move from a subsistence to a market economy can grow quickly by adopting technologies developed elsewhere (and adapting them to local conditions), but it is not true that the world's growth problems can be understood simply in terms of the conditions needed to invent technologies in rich countries and those needed to copy them in poor countries. Since many of the processes that govern the flow of technology and capital between rich and poor countries also govern the flows among rich countries (and among sectors in each rich country), it is clear that many problems will be similar in the two groups of countries. Of course, institutional arrangements will affect the diffusion and improvement of both major and minor innovations in developing countries. But they also do so in developed countries, where forces such as competition policy, industrial concentration, national attitudes to risk-taking, support of R&D, and the organization of university research are thought to influence the development and diffusion of new technologies.

work by developing the externalities that come from initial investment in the local economy, and that give benefits not captured by the firms that help to confer them. The policies also take account of the fact that technology is not bought in competitive markets and imported 'ready to go'. The recommended policies would thus do more than just attract FDI and create favourable market conditions. They would be designed to encourage the diffusion of technological capacities into the local economy so that all parts of the economy could benefit and grow. This requires the kind of public assistance that was provided in varying degrees by the governments of the Asian Tigers.

Experience suggests, however, that the appropriate set of policies is usually highly country-specific. What works well in one environment may fail in another. Many local details need to be assessed before appropriate policies can be designed for one country. These depend, among many other things, on location, size of economy, existing natural and human resources, infrastructure, social and cultural attitudes, and development stage.

Protection of the domestic market Such policies can work at the early stages by establishing a protected domestic market through tariffs and other import restrictions. Virtually every country that has moved to a sustained growth path in the past, including the United States, Canada, Japan, and all of the NIEs, has done so using import substitution in its early stages of industrialization. A protected home market provides a possible solution to the problem of coping with the enormous externalities involved in building up an infrastructure of physical and human capital as well as the required tacit knowledge and abilities. Even if not all the specific infants that are protected by the import-substitution policy grow into self-sufficient adults, the externalities may still be created and become available for a second generation of more profitable firms.

Protection of the home market from international competition can, however, pose serious problems unless it is selective and temporary. Investment may occur mainly in areas where comparative advantage never develops. High costs of protected industries may create a lack of competitiveness of other domestic industries whose inputs are the outputs of the protected industries. Potential comparative advantages may not be exploited because of the distorting effects of existing tariffs, and, as always, consumers bear much of the cost through high prices of protected outputs.

Innovation policies Other methods of building an industrial and R&D capacity include the much-needed public investment in infrastructure and human capital and many other things, such as the provision of adequate financial schemes to favour investment in physical and intangible assets; procurement and tax incentives; provision of technical and marketing information; consulting services for assisting firms in industrial restructuring and in the adoption of new technologies and organizational techniques; support services in design, quality assurance, and standards; schemes for training and retraining personnel; and facilities for start-up companies.

Those who advocate such a policy package stress the importance of having the above incentives operate as a part of a more general innovation and competition policy in order to encourage technological transfer to the local economy. Linkages among firms, and between firms and universities and research institutions, both within the country and in the rest of the world, are also important.

Policies that encourage the development of small and medium-sized enterprises are important to any development strategy. These tend to be locally owned and to be the vehicle by which know-how and best practices are transferred from TNCs to the local economy. They are also in the sector most vulnerable to excessive red tape, rules and regulations, profit taxes, and other interferences that raise the cost of doing business.

A cautionary note There is no doubt that the governments of many poor countries have been highly interventionist—and some still are. Thus a good first strategy is often to diminish the government's place in the economy. There is no point adopting a new, relatively rational, technology-promotion strategy if existing government interventions are irrational and heavy. What is needed is to clear away unproductive interventions first. This does not demonstrate, however, that if a government were starting from scratch, the best objective would be to minimize its place in the economy.

Whatever methods are chosen, selective intervention is a delicate instrument, highly dangerous when used by inept hands; even when it is used by practised hands, much damage can be done.

Even those who advocate it accept that the intervention needs to be carefully tailored to get specific results and to reduce the opportunities for small groups to gain at the expense of others. They also agree that most assistance should as a rule be terminated after a specified period. Others feel that the risks are too great and would not take government policy beyond the Washington Consensus.

Conclusion

The prospects for growth in developing countries looked much better at the end of the 1990s than they had twenty years before. Growth of real per capita GDP in developing countries averaged only 2 per cent between 1979 and 1988, and most of that growth was attributable to Asia. African developing countries experienced a fall of –0.6 per cent per annum, and those of the Middle East and Europe experienced a fall of –1.2 per cent per annum over the same period. However, between 1989 and 1998 developing countries experienced 3.6 per cent per annum real GDP growth per capita, and all regions showed, at worst, a modest rise in real GDP per capita. The International Monetary Fund assessed the prospects as follows:

The robust growth trend in the developing world and increasingly also in many transition countries can be attributed to the success of a growing number of economies in establishing and maintaining macroeconomic stability and in pursuing outward-oriented, market-based reforms that are enabling them to integrate rapidly into the global economic and financial system. For those developing countries in the Western Hemisphere, the Middle East, the Indian subcontinent, and Africa where living standards have been growing only modestly, and where recent improvements in growth performance may still be fragile, there is considerable urgency in the need to introduce more comprehensive economic strategies aimed at addressing key policy weaknesses. This also applies to those countries in transition that continue to lag behind in the transformation process. . . . While macroeconomic stability, trade liberalization, and the creation of the basic institutional framework of market economy are essential for stronger growth, and often sufficient to enhance economic performance for a time, broader-based reforms are necessary to sustain and enhance countries' longer-run growth performance and ensure that the benefits of reform are more widely shared. Such 'second-generation' reform requirements, which also apply in many instances to the advanced economies, include the need to accelerate social progress and invest in human capital by increasing the quality of public expenditures; strengthen the efficiency and robustness of the financial sector, including through appropriate prudential oversight; reform and eventually privatize state-owned enterprises and generally reduce government intervention in the economy in areas where market forces provide far greater efficiency; address corruption and improve governance; and enhance the transparency of government budgets, and generally strengthen the quality and timeliness of economic data to help reduce the risk of disruptive changes in investor confidence when economic or financial problems eventually appear.[8]

---

[8] *World Economic Outlook*, Oct. 1997, p. 17.

Summary

The uneven pattern of development

■ About one-quarter of the world's population still exists at a level of bare subsistence, and over 80 per cent live in countries with income per head at less than 20 per cent of the US level. Although some poorer societies have grown rapidly, the gap between the very richest and the very poorest remains large and is not decreasing.

Restraints on economic development

■ Impediments to economic development include excessive population growth; resource limitations; inefficient use of resources, particularly those that are related to X-inefficiency; inadequate infrastructure; excessive government intervention; and institutional and cultural patterns that make economic growth difficult.

Development policies

■ The older model for development policies included (a) heavy tariff barriers and a hostility to foreign direct investment to protect the home market for local firms; (b) many government controls over, and subsidization of, local activities; and (c) exchange rates pegged at overly high values with imports regulated by licences.

■ During the 1980s many governments became sceptical of this model after observing (a) the poor growth performances both of the planned economies and of those developing countries that adhered closely to this model; (b) the good performances of those who did not follow the model; and (c) the globalization of the world economy, which made transnational corporations and foreign direct investment increasingly important. Today no developing country can play a part in the global trading system without some significant presence of TNCs within its borders.

■ The newer view holds that (a) heavy indiscriminate protection of home markets should be avoided; (b) protection that does exist should be targeted to sectors that have a real chance of creating comparative advantage, and should be for only a moderate period of time so that market tests of success and failure can be allowed to operate; (c) competition is an important spur to efficiency and innovation; (d) quantitative controls should be avoided and exchange rates set at a market-clearing value; and (e) production of most goods and services should be in the private sector, except where there are strong reasons for preferring the public sector, as might be the case in, say, medical and health services.

■ Part of this new view is given in the Washington Consensus, which calls for (a) sound fiscal and monetary policies; (b) broadly based taxes, levied at moderate rates; (c) market determination of prices and quantities; (d) discriminating use of infant industry protection for moderate time-periods; (e) an acceptance of FDI and the presence of TNCs; (f) active government provision of education, health care, and infrastructure; and (g) anti-poverty programmes to help in human resource development and to aid those who are left behind by the growth process.

■ An active debate turns on whether the conditions of the Washington Consensus are sufficient, or just necessary, to establish a country on a sustained growth path. Those who regard them as sufficient feel that, once unleashed, natural market forces will create sustained growth.

■ Those who regard the conditions of the Washington Consensus as just necessary point to substantial externalities and pervasive market failures in the diffusion of technological knowledge from advanced to less advanced nations. They argue that foreign firms will not invest enough because they cannot capture in their profits many of the benefits they confer on the local economy (externalities) and that much of the technological know-how will not diffuse to local firms because such knowledge is not easy to transfer (market failure). These economists call for active government innovation policies to augment investment and to assist in the transfer of technological know-how and practice to the local economy.

Topics for review

■ Barriers to development
■ The vicious circle of poverty
■ The NIEs
■ TNCs and FDI
■ The Washington Consensus
■ Externalities and market failures in the diffusion of technology

Questions for discussion

1 Outline the factors that contribute to holding back the growth of some countries even though they are abundant in natural resources.

2 To what would you attribute the success of countries like Singapore and Taiwan that have grown rapidly in the last few decades despite a limited endowment of natural resources?

3 Why is foreign investment important in the development process?

4 Is growth in the developing world good or bad for the developed economies? (You might want to read Chapter 34 before answering this question.)

5 Critically assess the policies proposed under the Washington Consensus. Does the quote from the IMF on page 576 merely restate the consensus, or is there anything new being said?

Chapter 34
International Trade

Economic growth and development, topics that we have discussed in the two previous chapters, would be very hard to achieve if residents of an economy could not buy some goods from abroad and export other goods to generate revenue to pay for the imports. *International trade* refers to exchanges of goods and services that take place across international boundaries. The British, for example, buy BMWs made in Germany, Germans take holidays in Italy, Italians buy spices from Tanzania, Belgians import oil from Kuwait, Egyptians buy Japanese cameras, and the Japanese depend heavily on American soybeans as a source of food. Indeed, there is substantial evidence to show that international trade and economic growth are positively linked.

In this chapter we explain why trade increases output and incomes. We then ask why, if trade is generally beneficial, governments have often attempted to restrict the freedom to trade. Finally, we discuss some of the institutional arrangements that affect world trade.

Sources of the gains from trade

An economy that engages in international trade is called an **open economy.** One that does not is called a **closed economy.** A situation in which a country does no foreign trade is called **autarky.** The advantages realized as a result of trade are called the **gains from trade.** Although politicians often regard foreign trade as being different from domestic trade, economists from Adam Smith on have argued that the causes and consequences of international trade are simply an extension of the principles governing domestic trade. What is the benefit from trade among individuals, among groups, among regions, or among countries?

Interpersonal, interregional, and international trade

Consider trade among individuals. Without trade, each person would have to be self-sufficient; each would have to produce all the food, clothing, shelter, medical services, entertainment, and luxuries that he or she consumed. A world of individual self-sufficiency would be a world with extremely low living standards.

Trade among individuals allows people to specialize in those activities they can do well and to buy from others the goods and services they themselves cannot easily produce.

A good doctor who is a bad carpenter can provide medical services not only for his or her own family, but also for an excellent carpenter who lacks the training or the ability to practise medicine. Thus trade and specialization are intimately connected. Without trade, everyone must be self-sufficient. With trade, everyone can specialize in what he or she does well and satisfy other needs by trading.

The same principles apply to regions. Without interregional trade, each region would be forced to be self-sufficient. With trade, each region can specialize in producing goods or services for which it has some natural or acquired advantage. Plains regions can specialize in growing grain, mountain regions can specialize in mining and forest products, and regions with abundant power can specialize in manufacturing. Cool regions can produce wheat and other crops that thrive in temperate climates, and hot regions can grow such tropical crops as bananas, sugar, and coffee. Places with lots of sunshine and sandy beaches can specialize in the tourist trade. The living standards of the inhabitants of all regions will be higher when each region specializes in products in which it has some natural or acquired advantage and obtains other products by trade than when all regions seek to be self-sufficient.

The same principle also applies to nations. Nations, like regions or persons, can gain from specialization. More of the goods in which production is specialized are produced than residents wish to consume, while less domestic production of other goods that residents desire is available.

International trade is necessary to achieve the gains that international specialization makes possible. Trade allows each individual, region, or nation to concentrate on producing those goods and services that it produces efficiently while trading to obtain goods and services that it does not produce efficiently.

Specialization and trade go hand in hand, because there is no motivation to achieve the gains from specialization without being able to trade the goods produced for the different goods desired. Economists use the term 'gains from trade' to embrace the results of both. This was first discussed in Chapter 1, and it would be worth re-reading now pages 8–10 and Box 1.4.

We will examine two sources of the gains from trade. The first is differences among regions of the world in climate and resource endowment that lead to advantages in producing certain goods and disadvantages in producing others. These gains occur even though each country's costs of production are unchanged by the existence of trade. The second source is the reduction in each country's costs of production that results from the greater production that specialization brings.

The gains from specialization with given costs

In order to focus on differences in countries' conditions of production, suppose that each country's average costs of production are constant. We will use an example below involving only two countries and two products, but the general principles apply as well to the real-world case of many countries and many products.

Absolute advantage

Box 1.4 on page 9 showed the simple case of absolute advantage. One region is said to have an **absolute advantage** over another in the production of good X when an equal quantity of resources can produce more X in the first region than in the second. If we rename the individuals in the Box as countries we see what is obvious. Total production can be increased if each country specializes in producing the product for which it has an absolute advantage.

These gains from specialization make the gains from trade possible. If consumers in both countries are to get the goods they desire in the required proportions, each must export some of the commodity in which it specializes and import commodities in which other countries are specialized.

Comparative advantage

When each country has an absolute advantage over others in a product, the gains from trade are obvious. But what if one country can produce all commodities more efficiently than other countries? In essence this was the question English economist David Ricardo (1772–1823) posed nearly 200 years ago. His answer underlies the *theory of comparative advantage* and is still accepted by economists today as a valid statement of the potential gains from trade.

The gains from specialization and trade depend on the pattern of comparative, not absolute, advantage. Although this point was illustrated in Box 1.4, it is important enough to justify another example. Let us assume that there are two countries, the United States and the European Union. Both countries produce the same two goods, wheat and cloth, but the opportunity costs of producing these two products differ between countries. Recall from Chapter 1 that the *opportunity cost* in production is given by the slope of the production-possibility frontier, and it tells us how much of one good we have to give up in order to produce one more unit of the other. For the moment we assume that this opportunity cost is constant in each country at all combinations of outputs.

For the purposes of our example we assume that the opportunity cost of producing 1 kilogram of wheat is 0.60 metres of cloth in the United States, while in the European Union it is 2 metres of cloth. These data are summarized in Table 34.1. The second column of this table gives the same information again but expressed as the opportunity cost of 1 metre of cloth (so the numbers there are the reciprocals of the numbers in the first column).

The sacrifice of cloth involved in producing wheat is much lower in the USA than it is in the EU. World wheat production can be increased if the USA rather than the EU produces it. Looking at cloth production, we can see that the loss of wheat involved in producing one unit of cloth is lower in the EU than in the USA. World cloth production can be increased if the EU rather than the USA produces it. The gains from a US shift towards wheat production

Table 34.1 Opportunity cost of wheat and cloth in the USA and the EU

	Wheat (kg)	Cloth (metres)
USA	0.60m cloth	1.67kg wheat
EU	2.00m cloth	0.50kg wheat

Comparative advantages reflect opportunity costs that differ between countries. Column (1) expresses opportunity cost per kilogram of wheat. Column (2) expresses the same information in terms of metres of cloth. The USA has a comparative advantage in wheat production, the EU in cloth.

and an EU shift towards cloth production are shown in Table 34.2.

The gains from trade arise from differing opportunity costs in the two countries.

The slope of the production-possibility boundary indicates the opportunity costs, and the existence of different opportunity costs implies comparative advantages and disadvantages that can lead to gains from trade. Figure 34.1 illustrates how two countries can both gain from trade when they have different opportunity costs in production and the opportunity costs are independent of the level of production. An alternative diagrammatic illustration of the gains from trade appears in Box 34.1, where the production-possibility frontier is concave (which means that opportunity cost varies with the composition of output).

The conclusions about the gains from trade arising from international differences in opportunity costs are summarized below.

Table 34.2 Gains from specialization with differing opportunity costs

	Changes from each producing one more unit of the product in which it has the lower opportunity cost	
	Wheat (kg)	Cloth (metres)
USA	+1.0	−0.6
EU	−0.5	+1.0
Total	+0.5	+0.4

Whenever opportunity costs differ between countries, specialization can increase the production of both products. These calculations show that there are gains from specialization given the opportunity costs of Table 34.1. To produce one more kilogram of wheat, the USA must sacrifice 0.6m of cloth. To produce one more metre of cloth, the EU must sacrifice 0.5kg of wheat. Making both changes raises world production of both wheat and cloth.

(i) United States

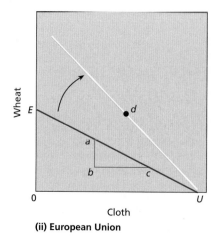

(ii) European Union

Figure 34.1 Gains from trade with constant opportunity costs
International trade leads to specialization in production and increased consumption possibilities. The blue lines in parts (i) and (ii) represent the production-possibility boundary for the United States and the EU, respectively. In the absence of any international trade these also represent each country's consumption possibilities.

The difference in the slopes of the production-possibility boundaries reflects differences in comparative advantage, as shown in Table 34.1. In each part the opportunity cost of increasing production of wheat by the same amount (measured by the distance *ba*) is the amount by which the production of cloth must be reduced (measured by the distance *bc*). The relatively steep production-possibility boundary for the United States thus indicates that the opportunity cost of producing wheat in the United States is less than that in the European Union.

If trade is possible at some terms of trade between the two countries' opportunity costs of production, each country will specialize in the production of the good in which it has a comparative advantage. In each part of the figure production occurs at *U*; the United States produces only wheat, and the EU produces only cloth.

Consumption possibilities are given by the yellow line that passes through *U* and has a slope equal to the terms of trade. Consumption possibilities are increased in both countries; consumption may occur at some point such as *d* that involves a combination of wheat and cloth that was not obtainable in the absence of trade.

Box 34.1 The gains from trade with varying opportunity costs

International trade leads to an expansion of the set of goods that can be consumed in the economy in two ways: by allowing the bundle of goods consumed to differ from the bundle produced, and by permitting a profitable change in the pattern of production. Without international trade the bundle of goods produced is the bundle consumed. With international trade the consumption and production bundles can be altered independently to reflect the relative values placed on goods by international markets.

The graphical demonstration of the gains from trade proceeds in two stages.

Stage 1: fixed production

In each part of the figure the yellow curve is the economy's production-possibility boundary. If there is no international trade, the economy must consume the same bundle of goods that it produces. Thus the production-possibility boundary is also the consumption-possibility boundary. (In contrast to Figure 34.1, opportunity cost here varies along the boundary.) Suppose the economy produces, and consumes, at point a, with x_1 of good X and y_1 of good Y, as in part (i) of the figure.

Next suppose that, with production point a, good Y can be exchanged for good X internationally. The consumption possibilities are now shown by the line tt drawn through point a. The slope of tt indicates the quantity of Y that exchanges for a unit of X on the international market.

Although production is fixed at a, consumption can now be anywhere on the line tt. For example, the consumption point could be at b. This could be achieved by exporting $y_1 - y_2$ units of Y and importing $x_2 - x_1$ units of X. Since

point b (and all others on line tt to the right of a) lies outside the production-possibility boundary, there are potential gains from trade. Consumers are no longer limited by their country's production possibilities. Let us suppose they prefer point b to point a. They have achieved a gain from trade by being allowed to exchange some of their production of good Y for some quantity of good X and thus to consume more of good X than is produced at home.

Stage 2: variable production

There is a further opportunity for the expansion of the country's consumption possibilities: with trade the production bundle may be profitably altered in response to international prices. The country may produce the bundle of goods that is most valuable in world markets. This is represented by the bundle d in part (ii). The consumption-possibility set is shifted to the line $t't'$ by changing production from a to d and thereby increasing the country's degree of specialization in good Y. For every point on the original consumption-possibility set, tt, there are points on the new set, $t't'$, which allow more consumption of both goods; compare points b and f, for example. Notice also that, except at the zero-trade point, d, the new consumption-possibility set lies everywhere above the production-possibility curve.

The benefits of moving from a no-trade position such as a to a trading position such as b or f are the gains from trade to the country. When the production of good Y is increased and the production of good X decreased, the country is able to move to a point such as f by producing more of good Y, in which the country has a comparative advantage, and trading the additional production for good X.

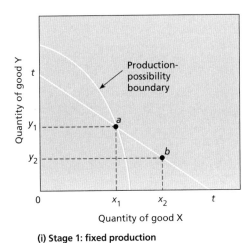

(i) Stage 1: fixed production

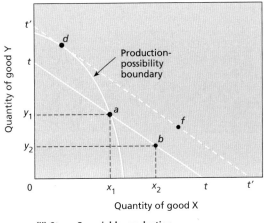

(ii) Stage 2: variable production

1. Country A has a *comparative advantage* over country B in producing a product when the opportunity cost (in terms of some other product) of production in country A is lower. This implies, however, that it has a comparative disadvantage in the other product.

2. Opportunity costs depend on the relative costs of producing two products, not on absolute costs.

3. When opportunity costs are the same in all countries, there is no comparative advantage and there is no possibility of gains from specialization and trade.

4. When opportunity costs differ in any two countries, and both countries are producing both products, it is always possible to increase production of both products by a suitable reallocation of resources within each country.

Gains from specialization with variable costs

So far, apart from in Box 34.1, we have assumed that unit costs are the same whatever the scale of output, and we have seen that there are gains from specialization and trade as long as there are interregional differences in opportunity costs. If costs vary with the level of output, or as experience is acquired via specialization, *additional* sources of gain are possible.

Scale and imperfect competition

Real production costs, measured in terms of resources used, often fall as the scale of output increases. The larger the scale of operations, the more efficiently large-scale machinery can be used and the more efficient the division of labour that is possible. Smaller countries such as Switzerland, Belgium, and Israel whose domestic markets are not large enough to exploit economies of scale would find it prohibitively expensive to become self-sufficient by producing a little bit of everything at very great cost.

Trade allows smaller countries to specialize and produce a few products at high enough levels of output to reap the available economies of scale.

One of the important lessons learned from patterns of world trade since the Second World War results from im-

perfect competition and product differentiation. Virtually all of today's manufactured consumer goods are produced in multiple differentiated product lines. In some industries many firms produce this range; in others only a few firms produce the entire product range. In both cases firms are not price-takers, and they do not exhaust all available economies of scale as a perfectly competitive firm would do. This means that an increase in the size of the market, even in an economy as large as the USA or EU, may allow the exploitation of some previously unexploited scale economies in individual product lines.

These possibilities were first dramatically illustrated when the European Common Market (now called the European Union, the EU) was set up in the late 1950s. Economists had expected that specialization would occur according to the classical theory of comparative advantage, with one country specializing in cars, another in refrigerators, another in fashion clothes, another in shoes, and so on. This is not the way it worked out. Instead, much of the vast growth of trade was in intra-industry trade. Today one can buy French, English, Italian, and German fashion goods, cars, shoes, appliances, and a host of other goods in the shops of London, Paris, Bonn, and Rome. Ships loaded with Swedish furniture bound for London pass ships loaded with English furniture bound for Stockholm; and so on.

What free European trade did was to allow a proliferation of differentiated products, with different countries each specializing in differentiated subproduct lines. Con-

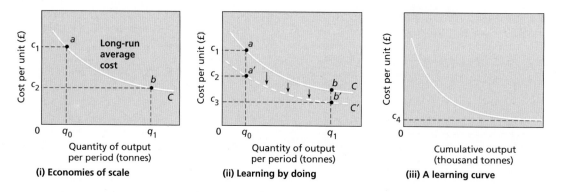

Figure 34.2 Gains from specialization with variable costs

Specialization may lead to gains from trade by permitting economies of larger-scale output, by leading to downward shifts of cost curves, or both. A country can produce output q_0 at an average cost per unit of c_1 and can export the quantity $q_1 - q_0$ if it produces q_1. This may lead to cost savings in two ways. (i) The increased level of production of q_1 compared with q_0 permits it to *move along* its cost curve, C, from a to b, thus reducing costs per unit to c_2. This is an economy of scale. (ii) As workers and managements learn, they may increase productivity and shift the cost curve from C to C'. This is learning by doing. The downward *shift*, shown by the arrows, lowers the cost of producing every unit of output. At output q_1 costs per unit fall to c_3. The movement from a to b' incorporates both economies of scale and learning by doing.

Part (iii) shows a learning curve. This shows the relation between the costs of producing a given output per period and the total output over the whole time during which production has taken place. When all learning possibilities have been exploited, costs reach a minimum level, shown by c_4 in the figure.

sumers have shown by their expenditures that they value this enormous increase in the range of choice among differentiated products. As Asian countries have expanded into European and American markets with textiles, cars, and electronic goods, European and American manufacturers have increasingly specialized their production, and they now export textiles, cars, and electronic equipment to Japan even while importing similar but differentiated products from Japan.

Learning by doing

The discussion so far has assumed that costs vary only with the level of output. They may also vary with the experience accumulated in producing a good over time.

Some economists place great importance on a factor that we now call *learning by doing*. They argue that as countries gain experience in particular tasks, workers and managers become more efficient in performing them. As people acquire expertise, costs tend to fall. There is substantial evidence that such learning by doing does occur.

The distinction between this phenomenon and the gains from economies of scale is illustrated in Figure 34.2. This is one more example of the difference between a movement along a curve and a shift of the curve.

Recognition of the opportunities for learning by doing leads to an important implication: policymakers need not accept *current* comparative advantages as given. Through such means as training and tax incentives, they can seek to develop new comparative advantages. Moreover, countries cannot complacently assume that their existing comparative advantages will persist. Misguided tax incentives and subsidies, or policies that discourage risk-taking, can lead to the rapid erosion of a country's comparative advantage in particular products. So, too, can developments in other countries.

The terms of trade

So far we have seen that world production can be increased when countries specialize in the production of the goods and services in which they have a comparative advantage, and then trade with one another. We now ask how these gains from specialization and trade will be shared among countries. The division of the gain depends on what is called the **terms of trade,** which measure the quantity of imported goods that can be obtained per unit of goods exported.

A rise in the price of imported goods, with the price of exports unchanged, indicates a fall in the terms of trade; it will now take more exports to buy the same quantity of imports. Similarly, a rise in the price of exported goods, with the price of imports unchanged, indicates a rise in terms of trade; it will now take fewer exports to buy the same quantity of imports. Thus the ratio of these prices measures the amount of imports that can be obtained per unit of goods exported.

Because actual international trade involves many countries and many products, a country's terms of trade are computed as an index number:

$$\text{Terms of trade} = \frac{\text{Index of export prices}}{\text{Index of import prices}} \times 100.$$

A rise in the index is referred to as a *favourable* change in a country's terms of trade. A favourable change means that more can be imported per unit of goods exported than previously. For example, if the export price index rises from 100 to 120 while the import price index rises from 100 to 110, the terms of trade index rises from 100 to 109.

At the new terms of trade, a unit of exports will buy 9 per cent more imports than at the old terms.

A decrease in the index of the terms of trade, called an *unfavourable* change, means that the country can import less in return for any given amount of exports or, equivalently, that it must export more to pay for any given amount of imports. For example, the sharp rise in oil prices in the 1970s led to large unfavourable shifts in the terms of trade of oil-importing countries. When oil prices fell sharply in the mid-1980s, the terms of trade of oil-importing countries changed favourably. The converse was true for oil-exporting countries.

There are two other concepts closely related to the terms of trade that we have come across before, especially in Chapter 28. These are the *real exchange rate* and *competitiveness*. They also are indexes of the relative prices of domestic and foreign goods. However, both competitiveness and the real exchange rate normally relate to the prices of domestic production relative to foreign production, while terms of trade apply just to the subset of outputs that are imported and exported.

Notice, however, an interesting ambiguity in terminology. We have said above that an improvement in the terms of trade is 'favourable'; but a rise in domestic prices relative to foreign prices could also be described as a *loss of competitiveness*. This would normally be considered 'unfavourable'. Clearly the same event cannot switch from good to bad just because of what we call it. The reality is that whether a relative rise in domestic prices is good or bad depends upon why it came about. If the prices of the things we produce and sell in world markets rise because they are in high demand, then this is a good thing and we are better off for it (even though it could be described as a loss of competitiveness). However, if our prices rise because of inefficiency or higher wages bills, *for a given level* *of world demand for our output*, then we will lose sales to foreign competitors and we will be worse off.

We now turn to a discussion of the arguments for and against government intervention in international trade.

The theory of commercial policy

Government policy towards international trade is known as **commercial policy.** Complete freedom from interference with trade is known as a **free trade** policy. Any departure from free trade designed to give some protection to domestic industries from foreign competition is called **protectionism.**

Today debates over commercial policy are as heated as they were 200 years ago when the theory of the gains from trade that we presented above was still being worked out. Should a country permit the free flow of international trade, or should it seek to protect its local producers from foreign competition? Such protection may be achieved either by **tariffs,** which are taxes designed to raise the price of foreign goods, or by **non-tariff barriers,** which are devices other than tariffs that are designed to reduce the flow of imports; examples of the latter include quotas and customs procedures deliberately made more cumbersome than is necessary.

The case for free trade

The case for free trade is based on the analysis presented above. We saw that whenever opportunity costs differ among countries, specialization and trade will raise world living standards. Free trade allows all countries to specialize in producing products in which they have a comparative advantage.

Free trade allows the maximization of world production, thus making it possible for each consumer in the world to consume more goods than he or she could without free trade.

This does not necessarily mean that everyone will be better off with free trade than without it. Protectionism could allow some people to obtain a larger share of a smaller world output so that they would benefit even though the average person would lose. If we ask whether it is possible for free trade to improve everyone's living standards, the answer is 'yes'. But if we ask whether free trade does in fact always do so, the answer is 'not necessarily'.

There is abundant evidence that significant differences in opportunity costs exist and that large gains are realized from international trade because of these differences. What needs explanation is the fact that trade is not wholly free. Why do tariffs and non-tariff barriers to trade continue to exist two centuries after Adam Smith and David Ricardo stated the case for free trade? Is there a valid case for protectionism?

The case for protectionism

Two kinds of arguments for protection are commonly offered. The first concerns national objectives other than total income; the second concerns the desire to increase one country's national income, possibly at the expense of world national income.

Objectives other than maximizing national income as reasons for protectionism

It is possible to accept the proposition that national income is higher with free trade, and yet rationally to oppose free trade, because of a concern with policy objectives other than maximizing income.

Non-economic advantages of diversification   Comparative advantage might dictate that a country should specialize in producing a narrow range of products. The government might decide, however, that there are distinct social advantages in encouraging a more diverse economy. Citizens would be given a wider range of occupations, and the social and psychological advantages of diversification would more than compensate for a reduction in living standards to, say, 5 per cent below what they could be with complete specialization of production according to comparative advantage.

Risks of specialization   For a very small country, specializing in the production of only a few products—though dictated by comparative advantage—may involve risks that the country does not wish to take. One such risk is that technological advances may render its major product obsolete. Everyone understands this risk, but there is debate over what governments can do about it. The pro-tariff argument is that the government can encourage a more diversified economy by protecting industries that otherwise could not compete. Opponents argue that governments, being naturally influenced by political motives, are in the final analysis poor judges of which industries can be protected in order to produce diversification at a reasonable cost.

National defence   Another non-economic reason for protectionism concerns national defence. It used to be argued, for example, that the United Kingdom needed an experienced merchant navy in case of war, and that this industry should be fostered by protectionist policies even though it was less efficient than the foreign competition. The same argument is sometimes made for the aircraft industry.

Protection of specific groups   Although free trade will maximize per capita GDP over the whole economy, some specific groups may have higher incomes under protection than under free trade. An obvious example is a firm or industry that is given monopoly power when tariffs are used to restrict foreign competition. If a small group of firms, and possibly their employees, find their incomes increased by, say, 25 per cent when they get tariff protection, they may not be concerned that everyone else's incomes fall by, say, 2 per cent. They get a much larger share of a slightly smaller total income and end up better off. If they gain from the tariff, they will lose from free trade.

Tariffs tend to raise the relative income of a group of people who are in short supply domestically and to lower the relative income of a group of people who are in plentiful supply domestically. Free trade does the opposite.

Conclusion   Other things being equal, most people prefer more income to less. Economists cannot say that it is irrational for a society to sacrifice some income in order to achieve other goals. Economists can, however, do three things when faced with such reasons for adopting protectionist measures. First, they can ask if the proposed measures really do achieve the ends suggested. Second, they can calculate the cost of the measures in terms of lowered living standards. Third, they can see if there are alternative means of achieving the stated goals at lower cost in terms of lost output.

Maximizing national income as a reason for protectionism

Next we consider five important arguments for the use of tariffs when the objective is to make national income as large as possible.

To alter the terms of trade   Trade restrictions can be used to turn the terms of trade in favour of countries that produce, and export, a large fraction of the world's supply of some product. They can also be used to turn the terms of trade in favour of countries that constitute a large fraction of the world demand for some product that they import.

When the OPEC countries restricted their output of oil in the 1970s, they were able to drive up the price of oil relative to the prices of other traded goods. This turned the terms of trade in their favour; for every barrel of oil exported, they were able to obtain a larger quantity of imports. When the output of oil grew greatly in the mid-1980s, the relative price of oil fell dramatically, and the terms of trade turned unfavourably for the oil-exploring companies. These are illustrations of how changes in the quantities of exports can affect the terms of trade.

Now consider a country that provides a large fraction of the total demand for some product that it imports. By restricting its demand for that product through tariffs, it can force the price of that product down. This turns the terms of trade in its favour because it can now get more units of imports per unit of exports.

Both of these techniques lower world output. They can, however, make it possible for a small group of countries to gain because they get a sufficiently larger share of the smaller world output. However, if foreign countries retaliate by raising their tariffs, the ensuing tariff war can easily leave every country with a lowered income.

To protect against 'unfair' actions by foreign firms and governments   Tariffs may be used to prevent foreign industries from gaining an advantage over domestic industries by use of predatory practices that will harm domestic industries and hence lower national income. Two common practices are subsidies paid by foreign governments to their exporters and price discrimination by foreign firms, which is called *dumping* when it is done across international borders. These practices are typically countered by levying tariffs called countervailing and anti-dumping duties.

To protect infant industries   The oldest valid argument for protectionism as a means of raising living standards concerns economies of scale. It is usually called the **infant industry argument.** If an industry has large economies of scale, costs will be high when the industry is small, but will fall as the industry grows. In such industries the country first in the field has a tremendous advantage. A newly developing country may find that in the early stages of development its industries are unable to compete with established foreign rivals. A trade restriction may protect these industries from foreign competition while they grow up. When they are large enough, they will be able to produce as cheaply as foreign rivals and thus will be able to compete without protection.

To encourage learning by doing   Learning by doing suggests that the pattern of comparative advantage can be changed. If a country learns enough through producing products in which it currently is at a comparative disadvantage, it may gain in the long run by specializing in those products, and could develop a comparative advantage as the learning process lowers their costs.

The successes of such newly industrializing countries (NICs) as Brazil, Hong Kong, South Korea, Singapore, and Taiwan seemed to many observers to be based on acquired skills and government policies that created favourable business conditions. This gave rise to the theory that comparative advantages can change, and that they can be developed by suitable government policies.

Protecting a domestic industry from foreign competition may give its management time to learn to be efficient, and its labour force time to acquire the needed skills.

If this is so, it may pay in the very long run to protect the industry against foreign competition while a dynamic comparative advantage is being developed.

Some countries have succeeded in developing strong comparative advantages in targeted industries, but others have failed. One reason such policies sometimes fail is that protecting local industries from foreign competition may make the industries unadaptive and complacent. Another reason is the difficulty of identifying the industries that will be able to succeed in the long run. All too often the protected infant grows up to be a weakling requiring permanent tariff protection for its continued existence; or else the rate of learning is slower than for similar industries in countries that do not provide protection from the chill winds of international competition. In these instances the anticipated comparative advantage never materializes.

To create or to exploit a strategic trade advantage An important recent argument for tariffs or other trade restrictions is to create a strategic advantage in producing or marketing some new product that is expected to generate profits. To the extent that all lines of production earn normal profits, there is no reason to produce goods other than ones for which a country has a comparative advantage. Some goods, however, are produced in industries containing a few large firms where large-scale economies provide a natural barrier to further entry. Firms in these industries can earn extra-high profits over long periods of time. Where such industries are already well established, there is little chance that a new firm will replace one of the existing giants.

The situation is, however, more fluid with new products. The first firm to develop and market a new product successfully may earn a substantial pure profit over all of its opportunity costs and become one of the few established firms in the industry. If protection of the domestic market can increase the chance that one of the protected domestic firms will become one of the established firms in the international market, the protection may pay off.

Many of today's high-tech industries have falling average total cost curves because of their large fixed costs of product development. For a new generation of civilian aircraft, silicon chips, computers, artificial-intelligence machines, and pharmaceuticals, a very high proportion of each producer's total costs goes to product development. These are fixed costs of entering the market, and they must be incurred before a single unit of output can be sold. In such industries there may be room for only a few firms.

The production of full-sized commercial jet aeroplanes provides an example of an industry that possesses many of these characteristics. The development costs of a new generation of jet aircraft have risen with each new generation. If the aircraft manufacturers are to recover these costs, each of them must have large sales. Thus the number of firms that the market can support has diminished steadily, until today there is room in the world aircraft industry for only two or three firms producing a full range of commercial jets.

The characteristics just described are sometimes used to provide arguments for subsidizing the development of such industries and/or protecting their home markets with a tariff. Suppose, for example, that there is room in the aircraft industry for only three major producers of the next round of passenger jets. If a government assists a domestic firm, this firm may become one of the three that succeed, and the profits that are subsequently earned may more than repay the cost of the subsidy. Furthermore, another country's firm, which was not subsidized, may have been just as good as the three that succeeded. Without the subsidy, however, this firm may lose out in the battle to establish itself as one of the three surviving firms in the market.

This example is not unlike the story of the European Airbus. The European producers received many direct subsidies (and they charge that their main competitor, the Boeing 767, received many indirect ones). Whatever the merits of the argument, several things are clear: the civilian jet aircraft industry remains profitable; there is room for only two or three major producers; and one of these would not have been the European consortium if it had not been for substantial government assistance.

Generalizing from this and similar cases, some economists advocate that their governments should adopt *strategic trade policies* more broadly than they now do. This means, for high-tech industries, government protection of the home market and government subsidization (either openly or by more subtle back-door methods) of the product development stage. These economists say that if their country does not follow their advice, it will lose out in industry after industry to the more aggressive Japanese and North American competition—a competition that is adept at combining private innovative activity with government assistance.

Opponents argue that once all countries try to be strategic, they will all waste vast sums trying to break into industries in which there is no room for most of them. Advocates of strategic trade policy reply that a country cannot afford to stand by while others play the strategic game.

Advocates also argue that there are key industries that have major 'spillovers' into the rest of the economy. If a country wants to have a high living standard, it must, they argue, compete with the best. If a country lets all of its key industries migrate to other countries, many of the others will follow. The country then risks being reduced to the status of a less developed nation.

Opponents argue that strategic trade policy is just the modern version of mercantilism, a policy of trying to enrich oneself at the expense of one's neighbours rather than looking for mutually beneficial gains from trade. They point to the rising world prosperity of the entire period following the Second World War, which has been built largely on a rising volume of relatively free international trade. There are real doubts that such prosperity could be maintained if the volume of trade were to shrink steadily because of growing trade barriers.

In today's world a country's products must stand up to international competition if they are to survive. Over time this requires that they hold their own in competition for successful innovations. Protection, by conferring a national monopoly, reduces the incentive for industries to fight to hold their own internationally. If any one country adopts high tariffs unilaterally, its domestic industries will become less competitive. Secure in its home market because of the tariff wall, the protected industries are likely to become less and less competitive in the international market. As the gap between domestic and foreign industries widens, any tariff wall will provide less and less protection. Eventually, the domestic industries will succumb to the foreign competition.

Although restrictive policies sometimes have been pursued following a rational assessment of the approximate cost, it is hard to avoid the conclusion that more often than not such policies are often pursued for political objectives, or on fallacious economic grounds, with little appreciation of the actual costs involved.

Methods of protection

We have now studied some of the many reasons why governments may wish to provide some protection for some of their domestic industries. Our next task is to see how they do it. What are the tools that provide protection?

The two main types of protectionist policy are illustrated in Figure 34.3. Both cause the price of the imported good to rise and its quantity to fall. They differ, however, in how they achieve these results. The caption to the figure analyses these two types of policy.

Policies that directly raise prices

The first type of protectionist policy directly raises the *price* of the imported product. A tariff, also often called an *import duty*, is the most common policy of this type. Other such policies include any rules or regulations that fulfil three conditions: they are costly to comply with; they do not apply to competing, domestically produced products; and they are more than is required to meet any purpose other than restricting trade.

As shown in part (ii) of Figure 34.3, tariffs affect both foreign and domestic producers, as well as domestic consumers. The initial effect is to raise the domestic price of the imported product above its world price by the amount of the tariff. Imports fall, and as a result foreign producers sell less and so must transfer resources to other lines of production. The price received on domestically produced units rises, as does the quantity produced domestically. On both counts domestic producers earn more. However, the cost of producing the extra output at home exceeds the price at which it could be purchased on the world market. Thus the benefit to domestic producers comes at the expense of domestic consumers. Indeed, domestic consumers lose on two counts: first, they consume less of the product because its price rises; and second, they pay a higher price for the amount that they do consume. This extra spending ends up in two places: the extra that is paid on all units produced at home goes to domestic producers (partly in the resource costs of extra production and partly in profit), and the extra that is paid on units still imported goes to the government as tariff revenue.

Policies that directly lower quantities

The second type of protectionist policy directly restricts the quantity of an imported product. Any implicit or explicit restriction on trade that does not involve a tariff is known as a **non-tariff barrier.** These can take various subtle forms including quality standards that are complicated to interpret or customs forms that take weeks to get approved. But many non-tariff barriers are more obvious and easy to understand. A common example is the **import quota,** by which the importing country sets a maximum on the quantity of some product that may be imported each year. Increasingly popular in the recent past, however, has been the **voluntary export restriction** (VER), an agreement by an exporting country to limit the amount of a good that it sells to the importing country.

The European Union and the United States have used VERs extensively, and the European Union also makes frequent use of import quotas. Japan has been pressured into negotiating several VERs with the European Union and the United States in order to limit sales of some of the

(i) Free trade

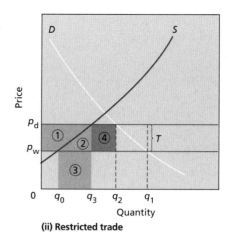

(ii) Restricted trade

Figure 34.3 Methods of protecting domestic producers

The same reduction in imports can be achieved by using either a tariff or a quantity restriction. In both parts of the figure D and S are the domestic demand and supply curves, respectively, and p_w is the world price.

Part (i) of the figure shows the situation under free trade. Domestic consumption is q_1, domestic production is q_0, and imports are $q_0 - q_1$.

Part (ii) shows what happens when protectionist policies restrict imports to the amount $q_2 - q_3$. When this is done by levying a tariff of T per unit, the price in the domestic market rises by the full amount of the tariff to p_d. Consumers reduce consumption from q_1 to q_2 and pay an extra amount, shown by the coloured areas 1, 2, and 4, for the q_2 that they now purchase. Domestic production rises from q_0 to q_3. Since domestic producers receive the domestic price, their receipts rise by the three medium blue areas, labelled 1, 2, and 3. Area 3 is revenue that was earned by foreign producers under free trade, while areas 1 and 2 are paid by domestic consumers because of the higher prices they now face. Foreign suppliers of the imported good continue to receive the world price, so the government receives as tariff revenue the extra amount paid by consumers for the $q_3 - q_2$ units that are still imported (shown by the dark blue area, 4).

When the same result is accomplished by a quantity restriction, the government—through either a quota or a *voluntary export agreement (VER)*—reduces imports to $q_2 - q_3$. This drives the domestic market price up to p_d and has the same effect on domestic producers and consumers as the tariff. Since the government has merely restricted the quantity of imports, both foreign and domestic suppliers get the higher price in the domestic market. Thus foreign suppliers now receive the extra amount paid by domestic consumers (represented by the dark blue area labelled 4) for the units that are still imported.

Japanese goods that have had the most success in international competition. For example, in 1983 the United States and Canada negotiated VERs whereby the Japanese government agreed to restrict total sales of Japanese cars to these two countries for three years. When the agreements ran out in 1986, the Japanese continued to restrain their car sales by unilateral voluntary action.

Fallacious trade-policy arguments

We saw above that there are gains from a high volume of international trade and specialization. We have also seen that there can be valid arguments for a moderate degree of protectionism. There are also many claims that do not advance the debate. Fallacious arguments are heard on both sides, and they colour much of the popular discussion. These arguments have been around for a long time, but

their survival does not make them true. We will examine them now to see where their fallacies lie.

Fallacious arguments for free trade

Free trade always benefits all countries This is not necessarily so. We saw above that a small group of countries may gain by restricting trade in order to get a sufficiently favourable shift in their terms of trade. Such countries would lose if they gave up these tariffs and adopted free trade unilaterally.

Infant industries never abandon their tariff protection It is argued that granting protection to infant industries is a mistake because these industries seldom admit to growing up, and will cling to their protection even when fully grown. But infant industry tariffs are a mistake only if these industries never grow up. In this case permanent tariff protection would be required to protect a weak industry never able to compete on an equal footing in the international market. But if the industries do grow up and achieve the expected scale and learning economies, the real costs of production are reduced and resources are freed for other uses. Whether or not the trade barriers remain, a cost saving has been effected by the scale economies.

Fallacious arguments for protectionism

To prevent exploitation According to the exploitation theory, trade can never be mutually advantageous; one trading partner must always reap a gain at the other's expense. Thus the weaker trading partner must protect itself by restricting its trade with the stronger partner. By showing that both parties can gain from trade, the principle of comparative advantage refutes the exploitation doctrine of trade. When opportunity-cost ratios differ in two countries, specialization and the accompanying trade make it possible to produce more of all products. This makes it possible for both parties to consume more as a result of trade than they could get in its absence.

To protect against low-wage foreign labour Surely, this argument says, in industrialized nations the products of low-wage countries will drive domestic products from the market, and the high domestic standard of living will be dragged down to that of its poorer trading partners. Arguments of this sort have swayed many voters through the years.

As a prelude to considering them, stop and think what the argument would imply if taken out of the international context and put into a local one, where the same principles govern the gains from trade. Is it really impossible for a rich person to gain from trading with a poor person? Would the local millionaire be better off if she did all her own typing, gardening, and cooking? No one believes that a rich person cannot gain from trading with those who are less rich.

Why then must a rich group of people lose from trading with a poor group? 'Well,' some may say, 'the poor group will price their goods too cheaply.' Does anyone believe that consumers lose from buying in supermarkets just because the prices are lower there than at the old-fashioned corner shop? Consumers gain when they can buy the same goods at a lower price. If the Koreans pay low wages and sell their goods cheaply, Korean labour may suffer, but the EU will gain by obtaining imports at a low cost in terms of the goods that must be exported in return. The cheaper our imports are, the better off we are in terms of the goods and services available for domestic consumption.

Stated in more formal terms, the gains from trade depend on comparative, not absolute, advantages. World production is higher when any two areas, say the EU and Japan, specialize in the production of the goods for which they have a comparative advantage than when they both try to be self-sufficient.

Might it not be possible, however, that Japan will undersell the EU in all lines of production and thus appropriate all, or more than all, the gains for itself, leaving the EU no better off, or even worse off, than if it had no trade with Japan? The answer is no. The reason for this depends on the behaviour of exchange rates, which were discussed in Chapter 28. As we saw in that chapter, equality of demand and supply in foreign exchange markets ensures that trade flows in both directions. The reason a country cannot import for long without exporting may also be stated intuitively as follows.

Imports can be obtained only by spending the currency of the country that produces the imports. Claims to this currency can be obtained only by exporting goods and services, or by borrowing. Thus, lending and borrowing aside, imports must equal exports. All trade must be in two directions; we can buy only if we can also sell.

In the long run trade cannot hurt a country by causing it to import without exporting.

Trade, then, always provides scope for international specialization, with each country producing and exporting those goods for which it has a comparative advantage and importing those goods for which it does not.

Exports raise living standards; imports lower them Exports create domestic income and employment; imports create income and employment for foreigners. Thus, other things being equal, exports tend to increase our total national income and imports reduce it. Surely, then, it is desirable to encourage exports by subsidizing them and to discourage imports by taxing them.

This is an appealing argument, but it is incorrect. Exports raise national income by adding to the value of domestic output, but they do not add to the value of domestic consumption. In fact exports are goods produced at home and consumed abroad, while imports are goods produced abroad and consumed at home. The standard of living in a country depends on the goods and services available for consumption, not on what is produced.

The living standards of a country depend on the goods and services consumed in that country. The importance of exports is that they permit imports to be made. This two-way international exchange is valuable because more goods can be imported than could be obtained if the same goods were produced at home.

To create domestic jobs and reduce unemployment It is sometimes said that an economy with substantial unemployment, such as Spain in the 1990s, provides an exception to the case for freer trade. Suppose that tariffs or import quotas cut the imports of Japanese cars, Korean textiles, US computers, and Polish vodka. Surely, the argument maintains, this will create more employment in local industries producing similar products. The answer is that it will—initially. But the Japanese, Koreans, Americans, and Poles can buy from Spain only if they earn pesetas by selling things to (or by borrowing pesetas from) Spain. The decline in their sales of cars, textiles, computers, and vodka will decrease their purchases of Spanish vegetables, fruit, and wine, and holidays in Spain. Jobs will be lost in Spanish export industries, and gained in those industries that formerly faced competition from imports. The likely long-term effect is that overall employment will not be increased but merely redistributed among industries. In the process, living standards will be reduced because employment expands in inefficient import-competing industries and contracts in efficient exporting industries.

Industries and unions that compete with imports often favour protectionism, while those with large exports usually favour more trade. Protection is an ineffective means to reduce unemployment.

Global commercial policy

We now discuss supranational influences on commercial policy in the world today. We start with the many international agreements that govern current commercial policies and then look in a little more detail at the European Union.

Before 1947 any country was free to impose any tariffs on its imports. However, when one country increased its tariffs, the action often triggered retaliatory actions by its trading partners. The Great Depression of the 1930s saw a high-water mark of world protectionism, as each country sought to raise its employment by raising its tariffs. The end result was lowered efficiency, less trade—but no increase in employment. Since that time, much effort has been devoted to reducing tariff barriers, on both a multilateral and a regional basis.

GATT and the WTO

One of the most notable achievements of the post-war era was the creation of the General Agreement on Tariffs and Trade (GATT). The principle of GATT is that each member country agrees not to make unilateral tariff increases. This prevents the outbreak of tariff wars in which countries raise tariffs to protect particular domestic industries and to retaliate against other countries' tariff increases. Such wars usually harm all countries as mutually beneficial trade shrinks under the impact of escalating tariff barriers.

There have been eight 'rounds' of global trade talks since 1948. The three most recently completed rounds of GATT agreements, the Kennedy round (completed 1967), the Tokyo round (completed 1979), and the Uruguay round (completed 1993), have each agreed to reduce world tariffs substantially, the first two by about one-third each, and the last by about 40 per cent.

The Uruguay round created a new body, the World Trade Organization (WTO), that superseded the GATT in 1995. It also created a new legal structure for multilateral trading. Under this new structure all members have equal mutual rights and obligations. Until the WTO was formed, developing countries who were in GATT enjoyed all the GATT rights but were exempt from most of its obligations to liberalize trade—obligations that applied only to the developed countries. Now, however, all such special treatments are being phased out over seven years from 1995. There is also a new dispute-settlement mechanism with much more power to enforce rulings over non-tariff barriers than existed in the past. In its first three years the WTO dealt with 132 complaints; while the GATT only heard 300 in forty-seven years!

In 1997 three strands of negotiation that had been left incomplete in the Uruguay round were completed, involving agreements to lower trade barriers in telecommunications, financial services, and information technology. These agreements were important because they greatly increase the amount of trade covered by WTO rules and dispute-settlement procedures, they may lead to larger trade volume gains than the entire Uruguay round, and they complete most of the unfinished business from Uruguay, clearing the way for a new global trade round.

By 1998 the WTO had 132 member countries, with a further 30 including Russia and China hoping to join.[1] It is thus growing into a truly global forum for the regulation of government involvement in world trade. Figure 34.4 shows that world trade has grown faster than world GDP since 1950. Indeed, while real GDP has grown sixfold, world export volumes have grown nearly twentyfold. It is hard to believe that this could have occurred without the liberalization of international trade brought about through successive rounds of tariff negotiation.

Types of regional agreement

Regional agreements seek to liberalize trade over a much smaller set of countries than the WTO membership. Three standard forms of regional trade-liberalizing agreement are free-trade areas, customs unions, and common markets.

---

[1] The latest information about the WTO can be found on the Internet at www.wto.org.

Figure 34.4 World real GDP and export volume, 1950–1997 (index: 1950 = 100)

Trade has grown more than GDP in the post-war period. Since 1950 world real GDP has increased sixfold while the volume of world trade has risen twentyfold.

Source: The Economist, 16 May 1998.

A **free-trade area** (FTA) is the least comprehensive of the three. It allows for tariff-free trade among the member countries, but it leaves each member free to impose its own trade restrictions on imports from other countries. As a result members must maintain customs points at their common borders to make sure that imports into the free-trade area do not all enter through the member that is levying the lowest tariff on each item. They must also agree on rules of origin to establish when a good is made in a member country, and hence is able to pass duty-free across their borders, and when it is imported from outside the free-trade area, and hence is liable to pay duties when it crosses borders within the free-trade area.

A **customs union** is a free-trade area plus an agreement to establish common barriers to trade with the rest of the world. Because they have a common tariff against the outside world, the members need neither customs controls on goods moving among themselves nor rules of origin.

A **common market** is a customs union that also has free movement of labour and capital among its members.

Trade creation and trade diversion

A major effect of regional trade liberalization is on resource reallocation. Economic theory divides these effects into two categories.

Trade creation occurs when producers in one member country find that they can undersell producers in another member country because the latter lose their tariff protection. For example, when the North American Free Trade Agreement (NAFTA) came into force, some Mexican firms found that they could undersell their US competitors in some product lines, while some US firms found that they could undersell their Mexican competitors in others, once

tariffs were eliminated. As a result specialization occurred and new international trade developed.

Trade diversion occurs when exporters in one member country replace foreign exporters as suppliers to another member country as a result of preferential tariff treatment. For example, US trade diversion occurs when Mexican firms find that they can undersell competitors from the rest of the world in the US market, not because they are the cheapest source of supply, but because their tariff-free prices are lower than the tariff-burdened prices of imports from other countries. This effect is a gain to Mexican firms but a cost to the United States—which now has to export more goods for any given amount of imports than before the trade diversion occurred.

From the global perspective trade diversion represents an inefficient use of resources.

From the narrower national points of view of Mexico and the United States, however, it brings some gain as well as some loss. In so far as there is a shared desire to increase domestic manufacturing production, trade diversion brings mutual benefit to both countries. It gives producers within the two countries an advantage over producers in the rest of the world, which has the effect of increasing the total amount of production and trade that occurs among the member countries while reducing what comes in from third countries.

EFTA, NAFTA, and other FTAs

The first important free-trade area in the modern era was the European Free Trade Association (EFTA). It was formed in 1960 by a group of European countries that were unwilling to join the European Economic Community as the EU was then called because of its all-embracing character. Not wanting to be left out of the gains from trade, they formed an association whose sole purpose was tariff removal. First, they removed all tariffs on trade among themselves. Then each country signed a free-trade-area agreement with the EEC. This made the EEC–EFTA market the largest tariff-free market in the world (over 300 million people). Three of the EFTA countries switched to full membership of the EU in 1995.

In 1988 a sweeping agreement was signed between Canada and the United States, instituting free trade on all goods and most non-government services, and covering what is the world's largest flow of international trade between any two countries. In 1993 this agreement was extended into the North American Free Trade Agreement (NAFTA) by renegotiation of the Canada–USA agreement to include Mexico. Australia and New Zealand have also entered into an association that removes restrictions on trade in goods and services between their two countries, and a group of countries in Southeast Asia have formed the ASEAN trade group.

The countries of Latin America have been experimenting with free-trade areas for many decades. Most earlier attempts failed, but in the last few years a more durable free-trade area has been formed, known as Mercosur. In April 1998 an initiative was taken to put in place a free-trade area for the whole of the Americas by 2005 which would in effect be based upon a merger of NAFTA and Mercosur. It remains to be seen if this will come to fruition. Currently the US legislature is blocking all efforts to extend NAFTA to other countries, beginning with Chile.

Common markets: the European Union

By far the most successful common market, which is now referred to as a single market, is the European Union. Its origins go back to the period immediately following the Second World War in 1945. After the war there was a strong belief throughout Europe that the way to avoid future military conflict was to create a high level of economic integration between the existing nation-states. Later the motivation switched to creating a powerful economic bloc which could be competitive with Japan and the USA.

In 1952, as a first step towards economic union, France, Belgium, West Germany, Italy, Luxembourg, and Holland formed the European Coal and Steel Community. This removed trade restrictions on coal, steel, and iron ore among these six countries. In 1957 the same six countries signed the Treaty of Rome. This created the European Economic Community (EEC), which later became the European Community (EC), and after 1993 the European Union (EU). In 1973 the United Kingdom, Denmark, and Ireland joined, and they were followed in 1981 by Greece and in 1986 by Spain and Portugal. Austria, Sweden, and Finland entered in 1995. Several other countries, such as Poland, Hungary, the Czech Republic, and Cyprus are hoping to join in the early twenty-first century.

In the first two decades of its existence the main economic achievements of the EEC were the elimination of internal tariff barriers and the establishment of common external tariffs (in other words the establishment of a customs union), and the establishment of the Common Agricultural Policy, which, for better or for worse, guarantees farm prices by means of intervention and an import levy (see Chapter 5). There were other significant EEC policies, such as regional aid and protection of competition, but they did not have great economic impacts early on.

By the mid-1980s it was clear that the intended 'Common Market' had not been achieved. There remained many non-tariff barriers to trade and to the mobility of labour. These included quality standards, licensing requirements, and a lack of recognition of qualifications. In financial services there were explicit exchange controls and other regulatory restrictions on cross-border trade. In response a new push to turn the customs union into a genuine common market began in 1985.

The Single Market Programme

The Single Market Act was signed in 1986. Its intention was to remove all remaining barriers to the creation of a fully integrated single market by the end of 1992. The Single Market Act did not in itself create the single market. Rather, it was a statement (or treaty) of intent which instituted a simplified administrative procedure whereby most of the single market legislation needed only 'weighted majority' support, rather than unanimity. The single market itself was to be created by a large number of Directives, which are drafted by the European Commission, the EU's civil service. These become Community law after they have been 'adopted' by the European Council (a committee of the heads of state or other ministers of member states). They then have to be ratified in the law of each member state. Once in force, they have precedence over the domestic laws of member states if there is a conflict.

Eliminating non-tariff barriers has been approached on a product-by-product basis. Only in this way could minimum quality standards be created which would permit cross-border trade without the threat of quality checks as a prerequisite to entry (a problem that plagues some branches of Canada–USA trade). This has required a complicated set of negotiations on quality standards relating to everything from condoms to sausages and from toys to telecommunications. There is even a quality standard for the bacterial content of aqueous toys—transparent plastic souvenirs containing, perhaps, a model of Big Ben or the Eiffel Tower, which, when shaken, create a snow scene.

All countries have such safety or quality standards for their products, and what has been happening is the harmonization of these standards, which is something that Canada and the United States have been trying to do since their Agreement was put into force in 1989.

The Single Market Programme is an ongoing process, not a discrete jump. Some of the intended measures have been implemented, but many are still in the pipeline. The process will continue well into the twenty-first century.

Many important steps were achieved by the end of 1992, including the removal of some border checks. (At UK ports and airports, this means a blue channel through which EU citizens are permitted to carry as many goods as they like, if bought in other EU countries, so long as they are for personal use.) But the process of increasing economic integration continued well after 1992.

The single market in financial services

Perhaps the most significant achievements of the Single Market Programme to date have been in the area of trade in financial services. Although the Treaty of Rome called for free movement of capital as well as goods, this was ignored until the mid-1980s. Most member countries had exchange controls on capital movements until recently. These controls prohibited residents of each country from investing in any other country.

The Capital Liberalization Directive required all member states to abolish exchange controls by June 1990. Some member states, such as the UK and Germany, had already abolished controls. France and Italy, which had not, were forced to do so by the Directive. Spain, Portugal, Ireland, and Greece were given longer to comply. All except Greece fully abolished their controls by the end of 1992, and Greece abolished most of its controls by 1994.

Once exchange controls were abolished, it could be argued that nothing else had to be done to create a single market in financial services. Certainly wholesale financial markets rapidly integrated with the global financial system, once they were free to do so. Indeed, this is one of the key elements of globalization, which was discussed in Box 29.1 on page 493.

However, agreement was still needed on how to facilitate greater cross-border competition in retail financial markets. Each country in isolation had already created a domestic regulatory regime designed, in part, to protect the consumer. How was the EU to encourage competition but maintain a sensible regime of consumer protection? Financial services are particularly prone to fraud, because the profit margin for a crook is 100 per cent—even a used car salesman has to show you a car, but the seller of an investment product offers only future promises!

The European Union adopted a pragmatic approach based upon assuming the competence of existing regulators. Firms in each sector were to be authorized as 'fit and proper' by their home country regulator, and they would then be presumed to be fit and proper to trade in any member state. In effect the home country gave a driving licence which then permitted an authorized company to 'drive' anywhere in the Union. This mutual recognition of regulators has been wrongly interpreted as permitting financial services firms to trade anywhere in the European Union on the basis of their home country's rules. A moment's thought will tell you why it has to be wrong. Imagine, for example, British drivers being permitted to drive on the left in France just because that is the law in Britain. It is just as disastrous to have banks in any one location trading under fifteen different legal structures.

The single market in financial services is built on a dual set of principles: home country authorization, and host country conduct of business rules. This means that a firm can be authorized to trade throughout the Union by the home regulator, but the trade itself must obey the local laws in the country concerned.

Allowing home countries to regulate entry and host countries to regulate performance is a simple application of the principle of *national treatment* that was developed in the context of the Uruguay round. It means that foreign firms get treated just the same as local firms.

The Cecchini Report of 1989 estimated that the completion of the Single Market Programme may increase the GDP of the European Union by up to 6 per cent. However, a well-known American economist, Richard Baldwin, has challenged that figure, suggesting that the gains could be at least twice as large (owing to economies of scale external to firms). And this is only the gain in one year. Similar gains will continue to flow in future years. Thus, while politically tortuous, the process of reducing trade barriers, even within groups of countries, is capable of creating considerable gains in economic efficiency.

The Maastricht Treaty

Signed in 1992, the Maastricht Treaty pushed the process of EU integration further. It included an agreement creating the common currency that came into being in January 1999. It is likely that the introduction of the single currency will do as much as any of the previous tariff reductions to integrate the economies of the European Union, as it makes the price system much more transparent and eliminates exchange rate risk. The implications of the single currency will be unclear until the early years of the twenty-first century.

The Maastricht Treaty also contained a Social Chapter, covering harmonization of policies with respect to labour markets and other social areas. The United Kingdom opted out of this Chapter initially, but opted back in in 1997.

The future of the multilateral trading system

At the end of the Second World War the United States took the lead in forming GATT and in pressing for reductions in world tariffs through successive rounds of negotiations. Largely as a result of this US initiative, the world's tariff barriers have been greatly reduced, while the volume of world trade has risen steadily (see Figure 34.4 on page 591).

The next few years will be critical for the future of the multilateral trading system, which has served the world so well since the end of the Second World War. The dangers are, first, a growth of regional trading blocs that will trade more with their own member countries and less with others, and second, the growth of state-managed trade.

The 1920s and 1930s provide a cautionary tale. Arguments for restricting trade always have a superficial appeal and sometimes have real short-term payoffs. In the long term, however, a major worldwide escalation of tariffs would lower efficiency and incomes and restrict trade worldwide, while doing nothing to raise employment. Both economic theory and the evidence of history support this proposition. Although most agree that pressure should be put on countries that restrict trade, the above analysis suggests that these pressures are best applied using the multilateral institution, the WTO. Unilateral imposition of restrictions in response to the perceived restrictions in other countries can all too easily degenerate into a round of mutually escalating trade barriers.

The European Union, although it has achieved something close to free trade within the Union, has been equivocal on free trade with the rest of the world. Anti-dumping duties, voluntary export agreements, and other non-tariff barriers have been used with effect against successful importers—particularly the Japanese. Although these measures may bring short-term gains, both economic theory and historical experience suggest that they will bring losses in the long term. Protectionism reduces incomes because low-priced goods are excluded to the detriment of current consumers, particularly those with lower incomes. It also reduces employment because restrictions on imports are sooner or later balanced by restrictions on exports as other countries retaliate. It also inhibits the technological dynamism that is the source of long-term growth, by shielding domestic producers from the need that free international competition forces on them: to keep up with all foreign competitors.

Summary

Sources of the gains from trade

■ Potential gains from trade exist when one country, region, firm, or individual has a comparative advantage in the production of some good or service.

■ Comparative advantage occurs whenever countries have different opportunity costs of producing particular goods. World production of all products can be increased if each country transfers resources into the production of the products in which it has a comparative advantage, which means those in which it has the lower opportunity cost.

■ The most important proposition in the theory of the gains from trade is that trade allows all countries to obtain the goods in which they do not have a comparative advantage at a lower opportunity cost than they would face if they were to produce all products for themselves; this allows all countries to have more of all products than they could have if they tried to be self-sufficient.

■ As well as gaining the advantages of specialization arising from comparative advantage, a nation that engages in trade and specialization may realize the benefits of economies of large-scale production and of learning by doing.

■ Classical theory regarded comparative advantage as being determined largely by natural resource endowments, and thus as difficult to change. Economists now believe that some comparative advantages are acquired and thus can be changed. A country may, in this view, influence its role in world production and trade. Successful intervention leads to a country acquiring a comparative advantage; unsuccessful intervention fails to develop such an advantage.

The terms of trade

■ The terms of trade refer to the ratio of the prices of goods exported to those imported, which determines the quantity of imports that can be obtained per unit of exports. The terms of trade determine how the gains from trade are shared. A favourable change in the terms of trade—that is, a rise in export prices relative to import prices—means a country can acquire more imports per unit of exports.

The theory of commercial policy

■ Protection can be a means to ends other than maximizing world living standards. It is also sometimes justified on the grounds that it may lead to higher living standards for the protectionist country than a policy of free trade would. Such a result might come about by developing a dynamic comparative advantage allowing inexperienced or uneconomically small industries to become efficient enough to compete with foreign industries. A recent argument for protection is to operate a strategic trade policy whereby a country attracts firms in oligopolistic industries that, because of scale economies, can earn large profits even in equilibrium.

■ Domestic industries may be protected from foreign competition by tariffs, which affect the prices of imports, or by non-tariff barriers, which affect the quantities of imports.

■ Some fallacious free-trade arguments are that (a) because free trade maximizes world income, it will maximize the income of every individual country; and (b) because infant industries seldom admit to growing up and thus try to retain their protection indefinitely, the whole country necessarily loses by protecting its infant industries.

■ Some fallacious protectionist arguments are that (a) mutually advantageous trade is impossible because one trader's gain must always be the other's loss; (b) our high-paid workers must be protected against the competition from low-paid foreign workers; and (c) imports are to be discouraged because they lower national income and cause unemployment.

Global commercial policy

■ The World Trade Organization (WTO) has taken over from GATT the role of policing world trade rules relating to government commercial policies and providing a forum for further international co-operation in evolving the global trade regime.

■ Regional trade-liberalizing agreements such as free-trade areas and common markets bring efficiency gains through trade creation and efficiency losses through trade diversion. The North American Free Trade Agreement (NAFTA) is the world's largest and most successful free-trade area, while the European Union is the world's largest and most successful common market (now called a single market).

Topics for review

■ Comparative advantage
■ Gains from trade
■ Terms of trade
■ Free trade and protectionism
■ Tariff and non-tariff barriers to trade

■ General Agreement on Tariffs and Trade (GATT)
■ World Trade Organization (WTO)
■ Common markets, customs unions, and free-trade associations
■ North American Free Trade Agreement (NAFTA)
■ European Union (EU)

Questions for discussion

1 It is quite common for governments from time to time to encourage their citizens to buy home-produced goods in preference to foreign-produced goods. (For example, in the United Kingdom a 'buy British' policy has been encouraged in the past.) In what ways if any could such encouragement be good for the domestic economy?

2 Outline the arguments for and against free trade.

3 Compare and contrast tariffs and quotas as methods of restricting trade.

4 Why does trading with countries where workers have lower real incomes *not* make us worse off?

5 Why is it that openness to foreign competition seems to be good for economic growth?

Chapter 35
Global Macroeconomics in Action

In this final chapter we use some of the economic analysis that we have developed in the last two parts of this book to help understand some events and policy issues that were current in the late 1990s. Many of these issues will continue to be important well into the twenty-first century, while others are sure to emerge. The point to notice is that the analytical tools we have set out above are relevant to understanding a wide range of economic phenomena *in all parts of the world*. There is no such thing as British economics or American economics. There is just economics, and it helps us to understand events anywhere. Of course, institutions and cultures differ around the world, and a well-trained economist needs to be able to incorporate these local differences into his or her analysis in order to derive correct conclusions.

We start in Japan, where the macro policy options were heavily constrained in the late 1990s by the fact that the economy was in recession but interest rates were already close to zero and so could not be set any lower. As we will see, this is not a new problem, but it is one that has not been experienced since the Second World War. Then we turn to Europe, where the creation of the single currency, the euro, in 1999 has created a whole new set of macro policy problems that have not been experienced in recent history in quite this form. Eleven countries have suddenly

become subject to a 'one-size-fits-all' monetary policy regime, and at the same time constraints have been imposed on fiscal deficits. In such circumstances can there be any stabilization policy at all?

A third event we look at is the introduction of the minimum wage in the United Kingdom in 1999. We have analysed the microeconomics of the minimum wage in Chapter 15. Here we look at the macroeconomics of this policy. How does the introduction of a minimum wage impact on output and the price level, and what should the response be of the monetary policymakers?

Fourthly, we investigate the financial crisis in Southeast Asia that broke out in late 1997 and continued in some parts into 1998 (and possibly longer). This illustrates the interaction of domestic economic management with the global capital markets, and it holds lessons for all economies in the modern world of internationally mobile finance.

Finally, we discuss some worldwide phenomena that are important for all countries. These include the trend to lower worldwide inflation that was evident at the end of the 1990s; the implications for world real interest rates of fiscal consolidation, that is, reduction or elimination of government budget deficits, in most of the major countries of the world; and the effects of globalization on the world business cycle.

Japan in the late 1990s: the liquidity trap revived

Japan has been one of the most successful economies of the post-Second World War period. It experienced spectacular growth rates of real GDP in the 1950s and 1960s, which averaged nearly 10 per cent. This rapid growth moderated somewhat in the 1970s, but in the ten-year period 1979–88 Japan still had the highest average growth rate of all the major industrial countries at 3.8 per cent, compared to an average for the seven major industrial countries (the G7) of 2.9 per cent. In the next ten years, 1989–98, however, Japanese economic growth at 2.4 per cent had fallen very close to the G7 average of 2.2 per cent, and in 1997 and 1998 Japan had the *lowest* rate of economic growth of all the major economies.

The general prospects for the Japanese economy in the medium term appeared quite good—by the late 1990s it had attained a level of real GDP per capita that was about 85 per cent of the US level, and it could expect to continue growing on average at rates no lower than those experienced by other mature economies, around 2.5 per cent— or better, given Japan's high saving rate. Rather, the problem for Japan was a cyclical one, compounded by problems in the financial system, partly associated with adjustments to the new slower growth environment.

We look first at the course of the Japanese economy in terms of its actual and projected output gap. We then consider some of the main elements of the 'shocks' that brought the problem about. Finally, we consider the difficulties faced by policymakers in trying to rectify the situation.

The output gap

Figure 35.1 shows IMF data for the GDP gap for Japan from 1983 to 2000, with the 1998–2000 figures being forecasts. The facts are clear. After a boom in the early 1990s Japan's GDP was below potential from 1993. It stayed below potential right through the rest of the 1990s, and was projected by the IMF to return to potential only in around 2003. A major increase in the GDP gap occurred in the 1997–2000 period, and it was expected to peak at 6 per cent of GDP in 1999, though this projection depended upon assumptions about policy reactions and the external environment that may turn out to have been wrong.

This created a serious economic crisis for a country that had experienced fast growth and high employment levels for the previous four decades. In May 1998 unemployment reached 4.1 per cent, the highest level since the Second World War, and it seemed to be heading higher still. This may not seem like a high unemployment rate by the standards of other countries, but disguised unemployment is thought to be high in Japan, so that its figures are difficult to compare with other countries', and the real level of unemployment was probably much higher.

Where did the crisis come from?

Asset prices The problems of the Japanese economy in the second half of the 1990s were a product of the extreme success of the Japanese economy in the previous four decades. Rapid real growth became the norm, and expectations of continued rapid growth got built into market prices. In 1991 the Japanese stock market index peaked at around 38,000, but in August 1998 it stood at around 15,000—well under half its peak value. This collapse of share prices was mirrored in property prices, which also fell dramatically in the second half of the 1990s.

Assets prices are an important influence on spending decisions. We discussed in Chapter 21 the importance of wealth effects on consumer spending. As wealth rose in the 1980s, Japanese consumers felt very well off, and they increased their spending on both consumer goods and property. However, a collapse of wealth had the reverse effect, causing them to cut their spending and feel increasingly cautious about the future.

Asset prices are also very important in spending decisions of companies and lending decisions by banks. Companies with a high stock market value find it easier to raise more capital, and banks are happy to lend on the basis of high property values or share holdings. Banks in Japan also hold shares in companies directly, so a fall in share values affects the capital of the banks, and thereby their ability to make further loans.

Figure 35.1 The Japanese GDP gap, 1983–2000
Japan had a large inflationary gap in the early 1990s and a large recessionary gap in the late 1990s.
Source: IMF, *World Economic Outlook*, May 1998.

Thus falling assets prices and falling spending and loss of confidence create a process that can spiral downwards for some time. Some elements of this downward spiral are evident in any recession, as discussed in Chapter 27. However, the situation was worse than a normal cyclical recession in Japan in the late 1990s because of the abnormally large falls in asset prices. This experience was labelled by American economist Irving Fisher (1867–1947) as a situation of **debt deflation**.

The process of debt deflation will not go on for ever, but it may take the economy into a very deep recession before it is reversed. At some stage, however, goods and asset prices fall to a level so low that they appear cheap. Consumers start spending again, and firms want to invest. Once confidence returns, the interaction of the multiplier and the accelerator help to run any initial increase in spending into an upturn as the spiral starts in an upward direction. In an open economy like Japan, this process can also be reinforced by swings in the exchange rate.

The exchange rate One further important element of the Japanese situation that we have not so far emphasized is the path of the Japanese real exchange rate. Figure 35.2 shows that the real exchange rate for Japan was on an upward trend from 1950 right up to 1996. This meant that Japanese goods were becoming more and more expensive relative to competitors' goods. This made it increasingly difficult for Japanese producers to compete in world markets, so they increasingly produced overseas and sourced their inputs in other countries.

In effect the high real exchange rate added to the deflationary forces in the domestic economy, as domestic firms switched their investments overseas and net exports were lower than they otherwise would have been.

In Chapter 28 we discussed the concept of purchasing power parity (PPP). There we argued that PPP was likely

Figure 35.2 The Japanese real exchange rate, 1950–1996

The Japanese real exchange rate showed a strong upward trend for four-and-a-half decades up to the mid-1990s.

Note: Based on consumer price indexes, 1951 = 100.

Source: IMF, *World Economic Outlook*, Oct. 1997.

Figure 35.3 The Japanese official interest rate, 1991–1998

The Japanese official discount rate was 0.5 per cent from the end of 1995 up to mid-1998.

Source: IMF, *World Economic Outlook*, Oct. 1997.

to hold approximately in the long run, because in a global economy one country's prices cannot diverge increasingly from prices elsewhere in the world. For a long time it seemed that this prediction did not apply to Japan, as the Japanese real exchange rate appreciated steadily through the 1980s and early 1990s. However, it now seems likely that Japan will not prove to be an exception once recent years are taken into account. Since 1995 the Japanese real and nominal exchange rates have fallen back sharply from their peak. In 1995 the nominal exchange rate of the yen reached a peak against the US dollar of about ¥85 per dollar. However, by August 1998 this had fallen to ¥145 per dollar, though it later recovered somewhat.

Just as the rise in the yen added to the deflationary forces, so the fall in the yen will undoubtedly help stimulate recovery. It will do this by making domestic goods cheaper relative to foreign goods and thereby inducing an upward shift in net exports.

Policy responses

Given the overall scenario of an economy exhibiting a large negative GDP gap, what could the Japanese authorities do to help improve the situation?

The main policy tools at their disposal are the monetary and fiscal policy instruments that we have discussed extensively in our analysis of macroeconomics.

Monetary policy A standard monetary policy intervention involves the authorities changing the interest rate at which they will lend to the money markets. In Japan this is the official discount rate. For an economy in recession, a

monetary policy reaction intended to stimulate the economy would involve lowering the interest rate.

Figure 35.3 shows that the Japanese monetary authorities did indeed lower their interest rate steadily from 1991. This was almost certainly an attempt to moderate the rise in the real exchange rate, rather than to stimulate output directly, as at that time the Japanese economy was above potential GDP. However, by 1995 the economy was running well below potential, so the rate cuts in that year were (at least partly) intended to stimulate output.

The important point to notice is that by the end of 1995 the Japanese official discount rate was as low as one half of one per cent, and it stayed at this level right through into 1998. At this stage the problem became a somewhat unusual one. *When interest rates have already been pushed down as low as they can go, what can the monetary authorities do then in order to stimulate aggregate demand?* The answer is: not much with monetary policy tools.

This problem was encountered during the recession of the early 1930s, and it was extensively discussed in debates associated with the Keynesian revolution. The problem was known as the **liquidity trap.** It arises when interest rates are so low that nothing else can be done to stimulate spending via even lower rates. If investors cannot be encouraged to invest when interest rates are close to zero, it is not clear what else the monetary authorities can do to increase aggregate demand.

Even if the government were simply to print more money and give it to people,[1] in a liquidity trap this does not necessarily increase spending, as people can simply save the money (owing to lack of confidence in the future). Keynes described this powerlessness of monetary policy in

---

[1] In practice the monetary authorities would not usually literally print money and spend it; rather, they would buy long-term government debt with high-powered money. This increases the liquidity of both the public and the banks with possible positive effects on spending.

a liquidity trap as being the same as trying to move an object by 'pushing on a string'.

In the post-war period most economists in the major economies had dismissed the liquidity trap as a phenomenon that was possible in theory but did not arise in practice. Clearly this is a rare occurrence, but it helps to explain the problems of Japan in the late 1990s.

Fiscal policy When monetary policy becomes powerless, fiscal policy is another possibility. Cuts in taxes and increases in spending by the government can be used as measures to create public demand where private demand is lacking.

Figure 35.4 shows the net impact of fiscal policy changes in Japan for each year from 1983 to 1999. In the 1980s fiscal policy was generally designed to reduce aggregate demand, but from 1992–6 fiscal policy was stimulatory. In 1997 fiscal policy was tightened sharply, but by late 1997, when the Asian crisis broke out (see below), it became clear that Japan was heading into a major slowdown. In April 1998 the Japanese government announced a package of fiscal stimuli that included public works spending of ¥7.7 trillion and tax cuts worth ¥4.6 trillion, in addition to some financial support for weak financial institutions. The net effect of the fiscal package was claimed to be a boost to demand by about 2 to 3 per cent of GDP, though some commentators thought that the effect would be less, and the net effect did little more than reverse the tightening of the previous year. This was unlikely to be a large enough boost to eliminate the forecast 6 per cent GDP gap in 1999, especially as the fiscal stance was forecast to tighten again in 1999.

Accordingly, at the time of writing it looks as though Japan will have to rely largely on the automatic stabilizing mechanisms discussed in Chapter 27 to return it to its potential GDP. However, the IMF forecast made in May 1998 predicts that the GDP gap will not be eliminated in Japan until around 2003. This forecast could be wrong if the exchange rate falls much faster than expected, thereby stimulating net exports. There may also be further fiscal stimuli that have not been built into this forecast, but it is hard to see that the monetary authorities can do anything to help stimulate demand.

The Japanese economy exhibited a severe recessionary gap in the late 1990s. Monetary policy actions were constrained by the fact that interest rates could go no lower, and the fiscal authorities felt unable or unwilling to introduce a major fiscal stimulus. Hence Japan seemed likely to rely on the automatic adjustment mechanisms to return it to potential output.

Structural reforms Monetary and fiscal policies are the main macro stabilization tools available, but many observers believe that some structural reforms in the Japanese economy could also be helpful, at least in the medium

Figure 35.4 The impact of fiscal packages in Japan
Fiscal policy in Japan was tightened in 1997 but was projected to boost GDP by 1–2 per cent in 1998.

Source: Financial Times, 3 June 1998, p. 19.

term. There are three main areas in which structural reforms have been suggested. First, the Japanese banking system needed reform because it had too many banks that had too many outstanding bad loans and low-valued assets, which put them in a weak position to finance new investment. This position was compounded by the complicated links between banks and industrial conglomerates that made it hard to assess the performance of banks independently of the corporation to which they were linked. Restructuring of banks would be politically difficult but beneficial to economic performance in the long run.

The second area of proposed structural reform is agriculture. The OECD estimated that in 1997 producer subsidies to agriculture in Japan amounted to about 70 per cent of the value of production. These subsidies included direct subsidies, cheap loans, and guaranteed prices. They benefited about 2 per cent of the population who worked on the land at the expense of the remaining 98 per cent of the population. Consumers would gain substantially from cheaper food prices if subsidies and protection were removed. Increases in food imports would also reduce the current account surplus and lower the exchange rate, thereby giving a stimulus to domestic industry.

The third area in which structural reform could help the Japanese economy is in distribution. Japan has a highly restricted and inefficient system of wholesale and retail distribution. If the authorities were to permit free entry into the distribution sector, this would lower consumer prices and stimulate domestic demand, improving the prospects for a return to more rapid GDP growth.

Of course, structural reforms take time, and they generate losers as well as winners. The net gains that they can bring are often not evident for many years or even decades. However, postponement can do little but add to inefficiencies in an already struggling economy.

Stabilization policy in the euro zone

In January 1999 eleven EU member states embarked upon a monetary experiment. They established a single common currency for all their countries, the euro, with a single common monetary authority, the European Central Bank.[2] We have discussed the monetary operations of the ECB in Chapter 25. Here we consider how monetary and fiscal policies can be used for stabilization of the euro zone economies under the new regime.

Monetary policy

As mentioned in Chapter 25, monetary policy is targeted on achieving price stability in the euro zone as a whole. Price stability is defined as inflation of 2 per cent or less in the HICP for the euro area as a whole, and there is a reference value for the growth rate of euro area M3 of 4.5 per cent. The ECB will aim to tighten monetary policy by raising interest rates when there is judged to be inflationary pressure, and it will aim to relax monetary policy by lowering interest rates when there is deflationary pressure.

In effect the ECB will try to assess whether there is an inflationary gap or a deflationary gap for *the euro zone as a whole*, and it will be responding accordingly with either policy loosening or policy tightening. In this way it will be performing the same exercise as monetary authorities individually (under floating exchange rate regimes) were performing, but now it will be doing it as if the euro zone were one country. Thus monetary policy will be an important tool for controlling aggregate demand across the whole euro zone, but it will be powerless to affect the relative aggregate demand of any one member state, just as the UK Monetary Policy Committee sets interest rates for the whole of the United Kingdom and is unable to exert any differential influence over monetary conditions in Yorkshire or Scotland.

This situation may be fine if the countries of the euro zone are hit by common shocks and move more or less together. However, monetary policy will be powerless to help correct the imbalance if one member country is in recession while other member countries are booming. Monetary policy in the euro zone will have to be aimed at the behaviour of euro zone aggregates and ignore individual country differences.

This may not be as bad as it seems, because it may be better than the situation that ruled under ERM, where monetary policy was in effect set by Germany with German conditions in mind. However, it does mean that some other method will be needed to cope with shocks to one country that do not affect others. Here one might think that fiscal policy could be used to fill the gap; however,

severe restrictions have been placed on fiscal policy discretion as well.

Fiscal policy: the Stability and Growth Pact

The Maastricht Treaty of 1992 required potential members of the euro zone to get their budget deficits below 3 per cent of GDP in order to qualify for membership. Subsequently an agreement was reached, known as the Stability and Growth Pact, that extended the commitment to keep deficits below 3 per cent indefinitely.

Countries will be allowed to breach the 3 per cent limit 'in exceptional and temporary circumstances'. A government deficit greater than 3 per cent of GDP will be considered exceptional and temporary if it results from an unusual event outside the control of the member state in question or from a severe economic downturn, provided also that once the temporary cause has passed, EU Commission projections for the following year forecast the deficit to be falling back to 3 per cent or less. A decline in GDP of 2 per cent or more in one year would as a rule be regarded as a severe downturn.

Countries that are identified as having excessive deficits are potentially subject to financial penalties, though they have a further year after being warned in which to remove the excess deficit. Sanctions would initially take the form of non-remunerated deposits, amounting to between 0.2 per cent and 0.5 per cent of GDP, depending on the size of the deficit. This deposit would be returned if the excessive deficit were corrected within two years; otherwise it would be converted into a fine.

IMF staff have calculated that an average EU country that had a fiscal balance when its GDP was at its potential level would tend to reach a 3 per cent deficit with a GDP gap of around 5 per cent of GDP. (Recall that taxes fall as GDP falls and some government expenditures, like unemployment benefit, rise.) This means that automatic stabilizers could accommodate a fluctuation of up to 5 per cent of GDP around trend while meeting the limits of the Stability and Growth Pact, and this is well within the normal range of business cycle fluctuations.

Thus so long as member states have a fiscal balance when the economy is at potential GDP—a situation referred to as one of *structural balance*—then budget deficits will be able to rise during recessions and fall during booms without breaching the 3 per cent limit. However, problems

---

[2] Strictly it is the European System of Central Banks (ESCB), which is made up of the central banks of each euro zone member plus the ECB; however, monetary policy is made by the ECB.

will be caused if member states change their fiscal stance, and it remains to be seen whether any member will really end up being fined or whether some political fudge will be resorted to. It would be ironic if the outcome were to increase political tensions when the aim of the single currency is to enhance the integration of EU member states.

It is tempting to conclude that the Stability and Growth Pact will leave member states with very severe restrictions on their fiscal freedom. However, the restrictions under the new regime may actually be less severe than in the recent past, when governments have been trying to eliminate high budget deficits in order to meet the Maastricht criteria. As an IMF assessment put it,

In any event, concerns about the potentially constraining effects on countries' abilities to pursue countercyclical fiscal policies need to be put into the perspective of the constraints imposed by large deficits in most EU countries over much of the past twenty-five years. From this viewpoint, the increased discipline involved in adhering to the pact may well permit a greater stabilizing role for fiscal policy than has been possible in most of these countries in many years. At the same time, the achievement of a high degree of price stability, together with the focus of the European System of Central banks on conditions throughout the euro area (in contrast to the dominant influence of German economic conditions on monetary policy in countries participating in the exchange rate mechanism (ERM)), should allow monetary policy to play a greater stabilizing role than in the past for the euro area as a whole.[3]

The single currency in Europe poses new challenges for monetary and fiscal policies. Monetary policy is 'one-size-fits-all', and fiscal policy is restrained by the Stability and Growth Pact. It remains to be seen whether the outcome will be better or worse than under the previous regime.

One reason why policy may be better in future than it has been in the past is that policymakers have often made mistakes. It would be an error to compare regimes on the assumption that policy changes in the past have always been stabilizing. In practice mistimed policy interventions have often made the business cycle worse. Hence the merging of monetary policy under the aegis of one authority and the restraints on budget deficits may improve the policy outcome *simply by making it harder for governments to get it wrong.* As US Nobel laureate Robert Solow once said, 'If you don't know what you're doing, don't do much of it!'

However, it is hard to believe that Europe will proceed for very long without some form of asymmetric shocks, that is, shocks that affect some countries more than others, or even affect countries in opposite ways. In a world of rapid technological change, for example, it is likely that there will be some 'technology shocks' that affect the more technologically advanced economies differently from the less advanced. Common responses will not occur if some countries are much more rigid in cost structures, prices, factor mobility, and industrial organization. In these cases the inability to adjust through exchange rate changes could cause the persistence of severe pockets of unemployment and stagnant growth—unfortunately 'pockets' could refer to whole countries.

[3] IMF, *World Economic Outlook*, Oct. 1997, p. 59.

The UK minimum wage

The Labour government elected to office in the United Kingdom in May 1997 was committed to the introduction of a statutory minimum wage. In June 1998 it was announced that there would be a minimum wage of £3.60 per hour for all workers over 22 years of age from April 1999. There was also to be a youth rate of £3.20 per hour for workers aged between 18 and 21.

In Chapter 15 we discussed the microeconomic effects of the minimum wage. Here we wish to use our macro model to see what impact it might have on the economy as a whole so that we can discuss macro policy implications. At £3.60 the Low Pay Commission estimated that 2 million workers would be affected and the national wage bill would rise by around 0.6 per cent, though some sectors would see rises of up to 3 per cent. These figures measure only the extra cost of those workers previously paid below the minimum wage. There may be further effects if workers on higher wages bargain for increases to preserve pay differentials.

These effects may be quite small in the aggregate. However, it is a useful exercise to see how such a shock to the supply side of the economy can be analysed using the framework of our macro model. So how do we analyse the impact of a minimum wage in a macroeconomic context?

Impact of higher wages

The increase in wages for some workers is an increase in input costs for firms, and this is represented in our macro model by a shift upward and to the left of the short-run aggregate supply curve. Slightly more open to debate is the issue of whether there will be an impact on the level of potential output, and thus on the position of the *LRAS* curve. Also, it might be argued that since some low-paid workers will see pay rises of around 25 per cent, this will also have an impact on aggregate demand as this higher pay leads to more consumer spending. We discuss each of these in turn.

Impact on potential GDP There is little doubt that an increase in wages will shift the *SRAS* curve upwards, but it is not so obvious whether there will be an effect on the position of the *LRAS* curve, that is, on potential output. If labour markets were previously competitive and labour could be thought of as a homogeneous and unchanging commodity, then a higher minimum wage would lower potential GDP, so long as we were prepared to assert that this would be a permanently higher real wage. This is because, in competitive markets, a higher real wage leads to lower employment, and lower employment in turn is associated with a lower potential GDP. Thus there would be a once-and-for-all drop in potential GDP, though the growth rate from then on may return to the same long-run level.

However, if labour markets were imperfect to start with (as discussed in Chapter 15), so that there was monopsony in the demand for labour, a minimum wage *could* in theory lead to increased employment, and in some cases little or no reduction in equilibrium output.

With or without competitive labour markets, a minimum wage lowers firms' profits and therefore lowers the return on capital. This will provide a disincentive to capital formation (however small), which may have a negative effect on trend growth. This will not lower potential GDP immediately, but it may lower its growth rate thereafter.

One possible flaw in this analysis is that it treats labour as a homogeneous commodity. But workers can acquire skills and they can work harder in the hours available if they feel they have the right incentives. It is *possible* that a higher minimum wage will both improve the motive to work hard and increase the incentives to acquire skills. The latter will take some time to change the quality of the workforce, but the former could have an impact quite quickly. Of course, the incentive to acquire skills could go either way. Those who now get the higher wage without doing anything different have *less* incentive to acquire skills, but those who are not sure if they can keep their job, or even get a job at all, at the higher wage do have an incentive to acquire skills in order to remain in their current job or get a new one.

These possibilities make the longer-term impact of the minimum wage harder to assess. However, we incorporate them into our analysis by assuming that the potential level of GDP is the same after the introduction of the minimum wage as before. On balance it is more likely to be slightly lower in the short term; but if there is any truth in the incentive and skills-acquisition argument in the longer term, the beneficial effect could eventually be big enough to offset the initial negative effect.

Effects on aggregate demand The other question we need to think about is whether the minimum wage will increase aggregate demand. It could be argued that higher wages will lead to more consumer spending in the economy, so that we should see a shift to the right of the *AD* curve. This may indeed happen, but it is more likely that there will be virtually no effect, or even a negative effect. The reason is that while some workers may have higher earnings, others may lose their jobs entirely. Also firms' profits will fall, so there may be a negative effect on dividend incomes as well as lower investment by firms. The balance of these conflicting effects is hard to judge, but our best guess is that in the absence of any policy response by monetary or fiscal authorities the *AD* curve will initially stay roughly where it was to start with.

Supply shock We show a diagrammatic analysis of the likely impact effect of the minimum wage in Figure 35.5. This shows the economy starting in an initial equilibrium

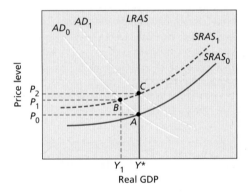

Figure 35.5 The macroeconomic effects of the minimum wage

The effects of the minimum wage depend upon whether the monetary authorities accommodate the supply shock. The initial situation is at point *A*, with price level P_0 and output at its potential level Y^*. The introduction of the minimum wage shifts the *SRAS* curve from $SRAS_0$ to $SRAS_1$. With a given *AD* curve the economy moves to point *B* with price level P_1 and output Y_1. If the monetary authorities adjust their interest rate policy so as to hold the money stock constant, the economy will stay at *B* until the automatic adjustment mechanism in the face of a recessionary gap puts downward pressure on wages and prices and the economy returns to point *A*. However, if the monetary authorities react to the fall in output by following interest rate policies that generate an increase in the money stock, the *AD* curve will shift from AD_0 to AD_1, and the economy will move to point *C*, where potential GDP has been restored but at a higher price level P_2.

situation with output at its potential level. This is not just a convenient analytical assumption—it is also the case that the IMF forecast (in 1998) that the UK economy would be more or less exactly at its potential level of output in 1999 when the new minimum wage was introduced.

According to the above discussion, the main effect of introducing the minimum wage in a macro context can be captured by a shift of the *SRAS* curve up to the left. With a given *AD* curve (that is, a given money stock and given exogenous expenditures) GDP will fall and the price level will rise. This is the scenario of *stagflation* that we discussed in the context of negative supply shocks in Chapter 27. The impact effect is thus to increase prices, as firms pass on some of their higher wage costs in higher goods prices, at the same time as output falls, as firms cut back employment and reduce output because of the higher real wage they face.

If the *AD* curve stays where it is, the automatic adjustment mechanism we discussed in Chapter 27 will eventually come into action as the recessionary gap puts downward pressure on wages in general (not just those of the low paid). Thus over time the *SRAS* curve will shift back down to the right and the economy will return to potential GDP. What happens to the price level in equilibrium depends on whether potential GDP is higher, lower, or the same as before. As we have discussed, it could be lower, but we are assuming that it is the same, so the price level will return to its original position.

Notice that the operation of this automatic adjustment mechanism will involve falls in real wages for the average worker but not for those on the minimum wage. This potential contraction of differentials between the lowest paid and the more skilled could have a disincentive effect on skill acquisition for those higher up the earnings ladder, though the impact is likely to be small in a world where skills are changing rapidly anyway.

Whether or not the automatic adjustment mechanism will have to be relied upon depends on the reaction of policymakers.

Policy reaction

As we discussed in Chapter 30, the inflationary impact of supply shocks depends to some extent on how policy-makers react. We analysed in that chapter how the outcome depends on whether or not the monetary authorities accommodate the supply shock. The same analysis applies here.

Given that the Bank of England sets interest rates and not the money stock, a policy in which the interest rate remained constant would accommodate the shock to some degree, whereas a non-accommodatory monetary policy would require some rise in interest rates. This is because with a constant money stock the interest rate would tend to rise (because with a higher price level the real money supply has fallen). Thus if the monetary authorities raise interest rates (by the appropriate amount), the money stock will remain constant and so the *AD* curve will remain at its initial position. However, if the monetary authorities resist a rise in interest rates and thereby permit the money stock to rise, the *AD* curve will shift to the right. The GDP gap will be closed faster, but the economy will move to a higher price level, rather than returning to its initial position.

What the monetary authorities will actually do in response to the imposition of a minimum wage will presumably depend upon how large the impact on prices is expected to be and whether this threatens to any significant degree the ability of the Monetary Policy Committee to keep inflation close to the inflation target that it has been given by the government.

Of course, the minimum wage will not be the only shock that policymakers have to react to, and, indeed, it may be swamped by other events. However, readers will be able to see what weight was given to this particular shock and how the Monetary Policy Committee chose to react to it by reading various issues of the Bank of England's quarterly *Inflation Report*, which sets out the thinking behind monetary policy in the United Kingdom.

The Asian crisis

In the summer of 1997 a major financial crisis broke out affecting several countries in Southeast Asia. This crisis was largely unforeseen, as many of the countries involved appeared to have rapidly growing economies and governments with sound fiscal positions. However, crisis there was, and at the time of writing (late 1998) the full impact had yet to unfold.

We first examine the nature of financial crises. We then look at the events before drawing some conclusions about the problems revealed.

Financial crises

There are four different types of economic or financial crisis, and any specific crisis situation may have elements of one, some, or all of these. We consider each in turn.

Currency crisis A currency crisis shows up when there is a speculative attack on the exchange rate of a country's currency, resulting in a devaluation of a pegged currency or sharp depreciation of a floating currency (see Chapter 28 for an analysis of currency pegging). Usually a currency crisis involves the domestic monetary authorities losing large amounts of their international reserves and/or raising interest rates very sharply in order to try to discourage capital outflows.

Banking crisis A banking crisis may occur because depositors lose confidence in the solvency of banks and attempt to withdraw their deposits, thereby causing a run on the banks. Alternatively it may occur because banks make so many bad loans and investments that they become insolvent without any depositors' panic. In either case they are forced to close or seek a bailout in the form of financial support from the government. Failure of one small bank might not produce a crisis, but failure of a bank that has a large share of deposits would, as would failure of a number of banks at the same time.

Systemic financial crisis The third type of financial crisis involves severe disruption in domestic financial markets that hampers the working of the real economy. Such a crisis would be harmful to real activity because it would disrupt the payments system and it would lead to a breakdown of all those markets that channel funds from savers to borrowers. Banking and currency crises may be components of a systemic financial crisis, but this is something bigger than either of these two, involving equity and bond markets as well as money market institutions.

Foreign debt crisis The final type of crisis arises when one or more countries find that they are unable to keep up the interest payments on their foreign debt. This situation may trigger loss of confidence in the economy or the government, and so could bring about a currency or banking crisis. It also frequently involves application to the IMF for financial assistance (which could happen in response to any of the other types of crisis, especially a currency crisis). The IMF in turn typically imposes some *conditionality*, or special terms, for the loan, which often involves monetary and fiscal policy tightening. There will also usually be some negotiation between debtors and creditors in order to reschedule the debt, that is, turn unpaid interest into a further loan. As the IMF reports,

Crises of all types have often had common origins: the build-up of unsustainable economic imbalances and misalignments in asset prices or exchange rates, often in a context of financial sector distortions and structural rigidities. A crisis may be triggered by a sudden loss of confidence in the currency or banking system, prompted by such developments as a sudden correction in asset prices, or by disruption to credit or external financing flows that expose underlying economic and financial weaknesses. Crises may involve sharp declines in assets, and failures of financial institutions and non-financial corporations. Of course, not all corrections of imbalances involve a crisis. Whether they do or not depends, apart from the magnitude of the imbalances themselves, on the credibility of policies to correct the imbalances and achieve a 'soft landing' and on the robustness of the country's financial system. These factors together determine the economy's vulnerability to crises. Crises may then be considered to be the consequence of financial or economic disturbances when economies suffer from a high degree of vulnerability.[4]

There have been many financial crises in recent history. There was a currency crisis in Europe in September 1992 when the United Kingdom and Italy were forced to leave the ERM, and there was another in the summer of 1993 when the remaining ERM members adopted wide fluctuation bands in order to accommodate exchange rate changes without destroying the principles of the exchange rate mechanism.

The most famous banking crisis of all time happened in the United States in the early 1930s when over 10,000 banks went bust. More recent examples include a crisis in Sweden in 1993, the secondary banking crisis in Britain in 1974, and the collapse of many savings and loans institutions (equivalent to UK building societies) in the United States in the 1980s.

Systemic financial crises have, fortunately, been less frequent, but they have arisen when there has been political breakdown, often associated with war or revolution. A recent example occurred in Serbia in 1993 where the breakdown of the financial system was accompanied by hyperinflation (see Box 30.1 on page 517).

Foreign debt crises have been all too frequent in the last two decades. A major crisis affecting many countries in Latin America, such as Mexico, Brazil, and Argentina, broke out in 1982. So severe was this crisis that it threatened the survival of many major US and UK banks which had lent large amounts of money to these countries. Mexico had a further severe debt crisis in 1994.

Events in Southeast Asia 1997–1998

The Asian crisis that broke out in the summer of 1997 had elements of a currency crisis, a banking crisis, and a foreign debt crisis, though the currency and banking crises were the dominant elements. The worst effects of the crisis were felt by five countries: Korea, Thailand, Malaysia, the Philippines, and Indonesia. Indonesia was affected worst of all, as the economic effects led to political turbulence which brought down President Suharto in May 1998, and at the time of writing it is not yet clear if the new government can restore confidence. While the situation was slightly different in each country, we concentrate on the common factors.

[4] IMF, *World Economic Outlook*, May 1998, p. 75.

The currency crisis The background to the crisis in this region, as with Japan, was a sustained period of high real growth. Collectively these economies, together with some others such as Singapore, Taiwan, and Hong Kong, were called the 'Asian Tigers', and through the early 1990s they were the success story of the world economy. In the 1980s their average real growth rate was 7.7 per cent, and in the 1990s it was still 6.4 per cent even including projections for a slowdown to 1.8 per cent in 1998 and a recovery to 4.5 per cent in 1999 (though at the time of writing these projections were being revised downwards).

Because this region was growing quickly at a time when many of the industrial countries were stagnating, or growing only slowly, it should not be surprising that financial capital was attracted to invest in these so-called emerging markets. Most of the countries involved pegged their exchange rates to the dollar, and the substantial inflows of capital during the first half of the 1990s meant that the monetary authorities were able to build up healthy reserves of foreign exchange. This increased both the confidence of foreign investors and the belief of domestic borrowers that they did not face any exchange rate risk on dollar debts.

Thailand was the first country to feel the buildup of a currency crisis. There had already been concerns in 1996 about the sustainability of the dollar peg, and there was renewed pressure on the currency in early 1997. Also there had been falls in equity prices from 1996 and a collapse of property prices. This was made worse by a growing current account deficit on the balance of payments and concerns that the short-term external debt was becoming excessive.

Capital flowed out of Thailand in increasing volume, and on 2 July 1997 the Thai authorities abandoned the exchange rate peg to the dollar. The value of the baht (the Thai currency) fell initially by 10 per cent but then continued to fall as concerns built up about the political situation and the delay by policymakers in taking corrective action. The stability of major financial institutions came into question as elements of a banking crisis started to take over.

The currency crisis in Thailand and the resulting collapse in the exchange rate turned the focus onto neighbouring countries. Speculative pressure forced the Philippines, Malaysia, and Indonesia to follow Thailand in floating their currencies, and all floated downwards by substantial amounts, as shown in Figure 35.6(i) for Korea, Thailand, and Indonesia. Last of the five most affected countries to be hit by a currency crisis was Korea, but its exchange rate fall, when it came, was as severe as any but Indonesia's. At the worst point the value of these five currencies had fallen by amounts ranging from around 40 per cent (for Malaysia and the Philippines) to over 80 per cent (for Indonesia).

Currency devaluations of such large size have one good effect—they lower domestic output prices relative to foreign goods and so boost net exports. However, they have several bad effects that tend to dominate in the short run. First, prices of imported materials rise, and this boosts domestic inflation—this effect alone led to riots in Indonesia as petrol and food prices rose very sharply. Second, the domestic value of foreign-currency debts rises sharply, putting the viability of companies and financial institutions at risk. Third, domestic authorities tend to

(i) **Dollar exchange rates of Korea, Thailand, Indonesia and Japan, July 1997–July 1998**

(ii) **Equity prices in Korea, Thailand, Malaysia, and Indonesia, Jan. 1997–June 1998**

Figure 35.6 Dollar exchange rates and equity prices during the Asian crisis

The exchange rate of Thailand was the first to fall, in July 1997. The Korean collapse started in October 1997. Equity prices also fell in late 1997, recovered temporarily in early 1998, but fell again in April–May 1998.

Sources: part (i): *Financial Times*, 1 July 1998, p. 23; part (ii): Datastream.

raise interest rates and taxes, both to defend the currency and to avoid further capital flight. This puts severe financial pressure on all those who have borrowed money at floating interest rates as repayments rise sharply. Fourth, the financial squeeze involved in all of this forces asset sales and lowers profits, which in turn leads to a collapse of equity and property prices (see Figure 35.6(ii) for equity prices). Domestic economic activity slows sharply as both consumer spending and investment spending are severely curtailed.

The banking crisis The currency crisis soon also developed into a banking crisis, as a result of which many banks were forced to close or to be restructured. There were three main components to the banking crisis in Asia in 1997–8.

First, the countries involved had experienced many years of high growth. It is easy to make good loans in such periods because profits are generally rising, as are equity prices and property prices. Loan defaults are a very small percentage of loans made, and so bankers tend to get overconfident that loans made will be repaid in due course. This is especially true of young bankers who have never known anything other than boom conditions. However, as time goes by, they start to make loans that are increasingly risky. Indeed, even safe loans in good times will turn out to be bad loans once a major downturn occurs. This tends to be reinforced by asset price bubbles in which speculators borrow money to buy assets, which in turn drives asset prices up further and feeds even more speculative buying. Widespread bankruptcies result when the asset price bubble bursts.

The second element behind the banking crisis was the false assumption by many banks that the currency would remain pegged to the US dollar. This encouraged many banks to borrow in dollars in order to make domestic currency loans. As US dollar interest rates were low relative to domestic interest rates, for a while this was a highly profitable strategy. However, once the exchange rate peg was broken, the true level of foreign exchange rate risk was revealed, making many banks insolvent in the process.

Finally, the rapid growth in these countries had disguised the fact that many banks were badly run and that the system of banking regulation was inadequate. The 1982 debt crisis had already led to the introduction of a new global bank regulatory regime from 1992. However, the crisis revealed inadequate application of these new prudential regulations in some of the countries of Southeast Asia. This served to make worse a crisis that would have brought down some banking institutions even under an adequate regulatory regime.

The currency and banking crises in Asia caused major disruption to the economies involved, imposing bankruptcy and financial hardship on millions of people.

As in the case of Japan, discussed above, there were also other structural problems in the economies involved. Many of these resulted from government intervention that led to inefficiencies and lack of international competitiveness in various sectors. However, the detail is different in each country, and a detailed examination of these issues is beyond our scope.

Economics of the global village

We conclude our study of macroeconomics by returning our attention to the main industrial countries and pointing out that they are all subject to some common trends. This is indicative of an increasing interdependence both through the increased integration of economies and through the commonality of ideas. The three phenomena to which we draw particular attention are the apparent conquest of inflation, the acceptance of fiscal consolidation as a policy goal, and the submergence of country-specific cycles under the world business cycle.

The death of inflation?

Figure 35.7 shows the path of inflation in many of the developed countries of the world. Inflation was generally low in the 1950s and 1960s, but it rose almost everywhere in the 1970s. By the mid-1990s, however, with remarkable

uniformity, inflation had fallen to very low levels, typically in the range of 1–3 per cent. The obvious question to ask is 'Has inflation gone for good, or could it return sometime soon?'

The answer to this important question is that inflation certainly *could* return, but that it is to be hoped that the makers of monetary policy have learned lessons from the mistakes of the 1970s so that they will be able to keep inflation under control in future. Indeed, in many countries central banks have been given an explicit target of price stability or low inflation and have been given a degree of independence from elected politicians. The new institutional structures in the United Kingdom and the euro zone were set out in Chapter 25.

The important lesson that was learned by most countries in the 1970s and 1980s is that higher inflation does not generate higher output growth. On the contrary, it

Figure 35.7 Inflation in twelve countries, 1960–1997
Inflation rose in all countries in the 1970s but had fallen universally by the mid-1990s.

Source: IMF, *World Economic Outlook*, May 1998.

became clear that once inflation is established in an economy, it is extremely costly in terms of lost output to get rid of it. Most agree that long-term economic growth is a desirable goal, and it is now widely accepted that an environment of low and stable inflation is most conducive to growth.

This seems almost a cliché today, but it would not have been widely accepted a few years ago. This is an illustration of how the study of economics advances our understanding of the world in which we live, and ultimately influences the policies of even non-economists. It is worth spelling out how perceptions of the nature of the problem have evolved since the Second World War.

Early Keynesian macroeconomics focused almost exclusively on the problem of unemployment. This was because the high unemployment of the early 1930s was fresh in everyone's thoughts. The cure for unemployment was for the monetary and fiscal authorities to maintain a high level of aggregate demand. However, even in the early post-war years some economists warned of the possibility of endemic cost-push inflation as a result of running the economy at a high level of demand. They worried that strong labour unions would force up wages even in the absence of a significant inflationary gap; that oligopolistic industries would pass these wage increases on as increased prices; and that the government's commitment to full employment would lead the monetary authorities to accommodate supply-side inflation.

As a solution to this problem, some recommended *incomes policies* that involved government control of wage increases, and in some cases price increases. Attempts at incomes policies always failed in their goal of controlling inflation, though they were tried repeatedly in several countries, including the United Kingdom in the 1960s and 1970s. But the very high inflation rates of the 1970s convinced many people that this approach was wrong.

By the early 1980s several things started to change. In the United Kingdom Prime Minister Margaret Thatcher committed herself to controlling inflation via strict monetary and fiscal policies. She also made a direct attack on the power of trade unions—most notably by refusing to give in to the coalminers in 1984—and she sold off the major state-owned industries so that government became a less significant employer. More generally, technological change led to fewer oligopolies and produced more small firms in highly competitive industries. Also governments around the world came to worry more and more about inflation, and abandoned their commitment to full employment at any price.

The inflation of the late 1970s to early 1980s was broken at substantial cost in terms of unemployment. In retrospect this high unemployment can be seen as the cost of gaining a new reputation for being willing to impose major sacrifices to eliminate inflation. All of these things combined to produce a more flexible private sector, and a public sector more concerned about stable prices and fiscal rectitude than unemployment. Ironically, this new approach of low inflation and fiscal conservatism may produce better prospects for employment and real growth than the old policy of full employment at any price.

Fiscal consolidation

The control of inflation can be thought of as the product of a greater understanding of what causes inflation and how to control it. Inflation is a fall in the value of money, so low inflation is inevitably the product of monetary policy. Fiscal policy is the other major instrument for controlling aggregate demand discussed extensively from Chapter 22 onwards. **Fiscal consolidation** refers to the process of governments reducing their budget deficits, and in many cases setting rules to limit future deficits.

Attitudes to fiscal policy have changed in the last decade

or so, just as radically as have attitudes to monetary policy. In the 1970s many governments ran substantial fiscal deficits and some built up substantial levels of debt. Again it was discovered that these fiscal deficits were not good for the healthy growth of the economy. High government borrowing crowds out private investment, and high debt interest payments restrict the ability of the government to spend on education, health, and infrastructure investments. Government subsidies to inefficient industries do not make them efficient; rather, they allocate resources to areas where their return is low.

In Europe many governments were forced by the Maastricht Treaty to change their attitude to deficits and debt. (Recall that this treaty placed an upper limit on deficit size of 3 per cent of GDP for any country wishing to join the single currency system.) Figure 35.8 shows how deficits have shrunk in relation to GDP in the EU as a whole. The Stability and Growth Pact seems likely to keep up pressure on all EU members to preserve a fiscal position close to structural balance for the indefinite future.

However, Europe is not the only area of the world in which fiscal consolidation is the order of the day. The United States was heading for a budget surplus in 1999 after two decades of severe fiscal deficits. Canada had a fiscal crisis in the early 1990s as its debt mushroomed. Fiscal tightening was instituted, and a large budget surplus was achieved in 1998. New Zealand offers a similar story, and a budget that is balanced on average over the cycle became the goal.

The impact of fiscal consolidation around the world is yet to be fully felt, but it could be beneficial to growth. In the short term fiscal cutbacks involve a fall in aggregate demand. The high unemployment in parts of the EU is evidence of this short-run cost. However, as government borrowing falls and tax burdens fall, there is a longer-term benefit. Governments borrow less and hence more of the world's savings is left to finance private investment expenditure. Investment gets crowded in rather than crowded out, and real interest rates fall.

Whether these beneficial effects will follow is speculation, though speculation based upon an economic model. However, what is not speculation is that semi-permanent structural fiscal deficits are a thing of the past. It is hard to believe that this big structural change will not have major implications for the world economy. However, only time will tell if higher growth is one of them.

A global business cycle?

Throughout this book we have repeatedly mentioned the important trend towards globalization. This means that goods markets and financial markets around the world are increasingly integrated. One implication of this trend is that the business cycle around the world has become an increasingly shared phenomenon. Throughout our discussion of macroeconomics we have talked as if a single country is the relevant entity for analysis. In reality the world economy may be sufficiently integrated that few countries can influence this global cycle by their own actions.

Figure 35.9 shows the growth rates of real GDP for three

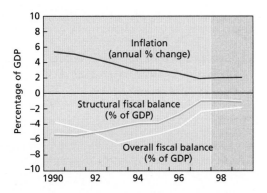

Figure 35.8 Average inflation and general government balance in the EU, 1990–1999

Since the signing of the Maastricht Treaty considerable progress has been made by the countries of the European Union in reducing inflation and fiscal imbalances. Actual fiscal deficits averaged about 2 per cent of GDP in 1997, down from around 7 per cent in 1993. The structural fiscal balance shows what the deficit would be if the economy were at potential GDP. This was about 1 per cent of GDP in 1997 and was projected to stay at this level for 1998 and 1999. The shaded area indicates IMF staff projections.

Source: IMF, *World Economic Outlook*, Oct. 1997.

Figure 35.9 The growth rate of real GDP, 1970–1998

Growth rates in many countries follow similar cycles. Most major countries had a recession in 1974–5, 1980–2, and 1990–2. The figure shows growth rates of real GDP for France, Canada, the UK, and the average of the seven largest industrial economies (G7).

Source: Datastream.

countries plus the average for the seven largest industrial countries. It is clear from the figure that there is a common pattern to the cycle. There was a general recession in 1974–5, 1980–2, and 1990–2. This is not just coincidence. All economies were affected by the oil price rises of 1973 and 1979, and all were affected by the slowdown in world demand in the early 1990s. It should not be surprising that economies substantially open to trade should be affected by supply shocks and demand shocks originating in the world economy.

The surprising feature is that most of the economies involved have looked for domestic explanations and policy remedies for their own cycle. The truth could be that if all these countries have imported their cycles from the world economy, there is not much any one acting alone can do to stop world influences dominating in future. If this is true, there may be very little that domestic monetary and fiscal policies can do to stabilize specific economies. Rather, only policies at the supranational level, or co-ordinated policies among a group of countries acting together, could be expected to carry sufficient weight to influence the world cycle.

Indeed, one interpretation of the incentives for the creation of the European Central Bank and the common monetary policy for eleven European countries is that acting alone they were at the mercy of world market forces, but acting together they may have some influence over their economic environment.

Conclusion

Macroeconomics as a subject is at the heart of many of the most interesting and important issues facing the world economy today. The analysis we have set out above is relevant to all economies; indeed the only truly self-sufficient macroeconomy is the world economy itself. Each nation-state within the world economy has some things that it can influence for itself, but it has many others, including the markets for its imports and exports, and for financial capital, that are world markets. Hence we cannot understand the macroeconomics of any single country by studying events in that country alone. But we can use the tools of macroeconomics that we have developed above to understand both the behaviour of the economy in which we live and the behaviour of the other economies that affect us.

Summary

- Macroeconomics can be applied to economies throughout the world, and to the world economy itself.

Japan in the late 1990s

- The Japanese economy suffered because its high growth rate and appreciating real exchange rate were unsustainable.

- At the end of the 1990s there was a major recession, and the monetary authorities were unable to lower interest rates because they were already close to zero.

- The fiscal authorities were reluctant to incur too great a deficit, and the politicians were slow to address structural problems in the economy.

Stabilization policy in the euro zone

- The creation of a single currency means that monetary policy will have to be targeted on the behaviour of the euro zone in general and so cannot influence demand conditions in any one country.

- Fiscal policy is constrained by the Stability and Growth Pact, which punishes member states for excessive deficits.

The UK minimum wage

- The introduction of the minimum wage is a supply shock to the UK economy. This shifts the *SRAS* curve to the left. Its effect depends on whether or not it is accommodated by the monetary authorities.

The Asian crisis

- Financial crises can be of four types: a currency crisis, a banking crisis, a foreign debt crisis, or a systemic financial crisis.

- The 1997–8 crisis in Asia was both a banking crisis and a currency crisis, with some elements of a foreign debt crisis.

Economics of the global village

- Inflation has been brought under control in most countries around the world.

- Many governments have chosen to reduce, or even eliminate, their budget deficits.

- Most economies are greatly affected by the global business cycle, and there is very little that any one country can do to influence it.

Topics for review

- The liquidity trap
- Monetary policy in the euro zone
- The Stability and Growth Pact
- Supply shocks
- The minimum wage
- Financial crises
- Death of inflation
- Fiscal consolidation
- Global business cycles

Questions for discussion

1 Collect the most recent information available on the Japanese economy from sources such as the IMF's *World Economic Outlook* and *The Economist* and assess how the Japanese economy has evolved since mid-1998 (when this book was written). Has Japan performed better or worse than the IMF projections reported in Figure 35.1? If better, to what is this improvement attributable—policy changes, changes in the world economy, or internal adjustment within Japan? If worse, what else went wrong?

2 Outline the policy targets that have been established by the European Central Bank. Does the ECB have an inflation or a money supply target? Assess the extent to which the ECB has been successful in hitting this target.

3 Did the implementation of the UK minimum wage in 1999 seem to have any significant effect on employment, wages, and inflation? If there was any effect, how did policymakers react? (*Hint*: You can find out what the UK Monetary Policy Committee said about the impact of the minimum wage from various issues of the Bank of England's *Inflation Report* in 1998 and 1999.)

4 Assess the extent to which the Asian crisis of 1997–8 is still affecting the economies of Thailand, Korea, Indonesia, and Malaysia. Was this just a temporary setback, or did it change the growth prospects of these countries for many years?

5 Is the world inflation environment still as benign as it was in 1998? Examine data for inflation in the major industrial countries. What is happening to commodity prices? Would it still be true to say that inflation is dead? If so, assess whether you expect this situation to continue.

6 Is there a global business cycle, or are major countries at different stages of the cycle? Collect data on the growth rates of GDP in the USA, Germany, Canada, and France. Do these countries have similar cycles? Explain what you have found.

Glossary

absolute advantage The advantage that one region is said to have over another in the production of some commodity when an equal quantity of resources can produce more of that commodity in the first region than in the second. Compare *comparative advantage.*

absolute price The price of a good or a service expressed in monetary units. Also called a money price.

accelerator theory of investment The theory that the level of investment depends on the rate of change of output.

accommodation Said to occur when the monetary authorities increase the money supply in response to a negative *aggregate supply shock.* Accommodation has the effect of offsetting the downward impact of the shock on real GDP at the cost of a permanently higher price level.

actual GDP The level of GDP actually produced over a given period.

AD curve See *aggregate demand curve.*

ad valorem tax A tax levied as a percentage of the value of some transaction.

adaptive expectations The expectation of the future value of a variable formed on the basis of an adjustment which is some proportion of the error in expectations made last period. The error is the difference between what was expected last period and what actually happened.

administered price A price that is set by the decisions of individual firms rather than by impersonal market forces.

adverse selection The tendency for people most at risk to insure, while people least at risk do not, so that the insurers get an unrepresentative sample of clients within any one fee category.

agents All decision-makers, including consumers, workers, firms, and government bodies.

aggregate demand (AD) The total desired purchases of all the nation's buyers of final output.

aggregate demand curve A curve that plots all combinations of the price level and national income that yield equilibrium in the goods and the asset markets—i.e. that yield *IS–LM* equilibrium.

aggregate demand shock A shift in the *aggregate demand curve* resulting from an autonomous change in exogenous expenditures or the money supply (or equivalently, a policy-induced change in interest rates).

aggregate (desired) expenditure (AE) The total volume of purchases of currently produced goods and services that all spending units in the economy wish to make.

aggregate production function The technical relation which expresses the maximum national output that can be produced with each possible combination of capital, labour, and other resource inputs. See also *production function.*

aggregate supply (AS) The total desired output of all the nation's producers.

aggregate supply curve A curve relating the economy's producers' total desired output, Y, to the price level, P.

aggregate supply shock A shift in the *aggregate supply curve* resulting from an exogenous change in input prices or from technical change (exogenous or endogenous). One example is the oil price shocks of the 1970s.

allocative efficiency Resources cannot be reallocated to produce a different bundle of goods which will then allow someone to be made better off while no one is made worse off.

allocative inefficiency Resources can be reallocated to produce a different bundle of goods which will then allow someone to be made better off while no one is made worse off.

appreciation When a change in the free-market exchange rate raises the value of one currency relative to others.

arbitrage Trading activity based on buying where a product is cheap and selling where it has a higher price (from the French word 'arbitrer': to referee or arbitrate). Arbitrage activity helps to bring prices closer in different segments of the market.

arc elasticity A measure of the average responsiveness of quantity to price over an interval of the demand curve: $(\Delta q/q) \times (p/\Delta p)$. See also *point elasticity.*

asymmetric information A situation in which some economic agents have more information than others and this affects the outcome of a bargain between them.

autarky Situation existing when a country does no foreign trade.

automatic fiscal stabilizers Stabilizers that arise because the value of some tax revenues and benefits changes with the level of economic activity. For example, income tax revenue rises as personal incomes rise, corporation tax revenue increases with company profits, and unemployment benefit falls as employment increases.

autonomous expenditures Expenditures that are determined outside the domestic economy or are independent of the current level of GDP.

autonomous variable See *exogenous variable.*

average fixed costs (AFC) *Total fixed costs* divided by the number of units produced.

average product (AP) Total output divided by the number of units of the *variable factor* used in its production.

average propensity to consume (APC) Total consumption expenditure divided by total national income, C/Y.

average propensity to import Total imports divided by total national income (or expenditure), IM/Y.

average propensity to save (APS) Total saving divided by total national income, S/Y. Also known as the savings ratio.

average propensity to tax Total tax revenue divided by total national income, T/Y.

average revenue (AR) *Total revenue* divided by the number of units sold.

average total cost (ATC) The total cost of producing any given output divided by the number of units produced, i.e. the cost per unit.

average variable cost (AVC) *Total variable cost* divided by the number of units produced. Also called unit cost.

balance of payments accounts A summary record of a country's transactions involving payment or receipts of foreign exchange.

balance of trade The difference between imports and exports.

balanced budget A situation in which current revenue is exactly equal to current expenditure.

balanced budget multiplier Measures the change in GDP divided by the balanced budget change in government expenditure that brought it about.

balanced growth Occurs when most major sectors of the economy grow together at similar rates.

barriers to entry Anything that prevents new firms from entering an industry that is earning profits.

barter The trading of goods directly for other goods.

base period A time-period chosen for comparison purposes in order to express or compute index numbers. Values in all other periods are expressed as percentages of the base-period value.

base rate The interest rate quoted by UK banks as the reference rate for much of their loan business. For example, a company may be given a loan at 'base plus 2%'. The base rate changes periodically when the monetary authorities signal that they wish money market rates in general to change. The equivalent term used by US banks is prime rate.

base year A *base period* that is a year.

basic prices Used in national accounts to refer to prices received by producers that exclude taxes on products, as in 'gross value added at basic prices'.

BB line The locus of levels of the interest rate and real GDP for which the desired current account balance of payments surplus (deficit) just equals the desired capital account deficit (surplus).

bill A tradable security, usually with an initial maturity of up to six months, which pays no explicit interest and so trades at a discount to its maturity value.

black market A market in which goods are sold at prices that violate some legally imposed pricing restriction.

bond In economic theory, any evidence of a debt carrying a legal obligation to pay interest and repay the principal at some stated future time. This concept covers many different debt instruments that are found in practice.

boom Period of high output and high employment. See also *slump*.

break-even price The price at which a firm is just able to cover all of its costs, including the opportunity cost of capital. See also *shutdown price*.

budget balance See *balanced budget*.

budget deficit The shortfall of current revenue below current expenditure, usually with reference to the government.

budget line Shows all those combinations of commodities that are just obtainable given a household's income and the prices of all commodities.

budget surplus The excess of current revenue over current expenditure, usually with reference to the government.

built-in stabilizer Anything that reduces the economy's cyclical fluctuations and that is activated without a conscious government decision. See also *automatic fiscal stabilizers*.

business cycles Fluctuations in the general level of activity in an economy that affect many sectors at roughly the same time, though not necessarily to the same extent. In recent times, the period from the peak of one cycle to the peak of the next has varied in the range of five to ten years. Used to be known as trade cycles.

buyout When a group of investors buys up a controlling interest in a firm.

capacity The output that corresponds to the minimum short-run *average total cost*.

capital All those man-made aids to further production, such as tools, machinery, and factories, which are used up in the process of making other goods and services rather than being consumed for their own sake.

capital and financial account Part of the balance of payments accounts that records international transactions in assets and liabilities.

capital consumption allowance An estimate of the amount by which the capital stock is depleted through wear and tear. Also called *depreciation*.

capital inflow Arises when overseas residents buy assets in the domestic economy or domestic residents sell foreign assets.

capital–labour ratio The ratio of the amount of capital to the amount of labour used in production.

capital outflow Arises when overseas residents sell assets in the domestic economy or domestic residents buy foreign assets.

capital stock The total quantity of physical capital in existence.

capital widening Increasing the quantity of capital without changing the proportions in which the factors of production are used.

cartel A group of firms that agree to act as if they were a single seller.

cash base See *high-powered money* and *M0*.

central authorities See *government*.

central bank A bank that acts as banker to the commercial banking system and often to the government as well. In the modern world it is usually a government-owned institution that is the sole money-issuing authority and has a key role in the setting and implementation of *monetary policy*.

centrally planned economy See *command economy*.

ceteris paribus 'Other things being equal', commonly used to describe a situation in which all but one of the *independent variables* are held constant in order to study the effect that a change in the remaining independent variable has on the variables of interest.

change in demand A shift in the whole demand curve, i.e. a change in the amount that will be bought at each price.

change in the quantity demanded An increase or decrease in the specific quantity bought at a specified price, represented by a movement along a demand curve.

circular flow of income The flow of expenditures on output and factor services passing between domestic (as opposed to foreign) firms and domestic households.

classical dichotomy Concept in *classical economics* that monetary forces could influence the general price level but had no effect on real activity. Related to the concept of *neutrality of money*.

classical economics Usually refers to the body of thought on economics which had built up in the hundred years or so before the 1930s; often associated (probably incorrectly) with the notion that government policy cannot influence the level of economic activity. Contrasted with *Keynesian economics*, which attempted to break down the *classical dichotomy*.

closed economy An economy that does not engage in international trade (*autarky*).

closed shop A firm in which only union members can be employed. Closed shops may be either 'pre-entry', where the worker must be a member of the union before being employed, or 'post-entry', where the worker must join the union on becoming employed.

Coase theorem The proposition that if those creating an externality and those affected by it can bargain together with zero transactions costs, the externality will be *internalized* independently of whether it is the creators of or the suffers from the externality who have the property rights.

collective consumption goods See *public goods*.

command economy An economy in which the decisions of the central authorities (as distinct from households and firms) exert the major influence over the allocation of resources and the distribution of income. Also called a centrally planned economy.

commercial policy The government's policy towards international trade, investment, and related matters.

commodities A term that usually refers to basic goods, such as wheat and iron ore, which are produced by the primary sector of the economy. Sometimes also used by economists to refer to all goods and services.

common market An agreement among a group of countries to have free trade among themselves, a common set of barriers to trade with other countries, and free movement of labour and capital among themselves.

common property resource A resource that is owned by no one and may be used by anyone.

comparative advantage The ability of one nation (or region or individual) to produce a commodity at a lower opportunity cost in terms of other products forgone than another nation (or region or individual). Compare *absolute advantage*.

comparative statics Short for 'comparative-static equilibrium analysis'; studying the effect of a change in some variable by comparing the positions of static equilibrium before and after the change.

competition policy Policy designed to prohibit the acquisition and exercise of monopoly power by business firms.

complements Two goods for which the quantity demanded of one is negatively related to the price of the other.

concentration ratio The fraction of total market sales (or some other measure of market occupancy) accounted for by a specific number of the industry's largest firms, four-firm and eight-firm concentration ratios being the most frequently used.

constant returns Situation existing when a firm's output increases at the same rate as all its inputs increase.

consumer An agent who consumes goods or services.

consumers' surplus The difference between the total value consumers place on all units consumed of a commodity and the payment they must make to purchase that amount of the commodity.

consumption The act of using goods and services to satisfy wants.

consumption expenditure The amount that individuals spend on purchasing goods and services for consumption.

consumption function The relationship between personal planned consumption expenditure and the variables that affect it, such as *disposable income* and wealth.

contestable market A market is perfectly contestable if there are no *sunk costs* of entry or exit, so that potential entry may hold the profits of existing firms to low levels—zero in the case of perfect contestability.

co-operative solution A situation in which existing firms co-operate to maximize their joint profits.

cost minimization An implication of profit maximization that the firm will choose the method that produces any specific output at the lowest attainable cost.

creative destruction Schumpeter's theory that high profits and wages earned by monopolistic or oligopolistic firms and unions are the spur for others to invent cheaper or better substitute products and techniques that allow their suppliers to gain some of these profits.

credibility The extent to which actors in the private sector of the economy believe that the government will carry out the policy it promises in the future. It is important in policy analysis in macro models which assume *rational expectations*, since expectations of future policy action influence current behaviour.

cross-elasticity of demand The responsiveness of demand for one commodity to changes in the price of another, defined as the percentage change in quantity demanded of one commodity divided by the percentage change in the price of another commodity.

cross-sectional data A number of observations on the same variable, such as individuals' savings or the price of eggs, all taken at the same time but in different places or for different agents.

current account Account recording all international transactions related to goods and services.

customs union A group of countries that agree to have free trade among themselves and a common set of barriers against imports from the rest of the world.

cyclical unemployment See *demand-deficient unemployment*.

debt deflation A fall in aggregate demand that is associated with falling asset values, causing a negative wealth effect on consumption. It could also involve a decline in investment as investors wait for asset values to stop falling.

debt instruments Any written documents that record the terms of a debt, often providing legal proof of the conditions under which interest will be paid and the principal repaid.

decision lag The time it takes to assess a situation and decide what corrective action should be taken.

decreasing returns to scale A situation in which output increases less than proportionately to inputs as the scale of production increases.

deflation A decrease in the general price level.

degree of risk A measurement of the amount of risk associated with some action such as lending money or innovating. When the nature of the risk is known, the degree can be measured by the variance of the probability distribution describing the possible outcomes.

demand The entire relationship between the quantity of a commodity that buyers wish to purchase per period of time and the price of that commodity, other things being equal.

demand curve A graphical relation showing the quantity of some commodity that households would like to buy at each possible price.

demand-deficient unemployment Unemployment that occurs because aggregate desired expenditure is insufficient to purchase all of the output of a fully employed labour force. Also called cyclical unemployment.

demand for money The amount of wealth agents in the economy wish to hold in the form of money balances.

demand for money function The relation between the quantity of money demanded and its principle determinants such as income, wealth, and interest rates.

demand function A functional relation between quantity demanded and all of the variables that influence it.

demand management Policies that seek to shift the aggregate demand curve by shifting either the *IS* curve (fiscal policy) or the *LM* curve (monetary policy).

demand schedule A numerical tabulation showing the quantities that are demanded at selected prices.

dependent variable The variable that is determined by the *independent variables*; e.g. in the consumption function consumption is the dependent variable.

depreciation (1) The loss in value of an asset over a period of time owing to physical wear and tear and obsolescence. (2) A fall in the free-market value of domestic currency in terms of foreign currencies. See also *capital consumption allowance*.

depression A prolonged period of very low economic activity with very high unemployment and high excess capacity.

derived demand The demand for a factor of production that results from the demand for the products it is used to make.

developed countries Usually refers to the rich industrial countries of North America, Western Europe, Japan, and Australasia.

developing countries See *less developed countries*.

development gap The gap between *less developed countries* and *developed countries*.

differentiated product A product that is produced in several distinct varieties, or brands, all of which are sufficiently similar to distinguish them, as a group, from other products (e.g. cars).

diminishing marginal rate of substitution The hypothesis that the less of one commodity is presently being consumed, the less willing will the consumer be to give up a unit of that commodity to obtain an additional unit of a second commodity; its geometrical expression is the decreasing absolute slope of an indifference curve as one moves along it to the right.

direct investment See *foreign direct investment*.

direct taxes Taxes levied on persons that can vary with the status of the taxpayer, e.g. income tax.

discount rate The difference between the current price of a bill and its maturity value expressed as an annualized interest rate.

discouraged worker Someone of working age who has withdrawn permanently from the labour force because of the poor prospects of employment.

diseconomies of scale See *decreasing returns to scale*.

disembodied technical change Technical change that is the result of changes in the organization of production that are not embodied in specific capital goods, e.g. improved management techniques.

disequilibrium A state of imbalance between opposing forces so that there is a tendency to change, as when quantity demanded does not equal quantity supplied at the prevailing price.

disposable income The after-tax income that individuals have at their disposal to spend or to save.

distribution of income The division of total national income among various groups. See also *functional* and *size distribution of income*.

distribution theory The theory of what determines the way in which the nation's total income is divided among various groups. See also *functional* and *size distribution of income*.

dividends Profits that are paid out to shareholders.

division of labour The breaking-up of a production process into a series of repetitive tasks, each done by a different worker.

double counting In national income accounting, adding up the total outputs of all the sectors in the economy so that the value of intermediate goods is counted both in the sector that produces them and every time they are purchased as an input by another sector.

dumping When a commodity is sold in a foreign country at prices below its domestic sale price for reasons not related to costs.

duopoly An industry containing exactly two firms.

economic growth The positive trend in the nation's total real output or GDP over the long term.

economic models A term used in several related ways: sometimes as a synonym for theory, sometimes for a specific quantification of a general theory, sometimes for the application of a general theory to a specific context, and sometimes for an abstraction designed to illustrate some point but not meant as a full theory on its own.

economic profits The difference between the revenues received from the sale of output and the full opportunity cost of the inputs used to make the output. The cost includes the *opportunity cost* of the owners' capital. Also called pure profits or simply *profits*.

economic rent Any excess that a factor is paid above what is needed to keep it in its present use.

economies of scale See *increasing returns to scale*.

economies of scope Economies achieved by a multi-product firm owing to its overall size not its amount of production of any one product; typically associated with large-scale distribution, advertising, and purchasing and lower cost of borrowing money.

economy Any specified collection of interrelated marketed and non-marketed productive activities.

effective exchange rate An index number of the value of a nation's currency relative to a weighted basket of other currencies. Whereas an *exchange rate* measures the rate of exchange of a currency for one other currency, changes in the effective exchange rate indicate movements in a single currency's value against other currencies in general.

efficiency wage A wage rate above the market-clearing level which enables employers to attract and keep the best workers as well as providing employees with an incentive to perform well and avoid being sacked.

elastic The percentage change in quantity is greater than the percentage change in price (elasticity is greater than 1).

elasticity of demand See *price elasticity of demand*.

elasticity of supply See *price elasticity of supply*.

embodied technical change A technical change that is the result of changes in the form of particular capital goods.

endogenous variable A variable that is explained within a theory. Also called an induced variable.

entrepreneur One who innovates, i.e. one who takes risks by introducing both new products and new ways of making old products.

entry barrier Any natural barrier to the entry of new firms into an industry, such as a large *minimum efficient scale* for firms, or any firm-created barrier, such as a patent.

envelope Any curve that encloses, by being tangent to, a series of other curves. In particular, the envelope cost curve is the *LRAC* curve, which encloses the *SRAC* curves by being tangent to each without cutting any of them.

equation of exchange $MV = PT$, where M is the money stock, V is the velocity of circulation, P is the average price of transactions, and T is the number of transactions. As usually defined, it is an identity which says that the value of money spent is equal to the value of goods and services sold. However, with additional assumptions it provides a basis for the *quantity theory of money*.

equilibrium A state of balance between opposing forces so that there is no tendency to change.

equilibrium differentials Differentials in the prices of factors that persist in equilibrium without generating forces to eliminate them.

equilibrium employment (unemployment) The level of employment (unemployment) achieved when GDP is at its potential level. Traditionally referred to as full employment. Equilibrium unemployment (*frictional* plus *structural*) is total unemployment minus *demand-deficient unemployment*.

equilibrium price The price at which quantity demanded equals quantity supplied.

equilibrium quantity The amount that is bought and sold at the *equilibrium price*.

equities Certificates indicating part ownership of a joint-stock company.

excess capacity theorem The prediction that each firm in a monopolistically competitive industry is producing below its minimum efficient scale and hence at an average cost that is higher than it could achieve by producing its capacity output.

excess demand The amount by which quantity demanded exceeds quantity supplied at some price; negative *excess supply*.

excess supply The amount by which quantity supplied exceeds quantity demanded at some price; negative *excess demand*.

exchange rate The rate at which two national currencies exchange for each other. Often expressed as the amount of domestic currency needed to buy one unit of foreign currency.

excludable The owner of an excludable good can prevent others from consuming it or its services.

execution lag The time it takes to initiate corrective policies and for their full influence to be felt.

exhaustible resource See *non-renewable resource*.

exhaustive expenditures Government purchases of currently produced goods and services. Also called government direct expenditures.

exogenous variable A variable that influences other variables within a theory but is itself determined by factors outside the theory. Also called an autonomous variable.

expectations-augmented Phillips curve See *short-run Phillips curve*.

expected value The most likely outcome of some procedure that is repeated over and over again; the mean of the probability distribution expressing the possible outcomes.

explicit collusion When firms explicitly agree to co-operate rather than compete. See also *tacit collusion*.

external economies Economies of scale that arise from sources outside the firm.

externalities Costs or benefits of a transaction that fall on people not involved in that transaction.

extrapolative expectations Expectation formation based on the assumption that a past trend will continue into the future. The simplest form of extrapolation would be to assume that next period's value of a variable will be the same as this period's.

factor markets Markets where factor services are bought and sold.

factor price theory The theory of the determination of the prices of factors of production.

factors of production Resources used to produce goods and services; frequently divided into the basic categories of land, labour, and capital. Sometimes entrepreneurship is distinguished as a fourth factor; sometimes it is included in the category of labour.

fiat money Inconvertible paper money that is issued by government order (or fiat).

final demand Demand for the *final goods and services* produced in the economy.

final goods and services The outputs of the economy after eliminating all *double counting*, i.e. excluding all intermediate goods.

financial capital The funds used to finance a firm, including both equity capital and debt. Also called money capital.

financial innovation Occurs when new products are introduced into the financial system, or when existing suppliers behave in new ways. Changes are often a complex interaction of regulatory changes, changing technology, and competitive pressures.

financial intermediaries Financial institutions that stand between those who deposit money and those who borrow it.

fine-tuning The attempt to maintain national income at, or near, its full-employment level by means of frequent changes in fiscal and/or monetary policy. Compare *gross-tuning*.

firm The unit that employs factors of production to produce commodities that it sells to other firms, to households, or to the government.

fiscal consolidation A situation in which governments that have been running substantial budget deficits decide to aim for a sustainable budgetary position, usually by getting their expenditure under control.

fiscal policy Attempts to influence the aggregate demand curve by altering government expenditures and/or taxes, thus shifting the *IS* curve.

fixed capital formation See *fixed investment*.

fixed cost A cost that does not change with output. Also called overhead cost, unavoidable cost, or indirect cost.

fixed exchange rate An exchange rate that is held within a narrow band around some pre-announced par value by intervention of the country's central bank in the foreign exchange market.

fixed factors Inputs whose available amount is fixed in the short run.

fixed investment Investment in plant and equipment.

floating exchange rate An exchange rate that is left free to be determined on the foreign exchange market by the forces of demand and supply.

flow variable See *stock variable.*

foreign direct investment (FDI) Non-resident investment in the form of a takeover or capital investment in a domestic branch, plant, or subsidiary corporation in which the investor has voting control. See also *portfolio investment.*

foreign exchange Foreign currencies and claims to them in such forms as bank deposits, cheques, and promissory notes payable in the currency.

foreign exchange market The market where foreign exchange is traded—at a price that is expressed by the *exchange rate.*

45° line Used in macroeconomics to indicate points where expenditures and output are equal, so that what firms produce is just equal to what agents wish to buy.

free-market economy An economy in which the decisions of individuals and firms (as distinct from the central authorities) exert the major influence over the allocation of resources.

free-rider problem The problem that arises because people have a self-interest in not revealing the strength of their own preferences for a *public good* in the hope that others will pay for it.

free trade An absence of any form of government interference with the free flow of international trade.

free-trade area An agreement between two or more countries to abolish tariffs on all, or most, of the trade among themselves, while each remains free to set its own tariffs against other countries.

frictional unemployment Unemployment that is associated with the normal turnover of labour.

function Loosely, an expression of a relationship between two or more variables. Precisely, Y is a function of the variables $X_1,\ldots,X_n$ if for every set of values of the variables $X_1,\ldots,X_n$ there is associated a unique value of the variable Y. Also referred to as a *functional relation.*

functional distribution of income The distribution of income among major factors of production.

functional relation A mathematical relation between two or more variables such that for every value of the independent variables there is one and only one associated value of the dependent variable.

gains from trade Advantages realized as a result of specialization made possible by trade.

GDP See *gross domestic product.*

GDP gap See *output gap.*

general price level Average level of the prices of all goods and services produced in the economy. Usually just called the price level.

Giffen good A good with a positively sloped demand curve.

gilt-edged securities UK government bonds; so called because they are considered to carry lower risk than private sector debt.

given period Any particular period that is being compared with a *base period* by an index number.

globalization The increased worldwide interdependence of most economies. Integrated financial markets, the sourcing of the production of components throughout the world, the growing importance of transnational firms, and the linking of many service activities through the new information and communications technologies are some of its many manifestations.

GNI See *gross national income.*

GNP See *gross national product.*

gold standard Currency standard whereby a country's money is convertible into gold.

Goodhart's law The view that many statistical relations (particularly those established by monetarists) cannot be used for policy purposes because they do not depend on causal relations and are, therefore, unstable.

goods Tangible production, such as cars or shoes. Sometimes all goods and services are loosely referred to as goods.

goods markets Markets where goods and services are bought and sold.

government In economics, all public agencies, government bodies, and other organizations belonging to, or owing their existence to, the government; sometimes (more accurately) called the central authorities.

government direct expenditures See *exhaustive expenditures.*

government failure Where government intervention imposes costs that would not have been accrued if it had acted efficiently.

Gresham's law Bad money (i.e. money whose intrinsic value is less than its face value) drives good money (i.e. money whose intrinsic value exceeds its face value) out of circulation.

gross capital formation See *gross investment.*

gross domestic product (GDP) The value of total output actually produced in the whole economy over some period, usually a year (although quarterly data are also available).

gross investment The total value of all investment goods produced in the economy during a stated period of time.

gross national income (GNI) A measure of what a nation earns from all its economic activity anywhere in the world. It differs from *gross domestic product*, which measures only what is produced in the domestic economy (some of which may generate income for non-residents). Used to be known as *gross national product.*

gross national product (GNP) A national accounts concept equivalent to *gross national income* used prior to 1998. It measures income earned by domestic residents in return for contributions to current production, whether production is located at home or abroad, and is equal to GDP plus net property income from abroad.

gross return on capital The market value of output minus all non-capital costs; the gross return is made up of depreciation, the pure return on capital, any risk premium, and the residual, which is *pure profit.*

gross-tuning Use of monetary and fiscal policies to attempt to correct only large deviations from potential national income. It is contrasted with *fine-tuning*, which aims to adjust aggregate demand frequently in order to keep national income close to its potential level at all times.

high-powered money The monetary magnitude that is under the direct control of the central bank. In the UK, it is composed of cash in the hands of the public, bank reserves of currency, and clearing balances held by the commercial banks with the Bank of England. Measured by M0.

hog cycles A term used to characterize cycles of over- and underproduction because of time-lags in the production process. For example, high prices for pork today lead many farmers to start breeding pigs; when the pigs mature there will be an increased supply of pork, which will drive down its price; so fewer farmers will breed pigs and the price will later rise again, starting the cycle over again.

homogeneous product A product is homogeneous when, as far as purchasers are concerned, every unit is identical to every other unit.

horizontal equity Treating similar groups equitably, which usually means treating them similarly. Compare *vertical equity*.

household All the people who live under one roof and who take, or are subject to others taking for them, joint financial decisions.

human capital The capitalized value of productive investments in persons. Usually refers to value derived from expenditures on education, training, and health improvements.

hyperinflation Episodes of very rapid inflation.

hysteresis The lagging of effects behind their causes. In economics the term has come to relate to persistence or irreversibility of effects. An example is the difficulty of returning the long-term unemployed to work because their skills have deteriorated. It also implies path-dependency, which means that the ultimate equilibrium is not independent of how the economy gets there (i.e. it is not unique).

identification problem The problem of how to estimate both demand and supply curves from observed market data on prices and quantities actually traded.

import quota A maximum amount of some product that may be imported each year.

imputed costs The costs of using factors of production already owned by the firm, measured by the earnings they could have received in their best alternative employment.

incidence In tax theory, where the burden of a tax finally falls.

income–consumption line On an indifference-curve diagram, a line showing how consumption bundles change as income changes, with prices held constant.

income effect The effect on quantity demanded of a change in real income, relative prices held constant.

income-elastic The percentage change in quantity demanded exceeds the percentage change in income.

income elasticity of demand The responsiveness of quantity demanded to a change in income as measured by the percentage change in quantity divided by the percentage change in income.

income-inelastic The percentage change in quantity demanded is smaller than the percentage change in income.

increasing returns to scale A situation in which output increases more than in proportion to inputs as the scale of a firm's production increases. A firm in this situation, with fixed factor prices, is a decreasing-cost firm.

incremental ratio When Y is a function of X, the incremental ratio is the change in Y divided by the change in X that brought it about, $\Delta Y/\Delta X$. The limit of this ratio as ΔX approaches 0 is the derivative of Y with respect to X, dY/dX.

independent variable A variable that can take on any value in some specified range; it determines the value of the dependent variable.

index number An observation in a given time-period expressed as a ratio to the observation in a *base period* and then multiplied by 100.

index of retail prices See *retail price index*.

indexation When a contract, for wages, pensions, or repayment of debt, is specified in real terms. Any specified money payment would be increased to compensate for actual inflation. More generally, the term applies to any contingent contract tied to an index number.

indicators Variables that policymakers monitor for the information they yield about the state of the economy.

indifference curve A curve showing all combinations of commodities that yield equal satisfaction to the consumer.

indifference map A set of indifference curves in which curves further away from the origin indicate higher levels of satisfaction than curves closer to the origin.

indirect tax A tax levied on a transaction that is paid by an individual by virtue of his or her association with that activity and does not vary with the circumstances of the individual who pays it, e.g. VAT on a restaurant meal.

induced Anything that is determined from within a theory. The opposite of autonomous or exogenous; also called endogenous.

induced expenditure Any expenditure flow that is related to national income (or to any other variable explained by the theory).

induced variable See *endogenous variable*.

industrial union A single union representing all workers in a given industry, whatever their trade.

industry A group of firms that sell a well-defined product or closely related set of products.

inelastic The percentage change in quantity is less than the percentage change in price (elasticity is less than 1).

infant industry argument The argument that new domestic industries with potential economies of scale need to be protected from competition from established low-cost foreign producers so that they can grow large enough to achieve costs as low as those of foreign producers.

inferior good A commodity with a negative *income elasticity*; demand for it diminishes when income increases.

inflation A positive rate of growth of the general price level.

inflationary gap A negative output gap, i.e. actual GDP exceeds *potential output* (GDP).

inflationary shock Any autonomous shift in aggregate demand or aggregate supply which causes the price level to rise.

information lag The time between an event happening and policymakers learning about it. For example, national accounts data for a quarter do not arrive until six weeks or so after the quarter ends and are then revised several times subsequently.

infrastructure The basic facilities (especially transportation and communications systems) on which the commerce of a community depends.

injections Exogenous expenditure flows into the home economy. The main injections in the macro model are government spending, exports, and investment.

innovation The introduction of something new, either a new product or a new way of making an old product. See also *entrepreneur*.

innovators Those who innovate. Also called *entrepreneurs*.

inputs The materials and factor services used in the process of production.

insider–outsider model An analysis of labour markets which gives more influence over market outcomes to those in employment (usually via trade union representation) than to the unemployed.

instruments The variables that policymakers can control directly. (In econometrics instruments are proxy variables used in regression equations because of their desirable statistical properties—usually independence from the equation error.)

interest The amount paid each year on a loan, usually expressed as a percentage (e.g. 5%) or as a ratio (e.g. 0.05) of the principal of the loan.

intermediate goods and services All goods and services used as inputs into a further stage of production.

internal economies Economies of scale that arise from sources within the firm.

internal labour market The market inside the firm in which employees compete against each other, particularly for promotion.

internalize an externality To do something that makes an *externality* enter into the firm's own calculations of its private costs and benefits.

inventories Goods and materials that are held during the production or distribution process. See also *stocks*.

investment The act of producing or purchasing goods that are not for immediate consumption.

investment demand function A negative relationship between the quantity of investment per period and the interest rate, holding other things constant. Used to be more commonly called the marginal efficiency of investment.

investment expenditure Expenditure on capital goods.

investment goods Goods produced not for present consumption, i.e. capital goods, inventories, and residential housing.

invisibles Services, especially in the context of the balance of payments accounts, that we cannot see crossing the frontier, such as insurance, freight haulage, and tourist expenditures.

involuntary unemployment Unemployment that occurs when a person is willing to accept a job at the going wage rate but cannot find such a job.

IS curve The locus of combinations of the interest rate and the level of real GDP for which desired aggregate expenditure equals actual national output. So called because, in a closed economy with no government, it also reflects the combinations of the interest rate and national income for which investment equals saving, $I = S$. In general it reflects points for which *injections* equal *withdrawals*.

IS/LM model A diagrammatic representation of a model of aggregate demand determination based upon the locus of equilibrium points in the aggregate expenditure sector (*IS*) and the monetary sector (*LM*). It is incomplete as a model of GDP determination because it does not include an aggregate supply curve.

isocost line A line showing all combinations of inputs that have the same total cost to the firm.

isoquant A curve showing all technologically efficient factor combinations for producing a given level of output.

isoquant map A series of *isoquants* from the same production function, each isoquant relating to a specific level of output.

J-curve Pattern usually followed by the *balance of trade* after a devaluation of the domestic currency. Initially the trade balance deteriorates, and then, after a lag, it improves.

joint-stock company A firm regarded in law as having an identity of its own. Its owners, who are its shareholders, are not personally responsible for anything that is done in the name of the firm. Called a corporation in North America.

Keynesian economics Economic theories based on *AE*, *IŠ*, *LM*, *AD*, and *AS* curves and assuming enough short-run price inflexibility that *AD* and *AS* shocks cause substantial deviations of real GDP from its potential level.

Keynesian revolution Adoption of the idea that government could use monetary and fiscal policy to control aggregate demand and thereby influence the level of GDP. For a while it was believed that Keynesian economics had found ways in which policymakers could smooth business cycles and eliminate unemployment.

Kondratieff cycles Long cycles in economic activity of around fifty years' duration. Sometimes referred to as long waves.

labour All productive human resources, mental and physical, both inherited and acquired.

labour force See *working population*.

labour force participation rate The percentage of the population of working age that is actually in the labour force (i.e. either working or seeking work).

labour productivity Total output divided by the labour used in producing it, i.e. output per unit of labour.

Laffer curve A curve relating total tax revenue to the tax rate.

land All free gifts of nature, such as land, forests, minerals, etc. Sometimes called natural resources.

law of diminishing returns Law stating that if increasing quantities of a variable factor are applied to a given quantity of a fixed factor, the *marginal product*, and the *average product*, of the variable factor will eventually decrease.

leakages See *withdrawals*.

learning by doing The increase in output per worker that often results as workers learn on the job through repeatedly performing the same tasks. It causes a downward shift in the average variable cost curve.

legal tender Currency that is recognized in law as the acceptable medium for payment of debts. Bank of England notes became legal tender in England and Wales in 1833. Euro notes issued by the European Central Bank are expected to become legal tender for members of the euro zone in 2002.

less developed countries (LDCs) The lower-income countries of the world, most of which are in Asia, Africa, and South and Central America. Also called underdeveloped countries and developing countries.

life-cycle theory A theory that relates a household's actual consumption to its expected lifetime income.

limited partnership A form of business organization in which the firm has two classes of owner: general partners, who take part in managing the firm and who are personally liable for all of the firm's actions and debts, and limited partners, who take no part in the management of the firm and who risk only the money that they have invested.

liquidity The ease with which an asset can be converted into money. Sometimes refers to money itself—*liquidity preference* used to be widely used in economics as an expression meaning demand for money.

liquidity preference The demand to hold wealth as money rather than as interest-earning assets. Also called the *demand for money*.

liquidity trap A situation that may arise when interest rates are so low that further reductions are either not possible or do not stimulate spending. In such situations the monetary authorities cannot stimulate aggregate demand by interest rate changes alone.

LM curve The locus of combinations of the interest rate and real GDP for which money demand equals money supply. So called because it represents the points where *liquidity preference* equals the money supply.

logarithmic scale A scale on which equal proportional changes are shown as equal distances (e.g. 1 cm may always represent doubling of a variable, whether from 3 to 6 or 50 to 100). Also called log scale or ratio scale.

long run A period of time in which all inputs may be varied but the basic technology of production is unchanged.

long-run aggregate supply (LRAS) curve A curve that relates the price level to equilibrium real GDP, after all input costs, including wage rates, have been fully adjusted to eliminate any excess demand or supply.

long-run average cost (LRAC) curve Curve showing the least-cost method of producing each level of output when all inputs can be varied. Also sometimes called the long-run average total cost curve.

long-run industry supply (LRS) curve Curve showing the relation between equilibrium price and the output that the firms in an industry will be willing to supply after all desired entry or exit has occurred.

long-run Phillips curve (LRPC) Curve showing the relation between unemployment and stable rates of inflation that neither accelerate nor decelerate (and therefore for which actual and expected inflation are equal). Usually thought to be vertical at the *natural rate of unemployment* or *NAIRU*.

long wave See *Kondratieff cycles*.

Lorenz curve A curve showing the extent of departure from equality of income distribution. It graphs the proportion of total income earned by all people up to each stated point in the income distribution, such as the proportion earned by the bottom quarter, the bottom half, and the bottom three-quarters.

Lucas aggregate supply curve An aggregate supply curve which is positively sloped for unexpected increases in the price level but vertical for anticipated increases in the price level. Also known as the 'surprise' aggregate supply curve.

Lucas critique The proposition that forecasts and simulations using empirical macro models will be inaccurate when used to predict the effects of changes in policy. This is because the behaviour of agents will be different under different policy regimes.

M0 Currency held by the non-bank public plus bankers' deposits with the central bank. Also known as the monetary base, the cash base, or *high-powered money*.

M1 A measure of the money stock which includes currency plus current account bank deposits. This measure is no longer reported by the Bank of England.

M2 Currency held by the public plus retail current and savings accounts in banks and building societies. Also known as 'retail M4'.

M3 Measure of broad money no longer used by the UK authorities. It was equal to M1 plus all savings deposits in banks. A harmonized measure of M3, *M3H*, is in use in the euro area as a monetary indicator; however, this has a different definition, as it is equal to M4 plus foreign currency and some other deposits.

M4 Currency in circulation plus all sterling deposits in banks and building societies.

macroeconomic policy Any measure directed at influencing such macroeconomic variables as the overall levels of employment, unemployment, GDP, and prices.

macroeconomics The study of the determination of economic aggregates and averages, such as total output, total employment, the general price level, and the rate of economic growth.

marginal cost (MC) The increase in total cost resulting from raising the rate of production by one unit.

marginal cost pricing A policy of setting the price of a product equal to its marginal cost.

marginal efficiency of capital The rate at which the value of the stream of output of a marginal unit of capital must be discounted to make it equal to £1.

marginal efficiency of capital schedule A schedule that relates the marginal efficiency of each additional £1 worth of capital to the size of the capital stock.

marginal efficiency of investment The relation between desired investment and the rate of interest, assuming all other things are equal.

marginal physical product (MPP) See *marginal product*.

marginal product (MP) The change in total product resulting from using one more (or less) unit of the variable factor. Also called marginal physical product. Mathematically, the partial derivative of total product with respect to the variable factor.

marginal productivity theory The demand half of the *neoclassical theory* of income distribution, in which the demand for any variable factor is determined by the value of that factor's *marginal revenue product*.

marginal propensity not to spend The proportion of any new increment of income that is not passed on in spending, and instead leaks out of (i.e. is withdrawn from) the circular flow of income. Also called the marginal propensity to withdraw and the marginal propensity to leak.

marginal propensity to consume (MPC) The proportion of any new increment of income that is spent on consumption, $\Delta C/\Delta Y$

marginal propensity to import The proportion of any new increment of income that is spent on imports, $\Delta M/\Delta Y$.

marginal propensity to leak See *marginal propensity not to spend*.

marginal propensity to save (MPS) The proportion of any new increment of income that is saved, $\Delta S/\Delta Y$.

marginal propensity to spend The ratio of any increment of induced expenditure to the increment in income that brought it about.

marginal propensity to tax The proportion of any increment in income that is taxed away by the government, $\Delta T/\Delta Y$.

marginal propensity to withdraw See *marginal propensity not to spend*.

marginal rate of substitution (MRS) The rate at which one factor is substituted for another with output held constant. Graphically, the slope of the *isoquant*.

marginal rate of transformation The slope of the *production-possibility boundary*, indicating the rate of substitution of production of one good for that of another.

marginal revenue The change in total revenue resulting from a unit change in the sales per period of time. Mathematically, the derivative of total revenue with respect to quantity sold.

marginal revenue product (*MRP*) The addition to a firm's revenue resulting from the sale of the output produced by an additional unit of the variable factor.

marginal utility The change in satisfaction resulting from consuming one unit more or one unit less of a commodity.

market An area over which buyers and sellers negotiate the exchange of a well-defined commodity.

market economy A society in which people specialize in productive activities and meet most of their material wants through exchanges voluntarily agreed upon by the contracting parties.

market failure Any market performance that is less than the most efficient possible (the optimal) performance.

market for corporate control Where potential buyers and sellers (both willing and unwilling) bargain about transferring ownership of firms.

market prices In national accounts refers to the fact that expenditures are measured in the prices actually paid by consumers and so include taxes on products. See also *basic prices*.

market sector That portion of an economy in which producers must cover their costs by selling their output to consumers.

market structure The characteristics of a market that influence the behaviour and performance of firms that sell in the market. The four main market structures are *perfect competition, monopolistic competition, oligopoly*, and *monopoly*.

maturity The length of time until the redemption date of a security such as a bond.

medium of exchange A commodity or token which is widely accepted in payment for goods and services.

menu costs Costs associated with changing prices, such as the costs of reprinting catalogues or menus. These costs make it rational for producers to keep output prices fixed until input prices have changed significantly, or to respond only periodically.

mercantilism The doctrine that the gains from trade are a function of the balance of trade, in contrast with the classical theory, in which the gains from trade are a function of the volume of trade.

merchandise account The part of the balance of payments accounts relating to trade in goods.

merchandise trade Trade in physical products. Same as *visible trade*.

merger The uniting of two or more formerly independent firms.

merit goods Goods which the government decides have sufficient merit that more should be produced and consumed than people would choose to purchase if left to themselves.

microeconomics The study of the allocation of resources and the distribution of income as they are affected by the working of the price system and by the policies of the central authorities.

minimum efficient scale (MES) The smallest level of output at which long-run average cost is at a minimum; the smallest output required to achieve all economies of scale in production.

mismatch See *structural unemployment*.

mixed economy An economy in which some decisions about the allocation of resources are made by firms and households and some by the government.

monetarism The doctrine that monetary magnitudes exert powerful influences in the economy and that control of these magnitudes is a potent means of affecting the economy's macroeconomic behaviour.

monetary base See *high-powered money* and *M0*.

monetary equilibrium A situation in which there is no excess demand for or supply of money.

monetary policy Policy of trying to control aggregate demand (and ultimately inflation) via the setting of short-term interest rates.

monetary transmission mechanism The mechanism that turns a monetary shock into a real expenditure shock and thus links the monetary and the real sides of the economy.

money Any generally accepted medium of exchange, i.e. anything that will be accepted in exchange for goods and services.

money demand function The function that determines the demand to hold money balances.

money income Income measured in terms of some monetary unit. See also *real income*.

money multiplier The ratio of the money stock to the monetary base (*high-powered money*).

money price See *absolute price*.

money rate of interest The rate of interest as measured in monetary units.

money stock See *supply of money*.

money supply See *supply of money*.

monopolist A single seller in any market.

monopolistic competition A market structure in which there are many sellers and freedom of entry but in which each firm sells a differentiated version of some generic product and, as a result, faces a negatively sloped demand curve for its own product.

monopoly A market structure in which the industry contains only one firm.

monopsonist A single purchaser in any market.

moral hazard Any change in behaviour resulting from the fact that a contract has been agreed. One example is drivers who drive more recklessly because they have accident insurance; another is employees who do not work hard because employers cannot monitor their performance effectively.

multinational enterprises (MNEs) See *transnational corporations*.

multiplier The ratio of the change in GDP to the change in autonomous expenditure that brought it about.

multiplier–accelerator theory An element of business-cycle dynamics caused by the interaction of the multiplier and the accelerator, which can make the economy follow a cyclical path in response to a one-off exogenous shock.

NAIRU The amount of unemployment (all of it *frictional* or *structural*) that exists when GDP is at its potential level and that, if maintained, will result in a stable rate of inflation. The acronym stands for 'non-accelerating-inflation rate of unemployment'. In the long run the NAIRU is equivalent to the *natural rate of unemployment*.

Nash equilibrium In the case of firms, an equilibrium that results when each firm in an industry is currently doing the best that it can, given the current behaviour of all other firms.

national debt The debt of the central government.

national income In general, the value of the nation's total output, and the value of the income generated by the production of that output. Measured in practice by *gross national income* and assumed in most of this book to be equivalent to GDP.

national product A generic term for the nation's total output, which might be measured more specifically by GDP. See *gross national product*.

natural monopoly An industry whose market demand is insufficient to allow more than one firm to cover costs at any positive level of output.

natural rate of unemployment The level of unemployment in a competitive economy that corresponds to potential GDP in long-run equilibrium and that is associated with stable inflation. For most purposes it is equivalent to the *NAIRU*, but the latter may differ when the economy is adjusting slowly back to full equilibrium following some large shock.

natural scale A scale on which equal absolute amounts are represented by equal distances. Compare *logarithmic scale*.

negatively related Refers to the relationship where an increase in one variable is associated with a decrease in the other.

neoclassical theory In general, a theory based on the maximizing choices of well-informed agents pursuing their own self-interest. In *distribution* it is a theory that factor incomes are determined by demand and supply, where demand depends on the value of the factor's marginal product and supply depends on the maximizing decisions of those who own the factors.

net exports Total exports minus total imports ($X - IM$).

net investment Gross investment minus replacement investment, which is new capital that represents net additions to the capital stock.

net taxes Total tax receipts net of *transfer payments*.

neutrality of money Hypothesis that the level of real national income is independent of the level of the money stock.

New Classical theory A theory that assumes that the economy behaves as if it were perfectly competitive with all markets always clearing; where deviations from full employment can occur only if people make mistakes and where, given rational expectations, these mistakes will not be systematic.

New Keynesian economics Recent research agenda which has focused on explaining why prices do not adjust to clear markets, especially the labour market. It differs from the traditional Keynesian approach in its concern for *equilibrium unemployment* as well as *demand-deficient unemployment*.

newly industrialized countries (NICs) Formerly *less developed countries* that have become major industrial exporters in recent times. Sometimes called newly industrialized economies (NIEs).

nominal interest rate Actual interest rate in money terms. It is contrasted with the real interest rate, which is the nominal interest rate minus the inflation rate (or expected inflation rate).

nominal money supply The money supply measured in monetary units.

nominal national product Total output valued at current prices and usually measured by 'money GDP'.

non-cooperative equilibrium The equilibrium reached when firms calculate their own best policy without considering competitors' reactions and without explicit collusion.

non-excludable A good or service is non-excludable if its owners cannot dictate who will consume it.

non-market sector That portion of an economy in which producers must cover their costs from some source other than sales revenue.

non-renewable (or exhaustible) resource Any productive resource that exists as a fixed stock that cannot be replaced once it is used, such as natural petroleum.

non-rivalrous A good or a service is non-rivalrous if a given unit of it can be consumed by everyone. Thus one person's consumption of it does not reduce the ability of another person to consume it, as with knowledge, national defence, police protection, and navigational aids.

non-strategic behaviour Behaviour which does not take account of the reactions of others, as when a firm acts in perfect or monopolistic competition.

non-tariff barriers Devices other than tariffs that are designed to reduce the flow of imports.

non-tradables Goods and services that are produced and sold domestically but do not enter into international trade.

normal good A commodity whose demand increases when income increases. Compare *inferior good*.

normative Things that concern what ought to be and thus depend on value judgements. Compare *positive*.

oligopoly An industry that contains only a few firms.

open economy An economy that engages in international trade.

open-market operations Sales or purchases of securities by the central bank aimed at influencing monetary conditions.

open shop A place of employment in which a union represents its members but does not have bargaining jurisdiction for all workers, and where membership of the union is not a condition of getting or keeping a job.

opportunity cost Measurement of cost by reference to the alternatives forgone.

optimum output See *profit-maximizing output*.

ordinary partnership An enterprise composed of a group of individuals who are all jointly liable for the debts and other obligations of that enterprise.

output The goods and services that result from the process of production.

output gap The difference between potential output and actual output ($Y^* - Y$); positive output gaps are called *recessionary gaps*; negative output gaps are called *inflationary gaps*.

overshooting Occurs when the impact effect of a shock takes a variable beyond its ultimate equilibrium level. Most widely applied to the exchange rate. A characteristic of a wide class of exchange rate models under rational expectations is that when monetary policy is, say, tightened, the exchange rate initially appreciates to a point from which it will depreciate towards its long-run equilibrium level.

Pareto optimality A situation in which it is impossible to reallocate production activities to produce more of one good without producing less of some other good, and in which it is impossible to reallocate consumption activities to make at least one person better off without making anyone worse off. Also called Pareto efficiency.

partnership An enterprise with two or more joint owners, each of whom is personally responsible for all of the partnership's debts.

paternalism The belief that the individual is not the best judge of his or her own self-interest; i.e. the belief that someone else knows better.

path-dependence Non-uniqueness of equilibrium resulting from the possibility that what happens in one period affects the stock of physical and human capital for a long time subsequently. Sometimes referred to as *hysteresis*.

per capita economic growth The growth of per capita GDP or GNI (GDP or GNI divided by the population).

per-unit tax See *specific tax*.

perfect competition A market structure in which all firms in an industry are price-takers and in which there is freedom of entry into, and exit from, the industry.

permanent income The maximum amount that a person can consume per year into the indefinite future without reducing his or her wealth.

permanent income theory A theory that relates actual consumption to *permanent income*.

perpetuity A bond that pays a fixed sum of money each year for ever and has no redemption date. Sometimes called a consol.

personal disposable income (PDI) The gross income of the personal sector less all direct taxes and national insurance contributions.

personal income Income earned by or paid to individuals, before deducting personal income taxes.

Phillips curve Relates the percentage rate of change of money wages (measured at an annual rate) to the level of unemployment (measured as the percentage of the *working population* unemployed).

point elasticity Uses the derivative at a point on the demand curve (dq/dp)×(p/q). See also *arc elasticity*.

political business cycles Cycles in the economy resulting from the political goals of incumbent (or potentially incumbent) politicians. The simplest form is the deliberate pre-election boom, though modern theories are more subtle.

poll tax A tax which takes the same lump sum from everyone.

portfolio investment Investment in bonds and other debt instruments that do not imply ownership, or in minority holdings of shares that do not establish legal control.

positive Refers to statements concerning what is, was, or will be; they assert alleged facts about the universe in which we live. Compare *normative*.

positively related Refers to the relationship where an increase in one variable is associated with an increase in another.

potential output (GDP), Y^* The level of output at which there is a balance between inflationary and deflationary forces. It is also the level of output at which there is no *demand-deficient unemployment* (the economy is at the *NAIRU*) and the existing capital stock is being run at its normal rate of utilization.

precautionary balances The amount of money people wish to hold because of uncertainty about the exact timing of receipts and payments.

present value The value now of a sum to be received in the future. Also called discounted present value.

price–consumption line A line on an indifference curve diagram showing how consumption changes as the price of one commodity changes, *ceteris paribus*.

price control Anything that influences prices by law rather than by market forces.

price discrimination Situation arising when firms sell different units of their output at different prices for reasons not associated with differences in costs.

price elasticity of demand The percentage change in quantity demanded divided by the percentage change in price that brought it about. Often called elasticity of demand.

price elasticity of supply The percentage change in quantity supplied divided by the percentage change in price that brought it about. Often called elasticity of supply.

price index A statistical measure of the average percentage change in some group of prices relative to some base period.

price level See *general price level*.

price-makers Firms that administer their prices. See *administered price*.

price system An economic system in which market-determined prices play a key role in determining the allocation of resources and the distribution of the national product.

price-taker A firm that can alter its rate of production and sales within any feasible range without having any effect on the price of its products.

principal (1) The amount of a loan, or (2) the unit that employs agents to work on its behalf.

principal–agent problem The problem of resource allocation that arises because contracts that will induce agents to act in their principals' best interests are often impossible to write or too costly to monitor.

principle of substitution Methods of production reflect the relative prices of inputs, with relatively more of the cheaper input and relatively less of the more expensive input being used.

prisoner's dilemma A term in game theory for a game in which the *Nash equilibrium* leaves both players less well off than if they co-operated with each other.

private benefits The benefits of some activity that accrue to the parties in that activity.

private consumption expenditure Spending for which the consumption of the goods bought is done by private individuals (even where payment may have been made by the government, such as on health services).

private cost The value of the best alternative use of the resources used in production as valued by the producer.

private sector That portion of an economy in which the organizations that produce goods and services are owned and operated by private units such as households and firms. Compare *public sector*.

pro-cyclical Positively correlated with the business cycle.

producer Any unit that makes goods or services.

producers' surplus Total revenue minus total variable cost; the market value that the firm creates by producing goods, net of the value of the resources currently used to create these goods.

production The act of making goods and services.

production function A mathematical relation showing the maximum output that can be produced by each and every combination of inputs.

production-possibility boundary A curve that shows the alternative combinations of commodities that can just be attained if all available productive resources are used; it is the boundary between attainable and unattainable output combinations.

productive efficiency Production of any output at the lowest attainable cost for that level of output; it is impossible to reallocate resources and produce more of one output without simultaneously producing less of some other output.

productivity Output per unit of input employed.

products A general term referring to all goods and services. Sometimes also referred to as *commodities*.

profit (1) In ordinary usage, the difference between the value of outputs and the value of inputs. (2) In microeconomics, the difference between revenues received from the sale of goods and the value of inputs, which includes the opportunity cost of capital. Also called *pure profit* or *economic profit*. (3) In macroeconomics it is a component of factor incomes (and thus income-based measures of national product) and is measured as trading surpluses plus a component of mixed incomes.

profit-maximizing output The level of output that maximizes a firm's profits. Sometimes also called the optimum output.

progressive tax A tax that takes a larger percentage of people's income the larger their income is. Compare *regressive tax*.

progressivity The general term for the relation between income and the percentage of income paid in taxes.

proportional tax A tax that takes the same percentage of people's income whatever the level of their income.

protectionism Any departure from free trade designed to give some protection to domestic industries from foreign competition.

public corporation A body set up to run a nationalized industry. It is owned by the state but is usually under the direction of a more or less independent, state-appointed board.

public goods Goods and services which, once produced, can be consumed by everyone in the society. Also called collective consumption goods.

public sector That portion of an economy in which production is owned and operated by the government or by bodies created by it, such as nationalized industries. Compare *private sector*.

purchasing power parity (PPP) exchange rate The exchange rate between two currencies that equates their purchasing powers and hence adjusts for relative inflation rates.

purchasing power parity theory The theory that the equilibrium exchange rate between two national currencies will be the one that equates their purchasing powers.

pure market economy An economy in which all decisions, without exception, are made by individuals and firms acting through unhindered markets.

pure profit Any excess of a firm's revenue over all opportunity costs including those of capital. Also called economic profit.

pure rate of interest See *pure return on capital*.

pure return on capital The amount that capital can earn in a riskless investment. Also called the pure rate of interest.

quantity actually bought and sold The amount of a commodity that consumers and firms actually succeed in purchasing and selling.

quantity actually purchased See *quantity actually bought and sold*.

quantity demanded The amount of a commodity that households wish to purchase in some time-period.

quantity supplied The amount of a commodity that firms offer for sale in some time-period.

quantity theory of money Theory predicting that the price level and the quantity of money vary in exact proportion to each other—i.e. changing M by X% changes P by X%.

ratio scale See *logarithmic scale*.

rational expectations The theory that people understand how the economy works and learn quickly from their mistakes, so that, while random errors may be made, systematic and persistent errors are not made.

rational ignorance This occurs when agents have no incentive to inform themselves about some government action because the costs of so doing greatly exceed the potential benefits of any action the agent could take as a result of having the correct information.

real business cycles An approach to the explanation of business cycles which uses dynamic equilibrium market-clearing models and relies on productivity shocks as a trigger. In such models all cycles are an optimal response to the real shock and there are no deviations from potential output: rather, it is the full equilibrium that fluctuates over time.

real capital Physical assets that include factories, machinery, and stocks of material and finished goods. Also called physical capital.

real exchange rate An index of the relative prices of domestic and foreign goods.

real income The purchasing power of *money income*, measured by deflating nominal income by an index of the price level.

real money supply The money supply measured in purchasing power units, measured as the nominal money supply divided by a price index.

real national product Total output valued at base-year prices, measured for example by GDP at 1999 prices.

real product wage The proportion of the sale value of each unit that is accounted for by labour costs (including the pre-tax nominal wage rate, benefits, and the firm's national insurance contributions).

real rate of interest The money rate of interest minus the inflation rate (or expected inflation rate), which expresses the real return on a loan.

real wage The money wage deflated by a price index to measure the wage's purchasing power.

reallocation of resources Some change in the uses to which the economy's resources are put.

recession A sustained drop in the level of economic activity.

recessionary gap A positive output gap, when actual national income falls short of potential national income.

redemption date The time at which the principal of a loan is to be repaid.

regressive tax A tax that takes a smaller percentage of people's incomes the larger their income is. Compare *progressive tax*.

relative price Any price expressed as a ratio of another price.

renewable resources Productive resources that can be replaced as they are used up, as with *real capital* or forests; distinguished from *non-renewable resources*, which are available in a fixed stock that can be depleted but not replaced, as with natural oil and coal.

replacement investment Investment which replaces capital as it wears out but does not increase the capital stock.

replacement ratio Benefits received by those out of work as a proportion of the wage of those in employment.

repo Short for a 'sale and repurchase agreement' whereby a firm sells a security (such as a gilt) to a bank and agrees to buy it back at some future time. The difference in price between sale and repurchase reflects the ruling rate of interest. The deal is a loan (usually short term) secured on the security involved. Central banks typically set the rate of interest in repo transactions for a specific term. In the UK the Bank of England sets the two-week repo rate.

reservation price The price below which some action will not be taken, such as selling a commodity or accepting a job.

resource allocation The allocation of the economy's scarce resources among alternative uses.

retail price index (RPI) An index of the general price level based on the consumption pattern of typical consumers.

reverse repo Similar to a *repo*, but here the bank sells the security to the firm and agrees to buy it back at some future date.

risk-averse Describes people who wish to avoid risks and so will only play games that are sufficiently biased in their favour to overcome their aversion to risk; they will be unwilling to play mathematically fair games, let alone games that are biased against them.

risk-loving Describes people who are willing to play some games that are biased against them, the extent of the love of risk being measured by the degree of bias that they are willing to accept.

risk-neutral Describes people who are indifferent about playing a mathematically fair game and so are willing to play games that are biased in their favour but not games that are biased against them.

risk premium The return on capital necessary to compensate owners of capital for the risk of loss of their capital.

rivalrous A good or service is rivalrous if, when one person consumes a unit of it, no other person can also consume that unit, as with all ordinary goods and services such as apples or haircuts.

saving Income received by individuals that they do not spend through *consumption expenditure*.

savings ratio See *average propensity to save*.

scatter diagram Plots a series of observations each made on two variables, e.g. the price and quantity of eggs sold in twenty different cities.

seigniorage The revenue that accrues to the issuer of money.

self-employed Those people who work for themselves.

sellers' preferences Allocation of a commodity that is in excess demand by the decisions of sellers.

services Intangible production that does not produce a physical product, such as haircuts and medical services.

shares See *equities*.

shifting The passing of tax incidence from the person who initially pays it to someone else.

short run The period of time over which the inputs of some factors cannot be varied.

short-run aggregate supply (SRAS) curve The total amount that will be produced and offered for sale at each price level on the assumption that all input prices are fixed.

short-run equilibrium Generally, equilibrium subject to fixed factors or other things that cannot change over the time-period being considered.

short-run Phillips curve Any particular Phillips curve drawn for a given expected rate of inflation.

short-run supply curve A curve showing the relation of quantity supplied to price when one or more factor is fixed; under perfect competition it is the horizontal sum of marginal cost curves (above the level of average variable costs) of all firms in an industry.

shutdown price The price that is equal to a firm's average variable costs, below which it will produce no output. See also *break-even price*.

simple multiplier Usually applies to the value of the *multiplier* in the aggregate expenditure system before any account is taken of the feedback from the monetary sector and from aggregate supply.

single proprietorship An enterprise with one owner who is personally responsible for everything that is done. More commonly called a *sole trader*.

size distribution of income A classification of income according to the amount of income received by each individual irrespective of the sources of that income.

slump A period of low output and low employment. See also *boom*.

small open economy (SOE) An economy that is a price-taker for both its imports and its exports. It must buy and sell at the world price, irrespective of the quantities that it buys and sells.

social benefits The value of an activity to the whole society, which includes the internal effects on those who are involved in deciding on it and the external effects on those who are not involved in the activity.

social cost The value of the best alternative use of resources that are available to the whole society.

sole trader A non-incorporated business operated by a single owner. Modern UK terminology for a *single proprietorship*.

specialization of labour The organization of production so that individual workers specialize in the production of particular goods or services (and satisfy their wants by trading) rather than producing everything they consume (and satisfying their wants by being self-sufficient).

specific tax A tax expressed as so much per unit, independent of its price. Also called a per-unit tax.

speculation Taking a financial position that will yield profits if prices move in a particular direction in future but will yield losses if they move the other way.

speculative balances Monetary assets held for their expected rate of return rather than for transactions purposes.

speculative motive The motive that leads agents to hold money in response to the risks inherent in fluctuating bond prices. More generally, it refers to the asset motive, as opposed to the transactions motive, for holding money.

spread The difference between the prices or interest rates on specific assets or loans, such as the spread between deposit and loan rates offered by banks.

SRAS curve See *short-run aggregate supply curve*.

stabilization policy The attempt to reduce fluctuations in GDP, employment, and the price level by use of *monetary* and *fiscal policies*.

stagflation The simultaneous occurrence of a recession (with its accompanying high unemployment) and inflation.

stock See *equities*.

stock variable A variable that does not have a time dimension. It is contrasted with a flow variable, which does.

stockbuilding The process of building *stocks* or inventories.

stocks Accumulation of inputs and outputs held by firms to facilitate a smooth flow of production in spite of variations in delivery of inputs and sales of outputs. Now called inventories in national accounts.

strategic Behaviour that takes into account the reactions of others to one's own actions, as when an oligopolistic firm makes decisions that take account of its competitors' reactions.

structural unemployment Unemployment that exists because of a mismatch between the characteristics of the unemployed and the characteristics of the available jobs in terms of region, occupation, or industry.

substitutes Two goods are substitutes if the quantity demanded of one is positively related to the price of the other.

substitution effect The change in quantity demanded of a good resulting from a change in the commodity's relative price, eliminating the effect of the price change on real income.

sunk costs of entry Those costs that must be incurred for a firm to enter a market and that cannot be recouped when the firm leaves.

supply The whole relation between the quantity supplied of some commodity and its own price.

supply curve The graphical representation of the relation between the quantity of some commodity that producers wish to make and sell per period of time and the price of that commodity, *ceteris paribus*.

supply function A mathematical relation between the quantity supplied and all the variables that influence it.

supply of effort The total number of hours people in the labour force are willing to work. Also called supply of labour.

supply of labour See *supply of effort*.

supply of money The total amount of money available in the entire economy. Also called the money supply or the money stock.

supply schedule A numerical tabulation showing the quantity supplied at a number of alternative prices.

supply shocks A shift in any aggregate supply curve caused by an exogenous change in input prices or technology.

supply-side policies Policies that seek to shift either the short-run or the long-run aggregate supply curve.

surprise aggregate supply curve See *Lucas aggregate supply curve*.

tacit collusion Occurs when firms arrive at the co-operative solution (which maximizes their joint profit) even though they may not have formed an explicit agreement to co-operate.

takeover When one firm buys another firm.

targets The variables in the economy which policymakers wish to influence. Typical policy targets might be inflation, unemployment, and real growth.

tariffs Taxes on imported goods.

term The amount of time between a bond's issue date and its redemption date.

terms of trade The ratio of the average price of a country's exports to the average price of its imports.

theory of games The study of rational decision-making in situations in which each player must anticipate the reactions of competitors to the moves that he or she makes. It can be applied to analysis of the strategic interaction of firms in oligopolistic markets.

third-party effects See *externalities*.

time-inconsistency Problem that arises in rational-expectations models when policymakers have an incentive to abandon their commitments at a later time. The existence of this incentive is generally understood by private sector agents, and it may influence their current behaviour.

time-series data Data on some variable taken at different, usually regularly spaced points in time, such as consumer spending in each quarter for the last ten years.

total cost (*TC*) The total of all costs of producing a firm's output, usually divided into *fixed* and *variable costs*.

total final expenditure The total expenditure required to purchase all the goods and services that are produced domestically when these are valued at market prices.

total fixed costs The total of a firm's costs that do not vary in the short run.

total product (*TP*) Total amount produced by a firm during some time-period.

total revenue (*TR*) The total amount of money that the firm receives from the sale of its output over some period of time.

total utility The total satisfaction derived from consuming some amount of a commodity.

total variable costs The total of those of the firm's costs that do vary in the short run.

tradables Goods and services that enter into international trade.

trade account The part of the balance of payments accounts relating to trade in goods.

trade creation Trade between the members of a customs union or free-trade area where previously protected industries served their own home markets.

trade cycles See *business cycles*.

trade diversion The diversion of the source of a member country's imports from other countries to union members as a result of the preferential removal of tariffs following the formation of a customs union or a free-trade area.

trade or craft union A union covering workers with a common set of skills, no matter where, or for whom, they work.

trade-weighted exchange rate The average of the exchange rates between a particular country's currency and those of each of its major trading partners, with each rate being weighted by the amount of trade with the country in question. Also called the *effective exchange rate*.

traditional economic system One in which behaviour is based primarily on tradition, custom, and habit.

transaction costs Costs involved in making a trade in addition to the price of the product itself, such as the time involved or the cost of transport.

transactions balances Holdings of money intended to be used for buying goods or services at some unknown future time.

transactions demand for money The amount of money that people wish to hold in order to finance their transactions.

transfer earnings The amount that a factor must earn in its present use to prevent it from moving (i.e. transferring) to another use.

transfer payments Payments not made in return for any contribution to current output, such as unemployment benefits.

transition economies Countries that abandoned central planning and have been making the transition to market economies, such as the countries of Eastern Europe and the former Soviet Union.

transmission mechanism See *monetary transmission mechanism.*

transnational corporations (TNCs) Firms that have operations in more than one country. Also called transnationals or multi-national enterprises (MNEs).

underdeveloped countries See *less developed countries.*

unit cost See *average variable cost.*

unit elasticity An elasticity with a numerical measure of 1, in-dicating that the percentage change in quantity is equal to the percentage change in price (so that total expenditure remains constant).

utility See *marginal utility* and *total utility.*

utils An imaginary measure of utility used in the exposition of marginal utility theory, which assumes that utility is cardinally measurable.

validation When the authorities sustain an ongoing inflation by increasing the money supply.

value added The value of a firm's output minus the value of the inputs that it purchases from other firms.

value added tax (VAT) Tax charged as a proportion of a firm's *value added.*

value of money See *purchasing power of money.*

variable Any well-defined item, such as the price of a commodity or its quantity, that can take on various specific values.

variable cost A cost that varies directly with changes in output. Also called direct cost or avoidable cost.

variable factors Inputs whose amount can be varied in the short run.

velocity of circulation The number of times an average unit of money is used in transactions within a specific period. Defined as the ratio of nominal GDP to the money stock.

vertical equity Equitable treatment of people in different income brackets. Compare *horizontal equity.*

very long run A period of time over which the technological pos-sibilities open to a firm are subject to change.

visible account The part of the balance of payments accounts relating to trade in goods.

visible trade Trade in physical products. Same as merchandise trade.

visibles Goods, i.e. things such as cars, aluminium, coffee, and iron ore, that we can see when they cross international borders.

voluntary export restriction (VER) Restriction whereby an ex-porting country agrees to limit the amount it sells to a second country.

voluntary unemployment Unemployment that occurs when there is a job available but the unemployed person is not willing to accept it at the existing wage rate.

winner's curse The possibility that the agent who wins the bidding on a contested takeover may pay more than the target firm is really worth because the winner is the one with the highest valu-ation of all bidders.

withdrawals Spending that leaves the economy and does not create further incomes for domestic residents. Import spending, for example, creates incomes overseas. Also called leakages.

working population The total of the employed, the self-employed, and the unemployed, i.e. those who have a job plus those who are looking for work.

X-inefficiency Failure to use resources efficiently within the firm so that firms are producing above their relevant cost curves and the economy is inside its production-possibility boundary.

yield curve A line on a graph plotting the yield on securities against the term to maturity.

Index

Headwords in green refer to subjects defined in the Glossary. Page numbers of subjects covered in boxes are shown in **bold** type; page numbers in *italic* are to references in the appendices.

Index compiled by Margaret Cronan